D0712670

WITHDRAWN
UTSA LIBRARIES

THE CAMBRIDGE HISTORY
OF THE ROMANCE LANGUAGES

This *Cambridge History* is the most comprehensive survey of the history of the Romance languages ever published in English, offering major and original insights into the subject. Informed by the latest advances in Romance linguistics and general linguistic theory, it engages with new and original topics that reflect wider-ranging comparative concerns, such as the relation between diachrony and synchrony; morphophonological persistence; form–function relationships; morpho-syntactic typology; pragmatic change; the structure of written Romance; and lexical stability.

Volume I is organized around the two key recurrent themes of *persistence* (structural inheritance and continuity from Latin) and *innovation* (structural change and loss in Romance). An important and novel aspect of the volume is that it accords persistence in Romance a focus in its own right rather than treating it simply as the background to the study of change. At the same time, it explores in depth the patterns of innovation (including loss) at all linguistic levels. The result is a rich structural history which marries together data and theory to produce new perspectives on the structural evolution of the Romance languages.

MARTIN MAIDEN is Professor of the Romance Languages and Director of the Research Centre for Romance Linguistics at the University of Oxford. He is also a Fellow of Trinity College, Oxford, and a Fellow of the British Academy. His recent publications include *A Reference Grammar of Modern Italian* (with Cecilia Robustelli, 2007).

JOHN CHARLES SMITH is Faculty Lecturer in French Linguistics and Deputy Director of the Research Centre for Romance Linguistics at the University of Oxford and a Fellow of St Catherine's College, Oxford. He has published widely on agreement, refunctionalization, deixis, and the evolution of case and pronoun systems, with particular reference to Romance.

ADAM LEDGEWAY is Head of the Department of Italian and Senior Lecturer in Romance Philology at the University of Cambridge, and a Fellow of Downing College, Cambridge. His recent publications include *Grammatica diacronica del napoletano* (2009).

THE CAMBRIDGE
HISTORY OF THE
ROMANCE LANGUAGES

VOLUME I   *Structures*

EDITED BY

MARTIN MAIDEN,
JOHN CHARLES SMITH
and
ADAM LEDGEWAY

CAMBRIDGE
UNIVERSITY PRESS

CAMBRIDGE UNIVERSITY PRESS

Cambridge, New York, Melbourne, Madrid, Cape Town, Singapore,
São Paulo, Delhi, Dubai, Tokyo, Mexico City

Cambridge University Press
The Edinburgh Building, Cambridge CB2 8RU, UK

Published in the United States of America by Cambridge University Press,
New York

www.cambridge.org
Information on this title: www.cambridge.org/9780521800723

© Cambridge University Press 2011

This publication is in copyright. Subject to statutory exception
and to the provisions of relevant collective licensing agreements,
no reproduction of any part may take place without the written
permission of Cambridge University Press.

First published 2011

Printed in the United Kingdom at the University Press, Cambridge

A catalogue record for this publication is available from the British Library

Library of Congress Cataloguing in Publication data
The Cambridge history of the Romance languages / edited by Martin Maiden,
John Charles Smith, and Adam Ledgeway.
    v.   cm.
Contents: v. 1. Structures – v. Context.
ISBN 978-0-521-80072-3 (hardback)
1. Romance languages – History.   I. Maiden, Martin, 1957–   II. Smith,
John Charles, 1950–   III. Ledgeway, Adam.   IV. Title.
PC45.C245   2010
440.09–dc22

                                                            2010039944

ISBN 978-0-521-80072-3 Hardback

Cambridge University Press has no responsibility for the persistence or
accuracy of URLs for external or third-party internet websites referred to
in this publication, and does not guarantee that any content on such
websites is, or will remain, accurate or appropriate.

In memoriam
Joseph A. Cremona 1922–2003

CONTENTS

CONTRIBUTORS

BRIGITTE L. M. BAUER *Associate Professor, The University of Texas at Austin*

STEVEN N. DWORKIN *Professor of Romance Languages and Linguistics, University of Michigan*

ADAM LEDGEWAY *Senior Lecturer in Romance Philology and Head of the Department of Italian, University of Cambridge*

MICHELE LOPORCARO *Professor of Romance Linguistics, Romanisches Seminar, Universität Zürich*

MARTIN MAIDEN *Professor of the Romance Languages and Director of the Research Centre for Romance Linguistics, University of Oxford*

MARIA M. MANOLIU *Professor Emeritus, University of California*

CHRISTOPHER JOHN POUNTAIN *Professor of Spanish Linguistics, Queen Mary, University of London*

GIAMPAOLO SALVI *Professor of Romance Linguistics, Eötvös Loránd University*

JOHN CHARLES SMITH *Faculty Lecturer in French Linguistics, Deputy Director of the Research Centre for Romance Linguistics and Fellow of St Catherine's College, University of Oxford*

ROSANNA SORNICOLA *Professore Ordinario di Linguistica Generale, Università di Napoli Federico II*

ARNULF STEFENELLI[†]

JOHN TRUMPER *Professor of Linguistics, Università della Calabria*

ABBREVIATIONS

Bibliographical abbreviations will be found under *References*, at the end of this volume.

*	unattested form or usage
**	ungrammatical form or usage
%	marginal form or usage
?	dubious form or usage; when used alone, form uncertain or unknown
??	highly dubious form or usage
=	cliticized to
$	syllable boundary
Ø	null argument (subject or object)
1	first person
1CONJ	first conjugation
1SW	one-syllable window
2	second person
2CONJ	second conjugation
2SW	two-syllable window
3	third person
3CONJ	third conjugation
3SW	three-syllable window
4CONJ	fourth conjugation
A	(i) adjective position (head of AP); (ii) subject of a transitive clause
ABL	ablative
Abr.	Abruzzese
Aca.	Acadian (French)
ACC	accusative

ACT	active
ADJ	adjective (category)
ADV	adverb position (head of ADVP)
ADVP	adverb phrase
Agr(S/O)	(subject/object) agreement
Agr(S/O)P	(subject/object) agreement phrase
Alb.	Albanian
Alg.	Algherese (Alguerès)
AP	adjective phrase
ARo.	Aromanian
Ast.	Asturian
AUG	augmentative
AUX	auxiliary
AUXP	auxiliary phrase
Bal.	Balearic (Catalan)
Bel.	Bellunese
Bol.	Bolognese
BrPt.	Brazilian Portuguese
C	(i) central; (ii) complementizer position (head of CP); (iii) consonant
Cal.	Calabrian
Cat.	Catalan
CLat.	Classical Latin
Cmp.	Campanian
coll.	colloquial
COMP	complementizer (category)
COND	conditional
ConF	contrastive focus
ContRo.	contemporary Romanian
Cor.	Corsican
Cos.	Cosentino
CP	complementizer phrase
Cpc.	Capcinese
Cst.	Castilian
CuSp.	Cuban Spanish
D	determiner position (head of DP)
DAT	dative
DEC	declension
DEF	definite

DEM	demonstrative
DET	determiner (category)
dial.	dialectal
DIM	diminutive
DO	direct-object
DoSp.	Dominican Republic Spanish
DP	determiner phrase
E	east(ern)
Egd.	Engadinish
Eml.	Emilian
Eng.	English
EuPt.	European Portuguese
Ext.	Extremaduran (Extremeño)
F	feminine
Fin	finiteness position (head of FinP)
FinP	finiteness phrase
Foc	focus
FocP	focus phrase
ForceP	(illocutionary) force phrase
Fr.	French
Frk.	Frankish
Frl.	Friulian
FUT	future
Gen.	Genoese
GEN	genitive
Ger.	German
Glc.	Galician
GR	grammatical relation
Grk.	Greek
Gsc.	Gascon
Hai.	Haitian
HPC	heavy penult constraint
HTop	hanging topic
IbR.	Ibero-Romance
IE	Indo-European
IMP	imperative
IND	indicative
IndefQ	indefinite quantifier
INDF	indefinite

INF	infinitive
InfF	informational focus
I(nfl)	(verb) inflection (head of IP)
INT	interrogative
IO	indirect object
IP	inflection phrase
IPF	imperfect
IPFV	imperfective
IRo.	Istro-Romanian
Ist.	Istrian
It.	Italian
Lad.	Ladin (ladino dolomitico)
Lat.	Latin
LD-Top	left-dislocated topic
Lec.	Leccese
Lig.	Ligurian
lit.	literally
Lmb.	Lombard (Italo-Romance)
Loc	Locative
Log.	Logudorese
Lvl.	Livinallonghese
Maj.	Majorcan
M	masculine
Mdv.	Moldovan
Mid.	middle
Mil.	Milanese
Mod., mod.	modern
ModFr.	modern French
ModOcc.	modern Occitan
ModPt.	modern Portuguese
ModSp.	modern Spanish
MRo.	Megleno-Romanian
Mtv.	Mantuan
MxSp.	Mexican Spanish
N	(i) north(ern); (ii) noun position (head of NP); (iii) noun
Nap.	Neapolitan
Neg	negator
NegP	negator phrase
NEUT	neuter

NOM	nominative
NP	noun phrase
Nrm.	Norman
O	(i) old; (ii) object
Ø	null argument (subject or object)
OBL	oblique (case)
OCat.	old Catalan
Occ.	Occitan
OFlo.	old Florentine
OFr.	old French
OIt.	old Italian
ONap.	old Neapolitan
OOcc.	old Occitan
OPrv.	old Provençal
OPt.	old Portuguese
ORo.	old Romanian
OSL	open syllable lengthening
OSp.	old Spanish
OSrd.	old Sardinian
OT	Optimality Theory
OTsc.	old Tuscan
PASS	passive
PAV	palatalization and affrication of velar consonants
PF	perfect
PFV	perfective
Pic.	Picard
Pie.	Piedmontese
PIE	Proto-Indo-European
PL	plural
PLPF	pluperfect
PP	(i) past participle; (ii) prepositional phrase
PRET	preterite
PRS	present
Prv.	Provençal
PST	past
Pt.	Portuguese
PW	phonological word
PYTA	*perfecto y tiempos afines*
Q	quantifier position (head of QP)

QP	quantifier phrase
QUANT	quantifier
Qué.	Québécois (French)
RæR.	Ræto-Romance
REFL	reflexive
Rmc	Romanesco
Ro.	Romanian
Ros.	Roussillonnais (Rossellonès)
Rov.	Rovignese
S	(i) south(ern); (ii) subject
$S_{A/O}$	intransitive subject of an unergative/unaccusative clause
Sal.	Salentino
SBJV	subjunctive
Sc-set	scene-setting adverb(ial)
Sen.	Sienese
SG	singular
Sic.	Sicilian
SIt.	southern Italian
Sp.	Spanish
Spec	specifier position
Srd.	Sardinian
Srs.	Surselvan
Srv.	Servigliano
t	trace of moved element
Tar.	Tarantino
TOP, Top	Topic
Tor	Turinese
Trn.	Trentino
Tsc.	Tuscan
UEgd.	Upper Engadinish
Umb.	Umbrian
V	(i) verb; (ii) vowel
Vgl.	Vegliote
Vnz.	Venetian
VOC	vocative
VP	verb phrase
VQ	vowel quality
VR	vowel reduction
Vto.	Veneto

V2	Verb Second (syntax)
W	west(ern)
Wln.	Wallon
WRæR.	western Ræto-Romance
X	unspecified element
YE	yod-effect

List of authors

Caes.	Caesar
Cat.	Catullus
Cic.	Cicero
Cor. Nep.	Cornelius Nepos
Enn.	Ennius
Hor.	Horace
Liv.	Livy
Naev.	Naevius
Oribas.	Oribasius
Ov.	Ovid
Petr.	Petronius
Pl.	Plautus
Sall.	Sallust
Ter.	Terence
Val. Max.	Valerius Maximus
Verg.	Vergil

INTRODUCTION

This *Cambridge History of the Romance Languages* stands on the shoulders of giants. A glance at the list of bibliographical references in this work should suffice to give some idea of the enormous body of descriptive and interpretative literature on the history of the Romance languages, both from the point of view of their structural evolution (the main focus of this volume) and with regard to the contexts in which they have emerged as distinct 'languages', and gained or lost speakers and territory, and come into contact with other languages (the focus of the second volume). This profusion of scholarship, adopting a multiplicity of approaches (synchronic, diachronic, microscopic, macroscopic) has more than once provided material for major, indeed monumental, comparative-historical synopses (e.g., Meyer-Lübke (1890–1902), Lausberg (1956–62), or the massively detailed and indispensable encyclopaedic works such as Holtus, Metzeltin and Schmitt (1988–96) and Ernst, Glessgen, Schmitt and Schweickard (2003–9)).

Much of the finest scholarship in Romance linguistics has, naturally enough, been conducted in Romance languages, or in German (the native language of some of the major founding figures of the discipline). One of our aims is to reach out to linguists who are not Romance specialists, and who may not know these languages. While the histories of some of the better-known major Romance languages (Italian, French, Spanish, Portuguese) have been treated in English, this work is certainly the first detailed comparative history of the Romance languages to appear in English.[1]

The aim of *The Cambridge History of the Romance Languages* is not to compete with or supersede the works mentioned above, but to complement them, by presenting both to Romanists and to historical linguists at large the major and most exciting insights to emerge from the comparative-historical study of Romance. With this in mind, we have deliberately attempted in the presentation and discussion of the material of the two volumes to adopt a more inclusive approach which, while not alienating the traditional Romanist, bears in mind the practical limitations and needs of an interested non-specialist Romance readership (witness, for instance, the extensive translation of Romance and Latin examples), though in no case is this done at the expense of empirical and analytic detail.

It is our firm belief that the richly documented diachronic, diatopic, diastratic, diamesic and diaphasic variation exhibited by the Romance family offers an unparalleled wealth of linguistic data of interest not just to Romanists, but also to non-Romance specialists. This perennially fertile and still under-utilized testing ground, we believe, has a central role to play in challenging linguistic orthodoxies and shaping and informing new ideas and perspectives about language change, structure and variation, and should therefore be at the forefront of linguistic research and accessible to the wider linguistic community.

The present work is not a 'history' of Romance languages in the traditional sense of a 'standard' reference manual ('vademecum') providing a comprehensive structural overview of individual 'languages' and/or traditional themes (e.g., 'Lexis', 'Vowels', 'Nominal Group', 'Tense, Aspect and Mood', 'Subordination', 'Substrate', 'Prehistory', etc.) on a chapter by chapter basis (cf., among others, Tagliavini (1972), Harris and Vincent (1988), Holtus, Metzeltin and Schmitt (1988–96)), but, rather, is a collection of fresh and original reflections on what we deem to be the principal questions and issues in the comparative internal (volume 1: Structures) and external (volume 2: Contexts) histories of the Romance languages, informed by contemporary thinking in both Romance linguistics and general linguistic theory and organized according to novel chapter divisions which reflect broader, overriding comparative concerns and themes (generally neglected or left untackled in standard works), rather than those which are narrowly focused on individual languages or developments. This is not to say that readers wanting to learn something about a classic topic of Romance linguistics such as the survival of the nominative vs. oblique case distinction in old French, for example, will not find the relevant information simply because there is no individual chapter on 'French' or 'The Nominal Group'. On the contrary, they will find, throughout, rich and diverse comparative discussions of this topic in relation to other Gallo-Romance varieties (not to mention non-Gallo-Romance varieties which preserve, to varying degrees, traces of case distinctions) from the perspective of: (i) the issues and questions it raises for the relationship between diachronic and synchronic analyses (see Sornicola, chapter 1: §3.1); (ii) its impact on the morphophonological exponence of nominal categories (see Maiden, chapter 4: §2) and the restructuring of the nominal paradigm (see Maiden, chapter 4: §§3–3.1); (iii) its refunctionalization as an agency opposition (see Smith, chapter 6: §2.2); (iv) its differential development and distribution in nominal and pronominal paradigms (see Salvi, chapter 7: §§2.1–2); and (v) its integration into an early Romance active vs. stative syntactic alignment (see Ledgeway, chapter 8: §6.2.2.2). Inevitably, this will mean that certain aspects of the history of the Romance languages or individual members thereof – though admittedly very few, as a thorough reading of the following pages reveals – may not be exhaustively covered. A case in point is the development of the Romance future and conditional paradigms derived from the infinitive and a weakened present/past form of HABERE 'have' (e.g., CANTARE + *-a/*-ia > Sp. *cantará/cantaría* 's/he will/would sing'), which although discussed in relation to other developments, such as the distribution of root-allomorphy (cf. Maiden, chapter 5: §6) or the directionality of the head parameter (cf. Ledgeway, chapter 8: §5), does not form the subject of a separate study in its own right. Nevertheless, we are convinced that the merits of the individual chapter divisions adopted here far outweigh any potential lacunae (for which, in any event, there exist in virtually all cases other reliable treatments; for the Romance future and conditional paradigms, see, among others: Valesio 1968; Coleman 1971; Harris 1978: ch. 6; Fleischman 1982; Green 1987; Pinkster 1987; Vincent 1987; Maiden 1996c; Loporcaro 1999; Nocentini 2001; La Fauci 2006).

This work is organized around four key recurrent themes: *persistence, innovation, influences* and *institutions*. Thus, much of the first volume dedicated to the linguistic 'Structures' of Romance juxtaposes chapters or chapter sections dealing with issues of persistence on the one hand and innovation on the other in relation to the macroareas of phonology, morphology, morphosyntax, lexis, semantics and discourse-pragmatics. It goes without saying that the Romance languages are the modern continuers of Latin and therefore many aspects of structure persist from that language into Romance. It is not usual, however, for works on the Romance languages to concentrate on these factors of inheritance and continuity, since they – understandably – prefer to comment on what is new and different in Romance by comparison with Latin. By contrast, we believe that it is an important and original aspect of the present work that it accords persistence in Romance (and hence inheritance from Latin) a focus in its own right rather than treating it simply as the background to the study of the changes.

At the same time, we devote considerable space to the patterns of innovation (including loss) at all linguistic levels that have taken place in the evolution of Romance. Thus, the chapters of the present volume equally address many of the most important changes in the history of the Romance languages, profitably marrying data and theory to create new perspectives on their structural evolution.

Structural persistence and innovation within Romance cannot, of course, be studied in isolation from the influences and institutions with which the Romance languages and their speakers have variously come into contact at different periods in their history. For this reason, the authors of individual chapters have been encouraged to consider, as far as possible, structural persistence and innovation in relation to these influences and institutions and the extent to which they may have helped in arresting or delaying them on the one hand and shaping or accelerating them on the other. It is, however, in the second volume dedicated to the 'Contexts' in which the Romance languages have evolved that the central role assumed by *influences* and *institutions* is investigated, as well as their bearing on questions of persistence and innovation (cf. the discussion of the Romance creoles). It is well known that the Romance languages have been subject in varying degrees to the effects of outside influences. In addition to contact and borrowing (e.g., from Germanic, Arabic, Slavic) and substrate effects (e.g., from Celtic), there is also the all-important role of Latin as a learnèd language of culture and education existing side by side and interacting with the evolving languages, as well as the role of contact and borrowing between Romance languages. When speaking of institutions, we have in mind both the role of institutions in the sense of specific organizations (the Church, academies, governments, etc.) in the creation of 'standard' languages and the prescription of norms of correctness, and also the language as an institution in society involved in, among other things, education, government policy, and cultural and literary movements.

Consequently, the focus throughout both volumes is on an integration of the internal and external perspectives on the history of the Romance languages, in part achieved through a multiauthor format which brings together the best of recent scholarship in the two traditions, and in part through careful editorial intervention and cross-referencing across chapters and volumes.[2] However, as editors we have been keen to impose as few constraints on our contributors as possible in order to create an opportunity for international scholars of stature and intellectual vision to reflect on the principles and areas that have been influential in a particular subarea, and to reassess the situation.

It is necessary here to mention, albeit briefly, the rationale behind a number of our decisions in representing, and referring to, Latin. It is customary (though in no way a universally accepted practice) in many works on Latin and Romance to cite Latin forms in small capitals. Although we recognize that there are, of course, no linguistic grounds for this choice of typographic representation, inasmuch as Latin forms could just as legitimately appear in lower-case italics on a par with any other language, we have chosen to follow here the (more or less) established convention of employing small capitals for cited examples. While it is true that the ancient Romans did not use small capitals to represent their language, it is equally true that they did not use lower-case italics either. However, we believe that the conventional practice of placing Latin forms in small capitals has the typographical advantage, especially in a work like ours, where reference to Latin forms is legion, of allowing immediate and efficient recognition of the two diachronic poles of our investigation, Latin (small capitals) and Romance (lower-case italics). Where we do depart, however, from current conventional practice is in our representation of the classical Latin high back vowel/glide [w], which is today usually represented as 'V' in syllable onsets (e.g., VIVO 'I live') and U in all other positions (e.g., HABUIT 'he had') or, according to another school of thought, as 'V' when it appears in upper case and 'u' when in lower case (e.g., *Viuo* 'I live'). By contrast, we have preferred to adopt U (lower case) / U (upper case) in all positions (hence, UIUO and HABUIT), which not only reflects the original practice of ancient Romans, but also makes the value of the grapheme more transparent in the discussion of Latin (morpho)phonology. One further departure from current typographical conventions concerns our decision to cite all non-attested forms, whether reconstructed for Latin or any other language (but in all cases preceded by a single asterisk) in phonetic transcription (e.g., *vo'lere 'to want' replacing classical UELLE), and not in small capitals (e.g., *UOLERE) as is frequently the case in other works.

Finally, although we do not wish to enter here into a discussion of the value or the appropriateness of such labels as 'vulgar', 'late', 'spoken', 'literary' and many others in relation to Latin (for which we refer the reader to the chapters in Volume II by Banniard, Varvaro and Wright), we are keen to point out that we do not consider Latin a monolithic variety, uniquely to be identified with the prescriptive norm passed down to us in the high literary and rhetorical models of the classical era. Rather, like any other natural language that has existed, we take Latin to be a rich and varied polymorphous linguistic system which was subject, both on the diachronic and synchronic axes, to the same kinds of diatopic, diastratic, diamesic and diaphasic variation as its modern Romance descendants. We therefore deliberately avoid capitalized epithets in such syntagms as 'Vulgar Latin' or 'Late Latin', which unreasonably suggest an ill-founded linguistic and psychological demarcation between one supposed language, Classical Latin on the one hand, and an autonomous derivative, 'Vulgar Latin' or 'Late Latin' on the other. Rather, in the same way that linguists regularly append descriptive labels like 'modern', 'spoken', 'popular', 'dialectal', 'journalistic', 'literary', 'Latin-American' and such like to the modern Romance languages to refer to a particular 'variety' of that language (e.g., '(spoken) Barcelona Catalan', 'popular French', 'journalistic Italian', 'literary Romanian', 'Latin-American Spanish'; see Wright, Volume II, for further discussion), we have left it to the discretion of individual authors to indicate and identify, where necessary, the particular register, style or variety of Latin intended by means of an appropriate non-capitalized epithet or periphrasis, be it 'vulgar Latin', 'spoken Latin' or 'the Latin of North-West Africa'.

To conclude, we should like to remember here Joseph Cremona, who died on 19 March 2003, and to whom the present volume of *The Cambridge History of the Romance Languages* is dedicated – fittingly so since Joe was the first to hold the post of Lecturer in Romance Philology (1955–89) in the University of Cambridge. During his long and eminent career, Joe firmly established, and when necessary, defended, the study of Romance linguistics in Cambridge, and inspired and encouraged successive generations of students to become specialists in Romance and/or general linguistics. Indeed, it stands as a testimony to his continuing legacy that a great many of those currently teaching the history and structure of Romance languages in British universities have been his students (or, latterly, have been taught by his students). Amongst them are two of the present editors and several of the contributors to the two volumes. The subject is buoyant and flourishing in Britain today, and a very large share of the credit goes to him. What he created was not so much a 'Cremona school' as a 'Cremona style': he argued that fruitful study of the structure and evolution of the Romance languages requires a thorough acquaintance with linguistic theory, and at the same time that the study of linguistics, and especially historical linguistics, needs mastery of the kind of comparative and historical data which can be gleaned abundantly from Romance languages. It is these same issues and principles which have guided and shaped *The Cambridge History of the Romance Languages*, a fitting tribute, we believe, to his memory.

I ROMANCE LINGUISTICS AND HISTORICAL LINGUISTICS: REFLECTIONS ON SYNCHRONY AND DIACHRONY[1]

Rosanna Sornicola

In remembrance of Eugenio Coseriu, József Herman, Yakov Malkiel

1 Introduction

I discuss here some problems of Romance diachronic morphosyntax in the light of theoretical and methodological considerations on the relation between diachrony and synchrony, and the question of linguistic change.

I first attempt to demonstrate a thesis that is perhaps not obvious, and rather goes against the grain of contemporary thinking: Romance linguistics has rather more to offer general linguistics in its thinking on the synchrony–diachrony relationship and the problem of language change than contemporary general linguistics has to offer Romance linguistics. Our discipline not only possesses an extraordinary stock of data, but also has long had a rich array of methodological and theoretical tools, which make it a particularly ideal platform for tackling the intellectual problem of diachrony. Romance linguistics foresaw aspects of the modern debate, and in some respects offered solutions ahead of that debate. In particular I shall be concerned with the following issues:

(a) 'Laws': are there laws of transformation through time, besides laws of analogy? In other words, do diachronic structures exist, in addition to synchronic ones?

(b) The form–function relation: does this relation have the same properties in diachrony as in synchrony?

(c) Syntactic factors in morphosyntactic change: is their role active or inert?

1

2 Between general and Romance linguistics

2.1 Introduction

Are the power and potential of Romance diachronic linguistics obvious? That they are not seems to me to be shown by the arguments that have arisen in recent years in North American Romance linguistics, as well as in schools of thought rooted in different theoretical and methodological approaches, such as diachronic typology, grammaticalization theory or generative diachronic syntax. Following a preoccupation dear to Yakov Malkiel, founder of an authoritative American school of Romance linguistics, Stephen Dworkin has repeatedly called for a 'rejuvenation' of Romance linguistics, through openness to new theories and methods, and promoted stimulating exchanges of views between Romanists from different countries (see also Malkiel 1988:20). But how feasible is this? And what should this rejuvenation consist of? Are we to rethink old problems and domains of enquiry, or should we identify new ones, from the perspective of recent theories? Theories, of course, are never neutral with regard to the data they assume. In fact, theories impose their own specific empirical domains.

This could be one of the crucial points of the question. Take the Chomskyan distinction between *E-language* ('External language') and *I-language* ('Internal language'), nowadays widely used in diachronic generative syntax. From the outset research has focused on changes in *I-Language*; moreover, the primary explanandum is taken to be changes in grammars, mental entities represented in the minds/brains of individuals. *E-languages*, and the changes they undergo, are of little import, being considered mere epiphenomena (see Lightfoot 1999:74; 2003). Typical issues are: Why do French children have V(erb)-to-I(nflection) raising, while English children do not, and lower their 'I' (Lightfoot 2003:499). Or: How does the category change from noun to preposition (e.g., Lat. CASA > Fr. *chez*) conform to an acquisitional principle such as 'Minimize feature content' (see Longobardi 2001:294f.)?

Such questions and the kind of data they involve are very different from what the traditionally trained Romanist is used to. To apply the Chomskyan distinction again, the data may be said to involve *E-language*, which look, to boot, like rather restricted technical questions which some may regard as unexciting, such as: If the medieval geographical extension of derivatives of IPSE in the function of 'nascent article' was much greater than today, how did it subsequently get reduced diachronically, both diatopically and diastratically? And how, conversely, did the continuants of ILLE in the same function gain ground, eventually establishing themselves over most of the Romània (see Aebischer 1948)? And are the plurals in -*i* of Italian and Romanian masculine nouns direct continuants of the Latin second declension nominative plural inflection -*i*, or must we postulate a more complex, less 'economical' and multi-staged, development (see Sabatini 1965)? Much of the strength of Romance linguistics resides in such questions, and in answers to them which harness together the multiple dimensions of spatial, social and historical enquiry, the interplay of which forms a leitmotif of the whole discipline (see Coseriu 1973; 1981; Malkiel 1988:20).

Yet further, more wide-ranging, issues have also been raised. In 1978, in an article on the problem of language change (reprinted in Herman 1990), the eminent Hungarian Latinist and Romanist József Herman had discussed some 'cluster changes', mainly morphosyntactic and syntactic, and datable between the second and seventh centuries, which had major repercussions on the structure of the noun phrase and the sentence. These phenomena appear to have occurred in parallel: (1) simplification of Latin declension; (2) replacement of some case forms with prepositions; (3) appearance of new prepositional elements with a more definite spatio-temporal meaning; (4) tendencies to changes in word order; and (5) loss or weakening of word-final, consonantal and vocalic, segments. Herman was convinced that what was particular to historical explanation lay in: (a) the interrelations and mutual causes of changes; and (b) the possible connections between linguistic change and the circumstances of linguistic transmission (Herman 1978a=1990:362). Of course, different models of diachrony contain the idea of interconnected clusters of changes, reflecting deep structural adjustments (in the language or the grammar), yet these models all share the aim of rationalizing change. Think, for example, of the typological representation of clusters of adjustments affecting languages understood as objects external to the speakers, or the generative models which hypothesize 'cascades of changes' which grammars may undergo (see Lightfoot 1999; 2003; Longobardi 2001). In a more or less direct way both hark back to the functionalist conceptions of the early twentieth century, according to which change is not made up of independent adjustments, but occurs as part of a system of interrelated changes. If Herman generally follows this point of view, his position is clearly distinguished by its distance from typological and generative conceptualizations of the past few decades.

I concur entirely with Malkiel, who held that Romance linguistics contains a 'reservoir of priceless data' and considered its diachronic domain one of 'truly inexhaustible possibilities' (Malkiel 1988:19). There is no reason to think that he was in any way calling for the abandonment of the traditional preoccupations of the discipline. This is clear from a dream he evoked, at the end of a resonant address in 1988 on the complex history of Romance linguistics, which appeared to him to take the form of a three-faced Janus. He called for the new generations of Romanists who had strayed away (to Malkiel's regret) into synchronic studies, to return with renewed interest to the classic themes of diachronic linguistics, but to do this without ignoring twentieth-century developments. In terms that, perhaps, reflected his direct exposure to the world of North American linguistics, where diachronic studies had been reshaped by synchronic studies, Malkiel (like Herman) focused our attention on the essentials of history and diachrony, asserting their specific and autonomous nature.

Yet is this wealth of data and historical problems, in space, society and time, of itself a strength of Romance linguistics, or is there a risk of its becoming a kind of locked strongbox, to which only tiny cliques of specialists hold the key, and whose treasures must lie largely unexploited? There is also the risk that diachronic Romance linguistics could become a mere auxiliary to diachronic speculation, a kind of 'empirical data dump', on which theories whose 'historical' nature is dubious could draw as they please. This risk may be emblematic of a new phase in the history of linguistics in which the unresolved contraposition of synchrony and dia-chrony in Saussurean structuralism, and the attempts to reconcile them within European and then North American functionalism, appear to have resulted in the abolition of both synchrony and diachrony, in favour of a universal grammar lying outside time, space and society.

2.2   *The riches of the historical world: new and*
        old paths in historical linguistics

The classical problems of Romance linguistics may still be valid, but how are they to be addressed from a novel perspective? The study by Herman mentioned above seems to me to offer an excellent vantage point from which to assess the distance between an authoritative point of view subscribed to by many Romanists, and some recognized approaches in diachronic linguistics which are conspicuously concerned with language as a whole.

One initial difference lies in the fundamentally sceptical view of diachronic theories manifest in Herman's work. This is not to say that he did not attempt to give an organic and coherent representation of change, but he did have a clear awareness of the limits of representations of historical facts. He may have hypothesized that the five (morpho)syntactic changes mentioned above were manifestations of a single complex structural change, involving encoding of NP-internal relations and the relation of the NP to the rest of the sentence, but he did not think that this was a matter of causal determination in one direction or another. He concluded therefore that 'there is no reliable and generally acceptable answer to the question of how these processes determine each other or indeed whether any of them takes priority of causal type over the others. We could refer, at most, to a negative conjecture: an old and simplifying causal solution can in all probabilities be excluded' (Herman 1978a; 1990:365). The point is that Herman was convinced that historical linguistics had to be found specific and adequate models, quite different from physical–causational ones, and that the very concept of 'historical explanation' in linguistics lay largely unexplored.

This fundamental scepticism also involves more specific but not unimportant issues, such as the chronological delimitation of changes. Herman makes extremely cautious use of periodizations, knowing that the date of first attestation is relative and that even frequent occurrence cannot be taken as evidence of the passage from one stage to another. The issue arises of interpretation of sources, especially written sources as reflections of spoken language – an exquisitely historical problem with enormous consequences for the analysis of change. For this reason, more or less accurate periodizations have for Herman a less central role than appears from some contemporary discussions, which retain the legacy of Neogrammarian-style positivist conceptions, apparent also in the widespread idea that the locus of change is language acquisition over successive generations of speakers (see Lightfoot 2003). Even further removed from Herman are models, such as diachronic typology and grammaticalization theory, which, in different ways, view change in terms of linear cycles. These are not historical cycles in the sense of modern historiographical debate, but rather evolutionary cycles. The concepts of 'evolution' and 'history', albeit often nowadays considered interchangeable, are profoundly different. Recall that in historical sciences this terminological fusion had already been successfully criticized, and superseded, in the final decades of the nineteenth century (see Tessitore 1991), as had the idea of the predictability of change, which in many theories was allied to a biological–evolutionary view of linguistic development. Herman's approach is concerned neither with the origin nor the future development of a given phenomenon. From its origins Romance linguistics has been aware that a truly historical conception of language is a very different matter from a biological–evolutionary one. Consequently, however much one might agree with some recent generative critiques of typological–evolutionary models (see Lightfoot 1999:210), they look like an extremely tardy recognition of ideas that have been argued for in the theory and practice of Romance linguistics for two centuries.

But the greatest split lies in the synchrony–diachrony relationship. Herman (1978a; 1990:357) rightly stressed an issue which still seems highly important twenty years on: the theoretical literature approached the problem of diachrony from the perspective of synchrony, 'either by applying theories established within synchrony to the history of language, or by denying the possibility of a substantial distinction between synchrony and diachrony with reference to obviously perceptible traces of historical changes in synchronic state'.

2.3   Synchrony and diachrony

The subordination of diachrony to synchrony (or their interchangeability, which is only apparently different) has deep roots, but emerges distinctly in various North American groups of scholars in the 1960s. A thesis such as Hoenigswald's (1960:3), that 'much time and effort could have been saved if historical theory had been built on more explicit synchronic foundations', although characteristic of conceptions of reconstructionist historical linguistics, has continued to this day to influence other domains of general linguistics concerned with diachrony (see Lightfoot 1999:266). At the Austin congress of 1967, Lehmann outlined the programme for a new diachronic linguistics, built on modern descriptive linguistics and concerned primarily not with structural units, or states, but the operations or processes which characterize the working of languages. Taking his inspiration from Praguean models of dynamic functionalism, he stressed the concept of the fluidity of languages with respect to synchrony and diachrony, a concept which, he held, emerges conspicuously if one looks at operations and not states. Yet the synchronic roots of such a programme are hard to deny, for various reasons: (a) it takes as basic the conception of an active 'participant' in change; and (b) the operations or processes are, after all, representations of events which express more or less broad movements in time, through descriptive schemas. In other words, the priority of synchrony over diachrony is reformulated as the priority of descriptive over truly historical linguistics (see Lehmann 1968; 1982). Such has been the mould of diachronic typology and, in different ways, other approaches to diachrony, over the last forty years.

The 'neofunctionalist' programme had to contend with some fundamental difficulties, and there may have been excessive optimism about solving them: (a) the problem of the metalanguage, i.e., of the comparability of different linguistic phenomena in terms of universal analytic categories; (b) the problem of how to treat the form–function relationship in diachrony; and (c) the problem of whether theoretical models and sophisticated philological practices were really compatible. Perhaps the greatest difficulties lurk in this last problem, which is only apparently methodological: theoretical paradigms (whatever their nature) and historical–philological paradigms are far from easy to mesh together, without banal (or distorted) treatment of one or the other set of paradigms.

At Austin, morphology and syntax, banished to the realm of synchrony by early structuralism, were put forward as new directions for research on language change: diachronic syntax was brought into the study of the impact of morphological paradigms on sound change, and both in turn were brought into the examination of the impact of sociolinguistic facts on linguistic structure. While Lehmann wanted wholesale transplantation of operational–descriptive models into diachrony, Malkiel's Austin speech pointed in the opposite direction, with a clear attempt to bend synchrony towards diachronic investigation, in line with the dream of grafting some new branches on to the sturdy roots and the trunk of the old tree of Romance linguistics. Analogical–synchronic factors are considered as the limit of regular diachronic development, bound by so-called sound laws. These factors present both a source of phonetic irregularity, on the historical level, and a structural explanation of diachronic irregularities, on the theoretical level (see Malkiel 1968). Yet it seems certain that for Malkiel the historical perspective was to remain central and unchanged, with all its attendant array of technical and methodological tools, and conceptual problems.

In a different way from typological and grammaticalization-based approaches, generativism has also defined a programme where synchrony (description) controls diachrony (historical representation). The study of diachrony is part of a broader programme of biological research on mind, centred on the theory of Universal Grammar (UG) and its relations with individual grammars (see Lightfoot 1999:266f.). The object of enquiry is change occurring in grammars as an effect of the 'resetting of parameters', on the basis of primary (external) linguistic data, which constitute the 'triggering experience', whilst changes in the external linguistic environment, considered accidental, are of secondary interest. Change is thus conceived as a different *setting* of parameters, occurring under particular conditions, which give rise to a discontinuity (or 'catastrophe' – see Thom 1975). The discontinuity is an event which occurs in synchrony, in individuals' minds.

In this mentalist framework the dependency of historical linguists on synchronic linguists is clearly spelled out. Only a synchronically based theory of grammar, a theory capable of accounting for the grammar of any natural language as emerging from normal childhood experience, would be able to explain which changes are fortuitous (i.e., attributable to environment) and which are necessary (i.e., grammatical and thus justifiable), while historians were bound to have but an uncertain answer (Lightfoot 1999:265f.). Possible change is therefore necessary change, imposed by the laws of UG. Whatever such laws are, there are good reasons to hold that change is only partially and perhaps marginally connected with such general principles.

Lightfoot's theory has some unresolved problems, such as the relation between ontogeny and phylogeny, which contains an unjustified leap of logic. The properties considered specific to phylogeny are defined in terms of a conceptual inheritance in historical linguistics which recycles late nineteenth- and early twentieth-century ideas. What sets off the trigger remains particularly obscure. Lightfoot (1999:266), well aware of these difficulties, sets out the possible contribution of historical linguistics to synchronic theories:

> Syntacticians are embarrassingly silent on what it takes to set the parameters which they define. What makes historical studies so interesting is that one can sometimes identify cases where grammars change at some stage in the history of the language. If we are lucky, we can then identify changes taking place in the language just prior to the emergence of the new grammar. In that case, if our records are good, we are in a position to identify just what it took to trigger the new grammar. In fact, it seems to me that we can learn more about the nature of the triggering experience from language change than in any other way. This is no small claim, because unless syntacticians start identifying how their parameters get set by children, somebody is going to call their bluff and show that the emperor has no clothes.

This places a heavy burden on historical linguistics, for which it does not seem to get due recognition. This theory still implies historical movement, albeit implicitly, but only insofar as it can rationally be represented within the grammar as a point of major change (catastrophe). A more radical theory is that of inertia or diachronic minimalism. According to the generativist Giuseppe Longobardi (2001:277):

> A priori […] the ideally restrictive theory of language change should probably claim that diachronic change does not exist. This is so because, if

diachronic change exists, we are faced with a dilemma: either one must assume that at least some primitive change is unmotivated (i.e. largely beyond the scope of scientific inquiry), which is incompatible with the ideal theory: or one loses any understanding of why the previous synchronic state was possible at all. Since it seems to be a fact that changes exist (and previous synchronic states, too, of course), the ideal (or perfectly minimalist) theory cannot be fully pursued.

Consequently, the number of primitive causes must be reduced to a minimum, some of them being cast out to the very edge of grammatical systems, or beyond. This logical operation is accompanied by another: the assignment of an explanatory role to social, material and cultural changes, which are external to or independent of the grammar. And it is a Romance phenomenon with which Longobardi shows this, namely the development of French *chez* as an element with a prepositional function. This is the type of change traditionally represented in terms of 'grammaticalization' (passage from one grammatical category to another: Lat. CASA(M) > Fr. *chez*), which within a generative framework constitutes a prime example of the problem of the *resetting* of parameters. Longobardi ingeniously attempts to combine etymological and general linguistic analyses. Drawing on numerous works in Romance historical linguistics, he describes a broad range of nominal constructions with continuants of Lat. CASA. His originality lies in comparing such Romance types with the Semitic 'construct state' type (cf. Hebrew *beyt ha-more*, 'the teacher's home', lit. 'the home of the teacher'), and deriving them from principles of UG. But the set of universal properties of the construct state is only the starting point, perhaps going back to a 'predocumentary common Romance stage', of a development that in the case of *chez* involves in all five diachronic changes:

(1) the two lexemes MANSIO 'abode, dwelling' and HOSPITALE 'abode, asylum' develop the meaning 'house' in the Gallo-Romance area;
(2) the noun *chiese*, the phonetically regular development of CASA, disappears;
(3) Lat. CASA(M) also follows a different phonetic development, representable as *kas> *chies* > *chez*;
(4) NOUN > PREP;
(5) the meaning 'house' is transformed into that of 'general and abstract position'.

Longobardi (2001:298f.) concurs with various Romanists in seeing a relationship between (1) and (2), which he expresses, however, in 'causal' terms ((1) caused (2)). His thesis is that change (2) is responsible for the whole set of changes (3)–(5) and that consequently (1) is the original change, external to the grammar, which gave rise to all the others.

The notion that the triggering condition is external to the grammar opens the way to conclusions laden with theoretical implications: in the syntactic history of *chez* there was no resetting of parameters, and even syntactic change (4) might be considered a secondary consequence of a semantic change which occurred in another lexeme (Longobardi 2001:297–99). In effect, at the syntactic level nothing happened. This representation invokes continuity, as more generally expressed in the theory of inertia: 'language is diachronically inert unless proved otherwise'. This model of reanalysis of a grammatical category has its attractions, especially when compared with the analyses offered by grammaticalization theory, which represent this type of change in terms of fluctuations – it matters not whether diachronic or synchronic – at the end of which there is a definitive 'leap' from one category to another. Neither approach is unproblematic. The analysis of the diachrony of *chez* is scarcely 'historical', in the sense, particular to Romance linguistics, of a systematic description of the characteristics of linguistic structures in their distribution in time, in space, in society and in the culture of individuals, and in the sense of an understanding of how such structures interact with external factors. The historical method adopted is really more of a typological–reconstructive one. And historical factors are exploited, simplistically, to demonstrate a given assumption. On the level of the diachronic model represented, the result is clever, rather than convincing (as I intend to show elsewhere).

It is in Romance linguistics that the idea of the non-existence of language change has received a major theoretical formulation, at the hands of Coseriu. But his argumentation is quite different, being of a historical–empirical nature. As for diachronic minimalism, some questions arise. If language is diachronically inert, what is the point of turning to diachrony, from the point of view of grammatical investigation? Does the theory of inertia not deliver the *coup de grâce* to what was left of the notion of diachrony as a process of historical transformation dominated by grammar? And does it not amount to an unconditional surrender to external factors, which on this account are still haphazard and accidental? In that case, grammatical rationalism, taken to its logical extremes, would give rise to an evident paradox: the belief that everything in diachrony is purely contingent.

The apparent supremacy of external factors in the generative theory of inertia is deceptive, for the logic of the theory does not favour the identification of such factors. Its ultimate aim is to represent grammar unaffected by the perturbations of change, so as to conform as far as possible to an ideally restrictive theory of change. Hence, unlike Lightfoot's proposals, the 'triggering' factors of change are banished to the periphery of the grammar and even beyond. It is remarkable that, once this is done, the grammar may become indifferently a synchronic or a diachronic model. Yet another paradox seems to be that this leads by another route to the same general conclusion as the functionalists on the non-distinctness of synchrony and diachrony. This conclusion is reached in many respects from the opposite direction: the diachrony of the inertia model is by definition static, while functionalistic models are based on the concept of the dynamic potential of the activity of speaking.

The difficulties of generative approaches show how difficult it is to reconcile biological and historico–cultural paradigms. They cannot simply be combined together and the historical is ultimately distorted by the predominance of the biological, and reduced to a mere epiphenomenon (see Lightfoot 1999:265). Many Romanists would find this worrying. Herman's concerns about the lack, since Saussure, of broad engagement with the historical dimension of language on its own terms, seems today more relevant than ever.

The 1980s have been said to mark a turning point in linguistics, with the attempt to bring down the wall between general and historical linguistics which had stood for the best part a century (see Matthews 1991:3f.). But this may be less straightforward than the collapse of the Berlin Wall. To grasp the potential of Romance linguistics, we need to examine why.

Saussure's reflection on synchrony and diachrony appears nowadays, thanks to the publication of notes from the *Cours*, edited by Constantin, Patois and Riedlinger (in Komatsu and Harris 1993; Komatsu and Wolf 1996; 1997), much more multifaceted and complex than what emerged from the edition edited by Bally and Sechehaye (Saussure 1922). The debate of the 1960s on new directions of research in diachrony may have been influenced by the earlier edition. We need to review the main points of this debate to assess the import of the critical revisions which were subsequently proposed, and to grasp what is specific and characteristic of the perspectives offered by Romance linguistics. Fundamental are: (a) the idea of the link between system and consciousness; (b) the problem of teleologism; and (c) reflection on the concepts of phenomenon and law.

The need to contrast synchronic and diachronic phenomena, as Saussure held (Riedlinger, Quire II [Komatsu and Wolf 1997:36f.]), is rooted in a theoretical conception born of thoroughgoing philosophical assessment of the notion of system and that of *événement*. Crucial is the idea of the speaker's linguistic 'feeling'. A synchronic fact exists only as an element in a network of psychological relations (dependencies) which lie in the consciousness of speakers in a collectivity (see Constantin, Quire IX [Komatsu and Harris 1993:120f.]). There, feeling and meaning are indissolubly linked (Riedlinger, Quire III [Komatsu and Wolf 1997:49]). In other words, for there to be a synchronic fact there must be speakers who perceive and feel it as an entity clear and distinct from other facts, which are nonetheless connected to it. Only such feeling gives value to synchronic facts.

The aspects of this model which post-Saussurean structuralism and functionalism in its various manifestations have most emphasized are the logical and formal ones, i.e., the logical, differential and oppositional relations between the elements of linguistic associative networks. Yet it is the relation between synchronic fact and individual speaker which has fundamental theoretical consequences. A synchronic fact is not a mere linguistic 'phenomenon' or 'event' in abstract space, divorced from any speakers for whom it has 'value',[2] and speakers' awareness stands as the only yardstick for determining the degree of reality of a phenomenon in synchrony and the possibility of representing it as a structure.

The epistemological status of diachronic facts is quite different. Such facts 'are opposed to synchronic facts as are events to a system, are only events' and 'we do not speak via events' (Riedlinger, Quire II [Komatsu and Wolf 1997:46]; see Herman 1978a; 1990:361f.). As an *événement*, every diachronic fact is determined and exists outside the loop of linguistic, logical and psychological relations which lies in the awareness of speakers in a collectivity. It is an independent fact, in series with other diachronic facts (Riedlinger, Quire II [Komatsu and Wolf 1997:45]). It is not brought alive by the speaker's feeling, and thereby lacks direct interpretation and structural value.

Yet the distinction between the two orders of facts raises a number of unresolved questions. The consequences for synchrony of the centrality of the speaker's perspective were not all followed through. For this point of view can be thoroughly and coherently applied only within a time frame in which observer and speaker coexist, and of which the linguist–observer is a direct witness. Saussure's thinking displays a rather blurred overlapping between the concept of 'observer' who infers the characteristics of a given *état de langue* and that of 'speaker' in whose feeling and consciousness they are reflected or experienced. The failure to think through the logical leap from speaker to linguist–observer prevents further exploration of a central question: the attribution of meaning and value for *états de langue* in the past which the observer does not witness can only be a matter of conjecture.

Moreover, the divorce between observer and speaker's feeling, with regard to past phases of the language, means that the description of past states may be considered more like the process whereby an observer infers (describes conjecturally) what caused the passage from one state to another. In other words, theoretically and methodologically, it is only the synchrony of the observer's present that is radically different from diachrony.

The centrality assigned to the speaker throws some light on the idea that the study of grammatical and semantic facts belongs to synchrony, while non-grammatical facts belong to diachrony (Riedlinger, Quire IV [Komatsu and Wolf 1997:67). Grammar and meaning live only in the consciousness of speakers. They decay and melt away into mere events if we try and study them from the perspective of the transformations they undergo in time, for which we generally have only the material documentation which survives individuals. There are problems and contradictions in this polarization, due to lingering nineteenth-century syntactic and phonological concepts, but the status of grammatical and non-grammatical facts in relation to the speaker's linguistic feeling and to the role of time in language retains its great interest. And all the more interesting are Saussure's doubts about the possibility of associative and syntagmatic facts having a history, and the implications for the separation of diachrony and synchrony, if indeed they did. The conclusion that synchrony and diachrony are harder to distinguish in the domain of meaning and syntax than in that of phonetics, points up an awkward theoretical problem.

In any case, the distinction mentioned above has an important theoretical corollary, frequently stressed by Coseriu: the notion of 'historical grammar' is a contradiction in terms, because 'no system can straddle a succession of periods' (Riedlinger, Quire IV [Komatsu and Wolf 1997:62). In other words, structural laws of change are unthinkable. Diachrony is the realm of *événements* occurring one after the other in an unstructured way and whose logical links only the speakers' linguistic feeling can provide. By the way, studying different *états de langue* one after the other does not mean that one is moving in the domain of diachrony (Riedlinger, Quire IV [Komatsu and Wolf 1997:48f.). This is a conclusion of major theoretical significance, which has been ignored in many subsequent models of dia-chrony. But Romance linguistics has never forgotten it.

Saussure's thinking also has major consequences for the relationship between the two dimensions, involving the paradox of a close mutual dependency alongside radical independence and irreducibility (Riedlinger, Quire IV [Komatsu and Wolf 1997:36f.). The two domains are incom-mensurable, and any attempt to reconcile them is chimerical and fraught with perennial pitfalls (Constantin, Quire IX [Komatsu and Harris 1993:112]). For example, a phonetic change might be considered a natural event in itself, lying outside speakers' consciousness, yet it becomes a synchronic fact when the resulting phonetic variants are assigned a meaning. But the synchronic fact is not explained by the diachronic one.

The conception summarized hereto goes hand in hand with a profoundly antiteleological outlook (Constantin, Quire IX [Komatsu and Harris 1993:111]):

> It is a mistaken idea we have that the language appears to be a mechanism created with a view to and in accordance with the concepts to be examined; we see how the state was never destined to express the meanings it acquires or to mark them according to a convention governing the terms employed. A fortuitous state occurs and is taken over. Nothing is more important from a philosophical point of view. But the state must be carefully distinguished from what changes it.

The antiteleological position has a significant link with ideas of the concept of law, and the need to distinguish between synchronic and diachronic laws (Constantin, Quire IX [Komatsu and Harris 1993:117f.]):

> In the diachronic domain a law is imperative and dynamic. It abolishes one thing and introduces another. It makes itself felt by its effect. It has a force. A diachronic law expresses an imperative which is carried out whatever the resistance. A synchronic law expresses an existing order. It is a law of the same kind as when one asks: on what plan were trees planted in the garden? This law captures a state of affairs, an arrangement.
> <Not imperative, not dynamic>

Two kinds of general problem emerge, which still deserve our attention today: the role of sound change in diachrony and the concept of the imperative nature of laws. In both cases the conclusions are of wider importance than may at first seem. This is apparent, for example, in the idea that the term 'law' should be applied with much greater care to diachronic than to synchronic facts (see Riedlinger, Quire III [Komatsu and Wolf 1997:48]). And the idea of a non-imperative, non-dynamic synchronic law, that merely describes a state of affairs, is not after all far removed from the concept of synchronic rule found in subsequent models of theoretical linguistics. But there remains a major difference: in these latter developments synchronic rules are *ipso facto* projectable onto diachrony, while for Saussure such an operation could by no means be taken for granted.

It is thus clear why one of the major critical points in diachronic theory is the problem of the postulability of structural laws of language change.

Recent typological and grammaticalization-based models answer in terms of structural cycles (or laws) of transformation, with an evident intellectual debt to the early twentieth-century thought of the Prague School, which stressed the complementarity of permanence and change, the interaction of synchrony and diachrony and the interchangeable nature of diachronic and synchronic laws themselves. Rejecting 'the sterile and fictitious method of the history of isolated facts'[3] (*Thèses* 1929:9), the Prague School had affirmed the need for historical linguistics (and other evolutionary sciences) to move from a conception of facts produced arbitrarily and accidentally, regular as they may be, to a nomogenetic conception of 'concatenation of evolutionary facts according to laws' (*Thèses* 1929:9). Not only synchrony, but also evolution is taken to have structural laws which can explain both phonological and grammatical changes (*Thèses* 1929:8). In this view, linguistic changes are indeed not destructive forces operating by chance and in an unstructured way, but often aim at stabilizing and rebuilding the system (*Thèses* 1929:8). On the other hand, synchronic description cannot entirely dispense with the concept of evolution, for 'even in a sector envisaged synchronically there exists an awareness of the stage which is disappearing, of the present stage, and of the stage which is coming into being'[4] (*Thèses* 1929:8). As in neofunctionalist diachronic models, in this approach there are no longer any insurmountable barriers between the synchronic model and the diachronic model. Moreover, the notion of functional system may be used, in different ways, in both dimensions (*Thèses* 1929:7–8). At the base of this conception is the idea that the foundation of movements in synchrony and diachrony is the speaker understood as a participant and protagonist in the functioning of the language. But this model has its theoretical problems: the actions of speaking individuals in the synchronic function and the diachronic transformations which affect language overall belong to mutually incompatible dimensions: the former are on a small scale, the latter on a large scale (see Herman 1978a; 1990:360).

In sum, even if Saussure's thinking bears the hallmark of an inheritance of opinions common in late nineteenth-century historical linguistics, his discussion of the concept of law, and particularly his rejection of the imperative nature of laws, shows that he has really advanced beyond a positivistic viewpoint which likened linguistic laws to those of physics. Actually, it might be better to say that in recognizing the importance of value/meaning as a guiding epistemological principle for the study of synchrony, Saussure already belongs to an age that has adopted function as the interpretative key in historical enquiry, but that in limiting this principle to synchrony he shies away from the conceptual leap that others were to make shortly after, that of using the concept of function as a tool for understanding how historical change happens. This is a major issue. It makes us face the daunting task of imagining, on the basis of sources which are perforce indirect, a complex of interrelated processes, with the aim of identifying an overarching reason for their development. It is the task of the 'resuscitation' of the past by historians. But at this point the problem is what 'resuscitation' means.

This difficulty is conspicuous in those parts of the *Cours* dealing with the prospective and retrospective viewpoint in diachrony – yet another issue which has retained its interest to this day. The former 'is equivalent, if we could apply it without difficulty, to the complete synthesis of all facts which concern the history, the evolution of language' (Riedlinger, Quire III [Komatsu and Wolf 1997:63a). The latter places the observer at a particular period of time and leads him to ask 'not what the result of a form is, but what forms gave rise to it' (Riedlinger, Quire III [Komatsu and Wolf 1997:64a). This is in effect the reconstructive method. The distinctions echoes that made some years earlier by Meyer-Lübke in his *Einführung in das Studium der romanischen Sprachwissenschaft* (Meyer-Lübke 1901), who distinguished in Romance linguistics a 'horizontal' method (synchronic, in Saussurean terms), from two 'vertical' methods, one from ancient to modern, the other from modern to ancient, and who considered the latter to be 'the real history of linguistics' (see Varvaro 1968:149 and n24).

The prospective approach is ideal, and difficult to apply, largely because 'here the document is no longer the observation of what is more or less present to speakers', but something indirect (Riedlinger, Quire IV [Komatsu and Wolf 1997:63]): 'We would need an infinite mass of photographs of the language, of exact notations from one moment to the next in order thus to move forward following the course of time' (Riedlinger, Quire IV [Komatsu and Wolf 1997:63]). Significantly, in observing that this methodology may be applied to some languages and not others, Romanists are cited as scholars whose field allows the best application of this approach:

> Romance scholars are in the best position imaginable because they have, in the slice of time which concerns them, the point of departure. But even in exceptional conditions, at every moment in an infinity of compartments there will be none the less enormous gaps which will have to be filled by abandoning narration and synthesis so as to give another direction to the investigation, and this investigation will generally fall within the retrospective point of view.
>
> (Riedlinger, Quire IV [Komatsu and Wolf 1997:64])

16

So the retrospective, or comparative, point of view is indispensable (Riedlinger, Quire IV [Komatsu and Wolf 1997:65). In Romance linguistics this conclusion, even at the time of the *Cours*, would not have been subscribed to by everybody (see Varvaro 1968:133–64).

Theoretical thinking on synchrony and diachrony in Romance linguistics has played an appreciable role in clarifying the terms of the early twentieth-century debate, with obvious consequences for the work of the Romanist. As early as the late 1950s Coseriu had rightly pointed out the confusion caused by greater stress being laid either on methodology, or on ontology or definition:

> What is independent of diachrony is synchronic description, not the *real state of* the language, which is always a 'result' of another earlier stage, and is even for Saussure a product of historical events. The problem arises because Saussure talks about description, even if he does not clearly distinguish the 'real' and the state of the language as projected. Thus the Saussurean antinomy when mistakenly transferred to the level of the object is quite simply the difference between description and history, and in this sense no longer has anything Saussurean about it except the terminology, and cannot be suppressed or annulled, because it is a conceptual necessity. (Coseriu 1973; 1981:13)

Of prime importance is the stress laid on the complementary, rather than antithetical, relation of description, history and theory and the fact that 'description and history are mutually exclusive not from the point of view of the object, but *as* operations; that is, they are *distinct operations*' (Coseriu 1973; 1981:18). In this sense, the idea of the non-separability of diachrony and synchrony seems to receive a more lucid formulation than the Prague version: the existence of a diachrony in synchrony and a synchrony in diachrony is a matter of the real state of the *langue*, not the method or the observer's point of view (see Coseriu 1973; 1981: ch. 6).[5]

Equally important is the central position given to the concept of linguistic 'tradition', defined as the 'transmission' of common and current modes of speaking which form the idiomatic inheritance of a language (Coseriu 1973; 1981:31, 34). This concept, profoundly imbued with a sense of history, has numerous implications. Insofar as it refers in turn to the idea of 'traditional knowledge', quite different from abstract universal knowledge (Coseriu 1973; 1981:38–40), it may offer a concrete historical point of contact between the fortuitous and irregular nature of diachrony, inaccessible to speakers' consciousness, and the array of associative relationships which define a language at a particular period and which exist only in the perception of speakers of that period. This traditional knowledge, inherited by speakers initially as an impenetrable linguistic tool to which they give new life, is a key to comprehending why the *I-language* and *E-language* dichotomy is ill-suited to an understanding of historical processes. This model artificially polarizes abstract and more or less universal mechanisms of linguistic knowledge and the textual objectification of languages as external products. But the concept of linguistic tradition also has a crucial theoretical implication for the modelling of change. Change does not concern phenomena taken as mere physical or mechanical facts, but the creation of linguistic traditions, defined as 'the historical objectivization of what has been produced in speech' (Coseriu 1988:149). Therefore 'linguistic change is the historical process by which a language disappears or arises, by which linguistic traditions die out or come into being, and by which often new traditions partially or wholly take the "place" of those dying out in the system of traditions which we call a language' (Coseriu 1988:150). For many Romanists, this viewpoint can hardly be avoided.

There is a final component characteristic of Coseriu's diachronic thinking which strikes a cord with many Romanists: the centrality (alongside traditional knowledge) of speech understood as textual production, in its multiple dimensions as general or historical activity, and as 'knowing how to speak' (Coseriu 1973; 1981:32, 38). It has long been a widely held conviction that studying the processes at work in spoken language at a particular synchronic stage may help linguistic change 'shed its contradictory nature and its alleged mystery' (Coseriu 1973; 1981:42).

3   Some case-studies

3.1   *Old French declension*

A prime showcase for the difference between the diachronic and synchronic perspectives, and the problematic interaction between them, involves a classic topic of Romance linguistics, the genesis of the nominal inflectional systems of old Gallo-Romance. The early Romance case systems show up as anything but homogeneous and regular. They appear to be constructions haphazardly cobbled together from the remains of an old, collapsed building. The continuities seem sometimes to involve phonetic form, sometimes morphological structure. Romance historical linguistics has variously stressed the role played by formal, or by functional, characteristics.

The relevant facts about the Latin case system (see also chapter 4: §3.1) are recapitulated here as they regard masculine and feminine nouns:

	First declension (F)		Second declension (M)	
	Singular	Plural	Singular	Plural
Nominative	ROSA 'rose'	ROSAE	MURUS 'wall'	MURI
Accusative	ROSAM	ROSĀS	MURUM	MURŌS
Genitive	ROSAE	ROSĀRUM	MURI	MURŌRUM
Dative	ROSAE	ROSIS	MURŌ	MURIS
Ablative	ROSĀ	ROSIS	MURŌ	MURIS

			Third declension	
	Singular	Plural	Singular	Plural
Nominative	CANIS 'dog'	CANĒS	HOMO 'man'	HOMINĒS
Accusative	CANEM	CANĒS	HOMINEM	HOMINĒS
Genitive	CANIS	CANUM	HOMINIS	HOMINUM
Dative	CANI	CANIBUS	HOMINI	HOMINIBUS
Ablative	CANE	CANIBUS	HOMINE	HOMINIBUS

Certain facts about this system are very salient in discussions of the evolution of the Romance case system, notably aspects of the distribution of the inflectional ending -s and the nature of the nominative and accusative forms:

- -s characterizes all accusative plurals;
- -s characterizes both nominative plural and accusative plural in the third declension;
- -s also characterizes nominative singular in second (and many third) declension nouns;
- many third declension nouns show formal distinctions between nominative singular and the rest of the paradigm. Notably, fewer syllables in nominative singular than elsewhere ('imparisyllabicity'), and sometimes differences of stress (e.g., NOM.SG IMPERÁTOR 'ruler' vs. IMPERATÓR- everywhere else);

- first declension nouns are predominantly feminine; second declension nouns predominantly masculine. The third declension contains both masculine and feminine nouns, without formal distinction of gender;
- -M, the marker of accusative singular, was early subject to deletion, leading, for example, to formal identity between the nominative singular and accusative singular in the first declension.

Over the final decades of the nineteenth century, and the beginning of the twentieth, the collapse of Latin declension and the transition to the nominal inflectional systems of Romance was discussed in detail by the major figures of Romance historical linguistics, who were aware, sometimes acutely, of the implications for linguistic theory. Aspects of this debate remain relevant to this day for our understanding of the relation between syntactico-semantic factors and formal (i.e., phonetic and morphological) factors in the relevant diachronic developments, and also have considerable implications for the thesis that the change brought about by the most widespread process of morphosyntactic change involved generalization of the accusative case form. Indeed, this issue was the arena for two opposing theories on the principles of linguistic change.

The first theory, asserted and defended by Diez and Meyer-Lübke, could be labelled 'hypostatization of form and predominance of mental processes'. In it, systemic changes are examined by taking the forms and functions of the CLat. case system as the terms of comparison, and focusing on any functional deviations with respect to each particular form. This approach was adopted towards both late Latin and Romance forms. The following are characteristic of this approach:

- Form is an absolute parameter, in terms of which comparability under change can be assured.[6]
- Mental processes are assumed to be a more characteristic aspect of change than are substantive phonetic changes associated with production.
- The perspective is 'teleological', in that various forces are assumed to be in play leading towards the emergence of a single universal case, the accusative. Teleologism often goes hand in hand with functionalist approaches, but in the present instance it seems rather to be associated with the sharp separation between form and function.
- Change is studied through the comparison of successive synchronic stages in each of which the system appears stable and fully articulated.

The second theory, maintained variously by D'Ovidio and Schuchardt, could be called the 'theory of transitional forms and functions'. The changes between Latin and Romance are considered as processes in which form and function maintain a certain degree of stability during the transformation, and form is taken as the 'external' locus (or symptom) of change.

Form and function are closely bound together, yet:

- In the processes of change, phonetics and morphological form are accordingly considered more influential than – or at any rate preconditions for – mental representation.
- There is wariness about the possible teleological implications of diachronic processes.
- The overall model focuses on the examination of individual facts, or the specific (accidental) characteristics of the transitional forms which gradually dismantle the Latin edifice.

The second theory in no way implies that the entire process is fortuitous. To follow the diachronic dismantling of a system requires an understanding of the incidence of certain forms as relics, each with its own *raison d'être*, which, like the remains of an older edifice, will form a new one, where the individual parts still bear the traces of their past, yet have been, or are being, reassembled into a new construction. The 'reasons' are inextricably bound up with the nature of the historical processes. In history nothing is created and nothing destroyed. Cataclysmic changes excepted (but not always, even then), innovation always passes through the remodelling of pre-existing structures: the material and the structures persist, albeit often in altered form, but their functions are redefined.

These principles are only apparently reflected in the first theory, which considers the persistence of forms from an absolute, rather than relative, stance and interprets functions exclusively in semantic terms. The two sides of the sign, the static signifier and the dynamic signified, are separated by diachrony. The accusative form is seen as having 'usurped' the functions of the other case-forms. But such an approach is profoundly anti-historical, in that entities are still postulated which exist only relationally (inasmuch as they are defined in relation to one another), when they no longer survive. Here all the unresolved contradictions of a structural diachrony are plain.

Characteristic of these problems are the kinds of methodological and theoretical positions assumed in a debate which involved many front-ranking Romanists (such as Schuchardt, Ascoli, Mussafia, Tobler, Meyer-Lübke), especially with regard to D'Ovidio's (1873) thesis on the origin of Latin nominal inflection. D'Ovidio had rejected Diez's thesis that the accusative was the basic form underlying the OFr. and OPrv. object case, as well as the single case form of Italian and Spanish. D'Ovidio had asked whether the two-case stage had occurred not just in French and Provençal, but also in Spanish and Italian.[7] His fundamental thesis, based on reflection on Italian, was that the simplification of Latin declension had been the product of a gradual reciprocal levelling of all the cases. A valuable article by Schuchardt gives a positive analysis of D'Ovidio's argument and all its implications, surveying each of the various positions in the ongoing debate at that time, and drawing a wide-ranging and sharply observed picture of the process by which the Latin declensional system disintegrated, and of the various stages in the development of the Romance inflectional system. His summary of D'Ovidio's thesis contains numerous pithy observations of considerable theoretical and methodological weight. Schuchardt observes (1874:167f.) that, in D'Ovidio's view, Diez was guilty of setting unadulterated Latin side by side with the Romance paradigm and seeking the most direct link between them, rather than patiently tracing the gradual dismantling of the Latin system. Schuchardt acknowledges that D'Ovidio's demonstration is seductively clear. Italian *campo* 'field' may derive from the nominative CAMPUS, accusative CAMPUM or dative–ablative CAMPO (but not from genitive CAMPI); *amore* 'love' only from accusative AMOREM, dative AMORI or ablative AMORE (but not from nominative ÁMOR or genitive AMORIS); *corpo* 'body' only from the nominative or accusative (both CORPUS),[8] but not from genitive CORPORIS, dative CORPORI or ablative CORPORE. So far as all three Italian forms have a common origin, they can only come from the accusative. Various sound changes – loss of Latin final -M, postulated loss of -S, merger of long ō with short ŭ – would have led to CAMPUM and CORPUS becoming *campo* and *corpo*. But in this case, D'Ovidio observes, *campo* can also come from CAMPUS: so is it really right to say that the accusative form *campo* usurped (replaced) both the nominative and the dative–ablative forms, which were identical in form (*campo*) to the accusative?

Schuchardt further synthesizes two important principles: that in change there are no mysterious forces at work inexorably leading towards definite results and that, in general, mental (functional?) processes are subordinate to physiological (phonetic) processes. He asks (1874:168) where the impulse to replace Latin cases with just one or two forms might come from, and suggests that it is rash to assume that such a mysterious linguistic impulse is really at work, for mental processes are subordinate to physiological ones. D'Ovidio is right in saying that there is always a mental process at work in morphological transformations, but (Schuchardt proposes) the 'tracks' along which the mind moves are laid down by phonetic transformations.

At this point we need to summarize the division into declensional classes common to many grammars, and reflecting the application of different criteria: gender, morphological structure (A, B, C, E, F, below) and declensional patterns (G, H, below). Yet the various accounts are noticeably heterogeneous, using these criteria in different ways, giving greater weight to synchronic and analogical aspects (such as classification on the basis of the morphological characteristics of word structure), or stressing a diachronic approach (by considering the original membership of a noun in a particular Latin declensional class). Some accounts interweave the various criteria and perspectives. In many, especially of the synchronic–structural type, gender acquires special importance not only descriptively, but also as a tool for explaining change on the basis of analogy. Actually, the role of gender evolved gradually and in a by no means linear fashion. There is a considerable diachronic continuity. The Latin first and second declensions, the lexemes which belonged to them and their respective inflectional patterns survived in an etymologically regular way in OFrench. They were already clearly linked with gender in Latin (the first declension was largely feminine, the second largely masculine), and therefore they could have exercised analogical attraction not only on Latin nouns belonging to other declensions, but also on French third declension F and M nouns. But the historical reality may have been much more complex. In any case, we see here another aspect of the clash between diachronic (see Paris 1872) and synchronic (see Meyer-Lübke 1894:§21–24) perspectives. This clash also brings out the important issue – often overlooked – of the mismatch between Latin and Romance cases: for example, it is inappropriate to label the 'subject' 'nominative', and 'subject' is itself an unsatisfactory label since the case-form in question encodes more than just the subject function.

Here are the basic facts about OFrench declension classes.

Class A. Feminine. Type *fille* 'daughter' (‹ FILIA/FILIA(M))

SG *fille*	PL *filles*

This class contains the continuants of the Latin first declension largely composed of feminines.

Class B. Feminine. Types *fin* 'end' (‹ FINIS/FINE(M)), *medre* 'mother' (‹ MATER/MATRE(M)), *cité* 'city' (‹ CIVITAS/CIVITATE(M))

SG *fin(s), medre*	PL *fins, medres*

This class contains the continuants (largely feminine) of the Latin third declension, comprising both originally parisyllabic and originally imparisyllabic forms. However, the latter had already been remodelled into a parisyllabic pattern in late Latin, through generalization of the oblique stem (such as *maison* 'house', from MANSIO/MANSIONE(M), *cité* 'city' from CIVITAS/CIVITATE(M), etc.). Nouns of this class do not consistently conform to the declensional pattern.

Class C. Feminine. Type *nonne/nonnain* 'nun', *suer/seror* 'sister' (‹ SOROR/SORORE(M))

SG	PL
S *nonne, suer*	S *nonnains, serors* (*suers*)
OBL *nonnain, seror* (*suer*)	OBL *nonnains, serors*

This class also comprises a number of proper names. It lumps together different patterns of case alternation (the Germanic type *-e/-ain* against the Latin type *-OR/-ORIS*). And there are some irregularities in the alternation between the subject stem and the oblique stem.

Class D. Masculine. Type *murs* 'wall' (‹ MURUS/MURU(M))

SG	PL
S *murs*	S *mur*
OBL *mur*	OBL *murs*

This class is generally characterized by the fact that its members have a rather regular and specific inflectional pattern for case. By synchronic and structural criteria this class might be described as that of masculine parisyllabics whose stem ends in a consonant, but it is in fact often defined by diachronic criteria: it comprises continuants of the Latin second declension, or of lexemes assimilated into that declension. The potential for clash between diachronic and the other criteria is clear from some accounts which include in this class continuants of the Latin third declension (parisyllables such as reflexes of CANIS, PANIS, or imparisyllables which have become parisyllables, such as the reflex of LEO/LEONE(M); see Brunot 1966, I:181). Clearly in this case the criterion for inclusion in class D is the fact that these nouns conform to the declensional pattern of the type *mur*, characterized not only by a particular structure but also by relative regularity. It must also be stressed that the overall inflectional structure of this class is an entirely etymologically regular development from Latin.

Class E. Masculine. Type *pedre* 'father' (‹ PATER/PATRE(M))

SG	PL
S *pedre(s)*	S *pedre*
OBL *pedre*	OBL *pedres*

This class can be defined, on structural criteria, as parisyllabic masculines whose stem generally ends in a vowel. Diachronically, these are continuants of Latin third declension parisyllabics, plus some continuants of nouns in -ER from the second declension and some from third declension imparisyllabics in -OR, which had developed as parisyllabics (e.g., *arbre* 'tree', from ARBOR/ARBORE(M)). Nouns of this class conform to the declensional pattern in an inconsistent fashion. Moreover, the plural subject case form is clearly not an etymologically regular development from Latin. To justify this pattern appeal has been made to analogical attraction by the subject case form of the class D masculine declension.

Class F. Masculine. Types *cons/conte* 'count' (‹ COMES/COMITE(M)), *ledre/ladron* 'thief' (‹ LATRO/LATRONE(M)), *enfes/enfant* 'child' (‹ INFANS/INFANTE(M))

SG	PL
S *cons ledre(s) enfes*	S *comte ladron enfant*
OBL *comte ladron enfant*	OBL *comtes ladrons enfanz*

This class comprises masculine nouns which have conserved the Latin alternation between parisyllabic and imparisyllabic stems, the former being specialized as the subject case form and the latter as the oblique. Nouns of this class may also show stress variation: invariant (e.g., *cóns/cómte*) vs. variant (e.g., *lédre/ladrón*). Where Latin stem alternants are thus preserved, structural and diachronic description coincide. But the picture is complicated by the fact that an originally second declension noun such as *prestare* (‹ PRESBYTER), and nouns derived from Germanic bases in -o, -óne [...] are included here. And the inflectional pattern is only partly etymological. Beside the lack of correspondence between the plural subject case-form and the Latin nominative forms (where once again analogical attraction by the masculine class D has been invoked), it needs to be stressed that many lexemes are notably erratic in their adoption of zero or -*s* as the singular subject case inflection.

Class G. Feminine indeclinables. Type *pais* 'peace', *voiz* 'voice'
Class H. Masculine indeclinables. Type *nes* 'nose', *sens* 'sense'

The unsystematic nature of OFrench declension is clear from many irregularities, involving various kinds of theoretical issues, which can be labelled as structural irregularities (lack of structural isomorphism between the various nominal classes) and empirical irregularities (the numerous cases of failure to conform to the paradigms, in the manuscripts which preserve the texts). Halfway between these are 'lexical singularities', where some lexemes constitute obvious exceptions within a paradigm which is otherwise clearly characterizable. For example, the MSG *fils* 'son' (< FILIUS), invariant for case and revealing lexicalization of the originally second declension nominative -*s*. These outcomes demonstrate that even continuants of the Latin second declension, which at every stage of OFrench constitute the most unwaveringly regular class of masculine nouns, do not form a unitary bloc.

Such anomalies are of considerable theoretical interest in that they allow us to induce more general developmental principles, with regard to semantic factors such as [+animate] and [+human]. But the role of such factors can hardly have been regular either. As Pope (1934:§805) notes, in the paradigm of parisyllabic nouns the appearance of -*s* and -*z* 'came to be regarded as the characteristic flexion of the Nom. Sing. Masc.', but this affected names of things somewhat earlier than proper names. Even more irregular is the development of proper names, making it difficult to invoke the influence of the Animacy hierarchy (Schøsler 2001b:174, 102).

There is also considerable case variation according to syntactic context. As Woledge *et al.* (1967) have shown for the *Chanson de Roland*, some syntactic structures, particularly those in apposition or lacking an explicit predicate, tend to favour the oblique case form over the subject form (see also Moignet 1966:346–49). Yet, in the same syntactic contexts, some noun classes (imparisyllabics) tend to stay closer to the regular use of case forms than others, while parisyllabics like *reis* 'king', and even more masculines in -*e*, and feminines, are less sensitive to the effects of syntactic context. Feminines are virtually indeclinable. These are idiosyncratic lexical developments, reflecting complex formal and semantic factors, at times collaborative, at times antagonistic (see Woledge *et al.* 1969). There is also evidence that metrical considerations could prevail over syntactic ones, case forms of a given noun being used (as already seen in the *Chanson de Roland*) indifferently, according to requirements of assonance and metre (Woledge *et al.* 1967:166f.; Vising 1882:6 for Anglo-Norman). Geographical differentiation is also important.[9] Indeed, Stanovaïa (1993) attributes the great variability of OFrench declension not to a 'system', but to remnants of a destroyed declensional system, preserved in some *scriptae*, and rearranged in others.[10]

Overall, we can hardly postulate a 'system'.[11] The hybrid nature of the case markers also shows that we are dealing not with a coherent system, but with relics of an older array of forms which have been extended and remodelled in different ways according to place and textual traditions. The inflectional system seems to have atrophied in the ending -*s*, which is associated with the singular subject function (originally mainly masculine, but later spreading into third declension feminines), or an oblique plural function, or simply plural. But in addition to case-endings there is also – diachronically notably persistent – allomorphy of the root, originating in Latin imparisyllabic masculine third declension animates.[12]

In all, case marking is better preserved in the singular than the plural (see Schøsler 2001b:170); and there is syncretism between the subject singular and oblique plural case forms in -*s*. Syncretism, like allomorphy, is inherited from Latin, but as fragments which are reorganized according to new patterns of paradigmatic relations. Comparison of the Latin and OFrench paradigms may show the extent of what has changed, but scarcely constitutes an explanation. Rather, we may perhaps say that the condition mentioned above resulted from and abetted greater unpredictability and instability. And the lack of alternation between subject and oblique case forms derived from the first declension, both in the singular and the plural (showing the characteristic western Romance opposition between zero in the singular and -s in the plural) constitutes a gap in the system.

The role of analogy in the relation between diachrony and synchrony is crucial and problematic. Analogy is really a synchronic factor whose diachronic use may clash with other mechanisms of transformation, and whose explanatory force remains very uncertain. Nor is it clear in what relation it stands to the various chronological sequences of events or exactly what its role was in the various diachronic stages under examination.

All scholars agree on the analogical nature of the neutralization of case distinctions in continuants of the Latin first declension, based on loss of singular -M and loss of case distinctions in the singular,[13] but not on the origins of plural -*s*. Some trace Gallo-Romance -*s* back to the Latin accusative plural -AS,[14] while others believe that this inflection cannot be connected with any Latin case form (see Schuchardt 1874:163).

The continuants of the Latin second declension with nominative -*s* are, on the whole, a rather regular and consistent locus of conservation of morphological and phonetic structure. Thus:

S SG -*s*	PL -Ø
OBL SG -Ø	PL -*s*

The major diachronic problem is the development of the Latin third declension (see Paris 1872:110). Diachronically, the main division is, in the singular, between nouns of imparisyllabic and parisyllabic origin. The former show different forms for subject and oblique singular (e.g., *cons/comte, hom/home*); the latter (e.g., the continuants of FRATER, PATER) lack case allomorphy, and some have invoked analogy and paradigmatic levelling to account for the remodelling of their inflectional pattern on class D (singular subject *murs* / oblique *mur*), giving rise to an alternation between subject *li peres, li freres* and oblique *le pere, le frere*.[15] Such levelling appears variably in Anglo-Norman texts.[16] Yet later -*s* was allegedly added even to imparisyllabic nouns which already displayed allomorphy for case (e.g., *homs, empereres, sires*; see Paris 1872:111f.). For some this addition of -*s* never took root in the French introduced into England (thus Paris 1872:111f.), but the available evidence shows a more problematic situation. In the Cambridge Psalter -*s* is usually lacking in the subject case form of imparisyllabic nouns, although there are a few counterexamples, especially *sires* 'sire'. See (Brekke 1884:8) for the *Voyage Saint Brandan*.

Other scholars hold that -*s* originally appears in the singular only in words where it is etymologically justified, its extension being a rather late phenomenon fundamentally due to analogical adjustments, and more characteristic of Anglo-Norman and western French texts, so that careful poets like Wace and Chrestien only knew forms without -*s*[17] – a view contradicted by Woledge's findings (1979:18f.) from the manuscript tradition of Chrestien de Troyes.

Contrary to what one would predict from Latin, from the very earliest Gallo-Romance documents we find no -*s* in the subject plural form. This does not necessarily mean that third declension subject plural -*s* had already been lost in the lower sociolinguistic registers of late Latin.[18] We could, again, be dealing with attraction by the Romance paradigm comprising nouns derived from the Latin second declension.[19] Clearly these are speculations which stress synchronic analogical mechanisms: Schuchardt

(1874:161, n1) saw that this could not be taken for granted. After all, in Merovingian documents both the nominative and accusative plural forms of the third declension are well preserved, and indeed the nominative has about a 10 percent higher rate of conservation than the accusative.[20] Problematic as the testimony of such documents may be, it is by no means proven that nominative plural third declension -*s* was lost in late Latin.

Even more problematic is the development of Latin third declension feminine nouns (OFrench class B) conserving Latin root-final consonants (*dolor(s)*, *genz/gent, flor(s), maison(s), vertet/vertez, defension(s)*). Here too we find marked inflectional variability according to region, period and text. As for second and third declension masculines (classes E and F), Chrestien de Troyes has a fairly regular two-case system: in the singular (with a few idiosyncratic exceptions) we have -*s* in the subject form and no -*s* in the oblique; in the plural, like First declension feminines (class A), -*s* appears in subject and oblique forms alike. The long-standing discussion as to whether this reflects an ancient state of affairs[21] has been complicated by competing etymological and analogical arguments, obscuring the fact that between Classical Latin and Romance multiple transformations – far from regular either in time or space – must have occurred.

Chrestien shows conspicuous changes with respect to Classical Latin. Firstly, levelling of Latin imparisyllabic stems on stems with a greater number of syllables, i.e., remodelling of the nominative stem on the basis of the oblique stem. So Latin allomorphy of the type

NOM FLO-S	GEN/DAT/ACC/ABL FLOR-
NOM MANSIO	GEN/DAT/ACC/ABL MANSION-
NOM UIRTU-S	GEN/DAT/ACC/ABL UIRTUT-

gives way to the stems FLOR-, MANSION-, UIRTUT-, whence nominatives FLOR(E), MANSION(E), UIRTUT(E), alongside oblique forms with the same stem. The documentation suggests that this phenomenon must already have been characteristic of late, and especially Merovingian, Latin.

The second change concerns non-etymological subject singular forms in -*s* and built on the oblique root (e.g., *flor, vertez* vs. Lat. FLOR, UÉRITAS). But is this an analogical development that arose during the twelfth century and established itself in Chrestien and others, or a survivor of late Latin popular forms? The picture has been further complicated by the discussion of the problem in the context of investigating the dissolution of the two-case system. In fact the earlier phases need to be examined on their own terms.

The direction of the diachronic process doses not emerge clearly from an examination of the documentation, highly variable both geographically and textually. But, despite appreciable differences both in and between texts, some Anglo-Norman texts actually do show a notable incidence of -*s*. The Oxford Psalter, and the Cambridge Psalter (mid twelfth century) have plenty of forms in -*s*, with some morphological distinctions: thus in the Cambridge Psalter subject -*s* occurs in 40 percent of derivatives of the Latin type -AS/-ATIS, and in nearly 80 percent of derivatives of the type -O/-ONIS. Much lower percentages are found in all other types (see Fichte 1879:81). Subject -*s* is frequent in later Anglo-Norman texts (see Vising 1882:96–98; Brekke 1884:21).

This textual and geographical distribution makes Meyer-Lübke's (1894:§ 21) and others'[22] division between an Anglo-Norman and a French and Provençal dialect area look implausible. The latter area, from antiquity, allegedly distinguished subject *flors* from oblique *flor*, held to conserve a vulgar Latin situation,[23] while Anglo-Norman deviated from it by keeping -*s*. This resurrects the thesis that Galloromania should be divided into areas that preserve the late Latin situation and those that rapidly broke away from it. The thesis (see Vising 1882:12f.; Schøsler 1984:171–73), that this situation is due to imperfect learning of French in England, has some sociolinguistic justification but should not be followed uncritically as an explanation of inflectional vacillations in the earliest Anglo-Norman texts.

The real interest of such vacillations is that they allow us to glimpse differences in the reorganization of the 'ruins' of an earlier inflectional system so that perhaps we should make a critical reappraisal both of the 'continuity' thesis (FSG.OBL -*s* in *fins* and *maisons* etc. goes back directly to late Latin types with remodelled subject -*s*)[24] and of the thesis which ascribes it to analogical innovation in OFrench Here, differing attitudes of the writers towards existing linguistic traditions might be decisive. That the Oxford and Cambridge psalters have many class B feminine forms with singular subject in -*s* might be related to their Latinizing orientation (see Trotter 2007). Similar considerations might hold for the regular presence of -*s* in Chrestien. Such orientations, characteristic of particular *scriptoria* or cultural environments, should not immediately be assigned to a particular area, let alone to a line of diachronic development.

Analogy has been extensively invoked. Both Paris and Meyer-Lübke concur that the singular subject case forms without -*s* in the second declension and third declension feminine, as found in the earliest Anglo-Norman texts and continental texts after Chrestien de Troyes, are due to the influence of the OFrench paradigm of first declension feminines (class A),[25] and both postulate analogical developments to justify forms in etymological or non-etymological -*s*.

Paris's model invokes analogical mechanisms in which gender is explicitly specified as a powerful attracting force. Analogy, which yielded a distinct plural subject case form in OFr. nouns of classes E and F, to make them like the plural of class D, also caused the disappearance of the singular subject case form of feminines of class B, bringing them in line with class A feminines, so that all feminine words declined in the same way, or rather that feminine declension consisted of no more than a gender distinction (see Paris 1872:114). This is strongly teleological, and it is not clear at what diachronic (or diastratic?) point such mechanisms might have operated. Latin or Romance? Moreover, Paris (1872:114) assumes that the spread of -*s* into OFr. feminine singular nouns of class B must have occurred late, according to an analogical influence exercised by masculine singulars in -*s* on feminine nouns, but this seems to involve a quite implausible inversion of the priority accorded to gender in the mechanism of the analogy (see Schuchardt 1874:161, n).

Yet the analogical model might have an interesting diachronic basis in the plural. Some have held (e.g., Paris 1872), that identity between feminine plural subject and oblique case forms (in -*s*) faithfully conserves the Latin morphological structures, while the masculines had deviated from their Latin antecedents. This view may have its attractions, but the differential role attributed to analogy in respect of gender seems excessive. On the other hand, the model itself implies that if 'attractors' were at work, these cannot have been purely semantic, but also formal (morphological).

To conclude, the limits to the analogical hypotheses seem to lie in the fact that they postulate abstract synchronic states which are difficult to determine historically, and cannot easily be reconciled with the actual complexity of the data. For example, on the analogical account, the spread of -*s* to feminine singular subjects with root-final consonants was due to the influence of the masculine singular subject form in -*s*. But we have seen that the ancient core of such forms comprised continuants of the Latin second declension, while continuants of the third declension underwent considerable vacillation in acquiring -*s*. So the hypothesis of simultaneous and identical analogical attraction on feminines and masculines alike seems even less satisfactory than a chain of analogies beginning with masculines and then affecting feminines. In any case, significant traces of forms in -*s*, for both masculines and third declension feminines, are already to be found in Anglo-Norman texts. Analogical explanations seem inadequate to account for the diachronic process.

The role of syntactic factors in these complex developments is equally controversial. For Schuchardt (1874:161), subject and oblique case forms were kept sharply distinct, in the respective functions of subject and object/complement, in the earliest French texts. Schuchardt (1874:162) also believed that since the oblique case form was gaining ground from the nominative in early medieval Latin documents, we have genitive, accusative and ablative case forms in place of the nominative. But it is hard to see that syntactic factors, let alone functional ones, such as differentiation of subject and object, had been at work here, for one would expect to see a much more regular paradigmatic distribution of case allomorphs. In fact, the two-term opposition is partial and asymmetrical. No such opposition had existed in feminine singular nouns derived from the Latin first declension since very early times (see Schuchardt 1874:163; Schøsler 1984; van Reenen and Schøsler 1988). There have also been considerable oscillations in nouns from the Latin third declension, both parisyllabic and imparisyllabic. In the plural, the two-way opposition is all but extinct except in forms derived from the second and third declensions (see Schøsler 2001b:170). But whatever the role of syntactic factors (see Moignet 1966; Woledge *et al.* 1967–69), they cannot have been the 'engines' of the construction of the precarious OFrench system: conservation of phonological structures and the attractive force of morphological patterns were also at work.

3.2   *The role of syntactic factors in the collapse of Latin declension*

The role of syntactic factors in determining other types of linguistic change is one of the most complex and controversial questions in diachronic linguistics. Once again, early twentieth-century thinking has implications which have still to be fully taken on board. Indeed, Saussure actually wonders whether syntagms and psychological associations, typically assigned to synchrony, do not also have their own history, and observes:

> As soon as we get outside of pure phonetics it is in fact much more difficult to draw the limit or to state a radical opposition. This is the most difficult part of the general division, but I cannot insist on it without getting into delicate considerations. However, in an infinity of cases we will see that facts we think are grammatical reduce to phonetic facts.
>
> (Riedlinger, Quire IV [Komatsu and Wolf 1997:67])

The fate of Latin declension is Saussure's main example. The thesis that the complex transformation of Latin declension in Romance can be reduced to a simplification due to confusion of final segments was as controversial then as today. For Saussure, this is hard to prove but not wholly implausible. He holds that one has at least to acknowledge an ordered sequence of two facts: the phonetic and diachronic confusion of final segments, and the introduction of a grammatical – hence synchronic – system (Riedlinger, Quire V [Komatsu and Wolf 1997:68]).[26] This model is consistent with the more general theory of the relation between synchrony and diachrony. Yet Saussure also seems to be trying, without success, to find a way out of a problem which he sees very clearly. If, as is the case, we can talk of a 'history of declension' (and more generally of the history of syntagmatic groups), we also have to recognize that it has an uneven hybrid quality, including 'a multitude of isolated facts some of which will be clearly phonetic and which will join others which have a different character' (Riedlinger, Quire V [Komatsu and Wolf 1997:68]). Phonetics intrudes at every turn, inevitably, yet there is a 'residue', 'which seems to justify a grammatical history' (Riedlinger, Quire V [Komatsu and Wolf 1997:69]). This contradiction cannot be resolved:

> Everything that is grammatical has to be referred to a state, and there is a contradiction in saying <that> a grammatical fact has a history in time. *The question of what to think of the evolutive view for things which are not purely phonetic is not clear; we will not find this to be a simple matter, and phonetics will have some role to play in it*
>
> (Riedlinger, Quire V [Komatsu and Wolf 1997:68f.], my italics)

This pithy conclusion might be shared by many Romanists, both of the old school and products of modern linguistic training.[27]

The transformation of Latin declension has long proved a rich and privileged testing ground for hypotheses about the relation between syntactic and phonetic factors in language change. A fine example is a work by Herman on structures apparently having accusatives instead of nominatives (see also the discussion of the extended accusative in Ledgeway, this volume, chapter 8, §6.2.2.1), in contexts where the relevant NPs are not governed by the verb, in which he discusses their implications in respect of the phonetic conditions governing vacillation in noun inflection. At issue are sequences of imprecations from the *Tabulae Defixionum* of Hadrumetum (short inscriptions containing curses) in which an optative mood predicate is expressed by the present subjunctive of intransitive (or intransitively used) verbs. Such predicates are preceded by proper names in -U (second declension) and -E (third declension). The second declension forms suggest accusatives,[28] but this is not uncontroversial.

As Herman himself recognizes, it is unclear whether these structures are subjects or accusatives of enumeration (a type of accusative used in lists of objects, particularly in agricultural or medical treatises). His conclusion that in the *Tabulae Defixionum* the accusative nominals are in an extra-syntactic position seems quite convincing. This position, like the enumerative structures, seem to have been the locus of functional alternation between nominative and accusative – for the late second century in the intensively Romanized areas of Africa. Structurally, this interchangeability cannot have applied to the traditional functions of the accusative or other oblique cases. Herman (1987:102) says that the alternations -US/Ø occurred with relatively high frequency only with nominative singular -US. Thus, with all due epigraphic caution, Herman states that rather than being an orthographical reflection of phonetic changes in the spoken language, this phenomenon corresponds to a more deeply rooted and complex morpho-syntactic conditioning. What is being suggested is that the variability in the occurrence of -S really reflected a functional perturbation in the use of case forms in -S, primarily in the nominative.

But what is the synchronic status of the execration tablets of Hadrumetum, within the wider diachronic development? At that time (late second to early third century) was -S-variation an African peculiarity, or is this impression a mere fluke due to the distribution of the texts that happen to have survived? And may we really assume that the rarer examples of -U for *-us* in 'popular' inscriptions of the imperial epoch, in Africa, Italy and elsewhere, are also nominative–accusatives with mobile -s? Herman says that we can but speculate. Given that in Africa length oppositions in vowels may have been lost earlier than in the rest of the Empire, and that this happened especially in unstressed (and particularly final) syllables, Herman speculates, with due caution, that complete homophony between SERVU(M) and SERVŌ, FILIA(M) and FILIĀ may have been relatively early in Africa.

Herman appears to give credence to the theory that the accusative became extended as the general case form, at least in the singular (Herman 1987:106). This allegedly began with the interchangeability of nominative and accusative, and gained momentum from the phonetic perturbations mentioned above, leading to homophony between the accusative and other case forms. The growing frequency in typically 'unmarked' contexts, such as detached, extra-sentential structures, then further facilitated the equivalence with the nominative (Herman 1987:106).

Herman's account fully displays the complexity of marrying a phonetic–phonological conception of change to a syntactic one, and more generally of reconciling historical and descriptive–synchronic models. He seems to have recourse to the theory of the accusative as universal case form, while giving chronological (and phenomenological?) and logical priority to phonetic and phonological aspects, arguing that since in the inscriptions most occurrences of nominatives are in syntactically independent positions, the -U of the accusative is there competing with and substituting the nominative form (Herman 1987:106). The Hadrumetum tablets are merely unusually clear and rich examples of a morphosyntactic vacillation which generally, a little later and perhaps less often, would also emerge elsewhere.

Whether forms resulting from phonetic erosion of classical case structures can be considered 'accusative' is doubtful. Recall D'Ovidio's and Schuchardt's criticisms of using classical forms as an absolute reference point for fully formed Romance forms, without interpreting the intermediate remnants of older forms according to different criteria, those of the processes of change. The fact that forms in mobile -s, typical of second declension nouns, appear in the same texts alongside third declension imparisyllabics in -E, whose case-value is even less certain, suggests that none of these forms can any longer be described in terms of 'nominative', 'accusative', etc.

At the end of his study, Herman asks a fundamental question: Is the morphosyntactic alternation -US/-U wholly unrelated to the later, phonetic, disappearance of all instances of final -s in the East and in most Italo-Romance dialects? Did the loss by final -s of its morphosyntactic function in nominal morphology contribute to the loss of -s elsewhere in the grammar? Herman admits he does not know, but could anybody ever really know? He has at least given us a way of framing the basic problem: What is the relation between phonetic and syntactic factors in the disappearance of Latin declension? We will never know if the supporters of the 'extended accusative' theory were right or whether some other theory is: for diachronic research deals perforce in hypotheses rather than certainties, thereby placing a limit on the observer's capacity to understand the historical processes. Once again we come up against the full force of the epistemological divide between synchrony, representable in terms of structure, and diachrony, where structure can be represented only in an uncertain and tentative way.

3.3   The prepositional object

The Romance prepositional object offers a further example of the need to distinguish the synchronic perspective associated with typology from the event-oriented perspective of diachrony. It has typological counterparts in numerous unrelated languages, leading some to establish actual patterns of formal correspondence across languages (see Bossong 1991; Nocentini

1992). The idea of a link between differential subject and object marking and syntactic type has been reinforced through typological approaches of this kind, but this may not help us much in our search for a diachronic 'explanation'. The semantic properties of the modern synchronic situation have simply been projected onto the past, both descriptively and in terms of explanation, often without asking whether the modern semantic properties have any real relevance to the diachronic explanation.

The early Romance situation must have been appreciably different from today. Fourteenth-century Sicilian and Neapolitan are illuminating in this respect (see Sornicola 1997). The object NP is by no means regularly [+human], [–referential]. If we seek a 'regular' occurrence of the semantic parameters found today, the medieval texts offer a confused and chaotic picture. But two sets of properties do stand out clearly: the lexical properties of the verb and the properties of the NP. And they seem to have not a semantic but a morphosyntactic basis. The verb, at some stage in the history of Latin, is one that took a dative complement (or the rival type AD + accusative) as an alternative to the accusative. The time-span ranges from archaic Latin to Christian Latin writers, and the Christian writers seem to play a decisive role in consolidating and generalizing the dative (or AD + accusative) complementation of numerous verbs. But there are also various cases of genuine 'karstification',[29] where the dative construction is documented for some verb in archaic Latin, yet is not attested in Classical Latin, only to reappear in Christian writers. And there is often an uninterrupted continuity with the relevant verb in old Tuscan texts, where it takes *a*; less frequently the *a* construction appears in Tuscan documents without any detectable Latin precursor. In Sornicola (1997) I made a lexical examination of these verbs, their Latin antecedents and their OTsc. counterparts. These are verbs such as *aiutare* 'help', *ascoltare* 'listen', *audire* 'hear', *clamare* 'call', *contraddire* 'contradict' and *confortare* 'encourage, console'.

Many such verbs take *a* not just in Italy but in other Romance languages. Even French, traditionally considered to lie outside the area of the prepositional object, shows uninterrupted series of verbs which may take *à* before a direct object: *prier* 'pray', *supplier* 'beseech', *requérir* 'request' and *aider* 'help' (see Lüdi 1978; 1981). These are the same lexical types as have shown the dative constructions in southern Italy since the earliest times.

The object NPs in southern Italy reveal the following crucial properties:

(1)   whenever it is a personal pronoun it is *always* preceded by a preposition;

(2)   if it is any other type of pronoun (relative, indefinite, etc.) it is *often, but not always* preceded by a preposition;

(3)   if its head is a full name, the preposition is not always present. Despite differences between texts, prepositional object marking is more common with NPs whose heads are proper names (and therefore [+human], [+referential]), than with those whose heads are [+human], [−referential]. But there are also many cases in which NPs with [+human], [−referential] heads are marked prepositionally.

This is exactly the situation that emerges for the Ibero-Romance area (Meyer-Lübke 1899:§50; Reichenkron 1951; Martín Zorraquino 1976; Villar 1983). Stimm (1986) shows that for Engadine Romansh, too, the phenomenon occurs with lexical verbs that took a dative construction (or AD + accusative) at some point in the history of Latin, or where the NP is a personal, relative or indefinite pronoun. There are therefore at least two different factors triggering the structure which appears at later synchronic stages: the constructional properties of certain verbs, and personal pronouns.

Traditionally, a great deal of emphasis has been put on the role of various functional factors, such as the need to differentiate subject and object (see, for example, Bossong (1991), who adopts in typological perspective an intuition already formulated by Diez in the *Grammaire des langues romanes*), and foregrounding of the object. These syntactic 'explanations' are multiply problematic. Both blithely project a synchronic structural model onto the past. In particular, the hypothesis of differential subject and object marking attributes to grammatical relations universal values which are far from being demonstrated, especially given that 'grammatical relations' are themselves one of the most controversial areas in modern syntactic theory. Even at the descriptive level for individual languages, one cannot always unequivocally assign a particular function, such as direct object or indirect object, to a given constituent (see Sornicola 1997). The government properties of the verbal lexemes have a crucial role here, for they may affect the structure of grammatical relations in ways incompatible with theoretical expectations. In recent years these problems have been addressed in some models (e.g., 'structural Case' and 'inherent Case' in generative grammar), which, as we shall see, have particular relevance for the study of the diachrony of the prepositional object.

Even if these problems were solved, could we really maintain that differentiating subject and object is the 'explanation'? Is it any more than a mere 'description' of a tendency present at a more or less recent synchronic stage? And as an explanation it is problematic even on the synchronic level. Typological studies have shown that morphological case marking is not essential to encode the subject–object relationship, given the availability of word order and semantic or contextual cues associated with the head of the NP. So the much-invoked role of ambiguity resulting from loss of case marking from Latin to Romance requires some caution. It seems a reasonable hypothesis that word order may have acted as a major synchronic differentiating factor of the subject and object relationship even in the past. In other words, appeal to ambiguity needs to be treated with the same caution for the past as for the present. Care may be needed with appeal to object foregrounding, which textual studies of various stages in the history of the Romance languages show to be not especially frequent.

What role has been played by the other triggering process, involving the pronominal properties of the NP? Here we have to consider the multiple successive layers of morphosyntactic properties of personal pronouns, over a long period stretching back perhaps as far as Latin, unfolding through the complex transition from Latin to Romance and reaching into the formative period of Romance literary languages. To simplify here greatly an extremely complex issue, we may identify at least three phases. The first may be described as late Latin, and shows a conservative tendency with regard to the declension of personal pronouns. In Romance languages pronouns have generally maintained declensional distinctions better than nouns (Löfstedt 1961:225). Thus in late Latin texts the functions we may label 'dative' were expressed synthetically in pronouns and analytically in nouns (using the AD + accusative construction). The survival of Classical Latin dative forms is confirmed by the fact that in many Romance languages the stressed oblique pronouns, whose formal development is more easily identifiable than for unstressed pronouns, have preserved a morphological structure which evidently goes back to a historically underlying dative form, as is apparent in the Spanish and northern Italian *mi* and *ti* (< DAT MIHI, TIBI) – see also the discussion in Smith, this volume, chapter 6. Romanian preserves a personal pronoun paradigm which distinguishes nominative/accusative/dative. Generalization of dative forms as stressed oblique pronouns, attested in some modern Romance areas, must have gone through periods of wavering between use and overuse of dative forms, endemic throughout the Romania between the sixth and the seventh century, the period of 'decadence' of Latin, but chiefly represented later by the Iberian area. Of the *Cartulario de San Vicente*, for example, Jennings (1940:150) observes that not only was the use of the dative conspicuous and well preserved in the expected contexts in

Latin, but that the pronominal paradigm shows dative case, even when the noun is preceded by AD.

The situation described by Jennings seems to characterize a more advanced phase of the development of the personal pronouns. This suggests a second phase which we will call 'pseudo-dative'. Oscillations between competing morphological types and the overuse of dative forms are also well attested by some relic stressed personal pronouns forms, both in Ibero- and in Italo-Romance. Such forms must have existed between the tenth and the thirteenth centuries, only to disappear almost everywhere. These relics are particularly interesting for an understanding of how the development of the pronouns may have come to bear on the formation of what we now call the 'prepositional object'. They have unequivocally 'dative' morphology, etymological in the second person, analogical in the first, but they are used in a general way for the oblique case. These forms are well documented by Menéndez Pidal. In tenth-century cartularies from Spain we frequently find the type 1SG *miue*, *mibe*, analogical on Latin 2SG TIBI, used as stressed oblique pronouns. Later this type is documented in the famously conservative Mozarabic and Sephardic Spanish varieties. The first person singular oblique form *myb* was still in use in the Mozarabic speech of Juda Ha-Leví around 1100; *a myby* 'to me' is still documented in the thirteenth-century Spanish of Don Todros, a rabbi at the courts of Alfonso X and then Sancho IV; *a myb* occurs in an Arabic *muwaššaha* by the 'blind man of Tudela' (died 1126). Note also the type *teue* (*cunteue* 'with thee') documented in 1034 in León, looking very much like the southern Italian forms *meve*, *teve*, *seve* (Menéndez Pidal 1956:340f.). These, too, show morphological continuity with Latin, the first person singular form being obviously analogically remodelled (see D'Ovidio 1905:50). For other Italo-Romance examples, see the references in Monaci (1955:639b). Although such forms survive to this day in some dialects of Salento and Basilicata (see Rohlfs 1968:139), they may, like the Ibero-Romance forms, be considered relics, supplanted in Italo-Romance by rival types which have existed since the earliest literary attestations. These are the pairs *mene*, *tene* and *mia*, *tia*, nowadays widespread in central and southern Italy. Whatever their etymology, they have presumably followed different developments: *mene* and *tene* come from accusative forms with the addition of -*ne*; *mia* and *tia* come from original dative forms (on this, see D'Ovidio 1905). What seems significant is that they share the property of being long, disyllabic forms. In the phase we are calling 'pseudo-dative', then, dative morphology had completely lost its old case value and had been refunctionalized in the light of a prosodic tendency to prefer longer forms over shorter ones.

The observation that in old Ibero- and Italo-Romance texts the preposition *a* (like *pe* in Romanian) is especially frequent with object NPs having first and second person pronouns as their heads may be viewed in a new light. The obligatory occurrence of prepositions before personal pronouns may be assigned to a third phase. While they are unlikely to have been exactly synchronous structural developments, the expansion of the prepositional structure may well have been a concomitant of the rise of the stressed monosyllabic pronouns *mi* and *ti*, which in Ibero-Romance took place at the expense of the pseudo-dative disyllabic forms. In Italo-Romance, the process must have been more complicated and locally differentiated – as witness, first, the notable polymorphism of early texts (e.g., copresence of Sicilian *mi* and *mia* even in the same text), and second, the modern differences between northern dialects where the type *mi*, *ti* is widespread, and central-southern dialects which display in some regards a more locally fragmented situation. The preposition *a* may initially have established itself before first and second persons stressed object pronouns as a mere expletive element, due to the prosodic lengthening of monosyllabic forms. This expletive element may then have been propagated, perhaps subsequently, to disyllabic pronominal forms, as is suggested by the fact that the preposition also occurs with the southern Italian types *mene* and *mia*. However that may be, the proliferation of the preposition could be taken to be a different effect of the same prosodic principle which was at work in the first two phases. So in all three phases a unitary principle could be said to have been at work, structurally realized in various different ways.

The hypothetical 'explanation' (better 'comprehension') offered here for the pronominal manifestation of the prepositional object in early Romance texts might be taken to imply an autonomous development of the *signifiant* with respect to the *signifié*. Yet during the long, multi-layered process described, semantic and referential factors may also have played a role, such as the person hierarchy. Both the southern Italian texts I have examined and the old Spanish texts examined by Reichenkron (1951), Martín Zorraquino (1976) and Villar (1983) clearly show that the object pronouns involved in prepositional structures are preponderantly first and second persons, something which may not be accountable for in purely 'formal' terms. Actually, it may be that semantic factors contributed more to the propagation than the genesis of the type. In Ibero-Romance and southern and central Italo-Romance, the fact that numerous verbs govern the dative, and the prosodic tendencies at work on personal pronouns, have gelled into a particular structural type due to the propagation of *a* into contexts with nouns specified as [+animate], [+human], [+referential], a phenomenon where semantic factors undoubtedly played some role.

We are now in a position to sketch out some further hypotheses on the diachrony of this syntactic type. Indeed, it seems that two phases ought to be distinguished: the genesis and the propagation of structural conditions. What in modern synchrony appears to us as a unitary type must have had a long and heterogeneous gestation, with multiple lines of genesis and development. In particular, while the two conditions identified for the initial phases (the verb governing the dative and prosodic tendencies at work on the personal pronouns) were presumably so widespread in the Romance world as to crystallize into manifestations which appear over wide areas separated by time and space, propagation itself may have followed different routes at different times. Thus in the French and northern Italian linguistic area, the initial conditions have always remained endemic and in some sense distinct from each other, without ever gelling into a unitary type, whilst in central and southern Italy the two initial conditions came together to form a structural type; finally, in some varieties of Spanish the preposition was generalized into contexts whose NP contains a noun with the features [–animate] and/or [–referential].

Of the two 'triggering' conditions, the prosodic factors acting on the personal pronouns must have been the strongest and most pervasive in the activation of the type, as witness the fact that it occurs in other Indo-European languages and even beyond.

Thus the modern synchronic description has a somewhat accidental, epiphenomenological, relation with the genesis of the type and is only partially linked to its propagation. This is perhaps unsurprising, given what the great general linguists and Romance linguists of the past used to say: that the synchronic dimension and the diachronic dimension involve different problems and methods.

But the diachrony of the prepositional object has further implications for the more general problems discussed in this chapter. What has emerged are conditions dependent on different textual and historical circumstances, at different periods in time. In addition, different 'principles', prosodic and semantic, have been hypothesized. Can these sets of conditions and principles really be considered 'causes'? The conditions are, precisely, no more than conditions, and the linguist can do no more than speculatively attempt to link them to historical sequences. As for the principles, their validity can only be discerned 'locally', in relation to the case in point. It does not seem logically valid to project a (universally active) global principle on the basis of these local contexts. Of course, general explanations of change will always be a generalization of particular explanations advanced for individual phenomena (see Coseriu 1973; 1981), but one has to admit that such a procedure still contains a good deal of approximation and uncertainty.

The conditions attending the 'origin' of the historic process which has shaped the Romance prepositional object type show remarkable stability, and confirm the force and permanence of certain structures through time. The dative-governing properties of some Latin verbs are continued through structures with AD + NP or through the refunctionalization of the debris of old pronominal forms. The 'propagation' phase, both to larger classes of verb lexemes and to NPs lacking the original semantic and referential features, is, of course, a different matter. Such analogical extensions or syntactic reanalyses can be brought about only within given synchronic states. But then, perhaps diachrony without change actually does exist?

4 Universal explanations and historical explanations

4.1 Laws, principles and explanations

The problems discussed so far raise anew the issue of the meaning and extent of recourse to 'laws', 'principles'[30] and 'explanations' in diachronic morpho-syntax. Actually a good many contemporary diachronic (and synchronic) models still bear traces, more or less explicitly, of notions of 'naturalness' and 'scientificness' which had already been the object of controversy in the early twentieth century.[31] Positivistic conceptions of forces or principles allegedly acting as causes of linguistic phenomena both in synchrony and in diachrony nowadays occur in various, and more or less subtle, guises. To simplify greatly, five groups of principles or causes are commonly invoked as explanatory factors:

(i) Reasons relating to the speakers' 'mind', meaning the capacity for understanding or an abstract mechanism underlying linguistic production. In addition to traditional principles of analogy, which level paradigms, there are also cognitive factors, of the type modelled in generative grammar (e.g., structural syntactic proper-ties assumed as abstract properties of the mind), or principles of various functional kinds, which project characteristics of the organ-ization of utterances (topic–focus structure, information structure) or characteristics of structural relations (e.g., subject vs. object) as explanatory generalizations.

(ii) Reasons relating to typological micro-parameters, such as patterns of linearization of constituents and their harmonization. The theoretical basis of such constructs is unclear, although they have been objectified and hypostatized as metahistorical entities overarching the classical framework of *langue* vs. *parole*, syntagmatic vs. paradigmatic, synchrony vs. diachrony.

(iii) Reasons relating to the degree of complexity or naturalness (markedness) of a given feature or phenomenon, on the basis of its cross-linguistic frequency.

(iv) Reasons which, while they bear on speakers, are of an eminently extrinsic, pragmatic nature (e.g., optimization of communication).

(v) External social reasons, which assume a more or less direct relationship between extra-linguistic characteristics and the presence or development of linguistic phenomena.

In any case it is worthy of note that recent years have seen a confluence of these principles in many studies of various theoretical and methodological stamps. Whether any of these principles has real explanatory power, rather than being essentially descriptive, is doubtful.

The risk of circularity is great. For example, are the harmonizations of linearization in structural configurations, defined on the basis of the synchronic states of individual languages (and with a degree of irregularity which simply cannot be ignored) really a 'causal' factor, or just a mere description imposed on diachrony? These are epistemological issues characteristic of so-called 'genetic explanations' (see Amsterdamski 1981:372; also Popper 1957). And the validity of general laws for languages has often been criticized with regard to synchronic states (see Matthews 1982). On top of these difficulties are others more specific to diachronic syntax: the transmission of syntactic traditions is unlike the transmission of traditions of other levels of analysis, in that extra-linguistic, historical factors, weigh more heavily on syntax (see Sornicola 1995).

4.2   *Diachronic explanations in Romance linguistics*

Before the North American developments discussed in §2, there had already been wide-ranging and penetrating reflection on the problem of diachronic explanation within Romance linguistics. For Coseriu (1973; 1981:80), 'explanation certainly goes beyond mere description, to motivate or justify changes, and find the reasons for them'. But Coseriu stresses that that these 'reasons' are not 'causes', in the sense of necessity, but conditions, circumstances or determining factors within which speakers have freedom to make linguistic choices. Such factors do not trigger change, but condition it and may help speed up or slow down what is improperly called the 'evolution of languages'. So the 'general problem of changes is [...] their conditioning'. The perspective of conditioning leads us to rule out the possibility that reasons (in the sense given above) could lie directly in the structure of society.[32] Coseriu holds that 'the historical problem of change is not a matter of establishing how a particular linguistic mode began (or how it could be initiated), but of establishing how it took shape or how it was able to take shape as a tradition, that is, how and under what cultural and functional conditions it entered or could have entered in a system of already traditional linguistic modes'.[33] The functional factors within the system (for example, its critical or weak points) and the cultural factors constitute multiple conditions for change and resistance to change. Under given historical conditions one group of factors may prevail over another. But the force of tradition has a major role: 'a vigorous cultural norm may mean indefinite stability for an "unbalanced" system'.[34] And the distinction between the general problem of change and the study of an individual change is an important one. In both cases we are dealing with various kind of historical explanation, distinct from the problem of the mutability of languages[35] – a problem which belongs purely to the theoretical dimension and which can be solved only if we recognize that mutability is not a bolt-on feature of linguistic systems, which needs to be explained, but a necessary, intrinsic, property, ultimately grounded in the historicity of the linguistic traditions on which the systems are built.[36]

Perhaps the most interesting point, especially in the light of diachronic models of recent decades, concerns the differentness of universal explanations and historical explanations. Coseriu observes that 'while we may know in general the causes of wars, of course we can only know the causes of the Peloponnesian war by studying them, because universal knowledge and generic knowledge are no substitute for specific historical documentation'.[37] Such documentation is an additional problem for the history of languages, being more difficult and elusive than in other disciplines, and lack of sources being a frequent problem to be faced. Our awareness of the technical difficulties of doing history, which are especially acute in linguistics, means that we have to take a highly hypothetical view of explanations, especially where the origins of a linguistic change are concerned, a viewpoint which in recent years has been reformulated as a diachronic 'scenario' (see Dressler 1997).

The formation of the Romance future is a case-study *par excellence* of the contrast between universal explanations and historical explanations. Earlier critical discussions have lost none of their theoretical interest but, over and above the phenomenon at issue, they bear directly on the logical structure of two types of argumentation perennially recurrent across different theoretical models. The morphological explanation holds that the lack of a regular paradigm of synthetic forms in the Classical Latin future led to recourse to periphrastic forms, especially bearing in mind that sound change in so-called vulgar Latin would have made the morphological patterns dysfunctional. The semantic/stylistic approach links the advance of the periphrastic future to an expressive need which conveyed modal affective values rather than temporal ones.[38] Both explanations have been reckoned inadequate and vulnerable.[39] Coseriu (1973; 1981:115) holds that:

> There are three facts to be explained: a) the general instability of the forms of the future (not of the category of future); b) the periodic re-formation of the future by forms with originally modal or prospective value which ultimately become 'temporal'; c) the re-formation of the Latin future at a particular point in history. The first two are not particular to one language or a particular point in history, and thereby require a universal explanation. Nothing is explained by stating that the forms of the future are re-formed because they are 'grammaticalized', because this is at best a mere attestation, which cannot account for the direction in which the re-formation of the future takes place.[40]

The dual nature of the future is a universal, intrinsic structural feature of this category, perennially wavering between the temporal and the aspectual (modal) poles: 'temporal forms are replaced by modal ones which in turn become temporal'.[41] Coseriu stresses that 'in any case a universal explanation is not of itself a historical one', for 'to explain why the Latin future was replaced by modal forms at one particular time, it is inadequate to assert that it is something which "usually happens", pointing to the universal reason for the phenomenon. You have to explain why this universal (and permanent) reason came to operate precisely in the period of so-called vulgar Latin: in other words, the universal expressive need must be justified as a historical need.'[42] For Coseriu, the determinant circumstance lies in attitudes and expressive needs brought to the fore by a phenomenon of great social cultural import – Christianity; Christianity marked a profound historical rupture with linguistic as well as other implications.[43] Note that this explanation is very different from those commonly used in sociolinguistics, which appeal to differences of social level. Such differences do not express causes but rather the point or direction of diffusion of a phenomenon.[44] What is being emphasized here is the role played by Christianity in bringing to the surface latent structural possibilities which predated any contemporary historical circumstances.

This approach has been criticized for its one-sidedness and for its down-playing of the question of when the periphrastic form emerged as such (see Fleischman 1982:50). The thesis that 'the primary causes of morpho-syntactic change must be sought in morphosyntactic factors' (Valesio 1969:192f; Fleischman 1982:50) may have its attractions, but appeal to 'multiple causation', postulating the joint influence of semantic, syntactic and morphological factors, as well as cultural factors (Fleischman 1982:50), has its problems too. On the one hand, it maintains, more or less implicitly, a naturalistic idea of the cause of diachronic processes; on the other, it places the onus of an elusive justification on a summary list of causes. It may be that the two approaches are just radically alien to each other. Attempts to establish the diachrony of periphrastic future (or past participle) constructions, based on the correlation between basic parameters, degree of 'boundness' and modal/aspectual/temporal[45] values are bold, but the resulting principles still require supplementary historical investigation (see Adams 1991).

More generally, grammaticalization models describe, in the best cases, successive cycles of structures, but it is doubtful whether these are truly explanatory, unless one follows the notoriously problematic principle of *post hoc, propter hoc.* The problem is that if one attempts to organize a series of changes into groups forming a genetically ordered system, the historical data are often incapable of refuting the model. Worse, as Amsterdamski observes, the causal nature of genetic explanations is doubtful 'because they do not generally formulate sufficient conditions for the emergence of the final state which requires explanation, or even for the intermediate states which make up the genetic sequence. So they fail to explain why the system evolved in the observed sequence, but only explain why it could have done so' (Amsterdamski 1981:372). The historicizing explanations of Coseriu are not, by definition, incontrovertible, but they have been put forward with a clear awareness that causal explanations in diachrony could lead us on an infinite wild goose chase.

5   Conclusions

It is almost a century since Saussure and the Prague School formulated models of diachrony. Their perspectives still reflected different stages in the wider debate about history. The terms of the debate within the humanities have since changed greatly and linguistics may have remained rather cut off from other disciplines and stranded on issues which are now outdated. Some contemporary diachronic linguists' (especially syntacticians') critiques of historical models as mere representations of single, accidental facts harks back to the old positivistic conception of history. Such critiques seem curiously ignorant of the wide-ranging debate about the intrinsically non-predictive and non-causal nature of historical explanations. For some, attempting to conceive a theory of history is a contradiction in terms. Central to this perspective is the role of different epistemological paradigms, founded on concepts of 'comprehension' and 'interpretation', on the ability to make sense of situations (see Momigliano 1974; 1987:22–23; Tessitore 1991). Others have argued that the leap from the documents of the past, which are never more than historical 'rubble', to making sense of them, can only be done by being something like a prophet, a medium or an interpreter of dreams (Benjamin 1997). Everyone recognizes that the unreliability of this type of knowledge and the scope for multiple and relativistic interpretations just come with the terrain. Yet such things form the basis of new models of genetic or historical explanation, which point up how 'even if the explanans of a genetic explanation seems to be a mere "historical narration" without mentioning any law linking the successive stages of the evolving system, it yet presents a theoretical structure' (Amsterdamski 1981:372). Freed of its causal value, the notion of 'theory' is here understood as a set of general but clearly delimited principles, justifying some of the major events in an evolutionary process.

This perspective does not claim to be a theory of history, but simply acknowledges the inevitably theoretical nature (that is, the fact that it is relative to a system of hypotheses) of any historical explanation. It transcends not only the positivistic conception of diachrony as the domain of the *événement* and the accidental, but also the functionalistic view of diachrony as a dimension in which there are at work principles of concatenation of phenomena belonging to successive diachronic stages, governed by teleological laws. The key issue is the representation of the passage from one state of a system to another. This idea of 'passage' centrally defined Saussure's and early structuralism's concept of diachrony. It was precisely in this respect that Saussure felt the need to differentiate the idea of diachrony from that of history, and to a lesser extent from that of evolution, both being considered not entirely suitable for use in linguistics (Riedlinger, Quire II [Komatsu and Wolf 1997:34]:81). On the other hand, some historians have criticized the appeal to both concepts of synchrony and diachrony because of their limited character, which misses the essential feature of historical research (see Braudel 1967–68; 1969). In effect, to this day diachronic linguistics and the history of the language present themselves as different domains with different presuppositions and methods. But both contain unresolved contradictions (these have been discussed for the history of the language by Varvaro 1972–3).

Saussure realized full well how difficult describing and justifying that 'passage' could be. He clearly perceived (without developing the point) the special diachronic status of syntax, where the passage from one diachronic state to the next is more strongly subject to the interaction of internal and external forces. He fought shy of developing theories on the subject and the best he could manage was to appeal to the concept of *événement* – which came down to admitting that there was an insuperable limit to explanation. Equally noteworthy is the fact that he was convinced of the need to avoid imposing a priori categories or units indiscriminately valid both for synchrony and diachrony (Riedlinger, Quire II [Komatsu and Wolf 1997:34f.]), a fact which may be considered another effect of the difficulty of modelling diachrony. The Prague School were prepared to envision explanations of the passage, but they were trapped inside a realistic, immanentist, ahistorical conception of the principles or laws regulating it, like many of the theorists who subsequently drew inspiration from the Prague School. Such mindsets, nowadays prevalent in many areas of linguistics, are very different from what emerges from theoretical thinking on contemporary historical research. Here, recognition of the intrinsically theoretical character of any historical narration or explanation has long been divorced from naively realist conceptions, and the discussion of the principles and models of analysis has reached a level of critical awareness which verges on ironic, disillusioned, detachment.

This is a standard to which modern diachronic Romance linguistics, caught as it is between the cognitive paradigms of history and diachrony, can come close to achieving. In their different ways, D'Ovidio, Schuchardt, Coseriu and Herman maintained the need to conceptualize the principles and 'causes' of the dynamics of change in a fashion opposed to any kind of metaphysical approach. In searching for the 'passage', they maintained a kind of sober equilibrium with regard to the possibilities and limits of diachronic research, which was perhaps due precisely to the fact that they were Romanists, and so researchers in a discipline distinguished by the most imposing 'mass of photographs of the past' of any linguistic domain, too imbued with the historical mentality to be oblivious to the razor's edge between history and diachrony. Even a scholar who, like Malkiel, had explored the more strictly diachronic end of this polarization had no doubts about the importance of the 'hard toil of historical preparation'.

At the close of the nineteenth century, Schuchardt held that a Romanist should be a general linguist before addressing problems of historical linguistics, an idea that was very modern at that time and long remained so. In the twentieth, in different ways, Coseriu and Malkiel attempted the difficult task of reconciling general linguistics and historical linguistics. But their work shows the importance of being a Romanist before being a general linguist. A Romance diachronic morphosyntax, just as much as a Romance diachronic linguistics, may be different from other diachronic syntaxes and other types of diachronic linguistics not so much because Romanists have available a mass of photographs of the past which lets them get closer to reality, but because they know that the photographs of the past and those of the present may let them dream a less fragmented, and rather richer, dream.

2   SYLLABLE, SEGMENT AND PROSODY

Michele Loporcaro

This chapter is concerned with some aspects of the evolution of prosody from Latin to Romance: prosody, specifically, is considered from the viewpoint of its effects at the segmental level. Thus, we do not deal with purely prosodic phenomena, such as intonation, but with the interplay between prosodic categories/domains, on the one hand, and segmental entities and processes, on the other, paying special attention to processes crucial to the transformation of Latin into Romance, and their reconstruction.

1   Vowel length, quantity and stress in Latin

To discuss the development of stress/accent from Latin to Romance we must address:

(1)   a. the phonetic implementation of prosodic (stress/accent) prominence;
      b. the phonological vs. morpho-lexical conditioning of stress placement;
      c. the position of stress (viz. its persistence vs. shift) from Latin to Romance;
      d. the domain of stress assignment.

(1a) is a much-debated issue touched upon for Latin in §3.1 and for Romance in §6. Our main concern will be (1b–d). It is uncontroversial that:

(2)   a. Latin stress was quantity-sensitive: in polysyllabic words of more than two syllables, it fell on a heavy (i.e., bimoraic) penult, otherwise on the antepenultimate (see the representations in (3));
      b. no Romance language has retained the Latin stress rule as such, due to the collapse of distinctive vowel quantity;
      c. nevertheless, exceptions aside, the stressed vowel of a Latin word remains the stressed vowel of its Romance continuant. For example,

in a form like CANTĀTUM 'sung', stress fell on the long /aː/ in the penult, and it is the continuant of that vowel that still carries stress in Sp./Pt. *cantado*, Fr. *chanté*, It. *cantato*, Ro. *cântat*, etc.

(2) shows that stress is inextricably intertwined with quantity. Latin stress depended on quantity (2a), not the reverse. But during the (pre)history of Latin several changes led to partial subordination of vowel quantity (VQ) to stress. While the VQ contrast was consistently preserved under stress, several shortening processes dramatically reduced its functional load in unstressed, especially final, position. The list includes *correptio iambica*, shortening of word-final vowels after a light syllable in words like BĔNĔ, MŎDŎ, CĂUĔ, PŬTĂ, which operated around 200 BC (Allen 1973:182). In the same period, there was shortening of unstressed vowels preceding a word-final consonant (except -S) in most endings: AMĂT, UIDĔT (≠ AMĀS, UIDĒS), ANIMĂL (≠ ANIMĀLIS), AMŎR (≠ AMŌRIS). Monosyllables are unaffected. Before -M, shortening was pre-literary, although not dating back to common Italic (Meiser 1998:77).

As a consequence of these changes, by the classical period the VQ contrast was largely limited to stressed syllables. In terms of text frequency, the counts in Herman (1968:197, n5, 199) show that the ratio of long to short vowels was 1:3 under stress, while the frequency of long vowels dropped (to 1:4) in unstressed syllables. This evolutionary trend contains the seeds of the Romance development, as quantity ceases to be, at least statistically, entirely independent of stress.[1]

However, in Classical Latin this process remained incomplete and VQ was still a crucial factor in stress assignment, since it concurred with syllable structure in determining syllabic quantity (or weight). As seen in (3), closed syllables count as heavy, whatever the VQ of the nucleus.

(3)

	open		closed	
a. light	b. heavy (no coda)		c. heavy (coda)	d. superheavy
CV	CVː		CVC	CVːC
RĬGĬDĂ,	PRĪUĀTŌ,		CŎNTĬNGĬT	STĒLLĀS,
FĂCĬLĔ	DĒPŌNŌ			TĒCTŌS

The difference between superheavy and heavy was not relevant for metre or stress. Furthermore, throughout the history of Latin there was a tendency to eliminate pattern (3d). An example is the deletion of final -D in the ablative ending. Deletion applied where -D followed a long vowel (e.g., PŌPLICŌD 'public' > CLat. PŪBLICŌ), whereas after a short vowel, -D was retained: APŬD.[2] Geminate -ss- was degeminated after a long vowel or diphthong: CĀSSUS 'fall' > CĀSUS, etc. A later development STĒLLA 'star' > *STĒLA can be reconstructed from Fr. *étoile* (and similar forms in NItalian dialects), with the same diphthong as in *toile* 'canvas'< TĒLA (vs. It. *stella* < STĒLLA). Arguably, the instability of (3c) was a harbinger of the Romance development (2b–c), by which VQ eventually became dependent on stress (cf. Meyer-Lübke 1920:145; Weinrich 1958:§40).

Through the above-mentioned conspiracy of changes in pre-literary and archaic Latin, length had gradually begun to retreat from unstressed position. Through the progressive elimination of (3c) it began to retreat from closed syllables even under stress. The final step in this development was the elimination (at the surface) of light syllables under stress and, consequently, of distinctive VQ. Pattern (3a) disappears through the establishment of a vowel lengthening process:

(4) $V \rightarrow V:/\_\_\_]\sigma$
      [+stress]

The ensuing situation is today best preserved in Italian and Sardinian, where vowel length occurs in complementary distribution, e.g., (5):

(5)   Italian   Sardinian
      a. ['kaːne] 'dog'   ['kaːna] 'grey-haired' FSG
      b. ['kanːe] 'reeds' ['kanːa] 'reed'

Despite many diverging ideas on this point (cf. §2), the complementary distribution in (5), and rule (4) generating it, have to be reconstructed for proto-Romance.[3] This does not hold for another aspect of open syllable lengthening (henceforth OSL) in these varieties, viz. the fact that it does not affect a word-final stressed vowel: e.g., It. [tʃiˈtːa] 'city'. This requires a complication of (4), to be discussed in §3.5, where a further important point will be addressed – the fact that OSL in Italian still depends on utterance prominence. Utterance prominence – it is suggested – may also have played a role in the rise of OSL in late Latin / proto-Romance.

Since the collapse of distinctive VQ left the consonant shell of the syllable unaffected, a part of the original quantitative motivation (or more precisely, heaviness-based motivation) of stress assignment persisted into (proto-) Romance (6):

(6)   HEAVY PENULT CONSTRAINT
      Stress cannot skip a heavy (i.e., checked) penultimate syllable.

While all Romance languages (except French) still have polysyllabic non-oxytonic words, and most still possess proparoxytones, whether inherited or borrowed, proparoxytones with a heavy penult are highly exceptional (see §4). Thus we may justifiably ask whether (6) (or some version thereof) still has to be assumed as a synchronically valid generalization for modern Romance languages.

Another constraint which (proto-)Romance inherited from Latin is (7):

(7) THREE SYLLABLE WINDOW (= 3SW)
     Stress cannot fall further back than the antepenultimate syllable.

Among Romance languages, only Romanian has acquired preantepenulti-mate stressed words, possibly under Slavic influence (see §4.2). In Italian, (7) shows exceptions in verb inflection and postlexically, in clitic clusters, while it is still active within lexical words. Most Gallo-Romance varieties, on the other hand, have restricted the window (see §4.3).

Before pursuing developments of the proto-Romance stress system into the daughter languages, we have to consider in detail the rise of the proto-Romance prosodic system.

2   Prosodic revolutions I: the collapse of distinctive vowel quantity

The exact path through which the Latin system, with distinctive VQ, gave way to the (proto-)Romance one, has been much debated. Crucial to our present concerns is the contention that this change was determined by the rise of OSL (4). This view implies that (4) has to be ascribed to proto-Romance, as maintained by Schuchardt (1866–68 III:43–44), Wartburg (1950:81f.), Weinrich (1958) and others. This was challenged with chronological and areal arguments. Meyer-Lübke (1890:524; 1920:142) proposed the sixth century as *terminus a quo*, on the evidence of the application of OSL to late Latin loans into Germanic and of the application of diphthongization to Frankish loans in OFrench: loans such as old High German *scuola* 'school', *fiebar* 'fever' and the others discussed in Mackel (1896), dating from between the sixth and ninth centuries, presuppose *schōla*, *fēbre* (with lengthened stressed vowel). The argument is flawed, however: Brüch (1921:574) points out that the dating of such loans into Germanic does not mean that the lengthening could not have occurred centuries earlier in vulgar Latin.

The same objection applies to the argument, also invoked by Meyer-Lübke, that diphthongization occurs in, for example, Frk. *bĕdi* > OFr. *bies*

53

'river bed', Frk. *hŏsa* > OFr. *huese* 'hose'. For some of these words there is evidence that the loan had already taken place in imperial Latin (Castellani 1985:17f.; 2000:48).

Another objection involves areal distribution. According to Schürr (1970:5f.) OSL (in Italian) or further developments thereof (in French) are limited to a central area, which by Bartoli's (1943) argument from the supposed conservative nature of 'lateral areas' must be regarded as innovative in this respect. OSL is not observed – Schürr claims – in the rest of the Romània (e.g., Portuguese, Spanish, Catalan, Occitan, Sardinian, southern Italian dialects, Romanian).

This list contains a number of errors. As shown in (5), Sardinian does display OSL: e.g., Log. [sa ˈðɔːmɔ] 'the house' vs. [ˈdrɔmːɔ] 'sleep.1SG'. The same goes for southern Italian dialects. Those spoken on the Adriatic coast, from southern Marche to Puglia, even show a dramatic development of the original allophonic difference, with the lengthened allophone further altered via diphthongization and/or colouring processes, a situation comparable with that of northern Gallo-Romance (see Merlo 1911–12: 908f., 919).

Thus, the whole central-southern part of the Romance world has to be annexed to the OSL area, *pace* Schürr, and there is compelling evidence that this isogloss stretched further south, including the African 'Romània submersa' (see below). The eastern and western peripheries must be addressed separately. Both Daco- and Ibero-Romance nowadays appear immune to OSL. The former became isolated from the rest of the Latin-speaking world in AD 271. Consequently, on the traditional view (e.g., Straka 1956:199; Nandriş 1963:16), depending on the absolute chronology of OSL dictated by the sources, we have to conclude either that Daco-Romance was not affected by the innovation or that it was, and lost OSL subsequently.[4] For the western periphery of the Empire the latter option gains plausibility a priori, since the Iberian Peninsula was never isolated from the rest of the Latin/Romance speaking world.[5] Note that under the hypothesis that OSL attained the Iberian Peninsula as well, its non-occurrence is explained by the demise of consonant gemination. This process, turning /ˈVCCV/ into /ˈVCV/, necessarily had an impact on OSL. Two opposite reactions are conceivable: suppression of OSL or lexicalization of its output giving rise to a novel VQ contrast. The latter option was taken by the northern part of western Romance (see §3.5), the former by Ibero-Romance.

Reconstructive arguments from loanwords and areal distribution can be complemented through the evidence of the Latin sources (8), showing that:

(8) a. OSL was at work at least by the early fifth century;
     b. it was directly related to the loss of distinctive VQ;
     c. both began in Roman Africa and gradually spread northwards to a substantial part (if not the whole) of the Latin world, before the collapse of the western Empire.

A selection of information available in the sources is provided in (9). To summarize, Augustine (AD 354–430), proclaiming the need for intellectuals to accommodate their lexical choices to be intelligible to the mass of uncultivated people, incidentally reports that VQ contrasts were not perceived by Africans, citing confusion between the vowel of os(sum) 'bone', which should be short, and that of os 'mouth', which should be long. Consentius (early fifth-century Gaul) mentions the 'African habit' of saying [ˈpiːper] for [ˈpiper] PIPER 'pepper', [oˈraːtor] for [oːˈraːtor] ORATOR 'orator'; also the 'barbarism' [ˈpiːkeus] for [ˈpikeus] PICEUS 'pitch-black', and [ˈpiːkes] for [ˈpikeːs] PICES 'pitch'.

(9) a. Augustine, *De doctr. christ.* IV,10,24: 'cur pietatis doctorem pigeat imperitis loquentem, *ossum* potius quam *os* dicere, ne ista syllaba non ab eo, quod sunt *ossa*, sed ab eo, quod sunt *ora*, intellegatur, ubi Afrae aures de correptione vocalium vel productione non iudicant?'
     b. Consentius, *Ars de barbarismis et metaplasmis* (Keil V 392): 'ut quidam dicunt *piper* producta priore syllaba, cum sit brevis, quod vitium Afrorum familiare est'.
     c. *Ibid.*: 'ut siquis dicat *orator* correpta priore syllaba, quod ipsum vitium Afrorum speciale est'.
     d. *Ibid.*: (exemplifying *barbarismus per immutationem syllabae*) 'ut si quis *piceus* dicens priorem extendat'.
     e. *Ibid.*: 'ut siquis dicens *pices* producta priore et correpta sequenti pronuntiet'.

Consentius complements this phonological observation with an observation on phonetic realization: that OSL is a peculiar feature of Africans' Latin pronunciation. Consentius' observations were taken at face value by Schuchardt (1866–68 III:44), who claims that in the earliest Romance the Africans had long stressed vowels before a short consonant, and short vowels in unstressed position.

More recently, much effort has been devoted to denying some or all of the conclusions in (8a–c). Schürr (1970:5f.) reduces Consentius' phonetic (allophonic) specifications to Augustine's phonemic ones, saying that they simply attest to the confusion about quantities prevalent among Latin-speaking Africans.[6]

According to Castellani (1991:20f.), on the other hand, both Augustine's and Consentius' remarks regard not vowel quantity but vowel timbre, in which case Consentius' example *orator* should be emended to *orat*. The reason for this claim is Castellani's *assumption* that by the second or at the latest the third century the non-quantitative pronunciation was universally prevalent all over the Empire. Note that the proposed emendation of *orator* into *orat* is not justified independently of this assumption.

Other scholars, while crediting Consentius' remarks as to the date of the rise of the allophonic distribution (4)–(5), do not give credit to the attribution of the merger to African Latin. His remarks are held to show only that 'in general the stressed vowel was lengthened in free position' (Wartburg 1950:81). The same argument appears more recently in Adams (2007:264f.). Mention of Africans in this connection is argued to have been motivated by the commonplace of Africans' Latin as representative of 'bad' pronunciation. As to the exact realization of the lengthening in *piper*, according to Wartburg Consentius must have meant [ˈpeːper], with the common Romance development (ĭ > /e/). Weinrich (1958:24) and Lausberg (1971:204), on the other hand, both assume that OSL was already established throughout the Empire by that time, and therefore take passages (9b–c) to prove (indirectly) that African Latin had a vowel system of the Sardinian type. Consentius' remark is argued to have been motivated by observation of the difference between his own pronunciation ([ˈpeːper]), characteristic of the Latin of Gaul, with ĭ > [eː] still identified phonemically with short /i/, and the African pronunciation [ˈpiːper], where /i/ was not lowered to [e], so that the deviation from the classical norm was interpretable only in terms of lengthening.[7]

Despite these interpretations, the most elementary reading of Consentius' observations still seems the right one. If he said *correpta* and *producta*, technical terms for shortening and lengthening, there is no compelling reason to take these terms to mean more (or less) than they usually do. They refer to quantity, not to quality, and to African Latin.

Herman's (1982) study of metrical inscriptions from Africa confirms the testimony of (9b–c). A corpus of 279 inscriptions dating from between the first century and the mid fourth is compared with two control corpora from Rome, one contemporary and one later, in order to ascertain similarities and dissimilarities in the patterns of deviation from the Classical Latin norm. The results are summarized in (10a–c):

(10) Errors on stressed vowels

		total	%
a.	Africa (first–early fourth century):	28	27%
b.	Rome (first–early fourth century):	7	8.6%
c.	Rome (late fourth–sixth century):	16	29%

Errors on stressed vowels consist, overwhelmingly, in the use of a short vowel in open syllables which should be heavy for the metre. Herman's method implies that the observed figures are contrasted with those that would be expected given a random distribution (i.e., in case the variable at issue – in this case stressed vs. unstressed – were uninfluential). Since in Latin texts the ratio stressed/unstressed vowel is 1:3 (Herman 1968:197, n5), the error rate in Africa (10a) closely approaches randomness, as opposed to the data from Rome in the same period, where the errors concentrate in unstressed vowels with more than chance frequency. This proves that the VQ contrast, in Rome, was endangered in unstressed position (see §1) but much better preserved under stress. The fact that no such difference is observed in Africa strongly suggests that distinctive VQ had been eliminated altogether. The situation changes radically, in Rome, after the mid fourth century, when the *urbs*, too, reaches 'African' figures, with confusions evenly distributed over stressed and unstressed vowels.

Herman also addresses the related issue of whether this epigraphic evidence supports the hypothesis that the merger of VQ co-occurred with the rise of OSL. Errors on stressed vowels mostly involve the erroneous occurrence of a short vowel where a long one would be required. Symmetrically, errors on unstressed vowels involve the replacement of long vowels with short ones with more-than-chance frequency: 68% in Africa, 47% in Rome, as against an expected random distribution of about 20% (the ratio of long to short vowels in unstressed position is 1:4; cf. Herman 1968:199). In sum, the results of the analysis of metrical evidence correspond exactly to Consentius' description (9b–e), and thus support the hypothesis of an early rise of OSL in the Latin of Africa and of its subsequent spread to the rest of the Empire, during the fifth century.[8]

Given the evidence in (10b–c), one can ask how so many scholars could maintain that contrastive VQ in (Roman) spoken Latin disappeared as early as, say, the third century BC (Pulgram 1975:287f.; Vineis 1984, at least for basilectal varieties), or the first century AD (e.g., Bonfante 1968; Castellani 1991:21; Väänänen 1966:18f.; etc.). The answer is disarmingly simple. Those scholars simply distrusted the testimony of Latin grammarians,[9] and relied, basically, on just one piece of evidence, the confusion, in the Latin sources, of <e>/<i> and <o>/<u>, which does occur in Rome as early as the third century BC and becomes more and more frequent during the Empire, in the epigraphical Latin of central and northern Italy and Gaul above all. From their occurrence, a 'transformation of Latin length into timbre'

(Straka 1956:199) was derived straightforwardly, as if the shift in quality automatically implied loss of the VQ contrast.

The argument is flawed. First, these documented deviations from the classical norm show only that the *quality* of short high vowels was already on its way to change, in the direction later taken by the further Romance development. However, as pointed out by Franceschi (1976:277), Herman (1998:9, n7), Loporcaro (1997:68f.) and Seidl (1995b:377), among others, even if short /i/ and /u/ changed to [ɪ]/[e] and [ʊ]/[o], this is in itself no proof that the VQ contrast was lost.

Further proof of the independence of the collapse of distinctive VQ and the qualitative mergers of ĭ vs. ē and of ŭ vs. ō is provided by Sardinian, which lost VQ, but did not merge ĭ vs. ē (e.g., [ˈpiːra] 'pear' < PĬRAM vs. [ˈsɛːrɔ] 'evening' < SĒRO) nor ŭ vs. ō (e.g., [ˈruːɣɛ] 'cross' < CRŬCEM vs. [ˈbɔːɣɛ] 'voice' < UŌCEM).

The available evidence supports Herman's (1998:21) placement of the VQ collapse within the first of the two main rounds of change he assumes to have taken place in the Latin–Romance transition. This first round was completed before the fall of the western Empire. It affected a linguistic system that was basically still unitary in speech, as well as in writing (though with diatopic, diastratic and diaphasic variation). Vowel quantity collapse, even though some harbingers of the change appear as early as the second to third centuries, was completed no earlier than the fifth.

At this point, inherited contrastive VQ plays no further role, either for stress assignment or for other aspects of the phonology: the proto-Romance system has arisen. After this stage, the second round of change began, with the application (or generalization) of several phonological processes that transformed the (unitary) system of proto-Romance into the systems of the individual Romance languages. Among these, those affecting vowels will be discussed in §3.

3   Prosodic revolutions II: syncope and apocope

The historical development of Romance syncope is a delicate, still controversial, issue. Syncope of the post-tonic vowel of proparoxytones, especially, clearly has a common (pan-Romance) core, rooted in (late) Latin, where it is massively attested: the *Appendix Probi* offers several examples of proscribed popular forms like *calda* for CALIDA 'hot', *oclus* for OCULUS 'eye', *veclus* for UETULUS 'old', *virdis* for UIRIDIS 'green', which must have been in common use in the spoken language of the time (probably mid fifth century, according to Flobert 1987) and underlie all Romance outcomes:

(11) CALIDAM 'hot' > CALDAM > Fr. *chaude*, It. *calda*, Log. (Srd.) *kalda*, Ro. *caldă*
FRIGIDAM 'cold' > FRICDAM > Fr. *froide*, It. *fredda*, Log. (Srd.) *fritta*
UIRIDEM 'green' > UIRDEM > Fr. *vert*, It. *verde*, Log. (Srd.) *bilde*, Ro. *verde*
OCULUM 'eye' > OCLUM > Fr. *œil*, It. *occhio*, Log. (Srd.) |*oːʒu*, Ro. *ochi*

On the other hand, syncope clearly developed at a different pace and to different extents in the individual languages (12):

(12) HEDERAM 'ivy' Sp. *hiedra*, Pt. *hera*, Cat. *eura*, Prv. *elra*, (OFr. *iere* >) Fr. *lierre* vs. It. *edera*, Ro. *iederă*

PŪLICEM 'flea' Sp. *pulga* (< PŪLICA), Fr. *puce*, It. *pulce*, vs. SIt. *pólice*, Log. (Srd.) |*puːliɣe*, Ro. *purice*

SŌRICEM 'mouse' Sp. *sorce*, (OFr. *surgier* 'catch mice'), It. *sorcio* vs. SIt. *sórice*, Log. (Srd.) |*soːriɣe*, Ro. *șoarece*

FRAXINUM 'ash tree' Sp. *fresno*, Pt. *freixo*, Fr. *frêne*, vs. It. *frassino*, Ro. *frasin*

A general tendency can be recognized, with western Romance displaying more extensive syncope than eastern, and Italy and Sardinian in between. Syncope also affected vowels preceding main stress, in this case, too, to an extent variable from language to language. The vowel most liable to syncope is the so-called 'intertonic', the foot-final vowel following secondary stress. Its deletion was regular in OFrench (CĪUITĀTEM 'city' > *citet*, LĪBERĀRE 'to free' > *livrer*), resulting in systematic reduction of pretonic bisyllabic feet to monosyllabic ones, but was quite widespread in the rest of Romance: e.g., Sp. *ciudad*, It. *città*, Ro. *cetate*, as against SEPTIMĀNAM 'week' > Sp. *semana*, Cat., Prv. *setmana*, Fr. *semaine* vs. It. *settimana*, Ro. *săptămână*.

As the last example shows, secondary stress generally protected vowels from being syncopated. Apart from secondary stress, the prosodic position most resistant to syncope is the initial unstressed syllable of trisyllabic paroxytones: e.g., DĪCĒBAT 'he said' > Sp. *decía*, Fr. *disait*, It. *diceva*, Ro. *zicea*; NEPŌTEM 'nephew' > Fr. *neveu*, It. *nipote*, Ro. *nepot*. Syncope in these contexts is highly exceptional. It occurs in northern Italian dialects of Emilia Romagna, where syncope went so far as entirely to destroy the pretonic foot: e.g., Bolognese [ˈstmɛːna] 'week', [ˈ(d)dʒeːva] 'said3SG.IPF' (Gaudenzi 1889; Coco 1970). In these varieties, syncope regularly deleted pretonic mid vowels, while /i a u/ were not affected, as seen in examples (13) and (14), respectively, from the dialects of Novellara (see Malagoli 1910–13a:107–28) and Lizzano in Belvedere (see Malagoli 1930:154–60). Where syncope has applied, standard Italian counterparts are added for comparison, as they coincide with the proto-Romance antecedents of the corresponding Emilian words:

(13)

/a i u/-preservation	[pa'gɛːr] *pagare* 'to pay', [ti'rɛːr] *tirare* 'to draw', [du'rɛːr] *durare* 'to last'
/e/-syncope	['zduː] *seduto* 'sat', ['vdeːva] *vedeva* '(he) saw', ['stãːŋta] *settanta* 'seventy', ['pkɛːr] *beccare* 'peck' vs. [ser'pẽːŋt] *serpente* 'snake', [teŋ'pesta] *tempesta* 'storm', [vres'pɛːr] *vespaio* 'wasps' nest'
/o/-syncope	['kvɛːrta] *coperta* 'blanket', ['klõŋb] *colombo* 'pigeon', ['pkõːŋ] *boccone* 'mouthful', ['plõːŋ] *pollone* 'side-shoot' vs. [for'miːga] *formica* 'ant', [roŋ'kiːna] *roncola* 'pruning-hook'

(14)

/a i u/-preservation	[gra'ŋaːre] 'hail', [kri'daːre] 'shout', [fu'maːre] 'smoke'
/e/-syncope	['mzuːra] *misura* 'measure', [med'doːri] *mietitori* 'harvesters', vs. [seŋ'tiːre] *sentire* 'feel'
/o/-syncope	['vreːre] *volere* 'want', ['kmãːŋda] *comanda* 'order3SG', ['dmeŋga] *domenica* 'Sunday' vs. [kor'tɛlːo] *coltello* 'knife'

As seen in these examples, syncope applied in open syllables (as well as in those that became open via degemination). Mid vowels in closed syllables, on the other hand, remained unaffected.

To a lesser extent, pretonic syncope is (or was) typical for rural Piedmontese, where it only affects proto-Romance /e/: ['zmija] 'resembles' < *SIMILIAT, ['fnɛstra] 'window' < FENESTRAM, ['stɛmbər] 'September' < SEPTEMBREM (Canavesano; see Zörner 1998:42). In modern French, /ə/ is deleted variably: [s(ə)krɛ] *secret* 'secret', [d(ə)mẽ] *demain* 'tomorrow'. In the Middle Ages, syncopated forms such as *fra* < *fera* '(he) will do' occur in Anglo-Norman texts. Modern Norman dialects delete pretonic /ə/ categorically: [dmøðɛ] *demeurer* 'to live', [dzastr] *désastre* 'disaster' (Montreuil 1998). Pretonic vowel reduction (VR) variably results in syncope in European Portuguese: e.g., *restaurantes* [Rəʃtau̯'rãtəʃ] 'restaurants' → [Rʃtau̯'rẽtʃ], *perfeito* [pər'fɐ̯itu] 'perfect' → [pr̩'fɐ̯it] (Parkinson 1988:141). This is but one manifestation of a recent shift in rhythmical structure, which transformed European Portuguese into a stress-timed language (§6).

While pretonic syncope is relevant only for secondary stress, post-tonic syncope in proparoxytones had a direct impact on primary stress assignment. Clearly, if post-tonic syncope applies across the board, proparoxytonic stress disappears and the 3SW, inherited from Latin, reduces to a 2SW. This happened most consistently in Gallo-Romance, where stress assignment has undergone the most radical restructuring (see §4.3).

Much effort has been devoted to establishing a precise chronology of French syncope, relative to the many other changes which transformed the sound shape of this language to an extent unknown elsewhere (e.g., UITELLU 'calf' > Fr. ['vo] vs. It. [vi'tɛlːo]). This has led to the assumption of several rounds of syncope, intertwined in relative chronology with other changes. For instance, retention of final -e in OFr. comte 'count' < COMITE vs. its deletion in pont 'bridge' < PONTE standardly led to the assumption that final vowel deletion applied after inherited clusters but not after clusters arising through syncope (e.g., Wüest 1979:146–68). The latter must be ordered before open syllable diphthongization for comte, not for jue(f)ne < *IUUENE. This observation, combined with the further asymmetries in the diphthongization of ŏ vs. ĕ (cf. OFr. friemte < FREMITU in the same prosodic and segmental context as COMITE), led scholars to postulate several rounds of syncope: cf. the different solutions proposed in Meyer-Lübke (1890) and Straka (1953), and the critical discussion by Morin (2003; with further references).

3.1   The Latin prehistory of Romance syncope

These and similar problems arise from a (conceptually) simple circumstance, which produced, however, a host of empirical complications: a tendency to syncope existed all along, from prehistoric Latin down to the development of the individual Romance languages. In the history of Latin, syncope was constantly present 'from prehistoric times down to the formation of the Romance languages' (Leumann 1977:95). Therefore, Pensado Ruiz (1984:234) is surely right in observing that one cannot speak of a 'start' to Romance syncope, but only of the generalization of a pre-existing phenomenon, given that cases of syncope have been appearing since archaic Latin.

Once this is admitted, some specific problems may be seen in a slightly different light. As for the comte vs. pont problem in the chronology of OFrench, Gsell (1996:560) assumes the coexistence of both syncopated and non-syncopated COM(I)TE, possibly specialized as allegro vs. lento forms, well into the history of French up to the age of the application of final vowel deletion.

Syncope in prehistoric Latin was the extreme result of a more general process of vowel reduction that affected short vowels after stress. In the period at which syncope applied (sixth–fifth century BC), primary stress consistently fell on the first syllable of the word, since the Classical Latin stress rule became operative only in about the fourth century BC. At this archaic stage, therefore, post-tonic vowel reduction could affect all non-initial syllables. It manifested itself in the form of short-vowel raising, and operated more radically in open than in closed syllables (15):

(15) F'ăCIO C'ONFĭCIO C'ONFĕCTUM

This tendency to vowel reduction was responsible for the deletion of final vowels in, for example, PARS 'part', MORS 'death', DŌS 'dowry' < *parti-s, *morti-s, *dōti-s. Both in the final syllable and word-internally, deletion applied only if its output was compatible with syllabification requirements: e.g., SĒSTERTIUS (a coin) < *sēmi-s-tertios, PERGO 'proceed' < *per-rĕgo, CULMEN 'roof' alongside COLUMEN, etc. In (15), on the other hand, *confĭcio could not possibly evolve to **CONFCIO: therefore only VR is observed, not syncope (cf. Leumann 1977:95–99; Meiser 1998:66). Thus, syncope and VR in prehistoric Latin were two sides of the same coin. Their application is usually held to have been dependent on the nature of stress. Latin stress remained dynamic all along: its chief acoustic correlate must have been amplitude, as opposed to classical Greek's 'melodic' accent, phonetically realized as a rise in pitch.[10] This dynamic nature did not change when, after the fourth century, protosyllabic stress yielded to the classical stress rule. This change probably coincided with a change in the degree of expiratory prominence: in the classical period, the dynamic strength was somewhat relaxed, at least in the acrolectal varieties reflected in the literary language (and in classical metrics, possibly under Greek influence), to crop up again in the late Empire when, for socio-political reasons, the standard progressively lost its force.

This historical development perfectly accounts for the relationship and continuity between early and late syncope, which is essential to the comprehension of later Romance evolution. This continuity, underscored in classical work on late Latin / early Romance (cf. Väänänen 1966:42; Straka 1964:227), has been recently questioned by Mester (1994:37–43), who sharply distinguishes 'early syncope', as exemplified by *per+regō > PERGŌ 'continue' (cf. perfect PERREXĪ), PORRIGŌ > PORGŌ 'stretch out', *jūrigō > IURGŌ 'quarrel', etc. from the 'late syncope' responsible for the Romance outcomes seen in (11). Assuming right-to-left foot formation and under the hypothesis that prehistoric and Classical Latin had a maximally bimoraic foot ('quantitative trochee'), early syncope is explained as the erasure of a 'trapped' (i.e., unmetrified) syllable. The examples in (11) do not match this pattern, since the first syllable is light. Therefore, they are taken to be instances of a structurally independent, later wave of (vulgar Latin) syncope that must have applied within a system which had become quantity-insensitive. Note, incidentally, that Mester restricts his discussion to post-tonic syncope, following antepenultimate stress, while claiming in a footnote that also pretonic cases of early syncope (as discussed, for example, in Burger 1928) 'mostly also occur in trapping configurations' (Mester 1994:39, n45).

Actually, closer inspection of the (archaic) Latin evidence shows that early syncope also applied to strings which could have been perfectly metrified, under Mester's assumptions (made explicit by bracketing in the following examples): e.g., $(călĕ)(făcĭ)<ō>$ > CALFACIO 'warm', $(sŭsĕ)<mō>$ > SŪMO 'eat', $*(dŏkĭ)<tos>$ > DOCTUS 'learnèd', $*(vĭrŏ)<tŭs>$ UIRTŪS 'virtue' (see Rix 1966; Lindsay 1894:185; Niedermann 1931:47; Leumann 1977:95–99; Meiser 1998:66). Syncope in what would have been the first foot, under Mester's assumptions, took place in BAL(I)NEUM 'bath' (syncopated from Varro and Cicero onwards), BAL(I)NEĀTOR 'bather' (in Plautus; cf. Väänänen 1974/82:43). Examples like MONSTRUM 'portent' < *monestrum (cf. MONEŌ 'I warn'), where syncope affected the nucleus of a closed syllable, fit Mester's picture even worse. Some such examples, like MŌNSTRUM, OFFICĪNA 'work-shop' (< *opificīna), SŪMŌ established themselves in the standard language. For others, vacillation is documented (e.g., COLUMEN/CULMEN), which, however, appears to have started much earlier than assumed by Mester: e.g., F'ENSTRA < F'ENESTRA 'window' (both documented in Plautus) (cf. Meiser 1998:66; Morani 2000:179); FRIGDARIA 'refreshing' (cf. FRIGIDUS 'cold'), CALDARIUM 'room for hot baths' (cf. CALIDUS 'warm'), in Lucilius (second century BC). The emperor Augustus reportedly dubbed as pedantic the pronunciation CALIDUS: clearly, then, by the late first century BC, syncopated CALDUS could not be qualified as 'low'. As Lahiri et al. (1999:387f., 394f.) point out, all of this evidence points to the early establishment of a quantity-insensitive initial foot. This is needed, in their view, for technical reasons related to secondary stress assignment. This evidence obviously supports the conclusion that the relevance of quantity for the linguistic system overall came to be threatened earlier in all or virtually all unstressed positions.

In conclusion, all claims of a sharp distinction between early and late syncope (à la Mester 1994) appear unwarranted. Once this is established, we can pursue further the evolution and consequences of syncope in Romance.

3.2 The spread of syncope

As we have said, long-term variation must be assumed well into the history of the individual languages. For French, in particular, this assumption is safer than several rounds of syncope intertwined with other changes (most notably, ĕ- and ŏ-diphthongization and final vowel reduction) postulated in Straka's (1953; 1956) relative (and absolute) chronologies.[11] Among the major Romance languages, French underwent VR and syncope in the most pervasive form, as is already apparent from the few examples provided above in (11). These changes led to a complete reshaping of the prosodic structure of words and to a radical change in the working of stress assignment. By the time of the earliest written records (the Strasbourg Oaths, 842), syncope had eliminated proparoxytonic stress in all words: e.g., OFr. *tendre* 'soft' < TENERUM, *moldre* 'to grind' < MOLERE, *estre* 'be' < ESSE(RE). This had the effect of reducing the 3SW: stress could fall, in OFrench, on either the final or the penultima, the latter option being subject to a segmental constraint, due to the weakening and/or loss of final vowels.

In no other Romance language did syncope set in so early and so pervasively as in Gallo-Romance. As for pervasiveness, even in Emilian, in which syncope affected not only pretonic (13)–(14) but also post-tonic vowels (e.g., Bolognese [ˈmɛːzna] 'grinder' < MACHINAM, [ˈdmaŋdʒa] 'Sunday' < DOMINICAM), this did not lead to a total elimination of proparoxytones (unlike French). Forms such as [ˈlɛːgr(u)ma] 'tear' < LACRIMAM, [ˈvep(e)ra] 'viper' < UIPERA survive, although subject to variable syncope synchronically (cf. Coco 1970:4, 14, 16). All dialects of Emilia show this co-occurrence: e.g., in Fiorenzuola (province of Piacenza), [ˈkudʒa] 'rind' < *CUTICAM, [ˈlaŋda] 'lamp' < LAMPADAM alongside [ˈsemula] 'bran (flour)' < SIMULAM, [ˈbarbura] 'Barbara' (Casella 1922:43).

As for the time at which syncope applied, for Castilian its ultimate phonologization in DOMINICUM > *domingo* must have followed lenition (as opposed to Fr. *dimanche*) and cannot have taken place prior to the eleventh century (when *dominigo* still occurs in texts; cf. Menéndez Pidal 1953:154). Loss of -*i*- in, for example, NOMINE > *nombre* 'name', PECTINE > *peine* 'comb' must have followed final -*e* deletion, which in turn 'was not yet generalized in the tenth century' (Menéndez Pidal 1953:80). Otherwise, after intervocalic -*n*-, final -*e* would have been deleted. The delay with respect to Gallo-Romance, for which the insurmountable lower limit is the end of the seventh century, is considerable. It testifies to a gradual spreading of this process from northern France, a pattern that will recur for other related processes (see §3.3).

3.3 Vowel reduction and apocope

As seen in section 1, pre-literary Latin had already undergone vowel reduction processes. These were part of a conspiracy that eventually resulted in the loss of the VQ contrast in unstressed position. We now return to the further (proto-)Romance development, limiting our scrutiny to final vowels which are relevant to stress assignment.

After the early processes discussed in section 1 (*correptio iambica*, third century BC), the shortening of unstressed vowels gradually proceeded. For instance, long -ŏ in the 1SG verbal ending was shortened, beginning in Augustan times, and shortened -ŏ was prescribed as standard for non-monosyllabic verbs by the fourth century AD (cf. Allen 1973:182, n2). As a result, the system of unstressed vowels inherited by all Romance languages maximally comprised five contrasting phonemes: /i e a o u/. If we concentrate on word-final position we see that Logudorese Sardinian and the dialects of central Italy preserve this situation best (16):[12]

(16)

a. Logudorese	ˈbeːni 'come.2SG'	ˈbɛːnɛ 'well'	ˈkraːβa 'goat'	ˈkantɔ 'sing.1SG'	ˈferːu 'iron'
b. Servigliano	ˈmitːi 'put.2SG'	ˈmeːte 'put.3SG'	ˈkoːsa 'thing'	ˈveŋko 'win.1SG'	ˈbonu 'good'

The two systems diverge in the treatment of -ĭ which, just as under stress, merges with -ī in Sardinian but with -ĕ in central Italy. This poses the problem of the relationship between the Sardinian vowel system and those of the remaining Romance languages (the issue is summarized for stressed vowels in this volume, chapter 3: §1.1), as apparent in the following tentative scheme, partially reproduced from Lausberg (1971:263) (17):

(17)

a. Classical Latin	ī	ĭ	ē	ĕ	A	ŏ	ō	ŭ	ū
b. Sardinian	i		ɛ		a	ɔ		u	
c. Vulgar Latin	i		e		a	o		u	
d. Southern Italian	i		e		a	o		u	
e. Tuscan	i		e		a	o			

Note that 'southern Italian' is here a reconstructive, rather than synchronic, label: while all southern Italian dialects in fact provide evidence (through metaphony, see chapter 3: §1.2.2) for the reconstructed five-way contrast in

Michele Loporcaro

(17d), only the dialects of central Italy (exemplified in (16b)) still preserve this system.[13]

Tuscan comes next (17e), in that all post-tonic back vowels merge into /o/: *bello* 'nice', *lupo* 'wolf' = *canto* 'sing.1SG', *quanto* 'how much'.[14] All remaining Romance varieties outside Italy display more radical reductions, which – as observed cross-linguistically for weakening processes – follow different phonetic routes. Final vowels may be peripheralized (*e > i, o > u*) or centralized and even deleted, /a/ being the most resistant, as shown in the following complementary overview (see Lausberg 1976:263; '–' = Ø):

(18)

a. Classical Latin	Ī	ĭ	Ē	ĕ	A	Ŏ	Ō	Ŭ	Ū
b. Romanian	i	e			ə	– (u)			
c. Portuguese	ə (–)			ɐ	u				
d. Spanish	e (–)			a	o				
e. Catalan	–			ə	– (o)				
f. Occitan	–			a	–				
g. French	–			ə, –	–				
h. Surselvan	–			ɐ	–				

Historically, all[15] these languages show traces of metaphony induced by (the outcomes of) -ī; Portuguese and Romansh (Surselvan), at least, also have reflexes of U-induced metaphony. Synchronically, the number of final vowels ranges from three to zero (French).[16] In between, and between all the stages in (17)–(18), a fine-grained variation is observable, that spans the whole documented history of Romance and is still partly reflected in dialect variation.

This variation is multi-dimensional. It may involve the quality of the final vowels (reduction) or result in their deletion, first context-sensitive and then context-free (with restructuring). Within Ibero-Romance, for instance, Castilian has shown system (18d) since the earliest texts, while north-west Leonese and western Asturian, like Galician, raise *e > i* and *o > u* (Menéndez Pidal 1953:79–81). Furthermore, Castilian deleted final -*e* (and, less commonly, -*o*) after most coronals, a process that was applied variably between the tenth century (the date of the earliest Castilian documents) and the twelfth. In Galician, this optional deletion started only in the eleventh century and was more constrained, not applying after -*d* (cf. Martínez Gil 1997b:304). In the twelfth century, Castilian went through a stage in which the constraints were relaxed and so-called 'extreme'

66

apocope took place: deletion was optionally possible in, for example, *nievel nief* 'snow', *adelant(e)* 'forward', *calient(e)* 'hot'.[17] The demise of extreme apocope, with the restoration of final vowels in the contexts in which they still occur today, happened in the second half of the thirteenth century. For this rise and fall, cultural influence from French and Catalan (and its decline) has been invoked. Along with this cultural factor, a common (western Romance) diachronic drift clearly also contributed. In this drift, northern Gallo-Romance is at the forefront.

In French, non-low vowels were first centralized (cf. Straka 1956:195, 198) and eventually deleted, a process completed around AD 700 (cf. Richter 1934:243f.; Sampson 1980b:30). At this point, word-finally, French only had a binary contrast Ø ≠ /ə/, the latter derived from -A. This state of affairs is mirrored in the earliest extant records, as shown by the vacillation between -*e* and -*a*: e.g., *domnizelle* 'maiden' < DOM(I)NICELLA (St Eulalia, about 880–900; see Hilty 2001:62–66) alongside *pulcella* 'maiden' < *PULICELLA (St Eulalia), both with a suffix pronounced [ˈɛlːə]. As for stress assignment, ə-ending polysyllables were the only paroxytones left in OFrench, after both syncope and VR had applied.[18]

The converging effect of syncope and final vowel deletion, thus, was a second prosodic revolution. Unlike the first one (§2), which can still be located within the history of spoken Latin (hence, proto-Romance), this second revolution belongs to the individual history of French, which underwent these changes at an earlier date and to a greater extent than other varieties.

If French was in the vanguard of the change, for VR as for syncope and many other processes, reconstruction of earlier stages of final vowel deletion must rely on evidence from other varieties. Dialects of northern Italy provide relevant evidence, as argued in Loporcaro (2005–6). Liguria and central Veneto have a four-vowel final system parallel to Tuscan (17e) (for Ligurian, with back vowels merged into /u/, rather than /o/: [ˈɔmu] < HOMO 'man', [ˈpɔrtu] < PORTO 'bring.1SG' like [ˈbaːʒu] < BASIUM 'kiss', [ˈœdʒu] < OC(U)LUM 'eye'; Toso 1997).

The remaining northern Italian dialects resemble OFrench in that they have deleted all final non-low vowels (see the Emilian data in (13) above), but final /a/ is preserved: e.g., Mil. [ˈnœːf] < NOUUM 'new' M vs. [ˈnœva] < NOUAM F. The stages in between can be reconstructed on the evidence of both medieval texts and modern dialect variation. Centralization of non-low vowels, which has to be reconstructed for a pre-literary stage of OFrench, is observable today in some Emilian dialects of the Apennines; e.g., Piandelagotti (province of Modena) (see (19)):[19]

(19)

-A	[aˈɡoc:a] < ACUC(U)LA 'needle', [saˈjøt:a] < SAGITTAM 'thunderbolt', [ˈʃɲu:ra] < *SENIORAM 'lady', [ɡaˈli:na] < GALLINAM 'hen', [eˈkat:a] < CAPTAT 'buys.3MSG'
-E	[ˈpɛv:rə] < PIPEREM 'pepper', [ˈsu:lə] < SOLEM 'sun'
-O	[mi a ˈkã:tə] < CANTO 'sing.1SG'
-I	[ti t ˈkã:tə] < *CANTI (CANTAS) 'sing.2SG'
-U	[ˈkar:ə] < CARRUM 'cart', [ˈɡal:ə] < GALLUM 'cock'

Dialects from the same area provide evidence for a further major path to vowel loss, as final non-low vowels can be optionally deleted (and most often are, in connected speech) when they do not occur prepausally (examples in (20a–b) from the dialect of Pianaccio, an outlying part of Lizzano in Belvedere, province of Bologna):

(20)

a. __ ##	b. __]PW [...]PW ...
[e ˈskris:e/**ˈskris]	[e ˈskris na ˈlet:ra] 'he wrote (a letter)'
[e j ˈa ˈskrit:o/**ˈskrit]	[e j ˈa ˈskrit na ˈlet:ra] 'he has written him (a letter)'

The same rule can be reconstructed for OMilanese (Contini 1935).

Further minor prosodically driven adjustments may result in final-/a/-deletion in all dialects of northern Italy preserving it. In the western Emilian dialect of Fiorenzuola, first conjugation imperatives have preserved etymological final /a/ (21a), which is however deleted under cliticization (cf. Casella 1922:43):

(21)   a. [ˈba:za] 'kiss', [ˈtrø:va] 'find'
      b. [ˈba:zla] 'kiss her', [ˈtrø:vla] 'find her'
      c. [ˈbazamla] 'kiss her for me', [ˈpagatla] 'pay it.F for yourself'

This prevents antepenultimate (21b) stress from being derived postlexically, in strings with one clitic, whereas with double clitics (21c) final /a/ in the verb is restored so as to allow syllabification of the ensuing consonant cluster. Anyway, preantepenultimate stress does not arise here, unlike Tuscan and standard Italian.

In sum, western Romance apocope appears as a differentiated process, which went through several intermediate steps and proceeded at a different pace in different varieties, as suggested by the following scheme (systems (22b–d) may also display synchronic rules of vowel deletion, of the sort shown in (20) and (21b), the latter also being found in systems of type (22e)):

(22)

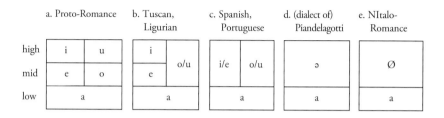

	a. Proto-Romance		b. Tuscan, Ligurian		c. Spanish, Portuguese		d. (dialect of) Piandelagotti	e. NItalo-Romance
high	i	u	i					
				o/u	i/e	o/u	ə	Ø
mid	e	o	e					
low	a		a		a		a	a

System (22e) coincides with those of Occitan and Romansh. The next step is qualitative reduction of /a/ > /ə/ (Catalan, OFrench), and finally deletion of /ə/ (as in modern French).

3.4   Syncope, apocope and the rise of Romance

The second prosodic revolution, which consisted of syncope and apocope (§§3.3–3.4) and was carried out earliest and in its fullest form in northern Gallo-Romance, had a great impact on the cultural history of the Latin–Romance speaking world. As we have seen, both changes were completed in OFrench before its earliest documentation in the ninth century: work on the chronology of phonological changes in pre-literary French, in the wake of the seminal study by Richter (1934:243f.), agrees in considering final vowel deletion as the last major change affecting the vowel system, after diphthongization, syncope, etc. It is supposed to have taken place between the seventh and the eighth centuries – shortly before French began to be used in writing. As Herman (1996) convincingly argued, this is not coincidental. On the contrary, the second prosodic revolution was the internal cause for this external (cultural) innovation.

Until the early seventh century, there is evidence that the acrolectal and basilectal varieties spoken in Merovingian Gaul (as elsewhere in the former territory of the western Empire) were still mutually intelligible (cf. Herman 1996:368–73, elaborating on Banniard 1992).[20] In particular, uneducated speakers could understand Latin as used by the Church and for other official purposes. By the mid eighth century, on the other hand, mutual intelligibility in Frankish Gaul had gone, as testified by

Pepin's and Charlemagne's constant preoccupation with the insufficient command of Latin by priests. This communicative breakdown is addressed in the resolution of the Council of Tours (AD 813), which prescribes that sermons have to be translated 'in rusticam Romanam linguam' (literally, 'into the rustic Roman tongue'). Thus, the crucial period in which the gap in intelligibility arose (between, roughly, 620/630 and the mid eighth century) coincides with the chronology of final vowel deletion, which was in turn preceded by syncope.[21] Thus, Herman concludes, unintelligibility was determined by the newly created prosodic mismatch between the oral performance of Latin – with internal and final syllables preserved, especially after the liturgical reform of Pepin (751–768) which replaced the *cantus Gallicanus* with the *cantus Romanus* – and the pronunciation of (Gallo-)Romance as modified by apocope and syncope. Thus, the fact that two breakpoints in Latin–Romance cultural history like the Council of Tours and the Strasbourg Oaths both took place in northern France is far from fortuitous. What we have termed the second prosodic revolution had far-reaching consequences for the cultural history of Europe.[22]

3.5 Proto-romance open syllable lengthening and secondary VQ contrasts

We saw in sections 1–2 that the rise of OSL was the main cause for the demise of contrastive VQ in late Latin / proto-Romance. OSL, however, was also the source of novel VQ contrasts that generally arose in northern Romance (i.e., the territory from the Apennines to northern France, or western Romance minus Ibero-Romance).[23] I now show how the evidence from geographical variation allows further reconstructive inferences as to the (early) history and development of vowel length.[24]

The VQ contrast is illustrated for some northern Romance varieties in (23)–(26):

(23) Milanese (Nicoli 1983:45, 49f.; Sanga 1984:60–64; 1988:291–93)[25]

a. CVCV	b. CVC:V	c. CVCV	d. CVCa
[ˈkaːl] 'loss'	[ˈkal] 'corn'	[ˈnøːv] 'new.M'	[ˈnøva] 'new.FSG'
[ˈnaːz] 'nose'	[ˈnas] 'be born'	[ˈsøːl] 'alone.M'	[ˈsøla] 'alone.FSG'
[ˈfyːz] 'spindle'	[ˈfys] 'be.3SBJV'	[ˈlyːz] 'light'	[ˈlyna] 'moon'

(24)   Friulian (Bender *et al.* 1952; Vanelli 1979; Frau 1984:18):

a. CVCV	b. CVC˙V	c. CVCV	d. CVCa
[ˈliːs] 'worn out'	[ˈlis] 'smooth.M'	[canˈtaːt] 'sung.MSG'	[canˈtade] 'sung. FSG'
[ˈlaːt] 'gone.MSG'	[ˈlat] 'milk'	[ˈkruːt] 'raw.MSG'	[ˈkrude] 'raw. FSG'
[ˈluːs] 'light'	[ˈlus] 'luxury'	[ˈloːf] 'wolf'	[ˈlove] 'she-wolf'

Friulian and Milanese have contrastive VQ in Romance oxytones only (23a–b), (24a–b), and neutralize the contrast elsewhere. Other varieties such as Emilian (including Cremonese, in southern Lombardy) and north-Alpine Provençal, on the other hand, also display the vowel quantity contrast in paroxytones:

(25)   Cremonese (Rossini 1975):
      [ˈpaːla] 'shovel' ≠ [ˈspala] 'shoulder'
      [ˈlaːna] 'wool' ≠ [ˈkana] 'reed'
      Bolognese (Coco 1970:88):
      [ˈfaːta] 'done.FSG' ≠ [ˈfaťa] 'slice'
      [ˈmeːter] 'metre' ≠ [ˈmeťer] 'put'

(26)   North-Alpine Provençal (Val Germanasca; Pons and Genre 1997; Morin
      2003:131):
      [ˈpeːno] 'punishment' ≠ [ˈpənːo] 'pen'
      [ˈpaːlo] 'shovel' ≠ [eiˈpalːo] 'shoulder'

Most current analyses of VQ in Friulian and Milanese argue that the rise of the VQ contrast must have been a (direct or indirect) consequence of apocope: Repetti (1992:175) proposes that Milanese contrastive length arose as a compensatory lengthening for the loss of final vowels. According to Baroni and Vanelli (2000), Francescato (1966:130–43), Hualde (1992b), Vanelli (1979) and Videsott (2001), lengthening compensated for the loss of voicing in the following consonant. Montreuil (1991:43–46) assumes the enforcement of a Strong Rhyme Constraint that requires that all stressed syllables be bimoraic and consequently triggers lengthening in (23a); for (Prieto 1993:91; 2000) lengthening is forced by the high ranking of a FOOT-BINARITY constraint, requiring that 'Feet should be analyzable as binary'.

These accounts have an obvious drawback: they destroy the link between the two kinds of VQ-systems (23–24 vs. 25–26). Even more seriously, they are at a loss to accommodate the occurrence of contrastive VQ in northern Italo-Romance varieties in which apocope did not occur, such as Ligurian (27a) or the southernmost Emilian dialects of the Apennines (27b):

(27) a. Genoese (see Forner 1975:50; 1988:458)
['pɔːsu] 'relax.1SG' < PAUSO ≠ ['pɔsu] 'can.1SG'< POSSUM
b. dialect of Lizzano in Belvedere (see Malagoli 1930:139–41)
[kaŋˈta] 'sung' ≠ [kaŋˈtaː] 'sing.2PL'
(no apocope: e.g., [aˈmiːgo/aˈmiːga] 'friend.MSG/FSG')

An alternative view, advocated in Morin (1992; 2003), and Loporcaro
(2005–6; 2007a), proposes that contrastive VQ throughout the northern
Romance domain arose not because of apocope but as a consequence of
degemination (see §2). Degemination, it is argued, transformed the allophonic distribution of length derived through OSL into a phonemic contrast, which subsequently retreated from paroxytones in Milanese and
Friulian while it was preserved in this prosodic context in the varieties in
(25)–(27).[26]

OSL clearly had a common core, which must be assumed for proto-
Romance and is reflected in the formulation given in (4). This common
core basically concerns paroxytones. As for both proparoxytones and oxytones, comparative evidence points to early differentiation. In northern
Italian dialects, OSL did not apply in the antepenultimate syllable. This is
exemplified with Milanese and Ligurian in (28):

(28) a. Milanese (Nicoli 1983:47–58):
['pegura] 'sheep', ['legura] 'hare', ['strɔlega] 'fortune teller.F', ['nivula]
'cloud' (also in etymological proparoxytones like ['azen] 'donkey');
b. Ligurian (Ghini 2001:171f.):
Genoese ['zuvenu] 'young man', ['karegu] 'load.1SG', ['navegu] 'be at
sea.1SG'; Savonese [u ˈnavega] 'he is at sea.3SG', ['avidu] 'greedy',
['arabu] 'Arab'.

This dispreference has a straightforward phonetic motivation: rhythmical
compensation. Experimental studies (cf. Marotta 1985; D'Imperio and
Rosenthall 1999:4–8, for modern standard Italian) have shown that
added phonetic material to the right of a stressed vowel within the same
foot induces shortening of the vowel. This is also sometimes reflected in
synchronic rules, even in northern Italian dialects where OSL gave way to a
VQ contrast. In the Emilian dialect of Fiorenzuola, the successors of Latin
proparoxytones all have a short vowel (['salaz] 'willow' < SALICEM, [salˈvadag]
'wild' < SILVATICUM, ['pasar] 'sparrow' < PASSER(UM), ['sabat] 'Saturday' <
SABBATUM) like ['gat] 'cat' < CATTUM, ['sapja] 'know.3SG.SBJV' < SAPIAT and
unlike ['aːla] 'wing' < ALAM, ['naːz] 'nose' < NASUM, ['laːg] 'lake' < LACUM. In
the same dialect, the constraint against long vowels in the antepenult is still
seen at work synchronically, when a verb with root /Vː/ is followed by two

clitics: [ˈbaːza] 'kiss.2SG', [ˈbaːzla] 'kiss her', as opposed to [ˈbazamla] 'kiss her for me', with shortening of the stressed vowel (Casella 1922:19).

On the other hand, in Romansh, proparoxytones must have been affected by OSL. This can be argued from data like the following, from the variety of the Tavetsch valley (western Surselvan) (Caduff 1952:33–37):

(29)   a.   [ˈeir̯] < HERI 'yesterday', [ˈleif̯] < LEUEM 'light.MSG', [ˈmeil̯] < MEL(E) 'honey'

   b.   [ˈmeid̯er] < METERE 'harvest', [ˈveid̯er] < UETERE 'old, used'

   c.   [ˈmjazɐ] < MEDIAM 'half.F', [ˈsjat] < SEPTEM 'seven', [ˈjarvɐ] < HERBAM 'grass'

   d.   [ˈpjarder] < PERDERE 'lose'

This dialect shows diphthongization of proto-Romance /ɛ/ to /ei̯/ in open syllables (vs. /ja/ in closed syllables, (29c–d)), both in original paroxytones (29a) and in original proparoxytones (29b) – which, incidentally, were all reduced to the 2SW through syncope and apocope (see §4.3).

As for OSL in proparoxytones, other Romance varieties are somewhat in-between. For Italian and French, this is shown by the variable application of diphthongization in, for example, It. *tiepido* 'lukewarm', *Fiesole* (placename) vs. *pecora* 'sheep', *medico* 'physician'. In OFrench as well, one finds diph-thongization in *œuvre* 'work' < OPERAM, *friemte* 'tumult' < FREMITUM, *fiertre* 'reliquary' < FERETRUM, along with the vacillation documented in, for example, *tiede/tede/tieve/teve* 'lukewarm' < TEPIDUM (see Morin 2003:137–49).

Cross-linguistic variation in the application of OSL is also observed for oxytones. The formulation in (4) refers to proto-Romance, on the testimony of Italian and Sardinian. However, for these varieties the OSL rule must be complemented with (30):

(30) $V \rightarrow V{:}/ \underline{}]_\sigma X]_{PW}$ [where 'X' is not phonetically empty]
       [+stress]

This condition mirrors the fact that OSL does not affect final vowels in Italian ([veˈrːa] 'will come.3SG') and Sardinian (Log. [gːaˈfːɛ] 'coffee'). This further specification, however, cannot be projected back onto proto-Romance, which is hardly surprising since final stressed vowels did not occur in Latin. The class of Romance oxytones was fed by several diachronic processes in the individual languages (a list of these conspiring changes, for Italian, is given in (35), section 4). And in fact the quantitative treatment of word-final stressed vowels diverges across Romance. Even for languages that no longer have OSL as a synchronic rule, this can be inferred from the outcomes of stressed vowels.

Northern Italian dialects as well as Raeto-Romance, prior to degemination, must have possessed the restriction, as testified by the fact that word-final stressed vowels follow the fate of stressed vowels in closed syllables. This is exemplified in (31) with the development of proto-Romance /i u/ in Bolognese (cf. Gaudenzi 1889; Coco 1970), and with the development of proto-Romance /e o/ in Fassano (see Elwert 1943:44f., 52f.):

(31) a. Bolognese

	a. 'V$	b. 'V#	c. 'VC$
/i/	['viːd] 'saw.3SG' ['spiːga] 'ear (of corn)'	['de] 'day' [akˈse] 'thus'	['desː] 'said.3SG' ['melː] 'thousand'
/u/	['kruːd] 'raw' ['luːz] 'light'	['pjo] 'more' [virˈto] 'virtue'	['brot] 'ugly.M' ['sot] 'dry.M'

b. Fassano

	a. 'V$	b. 'V#	c. 'VC$
/e/	['tɛila] 'cloth' ['mɛis] 'month'	['me] 'me' ['te] 'thee'	['sek] 'dry.MSG' [kaˈpeʃe] 'understand.1SG'
/o/	['krouʃ] 'cross' ['soula] 'alone.FSG'	[aˈlo] < ADILLŌC 'there' [ni ˈo] < NEC ŬBI 'nowhere'	['rot] 'broken.MSG' ['sort] 'deaf.MSG'

In southern Italo-Romance, and French, on the other hand, word-final open syllables pattern with word-internal open, not closed, syllables. This is evidence that OSL must have affected word-final stressed syllables, too, in these varieties, exemplified in (32) with the outcomes of proto-Romance /e/ in French and a Pugliese dialect (Altamura; Loporcaro 1988):

(32) a. Altamura (province of Bari)

	'V$	'V#	'VC$
/e/	['paip] 'pepper' ['mais] 'month'	['tai] 'thee' ['mai] 'me'	['pɛʃː] 'fish' ['sɛkː] 'dry.F'

b. French

	V'$	V'#	V'C$
/e/	*toile* 'canvas' *poil* 'hair'	*toi* 'thee' *moi* 'me'	*dette* 'debt' *vert* 'green'

Note, in passing, that the existence of the two different options is one manifestation of the conventionalization of OSL: there is an immediate phonetic reason for vowel lengthening under stress in open syllables, and it would be natural for this to also happen word-finally. The choice between application (southern Italian, French) vs. non-application (central and northern Italian) of lengthening in word-final stressed syllables is thus a purely phonological one.[27]

We have talked about OSL, hitherto, as though it were a strictly word-level process. However, the experimental evidence of modern standard Italian shows that this is not so. While there is abundant evidence for a roughly 1:2 ratio for stressed vowel durations in 'CVCCV vs. 'CVCV words, when uttered in isolation (Fava and Magno Caldognetto 1976; Farnetani and Kori 1986; D'Imperio and Rosenthall 1999:6), it has also been demonstrated that OSL is utterance-bound. Bertinetto (1981:132–37, 263) shows that the effects of OSL dramatically reduce (to a ratio very close to the threshold of perceptibility) when 'CVCV words are uttered in connected speech in non-prepausal position. The conclusions of D'Imperio's (2000:72) study on the acoustic–perceptual correlates of sentence prominence in Italian are in line with these findings.

These experimental results for standard Italian have a special value for the reconstruction of (variation in) vowel duration in proto-Romance, since Italian (the standard as well as its central and many of its southern dialects) is the only variety – with Sardinian – that retains OSL as a synchronically active allophonic process.

Is there reason to project back these conditions into proto-Romance? A general reason to envisage this possibility is that prepausal lengthening appears quite widespread cross-linguistically. Moreover, parallel to what we saw in (31)–(32), relevant evidence can be gathered from descriptions of Italo-Romance dialects in which the original (purely allophonic) lengthening evolved into phonemic changes. This happened in two different ways. In northern Italo-Romance, as a product of western Romance degemination and the deletion of final vowels except -A, a novel VQ contrast arose. Thus, the distribution of /Vː/ vs. /V/ provides (indirect) evidence as to the factors which constrained OSL in its original, allophonic form. In southern Italo-Romance, on the other hand, no VQ contrast has ever arisen, since degemination never applied. Nevertheless, in many SItalian dialects (especially on the Adriatic side of the Apennines), the output of OSL underwent further changes via diphthongization and/or various colouring processes.

Even for NItalian dialects, many of which retain distinctive vowel length to this day, some descriptions emphasize that length is perceptible when the word is uttered in isolation and/or prepausally, but heavily reduced elsewhere. Thus, for the Emilian dialect of Fiorenzuola, Casella (1922:51) observes that the long vowels in, for example, [aˈmiːk] 'friend', [ˈpaːga] 'pay.2SG.IMP', are shortened in [aˈmik kun tyt | aˈmik ku ˈnsõ] 'everybody's friend, nobody's friend', [ˈpag ti ˈto ˈdebit] 'pay your debts'. See also Rossini (1975:184f.) for Cremonese.

In south-eastern Italian dialects, prepausal position is where all diphthongization and/or colouring processes apply most systematically. In Bisceglie (province of Bari; see De Gregorio 1939), stressed -A- was coloured to [ɔ], whereas high vowels diphthongized (-ī- > [ø̯i], -ū- > [iu̯]) in open non-antepenultimate syllables: e.g., [ˈkɔpə] 'head' < CAPUT, [ˈfɔvə] 'bean' < FABAM; [gaˈdːø̯inə] 'hen' < GALLĪNAM, [ˈfø̯ikə] 'fig' < FĪCUM; [ˈkriu̯tə] 'raw' < CRŪDUM, [ˈmiu̯tə] 'funnel' < IMBŪTUM. All of these processes are blocked when the word concerned is not prepausal: e.g., [atːaˈkːːa la ˈmønə] literally, 'to attach the hand', [aˈsːi ˈforə] 'to get out', [ˈcːu ˈbːrutːə] 'uglier' vs. prepausal [atːaˈkːɔ], [aˈsːɔjə], [ˈcːiwə]. The same happens in nearby Bitonto: [rə ˈtʃø̯im] 'cauliflowers' vs. [rə ˈtʃimə də ˈreu̯p] 'turnips', [sə n ˈɛ ˈʃːiu̯t] 's/he went away' vs. [ˈɛ ˈʃːut a ʃːʊˈkwewə] 's/he went to play'. The Lucanian dialect of Matera displays similar alternations: e.g., [ˈɪ ˌdːʒːiːtə ˈfai̯ir] 'he went to the countryside' (lit. 'outside' < FORAS) vs. undiphthongized [ˈfoːrə ˈtarː] 'out of town', [nan dʒ ˈɪbːəˈnɪi̯t] 's/he didn't come' vs. [nan dʒ ˈɪ bːəˈnɪi̯tə nəˈʃːɪi̯n] 'nobody came'. In this variety, diphthongization under main utterance stress affected closed syllables too: [ˈla tʃəˈpau̯dː] 'the onion' vs. [na tʃəˈpɔdːa ˈbːjɔ̯ŋg] 'a white onion', [ˈjau̯ndʒ] 'smear' vs. [ˈjɔ̯ndʒə ˈbːø̯u̯n] 'smear well', [ˈstɔn: aˈsːɛ ˈkɛːn] 'there are many dogs' vs. [ˈna nːə ˈstau̯nː] 'there aren't any', [nʊ trasˈkɪrsə ˈlʊŋːə ˈlau̯nː] 'a very long discourse'. Similar examples of diphthongization are found, if less frequently, in the western part of southern Italy. Rohlfs (1938) discusses two such dialects, the Campanian variety of Pozzuoli (province of Naples; see now also Abete 2006) and the northern Calabrian variety of Belvedere Marittimo (Cosenza):

(33) a. Pozzuoli
    ['tai̯lə] 'cloth'   ['tɛla 'jaŋgə] 'white cloth'
    [a 'naṷtʃə] 'the walnut'   [na 'nɔtʃə 'rɔsːə] 'a big walnut'
    ['føi̯lə] 'thread'   [nu 'filə 'føi̯nə] 'a thin thread'
   b. Belvedere Marittimo
    ['vai̯nu] 'wine'   [u 'vinu 'jaŋku] 'white wine'
    ['lau̯na] 'moon'   [a 'luna 'nɔva] 'new moon'
    ['vau̯tʃe] 'voice'   [a 'bːutʃe 'avuta] 'aloud'

As Rohlfs points out, the diphthongizations under discussion are relatively recent processes (all over southern Italy, they must be placed in relative chronology after metaphony: see Weinrich 1958:175–77; Papa 1986; Loporcaro 1988:26). Therefore, they do not directly mirror a proto-Romance situation. Nevertheless, the fact that they first arise in – and, in some dialects, remain limited to – utterance-final position provides comparative evidence to be added to the fading of distinctive VQ in non-prepausal position in (some) northern Italo-Romance dialects and to experimental measurements for contemporary standard Italian. All of this evidence points to the same conclusion: OSL may well have been conditioned by prepausal position in proto-Romance too. This carries a further implication for the whole issue, discussed in section 2, of the loss of Latin distinctive VQ. This may well have been lost in prepausal position first, through OSL, in a conflict between word-level phonology, providing for VQ contrast (at least under stress), and sentence-level phonetics, with its tendency to enhance stressed segments occurring prepausally.

4   Prosodic revolutions and stress assignment

We now return to stress. Italian is most conservative in this respect, in that both proto-Romance phonological constraints (6)–(7), repeated as (34a–b), still operate:

(34)   a. HEAVY PENULT CONSTRAINT (HPC)
         Stress cannot skip a heavy (i.e., checked) penultimate syllable
     b. THREE SYLLABLE WINDOW (3SW)
         Stress cannot fall further back than the antepenultimate syllable

In Italian, apocope did not take place and syncope was not generalized, so that the 3SW was not reduced. One major innovation was the rise of word-final stress in polysyllabic words, virtually unknown to Latin, through a conspiracy of changes (35):

(35)

a. Univerbation	*però* 'however' < *PER+HOC *perciò* 'therefore' < *PER+ECCE+HOC *così* 'thus' < *ECCUM+SIC *canterà* 'will sing.3SG' < *CANTARE+HA(BE)T
b. Coalescence	*amò* 'loved.3SG' < AMAUT < AMAUIT
c. Apocope	*virtù* 'virtue' < UIRTUTEM *libertà* 'liberty' < LIBERTATEM *sentì* 'felt.3SG' < *sentìo* < SENTIUIT

This results in the range of primary word stress options in (36):[28]

(36)

a. #…ˈσ#:	*libertà* 'liberty', *però* 'but'
b. #…ˈσσ#:	*mangiˈare* 'to eat', *mangiˈando* 'eating'
c. #…ˈσσ_Lσ#:	*mˈestolo* 'ladle', *fˈacile* 'easy'

The stress patterns **#…ˈσσ_Hσ#, or **#…ˈσσσσ# do *not* occur, a fact which demonstrates that both (34a–b) are still significant generalizations about Italian stress placement in the lexical phonology. The former has a few exceptions, as is to be expected, being a generalization about the lexical phonology. The exceptions comprise a handful of Greek loanwords (e.g., *pˈolizza* 'insurance policy' and *mˈandorla* 'almond') and a handful of place-names, mostly of non-Latin origin (*Tˈaranto*, *ˈOtranto*, *Lˈepanto*, *Lˈevanto*, *ˈAgordo*, *ˈAgosta*).[29]

(34b) has no exceptions within lexical morphemes, the only instances of fourth-but-last stress being found in verb inflection, where a 3PL ending *-no* is affixed to a proparoxytonic root verb (37a) or under cliticization (37b) (in the latter case, when a proparoxytonic root verb combines with three clitics, stress goes as far as the sixth-but-last syllable). Since stress is not affected by cliticization, violations of the heavy penult constraint also arise (37c):

(37) a. *ˈindicano* 'point.3PL', *mˈacinano* 'grind.3PL', *rˈadicano* 'root.3PL'
   b. *ˈindicalo* 'point to it', *ˈindicamelo* 'point to it for me', *ˈindicamicelo* 'point to it for me there'[30]
   c. *pˈerderti* 'to lose you', *bˈatterlo* 'to beat him'

That (37a–c) are perfectly pronounceable for speakers of Italian shows that neither the 3SW nor the heavy penult constraint any longer represent genuine constraints on pronounceability, in terms of Stampe (1979). In other words, they are not active postlexically in standard Italian and can be overridden in the postlexical phonology deriving surface strings such as those in (37). (34a–b), however, still constrain the lexical shape of words fully integrated into the native lexicon, as shown by nonce words:[31]

(38) a. /defeferlo/, /barumasto/, /meretʃerno/
      b. ***d'efeferlo*/***def'eferlo*, ***b'arumasto*/***bar'umasto*, ***m'erecerno*/
          ***mere'cerno*
      c. *defef'erlo, barum'asto, merec'erno*

Given phonemic strings like those in (38a), no speaker of Italian would ever produce stress placements like (38b), violating either (34a) or (34b). The result will invariably be (38c), complying with both.

Statistically, penultimate stressed words (36b) are in the majority, so that penultimate stress can be taken to be assigned by default. For both final and antepenultimate stress (some form of) lexical specification is needed. This lexical specification is the ultimate effect on the stress system of the loss of Latin vowel quantity: Romance stress has ceased to be phonologically predictable (i.e., to be describable as a postlexical rule) and largely become a matter of lexical specification, while remaining subject to (lexical) phono-logical constraints (34a–b).[32]

Several scholars have objected to this position, claiming that in late Latin / proto-Romance the Latin stress rule changed, and no longer obeyed the HPC but rather a looser constraint prescribing that stress would be attracted by any consonant cluster between the penult and the last syllable, however syllabified (cf. Havet 1877:434; Pope 1952:100; Ward 1951:484; Tekavčić 1972 I:305f.; Steriade 1988:399; Lahiri *et al.* 1999:395; Bullock 2001:187).

This conclusion is forced on us by the unwillingness to admit that late Latin underwent a syllable structure change, by which heterosyllabicity was selected as the preferred option even for -C+*r*/*l*/*j*- clusters (discussed in §5.2). Actually, as Scheer and Ségéral (2003:4) put it, this alleged 'new accent rule [...] is nothing but a linear way of saying that *any* CC cluster has become heterosyllabic'. Under this view, the claim that the HPC (34a) was switched off completely in proto-Romance becomes devoid of empirical content. For standard Italian, it is also at odds with the evidence from nonce words in (38): since Italian has, to this day, words like *p'alpebra, c'attedra, p'eriplo* (like Spanish or Portuguese),[33] the non-occurrence of (38b) must be explained with reference to syllabification, along the same lines as for Classical Latin.

As for stress, Italian, not having undergone the conspiracy of changes labelled here the 'second prosodic revolution', is still basically like

'butterfly'. As in Italian, stress position is generally unaffected by clitics, so that (postlexical) PWs with preantepenultimate and even fifth-but-last stress occur, typically with the definite article: *t'impurile* 'times-the.NPL', *v'everiţele* 'squirrels-the.FPL'.[35] As apparent from the last example, however, Romanian is unique among Romance languages in possessing lexical words (about twenty) with preantepenultimate stress (Roca 1999:676; Chitoran 2002:78, 84–85):

(40) a. *b'ivoliţă* 'female buffalo', *l'ubeniţă* 'water melon', *pr'epeliţă* 'quail', *sl'iboviţă* 'brandy', *t'ântoriţă* 'lazy woman', *v'everiţă* 'squirrel'
       b. *d'octoriţă* 'woman doctor', *p'astoriţă* 'shepherdess'

Romanian stress therefore cannot be described in terms of the common (proto-)Romance 3SW (*pace* Steriade 1984): Romanian has widened the window to four syllables (Roca 1999:676).[36] This point is strengthened by external evidence adduced by Roca (1999:690): Romanian speakers are the only ones across Romance to countenance preantepenultimate stress in foreign placenames such as *Br'atislava, C'openhaga*.

Violations of the 3SW also occur with numerals: seven of those from eleven to nineteen carry preantepenultimate stress (*unsprezece* 'eleven', *doisprezece* 'twelve', etc.), and in the remainder primary stress falls on the fifth-but-last syllable: *şaptesprezece* 'seventeen', *nouăsprezece* 'nineteen'. True, this highly unusual pattern is restricted to a lexically closed series and appears somewhat unstable, as witness the reduced colloquial forms (*unşpe, doişpe*, etc.) as well as by the tendency to swap primary and secondary stress: [ˌ^{W}unsprɛˌzɛtʃɛ] → [ˌ^{W}unsprɛˈzɛtʃɛ] (Ulivi 1985:585; Daniliuc and Daniliuc 2000:14). Moreover, numerals are compound words, and compounds are generally taken to consist of two distinct PWs in Romance (Nespor and Vogel 1986; Nespor 1999:137). However, this analysis needs to be empirically motivated, as is the case for Italian, where it is supported by the non-application of mid vowel tensing: within the first, unstressed, member of compounds, [ɛ ɔ] occur, although they are otherwise banned from unstressed position. Clearly, though, no similar empirical argument can be appealed to for (the second member of) Romanian numeral compounds of the *-sprezece* type, since this string is lexically unstressed.[37] Since secondary stress is postlexical (cf. Chitoran 2002:86–93), the optional primary/secondary stress shift is, by definition, postlexical.

This deviant behaviour may be explained historically: this pattern of numeral composition may be borrowed from old Slavic (see Bauer, this volume, chapter 10: §3.2.2), and likewise the stress pattern. Yet synchronically, the stress placement in these words is part of the phono-logical system of Romanian. Borrowing has also fed the pattern of fourth-but-last stress, as all the words in (40a) are Slavic loans; those of Latin origin (in (40b), plus *ch'elnăriţă* 'waitress' from *chelner* German *Kellner*), and a few others, analogically acquired the same stress pattern.

Finally, borrowing also contributed to the relaxation of the heavy penult constraint (34a), which in Romanian displays about thirty exceptions, more than in the rest of Romance. Again, the words in (41) are all of Slavic origin (Roca 1999:686; Chitoran 2002:262):

(41)   *dr'agoste* 'love', *p'acoste* 'trouble', *st'aroste* 'abbot', *m'irişte* 'field', *p'ajişte* 'lawn', *priv'elişte* 'landscape'

4.3   Reduction of the 3SW

In Ibero-Romance, the application of syncope and apocope historically brought about a considerable quantitative reduction of the class of propar-oxytones, which are nowadays infrequent (hence marked) and mostly learnèd words. In Portuguese, for instance, one finds *víbora* 'adder' < UIPERAM, *érvodo* 'strawberry tree' < ARBUTUM, *pêssego* 'peach' < PERSICUM, *hóspede* 'host' < HOSPITEM, etc. Some of these coexist with syncopated popular variants (e.g., *bibra* 'viper'), which show the same process that turned, for example, TENERUM, CUMERUM, MANICAM, MEDICAM into *tenro* 'tender', *combro* 'hillock', *malga* 'soup pot', *melga* (a type of fish), etc. (Nunes 1975:68f.).

The same goes for Spanish, where most proparoxytones are learnèd words that failed to undergo syncope (e.g., *párroco* 'parish priest', *cónyuge* 'spouse', *autónomo* 'autonomous'), although for some no other cues point to their non-popular nature: e.g., *huérfano* 'orphan', *rábano* 'turnip', *espárrago* 'asparagus'.

In Catalan, the application of apocope (cf. 18e) further reduced the number of proparoxytones, even among learnèd words: ANGELUM > *àngel* 'angel', UTILEM >*útil* 'useful'. Antepenultimate stress remained in feminines ending in -/a/ like LACRIMAM > *llàgrima* 'tear' [ˈʎaɣrimə] (Badia i Margarit 1984:170).[38]

Other Romance areas have lost proparoxytones completely. In Romansh (see Roca 1999:668), antepenultimate stress only occurs in verb inflections, under circumstances reminiscent of those triggering preantepenultimate stress in Italian (37a–b). Consider the following (42) from Puter (Upper Engadine; Ganzoni 1977:16, 63):

(42)

	Unmarked order	Inversion	
a.	*ellas m'üdan*	*alura m'üdane*	'(then) they change.3PL'
b.	*ellas müd'aivan*	*alura müd'aivane*	'(then) they changed.3PL.IPF'
c.	*ellas müd'ettan*	*alura müd'ettane*	'(then) they changed.3PL.PRET'

The clitic *-e* occurs under inversion, due to the Verb-Second syntax of Romansh, and since it does not affect stress, penultimate stressed verb-forms (42a–c) turn into proparoxytones under inversion. As for the lexical phonology, however, Romansh can be said to have a 2SW.

The same applies to several varieties of Occitan and Franco-Provençal. The transition 3SW > 2SW, mirroring diachronic change (with the generalization of syncope, §3.2), is still reflected in geographical variation, on the Franco-Italian border. As one leaves Liguria and enters the Alpes Maritimes (see Dalbera 1994:55–58), the dialect continuum first presents a Ligurian-like area which has neither apocope nor generalized syncope and then preserves proparoxytones (Dalbera's 'A' area, comprising La Brigue, Menton, Breil, etc.). Further west, proparoxytones grow fewer ('B' area, around Nice), then become exceptional ('C' area, with Malaussène, Gilette, etc.), and finally disappear ('D' area: St Auban, Cagnes, Entraunes, Le Croix, Sigale, etc.). The continuum is exemplified in (43):

(43)		A. Breil	B. Peille	C. Malaussène	D. St Auban	
	a.	['manəga]	['manega]	['mãntʃɔ]	['mãntʃɔ]	'sleeve'
		[di'mɛnəga]	[di'mɛniga]	[di'mẽntʃe]	[di'mẽndʒe]	'Sunday'
	b.	['pɛrsəgu]	['pɛsəge]	[pe'sɛge]	[pe'sɛge]	'peach'
	c.	['fʀiguřa]	[fy'ygua]	[fe'rigulo]	[ferigu'letɔ]	'thyme'

There is little doubt that the increasing marginalization of proparoxytones, and finally the establishment of a 2SW, was induced by syncope, whose effects are seen in (43a). However, once this prosodic constraint was established, it became autonomous and, in turn, brought about further changes, such as stress shift (43b: C–D areas) or elimination of lexical residues through affixation and/or lexeme substitution (43c: D area).[39]

The strategy seen in (43b) is basically that which French adopted to cope with learnèd proparoxytones, reintroduced from Latin, like *fac'ile* 'easy', *ridic'ule* 'ridiculous' (contrast Italian *f'acile, rid'icolo*, which preserve Latin antepenultimate stress). Unlike French (and Oïl dialects), in Occitan and Franco-Provençal stress shift does not only apply to learnèd words and loans (e.g., [rədiˈkulːo] 'ridiculous', [faˈbrəkːa] 'factory', [koˈmɔdːo] 'comfortable', [sɛ̃ˈtəkːo] 'mayor', in the Franco-Provençal dialect of Sarre, Aosta; see Molinu and Roullet 2001:119–23). Rather, since syncope was not as pervasive as in the North of Gaul and did not eliminate proparoxytones altogether, residual proparoxytones such as *[ˈpɛsege] had to be restressed and thus became [peˈsɛge] (as for Occitan in 43);[40] for Franco-Provençal e.g., IUUENEM > [dzuˈveno] 'young', LACRIMA > [laˈgrema] 'tear' (Gardette 1983:572f.).

In the Franco-Provençal varieties of Dauphinois (spoken around Grenoble) and Haute Maurienne (Haute Savoie), in fact, the 2SW is threatened by the tendency to shift stress onto the last syllable: e.g., [faˈrina] > [far(i)ˈna] 'flour' (Martin 1990:681). This stress shift, which may be accompanied by syncope (cf. [farˈna]), arose between the seventeenth and eighteenth centuries (Tuaillon 2006:9f.). A much older (pre-literary) change, common to the whole Franco-Provençal domain, resulted in stress shift after an original intervocalic consonant had been deleted (cf. Duraffour 1932:6; Tuaillon 2006:8), as seen in the examples in (44a), from the Upper Valais dialect of Chermignon d'en Haut (Studer 1924:5):

(44)　a.　[ˈnwa] 'naked.F' < NUDA, [ˈtwo] 'kill.1SG' < *TUTO, [ˈtwi] 'all.PL'
　　　　　< TOTI
　　　b.　[ˈɛfɛ] 'thick'< SPISSU, [ˈʎapĩ] 'rabbit', [ˈfrumja] 'ant' < FORMICA
　　　c.　[ˈmɔsɛta] 'bee', [ˈɛseli] 'stairs' < SCALARIU

Examples (44b–c) from the same dialect paint, however, a puzzling picture. Stress retraction in bisyllables (44b) – whether original or syncopated, like [ˈfrumja] – suggests a generalization of a ′σσ]$_{PW}$ pattern, which would leave final stress for monosyllables only (44a). Polysyllables like [pɔˈmɛtɛ] 'potato' < POM(U D)E TE(RRA) would fit this pattern, but this is not the case for the (44c) words, displaying stress retraction on the first syllable (thus creating new proparoxytones). This contradictory picture is probably the product of language contact. While rightward stress shift is in keeping with the window reduction, stress retraction in (44c) may be due to neighbouring Alemannic dialects.

A similar impact on stress has been postulated for the Alemannic– Romance contact along the left bank of the Rhine south of Lake Constance, which set in during the ninth century as Alemans began to spread southwards. Hilty (2000:36) mentions the evidence of placenames such as *Gästela* (near Grabs), which goes back to CASTELLUM (cf. Stricker 1981:86), but cannot be simply explained as borrowed into Alemannic (otherwise it would begin with **[kχ]). The phonetic shape of *Gästela* rather points to a 'symbiosis between Romance and Alemannic' (Hilty 2000:37), with Romance speakers adopting retracted stress (i.e., *['kastelːu/-ə]) into their own pronunciation, before Romance was eventually abandoned through language shift. But, apart from these episodes of contact-induced stress change, the overall structural trend in Romansh as well as in Gallo-Romance is clearly towards reduction of the 3SW to a 2SW.

A further change of 2SW > 1SW took place in French (and Oïl dialects) when final schwas, the only vowels to occur in final unstressed syllables in old French (cf. §3.3), were eventually deleted. The change took place, in the standard language, between the sixteenth and seventeenth centuries (Zink 1999:47, 181–83): e.g., *homme* 'man' [ɔm] < ['ɔmə]. Deletion also applied after consonant clusters: e.g., *quatre* 'four' [kat(χ)], *vaincre* 'win' [vɛ̃ːkχ]. In this stage, thus, stress categorically falls on the last syllable and, having lost any contrastive function, remains phonetically unsignalled on all words except the last one in an utterance, or breath group (Pulgram 1975:122f.).

This is the traditional description of the standard system that originated from Francien. Regional varieties of French spoken in southern France, however, preserve final [ə], traditionally considered as a low-level epenthetic vowel. More recently, some analyses reconsider this southern French final [ə], claiming that it is present underlyingly (see Durand *et al.* 1987:986): consequently, in words like *quatr*[ə] 'four', stress falls on the penultimate syllable, so that a trochaic foot can be postulated to account for stress assignment. This behaviour of southern French is directly explicable as a substratum effect, as Occitan generally has a 2SW for stress assignment.

Similar analyses, assuming a trochaic foot, have been put forward for standard French as well. Bullock (1995a; 1995b), within Optimality Theory, proposes that in modern French the foot consists of a syllabic trochee, heavy and left-headed (Strong-Weak). Final [ə] deletion is accounted for by a constraint *FF/BIN, excluding the possibility that a f(inal) foot may be bin(ary). This leads to the selection of [kaχt] *carte* as the winning candidate, given the input /'kartə/. As is apparent, the evidence for assuming (final) trochees in French largely depends on general assumptions concerning the existence and status of final /ə/, a much-debated issue. In classical generative phonology, underlying final /ə/ is generally assumed to account for alternations such as [mɔχ]/[mɔχt] *mort/morte* 'dead.M/F' (see, e.g., Schane 1968). The same sort of (indirect) evidence is invoked in more recent analyses which assume (vestigial) trochees in contemporary (northern) Gallo-Romance. Montreuil (1998) assumes a word-final trochee for

Jersey Norman, based on segmental evidence such as the distribution of assibilated [ð] < -ʀ-, which developed in intervocalic position (cf. 45a vs. 45b) and subsequently became final through apocope (45c) so that it contrasts at present with [r] (45d), preserved as such where a following final consonant was deleted:

(45) a. [dyðɛ] *durer* 'to last', [maðɛː] *marée* 'tide'
      b. [i ʀɛstɛ] *il restait là* 'he stayed there', [dɛrni] *dernier* 'last', [i'vrõn] *ivrogne* 'drunkard'
      c. [nɛð] *noire* 'black.F', [mɛð] *mère* 'mother', [vɛð] *voire* 'yes'
      d. [nɛr] *nerf* 'nerve', [mɛr] *marque* 'marker', [vɛr] *vert* 'green'

Assuming the existence of a word-final trochaic foot (even if 'vestigial') for contemporary French boils down to claiming that, despite [ə]-deletion, its prosodic structure has not changed underlyingly since the time of OFrench, so that stress is still assigned within a 2SW, rather than falling just on the last syllable. Apart from morphonological alternations (*bon/bonne*, etc.) the evidence adduced to substantiate this claim is the emergence of [ə] 'only under a very specific set of circumstances' (Roca 1999:669). One of these is before an initial '*h* aspiré': *quell*[ə]/*auc'un*[ə] *hache* 'what/no axe'. However, in this and similar cases, [ə] surfaces in a context which is complementary to the only one in which a (phonetic) stress prominence is phonetically realized in modern standard French, viz. prepausal position (see the experimental evidence discussed in, for example, Robinson (1968:173); Wunderli *et al.* (1978:398–415); and Lacheret-Dujour and Beaugendre (1999:42)).

Somewhat paradoxically, thus, phonetic evidence from word-final alternations that never surface where stress is realized is adduced to decide where stress falls. A characterization of the French data closer to the phonetic evidence is that, ever since the seventeenth century, when final -[ə] was deleted (prepausally and in most other contexts), French has had iambic rhythm and utterance-final stress (e.g., Lacheret-Dujour and Beaugendre 1999:45). On this view, northern Gallo-Romance today has a 1SW.

4.4 *On the lexical nature of Romance stress*

Most recent analyses emphasize the claim that Romance stress is not 'a lexical property' (Serra 1997:195, on Catalan), not 'entirely lexical' (Chitoran 2002:51, on Romanian), etc.

Of course, these treatments do recognize the existence of surface variation in stress placement, due to the coexistence of 'regular' and 'marked' patterns. In what follows, I will exemplify this kind of approach by discussing the account of Catalan word stress by Serra (1997).[41] He starts from the following descriptive generalizations:[42]

(46) Regular pattern

    a. If a word ends in a consonant it is an oxytone: *llençʻol* 'sheet', *generʻal* 'general'

    b. If a word ends in a vowel it is a paroxytone: *casʻeta* 'little house', *resʻidu* 'residue'

    Marked patterns

    c. There are words that end in a vowel and are oxytones: *català* 'Catalan', *camí* 'path'

    d. There are words that end in a consonant and are paroxytones: *àrab* 'Arab', *llʻapis* 'pencil'

    e. Some words are proparoxytones: *Júpiter* 'Jupiter', *càrrega* 'load'

After noting this variation (and the statistical imbalance between the regular vs. irregular stress patterns) 'a relatively simple mechanism for the assignment of stress in Catalan is proposed' (Serra 1997:196). This relies on moraic structure and the metrical grid, and consists in the 'projection of the morae, construction of binary trochees from right to left, and finally, the assignment of a beat to the rightmost column to mark the prominence of the primary stress' (Serra 1997:202). This is exemplified in (47) with the regular patterns (46a–b):

(47) a.

		*		b.			*	
		*					*	
*	(*	*)		(*	*)	(*	*)	
μ	μ	μ		μ	μ	μ	μ
re	si	du		ge	ne	ra	l
Pa	l	ma		lle	n	ço	l

On this view, Catalan has a *phonological* mechanism assigning primary word stress to the last but one mora (for checked penults, as in *Palma*, a further assumption is needed, viz. that 'stress received by the lateral belongs to the whole syllable'; Serra 1997:203). In a further step, the marked patterns (45c–e) are explained away as 'only apparently exceptional'. To achieve this, a basic assumption plus some representational adjustments are needed. The assumption is that stress is assigned to (lexical) morphemes, not to (phonological) words. This directly explains the first set of exceptions (46c), as *català*, *camí* alternate with *catalana* 'Catalan.FSG', *caminar* 'to walk', etc. After this, 'a severely reduced number of words remains' (Serra 1997:204), whose roots do not end in a consonant, such as *cafè*, *sofà* (PL *cafès*, *sofàs*). For these, the substandard plurals *cafʻens*, *sofʻans* show that they tend to be reanalysed as involving a consonant final root, due to their stress pattern. For (46d–e), on the other hand, two different kinds of extrametricality are assumed, as shown in (48a–c):

(48)　a.　*　　　　　b.　*　　　　　　　c.　*
　　　　(*　*)　　　　(*　*)　　　　　　(*　*)
　　　　μ　μ　<μ>　　μ　μ　<μ>　　　μ　μ
　　　　à　*ra*　*b*　　[*fà*　*bri*　*c*]　+ *a*　　*Jú*　*pi* <*ter*>

In (48a) the final consonant is assumed to be extrametrical. (48b) is a vowel-final proparoxytone, but the general assumption that stress is assigned to morphemes allows one to neglect the ending and, again, to mark as extrametrical the root-final consonant. For (48c), which has no ending, the whole final syllable must be marked extrametrical.

The analysis has its merits: it sorts out the different stress patterns of Catalan and organizes them into classes which are formally defined. Some empirical inadequacies remain, though. For instance, the eradication of the irregular pattern (46c) is not complete, since the author does not address indeclinables such as *aixi* 'so', *això* 'this', for which there is no evidence of a consonant-final root. A further empirical problem, far more general, concerns the fact that similar structural descriptions must be assumed ad hoc to account for the Ibero-Romance (and Romanian) stress pattern. The exceptional extrametrical markings in (48) cannot be projected back onto prior stages of the Latin–Romance development, and this creates something of a paradox. The diachronic drift tended to reduce the class of proparoxytones, eliminating them altogether in some varieties (Romansh, Gallo-Romance). However, structural representations such as (48b–c), with their neat metrification, obscure the starting point for the (conspiracy of) changes. Had such metrification options been available from the outset, there would have been no structural motive for the changes reviewed in section 3. A view that is more respectful of (surface) phonetic facts consists, instead, in saying that this motive lies in (a) the existence of ternary feet, and (b) the fact that such feet became more and more marginal in the history of Romance.

A further problem with this analysis concerns the computation of stress on morphemes rather than words, implying the exclusion of desinences from the stress domain. This a step often taken in current analyses of Romance word stress: e.g., Roca (1999:670–74) in a comparative perspective, or Chitoran (2002:79f.) on Romanian, according to whom '[i]n the unmarked case stress falls on the rightmost syllable of the prosodic word, which corresponds to the root in monomorphemic forms'. Thus, *sare* 'salt' is underlyingly /[sar]$_{\text{PWd}}$e/.

However, in languages still possessing proparoxytones, this poses a problem. Consider the Italian examples in (49):

(49) a. *esp'erta* 'expert.F', *inc'olto* 'uncultivated.M'
      b. *c'attedra* '(teacher's) desk', *p'eriplo* 'circumnavigation'
      c. *es'edra* 'exedra', *ar'atro* 'plough'

The examples in (49a) have stress on the penult due to the HPC. Note that this heaviness, quite trivially, only arises *after* syllabification. Only once syllabification is performed do the words in (49a) differ from those in (49b), whose consonant cluster is a well-formed complex onset and, consequently, does not necessarily attract stress (as shown by comparison of (49b) and (49c)). But, if the domain for stress assignment is the morpheme, and if the prosodic word reduces to the root, then the syllabification contrast between [*esp'ert*]*a* and [*c'attedr*]*a* becomes irrelevant, and the generalization concerning the stress pattern in (49a) is lost.

In a more general perspective, the approach to Catalan stress discussed above, like most current treatments of (Romance) stress within generative phonology, rests on a basic ambiguity concerning the label 'lexical', insightfully discussed in Aronoff (1994:16–22). Aronoff shows that 'lexical' is used in the linguistic literature with two different meanings that should be kept distinct: *lexical₁* 'idiosyncratic' and *lexical₂* 'lexemic'. What analyses such as that summarized above show is that stress in Romance is not entirely idiosyncratic (i.e., lexical₁) but, rather, there are sub-regularities. But the very fact that these analyses have to refer to morphemes and to stipulate (different sorts of) extrametricality is in itself proof of the fact that Romance stress is indeed lexical₂ (i.e., lexemic). While Latin stress obeyed surface true phonological constraints, (Proto-)Romance stress does not.

This lexical nature is often recognized, at least for some subcomponents: thus, Roca (1999:729) analyses Spanish verb stress as non-metrical, but rather specified as a 'lexical asterisk'. But analyses building on metrical structure also rely heavily on lexical specification, through the notion 'extrametricality'. If applied to Latin, as, for example, in Mester (1994) and Roca (1999:660), it boils down to the (elegant) formalization of a truly phonological generalization: computation of stress placement always skips the last syllable (cf. Allen (1973:177) and the previous literature discussed there, which has long realized this fact). When applied to Romance, on the other hand, extrametricality reduces to a device 'to mark lexical exceptionality on stress placement' (Martínez Gil 1997b:295).

Hence Romance stress, synchronically, cannot be accounted for in purely phonological terms and the analyses of the kind discussed here actually confirm, rather than refute, that word stress has become lexical.[43] It is a feature which is specified on lexical morphemes, and is subject (variably) to some (residual) phonological constraints, viz. (1a–b), which are still at work in the lexical phonology of Romance languages (except French).

This is the ultimate combined effect of the two prosodic revolutions considered in sections 2–3, that gradually transformed the Latin stress rule into the more complex stress systems of the Romance languages.

5   Syllable structure in Romance diachronic phonology

The syllable and syllable structure were referred to in the foregoing sections inasmuch as they proved relevant to the statement of stress placement and the related topic of distribution of vowel length. This corresponds to an established practice in Romance studies. Going through reference work in the Neogrammarian tradition, first and foremost Meyer-Lübke's (1890) monumental compendium, one is struck by the fact that the syllable is constantly referred to in the illustration of changes undergone by vowels, but not explored in depth when talking about consonant clusters. A fortiori, no specific section is devoted to syllabification. This practice reflects a well-known analytical difficulty: while it is easy, for both speaker and linguist, to locate and count syllable nuclei, decisions about the syllabification of intervening consonants are often much harder.

When it comes to consonants, syllabification is less frequently addressed in the classical literature in Romance diachronic phonology. This is not accidental. Rather, it points to the fact that reference to syllable structure (in particular, to shifts in syllabification) as an explanatory tool in cases which seem obvious to present-day phonologists was not customary at the time. Lack of consideration of (re)syllabification as a possible source of change sometimes leads to striking conclusions. Thus, in Meyer-Lübke (1920:142) it is argued that the stress shift before C+*r* clusters (e.g., TENÉBRAS 'darkness'), evidenced by Romance outcomes such as Sp. *tinieblas*, is due to a lengthening of the stressed vowel ('tenébrae'), explained in turn by the sonority of the following liquid. Note that, in Meyer-Lübke's own reconstruction, this lengthening should have taken place at a stage when distinctive VQ was gone, and OSL was at work instead. A lengthening effect skipping the interposed obstruents appears implausible, though, and a much simpler explanation is available. Given that the heavy penult constraint was active all along, it is sufficient to assume that in TENEBRAS, just as in INTEGRUM 'whole', TONITRUM 'thunder', COLUBRUM 'grass snake', PAL-PEBRA 'eyelid', PULLITRUM 'foal', etc. (cf. Sp. *entero*, Fr. *entier*, *tonnerre*, *couleuvre*, *paupière*, It. *intero*, *puledro*, Log. Srd. [in'treu], [ko'lɔːra], etc.), resyllabification took place ($^{\$}$Cr > C$^{\$}$r) and the stress shift automatically follows.

The question is whether there is independent evidence for this assumption. But Meyer-Lübke did not ask and, to this day, there are scholars who are unwilling to resort to syllabification shifts in order to explain this or other aspects of the phonological development of Romance varieties. As for C+*r/l* clusters, the clearest statement of this stance is found perhaps in Steriade (1988:403), in whose view, C+*r/l* clusters were tautosyllabic all along, so that shifts in syllabification are not available as an explanatory device. This is an explicit reassertion of the principle that inspired, implicitly, Meyer-Lübke's description. It denies that readjustments in syllable structure played a significant role. In the following sections, we see strong evidence to the contrary, and that we are now in a better position to understand what happened to syllable structure and syllabification in late Latin and the transition period.

5.1   Coda weakening in (early) Romance

A widely held view, especially in structuralist diachronic phonology, claims that one of the main innovatory trends in the phonology of late Latin / proto-Romance was a sort of 'open syllable drift' (see Lausberg 1976:352). This position is maintained perhaps most consistently by Kiss (1972), who derives from this general principle empirical manifestations as diverse as the loss of final consonants. However this 'tendency' does not stand closer scrutiny. Recent analyses of the development of consonant clusters in late Latin / proto-Romance make it plausible that there *was* a systematic resyllabification in consonant clusters (see §5.3). These analyses imply that all word-internal open syllables except CV.CV were eliminated, an implication obviously incompatible with the alleged tendency towards open syllables.

As for western Romance degemination, it started from Gallo-Romance, where obstruents underwent it in the eighth century (Richter 1934:250; Politzer 1951:41). By that time, the generalization of syncope (see §3.2) increased dramatically the complexity of syllable structure (e.g., ARBOREM > OFr. [ˈarbrə] 'tree'). Obviously, no general drift or conspiracy can be assumed for western Romance at that time.

The same goes for the deletion of final consonants, which took place at a different pace in the different languages, and was also counterbalanced by apocope (and syncope) processes that constantly recreated (word-final) codas. But even if the early stages are considered, it is apparent that there was no generalized syllable opening in early Romance. Word-finally, Latin final -s is retained to this day in Raeto-Romance, Occitan, Catalan, Sardinian, (northern) Spanish and Portuguese, and not only -s but also -T were preserved in Gallo- and Ibero-Romance well into the period of their early documentation.

What is more, there is evidence that deletion went through a (late Latin) stage in which assimilation to a following consonant took place. For final -T in verb inflection this was shown convincingly by Fanciullo's (1997a) analysis of Pompeian Latin. A distich such as *quisquis ama valia, peria qui nosci amare / bis [t]anti peria, quisquis amare vota* (cf. CLat. AMAT, UALEAT, PEREAT, UOTAT), often quoted as an illustration of final -T deletion, shows metrical errors exclusively where final consonants are deleted, but is metrically perfect if we assume that the pronunciation was *quisquis ama* [b:]*alia,* [p:]*eria* [k:]*ui* etc., with that kind of gemination after third person verbs still found in conservative varieties such as Sardinian and the southern Italian dialects spoken on the Calabria–Lucania border (the 'Lausberg zone'): e.g., [ˈβɛːnə nːu ˈjurn] 'a day comes' (Nova Siri) vs. [ˈβɛːnəðə ##] < UENIT (Lausberg 1939:145); Logudorese [ˈbːeni ˈkustu] 'this (guy) comes' vs. [ˈbeːnið ˈisːɛ] 'he comes'. This assimilation process had existed for centuries in Italic and in rural varieties of Latin, and finally found its way into the spoken Latin of the Empire, as shown by epigraphic evidence such as *sud die* (= *sub die*), *at tuos* (= *ad tuos*). It is this sandhi assimilation that further developed into the process currently known as *raddoppiamento fonosintattico*, which is nowadays preserved by Italian only but must be assumed for proto-Romance (see discussion in Loporcaro 1997).

Such evidence, often neglected in surveys of late Latin readjustments of syllable structure, shows that the final syllable did not simply become open. What it shows is that consonants in syllable codas tended to become weakened, getting exposed to a replacement of their features through spreading from the following onset consonant. This is the very same syndrome which has long been recognized for word-internal consonant clusters, as testified by, e.g., Lausberg (1976:321–26), Väänänen (1974/ 1982:§§113–25) and Weinrich (1958:228f.). In late Latin / proto-Romance, syllable contacts were simplified through many segmentally different changes which all shared one and the same phonological essence: the weakening/simplification of the coda (e.g., Marotta 1995:445–56). Obstruent groups were simplified: SANCTUS, CINCTUS, DEFUNCTUS changed to *santus, cintus, defuntus* (often encountered, in inscriptions from all over the Empire), which developed into It., Sp., Pt. *santo,* Ro. *sânt,* etc. In general, all heterosyllabic clusters of non-homorganic consonants containing a coda obstruent were modified. Labials were assimilated: -PT-, -BT- > [tː], as in It. *rotto* 'broken', *sotto* 'under'; -PS- > [sː], as in *esso* 'it', -BV- > [vː], as in *òvvio* 'obvious', -MN- > [nː], as in *danno* 'damage'. Velars were either assimilated or vocalized (via a fricative stage): -CT- > [tː], as in It. *latte*/[i̯t], as in Fr. *lait* 'milk'; -G'D- > [dː], as in It. *freddo*/[i̯d], as in Fr. *froid* 'cold', etc.

All of the proto-Romance changes considered so far may be labelled 'weakening'. Weakening may take place through feature depletion, affecting the target segment, which thereby undergoes assimilation. This resulted in an increase in the number of geminates occurring in proto-Romance, with respect to Latin (both lexically and postlexically, through *raddoppiamento fonosintattico*). Alternatively, weakening may consist in a movement towards the vocalic pole of the scale of Consonantal Strength (reported in (50) in the version assumed by Vennemann 1988):

(50)   Scale of Consonantal Strength

vowels	vowels	glides	rhotics	laterals	nasals	fricatives	stops	stops
low	high	w j	r	l	m n	s z f v	b d g	p t k

Take the western Romance development of Latin -CT-: it first involved fricativization to [çt] (documented in Mozarabic <noxte>; see Corriente 1997:349), then vocalization to [i̯t] (OFr. *fait*, Pt. *feito*), that further evolved through palatalization ([i̯tʃ] > [tʃ]) in Sp. *hecho* (Menéndez Pidal 1953:143f.). This change matches the description of Vennemann's (1988:21) Coda Law (51):

(51)   *Coda Law*
       A syllable coda is the more preferred: (a) the smaller the number of speech
       sounds in the coda, (b) the less the Consonantal Strength value of its
       offset [= its last segment], (c) the more sharply the Consonantal Strength
       drops from the offset toward the Consonantal Strength of the preceding
       syllable nucleus.

The series of proto-Romance coda weakening processes conspired to the effect of radically constraining the distribution of consonants in coda position. In proto-Romance, heterosyllabic clusters (syllable contacts) reduced to only a subset of those admitted in Latin: homorganic nasal + obstruent, and to coronal codas (liquids and /s/) + C.

This is still the core of coda constraints found in individual Romance languages. For instance, Italian: ['kan̪to] 'sing.1SG', ['gamba] 'leg', ['karta] 'paper', ['kasta] 'chaste.FSG', ['sal̪ta] 'jump.3SG.PRS'. In Italian the coda can be occupied also by (the first portion of) a geminate (['faːʦo] 'done'). Elsewhere, with degemination, the inventory of admissible codas reduced to coronals /l r s/ and homorganic nasals. In Portuguese, coda nasals were deleted with accompanying nasalization of the preceding vowel (see (52) below) so that, at the surface at least, the coda position in this language may only be occupied by /l r s/ (Mateus and d'Andrade 2000:137).

Apart from /s/, obstruents could not occupy the coda in proto-Romance (as a product of the late Latin coda weakenings) and still cannot, in the indigenous lexicon, in a language such as Italian – although in Italian loanwords have introduced coda obstruents: *ritmico* 'rhythmic', *afta* 'aphthae' (likewise, Pt., Sp. *rítmico, afta*). Loanwords aside, violations of the original coda condition were introduced through vowel deletion (syncope and apocope). Here, individual languages diverge as to the degree of adaptation of the newly created clusters. Thus, Spanish acquired coda [θ ð] (word-finally, also [x]), as in *juzgar* 'to judge', *voz* 'voice', *sed* 'thirst', *reloj* 'watch', but did not admit non-homorganic nasals, adapting COM(I)TE into *conde* 'count'. Catalan and French are in the vanguard of innovation, in this respect, because of more extensive vowel deletion. After generalized [ə]-loss, French presents blatant violations of the sonority sequencing, at least at the surface: e.g., *arbre* ['arbʁ] 'tree'. Whether or not these strings are analysed as codas, however, depends on specific models. Theories such as Government Phonology (e.g., Lowenstamm 1996), for instance, would integrate (at least) an empty nucleus word-finally, owing to general principles governing phonological representations: the exception would thereby be destroyed.

Spanish depalatalization of [ɲ ʎ] offers a good illustration of how languages may react to violations of the coda constraints arising from vowel deletion. [ɲ ʎ] alternate with [n l] in for example *doña/don* 'lady/sir', *desdeñar/desdén* 'to disdain / disdain' and *ella/él* 'she/he', *bello/beldad* 'beautiful/beauty', *caballo/cabalgar* 'horse / to ride', etc. (see Pensado Ruiz 1997, with further references). The same depalatalization is found in Occitan (Bec 1973:45f.) and dialects of Catalan (Blasco Ferrer 1984a:52). Synchronically, this is due to a distributional constraint: palatal laterals usually occur in intervocalic or prevocalic position but are barred from consonant clusters altogether. The diachronic reason is simply that [ɲ ʎ] first arose through palatalization of clusters that were not exhaustively contained in a syllable coda. Therefore, in proto-Romance they could only occur intervocalically, and were always long, as a product of the syllable contact adjustments to be considered below. In this respect, too, Italian most faithfully preserves the original proto-Romance situation: LIGNUM > ['leɲːo] 'wood', UINEAM > ['viɲːa] 'vineyard', PALEAM > ['paʎːa] 'straw'.

Application of syncope and apocope, in western Romance, first created coda palatal sonorants and, with them, a new phonological difficulty, to which most varieties reacted through coda depalatalization. In this respect, too, standard Catalan is more liberal than Spanish, preserving word- and syllable-final [ɲ ʎ]: *puny* [ˈpuɲ] 'fist', *vell* [ˈbeʎ] 'old' (Badia i Margarit 1984:231, 249).

Codas can also become more complex through processes other than vowel deletion. In some areas of Raeto-Romance (Sotsés and Albula Valley), diphthongs were 'hardened', changing their offglide into a stop: e.g., Sotsés [durˈmekr] < DORMĪRE 'sleep', [ˈʃcikr] < OBSCŪRU 'obscure', [ˈvukʃ] < VŌCE 'voice', [ˈɟukf] < JUGU 'yoke' (cf. Liver 1999:157). On the whole, however, processes applying selectively to coda consonants more frequently effect weakening/simplification of this syllabic constituent, in compliance with the Coda Law (51). For instance, /l/ is realized as alveolar in syllable heads but velarized to [ɫ] in codas in European Portuguese (*mal* [ˈmaɫ] 'evil', *polpa* [ˈpoɫpɐ] 'pulp') and is further weakened to [w] in Brazilian Portuguese ([ˈmaṷ], [ˈpoṷpɐ]; see Mateus and d'Andrade 2000:138). A similar coda velarization /l/ → [ɫ] occurs in Catalan (cf. Recasens 1996:305f.). Symmetrical weakening via vocalization to [i̯] is also documented in several Italo-Romance varieties: e.g., ORmc. *voize* [ˈvɔi̯tse] 'wanted.3SG' < *VOLSIT.

Also recurrent is the weakening of coda nasals and sibilants. The former is widely attested in Romance varieties (see Tuttle 1992; Hajek 1997, for Italo-Romance) and is responsible for the rise of nasalized vowels in French and Portuguese:

(52)		Portuguese	French	
	CANTO	*canto* [ˈkɐ̃tu]	*chante* [ˈʃɑ̃t]	'sing.1SG'
	UENTUM	*vento* [ˈvẽtu]	*vent* [ˈvɑ̃]	'wind'
	SONUM	*som* [ˈsõ]	*son* [ˈsõ]	'sound'
	FĪNEM	*fim* [ˈfĩ]	*fin* [ˈfɛ̃]	'end'
	COMMŪNEM	*comun* [kuˈmũ]	*commun* [komœ̃)]	'common'
	PĀNEM	*pão* [ˈpɐ̃ṵ̃]	*pain* [ˈpɛ̃]	'bread'

Coda /s/ weakening is also attested in language after language. In the Spanish varieties of Murcia and Andalusia (as well as in South American Spanish), it undergoes aspiration ([h]) and deletion, triggering a laxing of the preceding vowel and the creation of vowel harmony; see Hernández Campoy and Trudgill (2002) for a recent discussion and survey of the literature on this topic. The authors underscore that the process actually involves not only /s/ but all coda consonants except nasals.

The weakening of coda consonants, obeying universal preferences, is a recurrent pattern throughout the history of the Romance languages. It appears to have been at work ever since proto-Romance, and accounts for several changes previously attributed to an alleged open syllable tendency. Further evidence against this 'tendency' is given in section 5.3.

5.2   The structure of syllable heads

On the whole, the structure of the syllable head (called 'onset' in other terminologies) remained more stable, especially in word-initial position, than that of codas.[44] A notable exception is northern Italian dialects in which pretonic syncope applied (cf. the Emilian data in (13) above) resulting in complex word-initial clusters: e.g., [ˈsptsaːvnə] 'were breaking.3PL', [ˈvdiːvnə] 'were seeing.3PL', [ˈʃcɛlːə] 'bucket.DIM', [ˈfcøtːa] 'old woman. DIM' in Piandelagotti (province of Modena). Apart from the mere occurrence in word-initial position, rule-based evidence (discussed in Loporcaro 1998b) shows that at least some of these newly arisen clusters are indeed syllabified as heads.

These exceptions aside, most changes affecting syllable heads proceeded in the opposite direction (i.e., simplification). Cross-linguistic differentiation in this domain mainly concerned the degree of preservation of less-preferred clusters, according to Vennemann's (1988:13) Head Law (53):

(53)   *Head Law*
        A syllable head is the more preferred: (a) the closer the number of speech sounds in the head is to one, (b) the greater the Consonantal Strength value of its onset [= its first segment], and (c) the more sharply the Consonantal Strength drops from the onset toward the Consonantal Strength of the following syllable nucleus.

While C+*r* clusters remained admissible all along, C+*l* clusters were variously modified in Italian, Spanish and Portuguese, while being preserved elsewhere (Lausberg 1976:281): e.g., It. *piano* 'flat', *chiave* 'key', *fiamma* 'flame', Sp. *llano*, *llave*, *llama* vs. Fr. *plain*, *clé*, *flamme*. However, this diachronic trend seldom resulted in complete eradication, as C+*l* clusters were constantly reintroduced in Latinisms.

Headless syllables also created difficulties for some (dialectal) Romance varieties, which repaired this through glide prosthesis. In some Daco-Romanian dialects, prosthesis not only occurs before /e/ as in the standard (e.g., [j]*el* 'he', [j]*este* 'is') but is generalized before all initial vowels (e.g., [ˈji]*nimă* 'heart', [ˈwu]*nghie* 'fingernail', [ɨa]*rc* 'bow' (Sala 1976:42f.).

Prosthesis is widespread in southern Italian dialects too: e.g., Pugliese [ˈjɛrf] 'grass' < HERBAM, [ˈjard] 'to burn' < ARDERE, [ˈjldː] 'he' < ILLUM in Altamura (Loporcaro 1988:196; see also Lausberg 1939:90–92).

Apart from language-specific changes, however, at least one common change in head structure can be reconstructed for proto-Romance. This concerns word-initial *s*+C clusters. Although many current theories disallow in principle their syllabification as complex heads (Kaye *et al.* 1990:204f.), for Latin there is evidence that this may indeed have been the case. Not word-internally, where metrical evidence unambiguously points to the syllabification *res.pi.ro* (see Allen 1973:139), but at word boundaries. In Greek, when a string -V̆ # *s*C- occurred in the metre, the syllable was normally measured as heavy, which is evidence for sandhi resyllabification. Latin poets, however, tend to avoid this collocation (see Hoenigswald 1949), which has been interpreted as sign of the conflict between the imitation of Greek practice and the light measurement (i.e., non-resyllabification). Since the latter runs counter to the Greek model, it must be seen as 'the native Latin treatment' (Allen 1973:140).

In late Latin (and proto-Romance), however, systematic heterosyllabication seems to have been extended to word-initial *s*C- clusters as well, as indicated by several pieces of evidence, the most important of which is *i*-prosthesis. This is widespread in Latin texts from Africa (see Acquati 1971:182f.; Kiss 1972:91–93; Kramer 1983:14; Fanciullo 1992:169), whence it seems to have spread to southern and central Italy (whereas it is virtually absent in Christian epigraphs from northern Italy and Gaul; Herman 2000b:125).

Prosthesis is best understood as a last resort strategy, applying when the context for sandhi resyllabification was not met. Thus, the prosthetic vowel must have been originally confined to utterance-initial and postconsonantal position (Weinrich 1958:232), a situation still preserved in early old French. Thus, in the *Alexis* (eleventh century), one finds verses like *(et) a la spusa qued il out espusethe* 'and to the bride that he had married' (Zink 1999[6]:67f.; Lausberg 1976:295f.); after a pause prosthesis also occurs regularly. Prosthesis was later generalized (with restructuring of the underlying form): cf. (later) OFr. *espus* (> *époux*), Sp., Pt. *esposo*, Srd. *ispozu* 'bridegroom'. For speakers of Ibero-Romance, prosthesis before *s*C- still mirrors a constraint on pronounceability, while this is no longer the case for French or Sardinian. In (Tuscan) Italian, on the other hand, prosthesis continued to be conditioned by sentence phonetics until not long ago, in many dialects at least (e.g., *in istrada* 'in (the) street' vs. *la strada* 'the street').

Many Romance varieties show traces of sandhi resyllabification of *s*C-, the most famous case being the old Tuscan selective replacement of the

MSG definite article *lo* < ILLUM through *(i)l* before singleton consonants and consonant clusters exhaustively syllabified as syllable heads but, crucially, not before *s*C. While most analyses regard the synchronic distribution of the articles in modern standard Italian as proof that word-initial *s*C- still is heterosyllabic (e.g., Davis 1990; Kaye *et al.* 1990:204f.; Marotta 1993). Bertinetto (1999) argues that this is no longer the case, and that the syllabification of *s*C- for speakers of modern standard Italian is underdetermined.

5.3   Syllable contacts and syllabification shift from Latin to Romance

Two seminal contributions (Pensado Ruiz 1988; Vennemann 1988) have drawn attention to syllabification shifts as an explanatory device for phonological change in proto- and early Romance. Before that, only some isolated and unsystematic attempts in this direction were made. In work on French and Italian, Salverda de Grave (1920; 1930) assumed that different syllabifications of consonant clusters should be assumed for proto-Romance, in order to account for French doublets such as *double, couple* continuing -PL-.

A further important aspect is *syllable contact*. Consider the following law (Murray and Vennemann 1983):

(54)   *Contact Law*
        A syllable contact A$^\$$B is the more preferred the less the consonantal strength of A and the greater the consonantal strength of B

This results from the convergence of the Coda Law (51) with the Head Law (53). Among diachronic illustrations of the Contact Law, Vennemann (1988:46) discusses gemination in Italian consonant clusters, as exemplified in (55):

(55)   a.   C$^\$$j *sappia* 'know.SBJV.3SG' < SAPIAT, *gabbia* 'cage' < CAUEAM, *vendemmia* 'vintage' < UINDĒMIAM, *faccio* 'I do' < FACIO;

        b.   C$^\$$w *acqua* 'water' < AQUAM, *volli* < 'I wanted' UOLUĪ, *gennaio* 'January' < IENUARIUM (for CLat. IĀNUĀRIUM);

        c.   C$^\$$r *labbro* 'lip'< LABRUM, *febbre* 'fever' < FEBREM, *Affrica* (Tsc.) 'Africa' < AFRICAM;

        d.   C$^\$$l *doppio* 'double' < DUPLUM, *fibbia* 'brooch' < FIB(U)LAM, *occhio* 'eye' < OC(U)LUM.

Assuming that the starting point for gemination was a 'bad' syllable contact with a weak consonant or glide in the onset ('head' in Vennemann's terminology) of the following syllable, it becomes possible to unify all geminations in (55a–b) under the same phonological process: they all created a better syllable contact, by filling in a stronger consonant in the syllable head ($C^\$j > C^\$Cj$, and the like).

In Italian, this gemination is still directly observable. Gemination induced by proto-Romance -i̯- (55a) regularly affected all consonants except -R-, -S- (Rohlfs 1966:385–414; Castellani 1965; Lausberg 1976:331), as testified by *cuoio* 'leather' < CORIUM, *muoio* 'I die' < MORIO(R), as well as *bacio* 'kiss' < BĀSIUM, *camicia* 'shirt' < CAMĪSIA (still pronounced ['baːʃo], [kaˈmiːʃa] in Florence), in spite of modern orthography; see Castellani (1952:28–34). Gemination was regular before -L-, much less so before -R-, where it never affected dentals or velars, which often show intervocalic voicing instead, implying occurrence in the syllable head (*padre* 'father' < PATREM, *madre* 'mother' < MATREM, *ladro* 'thief' < LATRO; *magro* 'thin' < MACRUM, *pigro* 'lazy' < PIGRUM). Labials too are affected only sporadically.

This irregularity is not disturbing, though: it suffices to assume that proto-Romance syllabification of the clusters in (55a–d) was variable. The problem is whether there is evidence for this assumed variability.

Note that this problem splits into two subproblems, concerning (55a–b) and (55c–d), respectively. For the latter, we have abundant evidence that they were tautosyllabic in CLat. (i.e., they built complex syllable heads). Thus, the question is: Is there evidence for an alternative (hetero)syllabification? For the former, the question is even more radical, as there were no such clusters in CLat. Consonantal /j/ occurred word- and morpheme-initially (IAM 'now', SUBIECTUS 'subject') or intervocalically, where it was geminated (PEIUS 'worse', phonetically ['pɛjːus], scanned with the first syllable long in verse). Thus, the $C^\$j$ syllabification assumed in, say, SAPIAT, forces us to assume that CLat. SA.PI.AT, trisyllabic, changed to SAP.JAT, with a syllabification shift, rather than categorically became SA.PJAT, since the latter could not possibly explain gemination, under the Contact Law hypothesis.

Note that that the proto-Romance change assumed (SA.PI.AT > SAP.JAT) seems to have worsened syllable structure in the first place: the syllable contact it created is bad because both the coda ($p^\$$) and the head ($^\$j$) are. (Recall that the Contact Law (54) results from the combination of the Coda and the Head Laws.)

Let us begin with the second puzzle, the rise of the 'unnatural' syllabifications $C^\$j$, $C^\$w$, etc., a problem discussed by Pensado Ruiz (1988). Pensado Ruiz combines the evidence from Romance developments of -C+*j/w*-, pointing to heterosyllabicity (see directly), with the evidence on Latin syllabification provided by classical metrics, as gathered and discussed especially in Allen (1973). In Latin verse, *i/u*+V could optionally become *j/w*+V, as testified by *Laviniaque venit / litora* (Verg., *Aeneid*), where *Laviniaque* counts four syllables. Since the preceding vowel is long, this [laːˈwiːnjakwe] does not provide any cues as to the syllabification of the resulting [nj] cluster. However, when a short vowel precedes, the syllable was measured as heavy, as in the following verses from the *Aeneid*:

(56)   *aedificant, sectaque intexunt abiete costas* ([ab.je.te]) (2.16)
        'they construct, and line the ribs with sawn fir'
        parietibus textum caecis iter ancipitemque ([par.je.ti.bus]) (5.589)
        'a path interwoven in its dark walls and a doubtful …'
        genua labant, vastos quatit aeger anhelitus artus ([gen.wa]) (5.432)
        'knees fail, a sickly panting shakes his vast joints'

This is evidence that, in case a glide occurred instead of a hiatus, the ensuing cluster was heterosyllabic. Consider further that Latin C*i*V strings derive from PIE *Cj*V through *i*-vocalization: e.g., SO.CI.US < *sok*ʷjos, A.LI.US < *aljos (Leumann 1977:125). Consequently, if SO.CI.US is an innovation, it is reasonable to suppose that SOC.JUS and parallel cases found in verse attest to the survival of a syllabification option otherwise banned from the standard language but which was carried on as a marginal option in verse and eventually generalized in late Latin / proto-Romance.

Thus, the metrical evidence and the Romance evidence in (55) can be easily accommodated under the assumption of a syllabification -C.*j*-.[45] There is evidence that this glide started to induce gemination of the preceding consonant – as preserved to this day in Italian – very early (according to Castellani (1965:121f.), as early as the first to second century). Spellings with gemination are reported in surveys focusing on the modifications of spoken Latin during the Empire (see Richter 1934:104). But it is hard to establish an upper limit: a *faccio* was recently discovered on a *defixio* dating from the first century BC in Iberia (see Agostiniani 1998). In all of these cases, gemination is evidence for consonantal /j/, because syllabic /i/ never induced it elsewhere. Under the Contact Law hypothesis, the two facts are connected and a conjoint explanation is provided.

The reflexes of the original heterosyllabicity (and gemination, possibly variable) in other Romance languages are not so clear as in Italian. Nevertheless, some evidence in this direction is available. Consider (57):

(57)   Pt.   Sp.   Fr.   Prv.   Rm.   It.
    SAPIAT *saiba*   *sepa*   *sache*   *sapcha*   *sapcha*   *sappia*

While only Italian preserves gemination, Gallo- and Raeto-Romance have glide hardening, pointing to a syllabification -C.*j*- that is confirmed by the non-application of /a/-palatalization in French. The Spanish and Portuguese examples in (57), on the other hand, show in this case the application of a conflicting process, viz. -C*j*/*w*- > -*j*/*w*C- metathesis, as further reflected in the outcomes of e.g., SAPUIT > Osp. *sope*, BASIUM > Sp. *beso* (see Rini 1991). While it is clear that metathesis, where it applied, bled gemination, the epigraphically documented *faccio* in Spain in the first century BC (cf. Agostiniani 1998) proves that, even there, the drift to gemination was present, whatever the final outcome.

Further evidence for the application of -C.*j*- > -C.C*j*- in (pre-literary) Ibero-Romance comes from the developent and distribution of palatal /ɲ/. Its distributional peculiarity, already mentioned in section 5.1, is straightforwardly explained under the hypothesis that its diachronic sources were not exhaustively syllabified as onsets. As is well known, these sources were manifold:

(58) a. geminates: *doña* 'lady' < DOM(I)NAM, *año* 'year' < ANNUM
   b. Latin consonant clusters: *ceñir* < CINGERE 'gird', *empeñar* 'pledge' < IMPEGNARE
   c. proto-Romance consonant clusters: *viña* 'vineyard' < UINEAM, señor 'sir' < SENIOREM

As for the Latin clusters in (58b), their heterosyllabicity is beyond any question. Since the same clusters gave rise to geminate [ɲː] still preserved in Italo-Romance, it is safe to assume that the same happened in the prehistory of Spanish as well, prior to degemination. Degemination, even for obstruents, had not begun yet by the time of the Arab invasion (711), as shown by the fact that Arabic geminates are treated differently, in loanwords, from their singleton counterparts (Pensado Ruiz 1993:197). And even when degemination applied, it did not bring about a merger of -NN- with -N-, since palatalization prevented it (cf. 58a; the same goes for /ʎ/). Now, for both (58a–b), the heterosyllabicity of the source is certain: assuming -N.I̯- (and, possibly, > -N.NI̯-) is, at this point, the null hypothesis, also on system-internal grounds.

As for the syllabification of *muta cum liquida* clusters (55c–d), evidence for variability in syllabification is available for several periods of the history of Latin. While Classical Latin stress in C'ONSĔCRO, P'ERPĔTRO, etc. testifies to an open penult, the occurrence of -ĕ- (not further reduced to -ĭ-; cf. (15) above) points to a closed penult in the pre-literary Latin stage (sixth–fourth centuries BC). Parallel to -C.j-, this earlier syllabification

(-C.r-) left traces in metrical practice, since before *muta cum liquida* a short vowel could occur in the *arsis* of the foot (by *positio debilis*, which means 'length by position', but 'weak', i.e., less consistent than before other clusters like -n.c-, -r.c-, etc.). The two possible measurements are seen in this verse of Lucretius: *quae patribus patres tradunt a stirpe profecta*. The most straightforward interpretation of this double possibility is to trace it back to a syllabification option (PĂ.TRI.BUS vs. PĂT.RES). The heterosyllabic option must have gained ground in the late Empire, as can be argued from the steep increase of long measurements (i.e., of the occurrences in which the syllable counts as heavy) in *positio debilis* documented by Timpanaro (1965:1082–83) and Viparelli (1990:26–33):

(59)	V in *positio debilis*:	heavy	light	(total hexameters)
	Ennius	3	37	(600)
	Lucretius	20	63	(600)
	Vergil	36	73	(600)
	Licentius, *Carmen ad Augustinum*	12	3	(154)
	Carmen de ponderibus	26	3	(208)

Since Vergil was the undisputed model of late hexametric poetry, this increase cannot be explained through imitation of literary models. Consequently, it must reflect phonological change, the same change that led to the syllable shift (considered above, in section 5) now observable in words like those in (60):

(60)		
*CA.THĔ.DRA	OFr. *chaiere*; OPrv. *cazeira*; NIt. *cadrega*;
CO.LŎ.BRA	Fr. *couleuvre*; OPrv. *coloura*; Log. *colóru/colòra*;
INTĔGRU	Sp. *entero*; Pt. *enteiro*; Fr. *entier*; It. *int(i)ero*; Log. *intréu*; Ro. *întreg*;
*PAL.PĔ.TRA	Fr. *paupière*, Venetian *palpiera*;
PULL ĬTRU	It. *puledro*;
TENĔBRAE/-AS >	Sp. *tinieblas*;
TON ĬTRU	Fr. *tonnerre*; Prv. *toneire*

The same stress shift in the spoken language is documented in the remark by Isidore of Seville (*Etym.* 32), who prescribes the paroxytonic pronunciation in *tenébra* and even condemns as *barbarismus* the (classical) *ténebra*.

To this evidence for heterosyllabication various objections have been raised: none of them, however, is conclusive (see Loporcaro 2005b). I mention here just the most frequent one, concerning Romance (Allen 1973:139, n2):

> In late Latin, as the evidence of Romance development shows, there was a shift of accent from, e.g., *ténebrae* to *tenébrae*. But this can hardly mean that the syllabification was then *te.neb.rae*, since the Romance evidence also indicates an *open* syllable. [emphasis added, M.L.]

This opinion, although quite common, is ill-founded. True, diphthongization in Tuscan and French consistently applies before *muta cum liquida* clusters: e.g., OFr. *piedre* 'stone' < PETRAM, *fievre* 'fever' < FEBREM, like *fier* 'proud' < FERUM and unlike *fer* 'iron' < FERRUM; likewise in Tuscan *pietra*, like *fiero* vs. *ferro*. But diphthongization is a later change, as it presupposes OSL that was generalized during the fifth century. This does not mean that heterosyllabicity is unavailable *in principle* in Romance (as implied, e.g., by Steriade 1988:403) as an option for the syllabification of -C*r*- clusters. This is evidenced by phonological processes such as obstruent vocalization in Chilean Spanish (see Martínez Gil 1997a:172), where *vi.na*[i̯].*re*/*vi.na*[u̯].*re* 'vinegar', *re*[i̯].*la*/*re*[u̯].*la* 'rule' occur, with coda vocalization, instead of standard *vi.na.gre*, *re.gla*; see Dalbera (1994:508–15) and Scheer and Ségéral (2003) for parallel Gallo-Romance evidence.

Not only is heterosyllabicity available in principle, but there is reason to believe that a substantial part of Italian dialects (those of southern Italy) preserve the situation inferrable from the stress shift in (60). This is testified by the outcomes of stressed vowels in the dialects from Abruzzo to Puglia. Whenever a change affected vowels in stressed open syllables, it did not apply before *muta cum liquida* clusters. This is exemplified in (61a–c):

(61)

	a. Loreto Aprutino (Pescara, Abruzzo)	b. Agnone (Isernia, Molise)	c. Cerignola (Foggia, Apulia)
	/ɔ/	/a/	/i/
open σ	[ˈrotə] 'wheel'	[ˈsɛanə] 'whole'	[ˈspoi̯kə] 'spike'
_ Cr	[ˈskɔprə] 'uncover.1SG'	[ˈlatrə] 'thief'	[pəˈdːitrə] 'colt'
closed σ	[ˈkɔrpə] 'body'	[ˈmaldə] 'mortar'	[ˈfirmə] 'steady.M'
	[ˈfɔsːə] 'hole'	[ˈkwaʎːə] 'rennet'	[ˈfiɟːə] 'son'

These dialects, in other words, never returned to the tautosyllabic option (unlike Tuscan or French) and thus bear direct evidence to the syllabification assumed for proto-Romance in (55c–d).

To sum up, the data from syllable contacts reviewed in this section converge with those from syllable codas inspected in section 5.1 and allow us to conclude that late Latin / proto-Romance had no 'tendency towards open syllables'. Quite the contrary, for stressed syllables, a 'tendency towards closed syllables' seems to have been in force. On the reasons why this might have been the case we will say something in section 6.

6   Rhythm as an explanatory factor for some major prosodic changes

Following a distinction originally proposed in these terms by Pike (1943:34), the languages of the world have been claimed to belong to either of two basic prosodic types: syllable-timed vs. stress-timed. While this bipartition has often been criticized for being too speculative and/or schematic, many studies over the last decade or so have provided a new thrust to this stream of research, developing several competing quantitative methods for assessing the rhythmic type to which a language belongs, based on experimental evidence (cf., e.g., Ramus *et al.* 1999; Ramus 2002; Grabe and Low 2002; Bertinetto and Bertini 2008a; 2008b). In this vein, Bertinetto and co-workers (cf. also Bertinetto and Vékás 1991) have proposed reinterpreting the traditional dichotomy syllable- vs. stress-timed in terms of 'control vs. compensation' (Bertinetto and Bertini 2008b:1):

> An ideally controlling [...] language should be conceived of as a language in which all segments receive the same amount of expenditure, i.e. articulatory effort, and (ideally) tend to have the same duration. This is obviously impossible, due to the varying points and manners of articulation; but this view acquires plausibility once we consider how languages do in fact differ in terms of the coupling of vocalic and consonantal gestures. Some languages admit a much higher segmental overlap (coarticulation) than others.

Thus, languages depart more or less strongly from the idealized controlling type, depending on the amount of coarticulatory overlapping they allow. Those allowing stronger overlap will be instances of the compensation type and show stronger compression of segments occurring in prosodically weak positions.

We cannot go into the technical details of any of the above-mentioned recent models here: the point is that for many specialists, still today, the classification of languages into two basic rhythmic types[46] appears a viable tool for characterizing cross-linguistic variation. This kind of classification has been applied to the Romance languages: most of the standard languages seem to be clear examples of the syllable-timed (or controlling) type: see, e.g., the early work by Bertinetto (1977) on Italian, or the comparative study of Italian, Spanish, Catalan and French, all featuring as syllable-timed among the languages, investigated by Ramus (1999); the same applies to Grabe and Low's results (2002:528–30), from which French and Spanish clearly differ from stress-timed German and Dutch.[47] European Portuguese, on the other hand, is stress-timed (or compensating). Thus, while unstressed syllables are (and have been) relatively stable in Spanish or Italian, they undergo massive reduction in, for example, Pt. *restaurantes* 'restaurants' [ʀəʃtauˈʀãtəʃ] → [ʀʃtauˈʀɐ̃tʃ], *perfeito* 'perfect' [pərˈfɐitu] → [pr̩ˈfɐit] (cf. Parkinson 1988:141). This seems to be a fairly recent development, as Brazilian Portuguese does not show those reductions and has much less tolerance for complex consonant clusters: e.g., *abstrato* 'abstract' [abiˈstratu], *advogado* 'lawyer' [adʒivoˈgadu].

While for living languages hypotheses, in this domain as elsewhere, can be tested experimentally, reconstruction (and specially reconstruction of prosody) rests on much more slippery ground: the evidence available is purely qualitative, reducing basically to documented segmental changes (e.g., vowel reduction, syncope and the like). Yet several scholars have put forward hypotheses invoking (changes in) rhythm as an explanatory factor in the history of the Romance languages. French is today syllable-timed (see, e.g., Lacheret-Dujour and Beaugendre 1999:37), but the massive application of weakening processes in unstressed position in old French was explained by assuming that the language went through a stage with stress-timing (cf. Richter 1911; Matte 1982:59; Palermo 1971:43; Dressler 1992:132). Indeed, the very shift back to syllable-timing was the endpoint of the segmental reductions in prosodically weak positions typical of a stress-timed language: once, say, DOMINĬCAM or OFFICĪNAM, through several steps, were restructured as [dimɑ̃ʃ] 'Sunday', [yzin] 'factory', there was subsequently little left for reduction to apply to synchronically, and syllable-timing was restored.

Matte (1982) outlines the changes in the overall rhythmical pattern through the history of French, using the terminological pair *mode décroissant* vs. *mode croissant*, in ways basically equivalent to the distinction between stress- and syllable- (or mora-)timing. This can be shown both extensionally (by the languages ascribed to one mode or the other, viz., e.g., English, *décroissant* vs. modern French, *croissant*) and intensionally (from the features used to diagnose the two types, viz. weakening vs. lack of weakening of unstressed vowels, C-V-C transitions showing more vs. less overlapping, etc.; cf. Matte 1982:59–60). From the Latin starting point (Latin was characterized by *mode croissant*), there emerged a gradual development towards the opposite rhythmic pole during the first to fourth centuries, culminating in the seventh.[48] By that time, OFrench was in Matte's opinion a clear case of *mode décroissant*. After a period of stability (ninth to thirteenth centuries), the *mode croissant* prosody progressively gained ground (thirteenth to seventeenth centuries), subsequently becoming firmly established.

Many aspects of this specific reconstruction, as of any other in this area, will have to remain purely speculative. Yet changes in the overall rhythmic pattern seem to offer an attractive unifying line of explanation for the prosodic revolutions in the history of Romance discussed in previous sections. If one (re)considers syncope, on the one hand (§§3–3.2), and shifts in syllable structure (§5.3), on the other, the curves seem to coincide pretty well. Archaic Latin (§3.1) went through a stage (sixth to fifth centuries BC) in which syncope applied and many distinctively long vowels in unstressed position were shortened; at the same time, there is evidence for heterosyllabication even of *muta cum liquida* clusters (§5.3: *consĕcro*, not **consīcro*). It is tempting to explain all these facts as epiphenomena of one single rhythmic principle: archaic Latin might have tended towards stress-timing. The reverse is true of the Latin language of the classical period, in which unstressed syllables remained stable and *muta cum liquida* clusters were tautosyllabic, betokening a lesser power of attraction on the part of the stressed nucleus.

Both reduction of unstressed segments and syncope are classic symptoms of stress-timing. Likewise, stress is commonly assumed to be able to influence syllabification: cf. Lutz's Law in Vennemann (1988:61) and the statement by Vennemann (1988:59) concerning the syllabification of [VdrV] strings in old English: 'an accented first syllable tends more strongly to attract part of the [following] cluster toward itself than an unaccented first syllable'. This tendency has direct consequences on syllabification in typical stress-timed languages such as English or German, not in typical syllable-timed languages such as Spanish or Italian. Thus, heterosyllabication in pre-literary Latin may receive a prosodic–rhythmical explanation (in terms of stress-timing). And since the same syndrome (intensification of syncope as well as heterosyllabication of -C+*r*/*l*/*j*- clusters) occurs again in the Latin–Romance transition, it seems possible to give the same explanation for what appear to be the same phenomena. Proto-Romance, therefore, might have shifted again towards the stress-timed pole. This cannot, however, be due primarily to the Gaulish (or any other specific) substratum, since it is by no means limited to northern Gaul.[49] In the conclusion to section 5.3 it was shown that central-southern Italian dialects have preserved heterosyllabic *muta cum liquida* clusters all along (-C+*j*- clusters were affected by several changes). It can now be added that there is evidence (cf. the experimental studies by Trumper *et al.* 1991; Schmid 2004) that those dialects have adhered to the stress-timed type down to this day.

3   PHONOLOGICAL PROCESSES[1]

Michele Loporcaro

The issue of phonological processes in Romance could be tackled in principle in at least two different ways, the synchronic–universalistic and the historical–inductive. One might consider, deductively, a general typology of phonological processes and exemplify them with Romance materials drawn from diachronic change as well as synchronic rules. At the present stage of the debate in theoretical linguistics, this kind of deductive approach would have the disadvantage that, with the blossoming of no-rule approaches to phonology since the 1990s, there is now little agreement upon the necessity of process-based descriptions for synchronic phonology. As Lass (1984:169f.) puts it, in his early discussion of the topic: 'the only case when process terms can be used in a relatively theory-neutral sense is [...] in describing historical change'. Historical change and its effects are the main focus of this chapter.

I shall first address the main changes that affected vowels (§1), starting from the most general context-free changes that reshaped the vowel system as a whole (§1.1). In section 1.2 I review two rather general sets of contextual processes, viz. diphthongization and metaphony. Section 1.3 considers some of the phonological processes that altered vowel qualities as successors to proto-Romance open syllable lengthening, and in section 1.4 I deal with a set of vowel-fronting processes which applied in several rounds over large Romance-speaking areas, especially A-fronting (> [æ] > [ɛ]) and the rise of the 'mixed' vowels [y] (< ū) and [ø] (< ŏ). Section 1.5 addresses vowel nasalization processes. Apart from section 1.5, all other sections on the development of vowels show a measure of overlap, since many of the processes under discussion intertwine in their motivations and/or effects. Apart from section 1.5, all sections concern exclusively the development of stressed vowels, since processes affecting unstressed vowels are dealt with in chapter 2. In section 2, I consider processes that affected consonants.

Section 2.1 reviews the different rounds of palatalization that affected most Romance varieties, and in section 2.2 I deal with weakening processes (lenition and degemination) in intervocalic position.

1 Vowels

1.1 The emergence of the Romance vowel systems

The most noteworthy property distinguishing all the vowel systems of the Romance languages from that of Latin is that none of them preserves the distinctive vowel quantity of the mother-language (see chapter 2). However, since loss of VQ resulted in different vowel systems in the different branches of Romance, Latin VQ has to be considered again while dealing with the differentiation of Romance vowel systems (indeed, the literature on the two topics is largely the same). As a starting point for the divergent developments of the Romance languages, the following system may be assumed for Classical Latin:[2]

(1)   Classical Latin vowel system

/ iː	i	eː	e	a	aː	o	oː	u	uː /
[iː	ɪ	eː	ɛ	a	aː	ɔ	oː	ʊ	uː]

FILUM	PIRA	SERA	UENIO	CANIS	AMATUM	COLLUM	UOX	CRUX	LUX
'thread'	'pear'	'evening'	'come.1SG'	'dog'	'loved'	'neck'	'voice'	'cross'	'light'

As witnessed by several passages in Latin grammarians, especially for mid vowels,[3] phonemic long vs. short vowels differed phonetically in tenseness/ height/peripherality (e.g., Straka 1959:181), along the lines usually described in the comparative literature in phonetics for languages such as English, German or Czech (see, e.g., Jakobson and Halle 1962; Lehiste 1970:30–33). Just as in, say, modern Standard German, Latin long /eː/, realized as [eː], was closer to short /i/ (probably realized as [ɪ]) in the acoustic–articulatory space than it was to short /e/ (pronounced [ɛ]). This phonetic circumstance must have favoured a tendency for long /eː/ (e.g., in CĒNA 'dinner') and short /i/ (e.g., in PĬPER 'pepper') to be treated at some point as members of a binary length contrast, a tendency reinforced by the fact that monophthongization of /ae̯/ (<archaic /ai̯/) had provided a new long counterpart /ɛː/ (e.g., in CÆLUM 'sky') to short (and phonetically lax) /e/ (as in UENIT 'come.3SG.PRS.IND'), which could at this point be reanalysed as /ɛ/, contrasting with both long /ɛː/ < /ae̯/ and short /e/ (< /i/).[4] A symmetrical tendency must have obtained on the velar side of the vowel system, with short /u/ (phonetically [xʊ]) tending to be reanalysed as the short counterpart of long /oː/, rather than of /uː/.

Both tendencies, for velar and for palatal vowels, were favoured by the Italic substratum, since Oscan-Umbrian (hence proto-Sabellian) had experienced a similar shift in vowel qualities long before Latin (Lejeune 1975; Seidl 1994). Note that, even with this rearrangement of the length-to-quality mapping, Italic had preserved contrastive VQ, albeit only under stress: e.g., Oscan *pís* 'who' [ˈpes], with the reflex of PIE *ĭ, vs. *tríibúm* 'house.ACC' [ˈtreːbom], with PIE *ē.[5] It is therefore unwarranted to take the changes in quality undergone by short vowels ([i] > [ɪ] > [e], [u] > [ʊ] > [o]) as sufficient evidence for the collapse of Latin VQ, as suggested by most reference works on the Latin–Romance transition (e.g., Lausberg 1976:202; Väänänen 1974/1982:30) with schemes such as that in (2), or with labels such as 'Italic qualitative system' for the output system (2b):

(2)   From the Classical Latin to the 'Italic qualitative system' (e.g., Lausberg 1976:202)

a.	iː	i	eː	e	a(ː)	o	oː	u	uː

b.	i	e	ɛ	a	ɔ	o	u	

Just as the Italic languages did not immediately become merely 'qualitative' despite the quality shifts, so contrastive VQ might well have persisted in spoken Latin – as argued, for example, by Franceschi (1976:277) – even in varieties displaying lowering of ĭ ŭ, until an independent change, viz. the rise of open syllable lengthening (OSL; see chapter 2, §2), caused the demise of the VQ contrast.

Against the received opinion that 'length opposition becomes quality opposition' (Straka 1959:180), a chronological argument can also be invoked. The traditional view assumes that this change started about the mid first century AD ('first sporadic examples of the opening [ɪ] > [e], [ʊ] > [o]', Straka 1959:180) and was completed for [ɪ] > [e] by the end of the second century (after what Straka calls the 'linguistic separation of Sardinia') and for [ʊ] > [o] around the end of the third century AD (after the 'linguistic separation' of Dacia). However, such sporadic attestations are indeed much earlier, as witnessed by examples like *tempestatebus* (for *tempestatibus*), carved on L. Cornelius Scipio's grave (consul in 259 BC) – in other words, preclassical Latin shows such a process at its highest sociolinguistic level. This is proof that the realization as [ɪ] (and perhaps, variably, already

[e]) of short ĭ had been around, in all registers of Latin, from very early. As a consequence, either one assumes that the qualitative change [i] > [ɪ] (> [e]), at the first stage, was carried over without abandoning vowel quantity, as proposed here, or one has to assume (like Pulgram 1975, for instance), that contrastive VQ was already lost in spoken Latin by the third century BC (at the latest) – an unsustainable claim, as shown in chapter 2, §2.

Note that while the allophonic tense vs. lax differentiation for long vs. short vowels can be reasonably assumed for spoken Latin as such, all subsequent developments which came to further modify the original picture in (1) must be placed within the structural histories of particular areas and/ or varieties of late Latin / early Romance. Adopting Herman's (1985a:88f.) tripartition, those changes can be ascribed to the 'second dialectalization', which took place during the Empire.

In Sardinia, the allophonic differentiation [iː/ɪ], [eː/ɛ], etc. was apparently given up, so that no reassociation of [ɪ] with [e(ː)] occurred. The final outcome (i.e., the Sardinian vowel system (3)) shows a plain merger of (Classical Latin) long and short counterparts into one phoneme, yielding a five-vowel system (examples from Logudorese; the first line displays the Latin source vowel):

(3)   Sardinian vowel system

iː	i	eː	e	a(ː)	o	oː	u	uː
i		ɛ		a		ɔ		u

ˈfiːlu	ˈpiːra	ˈseːrɔ	ˈbeːnɛ	ˈkaːnɛ	ˈbɔːna	ˈbɔːɣɛ	ˈruːɣɛ	ˈluːɣɛ
'thread'	'pear'	'evening'	'well'	'dog'	'good.FSG'	'voice'	'cross'	'light'

This kind of vowel system is shared today by Logudorese (the most conservative variety, spoken in the central-northern part of the island) and Gallurese (in the north-east), and the same development took place at first in Campidanese, in the southern half of the island, a variety which nowadays has, on some analyses, a seven-vowel system.[6] For the north-western Sassarese area, which displays an asymmetrical system, there is evidence for a more ancient stratum also manifesting the Sardinian system (3).[7] The Sardinian vowel system (3) stretches into southern Corsican, too (e.g., [ˈfilu] 'thread' = [ˈpilu] 'hair', [ˈmezi] 'month' = [ˈpedi] 'foot', [ˈkori] 'heart' = [ˈfjori] 'flower', [ˈfurːu] 'oven' = [ˈmulu] 'mule'; see Barbato 2008:145; Dalbera Stefanaggi 2001:99f.).

In southern Italy, the Sardinian-type vowel system occurs in the area covering the northernmost part of Calabria – north of the rivers Crati and

Coscile – and southern Lucania, south of the river Agri. The area was first described in detail by Lausberg (1939), who dubbed it *Mittelzone* ('Middle Zone'): e.g., in Trebisacce (province of Cosenza): [ˈtɛːʁə] < TĒLAM 'cloth' = [ˈtɛːnə] < TĔNET 'holds, has' ≠ [ˈpɪːpə] < PĬPER 'pepper' and, symmetrically, [ˈnɔːvə] < NŎUAM 'new.ꜰ' = [ˈsɔːʁə] < SŌLEM 'sun' ≠ [ˈnuːtʃə] < NŬCEM 'walnut' (see Pace 1993–94). It has been argued that this similarity is due to secondary convergence, unlike in Sardinia, based on the fact that the outcomes of ĕ ē and ŏ ō under metaphony do not merge in some dialects of the *Mittelzone*: e.g., in Senise (province of Potenza) non-metaphonic [ˈpɛrə] < PĔDEM 'foot' like [ˈmɛsə] < MĒNSEM 'month', but metaphonic [ˈpjerə] 'feet' ≠ [ˈmɪsə] 'months'; and symmetrically [ˈrɔtə] < RŎTAM 'wheel' = [nəˈpɔtə] < NEPŌTEM 'nephew' as opposed to the contrast between [ˈfwokə] < FŎCUM 'fire' vs. [nəˈputə] < NEPŌTES 'nephews' (Fanciullo 1988:676f.). This has been taken as evidence that the area might have gone through a stage with a vowel system of the common Romance type to be considered below in (6).[8]

As for Sardinia, that the situation observed today goes back to Latin in a straight line is demonstrated by the epigraphic evidence studied by Herman (1985c) (also Herman 2000b:131; Lupinu 2000:32f.). These studies show that graphic <i>/<e> confusions, frequent in the Italian peninsula, are virtually absent in Sardinia. This confirms that the vowel system observed today (3) is the endpoint of a straightforward development, which never experienced the *i/e* and *u/o* mergers. In other words, Herman was able to show that the information from inspection of Latin inscriptions is congruent with that coming from modern Romance dialects.

For those territories in which Latin/Romance died out, the latter type of evidence is not available, which makes any conclusion more debatable: for African Latin / early Romance it has been maintained that it might have developed a vowel system of the Sardinian type (see, e.g., Wagner 1941:10; Weinrich 1958:24; Lausberg 1976:204; Adams 2007:262), from evidence such as the testimonies of Augustine quoted in chapter 2, section 2, according to whom ōs 'mouth' and ŏs 'bone' had become homophonous for African speakers. Had the originally allophonic quality distinction been retained (as in Italy) and not lost (as in Sardinia), Augustine could not possibly have reported such a merger.[9]

A congruence of the two above-mentioned types of sources is observed also with regard to the asymmetry in the 'Italic' quality mergers. As shown in (4), Romanian has merged the outcomes of Latin ĭ and ē, but not those of ŭ and ō.[10]

(4)   Romanian vowel system

iː	i	eː	e	a	o	oː	u	uː
i	e		ɛ	a	ɔ		u	

fir	leg	cred	piatră	vacă	roată	soare	gură	cur
'thread'	'tie.1SG'	'believe.1SG'	'stone'	'cow'	'wheel'	'sun'	'mouth'	'arse'

This kind of asymmetrical merger is found not only in Daco-Romance (in all its branches) but also in a small area of western Lucania – a fact first revealed by the *AIS* and Lausberg (1939:44–46):[11]

(5)   Romanian vowel system (dialect of Castelmezzano, province of Potenza, *AIS* point 733)

iː	i	eː	e	a	o	oː	u	uː
i			e	a		o	u	

ˈfiːlə	ˈseːtə	ˈseːra	ˈmeːlə	ˈaːkə	ˈkoːrə	ˈsoːlə	ˈvuddə	ˈmuːrə
'thread'	'thirst'	'evening'	'honey'	'needle'	'heart'	'sun'	'boil.3SG'	'wall'

This prompted the inference that a substantial part of the Romance-speaking territory, apart from Sardinia (and possibly Africa), went through a 'Romanian' stage: this applies to southern Italy as a whole, according to Lüdtke (1956:97f.) – for whom 'Puglia and not the Balkans is the place of origin of the eastern vowel system' – and to the entire Peninsula for Bonfante (1983:417).[12] Further evidence for the broader geographic extension of the asymmetric vowel system (4) seems to come from Dalmatian, whose northern variety became extinct in 1898 with the death of the last speaker of Vegliote. In Vegliote, the outcomes of Ē and Ĭ merged in all syllabic contexts (e.g., [ˈmaik̯] < MĒCUM 'with me'= [ˈfaid̯] < FĪDEM 'faith'= [ˈstale] < STĒLLAE 'stars' = [ˈlaŋga] < LĬNGUAM 'tongue'), whereas Ō and Ŭ merged in open syllables, as they were both affected by diphthongization ([ˈbau̯d] < UŌCEM 'voice' = [ˈnau̯k] < NŬCEM '(wal-) nut'), but remained distinct in checked syllables ([ˈsamnŏ] < *SŎMNIUM instead of SŎMNIUM 'dream' vs. [ˈbuka] 'mouth' < BŬCCAM 'cheek'; cf. Bartoli 1906 II:336f.).[13]

Indeed, Latin epigraphic evidence confirms that the Ĭ/Ē merger spread earlier than the Ŭ/Ō one: drawing on an epigraphic corpus from the mid second until the fourth century, Herman (1985a:75f.) found that graphic confusions between <o/u> balance those between <e/i> only in north-eastern Italy (Regio X), and nearly so in parts of Campania, whereas in the rest of Italy and in Gaul <o/u> confusions occur more seldom than would be expected given a random distribution.[14] Furthermore, Herman (1985a:76) observes that on the Adriatic coast south of Ancona (the area including Puglia) such confusions do not appear before the Christian era. And, as expected, they never occur in the epigraphic materials from Dacia.[15]

The rest of the Romance-speaking world displays the merger of the outcomes not only of Latin ĭ and ē but also of ŭ and ō (as illustrated in (6a–c) with Italian, Spanish and French examples):

(6)   Common Romance vowel system

iː	i	eː	e	a	o	oː	u	uː
i		e		ɛ		a	ɔ		o		u

a.	It.	*filo*	*pera*	*stella*	*ferro*	*male*	*porco*	*voce*	*orso*	*duro*
b.	Sp.	*hilo*	*pera*	*estrella*	*hierro*	*mal*	*puerco*	*voz*	*oso*	*duro*
c.	Fr.	*fil*	*poire*	*étoile*	*fer*	*mal*	*porc*	*voix*	*ours*	*dur*

According to philological evidence, this vowel system was firmly established in the central and western regions (to the exclusion of the areas, already mentioned in (3)–(5), which attest to different vowel systems to this day) by the end of the western Empire. The *Appendix Probi*, probably written in Rome around the mid fifth century AD, shows instances of merger of both ĭ ē and ŭ ō.

The rise of this pattern, usually labelled the 'common Romance' (or even 'pan-Romance') vowel system, can be interpreted as follows. By the time the open syllable lengthening rule (cf. chapter 2: §2) spread (probably from Africa), to conquer the rest of the Latin-speaking world (with the possible exception of the eastern provinces), leading to the collapse of distinctive VQ, the outcome of Latin short ŭ had come to be pronounced /o/ in the whole area from the Adriatic sea (including Dalmatian; cf. Muljačić 1965:1190) to the Atlantic coast.[16] As eloquently shown by French, among the major literary languages, as well as by hundreds of other Romance dialects, the common core of the 'common Romance' vowel system is limited to the original mergers of ĭ ē and ŭ ō, which gave rise to a seven-vowel, four-height system, upon which a large array of later processes were superimposed (in French, for instance, /a/-palatalization and the (drag-)chain shift /u/ > /y/, /o/ > /u/

(cf. §1.3), as well as diphthogization of lower-mid vowels (cf. §1.2) (not visible in (6), either for French or Italian, since the examples do not occur in open syllables) and of higher-mid vowels, visible in *poire* and *étoile*. Such further developments, in many Romance varieties, resulted in (several different kinds of) vowel shifts, of which we cannot even sketch a typology here.

Some other types of vowel systems might appear at first glance to derive straight from the Classical Latin system (1), independently of the common Romance development (6). This has been maintained for the Sicilian system (7), which spreads from Sicily into the southernmost part of the Peninsula, up to the river Crati in central-northern Calabria, reappearing also further north in the coastal area of southern Campania (southern Cilento, province of Salerno, in an area south of Vallo; see Rohlfs 1937:84–86; De Blasi 2006:46f.), as well as in central and southern Salento (province of Lecce):[17]

(7)   Sicilian vowel system

iː	i	eː	e	a	o	oː	u	uː
	ɪ		ɛ	a	ɔ		ʊ	

'fiːlʊ	'nɪːvɪ	'tɪːla	'pɛːdɪ	'kaːsa	'kɔːrɪ	'vʊː tʃɪ	'nʊːtʃɪ	'mʊːrʊ
'thread'	'snow'	'cloth'	'foot'	'home'	'heart'	'voice'	'nut'	'wall'

For this kind of system, a direct merger of Latin Ī Ĭ Ē and Ū Ŭ Ō has been assumed by, e.g., Rohlfs (1966:10) and Lüdtke (1965b:1106f.; 2005:398, 409). However, it seems more appropriate to consider the Sicilian system (Lausberg 1976:206; Fanciullo 1984) a further development of the common Romance type, with merger of proto-Romance /u/ (< Lat. ū) and /o/ (< Lat. ŭ ō), and, respectively, /i/ (< Lat. ī) and /e/ (< Lat. ĭ ē), due to the superstratum influence of Byzantine Greek.

Still another type of system best explained as a further transformation of (6) – rather than as an independent evolution from Latin – is that occurring in an area of southern Italy stretching from northern Salento (with Taranto and Brindisi) into western and northern Basilicata (*AIS* points 735 Pisticci and 726 Ripacandida) down to the south-eastern part of the province of Salerno (Campania: Teggiano, *AIS* point 731, with some remnants further west in Omignano, point 740; cf. Avolio 1995:59f.). This area, christened by Lausberg (1939) as *Randgebiet der Nordzone* ('area on the periphery of the northern [i.e., 'Neapolitan'] one'), displays the following pattern (Lausberg 1939:50–54):

(8) 'Periphery' vowel system (*Randgebiet*; dialect of Carovigno, province of Brindisi, *AIS* point 729)

iː	i	eː	e	a	o	oː	u	uː
i		ɛ		a		ɔ		u

'fiːlᵘ	'pɛːpɔ	'sɛːra	'pɛːtɔ	'aːkᵘ	'kɔːrɔ	'sɔːlɔ	'krɔːʃɔ	'kruːtᵃ
'thread'	'pepper'	'evening'	'foot'	'needle'	'heart'	'sun'	'cross'	'raw.FSG'

The rise of this system has been explained in two opposite ways: according to Lausberg (1939:84) and Parlangeli (1960:29), in this area an original system of type (6) was influenced by the Sicilian vowel system (7) of the dialects spoken further south. More plausibly, according to Franceschi (1965:154) and Barbato (2002:40–44), in this area an originally Sicilian vowel system was reshaped, beginning with the late Middle Ages, due to the cultural prestige of Naples. When confronted with this prestige model, with /e o/ < Lat. ĭ ē and ŭ ō, the speakers of the local dialects, originally with Sicilian vocalism (7), reassigned their /i u/ in the corresponding lexemes to the mid vowels available in their original vowel system, viz. /ɛ ɔ/, through word-by-word substitution.

That a merger like that attested in (8) may be the product of a secondary modification is confirmed by the Corsican variety of Morsiglia (Cap Corse; Dalbera Stefanaggi 1995b:127–36), where proto-Romance /o/ and /ɔ/ (as well as /au̯/) have merged without residue (e.g., [la dʒi'bolːa] < CEPŬLLAM 'the onion', [la 'grodːʒe] < CRŬCEM 'the cross' = ['nosːu] < NŎSTRUM 'our(s).MSG', ['fogu] < FŎCUM 'fire'); [ɔ] occurs only, variably, before [R] and [n] (e.g., ['tɔRu]/['toRu] 'bull', ['bɔnu] 'good.MSG', ['sɔnːu] 'sleep'), but there are no minimal pairs; proto-Romance /ɛ/, on the other hand, largely merged with /e/ (e.g., [si ᶦʷestɛ] < UĔSTIT 's/he dresses him-/herself', [tʃɛR'belːu] < CEREBĔLLUM 'brain', like ['seRa] < SĒRAM 'evening', ['beðɛ] < UĬDET 'see.3SG'), although some minimal pairs are retained: ['bɛnɛ] < UĔNIT 'come.3SG' vs. ['benɛ] < UĒNAE 'veins'. Were it not for the latter, the system would appear identical to (8) and preserve no trace of a previous stage like (6).

Apart from the dialect of Morsiglia, the rest of the central and northern varieties of Corsica display a vowel system of type (6), in which, however, the qualities of the mid vowels have been reversed:

(9)   Central-Northern Corsican vowel system (Lentu, *NALC* point 13)

i:	i	e:	e	a	o	o:	u	u:
i	ɛ		e	a	o		ɔ	u

'rik:u   u'bɛlu   'bɛzu   u'beðɛ   'agu   'os:e   u'vjɔrɛ   u'vɔrnu   u'vjumɛ
'rich'   'the hair'   'weight'   'the foot'   'needle'   'bones'   'the flower'   'the oven'   'the river'

Thus, the system of Morsiglia, which still shows remnants of the original distribution Ĕ > [ɛ] vs. Ē > [e], can be interpreted as the product of (fairly recent) influence from the nearby area, from which the higher-mid realization of the outcomes of Ĕ ŏ is being imported on a word-by-word basis, eventually resulting (unlike in 9) in the loss of the original contrast (Barbato 2005–6).

The reversal in (9) has been explained by assuming that the proto-Romance lower-mid vowels were first diphthongized and raised and then finally monophthongized to /e o/ (Dalbera Stefanaggi 1990:141f.; 1991:548; 1995a:117; Barbato 2005–6:21). The same kind of explanation (diphthongization followed by monophthongization) has been invoked (by Fabra 1904; followed, e.g., by Rokseth 1921:533f.; Badia i Margarit 1984:131f., 138; Lausberg 1976:211, 213, 228) to account for the asymmetric reversal of proto-Romance /ɛ/ and /e/ in (eastern mainland) Catalan, where ['perə] < PĒTRUM 'Peter' vs. ['pɛrə] < PĬRAM 'pear' are kept distinct.[18]

Between (9) (reversed Tuscan vowel system) in the north and the Sardinian vowel system in the south-east (considered above while discussing 3), inspection of dialect variation in Corsica reveals yet another type of vowel system with inversion of the lower-mid and higher-mid vowel phonemes, for which Dalbera Stefanaggi (1991:480), Dalbera and Dalbera Stefanaggi (1998:154), who first identified it, entertain the hypothesis that it may represent a primary development from Latin. This is the system found in the south-western dialect belt (around the course of the Tàravu river), interposed between the two above-mentioned areas. In this system, illustrated in (10) with data from *NALC* point 47, Macà Croci, Ĭ Ŭ > [ɛ ɔ] are kept distinct from Ī Ū > [i u] as in the common Romance system, whereas Ĕ and Ē, ŏ and ō undergo phonemic merger, as in Sardinian, although becoming [e o], respectively:

(10) South-western Corsican vowel system (Taravese: Macà Croci, *NALC* point 47)

iː	i	eː	e	a	o	ɔː	u	uː
i	ɛ		e	a	o		ɔ	u
aˈmigu	ˈpɛlᵊ	ˈpezu	ˈpedi	ˈakːwa	ˈjogu	niˈpotᵊ	a ˈgrɔtʃᵊ	ˈjunⱼᵊ
'friend(M)'	'hair'	'weight'	'foot'	'water'	'game'	'nephew'	'the cross'	'June'

Barbato (2005–6; 2008) argues convincingly that Taravese, like Sassarese (see note 7), must also have originally possessed a Sardinian vowel system, which was then modified through word-by-word substitution due to pressure of the Tuscan system, also found in the dialects neighbouring to the north (9). Unlike in Sassarese, this replacement resulted in a symmetric system, which is, however – if Barbato is right – not a primary development of the Latin system (1), unlike the Sardinian (3), the Romanian (4) or the common Romance (6) ones.

Many other (synchronically wildly divergent) types of vowel systems are found across Romance. Yet, the above overview is limited to the originally distinct evolutions plus a few problematic cases for which the possibility of a primary development from Latin has been entertained by some scholars. In the following sections, we consider selected further changes in the stressed vowel systems, which had a significant impact on the shape of the vowel system of large areas of the Romance-speaking world.

1.2 *Diphthongization and metaphony*

This section is devoted to two sets of contextual processes which have further modified the vowel system of most Romance languages in addition to the context-free changes considered in section 1.1. Both diphthongization and metaphony occur in almost all Romance branches, in several different forms. In this section, we will not address the full array of diphthongization processes (some of which are mentioned in chapter 2, §3.5), but only those which enjoy a special status (and have been most intensively discussed in a pan-Romance perspective) given that they have recurred in the majority of Romance languages since their earliest documentation: diphthongization of Latin stressed ĕ ŏ.

1.2.1 Diphthongization of ĕ ŏ

Although this diphthongization seems to have occurred quite early, its placement as early as the third (ĕ > [jɛ]) and fourth (ŏ > [wɔ]) centuries

Michele Loporcaro

AD by, e.g., Straka (1953:268) and Zink (1999:53), following Richter
(1934:155f.), is unwarranted, since it is based on misreadings of Latin
inscriptions and incorrect interpretations of some passages by Latin grammarians.[19,20] For Tuscan, for instance, the earliest evidence for [wɔ] < ŏ
comes from Langobardic documents from the mid seventh century
(Castellani 1961:95). Italian – i.e., Florentine, together with most of western Tuscany, Sienese and Cortonese, as well as part of Umbria (Perugia and
Gubbio; see Castellani 2000:260) – patterns with French (i.e., Francien and
other Oïl dialects) in displaying diphthongization in open stressed syllables.[21] This led many (e.g., Bourciez 1937:94; Wartburg 1950:82, 141;
Castellani 1962; 1970a; 1970b; 1970c) to interpret this diphthongization
as one of the manifestations of the proto-Romance OSL (cf. chapter 2, §2).

In other varieties ĕ ŏ also diphthongized in checked syllables. This was
the case in Castilian (*nuevo* 'new.MSG', *fuerte* 'strong.SG', *tiene* 'have.3SG',
hierba 'grass'), and in Neapolitan, where the final outcome depends on the
following vowel (cf. De Blasi and Imperatore 2000:38–45, 79–88):

(11)

		before -A -E -O		before -I -U	
		open syllable	checked syllable	open syllable	checked syllable
a.	ŏ	['bːɔːnə] 'good.F'	['mɔrtə] 'dead.F'	['bːwoːnə] 'good.M'	['mwortə] 'dead.M'
b.	ĕ	['pjeːrə] 'feet'	['vjermə] 'worms'	['pɛːrə] 'foot'	['vɛrmə] 'worm'

This correlation – observed in Neapolitan as well as other Romance
varieties – led many scholars to discuss the relationship of Romance
diphthongization to metaphony, the latter being defined as a process
involving a change in the stressed vowel (fronting, raising or diphthongization) before a final (or also, in some varieties, word-internal) high vowel
(i.e., the outcomes of Lat. -ī -ŭ) or only before a front high vowel (Lat. -ĭ)
(possibly also before a palatal glide /j/).

Hitherto we have considered three different patterns with diphthongiza-
tion of ĕ ŏ conditioned by syllable structure (as in French or Standard
Italian: the Florentine type in (12a)) or by the following vowel (as in
Neapolitan (12c)) or by neither (the Castilian type in (12d)):

(12)

ĕ ŏ-diphthongization sensitive to:	a. Florentine	b. Old Aretine	c. Neapolitan	d. Castilian
i. syllable structure	+	+	–	–
ii. quality of the final vowel	–	+	+	–

Before considering the fourth possible combination (12b), let us elaborate on the relationship between type (12d) and the open syllable diphthongization shown by Florentine or French (12a). Generalized diphthongization of ĕ ŏ of the kind observed in Castilian can be considered the further evolution of a former stage in which the diphthong was conditioned contextually. The problem is whether this original conditioning can have been of type (12i) or (12ii) (or both). Although it has been argued that, in a pre-literary stage, OCastilian must have been of type (12c) (cf. §1.2.4), similar developments (i.e., 12c > 12d) are not documented with certainty in any Romance variety.

On the contrary, changes (12a) > (12d) are well attested in different Romance branches. In Rovigotto (southern Veneto; see Ascoli 1873:442f.), ĕ ŏ > [je wo] is found also in checked syllables: [ˈmjɛrkore] 'Wednesday', [aˈvjɛrto] 'open.MSG', [ˈwɔsːo] 'bone', [ˈkwɔrda] 'rope'. For this dialect, we must assume a previous stage of type (12a), like nearby Venetian (see below), modified via fairly recent generalization of the diphthongs, as proved by the fact that diphthongization also affects *[ɔ] < AU ([ˈwɔːro] 'gold' < AURUM, [ˈwɔːka] 'goose' < AU(I)CAM), which monophthongized only in the early Middle Ages throughout northern Italy.[22] The same holds for north-eastern Gallo-Romance (Wallon dialects), where ĕ ŏ also diphthongized in originally checked syllables: e.g., Liégeois *fièsse* 'feast' < FESTAM, *fiêr* 'iron' < FERRUM, *pwète* 'door' < PORTAM, *cwèsse* 'coast' < COSTAM (cf. Remacle 1948:49, 62f.). This was a later overgeneralization of the diphthong, according to Wartburg (1950:87). Likewise, the Castilian type can be considered a later development of a previous open syllable diphthongization.

As shown in (12b), the fourth logical combination is attested too, since the language of the medieval texts from an area comprising eastern Tuscany (Arezzo, Sansepolcro), northern Umbria (Città di Castello) and northern Marche (Urbino) systematically shows diphthongs from stressed ĕ ŏ only when both conditions are met: e.g., OAretine, until the early fourteenth century, *vieni* 'come.2SG' vs. *vene* 'come.3SG', *bu(o)no* 'good.MSG' vs. *bona* 'good.FSG' (Castellani 2000:368).

The occurrence of this fourth type has been taken as proof that all ĕ ŏ-diphthongization, even that of Florentine, was originally metaphonic in nature (e.g., Schürr 1965; 1970:32–141; 1972).[23] On this view, the Florentine distribution *buono,-a,-i,-e* vs. *grosso,-a,-i,-e* was created via super-imposing (an originally metaphonic) diphthongization, coming from either northern or central-southern dialects, onto a reconstructed proto-Florentine variety which had by hypothesis no diphthongs at all. When metaphonic diphthongization was imported, then, it became sensitive, only in Tuscany, to syllable structure, and analogical levelling took place, with [wɔ] (and [jɛ]) generalized to whole paradigms, provided that the (purportedly new) syllabic constraint (12i) was met, and eliminated, on the other hand, from all checked syllables. On this view, the OAretine pattern (12b) is a remnant of a transitional stage, still attesting to the first introduction of diphthongization (still subject, by hypothesis, to metaphonic conditioning) into Tuscany. In the same vein, lack of diphthongization in Florentine (and Standard Italian) *bene* 'well' (adverb), *nove* 'nine' has been interpreted as a relic of the original situation, left untouched by analogy since these morphologically invariant words were not part of any paradigm and consequently there was no allomorph from which the diphthong could spread. However, an alternative explanation is available: since these forms often appear non-prepausally (e.g., *nove giorni* 'nine days', *ben venuto / benvenuto* 'well come / welcome'), their vowels may well not have undergone a change that was crucially conditioned by main stress (as argued by Castellani 1970c:169; cf. also Sánchez Miret 1998:171f.).[24] What is more, diphthongs in *biene, nuove* are indeed attested in the medieval varieties from central Tuscany through northern Umbria showing diphthongization of the Florentine type (12a) (Sienese, Cortonese, Eugubino, Perugian; cf. Serianni 1999:109). There are also plenty of words which developed the diphthong despite their paradigmatic isolation (e.g., the placename *Fiesole* < FAESULAE).

The OAretine pattern lends itself equally to an interpretation diametrically opposed to Schürr's. If one assumes that open syllable diphthongization and metaphony arose as two distinct processes (as argued, e.g., by Wartburg 1950:122f.; Lüdtke 1956:82f.) in different areas – the former in central Tuscany, the latter both to the north and south-east of Tuscany – then OAretine, lumping together the two conditions, can be conceived as a compromise between the two, which fits well with the geolinguistic position of the dialect. On the contrary, if only metaphonic diphthongization had arisen initially, then one would have to assume (as Schürr does) that OAretine is more conservative than Florentine and that the open syllable restriction first arose in south-eastern Tuscany, to then spread gradually westwards so as to conquer Florence as well. This assumption is, however, at odds with what is independently known about the socio-geolinguistic situation of central Italy.[25]

A further argument against this assumption comes from the conclusion (reached in §1.2.4) that metaphony must have been realized originally, at least throughout Italo-Romance, as raising rather than diphthongization. This is at odds with Schürr's hypothesis, that needs an original stage with metaphonic *diphthongization*, rather than just metaphony.

All in all, the evidence seems to militate in favour of Castellani's (1970a:415) conclusion: '[c]learly, in Arezzo there is no preservation of a mythical palaeo-Tuscan stage. One simply finds a different type of development.'[26]

For other Romance varieties, the assumption that they have switched from one of the types in (12a–d) to another, in spite of lack of documentation, rests on firmer ground. Inversion of vowel heights of lower and higher-mid vowels in central-northern Corsican (see (10) above) and (for proto-Romance /ɛ/ and /e/) in Catalan (e.g., *herba* ['erbə] 'grass', *bec* ['bek] 'beak' vs. *cadena* [kə'dɛnə] 'chain', *sec* ['sɛk] 'dry') has been explained (see §1.1) by invoking an intermediate stage with diphthongization of proto-Romance /ɛ/ (as well as /ɔ/, for Corsican: e.g., in Bastia, *NALC* point 6, ['jogu] 'game', [len'tsolu] 'sheet' vs. [a 'ɔdʒɛ] 'the voice', [ni'pɔtɛ] 'nephew').

Some other languages have lost diphthongs in some contexts only, as was the case in Friulian and Dalmatian (Vegliote). Both, parallel to Corsican and Catalan, must have gone through a stage of type (12d), like Castilian, although both display diphthongs only in checked syllables: Vgl. ['pjal] 'skin' < PĔLLEM, ['bjal] 'beautiful.MSG' < BĚLLUM, ['kwal] 'neck' < CŎLLUM, ['nwat] 'night' < NŎCTEM (Bartoli 1906, II:333f.), Frl. ['pjardi] 'to lose', ['warfiŋ] 'orphan' (Frau 1984:32, 107). In open syllables, on the other hand, vowel qualities show that there has been monophthongization: Vgl. ['dik] 'ten' < DĔCEM, ['luk] 'place' < LŎCUM, Frl. ['piːt] 'foot' < PĔDEM, ['kuːr] 'heart' < CŎR[E].[27]

Northern Italo-Romance varieties present a much fuzzier picture, discussed in Rohlfs (1966:112–23, 139–50). Diphthongs from ĕ ŏ surface today in very few dialects: in the Ligurian dialect of Rovegno (*AIS* point 179) one has ĕ > [je] in open syllables (['djeʒe] 'ten', ['mjeve] 'honey') and ŏ > [wo] before a coda rhotic (['worbu] 'blind', ['mworti] 'dead.MPL'). In Venetian (Zamboni 1974:26), ĕ > [je] in open syllable occurs regularly (['djeze] 'ten', ['pjera] 'stone'), whereas [wɔ] is preserved only in some lexemes (['kwɔr] 'heart'), the most widespread outcome of ŏ being a raised [o] (['fora] 'ouside', ['fogo] 'fire'), standardly explained as a further development of a previous [wɔ]-diphthong, on a par with the third Venetian outcome of ŏ, viz. [jo] (e.g., ['njozer] 'to harm'). The examples mentioned show that Venetian diphthongization occurs in (originally) open syllables, like in Florentine (12a). Medieval documents from Venice, furthermore, show that open syllable diphthongization spread, for [je], not earlier than the mid fourteenth century, and even later for ŏ > [wɔ] (see Stussi 1965:xxxix–xlii; Formentin 2002:109), a late chronology that may suggest Florentine influence.

On the whole, in northern Italo-Romance it is much more frequent to encounter outcomes of ĕ ŏ which are not diphthongs, but which have often been interpreted as further developments thereof. For instance, [i] (< [je]) < ĕ in Milanese (cf. ['vitʃ] 'old.MPL', alongside ['vetʃ] 'old.MSG'; Salvioni 1884:63) and in many other dialects (e.g., ['sid] 'sit.2SG' in the Romagnol variety of Lugo; Schürr 1919:140).

As shown by the last examples, the open syllable condition (12i) is not the only one under which diphthongs have arisen from ĕ ŏ in northern Italo-Romance (and in the rest of Romance too). In fact, diphthongs, or what have been interpreted as further developments of previous diphthongs, also occur in many dialects of northern Italy in the context of a palatal(ized) consonant (e.g., ['pjentʃenu] 'comb', ['vjeɲɲu] 'come.1SG' in the dialect of the Gallo-Italian enclave of Sperlinga in Sicily, *AIS* point 836, imported there through migration in the twelfth century), or due to the application of metaphony.

Metaphony, in most of northern Italy, was caused by a final -ī which was then deleted (cf. chapter 2, §3.3) and affected all non-high stressed vowels (including -A-), as illustrated by the following examples from the dialect of Menzonio (a western Lombard variety of Canton Ticino; see Salvioni 1886:236–48): ['mar]/['mɛr] 'bitter.MSG/PL' < AMĀR(UM), ['ʃterlu]/['ʃtirli] '(of cattle) not producing milk(SG/PL)' < STĔRIL(EM), ['debul]/['dibul] < DĒBIL(EM) 'weak.MSG/PL', ['fɔrt]/['ført] 'strong.MSG/PL' < FŎRT(EM), ['long]/['løɲɟ] 'long.MSG/PL' < LŎNG(UM).

As already seen in these examples, in some dialects of Lombardy and Piedmont the change ŏ > [ø] (see below and §1.4) is also limited to the same context: e.g., in Villafalletto (*AIS* point 172) in the province of Cuneo (south-western Piedmont) ['ɔm]/['øm] 'man/men', ['ɔs]/['øs] 'bone/-s' (see Rohlfs 1966:141). In just a few alpine dialects metaphony was induced not only by -ī but also by -ŭ, as in Sardinian and in southern Italo-Romance: e.g., Ossolano (Alpine Lombard) ['øf] 'egg/-s', ['øtʃ] 'eye/-s' as opposed to non-fronted outcomes of Lat. ŏ in, e.g., ['rɔda] 'wheel', ['nɔva] 'new.FSG'.[28] Discussing these data, Rohlfs maintains that the change ŏ > [ø] went through an intermediate diphthongization: for (an older stage of) the dialects of these conservative areas, then, metaphonic rather than open syllable diphthongization has to be assumed. And, in his overall evaluation (Rohlfs 1966:121–23, 148–50) of the intricate situation in northern Italy, he concludes that, of the three conditions bringing about diphthongization in this area, metaphony and occurrence before a palatal consonant are more widespread and systematic than the open syllable environment.[29] Indeed, diphthongization before yod seems to be a common feature of the whole of western Romance but Castilian, which, as we saw in (12d), has diphthongs throughout except before a palatal consonant: e.g., *pecho* 'breast', *noche* 'night' (Hilty 1991:142).

The situation in French is fairly similar to that described for northern Italy. Here, too, one observes an asymmetry between retention of the diphthong from ĕ (*pied* 'foot') and monophthongization of the diphthong from ŏ (OF *cuer* > [ˈkœʁ]). Since this change, in Gallo-Romance as in north-western Italo-Romance, occurs in dialects also showing ū > [y], it has been supposed (first by Ascoli 1882:24–28) that the two changes were related and that ŏ-fronting went through the intermediate stages [wo] > [yo] > [yø] (cf. also Meyer-Lübke 1934:58, 85; Zink 1999:55). For old Provençal, the same palatal realization of the <u> occurring in the (graphic) diphthongs *uei uou* < ŏ has also been assumed (Schroeder 1932:174).

Open syllable diphthongization applied regularly in French, whereas this was not the case in Provençal, where outcomes with and without the diphthong coexist in medieval texts: e.g., *(u)ops* < OPUS 'work, need', *suegre/sogre* < SOCRUM 'father-in-law' (Anglade 1921:74; Sánchez Miret 1998:233).[30]

The whole Gallo-Romance area converges with northern Italy and Raeto-Romance, on the one hand, and Catalan, on the other, in also showing diphthongization of ĕ ŏ before palatal consonants: e.g., Fr. *mi* 'half.MSG', *vieil* 'old.MSG', Prv. *mieg*, *vielh*, Cat. *mig*, *vill*, Surselvan *miez* < MEDIUM VET(U)LUM (cf. Sánchez Miret 1998:213; Lausberg 1976:232).[31]

1.2.2 Metaphony

We have already spoken of metaphony as one conditioning factor for ĕ ŏ diphthongization. We now consider Romance languages which display metaphony but lack ĕ ŏ diphthongization. This is the case in Portuguese and Sardinian (on Catalan, for which diphthongization has been assumed for a pre-literary stage, see §1.1), both of which display metaphony, although with considerable differences. In Portuguese, proto-Romance /ɛ ɔ/ < Lat. ĕ ŏ were raised to [e o] before -ŭ: e.g., *gr[o]sso* 'big.MSG', *n[o]vo* 'new.MSG' vs. *gr[ɔ]ssa, -as, -os* 'big.FSG/FPL/MPL', *n[ɔ]va, -as, -os* 'new.FSG/FPL/MPL'. While proto-Romance higher-mid vowels were preserved in principle as [e o] (e.g., *qu[e]do, -a, -as, -os* 'calm.MSG/FSG/FPL/MPL' < QUĒTUM, *t[o]do, -a, -as, -os* 'all.MSG/FSG/FPL/MPL' < TŌTUM), in several cases they were subjected to the same metaphonic alternation originally affecting the outcomes of proto-Romance /ɛ ɔ/: e.g., *form[o]so* 'beautiful.MSG' (as well as all the adjectives in *-oso*) vs. *form[ɔ]sa, -as, -os* 'beautiful.FSG/FPL/MPL' (but still *form*[o]*sos* in the sixteenth century; cf. Williams 1962:129f.). This analogical levelling shows that metaphony has been morphologized: its context is opaque, as the alternants occur elsewhere as distinct phonemes (e.g., *s*[ɛ]*lu* 'stamp.1SG' vs. *s*[e]*lu* 'seal', *b*[ɔ]*la* 'a kind of cake' vs. *b*[o]*la* 'ball'; Mateus and d'Andrade 2000:17), and different alternants occur in what is today the same environment (e.g., due to merger of the vowels in inflections such as -ŭ and -ōs). The alternations originally created by metaphony have been redeployed to signal distinctions between different cells within paradigms: cf. non-alternating first conjugation *m*[ɔ]*ro/-a* 'reside.1/3SG' vs. differently alternating second and third conjugation *m*[o]*vo/m*[ɔ]*ve* 'move.1/3SG', *d*[u]*rmo/d*[ɔ]*rme* 'sleep.1/3SG' (Quicoli 1990:296–313).[32] Portuguese also possibly displays – but much less regularly – the effects of metaphonic raising of proto-Romance higher-mid vowels (e.g., *sirgo* 'raw silk' < SĒRICUM, *vindima* 'grape harvest' < UINDĒMIAM; Nunes 1975:48), although this is much more controversial.[33]

The situation is more regular in the northern varieties of Ibero-Romance: Asturian and Leonese display metaphonic raising to [i u] of both proto-Romance higher- and lower-mid vowels before (the outcomes of) Lat. -ī -ŭ: e.g., Leonese *ayiri* 'yesterday' < HĔRI, *timpu* 'time' < TĔMPU, *abirtu* 'open. MSG' < APĔRTUM (≠ *abierta, -os*), *tichu* 'roof' < TĒCTUM, *pilu* 'hair' < PĬLUM, *primiru* 'first.MSG' (≠ *primera, -os*), *trampusu* 'treacherous.MSG' (≠ *tramposa*); in the same environments, stressed -A- was raised to [e]: *pelu* 'post' < PALU (Zamora Vicente 1967:105–9; cf. also Hilty 1991, on Asturian). The metaphonic alternations thereby arising have been put to work to signal a contrast in gender (or, according to some, in number),[34] both on agreeing words (demonstratives, possessives, adjectives, etc.) and – in central Asturian – on nouns (overt gender): e.g., in the central *Bable* of Lena *isti quisu nigru* 'this (piece of) black cheese' (masculine) vs. *esto queso negro* 'this (sort of) black cheese' (neuter) (cf. Neira Martínez 1955:70–72; 1978).

As in Portuguese or Asturian-Leonese, in most of the languages in which it applied, metaphony gave rise to alternations which serve the expression of morphological categories: this was discussed in a rich literature on the so-called morphologization of metaphony (cf. Tuttle 1985; Fanciullo 1994; Maiden 1989; 1991a, especially focusing on Italian dialects, on which see below). As in Portuguese or Leonese, [±metaphonic] alternants can express the values of morphosyntactic features such as gender/number/person within verbal or nominal paradigms. Similar examples have been adduced above for northern Italo-Romance and more will be discussed for Romanian (in 13).

Another Romance variety which, like Portuguese and Sardinian, does not show diphthongization at all is OSicilian. Although central and southeastern Sicilian dialects nowadays do have metaphonic diphthongs (e.g., Ragusa [ˈnwoṵ] 'new.MSG' vs. [ˈnɔa] 'new.FSG', [ˈpɔnti] 'bridge' vs. [ˈpwonti] 'bridges'; Piccitto 1941:30f.), medieval texts are completely lacking in diphthongs (cf. Bruni 1984:343).

Among the modern Romance languages, Sardinian (in its Logudorese variety) is generally considered the variety in which metaphony has been preserved to this day in its most conservative form, as a purely allophonic process. Given the Sardinian five-vowel system (3), metaphony induces allophonic variation between [ɛ e], [ɔ o], with the higher-mid realization before high vowels and yod ([aˈbːɛldzɔ]/[aˈbːeˑrizi] 'open.1/2SG', [ˈsɔːla]/[ˈsoːlu] 'alone.FSG/MSG'), and the lower-mid elsewhere, including word-finally (e.g., [ɡːaˈfːɛ] 'coffee', [ɡːaˈtːɔ] 'almond cake'). That metaphony is still an allophonic rule is shown by the fact that it affects loanwords (e.g., [isˈtoːrja] 'story' < It. *st*[ɔ]*ria*) and constrains the Sardinian pronunciation of other languages (e.g., Sardinian regional Italian *st*[o]*ria*).[35]

To sum up so far, metaphony in some form or other is found in all Romance branches, and most Romance branches also show diphthongization of ĕ ŏ, in some context or other, preserving diphthongs up to now, or showing what have been interpreted, more (e.g., Northern Italian) or less (e.g., Catalan) consensually as further developments of diphthongs. This led many scholars to ascribe either (or both) to a very early stage of the Latin–Romance transition. As for the chronology of open syllable diphthongization, see the remarks at the beginning of section 1.2.1: a date earlier than the sixth century (for Gallo-Romance) or late sixth to seventh centuries (for central Italo-Romance) seems unlikely. As for metaphony, this is considered to have been at work already in (vulgar) Latin by, e.g., Schürr (1936), Lüdtke (1956:75–121), Lausberg (1976:228) and Krefeld (1999b: ch. 4).[36] While some of the arguments brought to bear to this purpose are dubious, the geographic spread of metaphony across the Romance territory is strong evidence in support of an early date.[37] This is not to say, however, that in this very early stage, metaphonic *diphthongs* had developed. And indeed, the placement of those diphthongs at a very early stage is crucial for those overall interpretations of the development of Romance vowel systems that establish a direct link between (the rise of) ĕ ŏ diphthongization and metaphony – or, to put it more generally (to include also, most notably, Sánchez Miret 1998) between diphthongization and the quality of final vowels.

1.2.3   On the non-relatedness of ĕ ŏ diphthongization and metaphony

There seems to be solid evidence in support of the opposite view (upheld, e.g., by Wartburg 1950:122f.; Lüdtke 1956:82f.) that regards metaphony and ĕ ŏ diphthongization as two originally distinct phenomena, that may have converged in several Romance varieties.

Romanian provides crucial evidence in this respect. In this language, the facts of diphthongization are particularly intricate and have been interpreted in several different ways. The relevant data, as for the modern language, can be summarized as follows:

(13)

		before -ᴀ	before -ᴇ	before -ɪ -ᴜ -ᴏ
a.	ŏ/ō	*poartă* 'brings' *coadă* 'tail'	*soare* 'sun' *noapte* 'night'	*port* 'bring.1SG' *nopţi* 'nights'
b.	ĕ	*iarbă* 'grass' *iapă* 'mare' *piatră* 'stone'	*iepe* 'mares' *pietre* 'stones'	*ieri* 'yesterday' *fier* 'iron' *piept* 'breast'
c.	ē/ĭ	*seară* 'evening' *neagră* 'black.FSG'	*vede* 'see.3SG' *leg* 'tie.1SG' *negri* 'black.MPL'	*lege* 'law' *cred* 'believe.1SG'

A first remark is that syllable structure is not relevant here to determining the different outcomes. Second, due to the asymmetric mergers illustrated in (4), Lat. ō was also affected by the same diphthongization process as ŏ, whereas on the palatal side diphthongization under the same contextual conditions affected not only ĕ but also ē/ĭ. Third, these contextual conditions clearly involve the quality of the final vowel.

Note that the seeming difference in the influence of final -ᴇ on the different stressed vowels in (13a–c) is illusory, and due to a more recent process of harmonization of the diphthongs from ĕ and ē/ĭ to the final vowel. Before its application, the same outcomes were observed in ORomanian before -ᴇ as before -ᴀ, as is still the case for the outcomes of ŏ ō in (13a): ORo. *veade* > *vede* 'see.3SG', *leage* > *lege* 'law', *piatre* > *pietre* 'stones' (cf. Lambrior 1878:85f., n4; Lausberg 1976:227f.). The older stage (['lɛadʒɛ] 'law', ['sɛatɛ] 'thirst') is still preserved in Macedo-Romanian. The (old) Daco-Romanian (and Macedo-Romanian) facts show that initially the same outcomes were found before both -ᴀ and -ᴇ, and were distinct from those found before -ɪ -ᴜ -ᴏ. Since in Romanian -ᴏ merged early with -ᴜ, let us call the two contexts, simplifying a little, 'before non-high vowel' vs. 'before high vowel'. Now, this is precisely the contrast found in the environment of metaphony, as exemplified in (11), except that ŏ ō and Ē ĭ diphthongize before non-high vowels, whereas metaphonic diphthongization of the Neapolitan type occurs before high vowels. Now, many scholars regard ŏ ō > [o̯a] and Ē ĭ > [e̯a] as conditioned diphthongization, calling it metaphonic (e.g., Sánchez Miret 1998:193, with a long list of predecessors starting with Mussafia 1868). However, it is easily objected that the same diphthongization takes place where no conditioning environment is detectable: e.g., *dea* < DĒT 'give.3SG.SUBJ', *stea* < STĒT 'stay.3SG.SUBJ'. This demonstrates, as argued by Nandriş (1963:212f.) and Sala (1976; 2004:272–74), that this diphthongization is not conditioned. But since [o̯a] and [e̯a] developed by default, then the complementary context must have been positively specified in the phonological rule which must have accounted for the distribution of the allophones prior to diphthongization: this is in fact what has been argued by the many who reconstruct for proto-Balkan-Romance and pre-literary Romanian a stage in which a final high vowel induced an allophonic realization [e o], in complementary distribution with [ɛ ɔ] occurring elsewhere (cf. Vasiliu 1968:40f.). Sala (2004:272) equates this reconstructed allophonic distribution with the working of metaphony in Galician-Portuguese.

Note that, at this stage, Ĕ diphthongization to [je] (13b) must already have applied. This must be assumed on two grounds. First, had this not been the case, the outcome of Ĕ would have merged with either *[ɛ] or *[e] from Ē/ĭ. Second, the output of Ĕ-diphthongization came to be subject to the same metaphonic variation, giving, e.g., *['fjeru] 'iron' (before high vowels) vs. *['jɛrba] 'grass' (elsewhere). The nucleus of the latter was then subject to the later diphthongization process affecting *[ɛ] from Ē/ĭ (Lambrior 1878:86f.). This yielded an intermediate *[je̯a], later reduced to [ja].

In conclusion, the Daco-Romance facts provide evidence for a process of Ĕ-diphthongization prior to and independent of the application of metaphony. This fact confirms that diphthongization of proto-Romance lower-mid vowels is old, a result independently arrived at from inspection of the Gallo- and Italo-Romance data, and is not compatible with an original metaphonic conditioning.

The Romanian facts naturally lead us to mention Sánchez Miret (1998), the most recent comprehensive reappraisal of dipthongization on a pan-Romance scale, based on a detailed sifting of virtually all of the available evidence (see also Sánchez Miret 2007). Contrary to Schürr, Sánchez Miret argues that common to all Romance languages was a non-conditioned (rather than metaphonic) tendency to diphthongize ĕ ŏ. In keeping with this basic assumption, considering Romanian he regards only ē dipthongization (13b) as part of this general Romance process, while excluding dipthongization of ŏ ō> [o̜a] and ē ĭ > [e̜a] as instances of a 'metaphonic' process conditioned by the following non-high vowel.[38] On the contrary, metaphonic diphthongization in languages such as Neapolitan, traditionally taken to be induced by final high vowels, is indeed – according to Sánchez Miret – an instance of the non-conditioned pan-Romance process. This, understood as a natural process motivated by the lengthening of a stressed vowel, was blocked by a following vowel of longer intrinsic duration. This is why -A, intrinsically longer, disfavours application of the process, whereas intrinsically shorter -I -U tend to favour it.

As argued in Loporcaro (2003a:86), a problem with this approach is that it treats diphthongizing metaphony (e.g., in Neapolitan, (11)) as completely unrelated to raising metaphony (e.g., in Sardinian): this point is elaborated in the next section.

1.2.4   Metaphonic diphthongization vs. raising

Metaphony occurs, throughout Romance, basically in the two forms of diphthongization and/or raising. In principle, the two could be independent developments (as argued, for Italian dialects, by Rohlfs 1966:128, 154f.) (14a), or one could argue that metaphony arose in only one form (14b) and that later changes brought about the distribution observed today:

(14) Metaphonic diphthongization and raising
    a. two unrelated processes
    b. different and successive steps in one and the same development
       i. diphthongization > raising
       ii. raising > diphthongization

This issue is deeply intertwined with that of the origin of ĕ ŏ diphthongization itself: assuming that the latter was determined by metaphony on a pan-Romance scale, as Schürr does, implies that metaphony must have occurred uniformly as diphthongization across Romance at a sufficiently remote pre-literary stage.

Proponents of this position (14bi) have to face several difficulties and are forced to make a number of unwarranted assumptions. The most striking one concerns (Logudorese) Sardinian, which shows no trace of diphthongization throughout its documented history and which, according to the *communis opinio* in Romance studies (but see the conclusion of this section), is alone in preserving metaphony as an allophonic phonological rule. By all standards in diachronic phonology (cf. Dressler 1980:117; Kiparsky 1995), this represents a stage logically prior to morphologization, as observed elsewhere in Romance. Ferguson (1976:126f.), however, simply assumes an 'incipient diphthongization' for Sardinian too, which 'was not continued'. Likewise, Schürr (1970:26f.) claims that Sardinian is not conservative and that Sardinian metaphony needs to be evaluated in the same light as metaphony in those mainland Italian dialects which have a Sardinian vowel system, which in his view presuppose an early monophthongization. As shown in section 1.1 (see note 8), the dialects of the Lausberg area have metaphonic dipthongization. However, whether those dialects did preserve Sardinian vocalism all along has been questioned: according to Fanciullo (1988:676f.), they went through a stage with common Romance vocalism, while Savoia (1997) follows Lausberg (1939) in maintaining that Sardinian vocalism is a primary development in that area. Now, if Fanciullo is right, then Schürr is wrong. But even if Lausberg and Savoia are right and the Lausberg area has an *original* Sardinian vocalism (which means a set of context-free diachronic correspondences as shown in (3)), this does not of itself require that Sardinian must have gone through such a stage with metaphonic diphthongization.

The same line of argument as for Sardinian is followed by Schürr (1970:100–2) for Galician-Portuguese. There are no traces of (metaphonic) diphthongization here either, yet Schürr claims that this should be assumed for a pre-literary stage. In Castilian, too, diphthongization is not conditioned by the final vowel, yet such a conditioning is postulated for pre-literary OCastilian (Schürr 1970:112–17) on such scanty evidence as the occurrence of unexpected diphthongs in, e.g., *cuerto* (Soria, Burgos), *cuerro* (valle de Losa, north of Burgos) instead of *corto* < CURTUM 'short', *corro* < CURRO 'run.1SG' (see García de Diego 1946:304).

Those irregular diphthongs are regarded as proof that OCastilian, prior to the Reconquest, had just metaphonic diphthongs, and that such 'accidents' occurred in the process of superimposing an originally metaphonic diphthongization onto dialects which were already in the process of generalizing diphthongs as in (12d), therefore displaying variation *o*/*ve* (or *vo*). This is sheer speculation, as unexpected isolated cross-overs in the outcomes of proto-Romance /o/ vs. /ɔ/ and /e/ vs. /ɛ/ are legion in all Romance languages, and some are even pan-Romance: e.g., ŏUUM (attested in Persius' adjective *ovato*) > It. *uovo*, Sp. *huevo*, etc. 'egg' for Classical Latin ōUUM. The facts here are simply that Galician-Portuguese and Sardinian show metaphony by raising, and no trace of diphthongization, whereas Castilian has ĕ ŏ diphthongization without metaphonic conditioning.

Inspection of southern Italo-Romance metaphony provides evidence in support of (14bii). All over southern and central Italy (apart from Tuscany), two basic patterns of metaphony are encountered, exemplified in (15)–(16) from the dialects of Naples and Servigliano (province of Ascoli Piceno), respectively:

(15) Neapolitan type (Naples; cf. Vignuzzi and Avolio 1994:644f.)

		before -A -E -O		before -I -U -O	
		open syllable	checked syllable	open syllable	checked syllable
a.	ŏ	['bːɔːnə] 'good.F'	['mɔrtə] 'dead.F'	['bːwoːnə] 'good.M'	['mwortə] 'dead.M'
b.	ĕ	['pɛːrə] 'foot'	['vɛrmə] 'worm'	['pjeːrə] 'feet'	['vjermə] 'worms'
c.	ō/ŭ	[nə'poːtə] 'nephew'	['sordə] 'deaf.F'	[nə'puːtə] 'nephews'	['surdə] 'deaf.M'
d.	ē/ĭ	['meːʃə] 'month'	['sekːə] 'dry.F'	['miːsə] 'months'	['sikːə] 'dry.M'

(16) Sabino type (Servigliano; cf. Camilli 1929:224–31)

		before -A -E -O		before -I -U -O	
		open syllable	checked syllable	open syllable	checked syllable
a.	ŏ	['mɔːre] 'die.3SG'	['mɔrta] 'dead.FSG'	['moːri] 'die.2SG'	['mortu] 'dead.MSG'
b.	ĕ	['pɛːde] 'foot'	[a'pɛrta] 'open.FSG'	['peːdi] 'feet'	[a'pertu] 'open.MSG'
c.	ō/ŭ	['loːpa] 'she-wolf'	['korsa] 'run.FSG'	['luːpu] 'wolf'	['kursu] 'run.MSG'
d.	ē/ĭ	['veːde] 'see.3SG'	['metːe] 'put.3SG'	['viːdi] 'see.2SG'	['mitːi] 'put.2SG'

Now, for Italy, both areal considerations and language-internal evidence suggest that dialects of type (15) went through a stage like (16). Geographically, as shown by Barbato (2009), the Neapolitan type centres on Naples and Rome,[39] two prestige centres which – given what is independently known – have influenced surrounding dialects over the centuries. The so-called Sabino/Ciociaresco type (with raising metaphony), on the other hand, is found in more conservative and marginal areas, which have resisted the spread of the innovation.[40]

The kind of system-internal evidence available in support of (14bii) can be illustrated with the Molisano dialect of Agnone. Here, diphthongization is sensitive to sentence phonetics, as exemplified in (17a) with the diphthong arisen from stressed ī in non-metaphonic context (more examples were provided in chapter 2, §5.3, (61b)):

(17)

	i. prepausal	ii. utterance-internal
a.	[ˈʃtamː a sːənˈdojːə] 'listen to me'	[ˈʃtamː a sːənˈdi ˈvuǫnə] 'listen to me carefully'
	[aˈuǫjə ˈtoːịrə] 'today it's windy'	[ˈtiːrə ruˈviǫndə] 'wind is blowing'
b.	[ˈmːiǫsə] 'in the middle of'	[ˈmːeːs a la ˈcɛtːsɐ] 'in the middle of the square'
	[ɲːa tə ˈsiǫndə] 'how do you feel?'	[n də ˈsendə ˈvuǫnə] 'don't you feel good?'
	[ruˈviǫndə] 'the wind'	[ruˈvendə ˈfɔrtə] 'strong wind'

Now, as shown in (17b), with the metaphonic outcomes of ĕ (before -ī/-ŭ) the same sensitivity is observed for metaphonic diphthongs as well. Crucially, as shown in the experimental study by Loporcaro *et al.* (2007), the non-diphthongized (higher-mid) variant of the metaphonic alternant is not identical to the (lower-mid) monophthong occurring in a non-metaphonic environment (e.g., in [ˈsɛndə] 'feel.1SG'). This can only mean that metaphony first caused raising of proto-Romance /ɛ/ (as well as /ɔ/) to [e] (and [o]), which subsequently diphthongized.[41]

The special fact about Agnone is that this diphthongization did not result in restructuring but got 'caught', as it were, in the overall pattern of sensitivity to sentence stress. Note that this reconstruction is consistent with the fact that, unlike the Tuscan diphthongs [wɔ jɛ], the metaphonic diphthongs found in southern Italo-Romance (exemplified with Neapolitan in (15)) almost everywhere display higher-mid [e o].[42]

Further evidence in favour of hypothesis (14bii) is provided by the experimental study of the dialects of southern Salento by Grimaldi (2003). Let us first summarize the traditional view, prior to Grimaldi's study. Metaphony, according to this view, is realized as diphthongization throughout Salento (e.g., Lec. [ˈtjeːni] 'keep.2SG' vs. [ˈtɛːne] < TENET 'keep.3SG'; [ˈseːni] 'play/sound.2SG' from previous [ˈsweːni], still preserved in rural Leccese dialects, vs. [ˈsɔːna] < SONAT 'play/sound.3SG'), just as in neighbouring central Puglia. This metaphonic diphthongization did not spread so far south as to cover the whole peninsula: ŏ > [we] stops at the line Nardò–San Cesareo–Vèrnole, whereas ĕ > [je] extends further south (Gallipoli). For historical and geographical reasons, it is clear that diphthongizing metaphony spread southwards during the early Middle Ages, possibly as one of the innovations favoured by the Langobardic conquest, as argued by Parlangeli (1953; 1960): the territories which resisted the innovation were the extreme strongholds of the area which remained under Byzantine rule at that time. Lacking metaphonic diphthongization, those southernmost dialects (near Capo di Leuca) have been commonly claimed not to display metaphony at all. So far the *science acquise*.

Grimaldi's study shows that this is, in fact, true only of the dialects of the south-western corner of Salento, from Gallipoli to Ugento. Here, experimental analysis reveals no significant coarticulatory effect of final high vowels on stressed [ɛ ɔ]. However, the dialects spoken further east do show a significant raising of stressed mid vowels either (according to the specific dialects) before high vowels or before -/i/ only. Furthermore, parallel to the asymmetry in diphthongizing metaphony in the dialects spoken a couple of miles to the north, in south-eastern Salentino, too, raising affects [ɛ] in more dialects and also [ɔ] in fewer. Thus, for instance, in S. Maria di Leuca one finds [ˈpeːdi] 'feet' vs. [ˈpɛ̣ːdɛ̣] 'foot', [ˈdentʰi] 'teeth' vs. [ˈdẹntʰɛ̣] 'tooth', but no allophonic variation for /ɔ/, whereas in Patù or Tiggiano one also finds [ˈʃoːki] 'play.2SG' vs. [ˈʃɔːka] 'play.3SG', [ˈkoːri] 'hearts' vs. [ˈkɔːrɛ̣] 'heart' (Grimaldi 2003:60–65). Grimaldi (2003:64) also shows that this kind of previously unnoticed metaphony carries over, just as we saw for Sardinia in section 1.2.2, to the local pronunciation of Italian: e.g., [paˈreːri] 'advices' vs. [paˈrɛ̣ːrɛ̣] 'advice'. This is proof of its being the effect of a synchronically active phonological rule.

These data lend themselves to a straightforward interpretation, which sheds crucial light on the whole issue of the relationship between diphthongization and metaphony. The dialects of south-eastern Salento, at the south-eastern corner of the whole Romània, were never reached by diphthongizing metaphony, but do show raising metaphony, just like Logudorese Sardinian. This confirms that the Sardinian situation has to be taken at face value, *pace* Schürr (1970:26f.) and Ferguson (1976:126f.): metaphony *in statu nascendi* was (and still is, in Logudorese as well as in south-eastern Salentino) a process of raising, not of diphthongization. In the many Romance varieties in which metaphony (induced by original -/i/, and sometimes also -/u/) occurs in a diphthongizing form (e.g., Romanian, (13), or Neapolitan, (15)), this is the product of a further development ([ɛ] > [e] > [je], [ɔ] > [o] > [wo]) as still arguable synchronically from data such as those from Agnone considered above in (17b).

With this demonstration, the whole edifice of assumptions concerning the origin of Romance (open syllable) diphthongization set up by Schürr (and his followers) collapses. It is thus shown that Romance ĕ ŏ diphthongization is a process which originated independently of any metaphonic conditioning. In fact, an independent diachronic motive is available for it, viz. open syllable lengthening (chapter 2, §2) and, conversely, no metaphonic explanation is at hand once the correctness of hypothesis (14bii) has been shown, dispelling the myth of a pre-literary, very old metaphonic diphthongization purportedly spanning the whole Romance-speaking territory.

1.3   *The qualitative fallout of the OSL*

As was shown in chapter 2, section 2, OSL can be ascribed to proto-Romance and be considered a straightforward cause for the demise of contrastive vowel quantity. Not all modern Romance varieties preserve it into the present, for reasons which may differ from language to language. In Daco- and Ibero-Romance, no trace of OSL can be detected. For scholars denying that OSL developed in proto-Romance – a stance taken by Schürr (1970:5f.) as a preliminary move for the hypothesis that open syllable diphthongization stems from metaphony (see §1.2), not from OSL – non-occurrence of OSL at the two extremes of the Romània is evidence for a conservative situation: those varieties have purportedly remained at a stage at which OSL had not yet arisen. Under the opposite scenario defended here, OSL might have arisen in proto-Romance as an allophonic rule, to be lost in Ibero-Romance when degemination obscured the difference in environment on which the selection of the lengthened vs. non-lengthened allophone previously depended – at least in a substantial proportion of the relevant cases (consonant clusters remaining unaffected). Either reconstructive view has, in itself, some plausibility. Note, however, that the geolinguistic arguments brought to bear by Schürr (1970:5f.) are inconclusive. Appealing to Bartoli's (1943) norm of lateral areas, he claims that OSL is restricted to a central area spanning from northern Gallo-Romance to central Italo-Romance and is unattested in the rest of the Romània.

Note first that there is evidence for innovations, consisting in common loss of an inherited feature that may happen polygenetically, that are shared by Daco- and Ibero-Romance. A case in point is the loss of past participle agreement in perfective periphrastics and of double perfective auxiliation (cf. Loporcaro 1998b:155, 171, 198; 2007b:179–81). Furthermore, the list is empirically incorrect: as observed in chapter 2, section 2, both Sardinian and southern Italo-Romance do display either OSL or diachronic successors thereof. The same holds for southern Gallo-Romance, since there are Occitan varieties which possess distinctive VQ which, as was shown in chapter 2, section 3.5, is a further development of OSL: cf., e.g., the north-alpine dialect of Val Germanasca (data from Pons and Genre 1997, discussed in Morin 2003:131), ['peːno] 'punishment' vs. ['pɔnːo] 'pen', ['paːlo] 'shovel' vs. [eï̯'palːo] 'shoulder', or the southern-alpine dialect of Breil and La Brigue (data from Dalbera 1994:126–28, discussed in Morin 2003:131), ['naːz] 'nose' vs. ['braʃ] 'arm', ['sek] 'dry.ᴍ' vs. ['tʃeːg] 'fold'. Since these are marginal and conservative dialects, it is fair to assume that Occitan as a whole, just like Oïl and Franco-Provençal dialects, did originally display OSL.

As for southern Italo-Romance, dialects split into two basic types, with those on the Tyrrhenian side of the Apennines mostly sharing with Tuscan and Sardinian an allophonic OSL rule (e.g., Neapolitan ['ʃtaːtə] 'been' vs. ['ʃtatːə] 'be.ɪᴍᴘ + 2SG enclitic'), and those spoken on the Adriatic side from Abruzzo to central Puglia and eastern Lucania displaying a series of processes affecting vowels in open syllables.[43] Some of them were reviewed in chapter 2, section 3.5, where it was emphasized that in many dialects those processes are sensitive to sentence phonetics, applying prepausally but not in utterance-internal position. This is the case in, for example, Bitonto (province of Bari), where Lat. ī ū evolved, respectively, to [ɔi̯] or [i], [iṷ] or [u] depending on syllable structure (Merlo 1911–12:908f., 919), but the diphthongs are found only prepausally.

However, in many other dialects from the same area open syllable diphthongization applied at word level and led to restructuring in the underlying representation: e.g., Altamurano ['vai̯t] 'see.3SG' < UĪDET, with a diphthong in all prosodic positions (e.g., [ʃə 'vai̯tə 'bːwei̯n] 'one sees well') vs. ['lɛɲː] 'tongue' < LĬNGUAM.[44] Many other processes obey the same conditions, affecting selectively open syllables (of oxytones and paroxytones) all over this southern Italian area, the simplest and more widespread one being raising of lower-mid vowels (e.g., ['rotə] 'wheel' < RŎTAM, ['detʃə] 'ten' < DĔCEM vs. ['kɔrpə] 'body' < CŎRPUS, ['mɛrlə] 'blackbird' < MĔR(U)LUM in Loreto Aprutino, Province of Pescara; see Parlangeli 1952), to which we may add various colouring processes (e.g., in Bisceglie, province of Bari, ['kɔpə] 'head' < CAPUT vs. ['catːə] 'square' < PLATEAM; see De Gregorio 1939).

Basically, the situation found in all those dialects is identical (abstracting away from variation in proparoxytones, see note 44), to that of French, Raeto-Romance or the northern Italo-Romance dialects considered in (31) (chapter 2, §3.5). The only crucial difference is the fact that western Romance degemination (cf. §2.2) has led to phonologization of vowel quantity in the latter varieties (which was possibly lost later, as was the case in standard French; cf. Morin 2006), whereas southern Italo-Romance

Adriatic dialects never went through such a stage: here, phonologization resulted exclusively from changes in vowel quality affecting the diachronic successor of the allophone originally lengthened via OSL.

Summing up, not only northern Gallo- and Italo-Romance, but rather the *whole* of Gallo- and Italo-Romance provide evidence for a proto-Romance OSL.[45]

1.4   Some widespread vowel-fronting processes

There is one process that naturally links the changes discussed in the previous section with those to be considered in this, viz. A-fronting, as instanced by, e.g., French *cher* < CARUM 'dear.M' vs. *char* < CARRUM 'cart'. This fronting, affecting stressed A in open syllables only, is found not only in northern Gallo-Romance but also in a conspicuous part of northern Italy, where the process occurs most pervasively in Emilia-Romagna (e.g., Bolognese ['tɛːvla] 'table' vs. ['vaːka] 'cow'; Coco 1970:4).[46] From the south-eastern corner of the Gallo-Italian territory (northern Marche: Urbino, Fano, etc.) open syllable fronting of A passes the Apennine to reach northern Umbria, eastern Tuscany (Arezzo, Cortona; e.g., ['æːpo] < APEM 'bee', ['kæːne] < CANEM 'dog' vs. ['kaldo] < CALIDUM 'hot.M' in Sansepolcro; cf. Merlo 1929a:67f.). Further north, in Piedmont and some dialects of Liguria, the change is subject to morphological conditions, as it occurs in selected morphemes (e.g., the -ARE first class infinitive ending: Turinese [maŋˈke] < 'to fail'). Open syllable fronting occurs also in rural dialects of Lombardy (e.g., in Vigevano, AIS point 271, ['næs] < NASUM 'nose', [aˈvær] < AUARUM 'greedy' vs. ['pasta] 'pasta'), whence it permeated lower-class urban varieties of Milanese during the seventeenth–eighteenth centuries, to be eventually lost with restoration of the original central vowel in, e.g., ['naːs] 'nose' (cf. Salvioni 1919:195). In the Alpine region, A > [ɛ] in open syllable is found in several dialects of Alpine Lombard: e.g., in Upper Leventinese (Airolo) ['cɛ] < CASAM.

In Swiss Raeto-Romance, the process occurs in upper Engadine (e.g., ['meːl] 'badly' < MALE, ['peːʃter] 'shepherd' < PASTOR, [tʃyˈreːr] 'to take care of' < CURARE vs. ['bratʃ] 'arm' < BRACHIUM in Zuoz) as well as in central Ladin (e.g., Gardenese ['nɛs] 'nose' < NASUM, ['tlɛr] 'clear' < CLARUM vs. ['paʃtər] 'shepherd'; Battisti 1926:53–57).

In south-eastern Italo-Romance as well, A-fronting occurs, among other processes considered in section 1.3: e.g., in Carbonara di Bari ['kɛᵃpə] 'head' < CAPUT, ['lɛᵃnə] 'wool' < LANAM vs. ['aɟːə] 'garlic' < ALLIUM (Merlo 1926:93f.).

The chronology of these changes may be quite different in the different areas. Thus, for Emilian, Bertoni (1909:584) suggests the twelfth century as a possible date for the A > [ɛ] change, whereas for central Ladin the same change is placed not earlier than the sixteenth century by Battisti (1926:77f.), Kuen (1923:68f.), Wartburg (1950:137). For French (i.e., northern Gallo-Romance), on the other hand, a much earlier chronology is assumed: e.g., sixth century A > [aɛ] > (seventh century) [ɛ] according to Zink (1999:57), late eighth century (through the same intermediate steps) according to Bourciez (1937:49). The latter is the latest possible chronology, since the change is already mirrored in the ninth century Sequence of St Eulalia (*spede, presentede, virginitet*; Hilty 2001:63).

This change, in both northern Gallo-Romance and northern Italo-Romance has been traced by Ascoli back to the Celtic substratum in the same way as the other vowel-fronting processes observed in (substantial parts of) the same areas, viz. ū > [y] and ŏ > [ø] (Ascoli 1864; 1882), which differ from A-fronting in not being conditioned by syllable structure.[47]

Felixberger (2003:596) reviews the respective positions of adherents (e.g., Wartburg 1950:37f.) and opponents (e.g., Meyer-Lübke (1920: 227–32)) of the substratum-based explanation of these processes. It is fair to say that scepticism about such explanation, in this specific case (and perhaps more generally), seems to prevail nowadays (e.g., Ternes (1998) for Gallo-Romance, and Di Giovine (2003) for Italo-Romance), for several reasons. On the one hand, the occurrence of those processes in Gaulish is not demonstrated, or has even been disproved, for ū > [y]: Ascoli based his argument on the (later) changes observed in insular Celtic (Ascoli 1882:22), while Gaulish has been since shown not to display fronting of Proto-Indo-European ū: e.g., *buei* 'be.SBJV.3SG' /bwei/, a cognate of Latin FUIT (Eska 2004:863–69). On the other hand, the application of ū-fronting, even in Gallo-Romance, seems to be quite late (not earlier than the seventh century – Bolelli 1940:203; Silvestri 1977–79:220),[48] at a time when Gaulish was probably already extinct (see Jackson 1953:317–19).

Furthermore, the processes at issue appear to obey different conditions in the different dialects in which they occur, and seem to be polygenetic, judging also from the chronology of documentation. A process of A--fronting, for instance, seems to occur in late Latin and is documented epigraphically all over the Empire (see Herman 1978b). This late Latin process, contrary to the Gallo-Romance one, is not conditioned by syllable structure, also occurring in checked syllables (e.g., *aenis* for ANNIS 'years. ABL.PL' in Africa), nor by stress, as it occurs not only in stressed (e.g., *stetim* for STATIM 'immediately'; Consentius, Keil V 392, 16) but also in unstressed syllables (e.g., *fetigati* for FATICATI 'tired'; Probus, Keil IV 212, 4). Since, however, this palatalization did not result in any generalized /a/ > /ɛ/ change, Herman (1978b:214f.) surmises that it might have not gone beyond the status of an allophonic (variable) process. The motivation proposed by Herman is based on the classical Martinetian argument of the 'asymmetry of articulators'. When the VQ contrast was lost, the number of vowel phonemes that had to be distinguished by quality increased. In this transition phase, given the lesser articulatory space in the back region, allophonic /a/-fronting helped avoid a clash with /ɔ/.

1.5   Vowel nasalization processes

Latin had no distinctive vowel nasalization. In Latin, 'universal phonetic nasality', involving a certain degree of physiological nasalization of vowels due to coarticulation with nasal consonants 'may be assumed to have operated as a default' (Sampson 1999:19).[49] A special case is that of word-final -M, which Latin sources attest to have been reduced to a nasalization of the preceding vowel. While it has been argued that this had phonological consequences for the vowels affected, in terms of length (e.g., Lüdtke 1965a) or nasality (e.g., Safarewicz 1974:185–87), no trace of those putative effects survive into Romance.[50]

From this common starting point, some Romance varieties then developed various allophonic nasalization processes, which eventually led, in French and Portuguese (among the standard languages), to the establishment of phonemic nasality. Most of those processes were originally triggered by nasal consonants, although some instances of non-conditioned allophonic nasalization are also reported. In this case, nasality sometimes serves grammatical purposes, typically the signalling of boundaries. Thus, in the Picard dialect of Santerre (cf. Flutre 1977:41, 55; Sampson 1999:19), high vowels are nasalized word-finally (e.g., [berˈbɛ̃] 'sheep', [perˈdœ̃] 'lost'; cf. Fr. *brebis*, *perdu*), and in the Franco-Provençal of Vaux all word-final unstressed vowels are nasalized phrase-finally: e.g., [ẽ ˈrevõ)] 'an oak tree' vs. [lo ˈrevo dy ˈbwaː] 'the oak in the wood' (Duraffour 1932:19f.; Sampson 1999:16). A similar process – although involving insertion of final [ŋ] rather than vowel nasalization – applies in the western Lombard dialect of Intragna (Centovalli, Canton Ticino), where a (non-phonemic) velar nasal is added to clause-final (or prepausal) stressed vowels: e.g., [u kaʃaˈdo l ɛ riˈvɔŋ] vs. [l ɛ riˈvɔ u kaʃaˈdoŋ] 'the hunter has arrived' (cf. Salvioni 1886:224f.; 1907:731). Besides, non-conditioned nasalization is sometimes reported as a sociolectally marked feature in one or the other speech community throughout the Romània (e.g., the Florentine middle-class accent).

Leaving aside non-conditioned processes, the rest of the phenomena touched upon in this section involve, at least in the beginning, assimilation of the vowel to an adjacent nasal consonant. This also involves languages for which traditional structuralist phonologists assume a phonemic contrast, based on minimal pairs such as French *fin* [ˈfɛ̃] 'end' vs. *fait* [ˈfɛ] 'done.M', *bon* [ˈbõ] 'good.MSG' vs. *beau* [ˈbo] 'beautiful.MSG' or Portuguese *sim* [ˈsĩ] 'yes' vs. *si* [ˈsi] 'oneself', *dom* [ˈdõ] 'gift' vs. *dou* [ˈdo] 'give.1SG'. Originally, what is today a contrastive [Ṽ] was a [VN] sequence. This has prompted analyses that contend that, underlyingly, nothing has really changed: e.g., Mateus and d'Andrade (2000:20–23) on Portuguese, or Schane (1968:48) on French. Such conclusions were often based on distributional arguments such as the following. After [Ṽ] in Portuguese one finds only [ʀ], which otherwise occurs after coda consonants (e.g., [ˈtɛ̃ʀu] *tenro* 'tender' like [palˈʀaɾ] *palrar* 'to chatter'), never [ɾ], which occurs intervocalically (e.g., [ˈpeɾɐ] *pera* 'pear'). Likewise in French, after [Ṽ] only voiceless [s] occurs (e.g., [ɛ̃siste] *insister* 'to insist'), never voiced [z], which occurs intervocalically (e.g., [reziste] *résister* 'to resist'). However, this distributional bias may be regarded as a diachronic leftover and need not have such dramatic consequences for synchronic analysis.

Portuguese and French are the only two standard Romance languages for which a phonemic nasality contrast has been assumed. Considering dialect variation, in addition to Portuguese, Oïl and Franco-Provençal dialects, contrastive (i.e., synchronically unconditioned) nasal vowels occur also in a small dialect area of Gascony (in Artix, ALF pt. 685, [ˈbĩ] 'wine' < VINUM, [ˈlỹœ] 'moon' < LUNAM, [ˈplɛ̃] 'full' < PLENUM; Sampson 1999:154), in some areas of northern Italy (especially Emilian: e.g., [ˈpɛ̃ː] 'bread', [ˈdmɛ̃ː] 'tomorrow' vs. [ˈvɛː] 'go.2SG', [ˈstɛː] 'stay.2SG' in Grizzanese, province of Bologna), Sardinia (many varieties of Campidanese) and north-western Corsica (cf. the map in Sampson 1999:351). In these areas too, the source of contrastive nasality historically is the deletion of a nasal consonant, which might have occurred in different contexts. In northern Italo-Romance it is usually found word-finally and preconsonantally, but not intervocalically: e.g., [ˈtɛ̃ː(ᵐ)pə] 'time' < TEMPUS, [ˈfɛ̃ː] 'hay' < FENUM, [ˈtrũː] 'thunder' < TONITRUM vs. [(al) ˈduna] 's/he gives' < DONAT, in the dialect of Piandelagotti (province of Modena).[51] In Campidanese Sardinian, on the other hand, nasal deletion and the subsequent rise of nasalized vowels has taken place only intervocalically: e.g., [ˈkãĩ] 'dog' < CANEM, [ˈsõũ)] 'sound' < SONUM, [ˈbĩũ] 'wine' < VINUM vs. [ˈkantu] 'sing.1SG' < CANTO, [ˈkontu] 'tell.1SG', etc. (Contini 1987:135, 453–61). Thus, Campidanese, on the one hand, and French and Northern Italian, on the other, display a mirror-image distribution of nasalization from nasal consonant deletion, whereas Portuguese has nasalization in all contexts: [ˈmẽw̃] *mão* 'hand', [ˈkẽtu] *canto* 'sing.1SG'. As Sampson (1999:286) observes, this means that no unitary implicational scale can be set up for contextual preferences for nasalization on a pan-Romance basis.[52]

Campidanese Sardinian nasalization differs from the nasalization patterns more often encountered across Romance in that it does not entail a change in vowel quality (except, trivially, for the effects of nasalization on formant structure and intensity documented by Contini 1987:460f.). Elsewhere in Romance, nasalization usually goes with appreciable changes in quality, as attested by lowering in French *fin* [ˈfɛ̃], *brun* [ˈbʁœ̃], etc. Changes in quality occur also in dialects in which nasalization remains an allophonic process, as in the dialects of the Sila area in northern Calabria, such as that of San Giovanni in Fiore (province of Cosenza), where just /a/ is affected, raising to a nasalized [ɐ̃] or even [ɨ̃]: [ˈmɨːnu] 'hand', [dʒuˈvɨ̃nːi] 'John', [ˈkɨ̃ntari] 'sing.3SG'. In several varieties, it is changes in quality (possibily combined with cross-dialectal comparison and philological evidence) that permit us to reconstruct nasal vowels for earlier stages of the language. This is the case in Romanian, where today's *lână* [ˈlɨnə] 'wool' < LANAM, *câine* [ˈkɨịnɛ] 'dog' < CANEM bear witness to a pre-literary stage with nasalization, for which Slavic influence has been envisaged (Sampson 1999:317–21). In other systems, however, nasalization, although reconstructible or documented for the past, left no traces in vowel quality, as seen in Milanese, which has restored syllable-final nasals in, e.g., [ˈpan] 'bread', [ˈvin] 'wine', but had deleted them, with subsequent (contrastive) nasalization (i.e., [ˈpãː], [ˈvĩː]) by the early nineteenth century, as evidenced by Cherubini (1839–43:xxxi), according to whom nasals in those words must be pronounced 'as the French do'. In eastern Lombard (Bergamasco), on the other hand, coda nasals have been deleted, rather than restored (e.g., [ˈpa] 'bread', [ˈtep] 'time'; cf. Sanga 1997:258): here, too, a previous stage *[ˈpãː], *[ˈtẽːp] is commonly assumed.

2 Consonants

The consonant systems of the Romance languages display a vast range of different patterns and processes. Some constraints on this variation are inherited. Thus, Latin contrasted four places of articulation (for obstruents), with the laryngeal represented only by the fricative /h/, deleted by the first century BC.[53] In proto-Romance, consequently, the furthest place back was the velar. Several diachronic processes, specific to one or another language, did lead to the rise of laryngeal and/or uvular allophones, like French /r/ realized as [ʁ R χ] (e.g., *rentrer* [ʁɑ̃tχe]), or Spanish /χ/ (from several diachronic sources, and with an articulation ranging from velar [x] to laryngeal [h] in different dialects). In several other cases, laryngeal allophones came to be derived via synchronic rules, as is the case for the coda weakening of /s/ → [h] in Andalusian Spanish (cf. Hernández Campoy and Trudgill 2002), or the weakening /s/ → [h] (when not adjacent to a consonant) in rural Bergamasco (e.g., ['hal] 'salt', but [ol 'sal] 'the salt'; cf. Bonfadini 1987).

For most cases in which phonemic laryngeals arose, contact can be traced as a determining factor in the change. Thus, OFrench acquired /h/ from Germanic (e.g., *honir* 'to shame' < HAUNIAN, *jehir* 'to force a confession' < IEHAN); that the consonant was indeed realized as [h] is demonstrated by the epenthesis in, e.g., *harangue* 'harangue' < HRING, *henap/hanap* 'chalice' < HNAPP (cf. Meyer-Lübke 1934:125). This phoneme even penetrated the inherited Latin lexicon (e.g., *haut* 'high' < Lat. ALTUM and Frk. HAUH-).

Contact with Arabic is responsible for the occurrence of a phoneme /h/ in the Sicilian dialect of Pantelleria: its realization can be either [h], [ħ] or [k], e.g., *hasíra/kasíra* 'doormat', but it does not merge with autochthonous /k/, which can never be realized as [h] (e.g., *kausi* 'trousers', never **hausi*; Tropea 1988:ix). Romanian is another case (cf. Nandriş 1963:156–58): /h/ occurs in words borrowed from Greek (e.g., *monarh* 'monarch'), Slavic (e.g., *duh* 'spirit') or Hungarian (e.g., *hotar* 'border'). Once it became available through borrowing, /h/ penetrated the native lexicon, especially as a hiatus-filler: e.g., *văduhă/văduvă* 'widow'.

Another innovation concerning places of articulation resulted from processes creating retroflex consonants in several varieties. The major Romance area displaying retroflex consonants extends from Sicily to the extreme south of Italy (Calabria and Salento), Sardinia and southern Corsica. The main diachronic source is Latin geminate -LL-, which gives rise to a retroflex lateral in only a few dialects of southern Calabria (e.g., [ka'val̢u] < CABALLUM 'horse'; see Rohlfs 1966:328), but most often is a postalveolar obstruent, either stop (e.g., Logudorese ['kaɖ̢u]) or affricate (e.g., Crotonese [ka'vaɖ̢zə]). In Sicily, Salento and Calabria (but not Sardinia and Corsica), dental stop + /r/ clusters also resulted in a retroflex affricate: e.g., Sicilian ['ma:t̢ʂɪ] < MATREM 'mother'. Some less extended areas are found in mountainous parts of mainland Italy (Abruzzese Apennines, e.g., ['b:ɛl̢:ə] 'handsome.MSG' in S. Andrea di Civitella del Tronto (see

Giammarco 1979:56); Lunigiana and upper Garfagnana, e.g., ['kweɖo] 'that.MSG', ['bɛɖo] 'handsome.MSG' in Corsano (see Savoia 1980:276) and in the Bay of Naples: e.g., [ka'ɖːiːnə] 'hen' (see Pianese 2002:246; also Como 2002; 2007 for nearby Monte di Procida)). There are also outcrops in the Iberian Peninsula.[54] Given this distribution, many have argued that retroflex consonants are due to a pre-Indo-European substratum (e.g., Merlo 1933:24; Millardet 1933). However, later research has shown that medieval texts, even those in Greek, Arabic or Hebrew characters which are not suspected of conservative spelling, show no trace of the phenomenon: for Sicily, Caracausi (1986:121–44) shows that retroflexion cannot be dated before the fourteenth century.

Detailed comparison of the phoneme inventories of the Romance languages would exceed by far the scope of the present section, which, like that on vocalism, will focus on processes that took place in many Romance dialects at an early date, thus contributing effectively to differentiate them from Latin. Some of these have been touched upon in chapter 2, section 5: in that section, we reviewed some changes affecting (proto-Romance) consonant clusters in many Romance languages, whose motivation can be traced back to adjustments in syllable structure: e.g., the gemination before -i̯- as exemplified by It. *sappia* 'know.PRS.SBJV', possibly related to the heterosyllabication documented by Provençal and Romansh *sapcha*, French *sache*, etc. The effects of -i̯- were also involved in a series of processes that applied generally and, although showing some intersection with the syllable-related ones, were not determined by syllable structure: Romance palatalizations. These processes, considered in section 2.1, were the main (most ancient, and most widespread) source of new consonants with respect to Latin, and first brought obstruents in this place of articulation into the phonological system.

2.1   Palatalizations and affrications

Several rounds of palatalization must be distinguished, based on the chronology of documentation and on the differences in areal diffusion.[55] For most of the processes involved, it can be observed preliminarily that they traditionally go under the label 'palatalization(s)' although the output of the change is not necessarily a palatal consonant: often it is a dental affricate (or fricative). Thus, a more accurate label would be 'palatalization/affrication'; however, for the sake of conciseness, we use the traditional label in what follows.

The oldest and most widespread process is the palatalization affecting the clusters -ci̯-, -ti̯-. The clusters themselves were an innovation with respect to Classical Latin, which probably broke through during the early Empire (cf. chapter 2, §5.3). Affrication of such clusters is documented as early as the second century AD, the first attestation generally pointed to (e.g., by Herman 1998:149) being *Crescentsianus* (*Corpus Inscriptionum Latinarum* (*CIL*) XIV 246, from Latium, AD 140). For -TI̯-, the affrication even made its way into normative prescription towards the end of the western Empire, when the spelling pronunciation of words like *etiam* and *Titius* is dubbed wrong by grammarians: cf. Servius (Keil V 445), Pompeius (Keil V 286), Papirianus (*apud* Cassiodorum, Keil VIII 216).[56] The early date of the process is confirmed by the fact that no branch of the Romance family appears immune from it. The affrication of -TI̯- must have preceded that of -CI̯-, because the former, not the latter, may result in a voiced affricate in intervocalic position via lenition (§2.2) in the medieval stages of the western Romance languages, which seems to imply that the change from cluster to plain consonant (via affrication) happened earlier (see Lausberg 1976:326f.): RATIONEM 'reason' > Sp. *razón*, Pt. *razão*, Occ. *razó*, all with [dz] in the (early) Middle Ages. Further developments then resulted in deaffrication: [dz] > [z] in the sixteenth century in Portuguese (Williams 1962:79f.), etc. Deaffrication combined with devoicing in Spanish (> [θ], e.g., in [ra'θon] 'reason'), as part of the general demise of the voicing contrast in non-plosives. When -TI̯- occurred postconsonantally (or geminate), voicing did not apply: e.g., *FORTIAM > Sp. *fuerza*, Pt. *força*, Fr. *force* 'strength', *MATTIAM > OSp. Pt. *maça*, Fr. *masse* 'club, mace'.

In western Romance, but more systematically in the eastern Romance languages, gemination affected this cluster. This explains why, in western Romance, some of the outcomes of -CI̯- and -TI̯- do not display voicing: e.g., Pt. *faço* < FACIO 'make.1SG', *face* < FACIAM 'face' (both with [ts] until the sixteenth century), Fr. *place* < PLATEAM 'square', *glace* < GLACI(AM) 'ice' (where also the non-application of A > [ɛ] confirms that the stressed syllable must have had a consonant coda: Meyer-Lübke 1934:124).[57]

A further change eventually resulting in the creation of palatal consonants, also very widespread across Romance, concerns voiced non-labial stops before yod: proto-Romance (-)GI̯- and (-)DI̯- merged with inherited (-)I̯- ultimately forming an affricate [d(ː)z] or [d(ː)ʒ]. At an early stage (up to the first century AD, according to Castellani 1965:113–18), -GI̯- -DI̯- -I̯- > [j(ː)]. The merger is reflected in spellings like *Aiutor* (Pompeii *CIL* IV suppl. I 7069), *Aiutoris* (Pompeii *CIL* X 8058) for *Adiutor,-oris*, and somewhat later by reactive spellings like *codiugi* (for *co(n)iugi*), with <di> instead of etymological -I̯- (Väänänen 1967:54). This outcome occurs to this day in most of southern Italo-Romance: e.g., Nap. ['jwoːkə] < IOCUM 'game', Sic.

['jɔːku], ['ɔːji] < HODIE 'today', Sic. and Cal. ['fuːju] < FUGIO 'flee.1SG' (cf. Rohlfs 1966:214, 393–95). This has been interpreted as uninterrupted preservation (Rohlfs) or as a regression from an earlier affricate (Väänänen 1967:55). Here, as elsewhere in Italo-, Gallo- and Ibero-Romance, the outcomes of -GI̯- -DI̯- -I̯- merged with that of -G$^{e/i}$-: Sic. [jiˈnɛʃtra], Nap. [jəˈnɛʃtə] < GINESTRAM 'broom', Cal. [jeˈlaːre], Nap. [jəˈla] < GELARE 'to freeze' (compare standard Italian [dʒ] in *ginestra, gelare = giorno, oggi*, Fr. [ʒ] (< Ofr. [dʒ]) in *geler = jour, janvier*, Sp. Ø in *helar = enero*; Lausberg 1976:282–86).

The further evolution of -I̯- (-GI- -DI-), eventually leading to results such as the western Romance ones just exemplified, went through subsequent stages with affrication and (possibly later) palatalization. Spellings with <z> for -I̯- appear from the mid second century: *azutoribus* 'helpers' (*CIL* VIII 18224) (for ADIUTORIBUS), *oze* 'today' (for HODIE from Carthage, second century; Audollent 1904:253), although the hypercorrect *Iosimus* (for *Zosimus*) occurring twice in Pompeii (*CIL* IV suppl. I 4599) suggests a still earlier date. In Christian inscriptions, in the following centuries, *zabolus* (= DIABOLUS) 'devil', *zaconus* (= DIACONUS) 'deacon' become frequent (see Väänänen 1967:54; Herman 1998:15). This brought Castellani to posit an intermediate step (first to second centuries AD) in which affrication ([j] > [d(ː) z]), but not yet palatalization, had taken place. The affricate realization [d(ː)z] came to be rivalled by [d(ː)ʒ] (< [dːj]), as attested by reactive spellings such as *geiunium* (= IEIUNIUM) 'fast' in the *Itala Bible*, *Giovi* (= IOVI) 'Jove' (*CIL* II 4972,47), *Magias* (= *Maias*) (*CIL* X 4545), etc. That palatalization did not at once oust the older dental affricate can be argued from variation still preserved in Romance. Both affricate outcomes co-occur in Tuscan (e.g., *raggio* 'ray', *razzo* 'rocket' < RADIUM), and this has been the case for a long time, as evidenced by Tuscan placenames such as *Orgiale/Orzale* < HORDEALEM.

The very occurrence of spellings with <ge> for etymological /je/ is evidence for the fact that original -G$^{e/i}$- had lost (or was losing, at first variably), its velar articulation, merging with original -I̯- (-GI-, -DI-) into a palatal sound, a merger already exemplified above for Gallo-, Ibero- and Italo-Romance. This widespread merger and the asymmetry with respect to the outcomes of -C$^{e/i}$- (see directly) in many languages suggests a different chronology for the palatalization of voiced vs. voiceless velar stops (by the latter, only -C$^{e/i}$- is meant, since -CI-, as shown above, was affected earlier). Väänänen (1967:54–56) and Herman (1998:13–15) place palatalization of -C$^{e/i}$- in a platoon of changes that spread approximately at the time of the fall of the western Empire, as opposed to the palatalization of the voiced counterpart -G$^{e/i}$-, which starts much earlier (first to second century AD) in central-southern Italy and Africa, although it only later spreads northwards and westwards. A conceivable phonetic path for this merger is that both -G- before palatal vowels and -ɪ- turned to [ɟ] as the first step (although this did not happen in all Romance languages: some exceptions are mentioned below). This stage is preserved in some Alpine dialects: in Val Bregaglia (dialect of Soglio) [(ɐl) ˈɟeːla] < GELAT 'it freezes', [ɟaˈnuil̯] < GENUCULUM 'knee' = [ˈɟuf] < IUGUM 'yoke', [ˈɟyɲ] < IUNIUM 'June' (Stampa 1934:111). An intermediate step is witnessed by Corsican and most dialects of southern Italy (with the sole exceptions of southern Lucania and part of Apulia) which still have [ɟ] as an allophone of /j/ postconsonantally or under *raddoppiamento fonosintattico*: e.g., Cor. [juˈdɛu] 'Jew', [un ɟuˈdɛu] 'a Jew', Nap. [joˈka] 'to play', [a ɟːoˈka] (the same form preceded by the preposition [a]) (Rohlfs 1966:214f.; Fanciullo 1997b:41). [ɟ] then developed into [dʒ] and then [dz], both of which are subject to deaffrication, at first variably in intervocalic position. Thus, Italian has *genero* < GENERUM 'son-in-law', *giacere* < IACERE 'to lie (down)', which is deaffricated intervocalically in Florentine (*il mi'* [ʒ]*enero* 'my son-in-law'). In Catalan, on the other hand, *gendre* and *jaure* sound [ˈdʒɛndrə], [ˈdʒau̯rə] only utterance-initially and/or in emphatic speech, whereas in connected speech [ʒ] occurs instead (Badia i Margarit 1984:181; Recasens 1996:285). Catalan remains closest to proto-Ibero-Romance [dʒ], which was altered one way or other in all other languages: Pt. [ʒ] (*gear* 'freeze' < GELARE, *jogo* 'game' < IOCUM) is not subject to allophonic variation, and Spanish has a fuzzy situation, with the two competing outcomes [j] and [x] (from earlier [ʃ] < [ʒ]). According to Menéndez Pidal (1953:124f.), the former is the regular outcome before (stressed) /i e a/ (e.g., *yace* 'he lies', *hielo* 'ice' – where *y* and *hi* are both pronounced [j] – < IACET, GELU), the latter before /o u/ (e.g., *juego* 'game'). However, a series of exceptions occurs, such as *yugo* 'yoke' < IUGUM and *jamás* 'never' < IAM MA(GI)S (alongside *ya* 'already' < IAM), which Menéndez Pidal ascribes to dialect mixture.[58] The same explanation is invoked by Lausberg (1976:286), who, however, does not entertain a conditioning by the following vowel.[59]

The stage [dʒ] developed into a dental affricate [dz] in most of northern Italo-Romance, where only some peripheral dialects preserve it at present: e.g., [ˈdzøgu] 'game' in the dialect of Fosdinovo (Lunigiana) or [ˈdzavu] 'yoke' in the dialect of Sanfratello (a Gallo-Italian enclave in Sicily; see Rohlfs 1966:214).[60] Elsewhere, [dz] was deaffricated to [z] (Genoese [ˈzeːna] 'Genua'; Toso 1997:47) or [ð] (rural Veneto [ˈðugo] 'game'). Those fricative outcomes occur in the Occitan and Raeto-Romance domains as well (Lausberg 1976:282).

Although the convergence just described in the affrication of (-)ɪ̯- and affrication/palatalization of (-)ɢ^{e/i}- is very widespread, there is a Romance area, viz. central Sardinia, which was not affected by either, and two more areas (Raeto- and Daco-Romance) that only underwent the former process, not the latter, thus providing evidence for a distinct chronology of the two. Central dialects of Sardinian, spoken in and around Nuoro, preserve initial [j] < ɪ̯- (Nuorese [ˈjuːvu] < IUGUM 'yoke', [ˈjɔʃːo] < DEORS(UM) 'down') as well as non-palatalized [ɡ] (Nuorese [ˈɡeneru] < GENERUM 'son-in-law', [ɡeˈlaːre] < GELARE 'to freeze'; Wagner 1941:84, 87).[61] The distinction has been preserved even after (-)ɢ^{e/i}- underwent palatalization, in Raeto- and Daco-Romance. In Romanian, one distinguishes between [dʒ] < (-)ɢ^{e/i}- and [ʒ] < (-)ɪ̯-: e.g., *genunchiu* 'knee' < GENUCULUM vs. *joc* 'game' < IOCUM.[62] As for Raeto-Romance, one finds, e.g., [ˈjo] < DEORSUM 'down', [ˈjaʒa] < IACET vs. [ˈʒɛndɐr] < GENERUM 'son-in-law', [ʒeˈlar] < GELARE 'to freeze' in the lower Engadinian variety of Sent (cf. Pult 1897:77, 79), or [ˈɟo] < 'down', [ˈɟjɛː] < IAM 'yes' vs. [ˈʒi̯ɛndɐr] < GENERUM, [ʒumˈblins] < GEMELL(OS)+INOS 'twins' in the Surselvan of Tavetsch (Caduff 1952:86, 91). This contrast stretches from Raeto-Romance to the border of northern Italo-Romance, in the Valtellinese dialect of Livigno: [ˈɟakom] < IACO(B)UM vs. [ˈʒemar] 'groan' < GEMERE (Rohlfs 1966:213).

Note that the central Alpine facts pose a problem of chronology, since they seem to require that palatalization of (-)ɢ^{e/i}- preceded the consonantization of (-)ɪ̯- (as claimed by Lausberg 1976:285), whereas the late Latin epigraphic evidence, as well as comparative evidence from central Sardinian, seems to testify to the reverse order. Apparently, while the general trend is largely the same, no one single chronology can be attained for the whole of Romance in this structural domain.

The chronological correspondence between philological and reconstructive evidence is clearer when it comes to the last palatalization process that affected almost all Romance languages, again with the exception of (central) Sardinia: the palatalization of voiceless velar stops before front vowels. Attestations are considerably later here than for the changes affecting (-)ɪ̯- and clusters with (-)ɪ̯- and (-)ɢ^{e/i}-. The earliest Latin loanwords into Germanic (e.g., CAESAR, CISTAM; cf. German *Kaiser*, *Kiste*), dating from the first centuries AD, preserve the velar consonant. The same holds for Latin loanwords into Celtic: e.g., Welsh *certh* 'right' < CERTUS, *plegyd* 'plea' < PLACITUM (Jackson 1953:402, n1).[63] There is evidence for at least partial preservation of velar stops in Afro-Romance as well (Fanciullo 1992:173).

Only in the last two centuries of the western Empire does one find some rare and late inscriptional evidence (Väänänen 1967:56) of

(-)c$^{e/i}$- palatalization, such as *intcitamento* CIL XIV 2165 (Italy), *dissessit* (for *discessit* CIL VIII 21801, Africa), both from the fifth century. An earlier clue (late fourth century) is provided by Ausonius (born in Burdigala, Bordeaux around 310), who alliterates *salo*, *solo* and *caelo* in his epigram on Venus's birth (52 Peiper). At any rate, there must have been a considerable period of variable application of palatalization of (-)c$^{e/i}$-, at a time in which the output of changes affecting -c$_I$- (and -t$_I$-) had long been phonologized.[64] This can be argued from the orthographic rendering of Latin names in the Greek writings of the Byzantine historian Procopius (born in Caesarea between 490 and 507). He still writes <k> indifferently for Latin (-)c$^{e/i}$- (e.g., *Loukernária*), whereas <tz> is employed to render -c$_I$- (e.g., *Moutziáni*; cf. Migliorini 1929:287).

This is the situation still preserved to this day by Logudorese Sardinian, which took part in the affrication of -c$_I$- and -t$_I$- (e.g., [ˈfatːo] < FACIO = [ˈputːu] < PUTEUM, with [tː] from an earlier [tθ] reflected in the medieval spelling: *fatho* = *puthu*; cf. Wagner 1941:109) but not in the palatalization of (-)c$^{e/i}$- and (-)G$^{e/i}$-: e.g., [ˈpaːɣɛ] < PACEM 'peace'. The only other Romance variety which was not affected by a full palatalization of (-)c$^{e/i}$- was Dalmatian (cf. Bartoli 1906, II:377f., 386f.; Migliorini 1929:287; Tuttle 1986a:319). In Vegliote, velar stops palatalized late enough to undergo the process before the outcome of Lat. ū (e.g., [ˈʃtʃor] < OBSCŪRUM 'dark') as well. For this to happen, palatalization must have applied later than ū fronting to [y]: -CŪ- > [ky] > [tʃy] > [tʃo]. Also the lack of palatalization before stressed Ē points in the same direction: CĒNAM diphthongized to [ˈkaịna] 'supper' before palatalization. The same goes for unstressed front vowels, which were lowered to [a], thereby bleeding palatalization: [karˈvjale] 'brains', [kaˈnaiʃa] < CINISIAM 'ash'. Only before stressed ī and ĕ did palatalization apply: [ˈtʃiŋko] < CĪMICEM 'bedbug', [ˈtʃil] < CAELUM 'sky'.

All over the rest of Romance, velar stops before front vowels were affected by palatalization, which eventually resulted in merger with the output of the earlier palatalization of -c$_I$-: e.g., Spanish *hace* 'does' < FACIT, *cielo* 'sky' < CAELUM with [ts] in OSpanish such as *brazo* 'arm' < BRACHIUM, *haz* 'face, side' < FACIEM. Yod-induced palatalization affected not only obstruents but also sonorants: before -$_I$-, most Romance branches have developed palatal sonorants like those still occurring in the outcomes of, e.g., UINEAM 'vineyard', PALEAM 'straw' in Cat. [ˈbiɲə], [ˈpaʎə], It. [ˈviɲːa], [ˈpaʎːa] (as well as in Portuguese, Occitan and Raeto-Romance). As with obstruents, partial or total loss of such sounds may have occurred in a further stage: French preserves [ɲ] (*vigne*), not [ʎ] (> [j], *feuille* < FOLIA), Romanian has turned both into [j]: *foaie* 'leaf', *vie* 'vineyard' (with [ɲ] still preserved in more conservative

Daco-Romance dialects; Ciorănescu 2002:834). Conversely, the same palatal sounds [ɲ], [ʎ] arose from other diachronic sources than ḷ-clusters through several distinct processes in different Romance branches: e.g., -GN- > [ɲ] in western Romance (Sp. *puño* 'fist', Pt. *punho*, Cat. *puny*, Occ. *ponh*, with the same pronunciation [ˈpoɲ] to be assumed for the OFr. predecessor of Fr. *poing*; see Lausberg 1976:325) and central Italo-Romance but not in southern Italo-Romance, Daco-Romance and Sardinian: cf., e.g., LIGNUM/-A 'wood' > Ro. *lemn*, Srd. [ˈlinːu], Pugliese [ˈlioːnə]. Geminate -LL- and -NN- palatalized in Ibero-Romance, as part of the chain shifts discussed in section 2.2.

Another process involving velars (both voiced and voiceless), which is not so general as those discussed thus far yet involves quite a substantial territory in central-northern Romance, is palatalization before -A-, found in the bulk of northern Gallo-Romance (Fr. *chien* 'dog' < CANEM),[65] Raeto-Romance and, formerly, probably in all of northern Italo-Romance. This change is also fairly old, although perhaps not as old as sometimes assumed: Zink (1999[6]:108f.) places it in the fifth century, while Meyer-Lübke (1934[5]:132f.), pointing to the first documentation of the phenomenon in the seventh century, adds that it is perhaps younger than the palatalization of velars before front vowels.

Northern Italy nowadays displays only scattered remnants of CA, GA > [ca ɟa] in areas which generally present /ka/ and /ɡa/ as outcomes of Lat. CA, GA: this is seen, for instance, in Alto Vicentino placenames such as *Chiampo* < CAMPUS or *(Contrada del) Chian* < CANEM (Vigolo 1992:13), or even in isolated lexical relics such as [ˈcaṵra] 'goat' < CAPRAM in Valfurva, [ˈco] 'tail' < CAUDAM in Livigno (upper Valtellina; see Salvioni 1925:215). Wherever sounds such as [c ɟ] resulted from this process, this was bound to introduce a further place of articulation in the palatal region. Thus, provided that (at least some of) the outcomes of -Cḷ-, -(C)ḷ-, (-)C[e/i]-, (-)G[e/i]-, etc. had retained the original palato-alveolar realization, the final result is a system in which not one but two distinct places of articulation are added, with respect to Latin.

In Raeto-Romance, actually, as shown earlier in this section, two distinct series of palatals already existed prior to palatalization of Lat. CA, GA, as the outcomes of velars plus front vowels were kept distinct from those of -ḷ-clusters. In those varieties, CA > [ca] GA > [ɟa] joined the latter series: cf. Schmid (2007) for lower Engadine [c ɟ] in *chan* 'dog' < CANEM, *giat* 'cat' < *GATTUM, identical with the outcomes of -ḷ- in, e.g., *gün* 'June' [ˈɟyn], *meg* 'May' [ˈmec], contrasting with [tʃ dʒ] from (-)C[e/i]-, (-)G[e/i]-, as in, e.g., *tschêl* 'sky' < CAELUM, *dschender* 'son-in-law'.

The foregoing discussion of the palatalization of ḷ-clusters and velar stops does not, of course, exhaust the set of palatalization processes found across

Romance: many others occurred on a language-specific basis. Some are fairly old and count among the defining isoglosses for certain dialect areas: palatalization of clusters of labial obstruents + -L- characterizes Ibero-Romance (e.g., Pt. [ʃiˈgaɾ] 'arrive' < PLICARE, [ˈʃamɐ] 'flame' < FLAMMAM, via OPt. [tʃ]) and, within Italo-Romance, it is distinctive of Ligurian: e.g., Genoese [ˈtʃyma] < PLUMAM 'feather', [ˈdʒaŋku] < BLANCUM 'white.M', [ˈdudʒu] < DUPLUM 'double', [ˈʃoṷ] < FLATUM 'breath' (Forner 1988:453). Some others are more pervasive in specific Romance branches: in Daco-Romance, palatalization of labials in secondary C+*j* clusters ([ˈcept] < [ˈpjept] < PECTUS 'breast', [ˈɲerkurʲ] < [ˈmjerkurʲ] < *MERCURIS 'Wednesday') is general in Macedo-Romanian and is also found less generally in Megleno-Romanian and sporadically in Istro-Romanian. It also occurs in several Daco-Romanian dialect areas, only Banat and Oltenia being immune from it (Macrea 1965:1220f.). A more recent palatalization process occurred in Acadian French, where velar stops palatalize before palatal glides and vowels, including those arisen via fronting ([ø y]): e.g., [tʃi] *qui* 'who', [tʃø] *queue* 'tail', [dʒɛte] *guetter* 'to watch for', [dedʒøle] *dégueuler* 'vomit (of animals)'. While this palatalization is a categorical allophonic process, the same outputs [tʃ] [dʒ] arise variably from /tj/ /dj/ as well: [tʃɛd] *tiède* 'lukewarm', [dʒø] *Dieu* 'God' (Lucci 1972:34, 95–100). Dental obstruents are regularly palatalized in Brazilian Portuguese, too: [ˈtʃiɐ] *tia* 'aunt', [ˈdʒiɐ] *dia* 'day' (Mateus and d'Andrade 2000:17).

The inventory of such palatalization processes could be expanded virtually ad infinitum, drawing on the detailed documentation available for all Romance branches. Yet virtually none of these parochial processes has the territorial spread and chronological depth of those considered earlier on in this section, which can be claimed to lie at the very core of Romance phonological history.

2.2 Lenition and degemination

Another family of diachronic processes affected the majority of the Romance languages, viz. lenition (used here as a cover term for voicing and/or frication) and degemination:

(18)

	Spanish	French	Italian	Romanian			Latin	
a.	*fuego*	*feu*	*fuoco*	*foc*	lenition	<	FOCUM	'fire'
b.	*vaca*	*vache*	*vacca*	*vacă*	degemination	<	UACCAM	'cow'

Like palatalization, lenition was conditioned contextually by the adjacent vowels, although here no specific vowel qualities were involved, but only the intervocalic context, as one favouring the weakening of intervening consonants. The same can be said for degemination, which in fact co-occurred with lenition throughout western Romance, sharing the same context and the same functional motivation. At the eastern end of the Romance-speaking world, Daco-Romance escapes the correlation, displaying only degemination (e.g., *vacă* < UACCAM 'cow') but no intervocalic voicing/frication (e.g., *a pleca* 'to leave' < PLICARE, *roată* 'wheel' < ROTAM). A similar situation is found in an area stretching across the Pyrenees, spanning the Gascon varieties of Béarn (Vallées of Aspes and Barétous) and Aragonese (cf. Elcock 1938; Rohlfs 1970:130–37): Béarnais [pleˈka] 'to fold' < PLICARE, [kriˈta] 'to scream' < QUIRITARE, Aragonese [saˈper] 'to know'. Given the adjacency to the Basque-speaking territory, and given the fact that this has shrunk considerably over the centuries, this preservation has been attributed to a Basque substratum (cf. the preservation of voiceless stops in Latin loans into Basque: e.g., *bake* < PACEM, *errota* 'mill' < ROTAM). Surely, it is an instance of preservation, in spite of Ronjat's claim (1930–41, II:77) to the contrary.

Central and southern Italo-Romance, south of the Apennines, is the only Romance area that remained unaffected either by lenition or degemination: this determined the synchronic situation described in chapter 2, section 1, since preservation of gemination prevented the phonologization of vowel quantity which is observed in northern Romance.

The chronology and mutual structural relationship of lenition and degemination have been intensively discussed. That the two represent a chain shift is evident for western Romance; cf. the French examples in (19):

(19) /pp/   /p/   /b/   /v/
      CUPPAM >   *coupe*   'cup'
      CŪPAM   > *cuve*   'vat'
                  HABĒRE   > *avoir*   'to have'
                  MOUĒRE   > *mouvoir* 'to move'

This was analysed as a push chain by Martinet (1955), with degemination forcing lenition.[66] Philological evidence points to the opposite chronology. In western Romance, degemination probably spread from Gaul, and first affected obstruents, for which there is evidence of the process in the eighth century (Richter 1934:250; Politzer 1951:41), whereas sonorants were affected considerably later.[67] In Spain, degemination had surely not applied by the time of the Arab conquest (AD 711), as testified by the different treatment of singleton vs. geminate consonants, both sonorant and obstruents, in Arabic loans (Pensado Ruiz 1993:197): final geminate -*bb*, for instance, regularly preserved its labial articulation, eventually yielding -*be* (e.g., Arabic *al-ǧubb* > *algibe* 'dungeon', Arabic. *šabb* > *(a)jebe* 'alum'), whereas final singleton -*b* was sometimes preserved (*árabe*), sometimes changed to some other consonant (*alacrán* 'scorpion', *almotacén* 'weights and measures officer'). A similar contrast is observed for sonorants: final geminate -*rr* receives an epithetic vowel (Arabic *ḥurr* > *hurro*), singleton -*r* does not (e.g., *alcázar* 'fortress', *aljófar* 'pearl'). Further Ibero-Romance evidence sifted by Pensado Ruiz (1993:201), apart from loans, shows that geminate sonorants survived in Spanish, however marginally, in the Middle Ages and beyond. According to Pensado Ruiz, this persistence was a phonetic fact, not the effect of a phonologically motivated resistance to giving up the contrasts, that were eventually rescued (for /l n r/) under the form of a qualitative difference, as argued by Martinet (1955).[68] Be that as it may, persistence of geminate sonorants into the twentieth century was reported for northern dialects of Spanish: cf., e.g., Belsetán [ˈpɛnːa] 'rock' (Sp. *peña*), [ˈbɛlːa] 'beautiful.F', recorded by Badia i Margarit (1950:87f.), who observed, however, that gemination was the most unstable of all the phonetic traits of Belsetán.[69]

In northern Italo-Romance, degemination spread gradually southwards, with some delay in comparison with Gallo-Romance.[70] The earliest extant texts show that degemination of obstruents was already accomplished whereas geminate sonorants were still preserved: e.g., *sepellir* 'to bury', *pelle* 'leather', *gonnelle* 'skirts' in the late twelfth-century Savonese declaration of Paxia (Castellani 1976:177). Evidence from Gallo-Italian enclaves in Sicily and Lucania shows that geminate -LL- was preserved well into the twelfth century: indeed, in those dialects this sound underwent retroflection (cf. §2), which affected only geminate laterals in neighbouring southern Italian dialects (e.g., [gaˈɖːiːna] < GALLINAM 'hen' in Trecchina, Lucania; Rohlfs 1966:323). We would not expect this development if degemination had already applied prior to the redeployment of the colonists to southern Italy in the first half of the twelfth century. A wealth of other traces of the longer preservation of geminate sonorants is to be found in northern Italo-Romance: in Venetian (Zamboni 1974:26), final mid vowels were in part deleted (e.g., [ˈpjeŋ] 'full.M', [ˈmal] 'evil'), but they were always preserved after original geminates ([ˈmie] 'thousand', [ˈpano] 'cloth'), which implies that by the time apocope applied (during the thirteenth century according to Pellegrini 1975:70; Zamboni 1976:326f.), geminate sonorants were still there.

A similar persistence of length contrasts, eventually yielding to differences in quality, and not merger, is reported for /r n l/ in Daco-Romance: sixteenth-century Romanian texts still distinguished /r/ vs. /r̄/ (the latter written <rr> or with Glagolitic <r>), and evidence for a contrast /n/ vs. /nn/ is provided by the lack of rhotacism in the latter (e.g., ORo. *anu* < ANNUM 'year' vs. *lîră* < LANAM 'wool' (Sala 1976:76–81)).

Several Romance varieties attest to intermediate stages on the path towards degemination. While the endpoint of the process is a system in which gemination is neither phonemically represented nor phonetically realized, some varieties show (de)gemination either only at the surface or only underlyingly. Several dialects of Franco-Provençal, of Alpine Lombard and of the Emilian Apennine area, show degemination before stress but retention (or even generalization) of geminates after distinctively short stressed vowels: e.g., in the Franco-Provençal patois of Hauteville ['gotːa] 'drop', ['papːa] 'pope', ['blətːa] 'wet.ꜰ', ['kabːra] 'goat' (Martinet 1956:56–59). Under such conditions, consonant length is an allophonic concomitant of distinctive vowel shortness (cf. Martinet 1956:75; 1975:205 on the distinctiveness of vowel quantity in Franco-Provençal).[71] Even learnèd words displaying stress shift are subject to gemination: e.g., Aostan [sə̄'təkːo] 'mayor' < It. *sindaco* (Molinu and Roullet 2001:124). Clearly, preservation of geminates just at the phonetic surface is an intermediate stage towards complete demise. Another possible (and symmetrical) intermediate step is documented by those dialects for which an (arguably underlying) geminate is degeminated by phonological rule. Cravens (2002:103) discusses the central Corsican dialect of Veru, where underlying /ll/ surfaces as [d] word-internally (e.g., ['badi] < /'balli/ 'valley' < UALLEM), whereas [lː] occurs at word boundary, for instance under *raddoppiamento fonosintattico* (['tre 'lːumi] 'three lamps').

As for the explanation of degemination, in studies in diachronic Romance phonology it has been customary to view it as one manifestation of a purported drift towards a CVCV structure. However, as shown in chapter 2, sections 5.3 and 6, proto-Romance was probably characterized by a 'tendency towards a closed syllable'. Nor can a conspiracy aiming at the generalization of CVCV structure be invoked for the later stages in which western Romance degemination applied; by that time, several changes (syncope, apocope) had multiplied closed syllables: Catalán (1989:78–80) observes for OSpanish, between the late eleventh and the thirteenth centuries, a 'proliferation of closed syllables'.

More to the point than the appeal to an open syllable drift is the framing of western Romance degemination in terms of a (drag) chain shift with lenition, as shown in (19) above. The absolute chronology of lenition is considerably earlier than that of degemination. Voicing of intervocalic stops is attested, albeit sporadically, in epigraphic documents from the whole territory of the western Empire since the first century[72] (see Weinrich 1960; Campanile 1971:59f.; Varvaro 1984). It grows more frequent in Gaul from the sixth century (Herman 1998:13), whereas Visigothic Spain (cf. Herman 1995:68f.) and Langobardic Italy (see Politzer and Politzer 1953:13) show a considerable delay.[73]

While at this time it is fairly clear that written attestations from France testify to a phonological change already accomplished in the spoken language, the earlier instances of voicing from the time of the western Empire pose a problem, since they crop up virtually everywhere in the Empire, including regions in which the further Romance development does not show lenition: compare, e.g., EXTRICADO, for -ATO (*CIL* III 3620), from Pannonia Inferior (AD 217), contrasting with the lack of lenition in Romanian *mâncată* 'eaten.FSG'. It has been argued (Cravens 1991; 2002) that the (epigraphic) Latin data can be reconciled with the Romance outcomes, under the assumption that an allophonic voicing process was at work in imperial Latin, and that this process was phonologized in the west, leading to restructuring, but was suppressed (with rule loss) in the east.

3 In lieu of a conclusion

With the foregoing discussion, I have reviewed, and – at times – cast new light on, some of the classic problems of Romance historical phonology, and the most significant phonological processes shaping the nascent Romance languages. The list of more localized and recent changes which one might also examine is daunting and endless: I hope at least to have shown (in this chapter and the preceding one) something of the richness and complexity of the historical phonological material which the Romance languages have to offer.

4   MORPHOLOGICAL PERSISTENCE

Martin Maiden

1   Introduction

This chapter aims to describe those aspects of Latin inflectional morphology which remain substantially intact from Latin into Romance, focusing especially on cases where the relation between grammatical or lexical meaning, on the one hand, and morphological form, on the other, is arbitrary and idiosyncratic. Much of Latin inflectional morphology is of the 'fusional' type, characterized by allomorphy (more than one form corresponds to one meaning), cumulativeness (one form simultaneously expresses more than one morphosyntactic property) and, sometimes, 'emptiness' (there are formatives to which no grammatical meaning can be independently ascribed). Studies of Romance historical morphology usually highlight what has *changed*, assuming tacitly or explicitly that the change is motivated, at least in part, by preference for formally simpler, more 'transparent', form–meaning relationships. It should be obvious, however, that the ancient Romans were no better endowed to cope with morphological complexity than any subsequent generation of native[1] speakers, and a priori there is no reason why morphology should get simpler. Overall, it does not. Some of the most eye-catching changes in inflectional morphology, such as the complete loss of the future imperfective inflections from Latin (see below), or the disappearance of the passive inflectional endings in favour of auxiliary + past participle constructions, probably have more to do with the existence of alternative structures, than with a move towards 'simplicity' (see Herman 2000a:71–74; also 59, 68f.). Indeed, the Latin imperfective passive inflections were (with the exception of second person endings -RIS and -MINI) characterized by an extremely transparent ending -(U)R,[2] yet such structural transparency did not impede their complete disappearance. The near-total elimination of an inflectional case system whose endings are characterized by extensive cumulativeness, syncretism and allomorphy (e.g., -O in DOMINO

155

'master' simultaneously signals dative and singular, is identical to the ablative singular case ending, and is restricted to second declension nouns, the same functions being performed by -I, -UI, etc., in other declensional classes), and its replacement in many Romance varieties by structures in which case is indicated configurationally or by means of prepositions, might suggest that the case system was lost, in part, because of sheer morphological complexity,[3] but one need only point to the verb to find a system of even more complex inflectional morphology preserved, substantially, intact.

My aim here is not to describe what might be seen as little more than uninteresting diachronic inertia but rather to identify areas where inertia might almost be described, paradoxically, as 'dynamic'. I have in mind structures in which the form–meaning relationship was and remains opaque, yet 'holds out', through time, despite clear potential for resorting to a more transparent structure. In certain cases we shall see that morphological structures which had well-defined functions in Latin lose their functional motivation yet persist. The phenomena I examine here – and especially my treatment of the remnants of the Latin perfective roots – are like many of the data presented in chapter 5 in indicating the importance of autonomously morphological structure as a driving force in morphological change. What emerges, especially in the verb, is not only the conservation of arbitrary and idiosyncratic features of inflectional morphology, but even their amplification and hypercharacterization.

2 Allomorphy and cumulativeness in person and number inflection

Overall, the typically cumulative inflectional endings of the Latin verb (in which person and number are indissolubly 'fused') are well preserved in Romance, disturbed only by phonological change or by analogies which overall do nothing to reduce their cumulativeness. Consider the present indicative, imperfective, of CANTARE 'sing' (1):

(1) 1SG   CANT-O
     2SG   CANTA-S
     3SG   CANTA-T
     1PL   CANTA-MUS
     2PL   CANTA-TIS
     3PL   CANTA-NT

Comparison of this paradigm with a few of its Romance outcomes shows that relatively little has changed, beyond the purely phonological: Pt. *canto cantas canta cantamos cantais cantam*; Sp. *canto cantas canta cantamos cantáis cantan*; Cat. *canto cantes canta cantem canteu canten*; Fr. *chante chantes chante chantons chantez chantent*; It. *canto canti canta cantiamo cantate cantano*; Ro. *cânt cânţi cântă cântăm cântaţi cântă*. It is nonetheless conceivable that speakers might tend towards a more 'transparent' structure, in which person and number were separately marked. On the basis of It. *canta* vs. *cantano*, it might have been deduced that '-*a* = third person and -*no* = plural', a reanalysis followed by reorganization of the paradigm along the following, 'transparent', lines with unique markers of person and number (2):

(2) 1SG   *canto*
     2SG   *canti*
     3SG   *canta*
     1PL   **cantono   (= 1SG + PL *no*)
     2PL   **cantino   (= 2SG + PL *no*)
     3PL   *cantano*   (= 3SG + PL *no*)

This example is invented, and 'agglutinative' reanalyses along such lines are rare.[4] In any case it is hard to see how such reanalyses could have been made, given that it is usually impossible to analyse the cumulative inflections into components each associated with a morphosyntactic property. The occasional emergence of inflections uniquely associated with one property seems to be accidental. Thus the Latin plural ending -s was cumulative in that it indicated not only number but also case (accusative in the first and second conjugations, nominative and accusative in the remainder), but the fact that in many Romance varieties -s becomes a unique marker of plural (e.g., Sp. *la rosa – las rosas*) is in large measure a fortuitous consequence of the loss of case-forms other than one whose original function was to mark the accusative.

Some of the inflectional person and number desinences of Latin were characterized not only by cumulativeness, but also by suppletion according to tense, mood and aspect. This was especially true of the first person singular and, to a lesser extent, of the second person (the corresponding personal pronouns are also suppletive). Such suppletion survives substantially intact into Romance. Consider first the following Latin first person singular forms of FACERE 'make' (3):

(3)   PRS.IND   PRS.SBJV   IPF.IND   PFV.IND   PLPF.IND   PLPF.SBJV

      FACI<u>O</u>   FACIAM   FACIEBAM   FECI   FECERAM   FECISSEM

Their Romance continuants, *modulo* certain sound changes (notably deletion of final -M and -T, which often leads to novel syncretism with the third person singular, as in Spanish first and third persons singular imperfect indicative *hacía*), preserve this situation pretty well intact (4):

(4) Spanish   *hago*   *haga*   *hacía*   *hice*   *hiciera*   *hiciese*
     French   *fais*   *fasse*   *faisais* *fis*   [...]   *fisse*[5]
     Italian   *faccio* *faccia* *facevo*   *feci*   dial. *fecera* *facessi*
     Romanian   *fac*   [...]   *făceam*   *făcui*   [...]   *făcusem*
                                               older *feci(u)*   *fecesem*

Modern standard Italian shows generalization of present indicative *-o* (e.g., *canto*) into the imperfect indicative (e.g., *cantavo* for older *cantava*), and apparently of the first person singular preterite ending *-i* (e.g., *feci*) into the imperfect subjunctive (e.g., *facessi* for original *facesse*). Romanian *-m* is apparently an extension from the first person plural (it cannot, on historical phonological grounds, continue the Lat. final -M); preterite forms such as *feciu* suggest generalization of the ORomanian first person singular present indicative ending *-u* (e.g., *facu*). But these rare local analogical adjustments merely serve to emphasize that virtually nowhere has the original suppletion actually been *eliminated*: it has at best been 'rearranged'. Gascon and certain other Occitan varieties stand out as an exception by having generalized *-i* as a first person singular ending in all tenses and moods.[6] The *-s* characteristic of the Latin second person singular continues across Romance (the *-i* ending found in Romanian and Italo-Romance is probably a phonetic reflex of an original thematic vowel + -s; see Maiden 1996a). However, the second person singular ending in the Latin perfect was -STI, which survives extensively as a distinct second person singular preterite ending in Ibero- and Italo-Romance: e.g., CANTAUISTI > Sp. *cantaste*, It. *cantasti*. The third person singular was stably marked by -T in all moods, aspects and tenses. In most Romance varieties (not Sardinian or parts of southern Lucania and northern Calabria), this inflection was deleted (although preserved in Gallo-Romance in certain postconsonantal environments).

Latin plurals displayed a relatively stable relationship between endings and person/number. All first person plural verbs end in -MUS, a state of affairs widely maintained, allowing for phonlogical adjustments (e.g., CANTAMUS > Sp. *cantamos*, Fr. *chantons*, It. *cantiamo*, Ro. *cântăm*). The second person plural is generally a regular continuant of Lat. -TIS (e.g., CANTATIS > Sp. *cantáis*, Fr. *chantez*, Lad. can'teis, Ro. *cântaţi*); in some varieties the Lat. second person plural imperative -TE is also preserved distinct (e.g., CANTATE > Sp. *cantad*, Lad. can'tede), while in Italian *-te* characterizes all second person plural endings (see Maiden 2007b). The third person plural was marked by -NT, again generally continued as -n or -nt into Romance (in Romanian and

some Italo-Romance varieties this ending was deleted): e.g., CANTANT > Sp. *cantan,* Fr. *chantent,* It. *cantano,* Ro. *cântă.*
The partly suppletive morphology of the Latin first and second person pronouns is also generally perpetuated in Romance (e.g., the first person singular pronoun NOM. EGO, ACC. ME > Sp. *yo, me*; Fr. *je, me,* It. *io, mi,* Ro. *eu, mă*; see Salvi, this volume, chapter 7).[7] The possessive adjectives also show suppletion for number: MEUM 'my', TUUM 'your. SG', NOSTRUM 'our', UESTRUM/UOSTRUM 'your.PL'> Sp. *mío, tuyo, nuestro, vuestro*; Fr. *mon, ton, notre, votre*;[8] It. *mio, tuo, nostro, vostro*; Ro. *meu, tău, nostru, vostru.* Romance third person pronouns generally derive from the Latin demonstratives ILLE (or IPSE), whose paradigms show relatively little root-allomorphy: e.g., Sp. MSG *él* MPL *ellos* FSG *ella* FPL *ellas*; Fr. MSG *il* MPL *ils* FSG *elle* FPL *elles*; Ro. MSG *el* MPL *ei* FSG *ea* FPL *ele.* The Latin third person object reflexive pronoun, SE, is continued throughout Romance (as *se,* It. *si,* Cat. *es*); the related possessive SUUS evolves as a third person possessive adjective (no longer necessarily coreferential with the subject): Pt./Cat. *seu,* Sp. *su(yo),* Fr. *son,* It. *suo,* Ro. *său.* In some varieties, the *s-* form is restricted to a singular possessor, plural possessors having acquired a suppletive form derived from Lat. GEN.PL ILLORUM (or IPSORUM): Cat. *llur,* Fr. *leur,* It. *loro,* Ro. *lor* (Srd. *issoro*). Romanian also has alternative singular possessives, *lui* (for masculine possessors) and *ei* (for feminine possessors). These are derived from (late) Latin M *ILLUI(US) and F *ILLEI(US) (Väänänen 1963:§276).

3   Declensional classes

Virtually every Latin noun and adjective belonged to one of five declensions, distinguished by the presence, in parts of the paradigm, of a semantically empty 'thematic vowel' immediately following the lexical root. As the examples below show, the identity of inflectional endings depended, in part, on declensional class. Three of these (conventionally labelled 'first', 'second' and 'third' declensions) comprised nouns and adjectives, the remainder only nouns. The first declension was populated almost exclusively by feminine nouns and adjectives, the second overwhelmingly by masculines and neuters (inflectionally distinct in the nominative and accusative only); the third and fourth contained both masculines and feminines, without inflectional distinction, and neuters, which were distinct only[9] in their nominative and accusative forms. The fifth contained mainly feminine nouns and no neuters. The inflectional paradigm of many adjectives (and of some nouns denoting living beings) conflated first and second declension forms. So a feminine adjective in first declension -A implied a masculine counterpart in second declension -US (and a neuter in second declension -UM), and vice versa (5).

(5)   First declension[10]

	SG	PL
NOM	ALTA (F) 'high'	ALTÆ
ACC	ALTAM	ALTĀS
GEN	ALTÆ	ALTĀRUM
DAT	ALTÆ	ALTĪS
ABL	ALTĀ	ALTĪS

Second declension

	SG	PL	SG	PL
NOM	ALTUS (M) 'high'	ALTĪ	ALTUM (NEUT)	ALTA
ACC	ALTUM	ALTŌS	ALTUM	ALTA
GEN	ALTĪ	ALTŌRUM	ALTĪ	ALTŌRUM
DAT	ALTŌ	ALTĪS	ALTŌ	ALTĪS
ABL	ALTŌ	ALTĪS	ALTŌ	ALTĪS
VOC	ALTE			

Third declension

	SG	PL	SG	PL
NOM	UIRIDIS (M/F) 'green'	UIRIDĒS	UIRIDE (NEUT)	UIRIDIA
ACC	UIRIDEM	UIRIDĒS	UIRIDE	UIRIDIA
GEN	UIRIDIS	UIRIDIUM	UIRIDIS	UIRIDIUM
DAT	UIRIDĪ	UIRIDIBUS	UIRIDĪ	UIRIDIBUS
ABL	UIRIDE	UIRIDIBUS	UIRIDE	UIRIDIBUS

NOM	PARS (F) 'part'	PARTĒS	MARE (NEUT) 'sea'	MARIA
ACC	PARTEM	PARTĒS	MARE	MARIA
GEN	PARTIS	PARTIUM	MARIS	MARIUM
DAT	PARTĪ	PARTIBUS	MARĪ	MARIBUS
ABL	PARTE	PARTIBUS	MARĪ	MARIBUS

NOM	TEMPUS (NEUT) 'time'	TEMPORA
ACC	TEMPUS	TEMPORA
GEN	TEMPORIS	TEMPORUM
DAT	TEMPORĪ	TEMPORIBUS
ABL	TEMPORE	TEMPORIBUS

Fourth declension

	SG	PL	SG	PL
NOM	ACUS (F) 'needle'	ACŪS	CORNU (NEUT) 'horn'	CORNUA
ACC	ACUM	ACŪS	CORNUM	CORNUA
GEN	ACŪS	ACUUM	CORNŪS	CORNUUM
DAT	ACUĪ	ACUBUS	CORNŪ	CORNUBUS
ABL	ACŪ	ACUBUS	CORNŪ	CORNUBUS

Fifth declension

	SG	PL
NOM	DIĒS (F) 'day'	DIĒS
ACC	DIEM	DIĒS
GEN	DIĒĪ	DIĒRUM
DAT	DIĒĪ	DIĒBUS
ABL	DIĒ	DIĒBUS

Lexical roots were generally phonologically invariant, except in some nouns and adjectives of the third declension (such as LATRO 'brigand' and PARS 'part'), where the nominative singular root (together with the accusative singular root, in neuters) was phonologically differentiated in a variety of ways from all other case-forms. It will be seen from the above that the inflectional system was multiply *opaque*: each case being expressed by an array of inflectional desinences varying according to number and gender; and most inflectional endings syncretistically expressing more than one case. Thus the genitive is expressed variously by -Æ, -ĀRUM, -Ī, -ŌRUM, -IS, -IUM, -UM, -US, -UUM, -ĒI, -ĒRUM; and several of these forms have multiple functions: for example, -Æ expresses genitive and dative singular, and nominative plural, while -Ī expresses genitive singular, dative singular, and nominative plural, etc.

The radical reductions of the Latin inflectional case system, the loss (discussed below) of the fourth and fifth declensions, and various phonological changes, carried with them a major reduction in the distinctiveness of declensional classes. Bearing in mind that most Romance nouns and adjectives continue a form historically identifiable with the accusative case form, the following would probably have been the historically expected results at some point in the very early history of Romance (6):

(6) SG   PL
     ˈalta   ˈaltas
     ˈalto [ˈaltu] ˈaltos
     ˈverde   ˈverdes
     ˈparte   ˈpartes

Traces of declensional class survive in the word-final vowel. Most Romance varieties conserve to this day a system in which nouns and adjectives have one of three distinct final vowels, e.g., (7):

(7) Spanish: *alta – altas, alto – altos, verde – verdes, parte – partes*
     Romanian: *înaltă – înalte, înalt*[11] *– înalţi, verde – verzi, parte – părţi*

In those varieties where final unstressed vowels other than [a] are generally deleted (e.g., Catalan, Gallo-Romance, Raeto-Romance, most of northern Italy: see further Loporcaro, this volume, chapter 2: §3) we obtain two classes: nouns and adjectives (of both genders) ending in zero, and those (overwhelmingly feminine) ending in -[a] (or a reflex thereof) (8):

(8) Catalan: *alta – altes, alt – alts, vert – verts, part – parts*
     French: *haute – hautes, haut – hauts, vert – verts, part – parts*

A shadow of the old declension class system survives,[12] in that adjectives (and some nouns denoting living beings) which originally belonged to the third declension do not inflectionally distinguish gender: e.g., Sp. *techo verde* 'green roof', *casa verde* 'green house'; It. *tetto verde, casa verde*; Ro. *acoperiş verde, casă verde*. In contrast, feminine adjectives in first declension -a have a masculine counterpart in -o, and vice versa (Sp. *techo blanco* 'white roof', *casa blanca* 'white house'; It. *tetto bianco, casa bianca*; Ro. *acoperiş alb, casă albă*). This vestigial declensional difference has been erased in many varieties where word-final -e and -o have been deleted (French, Occitan, Catalan, Raeto-Romance) by widespread extension of the feminine inflection to original third declension *adjectives*: Cat. *la casa verda*; Fr. *le toit vert* but *la maison verte*. Some traces of earlier gender-invariant third declension adjectives survive in modern French expressions containing feminine nouns, such as *grand-mère* 'grandmother', *avoir grand faim* 'to be very hungry' (but *la grande maison* 'the big house').

In general, the distinctive morphology of the fourth and fifth declensions was not continued in Romance. Fifth declension nouns, overwhelmingly feminine, were generally incorporated into the first declension (e.g., FACIE(M) 'face' > *ˈfakja > Fr. *face*, It. *faccia*, Ro. *faţă*), although some entered the third (e.g., FIDE (M) 'faith' > Sp., Cat. *fe*, Fr. *foi*, It. *fede*). Southern Italian dialects retained at least until the fifteenth century reflexes of the fifth declension derivational ending used in forming abstract nouns, -ITIE(S) (e.g., ONap. *recheze* 'wealth').[13] The close formal similarity (notably in nominative and accusative singulars, where both declensions had inflections -US and -UM) between the fourth and second declensions favoured reassignment of most fourth declension words to the second. Since the second declension was predominantly non-feminine, original fourth declension feminines were often assigned masculine gender (e.g., F.ACC ACU(M) 'needle' > It. M *ago*, Ro. M *ac*), feminine fourth declension nouns denoting persons were allocated to the (overwhelmingly feminine) first declension (e.g., SOCRU(M) 'mother-in-law' > Sp. *suegra*, It. *suocera*, Ro. *soacră*).[14] But remnants of the fourth declension do survive. In medieval Tuscan, and some modern central and southern Italian dialects, the feminine singular accusative MANU(M); FICU(M), plural MANUS; FICUS, appear as invariant *mano mano* 'hand'; *fico fico* 'fig'; modern Venetian plural *man* presupposes earlier *ˈmano. For the plurals we might reconstruct the phonetic development MANUS > *ˈmanui > *ˈmanu > *ˈmano (see Maiden 1996a for a more detailed account). Rohlfs (1968:17f.) shows that in southern Italian dialects a few non-fourth declension nouns were attracted into this pattern.

3.1 *Number and declensional class*

The expression of number in nouns (and agreeing adjectives) shows considerable continuity. The Romance languages maintain the Latin distinction between singular and plural, and continue to mark it inflectionally. In Latin, all noun and adjective plural inflections were predictable on the basis of the morphological structure of the singular (if gender was also known). This is largely true in Romance. Also, the plural inflections directly continue Latin (usually accusative) plural inflections. But although plural inflections are well preserved, we shall see that plural morphology is no longer always systematically predictable on the basis of the singular, especially in eastern Romance.

The main type of plural inflection historically underlying all Romance languages, independently of inflectional class, was -s, continuing the characteristic ending of the Latin accusative plural (CASA(M) 'house' – CASAS, ALTU(M) 'high' – ALTOS, NOCTE(M) 'night' – NOCTES, CANE(M) 'dog' – CANES, DIE(M) 'day' – DIES, MANU(M) 'hand' – MANUS). Simplifying somewhat,[15] Ibero-Romance, Gallo-Romance, Sardinian (and to a lesser extent Raeto-Romance) add -s to the singular stem (e.g., Sp. *casa – casas*; *alto – altos*; *noche – noches*; *can – canes*; *mano – manos*; *día – días*). It is true that in French phonetic deletion of word-final -s has led to invariance between singular and plural (e.g., ROSAM 'rose' – ROSAS > OFr. *rose – roses* > ModFr. *rose* [ʁoz] – *roses* [ʁoz]), but this does not make French plural formation any less 'predictable'. Italo-Romance, Dalmatian and Romanian also belong historically to the -s camp. Their plural inflections -i, and feminine -e, are widely taken[16] to continue, respectively, the masculine second declension nominative plurals (e.g., ALTUS – ALTI), and feminine first declension nominative plurals (CASA – CASÆ), but this is probably a mistake. Note that -i also continues third declension -ES, regardless of gender (9):

(9)   Italian *casa – case*; *alto – alti*; *notte – notti*; *cane – cani*; *mano – mani...*
      Romanian *casă – case*; *înalt – înalţi*; *noapte – nopţi*; *câine – câini*;
      mână – mâini...

Maiden (1996a) offers an array of historical and comparative evidence to suggest that -e does not in fact display the expected phonological properties of a reflex of -Æ; in particular, it shows complete absence in Italo-Romance of the expected palatalization of a preceding velar consonant (e.g., It. *le amiche* 'the (female) friends'), and absence of otherwise regular deletion of unstressed final -e in northern varieties. Rather, its development indicates a phonetic development of -AS (there are partially parallel developments for the second person singular present and imperfect indicative ending -AS), probably via a stage *-aï. There are similar arguments for -i having developed phonetically from -es, probably via *-eï. Nonetheless, it is certain that traces of the second declension masculine nominative plural -i do survive in some areas. In Gallo-Romance, which conserved a vestigial case system[17] distinguishing nominative vs. oblique forms, we have the OFrench type NOM.PL *mur* 'wall' OBL.PL *murs*, where the zero inflection in the nominative plural reflects historically regular deletion of unstressed final -i. This pattern was frequently extended to original third declension masculines (e.g., NOM.PL *chien* 'dog' OBL. PL *chiens*). Such a formal case system also persisted in Raeto-Romance, and Haiman and Benincà (1992:142f.) give an account of its partial persistence in Surselvan and older stages of Vallader. Loss of the case distinction in favour of the oblique form ensures the triumph of -s in Gallo-Romance, but in varieties of Ladin and Friulian the disappearance (in pre-literary times) of the case system is not accompanied by loss of case *forms*. Rather (and especially in original second declension words), masculine plurals reflecting original NOM.PL -i coexist with others continuing -s. The original presence of inflectional front vowel -i is usually reflected in *palatalization* of certain preceding root-final consonants, so that there are two modes of plural formation, whose distribution is often synchronically unpredictable. A good picture of the complexities of masculine plural formation can be gleaned from Elwert (1943:129–49) for Val Fassa and Belardi (1983) for Val Gardena (Belardi documents 'double' plural marking such that plural -s is itself palatalized). As a rule of thumb, it seems that if a root ends in a consonant originally susceptible to palatalization before [i], then it is likely to have a palatalized plural. But this rule is not absolute, as we see from Benincà and Vanelli's study (1978) of the Friulian of Clauzetto (10):

(10)	SG	PL	SG	PL
	foụk 'fire'	foụks	an 'year'	aɲ
	plomp 'lead'	plomps	nas 'nose'	naʃ
	prat 'meadow'	prats	kest 'this'	kesc
	armar 'cupboard'	armars	kaval 'horse'	kavại
	etc.		etc.	

Maiden (2000a) has argued that an '-i vs. -s' plural inflectional system may have survived widely also in Italo-Romance, in pre-literary times, and that the two plural forms coexisted after the collapse of the case system. While -i has triumphed as the masculine plural marker throughout

Italo-Romance, Maiden suggests that the frequent (but not absolute) failure of expected palatalization of root-final velars before -i (e.g., It. *lungo – lunghi, secco – secchi*) reflects the influence of original copresence of plurals originally ending in non-palatalizing *-os.[18]

The indeterminacies of Ladin and Friulian plural formation are the harbinger, if one moves eastwards across the Romance world, of increasing disturbance in the continuity of plural formation between Romance and Latin, particularly in *nouns*. Italian has a scatter of irregular noun plurals such as *ala* 'wing' – *ali, bue* 'ox' – *buoi, dio* 'god' – *dei*, for which there is probably semantic motivation (see Maiden 1995a:105f.), in that the plurals typically denote sets, or pairs, or cohesive entities whose constituent parts are not individually salient or easily differentiated.[19] A similar analysis also applies to most of the score or so of Italian masculine nouns whose plural is feminine and ends in -*a* (originating in the Latin neuter plural inflection, further discussed below), such as *osso* 'bone' – *ossa, uovo* 'egg' – *uova, braccio* 'arm' – *braccia*.[20]

The unpredictability of plural inflections derived from neuters, in southern Italy and especially in Romanian, will be treated under gender. The inflectional indeterminacy of plural formation is at its most acute in Romanian (see Graur 1968:80–158), where one suspects that many inflectional plurals must be fully specified in the lexicon alongside their singulars. Feminines in singular -*e*, together with all masculine animates, virtually always form their plurals in -*i* (e.g., M *băiat – băieți* 'boy', *lup – lupi* 'wolf'; F *mare – mări* 'sea', *carte – cărți* 'book'), but otherwise things are often chaotic. Many feminine nouns ending in -*ă* form their plural in -*e* (e.g., *casă – case* 'house', *englezoaică – englezoaice* 'Englishwoman', *apă – ape* 'water', *vână – vine* 'vein', *masă – mese* 'table'), but there is also -*i* (e.g., *vacă – vaci* [vatʃ] 'cow', *găină – găini* [gəˈinʲ] 'hen', *oglindă – oglinzi* 'mirror', *lună – luni* [lunʲ] 'month', *țară – țări* 'country', *groapă – gropi* 'pothole', *coadă – cozi* 'tail'); others vary (e.g., *roată – roți*, less commonly *roate*, 'wheel', *țigancă – țigănci* or *țigance* 'gypsy woman'). On the distribution of these rival inflections, see Graur (1968:106–27), who discerns a tendency to prefer -*e* in neologisms. The suspicion that the inflectional plurals of Romanian nouns usually must be specified in the lexicon together with their singulars (see also Graur 1968:66), is reinforced by the evidence of analogical changes affecting root-allomorphy and/or the singular inflectional ending. Byck and Graur (1967) list hundreds of examples of analogical remodelling of singular inflections and/or singular root-allomorphs *on the basis of the plural*, of a kind unparalleled elsewhere in the Romance-speaking world. Many Italo-Romance varieties have the *potential* for this kind of development, but creation of the 'wrong' singular on the basis of inflectional ambiguity in the plural is elsewhere extremely rare (see Rohlfs (1968:24) for some examples of analogical reformation of singulars based on -ora plurals).

Overall, while the plural inflections show substantial continuity with their Latin antecedents, there is a tendency as one moves eastwards through the Romance-speaking world for the systematic predictability of plural morphology on the basis of the singular, characteristic of Latin, to dissolve in favour of separate lexical storage of many plural and singular inflectional forms.

3.2   Gender and declensional class

Every Latin noun belonged to one of three grammatical gender classes (masculine, feminine or neuter). Adjectives agreed with nouns for gender. Some properties of the Latin gender system are listed below (11):

(11)

	Masculine	Feminine	Neuter
Animate	yes	yes	no
Inanimate	yes	yes	yes
Female	no	yes	no
Male	yes	no	no
1DEC	rare	yes	no
2DEC	yes	very rare	yes
3DEC	yes	yes	yes
4DEC	rare	yes	rare
5DEC	no (one exception)	yes	no

To summarize: neuters exclusively denoted inanimates (but by no means all inanimates were neuter);[21] animate masculines and feminines overwhelmingly denoted, respectively, males and females; nearly all first declension nouns were feminine, and nearly all second declension nouns were not feminine (being either masculine or neuter); the third declension was populated by nouns of all three genders. Vital to an understanding of the evolution of the Romance inflectional gender system is the incidence of neutralization of gender marking in Latin. In the second declension there is complete neutralization of masculine vs. neuter distinctions outside the nominative and accusative, and in the third declension all three genders are neutralized outside the nominative and accusative. There is evidence, in fact, for extensive confusion between masculine and neuter as early as in the preclassical and classical period (see Wilkinson 1985; 1986) (12):

(12) Second declension

	M	NEUT
NOM.SG	MURUS 'wall'	OUUM 'egg'
ACC.SG	MURUM	OUUM
NOM.PL	MURI	OUA
ACC.PL	MUROS	OUA

Third declension

	M/F	NEUT
NOM.SG	UIRIDIS 'green'	UIRIDE
ACC.SG	UIRIDEM	UIRIDE
NOM.PL	UIRIDES	UIRIDIA
ACC.PL	UIRIDES	UIRIDIA

The already compromised system of inflectional gender distinctions was further eroded in Romance because (a) it was normally the case form originally marking the accusative which survived and (b) loss of final -M removed the distinction in third declension words. Second declension masculines and neuters lose their distinctness in the singular, and inflectional gender distinctions disappear altogether from the third declension singular. By and large, what survives into Romance is the distinction between feminine and non-feminine (= masculine), while the partial correlation between gender and inanimacy is lost. Phonetically and structurally motivated loss of distinct neuter forms in the singular[22] was generally accompanied by loss of distinct neuter inflections in the plural, with originally masculine plural inflections prevailing in the second declension, and reflexes of masculine and feminine -ES in the third (e.g., OUUM – OUA 'egg' > Sp. *huevo* – *huevos*, Fr. *œuf* – *œufs*; MARE – MARIA 'sea' > Sp. *mar* – *mares*, Fr. *mer* -*mers*, It. *mare* – *mari*, Ro. *mare* – *mări*).

The persistence of fragments of neuter morphology will be the focus of this section, but it should be said first that, by and large, Latin feminine lexemes remain feminine in Romance, whilst Latin non-feminines remain non-feminine. Semantic or formal cues play a major role in this continuity: unsurprisingly, PATER 'father' stays masculine wherever it survives (e.g., Sp. *el padre*, Fr. *le père*, It. *il padre*), and MATER 'mother' remains feminine (e.g., Sp./It. *la madre*, Fr. *la mère*); the fact of ending in -a (from first declension -A(M)) generally ensures continuity of feminine gender (e.g., STELLAM 'star' > feminine Sp. *la estrella*, Fr. *l'étoile*, It. *la stella*, Ro. *steaua*), while -o (or -u), from masculine/neuter -U(M), generally ensures continuity of non-feminine (masculine) gender (e.g., FOCU(M) 'fire' > Sp. *el fuego*, Fr. *le feu*, It. *il fuoco*, Ro. *focul* 'the fire'). The role of inflectional cues in determining the maintenance of gender can be appreciated from the negative perspective of those instances where neither semantic function nor form assists speakers.[23] Third declension inanimate nouns offer neither inflectional nor semantic cues, and their development is correspondingly sometimes erratic, with genders varying from region to region (see also Lausberg 1976:§624). An idea of the vacillation between genders in such cases can be gained from considering the development of neuter[24] LAC 'milk', MEL 'honey', SAL 'salt', MARE 'sea', masculine DENTEM 'tooth', FLOREM 'flower', SANGUINEM or SANGUEN 'blood', PONTEM 'bridge', PANEM 'bread', PEDEM 'foot', feminine NIUEM 'snow', ARBOREM 'tree', UALLEM 'vale' (13):

(13)

	M	F
Pt.	*leite, sal, mel, mar, dente, sangue, pão, pé, vale*	*árvore, ponte, flor, neve*
Sp.	*diente, mar,*[25] *puente,*[26] *pan, árbol, pie, valle*	*leche, sal, miel, flor, sangre, nieve*
Fr.[27]	*lait, sel, miel, sang, pont, pain, arbre, pied, val*	*dent, mer, fleur*
It.	*latte, sale, miele, dente, fiore, mare, sangue, ponte, pane, albero, piede*	*neve, valle*
Srd.	*latte, sale, mele, sambene, frore, ponte, nie, pane, pede*	*dente, arbore, badde*
Ro.	*lapte, dinte, sânge, arbore*	*sare, miere, mare, floare, punte, nea, pâine, vale*

Of interest here is not so much that lack of inflectional indication of gender can lead to vacillation in the gender of individual lexemes but that, despite this, the Latin declensional distinctions remain substantially intact in the inflectional marking of gender. By and large, third declension nouns retain third declension morphology, and there is no general abolition of third declension endings in favour of the gender-unambiguous continuants of the first (feminine) and second (non-feminine) declensions. Nor is there any overall trend to assigning a single gender to all third declension inanimates (even if Italian shows a propensity for making them masculine). In short, the gender-neutral property of third declension morphology remains.

In second declension lexemes, masculine and neuter were inflectionally distinct in the nominative. In those Romance varieties in which a distinct nominative case remained intact, second declension masculine forms in -US (e.g., BONUS) were sometimes distinguished from original neuters in -UM (e.g., BONUM). In general, the fusion of original neuters with masculines meant that neuter nouns acquired the masculine nominative singular ending -s (e.g., neuter CASTELLUM > OFr. *chasteaus*), but in Gallo-Romance and Raeto-Romance predicative adjectives, a remnant of the neuter is used where the referent is 'indefinite': e.g., OFr. *Li pere est bons* 'The father is good' vs. *Ço est bon* 'That is good.' In Surselvan, the -s form is used with all predicative adjectives agreeing with masculine subjects, but an -s-less form is used in attributive adjectives, and where the referent is 'indefinite': *il um ej buns* 'the man is good', *il bien um* 'the good man', *il ei bien* 'it is good' (*bien* and *bun-* are allomorphs of the lexeme 'good'). What is unclear, however, is whether the -s-less form, when used with indefinites, continues neuter -UM, or continues simply the joint masculine/neuter accusative -UM.

Another possible remnant of a neuter inflection occurs in dialects of central and southern Italy (southern Marche and southern Umbria, Lazio south of the Tiber, western Abruzzo, northern Puglia, north-eastern Basilicata and northern Campania). Here masculine nouns are subdivided into two semantically based subclasses, according as the noun is 'mass'[28] (having abstract or generic referents), or 'count' (having 'countable' referents). This distinction is expressed principally through the inflectional morphology of determiners and pronouns. Generally, the 'count' determiners and pronouns are characterized by -[u] and their mass counterparts have -[o]: e.g., Ascrea (Lazio) [lu b'bellu] 'the beautiful one' vs. [lo b'bellu] 'beauty'; [lu 'filu] 'the thread' vs. [lo 'filu] 'thread'; [lu 'ferru] 'the iron (implement)' vs. [lo 'ferru] 'iron', [llu ko'noʃʃe] 'he knows him' vs. [llo 'itʃe] 'he says it'. In an area between Naples and Bari, mass determiners lengthen the initial consonant of a following noun. Bisceglie (Puglia) has [rə l'lattə] 'the milk', [rə p'pənə] 'the bread', etc. 'Mass' is only rarely expressed by an inflectional ending on the noun. In parts of Umbria and the Marche 'mass' nouns continuing second declension forms have -[o], but nowhere is this consistently the case. The origin of 'mass' morphology is problematic, but it probably continues a Latin neuter inflection peculiar to determiners and pronouns, characterized by nominative and accusative singular forms in -D – ISTUD and ILLUD vs. masculine ISTU(M) and ILLU(M) – as the source. These perhaps developed as *['estod], *['ellod] and *['estu], *['ellu] (-[u] is the usual development of -U(M) in SItaly), where [d] could subsequently have assimilated to a following consonant. Elsewhere, *-[d] was deleted, leaving -[o] as the ending. The association of neuter forms with 'mass' reference may reflect the fact that many Latin mass nouns were neuter: e.g., MEL 'honey'; SAL 'salt'; UINUM 'wine', etc., but Ojeda (1992) casts doubt on this view.

A similar phenomenon is encountered in Spain in dialects of Asturias (also Valladolid and Santander; see Ojeda 1992; also Fernández Ordóñez 2006–7; and Loporcaro, this volume, chapter 3: §1.2.2): e.g., *queso* 'cheese' (the substance)' vs. *quisu* '(a) cheese', *pan fino* 'fine bread' vs. *ceazu finu* 'fine sieve'. The distinction is also marked on pronouns and demonstrative adjectives but, unlike Italo-Romance, there is no restriction of the phenomenon to determiners and pronouns. The distinction also appears in adjectives and, most surprisingly, morphologically 'mass' adjectives can even be used with mass feminine nouns (e.g., *tela blanca* '(a piece of) white cloth' vs. *tela blanco* 'white cloth (in general)'). Restriction to determiners and pronouns does appear, however, in the standard Spanish definite article *lo* (used to create mass or generic nouns from adjectives:[29] e.g., *el blanco* 'the white one' vs. *lo blanco* 'that which is white, whiteness'), in the pronoun *ello*, and in the determiners *esto*, *eso* and *aquello* which can refer only to propositions or assertions (e.g., *esto es falso* 'this [statement] is false' vs. *éste es falso* 'this one is false'). Ojeda points out that in OSpanish the determiner and pronominal forms in -o could also have 'mass' reference (this applied also to adjectives modifying 'mass' feminine nouns). The consensus among Hispanists (e.g., Penny 1970; Ojeda 1992) is that this -o continues not a neuter inflection, but the old second declension ablative inflection -o, originally occurring in partitive constructions meaning 'some …' (e.g., DE CASEO 'some of the cheese'). Ojeda (1992) convincingly challenges the assumption (e.g., Alonso 1962) that mass reference was a particular characteristic of neuter nouns, thereby casting doubt on the plausibility of a development of neuter forms into mass forms. Although he alludes to the Italo-Romance domain as well, he overlooks the crucial fact that 'mass' determiners in Italo-Romance can cause *lengthening* of a following initial consonant – a detail compatible with original neuter forms such as ISTUD and ILLUD, but not with ablative -o. Since it seems unlikely that the resemblances between the Italo-Romance and Ibero-Romance phenomena are coincidental, the possibility that the mass-forms in the latter at least partly preserve neuter morphology should not, after all, be dismissed.

No Romance variety retains a morphologically distinct neuter gender, but most retain fragments of old neuter plural morphology,[30] and in many cases original neuter plural forms have acquired novel grammatical functions. The surviving neuter plural inflection is -a, which in Latin characterized all accusative and nominative neuter plurals regardless of declensional class, and was also immune from most neutralizing or deleting sound changes in Romance. In central and southern Italian dialects, and especially in Romanian, there has emerged a second (originally) neuter plural form -ora (which later becomes -uri in Romanian): the source of -ora is a morphological reanalysis of plurals of the type CORPUS – CORPOR-A 'body' and TEMPUS – TEMPOR-A 'time', where -OR-, originally a positional phonological variant of root-final -US, is interpreted as part of the inflectional ending, hence as CORP-ORA, TEMP-ORA. Survival of the neuter plural ending was by no means limited to original neuters: copious examples are given in Wilkinson (1985–91), but one has only to consider Italian *dito* – PL *dita* 'finger' (= Lat. M DIGITU(M) – DIGITOS), southern Italo-Romance a'nello – a'nɛlla 'ring' (= Lat. M ANELLU(M) – ANELLOS), or neologisms such as Ro. *lift* – *lifturi* 'lift, elevator', or *microfon* – *microfoane* 'microphone', to appreciate that these remnants of neuter morphology have a productive history, affecting words that were never neuter, nor even part of the inherited Romance lexicon.

What is common to all remnants of neuter plural -A (and -ORA), is that they were reanalysed as feminine: this is manifested in the fact that all adjectives and determiners modifying such forms are identical to feminine adjectives and determiners.[31] The basis for such reanalysis is that plural -A was formally identical to the inflectional ending of the characteristically feminine first declension nouns. The reanalysis is particularly observable with old neuter plurals of nouns whose referents typically occurred in groups or sets, and therefore had greater frequency of occurrence (and hence prominence) in the plural. Feminine singulars such as Pt., Sp., It. *arma*, Pt. *folha*, Sp. *hoja*, Fr. *feuille*, It. *foglia*, originate as Latin neuter plurals ARMA 'weapons', FOLIA 'leaves' (see also Wilkinson (1985:142, 144–46) for examples of such reanalyses already seen in Latin; also Wilkinson (1991) for a survey of the Romance data). The names of fruits were often neuter (e.g., PIRUM 'pear' – PL PIRA) but, since fruits typically occur in collectivities, they were more commonly referred to in their plural form in -A. The neuter plural was frequently reanalysed as a feminine singular (e.g., Fr. *la poire*, It. *la pera*), giving rise to new, 'regular', feminine plurals (e.g., Fr., *les poires*, It. *le pere*). While names of cultivated fruits were neuter, those of the trees on which they grew were normally feminine, with the peculiarity that these tree names had the morphological structure of second declension *masculines* (e.g., F PIRUS ALTA 'tall pear tree'). The unsurprising reanalysis of tree names as masculines,[32] and the reintrepretation of the original neuter plural fruit names as feminines, gave rise to a situation in Italo-Romance and Romanian in which a masculine form of the lexeme denoted the tree, and the feminine form the fruit:[33] e.g., It. *il pero* 'pear tree' vs. *la pera*, Ro. *părul* vs. *para*.[34]

In Sardinia (including Gallurese; see Mameli 1998:158f.), southern Basilicata and some Raeto-Romance varieties (see Lausberg 1939:139; 1976:§609), a kind of 'compromise' was attained, such that while old neuter plurals were reanalysed as singular, they often retained a collective 'plural' sense: e.g., Sardinian sa 'βira can mean 'pears generally', as well as 'the pear'; Surselvan *la bratscha* is the (pair of) arms on the body, while *ils bratschs* are indvidual arms (in earlier stages of the language, such singular forms could be accompanied by morphologically plural verbs; see Wilkinson 1986:165). Traces of this 'collective' sense can sometimes be seen in other Romance varieties: e.g., Sp. *huevo* 'egg' < OUUM vs. *hueva* 'roe, fish-eggs' < OUA, It. *legna* (Sp. *leña*) 'firewood' < LIGNA (see SG LIGNUM > It. *legno* 'wood'). For OProvençal examples, see Jensen (1976:32–38). Collectivities are necessarily larger than any of their component entities, and it may be that this fact explains why, in some Italo- and Ibero-Romance varieties, some lexemes have a feminine and a masculine form, with the feminine denoting a larger entity (e.g., It. *buco* 'hole' (usually small and two-dimensional) vs. *buca* 'large (and three-dimensional) hole', *cesto* 'basket' vs. *cesta* 'larger basket, panier'; Somiedo (Spain) *dida* 'toe', *didu* 'finger', *truena* 'thunderstorm' *truenu* 'thunder', *güertu* 'orchard', *güerta* 'large orchard'.[35]

In central and southern Italy, a different kind of 'compromise' operated: plurals in -a being reanalysed as feminine, but not always as singular. That such plurals are feminine[36] is clearly shown by agreeing adjectives and by pronouns, which are unambiguously feminine plural in form. As we saw above, Italian – and, far more abundantly, the dialects of southern and central Italy[37] – have a series of plural nouns which are feminine,[38] and characterized by inflectional -a, corresponding masculine singulars in -*o*: e.g., It. *l'uovo rotto* 'the broken egg' vs. *le uova rotte* 'the broken eggs'.[39] In some Italo-Romance dialects and, above all, in Romanian, there has also been analogical replacement of the plural inflection -a with the ending -e generally characteristic of feminine plural nouns and adjectives: e.g., Lat. OS – OSSA, CORNU – CORNUA > Ro. *os – oase, corn – coarne*.

Reflexes of the neuter plural inflections maintain a semantic characteristic of the old neuters, that of designating inanimates, but not always (see Maiden 1997:72f.; and especially Tuttle 1990). In SCorsica and parts of northern Umbria, the -a plural has percolated into some [+human] nouns, and has spread outside nouns originally belonging to the Latin second declension (in Umbria, this serves to disambiguate singulars from plurals where there has been phonological neutralization of the regular inflections). In parts of Puglia (e.g., Altamura; see Loporcaro 1988), the -ora ending has even extended to some feminine and animate nouns. In Romanian, -uri has acquired an additional function which seems more 'derivational' than 'inflectional', that of forming plurals of feminine 'mass' nouns (see Graur 1968:90–92), with the meaning 'different sorts of': e.g., *carne* 'meat' – *cărnuri* 'different sorts of meat', *mătase* 'silk' – *mătăsuri*.[40]

The survival of neuter plural inflections contributes considerably to the indeterminacy of plural inflectional morphology in the Romance languages of the east. In southern Italy (see Rohlfs 1968:35–41; Maiden 1997:71–73), and in Romanian, old neuter inflections are extensively used to form the plurals of masculine nouns denoting inanimates. It becomes difficult to predict whether a given inanimate noun will take a 'neuter' plural inflection and, if so, which inflection (the continuant of -A or the continuant of -ORA) it will take. In some cases, more than one inflection is possible for the same lexeme: thus Veroli in Lazio (Vignoli 1925:45f.) a'nɛllu 'ring' – PL a'nɛlla or a'nɛllǝra (or regular masculine a'neʎi), 'prato 'meadow' – PL 'prata, 'orto 'orchard' – PL 'ɔrtǝra. Romanian inanimates normally take the masculine inflection in -*i* in lexemes where the plural is used more frequently than the singular: e.g., *pumni* 'fists', *ochi* 'eyes', *cactuşi* 'cacti', or *kilometri* 'kilometres'. But this is not always so: cf. F.PL *degete* 'fingers', *picioare* 'legs', *grade* 'degrees [of temperature, etc.]') or *diamante* 'diamonds'. Overwhelmingly, however, the plural of an inanimate noun will be predictably[41] feminine. What is not predictable is its inflectional desinence: apart from a slight preference for -*e* in neologisms (see Graur 1968:127), it is usually[42] impossible to predict whether -*e* or -*uri* will occur: e.g., *ac – ace* 'needle', *fir – fire* 'thread', *nailon – nailoane* 'nylon', *loc – locuri* 'place', *abajur – abajururi* 'lampshade', *ton – tonuri* 'tone'.

4 The verb

4.1 The fate of the Latin perfective verb-forms

Aspectual differences (usually labelled 'imperfective' vs. 'perfective') were fundamental to the structure of the Latin verb, but are largely effaced in Romance. What is remarkable about the history of the Romance verbal paradigm is not so much that the distinction between perfective and imperfective persists in the inflectional system, despite general effacement of functional distinctions of aspect, but that the surviving, functionally incoherent (and phonologically disparate) perfective verb-roots remain intact, and retain exactly the pattern of paradigmatic distribution which they possessed when they signalled aspect. The fate of the perfective root has the same theoretical import as that described in chapter 5 for the fate of the so-called 'N-pattern' and 'U/L-pattern' of allomorphy. In fact, preservation of the perfective root is a prime diachronic example of 'morphomic' patterning (cf. Aronoff 1994; and the discusion in chapter 5 of this volume) in inflectional paradigms: a recurrent distributional pattern which is both phonologically and functionally incoherent, nonetheless emerges as a major force in the morphological history of Romance.[43]

In the Latin present, past, future and infinitive, an imperfective form was distinguished from a perfective one. In most first and fourth conjugation verbs, the perfective was characterized by a formative [w] immediately following the 'stem' (defined as 'lexical root + thematic vowel'). In some cases (notably second conjugation verbs), [w] appeared immediately adjacent to the root. The following examples contrast the third person singular imperfective and perfective (14):

(14)

First conjugation   Second conjugation

	IPFV	PFV	IPFV	PFV
PRS.IND	AMAT 'loves'	AMAUIT	TENET 'holds'	TENUIT
PRS.SBJV	AMET	AMAUERIT	TENEAT	TENUERIT
PST. IND	AMABAT	AMAUERAT	TENEBAT	TENUERAT
PST. SBJV	AMARET	AMAUISSET	TENERET	TENUISSET
FUT.IND	AMABIT	AMAUERIT	TENEBIT	TENUERIT

Fourth conjugation

	IPFV	PFV
PRS.IND	AUDIT 'hears'	AUDIUIT
PRS.SBJV	AUDIAT	AUDIUERIT
PST. IND	AUDIEBAT	ADIUERAT
PST. SBJV	AUDIRET	AUDIUISSET
FUT.IND	AUDIET	AUDIUERIT

The characteristic of third conjugation verbs (together with a good number of second conjugation members, and UENIRE 'come', in the fourth) was that their perfective[44] form was expressed by a motley array of root-allomorphs.[45] The irreducible phonological heterogeneity of these perfective roots (in part due to conflation of ancient 'aorist' and 'stative' roots; see Sihler 1995:579–90) is striking. In addition to partial reduplication (e.g., IPFV MORDET 'bites' vs. PFV MOMORDIT), of which a Romance remnant is It. *dà* 'give' – *diede* 'gave', ORo. *dă* – *deade* (< DAT – DEDIT), perfective roots could be differentiated from their imperfective counterparts by vowel quality or length (e.g., FACIT 'makes' – FECIT; UIDET 'sees' – UĪDIT, UENIT 'comes' – UĒNIT, LEGIT 'reads' – LĒGIT), changes in the root-final consonant (e.g., MITTIT 'sends' – MĪSIT; note also the difference of vowel length), addition of a sibilant to the root (e.g., SCRIBIT 'writes' – SCRIPSIT, DICIT 'says' – DIXIT, REMANET 'remains' – REMANSIT),[46] and sundry others (e.g., PONIT 'puts' – POSUIT, PREMIT 'presses' – PRESSIT, COQUIT 'cooks' – COXIT, TRAHIT 'pulls' – TRAXIT, FUNDIT 'melts' – FUDIT; EST 'is' – FUIT). Even though the reduplicating type effectively disappears, and the range of verbs involving differentiation of the root vowel becomes greatly curtailed (e.g., CURRIT 'runs' – CUCURRIT > It. *corre* – *corse*; MOUET 'moves' – MŌUIT > It. *muove* – *mosse*, LEGIT 'reads' – LĒGIT> It. *legge* – *lesse*), most types of perfective root survived intact into Romance (*modulo* sound changes) and, as the Italian examples just given show, those that were lost were often replaced by other perfect-root patterns.

The -IUI-/-EUE-, -EUI- elements of perfective verbs were already subject in imperial times to contraction:[47] e.g., DELEUISSET 'destroy.3SG.PST.PRF.SBJV' > DELESSET, DELEUERAT 'destroy.3SG.PST.PRF.IND' > DELERAT, DELEUEREUNT 'destroy.3PL.PRS.PRF.SBJV' > DELERUNT, DORMIUISSET 'sleep.3SG.PST.PRF.SBJV' > DORMISSET, DORMIUISTI 'sleep.2SG. PST.PRF.IND' > DORMISTI. This pattern spread analogically to the first conjugation (e.g., AMAUISSET 'love.3SG.PST.PRF.SBJV' > AMASSET, AMAUERAT 'love.3SG.PST.PRF.IND' > AMARAT, AMAUISTI 'love.2SG. PRS.PRF.IND'> AMASTI, AMAUERUNT 'love.3SG.PRS.PRF.SBJV' > AMARUNT). The fourth conjugation type AUDIRAT 'hear.3SG.PST.PRF.IND', AUDIRUNT 'hear.3PL.PRS.PRF.IND' is apparently a postclasscial development (although AUDIERAT, AUDIERUNT occurred), analogically modelled on the other conjugations (see Sihler 1995:586). One effect of these contractions was to blur the morphological marking of aspectual distinctions where these depended on [w] following the root vowel. The distinctive perfective stems became restricted just to roots, including those that ended in a consonant immediately followed by [w]. In Italo-Romance, [w] survived as [v] after a root-final -r or -l (e.g., PARUIT > It. *parve* 'it seemed'), but generally left a trace of itself in phonologically regular lengthening of the preceding root-final consonant: TENUIT > *tenne* 'he held', UOLUIT > *volle* 'he wanted', HABUIT > *ebbe* 'he had', *ᵛkadwit > *cadde* 'he fell', etc.; in Ibero-Romance and Gallo-Romance there is evidence that [w] underwent what is often described as metathesis, producing a diphthong in the root: e.g., SAP(I)UIT > *ᵛsapwit > *ᵛsauu̯pe > Pt. *soube* 'he knew', OSp. *sope*, OFr. *sot*. What the Romance languages inherit from Latin perfective marking is, then, a phonologically heterogeneous assemblage of root-allomorphs, augmented in some cases by the effects of [w] on a preceding root, and also by the effects of widespread assimilation of the root-final consonant to a following [s] (e.g., SCRIPSIT > It. *scrisse* 'wrote', OFr. *escrit*, OSp. *escriso*). Here are some representative samples of the range of such survivals from OSpanish, OFrench, ModItalian and sixteenth-century Romanian, contrasting the third person singular present indicative with its preterite counterpart. It is beyond the scope of this study to examine all the (largely regular) phonological developments, and many of the analogical changes, which underlie these forms. My aim, rather, is to show the phonological heterogeneity of the perfective roots surviving into Romance (15):

(15)   OSp. *ve* 'sees' – *vido*; *quiere* 'wants' – *quiso*; *viene* 'comes' – *vino*; *tiene* 'holds' – *tovo*; *haze* 'does' – *hizo*; *escribe* 'writes' – *escriso*; *conduce* 'leads' – *condujo*; *plaze* 'pleases' – *plogo*; *sabe* 'knows' – *sopo*; *pone* 'puts' – *puso*; *puede* 'can' – *podo*; *está* 'is' – *estovo/estido*; *ha* 'has' – *ovo*; *remane* 'stays' – *remaso*; *nasce* 'is born' – *nasco*; *vive* 'lives' – *visco*; *yaze* 'lies' – *yogo*; *trae* 'brings' – *trajo*; *ciñe* 'girds' – *cinxo*; *conoce* 'knows' – *conovo*; *mete* 'puts' – *miso*; *escribe* 'writes' – *escriso*; *es* 'is' – *fue*…

OFr. *veit* 'sees' – *vit*; *prent* 'takes' – *prit*; *quert* 'seeks' – *quist*; *vient* 'comes' – *vint*; *tient* 'comes' – *tint*; *met* 'puts' – *mist*; *fait* 'does' – *fist*; *escrit* 'writes' – *escrist*; *duit* 'leads' – *duist*; *ceint* 'girds' – *ceinst*; *mord* 'bites' – *morst*; *a* 'has' – *ot*; *plait* 'pleases' – *plot*; *sait* 'knows' – *sot*; *vuelt* 'wants' – *volt*; *maint* 'stays' – *mes*; *naist* 'is born' – *naquit*; *vit* 'lives' – *vesquit*; *est* 'is' – *fut*…

It. *vede* 'sees' – *vide*; *prende* 'takes' – *prese*; *chiede* 'asks' – *chiese*; *viene* 'comes' – *venne*; *tiene* 'holds' – *tenne*; *mette* 'puts' – *mise*; *fa* 'does' – *fece*; *scrive* 'writes' – *scrisse*; *piove* 'rains' – *piovve*; *conduce* 'leads' – *condusse*; *dice* 'says' – *disse*; *cinge* 'girds' – *cinse*; *morde* 'bites' – *morse*; *pone* 'puts' – *pose*; *fonde* 'melts' – *fuse*; *piace* 'pleases' – *piacque*; *ha* 'has' – *ebbe*; *sa* 'knows' – *seppe*; *vuole* 'wants' – *volle*; *rimane* 'stays' – *rimase*; *nasce* 'is born' – *nacque*; *vive* 'lives' – *visse*; *cuoce* 'cooks' – *cosse*; *nuoce* 'harms' – *nocque*; *cresce* 'grows' – *crebbe*; *cade* 'falls' – *cadde*; *trae* 'pulls' – *trasse*; *rompe* 'breaks' – *ruppe*; *dà* 'gives' – *diede*; *sta* 'stands' – *stette*, *è* 'is' – *fu*…

(O)Ro. *cere* 'asks' – *cerşii* (1SG); *face* 'does' – *feace*; *scrie* 'writes' – *scrise*; *zice* 'says' – *zise*; *coace* 'bakes' – *coapse*; *suge* 'sucks' – *supse*; *ajunge* 'reaches' – *ajunse*; *pune* 'puts' – *puse*; *rămâne* 'stays' – *rămase*; *aduce* 'brings' – *aduse*; *fierbe* 'boils' – *fiarse*; *scoate* 'removes' – *scoase*; *trimite* 'sends' – *trimise*; *dă* 'gives' – *deade*; *stă* 'stands' – *stătu*; *este* 'is' – *fu*

I do not mean that distinctive perfective roots survive always and everywhere. One reason for illustrating the diversity of perfective roots from older forms of these languages is that a long-standing tendency to eliminate the perfective root in favour of (original) imperfective roots seems to have accelerated greatly in recent centuries. For example, modern Spanish has preterite *escribió, nació, conoció, vivió, ciñó, metió*; French has *écrivit, conduisit, ceignit, mordit, voulut*; Romanian *ceru, făcu* – all remodelled on roots continuing Latin imperfectives.

Thus far it may seem that I have merely sketched the persistence of the Latin *status quo ante*, disturbed by a few relatively unremarkable phonological and morphological adjustments along the way. In fact, the survival of the 'perfective root' constitutes a remarkable and distinctive trait of Romance historical morphology – for morphological continuity is not accompanied by functional continuity. This can be best appreciated by comparing the paradigmatic distribution of Latin perfective word-forms with their continuants in Ibero-Romance, taking as our example third person singular forms of Lat. FACERE 'make' and its Spanish reflex *hacer* (16).

(16) Latin

IPFV				
PRS.IND	PRS.SBJV	PST.IND	PST.SBJV	FUT.IND
FACIT	FACIAT	FACIEBAT	FACERET	FACIET

PFV				
PRS.IND	PRS.SBJV	PST.IND	PST.SBJV	FUT.IND
FECIT	FECERIT	FECERAT	FECISSET	FECERIT

Spanish continuants (a blank means that the word-form in question is not continued) (17).

(17)

PRS.IND	PRS.SBJV	IPF.IND		
hace	*haga*	*hacía*		

PRT	FUT.SBJV	IPF.SBJV/PLP.IND	IPF.SBJV	FUT.SBJV
hizo	*hiciere*	*hiciera*	*hiciese*	*hiciere*

While the Spanish *forms* continue, more or less faithfully, their Latin antecedents, a glance at the 'function cells' in the above diagram shows dramatic functional discontinuity. There is no longer[48] a systematic morphological distinction between imperfective and perfective aspect. In fact, of the original perfective forms the only one which retains unambiguously perfective aspectual meaning is what we term the preterite. Moreover, this is the only remnant of the perfective which has an exclusively 'past' temporal value. The old perfect subjunctive, and future perfect, formally identical in Latin outside the first person singular, emerge in Ibero-Romance (and some Gascon dialects; see Rohlfs 1970:221) as a future subjunctive, devoid of aspectual connotations. This form has fallen into desuetude in modern Spanish, but still flourishes in Portuguese. The old pluperfect subjunctive FECISSET emerges in Ibero-Romance, as in most Romance varieties, as a so-called 'imperfect subjunctive', which again has no aspectual connotations and, despite its traditional classification as a 'past' tense, no necessary connection with past time (it functions also as a present or even future counterfactual, as in modern Sp. *Si lo hiciese ahora/mañana lo veríamos* 'If he did / were to do / were doing it now/tomorrow we'd see it'). The Latin pluperfect indicative, in addition to its past perfect value, could also function as a kind of past conditional (e.g., PERIERAT IMPERIUM [...] SI FABIUS TANTUM AUSUS ESSET, QUANTUM IRA SUADEBAT 'the empire would have perished, if Fabius had dared to do what his anger moved him to do' (Seneca)), and its appearance in conditional sentences may have favoured its later development in some Romance varieties as a conditional or subjunctive (see Togeby 1966:176). Its continuant appears in OSpanish as a past anterior form, a function which it retains vestigially today (see Lunn and Cravens 1991), particularly in Latin American varieties, and which continues in written Portuguese. It appears to have functioned principally as a conveyor of 'backgrounded information' (quite unlike the preterite, with which it shares a root) – a fact which apparently favoured its development (charted by Klein Andreu 1991) into an alternative form of imperfect subjunctive. For more illustration of the severe blurring of morphological marking of aspect in Romance, see Ledgeway, this volume, chapter 8.

Descriptive grammars of Spanish frequently label the set of forms continuing Latin perfective roots as 'perfecto y tiempos afines' ('perfect and related tenses'), without observing that the nature of the 'affinity' is, as we have seen, purely one of morphological structure. However, the label, reduced to the acronym 'PYTA', provides us with a conveniently opaque cover term for the continuants of Latin perfective roots, across the Romance languages, and regardless of their disparate functions. Henceforth I shall refer to them exclusively as 'PYTA' roots.

PYTA roots in other Romance varieties are also functionally heterogeneous, albeit sometimes in different ways. The function of the continuant of Latin perfect forms (e.g., Pt. *fez*, Cat. *feu*, Fr. *fit*, It. *fece*, ORo. *fece*) is much as in Spanish: exclusively perfective and past. The continuant of the pluperfect subjunctive (e.g., Pt. *fizesse*, Cat. *fes*, Fr. *fît*, It. *facesse*) also has much the same value as in Spanish, although in Ro. it survived as a pluperfect indicative (ORo. *fecese*). The fusion of the Latin perfect subjunctive and future perfect produced in the so-called 'rhotacizing' varieties of sixteenth-century Romanian (with Istro-Romanian and Macedo-Romanian dialects) a form of conditional (e.g., *fecere*) used, according to Ivănescu (1980:155f.), only in the protasis of those conditional sentences whose apodosis contained a verb in the future, imperative or present subjunctive. It may also be the source of future tense forms in -*re*/-*ro*/-*ra* found in Dalmatian (Bartoli 1906:§§482–83). Continuants of the Latin pluperfect indicative occur or occurred in most Romance varieties (although not in Romanian). I have already touched on their function in Ibero-Romance. They survive in OSardinian apparently with their original value (Wagner 1939:21f.), but in Italo-Romance (principally mainland southern Italy),[49] OCatalan, OOccitan (and OPiedmontese; see Gamillscheg 1912:186f., 242), they were typically used in the apodosis of non-past conditionals (e.g., ORoman *fécera* 'he would do'). In the history of French, the precise function of the corresponding forms – already obsolescent in the time of the earliest texts and largely restricted to northern and eastern varieties – is elusive (see Moignet 1959; Togeby 1966:178f.), and sometimes it seems close or identical in meaning to the preterite inherited from the Latin perfect (see Gamillscheg 1912:179f.; Lausberg 1976:§828). But it could also have a conditional, and clearly non-perfective, value (e.g., *Tel rien fiz que faire ne dure* 'I did something which I should not have done' – Roman de Thèbes), and could even serve, like the imperfect, to express a condition or state of affairs in the past (see Gamillscheg 1912:184). With the possible exception of old French, the reflexes of the Latin pluperfect indicative verb-forms are in no sense inherently perfective and, despite the Spanish label 'perfecto y tiempos afines', have remarkably little affinity with the preterite, either aspectually or in respect of tense.

It may still seem that what has been described is a matter of morphological inertia: the disparate perfective roots of Latin simply happen to remain intact, even though, so to speak, the functional 'rug has been pulled from under their feet'. But PYTA roots are much more than a fortuitous collection of fossils left over from a defunct *état de langue*. One might imagine that, once they became functionally incoherent, speakers made no further cross-paradigmatic generalizations about them. The fact that in, say, Ibero-Romance, the presence of a PYTA root in any one of preterite, pluperfect /past subjunctive or future subjunctive implied its presence in all of the others might be noticed by linguists, but not necessarily by medieval native speakers, who could simply have learned the pattern of root-allomorphy for each verb independently without ever 'recognizing the pattern'. There is no advantage, and some disadvantage, in trying to formulate this implicational principle as a 'derivational rule', which says that the root of the imperfect subjunctive etc. is 'derived' from that of the preterite. At best, this is simply a notational variant of the paradigmatic coherence of PYTA roots, and it entails the erroneous prediction that such a rule could be 'lost' while leaving the roots intact just in the preterite. In fact the presence of a PYTA root in the preterite always entails its presence elsewhere. Such possible examples of 'asymmetry' between the tense-forms as exist (see below) do not show the predicted directionality: sometimes the preterite appears to retain the PYTA root, at other times the imperfect subjunctive does (see also Morin 1990). In any case, the diachronic facts suggest a very different picture, which indicates that speakers have always been aware of the PYTA distributional pattern. This fact is manifested in two respects:

(i) *Coherence:* any morphological change affecting a PYTA root in one part of the paradigm of a given verb, always equally affects the PYTA root in all other parts of the paradigm of that verb.

(ii) *Convergence:* the phonological heterogeneity of PYTA roots tends to be reduced over time, so that PYTA roots converge on a common, characteristic, phonological form.

On all available evidence, the principle of coherence is overwhelmingly valid throughout the history of the Romance languages. There are virtually no 'mixed systems' such that, for example, the PYTA root appears in the preterite but not in the imperfect subjunctive or in the imperfect subjunctive but not in the preterite, or that a different kind of PYTA root appears in one of these categories from the other. It is important to stress that I am talking about the paradigmatic distribution of PYTA roots, not about the morphosyntactic categories with which they are associated. Most Romance varieties have lost the continuant of the Latin future perfect and future subjunctive and many no longer have a form continuing the pluperfect indicative. Istro-Romanian retains the continuant of the future perfect / perfect subjunctive, but loses the preterite and the continuant of the pluperfect subjunctive. Dialects of northern Italy, some Occitan varieties, spoken Catalan (excluding Valencia and the Balearics) and most of Romania have largely lost the preterite but retain the form continuing the Latin pluperfect subjunctive (which becomes the 'imperfect subjunctive', or in Romanian the pluperfect indicative). This relative incoherence of the morphosyntactic categories in which PYTA roots occur is an important guarantee against any suggestion that coherence is motivated by some underlying but elusive common property of semantic unity. Equally, it underscores the difficulty of trying to account for coherence by appeal to 'markedness': it is plausible that preterite and imperfect subjunctive are 'marked' categories in relation to, say, present indicative or imperfect subjunctive, but their coherence in respect of PYTA roots would only be explicable if they *both* bore *the same* markedness value in relation to the rest of the verb paradigm. Not only does this seem inherently unlikely, but the differential disappearance of the relevant morphosyntactic categories strongly suggests differentiation in markedness between them (a similar line of argumentation is put forward in chapter 5, à propos of 'N-pattern' allomorphy). Further evidence for the essential independence of preterite and imperfect subjunctive is the fact that they *are* sometimes differentiated in analogical change – when the change affects the inflectional endings. In most modern Languedocien varieties, the inflectional desinences of the preterite (with the frequent exception of the third person singular) are characterized by [r] (see also Bybee and Brewer 1980:211f.). The [r] element originates in the third person plural preterite and the old conditional (which had [r] throughout). In no Languedoc dialect does this [r] (which seems to have become a stable marker of the preterite) penetrate the imperfect subjunctive. In general (but see Alibèrt 1976:102; Ronjat 1937, 3:284), there is no convergence, even partial, between preterite and imperfect subjunctive desinences, in striking contrast to the systematic identity of the root.

Demonstrating the paradigmatic coherence of the PYTA root is a potentially endless task. My own extensive survey of dialect monographs, historical grammars and linguistic atlases across the Romance domain has evinced almost no unambiguous counterexamples (the status of which will be examined later). Coherence is apparent wherever the PYTA root is subject to analogical replacement by non-PYTA roots. Spanish (and Portuguese) has witnessed a notable replacement of PYTA roots since the Middle Ages, but such replacement operates equally on the preterite, the imperfect subjunctives and the future subjunctive: e.g., *escribir* 'to write': *escriso escrisiese escrisiera escrisiere* > *escribió escribiese escribiera escribiere*; *ceñir* 'to gird': *cinxo cinxese cinxera cinxere* > *ciñó ciñese ciñera ciñere*; *nacer* 'to be born': *nasco nasquiese nasquiera nasquiere* > *nació naciese naciera naciere*; *reír* 'to laugh': *riso risiese risiera risiere* > *rio riese riera riere*, etc. Similarly, in Occitan (Languedocien; Alibèrt 1976:110) levelling of PYTA roots in favour of a non-PYTA root never differentiates morphosyntactic categories: *cenhèri cenhèsse* (for older *ceis* etc.) 'gird', *jonheri jonhèsse* (for older *jois* etc.) 'join', *bevèri bevèsse* (for older *bec beguèsse* etc.) 'drink', *respondèri respondèsse* (for older *respós* etc.) 'answer'. Sometimes various different analogical influences have borne on the same PYTA root, but their effect is always symmetrical across the paradigm of the verbs affected (the relevant forms are in bold) (18):

(18)

PRS.IND	*recebi* 'I receive'	*sabi/sai* 'I know'	*som* 'I am'
IPF.IND	*recebiá*	*sabiá*	*èri*
PRT	*receupèri*	*saupèri*	*foguèri*
	receguèri	*saguèri*	*forèri*
	recebèri	*sabèri*	
		sachèri	
PRS.SBJV	*recepia/rececha*	*sàpia/sacha*	*siá*
IPF.SBJV	*receupèsse*	*saupèsse*	*foguèsse*
	receguesse recebèsse	*saguèsse*	*forèsse*
		sabèsse	
		sachèsse	

PRS.IND	*tòrci* 'I twist'	*vesi* 'I see'
IPF.IND	*torciá*	*vesiá*
PRT	*torceguèri*	*vegèri*
	torcèri	*veguèri*
		vejèri
PRS.SBJV	*tòrça*	*veja*
IPF.SBJV	*torceguèsse*	*vegèsse*
	torcèsse	*veguèsse*
		vejèsse

An interesting feature of some Occitan varieties is that the present subjunctive root is analogically extended to other parts of the paradigm.

This might create the expectation that speakers would seize the opportunity to create a 'common subjunctive' root, by limiting the extension just to the IPF.SBJV, but this does not occur at all, as is shown for example by PRS. SBJV *aja, veja, sacha* > PRT *ajèri* IPF.SBJV *ajèsse* 'have', *vejèri vejèsse* 'see', *sachèri sachèsse* 'know', etc., where the preterite is equally affected.[50]

In French, as in Spanish, there has been notable recession of PYTA roots in favour of non-PYTA roots since the Middle Ages, but this is always undifferentiated: e.g., *mors morsisse* 'bit' > *mordis mordisse, joins joinsisse* 'joined' > *joignis joignisse, repos reposisse* 'answered' > *répondis répondisse, escris escresisse* 'wrote' > *écrivis écrivisse*; there are no 'mixed systems' (say, ****mors mordisse* or ****mordis morsisse*). Ekblom (1908:111–13) and others have argued that such loss of PYTA roots was motivated by avoidance of homophony between preterite and present (e.g., *joins* was originally both first person singular preterite and first person singular present). In this case we might expect, contrary to fact, elimination of PYTA roots only from the preterite. Another interpretation of some replacements of PYTA roots is that of Wahlgren (1920; also Fouché 1967:300, 323, 330), who invokes analogical influences from the past participle (e.g., *voil* 'I wanted' > *voulus* under influence of past participle *voulu*). This could be predicted – again, contrary to fact – to affect the preterite but not the imperfect subjunctive, given the well-known structural parallelisms between *j'ai voulu* and *je voulus*, etc. (in modern spoken French the former type replaces the latter). Analogical replacements of the PYTA root since the earliest attestations of Romanian have been relatively few, but they are entirely consistent with coherence: *fece fecese* and *făcu făcuse* already coexisted in the sixteenth century.

Analogical changes internal to the PYTA root show the same coherence. Metaphony (assimilatory raising of stressed vowels before a high unstressed vowel; see chapter 3) was usually limited to the first person singular preterite (the only PYTA root in which a stressed root preceded a high vowel). Since it was peculiar to (one form of) the preterite, one might expect it to remain a specific marker of the preterite, thereby neatly delimiting this category against the rest of the paradigm. In fact analogical extension of the first person singular preterite root vowel always covers all PYTA roots in the paradigm of the relevant verb. Thus FECI > *ˈfeki > *ˈfiki > Sp. *hice* 'did', Pt. *fiz*; POSUI > *ˈposi > *ˈpusi > Sp. *puse* 'put', Pt. *pus*; QUAESIUI > *QUAESI > *ˈkesi > *ˈkisi > Sp. *quise* 'wanted', Pt. *quis*. In the pre-literary period the metaphonic vowel was already analogically generalized throughout the PYTA root, without differentiation of tense-form (although in Portuguese, and some western Spanish varieties, the third person singular preterite frequently escapes the analogy). Thus modern Spanish and

Portuguese: PRT 1SG *hice* 3SG *hizo* 3PL *hicieron* IPF.SBJV *hiciese*; PRT 1SG *fiz* 3SG *fez* 3PL *fizeram* IPF.SBJV *fizesse*; PRT 1SG *puse* 3SG *puso* 3PL *pusieron* IPF.SBJV *pusiese*; PRT 1SG *pus* 3SG *pôs* 3PL *puseram* IPF.SBJV *pusesse*; PRT.1SG *quise* 3SG *quiso* 3PL *quisieron* IPF.SBJV *quisiese*; PRT.1SG *quis* 3SG *quis* 3PL *quiseram* IPF.SBJV *quisesse*.

The earliest French texts testify to analogical generalization of the distinctive high vowel of the first person singular preterite, whose presence was due to metaphony triggered by the inflection -i. Initially, this extension affects only other stressed syllables, not just in the third person singular and third person plural preterite, but equally in the continuant of the Latin pluperfect indicative. Thus the phonetically regular, metaphonic, preterite 1SG *fis* 'I did', *vin* 'I came', *dui* 'I owed', *voil* 'I wanted'[51] < *^{l}feki, *^{l}veni, *^{l}dewwi, *^{l}vɔli subsequently extend their vowel (see Fouché 1967:276) to the third person singular and third person plural (e.g., *fist vint dut volt; fisdrent vindrent durent voldrent*), and also (see Fouché 1967:336f.) to the former pluperfects *fis(t)dra, vindre, firet, dure, voldra*. With the disappearance, by the fourteenth century, of the continuant of the pluperfect, the generalized vowel again became restricted to the preterite. Yet subsequent analogical change, operating chiefly from the fifteenth century onwards, and this time extending the vowel to unstressed syllables, affects not only the unstressed PYTA roots of the preterite, but equally those of the imperfect subjunctive (19):

(19)

	Old French		Modern French	
vin 'came'	*venisse*	*vins*	*vinsse*	
venist	*venissses*	*vins*	*vinsses*	
vint	*venist*	*vint*	*vînt*	
venimes	*venissiens*	*vînmes*	*vinssions*	
venistes	*venissiez*	*vîntes*	*vinssiez*	
vindrent	*venissent*	*vinrent*	*vinssent*	
fis 'did'	*fe(s)isse*	*fis*	*fisse*	
fe(s)is	*fe(s)isses*	*fis*	*fisses*	
fist	*fe(s)ist*	*fit*	*fit*	
fe(s)imes	*fe(s)issiens*	*fîmes*	*fissions*	
fe(s)istes	*fe(s)issiez*	*fîtes*	*fissiez*	
fistrent	*fe(s)issent*	*firent*	*fissent*	

There were other verbs in which (this time for purely etymological/phonological reasons) the vowel of the stressed syllable was distinct from that of unstressed syllables. Here, too, the stressed vowel was extended not only into unstressed roots of the preterite, but also into the imperfect subjunctive (20):

(20)

	Old French		Modern French	
vi 'saw'	*vëisse*	*vis*	*visse*
vëis	*vëisses*	*vis*	*visses*
vit	*vëist*	*vit*	*vît*
vëimes	*vëissiens*	*vîmes*	*vissions*
vëistes	*vëissiez*	*vîtes*	*vissiez*
virent	*vëissent*	*virent*	*vissent*
mis 'put'	*me(s)isse*	*mis*	*misse*
me(s)is	*me(s)isses*	*mis*	*misses*
mist	*me(s)ist*	*mit*	*mît*
me(s)imes	*me(s)issiens*	*mîmes*	*missions*
me(s)istes	*me(s)issiez*	*mîtes*	*missiez*
mistrent	*me(s)issent*	*mirent*	*missent*

The example of extension of the stressed vowel into the imperfect subjunctive of *venir* is particularly interesting. The imperfective and perfective roots of this verb were distinguished in Latin only by vowel length (UĔN- vs. UĒN-), and the regular neutralization of this distinction in unstressed syllables meant that the unstressed PYTA root became actually identical to the non-PYTA unstressed root (e.g., INF *venir*, 1PL.PRS *venons*, 1SG.IPF.IND *venais*, 1SG.IPF.SBJV *venisse*). The result was that in OFr. the inherently unstressed root of the imperfect subjunctive was identical to the present, imperfect indicative, etc., leaving the root *vin-* as a unique characteristic of the preterite. Nonetheless, so strong was the sense of formal identity between preterite and imperfect subjunctive that the distinctive identity of the preterite was sacrificed to the unity of the PYTA root, when *vin-* was extended to unstressed roots.

Coherence is, I repeat, a pan-Romance phenomenon, but there do exist some apparent counterexamples. Most, but not quite all, of these are poorly documented, or turn out to have non-perfective origins, or are merely tendencies, rather than absolutes. The crucial fact is that it is very rare for the unity of PYTA roots to be wholly broken. That the PYTA root is absent from the imperfect subjunctive of Sardinian is usually ascribed to the claim that the relevant forms directly continue the Latin imperfect subjunctive (see Wagner 1939:10). Berceo's use (attested only once; Alvarez Alvarez 1990:71) of preterite *andido* 'he went' vs. imperfect subjunctive *andasse* seems to be an exception that proves the rule in old Spanish. For French, Ekblom (1908:107) says H. Etienne *preferred* preterite *je lisi* 'I read' but imperfect subjunctive *je leusse*. Fouché (1967:348, 351) declares that it seems, according to a study by E. Dietz, that the type *fisse* 'I did' arose in imperfect subjunctives slightly earlier (early fourteenth century) than the preterite type *(tu) fis*, and that *venisse* 'I came' [beside *vins*] survived into the sixteenth century. Wahlgren (1920:218) says that in *vouloir* 'to want' the replacement of PYTA imperfect subjunctive was 'a little late' compared with the preterite (see also Nyrop 1960, II:149). In the Occitan of Gap, Ronjat (1937, 3:285) cites as preterites of the verb 'be' both *siguèrou* and *fouguèrou*, but the imperfect subjunctive is only given as *fóussi*. In Médoc (p. 284) we have preterite *fóuri* etc., but already see in the imperfect subjunctive *fouguèssi* alongside *foussi*. Béarnais (p. 294) has *aboui aboussi* 'have' but also, optionally, *oussi* when the verb is used as an auxiliary (but a preterite auxiliary is, as in French, very rare, and its equivalent may simply not have been recorded). A perhaps more serious counterexample is Ronjat's observation (p. 301) that in some varieties the preterite of the verb 'do', apparently homophonous with the present, has been 'almost completely' evicted by a form based on the non-PYTA root, while the imperfect subjunctive retains PYTA. In Béarnais, the older preterite of 'be' is stated (p. 289) to have been 'almost completely evicted' by a different root, whereas in the imperfect subjunctive the old PYTA root is 'not rare' alongside the innovating form. In both cases, however, the discrepancy is explicitly stated not to be absolute. In the Italo-Romance dialect of San Leucio del Sannio (Iannace 1983:78), 'be' displays a curious discrepancy between the preterite and the imperfect subjunctive: in the former it is *fugn-*, in the latter *foss-*. The source of the root-final *gn* ([ɲ]) in the preterite is obscure, but we should not exclude the possibility that it is a phonological linking element between the root *fu-* and the preterite inflection *-ietti*, etc. In any case, 'be' appears to be the *only* verb in this dialect which retains a preterite form. Three seemingly more serious classes of counterexample are constituted by Italian, Aromanian and Aragonese, all of which have a PYTA root in the preterite, but not in the other formerly perfective tense-forms. In fact, Italian is not a counterexample at all, and as for Aromanian, there are two possible lines of explanation compatible with coherence. Aragonese is, however, more problematic.

Italian has (3SG) preterite *fece* 'did', *disse* 'said', *cosse* 'baked', *crebbe* 'grew', *prese* 'took', *volle* 'wanted', *cadde* 'fell', *ruppe* 'broke', etc. vs. (3SG) imperfect subjunctive *facesse, dicesse, cuocesse, crescesse, prendesse, volesse, cadesse, rompesse*, etc. A different picture emerges, however, if we consider *essere* 'be' (21):

(21) Preterite Imperfect subjunctive Old conditional

Preterite	Imperfect subjunctive	Old conditional
fui	*fossi*	*fora*
fosti	*fossi*	
fu	*fosse*	*fora*
fummo	*fossimo*	
foste	*foste*	
furono	*fossero*	*forano*

Here, the *fu-/fo-* PYTA root occurs throughout the preterite and the imperfect subjunctive, and also appears in what is, in Italian, the sole (and archaic) remnant of the Latin pluperfect FUERAM, etc. The significant fact is that in this verb, and here alone, the PYTA root is always stressed. In medieval southern Italian dialects, the conditionals which continued the Latin pluperfect indicative had a stressed PYTA root (e.g., *fécera, vóllera, ábbera*), but in the modern dialects stress has shifted onto the ending. As the following examples from Veroli (Lazio) show, the PYTA root has disappeared (22):

(22) Preterite (1SG)   Conditional

Preterite (1SG)		Conditional
ˈdissi/diˈtʃii 'said'		diˈtʃɛra
ˈkosi/kuˈʎivi [*sic*] 'gathered'		kuˈʎɛra
ˈmɔrtsi/muˈrii 'died'		muˈrɛra
ˈputti/puˈtii 'could'		puˈtɛra
ˈʃoṵsi/ʃuˈʎii 'loosened'		ʃuˈʎɛra
ˈtinni/təˈnii 'held'		təˈnɛra
ˈviddi/vəˈdii 'saw'		vəˈdɛra
ˈvɔsi/vuˈlii 'wanted'		vuˈlɛra

We see that the preterite, too, has an unstressed variant and, when it is unstressed, the PYTA root is absent. Therein lies the explanation for the general Italo-Romance distinction between preterites with PYTA root and imperfect subjunctives without it (see Maiden (2000b) for a fuller account, and critique of earlier explanations): PYTA was reanalysed as an *inherently stressed* alternant, a fact which is apparent within the paradigm of the preterite itself, for in the second person singular, first person plural and second person plural, which are arrhizotonic, the non-PYTA root appears (e.g., Italian *féci facésti féce facémmo facéste fécero*). The dependency of PYTA on stress is further confirmed by the fact that in those southern dialects where the first person plural of the preterite happens to be rhizotonic (falls on the lexical root), it duly displays PYTA (e.g., ˈfetʃimo, ˈebbimo). The significance of the reanalysis of PYTA as a stressed alternant will be addressed further below. It is noteworthy that occasional analogical extension of PYTA roots into the past participle in Italo-Romance occurs only in those cases where the past participle has, exceptionally, an unstressed inflectional ending and therefore a stressed root: e.g., ONap. *vìppeto* 'drunk', *chiuòppeto* 'rained', *muòppeto* 'moved', *muòsseto* (also *muòsso, muovùto*) 'moved', *cùrzeto* (also *cùrzo, corrùto*) 'run'; see Ledgeway (2009). Italo-Romance is not, then, an exception to the coherence principle.

In Aromanian the PYTA root is present in the preterite but unexpectedly absent from the conditional, a form which appears to continue the Latin perfect subjunctive and/or future perfect. Various scholars have tacitly presupposed the principle of coherence by arguing that if the PYTA root is lacking in the conditional, then this must be because the conditional actually continues a non-perfective form, namely the Latin imperfect subjunctive (see Capidan 1932:473; Papahagi 1974:67; Ivănescu 1980:160). But there are grounds for scepticism about this account, since there are no other traces of the Latin imperfect subjunctive in Daco-Romance, and since the inflectional system of the Aromanian conditional displays a classic Daco-Romance characteristic of originally *perfective* forms (see Maiden 2009), namely the second person plural in *-t(u)* rather than *-ţ(i)*. Yet there is another line of explanation. It is striking that in Aromanian the PYTA root now only occurs before unstressed desinences. In the second person singular preterite, whose ending is stressed in all other Daco-Romance varieties, the PYTA root survives, but the stress has been moved onto the root. It is far from impossible (see Maiden (2004c) for further exemplification) that, as in Italo-Romance and as in some western Ibero-Romance dialects, the PYTA root has been hypercharacterized as selecting an unstressed ending. If so, the absence of the root from the conditional, whose endings are always stressed, falls out naturally, leaving the principle of coherence intact.

Certain Aragonese dialects have PYTA roots in the preterite, but not in the imperfect subjunctives. Or rather, the PYTA root *does* occur in the imperfect subjunctives, but only when these forms display the thematic vowel [je] (in the same dialects the PYTA root also turns up in the *gerund,*

189

if the gerund has thematic vowel [je]). Thus Panticosa (Nagore Lain 1986) (23):

(23) Preterite 1SG   Imperfect subjunctive 1SG
   estube   *estase*
   pude or *pudié*   *podese*
   quisié   *querese*
   supe   *sapese* or *supiese*
   tube   *tenese*
   binié   *benise* or *biniese*

Maiden (2001a) seeks to reconcile these facts with the general principle of coherence in the following way. Since there is nothing in the phonological system of Aragonese that could account in purely phonological terms for the appearance of the disparate set of PYTA alternants precisely before [je], we have an essentially morphological reanalysis of the original distribution, such that the PYTA root has been correlated with (no less arbitrary) 'preterite + forms in thematic [je]', resulting in extension of the PYTA roots into gerunds with [je], but also in loss of the PYTA root wherever [je] was not present. The difficulty[52] with Maiden's earlier account, however, is the probability that what we have here is not a matter of diachronic changes internal to Aragonese, but simply dialect-mixing, the imperfect subjunctive forms with PYTA roots and thematic [je] being *loans* from Castilian. The history of the Aragonese data clearly needs more extensive historical investigation. In the meantime, I take the position that it may constitute a real counterexample to the coherence of the PYTA root. If it does, it stands out precisely by being so rare. It bears repetition that over the vast majority of Romance languages there is remarkable coherence in the diachronic behaviour of the roots inherited from the Latin perfective, despite the collapse of their original functional underpinning.

Convergence of the PYTA roots towards a common phonological content is an essentially interparadigmatic phenomenon, in that the originally disparate PYTA roots of different verbs come to assume a common shape (mostly in respect of the root vowel). It is sometimes the case that one lexical verb provides the model on which other PYTA roots converge, but it is important to stress at the outset that such analogical coalescence, unless otherwise specified below, is always confined just to PYTA roots: the relevant 'leading verb' does not exercise analogical influence on other parts of the paradigm.

In modern Castilian (with some parallels in Portuguese),[53] all PYTA roots have acquired a high vowel. The sole exception is *traer* 'bring', whose

PYTA root *traj-* in fact appears as *truj-*, with a high vowel, in many Spanish dialects (see Malkiel 1983a). The spread of the metaphonic vowels [i] and [u] from the first person singular (however motivated)[54] tends to reduce further the range of root vowels. Such formal convergence goes even further in Spanish, where the [o] once characteristic of the series *ove* 'I had', *sope* 'I knew', *tove* 'I held' is completely replaced by [u]. In Portuguese, the reduction in the range of vowels is less extreme: verbs with *ou* remain unaffected (*ouve, soube,* etc.), but those originally having [e] and [o] have replaced these with [i] and [u]: *fiz fizeste fez fizemos fizestes fizeram; fizera* etc., *fizesse* etc., *fizer* etc.; *quis quiseste quis quisemos quisestes quiseram; quisera* etc., *quisesse* etc., *quiser* etc.; *tive* 'had' *tiveste teve tivemos tivestes tiveram; tivera* etc., *tivesse* etc., *tiver* etc.; *vim* 'came' *vieste veio viemos viestes vieram; viera* etc.; *viesse* etc., *vier* etc.; *pude* 'was able' *pudeste pôde pudemos pudestes puderam; pudera* etc., *pudesse* etc., *puder* etc.; *pus puseste pôs pusemos pusestes puseram; pusera* etc., *pusesse* etc., *puser* etc.

In medieval Portuguese, [i] had already spread throughout the PYTA root in *querer* but, otherwise, metaphonic [i] and [u] alternants were restricted to the first person singular, and it is widely accepted[55] that this metaphonic vowel was analogically propagated to the whole PYTA root. The sporadic resistance of the third person singular preterite is perhaps due to the particularly high frequency of this form. The spread of [i] and [u] may also have been determined by the fact that while there were no PYTA roots characterized exclusively by [e] or [o], there were some, like *adusse* 'brought' *adusse adusseste... adussesse,* etc., and *disse* 'said' *disseste ... dissesse,* etc., which had [i] and [u] throughout.

The same mechanism apparently operated in Spanish, although we cannot assume that the Spanish and Portuguese developments have a common historical origin, and there is a major difference in that in Portuguese the spread of [u] is restricted to verbs which originally had a metaphonized first person singular preterite (i.e., produced by regular assimilatory raising triggered by the inflection -i), whilst in Castilian PYTA roots in [o] (derived from *[au̯] and therefore exempt from meta-phony in the first person singular) also acquire [u] throughout. Some possible examples of generalization of [u] to PYTA roots in [o] occur (assuming that we can exclude later scribal influence) as early as Berceo and the Arcipreste de Hita (see Fouché 1929:82), but replacement of [o] is not complete until the sixteenth century. As for propagation of [i], Menéndez Pidal (1958:§120) states that *fezo, fezimos,* etc. persisted alongside *fizo, ficimos,* etc. into the late fifteenth century. In the thirteenth-century Aragonese *Flores de las leyes,* surveyed by Hanssen (1898:18), we find a stage where [i] and [u] have apparently spread throughout verbs which had metaphonic [i] and [u] in the first person singular (e.g., *pudo pudiere pudiesse*, etc.; *puso pusiestes pusiere*, etc.), but [u] has not spread to verbs in [o] < *[au̯] (e.g., *ovo* 'had' *oviere oviessemos*, etc.). In modern Aragonese, propagation of [u] seems complete.

The reasons for replacement of [o] by [u] in verbs in which there was no metaphonic vowel are unclear. Some invoke the analogical influence of verbs such as *poder* 'be able' or *poner* 'put' which had already generalized [u] in the PYTA root.[56] In this case, one is struck by the fact that the association between the PYTA root and high vowels had become strong enough to make all deviant verbs conform to the pattern. Others (e.g., Baist 1888:713; Hanssen 1898:32; Fouché 1929:70) invoke a specifically Castilian phenomenon of raising of unstressed vowels before [je] (which characterized the inflectional endings of non-present subjunctives and, in many varieties, all plural forms of the preterite). But in Castilian such raising systematically affected only the fourth conjugation, not the second (thus *durmieron* 'they slept' *durmiese*, etc., but *comieron* 'they ate' *comiese*, etc.), and since virtually all verbs with PYTA roots belong to the second conjugation, their apparent susceptibility to raising obliges us to say either (and arbitrarily) that PYTA roots 'belong to the fourth conjugation' or that they constitute a kind of 'conjugation class in their own right'. However that may be,[57] their differential susceptibility to raising would identify the verb-forms containing PYTA roots as an autonomous morphological class to which phonological change was differentially sensitive. One must disagree with Lloyd (1987:366) when he says that the spread of the high vowels[58] serves to contrast more clearly the difference between the perfective and imperfective aspects in the past, for the high vowels equally occur in the non-perfective non-present subjunctives. Yet the notion that the distinctive root might come to characterize all and only the preterite forms has, a priori, a certain plausibility, at least if we accept Bybee's view (1985) that aspect is highly 'relevant' to the verb and therefore highly likely to involve root-allomorphy. So having a distinctive preterite root is not only logically possible but arguably highly 'natural'. Yet speakers never exploit this possibility, and analogical change concerns not the morphosyntactic category of aspect, but the arbitrarily distributed PYTA root.

As early as in pre-literary Castilian an apparently counter-etymological vowel [o] and/or root-final consonant [v] appeared in the PYTA root instead of expected [e] + consonant: e.g., 1SG TENUI > *tove* 'held', *STETUI > *estove* 'stood', SEDUI > *sove* 'sat', CREUI > *crove* 'grew', CREDIDI > *crove* 'believed'. In dialects where the root is *tev-* and *estev-*, the root-final consonant alone has been analogically influenced. Hanssen (1898:29f.), Menéndez Pidal (1958:§120), Lloyd (1987:304) and Penny (2002:225) attribute these facts to the analogical influence of the PYTA root of *haber*, namely *ove* < HABUI, where the vowel [o] is uncontroversially the result of anticipation of the glide [w] in the preceding syllable, followed by mono-phthongization of the resulting diphthong; the same process is at work in SAPUI > *ˈsapwi > *ˈsau̯pi > *sope* 'I knew' and *ˈkapwi > *ˈkau̯pi > *cope* 'I fitted'. The influence of *ove* on *tove* might be ascribed (with Rini 1999:62f.) to their similarity of meaning (*tener* replaces *haber* as the lexical verb 'have'), but it is not clear that at the relevant stage in the history of Spanish *haber* and *tener* were significantly closer in meaning than are *avoir* and *tenir* in modern French. The rise of *estove* (in place of *estide*) is attributed by Rini to the influence of *ove*, again because they are both auxiliary verbs (but of very different kinds – this argument would be better supported if there were evidence for such analogical influence only in auxiliary uses of these verbs). It may be that, in turn, *seer* acquired *sove* because of a semantic similarity to *estar* ('sit' and 'stand'), and that *creer* got *crove* on the basis of structural similarity to *seer* (*crove* 'grew' from *creşçer* and *atrove* 'dared' from *atrever* are more problematic), but the salient and striking point remains that these formal convergences operate purely and exclusively in respect of PYTA roots. In OPortuguese there is clear evidence (Huber 1986:246; but see Malkiel 1983a:117, n93, 94) of analogical influence of *ouve* on other PYTAs, such as *jouve* 'lay' (< IACUI), *prouve* 'pleased' (< PLACUIT), *trouve* 'brought' (< TRAXI) (see also Malkiel 1983a:119).

Menéndez Pidal (1958:§120) attributes preterite forms such as *estude* and *andude* (also *tudiere* implying *?tude*) to the analogical influence of *pude* (the preterite form of *poder* 'be able'), a view shared by Lathrop (1980). *Estude* replaces earlier *estide*, whose high vowel is itself a substitute for expected *estiede* (< STETUI). The question why *pude* etc., should have imposed its vowel, and even its root-final consonant, on verbs such as *estar* 'be, stand' and *tener* 'hold' is, it must be said, obscure. It may simply be that the gradual replacement of the root-vowel [o] by [u] in this, after all very frequent, verb, established a model ('[o] tends to be replaced by [u] in the PYTA root'), such that other PYTA roots containing [o] followed suit. The model of verbs such as *venir* 'come', *hacer* 'do', *prender* 'take' in which a high vowel [i] had been generalized at an earlier date (e.g., *vino*, *hizo*, *priso*), may also have played a role. Some scholars have even invoked a 'socio-cultural preference for high vowels' (see Bustos Gisbert 1992:153f.). Attempts to find a semantic/functional motivation do not seem to me especially convincing. Rini's speculation (1999:62–66) that *poder* influences *estar* because they are both auxiliary verbs does not give due weight to the fact that they are auxiliary verbs of very different kinds occurring in different syntactic constructions (*poder* is really 'modal'), and that *estar* is not always an auxiliary. Rini proposes that *estove* (and *andove*) were blended with earlier *estude* and *andude*, to yield *estuve* and *anduve*, which in turn exerted pressure on *ove* to give *uve*. The form of *aver* then influenced *saber* 'to know' and *caber* 'to fit' because of 'structural similarities' (although how great these might have been before the merger of [b] and [v] is questionable). The majority [u] pattern thus established was then extended to other verbs.

There is also a chronological problem. According to Bustos Gisbert (1992), the extension of metaphonic [u] from the first person singular preterite is already general in mid fourteenth-century Alfonsine texts for *poner* 'to put' and *poder*, with the latter tending to lag behind somewhat in the arrhizotonic forms. Generalization of [u] into verbs in [o] and originally without metaphony is of later date (late fifteenth to mid sixteenth century; see Bustos Gisbert 1992:140–44), but seems to strike first and with most consistency in *plazer* 'please' (*plugo*). The earliest signs of extension into non-metaphonizing verbs in [o] affects stressed and unstressed forms indifferently (Bustos Gisbert 1992:143). Most strikingly, *haber* does not figure among the first verbs to be affected by [u] – in fact Bustos Gisbert shows that it brings up the rear. Nebrija systematically uses [u] in this group of verbs, with the signal exception of *haber*, for which both [o] and [u] appear, not only in Nebrija's own narrative, but even in expounding the paradigm of this verb.[59]

There is further evidence of convergence, in respect of the root-final *consonant*. Malkiel (1960) analyses the anomalous retention in OCastilian of intervocalic [d] in the preterite (and non-present subjunctive) of *ver* 'to see' (*vido vidiese*, etc.), which reflects the fortuitous fact that virtually all other preterite roots (and hence PYTA roots) end in a consonant, a pattern which would have been violated had intervocalic [d] been deleted. This implies that speakers postulated a root-final consonant as characteristic of PYTA roots, and, at least for a time this /d/ (it survives in Judeo-Spanish, some European dialects and throughout the Americas; see Espinosa 1946:302f.), resisted a sound change liable to violate that characteristic. Another phenomenon sometimes observed in OCastilian and preserved in some western Ibero-Romance (see Fouché 1929:71f.; Munthe 1887 = 1987:50f.) varieties is the substitution of [ʃ] (or [ʒ]) for [s] throughout the PYTA root. Old Castilian shows *cinxe, tinxe, raxe, rixe, tanxe, rixe, fuxe* for (regular, and sometimes attested) *cinse, tinse*, etc. In the dialect of Candamo (Díaz González 1979:70)

quixi 'wanted' … *quixera* …, *punxi* 'put' … *punxera* …, *fixi* 'did' … *fixera* …;
and in Alto Aller (Rodríguez Castellano 1951:147, 158f.): ˈpwenʃi, etc., ˈkiʃi,
etc., ˈfiʃi, etc. The source of [ʃ] is probably verbs originally in x (DIXIT > ˈdiʃe,
etc.). In OPortuguese, 'g' or 'x' spellings (representing a palatal) seem limited
to first person singular preterite forms (*fix fige; quix quige, maji* 'stayed' *magi*),
and Huber (1986:94) suggests that [ʃ] was the outcome of x only before
1SG -i (DIXI > *ˈdiksi > *dixe*, DIXIT > *ˈdikse > *disse*). If [ʃ] indeed originates
just in the 1SG preterite, its subsequent spread was a phenomenon exactly
like the extension of the metaphonic vowel, as described above. A further
example of analogical effects in root-final consonants are OCastilian *nasco*
'was born' and *visco* 'lived' (also sometimes *trasco* 'brought'), although the
direction of the analogy is debated; see, for example, Baist (1888:714);
Fouché (1929:84); Malkiel (1983a:111–13). It is noteworthy that all
PYTA roots which did not end in a single consonant have fallen out of use
since the Middle Ages, so that virtually all modern PYTA roots end in just
one consonant.

In Portuguese, convergence is also manifested in the vowel immediately
following the PYTA root. The normal endings of the second conjugation
preterite are: -ˈi, -ˈistə, -ˈeu, -ˈemus, -ˈestəs, -ˈerã. Their origin is problematic,
but broadly speaking it seems (see Williams 1962:194–96) they originate in
Latin verbs which were compounds of DARE (such as UENDO 'I sell' PERF
UENDIDI, cf. DO 'I give' DEDI). Shift of stress onto the second syllable,
regular opening of short i to [e], and various metaphonic effects produced
by a following -i, gave rise to the modern set of endings (e.g., UÉNDIDI >
*venˈde[d]i > *vendi*). The same vowel appears in the non-present
subjunctives: *beb*[e]*sse*, *beb*[e]*ra*, *beb*[e]*r*, etc. However, second conjugation
verbs with a PYTA root have the endings -[ə], -ˈistə (older and
dialectal -ˈestə), -[ə], -ˈɛmus, -ˈɛstəs, -ˈɛrã, with open [ɛ] rather than [e], and the
same vowel appears in the non-present subjunctives (e.g., *soub*[ɛ]*ra*, *soub*[ɛ]*sse*,
soub[ɛ]*r*). The most likely source for this development is the verb *dar* 'to give'
(see Gaßner 1908:418; Craddock 1983): Lat. DÉDI DEDÍSTI DÉDIT DÉDIMUS
DEDÍSTIS DÉDERUNT, with short E, regularly developed to [ɛ], whence *d*[ɛ]*i*, *d*
[ɛ]*mos*, etc., *d*[ɛ]*ra*, *d*[ɛ]*r* and also *d*[ɛ]*sse*, where [ɛ] is analogical. This, too, can
be viewed as a kind of 'convergence', for the analogical influence of *dar* seems to
have operated in such a way as to confer a unique and characteristic pattern on
PYTA roots, such that they are all marked by a distinctive thematic vowel.
A similar tendency is observable in OLeonese (Egido Fernández 1996:410).

The earliest French texts already attest to various convergences among
PYTA roots. A number of them converge on counter-etymological root-
final *s* [z], apparently attributable to the model of *mis mesist; mesisse* … 'put'

etc., and/or *pris presist*; *presisse* 'take' etc. (< MISI, MISISTI …; *ˈpresi *preˈsesti). From FECI, FECISTI, etc., one would expect (see Fouché 1967:276) *fiz *feisis (cf. PLACERE > *pleisir*), not *fis fesis*; *fesisse* (note that the root vowel is also analogically extended). From DIXI, etc. one should expect a unstressed root *deis-*, with voiceless [s] (Fouché 1967:287), yet we have *dis, desis*; *desisse*, etc., with voiced [z]; likewise *escresis* for expected *escressis* from SCRIPSISTI. Central varieties of OFrench, from the earliest records have *oi eus*; *eusse* 'have', *soi seu*; *seusse* 'know', *conui coneus*; *coneusse* 'know', *mui meus*; *meusse* 'move', etc. (< COGNOUI, COGNOUISTI; COGNOUISSEM, MOUI, MOUISTI; MOUISSEM) with a counter-etymological pretonic *e* ([ə]), instead of the expected regular *o*. These PYTA roots were either modelled on the type *deus, deusse*, etc., where *e* is the historically regular reflex of unstressed [e], or reflect the influence of the past participle *eu(t)* on the PYTA of *avoir*, creating a model which subsequently spread to other verbs (see Fouché 1967:317).

Towards the end of the twelfth century, many PYTA roots take on the root structure of *veoir* 'see' (see Fouché 1967:277; Pope 1952:377; Zink 1989:195), so that *mesis fesis*, etc. become *mëis fëis*, and later *mis fis* (24).

(24) Old French   Modern French

preterite	imperfect subjunctive	preterite	imperfect subjunctive
vi	*vëisse*	*vis*	*visse*
vëis	*vëisses*	*vis*	*visses*
vit	*vëist*	*vit*	*vît*
vëimes	*vëissiens*	*vîmes*	*vissions*
vëistes	*vëissiez*	*vîtes*	*vissiez*
virent	*vëissent*	*virent*	*vissent*
mis	*me(s)isse*	*mis*	*misse*
me(s)is	*me(s)isses*	*mis*	*misses*
mist	*me(s)ist*	*mit*	*mît*
me(s)imes	*me(s)issiens*	*mîmes*	*missions*
me(s)istes	*me(s)issiez*	*mîtes*	*missiez*
mistrent	*me(s)issent*	*mirent*	*missent*
fis	*fe(s)isse*	*fis*	*fisse*
fe(s)is	*fe(s)isses*	*fis*	*fisses*
fist	*fe(s)ist*	*fit*	*fît*
fe(s)imes	*fe(s)issiens*	*fîmes*	*fissions*
fe(s)istes	*fe(s)issiez*	*fîtes*	*fissiez*
fistrent	*fe(s)issent*	*firent*	*fissent*

It is difficult to say why, at a given point in history, a particular verb or cluster of verbs provide a model for the reformation of other PYTA roots. But the salient point is that this happens, and that the analogical attraction is restricted to PYTA. We do not find, for example, the past participle of *veoir* (*veu*) acting on that of *metre* (*mis*) to yield **meu, or the present *voit* transforming *met* into **moit. In fact, the analogy may be of a rather more abstract nature. Rather as Spanish showed signs of convergence on a (C)VC structure for PYTA roots, so French may have tended towards a (C)V structure, prompted by the fact that not only *veoir*, but also verbs like *avoir* (*oi, eus*; *eusse*, etc.), *savoir* (*soi, seus*; *seusse*, etc.), *être* (*fui, fus*; *fusse*, etc.) had such a root structure.

This discussion by no means exhausts the examples of convergence observable in the history of French. For example, alongside *pris presis*; *presisse*, etc. there emerged an alternative form *prins prenis*; *prenisse*, etc., modelled on *tenir*. As Fouché (1967:280) indicates, this may be partly due to the resemblance in the present tense between first and second persons plural *tenons tenez* and *prenons prenez*; but the analogical innovation is singularly limited to PYTA roots (we do not get an infinitive **prenir or a past participle **prenu). Similarly, Fouché (1967:301f.) observes that the verbs *seoir* 'sit' and *cheoir* 'fall' influenced the preterite of *gésir* 'lie', allegedly, in this case, because of a semantic resemblance – but the analogy only operates on PYTA roots.

Paradigmatic convergence effects are also apparent in the Italo-Romance and Romanian domains. In Romanian (Şiadbei 1930 and Frâncu 1980 offer useful overviews) there is a tendency to generalize a root-final [s] as characteristic of PYTA roots. In fact, modern Daco-Romanian has few PYTA roots that do not end in [s] (see Rothe 1957:103f.), usually because original non-sigmatic roots have been analogically replaced by a non-PYTA root (e.g., *fece* > *făcu* 'did'), while original non-sigmatic PYTA roots acquired [s] analogically (e.g., *rupe* > *rupse* 'broke'). Latin perfective roots in -x regularly yielded -[ps] in Romanian (e.g., COXIT > *coapse* 'baked', FRIXIT > *fripse* 'burned'), and there is some evidence for occasional convergence on this model (e.g., *fece* > *fepse*; Densusianu 1938:157). But there are far more cases of [s] appearing in place of expected [ps]. Compare Daco-Romanian DIXIT > *zise* 'said', DUXIT > *duse* 'brought', INTELLEXIT > *înţelese* 'understood', TRAXIT > *trase* 'pulled' with Aromanian *zipse, dupse, trapse*. Similar developments in Megleno-Romanian (Capidan 1925:166) seem to have been a little less far-reaching (INTELLEXIT > *anţilepsi*). Megleno-Romanian also has sigmatic *feasi*, etc. (Capidan 1925:131f., 166) alongside expected *feaţi*, etc.

At first sight, there is also relatively little sign of convergence in Italo-Romance PYTAs, although Magni (2001) has argued that the high incidence of root-final long consonants in Italian PYTAs (e.g., venni, mossi, caddi, etc.), usually attributed to purely phonological lengthening effects, may be what I would term 'convergence', involving attribution of a characteristic phonological shape to the root. As in Romanian, there has been generalization of root-final [(s)s] (e.g., It. 1SG *corsi* 'ran', *valsi* 'was worth', *presi* 'took', *risposi* 'replied'; cf. Lat. CUCURRI, UALUI, PREHENDI, RESPONDI) whose chronology is, however, difficult to determine. Almost certainly of more recent date are Sicilian forms (see Leone 1980:108f.) such as ˈkritti 'believed', ˈvitti 'saw' apparently remodelled on the type ˈpotti 'could'; ˈkjoppi 'rained', ˈvippi 'drank' and ˈippi 'had' formed on ˈsippi 'knew'; ˈkrissi 'believed' (in Buccheri; Mocciaro 1976:283) formed on ˈdissi; ˈvosi 'wanted', ˈdesi 'gave', ˈstesi 'stood' on ˈprisi. Similarly, It. *conobbi* 'knew', *crebbi* 'grew' are apparently influenced by *ebbi* 'had' (COGNOUI and CREUI should have given *conove and *creve); an even more extreme case is Corsican *pòbbe* 'was able'. Rohlfs (1968:326) documents further possible examples of analogical influence among PYTA roots. The non-etymological [e] which appears in It. *ebbi* (HABUI) and *seppi* (SAPUI) is most likely due to the influence of *stetti* 'stood', *detti* 'gave', *feci* 'did' – but these verbs also show mutual analogical influence in the present tense, so the convergence is here not strictly peculiar to the PYTA root.

The major type of convergence in Italo-Romance is not paradigmatic but syntagmatic. As we have already established, Italo-Romance PYTA roots became restricted to stressed positions only, and the association of PYTA roots with stress may be seen as a kind of hypercharacterization of the roots in terms of a characteristic feature to which I have so far alluded very little. All PYTA roots are associated, in all Romance languages, with unstressed inflections. In the typical case, the unstressed inflection occurs in the first person singular and third person singular preterite: Lat. DÍXI DIXÍSTI DÍXIT 'I/you/he said', FÉCI FECÍSTI FÉCIT 'I/you/he did', etc. > Sp. *díje dijíste dijo, híce hicíste hízo*; It. *díssi dicésti dísse, féci facésti féce*; ORo. *zísu ziséși zíse, féciu fecéși féce*. Most Romance varieties (not Ibero-Romance) have root-stress in the third person plural preterite too (see Ernout (1927:338f.) and Sihler (1995:589f.) for stress in the Latin third person plural preterite): DÍXERUNT, FÉCERUNT > It. *díssero, fécero*, ORo. *zíseră, féceră*. Some southern Italian varieties, with Romanian, also retain Latin rhizotonic stress in the first person plural (abandoned in most Romance varieties for arrhizotonic stress): Lat. DÍXIMUS, FÉCIMUS > SItaly ˈdissimo, ˈfetʃimo, ORo. *zísemu, fécemu*. Finally, Latin pluperfect indicatives containing perfective roots were also rhizotonic, and this stress pattern survived in the medieval Italian (and Gallo-Romance) conditionals derived from them (see Rohlfs 1968:346f.; Tekavčić 1980 II:315;

Maiden 2000b): Lat. DÍXERAM, FÉCERAM > *díssera, fécera*. Wherever PYTA roots do not appear, the endings are always stressed, and it is, to the best of my knowledge, a valid generalization about the Romance languages that, just as replacement of a PYTA by a non-PYTA root in one part of the paradigm implies its replacement everywhere else, so replacement of a PYTA by a non-PYTA root implies replacement of the unstressed inflections by stressed inflections. In other words, there are no cases in which the PYTA root disappears but the unstressed inflection remains. To those who would invoke supposed avoidance of potential homophonic clash with present tense-forms (cf. Sp. PRS.1SG *escribo* 'write' 3SG *escribe*, It. 2SG *scrivi* 'write' 3SG *scrive*) we can reply that, at least in Spanish, homophony has not obstructed the emergence of first person plural preterites such as *hablamos* 'we spoke' and *vivimos* 'we lived' identical to the present indicative, while in French *je finis tu finis il finit* 'I/you/he finishes', for example, can be either present or preterite. As for Italo-Romance, inflections such as unstressed 1PL *-imo*, 3PL *-ero* (and conditional *-era*) are distinct from all other inflectional endings, so that no risk of homophony appears – yet they are never preceded by a non-PYTA root. Maiden (2000b) suggests that the reason for the impossibility of non-PYTA root + unstressed ending may lie in a universal principle (the so-called 'No Blur Principle'; elaborated by Carstairs-McCarthy 1994; also Cameron-Faulkner and Carstairs-McCarthy 2000), disfavouring absolute synonymy among inflectional affixes. Indeed, there is apparently no case in Romance of non-optional, perfectly synonymous, inflection desinences in the verb. Now, if a non-PYTA root appeared before a stressless suffix, this principle would be violated, since it would then be the case that some verbs had in the preterite (and conditional) the unstressed endings, and others had stressed endings, without any functional differences between the rival sets of endings. One might imagine, that is, that Italian could have **scrívi scrivésti** **scríve scrivémmo** (or **scrívimo** in the relevant dialects) scrivéste **scrívero** 'write' but *ricevéi ricevésti ricevé ricevémmo ricevéste ricevérono* 'receive', showing the complete set of stressed preterite endings. In other words, the distribution of the inflectional endings of the first person singular, third person singular, (first person plural) and third person plural would be lexically unpredictable, and two perfectly synonymous suffixes would coexist, non-optionally, in the grammar. One of Carstairs-McCarthy's major insights is that autonomously morphological entities can function as the 'signata' of inflectional endings, and in our Romance case the PYTA root can be seen as serving as the 'signatum' of the unstressed desinences, the differentiatory factor which allows both *'-i '-e '-ero* and *-éi -é -érono* to coexist in Italian grammar (and, *mutatis mutandis*, in other Romance varieties). What Italo-Romance varieties have done, however, is to hypercharacterize this interdependency by making the unstressed desinence a unique defining characteristic of PYTA roots: 'no PYTA root without unstressed desinence, and no unstressed desinence without PYTA root'. Where other Romance varieties have tended to make PYTA roots converge paradigmatically, on a particular phonological shape within the root, Italo-Romance has made it converge syntagmatically – on a particular type of desinence. But everywhere there is convergence.

It is widely believed (e.g., Buchholtz 1889:134; Tekavčić 1980:298) that the Italian pattern, with PYTA roots restricted to rhizotones, is a unique distinguishing feature of Italo-Romance.[60] This is untrue, for in some dialects of north-western Spain a tendency to identify PYTA roots with atonic desinences also appears. Thus from the Montes de Pas (Penny 1969:132) (25):

(25)

1SG	2SG	3SG	1PL	2PL	3PL
ˈdixə 'said'	(d)iˈθistə	ˈdixu	(d)iˈθimus	(d)iˈθistəs	(d)iˈθjeịn
ˈkisə 'wanted'	kiˈristə	ˈkisu	kiˈθimus	kiˈθistəs	kiˈθjeịn
ˈpusə 'put'	puˈnistə	ˈpusu	puˈnimus	puˈnistəs	puˈnjeịn
ˈiθə 'did'	aˈæistə	ˈeθu or ˈiθu	aˈθimus	aˈθistəs	aˈθjeịn
ˈsupə 'knew'	saˈβistə	ˈsupu	saˈβimus	saˈβistəs	saˈβjeịn

The situation is rather different from Italo-Romance, in that some of these verbs may also retain PYTA roots throughout the paradigm (as is normally the case in Ibero-Romance), e.g., (26):

(26)   ˈdixə   (d)iˈxistə   ˈdixu   (d)iˈximus   (d)iˈxistəs   (d)iˈxjeịn
      ˈkisə   kiˈsistə   ˈkisu   kiˈsimus   kiˈsistəs   kiˈsjeịn
      ˈsupə   suˈpistə   ˈsupu   suˈpimus   suˈpistəs   suˈpjeịn

But if a non-PYTA root is introduced, then stress always shifts onto the ending (27):

(27)   (d)iˈθi   (d)iˈθistə   (d)iˈθjo   (d)iˈθimus   (d)iˈθistəs   (d)iˈθjeịn
      kiˈri[61]   kiˈristə   kiˈrjo   kiˈrimus   kiˈristəs   kiˈrjeịn
      saˈβi   saˈβistə   saˈβjo[62]   saˈβimus   saˈβistəs   saˈβjeịn

The imperfect subjunctive (Penny 1969:136) seems to show the same state of flux: but being arrhizotonic throughout, tends to undergo elimination of PYTA roots.

The PYTA root, like the phonologically created phenomena discussed in chapter 5, constitutes one of the distinctive 'hallmarks' of Romance languages precisely by virtue of its inherent arbitrariness. In a sense, it is an 'empty shell', a mere remnant of a once functionally motivated morphological structure, yet loss of functional coherence, as well as inherited absence of phonological coherence, have not prevented the survival and replication of its distributional patterning within the inflectional paradigm.

4.2   Conjugation

Another feature of the morphological structure of the verb – already arbitrary in Latin, yet remarkably well preserved throughout Romance – is 'conjugational class'. Nearly all Latin verbs each belonged to one of four arbitrary inflectional classes. These were principally characterized, synchronically, by 'thematic' vowels, immediately following the lexical root and appearing in a heterogeneous array of 'cells' within the paradigm. [a] is characteristic of the first conjugation, [e] of the second and [i] of the fourth: all of these may be short or long according to their place in the paradigm. The third is characterized by short [i] and [e]: an automatic consequence of the shortness of these vowels, following general principles of Latin stress placement, is that in the third conjugation stress is rhizotonic in the infinitive, and in the first and second persons plural. In addition to appearing as an 'empty morph', following the root, conjugation also manifests itself in the identity of inflectional elements (for example, the present subjunctives in [e] in the first conjugation, as opposed to those in [a] in the remaining conjugations). Here are some examples from a fragment of the Latin verb system (28):

(28)

	First conjugation	Second conjugation	Third conjugation	Fourth conjugation
Infinitive	AMĀRE 'love'	UIDĒRE 'see'	LÉGERE 'read'	AUDĪRE 'hear'
Gerund	AMÁNDUM	UIDÉNDUM	LEGÉNDUM	AUDIÉNDUM
Past participle	AMĀTUS	UĪSUS	LÉCTUS	AUDĪTUS

	Present indicative			
1SG	ÁMŌ	UÍDEŌ	LÉGŌ	ÁUDIŌ
2SG	ÁMĀS	UÍDĒS	LÉGIS	ÁUDĪS

3SG	ÁMAT	UÍDET	LÉGIT	ÁUDIT
1PL	AMĀMUS	UIDĒMUS	LÉGIMUS	AUDĪMUS
2PL	AMĀTIS	UIDĒTIS	LÉGITIS	AUDĪTIS
3PL	ÁMANT	UÍDENT	LÉGUNT	ÁUDIUNT

Present subjunctive

1SG	ÁMEM	UÍDEAM	LÉGAM	ÁUDIAM
2SG	ÁMĒS	UÍDEĀS	LÉGĀS	ÁUDIĀS
3SG	ÁMET	UÍDEAT	LÉGAT	ÁUDIAT
1PL	AMĒMUS	UIDEĀMUS	LEGĀMUS	AUDIĀMUS
2PL	AMĒTIS	UIDEĀTIS	LEGĀTIS	AUDIĀTIS
3PL	ÁMENT	UÍDEANT	LÉGANT	ÁUDIANT

Imperfect indicative

1SG	AMĀBAM	UIDĒBAM	LEGĒBAM	AUDIĒBAM
2SG	AMĀBAS	UIDĒBĀS	LEGĒBĀS	AUDIĒBĀS
3SG	AMĀBAT	UIDĒBAT	LEGĒBAT	AUDIĒBAT
1PL	AMĀBĀMUS	UIDĒBĀMUS	LEGĒBĀMUS	AUDIĒBĀMUS
2PL	AMĀBĀTIS	UIDĒBĀTIS	LEGĒBĀTIS	AUDIĒBĀTIS
3PL	AMĀBANT	UIDĒBANT	LEGĒBANT	AUDIĒBANT

Italian, like most Romance languages, has remained strikingly faithful to such patterning (29):

(29)

	Infinitive	amáre	vedére	léggere	udíre
	Gerund	amándo	vedéndo	leggéndo	udéndo
	Past participle	amáto	vísto	létto	udíto

Present indicative

1SG		ámo	védo	léggo	ódo
2SG		ámi	védi	léggi	ódi
3SG		áma	véde	légge	óde
1PL		amiámo	vediámo	leggiámo	udiámo
2PL		amáte	vedéte	leggéte	udíte
3PL		áma no	védono	léggono	ódono

Present subjunctive

1SG		ámi	véda	légga	óda
2SG		ámi	véda	légga	óda
3SG		ámi	véda	légga	óda
1PL		amiámo	vediámo	leggiámo	udiámo
2PL		amiáte	vediáte	leggiáte	udiáte
3PL		ámino	védano	léggano	ódano

Imperfect indicative

1SG	*amávo*	*vedévo*	*leggévo*	*udívo*
2SG	*amávi*	*vedévi*	*leggévi*	*udívi*
3SG	*amáva*	*vedéva*	*leggéva*	*udíva*
1PL	*amavámo*	*vedevámo*	*leggevámo*	*udivámo*
2PL	*amaváte*	*vedeváte*	*leggeváte*	*udiváte*
3PL	*amávano*	*vedévano*	*leggévano*	*udívano*

That there is no inherent obstacle to the complete loss of conjugational distinctions[63] is suggested by the fact that neutralizations do occur, sporadically, in some 'cells' of the verb paradigms. But these developments are, precisely, sporadic. Most Romance languages distinguish conjugation in first and second persons plural present indicative (e.g., Spanish *llevamos, lleváis* 'carry.1/2PL'; *vendemos, vendéis* 'sell.1/2PL'; *dormimos, dormís* 'sleep.1/2PL'), but French neutralizes conjugation in both: *levons, levez* 'lift.1/2PL'; *vendons, vendez; dormons, dormez*, where *-ons* is possibly a reflex of the ending of Latin SUMUS 'we are', and *-ez* is an originally first conjugation ending (a similar pattern is observable in Piedmontese). Standard Italian neutralizes conjugation in the first person plural present indicative and subjunctive by generalizing the originally subjunctive ending *-iamo* (*leviamo, levate; vendiamo, vendete; dormiamo, dormite*). Franco-Provençal and Friulian varieties also neutralize first person plural present (but not second person plural), while Catalan, some Occitan varieties and some central Italian dialects neutralize conjugation in the present subjunctive, by generalizing the first conjugation present subjunctive endings to all verbs. Conjugational neutralization in the present subjunctive is also widespread in Romansh and Friulian. French imperfect indicative (but not imperfect subjunctive) forms have a common set of endings for all conjugations, originating in the Latin -EBA- class (see Lausberg 1976:§807): see It. *levava; vendeva; dormiva* vs. Fr. *levait; vendait; dormait*. For examples of total neutralization in Italo-Romance imperfect indicatives, see Rohlfs (1968:290). Gerunds are also a locus of neutralization of conjugational distinctions. Many Gallo-Romance varieties, for example French and Franco-Provençal (see Fouché 1967:234; Iliescu and Mourin 1991:233), have generalized the first conjugation endings to all four conjugations (e.g., *parlant* 'speak', *voulant* 'want', *prenant* 'take', *dormant* 'sleep'), a development paralleled in much of northern Italy (see Rohlfs 1968:366) and in some varieties of Romansh (see Lausberg 1976:§819). Many southern Italian dialects generalize non-first conjugation -ˈεndo to all conjugations (Rohlfs 1968:366); there is a similar development in Sassarese (Wagner 1939:152) and in Valais (see Bjerrome 1957:35, 89f.).

The task of illustrating the neutralizations of conjugational distinction which have occurred in the history of Romance far exceeds the scope of this study, which is in any case concerned with the *persistence* of morphological structures. Very little neutralization is due to phonological change, even though the disappearance of the distinction between Latin unstressed short ĭ and ĕ does efface conjugational distinctions in the singular forms of original non-first conjugation verbs.[64] A survey of Romance verb morphology suggests the following generalizations about resistance to the elimination of conjugational distinctions:

(i) No Romance language reduces the number of distinct conjugation classes to fewer than three.[65]

(ii) The infinitive is where all Romance languages continue to distinguish at least three conjugational classes, and in no part of the Romance verb paradigm is the number of conjugational distinctions ever greater than in the infinitive.

The major distinction between Latin second and third conjugations lay in the infinitives, and the first and second persons plural present.[66] Only Romanian (and some varieties of Friulian) retain this characteristic in the first and second persons plural present, e.g., from UIDĒRE 'to see', TRANSMÍTTERE 'to send' (30):

(30)

	Second conjugation	Third conjugation
Infinitive	*vedeá*	*trimíte*
1SG	*văd*	*trimít*
2SG	*vézi*	*trimíți*
3SG	*véde*	*trimíte*
1PL	*vedém*	*trimítem*
2PL	*vedéți*	*trimíteți*
3PL	*văd*	*trimít*

There are few vestiges of rhizotonic first and second persons plural forms elsewhere in Romance. OSpanish *femos feches* continued FÁCIMUS FÁCITIS 'we/you do' (cf. Fr. *faites*). Wagner (1939:142) mentions traces of rhizotonic first and second persons plural forms in Logudorese. But while arrhizotony has prevailed in the finite forms, most Romance languages retain it in third conjugation infinitives (cf. UÉNDERE 'sell' > Ro. *vínde*, It. *véndere*, Fr. *vendre* – likewise Romansh, Franco-Provençal, Catalan, Occitan). Some third conjugation verbs shifted into the second in Romance, yielding arrhizotonic infinitives (e.g., SÁPERE > sa'pere 'know',

CÁDERE > ka'dere 'fall');[67] in Portuguese and Spanish all original rhizotonic infinitives have shifted to the arrhizotonic pattern (*vendér*, etc.). In Sardinian the reverse has occurred, so that all second conjugation infinitives become rhizotonic on the model of the third (e.g., UIDÉRE > *bíere*; see Wagner 1939:137). In many other Romance varieties there is a sporadic tendency for arrhizotonic infinitives to become rhizotonic: e.g., Venetian *véder* 'see', *tázer* 'be quiet' from UIDÉRE, TACÉRE; Ro. *rămâne* 'stay', *ţíne* 'hold' and sometimes *záce* 'lie' for older *rămâneá*, *ţineá*, *zăceá*. In some areas this development may affect not only second conjugation verbs but also those fourth conjugation verbs whose present tense is inflectionally identical to the third conjugation present: thus Sicilian (Leone 1980:30) vud'diri or 'vuddiri 'boil' (3SG.PRS 'vuddi). Azaretti (1982:192) and Griva (1980:65) mention similar cases of attraction of second and fourth conjugation verbs to rhizotonic stress (with corresponding third conjugation endings) in infinitives in Ligurian and Piedmontese; also Iannace (1983:85) for Campania.

(iii) All Romance languages distinguish at least two conjugational classes in the past participle.

In the arrhizotonic past participles (those comprising root + stressed thematic element + participial ending), most Romance languages maintain a three-conjugational distinction. Portuguese and Spanish, together with some southern Italian varieties, Surselvan and Engadine, oppose first and non-first conjugation verbs only (31):

(31)

French	*levé*	*vendu*	*dormi*
Catalan	*llevat*	*venut*	*dormit*
Italian	*levato*	*venduto*	*dormito*
Romanian	*luat*	*vândut*	*dormit*
Portuguese	*levado*	*vendido*	*dormido*
Spanish	*llevado*	*vendido*	*dormido*

The past participles in -u- (-*uto*, -*udo*, -*ut*, -*u*, etc.) are a Romance innovation involving the generalization (see Laurent 1999:92–94), among second and third conjugation verbs, of a participial ending originally limited to a small number of third conjugation verbs whose lexical root ended in U (e.g., -ŪTUS), to other verbs such as TENERE 'to hold' TENTUM (> *te'nutu), HABERE 'to have' HABITUM (> *a'vutu) – thereby associating a novel thematic vowel with second and third conjugation verbs. In Spanish and Portuguese an original series in -*udo* has been supplanted by -*ido* (see Laurent 1999:305–9), with the result that arrhizotonic past participles belong either to the first conjugation or to the non-first conjugation. Some southern Italian varieties (see Ledgeway 2009; Laurent 1999:183–94) generalize *-utu to the arrhizotonic past participles of all non-first conjugation verbs. Most Latin third (and some second) conjugation verbs have rhizotonic past participles, where the rhizotony often coincided with various idiosyncratic forms of root-allomorphy, and Romance languages generally conserve some trace of these rhizotonic participles (see Laurent 1999:194–200): e.g., FACERE 'to do', past participle FACTUS > Pt. *feito*, Sp. *hecho*, Cat. *fet*, Fr. *fait*, It. *fatto*; SCRĪBERE 'to write', SCRĪPTUS > Pt., Sp. *escrito*, Cat. *escrit*, Fr. *écrit*, It. *scritto*, Ro. *scris*; RŬMPERE 'to break', RŬPTUS > Pt., Sp. *roto*, It. *rotto*, Ro. *rupt*; DĪCERE 'to say', DĬCTUS > Pt. *dito*, Sp. *dicho*, Cat. *dit*, Fr. *dit*, It. *detto*, Ro. *zis*; UIDĒRE 'to see', UĪSUS > Pt., Sp., It. *visto*, Cat. *vist*. Sardinian, in addition to conserving rhizotonic past participles in third conjugation verbs, also favours rhizotonic second conjugation past participles (just as it favours rhizotonic second conjugation infinitives), and has extended the rhizotonic type ending in -itu: e.g., 'timitu 'feared', 'appitu 'had'.

(iv) All other parts of the verb paradigm display complete neutralization of conjugational distinctions in at least one Romance variety.

In general, the distinction between first and non-first conjugation verbs survives in the third person singular present indicative (It. *parla* 'speaks', *deve* 'must', *vende* 'sells', *dorme* 'sleeps'; Fr. *parle*, *doit*, *vend*, *dort*; Ro. *cumpără* 'buys', *vede* 'sees', *vinde*, *doarme*, etc.), but even here there is sometimes neutralization (e.g., in Romansh, Cosentino) in favour of the first conjugation ending -a. The distinction between first conjugation subjunctives in -e and those of other conjugations in -a is also generally well maintained, but both Catalan and several Italo-Romance varieties generalize the first conjugation-marker to all present subjunctives (see Alcover and Moll 1929–33; Rohlfs 1968:296–98, 301). In the imperfect indicative (see below) nearly all varieties distinguish at least two conjugations, but French is unusual in extending the same set of (originally) second and third conjugation endings to all verbs. Again, in the arrhizotonic preterite, Romance varieties preserve at least two conjugational distinctions, but Franco-Provençal varieties (e.g., Vaux) have generalized the same set of (non-first conjugation) endings to all conjugations. Note also in popular French, where the preterite is in any case obsolescent, a tendency to similar conjugational neutralization: e.g., *il parlit* 'he spoke', as well as *il vendit* 'he sold', *il dormit* 'he slept'. In many Occitan varieties (Alibèrt 1976) the preterite and imperfect subjunctive have generalized a non-first conjugation ending.

(v) Where conjugational distinctions are partially neutralized, neutralization nearly always affects non-first conjugation verbs, so
that the distinction between first and non-first conjugations is
more resistant to neutralization than that between non-first conjugation verbs.

By far the commonest type of partial conjugational neutralization involves loss of distinction between non-first conjugation verbs, resulting in a binary opposition between first conjugation and non-first conjuga-tion. There are also a few cases in which the fourth conjugation remains distinct, and the others are neutralized. I am unaware of any neutralization affecting first and fourth, and leaving second and third conjugations distinct.

In the first and second persons plural present indicative, some varieties have a binary distinction between first conjugation and the rest (e.g., Languedocien, Nuorese; also Franco-Provençal and Friulian in second person plural only). Many varieties of Catalan have extended second and third conjugation endings into the first, creating a binary opposition between the fourth and the rest. Surselvan, Upper Engadine, Gardenese and Valle d'Istria have a similar pattern of neutralization.

The imperfect indicative, continuing proto-Romance forms *-ava- (first), *-eva- (second and third), *-iva-[68] (fourth) survives in a few varieties (e.g., Italian, Gascon), but neutralization of the distinction between non-first conjugation verbs is very widespread (Ibero-Romance, Catalan, Languedocien, Surselvan, Piedmontese, Romanian and others), leaving an opposition between first and non-first conjugation verbs (32).[69]

(32)

Italian	*levava*	*vendeva*	*dormiva*
Spanish	*llevaba*	*vendía*	*dormía*
Romanian	*lua*	*vindea*	*dormea*

In contrast, the forms that continue the Latin pluperfect subjunctive (continued in most Romance varieties as the imperfect subjunctive; in

Romanian as a pluperfect indicative) preserve conjugational distinctions rather better. Spanish (but not Portuguese), French and Surselvan neutralize non-first conjugation verbs; elsewhere, three conjugations are generally distinguished. Catalan, some Occitan varieties and some varieties of the Upper Engadine, Upper Fassa, Piedmont and Valle d'Istria, neutralize the distinction between first and second conjugation (33).

(33)

Portuguese	*levasse*	*vendesse*	*dormisse*
Catalan	*llevàs*[70]	*perdés*	*dormís*
Italian	*levasse*	*vendesse*	*dormisse*
Romanian	*luase*	*vânduse*	*dormise*
Spanish	*llevase*	*vendiese*	*durmiese*
French	*levât*	*vendît*	*dormît*[71]

Where Latin pluperfect indicative forms survive (e.g., Pt. *levara, vendera, dormira*; Sp. *llevara, vendiera, durmiera*), the identical distribution applies. The same goes for the arrhizotonic preterites (34):

(34)

Portuguese	*levou*	*vendeu*	*dormiu*
Catalan	*llevà*	*vengué*	*dormí*
Italian	*levò*	*vendé*	*dormì*
Romanian	*luă*	*vându*	*dormi*
Spanish	*llevó*	*vendió*	*durmió*
French	*leva*	*vendit*	*dormit*

The history of conjugational distinctions in Romance deserves a more thorough comparative examination than is possible here, or than has been undertaken anywhere to date, and conclusions are perforce tentative. But that the infinitive and the past participle are the main loci of retention of conjugational distinctions probably reflects a tension between predominantly 'lexical' and predominantly 'inflectional' word-forms in the conjugational paradigm. In those parts of the paradigm that express tense, person, number and mood there is a potentially ambiguous segmentation between a lexical stem and an inflectional ending: is the A of Latin AMATIS 'you love' or the E of TENEBAM 'I held' part of the lexical root, or part of the inflectional ending? It is clearly reanalysis in the latter terms that explains later generalization of Fr. -ez and -ais as conjugation-independent markers of the relevant clusters of morphosyntactic properties. In the infinitive and past participle, in contrast, lexical content is pre-eminent and morphosyntactic content minimal. It would be hard to ascribe any independent function to the infinitive or past participle endings, because infinitives and past participles generally[72] convey no information about person, number, mood or tense. It is precisely the infinitive which in Romance languages traditionally serves as the 'basic', citation, 'dictionary-entry' form of the verb and provides verbal nouns (It. *il parlare* 'speaking', *il dovere* 'duty', *il finire* 'ending', etc.). In these circumstances, the conjugation-marking vowel is liable to be seen as an inherent, and arbitrary, element of the lexical stem. A similar lack of person, number, mood and tense marking inheres in the gerund. While it is true that some Romance varieties neutralize conjugation distinctions here (see above), the gerund also stands out as the one and only place in the Romance verb where originally neutralized conjugational distinctions between non-first conjugation verbs are actually disambiguated, with the [i] characteristic of the fourth conjugation infinitive and past participle occasionally being extended into the gerund in Portuguese, Istrian, Nuorese, Catalan, Aragonese and Gascon (cf. Sp. *vendiendo, durmiendo,* It. *vendendo, dormendo,* with inherited neutralization for all non-first conjugation forms vs. Pt. *vendendo, dormindo*).

In Gascon (Rohlfs 1970:212) there is a different type of conjugational differentiation, namely introduction of rhizotony into the third conjugation gerund: e.g., *en bènen* 'selling' vs. second conjugation *en boulén* 'wanting', on the model of the stress pattern of the corresponding infinitives. This Gascon example involves amplification of conjugational distinctions by marking directly on the lexical root a distinction that otherwise would have been neutralized in the relevant word-form. I am unaware of any other part of the verb in which neutralization of the characteristic conjugation-marking vowels is reversed. Where amplification does occur its locus is, significantly, the *lexical* root. The following three generalizations can be made about 'amplification' of conjugational distinctions (I shall focus on the last two):

- In many Romance varieties (except Portuguese, Spanish and Sardinian), the majority of fourth conjugation verbs are distinguished from others by the presence of an 'augment' (originally an ingressive affix) in the singular and third person forms of the present tense. In a subset of these varieties, many first conjugation verbs have another type of 'augment', in the singular and third person forms of the present. For further details, see chapter 5.

- First conjugation roots tend distinctively to resist allomorphy and favour invariance.
- In Ibero-Romance varieties, second conjugation verbs (in -er) and fourth conjugation verbs (in -ir) become differentiated according to the quality of the root vowel.

While the first conjugation subjunctive inflections in -[e] (e.g., Latin ROGEM 'I ask', ROGES, ROGET, ROGEMUS, ROGETIS, ROGENT) are inherited by all Romance varieties, there exists only one variety for which the phonologically expected palatalization/affrication of velar consonants before front vowels unambiguously occurs. This is OFrench, for which a few examples are available. Fouché (1967:202) cites *chevalzt* 'rides' < *ka'balliket, *juzt* 'judges' < *'judiket. True, Romanian has regular and systematic palatalization/affrication in the first conjugation (e.g., ROGET > *roage* [rọadʒe]), but it is not at all certain that Romanian always reflects the near-general 'Romance' palatalization of velars, rather than later, strictly local, developments.[73] There is simply no sign whatever, anywhere else in the Romance-speaking world, of the expected allomorphy in the first conjugation, despite the fact that in the relevant varieties palatalization/velarization occurred with absolute regularity outside the first conjugation. Thus Portuguese, Spanish, Catalan, Occitan and Italian present unpalatalized first conjugation subjunctives (where [g] before a front vowel is indicated variously by *gu* or *gh*, and [k] by *qu* or *ch*; the verbs illustrated are *rogar* 'ask', *pagar* 'pay', *tocar/toccare* 'touch') (35):

(35) Portuguese
rogue   rogues   rogue   roguemos   rogueis   roguem

Spanish
toque   toques   toque   toquemos   toquéis   toquen

Catalan
pagui   paguis pagui   paguem   pagueu   paguin

Occitan (Languedocien)
toque   toques   toque   toquem   toquetz   toquen

Italian
tocchi   tocchi   tocchi   tocchiamo   tocchiate   tocchino

These facts are usually interpreted (see Penny 2002:177) as evidence for a very early analogical replacement of the subjunctive root-allomorph by the unpalatalized alternant. Maiden[74] (1991b:n21), however, suggests that phonetic palatalization was resisted *ab initio* in the first conjugation, a resistance perhaps facilitated by the fact that the phonetic tendency to palatalization before [e] was weaker than that before [i] (cf. Dalmatian, where palatalization of velars occurred before [i] but not before [e]). Whatever the truth, it is striking that the tendency for invariant first conjugation roots asserts itself very early, while there is no sign whatever of such resistance in non-first conjugation verbs.

The allomorphy in the roots of verbs produced by differentiation of vowel quality due to the position of stress (described in detail in chapter 5) is almost totally eliminated in Italian and French first conjugations. In Italian (see Maiden 1992:293f.), such levelling is not unique to the first conjugation (cf. extension into unstressed syllables of the stressed syllable diphthong in *miéto* 'I reap' *miéti miéte mietiámo mietéte miétono*), but only in the first conjugation are there no longer any verbs in which stress-related alternation is obligatory (e.g., older *suóno* 'I sound' *suóni suóna soniámo sonáte suónano* is now superseded by *suóno suóni suóna suoniámo suonáte suónano*). And only the first conjugation has levelling in favour of the unstressed, as well as the stressed, alternants (e.g., *vólo* 'I fly' *vóli vóla voliámo voláte vólano; négo* 'I deny' *néghi néga neghiámo negáte négano*). The situation is similar in French: there are abundant traces of stress-related alternations in non-first conjugation verbs (e.g., *je meus – nous mouvons* 'I/ we move', *il doit – nous devons* 'he/we must'; see Fouché 1967:38–83), but in the modern language practically all stress-related alternations have been eliminated from the first conjugation,[75] so that, for example, *treuf – trouvons* 'I/we find' or *espoir – espérons* 'I/we hope' have given way to *trouve – trouvons* and *espère – espérons*. A further example of structural differentiation between first conjugation verbs and others appears in Galician (see Porto Dapena 1973; Santamarina 1974; Maiden 1991a). We shall see in chapter 5 that in Portuguese, verbs originally containing high mid vowels [e] and [o] in the root are subject to lowering to [ɛ] and [ɔ] in stressed syllables – thereby creating allomorphy between root-stressed and non-root-stressed verb-forms. The same is true for Galician, with the important difference that first conjugation verbs wholly resist this alternation-creating innovation. As for eastern Ibero-Romance varieties, Arnal Purroy (1998:355, 356) reports that in Baja Ribagorza all first conjugation verbs have invariant, non-diphthongized, roots (see also Alvar 1948:96; Nagore Lain 1986:137f.; Mott 1989:73). Castilian shows no overall root-invariance in respect of first conjugation root vowels. There is both elimination of alternation but equally extension of alternation into previously invariant roots (see Penny 2002:183f.). However, elimination appears to be principally a characteristic of first conjugation verbs, with few examples (e.g., *pretender* 'claim', *sorber* 'sip') from other conjugations.

How did the first conjugation acquire the apparent propensity for resistance to allomorphy? One might reverse the perspective and suggest that the retention of alternation in non-first conjugation verbs (which contain some highly frequent lexemes such as 'hold', 'come', 'be able', 'want') is a matter of token frequency (see Harnisch 1988:431), rather than conjugational class. However, *all* first conjugation verbs, regardless of their individual frequency, are subject to levelling, while many third and second conjugation verbs (including such relatively infrequent ones as Italian *solere* 'be wont') retain alternation, so that invariance is inescapably a general property of the conjugational class, rather than of the frequency of individual lexemes. For further discussion of this point, see Maiden (1992:296f.).

The fact that throughout the history of virtually all[76] Romance languages the first conjugation contains the overwhelming majority of lexical verbs, and is the predominant one used for derived forms, the production of neologisms, and borrowing (as was already the case in Latin; see Sihler 1995:528) might be considered relevant, but how? The characteristic invariance of the first conjugation might favour derivation/borrowing, etc., precisely because it allows retention of an invariant form of the lexical root of the source form; but this presupposes characteristic invariance, rather than explaining it. In any case, the Romanian first conjugation, which generally shows historically expected allomorphy patterns, also attracts neologisms. These new forms often show invariant roots, at least as far as vocalic alternation is concerned (e.g., the relatively recent loans, in infinitive and third person singular present indicative, *a costa* 'to cost' – 3SG *costă*, *a contesta* 'to contest' – 3SG *contestă* vs. inherited *a înota* 'to swim' – 3SG *înoată* 'swim', *a întreba* 'to ask' – 3SG *întreabă*, with regular mid-vowel diphthongization in the stressed syllable), so that it seems that the root-invariance of neologisms, on the one hand, and characteristic root-invariance of the first conjugation (in those languages where this is the case), on the other, are not necessarily closely linked. Another possibility it that the status of the first conjugation as the class to which derived forms are assigned, together with a tendency to maintain a transparent relationship between derived verb and the source lexeme, may have served to confer on this conjugation as a whole the property of root-invariance. For example, the failure of palatalization to appear in reflexes of subjunctive IOCET 'let him joke/play' might have arisen from a desire to preserve a transparent link with the noun IOCUM. But if this is correct, then what must originally have been a property of individual derived lexemes appears, in many Romance varieties, to have been reanalysed at an early date as a *general* property of first conjugation roots.

The first conjugation is not alone in acquiring characteristic properties of the root. Castilian second and fourth conjugation verbs have come to differ in the range of vowels which can occur in the root, in that high vowels [i] and [u] occur exclusively in the fourth conjugation, whereas these vowels are absent from the second (see Wilkinson 1971; Togeby 1972:263). In the fourth conjugation, the high vowel may be present throughout the paradigm (e.g., *cubrir* 'to cover'), or may appear only in parts of it (see the paradigms of *medir* 'to measure', *sentir* 'to to feel', *dormir* 'sleep') (36):[77]

(36)		Indicative	Subjunctive	Preterite
	1SG	*mído*	*mída*	*medí*
	2SG	*mídes*	*mída*	*medíste*
	3SG	*míde*	*mída*	*midió*
	1PL	*medímos*	*midámos*	*medímos*
	2PL	*medís*	*midáis*	*medísteis*
	3PL	*míden*	*mídan*	*midiéron*
	1SG	*siénto*	*siénta*	*sentí*
	2SG	*siéntes*	*siénta*	*sentíste*
	3SG	*siénte*	*siénta*	*sintió*
	1PL	*sentímos*	*sintámos*	*sentímos*
	2PL	*sentís*	*sintáis*	*sentísteis*
	3PL	*siénten*	*siéntan*	*sintiéron*
	1SG	*duérmo*	*duérma*	*dormí*
	2SG	*duérmes*	*duérma*	*dormíste*
	3SG	*duérme*	*duérma*	*durmió*
	1PL	*dormímos*	*durmámos*	*dormímos*
	2PL	*dormís*	*durmáis*	*dormísteis*
	3PL	*duérmen*	*duérman*	*durmiéron*
	1SG	*cúbro*	*cúbra*	*cubrí*
	2SG	*cúbres*	*cúbra*	*cubríste*
	3SG	*cúbre*	*cúbra*	*cubrió*
	1PL	*cubrímos*	*cubrámos*	*cubrímos*
	2PL	*cubrís*	*cubráis*	*cubrísteis*
	3PL	*cúbren*	*cúbran*	*cubriéron*

The phonological and morphological development of these forms is intricate and controversial (Penny (2002:185–90) gives a succinct survey of the Castilian facts; see also Togeby (1972); Bustos Gisbert (1992)). The salient point is that non-first conjugation verbs are distributed between conjugations according to characteristics of the height of the root vowel. The incidence of high vowels in the fourth conjugation is partly etymological, but significantly augmented by the fact that in this conjugation the first person singular and present subjunctive originally had yod following the root[78] (e.g., METIOR, METIAR > *ˈmetjo, *ˈmetja) and that this yod apparently exercised a raising effect on high mid vowels in the root (whence *mido, sintamos, durmamos <* METIOR, SENTIAMUS, DORMIAMOS). Some verbs which originally contained low mid front vowels in stressed syllables also show [i] rather than the expected diphthong [je]/[we] (e.g., SERUIO > sirvo 'I serve').[79] In Ibero-Romance, a process tending to raise unstressed [o] to [u] before stressed [i] (e.g., sofrimos > sufrimos) may also have contributed (see Penny 1972:334). In many fourth conjugation verbs, an [i] or [u] originally triggered by yod is subsequently spread to other parts of the paradigm (e.g., 3SG mide, cubre); in fact only two verbs survive (morir and dormir) in which [u] has not been generalized. The result of the frequent association between fourth conjugation and high vowels in Castilian is that all verbs containing such vowels are transferred to that conjugation (e.g., DICERE 'to say' > decir (digo, etc.), SCRIBERE 'to write' > escribir, UIUERE 'to live' > vivir, CONFUNDERE 'to confuse' > confundir, DIUIDERE 'to divide' > dividir, CONDUCERE 'to lead, drive' > conducir, DESTRUERE 'to destroy' > destruir; see Penny 2002:173; Togeby 1972:262; Wilkinson 1971). Moreover, analogical changes involving levelling of vocalic alternants in fourth conjugation verbs never lead to generalizations of the mid vowel alternants, and always favour the high vowel. The details are rather different in Portuguese: essentially, all verbs with original mid vowels in the root show raising to [i] and [u] in first person singular pesent and throughout the present subjunctive in the first conjugation wherever yod originally followed the root. But here, too, a link has emerged between conjugational class and the structure of the lexical root.

5   Conclusions

The asymmetries between form and meaning inherent in Latin inflectional morphology largely persist in Romance. In some parts of the verb they even expand. Where aspects of the Latin system disappear, the disappearance is typically not in the direction of greater inflectional transparency (e.g., reduction to a single stable inflectional marker for passive or future), but rather in favour of structurally quite different (e.g., analytic) modes of exponence. Where inflectional endings persist, their characteristic cumulativeness equally persists. The trend identified in chapter 5, towards the lexical root as an arena of autonomous paradigmatic structure, is also apparent in the conservation of morphological distinctions in the verb. All over the Romance world the remnants of aspectual root-allomorphy not only retain a diachronically coherent 'morphomic' paradigmatic distribution but, rather like the individual conjugations, tend towards characteristic shared phonological shapes, thereby amplifying allomorphic variation between PYTA and non-PYTA forms in individual lexical roots. Conjugational distinctions, too, are notably robust. The 'inflectional allomorphy' associated with conjugational class (e.g., first conjugation subjunctive 1SG AMEM 'love' vs. non-first conjugation UIDEAM 'see', LEGAM 'read', DORMIAM 'sleep') is overall well preserved. Despite a weak tendency in finite verb-forms to reanalyse conjugation-marking as an inherent part of the inflection, and thereafter to eliminate conjugation-dependent differences among inflectional desinences, there is also an innovatory tendency to manifest conjugational distinctions, as well as inherited remnants of aspectual distinctions, within the lexical root. In some varieties the first conjugation acquires a characteristically invariant root, so that *lack of root-allomorphy* becomes a characteristic of conjugational membership. The emergent Ibero-Romance dependency between the phonological shape of the root and conjugational class also has a clear paradigmatic dimension. As the Castilian examples show, it is not the case that the root must *always* contain a high vowel, nor that the high vowel must occur just where thematic vowel [i] follows the root. Rather, membership of the fourth conjugation means that there must be, in the paradigm of any given lexical verb, *some root-allomorph containing a high vowel*, while membership of the second conjugation entails there being no root allomorph containing a high vowel. Perhaps paradoxically, the widespread conservation of some of the most idiosyncratic features of Latin morphology actually manifests itself in novel, and autonomously morphological, forms of idiosyncrasy.

5 MORPHOPHONOLOGICAL INNOVATION

Martin Maiden

1 Introduction

This chapter explores the relationship between phonological change and inflectional morphology in Romance.[1] It focuses on three types of change whose interaction with morphological structure transcends the familiar scenario whereby alternations produced by sound change lose their phonetically motivated character and then become associated with the expression of morphosyntactic categories. Much of this study will be dedicated to cases in which the originally arbitrary and idiosyncratic nature, *from the morphological perspective*, of phonetic changes, is not only perpetuated in the morphology long after those changes are extinct, but is replicated and expanded. We enter the realm of paradigmatic structures that 'do not make sense', either functionally or phonologically, yet flourish as characteristic patterns in inflectional morphology.

My main concern is with allomorphy in the lexical roots of present tense verbs. This may seem excessively narrow, but amid the profusion of sound changes which have impinged on morphological structure these phenomena stand out, because they reflect phonetic processes ancestral to most Romance languages, but also because they delivered remarkable impetus to subsequent morphological evolution. In short, we shall deal with the emergence of patterns of paradigmatic structure which are highly arbitrary yet constitute a characteristic 'cut' (see Sapir 1921:62f.) for Romance morphology.

Recent years have seen growing theoretical interest (e.g., Aronoff 1994; Stump 2001; and, for Italo-Romance, Pirrelli 2000) in the existence of recurrent distributional regularities within inflectional paradigms which cannot be coherently represented, synchronically, either in phonological or functional terms. To take one of Aronoff's examples, Latin verbs sometimes display a special stem (the 'third stem'), which can vary completely in phonological form from verb to verb, and which appears in several parts of

216

the inflectional paradigm (supine, past participle future participle) which share no common morphosyntactic function, as well as in various forms in derivational morphology. The 'third stem' is subject to a distributional regularity (what Aronoff labels a 'morphome') in that its presence in any one of the 'cells' of the paradigm listed always implies its presence in all the others. Maiden (1992; 2000b; 2001a; 2001b; also Pirrelli 2000:156–95) argues that diachronic investigation of (Romance) inflectional morphology not only reveals phenomena which presuppose such morphomic structure (and thereby prove the 'psychological reality' of morphomes), but demonstrates the central role of morphomic structure in morphological change. In the present study, we shall see that a morphomic perspective is not only necessary to understand the evolution of Romance inflectional morphology, but can lead us to view with a fresh eye certain types of paradigmatic structure which seem, *prima facie*, unremarkable. The inflectional morphology of the Romance languages will turn out to be stranger than it seems.

2   Latin and Romance compared

Latin had virtually no allomorphy in lexical roots; Romance languages have it abundantly. Where French has M.SG *sec* 'dry' vs. F.SG *sèche*, Romanian *sec* vs. *seacă*, central Italian dialects ˈsikku vs. ˈsekka, Latin had just SICCUS – SICCA; where the present indicative reflexes of the Latin verb 'to hold' are conjugated in Spanish *tengo tienes tiene tenemos tenéis tienen*, in French *tiens tiens tient tenons tenez tiennent*, in Italian *tengo tieni tiene teniamo tenete tengono*, in (old) Romanian *țiu ții ține ținem țineți țin*, Latin had plain TENEO TENES TENET TENEMUS TENETIS TENENT.

True, a subset of Latin nouns and adjectives had, for historical phonological reasons (see Sihler 1995:204, 275f., 283f.), a nominative[2] singular root distinct from that of the rest of the paradigm (e.g., NOM.SG PES 'foot', GEN.SG PEDIS NOM.PL PEDES, NOM.SG FLOS 'flower', GEN.SG. FLORIS NOM.PL FLORES), but since the Latin nominative form does not generally survive in Romance, this allomorphy largely disappeared. In Latin polysyllabic roots of the third declension, stress sometimes fell on a different syllable in the nominative singular from that which it occupied through the rest of the paradigm: e.g., NOM.SG SÓROR 'sister', IMPERÁTOR 'commander', LÁTRO 'brigand' vs. SORÓR-, IMPERATÓR-, LATRÓN-. In Romance varieties which retained a vestigial case system, distinguishing 'nominative' from 'oblique' case (OFrench, OOccitan, Romansh, possibly OItalo-Romance; see Price 1971:97f.; Jensen 1976:53–76; Maiden 2000a), the stress alternations are sometimes continued and indeed amplified by differentiation of vowel quality (see section 5). Thus OFr. NOM.SG *suér*, 'sister', *emperére(s)* 'emperor', *lerre* 'thief', *ber* 'baron', OBL *serór*, *emperëór*, *larrón*, *barón*. Indeed, the LÁTRO – LATRÓNEM type, possibly assisted by the Frankish declensional type *baro – barun*, seems rather productive in early Gallo-Romance, not only in certain masculine personal names (e.g., *Charles – Charlon*), but also extending into various personal and other names denoting females in -a (e.g., OFr. *Eve – Evain*, *pute* 'whore' *putain*; see Jensen 1976:28–30; Jud 1907).[3]

Allomorphy in the Latin verb-root was restricted to a subset of mainly third conjugation verbs, and correlated with aspect. But allomorphy correlated with person, number and tense was nearly[4] absent in Latin, and the rise of such allomorphy is a major innovation in Romance.

3   Methodological preliminaries

In analysing the relationship between sound change and its morphological consequences, it is useful to distinguish 'impact' from 'impetus'. Consider this fragment of Italian morphology (1):

(1)   1SG.PRS.IND *leggo* ['lɛggo] 'I read'
        2SG.PRS.IND *leggi* ['lɛddʒi]

The alternation between root-final velar in the first person singular and palatal affricate in the second person singular is the effect of a (now long extinct) process palatalizing (and affricating) velar consonants before front vowels. The historically underlying root was invariant: LEGO – LEGIS ['lego – 'legis].

All this is unremarkable: a phonetic change creates variation in a morphological paradigm and, on ceasing to operate, leaves a 'morphologized' alternation. This is the 'impact' of the sound change, and it may create idiosyncratic patterns of alternation; thus the present (indicative and subjunctive) and imperfect indicative of *leggere* (2):

(2)

	1SG	2SG	3SG	1PL	2PL	3PL
IND	*leggo*	*leggi*	*legge*	*leggiamo*	*leggete*	*leggono*
	['lɛggo]	['leddʒi]	['leddʒe]	[led'dʒamo]	[led'dʒete]	['lɛggono]
SBJV	*legga*	*legga*	*legga*	*leggiamo*	*leggiate*	*leggano*
	['lɛgga]	['lɛgga]	['lɛgga]	[led'dʒamo]	[led'dʒate]	['lɛggano]

(IPF.IND.1SG *leggevo* [led'dʒevo], 2SG *leggevi* [led'dʒevi], etc.)

The second and third persons singular and the first and second persons plural present indicative all end up sharing one root-allomorph, while the non-palatalized alternant is shared by (most of) the present subjunctive and the first person singular and third person plural present indicative. There is no isomorphism with any natural class of morphosyntactic categories: rather, we have an arbitrary intersection of person, mood, number and tense: the [ddʒ] alternant has no particular correlation with any tense or mood (it also occurs in future, conditional, imperfect indicative, imperfect subjunctive, infinitive and gerund), and outside the present (with exceptions in the preterite) it occurs in all persons. The other alternant [gg] does not characterize 'subjunctive' in general, but only the *present* subjunctive – to which we must add the first person singular and third person plural indicative.

We may speak of 'impetus' when the change has morphological consequences extending beyond its regular and predicted impact. For example, the very morphological arbitrariness and idiosyncrasy which the sound change originally generated may be propagated into previously invariant verbs. *Fuggire* 'flee' (originally with *fuggi-* [fuddʒ] throughout) apparently[5] acquires the same alternation pattern as *leggere* (3):

(3)

	1SG	2SG	3SG	1PL	2PL	3PL
PRS.IND	*fuggo*	*fuggi*	*fugge*	*fuggiamo*	*fuggite*	*fuggono*
	['fuggo]	['fuddʒi]	['fuddʒe]	[fud'dʒamo]	[fud'dʒite]	['fuggono]
PRS.SBJV	*fugga*	*fugga*	*fugga*	*fuggiamo*	*fuggiate*	*fuggano*
	['fugga]	['fugga]	['fugga]	[fud'dʒamo]	[fud'dʒate]	['fuggano]

The 'impetus' of a sound change strikes yet deeper if, in addition to giving rise to alternations which are extended analogically to other verbs, the *pattern* of alternation created, *in abstraction from its phonological content*, is replicated with sets of alternants which were not those produced by the original change. *Credere* 'believe' has an invariant root [kred]. Yet in the history of Italian we find 1SG.PRS.IND and 3PL.PRS.IND *creggo creggono*, subjunctive *cregga*, etc., vs. *credi, crede*, etc. There is no precedent for an alternation [d] – [gg], and no sound change ever yielded such an alternant-pair. We shall see that the history of some Romance languages even reveals *conflation* of etymologically unrelated verbs into a single, suppletive, paradigm, with the alternants distributed according to patterns of alternation originally created by sound change.

A still deeper manifestation of the abstract paradigmatic patterns created by sound change appears when different pairs of alternants, all conforming to the same distributional *pattern*, show signs of formal *convergence*. In convergence, 'morphomic' structures lose some of their phonological heterogeneity, assuming, despite their *functional* heterogeneity and despite the semantically disparate range of lexemes in which they occur, a shared phonological shape. In Italian, not only do *fuggio -a*, and (at one historical stage) *credo -a* come to resemble *leggo -a*, by assuming root-final [gg], but even historically regular existing patterns of alternation, such as that in *vedere* 'see' (*veggio -a* ['veddʒo -a] vs. *vede-*, etc.), converge on this characteristic root-final shape, becoming *veggo -a*, etc.

Morphologically idiosyncratic distribution of alternants may also display a kind of diachronic diagnostic of morphomic structure which I term *coherence*. Under coherence, a mutually implicational relationship between paradigm 'cells' sharing the same alternant remains doggedly intact across time, despite the functional and phonological heterogeneity of that set of cells, and despite the potential for the content of those cells to become differentiated. For example (see Maiden 1992), when *veggio* is replaced by *veggo*, so equally is *veggiono* replaced by *veggono*, *veggia* by *vegga*, *veggiano* by *veggano*, and so forth. The change is 'coherent' in that the distribution seems to be an 'unbreakable whole', in which all of the cells involved move in step.

4   Sound change and the morphology of the noun and adjective

The Romance noun–adjective shows relatively little by way of allomorphy created through sound change. For example, expected, phonologically regular (see Loporcaro, this volume, chapter 3: §2.1), velar–palatal alternation triggered by front vowels in areas where the plural inflection is -i, or feminine -e, is actually rare.[6] In Italo-Romance it occurs only in a few nouns and adjectives preceding M.PL -i (e.g., *greco* ['grɛko] – *greci* ['grɛtʃi] 'Greek'), and *never* before F.PL -e (*greca* ['grɛka] – *greche* ['grɛke]). Such alternation occurs consistently only in Romanian (e.g., SG *mic* [mik] – PL *mici* [mitʃ] 'small', *italiancă* [italiˈaŋkə] 'Italian woman' – PL(+GEN.DAT. SG) *italience* [italiˈentʃe]). Romanian inflectional -*i* also produces palatalization of root-final [s], [n] and [l],[7] and affrication of root-final dentals: *rus* – *ruşi* [ruʃ] 'Russian', *an* – *ani* [aɲ] 'year', *rană* – *răni* [rəɲ] 'wound', *cal* – *cai* [kaj̣] 'horse', *cale* – *căi* [kəj̣] 'way', *crud* – *cruzi* [kruzʲ] 'raw', *rupt* – *rupţi* [ruptsʲ] 'torn', *roată* – *roţi* [rotsʲ] 'wheel'. It is a feature of the history of many northern Gallo-Romance and Raeto-Romance varieties that velar consonants were palatalized before [a] (see chapter 3: §2.1). This produced palatal alternation of root-final velars before the original feminine inflection -a: e.g., Fr. M.SG *sec* 'dry' F.SG *sèche* < ˈsekko – ˈsekka.

There are various types of allomorphy caused by assimilation of stressed root vowels triggered by following unstressed vowels. Romanian acquired a rule opening and then diphthongizing mid vowels principally before following non-high unstressed vowels (in Romanian, diphthongization of [e] later disappeared before unstressed [e]).[8] Thus *des* 'thick', *gros* 'thick' and *os* 'bone' (which is feminine in the plural, and ends in -*e*) (4):

(4)

	SG	PL	SG	PL	SG	PL
M	*des*	*deşi*	*gros*	*groşi*	*os*	
F.NOM-ACC	*deasă*	*dese*	*groasă*	*groase*		*oase*
F.GEN-DAT	*dese*	*dese*	*groase*	*groase*		

Metaphony, the assimilatory raising of stressed vowels (especially mid vowels, but sometimes also -a) before unstressed high vowels (see Maiden 1991a; Savoia and Maiden 1997; Loporcaro, this volume, chapter 3: §1.2) is, or was, present in probably all Italo-Romance varieties, and produced alternations between plurals in -i and singulars in -o (masculine) or -e (masculine and feminine). In central and southern Italy particularly, metaphony was also triggered by -u (a M.SG ending). From central Italy (5):

(5)

	SG	PL	SG	PL	SG	PL
M	ˈrussu 'red'	ˈrussi	ˈverde 'green'	ˈvirdi	ˈpɛde 'foot'	ˈpjedi
F	ˈrossa	ˈrosse	ˈverde	ˈvirdi	ˈvotʃe 'voice'	ˈvutʃi

In dialects of much of northern Italy, where final unstressed vowels other than [a] have been deleted, and in those parts of southern Italy where post-tonic vowels tend to merge as [ə], metaphonic alternation is sometimes the sole indicator of morphosyntactic category (e.g., ˈverde – ˈvirdi). In (central) Sardinian, the noun and adjective root is fundamentally invariant, except for allophonic metaphonic raising of mid vowels to [e] and [o], which can produce raised root vowels in the masculine singular (M.SG ˈnovu 'new' vs. M.PL ˈnɔvozo, F.SG ˈnɔva). Portuguese has lexically sporadic traces of metaphonic raising of low mid vowels in some masculine singulars in -*o* (-[u]), leading to root alternation between singular and plural (M.SG *n*[o]*vo* 'new' – PL *n*[ɔ]*vos*, F *n*[ɔ]*va*; *gr*[e]*go* 'Greek', *gr*[ɛ]*gos*, *gr*[ɛ]*ga*). This pattern is subject to analogical spread, for example to the suffix -*oso*, where, on etymological grounds, only [o] would be expected (e.g., *perig*[o]*so* 'dangerous', *perig*[ɔ]*sos*, *perig*[ɔ]*sa*). A similar pattern for low mid vowels can be found in Romansh.

In no Romance language is the invariance of the noun and adjective more prominent than in French (see Battye and Hintze 1992:156–64, 186–89). Historical deletion of word-final -s means that plurals are usually indistinguishable from singulars in speech: e.g., *chat* [ʃa] 'cat' – PL *chats* [ʃa]. Some nouns and adjectives in -*al* have plurals in -*aux* ([o]) as a result of vocalization of [l] before a following consonant (*-als > *-aṵs > -o), as in *cheval* – *chevaux* [ʃə'vo]). The type *œuf* [œf] 'egg' – *œufs* [œ] reflects earlier deletion of the root-final consonant before -s. Deletion of final unstressed vowels leads to invariance for gender in a great many nouns and adjectives (e.g., M.SG *mûr* 'ripe' F.SG *mûre* M.PL *mûrs* F.PL *mûres*, all pronounced [myʀ]). Many nouns and adjectives, however, display alternations between a root-final consonant (especially nasals, dentals, sibilants and sometimes [l], [r]) in the feminine, and the absence of that consonant in the masculine. This is the cumulative effect of at least two changes (see also Price 1971:45–48, 58f.):

(i)   deletion of final non-low unstressed vowels: e.g., M.SG *'totto 'all' F.SG *'totta M.PL *'tottos F.PL *'totto > *tot 'totə tots 'totəs; M.SG *'pleino 'full' F.SG *'pleina M.PL *'pleinas F.PL *'pleinas > *'plein 'pleina pleins 'pleinəs;

(ii) subsequent deletion of word-final consonants: *tout* [tu] *toute* [tut], *tous* [tu],[9] *toutes* [tut]; *plein* [plɛ̃] *pleine* [plɛn] *pleins* [plɛ̃] *pleines* [plɛn]. Notice also how the position, word-final or not, of the nasal consonant correlates with nasalization of the vowel (see Price 1971:82–87).

The type of consonantal voice-alternation for gender found in French M.SG *neuf* 'new' vs. F *neuve* and M.SG *vif* 'lively' vs. F *vive* reflects earlier *devoicing* of consonants in word-final position, a phenomenon widespread in Gallo-Romance, Raeto-Romance and much of northern Italy. Catalan also has variation between word-final consonants in masculines, and their non-word-final feminine counterparts, e.g., M.SG *viu* 'alive' F.SG *viva*, M.SG *tancat* 'closed' F.SG *tancada*.

A form of Latin allomorphy which persists only marginally into Romance concerns the comparative of adjectives and adverbs in -IOR (e.g., ALTUS 'high' ALTIOR 'higher'). In general, the synthetic Latin comparative has disappeared, in favour of analytic constructions (see chapter 7), and in Romanian it has disappeared entirely. But some examples persist, and in particular the suppletive comparative reflexes of BONUS 'good' – MELIOR 'better', MALUS 'bad' – PEIOR 'worse' and, rather less consistently, of MAGNUS 'great' – MAIOR 'greater', PARUUS 'small' – MINOR 'smaller, less, lesser', are widely attested (see Lausberg 1976:§§679–83). Interestingly, suppletion is often retained even though the lexical identity of the absolute form changes completely: Sp. *bueno – mejor, malo – peor, gran – mayor; pequeño – menor;* Fr. *bon – meilleur, mauvais – pire, grand – majeur,*[10] *petit – moindre;* It. *buono – migliore, cattivo* (OIt. *malo*) *– peggiore, grande – maggiore, piccolo – minore* (but Ro. *bun – mai bun* lit. 'more good', *rău – mai rău* lit. 'more bad'). There are parallels in the adverbs BENE 'well' – MELIUS, MALE 'badly' – PEIUS, MULTUM 'much' – MAGIS, PAUCUM 'little' – MINUS 'less' > Sp. *bien – mejor, mal – peor, muy – más, poco – menos;* Fr. *bien – mieux, mal – pis,* …, *peu – moins;* It. *bene – meglio, male – peggio, molto – più, poco – meno* (but Ro. *bine – mai bine, rău – mai rău,* etc.).

5 Sound change and the morphology of the verb

5.1 'L-pattern' and 'U-pattern'

The label[11] 'L-pattern' describes a type of alternation in which a distinctive root is shared uniquely by the present subjunctive and the first person singular present indicative. 'U-pattern' is the same, except that the distinctive root also appears in the third person plural present indicative. The L-pattern occurs throughout Romance (its U-pattern variant is restricted to parts of Italy, and Romanian), and arises from two sets of phonological changes (see further Loporcaro, this volume, chapter 3: §2.1). The first, ancestral to all Romance, is what I term the 'yod-effect' (YE), and principally involves palatalization and/or affrication of consonants immediately preceding yod. The second, common to all varieties (except Sardinian and partially Dalmatian) is palatalization and affrication of velar consonants (PAV) before a front vowel. Inscriptional evidence (Väänänen 1963:§§95–100) suggests that YE was operating by the second century AD, and PAV by the fifth.

The principal source of yod was Latin unstressed prevocalic E or I. In second and fourth conjugation (and some third conjugation) verbs, prevocalic E/I appeared after the root in the first person singular and throughout the present subjunctive; prevocalic I, but not E, also occurred in this position in the third person plural indicative: thus the present indicative (upper row) and present subjunctive (lower row) forms of Latin TENERE 'hold', FACERE 'make', UENIRE 'come' (6):

(6)

TENEO	TENES	TENET	TENEMUS	TENETIS	TENENT
TENEAM	TENEAS	TENEAT	TENEAMUS	TENEATIS	TENEANT

FACIO	FACIS	FACIT	FACIMUS	FACITIS	FACIUNT
FACIAM	FACIAS	FACIAT	FACIAMUS	FACIATIS	FACIANT

UENIO	UENIS	UENIT	UENIMUS	UENITIS	UENIUNT
UENIAM	UENIAS	UENIAT	UENIAMUS	UENIATIS	UENIANT

Prevocalic ɪ and ᴇ regularly became yod, probably yielding (7):

(7)

'tɛnjo	'tɛnes	'tɛnet	te'nemus	te'netes	'tɛnent
					['tɛnjunt]
'tɛnja	'tɛnjas	'tɛnjat	te'njamos	te'njatis	'tɛnjant

'fakjo	'fakes	'faket	fa'kemos	fa'ketes	'fakjunt
					['fakent]
'fakja	'fakjas	'fakjat	fa'kjamus	fa'kjates	'fakjant

'vɛnjo	'vɛnes	'vɛnet	ve'nimos	ve'nites	'vɛnjunt
					['vɛnent]
'vɛnja	'vɛnjas	'vɛnjat	ve'njamos	ve'njates	'vɛnjant

The evidence of most Romance varieties suggests early removal of yod from the third person plural indicative, creating an L-pattern distribution. In Ibero- and Gallo-Romance, indeed, the yodless -ent ending seems to have been extended into the other third person plurals. The exception is Italo-Romance in an area comprising Tuscany, northern Umbria, Lazio, the Marche and northern Abruzzo, which generally extend the third person plural type -junt, with yod, into the third person plural of verbs of the *ˈtɛnjo type as well (e.g., *ˈtɛnjunt), thereby giving rise to a U-pattern distribution.

The subsequent history of consonant +yod sequences constitutes an intricate chapter in Romance phonological history (see Lausberg 1976:§§451–78; Loporcaro, this volume, chapter 3: §2.1). Essential points are:

- In Italo-Romance and Sardinian (at least), yod lengthened most preceding short consonants.
- 'Consonant + yod' sequences fused and emerged as palatal, and sometimes affricate, consonants.
- Most widely affected are dentals and velars, which typically yield dental alveolar or palato-alveolar affricates (sometimes with merger between original dental + yod and velar + yod sequences).
- In most Romance varieties [n] and [l] fuse with yod, yielding [ɲ] and [ʎ], respectively (in Sardinian, typically [ndz] and [ldz]).
- Fusion of yod with preceding labials is rare, but in many Gallo-Romance varieties, and parts of southern Italy, a palato-alveolar affricate results (e.g., SAPIAT > ˈsapja 'know.PRS.SBJV' > OFr. [ˈsatʃə]). In some areas (e.g., Portuguese, Spanish), yod apparently undergoes metathesis with the preceding consonant: e.g., ˈsapja > ˈsai̯ba or ˈsaipa > Pt. saiba, Sp. sepa.
- In Tuscan, *[rj] sequences yield yod: e.g., *(MORIOR 'die.PRS.IND' > ˈmɔrjo > ˈmwɔjo). Elsewhere, yod either has no effect at all on [r], and disappears (SItaly ˈmɔro, Ro. mor), or sometimes metathesis occurs (OFr. muir < ˈmɔrjo, Pt. pairo 'I appear' < *ˈparjo).

What follows are examples of regular yod-effects, from a selection of Romance varieties. It should be remembered that subsequent sound changes may have denatured (in Romanian, even deleted) original palatal or affricate consonants, but everything here is, historically, quite regular. My concern is with the resultant alternation *patterns* (8). The fact that for some languages only one or two examples are given does not necessarily mean that there are few YE verbs. Rather, such verbs may have undergone significant developments to be reviewed later.

(8) Portuguese

tenho 'I have'	tens	tem	temos	tendes	têm
tenha	tenha	tenha	tenhamos	tenhais	tenham

vejo 'I see'	*vês*	*vê*	*vemos*	*vedes*	*vêem*
veja	*vejas*	*veja*	*vejamos*	*vejais*	*vejam*

faço 'I do'	*fazes*	*faz*	*fazemos*	*fazeis*	*fazem*
faça	*faças*	*faça*	*façamos*	*façais*	*façam*

venho 'I come'	*vens*	*vem*	*vimos*	*vindes*	*vêm*
venha	*venhas*	*venha*	*venhamos*	*venhais*	*venham*

meço 'I measure'	*medes*	*mede*	*medimos*	*medis*	*medem*
meça	*meças*	*meça*	*meçamos*	*meçais*	*meçam*

caibo 'I fit'	*cabes*	*cabe*	*cabemos*	*cabeis*	*cabem*
caiba	*caibas*	*caiba*	*caibamos*	*caibais*	*caibam*

Spanish

quepo 'I fit'	*cabes*	*cabe*	*cabemos*	*cabéis*	*caben*
quepa	*quepas*	*quepa*	*quepamos*	*quepáis*	*quepan*

Catalan

veig 'I see'	*veus*	*veu*	*veiem*	*veieu*	*veuen*
vegi	*vegis*	*vegi*	*vegem*	*vegeu*	*vegin*

Old French

vail 'I am worth'	*vaus*	*vaut*	*valons*	*valez*	*valent*
vaille	*vailles*	*vaille*	*vailliez*	*vailliens*	*vaillent*

tieng 'I hold'	*tiens*	*tient*	*tenons*	*tenez*	*tienent*
tiegne	*tiegnes*	*tiegne*	*tiegniens*	*tiegniez*	*tiegnent*

muir 'I die'	muers	muert	morons	morez	muerent
muire	?	?	muiriens	muiriez	muirent

Surselvan (Disentis)

ˈfɛtʃal 'I do'	fas	fa	fiˈɔin	fiˈɔis	fan
ˈfɛtʃi	ˈfɛtʃas	ˈfɛtʃi	fiˈejan	fiˈejas	ˈfɛtʃan

Sardinian (Nuorese)

bazo 'I am worth'	bales	balet	balímus	balíes	bálen
baza	bazas	bazat	bazamus	bazades	bázan

tenzo 'I hold'	tenes	tenet	tenímus	teníes	tènen
tenza	tenzas	tenzat	tenzamus	tenzades	tènzan

pottho 'I can'	podes	podet	podímus	podíes	pòden
pottha	potthas	potthat	potthamus	potthades	potthan

moryo 'I die'	moris	morit	morímus	moríes	mórin
morya	moryas	moryat	moryamus	moryades	moryan

Old Tuscan (*gli* = [ʎʎ], *gn* = [ɲ], *ggi* = [ddʒ], *cci* = [ttʃ])

vaglio 'I am worth'	vali	vale	valemo	valete	vagliono
vaglia	vagli	vaglia	vagliamo	vagliate	vagliano

rimagno 'I stay'	rimani	rimane	rimanemo	rimanete	rimagnono
rimagna	rimagni	rimagna	rimagnamo	rimagnate	rimagnano

veggio 'I see'	vedi	vede	vedemo	vedete	veggiono
veggia	veggi	veggia	veggiamo	veggiate	veggiano

piaccio 'I please'	*piaci*	*piace*	*piacemo*	*piacete*	*piacciono*
piaccia	*piacci*	*piaccia*	*piacciamo*	*piacciate*	*piacciano*

muoio 'I die'	*muori*	*muore*	*morimo*	*morite*	*muoiono*
muoia	*muoi*	*muoia*	*moiamo*	*moiate*	*muoiano*

(Old)[12] Romanian

văz 'I see'	*vezi*[13]	*vede*	*vedem*	*vedeți*	*văd*
——	——	*vază*	——	——	*vază*

auz 'I hear'	*auzi*	*aude*	*auzim*[14]	*auziți*	*aud*
——	——	*auză*	——	——	*auză*

țiu[15] 'I hold'	*ții*	*ține*	*ținem*	*țineți*	*țin*
——	——	*ție*	——	——	*ție*

sai 'I jump'	*sari*	*sare*	*sărim*	*săriți*	*sar*
——	——	*saie*	——	——	*saie*

PAV affected [k] and [g] where they were immediately followed by front vowels: e.g., DICIS 'you.SG say', LEGIS 'you.SG read' > It. *dici* [ˈditʃi], *leggi* [ˈlɛddʒi]; [g] sometimes resulted in yod in intervocalic position or after a sonorant: e.g., LEGIS > Sp. *ˈlejes > *lees*, COLL(I)GIT 'he gathers' > *ˈkɔlje > It. *coglie* ˈkɔʎʎe.

In the present tense of non-first conjugation verbs, the root-final consonant is immediately followed in Latin by a front vowel in the second and third persons singular and the first and second persons plural of the present indicative; in the first person singular and third person plural present indicative, and the entire present subjunctive, a non-front vowel follows the root (9):

(9)

DICO 'I say'	DICIS	DICIT	DICIMUS	DICITIS	DICUNT
DICAM	DICAS	DICAT	DICAMUS	DICATIS	DICANT

LEGO 'I read'	LEGIS	LEGIT	LEGIMUS	LEGITIS	LEGUNT
LEGAM	LEGAS	LEGAT	LEGAMUS	LEGATIS	LEGANT

After palatalization, the result – at least in Romanian and dialects of central Italy – is a U-shaped distribution. In central and upper southern Italy, this exactly replicates the distribution also and earlier created by yod. Elsewhere, the third person plural inflection (see above) was replaced by -ent, and as a result PAV also occurs in the third person plural present indicative, giving rise to a further L-shaped pattern: thus (10):

(10) Portuguese

digo	*dizes*	*diz*	*dizemos*	*dizeis*	*dizem*
diga	*digas*	*diga*	*digamos*	*digais*	*digam*

Spanish

digo	*dices*	*dice*	*decimos*	*decís*	*dicen*
diga	*digas*	*diga*	*digamos*	*digáis*	*digan*

crezco 'I grow'	*creces*	*crece*	*crecemos*	*crecéis*	*crecen*
crezca	*crezcas*	*crezca*	*crezcamos*	*crezcáis*	*crezcan*

Far-reaching deletions and mergers of intervocalic and syllable-final consonants, and various analogical adjustments, make it impossible to illustrate PAV from French without cumbersome digression (see Fouché 1967:111–21, 148). Occitan varieties often display a situation similar to Spanish, except that the velar has normally been eliminated from the first person singular present indicative: e.g., Gascon 1SG.PRS *disi* vs. PRS.SBJV *diga*, etc. For Italian and Romanian consider (11).

(11) Italian (NB: before [i] and [e], the letter *c* = [tʃ], *g* = [dʒ], *gl* = [ʎʎ], *sc* = [ʃʃ])

dico	*dici*	*dice*	*diciamo*	*(dite)*	*dicono*
dica	*dica*	*dica*	*diciamo*[16]	*diciate*	*dicano*

leggo	*leggi*	*legge*	*leggiamo*	*leggete*	*leggono*
legga	*legga*	*legga*	*leggiamo*	*leggiate*	*leggano*

cresco 'I grow'	*cresci*	*cresce*	*cresciamo*	*crescete*	*crescono*
cresca	*cresca*	*cresca*	*cresciamo*	*cresciate*	*crescano*

colgo 'I gather'	*cogli*	*coglie*	*cogliamo*	*cogliete*	*colgono*
colga	*colga*	*colga*	*cogliamo*	*cogliate*	*colgano*

Romanian (*c* and *g* = [tʃ] and [dʒ] before *i* and *e*)

zic 'I say'	*zici*	*zice*	*zicem*	*ziceți*	*zic*
——	——	*zică*	——	——	*zică*

împing 'I push'	*împingi*	*împinge*	*împingem*	*împingeți*	*împing*
——	——	*împingă*	——	——	*împingă*

In sum, most Romance varieties have the L-pattern, both as a result of YE and of PAV. Central and upper southern Italo-Romance has the U-pattern. Romanian has the L-pattern as a result of YE, but the U-pattern as a consequence of PAV. Central Sardinian lacks PAV.

That the L/U-pattern arises from historically separate and phonologically distinct sound changes (not to mention the disparate outputs of 'yod-effects'), guarantees that the alternants cannot be synchronically reduced to any underlying phonological unity. With YE, the fact that the triggering yod is frequently absorbed into the preceding consonant – yielding a set of palatal and affricate consonants unprecedented in Latin – means that the conditioning environment for the alternations disappears. Certainly, no Romance language has a rule palatalizing or affricating the relevant consonants before [o] or [a], so that OTsc. *rimagno – rimani*, *vaglio – vali*, *muoio – muori*, *piaccio – piaci* had no synchronic phonological motivation. Indeed, PAV alternations often show the reverse, where it is the non-palatalized alternant that appears before -o and -a, and the palatal before front vowel inflections (e.g., It. *piango* 'I weep' – *piangi*) – and even these alternations are 'opaque', in that there is no longer palatalization before front vowels.

The L/U-pattern does not correspond, either, to any coherent set of morphosyntactic properties.[17] 'Subjunctive' hardly forms a class with 'first person + singular' (in the L-pattern) or with '[+first person, + singular] + [+third person, +plural]' (in the U-pattern), and in any case the distinctive root does not characterize the 'subjunctive', but only the *present* subjunctive. The distributional patterns are as functionally idiosyncratic as they are phonologically irreducible. They are true morphomes: distributional patterns lacking any *raison d'être* outside the paradigm itself.

5.2 *Analogical generalization of U- and L-pattern alternants*

Analogical generalization of the U- or L-patterns into a previously invariant verb root also occurs in other Romance varieties. The L-shaped pattern associated with ORomanian verbs in which root-final dentals had undergone affrication, such as *simţ* 'I feel' and *au(d)z* 'I hear', had been systematically extended, in sixteenth-century Romanian (Densusianu 1938:205–7) to other non-first conjugation verbs with root-final dentals. Thus first person singular present indicative and third person subjunctive *prin(d)z*, *prin(d)ză* for *prind*, *prindă* 'catch'; *trimiţ*, *trimiţă* for *trimit*, *trimită* 'send'. In Istro-Romanian (Puşcariu 1926:173, 186) the rise of [g] – [z] alternations due to local depalatalization of [dʒ] (e.g., *trag* – ˈtradʒe > *trag* – ˈtraze 'pull') allows the verb *cuteza* 'dare' to acquire the innovatory alternation pattern 1SG.PRS *cuteg*, 3PL *cutegu*, vs. *cutez-* in the rest of the paradigm.

In old northern and eastern varieties of French (Gossen 1970:132f., 140–42; Fouché 1967:185, 207f.), YE produces regular *c(h)* [tʃ] in the first person singular present indicative and in the present subjunctive of various verbs: e.g., *mench-/ment-* 'lie', *tach-/tai-* 'be quiet', *parch-/part-* 'leave', *sench-/sent-* 'feel'. Root-final *-c(h)* is optionally but coherently generalized to the first person singular present indicative and present subjunctive of all conjugations (where they coexist with regular, unmodified, roots): e.g., PRS.IND *demanch* (or *demant*) 'I ask' *demandes*, etc.; SBJV *demanche* (or *demant*), etc. (cf. also *douc(h)* 'I doubt' *doutes* …, etc.). For dialects of the Alpes Maritimes, Dalbera (1994:614f.) reports the spread of an allomorph originally restricted to the present subjunctive into the 'first person singular present indicative as well.

In early French (Fouché 1967:93f., 113), a partial resemblance between *poeir* 'be able' (1SG.PRS.IND *puis*, 1PL.PRS.IND *poons*, PRS.SBJV *puisse*) and *ro(v)er* 'ask' (e.g., 1PL *roons*) generated an unprecedented (if short-lived) alternation in *ro(v)er*, *trover* 'find' and *prover* 'prove', e.g. (12):

(12)

truis	trueves	trueve	trovons	trovez	truevent
truisse	truisses	truisse	truissiens	truissiez	truissent

Verbs such as *manoir* 'stay' (1SG.PRS.IND *maing* SBJV *maigne*) seem to have exercised a similar analogical influence in OFrench on previously invariant first conjugation verbs such as *doner* 'give', *mener* 'lead' (Fouché 1967:144f.; Schmid 1949:140–46 gives similar Romance examples) (13):

(13)

doing	dones	done	donons	donez	donent
doigne	doignes	doigne	doigniens	doigniez	doignent

It is in the distribution of root *vowels* that the 'L-pattern' is most prominent in Portuguese. Virtually all Portuguese non-first conjugation verbs containing a mid vowel in the root display alternation between a closed mid vowel (in second conjugation) or a high, non-mid vowel (in third conjugation) in the first person singular present indicative and the present subjunctive, and an open mid vowel elsewhere (even where a closed vowel would be expected, as in *b*[ɛ]*be* or *t*[ɔ]*sse*, for expected **b[e]*be*, **t[o]*sse*) (for *beber* 'drink', *morder* 'bite', *tossir* 'cough', *servir* 'serve') (14):

(14)   Second conjugation

b[e]bo	b[ɛ]bes	b[ɛ]be	bebemos	bebeis	b[ɛ]bem
b[e]ba	b[e]bas	b[e]ba	bebamos	bebais	b[e]bam

m[o]rdo	m[ɔ]rdes	m[ɔ]rde	mordemos	mordeis	m[ɔ]rdem
m[o]rda	m[o]rdas	m[o]rda	mordamos	mordais	m[o]rdam

Third conjugation

tusso	t[ɔ]sses	t[ɔ]sse	tossimos	tossis	t[ɔ]ssem
tussa	tussas	tussa	tussamos	tussais	tussam

sirvo	s[ɛ]rves	s[ɛ]rve	servimos	servis	s[ɛ]rvem
sirva	sirvas	sirva	sirvamos	sirvais	sirvam

Whatever the historical mechanism, the outcome is undeniably an L-shaped distribution, in which roots have come to alternate in unexpected ways. Third conjugation verbs are especially odd in that they show the pattern of metaphonic alternation otherwise associated only with high mid input vowels. In other words, while we would expect *'tossjo -a to yield *tusso -a*, we would not expect *'sɛrvjo -a to yield *sirvo -a*, because the regular metaphonic output of low mid vowels in Portuguese nouns and adjectives is a high mid vowel (cf. *'fɔlja > f[o]lha* 'leaf', *'tɛrtju > t[e]rço* 'third'). The extent to which such verb allomorphy is a result of analogical adjustments or of sound change (a tendency to lower high mid vowels in verbs, *followed* by assimilatory raising before yod of the resultant low vowels, regardless of their etymological source, as proposed by Maiden 1991b) is debatable. We certainly have analogical creation of such alternation in at least one verb with originally invariant root in [i] (*frigir* 'fry'), and several originally in invariant [u] (e.g., *fugir* 'flee') (15):

(15)

frijo 'I fry'	*fr[ɛ]ges*	*fr[ɛ]ge*	(*frigimos*[18]	*frigis*)	*fr[ɛ]gem*
frija	*frijas*	*frija*	*frijamos*	*frijais*	*frijam*

fujo 'I flee'	*f[ɔ]ges*	*f[ɔ]ges*	(*fugimos*	*fugis*)	*f[ɔ]gem*
fuja	*fujas*	*fuja*	*fujamos*	*fujais*	*fujam*

5.3   Analogical creation of novel types of L- and U-pattern

The examples seen so far are phonologically 'concrete', in that their starting point is partial phonological identity between the alternating verb and the originally non-alternating verb. More remarkable are cases in which what is generalized is not the concrete alternation but merely the distributional pattern. Alternation-pairs which are not the product of the historical sound changes which generated the L/U-pattern, are nonetheless 'conflated' into that pattern. Latin POSSE 'be able' was one of the few verbs displaying root-allomorphy (POSS- vs. POT-) correlated with person, number and tense. Of Romance varieties retaining POSS- (e.g., Portuguese, northern and central Italo-Romance), none preserves the original distribution. Rather, it is redeployed in a way that replicates the locally[19] prevalent L/U-pattern (16):

(16) Old Tuscan (and other central Italian varieties)

posso	puoi	può	potemo	potete	possono
possa	possi	possa	possiamo	possiate	possano

Portuguese

posso	podes	pode	podemos	podeis	podem
possa	possas	possa	possamos	possais	possam

In OFrench *aler* 'go' there emerged in some varieties a 1SG.PRS.IND *voi(s)*. Although this allomorph has no historical *raison d'être* in the present subjunctive (see Fouché 1967:425–27), the subjunctive was reformed as *voise voises*, etc. Fouché (1967:35–37) documents a rather similar development in OBourguignon. In Genoese (Toso 1997:199f.), the verb 'to seem' has, alongside a phonetically regular root in *pä-*, an L-pattern root in *paggi-*, apparently modelled on forms such as *veuggio* 'I want' (17):

(17)

päo/paggio	päi	pä	paimmo	paei	pan
pagge	paggi	pagge	paggemmo	paggiœ	pàggian

A further example of creation of novel alternation appears in ORomanian (and modern dialectal) forms of *ucide* 'kill', which acquired 1SG *ucig* (vs. 3PL etc. *ucid*) and a SBJV *ucigă* (vs. IND *ucide*) (see also Maiden 1996b; Wilkinson 1981:80f.; 1982:115). There is simply no precedent for a [g] – [d] alternation: the appearance of [g] is probably an effect of another, unconnected, analogy, based on verbs like *ating atingi*, etc. 'I/you touch' – preterite *atinsei*, etc., such that verbs which, like *ucide*, also had perfects in root-final -s (e.g., *ucisei*), tended to generalize [g] *and* its palatalized alternant [dʒ] in the present (see Lombard 1955:1015f.). What is striking about this analogy in *ucide* is that it selects 'as a bloc' the forms in root-final [g], extending *just these*. In principle, all of the [dʒ] alternants might also have been introduced (into the relevant persons),[20] or both [g] and [dʒ] might have been extended piecemeal. But there arose within *ucide* an unprecedented alternation which nonetheless replicated exactly the L-shaped distribution.[21]

Portuguese tended to eliminate consonantal allomorphy, so that *paresco pareces* ...; *paresca* 'seem' and *jaço jazes* ...; *jaça* 'lie' gave way to *pareço pareces* ...; *pareça* and *jazo jazes* ...; *jaza*. There are, however, signs of formal reinforcement of L-shaped allomorphy: OPtortuguese had, alongside *jaço jaça*, also *jasco jasca*, but such a -*sc* vs. -*z* alternation (*jasco jazes*, etc.) was without precedent, and what appears to have happened is convergence of the first person singular present indicative and subjunctive root-final consonant with that of verbs such as *parescer, nascer* 'be born' *(paresco, nasco*, etc.). An enigma of Portuguese historical morphology is *perder* 'lose', modern *perco perdes* ...; *perca* ... which coexisted in the medieval language with *perço perdes* ...; *perça* ... and *pergo perdes* ...; *perga* ... . Lang (1909:310, n2) invokes the analogical influence of verb-forms such as OPt. *conhosco* 'I know' *conhoces* ...; *fingo* 'I feign' *finges* ...; *finga*, etc. The result was not only disruption of a previously invariant root, but creation of an upreceded alternation between [d] and a velar. Malkiel (1974b:353f.) even suggests influence from *buscar* 'seek'.

Sardinian has roots which should, etymologically, be invariant, yet acquire an analogical L-pattern (see Wagner 1939:154): e.g., Log. ˈdʒuɣere 'bring' (< Lat. ADDUCERE + IUNGERE) shows 1SG.PRS.IND and PRS.SBJV ˈdʒutto, -a on the analogy of ˈfaɣere 'do', which has 1SG and SBJV ˈfatto, -a (< ˈfakjo -a). But ˈpɛrdere 'lose' has 1SG ˈperdʒo 'I lose' in some localities (Wagner 1939: 154, n1), modelled on the type aˈperdʒo 'I open' (< aˈpɛrjo) and entailing a completely novel alternation between root-final [dʒ] and [d]. Equally unprecedented are alternations arising from analogical extensions of *preterite* roots into the present. These roots (e.g., ˈbalf- < UALU- 'be worth') were present in all persons of the preterite, and therefore had no prior association with the L-pattern, yet their introduction into the present follows precisely this distribution: 1SG.IND ˈbalfo 'I am worth', ˈkrɛtto 'I believe', ˈappo 'I have', subjunctive ˈbalfa, ˈkrɛtta, ˈappa vs. bal-, kre-, a-, etc. in the rest of the present indicative.

In some Romansh varieties, two distinct etyma meaning 'let', *laˈksare and *laˈkare (see Decurtins 1958:41–52), are conflated into an L-pattern distribution. The former (laʃ-) occurs in the subjunctive and and first person singular present indicative; the latter (lai-) occupies the rest of the paradigm (see section 5.7 below for first and second persons plural forms) (18):

(18) Sagogn

ˈlaʃel	ˈlais	ˈlai	ˈʃɛin	ˈʃeis	ˈlain
ˈlaʃi	ˈlaʃies	ˈlaʃi	ˈʃɛjen	ˈʃɛjes	ˈlaʃien

(IPF ˈʃeval, etc.)

Fouché (1967:168f.) suggests that the phonological development of parts of the paradigm of OFr. *faire* 'do' (*fais fait faimes faites font*) requires an etymon *fag- rather than *fak[j]-. If so, it is striking that the two roots were conflated in such a way that *fakj- appeared in 1SG.PRS.IND (*faz*) and in the PRS.SBJV (*face*), and opposed to *fag- elsewhere.

5.4   Novel allomorphy with velar alternants in L- and U-patterns

We have already seen examples from Romanian and OPortuguese of creation of novel allomorphy such that a velar[22] appears in first person singular present indicative, and subjunctive. Dramatic, and systematic, examples of creation of novel L- or U-pattern allomorphy of this kind (see Menéndez Pidal 1968:292f.; Maiden 1992), are observable[23] both in Ibero- and in Italo-Romance (19).[24] From the earliest records of Spanish expected *[ɲ] and *[ʎ], from *[nj] and *[lj] and alternating with [n] and [l], are replaced by [ŋg], [lg]. And instead of expected *ʦ ([ts]) from *[kj], there is [g] (e.g., *fago* for **faço*).[25]

(19) OSpanish

valgo 'I am worth'	*vales*	*vale*	*valemos*	*valedes*	*valen*
valga	*valgas*	*valga*	*valgamos*	*valgades*	*valgan*

vengo 'I come'	*vienes*	*viene*	*venimos*	*venides*	*vienen*
venga	*vengas*	*venga*	*vengamos*	*vengades*	*vengan*

salgo 'I go out'	*sales*	*sale*	*salimos*	*salides*	*salen*
salga	*salgas*	*salga*	*salgamos*	*salgades*	*salgan*

fago 'I do'	*fazes*	*faze*	*fazemos*	*fazedes*	*fazen*
faga	*fagas*	*faga*	*fagamos*	*fagades*	*fagan*

One model for the innovatory [g]-alternant is probably verbs such as *decir* 'to say' (*digo, dices* ...; *digas*), etc., in which the velar occurs in first person singular present indicative, and present subjunctive. Menéndez Pidal (1968:286f.) suggests that the [ŋg] – [n] alternations originate, paradoxically, in analogical levelling. Verbs like (20):

(20)

plango 'I cry'	*plañes*	*plañe*	*plañemos*	*plañedes*	*plañen*
planga	*planga*	*planga*	*plangamos*	*plangades*	*plangan*

with phonologically regular alternation, were early subject to levelling in favour of *-ñ-*, so that *plango, planga*, etc. coexisted with levelled *plaño, plaña*, etc. This equivalence of *ñ* with *ng* is supposedly the pivot on which turned substitution of **veño -a* with *vengo -a*. So where one, regular, alternation disappears, another, wholly novel, emerges. From verbs in root-final [n], the velar seems to have spread to other roots ending in other sonorants, whence *duelgo – dueles* …; *duelga* 'grieve' (and also in OSp. *fiergo – fieres* …; *fierga* 'strike').[26] Whatever the exact mechanisms (see Elvira 1998:194; Penny 2002:179), almost *all* Spanish L-pattern verbs – whether originally invariant or with existing root-final alternations – have ended up being characterized by root-final [g] in first person singular present indicative, and present subjunctive. A more gradual process, complete in the sixteenth century, was introduction of root-final [g] into the first person singular present indicative, and present subjunctive of most verbs in place of root-final yod. Verbs originally in **[gj]* or **[dj]* yielded [j], which was deleted after a front vowel (e.g., **ˈvedjo > veo*). Thus, from **ˈaudjo*, *ˈaudes* …: (21):

(21)

oyo 'I hear'	*o(d)es*	*o(d)e*	*o(d)imos*	*o(d)ides*	*o(d)en*
oya	*oya*	*oyas*	*oyamos*	*oyades*	*oyan*

This yod was analogically extended to other verbs with root-final vowels, e.g., (22):

(22)

trayo 'I bring'	*traes*	*trae*	*traemos*	*traedes*	*traen*
traya	*trayas*	*traya*	*trayamos*	*trayades*	*trayan*

Subsequently, this type of alternation gave way to the pattern in (23), which is continued into modern Spanish:

(23)

oigo	*oyes*	*oye*	*oímos*	*oídes*	*oyen*
oiga	*oigas*	*oiga*	*oigamos*	*oigades*	*oigan*

traigo	*traes*	*trae*	*traemos*	*traedes*	*traen*
traiga	*traigas*	*traiga*	*traigamos*	*traigades*	*traigan*

caigo	*caes*	*cae*	*caemos*	*caedes*	*caen*
caiga	*caigas*	*caiga*	*caigamos*	*caigades*	*caigan*

(etc.)

Espinosa (1946:244–47) details other extensions of [g] in American and European dialects. It is perhaps significant that introduction of [g] into verbs whose present subjunctive did *not* share a root with the first person singular (and therefore did not conform to the L-pattern) actually failed in Spanish (but cf. Malkiel 1974b:340): *haiga* 'have', *vaiga* 'go' for *haya*, *vaya* did not survive, perhaps because the corresponding first person singular present indicative was *he*, *voy*.

There are clear parallels to the Ibero-Romance developments in Italy (although mechanisms and chronology are partly different), where the velar also replaces historically regular alternants, yielding novel alternant-pairs such as [ŋg] – [n], [lg] – [l] and [gg] – [d] (24):

(24)   Old Tuscan

vegno 'I come'	*vieni*	*viene*	*venimo*	*venite*	*vegnono*
vegna	*vegni*	*vegna*	*vegnamo*	*vegnate*	*vegnano*

veggio 'I see'	*vedi*	*vede*	*vedemo*	*vedete*	*veggiono*
veggia	*veggi*	*veggia*	*veggiamo*	*veggiate*	*veggiano*

vaglio 'I am worth'	*vali*	*vale*	*valemo*	*valete*	*vagliono*
vaglia	*vagli*	*vaglia*	*vagliamo*	*vagliate*	*vagliano*

saglio 'I go up'	sali	sale	salimo	salite	sagliono
saglia	sagli	saglia	sagliamo	sagliate	sagliano

(Early) Modern Italian

vengo	vieni	viene	veniamo	venite	vengono
venga	venga	venga	veniamo	veniate	vengano

veggo	vedi	vede	vediamo	vedete	veggono
vegga	vegga	vegga	vediamo	vediate	veggano

valgo	vali	vale	valiamo	valete	vagliono
valga	valga	valga	valiamo	valiate	valgano

salgo	sali	sale	saliamo	salite	salgono
salga	salga	salga	saliamo	saliate	salgano

Both the [ddʒ] – [d] pattern, and the [gg] – [d] alternation which succeeded it, found themselves occasionally extended to verbs with previously invariant roots in [d]: *chiuggio* 'I close' /*chiuggo – chiudi* ...; *chiugga* ...; *chieggio* 'I ask' / *chieggo – chiedi*, etc.; *chieggia/chiegga*, etc.[27] A further example of the emergence of novel alternation is found in *trarre* 'bring, draw', which probably conflates two originally distinct alternative roots, from TRAHERE and *ᵗtragere (see Malkiel 1974b:335). The result is (25):

(25)

traggo	trai	trae	traiamo	traete	traggono
tragga	tragga	tragga	traiamo	traiate	traggano

According to Tekavčić (also Meyer-Lübke 1972:177f.) substitution of [gg], [ŋg], [lg], for [ddʒ], [ɲɲ], [ʎʎ], pivots on an early analogical levelling, such that palatalized roots in -[ddʒ], -[ɲɲ], -[ʎʎ], produced by PAV, optionally extend into the first person singular and third person plural present indicative, and present subjunctive (e.g., 1SG *leggio* 'I read' or *leggo, coglio* 'I gather' or *colgo, pugno* 'I prick' or *pungo* – based on *legge, coglie, pugne,* etc.). The 'correct' forms, with final velars, ultimately prevail, but the velar extends, 'hypercorrectly', to *vengo* for *vegno, salgo* for *saglio,* etc.

Old Sienese, and some modern Umbrian and south Tuscan varieties (see Hirsch 1886:435f.; Rohlfs 1968:260) go further, adding novel velar alternants to verbs with root-final [r]: Sienese 1SG *corgo* 'I run' – 2SG *corri* etc., Pietralunga 1SG ˈmɔrgo, 3SG ˈmɔre, 3PL ˈmɔrgono. At Civitella Benazzone (Perugia), the *AIS* even records [ɡɡ] – [v]: 1SG ˈbeggo 3SG ˈbeve 1PL baˈveno 3PL ˈbeggano. More unprecedented alternations involving velars occur in southern Italy. In the Bay of Naples area[28] there are novel alternations such as (26):

(26)

First person singular	Third person singular
ˈmɛkkə 'put'	ˈmɛttə[29]
attˈʃikə 'kill'	attˈʃirə
ˈʃɛŋgə 'descend'	ˈʃɛnnə
ˈparkə 'leave'	ˈpartə
ˈsɛŋgə 'feel'	ˈsɛndə

First conjugation verbs are affected, too (27):

(27)

ˈpɔrkə 'carry'	ˈpɔrtə
ˈmaŋgə 'send'	ˈmannə
ˈmeŋgə 'lead'	ˈmenə
aˈʃpɛkkə 'wait'	aˈʃpɛttə
ˈrakkə 'scratch'	ˈrattə

Corsican has novel alternations in the first conjugation of the sort ˈpilgu 'I take' – ˈpiʎa, parˈdoŋgu 'I forgive' – parˈdona, miˈʎurgu 'I improve' – miˈʎura. The analogical spread of such allomorphy need not involve a velar alternant: in Calabria and Salento 1SG ˈmiɲu 'beat' alternates with, e.g., 3SG ˈmina.[30]

5.5   Abstract paradigmatic structure or 'phonological' conditioning?

My interpretation of the changes involving velar consonants, as with the other extensions and convergences of the L- and U-patterns described, is that they involve not only the maintenance and spread of an abstract pattern of alternation, but its phonological 'convergence' (see chapter 4), in that the roots of the first person singular (and third person plural) present indicative, and present subjunctive come to share a characteristic phonological shape (the root-final velar). We have, in effect, an analogical levelling of the 'one meaning – one form' type. Yet the 'meaning' is not an extramorphological entity, but the characteristic L/U-pattern itself. It is possible that the velar alternant was preferred because it involves greater phonological differentiation between alternants: whereas [l] – [ʎʎ] and [n] – [ɲɲ] merely involve palatal alternation of sonorants (the lengthening is allophonic), [l] – [lg] and [n] – [ŋg] involve both a sonorant and a velar obstruent. In other words, the contours of the pattern are being accentuated.

The claim that the L/U-pattern is a purely *morphological* phenomenon, and not the result of synchronic phonological or morphosyntactic conditioning, is unorthodox. Indeed, Fanciullo (1998) raises the superficially alluring possibility that the generalization and distribution of the velar might be explained phonologically, as a kind of 'allophonic' rule selecting non-palatal alternants before a non-front vowel. A detailed reply to this claim appears in Maiden (2001b) (also Pirrelli 2000:79f., 178–84), but Fanciullo's account is undermined particularly by the existence of clear counterexamples in the verb, such as *voglio, soglio* + dialectal *coglio, leggio,* and past participles such as *conosciuto, venuto* (not **conoscuto*, **venguto*) with dialectal *leggiuto, sagliuto,* etc. Also, the non-palatal alternant may appear before front-vowel desinences, as in OUmbrian subjunctive *morghe* 'you die', Tuscan *finischiamo* 'we finish', etc. Further powerful evidence against Fanciullo's assumption is Bybee and Pardo (1981:956f.), who demonstrate experimentally that speakers of Spanish do not make a phonological analysis of the distribution of velar-final roots as occurring before back vowels ([a] and [o]).[31]

In sum, both the internal details of the Ibero- and Italo-Romance velars, and the evidence of parallel L/U-pattern changes elsewhere, show that speakers make structural generalizations (see also Elvira 1998:85) over a disjunct set of morphosyntactic categories, in which first person singular present indicative, and present subjunctive (+ third person plural present indicative) share a distinctive root.

5.6   *The N-pattern*

'N-pattern'[32] denotes a pattern of alternation, recurrent across Romance, such that the present tense first, second and third persons singular, the second person singular imperative, and the third person plural share a root distinct from that of the remainder of the paradigm (28):

(28)

1SG	2SG	3SG	1PL	2PL	3PL
	+imperative		+ rest of	paradigm	

The principal source of the N-pattern is historical differentiation in quality between stressed and unstressed vowels (see also Loporcaro, this volume, chapter 2). In general, the range of vowel qualities present in Romance stressed syllables is greater than that found in unstressed syllables. This fact has particular impact on verbs, all of which were characterized by alternating stress falling in some parts of the paradigm on the root ('rhizotony') and elsewhere on the ending ('arrhizotony'). In Latin, the position of stress depended on principles of prosodic phonology such that stress usually fell on the antepenultimate syllable, but on the penultimate when the latter was 'heavy' (i.e., had a rhyme comprising a long vowel or vowel + consonant). In the present, stress generally fell on the root in the three persons of the singular, and in the third person plural (in the third conjugation it fell on the root throughout the present – a state of affairs continued in Romanian, and some varieties of Friulian) (29):

(29)

First conjugation	Second conjugation	Third conjugation	Fourth conjugation
PÓRTO 'I bear'	UÍDEO 'I see'	LÉGO 'I read'	DÓRMIO 'I sleep'
PÓRTAS	UÍDES	LÉGIS	DÓRMIS
PÓRTAT	UÍDET	LÉGIT	DÓRMIT
PORTÁMUS	UIDÉMUS	LÉGIMUS	DORMÍMUS
PORTÁTIS	UIDÉTIS	LÉGITIS	DORMÍTIS
PÓRTANT	UÍDENT	LÉGUNT	DÓRMIUNT

The predominant[33] pattern – massively amplified in Romance by stress-related vowel differentiation – is that first, second and thid persons singular, and third person plural present are opposed, by virtue of their rhizotony, to the rest of the paradigm.

The Romance of most of Italy and the remainder of western Europe (except Sardinia) developed a system such that seven vowels [i e ɛ a ɔ o u] appeared in stressed syllables and five in unstressed [i e a o u]. The 'deficit' in the unstressed vowels arises because continuants of Latin short Ĕ and Ŏ remain distinct from those of long Ē and Ō. In stressed syllables the former yield [ɛ] and [ɔ], the latter [e] and [o]; in unstressed syllables they merge as [e] and [o]. This early differentiation is well preserved in Italian: for example, from the present indicative (30):

(30)

1SG	ˈpɔrto	ˈlɛggo
2SG	ˈpɔrti	ˈlɛddʒi
3SG	ˈpɔrta	ˈlɛddʒe
1PL	porˈtjamo	ledˈdʒamo
2PL	porˈtate	ledˈdʒete
3PL	ˈpɔrtano	ˈlɛggono

Note that this entails 'opacity' and unpredictability, for while the quality of unstressed mid vowels is predictable from that of stressed mid vowels, the reverse is not true (e.g., ledˈdʒete – ˈlɛddʒe, but veˈdete – ˈvede).

There were countless subsequent, localized, stressed-based vowel differentiations, of which only the most superficial sketch is possible here (see Lausberg 1976:§§154–296; also Loporcaro, this volume, chapter 3: §1), but among the occurrences directly relevant to the emergence of N-patterns are:

(i)   diphthongizations of stressed [ɛ] and [ɔ] to *[jɛ], *[wɔ] (restricted to open syllables in Gallo-, Raeto-, northern Italo-Romance, Tuscan, and to [ɛ] in Romanian);

(ii) diphthongizations of *[e], *[o] (+ raising and fronting of *[a]) in stressed open syllables in Gallo-Romance, Raeto-Romance, much of northern Italy;

(iii) raising of pretonic mid vowels to [i] and [u] (systematic in Sicilian and the dialects of the far south of Italy, sporadic in many other Italian dialects, applies to back vowels in French, Romanian, Portuguese);

(iv) centralization (usually as [ə]) of pretonic vowels, especially [e] and [a] (French, Catalan, Portuguese; Romanian, upper southern Italy for [a]), sometimes followed by deletion (N Italian dialects, Raeto-Romance varieties, French).

Examples of these, and other changes creating N-pattern allomorphy, are given below (the forms presented are the present indicative, and the first person singular imperfective indicative as representative of non-present tenses) (31):

(31) Romanian

mor 'I die'	*mori*	*moare*	*murim*	*muriţi*	*mor*
vin 'I come'	*vii*	*vine*	*venim*	*veniţi*	*vin*
plac 'I please'	*placi*	*place*	*plăcem*	*plăceţi*	*plac*
mănânc 'I eat'	*mănânci*	*mănâncă*	*mâncăm*	*mâncaţi*	*mănâncă*
usuc 'I dry'	*usuci*	*usucă*	*uscăm*	*uscaţi*	*usucă*
iau 'I take'	*iei*	*ia*	*luăm*	*luaţi*	*iau*

IPF.IND *muream, veneam, plăceam, mâncam, uscam, luam*

Sicilian

ˈpɛrdu 'I lose'	ˈpɛrdi	ˈpɛrdi	pirˈdimu	pirˈditi	ˈpɛrdunu
ˈpɔrtu	ˈpɔrti	ˈpɔrta	purˈtamu	purˈtati	ˈpɔrtanu

IPF.IND pirˈdia, purˈtava

Italian

muoio 'I die'	*muori*	*muore*	*moriamo*	*morite*	*muoiono*
siedo 'I sit'	*siedi*	*siede*	*sediamo*	*sedete*	*siedono*
odo 'I hear'	*odi*	*ode*	*udiamo*	*udite*	*odono*
devo 'I must'	*devi*	*deve*	*dobbiamo*	*dovete*	*devono*

IPF.IND *morivo, sedevo, udivo, dovevo*

Modern French

meurs 'I die'	*meurs*	*meurt*	*mourons*	*mourez*	*meurent*
dois 'I must'	*dois*	*dois*	*devons*	*devez*	*doivent*

IPF.IND *mourais, devais*

Medieval French was richer in examples (see Fouché 1967:8–61):

lef 'I wash'	*leves*	*leve*	*lavons*	*lavez*	*levent*
crief 'I burst'	*crieves*	*crieve*	*crevons*	*crevez*	*crievent*
peis 'I weigh'	*peises*	*peise*	*pesons*	*pesez*	*peisent*
mein 'I lead'	*meines*	*meine*	*menons*	*menez*	*meinent*
parol 'I speak'	*paroles*	*parole*	*parlons*	*parlez*	*parolent*
manju 'I eat'	*manjues*	*manjue*	*manjons*	*mangiez*	*manjuent*

IPF.IND *levoie, crevoie, pesoie, menoie, parloie, manjoie*

Catalan

p[a]*sso* 'I pass'	*p*[a]*sses*	*p*[a]*ssa*	*p*[ə]*ssem*	*p*[ə]*sseu*	*p*[a]*ssen*
pl̠[ɛ]*go* 'I fold'	*pl̠*[ɛ]*gues*	*pl̠*[ɛ]*ga*	*pl̠*[ə]*guem*	*pl̠*[ə]*gueu*	*pl̠*[ɛ]*guen*
pl̠[o]*ro* 'I weep'	*pl̠*[o]*res*	*pl̠*[o]*ra*	*pl̠*[u]*rem*	*pl̠*[u]*reu*	*pl̠*[o]*ren*
neixo 'I am born'	*neixes*	*neix*	*naixem*	*naixeu*	*neixen*

IPF.IND *p*[ə]*ssava, pl̠*[ə]*gava, pl̠*[u]*rava, neixía*

Spanish

muero 'I die'	*mueres*	*muere*	*morimos*	*morís*	*mueren*
pierdo 'I lose'	*pierdes*	*pierde*	*perdemos*	*perdéis*	*pierden*

IPF.IND *moría, perdía*

Portuguese

j[ɔ]*go* 'I play'	*j*[ɔ]*gas*	*j*[ɔ]*ga*	*j*[u]*gamos*	*j*[u]*gais*	*j*[ɔ]*gam*
ap[ɛ]*go* 'I sink'	*ap*[ɛ]*gas*	*ap*[ɛ]*ga*	*ap*[ə]*gamos*	*ap*[ə]*gais*	*ap*[ɛ]*gam*
f[a]*lo* 'I speak'	*f*[a]*las*	*f*[a]*la*	*f*[ɐ]*lamos*	*f*[ɐ]*lais*	*f*[a]*lam*

IPF.IND *j*[u]*gava, ap*[ə]*gava, f*[ɐ]*lava*

5.7 Analogical changes replicating the N-pattern

Various linguists (e.g., Matthews 1981; Dressler 1985:335; Vincent 1988b:297f.) observe that Romance languages have acquired N-pattern alternations which are not the product of sound change. In what follows we see that a disparate range of alternations has arisen conforming to the fundamental template whose starting point was the distributional pattern of allomorphy created by stress-related vowel differentiation.

A remarkable feature of Portuguese is wholesale generalization of the N-pattern vowel alternations into verbs historically containing high mid vowels, for which no such alternation is predicted. In fact almost all verbs lower[34] [e] and [o] in stressed syllables. Thus, from *'bevo, etc. 'drink', *'ploro, etc. 'weep' (32):

(32)

$(b[e]bo)^{35}$	$b[\varepsilon]bes$	$b[\varepsilon]be$	bebemos	bebeis	$b[\varepsilon]bem$

$ch[\mathfrak{o}]ro$	$ch[\mathfrak{o}]ras$	$ch[\mathfrak{o}]ra$	choramos	chorais	$ch[\mathfrak{o}]ram$

Romanian sometimes generalizes the N-pattern originally created by raising of a back vowel to [u] in pretonic syllables (e.g., *port* 'I wear' vs. 1PL *purtăm*) into verbs where [u] was originally present throughout the paradigm (e.g., *măsor* 'I measure' *măsurăm*). Dauzat (1900:155) gives Occitan examples of spread of N-pattern vocalic alternation into verbs where there was originally no such alternation.

The N-pattern can also impinge on the (consonantal) L/U-pattern root of the present subjunctive. In French *vouloir* 'want', *valoir* 'be worth', *aller* 'go', *tenir* 'hold' and *venir* 'come', there has been introduction of the N-pattern by eliminating the characteristic subjunctive root from first and second persons plural (see Fouché 1967:88, 173f., 426f.; also Aski 1995:421) (33):

(33)

vaille	vailles	vaille	valions	valiez	vaillent
veuille	veuilles	veuille	voulions	vouliez	veuillent
aille	ailles	aille	allions	alliez	aillent

Similar developments are widely observable in Raeto- and Italo-Romance. In Italian,[36] the subjunctive root is sometimes abolished from first and second persons plural present, at least for verbs with velar-final roots, e.g., in *rimanere* 'to stay' (34):

(34)

rimanga	rimanga	rimanga	rimaniamo	rimaniate	rimangano

Catalan, and some Romansh varieties, vocalized or deleted syllable-final consonants. This created consonantal alternations between the singular and plural in the present. When there is analogical levelling of the root-final consonant, however, it affects the third person plural present, but *not* first or second persons plural, *nor* the rest of the paradigm (35):

(35)   Catalan

| *bec* 'I drink' | *beus* | *beu* | *bevém* | *bevéu* | ***beuen*** |
| *moc* 'I move' | *mous* | *mou* | *movém* | *movéu* | ***mouen*** |

In the following example, a 3PL **ˈpodan would be expected (36):

(36)   Sedrun (Surselvan)

| pos 'I can' | pos | po | puˈdain | puˈdais | **pon** |

Some Surselvan dialects have apparently integrated an original third person singular present subjunctive form (characterized by root-final [t] see Lüdtke 1959:24–26, but cf. Decurtins 1958:197, 200f.) into the present subjunctive of dar 'give' and ʃtar 'stand', following the N-pattern. For example: (37):

(37)   Sagogn

| ˈʃtɛti | ˈʃtɛties | ˈʃtɛti | ˈʃtæjan | ˈʃtæjas | ˈʃtɛtien |

Romansh developed two alternants in the verb 'sit', se- (< *sɛd-) vs. sez-/saz- (< *sɛdj-), the latter originating in the first person singular present indicative and in the subjunctive (following the L-pattern). There has been analogical generalization of this alternant in the present indicative, but in such a way that only first and second persons plural are affected. Surselvan (Riein):

Present indicative

ˈseza | ses   se | saˈzein   saˈzeis | sen

Present subjunctive

ˈsezi   ˈsezias   ˈsezi   saˈzejan   saˈzejas   ˈsezian

In many Ladin dialects the [r] characteristic of the Romance infinitive has been deleted, with the exception of a handful of verbs where the ending was, at one time, preceded by [v].[37] For example, UENDERE > *'vender[e] > 'vəne 'sell'; BIBERE > *'bevre > 'bəire 'drink'. The [r], thus isolated, lost its association with the infinitive and was reanalysed as part of the root. From the infinitive it was analogically extended to other parts of the verb, but according to the N-pattern (38):

(38)

At Sonnino in Lazio (*AIS*), a vocalic alternant [i] originally restricted to the second person singular present of the verb (due to metaphony) is analogically extended, replacing the expected vowel [e], in ve'te 'see', but following the N-pattern (39):

(39)

A feature of Catalan dialects is analogical generalization of a morph containing [g] into the subjunctive of verbs where no [g] was originally present. Wheeler (1993:197f.) notes that the [g] element does not always affect all persons: in some dialects it appears in first, second and third persons singular and third person plural, and in others it appears only in first and second persons plural (see Ronjat 1930–41, III:162, for Occitan): either way, the result is 'N-pattern'. Similarly, many Italo-Romance varieties introduce root-final [g] into the subjunctive of certain verbs. But this [g] is frequently restricted to the N-pattern (40):

(40)   Prignano (*AIS*)

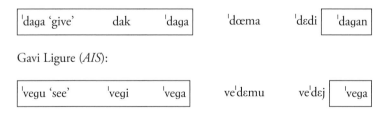

Gavi Ligure (*AIS*):

Various Italian dialects (see *AIS* map 1695) have a root-final consonant in the verb 'say' which is absent (for non-phonological reasons) in first and second persons plural present. Thus (41):

(41)   Montecatini (*AIS*):

ˈdiho	ˈdiʃi	ˈdiʃe	ˈdimo	ˈdithe	ˈdihano

Arnal Purroy (1998:384) gives a similar example for the Aragonese of Baja Ribagorza.

We saw (§5.3) that roots characteristic of the preterite were (in Sardinian) introduced into other tenses according to the U/L-pattern. There is also extension of preterite roots according to the N-pattern in the verbs descended from Latin STARE 'stand' and DARE 'give' in Sardinia (at Escalaplano) and here and there on the Italian mainland (Schmid 1949:33, 35). Teramo (Abruzzo) has a CV root in the singular and third person plural present forms of *ˈstare, but (optionally) 1/2PL.PRS ʃtaˈtemə ʃtaˈtetə, imperfect indicative ʃtaˈtevə, etc., future ʃtataˈrajə, etc., with the final dental consonant originally characteristic of the preterite. At Paliano (Lazio; Navone 1922:100), the preterite root of reflexes of FACERE 'make' appears to have spread according to the same pattern.

Castilian has a historically regular alternation in *jugar* 'play' between [we] in stressed syllables (*juégo*, etc.) and [u] in unstressed syllables (*jugámos*, etc.). The alternation is different from hundreds of other 'radical changing verbs' only in the marginal respect that [we] is normally the stressed counterpart of unstressed [o], rather than [u]. In other dialects there has been levelling variously in favour of [we] or of [u] in this verb. I surmise that the coexistence of both types of levelling underlies their subsequent integration into a single paradigm in Leonese dialects of the Maragatería area,[38] resulting in actual *reversal* of the etymological distribution of the alternants, despite the fact that Maragatería dialects have many other verbs in which [we] still regularly appears just in *stressed* syllables (42):

(42)

júgo	*júgas*	*júga*	*juegámos*	*juegádes*	*júgan*

(IPF.IND *juegába*, etc.)

What this shows is that distribution of alternation according to a familiar, abstract, morphomic patterning can operate independently of any association between phonologically concrete alternants (in this case [we]) with stress, or with any particular set of cells within the paradigm.

5.8   Root-augments and N-patterns

In many Romance varieties, N-pattern distribution is also displayed by 'root-augments'. These are semantically empty[39] formatives affixed immediately

Martin Maiden

after the root, and before inflectional endings. The most perspicuous of these appears throughout Romance, arises from protoforms *-isk- (or *-esk-), and characterizes fourth conjugation verbs (those with thematic vowel [i]). Some dialects with the augment (Lucanian in southern Italy, Corsican, northern Venetan, Ladin, Istrian, Dalmatian and Romanian, as well as eastern Gallo-Romance), display a second type,[40] usually restricted to the first conjugation, and continuing protoforms *-edj- (or *-edz-) (43):[41]

(43) *-isk- (or *-esk-)
      Present indicative

Catalan	Gascon	Surselvan	Italian	Istrian	Romanian
servéix	orbéishi	finéschel	finísco 'end'	fi'nisi	iubesc
'serve'	'open'	'end'		'end'	'love'
servéixes	orbéishes	finéschas	finísci	fi'nisi	iubéşti
servéix	orbéish	finéscha	finísce	fi'niso	iubéşte
servím	orbím	finín	finiámo	fi'nimo	iubím
servíu	orbítz	finís	finíte	fi'ni	iubíţi
servéixen	orbéishen	finéschan	finíscono	fi'niso	iubésc

Imperfect indicative first person singular (and other tenses)

| servía | orbívi | finével | finívo | fi'nivi | iubeám |

      -edj-/-edz-
      Present indicative

Tursi (Lucania)	Valle d'Istria	Romanian
mattsə'kij 'I chew'	maze'neji 'I grind'	lucréz 'I work'
mattsə'kijəsə	maze'neji	lucrézi
mattsə'kijətə	maze'neja	lucreáză
mattsə'kæmə	maze'nemo	lucrăm
mattsə'kasə	maze'ne	lucráţi
mattsə'kijənə	maze'neja	lucreáză

Imperfect indicative first person singular (and other tenses)

| mattsə'kæβə | maze'navi | lucrám |

There exists an extensive literature on the origins of *-isk-/*-esk-.[42] Suffice to say that some Latin verbs displayed an affix -sk-, which generally marked 'ingressive' meaning (e.g., FLORET 'it flowers' vs. FLORESCIT 'it's coming into bloom'). Such forms were most numerous in the second conjugation, less so in the fourth, and rare in the first. In most Romance varieties, the augment becomes characteristic of the fourth conjugation, as a consequence of structural mergers between the second and fourth conjugation. In most areas, it retains the second conjugation thematic vowel [e], yielding -esk-; in Gallo-Romance and Italo-Romance varieties (with islands of -esk-), the fourth conjugation theme vowel [i] prevails, yielding -isk-.[43]

In Sardinian, Portuguese and Spanish, *-esk- is present *throughout* the verb. In the remaining areas, the augment appears in parts of the paradigm only. The predominant distribution in Catalan, Gascon, Romansh, Italy and the Balkans, is the N-pattern. A different, though still paradigmatically restricted, pattern prevails in Gallo-Romance, where -isk- is typically found throughout the present, in the imperfect indicative, and in the present participle, and not elsewhere (but see Ronjat 1930–41, III:149f.) A few Italo-Romance localities (Sant'Elpidio a Mare, Serrone, Nemi, Teggiano, Serrastretta, San Chirico Raparo; see *AIS* map 1687) display the augment not only in the first and second persons plural present, but also in other tense-forms.[44]

The *-edj-/*-edz- augment originates[45] in the Greek verbal derivational affix -ιζ-, and entered Latin especially in Christian vocabulary. In most Romance varieties, reflexes of this element, which is especially prominent in the formation of denominal verbs and neologisms, occur *throughout* the paradigm (e.g., It. *guerreggiare* 'I make war', *guerreggio*, *guerreggiamo*, etc.).

Various scholars[46] have suggested that the motivation of N-pattern distribution of the augments is to produce 'columnar' stress throughout the paradigm (i.e., stress falls consistently on the penultimate syllable). This explanation is unsupported by any independent evidence. Indeed, given that in all Romance languages the overwhelming majority of verbs continue to show alternating stress in the present, it assumes that stress had been 'regularized' at the expense of making one subclass of verbs 'irregular' with respect to all others (see Wolf 1998:442f.). Zamboni's[47] view (1983) that *-isk- is 'inherently' stressed – and therefore cannot be combined with inflections which are also inherently stresssed – might (perhaps) be true synchronically, but does not explain how the augment *became* inherently stressed. Romanian presents an additional problem. The *-esc-* forms originally belonged to the third conjugation, which was root-stressed in first and second persons plural present indicative, a state of affairs which persists in

Romanian. Therefore, had the augment been preserved in the first and second persons plural, we would expect *iubésc iubéşti iubéşte **iubéştem **iubéşteţi iubésc*. Loss of the augment in first and second persons plural present therefore cannot be due to its elimination when unstressed.

Another line of thinking appeals to the 'transparency' obtained by making the root uniformly unstressed throughout the paradigm. Elwert (1943:144) argues that the stressed augment [e] in Val Fassa obviates the need for the root vowels to undergo regular stress-related vocalic alternation in denominal verbs and neologisms, but his appeal to transparency in the relationship between the derivational verb and its base word has a flaw: if the base word is a noun, it will have an inherently stressed root; but if in the verb it is *always* unstressed, this means that the verbal root will perforce be *differentiated* from its base form by the effects of unstressed vowel reduction (cf. ta'mɛiʃ 'sieve' and tame'ʒea 'he sieves', as opposed to a conceivable and more transparent **ta'mɛiʒa).

Lausberg (1976:§§801, 921) proposes that the alignment of stress differentiates stem and ending, thereby guaranteeing identical phonological treatment of the stem in all forms and the *transparency* of all forms, free from the differentiatory effects of stress alternation. The problem, once again, is that this does not explain why the augment becomes restricted to the N-pattern. The fact that it is stressed in the relevant parts of the verb may confer an advantage, but its retention elsewhere would confer no disadvantage; indeed, such retention would, by Lausberg's own logic, actually have the virtue of avoiding paradigmatic alternation.[48] Explanation in terms of 'root-allomorphy-avoidance' also entails a prediction which, to my knowledge, is not satisfied anywhere: we would expect the lexical distribution of the augment to tend to coincide with those verbs whose root was potentially susceptible to vocalic allomorphy. Since in Italo-Romance, Romanian and Catalan [i] and [u] (to a lesser extent [a]) are generally immune from such allomorphy, reflexes of verbs with mid vowels in the root should attract the augment, whilst reflexes of verbs with peripheral vowels should not. Yet the muster of verbs in the relevant languages which do not display the augment shows no particular predilection for peripheral root vowels (e.g., Italian *capisco* 'I understand', *finisco* 'I end', *unisco* 'I unite'), while a number of verbs which have root-allomorphy (e.g., *muoio* 'I die', *esco* 'I go out', *odo* 'I hear') lack the augment. In Romanian, speakers would seem, indeed, to have chosen the 'wrong' augment, if the motivation is elimination of allomorphy: [i] is generally invariable in Romanian, whilst [e] is subject to diphthongization before unstressed [ə] (historically, also before [e]), so that first person singular indicative *-esc* would have alternated originally with 3SG.PRS.IND *-eaşte* and subjunctive *-ească*, whereas no such alternation would have arisen had the augment contained [i].

The fact that in Lucanian dialects the augment seems to occur (see Lausberg 1939:156) in verbs whose first, second and third persons singular, and third person plural would otherwise carry proparoxytonic stress (compare 1SG mattsə'kij with Italian *màstico* 'I chew'), and that similar patterning is observable in OVenetian, Istrian and Corsican, might support the view that the distribution of the augment is motivated by stress. But appeal to stress completely fails to explain the augment's *absence* from the rest of the paradigm. An 'optimal' solution, avoiding proparoxytonic stress *and* allomorphic distribution of the augment, would show the augment throughout the paradigm.

Native learners of early Romance would have encountered a particularly bewildering situation in which an element of morphological structure not only had lost clearly discernible[49] semantic content but could not be uniquely correlated with any morphosyntactic property: it appeared in the present tense, the infinitive, the imperfect, the present participle, but not – for reasons of original incompatibility in Latin between an ingressive form and perfectivity – in any of the tense-forms inherited from the old perfective (preterite, imperfect subjunctive, various conditional and subjunctive forms derived from the perfect subjunctive and pluperfect), nor in the past participle. One solution, adopted by Portuguese, Spanish and Sardinian, was simply to reanalyse the augment as an inherent part of the root, and generalize it to the whole verb. Another, chosen by speakers of the remaining Romance varieties, also involves lexicalization of the augment, but in this case both augmented and augmentless alternants are preserved (e.g., fin- alongside finisk-), and speakers redeploy the rival forms according to the idiosyncratic template previously created by stress differentiation. The *-edj-/*-edz- type never displayed the type of idiosyncratic paradigmatic restrictions found in the early history of *-isk-/*-esk-, but it is surely significant that this type of augment always *presupposes* the presence of the *-isk-/*-esk- type: once speakers had deployed the *-isk-/*-esk- augment according to the N-pattern, it appears that the other augment simply followed suit.

5.9   The attractive force of the N-pattern

The N-distribution produced by stress differentiation is strikingly replicated by a number of verbs where etymologically distinct lexemes have been conflated suppletively. Most prominent is 'go'. IRE was one of few Latin verbs which displayed root-allomorphy correlated with person, number and tense. In most of the paradigm the root was I-, in the present subjunctive and in the first person singular and third person plural present indicative, E- (44):

(44)

EO	ĪS	IT	ĪMUS	ĪTIS	EUNT
EAM	EAS	EAT	EAMUS	EATIS	EANT

This alternation is nowhere preserved intact, and generally these roots are wholly or partly eliminated from the present (although in Vegliote a reflex of the I- root seems to be present throughout the paradigm,[50] and in the Basses Pyrénées the present subjunctive forms from EAM, etc., survive intact in all persons).[51] Almost all Romance varieties suppletively conflate two, sometimes three, etymologically different lexemes,[52] deriving from IRE, UADERE, AMBULARE. Repeatedly, such conflation takes on an N-shaped distribution (Aski 1995 gives more detailed treatment).[53] A common scenario is that original I:- roots survive outside the present, and in first and second persons plural present indicative (45):

(45)   Old Tuscan

(INF *gire*)

AIS map 1692 shows that this pattern remains widespread throughout central and southern Italy. Likewise in Iberia (although Spanish has extended *v-* throughout the present, and Portuguese has it in first person plural present indicative) (46):

(46)   Old Spanish

(INF *ir*)

In an area comprising northern Italy, Catalan, Gallo-Romance and western Romansh, verbs derived from AMBULARE (> Fr. *aller*; It. *andare*) supplant earlier i- forms, yet the N-distribution remains undisturbed (47).

(47)

French[54]

(INF *aller*)

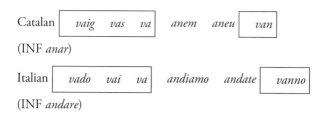

Catalan | *vaig* *vas* *va* | *anem* *aneu* | *van*

(INF *anar*)

Italian | *vado* *vai* *va* | *andiamo* *andate* | *vanno*

(INF *andare*)

There are many other examples of the force of the N-pattern in conflating suppletive allomorphs. The unique pair of alternants encountered in Tuscan *uscire* 'go out' follows the N-pattern (48):

(48)

| *esco* *esci* *esce* | *usciamo* *uscite* | *escono* |

Maiden (1995b) argues that this alternation arises from conflation of a reflex of EXIRE (OIt. *escire* 'go out') with *uscio* 'doorway'.

In Dalmatian,[55] the verb 'eat' has the root mantʃ- (3SG.IPF.IND manˈtʃua) *except* in the first person singular and third person singular present (second person singular and third plural are unattested), where the root is maˈnaɨk- (3SG maˈnaɨka). Both forms descend from *maniˈkare, but mantʃ- is probably an Italo-Romance loan, while maˈnaɨk- is indigenous. Apparently an 'etymological doublet' has merged into a suppletive paradigm following the N-pattern.

Numerous northern Italian dialects (see *AIS* 1664) show influence of the root-final [l] of *voˈlere 'want' on the present of *poˈtere 'be able', but usually not in the first and second persons plural present, nor in other tenses.[56] A typical example is Roncone (*AIS*) (49):

(49)

| pos pœl pœl | poˈdom poˈde | pœl |
| vœj vœl vœl | voˈlom voˈle | vœl |

At Minerbio (*AIS*) the present subjunctive of 'be' has acquired root-final [p], otherwise characteristic of the subjunctive of ʃaˈvɛr 'know', but shows no such influence in first and second persons plural (50):

(50)

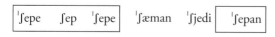

| ˈʃepe ʃep ˈʃepe | ˈʃæman ˈʃjedi | ˈʃepan |

In some Romansh varieties, reflexes of *ˈtragere and *tiˈrare, both meaning 'pull', have been conflated[57] into a single paradigm according to the N-pattern (51):

(51) Prez (Grigioni)

tir	ˈtiras	ˈtira	tarˈɟaɲ	tarˈɟes	ˈtiran

In Muras (Galicia; Otero Alvarez 1952), in the verb *traguer* 'bring', alternative roots tra- and trag- seem to have been paradigmatically integrated according to the N-pattern (first person singular present, and the present subjunctive have an L-pattern alternant) (52):

(52)

traigo	*tras*	*tra*	*traguemos*	*traguedes*	*tran*
traiga	*traigas*	*traiga*	*traigamos*	*traigades*	*traigan*

(IPF.IND *traguía*)

Descendants of STARE 'stand' and DARE 'give' have a CV-shaped root throughout the present. Thus old Tuscan (53):

(53)

do	*dai*	*dà*	*damo*	*date*	*danno*
sto	*stai*	*sta*	*stamo*	*state*	*stanno*

This led to loss of root-final consonants in some other verbs, in many Romance varieties, but *only* in the singular and third person plural present (the present subjunctive often retains a distinctive root-allomorph). Thus in reflexes of HABERE 'have' (54):

(54) Portuguese

hei	*has*	*ha*	*havemos*	*haveis*	*hão*

(INF *haver*)

French

ai	*as*	*a*	*avons*	*avez*	*ont*

(INF *avoir*)

Susch (Engadine)

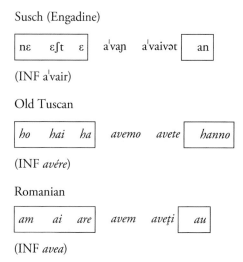

(INF a'vair)

Old Tuscan

| ho | hai | ha | avemo | avete | hanno |

(INF avére)

Romanian

| am | ai | are | avem | aveți | au |

(INF avea)

Over a smaller area reflexes of SAPERE 'know' receive similar treatment (55):

(55) Lags (Surselvan)

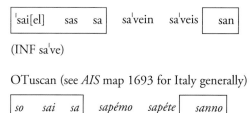

(INF sa've)

OTuscan (see *AIS* map 1693 for Italy generally)

| so | sai | sa | sapémo | sapéte | sanno |

(INF sapére)

and in various Romance varieties reflexes of FACERE 'do' are similarly affected (56):

(56) Muras (Galicia; Otero Alvarez 1952)

(INF facer)

Azaretti (1982:198) quotes the curious case of *paresce* 'seem' in Ventimigliese, where the CV model prevails optionally in second and third persons singular and third person plural (he does not mention the first person singular) but apparently not in first or second persons plural (57):

(57)

?	paresci/pai	paresce/pa	pariscèmu	pariscèi	paresce/pan

A number of dialects in Calabria and Sicily conflate reflexes of DONARE with DARE 'give' according to the N-pattern.[58] Leone (1980:36–39, 91f.) also documents an N-pattern conflation of *afflare (> [a]ʃʃare) with *troˈvare, both 'find', in south-eastern Sicily[59] (58):

(58)

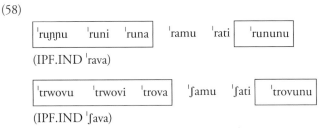

ˈruɲɲu	ˈruni	ˈruna	ˈramu	ˈrati	ˈrununu

(IPF.IND ˈrava)

ˈtrwovu	ˈtrwovi	ˈtrova	ˈʃamu	ˈʃati	ˈtrovunu

(IPF.IND ˈʃava)

In the same area, reflexes of SAPERE 'know' (see Schmid 1949:115) or, according to locality, FACERE 'do', exercise a partial influence on STARE 'stand' (59):

(59)

ˈstaju	staị	sta	staˈpjemu	staˈpiti	stanu
			or	or	
			staˈcimmu	staˈciti	

(IPF.IND staˈpia or staˈcia)

Schmid (1949:120–24) finds evidence for a similarly suppletive distribution of the first two verbs in old Occitan, and some varieties of Catalan.[60] In Limone (Schädel 1903:108), we have the same paradigmatic distribution, except that here DARE occurs in the singular and third person plural present and (apparently) DONARE elsewhere. A similar pattern is indicated for the Occitan dialects of the Po valley by Zörner (2008:158f.).

In short, the N-pattern plays a major role, repeatedly and across the Romance languages, as a 'template' for paradigmatic conflation of distinct root allomorphs.[61]

5.10   What is the N-pattern?

An initially seductive interpretation of the N-pattern is that it is semiotically motivated by 'markedness'. After all, 'present tense' is 'unmarked' with respect to other tenses, singular with respect to plural, and third person with respect to other persons. Could it be that the N-pattern 'diagrams' marked-ness relationships, given that singular, third person and present tense-forms are 'unmarked' in relation to the rest of the paradigm?

The problem is that appeal to 'markedness' paints a deceptive veneer over the real arbitrariness of the phenomenon. We have seen that *three* parameters of markedness are involved, and nothing explains why they intersect in the way they do. If plural is marked with respect to singular, why should the diagrammaticity of that relationship be disrupted by the fact that the third person plural present usually shares a root with all three persons of the singular? If third person is unmarked with respect to other persons, why should first, second and third persons share an alternant in the singular but not in the plural? If present is unmarked in respect to other tenses, why should the diagrammaticity of that relationship be disrupted by the fact that first and second persons plural present share a root with other tenses? And why are other possible parameters of markedness not involved? If subjunc-tive is marked with respect to indicative, why does the allomorphy not diagram *that* relationship? Above all, if the N-pattern diagrams some 'natural', and presumably therefore universal, markedness relationship, how is it that this pattern seems not to recur repeatedly in other languages? Bybee and Brewer (1980:224) find for Spanish that the frequency marking for persons of the present tense of the verb are, in order, third person singular, first person singular, first person plural, third person plural, second person singular, second person plural. Insofar as frequency is correlated with markedness, this hierarchy is patently unlike the N-pattern, for first person plural is considerably more frequent than second person plural and the two categories are not adjacent.

As with L- and U-patterns, we have to ask to what extent the N-pattern might actually be attributed to phonological, rather than morphological, factors. Should we say, as I propose, that the N-pattern is a functionally arbitrary paradigmatic accretion of first, second and third persons singular and third person plural in the present tense or, since precisely these roots are the ones that bear tonic stress, that N-pattern distributions are 'phonolog-ically' conditioned[62] by stress?

The first objection to the 'stress-based' analysis is that it would be a mere 'notational variant' of the purely morphological distribution, since that distribution is independently needed to state where stress falls in the paradigm. On this point see also Pirrelli (2000:12f.). It is most significant that original N-pattern alternants can be generalized *independently of stress*. Laredo in northern Spain[63] has 1SG present indicative ˈgwelo 1PL oˈlemos, but 1SG subjunctive ˈgwela 1PL gweˈlamos 'smell'; Sobrescobio has 1PL indicative *dormín* 2PL *dormíz* but the corresponding subjunctives *duermán duermáz* 'sleep', etc. In some varieties of Tuscan (Rohlfs 1968:243), and in various northern Italian varieties such as Piedmontese (see Brero 1971:70), the augment has N-pattern distribution in the indicative, but appears in all persons of the present subjunctive, again independently of stress. In the verb 'go' in some Occitan varieties, the 'unstressed' alternant an- appears throughout the present subjunctive (see Quint 1998:61). The explanation for this is not hard to see, for it is a matter of analogical extension of a pattern of distribution of alternants characteristic of the L/U-pattern: just as these typically involve formal identity between the root of the first person singular (and third person plural) present indicative and that of the whole of the present subjunctive, so what are in origin N-pattern alternants may be subject to the same analogical distribution with, for example, diphthongs and augments appearing in the first and second persons plural present subjunctive. That such changes can occur suggests that the N-pattern alternants are not 'conditioned by stress' but rather directly associated with an array of paradigmatic cells. It is their direct association with such cells which makes it possible for the L/U-pattern (itself defined over the set of cells present subjunctive + first person singular present indicative [+ third person plural present indicative]) to have access to them, and to 'redeploy' them.

The fact that stress itself is associated with the 'N-pattern' array of cells is what makes it possible, also, for stress to be redistributed according to the L/U-pattern. First and second persons plural present subjunctive display the same root stress as all other forms of the present subjunctive – especially in Romansh and a number of northern Italian dialects, but also beyond. Thus Ventimigliese (Ligurian) 1PL *càntimu*, 2PL *cànti* 'sing'. Corsican, Galician and some Spanish dialects,[64] show extensive retraction of stress onto the first and second persons plural root in the present subjunctive, accompanied by the appearance of the allomorph found in the stressed forms of the present subjunctive (e.g., Somiedo *puédamus, puédais*). The fact that in Ventimiglia the *-isk- augment[65] *also* appears in the first and second persons plural subjunctive (*finìscemu, finìsci* vs. indicative *finìmu, finì* 'finish') leads Azaretti (1982:200) to conclude that the distribution of the augment is an *effect* of stress. But the evidence we have been reviewing here suggests that this is an error of perspective: stress is simply a 'fellow passenger' in a general tendency for features of the present subjunctive and 1SG present indicative root to assume an L/U-pattern distribution.

Yet another pointer comes from Italian, where it is precisely those verbs that deviate from the N-pattern by also having the diphthong in their infinitives (e.g., *cuòcere, chièdere, muòvere*) which tend to remove allomorphy by generalizing the diphthong (e.g., *chiede chiedeva, muove muoveva,* etc.), whereas *solère, volère, sedère, tenère, morìre,* which generally conform[66] to the N-pattern, tend to retain N-pattern alternation (*suole – soleva,* etc.). If the N-pattern were a matter of stress, then the presence of the diphthong in root-stressed infinitives would not be expected to cause differentiation between the two sets of verbs. If, however, the N-pattern is specified over a set of paradigmatic cells excluding the infinitive, then verbs with diphthongs in the infinitive are deviant.

Further evidence for the independence of the N-pattern from stress occurs where stress shifts onto the root, but the vocalic N-pattern persists. It is a characteristic of some Occitan varieties that the (unstressed) root of the preterite and imperfect subjunctive is analogically extended into the (N-pattern root-stressed) present subjunctive; but the originally unstressed vocalic alternant now appears in the stressed root. Thus the verb 'want' in the Pays de Seyne (Quint 1998:55) (60):

(60)

PRS.IND	ˈvwɔlu	ˈvwɔs	vwɔ	vuˈlẽ	vuˈlɛs	ˈvwɔn
PRS.SBJV	ˈvuge	ˈvuges	ˈvuge	vuˈgen	vuˈges	ˈvugen
IPF. SBJV	vuˈgɛse					

Occitan also occasionally shifts stress form the ending onto the root in infinitives, but the original 'unstressed' vowel alternant still persists in the newly stressed root: accordingly in the Basses Pyrénées (Bendel 1934:97f.) we have, in the verb 'to be able' (table 61):

(61)

PRS.IND	pœts	pots	pot	puˈðem	puˈðets	ˈpoðen
INF	ˈpuðe					

Infinitive ˈbule 'want' arises in the same way. Ronjat (1930–41, II:245)[67] gives Occitan examples in which the introduction of rhizotonic stress in the imperfect had not led to loss of the 'unstressed' vocalism of the root: e.g., inf. *voulhí,* 1SG.PRS *vóle,* 1SG imperfect *vóulio.* In contrast, in the dialect of Nice (Toscano 1998), the vocalism of the stressed root of the present tense is (optionally) extended into the unstressed root of future and conditional, but not elsewhere.

In some Romance languages which fuse UADERE and IRE in the verb 'go', the N-pattern is not conditioned by stress, because the root is stressed throughout the present tense. Thus old Spanish (62):[68]

(62)

If the N-pattern alternants are conditioned by stress, one would expect the 'unstressed' alternants if the verb were used as a clitic (hence inherently unstressed) auxiliary. Some Romance languages, such as Romanian, Occitan (Ronjat 1930–41, III:294) and Sicilian (Leone 1980), have reduced atonic (clitic) forms of the verb 'to have' when it is used as an auxiliary: but nowhere does the form used correspond to the 'unstressed' form of the lexical verb. In fact, it is the apparently 'stressed' root (characterized by lack of a labial consonant) which appears in the auxiliary. Thus Romanian: *am ai áre avém avéţi au o carte* 'I/you, etc. have a book' vs. *am ai a am aţi au citit o carte* 'I/you, etc., have read a book.'

As for augments, it is an inherent feature of all augmented forms that the lexical root is *unstressed*, yet all other existing patterns of stress-related allomorphy involve stressed lexical roots. Were the distribution of allomorphs directly mediated by root-stress, one would expect the augmented forms to become restricted to positions where the lexical root was already unstressed – in other words, the reverse of what actually happens in Romance.

Another major objection to the stress-conditioned account of the N-pattern is its phonological unnaturalness. The point is not simply that most of the alternants would be, by universal phonological criteria, utterly bizarre outputs of a process effected by stress, but rather that they are 'unnatural' even in terms of the phonological systems of the languages in which they occur – for they do not find any independent support outside the verbs in which they occur. The stress-conditioned account predicts that if the lexical root also occurs outside the verb paradigm, it should be subject to the same phonological principles. Appropriate examples are elusive, but an empirically testable intuition is that a noun ˈrunu 'gift' in south-eastern Sicilian dialects, sharing a root with ˈruna 'he gives', etc., will be ruˈnuttsu, not **ruttsu, despite the type of allomorphy found in the verb. The unstressed [uʃʃ-] alternant of Italian *uscire* 'to go out' actually comes from the *stressed* root of the noun *uscio* 'doorway'.

Finally, some very common Romance verbs show special allomorphy in the second person singular imperative (e.g., It. 2SG.PRS.IND *hai* 'have', *sai* 'know', *sei* 'be', IMP *abbi, sappi, sii*; Ro. 2SG.PRS.IND *duci* 'take', *faci* 'do', *vii* 'come', *eşti* 'be', IMP *du, fă, vino, fii*). It is not then particularly surprising that virtually all Sicilian dialects which have an N-pattern distribution of reflexes of *do'nare and *'dare nonetheless preserve an imperative da, rather than **'duna (see Schmid 1949:118, n3), but this is a detail which rather clearly shows the independence of the N-pattern from stress.

To conclude, any attempt to tie the N-pattern to stress would not only be otiose, in that stress itself requires specification in terms of 'cells' in the morphological paradigm, but is widely contradicted by a range of diachronic facts from Romance. In fact, stress has become simply one of a heterogeneous range of types of alternation correlated with the N-pattern.[69]

5.11   Indo-European, Sardinian and the N-pattern

My hypothesis is that a phonological process of vocalic differentiation 'etched' into the paradigmatic system of the Romance verb an abstract, autonomous, configuration which attracted and channelled other kinds of allomorphy, and which is not determined by any extramorphological factor. The claim that the N-pattern is an idiosyncrasy of Romance entails two predictions: nothing like the N-pattern should occur in other languages even if their verb paradigm, like Romance, expresses inflectionally two numbers, three persons and the present tense; and any Romance variety that had escaped stress-conditioned vowel differentiation should not show the N-pattern.

My preliminary enquiries about other Indo-European varieties (Albanian, Germanic, Slav, Greek, Indo-Aryan and, not least, Italic itself), similarly structured in the relevant respects, reveal nothing like the N-pattern. No Romance variety escaped stress-related vowel differentiation, but there is one, Logudorese (Sardinian), where such differentiation was, and remains to this day, minimal – involving an *allophonic* variation such that /ɛ/ and /ɔ/ become [e] and [o] when unstressed (or followed by an unstressed high vowel). And precisely in Logudorese there are simply no N-pattern verbs:[70] even 'go' and 'have', loci of allomorphy elsewhere, show no sign (see Wagner 1939:156–60). Thus (where *app-* in the first person singular reflects an L-pattern allomorph, shared with the subjunctive) (63):

(63)

ando	andas	andat	andamus	andáes	andan
appo	as	at	amus	azes	an

These comparative data, both from outside and within Romance, are, then, consistent with my hypothesis.

6   Conclusion

What I have established is that synchronically arbitrary abstract distribution classes can condition and channel change in morphological paradigms. This leaves unresolved the question why, in Romance languages, these rather than any other patterns function in this way, and the even more fundamental question why such patterns play a role in morphological change at all.

The reason why so many Romance languages follow N-pattern and L/U-pattern distributions may be straightforward: these were originally (with the old perfective root, discussed in chapter 4), the *only* sources of root-allomorphy in the verb, so they were the only model of root-allomorphy for person, tense and number available. However, conflation of suppletive allomorphy is almost exclusively the domain of the N-pattern. I suspect that this is explicable by reference to the set of paradigmatic cells which the N-pattern specifies and which, unlike L/U, includes the *third person present tense*. Given that third person present forms tend to be the most frequent, and thereby most salient, it is precisely in these forms that variant verb-roots are likely to be most prominent, and conflation of alternative forms into a single paradigm is therefore likely to follow a pattern (the N-pattern) in which third person present forms are specified.

Undoubtedly there are other types of 'morphomic' change peculiar to subvarieties of Romance and dependent on 'local' phonological and other changes. For example, in Occitan a phonologically motivated coalescence, in certain verbs, of the roots of the present subjunctive and preterite seems to have favoured a general analogical tendency to identity between the subjunctive and preterite roots (see Maiden 1996b). In such cases, which occur in languages which already have a rich array of patterns of root-allomorphy, the problem of explaining why a given pattern, rather than any other, should serve as a template for subsequent paradigmatic change becomes greater. For the time being, we may have to limit ourselves to observing that such phenomena can and do occur, and that the historical linguist should be alert to them. But this alertness should extend not merely to cases in which there is clearly no extramorphological motivation for a pattern of change, but even to cases where, apparently, there is such a motivation.

Consider the morphology of the future tense in those Romance languages of Italy, France and the Iberian Peninsula with a future derived historically from a fusion of the infinitive with a stressed auxiliary form of the present indicative of HABERE 'to have' and a conditional, or 'future-in-the-past' composed of the infinitive plus a stressed form of the imperfect (or in Italian the preterite) indicative of HABERE. Various regular sound changes (particularly involving syncope[71] of the unstressed thematic vowel of the infinitive, and subsequent consonantal assimilations or epentheses) often led to the rise of root-allomorphs which were not only distinct from the infinitive, but unique to the future and conditional. For example (64):

(64)

				Sp.	Fr.	It.
INF	UALERE 'be worth'	>	*va'lere	>	*valer*	*valoir*	*valere*
FUT	UALERE+HABET	>	*vale'ra	>	*valdrá*	*vaudra*	*varrà*
COND	UALERE+HABEBAT	>	*vale're ßa	>	*valdría*	*vaudrait*	
	UALERE + HABUIT	>	*vale'rabbe	>			*varrebbe*
INF	UENIRE 'come'	>	*ve'nire	>	*venir*	*venir*	*venire*
FUT	UENIRE + HABET	>	*veni'ra	>	*vendrá*	*viendra*	*verrà*
COND	UENIRE+HABEBAT	>	*veni're ßa	>	*vendría*	*viendrait*	
	UENIRE+HABUIT	>	*veni'rabbe	>			*verrebbe*

The special shared root of the future and the conditional appears to be *coherent* throughout the Romance languages. In French the diphthong *ie* has been extended analogically from the present into the future root: wherever this occurs, it occurs in future and conditional alike. In Italian there is a similar development in the verb *sedere* 'sit', with future *siederà* and conditional *siederebbe*. The elimination of remnants of the Latin IRE from the French verb 'go' leaves untouched the future and conditional *together* (*ira, irait*). Remnants of the -ISC/ESC- augment were generally eliminated in Gallo-Romance from the infinitive (where by regular sound change is yielded -i[s]t- or -e[s]t-), but in certain varieties (see Keller 1928:147) the -e(s)t- form of the augment has survived in the future *together with* the conditional. There are also signs that the future/conditional root acts as an 'attractor' of allomorphy. The forms [so] and [o] which replace the future/conditional roots of the French verbs *savoir* 'to know' and *avoir* 'to have' (*savra/avra, savroit/avroit > saura/aura, saurait/aurait*) are of unexplained origin (see Maiden 1992). Possibly they reflect a sporadic or dialectal sound change, but what is striking is that they establish themselves precisely in the future/conditional of these two verbs, thereby adding a new allomorph to them. In certain Occitan and French varieties which have generally replaced reflexes of DARE 'give' with those of DONARE, the future and conditional together still retain DARE (see Schmid 1949:123, 126f.). In the future/conditional *andrà/andrebbe* of Italian *andare* 'go' there is deletion of [e] – a change sporadically attested elsewhere in the grammar, as in *compero* or *compro* 'I buy', *sgombero* or *sgombro* 'clear, empty', but not found in any other first conjugation verb.

It might be thought that the coherence of the future/conditional root merely reflects their common function of indicating 'future time'. But I would suggest that even in cases of apparent functional motivation, the distribution of an alternation may still have a high degree of arbitrariness. In fact, there is a possible exception to the 'coherence' of future and conditional in an Occitan dialect[72] of the Corrèze area (Monteil 1997), where some future and conditional roots are distinct: for example, the verb ʃoụbi 'know' has (1SG) FUT ʃoụrɛị, but conditional ʃoụbri'jo. Assuming that there is no phonological explanation, this is an exception which 'proves the rule', in that it shows that there is no reason in principle why future and conditional must share the same root and makes all the more remarkable the fact that everywhere else they continue to do so. And even though future and conditional usually share future-time reference, they each have additional functions which are not shared: for example, the conditional can have past-time reference, unlike the future, and it can have evidential value (e.g., *Il y aurait une grève* 'There is [reportedly] a strike') not shared by the future. Indeed, in Italian since the seventeenth century (see Maiden 1996c), the conditional has lost the function of indicating 'future in the past', and is now fundamentally restricted to non-past counterfactual constructions; yet analogical extension of the diphthong *ie* into the future/conditional *siederò/siederei* operates regardless of any such distinction. The coherent behaviour of the future/conditional root, generally treated as unremarkable in discussions of Romance historical morphology, may be a good deal stranger than we commonly think.

We have still not addressed the utterly fundamental question of why unmotivated allomorphy should survive and prosper at all. It seems, after all, to be in fundamental contradiction to a universal property of linguistic signs, namely that a single meaning should correspond to a single phonological form. Not only is this intuitively true, but its truth is manifest over and over again in the history of all Romance languages in the phenomenon of 'analogical levelling', such that allomorphy is eliminated in favour of invariance (cf. It. *chiedere* 'ask', where the diphthong *ie* is now present throughout the paradigm, but was originally distributed only in stressed open syllables). In fact, 'analogical levelling' and the various phenomena of coherence, convergence and attraction surveyed in this chapter are at root *one and the same thing*.

There is a universal semiotic principle favouring biunique matching of lexical signata and signantia. The L/U- and N-patterns, so far from being 'antisemiotic' (cf. Pirrelli 2000:102), are in fact local, Romance, variants of this same universal principle. There is no sharp dichotomy between universal, 'system independent', naturalness and local 'system-dependent naturalness', which in 'Natural Morphology' seems to be viewed as a function of the fortuitous presence of numerically overwhelming types of deviation from form–meaning biuniqueness (see Wurzel 1987). Maiden (1996b; 1998a) illustrates that non-iconic and anti-iconic developments actually follow patterns which were originally in a small numerical minority. In plain terms, coherence, convergence and conflation of suppletive allomorphs are 'reserve strategies' for ensuring the biuniqueness of lexical signs. The 'default' is paradigmatic invariance. Predicting when and why allomorphy is *not* eliminated remains a problem, but for my present purposes what is important is simply the fact that allomorphy often *does* survive. Coherence and convergence are alternative strategies by which speakers, so to speak, 'minimize the damage', constraining deviations from biuniqueness in recurrent sets of paradigmatic cells and, in the case of convergence, making the phonological content of deviation maximally systematic and predictable. The very fact that speakers make 'morphomic'[73] generalizations about the structure of paradigms, abstracting away from extraparadigmatic functional or phonological details, suggests that they seek out, and seek to reinforce, paradigmatic patterns of maximal generality.[74]

6 CHANGE AND CONTINUITY IN FORM–FUNCTION RELATIONSHIPS

John Charles Smith

1 Introduction

In this chapter, I shall motivate and discuss a typology of changes in the relationship between linguistic form and linguistic function, with reference to the Romance languages, and attempt to elucidate some general principles which may underlie the developments described.[1] It will be useful to distinguish four types of change.

- **Refunctionalization** is the acquisition of a new value or function by an existing morphological opposition (the phenomenon which Lass (1990), borrowing a term from the evolutionary biologists Gould and Vrba (1982), refers to as 'exaptation'). However, the terms 'refunctionalization' and 'exaptation' have often been used without distinction to refer both to instances in which the original value of the formal opposition has disappeared and to those in which this original value has been retained alongside the new meaning (indeed, in subsequent work, Lass (1997) explicitly envisages both possibilities). I propose that the notion of 'refunctionalization' should be limited to the former case, in which the new function replaces (or displaces) the old one. A good example of this development is the evolution of some Latin accusative pronouns into conjunctive (clitic) forms and their dative counterparts into disjunctive forms in a variety of Romance languages.

- **Adfunctionalization** is the term I shall use to designate the second state of affairs outlined above, in which the new value or function is added to the existing one. As an example, we may take many of the Romance masculine/feminine doublets which derive from the singular/plural opposition in the Latin neuter; in these cases, not only do the nouns exhibit distinct genders, but, additionally, it is the feminine which retains the original literal meaning and the masculine which comes to encode a derived figurative meaning.

- **Functionalization** occurs when an opposition which has not previously had a morphological or lexical value or function comes to encode one. This development may take place as the result of differential phonological change; compare the creation of doublets in French as a result of the lexically diffuse evolution of the diphthong [oi] (for instance, *François* vs. *Français*). It may also arise (as it does in Istro-Romanian) from the redistribution, within a single linguistic system, of originally 'synonymous' items in the two languages of a bilingual (and diglossic) speech community.
- **Defunctionalization** is the loss of value or function of an opposition. This may happen in a variety of ways. One of these is for the two forms to survive as quasi-synonymous stylistic or sociolinguistic variants; sometimes (but not always), one of the forms is perceived as more archaic than the other. Another possibility is the reduction of what was previously a meaningful (lexical or morphological) opposition to the status of mere phonological variation (more accurately, a variation in pronunciation, as defined by Chambers and Trudgill 1998:97). One possible example of such a development is the alleged conflation in old French of the verbs *amer* and *esmer*.

Within refunctionalization (and adfunctionalization), we may distinguish between intramorphological change, lexical to morphological change (e.g., suppletion), and morphological to lexical change (e.g., the existence in modern French of doublets where one of the items derives from the old French nominative case and the other derives from the old French oblique case). I have claimed in recent work (Smith 2005; 2006) that refunctionalization and adfunctionalization are not random, but involve a principle of 'core-to-core' mapping, whereby some element, however abstract, of the original opposition survives in the new one. It may be that a similar process is at work even in some cases of functionalization, although the evidence does not for the moment justify such a claim.

The data presented will provide some (though by no means all) of the answers to Joseph's question (Joseph 1998): 'Where does morphology come from?' Morphological oppositions may arise from existing morphology (although this is something of a *mise en abyme*), from phonology and from the lexicon. In addition, a (similarly non-exhaustive) answer is given to the question 'Where does morphology go to?' – it may become lexicalized or phonologized, or remain as sociolinguistic or stylistic variation. My hypothesis is that the general principles here adumbrated from Romance are applicable more generally.

2   Refunctionalization

2.1   *Accusative vs. dative participant pronouns from Latin to Romance*

In Smith (1999a; 2006), I discuss the evolution of the accusative and dative forms of the first- and second-person singular pronouns from Latin to Romance in the light of Lass's original paper on 'exaptation'. There, as here, the arguments are exemplified from the first-person forms ME (accusative) and MIHI, reduced to MI (dative); the same arguments will apply, *mutatis mutandis*, to the second-person forms.[2] Lass (1990:81f.) begins: 'Say a language has a grammatical distinction of some sort, coded by means of morphology.' Clearly, one option is for this form–function relationship to survive intact, and this is what we find in Romanian, at least with regard to pronouns which are complements of verbs (see Poghirc 1969:239) – thus, accusative clitic *mă* < ME; dative clitic *mi* < MI; both forms have phonotactic variants which will not concern us here. For ease of reference, we may label languages which retain the form–function relationship in this way 'Type A' languages. Another example of a 'Type A' language is old Sardinian, which distinguishes between an accusative conjunctive form *me* (<ME) and a dative conjunctive form *mi* (<MI(HI)); see Wagner (1960–64:II, 57), s.v. *mè*.

Lass (1990:81f.) continues: 'Then say this distinction is jettisoned, PRIOR TO the loss of the morphological material that codes it. This morphology is now, functionally speaking, junk; and there are three things that can in principle be done with it: (i) it can be dumped entirely.' This first option is the course taken by standard French and many French dialects. There is no reflex of the Latin dative MI, but the accusative ME survives, yielding two forms: *moi* when tonic and *me* when atonic. The distribution of the two forms is no longer determined by stress, and the conventional labels are 'disjunctive pronoun' for the original tonic form and 'conjunctive pronoun' for the original atonic form. I shall return to the division of labour between these two items in the section below on functionalization. We might use the shorthand expression 'Type B' language to describe a language in which one of the forms of the original opposition disappears whilst the other survives. Let us call languages where one of the Latin case forms is lost 'Type B' languages, and the subset of this group which dispense with the dative 'Type B1' languages. Interestingly, there appear to be no 'Type B' languages in which it is the accusative and not the dative which has disappeared. Clearly, the non-existence of such languages is not axiomatic, and has to be explained; I shall return to this point below. For the moment, I shall designate them 'Type B2' languages, and distinguish them from 'Type B1' languages, such as French, which **are** attested.

Lass's next scenario (1990:81f.) is: '(ii) it [the distinction] can be kept as marginal garbage or nonfunctional/nonexpressive residue (suppletion, "irregularity")'. We appear to have an instance of this type of development in old Occitan, where both *me* < ME and *mi* < MI survive as both conjunctive and disjunctive pronouns in both accusative and dative cases. I shall return to this example in the section on 'defunctionalization' below. We may term languages which exhibit this type of development 'Type C' languages.

Finally, according to Lass (1990:81f.): '(iii) it [the distinction] can be kept, but instead of being relegated as in (ii), it can be used for something else, perhaps just as systematic. [...] Option (iii) is linguistic exaptation.' There are some good apparent examples of this process involving the oblique forms of the first- and second-person singular pronouns in Romance. Spanish (Lloyd 1987:278; Penny 1991:119f.), Portuguese (Mattoso Camara 1972:82–84), Galician (García de Diego 1909:108f.), northern dialects of French (i.e., the dialects of Picardy, Wallonia and Lorraine (Gossen 1951:101)) and most Italo-Romance dialects (Rohlfs 1968:§§442, 454) exhibit a conjunctive form derived from the Latin accusative (e.g., Lat. ME > Sp., Pt., Pic. *me*), and a disjunctive form derived from the Latin dative (e.g., Lat. MI > Sp. *mí*, Pt. *mim*, Pic. *mi*). This looks like a clear-cut case of 'exaptation' – the original distinction (accusative vs. dative) has been discarded, but the morphological opposition has not withered away; rather it has been pressed into service to encode something else.

If the morphology really has become 'junk', then, logically, we might expect to find languages which are mirror-images of the ones just discussed; that is, languages in which the **dative** yields the conjunctive form and the **accusative** the disjunctive form. A widely held opinion amongst Romance linguists is that Tuscan and its derivative, standard Italian, follow such a pattern; for instance, Melander (1928:146–50), Moignet (1965:55), Bourciez (1967:§221c) and Tagliavini (1972:257) all make this claim (Lat. ME > Tsc., It. *me*; Lat. MI > Tsc., It. *mi*). For ease of reference, I shall term languages which refunctionalize the Latin distinction 'Type D' languages, further distinguishing between 'Type D1' languages (the Spanish type, in which the conjunctive derives from the accusative and the disjunctive from the dative) and 'Type D2' languages (the standard Italian type, in which the reverse apparently happens).

So far, the data seem to bear out Lass's analysis. We have four basic language types, one of which maintains the original Latin opposition in both form and function, the others of which reflect each of the various possible developments outlined by Lass, including 'exaptation'.[3] The fact that the 'junk' morphology can apparently be refunctionalized in random ways (compare the difference between languages of types D1 and D2) would argue strongly that the formal opposition had, in late Latin or early Romance, become precisely that – junk.[4]

However, we are still left with the need to explain the absence of 'Type B2' languages (that is, languages in which the accusative form has disappeared without trace, but the dative has gone on to great things). More problematic for the notion of 'exaptation' is a related issue. I want to claim that, despite much received wisdom, there are, in fact, no languages of Type D2, either. If this is true, it means that the languages which employ the opposition between original Latin accusative and dative forms to encode a distinction between conjunctive and disjunctive pronouns all do so in the same way – the development is systematic and not random. We should therefore try to find some motivation (or better, some rationale) for it; but, of course, if we can do so, then we cannot be dealing with true 'junk'.

Let me first deal with the evolution of the first- and second-person singular pronouns in Tuscan and Standard Italian. There is an alternative to the widespread analysis referred to above. D'Ovidio (1886:68), Lausberg (1956:§255), Rohlfs (1968:§454), Tekavčić (1972:§§119, 764), and Elcock (1960:78, n1[5]), amongst others, note that [i] is the normal Tuscan development of late Latin pretonic [e] (just as [ə] is the normal outcome of this vowel in pretonic position in French). Some uncontroversial examples of these developments in standard Italian and French are given below.

Late Latin	Tuscan/Italian	French	
[meˈnakja]	[miˈnattʃa]	[məˈnas]	'threat'
[de ˈnɔkte]	[di ˈnɔtte]	[də ˈnɥi]	'by night'

As the second of these examples shows, 'pretonic' is defined with reference to the clitic group (in the sense of Nespor and Vogel 1986:145–63). But, of course, *me*, when proclitic to a verb (a possible position of the atonic pronoun complement of a verb during the late Latin and early Romance period; see Ramsden 1963:119f. and Salvi, this volume, chapter 7), will constitute a pretonic syllable; consequently, the accusative form of the pronoun in this position will develop to *mi*, just as it develops to [mə] in French.

Late Latin	Tuscan/Italian	French	
∴ [me ˈtrɔpat]	[mi ˈtrɔva]	[mə ˈtʁuv]	'finds me'

We still have to explain **enclitic** *mi* (here, [me] would be the expected development, and is in fact found in some Tuscan texts of the Renaissance, especially in rhyming contexts; see Rohlfs 1968:§454, n1); but, given that enclisis of pronouns gave way to proclisis in Tuscan in most circumstances (Rohlfs 1968:§469; see also the discussion and references in Ramsden 1963:112–33), it is not unreasonable to suppose that the enclitic form *mi* is an analogical extension of the commoner proclitic form (D'Ovidio 1886:70 and Rohlfs 1968:§454 both countenance this possibility).

There is strong circumstantial evidence to support the derivation of Tuscan *mi* from ME. Other Italian varieties seem to belong to either Type B1 (languages which have abandoned the Latin dative form) or Type D1 (the Spanish type, in which the Latin accusative has yielded the conjunctive form and the Latin dative the disjunctive form) (see Rohlfs 1968:§§442, 454). Of course, there is no a priori reason why Tuscan should conform to the pattern found elsewhere in Italy; but, even in Tuscan, the conjunctive pronoun assumes the form *me* when it is the first element of a clitic cluster – thus *me lo*; *me la*; *me ne*, etc. This form cannot be derived from Latin MI(HI); it is normally assumed to be the outcome of ME with secondary stress (Rohlfs 1968:§466), although Melander (1929:188) claims that it is a borrowing from one or more neighbouring dialects. The secondary stress argument receives some support from a parallel development: Latin DE 'down from', 'about' and subsequently 'of', which normally develops to Italian *di*, yields *de* when it is compounded with a following definite article – thus *della*, *dello*, *degli*, etc. 'of the'. Camilli (1946:90, n3), drawing attention to this parallel, refers to the contrast between the 'deboli' (weak) forms *mi* and *di* and the 'semiforti' (semi-strong) forms *me* and *de*.[6] It seems desirable, other things being equal, to postulate a common origin for the clitic forms *mi* and *me*. For all the above reasons, it is plausible to argue that Tuscan, and therefore Standard Italian, are 'Type B1' languages, like French.

Sardinian also provides some problematic data. As noted above, old Sardinian, like modern Romanian, was a 'Type A' language, maintaining the Latin opposition between accusative *me* and dative *mi* as conjunctive pronouns. However, in modern Sardinian, the case distinction has disappeared, and *mi* is now the sole form of the conjunctive pronoun, whilst a number of disjunctive forms exist (depending on the function of the pronoun and the variety involved), including *me* (for fuller discussion, see Jones 1993:199–200, 213). Blasco Ferrer (1984b:96) draws the superficially attractive conclusion that the dative has been generalized at the expense of the accusative; according to this analysis, Sardinian would be a 'Type B2' or a 'Type D2' language. The true position is, in fact, more complicated. Although [e] > [i] is not a widespread change in Sardinian, Wagner (1941:§59) notes that pretonic [e] can develop to [i] or [j] before a vowel, and that *mi* is thus a common development of the accusative pronoun in this position (Wagner 1960–64:II, 57, s.v. *mè*). We therefore have the situation in old Sardinian that *me* can only be the exponent of the accusative (in preconsonantal position), whilst *mi* can be the exponent of the dative or (in prevocalic position) the accusative. In these circumstances, the generalization of *mi* to become the sole first-person oblique clitic may well have an element of analogy; it could be misleading to regard the form which is generalized simply as a dative pronoun. Wagner (1951:328) further suggests that the generalization of the form *mi* may be due to Italian influence. It may be that some varieties of Sardinian are 'Type B2' or 'Type D2' languages and constitute an exception to the claim I am making; but, in this instance, where analogy and language contact may have played a significant role in the change, we are probably not dealing simply with a refunctionalization of the Latin distinction. In any case, the developments just described are subsequent to the initial developments in late Latin/early Romance which are the focus of this section.

The next question we have to ask is: Can the ME/MI(HI) opposition really be regarded as 'junk'? It is true that in late Latin we find both an increase in the use of the dative case and a tendency for the accusative and dative forms of pronouns to encroach on each other's traditional territory. Bonnet (1890:536), discussing nouns and pronouns as complements of verbs in the sixth-century Latin of Gregory of Tours, observes that the dative had been gaining ground since Cicero; whilst varying degrees of apparent interchangeability between the accusative and dative cases of pronouns are noted by Pei (1932:224, 167), Norberg (1943:171f.) and Wanner (1987:87). But it should be stressed that the increase in the use of the dative case of both nouns and pronouns and the overlapping use of the accusative and dative of pronouns, where it is attested, is limited to the complements of verbs. The development appears to have been driven by a semantic or thematic analogy involving verbs whose patient could also be construed as a beneficiary, and hence be encoded in the dative (for discussion and examples, see Löfstedt 1942:200–8). There is little or no evidence that the dative expanded its role to the point where it could serve as the complement of a preposition. So the data do not justify the claim that the ME/MI(HI) opposition really is 'junk' at any stage of Latin. But there is also an important a posteriori consideration: if there is no longer any contrast between the two items (other than the obvious phonological one), then we are a priori unable to explain the two lacunæ noted above, to wit:

(i) Why should it always be the original dative form that vanishes? In other words, why are there no languages of Type B2?

(ii) Why, when the distinction is refunctionalized, should the original accusative systematically yield the conjunctive form and the original dative the disjunctive form? In other words, why are there no languages of Type D2? There is a particular problem here, as intimated earlier. The characteristic use of the disjunctive form is as the complement of a preposition; but the dative is unattested in such a function in Latin.[7] There is thus no precedent for the subsequent Romance development (described by Penny (1991:120) as 'an early innovation of obscure motivation') – the disjunctive pronoun (a sort of prepositional case) is created *ex novo*, and its combination of form and function cannot be traced back to Latin in any concrete sense.

In Smith (2006), I claimed that, in the present instance, the opposition between the two pronominal forms has not been completely obliterated, but has rather been reduced to that between a 'core' term on the one hand, and a 'non-core' term on the other. To describe the state in which an opposition has been evacuated of all or almost all its concrete functional content (i.e., its exponence), but in which a residual, arguably more abstract, dichotomy remains – that is, an identity which, however diminished, is not yet junk – I followed Lass in borrowing a concept from a different discipline (hoping to avoid the pitfall pointed out by Lass (1990:79), that 'Such borrowings often turn from theoretical claims into sloppy metaphors'!). In this case, the discipline is art history, and the concept is that of 'skeuomorphy'. The term 'skeuomorph' appears to be a coinage of March (1889:166); compare the *OED*, second edition (1989), s.v. *skeuomorph* (vol. 15, p. 594). However, perhaps the best discussion of the notion of skeuomorphy is found in the work of the architectural historian Philip Steadman (1979:103–23). Amongst other examples, Steadman discusses the fact, originally noted by Lang (1887), that potters in the Cypriot village of Lithrodonto will add two blobs of clay to a newly finished jug, and, when asked to explain why they do this, can state only that it is part of the traditional design – 'We've always done it this way.' It turns out that similar vessels dating from about 500 BC excavated by archæologists in the same area are modelled in the form of female figures. The jugs are no longer modelled in female form, but a comparison of the classical version and the modern one shows quite clearly that it is the breasts of the original figure that have been retained as the two blobs of clay – they no longer represent anything concrete, but now have a more abstract function: that of being part of the traditional design. The concept of skeuomorphy is subsequently seized upon and elaborated by Humphrey (1992:185f.).

> Design features that were once of practical importance but have later become mainly if not wholly decorative – and no longer subject to selection on utilitarian grounds – are given the name 'skeuomorphs' (from the Greek 'utensil' 'form'). Examples are widely found in clothing (e.g. the buttons on the cuffs of men's coats), in engineering (e.g. the running boards on early motor cars), and on a grander scale, in architecture. In classical Greek temples (and their descendants right up to the present day) many of the decorative features of the stone buildings hark back to the structural features of the wooden buildings that preceded them: the dog-tooth Doric frieze, for example, comes originally from the pattern made by the exposed ends of timber roof-supporting beams, and the earliest stone temples even had stone reproductions of the wooden pins.
>
> Craftsmen tend to *copy* pre-existing models. And the reasons for copying are several. Partly it is that copying is easy: the selection or planning that went into the development of the earlier version is now inherent in the structure, and the copy can be made without having to work through this again. Partly it is that copying is safe: the earlier version did the job required of it, and the copy can be trusted to do the job at least as well. And partly it is that copying creates objects that are in tune with what people expect: the earlier version has set the standard for what the design 'ought to' look like, and the copy ends up looking comfortably familiar. This latter factor is likely to have been especially powerful when, as must often have happened, the old and the new versions have coexisted in the same environment and there has been a need to avoid a clash of styles (a stone temple, say, being built next door to a wooden one).[8]

Humphrey goes on to suggest that the notion of skeuomorphy can be applied to biological systems. *Mutatis mutandis*, it may also be richly relevant to linguistic change. In the account given by Humphrey and quoted above, a feature which starts off as functional loses its functionality and becomes decorative – that is, in some sense, cultural. I would want to argue strongly that it still has a content (in the appropriate parts of Cyprus, after all, pots without bumps would initially be regarded as a solecism), but that this content is a highly abstract one. 'Decorative' is not a term usually associated with serious studies of language,[9] and I don't mean it to be taken literally here; but the analogy will work, I think – even when evacuated of its concrete functional value or exponence, a morphological opposition can encode something more abstract.[10]

I have suggested (Smith 1999a; 2006) that the notion of 'core' value, alluded to above, is associated with one or more of at least the following: qualitative unmarkedness; quantitative unmarkedness (higher frequency); default status. Often, these criteria will yield identical results; but not always.[11] For this reason, I prefer not to use 'unmarked' as a cover term, leaving open the possibility that a particular criterion may dominate in particular circumstances (in keeping with the opinion expressed by Haspelmath (2006:63) that the term 'markedness' 'can be readily replaced by other concepts and terms that are less ambiguous, more transparent and provide better explanations for the observed phenomena').

- **Qualitative unmarkedness** is defined by a number of well-known criteria, summarized by Battistella (1990:26) as 'optimality, breadth of distribution, syncretization, indeterminateness, simplicity, and prototypicality'. Optimality refers to the fact that 'When certain segments or certain feature values imply others in language after language, those values are taken to be unmarked' (p. 26). As far as distribution is concerned, 'Unmarked terms are distinguished from their marked counterparts by having a greater freedom of occurrence and a greater ability to combine with other linguistic elements' (p. 26) – the characteristic referred to by Croft (1990:77) as 'versatility'. The unmarked term is also the one that occurs in positions of absolute neutralization. Syncretization means that 'Unmarked categories tend to be more differentiated than marked ones' (Battistella 1990:27). By the criterion of simplicity 'unmarked elements are less elaborate in form than their [marked] counterparts', and by that of prototypicality, they are 'experientially more basic' (p. 27).
- **Higher frequency** is generally assumed to be a quantitative indicator of unmarkedness (see especially the discussion in Greenberg 1966:64). Bybee (1985:117f.) further suggests that items which

occur more frequently in texts or discourse have greater 'lexical strength' – that is, they are more firmly entrenched in the mental representation of the lexicon.

- A **default form** is the one which occurs when there are no obvious criteria for selecting a particular item.

So, returning to the oblique forms of the first- and second-person singular pronouns in Latin, I shall maintain that the 'core' form is the original accusative, and that the 'core' function is that of conjunctive pronoun. Uncontroversially, if one of the terms disappears, it will tend to be the 'non-core' term. Winter (1971:61), for instance, in a discussion of the evolution of case systems, claims: 'If, in the course of its development through time, a system suffers a loss of forms, the more prominent form is likely to survive.' (He recognizes both quantitative prominence, straightforwardly definable in terms of frequency, and qualitative prominence, which is more difficult to define, but which corresponds to the commonly held views of qualitative unmarkedness referred to above.) Hence, no languages of Type B2. If the opposition is refunctionalized, the 'core' term will assume a 'core' function, whilst the 'non-core' term will assume a 'non-core' function. Hence, no languages of Type D2.

How might such a claim be justified by the data? First of all, can we reasonably maintain that the Latin accusative is the 'core' term and the dative the 'non-core' term in opposition to it? There is substantial evidence for this hypothesis. Vincent (1994; 1997d) argues convincingly for the view that the accusative was a default case in Latin; in contexts where case can neither be assigned structurally nor supplied by perseveration or 'echoing' of an NP in a previous sentence, it is the accusative that surfaces (compare isolated exclamations, such as *O me miserum!* see Blake 2001:9). Adams (2003:62–63, n146, 227, 477) discusses the so-called 'accusative of apposition' and suggests that this, too, may represent the use of the accusative as a default form. Winter (1971:55), arguing that 'the relative frequency of a form has some significance in determining its chances for survival or even adoption outside its original range of usage', presents figures showing that the accusative was also the most frequent case in Latin: 35.8% of 18,889 Latin noun forms taken from Plautus, Cæsar, Sallust, Vergil and Petronius (a corpus encompassing prose, poetry and drama written between the third century BC and the first century AD) are in this case. In contrast, the dative accounts for only 4.2% of Winter's sample, in penultimate place, ahead only of the vocative (2.2%).[12] The ratio of accusative to dative is 8.52:1. The Latin frequency dictionary of Delatte *et al.* (1981:220–22) confirms that the accusative is the most frequently occurring case in both prose (51,438 substantives out of 161,652, or 31.8% of occurrences) and poetry (21,598 substantives out of 68,600, or 31.5% of occurrences) and that (setting aside the rare locative case, which is absent from Winter's corpus) the dative is also the second least frequent case (9,527 tokens, or 5.89% of the total, in prose; 3,751, or 5.47% of the total, in poetry), ahead of the vocative. These figures yield a ratio of accusative to dative of 5.40:1 in prose and 5.76:1 in poetry. The function of the accusative is also less marked than that of the dative. The evidence presented by Pinkster (1990:40–48), on the basis of an examination of the first seventy-three chapters of Cicero's *De Oratore* (first century BC), does not enable any qualitative statement to be made concerning the dative; he can conclude only that this case 'occurs relatively infrequently' (p. 43). The accusative, on the other hand, has a well-defined function: it 'is pre-eminently the case for the marking of constituents which form part of the nuclear predication' (1990:40–48). But the Latin form ME is also the exponent of the ablative case of the first-person singular pronoun. According to the figures presented by Winter (1971:55), the ablative is the second most frequently occurring case of Latin, after the accusative, accounting for 24.7% of his sample of 18,889 noun forms (see above). Delatte *et al.* (1981:220–22) likewise find that the ablative is the second most frequent case in prose texts (38,931 substantives out of 161,652, or 24.1% of occurrences); although in poetry, this case is pushed into third position (14,854 substantives out of 68,600, or 21.7% of occurrences) by the nominative. As for the function of the ablative, for Pinkster (1990:43) it is 'pre-eminently the case for the marking of satellites, i.e., constituents in the periphery'. Seen in this light, the ME/MI(HI) contrast is an opposition between, on the one hand, a 'core' form which syncretizes the two most commonly occurring cases (or, at least, the two most commonly occurring oblique cases) and is the unmarked form for encoding both internal arguments/complements (Pinkster's 'constituents which form part of the nuclear predication') and non-arguments/adjuncts (Pinkster's 'satellites, i.e., constituents in the periphery'), and, on the other hand, a much less common case form with an exponence about which it is difficult to make any qualitative generalization, and which may therefore be regarded as marked.

The frequency of the pronominal forms themselves confirms this view. Figures derived from Delatte *et al.* (1981:260, 277, 278, 283, 288, 291, 497) yield a ME to MI(HI) ratio of 1.15:1 and a TE to TIBI ratio of 1.29:1.[13]

Turning now to the distinction between conjunctive and disjunctive pronouns, we may note that the function of the conjunctive pronoun is to be the complement of a verb, whilst the (original) function of a disjunctive pronoun is to be the complement of a preposition (Moignet (1965:56) usefully defines the contrast as being between a 'prédicatif' pronoun and its 'non prédicatif' counterpart).[14] Assuming the (un)markedness or 'coreness' of a subcategorized complement-type to be related to that of the item that subcategorizes it, we can start by making some cross-linguistic observations about the two syntactic categories involved. Verb is arguably a universal category (Croft 1990:46), Preposition (or Adposition) is not. On the basis of this evidence, Verb would seem to qualify as the 'core' or 'unmarked' of the two categories. Likewise, in many theories of syntax, Verb (or an equivalent feature) is a categorial primitive; no theory makes a similar claim about Prepositions. As regards the specifics of Latin, we find that Verbs exhibit the characteristics of an unmarked category (see above) relative to Prepositions. Verbs are more frequent than Prepositions in terms of both types and tokens – there are many more members of the category Verb, and they occur more frequently in texts. Of the total of 794,662 Latin word tokens (582,411 in prose; 212,251 in poetry) examined by Delatte *et al.* (1981:220–22), 182,070, or 22.91% of the total corpus, are verbs (134,229 (23.05%) in prose; 47,841 (22.54%) in poetry), and only 42,696, or 5.37%, are prepositions (35,722 (6.13%) in prose; 6,974 (3.29%) in poetry). Related to type frequency is the fact that Verbs constitute an open class, whilst the class of Prepositions is a (virtually) closed one. Verbs are also more 'versatile' than Prepositions (in the sense of Croft 1990:77); they may be inflectionally marked for person, number, tense, aspect, mood and voice, whilst Prepositions generally carry no inflectional marking at all.[15] Moreover, viewed as a class, Verbs may occur in a large number of syntactic environments (transitive sentences, intransitive sentences, passive sentences, etc.), and may take practically any phrasal category (including zero) as their complement; the distribution of Prepositions, on the other hand, is much more restricted. On the basis of these data, 'complement of verb' qualifies as a 'core' value in Latin with respect to 'complement of preposition'. The view that the conjunctive pronoun is the 'core' form relative to the disjunctive pronoun is also supported by frequency data from Romance. For Spanish, we have relevant information from Juilland and Chang-Rodriguez (1964:364, 380), whose figures yield a conjunctive to disjunctive ratio of 6.59:1 in the first-person singular and 24.8:1 in the second-person singular, and, more recently, Alameda and Cuetos (1995:352, 356, 462,

465) (first-person singular 9.19:1; second-person singular 8.86:1). In Italian, too, the conjunctive form is more frequent than its disjunctive counterpart, in this case by a ratio of between two and four to one, as shown by Bortolini *et al.* (1972:393, 684) (the ratio of conjunctive to disjunctive is 3.29:1 in the first-person singular and 3.13:1 in the second-person singular), Juilland and Traversa (1973:212, 217, 366, 370) (2.33:1 and 3.93:1) and De Mauro *et al.* (1993:280, 387) (2.78:1 and 1.95:1). In French, the disjunctive pronoun has expanded into a variety of new functions (notably that of emphatic subject-, object- or topic-marker), and, in the persons under discussion, is identical to the form assumed by a conjunctive pronoun when it bears stress (compare *Dis-moi*, *Réveille-toi*); although frequency dictionaries do not distinguish this conjunctive use from the disjunctive form. The figures found in word counts of French may therefore overestimate the frequency of the disjunctive pronouns. However, this potential inflation is not a practical problem, for the forms *me* and *te* are in any case more frequent than the forms *moi* and *toi*. From Juilland *et al.* (1970:218, 225, 350, 355), we derive a conjunctive to disjunctive ratio of 2.52:1 in the first-person singular and 2.31:1 in the second-person singular, whilst the frequency dictionary of Imbs (1971:1259, 1306, 1339, 2026, 2044, 2068) yields figures of 2.86:1 and 2.80:1, respectively.

On the basis of both qualitative and quantitative evidence, then, it seems plausible to maintain that 'accusative' and 'conjunctive pronoun' are 'core' values in Latin and Romance with respect to 'dative' and 'disjunctive pronoun' and that the change discussed in this section takes place according to a principle of 'core-to-core' mapping.

2.2   Nominative vs. accusative in Gallo-Romance nouns

I turn now to a second case-study: the fate of the case forms in Gallo-Romance nouns. Alone amongst the Romance languages, Gallo-Romance and Ræto-Romance maintained a nominal case system deriving from the distinction between the nominative and the accusative of Latin.[16] (In what follows, I shall limit my discussion to French and Occitan.) This is not the place to give a detailed account and analysis of the Latin and old Gallo-Romance case systems (for which see Sornicola, this volume, chapter 1: §3.1); I shall merely survey the data which relate to the arguments about refunctionalization. The case system of Latin is presented in Kühner and Stegmann (1912–14:II, 252–487) and Hofmann and Szantyr (1965:21–151).[17] Its fate in later stages of the language is outlined by Väänänen

(1981:110–15) and Herman (2000a:49–63). Succinct descriptions of the old French system are given by Pope (1934:310–14) and Zink (1997:27–38), whilst old Occitan is dealt with by Jensen (1976) and Skårup (1997:61–72). A detailed conspectus of old French declension is provided by Nyrop (1924:174–209), and an extensive discussion of the forms and functions of the old French cases has recently been undertaken by Buridant (2001:62–104). A comparable, although briefer, treatment of form and function in the case system of old Occitan can be found in Jensen (1994:2–18).

In most nouns, the morphophonemic realization of the case system was nugatory; in most feminines it was non-existent. The fact that the only inflection was -s, that it served as a case inflection in only a subset of masculine nouns, and that, even here, it could mark either case (nominative in the singular, oblique in the plural), ensured hesitation and confusion through most of the old French and old Occitan periods, and led to the ultimate demise of the system. In French and in some varieties of Occitan, the progressive disappearance of final [-s] left the inflection as a purely orthographical device and may have sealed its fate. The existence in both languages of a small imparisyllabic declension, in which the exponence of morphological case (albeit only in the singular) rested on something more substantial, did not prevent the system from collapsing. Bédier (1927:248) in a celebrated barb, claims that, if we set aside the oldest texts, those which date from the ninth and tenth centuries, such as the Eulalia Sequence and the *Vie de Saint Léger*, the rules governing declension manifest themselves in their purest form only in modern grammars of old French,[18] although this is something of an exaggeration (see Ashdowne and Smith 2007:195). Northern French authors and scribes, at least, show some consistency in case usage into the very late fourteenth century, or even a little beyond (Pope 1934:§806; Zink 1990:31; Marchello-Nizia 1997:121–25; van Reenen and Schøsler 2000b). However, here, as elsewhere, dating changes on the basis of the literary language in all likelihood leads us to conservative conclusions. Gardner and Greene (1958:4) claim (almost certainly over-simplifying) that 'the declension system was not moribund at the beginning of the fourteenth century; it was in actual fact dead'; whilst Zink (1990:30) plausibly suggests that the nominal case system had disappeared from spoken French by 1250. For detailed discussion, see Schøsler (1984). Similar considerations apply to Occitan, although nominal case may have survived slightly longer in this language (see Ronjat 1937:4f.; Jensen 1976:123–37; 1994:17f.).

Modern noun-forms are generally derived from the oblique case (usually the more frequent); but occasionally the nominative is the case which provides the modern form, e.g., Fr. *peintre* < NOM *PINCTOR 'painter' (*peinteur* < ACC *PINCTOREM); Fr. *prêtre* < NOM PRESBYTER 'priest' (*provoire* < ACC PRESBYTERUM); Fr. *ancêtre* < NOM ANTECESSOR 'ancestor' (*ancesseur* < ACC ANTECESSOREM); Fr. *sœur* < NOM SOROR 'sister' (*sereur* < ACC SOROREM); Fr. *traître* < NOM TRADITOR 'traitor' (*traiteur* < ACC TRADITOREM); Fr. *fils* < NOM FILIUS 'son' (*fil* < ACC FILIUM). Personal proper names may also be derived from the nominative, thus: Fr. *Sartre* < NOM SARTOR 'tailor' (*Sarteur* < ACC SARTOREM); Fr. *Charles* < NOM CAROLUS (%*Charle* < ACC CAROLUM); Fr. *Georges* < NOM GEORGIUS (%*George* < ACC GEORGIUM) (the forms *Charle* and *George* are occasionally attested in literary usage, especially in verse, for reasons of scansion; see Nyrop 1924:205–6); Fr. *Louis* < NOM LUDOUICUS (*Loui* < ACC LUDOUICUM); but also from the oblique, thus: Fr. *Pierre* < ACC PETRUM (*Pierres* < NOM PETRUS); Fr. *Martin* < ACC MARTINUM (*Martins* < NOM MARTINUS); Fr. *Étienne* < ACC STEPHANUM (*Étiennes* < NOM STEPHANUS). As a rule, animate nouns are more likely than inanimate nouns to appear as the subject of a sentence and hence to occur in the nominative case; inanimates are less likely to assume this role. This fact may explain the developments noted above, although it is then difficult to see why only a small subset of animate nouns should have survived in the nominative. In any case, even animate nouns are generally more likely to occur in the oblique case; as Foulet (1930:32) points out, a clause normally has only one subject, but may contain a large number of complements and adjuncts. It has been suggested (for example, by Zink 1997:37) that the frequency of vocative use of certain animate common nouns and proper names may have favoured the survival of the nominative case form (which was commonly used as a form of address), although, once again, it is not easy to establish principles which might account for the subset of nouns which continue this form. And, although grammars of old French and old Occitan generally state that the nominative was the case used as a form of address (see, for instance, Buridant 2001:54), the oblique case was also frequent in this function (as noted by Foulet 1930:8 and Ménard 1994:20, amongst others, for French, and Jensen 1976:126–29; 1994:6f., for Occitan). For general discussion of animacy and frequency as factors influencing the evolution of case systems, see Winter (1971:55–61); for specific discussion of the survival of the nominative in French, see Mańczak (1969) and Spence (1971); for a pan-Romance survey, arguing that the phenomena observed are the reflex of an early active/stative alignment, see Ledgeway (this volume, chapter 8: §6.2.2.2).

The evolution of the case system between Latin and Gallo-Romance is usually presented as a reduction in the number of forms (see, for instance, Pope 1934:302f. for French and Anglade 1921:215 for Occitan). However, assuming that the number of grammatical functions remains approximately constant, it also represents a refunctionalization, inasmuch as there are now fewer forms to express a similar range of functions. Specifically, the Latin nominative yields an old Gallo-Romance case, likewise known as the nominative, which fulfils the functions of the Latin nominative and vocative (the disappearance of the distinct vocative form, which in Latin existed only in masculine nouns of the second declension, and its replacement by the nominative form was already well under way in Latin; see Väänänen 1981:111); whilst the Latin accusative form gives rise to an oblique case, which subsumes the functions of the four remaining cases (accusative, genitive, dative, ablative), and which is not infrequently used as a form of address.[19] In other words, the former nominative comes to encode an external argument (i.e., a subject), whilst the former accusative comes to encode an internal argument or adjunct (the complement of a verb, be it direct object or indirect object, a measure phrase, the complement of a preposition, the possessor, etc.), and both forms are found as vocatives – a function which arguably lies outside the case system (see note 15).

Although this section is essentially concerned with nominal case, we should note an interesting development in the 1SG and 2SG pronominal subsystems of some Gallo-Romance varieties, such as Picard, a northern dialect of French, where the nominative assumes (or retains) the role of verbal subject, the accusative comes to represent any complement of the verb, and a form deriving from the Latin dative – the so-called 'disjunctive' pronoun – is used in an 'elsewhere' function (most commonly, as the complement of a preposition). (The latter two developments are discussed in section 2.1, above.) This represents both a partial extension and a partial contraction of the role of the Latin accusative (which, for instance, could not encode an indirect object, but which could serve as the complement of a preposition) (see Table 6.1). (On the pronominal system of old Picard, see Gossen 1970:123–25.) However, the refunctionalizations of the Latin case system which will be the chief concern of this section are lexical rather than paradigmatic. It is to these lexicalizations that I now turn.

There are a number of lexicalizations of the nominative–accusative/oblique opposition – that is, instances in which each of the case forms has survived, but as a separate lexical item. (It might be noted in passing that, within a typology of refunctionalization, such a development may be seen as the antithesis of suppletion, in which items with different lexical etyma

Table 6.1 *The evolution of the first-person singular pronoun between Latin and Picard*

Latin			Picard
NOM	EGO	> *je*	subject of verb
ACC	ME	> *me*	complement of verb
(DAT	MI(HI)	> *mi*	elsewhere)

come to form part of the same paradigm; see below, §2.3.[20]) Perhaps the best known and most often cited example is Lat. NOM HOMO 'human being' yielding Fr. *on*, Occ. *on, om* 'one' (indefinite pronoun), with Lat. ACC HOMINEM yielding Fr. *homme*, Occ. *ome* 'man'; see Nyrop (1924:208f.); Ronjat (1937:6). The refunctionalization here is not simply a lexicalization; it also involves a categorial split. Of the two case forms of the original Latin noun, the accusative continues to encode a noun, whilst the original nominative now serves as the exponent of the indefinite subject pronoun. Despite the close contact between the two languages, this development appears to be an independent parallel evolution in Occitan rather than an influence from French (see Jensen 1994:154f.).

Other examples abound.

- Lat. NOM ÆGIDIUS [personal proper name] > Fr. *Gilles* [personal proper name] vs. Lat. ACC ÆGIDIUM > Fr. *gille* 'carnival clown', 'simpleton'; see *TLF* (Imbs 1971–94), s.v. *gille* (IX, 244). In this example, the nominative remains in the function of proper (fore)name, whilst a common noun with human reference is derived eponymically from the accusative.
- Lat. NOM UASCO 'Gascon' > Occ. *Gasc* [personal proper name] vs. Lat. ACC UASCONEM 'Gascon' > Occ. *gascoun* 'Gascon'; see Ronjat (1937:6). Here, it is the accusative which continues the original meaning of 'person (or language) from Gascony'. The nominative, on the other hand, gives rise to a family name, presumably via metonymy.
- Lat. NOM BRITTO 'Breton' > Occ. *Bret* [personal proper name], *bret* 'stammerer, stutterer' vs. Lat. ACC BRITTONEM 'Breton' > Occ. *bretoun* 'Breton'; see Ronjat (1937:6). Once again, the accusative continues the original meaning – in this instance, 'person (or language) from Brittany' – whilst the nominative gives rise to a metonymic family name. This development is exactly analogous to

the *Gasc* vs. *gascoun* development discussed in the previous section. However, in this case there is an additional development, in that the nominative also gives rise to a common noun meaning 'stammerer' or 'stutterer', presumably by way of a metaphor (or possibly another metonymy) equating foreign speech with linguistic ignorance or incompetence (in much the same way as the word for 'German' in Slavonic languages is cognate with the word meaning 'dumb' or 'mute' – see, for instance, Vasmer (1971:62), s.v. *немец* – although in the present case the image takes the foreignness as its starting point rather than the disability). A semantic characterization of the difference between the two common nouns might include some reference to the role of agentivity in the definition of each: a stammerer or stutterer is recognizable as such on the basis of a specific action or activity, whilst the notions of nationality or ethnicity involved in being Breton are defined more statically, or even passively, primarily in terms of set-membership. Correspondingly, one may speak of taking action to 'cure', or 'curb', or 'correct' a stammer; these concepts are inapplicable to ethnicity, even in the case of people who seek to deny their origins.

- Lat. NOM DRACO 'serpent, dragon' > Occ. *dra(c)* 'imp, sprite, goblin' vs. Lat. ACC DRACONEM 'serpent, dragon' > Occ. *dragoun* 'dragon'; see Ronjat (1937:6). Here, the original nominative undergoes a metonymic shift and comes to refer to a mythical being with human characteristics, whilst the accusative retains the approximate meaning of the original item, yielding the name of a likewise mythical animal.

- Lat. NOM IACOBUS [personal proper name] > Fr. *Jacques* [personal proper name]; 'peasant', 'bumpkin'; 'jay' vs. Lat. ACC IACOBUM [personal proper name] > *ja(c)que* 'jerkin'; see *TLF* (Imbs 1971–94), s.v. *jacques* (X, 627), *jaque, jacque* (X, 653). This lexicalization has similarities with the *Gilles* vs. *gille* development discussed above, except that there is an eponymic split. Whilst the nominative is once again the origin of the proper (fore)name, it also yields two types of animate eponym: human ('peasant', and, by metonymic extension, 'bumpkin'), and non-human (the ornithonym 'jay'). The accusative, on the other hand, gives rise to an inanimate eponym, also derived metonymically ('jerkin' – a garment traditionally worn by peasants).

- Lat. NOM *CAPTIATOR 'hunter' > Occ. *cassaire* 'hunter' (professional or in general) vs. Lat. ACC *CAPTIATOREM 'hunter' > Occ. *cassadou* 'hunter' (professional), 'hunter's hide', 'hoop-driver'; see

Mistral (1932), s.v. *cassaire, cassadou* (I, 486). Although both the original nominative and the original accusative yield nouns with human reference, the latter additionally gives rise to inanimate nouns denoting equipment used by hunters and coopers.

- Lat. NOM RES 'thing' > Gsc. *arrés* 'no one' vs. Lat. ACC REM 'thing' > Gsc. *arré, arrén* 'nothing'; see Rohlfs (1977:175), Palay (1961:58, 66). Here, the lexicalization is accompanied by a change of category, but there is no categorial split, inasmuch as each of the original cases of the Latin noun comes to serve as a pronoun in Gascon. The original nominative yields an animate pronoun (a striking development, as the Latin word is almost prototypically inanimate), whilst the original accusative gives rise to an inanimate pronoun.

- Lat. NOM CANTOR 'singer' > Fr. *chantre* 'cantor', 'choirmaster'; 'bard' vs. Lat. ACC CANTOREM > *chanteur* 'singer'; see *TLF* (Imbs 1971–94), s.v. *chantre* (V, 517), *chanteur* (V, 514).[21] In this example, the nominative and accusative forms of the same common noun have given rise to two lexically distinct common nouns. The nominative maps on to a semantically more agentive noun and the accusative maps on to a semantically less agentive noun. Specifically, we may distinguish here between individual and group control. When an individual *chanteur* is singing alone, he controls both his own voice and the overall sound; these are the same. When a *chanteur* is singing as part of a group, he controls his own voice, but has little control over the sound of the ensemble. The *chantre*, on the other hand, controls the choir or the congregation; he is responsible for the overall sound in a way that an individual *chanteur* in an ensemble is not and cannot be. It is in this sense that the *chantre* is clearly a more involved participant than the *chanteur*. A picture of a *chantre* as more agentive than a *chanteur* also emerges clearly from the extended use of the former term to refer to a leading figure who serves as the mouthpiece of a cause or country; see *TLF* (Imbs 1971–94), s.v. *chantre* (V, 517).

Is it possible to make any generalization about this at first sight somewhat disparate set of data? I think that it is, and that an important clue to what is going on is to be found in an apparently unrelated area. In a celebrated paper, Silverstein (1976) discusses the phenomenon of 'split ergativity', whereby, in a number of languages (including many spoken in Australia and the Americas), some types of NP behave accusatively (that is, they exhibit the nominative vs. accusative case marking found in accusative languages, in which intransitive and transitive subjects pattern together), whilst others behave ergatively (that is, they exhibit the ergative vs. absolutive case marking found in ergative languages, in which intransitive subjects pattern with direct objects). After surveying the data, he concludes that an item is more likely to exhibit nominative vs. accusative case marking the higher its position on the following hierarchy (Silverstein 1976:122):

first- and second-person pronouns
> third-person pronouns
> proper names
> nouns with human reference
> non-human animate nouns
> inanimate nouns

On this issue, see also Dixon (1994:83–97), who remarks that Silverstein's hierarchy 'relates to the fact that certain kinds of NPs are very likely to be the controller of an event, others less likely, others most unlikely' (p. 84). Silverstein's analysis is synchronic rather than diachronic, and the languages he examines are typologically, as well as geographically, remote from Gallo-Romance. Nonetheless, he is concerned with the relation of agency and animacy to case marking, and the categories he establishes are, I suggest, highly relevant to the data under discussion here. It has been observed that considerations of agency and animacy were relevant factors in the disappearance of the old Gallo-Romance case system – Schøsler (2001b:174), for instance, observes that proper nouns lose the distinction of case earlier than other items in old French (see also Ménard 1994:20, Ashdowne and Smith 2007, and, for a similar development in old Occitan, Jensen 1976:127); whilst Buridant (2001:77) notes that the -s inflection serves as the characteristic marker of an animate subject with determined reference in the role of agent,[22] and that nominative case marking disappears earlier from items which do not fulfil these criteria. I suggest that these factors are also at work in the refunctionalization of the system, and that Silverstein's hierarchy provides a framework within which to view the changes involved. The examples above show that, when the opposition between nominative and accusative/oblique has been refunctionalized in Gallo-Romance, it has come to encode, *inter alia*, the following dichotomies:

subject vs. complement/adjunct
(Lat. nominative vs. accusative becomes OFr., OOcc. nominative vs. oblique)

verbal subject vs. verbal complement (regardless of type)
(compare Pic. *je* vs. *me*)

pronoun vs. noun

> (compare Fr. *on* vs. *homme*, Occ. *on, om* vs. *ome*)

proper name vs. common noun

> (compare Fr. *Gilles* vs. *gille*, Occ. *Gasc* vs. *gascoun*, Occ. *Bret* vs. *bretoun*)[23]

human (or parahuman) referent vs. non-human referent

> (compare Occ. *dra(c)* vs. *dragoun*)

animate referent vs. inanimate referent

> (compare Fr. *Jacques* vs. *ja(c)que*, Occ. *cassaire* vs *cassadou*, Gsc. *arrés* vs. *arré/arrén*)

more active or involved participant vs. less active or involved participant

> (compare Occ. *bret* vs. *bretoun*, Fr. *chantre* vs. *chanteur*)

The refunctionalization may result in a straightforward subject–non-subject split: in the reduction of the five or six cases of Latin to the two cases of old Gallo-Romance, the nominative provides the subject form and the accusative a generalized complement and adjunct form; in the evolution of the Picard personal pronouns, the nominative yields a subject form and the accusative a verbal complement form. Such developments are rather unsurprising, as, at one level, they represent continuity: the more agentive case continues to encode the more agentive function.[24] I suggest that a similar principle is at work in cases of lexicalization. When lexicalization of the opposition between nominative and accusative/oblique yields items which can be related to different positions on Silverstein's hierarchy, the original nominative serves as the exponent of the item or group of items which is higher on the scale. The 'cut-off' point may vary (a fact which is itself of interest); but there are no counterexamples to this principle. When lexicalization yields results which lie outside or beyond Silverstein's hierarchy (as is the case with *bret* vs. *bretoun* or *chantre* vs. *chanteur*), the hierarchy nonetheless provides a pointer to the analysis of the change: the original nominative comes to encode the participant with greater involvement in or control over some action.

It is clear, therefore, that the original nominative case form consistently comes to encode the more agentive member of the opposition, whilst the original accusative or oblique case form comes to encode the less agentive one. In other words, although the opposition is refunctionalized, the basic distinction between a more agentive item and a less agentive item is retained. This process is in keeping with the proposal that morphological refunctionalization involves a process of 'core-to-core' mapping.[25]

John Charles Smith

2.3 Suppletion as refunctionalization

So far, we have examined an instance of intramorphological refunctionalization (the accusative and dative pronouns of Latin), and an instance
of morphological-to-lexical refunctionalization (doublets arising from the
continuation of both case forms of old Gallo-Romance). Both of these
examples have involved case morphology;[26] in each instance, I have tried to
demonstrate that the refunctionalization involves 'core-to-core' mapping.
We should also consider lexical-to-morphological refunctionalization, commonly known as 'suppletion'. In Romance, this type of change is particularly associated with the verb. It is discussed in detail by Maiden (this
volume, chapter 5), and I shall here refer only to some aspects of the process
which are relevant to the claims I am making about refunctionalization.

If we begin by taking one the best-known examples of suppletion in the
Romance verb – the forms of 'to go' in French, Italian and Spanish (for full
details, see Aski 1995) – we find the distribution of Latin etyma shown in
Table 6.2.

Is 'core-to-core' mapping at work in this case? In other words, can we
discern some sort of continuity (in terms of markedness, frequency, default
status or anything else) in order to account for the distribution of the etyma?
The notion of 'unmarked person' is not straightforward. Greenberg
(1966:84f.) examines data from a number of languages which 'lead one to
posit, tentatively at least, a hierarchy in which the third person [is] the least
marked, and the second person the most marked, with the first person
intermediate'. He bases this conclusion on frequency and on morphological
structure. However, an alternative, discourse-based, view might be put forward, in which discourse participants are less marked than non-participants,
and in which the speaker, as the necessary participant in every utterance, is
less marked than the hearer, yielding a hierarchy 'first person > second person
> third person'. Such a view underlies the work of Bühler (1934:79–148) and
Benveniste (1956), and is explicitly articulated by Dixon (1994:84–90).
Possibly the most detailed statement of such a hierarchy is by Silverstein

Table 6.2 *Latin etyma of the verb 'to go' in French, Italian and Spanish*

	IRE	UADERE[27]	[?]AMBULARE
French	FUT & COND	PRS IND: 1, 2, 3 SG; 3 PL	'elsewhere'
Italian	–	PRS IND & SBJV: 1, 2, 3 SG; 3 PL	'elsewhere'
Spanish	'elsewhere'[28]	PRS IND & SBJV: all persons	–

(1976), whose work on agentivity has already been referred to (see §2.2 above); he further draws attention to the fact that some languages may invert the order of first and second persons in this hierarchy, apparently treating the second person as more animate or agentive than the first.

What does seem clear is that the unmarked person may vary from one text-type to another, and even, perhaps, from one society to another. In personal narratives, we expect to find a large proportion of first-person forms, given the central role of the narrator. Interpersonal texts, such as instruction manuals, pedagogical textbooks or love poetry, will likewise be orientated towards the hearer/reader, and will in consequence contain large numbers of second-person forms. Finally, a descriptive text is likely to be written mainly in the third person. It is, moreover, probable that the social norms of particular societies will favour some types of discourse over others (compare some of the comments made by Manoliu, this volume, chapter 9). In these circumstances, it is extremely difficult to make objectively verifiable (or falsifiable) statements about the unmarkedness or 'coreness' of particular person forms.

Whatever the arguments about the unmarked person in the singular, we may be on firmer ground when claiming that the third person is unmarked in the plural. Whilst second- and third-person plurals correspond straightforwardly to the existence of more than one (potential) addressee or of more than one non-discourse participant, respectively, a plurality of first persons is a much more problematic notion. So-called first-person plurals are rarely, if ever, unalloyedly first person – they encode composite reference to the speaker and some other person or persons, including or excluding the addressee. It is true that an addressee may be confronted by a number of speakers using the same words simultaneously; but this is not the normal context in which first-person plural forms are used. And for any individual speaker, a 'plurality of first persons' interpretation is impossible, except perhaps in highly metaphorical contexts or in science fiction.[29] In this sense, then, the first-person plural may be considered as an abnormal, or at least atypical, plural and hence as marked. Frequency data tend to support this view. Greenberg's statistics on pronominal forms in the work of the second-century BC Latin playwright Terence (Greenberg 1966:78) give the following descending order of frequency (with the number of tokens in brackets): first person (1786), third person (1369), second person (1267). However, in the plural, the order is: third person (197), first person (146), second person (98). Of course, these figures are small, and have no more than a heuristic value. But they are suggestive, nonetheless. I here supplement them with data obtained from a search for present-tense forms on World Wide Web pages written in Italian, using the Google search engine, in February

2009. Once again, this method yields very approximate results, and must therefore be treated as no more than a heuristic. For a start, the larger numbers returned by the search engine are grossly rounded. It is important to use verb-forms which are as unambiguous as possible, and this rules out many regular verbs, where, for instance, the second-person plural of the present indicative is identical to the feminine plural form of the past participle (*portate* from *portare* 'carry', *finite* from *finire* 'finish', etc.). Likewise, short verbs must be eschewed, to avoid clashes with possible homographs, including acronyms. One ambiguity which is unavoidable in Italian is the syncretism between indicative and subjunctive in the first-person plural of the present tense of all verbs. This problem was dealt with by counting occurrences of both indicative and subjunctive forms in the second- and third-person plural. The inclusion of the third-person plural subjunctive form (which can serve as the equivalent of an imperative) also avoided any overestimate of the numbers for first- and second-person plural forms resulting from the syncretism between indicative and imperative in these persons. However, subjunctive forms were not counted in the singular, as this number exhibits syncretism of all three persons in the present subjunctive. The verbs selected were *conoscere* 'to know' and *riconoscere* 'to recognize'.[30] Although cognate, these verbs present significant semantic differences, which might affect the frequency of the various persons. In the singular, the first person of *conoscere* is most frequent (in keeping, perhaps, with its identity as a 'private' verb), whereas the most frequent person of *riconoscere* is the third. On the other hand, in the plural, it is always the third-person form which is the most frequent – and, strikingly, this remains the case even if the specific plural subjunctive forms are omitted from consideration (thereby leading to a potential overestimate of the occurrence of first-person plural indicatives) (see Tables 6.3 and 6.4).

Table 6.3 *Frequency of present tense forms of* conoscere

SG	IND			SBJV		TOTAL	
1	*conosco*	8,800,000	51.5%				
2	*conosci*	3,980,000	23.3%				
3	*conosce*	4,310,000	25.2%				
PL							
1	*conosciamo*	1,690,000	34.4%			1,690,000	32.4%
2	*conoscete*	1,470,000	29.9%	*conosciate*	131,000	1,601,000	30.7%
3	*conoscono*	1,750,000	35.6%	*conoscano*	180,000	1,930,000	37.0%

Table 6.4 *Frequency of present tense forms of* riconoscere

SG	IND			SBJV		TOTAL	
1	*riconosco*	538,000	17.8%				
2	*riconosci*	338,000	11.2%				
3	*riconosce*	2,140,000	71.0%				
PL							
1	*riconosciamo*	161,000	12.5%			161,000	11.5%
2	*riconoscete*	276,000	21.5%	*riconosciate*	739	276,739	19.8%
3	*riconoscono*	847,000	66.0%	*riconoscano*	116,000	963,000	68.7%

It is easier to make generalizations about number, tense and mood in this context. Greenberg (1966:75–80) discusses number in both nouns and verbs, concluding, on the basis of frequency and syncretization, that the singular is less marked than the plural (which is in turn less marked than other numbers, such as the dual and the trial). As far as tense is concerned, the same author (Greenberg 1966:87) rehearses a number of reasons for regarding the past as quasi-universally marked with respect to the present; these include its lower frequency and its greater morphological complexity. By the same token, the future is more marked than either present or past. On the basis of similar considerations, he also claims (Greenberg 1966:86) that 'the indicative may be considered the unmarked category as against the marked character of the one or more hypothetical modes'.[31] Of course, text-type will not be without influence on the latter two categories: historical narrative may favour the past tense (although the 'historic present' may well be used in this context), and prayers, imprecations and directive texts are perhaps more likely to use non-indicative forms (subjunctives, optatives, hortatives, imperatives). Nonetheless, there is a strong case for regarding singular number, present tense and indicative mood as the unmarked terms in contexts which are themselves unmarked. For further discussion of all these issues, see Croft (1990) and Battistella (1990).

Looking at the data on the verb 'to go' in French, Italian and Spanish, presented above, we may at least investigate the possibility that suppletion takes place in keeping with a principle of 'core-to-core' mapping. In all three languages, the distribution of the etyma is complex, but coherent, and this gives initial grounds for optimism. The reflex of UADERE is found in French throughout the unmarked number and in the least marked person of the marked number in the least marked tense and mood; that of IRE in the most marked tense(s); and that of AMBULARE in all other forms. In Italian, the reflex of UADERE is found throughout the unmarked number and in the least marked person of the marked number in the least marked tense and regardless of mood; the reflex of AMBULARE is found elsewhere. Finally, in Spanish, the reflex of UADERE occurs throughout in all persons of the unmarked tense, regardless of mood, whilst that of IRE is found elsewhere. Of course, in order to demonstrate that 'core-to-core' mapping was at work, we would have to establish the relative markedness or 'coreness' of the three Latin etyma, and demonstrate that the descending order of 'coreness' was UADERE, AMBULARE, IRE, and it is here that the problem lies, for this would require data concerning usage in late Latin which we do not currently possess and which may in principle be inaccessible to us. I return to this issue briefly below.

Other instances of suppletion can be analysed in a similar way. Maiden (2005b; see also this volume, chapter 5: §6) points out that many morphological patterns in Romance, although they may have arisen through sound change or originally had a semantic unity, are now autonomously morphological, as the result of formal convergence or functional divergence – they have become 'morphomes' (Aronoff 1994): systematic formal regularities with no synchronic phonological motivation and no unique functional correlate. One of the morphomes proposed by Maiden is the so-called 'N-pattern', whereby one stem is found in the first three persons singular and the third-person plural of the present tense, and another stem in other forms of the verb. In the light of the data and arguments presented above, Maiden's 'N–pattern' might be seen (*pace* Maiden himself; see this volume, chapter 5: §5.10) as a contrast between less marked forms (the unmarked number, and the unmarked person in the marked number, of the unmarked tense) and more marked forms. Although Maiden's 'N–pattern' does not normally involve suppletion, it is important for our present discussion because suppletion commonly takes place in accordance with it. Significantly, we do not find that the other morphomic patterns proposed by Maiden (such as the 'L-pattern' and the 'U-pattern'; see, once again, this volume, chapter 5) generally serve as a template for suppletion. Since it is also the case that these patterns, unlike the 'N-pattern', cannot easily be defined in terms of markedness, we may tentatively suggest that suppletion may involve some sort of 'core-to-core' mapping.

One example of 'N-pattern' suppletion concerns the verb 'to give'. Spanish, Portuguese, Italian and Romanian derive this verb (Sp., Pt. *dar*; It. *dare*; Ro. *a da*) from Lat. DARE 'to give', whereas this etymon has left no trace in French, where the corresponding verb *donner* is derived from what was originally a more specialized verb – Lat. DONARE 'to present, bestow'. However, not all Romance varieties use a single etymon uniformly. Maiden (2004d; personal communication) reports suppletion in the verb 'to give' involving these two etyma according to an 'N-pattern' morphome (i.e., one stem is found in the first three persons singular and the third-person plural of the present, whilst the other stem is found in other contexts), but otherwise unpredictable. Thus (in terms of the Latin etyma) one set of dialects (such as the dialect of Limone, on the borders of Liguria and Piedmont: hereafter 'Type I' dialects) exhibit a present indicative which corresponds to DO, DAS, DAT, DONAMUS, DONATIS, DANT, whilst another set of dialects (spoken in parts of Sicily and Calabria: hereafter 'Type II' dialects) exhibit the reverse distribution: DONO, DONAS. DONAT, *DAMUS*, *DATIS*, DONANT. These data might seem to demonstrate that, whilst the 'N-pattern' is robust, the distribution of the two etyma is random (Lass might have said that the opposition was 'junk'), and therefore that there is no evidence for 'core-to-core' mapping.

However, more careful consideration reveals that this need not be the case. Presumably (in fact, axiomatically) DARE survived in Spanish and Italian and DONARE in French because these were the forms which were most frequent in the Latin spoken in the relevant areas. We can make this claim with some justification, given that one of the forms ousted the other completely. It is tempting (although completely speculative, given the absence of concrete evidence) to suggest that something similar must be true in the examples of suppletion – i.e., that DARE was more frequent than DONARE in dialects of Type I, whilst the reverse was the case in dialects of Type II. When suppletion took place according to Maiden's 'N-pattern', the more frequent verb then filled the less marked slots in the paradigm. However, in suggesting that this may have been the mechanism involved, we encounter the same problem alluded to above in the discussion of the verb 'to go' in French, Italian and Spanish. Without observed data (which we will doubtless never have), the argument is completely circular (we derive our claim about frequency from the suppletion patterns, and we justify the suppletion patterns on the basis of our claim about frequency), and cannot be accepted as an account of these particular facts. I present it nonetheless as an example of the sort of consideration which should guide research in similar cases where we do have access to relevant data.

3   Adfunctionalization

3.1   *Singular vs. plural number in Latin neuter nouns*

I turn now to a diachronic process which resembles the refunctionalizations discussed in the previous section, but which, on inspection, turns out to be rather different. As is well known (see, for instance, Väänänen 1981:101–5, and, for discussion, Ramat 1998; see also Maiden, this volume, chapter 4: §3.2), with the loss of the neuter gender from Latin, many neuter nouns were assimilated to the masculine gender, whilst a number of neuter plurals in -A were reinterpreted as feminine singulars, presumably on the basis of their inflectional ending. What interests me here is the situation in which both developments occurred, giving rise to a refunctionalization of the singular/plural opposition. A fact which tends not to be pointed out is that a further shift may take place, whereby the masculine noun generally assumes a figurative meaning, whilst the feminine noun retains the original literal meaning. In these cases, we therefore have a two-stage apparent refunctionalization, according to the following pattern:

singular   >   masculine   >   metaphorical reading
plural   >   feminine   >   literal reading

Compare:

- Lat. FOLIUM 'leaf' > FOLIUM > OFr. *fueil*, Cat. *full*, It. *foglio* 'leaf (of book)'
  vs. Lat. FOLIA 'leaves' > FOLIAM > Fr. *feuille*, Cat. *fulla*, It. *foglia* 'leaf (of tree, etc.)';
- Lat. CORNU 'horn' > CORNUM > Fr. *cor* '(hunting) horn'
  vs. Lat. CORNUA 'horns' > *CORNAM > Fr. *corne* 'horn (of animal)';
- Lat. GRANUM 'seed' > GRANUM > Fr. *grain* 'grain, small quantity'
  vs. Lat. GRANA 'seeds' > GRANAM > Fr. *graine* 'seed';
- Lat. UASCELLUM 'small vase' > UASCELLUM > Fr. *vaisseau* 'ship, (etc.)'
  vs. Lat. UASCELLA 'small vases' > UASCELLAM > Fr. *vaisselle* 'crockery; washing-up';
- Lat. CEREBELLUM 'brain' > CEREBELLUM > Fr. *cerveau* 'brain (power, etc.)'
  vs. Lat. CEREBELLA 'brains' > *CEREBELLAM > Fr. *cervelle* 'brain (physical matter)'.

At first sight, this development is simply described.

(i)   The distinction of number is refunctionalized as a distinction of gender. The singular/plural opposition continues to exist, but it is no longer expressed by the original neuter morphology. Instead, the original neuter singular gives rise to a masculine singular, which develops an analogical masculine plural, whilst the original neuter plural yields a feminine singular, which develops an analogical feminine plural. At some stage (possibly from the outset), this gender split comes to correspond to a lexical split. This initial refunctionalization, of singular to masculine and plural to feminine, for all that it is presumably driven by considerations of formal similarity, does seem to be a 'core-to-core' mapping, in that markedness relations are maintained – the unmarked number becomes the unmarked gender, and the marked number becomes the marked gender.

(ii) However, the subsequent development, whereby the **masculine** form acquires a **metaphorical** meaning, whilst the **feminine** retains the **literal** meaning of the original item, appears to contradict the 'core-to-core' principle in the most striking way. Metaphorical meaning is, in an obvious sense, more marked than literal meaning – and yet it is precisely the unmarked singular number and masculine gender which come to encode this type of meaning. Does this mean that we have to reject the 'core-to-core' principle, or can we find some explanation for this phenomenon which is consistent with it?

We might begin by looking at other examples of masculine/feminine oppositions in Romance in search of clues that might help explain the development just noted. Most leads are unhelpful. It is clear that the morphological convergence of non-cognate items, such as Fr. *le tour* (M) (by back-formation from *tourner* < TURNARE) 'turn, tour, revolution' vs. *la tour* (F) (< TURREM) 'tower', tells us nothing about the present case. Nor do gender oppositions which arise from metonymy, such as French *la crème* (F) 'cream' vs. *le crème* (M) = *le café à la crème* 'coffee made with cream'. In many Romance languages, the referents of cognate masculine/feminine pairs are distinguished by size; however, there is little consistency in the relationship between gender and dimensions, as witness Sp. *barco* (M) 'ship' vs. *barca* (F) '(small) boat', but Sp. *charco* (M) 'puddle' vs. *charca* (F) 'pond'. Compare, too, Sp. *cesto* (M) 'basket taller than it is wide' vs. *cesta* (F) 'basket wider than it is tall'. A possibly related phenomenon is the 'masculine tree, feminine fruit' pattern found in some varieties; compare It. *melo* (M) 'apple tree' vs. *mela* (F) 'apple', Sp. *manzano* (M) 'apple tree' vs. *manzana* (F) 'apple'. None of these gender doublets sheds any light on the problem we are dealing with here.

However, there is one type of gender opposition in Romance which is relevant to the present discussion – the so-called 'double plurals' of Italian. As an example we may take It. *corno* 'horn', which exhibits two

Table 6.5 *Concepts without individual properties (adapted from Acquaviva 2005)*

non-discrete entities	homogeneous masses	*sand, water*
	collective masses	*furniture*
	activity predicates	*running*
	abstract nouns	*friendship*
equivalence classes	abstract units	*part*
	measures of quantity and amounts	*dozens, tons*
weakly individuated entities	members of cohesive collections	*fingers, stars*
	objects without salient distinctive properties	*eggs, times*

plurals – *corni* (M) 'animal horns separated from the animal', 'musical horns', 'horns of a dilemma' vs. *corna* (F) 'animal horns still on the animal', 'horns of the moon', etc. The properties of such plurals are discussed by Ojeda (1995) and Acquaviva (2005; 2008:123–61). In general, the feminine plural form may be construed as more 'weakly individuated' (Acquaviva 2005:259) or 'undifferentiated' (Acquaviva 2008:153) than its masculine plural counterpart. Of weakly individuated entities, Acquaviva (2005:259f.) states: 'These concepts are discrete and refer to actual entities, but these entities are conceptualized as interchangeable or weakly individual. […] In some cases, the lack of distinctive individuality has a basis in the lack of perceptual salience of the objects involved […]. In other cases, it depends on the cohesiveness of aggregates: in the singular, a concept like "finger" or "star" clearly refers to an individual entity, but the plural of such concepts is easily conceptualized as a cohesive aggregate, a larger structure in which each part presupposes the others. And obviously, the greater the cohesion of parts in a whole, the lesser their individuality. [The plural forms of these nouns] mean something different from just a plurality of singulars.' See also Tiersma (1982), Maiden (1995a:105f.) (and see Table 6.5).

In the light of Acquaviva's analysis, we may speculate that the Latin neuter nouns in question may have evolved in the following way. In Latin, the singular will have been interpreted as a strongly individuated item, whilst the default interpretation of the plural will have involved a collective meaning, as described by Acquaviva, and will therefore have been weakly individuated (see (A) in Table 6.6). However, alongside this collective interpretation, an interpretation of the plural as a 'plurality of singulars' may also logically exist. With the loss of the neuter gender and the absorption of neuter singulars into the masculine declension, a new analogical plural, with masculine inflectional endings, commonly arose, which presumably existed alongside the older plural in -A, at least for a time. The new plural form might supplant the older one, yielding the pattern found in Spanish (see (D) in Table 6.6). But the existence of two plurals also offered scope for semantic differentiation (in other words, the distinction could be functionalized),[32] with the older -A plural (which was now morphologically irregular) retaining its collective, weakly individuated, meaning, and the newer, masculine plural encoding the 'plurality of singulars' interpretation in a quasi-iconic way – i.e., as the regular plural of the individuated singular (see (B) in Table 6.6). If this weakly individuated plural came to be reinterpreted as a (feminine) singular (I shall discuss a possible mechanism for this process shortly), then it might acquire an analogical plural, yielding the pattern in (C) in Table 6.6. Finally, it would be possible for this new feminine, rather than surviving alongside the masculine, to oust it (as in (E) in Table 6.6). This seems not to have happened with the word for 'horn' – but did happen in some other instances (and at various stages, sometimes after the Latin period), to yield French *feuille* 'leaf', *arme* 'weapon', etc.

We should also discuss the mechanism whereby the collective plural could be reinterpreted as a singular. There is, of course, an obvious semantic vagueness about a collective concept, which at one level is clearly plural,

Table 6.6 *The fate of* CORNUM < CORNU

	singular	plural
(A) Latin		
strong individuation	CORNUM[33]	–
weak individuation	–	CORNA
(B) Distinction in plural but not in singular (Italian corno; corni, corna*)*		
strong individuation	CORNUS, CORNUM	CORNI, CORNOS
weak individuation	–	CORNA
(C) Distinction in singular and plural (French cor *vs.* corne; cors *vs.* cornes*)*		
strong individuation	CORNUS, CORNUM	CORNI, CORNOS
weak individuation	CORNA, CORNAM	CORNÆ, CORNAS
(D) No distinction in either singular or plural (< strong) (Spanish cuerno; cuernos*)*		
strong individuation	CORNUS, CORNUM	CORNI, CORNOS
weak individuation	–	–
(E) No distinction in either singular or plural (< weak) (not found?)		
strong individuation	–	–
weak individuation	CORNA, CORNAM	CORNÆ, CORNAS

Table 6.7 *The progress of individuation*

	singular	plural
I		
strong individuation	FOLIUM	–
weak individuation	–	FOLIA
II		
strong individuation	FOLIUS, FOLIUM	FOLII, FOLIOS
weak individuation	–	FOLIA
III		
strong individuation	FOLIUS, FOLIUM	FOLII, FOLIOS
weak individuation	FOLIA	
IV		
strong individuation	FOLIUS, FOLIUM	FOLII, FOLIOS
weak individuation	FOLIA, FOLIAM	FOLIÆ, FOLIAS

because it is made up of a plurality of entities, but in which, to recall Acquaviva's comment (Acquaviva 2005:259f.), quoted above, the plurality of weakly individuated concepts 'is easily conceptualized as a cohesive aggregate' and therefore lends itself to interpretation as a more or less strongly individuated singular.[34] Using FOLIUM as our example, we may therefore speculate that the change took place in stages corresponding to I–IV below. I, II and IV in Table 6.7 all represent putative stages in the development which have already been discussed. III postulates an inter-mediate stage between the asymmetrical distribution which must be the origin of Italian *corno, corni, corna* (see (B) above) and the symmetrical distribution underlying French *cor, cors; corne, cornes* (see (C) above) in which the form in -A may be interpreted as indifferently singular or plural (or perhaps as simultaneously singular and plural).

In support of stage III, in which the number of a form such as FOLIA is essentially vague or ambiguous, we may cite Niedermann (1943–44), who, in his study of the medical sections of the *Liber glossarum* or *Glossarium Ansileubi*, a compendium of earlier texts compiled in the late eighth century, suggests that the fact that FOLIA (etc.) often appears with a singular verb in Latin does not justify the claim that it is a feminine singular noun – rather, it could still be a plural collective noun triggering singular semantic agree-ment. He sees this as representing a transitional stage between FOLIA as a plural and as a true singular.[35] This transitional stage leads finally[36] to the pattern underlying the situation we find in old French and in modern

Italian and Catalan, whereby the weakly individuated term, originally plural, and subsequently unmarked for (or ambiguous as to) number, acquires normal number morphology, as in IV.

Such a development, it should be pointed out, is not an idiosyncrasy of Latin/Romance, but has parallels in other languages – compare Eng. *grape*, from OFr. *grap(p)e* 'bunch of grapes': 'first adopted in plural and collective uses, from which a new sense of the sing[ular] was afterwards evolved' (*OED*, s.v. *grape*, VI, 761–2). It also seems clear that 'strong' and 'weak' individuation are to be understood as relative terms. For instance, Lat. OUUM 'egg' undergoes development (C) in Spanish, yielding two cognates – *huevo, huevos* 'egg/s' (already a 'weakly individuated entity' in Acquaviva's terms; see above) and *hueva, huevas* 'roe, spawn' (an even **more** weakly individuated entity).

Key to an analysis of these developments is the understanding that the change under discussion is not refunctionalization as we have hitherto defined it.

First, in the cases discussed earlier (in §2), under the heading of 'refunctionalization', the distinction originally encoded by the refunctionalized morphology has disappeared completely – there is no distinction between accusative and dative forms of the first- and second-person singular pronouns of Spanish, Portuguese and Picard; nouns in modern French and Occitan do not exhibit different case forms, and so on. Indeed, the disappearance – or perhaps the decline – of these distinctions is arguably what triggers the refunctionalization of the morphology. The present instance is different. The distinction of number has not disappeared; at no stage does it seem not to have been possible to distinguish between, say, 'leaf' and 'leaves' in Latin or Romance. Although the morphology has acquired a new function, this change in function cannot have been triggered by the disappearance from the language of the distinction which it originally encoded, because that distinction did not disappear.

Second, the functional change which concerns us here can be broken down into two reinterpretations of an inflectional ending – -UM (the original neuter singular) as masculine singular and -A (the original neuter plural) as feminine singular. Contrary to the earlier cases discussed, these two reinterpretations are quite independent of each other. A Latin neuter noun may survive into Romance simply as a masculine (e.g., Fr. *étain* 'tin' < STAGNUM < STANNUM) or simply as a feminine (e.g., Fr. *arme* 'weapon' < ARMA). The apparent refunctionalization is merely a conflation of these two reinterpretations; whilst in the examples discussed earlier it is the opposition as a whole which is subject to reinterpretation.

Third, unlike the cases examined earlier, morphophonology plays a crucial role in the emergence of the new function. In the earlier examples, the refunctionalization yields either items which are not distinguished inflectionally (but rather lexically) or items in which the inflection is redeployed in a novel way. In the first case, we might speak of the original morphology being deflectionalized; in the second, of a completely new form–function relationship being created. In neither case is the particular morphophonological structure of either the old or the new forms of any significance. However, the number-to-gender change under discussion is different, in that there is already syncretism between the 'before' and 'after' forms prior to the reinterpretation taking place. The (accusative) masculine singular inflection -UM is already identical to its neuter counterpart. More significant is the syncretism between the neuter plural inflection -A and the feminine singular inflection -A, and it is precisely this syncretism which appears to be a necessary condition for items to move from one category to the other. In other words, the change is essentially an analogy. It is made possible by an indeterminacy of individuation, together with a chance (morpho)phonological resemblance. (In fact, the resemblance is not coincidental if we take a long-term view, because the neuter plural -A and the feminine singular -A have the same origin, in the Indo-European collective *h; see, for instance, Schmidt (1889). But this fact would not, of course, have been part of the linguistic awareness of Latin or Romance speakers.)

Similar examples may be found in other languages: compare English 'back-formed' singulars: *pea* from *pease* (OFr. *peis*); *cherry* from *cherise* (OFr. *cerise*); *Chinee* from *Chinese*; *Maltee* from *Maltese*; *Portuguee* from *Portuguese* (see *OED*, s.v. *cherry* (III, 89); *Chinee*, *Chinese* (III, 128–29); *Maltese* (IX, 276); *pea* (XI, 381), *pease* (XI, 404); *Portuguee*, *Portuguese* (XII, 161)), and South German (Bavarian and Austrian) *Watsche* 'slap round the ears', back-formed from original feminine singular *Watschen*, which has characteristic feminine plural morphology – compare *Bratsche/Bratschen* 'viola/violas' (Radden and Panther 2004). Here, the change operates in the opposite direction – in Latin/Romance, an original plural becomes a singular; in the Germanic examples, an original singular becomes a plural. If we were simply dealing with refunctionalization, it would indeed be worrying (in the context of the theory outlined above) that the change could go in either direction – it would seem that Lass was right to refer to 'junk' (i.e., random refunctionalization), and that the principle of 'core-to-core' mapping could not be maintained. However, as already noted, what we have here is a reanalysis guided by analogy. It is clear that this development is not straightforward refunctionalization, but a different type of change, and that it may therefore present a different outcome. Smith (2006) discusses further the notion that 'pseudo-refunctionalizations' may result from processes such as analogy and language contact, which can violate or override the 'core-to-core' principle (and see also the discussion of Sardinian first-person pronouns in § 2.1 above).

I turn now to the question of why the original singular > masculine should generally yield an item with metaphorical meaning, whilst the plural > feminine retains the literal meaning of the original word.

It is beyond the scope of this chapter to propose and motivate a theory of metaphor (for an attempt to do so, see MacCormac 1985); I am essentially concerned with how metaphors may come into being. Searle (1993:103) offers a relevant comment, claiming that, in computing the possible value of a metaphorical interpretation, speaker–hearers 'look for salient, well known, distinctive features' of the literal referent. I suggest that such features will be more readily identifiable in the case of a strongly individuated referent, by virtue of the fact that it is itself more salient and distinctive. It is perfectly possible for weakly individuated items to surface figuratively, as metaphors or similes, as in the following example, where *foliage* serves as a simile for *love*:

> My love for Linton is like the foliage in the woods. Time will change it, I'm well aware, as winter changes the trees – my love for Heathcliff resembles the eternal rocks beneath – a source of little visible delight, but necessary. (Emily Brontë, *Wuthering Heights* (1847), I, ix)

However, if we accept Searle's hypothesis, then the more strongly individuated an item is, the greater will be its propensity for figurative use.

There is thus a tendency for the (more individuated) masculine forms to encode figurative meaning, but this is not an absolute principle. To begin with, we do in fact find metaphorical uses of the feminine forms. This should not surprise us. Once the 'literal–metaphorical' split has taken place, and the two items have acquired lexical autonomy, there is nothing to stop either of them developing further metaphorical extensions, which a priori tell us nothing about the original split. For example, in English, *horn* referring to a protuberance on an animal's head and *horn* referring to a musical instrument, even though etymologically and phonologically identical, are generally perceived as completely separate lexical items. The metaphor is essentially dead. A fortiori, there is nothing to indicate that the French words *cor* and *corne*, which exhibit some phonological similarity but are not identical (indeed, *corne* is no closer phonologically to *cor* than is the etymologically unrelated *corde* 'rope'), are perceived as anything other than unrelated lexical items by contemporary French speakers. Moreover, the impetus for the original metaphorical extension may well still be present (perhaps as a cognitive quasi-universal; see, for instance, Lakoff and Johnson 1980). It is therefore not surprising to find more recent uses of *corne* in the sense of 'instrument made from horn', and thence 'warning device' (compare *corne de brume* 'fog horn' and *corne* in the obsolete sense of 'motor horn').

More significantly, the distinction in meaning between masculine and feminine items is often a good deal less clear cut than it might at first sight appear. For instance, a 'pocket-dictionary' approach to the meanings of *cerveau* and *cervelle* would yield something like the following: *cerveau* 'brain (as organ)' vs. *cervelle* 'brain (as physical matter)'.[37] However, the reality, as represented by the definitions to be found in the *TLF* (Imbs 1971–94), is much more complex, and may be summarized as follows: *cerveau*: 'brain (as an organ), whether human or animal, but especially human; intelligent machine; centre of intellectual life; hook at top of bell to attach clapper to; etc.'; *cervelle*: 'human brain (as physical stuff); animal brain (whether as physical stuff or as an organ); centre of intellectual life; hook on boat to attach rudder to; etc.'. Nonetheless, there is no doubt that, in these clusters of definitions, too, despite a certain overlap between the two items, *cerveau* tends to have meanings which are more salient, and hence more compatible with individuation, than does *cervelle* – function as opposed to substance, human as opposed to animal, and vertical ('hook at top of bell') as opposed to horizontal ('hook at end of boat').[38]

3.2   Refunctionalization vs. adfunctionalization

The developments outlined in this section may be schematized as follows:

I	II
analogical change rather than 'true' refunctionalization	*'true' refunctionalization: 'core-to-core' mapping, contrast of salience maintained*
singular >	masculine > metaphorical reading
plural >	feminine > literal reading

For ease of exposition, I have labelled the second process 'refunctionalization'; but, of course, there is a crucial difference between this change and the examples of refunctionalization discussed in §2, in that here the forms assume a value in addition to, not instead of, their original value. This possibility is envisaged by Lass (1997:320), who revises his earlier notion of exaptation as follows: 'In a typical case, the material exapted is at the point of exaptation doing something else (which it may continue to do); but it is still capable of being remanufactured or restructured, and still exapted, in a sense, as part of a different kind of coexisting structure.' In contrast to his earlier paper, Lass now makes no distinction between instances in which the original function of the refunctionalized material disappears and those in which it is retained alongside the new function – in other words, '[e]xaptation does not presuppose [...] "emptiness" of the exaptatum' (Lass 1997:318). But there is a clear and conceptually significant distinction between refunctionalization which goes hand in hand with loss of the original function and refunctionalization which is grafted on to the original function. Moreover, Lass's later account loses one of the attractions of his original proposal – it pinpointed a class of morphosyntactic changes in which a particular relationship between form and function obtained (see Vincent 1995). 'Exaptation' has indeed become established in the literature in this more restricted sense. If we are to accept the superordinate definition of 'exaptation', then we shall need words for the two types of change it covers: in the spirit of Gould and Vrba (whose 1982 paper was motivated by the ambiguity of the term 'adaptation'), we might reserve the term 'refunctionalization' for the process whereby a form loses its original function and takes on a new function, and coin the term 'adfunctionalization' for the process in which a form assumes a new function alongside or in addition to its original function. Gould and Vrba's original definition of exaptation referred to (biological) adfunctionalization. Lass borrowed the term and applied it to linguistic change in the sense of 'refunctionalization', but subsequently used it to refer to both refunctionalization and adfunctionalization.

3.3   Further examples of adfunctionalization

There are other examples of adfunctionalization in Romance. 'Social deixis' (see, for instance, Fillmore 1997) in French emerged from the opposition between the second-person singular pronoun *tu* and the second-person plural pronoun *vous* (together with the associated verb morphology); but this value has been grafted on to the original opposition of number – it has not displaced it.[39] More generally, the use of a marked item to encode deference, politeness or social distance is found in other contexts as well – for instance, the 'attenuative' use of the imperfect, as in Fr. *Je voulais vous poser une question*, It. *Volevo farLe una domanda*, Sp. *Quería hacerle una pregunta* 'I wanted to ask you a question.' We might also mention the evaluative (hypocoristic, affective, pejorative, etc.) use of diminutives and augmentatives in languages such as Spanish and Italian (see, for instance, Náñez Fernández 1973:376f. and Tekavčić 1972:III,178–96), although here the waters are murky. Jurafsky (1996) suggests a number of allegedly universal pathways which may lead to such adfunctionalizations. However, it is not always clear how the evaluative meaning arises from the diminutive or augmentative one, or even whether this is necessarily the process involved (the two meanings may always have coexisted). For further discussion, see Dressler and Merlini Barbaresi (1994).

The existence of these further examples (or possible examples) of adfunctionalization raises the additional question of the synchronic relationship between the original opposition and the new one. They may be superimposed or they may exist side by side – in other words, whilst the type encodes both functions, a given token may either likewise combine both functions (as occurs systematically with the masculine = metaphorical / feminine = literal lexical split which has been the main focus of this section), or it may encode only one of them (for instance, in French, a token of the second-person pronoun *tu* will always encode both singular number and 'familiarity' (so exhibiting both old and new functions simultaneously), whilst a given token of the second-person pronoun *vous* may encode plural number and 'formality' (also exhibiting both old and new functions simultaneously); but other tokens of *vous* may encode plural number and 'familiarity' (old function only) or singular number and 'formality' (new function only)).[40] Further research is required on this issue.

4 Functionalization

The process of functionalization, in which an opposition which has not previously had a morphological or lexical value comes to encode one, can be seen in the creation of many doublets – forms with the same etymology but different meanings. A caveat should be entered here: probably most doublets have not arisen as a result of functionalization – we may quote well-known examples such as Fr. *métier* 'trade, profession, job; loom' vs. *ministère* 'ministry', both from Lat. MINISTERUM, and Fr. *frêle* 'frail' vs. *fragile* 'fragile', both from Lat. FRAGILEM, and a host of others (for further examples, see Pope 1934:§§657–60; Nyrop 1914:§39). Here, one of the items is essentially a loan; the doublet arises through language contact, not through continuous evolution. However, there are some rather similar pairs in which a possible functionalization cannot be ruled out: compare Pt. *chaga* 'wound' vs. *praga* 'curse, nuisance, misfortune', both from Lat. PLAGAM; Pt.

chumbo 'lead' vs. *prumo* 'plumb-line', both from Lat. PLUMBUM; Sp. *lleno* '[literally] full' vs. *pleno* '[metaphorically] full, complete', both from Lat. PLENUM; Sp. *llave* '(literal) key' vs. *clave* 'key (to problem, etc.), code, clef', both from Lat. CLAUEM. Cases such as this are more difficult to assess; the more Latinate term may not be a loan as such, but a semi-learnèd item, which has a continuous history in the language, but which has resisted some sound change on account of the frequent use of its Latin form (for discussion of some of these issues and further references, see Pountain, this volume, chapter 13: §3.4.1). In each case, the semi-learnèd form has a less basic (in some sense derived) meaning – one which is metaphorical or more specific.

There are, however, some doublets which have incontrovertibly arisen through functionalization. One example is the 'Type B' pronominal distinction discussed in section 2.1 above, in which a single Latin etymon yields functionally distinct forms, according to whether or not it bears stress – compare Lat. ME (unstressed) > It. *mi*, Fr. *me* vs. Lat. ME (stressed) > It. *me*, Fr. *moi*. Here, the purely phonological distinction between a tonic and an atonic form has been functionalized as a grammatical distinction.

In Italian, the division of labour between the two forms is simple: *mi* is the conjunctive (adverbal clitic) form, whilst *me* is the disjunctive form (used with prepositions, in isolation or with contrastive focus). (Enclitic *mi* arguably results from analogy – see the discussion in section 2.1 above.) French is a little more complicated. In the standard language, *me* is the conjunctive (adverbal clitic) form, except when it would be the final element in an enclitic cluster, when we find *moi*: thus *il me le donne* 'he gives it to me' and *donne-m'en* 'give me some', but *donne-le-moi* (*donne-le-me) 'give it to me'. This is not the result of a synchronic restriction on weak/unstressed forms occurring cluster-finally *per se*, as witness the acceptability of *dis-le* 'say it', etc. (but note Qué. *dis-les* 'say it [*sic*]', etc., where the plural third-person pronoun appears to be used in avoidance of *le*; Gillian Sankoff, personal communication). Rather it arises from a diachronic constraint: if a distinction between stressed and unstressed object pronouns existed, then, regardless of their subsequent evolution, the original stressed form remains in stressed environments. In this sense, standard French has retained something of the original stressed/unstressed distinction, and it is difficult to speak of a clear pattern of functionalization. However, some (mainly colloquial) varieties of French have regularized the distribution of the two forms as follows: *me* is the adverbal (proclitic) form, *moi* is the 'elsewhere' form – enclitic, disjunctive (used with prepositions) and free-standing. Thus, these varieties have *donne-moi-z-en* (rather than *donne-m'en*), and some of them also have *donne-moi-le*, rather than *donne-le-moi* (see Grevisse and Goosse 2007:§683). This is a much clearer case of functionalization.

Another example of functionalization concerns the lexicalization of what was originally a purely phonological distinction in doublets arising from the differential development of MidFr. [wɛ] (from an earlier diphthong [oi]; see Pope 1934:§§518–26; Price 1971:§§4.5.4.3, 4.10; Zink 1996:57–9, 134). This sequence had two outcomes, more commonly lowering to [wa] during the seventeenth and eighteenth centuries, but also, in some cases, losing its first element (probably as early as the sixteenth century) and becoming [ɛ]. Each change was lexically diffuse; but, sometimes, both developments affected a word – compare Lat. SETAM > MidFr. *soie* [soiə] > [swɛə] > ModFr. *soie* [swa] 'silk; pig's bristle' and *soie* [sɛ] > *saie*[41] 'small brush made from pig's bristle used by goldsmiths' (see Price 1971:§4.10). However, this example is disputed. The *TLF* (Imbs 1971–94: vol. 14, p. 1415, s.v. *saie*), for instance, considers *saie* to be a loanword from a Norman or Picard dialect. If this is the case, then the apparent split would not be a case of functionalization, but simply a case of a doublet arising through borrowing (as in the examples given at the start of this section). More telling is the following example: (late) Lat. (< Frk.) FRANCISCUM > MidFr. *François* [frãsois] > [frãswɛ] > ModFr. *François* [frãswa] 'François [proper name]' and *François* [frãsɛ] > *Français* 'Frenchman'.

More generally, [oi] > [wɛ] > [ɛ] seems to have been a particularly prevalent change in **systematic** inflectional endings: all the singular persons and the third-person plural of the imperfect and conditional forms of verbs – thus from *porter* 'to carry', imperfect *je portais, tu portais, il portait, ils portaient* 'I (etc.) carried'; conditional *je porterais, tu porterais, il porterait, ils porteraient* 'I (etc.) would carry', where there is only one set of inflections for that tense/aspect form across all conjugations – but not **unsystematic** cases, such as the present indicative and subjunctive of *croire* 'believe' (*je crois*, etc.) vs. *connaître* 'know' (*je connais*, etc.) and the present subjunctive of *être* 'be' (*je sois*, etc.), which constitute but one of a large number of possible inflectional realizations of the present tense, alongside, for example, *je porte* 'I carry', *je finis* 'I finish', *je vends* 'I sell', and so on; and many (but by no means all) gentilic adjectives or nouns (as in *Français*), where, once again, the inflection is not systematic (it contrasts with *-ien, -an*, etc.). (The *Petit Robert* lists 166 such forms in *-ais* as against 199 in *-ois*; four forms may exhibit either ending. Of course, not all of these forms can be traced back to Middle French. Interestingly, possible functionalizations in these contexts seem not to have occurred: thus the adjective corresponding to both *Vienne* 'Vienna, Austria' and *Vienne* 'Vienne, France' is *viennois*, rather than *viennois* vs. **viennais*.)

A further interesting case of a doublet arising through functionalization is purely orthographic. Lat. COMPUTARE 'to count' uncontroversially yields OFr. *conter*. In addition to its numerical meaning, this verb came, by extension, to mean 'to tell, relate'.[42] From the thirteenth century onwards, we find the Latinizing orthography *compter* used alongside the more phonographic spelling in both senses; but each spelling gradually becomes specialized in one of the two meanings, until, by the early seventeenth century, the division of labour between the two is fixed. In this way, what was originally free variation (or possibly a distinction between a learnèd and a popular way of writing the same verb) is functionalized, and yields two distinct (albeit homophonous) lexical items – *compter* 'to count' and *conter* 'to tell, relate'. See *TLF* (Imbs 1971–94), s.v. *compter* (V, 1218–21) and *conter* (VI, 41).

Finally, Michael Friesner (personal communication) has pointed out to me a possible example of functionalization in contemporary Montréal French. As in colloquial European French, the word *voilà* [vwala] 'here is, there is' has a reduced form *v'là* [vla]. However, the distinction between the two, for at least some French speakers in Montréal, is no longer stylistic or sociolinguistic, but has been lexicalized, with the reduced form introducing temporal expressions (e.g., *V'là trois ans que je travaille ici* 'That's three years now I've been working here') and the unreduced form being found in other contexts (e.g., *Voilà le bus qui arrive* 'Here's the bus [coming]').

So far, we have mainly been discussing the functionalization of phonological or orthographic distinctions. It is almost certain that phonological variants are sociolinguistically significant before they become functionalized, although further work is needed to determine whether there is any consistent relationship between this sociolinguistic opposition and the functional distinction which emerges. I turn now to a type of functionalization which is more overtly sociolinguistic in origin – the redistribution, within a single linguistic system, of originally 'synonymous' items in the two languages of a bilingual speech community.[43] Unlike the creation of doublets by borrowing, which I have claimed does not constitute true functionalization, this process, whereby forms which already exist side by side in the speech community, with the same or similar meaning but as part of different linguistic systems, each with its own sociolinguistic status,[44] come to form part of the same linguistic system, where they enter into a structural opposition, does seem to represent functionalization. Maiden (2006b), drawing on work by Kovačec (1963; 1966; 1968), discusses the situation of Istro-Romanian, where, he notes, 'it is likely that there has been a stable coexistence of the two languages over several centuries, with

Istro-Romanian limited to village and family life, and Croatian being employed in wider public spheres'. In his discussion, he focuses on 'what one might term "structured accommodation", whereby the penetration into Istro-Romanian of a Croatian word or grammatical phenomenon is systematically attached to a particular semantic or structural context, giving rise to distributional patterns which are native neither to Istro-Romanian nor to Croatian, but a product of the encroachment of the latter'. He gives three examples.

- For numerals between 'five' and 'eight', Istro-Romanian uses both the 'indigenous' Romance items and items borrowed from Croatian, but there is a strict division of labour between the two sets of terms: the Croatian numerals must be used in what he terms 'lexical measure phrases' – that is, with a noun indicating time, weight, distance, etc. (Moreover, they must occur with an etymologically Croatian noun, if one is available with the relevant meaning.) Romance numerals appear to be ungrammatical when used in this type of phrase; Croatian numerals are ungrammatical in any other context. Thus (to quote one of Maiden's examples) /ʃɑpte kɑse/ – */sedəm kɑse/ 'seven houses' vs. /sedəm let/ – */ʃɑpte let/ 'seven years'.

- Istro-Romanian has acquired the extensive aspect marking which is typical of Slavonic languages (and not usual in Romance), whereby each verb has both perfective and imperfective aspect forms (which, in Slavonic generally, may be distinguished in various ways: by conjugation class, by prefixation or even lexically). Sometimes, both forms are borrowed from Croatian; in other instances, a Romance root is common to both forms, but the perfective is formed by adding a Croatian prefix to this root. However, in many cases, the Romance root provides the imperfective aspect form and the Croatian root the perfective: examples are 'to sleep' (imperfective /durmi/, perfective /zaspi/) and to drink (imperfective /bɛ/, perfective /popi/). As Maiden comments with regard to this last category, '[a]t one level, all that has happened is that a typically Romance system of limited aspect marking has been effaced by the more extensive Slav one, but what is remarkable is that speakers have, in a sense, "grammaticalized" the difference between the dominant and the recessive language, by effectively expressing perfectives in one language and imperfectives in the other'.

- Finally, Istro-Romanian, alone amongst Romanian varieties, has acquired a morphological distinction between adjectives and adverbs. In both Romanian and Croatian, adverbs are normally identical to some form of the adjective (the masculine singular in Romanian, the nominative/accusative of the neuter singular in Croatian). In addition to borrowing some Croatian neuter singular adjectival forms as adverbs corresponding to etymologically Romance adjectives (e.g., /teʃko/ 'heavily', alongside, /ɣrev/ 'heavy'), Istro-Romanian has also taken the final -o which is characteristic of Croatian neuter singulars and added it to native Romance adjective stems to form an adverb (e.g., /plin/ 'full', /plino/ 'fully').

What is not clear in all the above is the relevance or otherwise of the concept of 'core-to-core' mapping to functionalization. When our starting point is not a grammatical function or a lexical distinction, but rather a phonological contrast or the difference between a recessive and a dominant language, then 'coreness' is more difficult to define. In principle, the considerations of frequency, markedness and default status invoked in earlier sections may apply in these circumstances, too, but it is not clear exactly how; and a variety of other factors, ranging from phonæsthesia to language attitudes, may play a role as well. Any elucidation of these issues must await further research.

5   Defunctionalization

We may define defunctionalization as the retention of a formal opposition alongside the loss of the functional correlate of that opposition. This is presumably what Lass (1990:81f.) was referring to when he claimed that a formal distinction which had lost its functional value 'can be kept as marginal garbage or nonfunctional/nonexpressive residue'. It is perhaps the closest linguistic analogue of the 'decorative' value associated with skeuomorphy in art history.[45] I have already alluded to the fact that in old Occitan both *me* < ME and *mi* < MI survive as both conjunctive and disjunctive pronouns in both accusative and dative cases (although detailed analysis of texts might reveal different stylistic values for each form and access to native speakers would almost certainly have revealed sociolinguistic differences, the two pronouns are, grammatically speaking, in free variation). A possible further example of this type of process is represented by the contrast between the *passé simple* (e.g., *je fis*) and the *passé composé* (e.g., *j'ai fait*) of French, where what was originally a contrast between a punctual past and a present perfect has come to encode a number of distinctions at the levels of semantics, pragmatics, style and register, representing at least a partial defunctionalization of the opposition.[46] (For some discussion, see Wilmet 1976:61–82. Comparable developments have taken place in many varieties of Romanian (Graur 1968:318–21) and Italian (Rohlfs 1969:§§672f.; Tekavčić 1972:III, 515; Bertinetto 1991:88–101).)

A further striking example of defunctionalization is provided by the hypothesized mutual influence of the Middle French verbs *aimer* < AMARE and *esmer* < ÆSTIMARE, according to an argument put forward by Gilliéron (1918:267) and Orr (1951; 1953:113–19, 141–53). In this view, the homophony of the two verbs in 'N-pattern' forms (see the discussion in §2.3 above) led ultimately to their complete merger. If this account is correct (and it is contested; see, for instance, Robson 1954:57f.), we have what was originally a lexical opposition being reduced to a difference with no functional value; in particular, before the complete merger of the two items, one can envisage a stage in which the infinitive and the first- and second-person plural forms may have been realized with either stem vowel, without any corresponding difference in meaning (as shown in Tables 6.8 and 6.9). Of course, the two variants may not have been sociolinguistically equivalent – in particular, the realization with [a] may have been seen as more conservative – but, in terms of the typology established by Chambers and Trudgill (1998:97), they will simply have represented a difference in pronunciation, like that found in English *either* ([aɪðə] vs. [iːðə]) or *scone* ([skɒn] vs. [skəʊn]). The original formal opposition will have been retained, but will have been defunctionalized.

For a final example of defunctionalization, I return to the loss of the case system in old French, the aetiology of which was briefly outlined in the

Table 6.8 *The present indicative of* amer *and* esmer *in Middle French*

	AMARE			ÆSTIMARE	
	amer	[amer]		*esmer*	[ɛmer]
(*j'*)	*aime*	[ɛmə]	(*j'*)	*esme*	[ɛmə]
(*tu*)	*aimes*	[ɛməs]	(*tu*)	*esmes*	[ɛməs]
(*il*)	*aime*	[ɛmə]	(*il*)	*esme*	[ɛmə]
(*nous*)	*amons*	[amɔ̃]	(*nous*)	*esmons*	[ɛmɔ̃]
(*vous*)	*amez*	[ames]	(*vous*)	*esmez*	[ɛmes]
(*ils*)	*aiment*	[ɛmə]	(*ils*)	*esment*	[ɛmə]

Table 6.9 *The postulated present indicative of* amer/ aimer *in later Middle French*

	AMARE	
	amer/aimer	[amer]/[ɛmer]
(*j*)	*aime*	[ɛmə]
(*tu*)	*aimes*	[ɛməs]
(*il*)	*aime*	[ɛmə]
(*nous*)	*amons/aimons*	[amɔ̃]/[ɛmɔ̃]
(*vous*)	*amez/aimez*	[ames]/[ɛmes]
(*ils*)	*aiment*	[ɛmə]

section on refunctionalization above (§2.2). It should be stressed that case loss took place gradually. Before disappearing completely, the nominal case system went through a period of instability, with the form–function relationship showing signs of collapse before any reduction in morphological case marking. A parallel might be drawn here with syntactic change, in which a distinction is often drawn between 'reanalysis – the formulation of a novel set of underlying relationships and rules – and actualization – the gradual mapping out of the consequences of the reanalysis' (Timberlake 1977:141; see also Langacker 1977:58 and Harris and Campbell 1995:61, 97). The loss of the form–function relationship – the reanalysis – is difficult to date, although there is evidence for it in texts at least as early as the twelfth century (Schøsler 1984:171–76; Buridant 2001:75). However, the distinct case forms remained but were used in a less and less systematic way, until finally, in most instances, the formal distinction was lost too (the actualization).

It is the very end of this process that is relevant here. By the mid fifteenth century, awareness of the distinct case forms was limited to the fact that they had once existed, and, if they were used at all, it was as a grammatically unmotivated marker of archaism. For instance, as part of his *Testament*, most of which was composed in 1461–62, the poet François Villon wrote a 'Ballade en vieil langage françoys' (see Longnon 1977:24f.), in which he simply adds a final -*s* to a variety of nouns, regardless of their identity or function. Pope (1934:§806) observes that this attempt at pastiche 'shows clearly that he had no understanding of the rules at all' (see also Marchello-Nizia 1997:122). Here, then, a formal opposition with a grammatical function has been reduced to an opposition between a 'normal' form and an 'archaic' (or 'quaint') form.[47]

6   Conclusion

In this chapter, I have attempted to define a typology of changes in form–function relationships in Romance. In functionalization, an opposition acquires a linguistic function where none existed before; in refunctionalization, an opposition acquires one linguistic function in place of another; in adfunctionalization, an opposition acquires a linguistic function in addition to another; and in defunctionalization, an opposition loses all linguistic functions. (I do not, of course, mean to imply that any of the above processes are discrete or sudden.) The birth and death of functionality remain largely mysterious – much more work is required before we can make generalizations about, say, the origin of morphological and lexical oppositions in what was originally purely phonological variation and about the reduction of a meaningful opposition to mere stylistic variation. However, we can entertain hypotheses about refunctionalization and adfunctionalization. Specifically, it seems at least plausible to claim that these processes are guided by the principle of 'core-to-core' mapping which I have outlined above.

In making this proposal, I am not suggesting that linguistic 'junk' cannot exist (a claim which Lass (1990:100, n13) refers to as the 'semiotic fallacy'[48]). What I am saying is that the notion of 'junk' does not seem an especially appropriate or enlightening one to use when discussing the refunctionalizations discussed in this chapter. Whilst the original functional distinctions disappear, the formal oppositions which used to express them seem to retain a vestige of abstract content – they become, in the terminology introduced earlier, skeuomorphy, not junk – and, where one of the items is discarded or the opposition assumes a new function, it is this vestigial content which seems to determine what developments take place. Adfunctionalization, a fortiori, at no stage involves 'junk', as a new opposition is grafted on to an existing one rather than replacing it.

In a critique of Lass's views, Heath (1998:755f.) suggests that 'applying the notion of exaptation to language is questionable, since long-term retention of morphemes which have lost their original function (the "junk" phase) exacts a cost' (presumably in the form of excessive redundancy). Similarly, in the scheme of things which I have tried to sketch, 'junk' would not be essential to exaptation/refunctionalization, and could even be incompatible with it. Even after a morphological opposition has ceased to encode a particular functional opposition, it can still retain a more abstract value which can guide its refunctionalization; and it might well be the case that it cannot be refunctionalized unless this residual opposition is present. There are interesting parallels between morphosyntax and phonology in this respect, especially in the light of recent advances in our understanding of splits and mergers in sound systems (for a survey, see Labov 1994:293–418). 'Junk', in the Lassian sense, understood as the functional merger of originally separate morphosyntactic items which retain a separate formal identity, presents analogies with phonemic merger. The observation by Garde (1961:38f.) that innovations can create homonymy, but cannot destroy it, and that if two items become phonetically identical as a result of sound change, then sound change will never be able to separate them again,[49] leads Labov (1994:311) to formulate what he dubs 'Garde's Principle', whereby '[m]ergers are irreversible by linguistic means'. Skeuomorphy, on the other hand, shows similarities with the 'near-mergers' reported by Labov (1994:349–70), in which speakers systematically maintain an instrumentally detectable difference between two sounds without being able to perceive that they are making any distinction at all. In these cases, it is possible for awareness of a distinction to be re-established by 'retreating' from the 'near-merger'. Clearly, in the cases of skeuomorphy under discussion in this chapter, speakers would be able to perceive a distinction between the two members of an opposition at the level of phonetics or phonology; but, during an intermediate stage, when the original opposition had waned but the new opposition had not yet been established, they might claim that there was no difference in their meaning or function, that they were in 'free variation', even if they were not. In this view, 'junk' would amount to or be a consequence of complete defunctionalization, and skeuomorphy might be regarded as 'near-defunctionalization'. Just as in sound change, true mergers cannot be reversed, but near-mergers can give rise to a renewal or revival of a distinction which speakers perceive, so, I would claim, 'junk' cannot be refunctionalized, whereas skeuomorphic oppositions can.

As noted above, Lass (1997:320) refers to 'the point of exaptation', which implies that, for him, the process is a discrete or sudden one. But the continuity of adfunctionalization is not in doubt; and in this chapter I have sought to show that the refunctionalization of morphological oppositions is also a gradual and continuous process, and involves a transitional stage of skeuomorphy, or 'near-merger', resulting in a 'core-to-core' mapping from the old function to the new one. Couched in similar terms to Lass's, the claim I am making in respect of the examples analysed above might run: 'linguistic exaptation presupposes non-emptiness of the exaptatum'. I suggest that there is a close biological analogue of refunctionalization, in the form of the pupation of certain insect orders (such as

Lepidoptera): the components of the coherent larval system (the caterpillar), which has the well-defined function of eating and growing, turn into those of the quite distinct but equally coherent imaginal system (the butterfly or moth), which has the well-defined function of reproducing, by passing through a relatively incoherent stage (the chrysalis), whose sole function is to make the transition from the first state to the second; for some relevant discussion, see Truman and Riddiford (1999). However, despite the huge apparent differences between them, the larva and the imago are 'the same' in the sense that they share identical DNA. Moreover, although the chrysalis phase sees the total resorption of old tissues and the construction of new ones, parts of the nervous system remain intact, resulting in some maintenance of identity of the individual organism. It has been shown, for instance, that learning (specifically the association of an odour and an electric shock) which takes place in larval Drosophilidæ is retained into the adult stage, despite the major reorganization which occurs during pupation (see Tully *et al.* 1994). Thus, however distinct the two states which are mediated by the chrysalis phase, there is a fundamental continuity between them; and it would be quite erroneous to regard the pupa as in any sense unstructured or 'junk'.

As stated in the Introduction, my hypothesis is that the general principles here adumbrated from Romance are not idiosyncratic to that group of languages, but are applicable more generally – for instance, to such phenomena as the recasting of the opposition between inclusive and exclusive first-person plural pronouns as an distinction of number in some Austronesian languages (see Donohue and Smith 1998) or as a distinction of tense in Tiwi, a language of northern Australia (see Smith 2008). More fundamentally, these principles are relevant to the debate initiated by Heath (1998:756), who states, in a critique of Lass's original paper:

> Lass's metaphorical assemblage […] is ambivalent on the crucial matter of whether (non-contact-induced) grammatical evolution is basically continuous (the inherited formal and categorial system is regularly patched up with new material) or basically discontinuous (old structures periodically collapse, and entirely new ones are created out of the rubble). This must be the central issue of historical grammar, and of all historical scholarship, and our terminology and tropes should force us to confront it.

I believe that the evidence presented in this chapter argues for the essentially continuous nature of much morphosyntactic evolution, and that the terminology I have used (in particular, the use of the terms 'refunctionalization' and 'adfunctionalization' in preference to 'exaptation') and the 'trope' of skeuomorphy draw attention to this fact in the way Heath deems desirable, bolstering his view that 'in the absence of unusual contact situations […] the "old" grammatical patterns (categories and forms) are always decisive in shaping the way "new" patterns fit into the system' (Heath 1998:730) and that 'we need frameworks that give due weight to the restorative and conservative nature of much grammatical change' (Heath 1998:757).

7 MORPHOSYNTACTIC PERSISTENCE[1]

Giampaolo Salvi

1 Preliminaries and introduction

The continuity examined here[2] involves the system of oppositions realized by the morphology and by syntactic construction types, independently of the realization of individual morphemes.

Given that Latin covered an extensive diachronic (and to some extent diastratic) span, part of what survives in Latin texts prefigures in some respects the Romance type. For the Romance languages were not born overnight, but after a long gestation which had already commenced in the period traditionally classified as Latin, and was generally masked by the 'official' literary and grammatical language. This tradition did, however, allow fleeting glimpses of innovative phenomena in the written documentation. And even what is justifiably considered an innovation has its roots in earlier linguistic usage: syntactic innovations often involve extension of existing structures to a wider range of contexts or are the result of more or less direct reinterpretation of the semantic value of an existing construction.

These difficulties in identifying the main points of continuity between Latin and Romance mean that we shall compare Classical Latin (not all *attestations* of Latin) with Romance (focusing on early varieties). Note also that continuity is sometimes only apparent: constructions may be reintroduced into the written language in imitation of Latin (see Pountain, this volume, chapter 13), or a subsystem or construction may change first and then be restructured, returning spontaneously to the original system.

Continuity may vary according to language. Indeed, different degrees of continuity have been used as one possible parameter for typological classification of Romance languages on a scale of innovativeness vs. conservativeness (Vidos 1959 II: ch. 5; Renzi 1994: ch. 8). The degree of continuity shown by individual languages is in principle unpredictable, but some conservative features may have been favoured by the constant presence of a high culture based on Latin or by the continued presence of a literary written variety. Thus, while the western literary languages emerged under the aegis of Latin, Romanian remained outside its cultural reach for centuries; likewise, dialects or languages which have only recently acquired (or reacquired) a written form (e.g., Catalan), often show more innovative features in syntax than varieties with a continuous written tradition since the Middle Ages. Moreover, contact with other languages or (semi-) creolization, favour divergence from the common stock.

2 Grammatical categories

2.1 The nominal system

We focus here on case.[3] Latin had five cases (nominative, genitive, dative, accusative, ablative), plus a vocative form. In noun and adjective morphology, Romance has simplified this system (see also Maiden, chapter 4, this volume). In the historically attested languages we find two kinds of system, with at most two cases: nominative vs. oblique in old French and old Provençal, and in Romanian nominative/accusative vs. genitive/dative. The other languages eliminate case completely, but all varieties conserve traces of a case system in pronouns.

Romance case systems are all derivable from an original three-case system, where accusative and ablative, on the one hand, and genitive and dative, on the other, were no longer distinguished (Dardel 1964). For further discussion of the nature of the early Romance case system, see, for example, La Fauci (1997:37–53); Zamboni (1998:137–42; 2000:93, 110–15) and also Ledgeway, this volume, chapter 8, note 69). In discussing Romance we shall speak therefore of nominative, accusative (the latter incorporating the functions of ablative) and genitive/dative; 'oblique' designates forms which merge the functions of accusative with those of genitive/dative.

In old French and old Provençal most nouns, adjectives and determiners present two distinct case forms: a nominative continuing the subject functions of the Latin nominative (1), and an oblique continuing the functions of the other cases: accusative as direct object and complement of a preposition (2a–b, respectively); ablative as complement of a preposition and temporal or mood complement (3a–c, respectively); genitive for possessor, in some special circumstances (4a), competing with the prepositional phrase introduced by *de* (4b); dative as indirect object, at least in

certain cases (5a), and in competition with the prepositional phrase introduced by *a* (5b):

(1) OFr. *com* cist pains (NOM) *me dehaite!* (*Courtois d'Arras*)
'how this bread makes me ill!'

(2) a. OFr. *Por moi [...] ne tueriés pas* un poulet (OBL) (*Courtois d'Arras*)
'For me you wouldn't kill a chicken'
b. *Ainc en* point (OBL) *n'en* lieu (OBL) *n'en vint / tant que la Pentecouste*
vint (*La Chastelaine de Vergi*)
'He did not reach any spot or place until Whitsun came'

(3) a. OFr. *Si est en* si grant desconfort (OBL) / *qu'a mort se tient et a trahi* (*La*
Chastelaine de Vergi)
'He is in such distress that he holds himself dead and betrayed'
b. *en arés grant piece entiere /* cascun jor (OBL) *en vo pannetiere* (*Courtois*
d'Arras)
'you will have large piece of it every day in your pantry'
c. *la vient* le trot (OBL) (Chrestien de Troyes, *Li Contes del Graal*)
'There he comes at a trot'

(4) a. OFr. *ou la niece* le duc (OBL) *manoit* (*La Chastelaine de Vergi*)
'where the duke's niece dwelt'
b. *l'ame* de ten pere et de te mere *soit en benooit repos!* (*Aucassin et Nicolette*)
'thy father's and thy mother's soul be in blessed rest!'

(5) a. OFr. Son oncle (OBL) *conta bonement / son couvenant et son afere*
(Huon Le Roi, *Le Vair Palefroi*)
'He told his uncle sincerely of his agreement and dealings'
b. *Droit* a mon oncle *le dirai* (Huon Le Roi, *Le Vair Palefroi*)
'I'll tell my uncle immediately'

Note, however, that the oblique covers only a small part of the uses of the
Latin genitive and dative, and basically only the prepositional uses of the
ablative; remaining functions were expressed by prepositional phrases.

Some Franco-Provençal dialects of the Valais retain the two-case distinction in the masculine article, and indeed have extended it to the feminine
singular article, unlike old French and old Provençal (Schmid 1951:80).
Surselvan also preserves a trace of this type of declension, using -*s* (the
nominative singular marker in old French and old Provençal) to mark
masculine singular adjectives and participles in predicative position: *il tschiel*
*era staus cuvretg*s 'the sky had been cloudy'.[4] Predicative *il tat ei* vegls 'the
grandfather is old' is opposed to attributive *in um* vegl 'an old man'. The
ending -*s* no longer marks nominative, but has been reinterpreted as a

predicative marker, appearing even when the predicate refers to the direct object: *render enzatgi* ventireivels 'to make somebody happy' (in old French an oblique case would have been used). Predicative -*s* is not used if the subject is a semantically neutral pronoun: e.g., *ton fuva* cert 'that much was certain'. In feminine singular nouns and adjectives, and in the determiner system, Romanian keeps a two-case distinction: 'nominative/accusative' continues the functions of Latin nominative, accusative and ablative, namely subject (6a), direct object (6b), complement of a preposition (6c) and temporal complement (6d); and 'genitive/dative' continues the functions of Latin genitive to indicate possessor (7a) and of dative to express indirect object (7b) (examples from Ispirescu):

(6) a. Ro. *A fost* un împărat (NOM/ACC) *şi* o împărăteasă (NOM/ACC)
      'There was a king and a queen'
     b. *Ei aveau* o grădină foarte frumoasă (NOM/ACC)
      'They had a very beautiful garden'
     c. *într*-o zi (NOM/ACC) *văzu că* ...
      'one day he saw that [...]'
     d. A doua zi (NOM/ACC) *pîndi şi cel mijlociu*
      'The next day the middle one was on guard too'

(7) a. *în fundul* acestei grădini (GEN/DAT)
      'at the bottom of this garden'
     b. *Făt-Frumos zise* tatălui său (GEN/DAT) *să* ...
      'Prince Charming told his father to [...]'

The other case functions are performed by prepositional phrases, especially direct object with animate reference, e.g., *Împăratul adună numaidecît* pe sfetnicii săi 'The king assembled forthwith his advisors' (lit. 'on his advisors'). Some Raeto-Romance dialects have a dative form of the article (SG *li* < ILLI, PL *lis* < ILLIS) and in some varieties dative case is accompanied by the preposition *a* (Schmid 1951:68–79; Linder 1987:205–32):

(8) a. Obervaz (Graubünden) ˈʒi ˈkwiʎ li (DAT) ˈmamə 'tell the mother'
     b. Alvaneu (Graubünden) ˈʒoj ˈkwiʎ a li (DAT) ˈmamə

In the past, this phenomenon had a greater territorial extent and involved other determiners. Here, as in Romanian, preservation of Latin case-forms was probably favoured by contact with languages having case systems (German for Raeto-Romance, other Balkan languages for Romanian). Romanian also has a vocative form. Masculine singular -*e* might preserve the Latin form: *doamne* 'lord' < DOMINE; but it could also be of Slav origin, as feminine singular -*o* (*fato* 'girl') definitely is. The most widespread masculine singular form -*ule* (*domnule*), of debatable origin, is a later innovation. In the plural the genitive/dative form of the article is used to express vocative (*domnilor*), a Romanian innovation.

2.2 Case in pronominal systems

All Romance languages preserve some case-forms in their pronominal system. There are separate systems for clitics and other pronominal forms. The clitic systems everywhere continue the categories accusative and dative. But despite the many functions performed by these cases in Latin, Romance clitics express only the central actants of the verb: accusative clitics function only as direct object, and dative forms are only indirect object. This restriction is certainly linked to the fact that Romance clitics are adverbal particles whose range extends to the arguments of the verb, but only exceptionally to the complements of other main syntactic categories, nor to the modifiers of the VP and the sentence. Subject clitics are Romance innovations found only in French, part of Occitan, NItalian dialects (see Spiess 1956; Vanelli 1987).

The formal distinction between accusative and dative is everywhere neutralized in 1PL and 2PL (9), and in 1SG, 2SG and in the reflexive everywhere, except Romanian (10):[5]

(9) Fr. *nous/vous* (ACC/DAT)

(10) a. Fr. *me/te/se* (ACC/DAT)
      b. Ro. *mă/te/se* (ACC) – *îmi/îţi/îşi* (DAT)

In the third person the distinction persisted in old Romance (e.g., OFr. *le/la/les* (ACC) – *li/lor* (DAT)), but is lost in some varieties, such as Surmiran and Engadine (11a), and (in part) Spanish for personal direct object (11b):

(11) a. upper Engadine *al/la/als/las* (ACC/DAT)
      b. Sp. Le *vi (a Juan)* / Le *dije (a Juan) que ...*
         'I saw him (Juan)' / 'I told him (Juan) that [...]'

In non-clitic pronouns, all old Romance languages distinguish at least a nominative and an oblique form in 1SG and 2SG forms (12a), but not in 1PL and 2PL (12b):

(12) a. (O)It. *io/tu* (NOM) – *me/te* (OBL)
      b. *noi/voi* (NOM/OBL)

In Romanian there is a three-way distinction in 1SG and 2SG: nominative – accusative – dative (13a), but in 1PL and 2PL there is just nominative/accusative – dative (13b):

(13) a. Ro. *eu/tu* (NOM) – *mine/tine* (ACC) – *mie/ţie* (DAT)
      b. *noi/voi* (NOM/ACC) – *nouă/vouă* (DAT)

This three-way distinction in 1SG and 2SG also characterizes Friulian and various Ladin and Raeto-Romance dialects,[6] where however the dative form must be accompanied by the preposition *a* (14a,b); likewise Sardinian, where dative is also used for the direct object (14c) (Loporcaro 2001):

(14) a. Friulian *jo/tu* (NOM) – *me/te* (ACC) – *mi/ti* (DAT)
 b. *Damile* a mi 'Give it to me' (cf. *Lu fas* per me 'She does it for me')
 c. Bonorva (Sassari) am ˈbiðu a tˈtiɛ 'They've seen you'; su iˈnari ði lu ˈðaɔ a tˈtiɛ 'The money, I give it to you' (cf. daɛ ˈðɛ 'by you')

In old Italian, old Provençal and old French, the third person behaves like 1SG and 2SG (15), while in Romanian, Catalan, Spanish and Portuguese it behaves like 1PL and 2PL (in Romanian the third person forms also function as genitive) (16):

(15) OIt. *egli, ella / egli, elle* (NOM) – *lui, lei / loro* (OBL)

(16) a. Ro. *el, ea / ei, ele* (NOM/ACC) – *lui, ei / lor* (GEN/DAT)
 b. Sp. *él, ella / ellos, ellas* (NOM/OBL)

Modern varieties have frequently abandoned the case distinctions (French, Occitan, NItalian dialects), or limit them to 1SG (Catalan, parts of Galician) or to 1SG and 2SG (Italian), a process already underway at the earliest stages, e.g., in the third person in old Provençal (*el* replaces *lui*, etc.) or 2SG in old Catalan (*tu* replaces *ti*). Some varieties (old Italian, central and southern Italian dialects, Sardinian, Spanish, Portuguese) also preserve the postpositional 'comitative' type MECUM 'with me', etc. (Loporcaro 2001), literally 'me-with', to which they often (redundantly) prefix CUM, yielding a special form beginning with *co(n)-*:

(17) OPt. *migo*, MPt. *comigo*

The case distinction found in Romanian third person pronouns characterizes the whole nominal system, including other pronouns and determiners: e.g., *acest* (NOM/ACC) – *acestui* (GEN/DAT) 'this'. In old Provençal and old French, the distinction is between nominative and oblique (Renzi 1993). In demonstratives (and in the form meaning 'other') referring to animates, old French and old Italian made a three-way distinction, similar to that which in Romanian characterizes 1SG and 2SG pronouns (Renzi 1998):

(18) a. OFr. *cist* (NOM) – *cest* (ACC) – *cestui* (GEN/DAT)
 b. OIt. *quegli* (NOM) – *quello* (ACC) – *colui* (GEN/DAT)

The distinction between the two non-nominative forms was unclear from the earliest times and the *-ui* form tends to encroach on the functions of the accusative, producing a two-term system.

The relative pronoun is different. Some uses of *que/che*, traditionally considered a relative form, are better regarded as complementizer *que/che* (Kayne 1976), especially in subject and direct object relativization. This means that in relative structures some functions are simply unexpressed and the paradigms are not necessarily complete (or the case-forms are not used in every possible syntactic context). For simplicity we consider here only restrictive relatives with overt heads and animate referents. In Romanian the distinction is also nominative/accusative – genitive/dative (19a); in Portuguese and Spanish there is an oblique form and a special fossilized adjectival genitive (19b); old French (and some old Italian dialects; cf. Ledgeway, this volume, chapter 8: §6.2.4) has the distinction nominative – oblique here as well (19c), lost in modern French (19d), plus a special form (of adverbial origin) for prepositional phrases introduced by *de*, whose use partly overlaps that of the oblique; Italian has only one oblique form (19e):

(19) a. Ro. *care* (NOM) / *pe care* (ACC) – *căruil/căreil/căror* (GEN/DAT)
  b. Sp. *quien* (OBL) (– *cuyo* [possessive ADJ])
  c. OFr. *qui* (NOM) – *cui* (OBL) (– *dont*)
  d. MFr. *qui* (– *dont*)
  e. It. *cui* (OBL)

So OFr. *qui* functions as subject (20a), *cui* as DO (20b), as complement of a preposition (20c), as IO (20d) and Possessor (20e); but for DO, instead of *cui*, we normally have the simple complementizer (20f):

(20) a. OFr. *le plus debonere* / *chevalier* qui (NOM) *onques fust nez* (Chrestien de Troyes, *Li Contes del Graal*)
    'the noblest knight that was ever born'
  b. *celui* / cui (OBL) *j'amoie* (*La Chastelaine de Vergi*)
    'the one whom I loved'
  c. *la blondette* por cui (OBL) *je morrai* (Colin Muset, *Les Chansons*)
    'the little blonde for whom I'll die'
  d. *celui [...]* cui (OBL) *de sa fille avoit don fet* (Huon Le Roi, *Le Vair Palefroi*)
    'the one to whom he had made a gift of his daughter'
  e. *cele* cui (OBL) *sans gist en l'araine* (*Piramus et Tisbé*)
    'she whose blood lies in the sand'
  f. *son ami* que (compl) *dui jaiant* / *avoient pris* (Chrestien de Troyes, *Erec et Enide*)
    'her friend whom two giants had taken'

2.3 Deictic distinctions in demonstratives (and locative adverbs)

The tripartite Latin deictic system (near speaker / near addressee / neither) survives in most languages, although the *forms* differ: Portuguese, Spanish, Valencian (in part), Occitan (in part) (21) (see Ledgeway 2004b for the position in central and southern Italian). The remainder have two terms: old French, spoken Catalan, Occitan (in part), northern Italy and standard Italian, Romanian (22) or supplement the distinctions syntactically: MFr. (23):

(21)   Pt. *este/esse/aquele*

(22)   OFr. *cist/cil*

(23)   MFr. *ce [...]-ci / ce [...]-là*

It is not always clear that the modern tripartite system directly continues Latin. In old Portuguese, locative adverb systems are binary (24a); one of these remains binary today, while the other became tripartite only after the Middle Ages (24b) (see Teyssier 1982:31f., 67):

(24)   a. OPt. *acá/alá, aqui/ali*
       b. MPt. *cá/lá, aqui/aí/ali*

In demonstratives, the earliest attestations of *esse* are anaphoric ('the said'), which may mean that the three-term system is a late medieval innovation (Teyssier 1982), but the addressee-oriented demonstrative is extremely rare in written texts. Likewise the tripartite system of some modern Occitan varieties is unmatched in old Provençal.

2.4 Free and clitic pronouns

Unlike Latin, all Romance languages, at least in their early stages, distinguish two sets of pronouns: free, behaving syntactically like Noun Phrases, and clitic, with restricted distribution (in modern Romance they are adjacent to the verb and, when they follow the verb, have the characteristics of inflectional affixes). This continues the Latin distinction between weak and strong uses of pronominal forms (Salvi 2001a):

Latin	strong	weak
phonetics	stressed	unstressed
syntax	all possible positions for an NP	fixed position
semantics	theme, new or contrastive theme, focus	pure anaphora

This distinction corresponds grosso modo to that between free and clitic forms in Romance: the former are stressed, the latter lack inherent stress (cf. *me* and *mi* in 25); the former have the same freedom of syntactic distribution as NPs (e.g., after preposition in 25), the latter have fixed position (immediately preverbal in 25); the former may have thematic (25) or focus value (beside anaphoric), the latter are exclusively anaphoric (*(quanto a) me* vs. *mi* in 25):

(25) It. *Quanto a* me, *queste minacce non* mi *spaventano*
       'As for me, these threats do not scare me'

But there are differences: Latin weak pronouns are variants of strong pronouns and have the same range of syntactic functions; in Romance, clitics can only express the central actants of the verb, except the subject. Since some uses of Romance free pronouns have no functionally equivalent clitic forms, in such cases the free forms combine all the possible semantic functions, and may therefore simply be anaphoric, e.g., as complement of a preposition (26):

(26) It. *Ho invitato Giovanni e più tardi sono andato con* lui *da Maria*
       'I invited Giovanni and later I went with him to Mary's'

In Latin, pure anaphora could be expressed not only by a weak pronoun but by zero (see Vincent 2000). In early Romance, the expression of anaphora was normally obligatory for the direct and indirect object, and realized by a clitic (27):

(27) OPt. *Entom tomou o moço o meestre nos braços, e teendo-*o *em elles* lhe *cingeo el-rrei a espada e* ho *armou cavalleiro, e beijou-*ho *na boca lançando-*lhe *a beençom, dizendo que Deus* o *acrecentasse de bem em melhor e* lhe *desse tanta honrra ...* (Fernão Lopes, *Crónica de Dom Pedro*)

       'Then the master took the boy in his arms and, while he held him thus, the king girded him with a sword and armed him as a knight, and kissed him on the mouth, giving him the blessing, saying that god should make him grow better and better and give him so much honour [...]'

The fixed position of Latin weak forms and Romance clitics is not the same either; but we shall see later that the latter derives from the former.

On the phonetic side, Latin weak pronouns were independent enclitic words which did not modify the stress of their host words, while Romance enclitics behave like affixes and in some languages may carry the main stress of the phonological word formed with their host. Thus French, where stress is always on the final syllable of a word (28):

(28) Fr. *dis* ['di] + *le* [lə] → *dis-le* [di'lə] 'say it'

Despite all these differences, and the fact that clitics as a morphosyntactic category are a Romance innovation, the distinction between free and clitic forms in Romance may be seen as continuing the Latin distinction between strong and weak personal pronouns, of which Romance preserves some fundamental characteristics.

2.5   *The verb system*

Latin verb morphology distinguished Aspect, Tense, Mood, Voice and Person. All of these, except Voice, have formal continuants in Romance, even if the expression of particular properties may be realized syntactically.

The formal distinction of aspect between perfectum and infectum in Latin was organized as follows:

	infectum	perfectum
present	present LAUDO	perfect LAUDAUI
past	imperfect LAUDABAM	pluperfect LAUDAUERAM
future	future LAUDABO	future anterior LAUDAUERO

The distinction already had a limited morphosyntactic role, and did not mark a coherent opposition between perfective and imperfective aspect (Ronconi 1946: ch. 4): present and future in particular may have perfective and imperfective value. Moreover the perfect not only indicates completedness (29) with respect to the present, but also has aorist value (30), which *is* perfective, but does not fit easily into this scheme of oppositions, indicating as it does a past event without temporal links to the present:

(29)   Lat. *quid mihi [...] quod dici possit,* reliquisti? (Cic.)
       'What have you left for me to say?'

(30)   Lat. *Orgetorix [...] suam familiam [...]* coegit *et omnes clientes [...]*
       conduxit (Caes.)
       'Orgetorix gathered his retinue and brought together his *clientes*'

The temporal links of the aoristic use of the perfect are if anything with the imperfect, which may form the background (imperfective) to the events expressed by the perfect as completed (31):

(31)   Lat. *ipsi ex silvis rari* propugnabant (IPFV) *nostrosque intra munitiones ingredi* prohibebant (IPFV). *At milites legionis septimae [...] locum* ceperunt (PFV) (Caes.)

'they themselves were coming out to fight in small numbers from the woods and were trying to prevent our men entering the fortified camp. But the soldiers of the Seventh Legion occupied the place'

In (31) we have a real opposition between perfective and imperfective aspect, but this is the sole case where the oppositon is realized by two forms that also have the same time reference. Otherwise, the expression of a given aspect is accompanied by marking of a different point on the temporal axis. In particular, forms such as the pluperfect and future anterior do express perfective aspect, but also indicate a moment prior to that indicated by the (im)perfect or future. Thus in (32) pluperfect *venerant* expresses not only persistence of the effects of a past event at the reference point (completed aspect), but primarily that the event occurred before the reference point instantiated by the tense of the main event, represented here by *stabat* (anaphoric tense):

(32) Lat. *ad rivum eundem lupus et agnus* venerant (PLPF) *[...] superior* stabat (IPF) *lupus* (Ph.)
'a wolf and a lamb had come to the same stream [...] the wolf was above'

So the Latin verb system is essentially organized around tense, and expression of deictic and anaphoric time is fundamental, while expression of aspect is secondary and independently manifested only in the opposition between imperfect and perfect. This state of affairs is faithfully continued in Romance, where the morphological opposition of aspect is found only between imperfect and perfect (33):

(33) It. *Mentre Piero* dormiva (IPF), *il telefono* suonò (PF) *più volte*
'While Piero was sleeping, the phone rang several times'

The distinction between the use of perfect and imperfect was more faithfully preserved in older varieties, where the perfect had a rather wider range of use than today, corresponding exactly to that of Latin. It could present an event in its entirety even if it had a temporal extension greater than concomitant events expressed in the imperfect (serving as a frame to the focalized event; see Maiden 1998c:4.8.3). So in (34) the existence of the king is presented at the beginning as a total, concluded event, while his characteristics, which frame the event to be narrated, are presented in the imperfect, as being in progress, while their final point is not focalized, because what matters is that they be valid at the moment of the main action. The same system existed in Latin (35), while modern Romance would have the imperfect in both (36):

(34) OIt. *uno re* fu (PRF) *nelle parti di Egitto, lo quale* avea (IPF) *uno suo figliuolo primogenito* (*Novellino* 4)
'there was a king in Egypt who had a first born son'

(35) Lat. *Samia mihi mater* fuit (PRF); *ea* habitabat (IPF) *Rhodi* (Ter.)
'My mother was from Samos; she lived in Rhodes'

(36) ModIt. *In Egitto c'*era (IPF) *un re che* aveva (IPF) *un figlio*

Yet the Romance imperfect is no longer a purely imperfective tense: because of the spread of complement clauses in the indicative (replacing subjunctive and accusative and infinitive), the imperfect indicative extends its range of use as an anaphoric tense and thereby can express posteriority so that (like the future) it can also have perfective value (37):

(37) OIt. *E de dare s. xx, che lli prestai* [...] *disse che nne paghava la libra del chomune* (Florentine document 1275)
'And he must give (me) 20 soldi, which I lent him [...] he said that with this he would pay off the commune's direct tax'

Here the imperfect behaves like the imperfect subjunctive, which as an anaphoric tense could already express in Latin posteriority, and could therefore have perfective value (38):

(38) Lat. *tantus in curia clamor factus est ut populus* concurreret (Cic.)
'such a hubbub arose in the curia that the people came running'

Yet we should remember that, although the presence of the morphosyntactic category of aspect does not change from Latin to Romance, the creation of various aspectual periphrases allows Romance a more varied expression of aspect than in Latin. The creation of the perfective periphrasis (see Ledgeway, this volume, chapter 8: §6.2.1.1) allows differentiation of aorist, completed and inclusive aspect (where the duration of an event includes the time of utterance): normally aorist aspect is expressed by the old perfect, and completed and inclusive aspect by the new periphrasis (39a), but in Galician-Portuguese (at least in modern varieties), as well as SCalabrian and Sicilian, and many Latin American Spanish varieties, the old perfect expresses aoristic and completed aspect, while the new periphrasis is limited to inclusive aspect (39b) (Sten 1973: chs. 4, 10; Ilari 1999): [7]

(39) a. It. *cantai* (aoristic) 'I sang' – *ho cantato* (completed + inclusive)
'I have sung + I have been singing'
     b. Pt. *cantei* (aoristic + completed) 'I sang + I have sung' – *tenho cantado* (inclusive)
'I have been singing'

Likewise, creation of an analytic tense linked to the simple perfect (*pluperfect*) allows expression of a particular value of aorist aspect, immediate completion of the event (40):

(40) a. OIt. *Il lupo disse: «Andianvi».* Furono giunti *a lui* (*Novellino*)
          '[No sooner had] the wolf said: "Let's go there" [than] they reached him'
     b. classical Fr. *La cigogne au long bec n'en put attraper miette et le drôle* eut
          lapé *le tout en un moment* (La Fontaine)
          'The long-beaked stork couldn't catch a bit of it and the joker had
          lapped it all up in a trice'

Romance *tense* shows considerable continuity with Latin: all languages preserve present (though in Sardinian and often in SItaly it now only has 'generic' and 'atemporal' functions – the real present now replaced by *èssere* + gerund), imperfect and (at least originally) perfect indicative with their original temporal functions; Spanish and Portuguese long retained the pluperfect as well (which survives with other values in many other varieties), while the remaining languages replace it with a periphrasis, and Romanian with the pluperfect subjunctive form; the lost forms of the future are largely replaced by a periphrasis. These formal reshufflings leave the Romance languages able to express the same temporal relations as Latin, i.e., the three fundamental tenses present, past, future and the anaphoric tenses indicating anteriority with respect to a reference point other than the time of utterance. Taking Spanish as our principal example:

Latin		Romance
Deictic tenses		
Present	PRS CANTO >	PRS *canto*
Past	IPF CANTABAM > PRF CANTAUI >	IPF *cantaba* PRF *canté* (PRF periphrasis *he cantado*)
Future	FUT CANTABO	(periphrasis *cantaré*)
Anaphoric anterior tenses		
Past	PLPF CANTAUERAM >	PLPF (Pt. and classical Sp.) *cantara* (Ro. *cântasem* from Lat. PLPF.SBJV CANTAUISSEM) (perfective periphrasis *había* / *hube* *cantado*)
Future	FUT anterior CANTAUERO	(perfective periphrasis *habré cantado*)

The anaphoric relation of posteriority in the past was already expressed in Latin by a periphrasis (future participle + ERAM), generally replaced in Romance by an (originally) periphrastic structure parallel to that of the future (the so-called *conditional*) (41):

(41) Sp. *Dijo que* vendría
      'He said he would come'

In some varieties (French, Italian), the future periphrasis became a synthetic form at early date, thereby reinforcing the structure of the paradigm, whose deictic tenses are basically expressed morphologically by simplex forms, and whose anaphoric tenses are expressed syntactically by periphrases. On the same principle, the simplex form of the pluperfect tends to be eliminated.

Likewise in the subjunctive: the present is pan-Romance (it has generally disappeared from modern SItalian dialects), the imperfect survives in Sardinian (but not all modern varieties), while elsewhere it has been replaced in its functions by the pluperfect. The anteriority forms have been replaced by periphrases, as in the following schema (where *present/past* and *realizable/non-realizable* approximately indicate the functions that the subjunctive had in Latin subordinate clauses as the expression of sequence of tenses, and in Latin main clauses, as the expression of modality; see Kiss 1982: ch. 3). Exemplifying again mainly from Spanish:

	Latin	**Romance**
Present/realizable	PRS CANTEM >	PRS *cante*
Past/non-realizable	IPF CANTAREM >	IPF (Sardinian) *kantare* (PLPF CANTAUISSEM > IPF *cantase*)
Anteriority		
Present/realizable	PRF CANTAUERIM	(perfective periphrasis *haya cantado*)
Past/non-realizable	PLPF CANTAUISSEM	(perfective periphrasis *hubiese cantado*)

In Latin, posteriority was unexpressed, or expressed by a periphrasis (future participle + subjunctive present SIM / imperfect ESSEM). Romance languages in general have no separate form for posteriority, but sometimes resort to (originally periphrastic) forms of the future and conditional/future-in-the-past indicative (42):

(42) a. It. *Spero che* venga (PRS.SBJV) / verrà (FUT.IND)
          'I hope he'll come'
      b. Pt. *Esperava que me* convidassem (IPF.SBJV) / convidariam (COND)
          'I was hoping they would invite me'

Spanish had, as Portuguese still does, a future subjunctive (and future anterior) form, derived etymologically from the future anterior indicative and the perfect subjunctive, but the use of this tense is limited to certain types of adverbial and relative subordinate clause.

The distinction between present and future imperative is nowhere preserved.

Despite the notable continuity with the Latin tense system, there are systems with fewer distinctions: e.g., modern French, having lost the imperfect subjunctive, neutralizes the present and past forms (43a); likewise Romanian, which has not developed replacements for the Latin imperfect subjunctive (43b):

(43) a. classical Fr. *Il fallait qu'il se* levât (IPF.SBJV) / MFr. *...qu'il se* lève
          (PRS.SBJV)
          'It was necessary that he should get up'
      b. Ro. *Nu ştia bietul împărat pe care să îmbrăţişeze* (PRS.SBJV) *mai întîi*
          (Ispirescu)
          'The poor king didn't know which one to embrace first'

Some SItalian dialects have no morphologically distinct future form, and use the present to express the future, e.g., Cal. *lu fazzu* PRS *crai* 'I'll do it tomorrow' (while present time is usually expressed with a periphrastic construction with auxiliary + gerund: Cal. *ste faciennu* lit. 'I am doing' = 'I do'). Raeto-Romance and Ladin dialects which have acquired no conditional/future-in-the-past, or where the conditional is only modal, neutralize imperfect and conditional, as does Romanian: *Am prins trenul care* pleca (IPF) *peste 5 minute* 'I caught the train that was leaving / would leave 5 minutes later.'

The three Latin *moods*, indicative, subjunctive and imperative, are retained throughout Romance, but the division of labour may vary locally, not least because the creation of a new *conditional* (not pan-Romance) encroaches on the range of uses of the subjunctive.

Romance maintains the distinction between imperative and subjunctive in direct (second person) and, respectively, indirect (third person) and exhortative (1PL) orders (but in Modern French and in many Occitan and Catalan dialects the exhortative form now coincides with that of the indicative). This distinction assumes particular importance in languages such as Portuguese, Spanish and Italian that adopt third person forms for formal address:

(44) a. Lat. FAC/FACITE (IMP) – FACIAT/FACIANT – FACIAMUS (SBJV) 'do'
      b. Sp. *haz/haced* (IMP) – *haga/hagan* – *hagamos* (SBJV) 'do'

Of the various Latin second person prohibitive forms, negator + subjunctive survives in Portuguese, Spanish, Catalan, Occitan, Sardinian: Languedocien *Vengas pas* 'Don't come.' Second person plural negative imperative comprising negator + positive imperative, found in Romanian, Italian, French (e.g., Ro. *nu cântaţi* 'don't sing'), might continue Latin *ne cantate*, but the same phenomenon in second person singular (modern French, Surselvan, some NItalian dialects: e.g., ModFr. *ne chante pas*) is certainly an innovation – old French had negator + infinitive. It is uncertain whether this latter construction continues Latin negator + perfect subjunctive (NE CANTAUERIS > NE CANTARIS > OFr. *ne chanter*), or is a construction created analogically on the basis of Latin NOLI CANTARE 'don't sing' (lit. 'do not want to sing').

Subjunctive with optative value appears throughout Romance, e.g., OFr. *Or* aït *Diex Guillaume le marchis* (*Le Moniage Rainouart*) 'Now God help the marquis Guillaume.' But survival of the dubitative/potential use is more limited, and mainly found in a kind of interrogative sentence (45) and in Spanish and Portuguese in sentences with (Spanish) *quizás, tal vez* and (Portuguese) *talvez* (46). Romanian uses it where other Romance languages would use the future (47):

(45) a. Ro. Să fi adunat *el atâţia bani?*
          'Has he [really] amassed all that money?'
      b. It. *Che* facesse *per scherzare?*
          'Was he [really] joking?'

(46) Pt. *Talvez não* venham
      'Maybe they won't come'

(47) Ro. Să *tot* fie *cinci ani* (cf., e.g., It. Saranno *cinque anni*)
      'It must be five years'

Use of the imperfect/pluperfect subjunctive in this function was more widespread in the early varieties, and survives in those varieties (Raeto-Romance, Ladin, some NItalian dialects) which did not develop a conditional form: e.g., OFr. *A cui* demandasse (SBJV) *congié [...]?* (*Partonopeu de Blois*) 'From whom could I have sought leave [...]?' (cf. ModFr. *À qui* aurais *-je* pu (COND) *demander congé [...]?*). The present/perfect subjunctive is not maintained in hypothetical sentences, but in some varieties (old French and classical French, Italian dialects, Raeto-Romance, Ladin) the imperfect/ pluperfect subjunctive survives (48):

(48)　a.　OFr. *se j'osasse parler / Ge* demandasse *de quel tere estes nez* (*Le Couronnement de Louis*)
'If I durst speak, I should ask in what land you were born'

　　　b.　Surselvan *Sche jeu vess temps e daners*, mass *jeu ell'Italia*
'If I had time and money, I'd go to Italy'

　　　c.　Abruzzese sə mm a'vessə tə'nutə 'famə, a'vessə maɲ'ɲatə
'If I'd been hungry I would have eaten'

Note that the imperfect subjunctive initially has its (original) pluperfect meaning (49a), and was only later replaced by a periphrastic form (49b):

(49)　a.　OFr. *Ne ce ne li* deïst *il ja / S'a li n'eüst grant acointance* (*La Chastelaine de Vergi*)
'And he would not have told her even that had he not been very well acquainted with her'

　　　b.　Fr. *Je n'eusse pas été femme, si le visage de ma rivale n'eût pas excité ma curiosité* (P. Loti)
'I should not have been a woman if my rival's face had not excited my curiosity'

Elsewhere and in Modern French there is normally a conditional: ModFr. *Si j'osais parler, je vous* demanderais *de quel pays vous êtes originaire* 'If I dared speak, I should ask you from what land you hail.'

The *person* distinction between some forms may be neutralized. In Italian, all three singular persons of the present subjunctive, and the 1SG and 2SG imperfect subjunctive, are neutralized. In *spoken* French there is extensive (phonologically caused) person neutralization, in particular between all singular persons and the third person plural in the present and imperfect indicative, present subjunctive and conditional. In Portuguese and much of the Hispanophone world (Latin America, Canaries and part of Andalusia), the 2PL form has been replaced by the 3PL, originally used as a 'distant' address form.

3　Constructions

3.1　The noun phrase

In Latin the main element of cohesion in the NP was gender, number and case agreement of adjectival elements with the head. This agreement allowed non-adjacency of the elements, at least in some styles. Romance languages largely lose this possibility. In early Romance it was still possible to focalize part of the NP in preverbal position, leaving the rest in postverbal position (50):

(50) a. OFr. asez *i ot* contes e rois (Chrestien de Troyes, *Li Contes del Graal*)
          'There were many counts and kings'
     b. OIt. Neuna *è* maggiore forza *che la pietà* (*Fiori e Vita di Filosafi*)
          'There is no power greater than piety'

Nowadays such focalization is limited to non-adjectival quantifiers – see (51), where preposition *de* creates the possibility of separation:

(51) a. Fr. Combien *Pierre a-t-il perdu* d'argent?
          'How much money has Pierre lost?'
     b. *Charlotte a* assez *accepté* d'invitations
          'Charlotte has accepted quite a few invitations'

In contrast, gender, number and (where applicable) case agreement survives throughout Romance (see chapters 4 and 5 of this volume for inflectional morphological aspects).

In Latin, the unmarked expression of the complement of a nominal head was genitive case (or a possessive adjective). The genitive performed a wide range of functions: possessor (anything from true possession to a much vaguer relationship – see (52a)); with nouns with argumental structure it could indicate either the subject (52b) or the object (52c) of the nominalized predicate; it could also express a modifier of quality (52d) or specify the content of the head (52e); also subject–predicate relationships (52f) and partitiveness (52g):

(52) a. DOMUS PATRIS 'father's house'
     b. FLETUS OMNIUM 'the crying of everyone'
     c. CUPIDITAS REGNI 'the desire to rule'
     d. HOMINES MAGNAE UIRTUTIS 'people of great courage'
     e. URBS ROMAE 'the city of Rome'
     f. MONSTRUM MULIERIS 'that monster of a woman'
     g. PARS EQUITUM 'part of the knights'

All the functions of the genitive within the NP are performed in modern Romance (with the partial exception of Romanian), by *de/di* + NP. Substitution of the genitive with the periphrasis was already under way in Classical Latin for partitives, where DE or EX + ablative NP was used: e.g., *si quis [...]* de nostris hominibus (Cic.) 'If any of our men [...]'. DE + NP then gradually gains ground, eventually replacing all uses of the adnominal genitive (and going beyond). The syntactic genitive is thereby preserved in Romance, albeit under a new guise.

Comparison with languages which keep genitive or oblique case is interesting. Romanian uses either the genitive, or *de* + NP: apart from the partitive, where the preposition continues Latin usage (53g), note that where the genitive expressed a qualifying modification (53d, f), we have the prepositional construction; where there is a relation between two entities (possession (53a) or argumental (53b–c)) both solutions seem allowed, but *de* cases should be interpreted as a kind of compound noun where the noun introduced by *de* is not normally referential; so as a rule, in Romanian, possessive and argumental relationships are expressed by the genitive, but otherwise *de* is used (or *dintre* < DE + INTER 'between' for the partitive):

(53) a. *casa* mamei 'mother's house'
　　 a'. *casă* de oameni 'house of people/human habitation'
　　 b. *trecerea* timpului 'the passing of time'
　　 b'. *explozie* de mânie 'explosion of rage'
　　 c. *citirea* contorului 'the reading of the meter'
　　 c'. *strângere* de semnături 'gathering of signatures'
　　 d. *om* de ispravă 'person of achievement'
　　 e. *luna* lui aprilie 'the month of April'[8]
　　 e'. *ziua* de joi '(the day of) Thursday'
　　 f. *ticălosul acela* de Toma 'that rascal (of) Toma'
　　 g. *unii* dintre tovarăşi 'some of the comrades' / *un kilogram* de unt 'a kilo of butter'

Old Romanian could use *de* even where the modern literary language would use the dative–genitive: *pren mijloc* de băsērecă (in various translations of the psalms) 'in the midst of the congregation'; the preposition *a* could also be used: *împăratul* a toatâ lumĭa (*Codicele Todorescu*) 'king of the whole world' (Iliescu 2008).

In old French too, the oblique (as genitive) is restricted to possessors and nominal arguments (54a, b, c), while the other functions are performed by *de* (54d–g). As in Romanian, the modifier use is the preserve of *de* (54a'''), which also rivalled the oblique in possessor and argumental functions (54a', b', c'). Use of the oblique was actually very limited, being mainly found with proper nouns and NPs with proper noun status, otherwise *de* was used (also *a*, which survives in modern French, but with more restricted usage – 54a''):

(54) a. OFr. *la bouche* le roi (*La queste del Saint Graal*)
　　　 'the king's mouth'

a′. *l'ame* de ten pere et de te mere (*Aucassin et Nicolette*)
'your father's and mother's souls'

a″. *la chanbre* a la pucele (Chrestien de Troyes, *Li Contes del Graal*)
'the maiden's chamber'

a‴. *cort* de roi (Chrestien de Troyes, *Li Contes del Graal*)
'king's/royal court'

b. *la traïson* Lancelot (*La Mort le Roi Artu*)
'the betrayal by Lancelot'

b′. *la douçor* de ma nacion (*La queste del Saint Graal*)
'the gentleness of my native land'

c. *les traïtors* le roi (Béroul, *Le roman de Tristan*)
'the betrayers of the king'

c′. *une amorette* / d'une jone pucelette (Colin Muset, *Les Chansons*)
'a love for a young girl'

d. *chevalier* de grant proesce (*La Mort le Roi Artu*)
'knights of great prowess'

e. *la cité* de Kamaalot (*La Mort le Roi Artu*)
'the city of Camelot'

f. *cel fellon* de borjois (*Parise la duchesse*)
'that felon of a city-dweller'

g. *Molt en i ot* d'ocis et de navrés (*La Mort le Roi Artu*)
'There were many of them killed and wounded'

Within the Latin NP, the unmarked possessive adjective position was postnominal. Only Romanian and Sardinian retain this characteristic (55) (Renzi 2001); elsewhere the possessives come before the noun, after the determiners in Italian and Portuguese (56a), in complementary distribution with determiners in French and Spanish (56b):

(55) a. Ro. *prietenul* meu 'my friend'
　　　b. Srd. *su libru* meu 'my book'

(56) a. It. *i miei amici / alcuni* miei *amici* 'my friends / some of my friends'
　　　b. Fr. mes *amis* / **les mes *amis* 'my friends'

In Romanian, and central and southern Italian dialects, names of relations may have an enclitic possessive (without article) (57):

(57) a. Ro. *sorǎ*-ta 'your sister'
　　　b. Subiaco (Lazio) ˈnɔrema 'my daughter-in-law'

3.2　Comparative constructions

In Latin the comparative of adjectives was formed with a suffix -IOR (see also chapter 5), but with adjectives in -EUS, -IUS and -UUS, MAGIS + adjective was used, a structure available also for forms which could take the suffix; cf. *quid magis est saxo durum, quid mollius unda?* (Ov.) 'What is harder than a rock, what softer than a wave?' Beside MAGIS there was PLUS, which was alien to the educated norm until Christian Latin. Romance continues and generalizes MAGIS in peripheral areas (Portuguese, Spanish, Romanian – 58a) and PLUS in central areas (French, Italian – 58b), although Occitan has both:

(58) a. Pt. mais *bonito*
      b. Fr. plus *beau* 'more beautiful'

The second term of comparison was expressed in Latin with QUAM + phrase/sentence (or sometimes by the ablative) (59):

(59) a. Lat. *cum possit* […] *clarius dicere* quam ipse (Cic.)
          'since he can say it more clearly than the man himself'
      b. *tibi multo maiori* quam Africanus fuit (Cic.)
          'to you, who are much greater than the African was'

The construction is continued in old Portuguese, Galician old Sardinian, old Italian dialects and Romanian, where *quam > ca* (Herman 1963:150–60) (60):

(60) a. OPt. *Mais quero que mates mim* ca o veer matar ante mim (*A Questa do Santo Graal*)
          'I'd rather you kill me than to see him killed before me'
      b. Glc. *É máis listo o pai* ca non o fillo
          'The father is cleverer than the son'
      c. Ro. *Avea o pieliţă mai albă* ca spuma laptelui (Ispirescu)
          'Her skin was whiter than the foam of milk'

Elsewhere *quam* is generally replaced by *que/che* and *de/di* (or analytic forms: Ro. *decât*, It. *di quanto*, Sp. *de lo que*, Pt. *do que*), with various distributions.

3.3   The prepositional phrase

Latin was already largely a prepositional language, a situation continued in Romance. Some postpositional uses are actually prepositional phrase + adverb, with preposition (and article) suppressed: e.g., Pt. *rio acima < pelo rio acima* 'up river'. While in Latin part of the NP complement of the preposition could precede the preposition (generally adjective–preposition–noun: e.g., MAGNA CUM CURA 'with great care'), in Romance the NP always follows it (It. *con grande cura*).

From a functional point of view, in the evolution from Latin to Romance PPs often replace case-marked NPs, extending uses already present in

Classical Latin: we have seen DE + NP(ABL) alternating with the genitive in partitives. Similarly, AD + NP(ACC) alternated with the dative in verbs of movement: the dative was used with persons as an indirect object indicating destinatee / beneficiary of the event (61a), AD with things, as an indicator of place (61b); but the sense of place could prevail and so there was AD with persons too (62) – hence the use of AD to express indirect object:

(61)   a. *hominem* alicui *adducere* (Pl.)
          'to take a person to someone'
       b. *adducere exercitum* ad urbem (Cic.)
          'to lead the army up to the city'

(62)   *hunc* [...] ad carnificem *dabo* (Pl.)
       'I'll give this fellow to (into the hands of) the executioner'

3.4   The Sentence

3.4.1   Grammatical functions

The fundamental syntactic properties of the Latin *subject* survive, in that subject has nominative case and finite forms of the verb agree for person/ number with the subject (the participle agrees for number and gender) (63):

(63)   a. Lat. Pueri (M3PL) laudati (MPL) sunt (3PL) 'The boys were praised'

       b. It. *I ragazzi* (M3PL) *sono* (3PL) *stati* (MPL) *lodati* (MPL)

Moreover, with non-finite forms in control constructions, the 'suppressed' argument (coreferential with one of the arguments of the main verb) is the subject: so in *loqui omitto* 'I stop speaking', the subject of the infinitive *loqui* cannot be expressed, as in the corresponding Romance type, e.g., It. *smetto di parlare*. But there are differences. As we have seen, nominative case marking in modern varieties is generally reduced to a few pronominal forms and in some varieties is wholly absent. Even where it is marked morphologically, it tends to be restricted to instances where there is a precise correspondence between person/number expressed by the subject and that expressed by the verb. Thus in old NItalian varieties, the pronoun with subject function is always nominative when it is the subject of a finite verb, but may be either nominative or oblique when it is the subject of a gerund (Benincà 1994:171f.). In late old French, two coordinated pronouns in subject function may appear in the oblique (for here the verb is of a different person from the two pronouns): compare (64a) with older (64b):

(64) a. OFr. Moi (OBL) et voz *fumez en une hore engendré* (*Ami et Amile*)
      'you and I were begotten at the same time'
   b. *e* jo (NOM) e vos *irum* (*Chanson de Roland*)
      'you and I will go'

As for agreement, in *français avancé* and some NItalian dialects, it is also marked with a preverbal agreement particle (65a) or with this particle alone, if the verb does not have distinct person/number marking (65b) (Renzi 1992a):

(65) a. Mendrisio *lur i* (3PL) *cantan* (3PL) 'they sing'
   b. Locarno *lor i* (3PL) *canta* (unmarked form)

More important from a structural point of view is the fact that in many varieties the verb does not agree with a rhematic subject, in certain constructions. These generally involve change-of-state or change-of-place verbs or passive structures (so-called *unaccusative constructions*; see Burzio 1986: ch.1), where the subject is usually postverbal. Thus in (66a) the verb remains in the unmarked 3SG form, even though the subject is plural, and in (66b) the participle remains in the unmarked masculine, although the subject is feminine:

(66) a. OFr. Aparut *sor l'autel* les mains / Nostre Seignor (*La Vie de saint Josse*)
      'The hands of Our Lord appeared on the altar'
   b. *Onques ne* fu dit tel maniere / Tant dolereuse ne tant fire (Béroul, *Le Roman de Tristan*)
      'Never was such a kind (of punishment) so grievous and so fierce told of'

The lack of agreement, not unknown in archaic Latin but absent from the Classical Latin norm, treats the subject as the direct object of the verb, and such subjects show other points in common with direct objects, such as oblique case (67), alternating with nominative, or possible use of partitive/genitive clitic *en/ne* (68a), characteristic of direct objects (68b). Example (68a) also shows how the partial direct object characteristics of the postverbal subject can lead to insertion of a 'neuter' expletive pronominal subject (*il*):

(67) OFr. *N'i remaint* chevalier (OBL) *ne dame / qui ne s'atort* (Chrestien de Troyes, *Erec et Enide*)
   'There is no knight or lady left who is not preparing'

(68) a. ModFr. *Il* en *a été envoyé* un grand nombre
      'A large number of them were sent'
   b. *Pierre* en *a envoyé* un grand nombre
      'Pierre sent a large number of them'

So while Romance languages remain substantially nominative–accusative like Latin, there has evolved an ergative subsystem which treats the direct object of transitive verbs and the (rhematic) subject of certain predicates in like fashion. But subject pronouns are always excluded, thereby giving rise to a *split ergativity pattern* (Comrie 1981: chs. 5, 9): a nominative–accusative system for pronouns and an ergative–absolutive one (in certain respects) for ordinary NPs (see La Fauci 1988; 1997). Compare also the use of the extended accusative (with unaccusatives) in late(r) Latin, discussed, among other relevant issues, in Ledgeway, this volume, chapter 8: §6.

The *direct object* remains essentially a non-prepositional argument, as in Latin. An important innovation of some languages (in particular Spanish, SItalian dialects, Romanian, with traces in other varieties) is the use of a preposition to mark human and/or definite/specific direct objects (see Zamboni 1992; also Rohlfs 1971a).

A remnant of Latin structure is agreement of the participle with the direct object in analytic structures with auxiliary 'have' (Loporcaro 1998a). In Latin, the participle was a predicative complement of the direct object, and therefore agreed with its semantic subject: hasce aedes (FPL) conductas (FPL) *habet* (Pl.) 'He has this house rented/on rent.' Participial agreement was normal (if not usually obligatory) in the Middle Ages (69), and is robust to this day in some varieties (see, for example, Smith 1995a), although it has disappeared from Spanish, Portuguese and Romanian. In Catalan and Italian its survival is generally limited to some pronominal direct objects (70):

(69) a. OIt. *le pietre* [...] *avevano* perduta (FSG) loro virtude (FSG) (*Novellino*)
          'The stones had lost their power'
      b. *giamai non avea* veduto (unmarked) niuna fanciullezza (FSG) (*Novellino*)
          'He had never known any youth'
      c. *avendo*le (FPL) tese (FPL) (*Novellino*)
          'having spread them out'

(70) a. It. Li (MPL) *ho* visti (MPL)
          'I've seen them'
      b. Mi *ha* visto (unmarked) / vista (F) (with a feminine referent)
          'He's seen me'

Romance generally makes the distinction between dative and genitive, i.e., between indirect object as central actant of the sentence (preposition *a/à*) and complement of a nominal head (preposition *de/di*). Exceptions are Romanian, where the formal merger between genitive and dative is shared with other Balkan languages, and in part French, where, within the NP, the possessor may also be introduced by the preposition *a* (for

SItalian dialects, see Loporcaro and Limacher-Riebold 2001). Genitive and dative merger in Romanian does not imply lack of a distinction between indirect object and complement of a nominal head, for we have seen that the latter can also be introduced by *de* while the indirect object could be introduced in old Romanian by the preposition *a*: *o dĕde el a lucratori* (Coresi, *Tetraevanghelul*) 'he gave it to the workers'; even today it may be introduced in various cases by the preposition *la*, the modern counterpart of *a*: e.g., Ro. *Cui? Cui ai dat-o, nenorocito!* – La o chivuţă (Caragiale) 'Who to? Who did you give it to, wretch! – To a hawker woman'.

But is the Romance distinction really the continuation of the Latin one, especially bearing in mind that the oblique case in early Romance seems to subsume all functions other than the nominative, including genitive and dative? We have seen that the use of the oblique as indirect oject and complement of a nominal head is always just an alternative, in the attested early varieties, to the prepositional use, and this is confirmed by late and vulgar Latin texts, where the prepositional use is abundant, at least for AD. Probably in late Latin, prepositional constructions developed in competition with case constructions, and both coexisted over a long period, even after case distinctions have fused into a single oblique case form, until eventually only the prepositional forms survive:

Classical Latin	Late Latin	Early Romance	Modern Romance
Dative	Dative / AD + NP	*a* + NP / Oblique	*a* + NP
Genitive	Genitive / DE + NP	*de* + NP / Oblique	*de* + NP

We may conclude that the distinction in the expression of indirect object and the complement of a nominal head effectively continues the Latin distinction between dative and genitive.

A striking use of the Latin dative that is continued throughout Romance is the so-called possessive dative. This is a benefactive use expressing the person affected by the event; should things pertaining to that person also figure in the event (body parts, intellectual faculties, items of clothing, etc.), they are automatically attributed to that person and there is no need to specify the possessor. Thus in (71), dative *Caesari* expresses primarily the person to whom the action of throwing themselves on the ground is addressed, and that person is secondarily interpreted as possessor of the feet; likewise in Romance (72):

(71)   Lat. *sese* […] Caesari *ad pedes proiecerunt* (Caes.)
       'They threw themselves at Caesar's feet'

(72)   a. Sp. Le *duele la cabeza* a Mafalda
          'Mafalda's head aches'
       b. It. *Piero ha accarezzato la guancia* a Noriko
          'Piero stroked Noriko's cheek'
       c. OIt. *gittatelevi a' piedi umilemente* (Dante, *Rime*)
          'Throw yourself humbly at her feet'

The predicative complement, referring to the subject (73) or the direct
object (74) remains fundamentally a non-prepositional complement in
Romance, as in Latin:

(73)   a. Lat. *T. Albucius* […] perfectus Epicureus *evaserat* (Cic.)
          'T. Albucius had become the perfect epicurean'
       b. It. *Ne uscì* vincitore
          'He emerged the victor'
       c. Ro. *S-a întors* bolnavă *şi plângând la părinţii săi*
          'She returned sick and weeping to her parents'

(74)   a. Lat. *malitiam* sapientiam *iudicant* (Cic.)
          'They think that cunning is wisdom'
       b. Fr. *On le croyait* malade
          'One believed him (to be) ill'
       c. BrPt. *Todos acharam esse livro* uma droga
          'Everyone found this book dead boring'

All Romance languages also developed predicative complements introduced by a preposition (75) or by 'like', etc. (76), dependent on the
individual verb:

(75)   a. Ro. *L-a declarat* de vinovat
          'He declared him guilty'
       b. It. *Passa* per un gran fannullone
          'He passes for a complete idler'
       c. Cat. *L'han tractat* d'impostor
          'They treated him as an impostor'

(76)   a. Ro. *Şi alesese* drept profesor *pe verişorul ei* (Alecsandri)
          'And she'd chosen her cousin as teacher'
       b. It. *L'hanno scelto* come rappresentante del condominio
          'They chose him as condominium representative'
       c. Cat. *Tothom té en Malats* com un excel·lent pianista
          'Everyone regards Malats as an excellent pianist'

In Latin, expression of the subject in finite sentences was marked by the person/number ending of the verb, making specification of pronominal subject unnecessary. However, not only could *stressed* subject pronouns be used for textual reasons but even unstressed pronouns could appear, without any particular reason. Some medieval, and modern, languages (Portuguese, Spanish, Catalan, some Occitan varieties, central and southern Italian varieties, Romanian) retain this system in which the pronominal subject is not normally expressed. In the Middle Ages, French, Provençal, NItalian dialects and Florentine presented a system in which, simplifying somewhat, main clauses continue Latin usage, while subordinates have obligatory subject pronouns (Vanelli *et al.* 1985):

(77) a. OPrv. *E si acorda Ø, en son fol cor, qu'el fezes semblan qu'el s'entendes en autra dona* (*Vidas*)
          'And he decided, in his foolish heart, to feign courting another lady'
      b. OFlo. *ben ti dico Ø che* io *li mangiai io: ché* io *sono di tanto tempo, ch'*io *non debbo ormai dir bugia* (*Novellino*)
          'I tell you I did eat them; I'm old enough not to have to tell lies any more'

These varieties develop subject clitic pronouns in the late Middle Ages and, later, agreement particles (see above, and Vanelli 1987; Poletto 1993). A similar phenomenon is happening today in spoken Brazilian Portuguese (Roberts and Kato 1993; Kato and Negrão 2000).

Subject pronouns in old French and other varieties could be stressed and unstressed (modern clitics descend from the unstressed variants). The unstressed forms had a different position within sentence structure (Vance 1997: ch. 3–4): in postverbal position they immediately followed the verb and preceded the negative adverb *pas* (78a), while normal nominal subjects and stressed pronouns followed *pas* (78b); in subordinate clauses they immediately followed the complementizer, preceding certain temporal adverbs (79a), while nominal subjects and stressed pronouns followed these adverbs (79b):

(78) a. OFr. *Ja n'es tu pas filz de putain* (*Le Roman de Thèbes*)
          'You are certainly not the son of a whore'
      b. *Ne het* pas Deus *les humes* (Guernes de Pont-Sainte-Maxence, *La Vie de saint Thomas Becket*)
          'God does not hate men'

(79) a. OFr. qu'il onques *eüst veü* (*Le Roman de Tristan en prose*)
          'that he had ever seen'

b. *dont* onques chevaliers *n'avoit gueres veu a celui tens* (*La Queste del Saint Graal*)
'[the great secrets] of which a knight had hardly ever seen anything at that time'

These distributional properties are the same as for the weak use of pronouns in Latin: in verb-initial main clauses (the root of Romance word order – see below) they immediately followed the verb; in subordinates they immediately followed the complementizer. Old French unstressed subject pronoun forms can therefore be seen as directly continuing the weak use of pronouns in Latin.

3.4.2   Passive, impersonal, unaccusatives

The so-called Latin passive form entered into three basic types of construction:

(i)   the passive construction, involving demotion of the lexical ('deep') subject of the verb and promotion to subject of direct object (the lexical subject could be unexpressed or appear as a complement);

(ii) the impersonal construction, involving only demotion of the lexical subject (which could appear as a complement (80b)) and therefore normally operated with intransitive verbs; lacking a syntactic subject, the unexpressed lexical subject received a generic or indefinite interpretation:

> (80)   a. Lat. ITUR (passive) 'One goes' cf. Ø (SBJ) it (active)
> 'he goes'
> b. *cum* a Cotta (complement) [...] resisteretur (passive) (Caes.)
> 'since there was resistance from Cotta' (cf. *cum* Cotta (SBJ) resisteret (active) 'Since Cotta resisted')

(iii) the unaccusative construction (traditionally called 'middle'): the passive form represented the intransitive variant of a transitive verb, where the lexical direct object was promoted to subject (81a); this subject was typically non-agent; there was also a group of so-called 'deponent' verbs which had only a passive form and which were, by and large, semantically akin to the intransitive variants of the other verbs in this group (81b):

> (81)   a. Lat. X_S Y_{DO} MOUET (active) 'X moves Y' / Y_S MOUETUR (passive) 'Y moves'
> b. IRASCOR 'get angry', OBLIUISCOR 'forget', etc.

The function of the Latin passive is principally performed in Romance by the reflexive (Reichenkron 1933; Michaelis 1998; Selig 1998; Cennamo 1999). The link lies in unaccusative constructions and especially in cases where the event could be conceived either as an action or as a process or state: SANO ME 'I heal myself' is initially an action in which the subject heals itself, while SANOR 'I heal, I'm healed' is the process undergone by someone being healed through external intervention (physician or medicines – passive construction) or by spontaneous development (unaccusative). The latter interpretation is very close, however, to that of the reflexive: the cause of the healing, which cannot be objectively identified, is identified with the patient subject itself. Thus the reflexive construction beside the original action meaning also gets the process or state meaning corresponding to the passive form:

	'I heal myself'	
	'I'm in the process of healing'	
SANOR		SANO ME
	'I get healed'	

The reflexive construction in fact becomes the marker of the non-agentive interpretation and its use is extended to verbs which in Classical Latin had non-agentive meaning, but active form: *vadent se* (*Itinerarium Egeriae*), for classical UADENT, IBUNT 'they'll go'. But the substitution is not systematic, and in Romance, as in Latin, unaccusatives do not necessarily have a distinct form from corresponding transitives (cf. Lat. UERTO [transitive/intransitive] 'turn/turn round' (beside UERTOR 'turn round'), and Fr. *tourner* [transitive/intransitive]).

In the third person, the ambiguity between reflexive proper and unaccusative affects even the passive interpretation of the passive form, so that *sanat se* 'he heals (himself)' also assumes the interpretation 'he gets healed' (an external cause is attributed to the healing); this extension probably occurred first with non-human subjects (as the earliest attested examples show), which would explain why this usage did not extend to the first and second persons:

| | 'he heals himself' | |
| SANATUR | 'he's in the process of healing'

'he gets healed' | SANAT SE |

Once it has assumed passive meaning, the reflexive extends with its new meaning to intransitive verbs as well, yielding an impersonal interpretation.

The new uses of the reflexive, corresponding to the uses of the Latin passive, are well attested in early Romance (82–84); only the impersonal interpretation is somewhat later (85) (Salvi 2008):

Unaccusative

(82) a. ORo. *Şi* deschiseră-se *ochii amândurora* (*Palia de la Orăştie*)
          'And the eyes of both opened'
      b. OIt. … si raunaro *i demonî di ninferno* (Bono Giamboni, *Libro de' Vizî e delle Virtudi*)
          'the demons of hell gathered'
      c. OFr. *Por coi li rois ne* se levoit […]? (Chrestien de Troyes (?), *Guillaume d'Angleterre*)
          'Why was the king not getting up?'
      d. OPt. *adormeceu, / e* espertou-s' (Fernan Garcia Esgaravunha)
          'he fell asleep and woke up'

Passive

(83) a. ORo. său început *această carte a* se tipâri … (Coresi, *Evanghelia cu învăţătură*)
          'this book began to be printed', lit. 'to print itself'
      b. OIt. *i regni non* si tengono *per parole* (*Novellino*)
          'kingdoms are not held by words'
      c. OFr. *toutes les choses* […] se *peuvent* faire *de l'un l'autre* (Mahieu le Vilain, *Les Metheores d'Aristote*)
          'all things […] may be made one from the other'
      d. OPt. *esto* se *poderia bem* fazer (Fernão Lopes, *Crónica de D. João I*)
          'this could well be done'

Passive with agent complement

(84) a. OIt. *Lo vostro presio fino / in gio'* si rinovelli / da grandi e da zitelli (Guido Cavalcanti)
'May your fine valour be joyfully celebrated by young and old'

   b. OFr. par lui se desconfirent *la gent le roi Artu* (*La Mort le Roi Artu*)
'thanks to him the people of King Arthur were defeated'

   c. OPt. *a quall numqua* se quebrantasse por nem hum (*Portugaliae Monumenta Historica*)
'which should never be broken by anybody'

Impersonal

(85) a. OIt. *Per me* si va *ne la città dolente* (Dante, *Commedia*)
'Through me the way is to the city dolent'

   b. OFr. *Or* se cante (*Aucassin et Nicolette*)
'Here one sings'

   c. Pt. *é fraqueza* desistir-se *da cousa começada* (Camões)
'It is weakness to desist from an enterprise begun'

Romance still preserves some periphrastic Latin passive forms, comprising past participle and the auxiliary SUM. In Latin these expressed perfectum tenses, e.g., SANATUS SUM 'I have been healed (PASS) / I am healed (unaccusative).' The periphrasis is preserved primarily with unaccusative verbs (Tuttle 1986b), which in old Romance formed analytic tenses with auxiliary 'be': while *infectum* forms like LAUOR 'I wash [myself]' are replaced by reflexives (LAUO ME), the perfect forms are initially continued unchanged and LAUATUS SUM functions as the analytic counterpart of *lavo me* (but without the aoristic meaning of the Latin form, which in Romance is always expressed by the simple perfect). This state of affairs is attested in old Romance (86) (Ageno 1964: ch. 4) and survives in some modern varieties (87a), even if in most languages the use of the reflexive has been generalized throughout the paradigm (87b) (see also Cennamo 1999):

(86) a. OIt. *che·lli* erano rubellate [rubellarsi] (*Cronica fiorentina*)
'who had rebelled against him'

   b. OFr. *quant vers lui* fu tornez [se torner] (*La chevalerie Vivien*)
'when he turned towards him'

   c. OPt. *A alma non* era partida *ainda do corpo* [partir-se] (*Diálogos de São Gregório*)
'the soul had not yet departed the body'

(87) a. Brione sopra Minusio (Canton Ticino) a ˈsoŋ diseˈdaːt
'I've woken up'

   b. It. *Questa mattina* mi sono svegliato *presto*
'This morning I awoke early'

The same type of analytic form appears with those unaccusatives which have not become reflexives: MORIOR (passive) 'I die' becomes active in the infectum tenses (MORIO), but the Latin (passive) periphrasis survives in the perfectum MORTUUS SUM (88), and this type spreads to unaccusatives which in Latin had active forms (89):

(88) a. OIt. *la destriera* era morta (*Novellino*)
          'the mare had died'
      b. OPt. *O meu filho* he morto (*Diálogos de São Gregório*)
          'My son has died'

(89) OFr. *Cuntre Franceis li* sui venut *aidier* (*Chanson de Roland*)
      'I came to help him against the French'

Not all modern varieties keep the perfect periphrasis with SUM: Spanish, Portuguese, Catalan (except most Balearic varieties) and some SItalian dialects have generalized 'have' to all verbs. Romanian only has 'have' in the analytic perfect indicative, while *a fi* 'be' is used elsewhere, a usage sometimes attributed to Slav influence.

The absence of the reflexive in analytic forms with the participle extends, at least in old Italian and old French, to non-finite forms in general (Ageno 1964: ch. 4):

(90) a. OIt. *che io non possa* smarrire [smarrirsi] (Iacopone da Todi, *Laudi*)
          'that I may not lose myself'
      b. OFr. *Il ne pooit* lever [se lever] (*Aiol*)
          'He couldn't get up'

(91) a. OIt. *ed aiutan l'arsura* vergognando [vergognarsi] (Dante, *Commedia*)
          'and add unto their burning by their shame'
      b. OFr. *.iiii. leiues en vet la mer* covrant [se covrir] (*La chevalerie Vivien*)
          'the sea is covered with it for four leagues'

This phenomenon has been attributed to the fact that in Latin some non-finite moods lacked a passive and in these cases unaccusative verbs had to resort to the active form. This voice neutralization then supposedly spread to all non-finite forms and survived even after the passive was replaced by reflexives. Nowadays, this phenomenon has only isolated continuants, such as the Italian causative, e.g., It. *Lo faremo* pentire *di quel che ha detto* [for reflexive *pentirsi*] 'We'll make him repent for what he said.'

The Latin periphrastic passive construction also survives in the passive itself, although things are rather more complicated in this case. In Latin, the periphrasis expressed anteriority with respect to the reference point marked by the auxiliary: LAUDATUS SUM meant 'I have been praised' or 'I was praised', LAUDATUS ERAM 'I had been praised', etc. Past participle and 'be' also expressed state in resultative verbs: DOMUS CLAUSA EST 'the house is closed' (state), beside 'it has been closed' (past passive): obviously, the two expressions may be equivalent: if a house *is closed*, it must *have been closed*.

Since in the stative interpretation there were no limits on the tenses in which the copula could occur, there could also be tenses of the perfectum, indicating anteriority (not required by the passive periphrasis, where the auxiliary indicated the reference time for anteriority and anteriority was a property of the periphrasis as a whole), e.g., *arma quae* fixa *in parietibus fuerant, ea sunt humi inventa* (Cic.) 'the weapons which had been fixed on the walls, were found on the ground'. Given the equivalence of reference in the case of resultative verbs, here *fixa fuerant* could be replaced with *fixa erant*: for the discovery of the weapons on the ground follows the period in which they were attached to the walls (*fixa fuerant*), but it also follows the point at which they were fixed there (*fixa erant*). Given this equivalence, perfectum tenses begin to be used as alternative auxiliaries to infectum tenses in the passive construction expressing anteriority, e.g., *picturae* [...] *inclusae sunt in ligneis formis et in comitium* [...] *fuerunt adlatae* (Vit.) 'pictures [...] were placed in wooden frames and were taken to the assembly'.

Note that in the case of perfectum tenses the time reference of the auxiliary corresponds to that of the periphrasis, which is not true of the *infectum* forms. This correspondence between tense of the periphrasis and tense of the auxiliary is probably the basis of the Romance extension whereby analytic forms with an infectum auxiliary begin to refer to deictic tenses: LAUDATUS SUM is interpreted as a present, LAUDATUS ERAM as a past (imperfect), etc.: late Lat. *tantus mugitus et rugitus totius populi est cum fletu, ut forsitan porro ad civitatem gemitus populi omnis auditus sit* (*Itinerarium Egeriae*) 'so great are the bellows and yells of all the people, accompanied by wailing, that the groans of all the people are heard perhaps as far as the city'. Thus, when the synthetic forms of the Latin passive disappear, Romance already has a substitute to hand (92):

(92) a. OIt. *domanda che lli* sia perdonato (Brunetto Latini, *Rettorica*)
        lit. 'he asks that it should be forgiven to him'
      b. OFr. *j'ai a non Berte, si* soit *m'ame* assolue (Adenet le Roi, *Berte aus grans piés*)
        'my name is Bertha, may my soul be saved'
      c. OPt. *A alma* he atormentada *daquel fogo en que jaz e de que* he retheuda (*Diálogos de São Gregório*)

'The soul is tormented by the fire in which it lies and by which it is trapped'

However, in earliest Romance these forms maintained the ambiguity they had had in late Latin, so that (OIt.) *sono lodato* still had both the innovative meaning 'I'm praised' and the older 'I've been praised' (93):

(93) a. OIt. *Questi, dopo molto trattamento ch'era* fatto *di fare pace* [...], *celatamente n'andò in Francia* (*Cronica fiorentina*)
'He, after much negotiation which had been made to make peace, secretly went off to France'

b. OFr. *a l'endemain vint la novele laienz que li set frere* estoient ocis (*La Queste del Saint Graal*)
'on the morrow news came that the seven brothers had been killed'

These forms were subsequently joined by those based on the new perfective periphrases which replaced the old forms of the perfectum: It. *sono stato lodato, era stato lodato*, etc. In the earliest phase of Florentine these innovative forms are in a distinct minority beside the inherited forms, but eventually establish themselves as the sole forms for expression of anteriority.

The old Romance languages also present the impersonal variant of the passive construction, albeit to a rather limited extent: OIt. *fue consilglato per certi huomini ch'a llui* fosse dato *d'uno bastone* (*Cronica fiorentina*) lit.: 'it was suggested by certain persons that it should be given to him with a stick', i.e., '... that he should be beaten with a stick'.

Note that the survival of the passive construction with 'be' + participle seems to have been favoured by Latin–Romance diglossia; in Romanian, where such diglossia was absent, the normal form for expression of the passive was originally the reflexive, while the construction with *a fi* 'be' is a later development probably modelled on other Romance languages.

3.4.3   Indefinite subject

In verbs of saying, Latin could express a generic subject not only with the impersonal construction, but also by using the third person plural: DICUNT, NARRANT 'they say', etc. This possibility has been retained and extended in Romance (except French and Raeto-Romance) which can use third person plural to express a generic subject (*people*) and an indefinite subject (*someone*), generally with action verbs, e.g., It. Dicono (generic) *che* hanno ammazzato (indeterminate) *compare Turiddu* 'They say they have killed *compare* Turiddu' [i.e., 'Turiddu has been killed (by someone)']. In many

Romance languages, in verbs of communication the third person singular is also used for generic subject, e.g., Pt. Diz *que há na nossa gente [...] uns senhores...* (Garrett) 'It is said [lit. 'says'] that there are among our people some gentlemen ...' This was possible also in Latin INQUIT, late Latin DICIT.

3.4.4 Negation

Latin had two sentential negators: NE, used with volitive subjunctive and imperative, and NON, used elsewhere; it also had the phrasal negator HAUD (plus many negative conjunctions and adverbs). Of these, only NON survives in Romance, taking over the functions of the extinct forms. Syntactically, NON could occur immediately before the verb (94a) or be focused in sentence-initial position (94b):

(94) a. Lat. *Haec tibi antea* non *rescripsi, non quo...* (Cic.)
     'If I did not send you this reply before, it is not that [...]'
  b. non*ne hic homo modo me pugnis contudit?* (Pl.)
     'didn't this man beat me up with his fists only just now?'

In Romance, these two positions are neutralized because, in the formation of Romance sentence structure, the verb is moved to sentence-initial position, immediately after the focalized element. Consequently, negation, whether focalized or not, must always be immediately preverbal. A trace of the distinction between the two uses of negation is perhaps discernible in the fact that negation in old Romance shows two kinds of behaviour in sentence structure. It may behave as an element of the preverbal clitic cluster and therefore does not count as an independent position from a syntactic point of view: see (95), where negation is preceded by a thematic element, and (96), where it is preceded by a focalized element in first position; on the other hand, if there is no other preverbal element, negation counts as the first element of the sentential core, causing by itself proclitic position of the clitics (due to the Tobler–Mussafia Law, see below) (97):

(95) a. OIt. *'l fallo* non *vuol più che pentimento* (Rinuccino, *Rime*)
     'error requires no more than repentance'
  b. OFr. *tu* n'*iés mes hom* (*Chanson de Roland*)
     'thou art not my vassal'

(96) a. OIt. *già mai* non *averaggio 'n altra 'ntenza* (Rinuccino, *Rime*)
     'I shall never love another'
  b. OFr. *Niule cose* non *la pouret omque pleier* (*Eulalie*)
     'Nothing could ever sway her'
  c. OSp. *nada* non *perdera* (*Cantar de Mio Cid*)
     'he'll lose nothing'

(97) a. OIt. Non *si conviene estimare di che etade l'uomo sia* (*Fiori e Vita di Filosafi*)
'It is wrong to judge people by their age'
b. OFr. no *s defended* (*Passion de Clermont-Ferrand*)
'he did not defend himself'
c. OSp. non *se puede fartar del* (*Cantar de Mio Cid*)
'he cannot get tired of him'

The usage exemplified in (95)–(96) appears to continue Latin preverbal negation, where the negator was not an independent word but an accessory of the verb, and therefore did not occupy an independent position; the usage exemplified in (97) could continue that of the negator as an independent (and therefore focalizable) element: in this respect it could occupy in (97) the first position in the sentential core, the preserve of thematic or focalized elements, thereby allowing clitics in preverbal position and preventing that position from being occupied by other constituents; thus, for example, the subject appears in postverbal position in (98):

(98) a. OIt. Non *si turba il savio di perdere figliuoli o amici* (*Fiori e Vita di Filosafi*)
'The wise man is not troubled by the loss of children or friends'
b. OFr. *Toz i fu ars,* ne *l'i pot on aidier* (*Le Couronnement de Louis*)
'Everything was burned there, and one could not help him'

In any case, throughout early Romance, phrasal negation is represented by a preverbal particle from Latin NON. This picture was to change (Vai 1996), some languages (French, Occitan, some NItalian and Raeto-Romance dialects) introducing a postverbal adverb as an obligatory part of negation (Fr. *il ne vient* pas), and some of these varieties later eliminating the preverbal particle (spoken Fr. *il vient* pas). Other varieties (e.g., Brazilian Portuguese) repeat negation at the end of the sentence, sometimes suppressing the preverbal particle (BrPt. *(num) vi ele* não 'I didn't see him').

3.4.5   Subject–Predicate agreement

As with the NP, agreement between subject and predicate is inherited by all Romance languages. We saw above the case of agreement with the verb, but this also holds for nominal predicates referring to the subject (99a) and the direct object (99b):

(99) a. It. Le ragazze (FPL) *parevano* stanche (FPL)
'The girls seemed tired'
b. Li (MPL) *ritenevamo* belli (MPL)
'We considered them beautiful'

But in modern French predicates tend not to agree, e.g., Elle (F) *est devenu fou* (unmarked) 'She went mad' (Guiraud 1965:36).

3.4.6   Questions and answers

Latin formed *wh*-questions by moving the constituent subject to interrogation to the beginning of the sentential core. Throughout Romance this remained the model for this type of question (100):

(100) a. Ro. Pe care vecine *le-ai văzut?*
       'Which neighbours did you see?'
   b. Fr. À qui *as-tu donné ta serviette?*
       'Who did you give your briefcase to?'
   c. Sp. ¿Para qué *necesitas el dinero?*
       'Why (lit. 'for what') do you need the money?'

In some modern varieties (spoken French, some NItalian dialects, Brazilian Portuguese) the *wh*-phrases may remain in the position they normally occupy in declarative sentences (BrPt. *A senhora veio fazer* o que *aqui?* 'What have you come to do here?'; see Rossi 1993; Munaro 1999).

In yes/no-questions Latin had two strategies: normal verb-final declarative sentence structure (101), or movement of the verb to sentence-initial position (102); in both cases it usually also employed interrogative particles (see (101b) and (102)):

(101) a. Lat. *Tuae fidei credo?* (Pl.)
       'Can I trust you?'
   b. an *patris auxilium sperem?* (Cat.)
       'Can I hope for my father's help?'

(102) a. Lat. Estne *haec patera qua donatu's illi?* (Pl.)
       'Is this or is this not the bowl that was given you there?'
   b. Aspexitne *matrem exanimem Nero?* (Tac.)
       'Did Nero look at his dead mother?'

In old Romance languages, whose innovative word order is based on the Latin order with fronting of the verb, if no constituent is focalized, yes/no-questions are formed with the verb in initial position – a direct continuation of the construction in (102). Since the finite verb ends up before the subject, this is traditionally described as an inversion: Subject–Verb > Verb–Subject (103):

(103) a. OIt. Vuo' (V) tu (S) *diventar nostro fedele* [...]? (Bono Giamboni, *Libro de' Vizî e delle Virtù*)
       'Do you want to become one of our followers [...]?'

b. OFr. Sont (V) vostre panel (S) *aborré?* (Chrestien de Troyes, *Yvain*)
'Are the cushions of your saddle well padded?'

c. OPt. Diremos (V) nós (S) *ora, padre, que* […]? (*Diálogos de São Gregório*)
'Shall we now say, father, that […]?'

With the establishment of a more rigid SV… word order, Romance generally abandons this type of yes/no-question, which remains only in Raeto-Romance, in some Ladin varieties and, optionally in certain interrogatives, in Portuguese (104) (for Portuguese, see Âmbar 1988: ch.4); interrogative inversion also remains in part in varieties which have developed subject clitic pronouns, but only with these pronouns (105):

(104) a. Surmiran Vessan (V) igls paslers (S) *forsa svido el?*
'Have the sparrows perhaps emptied it?'

b. Pt. Terá (V) a Joana (S) *encontrado os óculos da mãe? / A Joana terá encontrado os óculos da mãe?*
'[I wonder if] Joana has found her mother's glasses?'

(105) Fr. As (V)-tu (clitic S) *vu Marie? /* **A (V) Pierre (S) *vu Marie?*
'Have you seen Marie?'

In answers to yes/no-questions, for affirmative replies Latin normally repeated the term which was the focus of the question (so that in questions without focalized elements it repeated the verb, which expressed the asseverative value of the utterance), and in the case of a negative reply it placed a negator before the focalized element or the verb; affirmative (ITA, SIC, CERTE, etc.) or negative adverbs (NON) could also be used as a reply. Early Romance languages keep repetition of the verb as their main means of answering a question (106). In some languages, such as French and Italian, the verb had to be accompanied by *sì/si* (< SIC) in affirmative replies (106a,b); and in Italian verbs other than *essere* and *avere* could be replaced by the pro-verb *fare* (107a), while in French such substitution was obligatory (107b):

(106) a. OIt. *darebbel·m'egli?* – Sì darebbe (*Novellino*)
'would he give it to me? – Yes'

b. *Ond'io non ne credo avere peccato* […] – *Certo* sì ài (*Novellino*)
'Hence I believe I have no sin in this. – Oh yes you do'

c. OSp. *Quiéreslo saber?* – Quiero (Fernando de Rojas, *La Celestina*)
'Do you want to know? – Yes'

d. OIt. *darebbel·m'egli?* […] – Non darebbe (*Novellino*)
'would he give it to me? – No'

(107) a. OIt. *Udistù mai di quel Guido novella?* – Sì feci (Bernardo da Bologna)
'Did you ever hear news of that fellow Guido? – Yes I did'

b. OFr. *Nel sai?* Si faz (Chrestien de Troyes, *Cligès*)
   'Do I not know it? Yes I do'

This construction survives today only in Galician-Portuguese (Sten 1936; Spitzer 1937): Pt. *Deste-lhe o livro?* – (Sim,) dei / Não dei 'Did you give him the book? (Yes) I did / No I didn't.' The other languages have generalized *non* for the negative reply, and various kinds of pro-form for a positive reply (Sp., Cat., It. *sí/si/sì*, Fr. *oui* (< HOC ILLE), Occ. *ò/òc* (< HOC), Ro. *da* (< Slav da), Srd. *e(m)mo*). These forms of response were already widespread in early Romance, e.g., OFr. *irai je donc toz sols?* – Oïl, *bels frere* (*Le Couronnement de Louis*) 'so must I go all on my own? – Yes, dear brother.' The Romanian phenomenon whereby the answer may repeat an element of the question (108a), and therefore the verb (108b), is separate; in Romanian, with analytic forms, one repeats both the auxiliary and the participle (108c) or just the participle (108d), unlike other (early) Romance languages and modern Portuguese, where only the auxiliary is repeated:

(108) a. Ro. *Tu ești?* – Eu (Sadoveanu)
         'Is it you? – Yes (lit. 'I')'
      b. *Cutezi să mă înfrunți?* – Cutez (Stancu)
         'Dare you defy me? – I do'
      c. *Am făcut bine?* – Ai făcut bine (Sadoveanu)
         'Did I do well? – You did'
      d. *Ați adus ceva coniac?* – Adus (Sadoveanu)
         'Have you brought any cognac? – I/We have'

3.4.7   Word order

In the transition from Latin to early Romance, word order (and the sentence structure on which this order is based) was radically transformed: while Latin was verb-final, medieval Romance is (almost) verb-initial, or more exactly it has an order with the verb in second position (V2 – although not uniformly so in the attested languages; see also Ledgeway, this volume, chapter 8: §§3.2.1–2). But there is also continuity with Latin, and traces of the old word order survive into earliest Romance (see Salvi 2000; 2004). The Latin sentence had the following syntactic positions:

Left periphery | (Focus) / (V) [SOXV] | Right periphery

The left periphery hosts any number of constituents with theme or frame functions, and the right periphery various types of heavy constituents and 'afterthought' elements. The central part of the sentence (sentential core) contains a verb-final nucleus and two positions, the first of which hosts focalized constituents, and the second the verb, which may be preposed in certain constructions. In Classical Latin, focalized constituent and preposed verb are in complementary distribution, yet we can assume them to occupy different syntactic positions because they belong to different categories: focalized constituents are phrases, while the verb is a syntactic head.

In the passage to Romance, there is further extension in the semantic range of the preposed verb, and verb-initial order becomes unmarked; even structures with focalization of a constituent conform to this general pattern (as noted, at first they lacked pre-position of the verb, because focalization of a constituent and pre-position of the verb were in complementary distribution): once pre-position of the verb is general, it automatically applies even where Focus position is occupied; thus (Phase 1):

Left periphery | (Focus) V [SOX] | Right periphery

In this first phase, the existence of a peripheral portion with frame and theme function guarantees that verb-initial sentences may be preceded by a theme; the consistent theme–predicate relationship subsequently leads to syntactic reanalysis: an element in the preliminary part is reanalysed as a (thematic) constituent of the sentential core, alternating with a focalized element; thus the following early Romance sentence structure (Phase 2) (Benincà 1994):

Left periphery | (Theme/Focus) V [SOX] | Right periphery

What of unstressed words? Latin weak forms appeared after the first phonetically realized position of the sentential core, thus after any focalized costituent or preposed verb; otherwise after the first constituent of the nucleus of the sentence:

Focus *pro* [SOXV] / V *pro* [SOX] / [X *pro* XV]

In early Romance the rule is unchanged, but it applies to a partly different word order: clitics are placed after the first realized constituent of the sentential core, thus after any thematic/focalized element, or after the verb:

Theme / Focus *cl* V [SOX] / V *cl* [SOX]

So early Romance did preserve many aspects of Latin word order, and I now review some major areas of conservation.

In Latin the left periphery hosted pragmatic theme/frame constituents. Often subordinate clauses were involved (109a), but also phrases marked with DE 'as for' (109b), or marked for the function that they perform within the sentential core (109c); the thematic element could also appear in the nominative (so-called *nominativus pendens* – (109d)). In the following examples we use weak pronoun position as a diagnostic of the boundary between peripheral and core parts of the sentence:

> (109) a. Lat. *si proficiscerer ad bellum, / periculum* te *meum commovebat* (Cic.)
> 'if I set out for the scene of war, you were appalled at the thought of my danger'
>
> b. *De Aufidiano nomine / nihil* te *hortor* (Cic.)
> 'In the matter of Aufidius' debt, I put no pressure upon you'
>
> c. *(cum) consili tui bene fortiterque suscepti / eum* tibi *finem statueris quem...* (Cic.)
> 'seeing that you have resolved that the policy you so honourably and gallantly adopted should cease from the very moment when ...'
>
> d. *familia vero* [...] / *non* mehercules *puto decumam partem esse quae dominum suum noverit* (Petr.)
> 'as for slaves [...], I don't believe, by Hercules, there's a tenth of them who know their own master'

The peripheral element was not normally repeated by an anaphoric pronoun within the sentential core, because Latin preferred zero anaphora for easily recoverable antecedents; but it could sometimes be picked up by a weak pronoun or by a stressed pronoun in cases of focalization or contrast.

Early Romance languages, too, make extensive use of the left periphery, which may be occupied by a subordinate sentence (110a), by a dislocated phrase introduced by a specialized preposition (110b), or marked by its function within the sentential core (110c). But marking is not necessary, and the peripheral element may be unmarked, especially for the indirect object (110d):

> (110) a. OFr. *quant li reis out enquis des nuveles de Uríe, / cumandad* lui *qu'...* (*Li Quatre Livre des Reis*)
> 'when the king had asked for news of Uriah, he ordered him to ...'
>
> b. *de mon cuer / comme est iriez!* (*Piramus et Tisbé*)
> 'my heart, how it is afflicted!'
>
> c. OPt. *a Santa Maria / mercee* lle *foi pedir* (Afonso X o Sabio, *Cantigas de Santa Maria*)
> 'of Saint Mary, he went and asked grace of her'
>
> d. *o padre, que o mal fezera per sa folia, / deron*-ll' *enton morte* (Afonso X o Sabio, *Cantigas de Santa Maria*)
> 'as for the father, who had done evil through his folly, they then killed him'

If the function expressed permits, the peripheral element is generally repeated by a clitic within the sentential core (110c,d), (111a); in focalization a stressed element may appear (111b):

(111) a. OFr. *Ceste bataille, / veirement* la *ferum* (*Chanson de Roland*)
'This battle, we really shall do it'
  b. *En un val grant et lé, dejoste un desrubant, /* illuec *vaurent torner li cuvert mescreant* (*La Chanson d'Antioche*)
'In a great wide valley, by a cliff, that is where the impious infidels wished to return'

These constructions continue in modern Romance (except Raeto-Romance and Ladin varieties where the medieval Verb-Second order has become more rigid); indeed use of the left periphery has spread widely even in languages which originally made only moderate use of it: the construction with theme preposed to the verb (131) is lost in most modern varieties and the periphery has assumed many of its functions (Vanelli 1986). In (112), clitic repetition is not always obligatory:

(112) a. Pt. *A raposa, o corvo viu(-a)*
'The fox, the crow saw (him)'
  b. Fr. *Pierre, je l'ai vu hier*
'Pierre, I saw him yesterday'
  c. It. *I giornali, non li ho comprati*
'The papers, I didn't buy them'

As for the dislocated element, in modern Romance, languages with some freedom of word order, such as European Portuguese, Spanish and Italian, prefer the prepositional variant (113a,b), while those with rigid Subject–Verb–Object order, such as French and Brazilian Portuguese, prefer the prepositionless variant (113c, d):

(113) a. Pt. *À raposa, o corvo roubou(-lhe) um queijo*
'From the fox, the crow stole a cheese from him'
  b. It. *A Maria, non (le) hanno detto niente*
'To Maria, they didn't tell (her) anything'
  c. Fr. *Cette affaire, on n'y pense plus*
'This business, we no longer think about it'
  d. BrPt. *Essa moça, eu (lhe) falei ontem*
'This girl, I spoke (to her) yesterday'

The explanation may be that structures like those in (113c,d) are interpreted as SUBJECT–PREDICATE, as happens with NP SUBJECT + VP

PREDICATE: in these languages the order Subject–(PREDICATE Verb–Object) may be so well established that even in sentences with dislocated elements, a SUBJECT–PREDICATE structure has to be superimposed in order for them to be acceptable (Galves 1993); and for this to happen, the dislocated element has to be an NP. The semantic structure of (113d) must be:

[SUBJECT*Essa moça*] [PREDICATE [SUBJECT*eu*] [PREDICATE*lhe falei ontem*]]

In languages with freer word order, dislocated elements, since they do not have to functions as SUBJECT, may appear with a preposition indicating their grammatical function.

As for the right periphery, it was reserved in Latin for heavy constituents (subordinate clauses, phrases containing relative clause, lists, etc.) and 'afterthought' constituents. This situation persists in Romance (114)–(115). With the change in the system of pronominal reference in Romance, peripheral phrases are normally represented, in the core sentence, by clitic pronouns (115) (see Riiho 1988):

(114) OPt. *Desto sentem o contrairo / os que continuadamente tragen ante os olhos da sua memoria como som boos em virtudes* (Dom Duarte, *Leal Conselheiro*)
Lit. 'On this take a contrary view those who continually evoke before the eyes of their memory how good they are with regard to virtues'

(115) a. OFr. *Pur quei l'avez ocis, / Cel saintisme arceveske?* (Guernes de Pont-Saint-Maxence, *La vie de Saint Thomas Becket*)
'Why have you killed him, that most holy archbishop?'
b. OSp. *Mostraron ge*la luego / *la fermosa donzella* (*Poema de Fernán González*)
'They showed her to him immediately, the beautiful maiden'

Verb-initial sentences represented in Latin a marked order bearing special meanings, such as jussive, concessive, presentative or representative of an event as a causal or temporal consequence of preceding events (eventive). They also characterized yes/no-questions. In these sentences, the different possible interpretations signalled by movement of the verb to first position were obtained from morphological information (e.g., use of the subjunctive or imperative), from context, and probably also intonation. In some cases the verb movement was optional (e.g., in jussives or questions). In early Romance, verb-initial order becomes unmarked, but without necessarily losing the original interpretations that this order had in Latin, particularly when supported by the accompanying factors listed above. We find jussive (116a,a'), presentative (116b,b'), eventive (116c,c') values (as well as yes/no questions). Verb-initial position was not the only possibility, as we see from the jussive (117a); in presentatives and eventives, the Verb-Second variant was used too, the circumstances of time or place relative to which the new referent is introduced, or of which the event is a consequence, being made explicit (117b, c):

(116) a. OFr. *De vostre fiz* [...] / *prengne vos en pitié!* (*Floovant*)
'Of your son, may pity take you!'
a′. bailliez *le moi* (Beroul, *Le Roman de Tristan*)
'Give it to me'
b. *El fons d'un val desos un olivier* / Sort *i fontainna* (*La Chanson d'Aspremont*)
'At the bottom of a valley, under an olive tree, comes forth a spring'
b′. *Li reis tint sa carue pur sun iur espleiter* / *E* vint *i Carlemaines tut un antif senter* (*Pèlerinage de Charlemagne*)
'The king steered his plough to finish off his day and Charlemagne arrived there along an old path'
c. *N'en ad vertud, trop ad perdut del sanc* [...] Falt *li le coer* (*Chanson de Roland*)
'He has not the strength, he has lost too much blood [...] His heart fails'
c′. *Ensi fu dessiegie Andrenople; et* torna *s'en li marchis arriere al Dimot a tote sa gent* (Villehardouin, *La Conquête de Constantinople*)
'So the siege of Adrianople was lifted and the marquis returned to Demotika with all his men'

(117) a. OFr. *quar t'en* vas *colcer* (*La Vie de saint Alexis*)
'so, go to bed'
b. *Forz Renouart* / *ainz ne* fu *si fort home* (*Aliscans*)
'Apart from Renouart, never was there so brave a man'
c. *cil revient a Sagremor, si li dist ce que sa dame li mande. Et lors se* part *Sagremors de la porte* (*La Mort le roi Artu*)
'he goes back to Sagremor and reports to him what his lady bids. Then Sagremor goes away from the door'

In modern Romance in general, the range of verb-initial sentences has become limited to jussives (118a) and presentatives (118b), but lost in eventives (although Spanish and Portuguese preserve these in some styles – see (119)):

(118) a. It. Da*llo a Maria*
'Give it to Maria'
b. È arrivato *Giovanni* / Ha telefonato *Giovanni*
'Giovanni has arrived / Giovanni has phoned'

(119) Pt. *começaram a cair muitas moedas de ouro*. Ficou *o rapaz admirado* (folk tale)
'many gold coins began to fall. The boy was astonished'

French has further restricted the range of presentatives: these no longer have an initial verb, because of the obligatory use of the expletive subject, already attested in the early language (120); and they are possible only with unaccusative verbs and indefinite subjects (121) (Pollock 1981; Willems 1985):

(120) OFr. Il *i corurent .vii. roi et .xv. duc* (*Le Couronnement de Louis*)
'Seven kings and fifteen dukes ran there'

(121) Fr. *Il est arrivé des filles* / ***Il est arrivé Jean* / ***Il a téléphoné une fille*
'Some girls have arrived / Jean has arrived / A girl has phoned'

In Latin one focalization strategy involved moving the focalized constituent to the beginning of the sentential core (cf. also *wh*-questions above) (122):

(122) a. Lat. nihil *te omnino fefellit* (Cic.)
'nothing whatever escaped your notice'
   b. ita *se cum multis conligavit* (Cic.)
'so inextricably has he tied himself up with his multitude of counsellors'

Often only a part of the constituent was focalized, while the rest remained in its position in the nucleus (123a), or was added as an 'afterthought' in postverbal position (123b):

(123) a. Lat. Magnam *haec res Caesari* difficultatem *ad consilium capiendum adferebat* (Caes.)
'This action of Vercingetorix caused Caesar great difficulty in forming his plan of campaign'
   b. magna *inter eos exsistit* controversia (Caes.)
'and a great dispute arose among them'

In old Romance, too, initial position remains a focalizing position. But the verb now occupies the immediately following position, so that focus immediately precedes the verb (as with *wh*-questions) (124):

(124) a. OPt. da mesa *se levantava, se chegavom a tempo que el comesse* (Fernão Lopes, *Crónica de Dom Pedro*)
'he would get up from the table, if they came while he was eating'
   b. OIt. di grande scienzia *ti tegnio* (*Novellino*)
'I hold that you are endowed with great wisdom'

And, as in Latin, just part of the constituent could be focalized too (cf. 50). But the focalization types available in Latin were more limited than in Romance: in Latin focalization involved quantifiers or was emphatic (underscoring, for example, scalar elements like the adjective *magnus* in (123)); in early Romance these values remain (quantificational focus in (50) and *wh*-questions, emphatic focus in (124) – in (124a) the scalar element is implicit), but the preverbal element could simply be a rhematic constituent (125) (informational focus; see Vanelli 1999):

(125) a. OFr. Messe e matines *ad li reis escultét* (*Chanson de Roland*)
'The king has heard mass and matins'
b. OIt. in concordia *fu con tutti li signori* (*Novellino*)
'he was in concord with all the lords'

Only to a limited extent does modern Romance generally preserve this array of focalizations in immediate preverbal position: in *wh*-questions, and (except French) in constructions with contrastive focalization (a type of quantificational focalization by which, for a predicate, one value is selected to the exclusion of all others), e.g., Italian A MARIA *ha dato il libro Piero* 'Piero gave the book to *Maria* (and to nobody else).' Sardinian and some SItalian dialects (notably Sicilian; see Cruschina 2006) are exceptions, and focalization conditions remain similar to the medieval ones (126):

(126) a. Srd. su duttore *appo vistu*
'I've seen the doctor' (as a response to 'Whom did you see?')
b. troppu grassu *est*
'he's too fat'

3.4.8 Position of clitic pronouns

Latin weak pronouns were placed, following a variant of the Wackernagel Law, after the first constituent of the core sentence, and therefore after the focalized constituent or after the preposed verb or, if these were missing, after the first constituent of the nucleus. In the V2 system of early Romance languages the clitics, continuing weak forms of Latin pronouns, are still placed after the first constituent of the sentential core (Renzi 1987): i.e., after a thematized (127a) or focalized (127b) phrase in preverbal position or, failing that, after the finite verb (127c), a rule known as the Tobler–Mussafia Law. Given the new position of the verb in the Romance sentence, clitics always appeared adjacent to the verb:

(127) a. OIt. *Allora / lo re si rinchiuse in una camera con questo greco* (*Novellino*)
'So the king shut himself in a room with this Greek'

b. *che domanda* mi *fate voi?* (*Novellino*)
   'what question are you asking me?'
c. *fu*li *detto che…* (*Novellino*)
   'it was said to him that […]'

Latin weak pronouns were enclitic elements, as Romance clitics must have been (Melander 1928), at least at first: their vowels could be deleted if preceded by a vowel-final word, a sign that they were phonetically dependent on the preceding word (128):

(128) a. OSp. *Aqui*m *parto de vos* (*Cantar de Mio Cid*)
        'Here I depart from you'
      b. OFr. *por quei*t *portat ta medre?* (*La Vie de saint Alexis*)
        'why did thy mother bear thee?'

This situation soon changes. While Latin weak pronouns were independent words, Romance clitics are reinterpreted as accessory elements of the verb, and so when they precede the verb they become proclitic to it, e.g., OFr. *qui* le *dira* (Chrestien de Troyes, *Yvain*) 'who will say it' (where the clitic keeps its vowel because its host begins with a consonant). This change initially has no effect on the Tobler–Mussafia Law, but most Romance languages gradually abandon it and begin to allow preverbal clitics even when no constituent precedes the verb in the sentential core. Relaxation of the Tobler–Mussafia Law begins very early (twelfth century) in old French in the context of yes/no-questions (129a), subsequently extending to the other contexts (129b) (de Kok 1985: chs. 3, 13):

(129) a. OFr. Te *tindrent onques Sarrazin en prison?* (*La prise d'Orange*)
        'Did the Saracens ever hold you in prison?'
      b. Se *appensa de faire ung amy qui* … (*Nouvelles françaises inédites du quinzième siècle*)
        'He thought of getting a friend who […]'

Only Galician-Portuguese (but not Brazilian Portuguese) and part of Asturo-Leonese retain to this day a modified form of the older situation (Salvi 1990): clitics remain postverbal if the verb is in absolute first position (130a) and preverbal if the verb is preceded by constituents with focus value (130b); otherwise they are postverbal (130c):

(130) a. Pt. *Viu*-me
        'He saw me'
      b. *Ninguém* o *sabia*
        'Nobody knew it'
      c. *O Pedro viu*-me
        'Pedro saw me'

In the other languages, the position of clitics becomes dependent on the finiteness of the verb: proclisis with finite forms and enclisis with non-finites and imperatives (Spanish, Catalan, part of Occitan, Italian, Romanian with some exceptions), but some languages extend proclisis to non-finite forms (part of Occitan, French) or to all cases (Brazilian Portuguese).

3.4.9   Archaic word orders

We saw above that we may assume an intermediate phase in the formation of Romance word order in which in unmarked order the verb was in first position. At this stage, thematic preverbal constituents find a place in the left periphery. By the earliest records of Romance this phase is generally over, and thematization makes use of the first (preverbal) position of the core sentence (V2 system); see (131a), where the theme is the direct object, and (131b–d), where the theme is the subject (the preverbal position of the clitic ensures that the theme is within the core sentence):

> (131) a. OPt. *(damos a uos* [...] *a nossa uina* [...]*) et* esta uina *uos damos per taes cõdições que...* (*Documento [1312]*)
> '(we give you [...] our vine [...]) and we give you this vine on the following conditions ...'
> b. OSp. Hyo *lo veré con el Çid* (*Cantar de Mio Cid*)
> 'I'll see about it with the Cid'
> c. OFr. Deus *les ad á mort livrez* (*Li quatre Livre des Reis*)
> 'God has consigned them to death'
> d. OPrv. lo reis *lo pres de felni' a reptar* (*Boecis*)
> 'the king began to accuse him of felony'

In old Portuguese and old Spanish there are still many traces of the older situation: thematic subjects (132) and direct objects (133) are often, if not principally, in peripheral position, as is shown by the position of the clitic in the following:

> (132) a. OPt. el-rrei | *mandou-ho assi fazer* (Fernão Lopes, *Crónica de Dom Pedro*)
> 'the king commanded that it should be done so'
> b. OSp. ella | *cogiol so el su manto* (*Primera crónica general de España*)
> 'she took him under her mantle'

> (133) a. OPt. a donzela | *leixarom-na* (*A Demanda do Santo Graal*)
> 'the maiden they abandoned her / the maiden was abandoned'
> b. OSp. este Allor | *enbiolo Miramolin por veedor* (*Texto español de la Crónica de 1344*)

'this Allor, Miramolin sent him as overseer. / This Allor was sent by Miramolin as overseer'

Beside the prevalent order with verb in second position, the early Romance languages also show clear traces of a more archaic ordering, possibly identifiable as a variant of Latin word order. From the languages that have been studied from this point of view (old French, Skårup 1975:ch. ix; old Portuguese, Salvi 1995), this word order, especially common in subordinate clauses (Salvi 2001b), has the following positions:

(1) after the element introducing the subordinate clause we find a pronominal form: in Portuguese these are clitics (not necessarily adjacent to the verb), in French the weak form of the subject pronoun);

(2) following a temporal adverb (Pt. *logo/nunca*, Fr. *ja/onques*);

(3) following a certain number of preverbal constituents including nominal subject and any adverbs; the subject is usually preverbal and precedes other constituents, but DO-subject order is also possible: in this case the DO lacks the characteristic properties of peripheral elements which it would have in a V2 system when it did not immediately precede the verb, i.e., we do not have the resumptive clitic. Thus (134)–(135):

(134) a. OFr. *que* [il]1 [jamais]2 [de ces mesons]3 *n'istroit* (Chrestien de Troyes, *Li Contes del Graal*)
'that he would never leave these houses'

b. *que* [onques]2 [hom en si grant beneurté]3 *ne mourut* (*La Queste del Saint Graal*)
'that never did a man die in such great happiness'

(135) a. OPt. *que* [lhe]1 [logo]2 [el-rrei]3 *nom mandou cortar a cabeça* (Fernão Lopes, *Crónica de Dom Pedro*)
'that the king did not immediately order his head to be cut off'

b. *Quando* [lhe]1 [aquello el rey]3 *ouvyo dizer* (*Crónica Geral de Espanha de 1344*)
'When the king heard him say that'

Note particularly that in (135b) the direct object (*aquello*) does not immediately precede the finite verb, but is not doubled by a clitic. Similar facts occur more rarely in the main clause, in the form:

(1) focalized element;

(2) pronominal form (clitic in Portuguese, weak subject pronoun in French);

(3) several constituents, without the characteristics of the peripheral elements:

(136) a. OFr. [Voir]1 [vos]2 *avez dit* (Chrestien de Troyes, *Li Contes del Graal*)
'You have told the truth'

b. [Reis de Westsexe]1 [cil]3 *esteit* (Geffrei Gaimar, *L'Estoire des Engleis*)
'That was the king of Wessex'

c. [Ja mais]1 [Karlon de nus]3 n'avrat servise (*Chanson de Roland*)
'Never again will we serve Charles'

(137) a. OPt. [logo]1 [lhe]2 [el-rrei]3 *taxava que* […] (Fernão Lopes, *Crónica de Dom Pedro*)
'immediately the king imposed on him as punishment that […]'

b. [tanto]1 [vos]2 [eu mui máis]3 *precei des i* (Joan Airas)
'so much more did I appreciate you thereafter'

Cases of non-finite forms preceded by one or more constituents probably also belong here:

(138) a. OPt. *pera* em ella *fazer as sepulturas suas* (*Crónica Geral de Espanha de 1344*)
'to make in it his tomb'

b. *ouve* todo esto *guisado* (*Crónica Geral de Espanha de 1344*)
'he had fixed all this'

These sentence schemes are clearly analogous to Latin word order. Weak elements follow the first element in the sentence: after the complementizer or the relative/interrogative phrase in subordinate clauses and after the sentence-initial focalized phrase in main clauses, and are not adjacent to the verb; this was the situation in Latin. Second, we find several constituents before the finite verb and there are no traces of a distinction between peripheral elements (with resumptive clitic) and constituent in first position: all the constituents belong to the core sentence; this again is the situation of Latin, which had all constituents before the verb. So this type of example represents survival of Latin word order beside the more widespread Verb-Second order of early Romance, destined to disappear definitively from written use in French already by the beginning of the fourteenth century, in Portuguese a couple of centuries later.

This is not just Latin word order *tout court*: in these sentences the finite verb is not normally in last position. This type of sentence may have represented an alternative grammar to the innovative V2 system in the long transition from Latin to Romance: in this grammar the onset is of the Latin type, while in the second part the constituents could freely be placed before the verb (as in Latin) or after the verb (as in the Romance V2 system).

3.4.10   Infinitive constructions; gerund; participle

Infinitive constructions with overt subject (Accusative and Infinitive) disappear, being generally replaced by finite constructions:

(139) Lat. ... *scripserunt ad eum sui...* [*multos ei molestos fore ...*] (Cic.) '... his friends wrote [...] to him [...] that many people there would [...] be an annoyance to him'

(140) It. *I suoi amici gli hanno scritto [che molti lo avrebbero importunato]*
'His friends wrote to him that many people would bother him.'

An apparent case of conservation is the construction with perceptual verbs, but cases of Accusative and Infinitive with perceptual verbs, in Latin (141a), do not refer to perception of a process in progress, as in Romance (142b), but to recognition of a fact, a relation which in Romance is expressed by a finite complement clause (142a); perception of the process in Latin was expressed by the present participle (141b):

(141) a. Lat. *audivistin tu* [*hodie me illi dicere ea quae* [...]]*?* (Pl.)
'did you hear that I was telling her today that [...]?'
b. [*Hinc ex hisce aedibus*] *paulo prius / vidi* [*exeuntem mulierem*] (Pl.)
'Just now I saw a woman come out of this house'

(142) a. It. *Hai sentito che le raccontavo queste cose?*
'Did you hear that I was telling her these things?'
b. *Ho visto una donna uscire da questa casa*
'I saw a woman coming out of this house'

While (141b) requires direct perception of an event, this is in theory unnecessary in (141a), where *audivisti(n)* could also mean 'you heard it said'. In such an example, where knowledge of context imposes the interpretation of knowledge in terms of direct perception (the addressee was present at the event), the boundary between the two interpretations may be dissolved and we could also translate it into Italian as *mi hai sentito raccontarle.* This referential indeterminacy might have favoured reinterpretation of the construction as a perceptual one and its survival in Romance.

Structurally, however, the Romance construction has different properties: while in Latin the constituent in the accusative is part of the subordinate clause (in (141a), e.g., being a weak pronoun, it follows the first constituent of the subordinate clause, *hodie*), in Romance accusative constituent and infinitive never behave as a unit (143), but the accusative constituent is rather the direct object of the perceptual verb and the infinitive represents a subordinate clause with predicative value (alternating with a finite complement and, in various languages, with the gerund (144)):

(143) It. **È [*una donna uscire*] *che ho visto*
  'It is a woman come out that I saw'

(144) Fr. *Je l'ai vu* aller à la gare / qui allait à la gare / allant à la gare
  'I saw him going to the station'

This is obviously a construction closer to that represented in Latin by the present participle, where the non-finite form functioned as a predicative modifier of the direct object of the perceptual verb (cf. 141b). The Romance perceptual construction is therefore probably not so much a direct continuation of the Latin accusative and infinitive as an extension of the use of the infinitive to contexts where Latin used the present participle, an extension favoured by the referential indeterminacy of examples like (141a).

In any case, in Romance the use of the infinitive *without* overt subject does survive, and indeed spreads at the expense of other nominal forms (Norberg 1943: ch. 14): it particularly replaces gerund/gerundive in its non-ablative uses (accusative after preposition / dative: AD DICENDUM / It. *a dire* 'to say', genitive: DICENDI / It. *di dire* 'of saying'), the supine (IRE DORMITUM / It. *andare a dormire* 'to go to sleep') and the present participle in perceptual constructions.[9]

In Latin, the infinitive without overt subject could be governed by various verbs, including modals (POSSUM 'be able', DEBEO 'must', UOLO 'want', etc.), aspectuals (SOLEO 'be wont', INCIPIO 'begin', DESINO 'stop', etc.) and many other verbs expressing the will or attitude of the subject. This type of construction is continued in Romance with the same semantic classes of verbs. In many cases, unlike Latin, the Romance infinitive is introduced by a preposition (see above).

In Latin, in this construction the infinitive and its complements did not constitute a unitary bloc with regard to the governing verb: matrix and subordinate clause constituents followed each other fairly freely in linear order: Lat. *si* te victori *nolles aut non auderes* committere (Cic.) 'if you had neither the will nor the courage to throw yourself on the mercy of the conqueror'. An important aspect of this permeability between matrix and subordinate clause is that weak pronouns dependent on the infinitive were always placed after the first constituent of the matrix clause. In early

Romance we find the same situation: with a good number of verbs governing the infinitive the clitics dependent on the infinitive occur obligatorily
with the governing verb (*clitic climbing*):

(145) a. OPt. *começou*-hos *de preguntar como...* (Fernão Lopes, *Crónica de
Dom Pedro*)
'he began to ask them how [...]'
b. OSp. *quel puede venir muy grand danno* (Don Juan Manuel, *El Conde
Lucanor*)
'for a very great harm may befall him'
c. OFr. *nus* le *irrums ásaillir fierement ú qu'il seit* (*Li Quatre Livre des Reis*)
'we shall go and attack him fiercely wherever he is'
d. OIt. *Voglio*lo *sapere da mia madre* (*Novellino*)
'I want to hear it from my mother'

In modern Romance, this possibility has remained with a limited number of verbs, which generally also admit collocation beside the infinitive
(146); French, Brazilian Portuguese and generally NItalian dialects allow
only collocation with the infinitive:

(146) a. Pt. *Não o pode saber / Não pode sabê*-lo
'He cannot know it'
b. It. Lo *vuole sapere / Vuole saper*lo
'He wants to know it'

Latin distinguished, beside the infinitive, two parallel nominal forms,
declinable for case, which replaced the infinitive in various contexts: the
gerund, with verbal properties, and the gerundive, with adjectival properties, exemplified here as complements of the adjective CUPIDUS:

(147) a. Lat. CUPIDUS <u>UIDENDI URBEM</u>
'desirous of seeing the city'
b. CUPIDUS <u>UIDENDAE URBIS</u>
'desirous of seeing the city'

The type of construction represented by the gerundive disappears completely from Romance. Even if in many uses it is substituted by the
infinitive, the gerund survives mainly in its ablative use, in which its
function in Latin was instrumental (148) or, more rarely, that of indicating
an accessory circumstance (149):

(148) a. Lat. *hominis mens* discendo *alitur* et cogitando (Cic.)
'the mind of man is nourished by studying and reflecting'
b. It. *Ho ottenuto questi risultati* lavorando sodo
'I obtained these results by working hard'

(149) a. Lat. *mori* [...] falsum fatendo (Cic.)
'to die confessing a falsehood'
b. It. *È uscito* correndo
'He went out running / He ran out'

In the use represented in (149a), the gerund replaces, already from the classical period, the present participle, many of whose functions it eventually assumes, including the perceptual construction (cf. 144). Some prepositional uses of the gerund are conserved, in particular that with IN, which assumes a temporal meaning (Spanish, Portuguese) and in French becomes the only possible form of the gerund: Fr. *Il est sorti* en chantant (< IN CANTANDO) 'He went out singing.' Many uses of the gerund attested in written Romance varieties derive from conscious imitation of Latin syntax, where the gerund is used as the counterpart of the present participle. Thus in old French the absolute construction (with overt subject) was limited to a certain number of lexicalized expressions (150), while more complex examples, like (151), normally appear only in translations from Latin:

(150) OFr. tot vëant mes iauz *l'ocist* (Chrestien de Troyes, *Yvain*)
'he killed him before my very eyes'

(151) OFr. *Tot issi fut rois par covent / Salemons* son pere vivent (*La Bible de Macé de la Charité – Rois*)
'Just so did Solomon become king according to the agreement, with his father living'

This also holds for many uses of the past participle: the only use that seems to be directly inherited from Latin is the attributive/predicative (It. *le cose dimenticate* 'things forgotten', *ne è uscito* sconfitto 'he emerged defeated'), while absolute constructions must be learnèd imitations of Latin. In grammars of old French (Moignet 1973; Jensen 1990; Buridant 2001), we find examples of the attributive (152) and predicative (153) use, while examples of the absolute construction are all of the type exemplified in (154), a variant of the construction 'with'+ NP + predicate, common in Romance; exceptions, like (155), are all in texts translated from or modelled on Latin:

(152) OFr. *il prist Nymes par le charroi* mené (*Le Charroi de Nîmes*)
'he took Nîmes with the cart he had brought there'

(153) OFr. *il se vit* desconfit (*La Queste del Saint Graal*)
'he saw himself defeated'

(154) OFr. Juntes ses mains *est alet a sa fin* (*Chanson de Roland*)
'he went to his end with his hands joined [in prayer]'

(155) OFr. Tel duel et tel priiere faite, / *Par grant ire a l'espee traite* (*Piramus et Tisbé*)
'This show of grief and these prayers having been made, in great despair he drew his sword'

3.4.11 Finite subordinate clauses

In Classical Latin, there were four main types of complement clauses: (i) accusative and infinitive; (ii) subjunctive subordinate clauses introduced by UT, NE, QUIN, etc.; (iii) finite subordinate clauses, basically in the indicative, introduced by QUOD (var. QUIA); and (iv) indirect question clauses (see below).

The accusative and infinitive construction was the unmarked type and used as the complement of declarative (156a), volitive (156b), dubitative and potential (156c) and factive (156d) predicates:

(156) a. Lat. *omnes in iis sedibus quae erant sub platano consedisse dicebat* (Cic.)
'he said that they had all sat on the chairs which were under the plane tree'
b. *liberos suos* [...] *beatos esse cupiat* (Cic.)
'he wants his children to be happy'
c. *nec verum est* [...] *idcirco initam esse cum hominibus communitatem* (Cic.)
'nor is it true that for this reason there arose a community among men'
d. *venire tu me gaudes* (Pl.)
'you're happy that I'm coming'

Subjunctive subordinate clauses were used with volitive predicates (157a) (final UT) and potentials (157b) (consecutive UT):

(157) a. Lat. *tu malim* [...] *actum ne agas* (Cic.)
'as for you, I'd rather you didn't concern yourself with matters that are closed'
b. *si verum est – quod nemo dubitat – ut populus Romanus omnes gentes virtute superarit* (Cor. Nep.)
'if it is true – and nobody doubts it – that the Roman people has surpassed all peoples in valour'

The construction with QUOD was used with factive predicates, often with the proleptic element ILLUD 'the fact': *illud gaudeo, quod* [...] *aequalitas vestra* [...] *abest ab obtrectatione et invidia* (Cic.) 'I am happy that the equality of your age is exempt from denigration and envy.' Fairly early, already in the classical norm, QUOD extends to the semifactive SCIO 'know' (158) and in popular language also to declarative verbs (159):

(158) Lat. *quod multa milia ipso die* [...] *ceciderunt et ceperunt, hoc, si ipsi tacuerint, vos scituros* [...] *non credunt?* (Liv.)
'that in that very day they slew and captured many thousands of men, do they not believe that, even if they kept it quiet, you will know it?'

(159) Lat. *dixi quia mustella comedit* (Petr.)
'I said the weasel ate them'

These are the first steps in a generalization which will lead to the elimination of the Accusative and Infinitive (Cuzzolin 1994) and the various types of subjunctive subordinates, in favour of a single construction introduced by *que/che*, functionally equivalent to QUOD (with indicative or subjunctive according to the governing predicate):

(160) a. Pt. *Disse-me* que *não o convidaria* (declarative predicate)
'He told me he wouldn't invite him'
   b. Sp. *Te ruego* que *me digas la verdad* (volitive predicate)
'I'm asking you to tell me the truth'
   c. Fr. *Il paraît* qu'*ils ont faim* (dubitative predicate)
'It seems they're hungry'
   d. It. *Sono contento* che *vengano* (factive predicate)
'I'm happy they're coming'

Romanian offers a different solution (Motapanyane 1995); subordinates in the indicative are introduced by *că* (< QUIA; see Herman 1963:165f.; use of *de* is a later innovation): *Maria spunea că studenţii pregătesc o grevă* 'Maria said the students were preparing a strike', while subordinate clauses in the subjunctive are introduced by the preverbal particle *să* (< SI) or by *ca* (+ preverbal *să*):

(161) a. Ro. *Doream* să *vină Ion*
'I wished *Ion* to come'
   b. *Doream* ca *Ion* să *vină*
'I wished Ion to come'

For the southern Italian dialect situation, see Ledgeway (2003b; 2005; 2006).

Subordinate *wh*-questions were characterized in Latin by pre-positioning of the interrogative phrase (162a), a construction which survives in Romance (162b); in yes/no-questions, normally the particles NUM, -NE, AN were used, as in direct questions (163a), but already in the classical period some constructions admitted SI 'if, whether' (163b), which becomes general in Romance (163c) (Ro. uses *dacă* 'if'):

(162) a. Lat. *miror* quid *hoc sit negoti* (Pl.)
'I wonder what this is'
b. Fr. *Je me demande* quand *il va arriver*
'I wonder when he'll arive'

(163) a. Lat. *dubitabunt sit*ne *tantum in virtute ...* (Cic.)
'they'll wonder whether there's such force in virtue ...'
b. *vide* [...] si *quis forte est* [...] *qui te nolit perisse* (Cic.)
'see whether by any chance there's someone who doesn't wish you died'
c. Fr. *Il ne sait pas* si *Pierre est à la maison*
'He doesn't know whether Pierre is at home'

In embedded *wh*-questions, the boundary between them and relatives is already blurred in early Romance: see (164), where the interpretation is that of an indirect question, but the structure is that of a relative with antecedent; in some cases the relative structure is grammaticalized in modern varieties (165):

(164) a. OIt. *voi di costà siate certi da que' di Chirchistede,* quello che *volessero che vi si spendesse* (*Lettera fiorentina,* 1291)
'you over there find out from Kirkstead's men how much they would like spent'
b. *non so* là dov'*io mi nasconda* (*Novellino*)
'I don't know where to hide'

(165) a. Pt. *Não sabia* o que *queria*
'He didn't know what he wanted'
b. Sp. *Ya verás* lo bien que *trabaja*
'You'll soon see how well he works'
c. Fr. *Je ne sais pas* ce que *maman a dit*
'I don't know what mum said'

Romance languages generally retain some relative pronoun forms (see above), so that the structure of attributive subordinate clauses continues that of Latin, with the relative pronoun at the head of the subordinate clause as an anaphoric doubling of the antecedent (cf. 20). Romance also shows a structure without relative pronoun: the attributive clause is introduced by the complementizer *que/che* and the function of the relativized element is expressed by verb agreement (for the subject), by a clitic (where the function in question can be expressed by a clitic) or is not expressed. Thus, while in (20b) relativization of the direct object is expressed with a relative pronoun, in (20f) there is only the complementizer and the function of the relativized element is unexpressed. Compare also (20a), with the subject expressed by a relative pronoun, and (166), with the complementizer and verb agreement expressing the function subject; also (167a), with a relative pronoun in indirect object function, and (167b), with the complementizer and a dative clitic; and (168a), with a prepositional complement expressed by the relative, and (168b), with the complementizer, and the grammatical function unexpressed:

(166) OFr. *mescroit les barons du reigne, / que li faisoient chose acroire / que il set bien que n'est pas voire* (Béroul, *Le Roman de Tristan*)
'he distrusts the great barons of the realm, who made him believe what he knows is not true'

(167) a. OIt. *l'altro, cui pareva tardar troppo* (Dante, *Commedia*)
'the other one, to whom it seemed he was going too slowly'
b. *un spirto* che *'n pensieri / gravi a morir* li *parve venir tardo* (Dante, *Commedia*)
'a spirit to whom, being immersed in grave thought, it seemed that death tarried in coming'

(168) a. OIt. *quel suono / di cui* le Piche *misere sentiro / lo colpo* (Dante, *Commedia*)
'that sound of which the wretched magpies felt the blow'
b. *le foglie* che *la materia e tu mi farai degno* (Dante, *Commedia*)
'those leaves of which the theme and thou shall make me worthy'

3.4.12 Indicative and subjunctive in subordinate clauses

Latin made extensive use of the subjunctive in subordinate clauses. Unlike main clauses, where it always has a distinct meaning from the indicative, in subordinates this value is often redundant (e.g., after volitive verbs) or wholly opaque (e.g., in consecutive clauses). Thus the subjunctive has been described as the mood of subordination, or the unmarked mood in subordinate clauses (Kiss 1982:42–48). In the evolution to Romance there is notable stability in semantically motivated subjunctives, while the opaque uses tend to be replaced by the indicative (Kiss 1982:77), which, with the ground it gains also from the accusative and infinitive (see above), becomes the unmarked mood in subordinate clauses too.

In summary, the subjunctive remains in complement clauses dependent on verbs of volition (169) and in final clauses (170) (*volitive subjunctive*); it also survives in the domain of negation, e.g., in causal subordinate clauses (171) which, if not negated, would be in the indicative, or in relative clauses when the existence of the antecedent is negated (172) (Farkas 1982):

(169) a. Lat. *hodie uxorem* ducas [...] *volo* (Ter.)
'I want you to take a wife today'
   b. Pt. *Queria que* viesse *comigo*
'I wanted him to come with me'

(170) a. Lat. *esse oportet ut* vivas (Ter.)
'you must eat to live'
   b. Fr. *Il parle hongrois pour que vous ne le* compreniez *pas*
'He speaks Hungarian in order that you should not understand him'

(171) a. Lat. *ingemescunt, non quod* doleant [...] (SBJV) , *sed quia* [...] *omne corpus* intenditur (IND) (Cic.)
'they moan not because they are in pain but because their whole body is stretched'
   b. Pt. *Fui-me embora não porque* estivesse (SBJV) *cansado, mas porque* tinha (IND) *que ir ao cinema*
'I left not because I was tired, but because I had to go to the cinema'
   c. Fr. *Ce n'est pas qu'il* soit *méchant*
'It's not that he's naughty'

(172) a. Lat. *nihil est quo me* recipiam (Pl.)
'there is nowhere where I can take shelter'
   b. Pt. *Não conheço ninguém que* seja *tão antipático*
'I don't know anyone who's so unpleasant'
   c. Fr. *Il n'y a pas un individu dans tout le pays qui* ait lu *ce livre*
'There's not a soul in the whole country who's read this book'
   d. Ro. *N-am văzut nimic care* să-mi placă
'I've seen nothing I like'

Among adverbial subordinates, it survives in concessives (173) (except in Romanian) and some temporals (174):

(173) a. Lat. *quamvis res mihi non* placeat (Cic.)
'although I dislike the matter'
   b. Pt. *Embora não* gostem *disso*
'Although they don't like this'
   c. Fr. *Quoiqu'il* fasse *froid*
'although it's cold'

(174) a. Lat. *is videlicet, antequam* veniat *in Pontum, litteras ad Cn. Pompeium mittet* (Cic.)
'indeed, before going to Pontus, he'll sent a letter to Gn. Pompeius'
   b. Pt. *Dá-lhas antes que se* murchem
'Give them to them before they fade'
   c. Fr. *Il est parti avant que j'*aie pu *lui parler*
'He left before I could speak to him'

d. Ro. *Înainte ca Ion* să fi intrat, *Maria a închis cartea*
'Before Ion entered, Maria shut the book'

In early Romance conditional subordinate clauses there is generally retention of the imperfect and pluperfect subjunctives (175), expressing low probability, with neutralization of the Latin distinction between present/perfect (potential) and imperfect/pluperfect (irrealis). In some languages, the subjunctive is replaced by the indicative (176a) or the conditional (176b):

(175) a. Lat. *possesne, si te* [...] *contio reliquisset?* (Cic.)
'could you (go on speaking), if the audience deserted you (lit. had deserted you)?'
   b. OFr. *L'en me devroit coper la teste / S'* [...] */ Eüsse fet tel deshonur* (Marie de France, *Fables*)
'One should cut off my head, if I had committed such an outrage'
   c. OIt. *Se voi* sentiste *come 'l cor si dole, / dentro dal vostro cor voi tremereste* (Guido Cavalcanti)
'If you could hear how the heart laments, you would tremble within your heart'

(176) a. Fr. *Si je l'avais vu, je te l'aurais dit*
'If I'd seen it, I'd have told you'
   b. Ro. *Dacă aş fi ştiut, aş fi venit şi eu*
'If I'd known, I'd have come too'

Among recessive or disappearing uses of the Romance subjunctive is its use in indirect questions, which is only partially preserved (177), its use in consecutive clauses, substituted by the indicative (178), and the *cum historicum* use (179), which has completely disappeared, being replaced by various circumstantial constructions:

(177) a. Lat. *quid* agatis [...], *fac* [...] *sciam* (Cic.)
'tell me how you are'
   b. OIt. *sì mi domandò che io* avesse (SBJV) (Dante, *Vita Nuova*)
'he asked me what was wrong with me'
   c. OIt. *lo duca il domandò poi chi ello* era (IND) (Dante, *Commedia*)
'my guide then asked him who he was'

(178) a. Lat. *scripta lex ita diligenter est ut* [...] appareat (Cic.)
'the law has been so carefully written that it appears [...]'
   b. It. *Il manoscritto è stato controllato così minuziosamente che non vi è* rimasto (IND) *nessun errore*
'The manuscript has been so minutely checked that no error has remained in it'

(179) Lat. *cum Argos oppidum* oppugnaret *in Peloponneso, lapide ictus interiit* (Cor. Nep.)
'while he was besieging Argos in the Peloponnese, he was hit by a stone and died'

But the major restructuring of subordination in Romance opens up new potential for expansion of the subjunctive: opinion verbs (with accusative and infinitive in Latin) often take the subjunctive (180), probably as an extension of the use of the subjunctive in reported speech (181):[10]

(180) a. Pt. *Cuidava que ele* estivesse *em casa*
   'She thought he was at home'
   b. OFr. *Einz quidoit que ce* fust *le ber* (*Roman de Renart*)
   'Rather he believed it was the husband'
   c. It. *Credeva che glielo* avesse spedito *Piero*
   'He thought Piero had sent it to him'

(181) Lat. *Phalereus Demetrius* [...] *Periclem vituperat quod tantam pecuniam* [...] coniecerit (Cic.)
   'Demetrius of Phaleron blames Pericles for wasting so much money ...'

In other cases, Romance generalizes the use of the subjunctive in certain syntactic contexts, while in Latin its use was at least in part determined semantically. Latin temporal subordinate clauses with ANTEQUAM and PRIUSQUAM could take the indicative, especially where the event had really occurred (182), while Romance has generalized the subjunctive (183) (cf. 174d):

(182) Lat. *neque prius fugere destiterunt quam ad flumen Rhenum* [...] pervenerunt (Caes.)
   'and they did not stop running until they reached the river Rhine'

(183) a. OFr. *Ainz quet* vedisse, *sin fui mult desirruse* (*La Vie de saint Alexis*)
   'Before I saw you, I was very desirous of it'
   b. OIt. *assai prima / che noi* fossimo *al piè de l'alta torre, / li occhi nostri n'andar suso a la cima* (Dante, *Commedia*)
   'long before we were at the foot of the high tower, our gaze went up to the top'

A later innovation is extension of the subjunctive to complement clauses governed by factive predicates, which still took the indicative in old Romance (184), as in Latin, while in modern Romance (except Romanian (186)) they usually take the subjunctive (185) (Gsell and Wandruszka 1986:§2.3.2):

(184) OFr. *Qued enfant n'ourent peiset lur en fortment* (*La vie de saint Alexis*)
'It grieves them greatly that they did not have a child'

(185) a. Pt. *Admirava-me que me* reconhecesse
'I was surprised he recognized me'
   b. Fr. *Je suis content que tu aies réussi*
'I'm happy you've succeeded'
   c. It. *Mi dispiace che tu* abbia perso *il treno*
'I'm sorry you missed the train'

(186) Ro. *Se bucura mama că-i* veneau *neamurile*
'Mother was glad her relatives were coming'

3.4.13   Sequence of tenses

In Latin, the temporal relation between different events, and in particular within the same sentence, was expressed with a complex system of tense harmonization such that the anteriority, simultaneity and posteriority of an event with respect to another event situated in the past or the future was not generally expressed by the same tense used to express anteriority, simultaneity and posteriority with regard to the moment of utterance. In a nutshell, in clauses with the subjunctive, while the relationship of (a) anteriority, (b) simultaneity and (c) posteriority with respect to the moment of utterance was generally expressed (a) by the perfect, (b) by the present and (c) by the present or future:

(a)		FECERIT (PRF)		he has done'
(b)	DICO QUID	FACIAT (PRS)	'I say what	he is doing'
(c)		FACIAT (PRS) / FACTURUS SIT (FUT)		he will do'

the same relationships in relation to a past event were expressed (a) by the pluperfect, (b) by the imperfect and (c) by the imperfect or future in the past:

(a)		FECISSET (PLPF)		he had done'
(b)	DIXI QUID	FACERET (IPF)	'I said what	he was doing'
(c)		FACERET (IPF) / FACTURUS ESSET (FUT)		he would do'

This system of tense harmony is essentially maintained in Romance (see Vanelli 1993). But early Romance languages also show lack of harmonization, as in the following, where the preterite, present and future express anteriority, simultaneity and posteriority independently of the reference time:

(187) a. OIt. *(una sposa novella,) alla quale voleano fare dire com'ella* fece (PRF) *la prima notte (Novellino)*
'(a new bride) whom they wanted to get to tell what she had done on her wedding night'

b. OFr. *Si leur dist que li rois Artus estoit a demie liue de la cité et que l'en puet* (PRS) *ja veoir plus de dis mile homes des lor (La Mort le roi Artu)*
'He told them that king Arthur was half a league from the city and that over 10,000 men could already be seen'

c. OIt. *l'altra partita dicea [...] come il Filgluolo di Dio* nascerà (FUT) *d'una pulçella sancta vergine ch' averà nome Maria (Cronica fiorentina)*
'the other part said how the Son of God would be born of a holy virgin maiden whose name would be Mary'

In languages which have developed outside the sphere of influence of Latinity, like Romanian or Surselvan, the unharmonized system is normal (although harmonization is possible). Romanian:

(188) a. *Mi-a spus că* a fost (PRF) *bolnav*
'He told me he'd been ill'

b. *Mi-a spus că* e (PRS) *bolnav*
'He told me he was ill'

c. *Mi-a spus că* va pleca (FUT)
'He told me he would leave'

Apparent lack of harmonization is also found in the subjunctive in spoken French, Romanian and dialects of the far south of Italy, where synthetic tense-forms of the subjunctive other than the present have been lost.

4   Conclusion

It would be wrong to think that little has changed in the Latin–Romance transition: the Romance languages are very different from Latin and they all resemble each other much more than they resemble Latin (Renzi 1984). Yet it must be stressed that, if the Romance languages have moved far from Latin, this had not happened in the radical way it might have – especially, of course, in the early varieties. In other words, the Romance languages have basically remained within the inflecting type: in the nominal system, while case has been drastically reduced, gender and number have remained robust; in the verb, the mood and tense system is preserved, indeed sometimes enriched – even where synthetic expression of categories is replaced by analytic structures, this has not changed the fundamental nature of the categories expressed (e.g., syntactic agreement, basically nominative–accusative sentence structure; active vs. passive distinction; elaborate system of subordination).

The Romance creoles show that things could have gone differently. True, the Latin–Romance transition occurred under very different conditions, but the fact that Latin was a secondarily acquired language for most speakers (under 'spontaneous' conditions) did play a fundamental role in many aspects of the evolution of Romance (e.g., replacement of synthetic by analytic structures). However, all this was tempered by the long period of diglossia (Latin/institutional language and Latin–Romance/spoken language) which guaranteed considerable structural continuity between Latin and Romance, eliminating many of the structures characteristic of the interlanguage we may hypothesize as a consequence of Latinization. Indeed, the most innovative Romance language (at least in its formative phase), and in any case the most eccentric one, is the one that was cut off earliest from this community: Romanian.

Moreover, in the Latin–Romance transition the process of loss of Latin morphosyntactic categories and syntactic structures was drawn out over several centuries. At their first appearance, Romance languages were already essentially different from Latin, but the conservative features attested in their earliest phases are much more numerous than later on (e.g., the case system, negation in French, Occitan and some NItalian dialects, word order, clitic placement, expression of the subject in French, and NItalian dialects). From the written tradition, these progressive losses can be reconstructed as a series of successive waves of losses/innovations, the first of which, fundamental for the formation of the Romance linguistic type, is probably datable between the sixth and seventh centuries (Herman 1998). Another is roughly datable to the late Middle Ages (dates vary somewhat according to geographical area) and separates old from modern Romance: in old Romance shared characteristics abound, both at the grammatical and lexical levels (Renzi 1994: ch. 12; Stefenelli 1998) due also to the wholesale preservation of Latin morphosyntactic and syntactic constructions; in modern Romance individual languages go their own way, albeit often showing striking parallels (Salvi 1997).

8   SYNTACTIC AND MORPHOSYNTACTIC TYPOLOGY AND CHANGE[1]

Adam Ledgeway

1   Introduction

There is general recognition among Romanists of all theoretical persuasions (see Harris 1978:5f.; Bauer 1995:5; La Fauci 1997:11f.; Zamboni 1998:128) that, in the passage from Latin to Romance, the morphosyntax of the emerging languages underwent significant changes in three fundamental areas of the grammar involving: (i) the nominal group; (ii) the verbal group; and (iii) the sentence. At a superficial level, the impact of such changes is most readily observable in: (i) the gradual reduction (e.g., medieval Gallo-Romance, Romanian) and/or eventual loss (e.g., Ibero-Romance, central-southern Italo-Romance) of the Latin morphological case system (see §6.2.2, and Sornicola, this volume, chapter 1: §3.1); (ii) the profusion of auxiliary verb structures (see §3.3.2) to mark such categories as tense (e.g., present perfectivity: Occ. *ai dormit* 'I have slept'), aspect (e.g., continuous aspect: Srd. *so kredende* lit. 'I am believing'), mood (e.g., epistemic modality: Cat. *La pipa deu valer molt* 'the pipe must be worth a lot') and voice (e.g., passive: Ro. *sînt invitaţi la un cocteil* 'they are invited to a cocktail party'); and (iii) the gradual shift from an original unmarked (S)OV word order (e.g., Lat. PAULUS LIBRUM SCRIPSIT 'Paul wrote a book') towards a fixed (S)VO (/V(S)O) order (e.g., Sp. *(Pablo) escribió (Pablo) un libro*; see §3.2.2, and Salvi, this volume, chapter 7: §3.4.7).

Moreover, in many historical treatments of Romance morphosyntax it is commonplace to interpret such changes as interrelated phenomena, rather than independent developments. For example, the loss of morphological case and the progressive establishment of (S)VO word order are frequently, albeit erroneously (Sasse 1977; Bichakjian 1987:89; Bauer 1995:7f.; La Fauci 1997:41), viewed as complementary developments in the restructuring of the original system of argument marking: on the one hand the weakening of the Latin case system necessitates a more rigid word order to distinguish crucially between subject and object (Vennemann 1974; Bauer 1995:5f.), while on the other hand a growing rigidification of word order renders the original case system increasingly redundant (Bourciez 1956; Zamboni 2000:102). In a similar fashion, the gradual erosion of the case system, with its concomitant effects on word order, is also held to be responsible, according to one frequent view (Grandgent 1907:42–48; Muller and Taylor 1932:65; Väänänen 1966:115–19; 1974/82:195–97; Lakoff 1972:189; Bauer 1995:137–39), for the increased use of prepositions, part of a more general typological shift from synthetic to analytic structures also reflected in the frequent recourse to auxiliaries within the verbal group (Harris 1978:15; Tekavčić 1980:15; Schwegler 1990).

Now, while the specific details of the complex morphosyntactic changes affecting the three key areas of the grammar hinted at above are relatively well known, scholars are still very much divided as to their correct interpretation, and how they are to be integrated within the overall typological change(s) witnessed in the passage from Latin to Romance. In what follows, we shall review several of these competing approaches, comparing how individual developments can best be accounted for across different theories and, in particular, how a number of traditional ideas can be profitably reinterpreted in the light of recent theoretical developments highlighting what further insights, if any, they provide for our overall understanding of the nature of the broad typological and structural changes that characterize the syntax and morphosyntax of the Romance languages with respect to Latin. Perhaps somewhat surprisingly, it will be shown that many of the conclusions reached within one particular theory often find immediate parallels in competing and otherwise seemingly incompatible theories, revealing the unmistakable merits of a complementary and integrated approach to old questions.

2   Syntheticity and analyticity

The principal differences in the morphosyntax of Latin and Romance have long been, albeit somewhat simplistically, viewed as representing two opposite poles of a syntheticity–analyticity continuum (Bourciez 1956:23; Harris 1978:15f.; Tekavčić 1980:15; Schwegler 1990; Posner 1996:156f.). This synthetic–analytic dichotomy, which goes back to the pioneering work of August Wilhelm von Schlegel (1818),[2] points to a Sapirian 'drift' from the predominantly synthetic structures of Latin towards the characteristically analytic structures of Romance or, as Harris

(1978:15) succinctly puts it, 'a tendency for syntax to take over a number of functions previously within the domain of morphology' such that 'an element of meaning previously conveyed by a stem and an affix is now expressed by a syntagm, that is, a combination of two or more elements that would traditionally be labelled words'. The examples are numerous and so well documented in the literature (see, for example, Schwegler 1990; Vincent 1997a:102f.) that they hardly need repeating here; suffice it to recall such classic examples as the replacement of: (i) the Latin suffixal comparative in -IOR '-er' (e.g., ALTUS : ALTIOR 'tall : taller') with a reflex of PLUS or MAGIS 'more' followed by the ungraded adjective or adverb (e.g., Fr. *plus haut*, Pt. *mais alto*; Zamboni 2000:121f.); (ii) the Latin synthetic future (e.g., PLUET 'it will rain') with an auxiliary + infinitive construction (e.g., Srd. *at a próere* lit. 'it has to rain'); and (iii) the accusative with infinitive construction, in which the sole marker of subordination lies in the 'exceptional' accusative marking of the infinitival subject (e.g., CREDO EUM FLERE 'I believe him to be crying'),[3] with a (non-)finite subordinate clause introduced by an overt complementizer (e.g., Cos. *criju ca chiangia* 'I believe that he is crying').

This traditional interpretation of the synthesis–analysis cycle proves, however, problematic on a number of accounts, as does the fundamental typological distinction on which it crucially rests (Schwegler 1990:4f.; Bauer 1995:10f., 138, 166; Vincent 1997a:99f., 105). Above all, one observes, with Schwegler (1990:193), a 'striking vagueness and ambiguity with which the terms ANALYTIC and SYNTHETIC, hence the concepts themselves, are used and understood in the literature'. Exemplary in this respect is the erroneous tendency to define Latin and Romance as synthetic and analytic languages, respectively, although both languages clearly also display, albeit in smaller measure, tendencies in the opposite direction (Schwegler 1990:28; Vincent 1997a:99). For instance, among other things Latin boasts numerous prepositions (including, AD 'to(wards)', EX 'out of', IN 'in, on', POST 'after', PROPTER 'on account of', SUB 'under'), a perfective passive periphrasis consisting of ESSE 'to be' + PP (e.g., PERICULUM NON UISUM ERIT 'the danger will not have been seen'), and a number of overt markers of subordination, including the subjunctive purposive complementizers UT/NE 'in order that (/not)' (e.g., HOC DICIT UT/NE EOS IUUET 'he says this in order it will (/not) help them'). Conversely, in Romance number and gender marking on nouns and adjectives is still typically suffixal (e.g., Glc. *vecĩn-o(s)/-a(s)* 'neighbour.M(PL)/F(PL)'), as are person/number and temporal/aspectual/modal categories on finite verbs (e.g., Gsc. *parti-vi/-vas/-va/ -vam/-vatz/-van* 'I/you (SG)/(s)he/we/you (PL)/they was/were leaving'). Thus, to the extent that any generalizations can usefully be made in relation to the synthetic and analytic parameter, they must be made in relation to specific construction types, rather than individual languages.

A further serious problem with the synthetic–analytic parameter is that it is frequently applied in absolute terms, whereas individual constructions can ostensibly display varying degrees of syntheticity and analyticity (Vincent 1997a:100). A case in point concerns what is called 'mesoclisis' in the (literary) European Portuguese future or conditional (e.g., *falar-me-ão* 'they will speak to me'), where the possibility of separating the person/ number inflection (e.g., *-ão* '3PL') from the future/conditional stem (e.g., *falar-* 'speak') with an intervening object clitic (e.g., *me* 'me.DAT') casts some doubt on the simple suffixal nature of the former. Similar problems arise for diminutive forms like Pt. *pãozinho* 'roll' (< *pão* 'bread' + DIM *-zinho*), which in the plural are marked not only in the desinence of the diminutive, but also on the nominal stem (e.g., *pãezinhos*). Examples like these, coupled with the thorny problem of how one is correctly to measure the autonomy of linguistic units (Schwegler 1990: ch. 2), frequently obscured by conventional, yet non-systematic, orthographic representations of the 'word' (cf. Sp./Cat. *¿Por qué?/Per què?* 'why?' vs. *porque/ perque* 'because', It. *da capo/daccapo* 'from the beginning', Fr. *bien que* vs. It. *benché* 'although', Sp. *sin embargo* vs. It. *tuttavia* (not **tutta via*) 'however', Fr. *Est-ce que ...?* [ɛs(ə)kə] 'Is it that ...?', an erstwhile morphosyntactically complex interrogative cleft synchronically reduced to a morphosyntactically simplex polar interrogative particle [(ə)sk]) lead Schwegler (1990:193) to conclude, somewhat unsatisfactorily, that the labels 'synthetic' and 'analytic' can, at best, be understood as nothing more than 'the *rough* measure of the morphemic interdependence of speech units' [italics A.L.].

Yet even adopting a relativized interpretation of the traditional usage still fails to make any intuitive sense of many developments. For example, in the wake of Schwegler (1990), Vincent (1997a:99f.) proposes a scalar definition of the synthetic–analytic parameter in terms of the degree of phonological and morphosyntactic autonomy borne by the constituent grammatical properties of a given construction. On this view, however, one of the most important consequences of the presumed synthetic to analytic drift, manifested in the gradual replacement of an original 'free' word order with a 'fixed' (S)VO order (see §3.2.2), must now, despite the obvious contradiction, be treated as a synthetic development. In particular, the remarkable syntactic autonomy and independence of the core constituents of the Latin sentence which could, in accordance with pragmatic principles, not only occur in all possible permutations (see §3.2.1), but whose internal structure, when complex, could, in certain cases and in specific registers, be scattered discontinuously across the sentence (see §3.1.1), must be taken as an indication of greater analyticity. By the same token, the greatly reduced positional autonomy, coupled with the increased semantico–syntactic interdependence, of the core constituents of the Romance sentence which can now only be interpreted relative to each other, and whose constituent parts are cohesively bound together, are to be understood within the current approach as a synthetic development.

Without doubt, however, the biggest problem for the traditional synthetic–analytic interpretation of the Latin to Romance development is that it offers no explanation whatsoever for the observed changes. In short, the predominant analytic patterns noted in Romance are nothing more than the partial surface reflex of a more deep-rooted structural change, variously interpreted below as the result of the emergence of full configurationality and related functional structure (§3), a move from dependent- to head-marking (§4), a change in the head/branching parameter (§5) and the resolution of a centuries-old conflict between accusative–nominative and active–stative alignments in the nominal and verbal domains (§6). By way of illustration, one only has to consider the parallel analytic developments in the nominal and verbal domains such as the use of prepositions and auxiliaries replacing earlier inflections: here the chief issue is not the replacement of synthetic forms with analytic ones, but, rather, a structural change in linearization involving the head or branching parameter that affects both inflectional morphology and syntax alike (von Wartburg [1934] 1971:256; Harris 1978:6; Bauer 1995:10, 24, 166; Oniga 2004:52, 75).[4] Thus, the principal innovation in inflectional morphology has been the move away from structures in which grammatical modification (head) follows the lexical element (modifier) to structures in which the relevant grammatical modification (head) precedes the lexical element (modifier): MARC-O > Fr. *à Marc* 'to Marcus', COGITAUERAT > Cat. *havia pensat* 'he had thought'. In syntax too, verbal and nominal heads, once frequently preceded by such modifiers as direct objects/genitives and manner adverbs/adjectives, come instead to precede all such modifiers (e.g., MORTEM METUIT : It. *teme la morte* 'he fears death', MORTIS METUS : *il timore della morte* 'fear of death', LIBERE UIUIT : *vive liberamente* 'he lives freely', LIBER HOMO : *un uomo libero* 'a free man'). These latter examples, which clearly do not involve analyticity, therefore highlight that the relevant change in linear order in syntax is consistent with that observed in inflectional morphology, ultimately both derivable from a single integrated and comprehensive structural change.[5]

By way of conclusion, we should also note that the postulation of an independent synthetic–analytic parameter is further undermined by the observation that all the presumed cases of analytic development can be otherwise independently subsumed within the general theory of grammaticalization (Hopper and Traugott 1993:17). In particular, the analytic developments witnessed in the history of Romance are not in any way exclusive to the Romance family, but simply exemplify a cross-linguistic tendency for synthetic structures, once weakened through phonetic erosion or other forces within the system, to be progressively replaced by new competing structures which 'given the nature of syntactic change, cannot help but be analytic' (Vincent 1997a:101). Once again, analyticity turns out to be a secondary or epiphenomenal development, ultimately the manifestation of a deeper change but not, significantly, its cause.

3   Configurationality

Developments traditionally falling within the realm of the synthesis–analysis parameter, as well as many more far-reaching and significant syntactic changes, find a much more promising and comprehensive explanation in terms of the rise of configurationality and, in particular, the concomitant emergence of functional structure. It has long been noted, although not formalized as such, that there is little evidence in Latin for a fixed constituent structure. For example, Meillet (1977:156), discussing the nominal group, observes that in Romance 'what marks an attributive adjective, a noun in apposition and a complement as being semantically bound together is their juxtaposition, their formation of a group', whereas in Indo-European 'groups were not bound together in this way. Each of the constituent elements, which were independently inflected for their own particular function, could be separated from the others. While it was natural to say TOGAM NOUAM INDUE [lit. 'toga.F.ACC new.F.SG.ACC put-on.IMP'], nothing ruled out such sequences as NOUAM INDUE TOGAM [lit. 'new.F.SG.ACC put-on.IMP toga.ACC'], or TOGAM INDUE NOUAM [lit. 'toga.F.ACC put-on.IMP new.F. SG.ACC'] [translation A.L.]. In a similar vein, Herman (2000a:84) goes so far as to claim that the establishment of fixed positions for the constituent parts of the nominal group represents 'one symptom of a wider change in the nature of the grammar, a change that is indeed one of the most far-reaching in the transition from Latin to Romance'.

In the light of such considerations, some researchers (e.g., Vincent 1988a:53f., 62f.; 1997c:149, 163; 1998:423f.; Lyons 1999:154f., 305f.), though not without their opponents (e.g., Pinkster 1990:186; Oniga

2004:100f.), have claimed that the most significant innovation characterizing the transition from Latin to Romance is to be sought in the move away
from a non-configurational syntax, in which the relationships between
individual linguistic items are signalled through the forms of the items
themselves (case inflections, agreement), towards an increasingly configurational syntax, in which the relationships between related linguistic items are
encoded by their fixed positions relative to each other. From this perspective, traditional generalizations about Latin's prevalent recourse to synthetic, or rather morphological, strategies, in contrast to those of a
predominantly analytic, or rather syntactic, nature in Romance can now
be subsumed naturally within the configurationality parameter (cf.
Bresnan's (2001:6) slogan '[m]orphology competes with syntax'). Below,
we examine these developments in configurationality in relation to the three
principal domains of the grammar: the nominal and verbal groups, and the
sentence.

3.1   The nominal and verbal groups

Quintilian's oft-quoted observation 'NOSTER SERMO ARTICULOS NON
DESIDERAT' ('our language does not require articles') can be taken to
mean not simply that Latin lacked articles, but, more fundamentally, that
it lacked a dedicated position for articles and other types of determiner.
Indeed, this implication is explicitly assumed by Lyons (1999:155),
who interprets the lack of definiteness marking in languages with
non-configurational nominal syntax as the absence of a corresponding
D(eterminer) position (see also Gil 1987). Consequently, the absence of
an article in Latin and its presence in Romance can be taken as compelling
evidence for the emergence of NP structure in the latter. This view is
further supported by the observation that other determiner-like elements
such as demonstratives and possessives, which fill the same syntagmatic
slot as the article, also typically come to fill the prenominal determiner
position in Romance (e.g., Sp. *el/este/su mechero* 'the/this/his lighter'),
whereas in Latin they could occur in either pre- or postnominal position
just like adjectives (e.g., (ILLE/SUUS) CANIS (ILLE/SUUS) '(that/his) dog
(that/his)').

The Romance VP sees a parallel development in the emergence of a
profusion of auxiliaries associated with a dedicated structural position
situated to the immediate left of the VP (e.g., Cat. *l'Enric va passar un
any a Londres* 'Enric spent (lit. **goes** spend.INF) a year in London'), Ro. *vor
da banii orfelinatului* 'they **will** give the money to the orphanage').[6]

Significantly, Latin, by contrast, had very few auxiliaries, with verb categories such as tense, aspect and mood, as well as person and number, overwhelmingly marked inflectionally. The chief exception was the perfective
passive auxiliary ESSE 'to be' which, unlike its Romance counterparts, could
occur both in pre- and postverbal position (Bauer 1995:104f.; Vincent
2007a:65; e.g., EPISTULA SCRIPTA EST/EPISTULA EST SCRIPTA 'the letter (has
been) written (has been)').[7] Its presence within the verb system can be
readily compared to that of demonstratives in the Latin nominal group:
both marked grammatical categories but, in the absence of a VP/NP
constituent, neither had yet been formalized by way of a dedicated functional position. This view is echoed by (Bauer 1995:106), who underlines
how '[t]he evolution of Latin shows not the creation of the auxiliary as such,
but rather a change in the nature of the auxiliary element and in the place it
occupied'.

The overall conclusion to be drawn from these preliminary observations
is that marking of definiteness and various verb categories in Romance
increasingly becomes associated with specific positions, namely the left edge
of the NP (even in Romanian which has an enclitic definite article; see
§3.3.1.2) and the left edge of the VP, whereas in Latin, in which the
nominal and verbal groups were not configurationally structured, such
categories were either not explicitly marked or had no fixed position
(Vincent 1988a:52f.).

3.1.1   Latin

Now, if we take a closer look at the Latin nominal and verbal groups, we
soon come to realize that not only did Latin lack dedicated positions for
marking definiteness and various verb-related grammatical categories, but it
proves extremely difficult to justify the existence of any fixed positions for
any constituent parts (Vincent 1988a:53, 60f.). By way of illustration,
consider the examples in (1a–i) and (2a–d):

(1)   a. **HAEC**   CIUITAS   / **STATUS**   **HIC**   RERUM
          this.NOM   city.NOM   / state.NOM   this.NOM   things.GEN
          'this city' (Cic.) / 'this state of affairs' (Cic.)

       b. **NULLUM**   MALUM   / HORA   **QUOTA**   EST?
          no.NOM   evil.NOM   / what.NOM   hour.NOM   is-it?
          'no evil' (Cic.) / 'What time is it?' (Hor.)

       c. **IPSUM**   ME   EXCOLO   /CATILINA   **IPSE**   PROFUGIT
          self.M.ACC   me.ACC   I-cultivate /Cataline.NOM   self.NOM   has.fled
          'I cultivate myself' (Pl.) /'Catiline himself has fled' (Cic.)

d. NON EST ISTA **MEA**   CULPA   / PRAEDIA   **MEA**
   not is   this my.NOM guilt.NOM / estates.ACC my.ACC
   'this is not my fault' (Cic.) / 'my estates' (Cic.)

e. **PUERILI**   SPECIE   / AETAS   **PUERILIS**
   boyish.ABL aspect.ABL / age.NOM boyish.NOM
   'of boyish appearance' (Cic.) / 'the age of boyhood' (Cic.)

f. PRO **UITA**   **HOMINIS** NISI   **HOMINIS** UITA   REDDATUR
   for life.ABL man.GEN unless man.GEN life.NOM is.returned
   'unless for the life of a man a man's life be paid' (Caes.)

g. **TESTIMONI**   FIDEM   / FIDES   **ERGA**   **PLEBEM**
   testimony.DAT faith.ACC / faith.NOM towards   people.ACC
   'confidence in the testimony' (Cic.) /'confidence towards the people'
   (Cic.)

h. **HAUD**   **DUBIE**   UICTOR   / **TRIDUI**   UIA
   no   doubt   victor.NOM / three.day journey.NOM
   'beyond doubt a victor' (Sall.) /'a three-day journey' (Caes.)

i. **UNA**   **EXCELLENTISSIMA** **UIRTUS,**   IUSTITIA   / CNIDUS
   one.NOM excellent.NOM   virtue.NOM   justice.NOM / Cnidus.NOM

   ET   **COLOPHON,**   **NOBILISSIMAE**   **URBES**
   and   Colophon.NOM most.noble.NOM cities.NOM
   'an excellent virtue, justice' (Cic.) / 'Cnidus and Colophon, most
   noble cities' (Cic.)

(2) a. ILLA   QUAE   CUM REGE   EST PUGNATA / DIU
       that.NOM which.NOM with king.ABL is fought   / long.time
       PUGNATUM **EST**
       fought   it-is
       'that (battle) which was fought with the king' (Cic.) / 'there was a long
       battle' (Caes.)

    b. UINUS   **MIHI**   **IN**   **CEREBRUM** ABIIT/ ONERARIAE
       wine.NOM me.DAT in   brain.ACC   left   / transport.ships.NOM
       ONUSTAE   STABANT   **IN**   ⁻USTRIS
       laden.NOM stood   in   calm.waters.ABL
       'The wine has gone to my head' (Petr.) / 'The laden transport ships
       stood in calm waters' (Naev.)

    c. **BENE**   MORI   QUAM **TURPITER** UIUERE   / **UIXIT**   **BENE**
       Well   die.INF   than dishonestly live.INF   / he.lived   well
       'it is better to die well than to live dishonestly' (Val. Max.) / 'he lived
       well' (Ter.)

    d. CAESAR   **LEGIONIBUS TRADUCTIS**   AD OPPIDUM CONSTITIT / TREMO
       Caesar.NOM legions.ABL ferried.PL.ABL to city.ACC stopped   / I.tremble
       HORREOQUE   **POSTQUAM**   **ASPEXI**   **HANC**
       I.shiver=and after   I.saw   her
       'Caesar, after the legions had been taken over the river, stopped
       outside the town' (Caes.) / 'I quiver and shiver since I have seen her'
       (Ter.)

What the linear alternations in these examples demonstrate is that the various elements that make up the nominal and verbal groups – including demonstratives (1a), quantifiers (1b), intensifiers (1c), possessives (1d), adjectives (1e), genitives and other adnominal complements (1f–g), adjuncts (1h) and appositions (1i); auxiliaries (2a), complements (2b), adverbs (2c) and adverbial adjuncts (2d) – may occur either to the left or the right of their associated nominal or verbal predicate. Admittedly some of these elements are reported to display an unmarked order, such that demonstratives, quantifiers and intensifiers normally precede their associated nominals,[8] whereas the postnominal position is favoured by possessives, appositions, genitives and other adnominal complements.[9] Similarly, grammatical tradition has it that (Classical) Latin preferred verb-final structures, as noted by Quintilian (*Institutio oratoria* IX 4, 26), who claimed that 'UERBO SENSUM CLUDERE, MULTO, SI COMPOSITIO PATIATUR, OPTIMUM EST' ('it is far better to end a sentence with a verb if the composition so permits'), and 'the older the text, the more regular this appears' (Watkins 1964:1039). Thus, while there would appear to be general consensus that the unmarked position of the verb in Classical Latin, particularly in the highest literary registers, is clause-final,[10] hence typically preceded by all other elements of the verbal group, the verb may also occur in clause-medial position (Ernout and Thomas 1953:161; Adams 1976; Väänänen 1974/ 1982:259f.; Vincent 1988a:61; Oniga 2004:98f.). As various scholars have noted (Linde 1923; Feix 1934:13–15; Marouzeau 1938:87f.; Bauer 1995:87–98), this latter option is most common when the postposed elements are complements of the verb.

Crucially, though, in none of the cases considered above is the opposite, albeit marked, order ever excluded (Vincent 1988a:60), thereby providing significant proof for the absence of a predetermined positional template within the Latin nominal and verbal groups. This view finds further support in the observation that in some cases there is little agreement in the literature as to whether it is at all possible to identify an unmarked position for some elements and, if so, which of the two positions should be considered unmarked. For example, despite the frequent claim reported above (together with associated references) that genitives tend to favour the postnominal position, Bauer (1995:55–59) notes, chiefly on the strength of the evidence of Adams (1976), that in Classical Latin preposed and postposed nominal genitives occur in equal number (a view echoed by Oniga 2004:76) and, indeed, that preposed pronominal genitives outnumber their postposed equivalents. Even greater uncertainty surrounds the question of adjective placement in Latin. For example, Herman (2000a:83) reports that 'either order was possible in Classical Latin, and this remained the case in Late Latin too', as well as in vulgar texts where 'it is just as common to find the adjective first as it is to find the noun first' (see also Feix 1934:27; Vincent 1988a:54; Oniga 2004:95). Others, by contrast, variously identify the prenominal position (e.g., Gildersleeve and Lodge [1895] 1997:430) or the postnominal position (e.g., Hale and Buck ([1903] 1994:§624; Coleman 1991b:326; Lehmann 1991:223) as unmarked. Yet others recognize a semantic opposition in the interpretation of the pre- and postnominal positions, including such values as affective/qualifying vs. intellectual/distinguishing (Marouzeau 1922:15/1953:1), epithetical vs. attributive (Ernout and Thomas 1953:162), qualifying vs. determinative (Väänänen 1974/1982:260), focused vs. non-focused (Pinkster 1990:185), descriptive vs. distinctive (Bauer 1995:67–72), intensional vs. extensional (Devine and Stephens 2006:481f.), according to a distinction which, despite the terminological variation, Vincent (2007a:64f.) convincingly argues to be the precursor of the modern Romance situation.

Similar ambiguity in opinions and analyses can be found in relation to the verbal group. Above, we noted that the verb may also occur in clause-medial position, especially when it co-occurs with a complement. Marouzeau (1938:82), however, goes so far as to claim that the choice between verb-final and verb-medial position was indiscriminately free, the latter frequently proving almost as common as the former in some texts, a view echoed by Bauer (1995:97), who concludes that the verb-medial position was never stylistically marked.[11] Indeed, it has been frequently pointed out (Linde 1923:154f.; Elerick 1989b:1; Pinkster 1990:168f.; Bauer 1995:90f.; Herman 2000a:86; Zamboni 2000:102) that while the verb-final position prevails in main clauses in the prose of such authors as Caesar, accounting for around 80–90 percent of all cases, this percentage lowers to 59 percent in Plautus (Adams 1976:90–98), varies between 32 percent and 52 percent in Cicero, and is as low as 33 percent in Varro. Herman (2000a:86) goes even further, maintaining that the 'categorization of the language as basically having SOV order is exaggerated, even as regards the Classical language; we can tell that in other genres of a less-elevated nature than historiography, such as in Cicero's Dialogues, for example, the statistics are not the same as in Caesar: here, verb-final sentences are not the dominant type'. A similar degree of freedom is also reported for adverbial adjuncts (Kühner and Stegman 1912–14 II:6113; Pinkster 1990:168), whose position in relation to the finite verb appears to be the least fixed.

In view of these facts, it would not appear rash to interpret the Latin data as indicative of an early stage (see further §3.3.3), inasmuch as the older

Indo-European tendency to prepose nominal and verbal modifiers, as particularly evidenced by early Latin and comparative Oscan and Umbrian evidence,[12] shows a progressive weakening through time. In particular, we witness a steady increase in postnominal and postverbal positioning of particular elements (especially dependent genitives and complements of the verb) of the nominal and verbal groups, whilst other elements (e.g., adjectives and adverbs) appear to freely oscillate between both positions (Pinkster 1990:168; Bauer 1995:166). The result is a loosely defined nominal and verbal group with an incredibly free word order. Indeed, the loose organization of both groups is further substantiated by the existence of discontinuous structures,[13] 'one of the most distinctive features of Latin with regard to Romance' (Väänänen 1974/1982:259), in which the expected logical contiguity between dependent elements (heads and modifiers) is interrupted:

(3) a. **INFESTAM**   REI   PUBLICAE   **PESTEM**
       dangerous.F.ACC thing.F.DAT public.F.SG.DAT plague.F.ACC
       'a plague dangerous to the state' (Cat.)

    b. **COMPLURES**   EIUSDEM   AMENTIAE   **SOCIOS**
       many.M.PL.ACC same.F.SG.GEN madness.F.GEN associates.M.PL.ACC
       'many associates in the same madness' (Cic.)

In (3a) the adjective INFESTAM 'dangerous', although directly modifying the noun PESTEM 'plague', is separated from the latter by its own dative complement REI PUBLICAE 'to the state'. Similarly, in (3b) the quantifier COMPLURES 'many' is separated from the noun SOCIOS 'associates' over which it ranges by the intervening genitive modifier EIUSDEM AMENTIAE 'of the same madness'. This same discontinuous pattern proves particularly common in sequences with nominals governed by prepositions (see 4a–c), in which an accompanying modifier (e.g., adjective, adverb, adnominal genitive) is placed before the preposition, thereby stranding its associated noun.[14] More rarely, the noun itself can be placed before a governing preposition, stranding any accompanying modifiers (See 4d), a usage principally limited to verse (Leumann and Hofmann 1928:495; Marouzeau 1953:67; Bauer 1995:136):

(4) a. **MAGNO**   CUM   **DOLORE**
        great.M.SG.ABL with   pain.F.ABL
        'with great grief' (Cic.)

     b. **PAUCA**   IN **UERBA**   CONFER
        few.NEUT.PL.ACC   in words.NEUT.ACC   condense.IMP.2SG
        'condense in a few words' (Pl.)

c. **QUEM**   AD   **NEM?**
which.M.SG.ACC   to   end.M.SG.ACC
'to what end?' (Cic.)

d. **ARBUSTA**   PER   **ALTA**
timber.trees.NEUT.ACC   through   tall.NEUT.PL.ACC
'through tall timber-trees' (Enn.)

Similar examples of discontinuous structures are found within the verbal domain. For instance, in (5a–b) the constituent parts of the prepositional complement IN DUAS PARTES 'in two parts' and the direct object NOSTRAM INUIDIAM 'our unpopularity' are variously divided between the pre- and postverbal positions. It is also possible to find mixed structures, in which some elements of the verbal group precede the verb while others follow it. For example, in (5c) the verb follows the frequentative adverb SAEPE 'often' but precedes its complement OMNIA 'all things', and similarly in (5d) the verb again precedes its complement UENIAM 'pardon' but follows the adverbial PETENTIBUS AEDUIS 'on the request of the Aedui':

(5)   a. ANIMADUERTI ... ORATIONEM   **IN   DUAS**   DIUISAM
         I.realized   accusation.F.SG.ACC in   two.F.PL.ACC divided.F.SG.ACC
         ESSE   **PARTES**
         be.INF   parts.F.PL.ACC
         'I realized ... that the accusation is divided in two parts' (Cic.)

      b. **NOSTRAM ...**   RIDEBANT   **INUIDIAM**
         our.F.SG.ACC   they.laughed   unpopularity.F.SG.ACC
         'they mocked at our unpopularity' (Petr.)

      c. DIES   INTERMISSUS   AUT   NOX
         day.M.SG.NOM   suspended.M.SG.NOM or   night.F.SG.NOM
         INTERPOSITA   **SAEPE**   PERTURBAT **OMNIA**
         interrupted.F.SG.NOM often   disturbs   all.things.ACC
         'Often a day or night's delay disrupts everything' (Cic.)

      d. LIBENTER CAESAR   **PETENTIBUS**   **AEDUIS**   DAT   **UENIAM**
         freely   Caesar.NOM requesting.PL.ABL   Aedui.PL.ABL   gives pardon
         'Willingly Caesar, upon the request of the Aedui, grants the pardon' (Caes.)

Now, while such discontinuous structures within the nominal and verbal domains undoubtedly prove most frequent in early Latin and, in the classical period, in deliberately archaic styles or poetry (Leumann and Hofmann 1928:495; Marouzeau 1949:42; 1953:62; Ernout and Thomas 1953:162; Bauer 1995:131f.), Oniga (2004:101f.) nonetheless reports that they occur in all linguistic registers of all periods and, according to Vincent (1988a:54), even 'in mundane prose' and are hence 'not unrepresentative of ordinary usage'. A similar conclusion is reached by Herman (2000a:82), who calculates that the contiguity of noun and associated adjective is frequently interrupted in classical prose texts (about 30 percent of cases in Caesar and 15–20 percent of cases in the philosophical works of Cicero).[15] Consequently, it would be incorrect to dismiss discontinuous structures as a purely literary artifice, especially since typologically their presence is entirely consistent with the other types of positional freedom in the nominal and verbal groups witnessed above. Indeed, identical discontinuous patterns are far from uncommon in many of the world's non-configurational languages, even those that lack a written tradition, such that 'we must be on our guard against ruling out all poetic usage simply on the grounds that it is poetic' (Vincent 1988a:28).

To conclude, we have established that within the nominal and verbal domains there is no evidence for a fixed constituent structure: not only can the constituent parts of the nominal and verbal groups occur both to the left and to the right of their associated noun/verb, but that even such 'relaxed' contiguity is not a necessary condition, insofar as semantically dependent constituent parts can be scattered discontinuously across the group. Naturally, such positional freedom is afforded by the rich case and agreement inflections of the Latin nominal and verbal domains, which ensures that dependencies between all constituent parts, whatever their position and whether contiguous or not, are readily identified by their morphological shape and not exclusively, if at all, by linear syntactic arrangement. For this reason, we claim that the Latin nominal and verbal groups have a 'flat' or non-configurational structure, in which the various dependencies between the constituent parts of nominal and verbal structures such as 'an author of a great book' (namely SCRIPTOR 'author.M. NOM', MAGNI 'great.M.SG.GEN', LIBRI 'book.M.GEN') and '(he) wrote a great book' (namely SCRIPSIT 'he.wrote', MAGNUM 'great.M.SG.ACC', LIBRUM 'book.M.ACC') are not signalled by their respective positions, witness the grammaticality of just some of the possible permutations illustrated in (6a–d) and (7a–d).

(6)   a. SCRIPTOR MAGNI LIBRI
        b. SCRIPTOR LIBRI MAGNI
        c. MAGNI LIBRI SCRIPTOR
        d. MAGNI SCRIPTOR LIBRI

(7)   a. SCRIPSIT MAGNUM LIBRUM
        b. SCRIPSIT LIBRUM MAGNUM
        c. MAGNUM LIBRUM SCRIPSIT
        d. MAGNUM SCRIPSIT LIBRUM

Adopting a tree-based representation, it is not possible therefore to assign to the Latin nominal and verbal groups a hierarchically organized constituent structure based on the notions of precedence and dominance. Rather, the only representations possible are the corresponding 'flat' structures in (8a–d), in which all constituent parts are assigned equal status:[16]

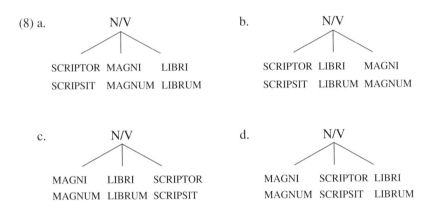

(8) a.   N/V

SCRIPTOR MAGNI   LIBRI
SCRIPSIT MAGNUM LIBRUM

b.   N/V

SCRIPTOR LIBRI MAGNI
SCRIPSIT LIBRUM MAGNUM

c.   N/V

MAGNI   LIBRI   SCRIPTOR
MAGNUM LIBRUM SCRIPSIT

d.   N/V

MAGNI   SCRIPTOR LIBRI
MAGNUM SCRIPSIT LIBRUM

3.1.2   Romance

As early as late Latin there is considerable evidence that the more flexible linearizations of the classical period were rapidly giving way to a more fixed ordering of the internal components of the nominal group and the verbal group.[17] This transferral of functional load from the morphological inflections of the constituent parts of the nominal group to the relative positions in which they occur is increasingly betrayed in late Latin texts in the weakening of agreement relations, with the consequence that '[m]ore and more we notice the use of a nominative inflection in an adjective or in a noun in apposition, which should strictly have the same inflection as the noun to which it is allied' (Herman 2000a:84; see also Väänänen 1974/1982:253f.). In the verbal domain, we witness a parallel growth in the generalized use of the accusative, the so-called extended accusative (see §6.2.2.1), to mark all nominals in addition to direct objects.[18] In the transition to Romance, this development is taken to its ultimate conclusion with the establishment of fully-fledged NP and VP structures, in which there is a one-to-one, isomorphic mapping between grammatical functions and dedicated syntactic positions.[19] In particular, the basic structure of the Romance NP and VP can be summarized by way of the linear templates in

(9a–b), where parentheses indicate optional elements and asterisks indicate possible recursion:

(9) a. NP: (DET) (QUANT) (*ADJ) N (*ADJ) (*PP)
     b. VP: (AUX) V (*ADV) (*OBJ) (*ADV)

However, the template is not simply linearly ordered, but is also subject to internal hierarchical ordering of its constituent parts. By way of example, consider the representative French NP in (10a) and its representation in (10b), which reveals, in contrast to the flat structure of Latin in (8a–d), a layered configurational constituent structure:

(10) a. *la   vieille   dame fatiguée   aux   lunettes   noires*
         the.F.SG old.F.SG lady.F tired.F.SG to-the.F.PL glasses.F.PL black.F.PL
         'the tired old lady with black glasses'

b.

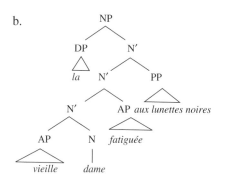

The nominal head *dame* 'lady' first combines directly with the prenominal adjectival phrase (AP) *vieille* 'old' to form the intermediate nominal constituent, here labelled as N' (namely [$_{N'}$ *vieille* [$_N$ *dame*]]). In turn, this newly created constituent combines with the postnominal AP *fatiguée* 'tired' to form an even larger intermediate constituent [$_{N'}$ [$_{N'}$ *vieille* [$_N$ *dame*]] *fatiguée*]. In turn, the PP adjunct *aux lunettes noires* 'with black glasses' combines with this newly formed N' constituent to form another intermediate constituent (namely [$_{N'}$ [$_{N'}$ [$_{N'}$ *vieille* [$_N$ *dame*]] *fatiguée*] [$_{PP}$ *aux lunettes noires*]]), which, once combined with the determiner phrase (DP) *la* 'the', which assigns a definite interpretation to the whole string, forms a semantically complete conceptual unit and hence an NP. Note that, in principle, it would be possible to have the nominal head first combine with the postnominal adjective and then, in turn, with the prenominal adjective (namely **[$_{N'}$ *vieille* [$_{N'}$ [$_N$ *dame*] *fatiguée*]]), but this possibility is ruled out, among other things (see below), for the reason that it would reverse the scope properties of both adjectives (incorrectly yielding the reading 'the old, tired lady', instead of 'the tired, old lady'). It is also interesting to note at this point that, although the relevant adjectives agree in gender (feminine) and number (singular), albeit only orthographically in some cases, with the nominal head, their differing degrees of syntactic cohesion with the latter are encoded, not by this residual agreement, but by their relative locality to the head. Consequently, we can say that the prenominal adjective *vieille* is a 'sister' to the nominal head *dame*, forming an intermediate N′ constituent which dominates both AP and N, whereas the postnominal adjective *fatiguée* is a sister to this latter intermediate N′ constituent.

Significantly, this representation highlights how, in the passage from Latin to Romance, the emergence of NP constituent structure gives rise to two dedicated adjectival positions, the prenominal position licensing given/non-contrastive readings and the postnominal position licensing new/contrastive readings.[20] Thus, in a sequence such as Sp. *una joven secretaria inteligente* lit. 'a young secretary intelligent (= an intelligent young secretary)', the secretary is identified by her intelligence and not her youthfulness, which is simply taken to be a known and, in this case, non-distinguishing quality of the individual concerned. Conversely, in the sequence *una inteligente secretaria joven* lit. 'an intelligent secretary young (= a young intelligent secretary)', the readings are reversed and we are talking about 'an intelligent secretary' about whom we want to convey that she is young.[21] Oversimplifying somewhat, the properties of the prenominal and postnominal positions of the adjective can be summarized as follows.[22] Contrary to what is claimed, at least in part (see discussion above in §3.1.1), for Latin, the prenominal position constitutes in Romance a marked position (Badia i Margarit 1962 I:150; Stati 1989:123; Ledgeway 2007a:105; Vincent 2007a:58f.), not only in terms of the specialized readings it licenses, but also in terms of its greater frequency in formal registers. Putting such considerations aside, however, we note that adjectives in prenominal/postnominal position typically correlate with the following respective interpretations: (i) inherent/non-inherent (e.g., Fr. *la blanche neige* 'white snow' vs. *la voiture blanche* 'the white car', It. *l'inglese eleganza* '(typical) English elegance' vs. *la moneta inglese* 'English currency', Sp. *su británica reserva* 'his British reserve' vs. *la Embajada británica* 'the British Embassy'); (ii) descriptive/distinguishing (e.g., Fr. *une courte lettre* 'a short letter' vs. *une jupe courte* 'a skirt that is short', It. *una vecchia scrivania* 'an old desk' vs. *una scrivania vecchia* 'a desk which is old'); (iii) subjective/objective (e.g., Cat. *(llunyanes) terres (llunyanes)* '(distant) lands', Vgl. *jójna biála béstia* 'a beautiful animal' vs. *un vestáit **bil*** 'a fine dress', Fr. *un (adorable) enfant (adorable)* 'a (charming) child', Ro. *un (formidabil) om (formidabil)* 'a (tremendous) person'; and (iv) figurative/literal (e.g., Cat. *la **grisa** quotidianitat* 'the grey (= dull) daily routine' vs. *la camisa **grisa*** 'the grey shirt', Pt. *um **antigo** patrão meu* 'an old (= former) boss of mine' vs. *Lisboa **antiga*** 'old Lisbon', Ro. *dulcele vis* 'the sweet dream' vs. *o cafea **dulce*** 'a sweet coffee').

As formalized in (10b) above, the two positions are also differentiated by their respective degree of integration with the nominal head, which in turn correlates with their differing degrees of semantic autonomy: whereas postnominal adjectives are semantically autonomous and enter into a looser structural relation with their noun, witness their ability to license the same readings in predicative function (e.g., Pt. *a rapariga **pobre*** 'the poor (= destitute) girl' = *a rapariga é pobre* 'the girl is poor'), prenominal adjectives enter into closer nexus with their associated noun, ultimately producing a marked reading only licensed in that particular configuration (e.g., *a **pobre** rapariga* 'the poor (= wretched) girl' ≠ *a rapariga é pobre*). It is for this reason that it has often been claimed that adjective + noun sequences behave like, and frequently correspond to, single lexemes or compound nouns (Gildersleeve and Lodge [1895] 1997:431; Radatz 2001: ch. 5; Ledgeway 2007a:114f.; Vincent 2007a:59): Cal. *mala parola* 'swear word' (cf. Cat. *renec*, Fr. *juron*, Sp. *taco*), Fr. *grand-mère* 'grandmother' (cf. It. *nonna*, Ro. *bunică*, Sp. *abuela*), Fr. *un petit pain* 'a (bread) roll' (cf. Cat. *panet*, It. *panino*, Pt. *pãozinho*), Nap./Sp. *bona fémmena/buena mujer* 'prostitute' (cf. Fr. *putain*, It. *puttana*), Fr./Pt. *petit déjeuner/pequeno almoço* (cf. Cat. *esmorzar*, It. *colazione*, Ro. *dejun*, Sp. *desayuno*). Above, this distinction was formally interpreted by treating prenominal adjectives on a par with complements insofar as they are generated as sisters to N, whereas postnominal adjectives are treated as adjuncts and generated as sisters to N′. This conclusion is further supported by the observation that the greater cohesion between prenominal adjective and noun gives rise to a number of phonomorphological processes of a strictly local nature. For instance, in French the prenominal adjectival position is one of the contexts in which *liaison* is still productive even in colloquial usage (Battye and Hintze 1992:140; Fagyal *et al.* 2006:67; e.g., *un lége*[ʁ] *incident* 'a slight incident'), and in Provençal (Wheeler 1988b:256f.; Lafont 1991:10) and many upper southern Italian dialects (Ledgeway 2007a:105–7) it is only the prenominal adjective which displays overt (plural) agreement (e.g., Prv. *aquest*[ej] *polid* [ej] *raub*[o] vs. *aquest*[ej] *raub*[o] *polid*[o] 'these (pretty) dresses (pretty)'; Nap. *brutti*[i] *cos*[ə] vs. *cos*[ə] *brutt*[ə] '(horrible) things (horrible)'). Similarly, Romance reflexes of BELLUS 'beautiful', BONUS 'good', GRANDIS 'big, great', MALUS 'evil' and SANCTUS 'saint, holy' commonly present apocopated forms in prenominal position (namely Fr., It. and Pt./Fr. *bel/ beau*, It./Sp. *buon/buen*, It. and Sp/Pt. *gran/grã(o)*, Sp. *mal* 'bad', It. and Sp./ Pt. *san/são*), morphophonological reductions which can now be straightforwardly derived from their status as sisters to N (e.g., Fr. *un beau souvenir* 'a fine memory', Pt. *bel-prazer* 'pleasure', It. *un buon ritorno* 'a pleasant return', Pt. *grã pressa* 'considerable haste', Sp. *un mal ingeniero* 'a bad engineer', *san Miguel* 'Saint Michael').

This structural distinction between pre- and postnominal adjectives equally proves essential in distinguishing between complements and adjuncts. Consider, for example, the Portuguese nominal and verbal sequences in (11a–c):

(11) a. um   estudante [PP *de física*]/ vai   estudando [NP *a   física*]
          a   student   of physics / he.goes studying   the physics

      b. um estudante [PP *de cabelo louro*]   / vai   estudando [NP *cada dia*]
          a   student   of hair   blond   / he.goes studing   each day

      c. um estudante [PP *de Lisboa*] / vai   estudando [PP *por causa do   prêmio*]
          a student   of Lisbon / he.goes studying   on account of.the prize

On the surface, the bracketed prepositional/nominal strings appear to be of equal status in that they all directly follow their nominal/verbal head. In (11a), however, the relevant PP/NP functions as the complement of the head *estudante/estudando* 'student/studying', whereas in (11b–c) the PPs/ NPs are optional modifiers of the nominal/verbal head, hence adjuncts. This difference can be seen in the grammaticality judgements associated with the strings in (12a–c), in which all three PPs and NPs are combined (and intonation is assumed to be neutral, excluding such marked processes as narrow focus and extraposition):

(12) a. um estudante[*de física*][*de cabelo louro*][*de Lisboa*]/ um estudante
          [*de física*][*de Lisboa*][*de cabelo louro*]

      a'. vai estudando[*a física*][*cada dia*][*por causa do prêmio*]/vai estudando
          [*a física*][*por causa do prêmio*][*cada dia*]

      b. **um estudante[*de cabelo louro*][*de física*][*de Lisboa*]/**um estudante
          [*de Lisboa*][*de física*][*de cabelo louro*]

      b'. **vai estudando[*cada dia*][*a física*][*por causa do prêmio*]/**vai estudando
          [*por causa do prêmio*][*a física*][*cada dia*]

      c. **um estudante[*de cabelo louro*][*de Lisboa*][*de física*]/**um estudante
          [*de Lisboa*][*de cabelo louro*][*de física*]

      c'. **vai estudando[*por causa do prêmio*][*cada dia*][*a física*]/**vai estudando
          [*cada dia*][*por causa do prêmio*][*a física*]

What these examples clearly illustrate is that complements like [*de física*] and [*a física*] enjoy a privileged position with respect to their selecting head, in that they combine directly with the latter to form an N'/V' constituent, hence the ungrammaticality of separating head and complement as in (12b–c). In contrast, adjuncts like [*de cabelo louro*], [*de Lisboa*] and [*cada dia*] and [*por causa do prêmio*] are less deeply embedded and as such are essentially unordered with respect to one another (12a, a'), attaching at the N'/V' level as illustrated in (13a–b):[23]

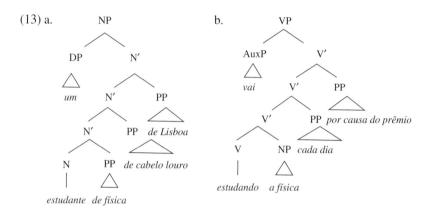

3.2   *The sentence*

3.2.1   Classical Latin

Traditional wisdom has it that in the transition from Latin to Romance sentential word order underwent a steady progression from SOV to SVO (Bauer 1995:7; Vincent 1997c:166; 2007a:65), 'a process already well under way in Latin' (Harris 1978:5).[24] On this view, word order in Latin is not absolutely free (*pace* Weil [1844] 1978:53f.), although enjoying considerably greater freedom than in Romance (Pinkster 1990:163; Bauer 1995:6), inasmuch as SOV order occurs with far greater statistical frequency than all other competing orders in most texts of the classical period (Hale and Buck [1903] 1994:§623; Linde 1923; Marouzeau 1938:106; Pinkster 1990:180, 187; Oniga 2004:97). Indeed, SOV order would appear to be a conservative feature of Latin syntax directly retraceable to Indo-European (Ernout and Thomas 1953:161; Lehmann 1972; 1974:114; Konneker 1975:367; Bauer 1995:86–89). The overall conclusion then is that SOV is the most frequent, hence unmarked, word order, but that all other orders are equally possible, although never entirely synonymous in that they convey some marked interpretation (Bauer 1995:6). This is essentially the view espoused by such scholars as Marouzeau (1922), Panhuis (1982), Pinkster (1990:181), Ostafin (1986), Vincent (1998:418f.), Oniga (2004:97) and Polo (2004), who see all orders other than SOV as the result of pragmatic factors and the organization of informational structure (e.g., OSV would be derived from SOV via topicalization of the object).

This view of Latin word order, though undoubtedly the most common, is not universally accepted (see Pinkster 1990:187f.). A number of scholars have claimed that Latin word order was essentially unstable (Ramat 1980:189), and that as early as Plautus SVO was already a frequent rival to SOV as the unmarked order, especially, though not exclusively, in lower and spoken registers (Lakoff 1968; Adams 1976; Panhuis 1982; Vineis 1993:LII–III; Oniga 2004:99). We have already seen above in §3.1.1 that, in the face of a frequent verb-medial position, many scholars have questioned the unmarked nature of the verb-final position, Herman (2000a:85) even arguing that the 'categorization of the language as basically having SOV order is exaggerated, even as regards the Classical language'. On this view, SOV as found in classical prose (notably in Caesar) and in formulaic inscriptions is often considered a more conservative and stylistic order with little or no relation to spoken usage, such that it is appropriate to speak of grammars in competition (Kroch 1989; Polo 2004). In this respect, it is often noted that one of the probable sources for the steady growth of unmarked SVO, alongside SOV, was complement clauses (Pinkster 1990:187; Oniga 2004:99): on account of their 'heavy' nature and concomitant perceptual complexity (Vincent 1976), preverbal complement clauses had already proved relatively infrequent in classical times (e.g., ARIOUISTUS UT CONLOQUERENTUR POSTULAUIT (Liv.) lit. 'Ariovistus, that they should enter into discussions, asked') and more frequently extraposed to a postverbal position (e.g., SENATUS DECREUIT UT CONSULE DUAS GALLIAS SORTIRENTUR (Cic.) 'the senate decreed that the two Gauls should be assigned arbitrarily by the consul'). Complement clauses thus provided a frequent context for SVO, readily reanalysed in time as a non-derived order.

Despite the differences in the two principal positions outlined above, the upshot is that, although one (SOV) or more (SOV, SVO) unmarked orders can be recognized, word order in Latin was nonetheless considerably free, albeit conditioned by pragmatic considerations. From this it follows that grammatical functions within the Latin sentence could not invariably, nor necessarily, be read off surface linear order but, rather, were typically identified by the morphological form of individual items. Thus, given a simple transitive sentence such as 'the boy calls the girl' (PUER 'boy.NOM', UOCAT 'calls', PUELLAM 'girl.ACC'), all six possible permutations are possible, namely SVO (PUER PUELLAM UOCAT), OSV (PUELLAM PUER UOCAT), SVO (PUER UOCAT PUELLAM), OVS (PUELLAM UOCAT PUER), VSO (UOCAT PUER PUELLAM) and VOS (UOCAT PUELLAM PUER). Once again it emerges that even in the domain of the sentence we are obliged to assume a flat structure, identical to that observed above in (8a–d) for the nominal and verbal groups:

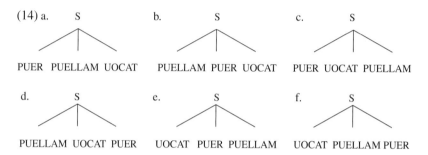

(14) a. S   b. S   c. S

PUER PUELLAM UOCAT   PUELLAM PUER UOCAT   PUER UOCAT PUELLAM

d. S   e. S   f. S

PUELLAM UOCAT PUER   UOCAT PUER PUELLAM   UOCAT PUELLAM PUER

Moreover, it is not always even possible to exhaustively identify one specific position within the sentence with a particular grammatical function. Not only can semantico–syntactic dependencies within the nominal and verbal groups be locally disrupted by placing logically contiguous elements in discontinuous positions within their group (e.g., MAGNAE UIR SAPIENTIAE great.F.SG.GEN man.NOM knowledge.F.SG.GEN ('a man of great knowledge'), BIBERE UOLO AQUAM drink.INF I.want water.ACC ('I want to drink some water')), but entire groups can be broken up and given discontinuous expression globally across the sentence.[25] For example, in (15a) the subject of the sentence 'the radiant Zephyrs' does not form a single syntactic phrase but is realized partly before the verb (CANDIDI 'radiant') and partly following the verb (FAUONII 'Zephyrs'), therefore making it impossible to talk about a (single) subject position. Analogous considerations carry over to the examples in (15b–d), where the elements that make up the (in)direct object argument are scattered discontinuously across the sentence, including, in the case of (15c–d), at the beginning (MEO, TUAM) and at the end (SERUO, UOLUNTATEM) of their clause. Particularly illustrative of the difficulty in identifying canonical argument positions are the two final examples, where the constituent parts of the subject and object arguments (see 15e) and the subject and locative arguments (see 15f) are intertwined and blended discontinuously among themselves.

(15) a. QUEM   TIBI   **CANDIDI**   PRIMO
       who.M.SG.ACC   you.DAT   radiant.NOM.PL   first.NEUT.SG.ABL
       RESTITUENT   UERE   **FAUONII...**   BEATUM
       return.3PL   spring.NEUT.ABL   Zehpyrs.NOM   happy.M.SG.ACC
       'Whom the radiant Zephyrs will give back to you happy ... at the beginning of the spring' (Hor.)

     b. HIC **OPTIMUS**   ILLIS   TEMPORIBUS EST **PATRONUS**   HABITUS
       he   best.M.SG.NOM those.ABLtimes.ABL is   lawyer.NOM   had
       'In those days he was considered the best lawyer' (Cic.)

     c. DEDI ... SYMBOLUM   SERUO   TUO ...   EPISTULAM...:
       I-gave symbol.NEUT.ACC   servant.M.DAT   your.M.SG.DAT   letter.F.ACC
       MEO   TU   EPISTULAM   DEDISTI   **SERUO?**
       my.M.SG.DAT   you   letter.F.ACC   you-gave   servant.M.DAT
       'I gave ... a token to your slave ... a letter: To *my* slave you gave a letter?' (Pl.)

     d. NONSATIS   CREDIDI,   **TUAM,**   HOMINIS   PRUDENTIS,   TAM
       not enough I.believed your.F.SG.ACC   man.GEN   prudent.M.SG.GEN   so
       UALDE   ESSE   MUTATAM   **UOLUNTATEM**
       great be.INF   changed.F.SG.ACC   intention.F.SG.ACC
       'I could not believe that you, as a prudent man, had so radically changed your intention' (Cic.)

     e. **AMISSOS**   LONGO   **SOCIOS**   SERMONE   REQUIRUNT
       lost.ACC   long.F.SG.ABL   companions.ACC   call.F.SG.ABL   they.search
       'they search for their lost companions with long calls' (Verg.)

     f. **GRANDIA**   PER   MULTOS   TENUANTUR ¯UMINA
       great.NEUT.PL.NOM   through   many.M.PL.ACC   are-
       reduced   rivers.NEUT.NOM
       RIUOS
       brooks.ACC
       'Great streams are channelled into many brooks' (Ov.)

Strong empirical evidence such as this highlights how it makes little sense to posit the existence of phrasal lexical categories like NP, AP, AdvP and VP in Latin, inasmuch as the elements that would conceptually make up these phrases need not cluster in cohesive groups but, rather, are free to occur individually in discontinuous strings across the sentence, ultimately bound together by their forms (inflection, agreement) rather than by means of word groups. This view is further substantiated by examples like those in (16a–d) below:

(16) a. **HUIC**   **EGO**   **ME**   **BELLO**
this.NEUT.SG.DAT   I   myself.ACC   war.NEUT.DAT
DUCEM   **PROFITEOR**
leader.M.SG.ACC   I.announce
'for this war I announce myself as leader' (Cat.)

b. **MAGNO**   **ME**   **METU**   **LIBERABIS**
great.M.SG.ABL   me.ACC   fear.M.ABL   you.will.free
'you will relieve me of great fear' (Cat.)

c. **PER**   **EGO**   **HAS**   **LACRIMAS**   **TE**   **ORO**
through   I   these.F.PL.ACC   tears.F.ACC   you.ACC   I.pray
'by these tears I beseech you' (Verg.)

d. **DE**   **CIUITATIS**   **ENIM**   **IURE ...**   **DISCEPTAMUS**
regarding   city.F.GEN   for   law.F.ABL ...   we.discuss
'For we are discussing civil law' (Cic.)

The underlined elements of the four sentences above illustrate the Wackernagel tendency of Latin weak pronouns and particular connectors (e.g., ENIM 'for', AUTEM 'however', UERO 'indeed') to occur in the second position of the clause (Hale and Buck [1903] 1994:§627; Ernout and Thomas 1953:161; Pinkster 1990:164; Vincent 1998:420–42; Salvi 2004; this volume, chapter 7: §3.4.8), sometimes in groups as in (16a) and sometimes even in the third position if monosyllables precede (see 16d). Significantly, such sentences reveal that, in computing second position, the Wackernagel rule does not necessarily make reference to word groups (cf., however, examples like **AD MORTEM** TE, CATILINA, CONSUL ET SENATUS DUCERE DEBENT (Cic.) 'to **(your) death** you, Catilina, the consul and senate must lead (you)'), but simply to individual words. This explains why the relevant Wackernagel elements in (16a–d) can split up what would otherwise be a contiguous nominal or prepositional group, since the syntax of the language is essentially not sensitive to such groups.[26]

3.2.2 Late Latin and Romance

Contrary to what was noted above for the nominal and verbal groups, which already display early yet significant signs of an emergent configurational structure in late Latin with the increasing contiguity and rigidification of their constituent parts, the sentence continues to exhibit considerable freedom even in the late Latin period (Herman 2000a:85–87), although verb-final orders are now very much diminished (Muldowney 1937: 120–28; Adams 1976; 1977; Bauer 1995:98–102), accounting for as little as 30 percent, for example, in the fifth-century *Peregrinatio Aetheriae* (Linde

1923; Harris 1978:19; Väänänen 1987:106). Such continued freedom in the positioning of the subject and object was no doubt made possible by the survival of core case inflections which, even after the start of the decline of case morphology in the late Latin period, remained distinct in the nominative and accusative for a number of centuries (witness their survival in early Gallo-Romance; see §6.2.2.2; and see Smith, this volume, chapter 6: §2.2; Sornicola, this volume, chapter 1: §3.1).[27] On this point, Herman (2000a:86) perceptively concludes that '[s]tatistically, the characteristic feature of late Latin texts seems to be to have the verb between the two noun phrases if two are there (including prepositional phrases) – that is, either SVO or OVS. Both these orders seem to have gained ground statistically since Classical times, and in some texts they form the clear majority.'

Significantly, it is precisely this predominant verb-medial order identified above by Herman for late Latin that, under the more usual label of Verb Second (V2), has been frequently claimed to constitute the transitional phase between an original Latin SOV order and the modern Romance SVO order (Harris 1978:20f.; Renzi 1985:267–75; Vincent 1988a:62; 1998:422f.). This V2 syntax is particularly well preserved in medieval varieties, especially, though not exclusively, in Gallo-Romance and Raeto-Romance (where it survives to the present day in Swiss varieties and in Ladin spoken in the province of Bolzano; Haiman 1988:368f.; Haiman and Benincà 1992:167–75).[28] During this V2 stage, sentences consist of two principal parts (see 17a), a sentential core with fixed S V O ADV order, and a left edge consisting of a COMP(lementizer) position to which the finite verb is raised in root clauses (see §3.3.3.1 below, and Salvi, this volume, chapter 7: §3.4.9), where it is preceded by one or more elements fronted from the sentential core to be assigned a pragmatically salient (Foc(us), Top(ic)) reading. In embedded clauses, by contrast, the left edge generally hosts an overt COMP and the finite verb is forced to remain within the sentential core, yielding the order S+V+O+ADV (see 17b). Thus, as the following representative early Romance examples demonstrate, alongside S +V+X (see 17c) we also frequently find in main clauses O+V(S) (see 17d), IO+V(S) (see 17e), O_{PP}+V(S) (see 17f) and ADV+V(S) (see 17g):

(17) a. [Top / Foc V [S t_V O ADV]]
    b. ...[COMP [S V O ADV]]
    c. [*Lo cavaliere* *prese* [$t_{Lo\ cavaliere}$ t_{prese} *i marchi*]]
       the knight took the marks (OTsc. *Novellino*)
    d. [*Autre chose* *ne* *pot* [*li roi* $t_{ne\ pot}$ *trouver* $t_{autre\ chose}$]]
       other thing not could the king find.INF
       'the king could not find anything else' (OFr. *Mort le Roi Artu*)

e. [*A questo*   *responsse*   [*Iasone* t*responsse* t*a questo*]]
   to this   replied   Jason
   'Jason replied to this' (ONap. *Libro de la destructione de Troya*, De
   Blasi 1986)

f. [*D'alguñas*   *cousas* me   *calarei* [t*me calarei* t*d'alguñas cousas*]]
   of.some   things   myself=I-shall-remain-quiet
   'I shall remain silent about certain matters' (OPt. *Diálogos de São
   Gregório*)

g. [*Molt* se maravellà   [*tota la*   *gent* t*se maravellà* t*molt*   *de*   *la*   *gran*   *humilitat*]]
   much   self=marvelled all   the   people   of   the   great   humility
   'All the people were very surprised at their great humility' (OCat.
   Ramon Llull)

Examples like these illustrate an early stage in the passage from Latin to postmedieval Romance: as in Latin, word order is free, though pragmatically conditioned, in the left edge, but is fixed, as in modern Romance, within the sentential core. Similarly, although pragmatic fronting to the left edge generally targets entire phrases as in (17c–g), a hallmark of a configurational Romance-style syntax, it can also frequently target individual elements of a given phrase, a hallmark of a non-configurational Latin-style syntax, yielding discontinuous structures (e.g., ONap. *ma **multo plu** me reputo **gloriuso** …* 'but **much more** I consider myself **glorious** (= much more glorious)'; see Poletto 2005a:210f.; 2005b; in press; Ledgeway 2007b:126–28; 2009: §21.1.2.2.2). The emergence of a late Latin / early Romance V2 syntax clearly represents the outcome of an unmistakable compromise between two competing grammars, combining aspects of an earlier non-configurational syntax on the one hand and aspects of an innovative configurational syntax on the other. Eventually the new configurational pattern comes to prevail: on account of the high frequency of subject fronting to the sentential left edge as the default topic within the older V2 system, preverbal subjects are progressively reanalysed as occupying a non-derived position within the sentential core (namely [$_\text{left periphery}$ S$_\text{Topic}$ V$_\text{finite}$ [$_\text{Core}$ t$_\text{S}$ t$_\text{V}$ X]] $\Rightarrow$ [$_\text{left periphery}$ Ø [$_\text{Core}$ S V$_\text{finite}$ X]]). The result is the unmarked SV(O) order of modern Romance, where all but UNDERGOER subjects are now associated with, and licensed in, a dedicated position within the configurational structure of the sentential core (e.g., Pt. *o **João** abriu a janela* 'João opened the window' vs. *abriu-se **a janela*** lit. 'opened=itself the window').[29] In many Gallo-Romance varieties grammaticalization of this subject position has run its full course, such that even UNDERGOER subjects are now attracted to the preverbal position (e.g., Fr. ***Jean** a ouvert la fenêtre* vs. ***la fenêtre** s'est ouverte*), thereby erasing an earlier reflex of an active/stative distinction (see §6.3).

Oversimplifying somewhat and putting aside some minor exceptions, Romance sentential word order can be said then to have converged in the modern languages towards a predominantly SVO order (e.g., Ro. *Ana a rezolvat problema* 'Ana has solved the problem'), in which the grammatical functions of subject and object are unambiguously marked by their respective positions to the left and the right of the verb.[30] In short, the Romance sentence provides dedicated positions for the verb, its arguments and any accompanying adjuncts, whose fundamental structure can be summarized according to the following linear template: S (AUX) V (*ADV) (O) (IO) (*ADV). Given this configurational structure of the sentence, in which the subject in its preverbal position hierarchically dominates the object in its more deeply embedded postverbal position, there follow a whole series of subject–object asymmetries often absent from non-configurational languages (Lyons 1999:154). For instance, a reflexive anaphor can be an object whose reference is controlled by a preceding subject (e.g., Sp. [*Ana*]ᵢ *crítica [a sí misma]*ᵢ 'Ana criticizes herself'), but it cannot be a subject referentially controlled by an object (e.g., **[*sí misma*]ᵢ *crítica [a Ana]*ᵢ 'herself criticizes Ana'). In Latin, by contrast, which we have argued lacks hierarchical constituent structure, subject and object do not enter into an asymmetrical relation of dominance and precedence at the structural level. Consequently, as Vincent (1997c:163) highlights, the Latin reflexive anaphor may precede its antecedent (see also Bertocchi 1989), as in the Plautine example [SUUS]ᵢ REX [REGINAE]ᵢ PLACET 'her king is pleasing to the queen'. If we were to assume a configurational structure of this Latin sentence, it would be impossible for the possessive anaphor SUUS 'her' from the higher subject position to be bound by its dative object antecedent REGINAE 'to the queen' situated in its more deeply embedded position. Similar considerations apply to control structures where an anaphoric implicit subject (here represented as Ø) can precede its antecedent (e.g., in Plautus [Ø]ᵢ REDDERE HOC, NON PERDERE ERUS [ME]ᵢ MISIT '[Ø]ᵢ return.INF this not lose.INF master [me]ᵢ sent' ('my master sent me to pay this back, not to lose it')). Evidence like this suggests that the correct interpretation of (Latin) anaphors cannot be simply read off surface syntactic structures, but follows from predication relations mapped between functional and constituent structures (Bresnan 2001:7–10; Mereu 2004:137–39).

A further indication of the emergence of subject–object asymmetries in the development of Romance comes from the way the deictics IPSE and ILLE have become associated with subjects and objects. On this point, Vincent (1997c) convincingly demonstrates how the definite article was originally limited to marking subject NPs (or, more generally, external arguments) via the grammaticalization of topics (hence the sources of the Romance article ILLE, originally a first-mention cataphor, and IPSE a second-mention anaphoric topic marker), whereas object NPs frequently occurred without an article, even when fully individuated. On the other hand, objects (or, more generally, internal arguments) came to be marked by clitics, which, by virtue of being prosodically weak, were not suited to marking informationally prominent referents and incompatible with the topic-marking value of IPSE.

3.3   Functional categories

As a concomitant of the emergence of hierarchical constituent structure in the nominal, verbal and sentential domains, we have seen how the left edge of the phrase in all three cases provides for a dedicated position for functional elements, namely D(eterminers), AUX(iliaries) and COMP(lementizers), the latter also hosting the finite verb in V2 contexts. This reflects the traditional intuition popularized within the synthesis–analysis approach that highlights the emergence in Romance of articles and clitics, auxiliaries and a whole host of finite and non-finite complementizers, all generally absent from Latin. In current theory, grammatical elements of this type are generally considered to head their own functional projections, namely DP, I(inflectional)P and CP, which represent the locus of grammatical information relating to the nominal group, verbal group and the sentence, respectively. On this view, one of the most significant generalizations of the traditional synthesis–analysis approach can now be elegantly and simply rephrased in terms of the emergence of the functional categories DP, IP and CP and eventual splits thereof (Vincent 1997a:105; 1997c:149; Lyons 1999:322f.), which were either entirely absent from Latin (e.g., DP, IP) or only present in incipient form (e.g., CP).

3.3.1   The DP

3.3.1.1   The indefinite article
The clearest evidence for the rise of DP structure in Romance comes from the universal appearance in all Romance varieties of the indefinite and definite articles. The former continues a weakened form of the Latin numeral for 'one' UNUM/-AM (> e.g., Cat./It./Sp. *un/una*, Fr. *un/une*, Pt. *um/uma*, Ro. *un/o*), and in some varieties now formally contrasts with the numeral for 'one' (e.g., Cal. *unu/una guagliune/-a* 'one boy/girl' vs. *nu/na guagliune/-a* 'a boy/girl'). Plural forms from UNOS/-AS (see also Bauer, this

volume, chapter 10: §3.2.1), best considered indefinite quantifiers rather than plural articles given that, unlike the corresponding singular articles, they generally prove optional (e.g., Cat. *vaig comprar (unes) taronjes* 'I bought (some) oranges'), are found in Ibero-Romance (Cat. *uns/unes xicots/xicotes* 'some boys/girls', Pt. *uns/umas senhores/senhoras* 'some men/women', Sp. *unos/unas socios/socias* 'some partners (M/F)') and, until the sixteenth century, also in French (viz. *uns/unes*), where they were principally employed with collective plurals (Price 1971:120): *uns guanz* '(a pair of) gloves', *unes brayes* '(a pair of) breeches', *unes joes* '(a pair of) cheeks', *uns ciseaulx* '(a pair of) scissors', *uns gran dens* '(a set/mouth of) large teeth'). It is these *pluralia tantum* that most frequently, though not exclusively, select the plural form of the indefinite article in Occitan varieties (Wheeler 1988b:260; Lafont 1991:9): *unis esclòps* '(a pair of) clogs', *unas cauças* '(a pair of) trousers', *uns caçaires* 'some huntsmen'. In Romanian, the plural form is only available in the dative/genitive, namely UNORUM > *unor*, with a zero form or the lexical quantifier *nişte* 'some' being employed in all other cases (e.g., *o să scriu (nişte) scrisori unor prieteni* 'I'll write (some) letters to some friends'). More rarely, in the nominative/accusative the articulated plural forms *unii/unele* are found, although in such cases the determiner is stressed (e.g., UNII ENGLEZI ŞTIU PUŢIN ROMÂNEŞTE 'SOME English people know a little Romanian').

Contrary to the early emergence and grammaticalization of the definite article, whose origins, albeit at first as an 'articloid', have been traced back to as early as between the third and eighth centuries AD (Lyons 1999:333), the indefinite article emerges much later in Romance and its usage does not become systematic in most Romance varieties until around the fourteenth century (Rohlfs 1968:38f.; Pozas-Loyo 2008; Maiden 1995a:121; 1998c:131). Before then, the use of the indefinite article is usually reserved for particularized new referents, presumably a residue of its numeral origin, whereas a bare NP is still generally employed for non-particularized referents (Price 1971:118f.; Lapesa 1974:453; Elvira 1994; Parry and Lombardi 2007:91f.; Pozas-Loyo 2008). For example, in the eleventh-century French text *Vie de St Alexis*, the article is not employed in the prayer of a desperate childless couple in their request to God, **Enfant** *nos done* 'Give us (a) child', since the meaning of the NP is 'any child'. When, however, God blesses them with a child, this is reported with the use of the indefinite article, namely **Un fi** *lor donet* 'He gives them a son', since the NP now picks out a specific individual (although the article could still be omitted even in such cases of high individuation, witness the following line from the same text: **Bel nom** *li mistrent* '(A) fine name they gave him'). This early restriction on the distribution of the indefinite article is clearly revealed in the following examples, where the modern Romance translation or equivalent would now require the use of the article: *Veïz tu **home** qui me puist resambler?* 'Have you seen (a) man who might resemble me?' (Fr., *Ami et Amile*), *donami **kavallo** da cavalcare* 'give me (a) horse to ride' (Tsc., *Novellino*), ***Grande duelo** avien las yentes cristianas* 'the Christian people felt (a) great sorrow' (Sp., *Cid*), ***Mal conselh** donet Pilat* 'Pilate gave (a) bad piece of advice' (Occ., *Venjansa*). Indeed, relics of this early usage still abound in the modern languages in proverbs and fixed expressions such as Ast. *(ta) en coche* '(he is) in (the) car', *(ponlo) en suelu* '(put it) on (the) floor'; Fr. *rendre **service*** 'to do (a) favour', *prêter **serment*** 'to swear (an) oath', *à **cheval*** 'on (a) horse', *sous **clef*** 'under (a) lock and key'; It. *portare **giudizio*** 'to pronounce (a) judgement', *aver **fame*** 'to be hungry (lit. to have hunger)', *in **mano*** 'in one's hand', *in **carrozza*** 'in (a) carriage'; Occ. *aver **fam*** 'to be hungry', *cantar **messa*** 'to sing (a) mass'; Sp. *sentirse como **pez** en el agua* 'to feel like (a) fish in water', *con **mujer nueva*** 'with (a) new wife', *querer por **esposa*** 'to want/take for (a) wife', *tener **dolor de cabeza*** 'to have (a) headache'. In the modern languages, by contrast, indefinite NPs, whether particularized or not (witness the indicative/subjunctive alternation in the following example), now generally require the article (e.g., Cat. *busco **una minyona** que em neteja* (IND)/*netegi* (SBJV) *la casa* 'I am looking for a maid that cleans/to clean the house for me').

3.3.1.2 The definite article

Turning now to the definite article (see Vincent 1997c; 1998; Zamboni 2000:115–18), this continues a weakened form of the Latin distal demonstrative ILLE 'that' (> Cat./Sp. *el/la*, Fr./Occ. *le/la*, It. *il/la*, Pt./SIt. dials *o/a*, Ro. *-(u)l/-a*) or the Latin intensifier IPSE 'same, -self', now with a limited areal distribution (> Bal./Costa Brava Cat. *es/sa*, Srd. *su/sa*) but in the past much more widely attested, including Gascon, Languedoc, the Alps and large areas of southern Italy (Aebischer 1948:193; Ravier 1991:89; Rohlfs 1968:112).[31] As is well known (Väänänen 1987; Renzi 1985:144–47; Nocentini 1990; Vincent 1997c; 1998), in many late Latin texts both ILLE and IPSE, the latter especially in areas of southern Romània (Vincent 1997c:154), frequently occur in contexts in which their spatial deictic function is considerably weakened,[32] and their principal role appears to be one of marking nothing more than definiteness, a precursor to the modern article which Aebischer (1948) famously terms an 'articloid'. Traditionally, then, the principal question has been whether the latter is a demonstrative with a much increased frequency (Herman 2000a:84f.) or indeed an article, but with a still limited range of use (Lyons 1999:333). Clearly, there are elements of truth in both positions, which should not be seen as mutually exclusive solutions to the question, but simply as the start and the end points in an unresolved and ongoing process of grammaticalization. In terms of their distribution, Renzi (1976), Selig (1992) and Zamboni (2000:116) argue that IPSE was predominantly used anaphorically in conjunction with second-mention items (hence largely equivalent to 'the aforementioned', e.g., from the *Peregrinatio Aetheriae*: MONTES ILLI ... FACIEBANT UALLEM INFINITAM INGENS, PLANISSIMA ET UALDE PULCHRAM ... UALLIS AUTEM IPSA INGENS EST UALDE 'the mountains ... formed an endless **valley**, huge, very flat and very beautiful ... **The** (= aforementioned) **valley** is indeed truly huge'), whereas ILLE could be used both anaphorically with second-mention items, as well as cataphorically with first-mention items including, for example, restrictive relatives (e.g., *Peregrinatio Aetheriae*: MONTES ILLI, INTER QUOS IBAMUS, APERIEBANT '**the mountains**, between which we were going, opened out'). To this picture we can add, following Vincent (1997c), that IPSE, unlike ILLE, performed a topic-marking function, only picking out informationally prominent second-mention items (hence an unsuitable candidate for the object clitic paradigm).

In early Romance the definite article displays considerable attenuation of its original deictic force, in that reflexes of ILLE and IPSE in their article function no longer situate a referent negatively with regard to the deictic sphere of the speech act participants (ILLE) or positively with regard to the deictic sphere of the addressee(s) (IPSE), but increasingly come to mark shared cognition between speaker(s) and addressee(s). Nonetheless, the article still retained considerable identifying force, as witnessed by the fact that in early texts it is generally excluded with unique, abstract and generic referents (Parry and Lombardi 2007:83f.) which, by definition, cannot be singled out (e.g., Fr. *Paien unt tort e chrestïens unt dreit* 'Pagans are wrong and Christians are right' (*Chanson de Roland*); Gsc. *leichatz estar ypocresie. Pocresie es tant a dire cum fengir de Diu amar* 'Let hypocrisy be. Hypocrisy is like pretending to love God' (*Disciplina clericalis*); Tsc. *giustizia mosse il mio alto fattore* 'Justice moved my lofty maker' (*Inferno*); Sp. *De qui crebanta camino del rey* 'About those who commit assaults on the highway of the king' (*Los fueros de la Novenera*)). In a number of cases, this early usage has been fossilized in the modern languages in proverbs and certain set expressions (e.g., Cat. *carrer amunt/avall* 'up/down (the) street', *nedar dins mar* 'to swim in (the) sea', *parar/desparar taula* 'to lay/clear (the) table'; Fr. *noblesse oblige, pauvreté n'est pas vice* 'poverty is not a vice', *blanc comme neige* 'white as snow', *fermer boutique* 'to shut up shop', *par terre* 'on (the)

Table 8.1 *Forms of article with proper names in Catalan*

	Standard Catalan		Substandard Catalan		Balearic Catalan	
	M	F	M	F	M	F
+C	*en Joan*	*la Joana*	*el Joan*	*la Joana*	*en Joan*	*na Joana*
+V	*l'Eduard*	*l'Alícia*	*l'Eduard*	*l'Alícia*	*n'Eduard*	*n'Alícia*

floor'; It. *cosa fatta capo ha* 'what's done is done (lit. **thing** done **head** has)', *gatta ci cova* 'something's up (lit. **cat** is brooding over it)', *in giardino* 'in the **garden**'; Sp. *gato escaldado del agua fría huye* 'once bitten twice shy (lit. scalded **cat** flees from cold water)', *Ausencias causan olvido* 'long absent, soon forgotten (lit. **absences** cause **oblivion**)', *en camino* 'on (the) **road**', *en dicho mes* 'in (the) said **month**').

In the modern languages, by contrast, shared cognition between speaker(s) and addressee(s) has come to assume increasing importance in the selection of the article, such that if a referent can be considered to form part of the interlocutors' common universe of experience, then the article is employed. Thus, the article is now generally required with unique, abstract and generic referents (e.g., Cat. *la vida i la mort* 'life and death', *els gats i les rates són animals* 'cats and rats are animals'; Ro. *îmi plac florile* 'I like flowers', *dreptatea este lumina vieții* 'justice is the light of life'), as well as with inalienable possessa (e.g., Fr. *je m'étais cassé la jambe* 'I had broken my leg', It. *Ida ha perso il portafogli* 'Ida has lost her purse') and proper names. The latter, which are by definition intrinsically referential, include non-modified countries (though generally not in Spanish and, to varying degrees, in Catalan (Wheeler *et al.* 1999:57), e.g., Sp. *España linda con Portugal y Francia* 'Spain shares borders with Portugal and France'), large islands, lakes, rivers and mountains (e.g., Pt. *o Brasil*, (but *Portugal* without the article), *a Madeira* '(the island of) Madeira', *o Titicaca* 'lake Titicaca', *o Tejo* 'the Tagus', *os Andes* 'the Andes'), as well as, in some areas, first names (e.g., Cat. *l'Artur*, *la Carme*; CNIt. *la Francesca* (but not with male names: *Francesco*), Occ. *lo Pèire*; EuPt. *o Armando*, *a Marinha*; Sal. *'u Francu*, *'a Paola*). Catalan, though not Valencian (e.g., *ha vingut Maria* 'Maria has arrived'), has moved the furthest in this direction (Wheeler *et al.* 1999:67f.), having developed a specialized paradigm (see Table 8.1) which, in the standard language, blends ILLE-derived forms (female names, vowel-initial male names) with a reflex of DOMINUS > *en* (consonant-initial male names),[33] but in the colloquial language, especially in the north-western dialects, often extends ILLE forms to the whole masculine paradigm (Badia i Margarit 1962 I:158; 1995:446f.; Veny

Table 8.2 *Catalan articles derived from* IPSE

	Costa Brava				Balearic Islands			
	M.SG	M.PL	F.SG	F.PL	M.SG	M.PL	F.SG	F.PL
+C	*es*	*es*	*sa*	*ses*	*es*	*es*	*sa*	*ses*
+V	*s'*	*ses*	*s'*	*ses*	*s'*	*e(t)s*[34]	*s'*	*ses*
amb 'with' +					*so*	*sos*	*sa*	*ses*

1998:36, 95). In Balearic varieties, by contrast, forms derived from DOMINUS/
DOMINA are extended to the whole paradigm (Veny 1998:67).

Catalan is also of interest in that the varieties spoken in the Balearics and
in some areas of the mainland (principally in and around Cadaqués, with
some receding pockets to the south along the Costa Brava between the Ter
and Tordera rivers) combine and productively contrast reflexes of both IPSE,
the so-called *article salat* (cf. *salar* 'to use the *sa* form of the article'), and ILLE
(see Table 8.2).[35]

While both forms have definite reference, only the former has truly
deictic force and is able to identify both anaphorically and cataphorically
definite referents (e.g., Maj. *la fan pujar damunt sa mula* 'they make her get
on **the** mule', *tu éts sa dona que jo vaig tirar anita passada per aquesta finestra?*
'Are you **the** lady that I threw out of this window last night?'), whereas the
latter is confined to marking unique referents, hence already fully identifiable (e.g., *el dimoni* 'the devil', *el rei* 'the king', *la reina* 'the queen', *el Papa*
'the pope', *el Bon Jesús* 'the Christ child', *la Mare de Déu* 'the mother of God
(= Virgin Mary)', *la Cúria* 'the Curia', *el cel* 'the sky', *l'infern* 'Hell', *el
purgatori* 'Purgatory', *la mar* 'the sea', *la terra* 'the earth', *la una* 'one
o'clock', *la vera creu* 'the true cross').[36] In a number of contexts, one can
therefore construct minimal pairs based around this [±deictic] contrast (e.g.,
Bal. *la Sala* 'the town hall' vs. *sa sala* 'the large (public) room', *pensam en la
mort* 'we're thinking of death' vs. *sa mort d'en Joan* 'Joan's death', *l'Església*
'the (institution of the) Church' vs. *s'església del poble* 'the village church', *el
món* 'the world' vs. *es meu món és sa música* 'music is my world', *el bisbe* 'the
Bishop (of Majorca)' vs. *tots es bisbes de Mallorca* 'all the (past) bishops of
Majorca').

To sum up, the DP can be seen to provide the relevant (in)definiteness
marking of its associated NP,[37] as illustrated in the simplified representation
of the Spanish example in (18a), and in some languages such as French (see
18b), where original final inflections for number and gender on nouns and
adjectives have been drastically eroded, the accompanying determiner is not

simply a spell-out of (in)definiteness, but is now also a quasi obligatory element of the nominal group as the sole exponent, in most cases, of number and gender:[38]

(18) a.   b.

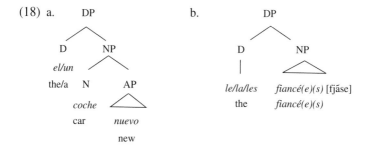

Even Romanian readily fits into this same pattern.[39] It displays a suffixal definite article (e.g., *fiu* 'son' + **-ul/-lui** > *fiul/fiului* 'son=the.NOM–ACC/=the.DAT–GEN', *fii* 'sons' + **-i/-lor** > *fiii/fiilor* 'sons=the.NOM–ACC/=the.DAT–GEN', *casă* 'house' + **-a/-ei** > *casa/casei* 'house=the.NOM–ACC/=the.DAT–GEN', *case* 'houses' + **-le/-lor** > *casele/caselor* 'houses=the.NOM–ACC/=the.DAT–GEN'), but a prenominal indefinite article (e.g., **un** *fiu* 'a son', **o** *casă* 'a house'). More specifically, we can assume that, as a suffixal element, the Romanian definite article must incorporate with an appropriate head to form a well-formed word (see Grosu 1988; 1994; Cornilescu 1992; Giusti 1993; 1997:102–06; 2002:57–70; Motapanyane 2000:3f., 8), be that a nominal head (**fiul** *bun* 'son=the good'; see 19a) or an adjectival head (**bunul** *fiu* 'good=the son'; see 19b) raised from within the NP to adjoin to the D position (*fiu* 'son', *bun* 'good', *-(u)l* 'the'):

(19) a.   b.

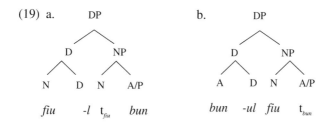

3.3.1.3   Other determiners

With the rise of the DP, other categories with determiner-like properties which in Latin had adjectival status are attracted to the D position. The

Table 8.3 *Tonic / Clitic possessive paradigms*

	Spanish		Occitan		Catalan		Romanian	
	Tonic	Clitic	Tonic	Clitic	Tonic	Clitic	Tonic	Clitic
1SG	*mío*	*mi*	*mieu*	*mo(n)*	*meu*	*mon*	*meu*	*mu*
2SG	*tuyo*	*tu*	*tieu*	*to(n)*	*teu*	*ton*	*tău*	*tu*
3SG	*suyo*	*su*	*sieu*	*so(n)*	*seu*	*son*	*său*	*su*
1PL	*nuestro*	*nuestro*	*nòstre*	–	*nostre*	–	*nostru*	–
2PL	*vuestro*	*vuestro*	*vòstre*	–	*vostre*	–	*vostru*	–
3PL	*suyo*	*su*	*sieu*	*so(n)*	*seu*	*son*	*lor*	–

main categories involved here are two, namely demonstratives and possessives. In both cases we find that some Romance varieties preserve two complementary paradigms, one related to the adjective and the other to the determiner. For example, in Catalan, Occitan, Romanian and Spanish, demonstratives canonically behave like determiners, lexicalizing the prenominal D position and hence in complementary distribution with the definite article. However, their original adjectival status has not been entirely jettisoned in these same varieties, inasmuch as they may still occur in the canonical postnominal adjectival position (typically with a pejorative reading in Ibero-Romance and Occitan, but with an emphatic reading in Romanian), in which case the D position is filled with the definite article (see 20a–d). In other varieties such as Portuguese and Italian (see 20e), by contrast, only the determiner use of the demonstrative is attested:

(20) a. **aquestes** / *aquelles opinions* vs. **les** *opinions* **aquestes** / *aquelles* (Cat.)
        these   / those opinions   the opinions these   / those

    b. **aqueste** / *aquel* **brave òme** vs. **lo** *brave òme* **aqueste** / *aquel* (Occ.)
        this   / that   good man   the good man this   / that

    c. **acest** / *acel program* vs. *program***ul**   **acesta** / *acela* (Ro.)
        this / that programme programme-the this   / that

    d. **este** / *ese* / *aquel país* vs. **el** *país*   **este** / *ese* / *aquello* (Sp.)
        this / this / that country the country this / this / that

    e. **esta / essa / aquela** *mentira* (Pt.) / **questi** / *codesti* / *quei* *cappelli* (It.)
        this / this / that   lie   these   / these   / those hats

Similarly, the possessive in these same varieties shows a formal contrast between a tonic adjectival paradigm (postnominal in Spanish and Romanian, but pre- and postnominal in Occitan and Catalan) and a clitic determiner paradigm generally limited to the singular persons (prenominal in all but Romanian; see Lyons 1986; Lombardi 2007b), as illustrated in Table 8.3.

In all cases, the clitic determiner forms are inherently definite on account of their lexicalization of the D position, whereas the tonic adjectival forms are underspecified for definiteness, hence their associated noun occurs with a determiner (e.g., Sp. *mi hija* 'my daughter' vs. *una/esta/ninguna hija mía* 'a/this/no daughter of mine', Occ. *son gat* 'his cat' vs. *lo/aquest sieu gat* or *lo/ aquest gat sieu* 'his cat/this cat of his', Cat. *ton cosí* 'your cousin' vs. *un/aquell cosí teu* 'a/that cousin of yours', Alg. *mos txius* vs. *los txius meus* 'my uncles', Ro. *socru-su* 'his father-in-law' vs. *socrul său/acest socru al său* 'his father-in-law/this father-in-law of his'). As with the definite article, the clitic determiner possessive in Romanian is also suffixal and hence attracts its associated nominal head to the D position. With the exception of Spanish and Occitan, in which the clitic determiner forms are not lexically restricted, the determiner clitic forms in the other languages characteristically have a more restricted distribution in that they are limited to singular, unmodified kinship terms (e.g., Cat. *la teva/**ta butxaca* 'your pocket', but *ta germana* 'your sister'), a distribution also found in the dialects of upper southern Italy (e.g., Nap. *'o vraccio tuoio* 'the arm your' vs. *sòrata* 'sister=your').

Although this dual adjectival–determiner paradigm can be assumed to underlie all Romance varieties historically, it has been lost in most varieties in favour of the generalization of one of the two paradigms. For instance, in Asturian, Italian and European Portuguese it is the adjectival paradigm which has prevailed (e.g., EAst. *los sos llibros* '(the) his books', It. *la nostra città* '(the) our city', EuPt. *a minha loja* '(the) my shop'), whereas in French and Brazilian Portuguese (Thomas 1969:80; Teyssier 1984:105) the determiner paradigm has generalized (e.g., Fr. *ses enfants* 'her children',[40] BrPt. *nosso vizinho* 'our neighbour'). In Asturian, Italian and European Portuguese, however, the adjectival possessives exceptionally appear to function as determiners when employed in conjunction with singular, unmodified kinship terms, since the determiner is excluded in such contexts (e.g., EAst. *(**lu) to pa* 'you father', It. *(**il) mio fratello*, EuPt. *(**o) meu irmão* '(**the) my brother').

To conclude this section, we must briefly discuss two other article types limited to Romanian, namely the so-called demonstrative article ECCE ILLE > *cel* (M.PL *cei*, F.SG *cea*, F.PL *cele*) and the possessive article (AD 'of' >) *al* (M.PL *ai*, F>SG *a*, F.PL *ale*). Both of these have received various interpretations in the literature,[41] the technical details of which need not concern us here. Suffice it to note that, in essence, both articles can be considered expletives which 'fill' an otherwise empty D slot. For example, one of the principal uses of the first is to replace the canonical article when the NP occurs with a cardinal quantifier (e.g., *cei trei copii* 'the three children') or when the cardinal selects for a null NP (e.g., *cei trei* [$_{NP}$ Ø] 'the three'). Given the strict complementary distribution of the demonstrative and canonical articles in this context (see **copiii trei 'the three children', **cei copii 'the children'), it is logical to interpret the presence of the cardinal quantifier as the element that excludes the canonical article. In the context of our analysis of the canonical article in (19a–b), this intuition finds an immediate answer. In particular, we can hypothesize that in examples like *cei trei copii*, raising of the nominal head *copii* to the D position to incorporate with the suffixal article *-i* is not possible, since its passage to the D position is blocked by the intervening quantifier position lexicalized by the cardinal *trei* (a classic case of the Head Movement Constraint).[42] To rescue the suffixal article *-i*, its empty nominal slot is lexicalized directly by the reflex of ECCE, namely *ce-* + *-i*, giving rise to the morphologically complex expletive determiner *cei*. Similarly, in examples like *cei trei* 'the three (ones)', where the NP contains a null nominal head, there can be no N-raising to D. Consequently, once again we see that whenever the movement strategy is blocked, stranding of the suffixal article under D is rescued by the last resort strategy of directly lexicalizing the empty N slot under D with the erstwhile presentative ECCE.[43]

Turning finally to the possessive article, this is employed in nominal possessive constructions whenever the D position of the possessee phrase is not immediately adjacent to the possessor phrase, hence absent in [*câinele*] [*fetei*] 'the girl's dog (lit. dog=the girl=the.GEN)', but obligatorily present in sequences such as [*câinele frumos*] *al* [*fetei*] 'the girl's pretty dog (lit. dog=the pretty *al* girl=the.GEN)', [*frumosul câine*] *al* [*fetei*] 'the girl's pretty dog (lit. pretty=the dog *al* girl=the.GEN)' or [*acest/un câine*] *al* [*fetei*] 'this/a dog of the girl (lit. this/a dog *al* girl=the.GEN)'. Superficially, then, the possessive article can be analysed as an expletive determiner which is exceptionally pressed into service to mark the gender and number of the possessee phrase in a position immediately adjacent to the possessor,[44] whenever the determiner of the possessee phrase is realized in a higher position.

3.3.2 The IP

One of the most salient developments of the verb system in the passage from Latin to Romance has been the large-scale transferral of many verb-related inflectional categories to preverbal auxiliaries. As the overt realization of a functional category Infl(ection) spelling out grammatical information relating to the VP, it is this same category which, as the locus of verb agreement, licenses nominative-marked subjects in its associated specifier position (SpecIP), the Romance dedicated preverbal subject position (see §6.3). This is exemplified below in (21) with the representative Catalan example *en Dominic estava aprenent la guitarra* 'Dominic was learning the guitar', where the progressive auxiliary *estava* 'was' spells out the Infl head that selects for the VP constituent headed by the gerund *aprenent* 'learning':

(21)

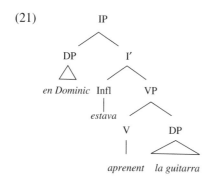

The emergence of an IP projection thus correlates directly with the grammaticalization of a number of originally lexical verbs to produce a wide range of auxiliaries, a process whose effects are not uniformly mapped onto the semantic, phonological, morphological and syntactic structures of the various Romance languages, which not only show considerable differences among themselves in relation to otherwise similar constructions (Green 1982; 1987; Pountain 1982; Vincent 1987; Remberger 2006), but which individually also display considerable variation from one auxiliary construction to another (Pottier 1961; Jones 1988b; Motapanyane 2000:14–20). Indeed, attempts to establish a pan-Romance definition of the linguistic category of auxiliary verb are notoriously riddled with difficulties, unlike the Germanic languages where it proves easier, though not entirely straightforward, to set up a number of formal criteria (cf. the NICE properties of English auxiliaries; see Steele *et al.* 1981; Harbert 2007:285–92) to identify a common class of auxiliaries (e.g., Eng./Ger. *can/können, must/müssen, will/wollen, may/mögen*, etc.). For example, in English and in German auxiliaries can consistently be identified, among other things, by their selection of an infinitival complement (rather than a past participle or gerund) and their incompatibility with the infinitival marker *to/zu* (e.g., *I must (**to) leave / Ich muß ab(**zu)fahren*), and their lack/avoidance of a past participle (e.g., *I have **had to** (**musted) leave / Ich habe abfahren **müssen** (**gemußt)*). In Romance, by contrast, all such generalizations present numerous exceptions. For example, just limiting ourselves to the reflexes of the modals *po'tere (< POSSE), DEBERE and *vo'lere (< UELLE) / QUAERERE in French, Italian and Spanish, we can note, among other facts, that: (i) clitic climbing in the modern languages is only permitted, but not obligatory, in Italian and Spanish (e.g., Fr. *je peux* **me** *l'imaginer* vs. It./Sp. **me lo** *posso immaginare* / **me lo** *puedo imaginar* 'I can imagine it'); (ii) in compound forms the auxiliary must be realized on the modal in French (e.g., *elle* **a dû** *sourire*), on either the modal or the infinitive indifferently in Spanish (e.g., *ella* **ha debido** *sonreír* / *debe* **haber sonreído**), and on either the modal or the infinitive in accordance with a deontic/epistemic distinction in Italian (e.g., *Lei* **ha dovuto** *sorridere* / *deve* **aver sorriso** 'she had to smile / must have smiled'); (iii) only in Italian, but not in French (Spanish has long lost all traces of perfective 'be'; see §6.2.1.1), is the auxiliary selection of the modal sensitive to the transitive/unaccusative nature of the embedded infinitive (e.g., It. **sono/ho** *voluto ritornare/aspettare* lit. 'I am/have wanted to return/wait' vs. Fr. *j'ai voulu retourner/attendre* 'I have wanted to return/wait'); and (iv) besides an infinitival complement, reflexes of *vo'lere/QUAERERE, but not *po'tere and DEBERE, may take a finite complement and, in certain contexts, also a participial complement (e.g., Sp. *quería* **que preparasen todo** / **todo preparado** 'I wanted that they prepare everything / everything prepared').

While acknowledging the absence of a discrete class of Romance auxiliaries, we may nonetheless identify a number of general cross-linguistic properties or parameters of auxiliation (see Heine 1993), which characterize to varying degrees those Romance verbs which realize verb-related categories such as tense, aspect, mood and voice. For instance, in the area of semantics it is a fairly easy task to recognize a number of verbs which have undergone various degrees of semantic impoverishment, including such cases as IbR. *seguir* 'to follow', whose original lexical meaning is clearly still transparent, though weakened, in the continuous/iterative aspectual periphrasis with a following gerund (e.g., Pt. **sigue** *estudando* 'he is still/goes on studying'), and It. *venire* 'to come', which has been completely desemanticized (or semantically bleached) in its dynamic passive auxiliary function with the participle (e.g., *le bozze* **venivano** *corrette* 'the proofs were being (lit. came) corrected'). In accordance with well-attested cross-linguistic pathways of auxiliation (Heine 1993:45–48), the core Romance verb-related grammatical categories are thus derived from original lexical predicates indicating:

(i) location (ESSE, STARE, SEDERE): passive (see 22a), progressive/continuous aspect (see 22b–d) and present perfectivity (see 22e):

(22) a. *El   pantalón   era/estaba   planchado* (Sp.)
       the   trousers   was/was   ironed
       'The trousers were being (dynamic)/were (stative) ironed'

    b. *vous êtes éternellement créant   tout ce   qu' il vous plaît   de créer* (OFr.)
       you are eternally   creating all this that it you=pleases of create.INF
       <small>'You are continually creating all that …'</small>

    c. *Era   a   se passejar* (Occ.)
       she.was to   self=walk.INF
       'She was taking a walk'

    d. *Está   a   cantar   / Está cantando* (EuPt./BrPt.)
       he.is   to   sing.INF / he-is singing
       'He is singing'

    e. *Sono   rimasti   in montagna* (It.)
       they.are remained   in mountain
       'they have remained in the mountains'

(ii) motion (IRE, UENIRE, AMBULARE): iterative aspect (see 23a), progressive/protracted aspect (see 23b–c), retrospective aspect (see 23d), future time (see 23e–f) and past time (see 23g):

(23) a. *An   pas tornadas   trobar   sas   amigas* (Occ.)
       they.have not returned   find.INF   their friends
       'They haven't found their friends again'

    b. *Es va   posant   bé* (Cat.)
       self=she.goes placing   well
       'She is (progressively) getting better'

    c. *Há quatro anos que ando/vou/venho   vendendo   automóveis* (BrPt.)
       has four   years that I.walk/I.go/I.come selling   cars
       'I've been selling cars for four years'

    d. *Je viens de me laver* (Fr.) / *Venh de me lavar* (Occ.)
       I   come of me=wash.INF / I.come of me=wash.INF
       'I have just washed'

    e. *Vegnel a   lavá* (Srs.)
       I.come to   wash.INF
       'I shall wash'

    f. *Van   a comer   con los   otros* (Sp.)
       they.go to eat.INF with the   others
       'They'll eat with the others'

    g. *Vaig anar al   mercat ahir* (Cat.)
       I.go go.INF to.the market yesterday
       'I went to the market yesterday'

(iii) possession (HABERE, TENERE): iterative aspect (see 24a), resultative aspect (see 24b–c) and present perfect (see 24d):

(24) a. [ˈkoza ˈteŋstu fajt]? (Pie.)   /   *lo tenh*   *de velhat* (Occ.)
     what hold.you done   /   him=she.holds of watched
     'what have you been doing?' / 'she keeps watching him'

    b. *Tinc*   *preparat el*   *sopar* (Cat.)
     I.have prepared the dinner
     'I have got dinner ready/prepared'

    c. *Tengo pittate*   *'e*   *parete* (Nap.)
     I.have painted the walls
     'I've got the walls painted'

    d. *El*   *ga*   *invecià*   *tanto* (Vnz.)
     'He has aged a.lot'

(iv)   volition (*voˈlere): future time (see 25a–b), deontic passive (see 25c):

  (25) a. *Avionul*   *va*   *pleca*   *dimineaţa* (Ro.)
     plane=the wants leave.INF morning-the
     'The plane will leave in the morning'

    b. *Voj*   *parti* (Frl.)
     I.want leave.INF
     'I will leave'

    c. *'i*   *lenzola*   *vulianu*   *cangiate* (Cos.)
     the sheets wanted changed
     'the sheets had to be changed'

(v)   obligation (DEBERE, HABER DE/AD): future time (see 26a–d):

  (26) a. *Je*   *ne*   *pense pas*   *qu'*   *elle*   *doive*   *venir* (Fr.)
     I not think not that she must.SBJV come.INF
     'I don't think she will come'

    b. *Sos óspites den*   *éssere*   *thuccatos prima de arrivare*   *nois* (Srd.)
     the guests must be.INF left   before of arrive.INF we
     'The guests will have left before we arrive'

    c. *Prometo-lhe*   *que hei-de*   *recusá-lo* (Pt.)
     I.promise=you that I.have-of refuse.INF=it
     'I promise you that I shall refuse it'

    d. *Aju*   *a*   *turnari*   *subbitu* (Sic.)
     I.have to return.INF at.once
     'I'll come back at once'

In the area of morphosyntax, Romance auxiliation is clearly visible in the process of decategorialization, whereby the emergent auxiliary progressively jettisons the typical morphosyntactic properties of its erstwhile lexical verb status. For instance, the auxiliary typically loses the ability to select its own arguments, simply inheriting and governing the syntax of its lexical verbal complement (see Harris and Campbell's (1995:193) *Heir-Apparent Principle*; see also Ramat 1987:16). Hence, unlike lexical verbs, auxiliaries impose, for example, no restrictions on the animacy or otherwise of their subject (e.g., Sp. *el alcalde **podría** dimitir* 'the mayor could resign', *el libro **podría** costar poco* 'the book could cost little'). Other reflexes of decategorialization include: (i) the emergence of gaps in the verb paradigm, such as the lack of an imperative for the reflex of perfective HABERE (e.g., Fr. ***aie fini la tâche avant midi!* 'have the task finished by midday!') or the incompatibility of Italian progressive *stare* + gerund with the preterite (e.g., **stette studiando, but Sp. *estuvo estudiando* 'he was studying'); (ii) the inability to form passives (e.g., felicity of Sp. progressive aspectual periphrasis *andar* + gerund in the active *el tendero ha andado aumentando los precios* 'the shopkeeper has been progressively increasing the prices', but not in the passive ***los precios han sido andados aumentando* 'the prices have progressively been increased'); (iii) the inability to take a nominal complement, as exemplified by Sp./Pt. perfective *haber/haver* 'to have' (e.g., **he dos hijos / **hei dois filhos 'I have two children'), now replaced by a reflex of TENERE (e.g., *tengo dos hijos* / *tenho dois filhos*); and (iv) the reduction and loss of verb inflection, as exemplified by the fossilization of Lat. UULT > *o* 'he wants' in the Romanian future construction *o să* + subjunctive (e.g., *o să laud/lauzi/ laude/ lăudăm/lăudaţi/laude* 'I/you(SG)/(s)he/we/you(PL)/they will praise') and the southern Apulian progressive aspectual marker *sta* (< *stare* 'to stand'), now used in all six grammatical persons (e.g., Lec. *sta* + *pperdu/pperdi/pperde/pperdimu/ pperditi/pperdenu* 'I am/you(SG) are/he is/we/you(PL)/they are losing').

With the increased semantic integration and grammatical dependency between auxiliary and verbal complement (namely [VERB] + [VERB] ⇒ [AUX + VERB]), the auxiliary construction comes to license a range of 'local' syntactic phenomena generally assumed to hold exclusively of mono-clausal constructions, including, for example, the attraction of negators and clitic pronouns to the auxiliary (e.g., Cat. *no ha (**no) vingut* 'he has not come', *la temperatura **no** va (**no) disminuint* 'the temperature is not going down'; It. *mi ha visto (**mi)* 'he has seen me', *mi vuole rivedere* 'he wants to see me again') and, in Ibero-Romance (including Catalan in this instance), the impossibility of intervening adverbs between perfective auxiliary and participle (e.g., Cat. *ja havia (**ja) parlat*, Pt. *já tenha (**já) falado*, Sp. *ya había (**ya) hablado* 'he had **already** spoken').

In many cases, this increased integration between auxiliary and dependent verb is translated morphophonologically into the creation of morphologically specialized (and often synchronically irregular) auxiliary paradigms displaying phonologically reduced (typically clitic) forms, which, in certain cases, contrast with morphophonologically regular and full paradigms preserved for the

Table 8.4 *Morphophonological specialization in auxiliary paradigms*

Haver(/Heure)		Avea		Anar		Dévere	
Lexical	Aux	Lexical	Aux	Lexical	Aux	Lexical	Aux
heig	*he*	*am*	*am*	*vaig*	*và(re)ig*	*devo*	*devo*
has [as]	*has* [əs]	*ai*	*ai*	*vas*	*va(re)s*	*deves*	*des*
ha [a]	*ha* [ə]	*are*	*a*	*va*	*va*	*devet*	*det*
havem	*(h(av)em)*	*avem*	*am*	*anem*	*và(re)m*	*devímus*	*demus*
haveu	*(h(av)eu)*	*aveţi*	*aţi*	*aneu*	*và(re)u*	*devítes*	*dedzis*
han[an]	*han* [ən]	*au*	*au*	*van*	*va(re)n*	*deven*	*den*

original lexical meaning of the same verb (cf. UADO > Cal. *ve* (+ *rapu*) 'I'm gonna (open up)' vs. *vaju* (+ *a ra casa*) 'I go (home)'). For example, although historically both derived from HABERE 'to have', in the present tense Cat. perfective *haver* differs from lexical *haver/heure* 'to receive' not only in exhibiting distinct morphologically reduced forms in specific persons (e.g., 1/2SG AUX *he/has* vs. lexical *hec/heus*), but also in the reduction of vowels to schwa in otherwise identical forms (e.g., ***ha*** [a] 'he receives' (also *heu*) vs. ***ha*** [ə] 'he has'). Also exemplary in this respect is Ro. *(a) avea* 'have', which in its grammatical uses as perfective auxiliary has developed specialized, reduced forms in a number of persons (e.g., ***avem*** *un dicţionar* 'we have a dictionary' vs. ***am*** *mâncat* 'we have eaten'). Similarly, Catalan and Sardinian contrast a regular, full lexical paradigm for 'to go' (*anar*) and 'to owe' (*dévere*), respectively, with a morphophonologically reduced paradigm of the same now specialized as preterite and future auxiliaries (e.g., Cat. ***anem*** *al mercat* 'we're going to the market' vs. ***va(re)m*** *anar al mercat* 'we went to the market'; Srd. *mi* ***devet*** *meta vinu* 'he owes me a lot of wine' vs. ***det*** *éssere issitu* 'he will have gone out'). The paradigms of all five verbs are given in Table 8.4.

Finally, we must observe that, in accordance with current theoretical assumptions, the availability in Romance of a dedicated auxiliary position Infl gives rise to a further dimension of variation across Romance. In particular, not only can the Infl position be lexicalized by distinct auxiliaries (cf. epistemic use of Cat. auxiliary *deure* 'must' to express supposition in [Infl ***deu*** [VP *tenir raó*]] 'he **must** be right') but, in the absence of the latter, may be overtly filled by the raised lexical verb where its finite inflectional features can be licensed (cf. epistemic use of future in substandard Cat. to express supposition in [Infl ***tindrá*** [VP t*tindrá* *raó*]] 'he must be right'; see Badi i Margarit 1962 I:391). This apparently explains the observed differences in the (unmarked) position of the verb in languages like French and Italian (see 27a–b) on the one hand and Spanish and Calabrian (see 27c–d) on the other:[45]

(27) a. *Jean*   [$_{I'}$ ***fumait***   [$_{VP}$ *toujours* t$_{fumait}$]] (Fr.)
     b. *Gianni* [$_{I'}$ ***fumava***   [$_{VP}$ *sempre* t$_{fumava}$]] (It.)
     c. *Juan*   [$_{I'}$ Ø   [$_{VP}$ *siempre* ***fumaba***]] (Sp.)
     d. *Gianni* [$_{I'}$ Ø   [$_{VP}$ *sempa* ***fumava***]] (Cal.)
     John   (smoked)   always (smoked)
     'John always smoked'

Exploiting the fixed positions of VP-adverbs like 'always' as a diagnostic
indicator of the left edge of the VP (Cinque 1999), we can now straightforwardly distinguish between overt verb-raising languages like French and Italian,
where the finite verb raises to the Infl position to the left of VP-adverbs, and
languages like Spanish and Calabrian, where the verb remains *in situ* to the right
of such VP-adverbs and Infl is not overtly lexicalized in the syntax.

3.3.3   The CP

In the same way that the heads D and Infl constitute the spell-out of
grammatical categories related to their associated NP and VP complements,
the sentential core too, now formally represented by IP, can be considered
to be embedded within a further layer of functional structure CP, the clausal
left periphery. In accordance with parametric variation, the left periphery
may spell out fundamental clausal distinctions such as finiteness, illocutionary force and other discourse-related categories (e.g., Topic, Focus), as
well as indirectly replicating information encoded within IP (see Rizzi
1997). Unlike DP and IP, however, there is already extensive evidence in
archaic Latin for the structure of CP (Vincent 1998), which exceptionally
constitutes a significant precursor to the later widespread extension of
configurational and functional structure to other areas of the grammar
(see §3.3.3.2 below).

3.3.3.1   Evidence for Latin CP structure

Above in §3.2.1, we noted that unmarked word order in Latin is predominantly considered to be SOV and that all other permutations, rather than
being 'free', are pragmatically determined orders derived from underlying
SOV.[46] On this view, V-initial orders (see 28a) involve fronting of the verb
to the left periphery, and XVS(X) orders (see 28b) involve the additional
step of fronting some other pragmatically salient element to the left periphery under topicalization or focalization (see also 17a above). More specifically, we take fronting of the verb to target the vacant C(omplementizer)
position and fronting of any accompanying topicalized or focalized element
to target its associated specifier position (see 29):[47]

(28) a. **MISERAT** ENIM   EI   PHARNACES   CORONAM   AUREAM
     had.sent indeed him.DAT Pharnaces.NOM crown.F.ACC golden.F.SG.ACC
     'Pharnaces had indeed sent him a golden crown' (Caes.)

    b. IDEM   **FACIT** CAESAR
     same.NEUT.ACC did   Caesar.NOM
     'The same does Caesar' (Caes.)

(29)

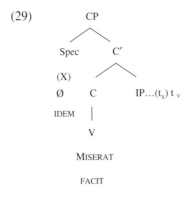

Thus, although preposed V orders still constitute a marked word order at this stage, often claimed to be a stylistic and/or pragmatic device serving to emphasize the verb of the utterance and licensing narrative functions such as introducing description and marking progress of action of narration (Marouzeau 1938:81f.; Ernout and Thomas 1953:161; Bauer 1995:93–95), there is clear evidence that they are also syntactically motivated. Following Kroll (1912) and Möbitz (1924), Bauer (1995:95f.) observes that fronting of the verb in main clauses frequently occurs whenever preceded by a subordinate clause (especially conditional and temporal types), an ablative absolute, a negation, an adverb or an adverbial phrase. In short, there can be no doubt that these syntactically determined contexts of verb fronting represent an unmistakable precursor to the fully-fledged V2 syntax of late Latin / early Romance outlined above in §3.2.2, which in the fullness of time would generalize as the unmarked word order replacing earlier SOV. Indeed, this conclusion is further confirmed by the observation that verb fronting in Latin rarely occurs in subordinate clauses (Bauer 1995:96), since in these cases the C position would typically already be lexicalized by an overt complementizer (e.g., UT, NE, QUIN, SI, CUM, QUOD, QUIA) and hence unavailable to host the fronted verb.

    In a similar vein, Vincent (1998:418–23) finds convincing evidence for the presence and structure of CP outlined above not only in late Latin texts such as the *Peregrinatio Aetheriae* (see 30a), but also in Golden Age authors such as

Cicero (see 30b) and early, non-literary Latin authors such as Cato (see 30c), where the finite verb and complementizer compete for the C position and SpecC hosts topicalized or focalized elements (see also Vincent 1997c:169, n17):

(30)

	SpecC		C	IP	
a.	TRANS	UALLEM	APPAREBAT	MONS	SANCTUS
	across	valley.F.ACC	appeared	mount.M.NOM	holy.M.SG.NOM

'across the valley there appeared the holy mount'

b.	DOMUS		UT	PROPUGNACULA	ET	PRAESIDIUM	HABEAT
	house.F.NOM		that	defences.NEUT.ACC	and	protection	has.SBJV

'in order that the house may have defences and guards'

c.	AD	UILLAM	CUM	UENIES	
	to	estate.F.ACC	when	you-come	

'when you arrive at the country house'

From examples like these, Vincent (1998:422) concludes that, despite an otherwise non-configurational syntax in which word order is constrained only by pragmatic principles, Latin exceptionally provides for a configurational suprastructure at the level of the clause. The latter provides for two fixed positions, C and SpecC, the latter filled by topicalized and focalized elements and the former increasingly targeted not just by complementizers in embedded clauses, but also by the finite verb in main clauses according to a pattern which would generalize in time, producing a V2 syntax (for more details, see Vincent 1998:422f.; Salvi this volume, chapter 7: §3.4.7).[48]

Although the early signs of the emergence of a CP projection in Latin are undeniable, the language still preserves evidence of an earlier archaic stage predating the emergence of CP structure. In Indo-European, complex sentences did not involve subordination, namely a CP structure with an overt subordinator, but, rather, were constructed on a simple paratactic or correlative relation (Palmer [1954] 1990:328; Haudry 1973; Bichakjian 1982; Bauer 1995:159f.). Indeed, evidence of the archaic pattern is still evident in Latin, where alongside hypotactic subordination structures like ROGO UT UENIAS 'I ask that you come', we still find the paratactic pattern involving simple juxtaposition of the two clauses (e.g., ROGO UENIAS, TU UELIM ANIMO FORTIS SIS 'I should like you to be of brave heart', FAC FIDELIS SIS 'see (that) you are faithful', SCRIBAS UIDE PLANE ET PROBE 'see (that) you write clearly and properly', TACEAS OPORTET 'it behoves (that) you remain silent'). Similarly, the accusative and infinitive construction, arguably the most important complementation pattern of the classical language, demonstrably does not involve an embedded CP structure. For example, in a sentence such as CAESAREM PROFICISCI CREDO 'I believe that Caesar is setting out', the infinitival clause (CAESAREM PROFICISCI 'Caesar.ACC leave.INF') and the finite clause (CREDO 'I.believe') are simply juxtaposed, the only marker of subordination appearing indirectly on the accusative-marked infinitival subject CAESAREM. More specifically, the accusative marking of the infinitival subject cannot be determined by the matrix predicate, since CREDO canonically assigns dative to its complement. Rather, the accusative case of the subject must be seen as a global property of the construction, ultimately the sole marker of the logical relationship between both clauses.

To conclude, from as early as the archaic Latin period there is extensive evidence of two conflicting patterns in the marking of the clause. The first represents an archaic non-configurational pattern inherited from the Indo-European parent language, in which a number of core complementation structures without overt subordinators, notably the accusative and infinitive construction, manifestly do not involve a CP projection. The second constitutes an innovative configurational pattern, albeit attested since the archaic Latin period, in which a number of subordination types with overt complementizers (e.g., UT, NE, QUIN, SI, UBI, QUOD, QUIA), as well as an incipient V2 syntax, both frequently preceded by fronted topics and foci, make recourse to an articulated CP structure.

3.3.3.2 Evidence for Romance CP structure

The CP structure reviewed above for Latin is further reinforced and extended in the transition to Romance, coming to permeate all structures of the emergent languages. In the first instance, as already outlined above in §3.2.2 and §3.3.3.1, this development most noticeably surfaces in the generalization of verb fronting to C in main clauses as part of the late Latin / early Romance V2 syntax, generally accompanied, in turn, by fronting of one or more pragmatically salient constituents to the left periphery. However, it also surfaces indirectly in the loss of the accusative and infinitive construction, one of the most notable casualties of the widespread development of CP structure. From an early date among non-literary authors (Perrochat 1932), but not until the postclassical period in other text-types, especially among Christian writers, the accusative and infinitive construction was commonly replaced by a finite complement clause introduced by the complementizers QUOD and QUIA, a usage finally consolidated as the core complementation pattern in vulgar texts after the fall of the Empire.[49] Clearly, there was no place in an emerging linguistic system with full configurational structure for a non-configurational complementation pattern such as the infinitive and accusative, hence its eventual demise.

A further area highlighting the consolidation of the CP projection is evidenced by the emergence in Romance of non-finite complementizers derived from the prepositions DE and AD to introduce infinitival clauses (see 31b, 32b), which to all intents and purposes parallel the use of finite complementizers derived from QUOD(/QUID) and QUIA to introduce tensed clauses (see 31a, 32a):

(31) a. *Digues-li* [CP [C′ ***que*** [IP *vingui*]]] (Cat.)
         tell=him   that   he.comes.SBJV
      b. *Digues-li* [CP [C′ ***de*** [IP *venir*]]] (Cat.)
         tell=him   of   come.INF
         'Tell him that he come / to come'

(32) a. *Convinsi*   *Ugo* [CP [C′ ***che*** [IP *tornasse*]]] (It.)
         I.convinced Ugo   that   he.return.SBJV
      b. *Convinsi*   *Ugo* [CP [C′ ***a*** [IP *tornare*]]] (It.)
         I.convinced Ugo   to   to-return
         'I convinced Ugo that he should return / to return'

It is evidence like this which has led many researchers investigating the structure of the left periphery in Romance to propose a richly articulated C-domain,[50] the fine structure of which can be represented schematically as in (33):

(33) [ForceP QUE/CHE [FrameP HTop, Sc-set [TopP LD-Top [FocP ConF, InfF, IndefQ [FinP DE/AD [IP…]]]]]]

| Theme | | Focus |

In particular, the left periphery, traditionally defined in terms of CP and its associated specifier and head positions (Chomsky 1986:§1), is now conceived as a split domain, hierarchically articulated into several fields and associated projections. Simplifying somewhat and leaving aside many of the language-specific details (for which, see, in particular, Benincà and Poletto 2004), we can identify from left to right at least two fields termed Theme and Focus, respectively. Whereas the Focus field hosts fronted indefinite quantifiers (IndefQ; see 34a), contrastively focused phrases (ConF; see 34b) and informationally focused phrases (InfF) – once widely attested in the V2 phase of early Romance (see 34c; Skårup 1975; Vanelli 1986; 1998) but now chiefly limited to Sardinian and southern Italian dialects like Sicilian (see 34d; Jones 1993:332–45; Cruschina 2006; Bentley 2007)[51] – the Theme field can be further divided into two subfields: Frame, hosting hanging topics (HTop; see 34e) and scene-setting adverbials (Sc-set; see 34f), and Topic, hosting left-dislocated topics (LD-Top; see 34g):

(34) a. **A**LGO   *habrán*   *comprado* (Sp.)
         something   they.will.have   bought
         'They surely must have bought something'

     b. *I*L   RUSSO   *insegna (, non* *lo* *svedese)* (It.)
         the Russian he.teaches not   the Swedish
         'RUSSIAN he teaches (, not Swedish)'

     c. **C**OM TANTA   PACEEN*ç*A *sofria*   *ela esta enfermidade* (OPt.)
         with so.much patience   suffered she this illness
         'She suffered this illness with great endurance'

     d. **S**ORDATU *es*   *diventatu* (Sa)   / NA MACHINA *accattai* (Sic.)
         soldier   he.is become   / A car   I.bought
         'He became a soldier' / 'I bought a car'

     e. ***Ta   frangine***, *je* *vais* *lui téléphoner* (Fr.)
         your sister   I go   to.her=telephone.INF
         'Your sister, I'll ring her later'

     f. ***Después de la guerra***, *ya*   *no* *volvió*   *a Madrid* (Sp.)
         after of the war   already not he.returned to Madrid
         'After the war he no longer returned to Madrid'

     g. ***Pe ea*** *o văd*   *mâine* (Ro.)
         on her her=I.see   tomorrow
         'I'll see her tomorrow'

It is interesting to observe at a pragmatico–semantic level that, whereas elements appearing in the two leftmost subfields are generally interpreted as 'old' or 'given' information, the Focus field is typically associated with informationally 'new' elements (Benincà and Poletto 2004:71). Also, at the syntactic level the three (sub)fields are distinguished: in contrast to elements appearing in Frame and Topic which often call for a resumptive pronominal clitic (see *o* 'her' (34g)), those appearing within Focus typically prove incompatible with a pronominal copy. Furthermore, in the V2 phase of medieval Romance, the distinction between the Theme and Focus fields is additionally signalled by the Tobler–Mussafia Law (ultimately a Romance-specific reanalysis of the Wackernagel Law; Benincà 1995; Wanner 1996; Vincent 1998:422), one of the principal generalizations of which states that enclisis obtains whenever the verb occurs in clause-initial position. Thus, in the case of focus fronting (see 35a), proclisis invariably obtains since the verb (raised to C-Fin) occurs in second position preceded by a fronted constituent in the Focus field. However, whenever the Theme field hosts a hanging topic and/or a left-dislocated constituent and the Focus field remains empty (see 35b), only enclisis is possible because the verb now raised to C-Fin technically occurs in clause-initial position, inasmuch as elements contained within the topicalization space are considered to be extra-sentential, hence invisible to the Tobler–Mussafia generalization which only makes reference to the Focus field. These facts are illustrated in the following minimal pair taken from ONeapolitan (*Libro de la destructione de Troya*):

(35) a. [FocP *si*   FUORTI   CUOLPI [FinP *li*   *donava* [IP …]]]
         such   strong   blows   to.him= he.gave
         'he gave him such strong blows with his sword'

    b. [TopP ***de queste toy promissiune*** [FocP Ø [FinP *voglyonde* [IP
         of   these   your   promises   I-want=thereof
        essere   *certa*]]]]
        be.INF   certain
        'I want to be entirely sure of these promises of yours'

Finally, we note that the three syntactic spaces outlined above are, in turn, closed off upwards by a complementizer position Force marking the illocutionary force of the clause, hosting such items as the Italian finite declarative complementizer *che* 'that' (see 36a), and downwards by a complementizer position Fin(iteness) specifying the modality and/or finiteness of the clause (hence also the position targeted by the finite verb under V2 as in (35a–b); see Ledgeway 2008), hosting such items as the Italian infinitival complementizer *di* 'of' (see 36b).[52] This explains their respective positions to the left and to the right of topics (Rizzi 1997):

(36) a. *So*   ***che***,   *la*   *data,*   *l'ho*   *sbagliata*
       I-know   that,   the   date,   it=I.have   mistaken

    b. *So,*   *la*   *data,*   ***di***   *averla*   *sbagliata*
       I.know,   the   date,   of   have.INF=it mistaken
       'I know (that), the date, I got (it) wrong'

Indeed, some Romance varieties present dual finite complementizer systems which appear to exploit both the higher and lower complementizer positions within the left periphery. Such is the case in many southern Italian dialects and Romanian,[53] which contrast an indicative complementizer that lexicalizes the highest Force position, and therefore precedes topics and foci (see 37a), and a subjunctive complementizer that lexicalizes the lower Fin position, and therefore follows topics and foci (see 37b), as illustrated by the following Salentino examples:

(37) a. *aggiu tittu* [ForceP ***ca*** [TopP/FocP *lu libbru/*   CRAI [IP   *lu kkattu*]]]
       I.have said   that   the book   tomorrow it=I.buy
       'I said that the book/TOMORROW I'll buy it'

    b. *ojju* [TopP/FocP *lu libru/* CRAI   [FinP ***cu*** [IP *lu kattu*]]]
       I.want   the book tomorrow   that   it=I.buy
       'the book/TOMORROW I want to buy it'

In a number of these same varieties it is possible to simultaneously realize both higher and lower complementizer positions when the left periphery hosts a topicalized or focused constituent, as in the following Romanian (see 38a) and OLaziale (see 38b) examples:

(38) a. *Vreau* [$_{ForceP}$ ***ca***   [$_{FocP}$ MÂINE   [$_{FinP}$ ***să*** [$_{IP}$ *meargă*]]]]
I.want   that   tomorrow   that he.go.SBJV
'I want him to go TOMORROW'

   b. *È   da   sape(re)*   [$_{ForceP}$ ***ch(e)*** [$_{TopP}$ *lu   cavallo b(e)n   et   diligentem(en)te*
it.is from know.INF   that   the horse   well and diligently

custodito ... [$_{FinP}$ ***ch(e)*** [$_{IP}$ *illo no(n) sia fatigato de grande et   sup(er)flua*
cared.for   that   it not be tired of big   and   superfluous

travaglia]]]]
work
'It is to be noted that, a horse (which is) well and attentively cared for ... should not be overburdened with too much unnecessary work'

3.4   Configurationality: concluding remarks

Although the existence or otherwise of non-configurationality is a controversial issue which still divides linguists,[54] we have seen that there is nonetheless an inescapable fundamental difference in the grammatical organizations of Latin and Romance syntax: whereas in the former, grammatical relations are encoded by the forms of words themselves through case and agreement morphology, so-called lexocentricity (Bresnan 2001:109–12), in the latter, grammatical relations are encoded through the syntactic context of individual words organized into distinct hierarchical phrase structure configurations. Indeed, as Vincent (1998:423f.) notes, (Classical) Latin presents all of Hale's (1983) classic tests for non-configurationality originally established on the evidence of Warlpiri (see also Mereu 2004:119): (i) word order determined by pragmatic, and not syntactic, properties (yielding so-called 'free word order'); (ii) discontinuous constructions; (iii) absence of a VP constituent; (iv) absence of expletive elements; (v) null arguments; (vi) rich case system to encode argument structure; (vii) backwards reflexivization; and (viii) absence of subject–object asymmetry.

With the exception of (iv) and (v), all the other criteria have already been extensively described and richly exemplified in the preceding discussion. The validity of (iv) and (v) for Latin are also relatively easy to prove: not only did Latin lack expletive subjects with impersonal verbs (e.g., Ø PLUIT '(it) rains'), but it also readily dropped referential subjects as well as objects (Vincent 1988a:59; 2000:38–40, 43f.; van de Wurff 1993; Oniga 2004:58f.), when these could be readily recovered from the pragmatic context (e.g., SI $\emptyset_i$ IN IUS UOCAT $\emptyset_j$ ITO. NI $\emptyset_j$ IT, $\emptyset_i$ ANTESTAMINO. IGITUR $\emptyset_i$ EM$_j$ CAPITO 'If (the accuser) sues (the accused), (the accused) must attend. If (the accused) does not attend, (the accuser) should call witnesses. In that case (the accuser) should have him arrested' (*Lex XII Tabularum*)). By contrast, the Romance languages are generally specified negatively in relation to these same criteria or, at most, present only partially positive specifications for some of them. For example, while many Romance languages license referential and expletive null subjects (e.g., Sp. $\emptyset$ *vienen* '(they) come', $\emptyset$ *llueve* '(it) rains'), others, especially Gallo-Romance, obligatorily realize both referential and expletive subjects (e.g., Fr. *ils viennent* 'they come', *il pleut* 'it rains'). Null objects, on the other hand, are even more restricted: fully referential null objects are principally limited to Brazilian Portuguese,[55] where the construction appears to be an innovation and related to the increase in overt subject pronouns (Galves 1993; Morais 2003; e.g., *Você não trouxe [passaporte]$_i$? – Aí é que está, eu trouxe $\emptyset_i$ mas como não precisei mostrar $\emptyset_i$ deixei $\emptyset_i$ no hotel* 'Didn't you bring your passport? – That's the point, I did bring (it), but since I didn't need to show (it), I left (it) at the hotel'), while generic null objects are more widely found (e.g., It. *Ciò induce $\emptyset$ a sospettare che …* 'This leads (us/people) to suspect that …' (see Rizzi 1986); Fr. (inanimates only) *Tu aimes [le porc]$_i$? – Oui, j'adore $\emptyset_i$* 'Do you like pork? – Yes, I love (it)' (see Zribi-Hertz 1984; Rowlett 2007:183)).

However, we have seen in §3.3.3.1 that, since its earliest attestations, Latin presents extensive evidence of a non-configurational syntax built around an otherwise isolated configurational CP superstructure, which affords the language a fixed point of reference within an otherwise free, non-configurational syntax.[56] Perceptively, Vincent (1998:424) relates this limited configurationality of Latin to a similar limited configurationality in Warlpiri, where the only fixed position in the clause is the obligatory second-position AUX (with Focus position to its immediate left), evidence which many have taken to be indicative of a fixed, configurational structure at the IP level (Bresnan 2001:6–10; Austin and Bresnan 1996; Mereu 2004:120, 123–26). Quite naturally, this leads us to the conclusion that configurationality is not strictly a binary parameter, but rather a scalar property of languages which can show varying degrees of (non-) configurationality in different areas of the grammar (Hale 1994; Lyons 1999:154; Mereu 2004:134), variously mixing endocentrically organized functional projections with exocentrically organized lexical projections

(Bresnan 2001:113f.; Mereu 2004:161). Thus, Latin displays a fixed hierarchical arrangement of discourse functions at the level of the clause (CP), but a non-configurational, 'flat' arrangement in verbal and noun phrase structure (see 39a), whereas in Warlpiri the core of configurationality is located at the level of the AUX (IP), with verb and noun phrases displaying a flat structure (see 39b):[57]

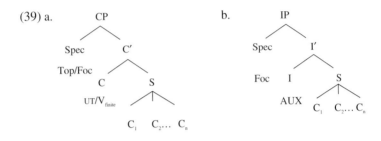

At the appropriate level of abstraction, the difference between Latin and Warlpiri is not whether one is more or less configurational than the other, but at what level configurationality, a minimum of which would appear to characterize all languages (Hale 1994; Mereu 2004:134, 139), is located: CP in Latin and IP in Warlpiri. This naturally explains why (late) Latin eventually develops a C-oriented V2 syntax whereas Warlpiri displays an I-oriented V2 syntax, since the finite verb is attracted to C in the first case and I(nfl) in the second. At the same time, we can now formalize the passage from Latin to Romance in terms of a gradual top-down development of configurationality from CP downwards, such that, following the emergence of IP and concomitant configurational structure, the locus of verb inflection slowly but steadily shifts from C to I(nfl) and the subject acquires a dedicated position in the latter's associated specifier position.

4   Head- and dependent-marking

Following the seminal work of Nichols (1986), a useful and insightful typological distinction is that between head-marking and dependent-marking (see also Vincent 1993; 1997c:164; Bresnan 2001:111–13; Mereu 2004: 63–72). In dependent-marking constructions, the relation between head and dependent is marked directly on the dependent itself, as in the Latin example EPISTULAM SCRIPSIT 'he wrote the letter', where the accusative case marking borne by the noun EPISTULAM 'letter' immediately identifies its syntactic function as direct object. In head-marking constructions, by contrast, the relation between head and dependent is marked on the head, as in the corresponding colloquial Spanish example *la escribió la carta*, where the verbal head *escribió* 'he wrote' bears a 3F.SG accusative clitic *la* that spells out the direct object function of the DP *la carta* 'the letter' with matching number and gender features. In this light, Romance clitics, often viewed as the spell-out of the verb's Case feature (see Borer 1984), receive a highly natural interpretation, if they can now be understood as the overt realization of such a feature on an independent D-head adjoined to the verb.

Contrasting examples like these highlight an important typological shift in the marking of grammatical relations in the transition from Latin to Romance, involving a gradual move away from dependent-marking towards head-marking (Vincent 1997c:164). Furthermore, this typological distinction is entirely compatible with, and provides additional support for, our preceding discussion of the rise of configurationality and functional structure in the passage to Romance. Indeed, Nordlinger (1998) and, in turn, Bresnan (2001:113f.) integrate the head-/dependent-marking distinction with that of (non-)configurationality to yield four basic language types: head-marking, configurational/non-configurational languages (e.g., Navajo/Mohawk), and dependent-marking configurational/non-configurational languages (e.g., Icelandic/Dyirbal). Within this typology, Latin is then similar to Dyirbal, marking within a predominantly non-configurational syntax grammatical dependencies lexocentrically through the distinct inflectional forms assumed by its dependents, whereas in the configurational syntax of Romance, grammatical dependencies, as in Navajo, are marked partly endocentrically through fixed, hierarchical structure and partly through head-marking.

As with the synthesis–analysis distinction, however, it is not appropriate to talk of head-marking and dependent-marking languages; rather, this distinction must be predicated of particular constructions, although it cannot be denied that, when considered from this dichotomy, individual languages show an overwhelming tendency to consistently employ one type over the other. Thus, although 'Latin is a prototypical example of a D[ependent-]M[arking] language' (Vincent 1997c:164), it does nonetheless exhibit some head-marking strategies, as in the referencing of nominative subjects through person and number agreement on the finite verb (e.g., AGRICOL-A/-AE LABORA-T/-NT '(the) farmer.NOM.SG/PL work.3SG/PL'). Similarly, although modern Romance varieties show a strong tendency towards head-marking, there are still a number of core dependent-marking strategies in evidence, including, for example, the differential marking of specific, animate objects with reflexes of the preposition AD 'to' (Ibero-Romance, southern Italian dialects; e.g., Abr. *vulem'accid' a ffratete* 'we want to kill (lit. to) your brother') or PER 'through' > 'on' (Romanian, e.g., *le-am întâlnit **pe fete*** lit. 'we them=have met on girls'),[58] although, paradoxically, as illustrated in the latter Romanian example, this dependent-marking strategy frequently calls for and licenses a corresponding head-marking construction, namely clitic-doubling.[59]

With this caveat in mind, the head-/dependent-marking distinction provides us with an immediate and complementary account for our previous discussion (§3.3) of the emergence of the functional heads D, I and C (and their associated projections) in Romance which, with the shift from dependent-marking to head-marking, make available the means to directly encode grammatical information relating to nominal, verbal and clausal dependents. Beginning with the first of these, the widely noted erosion of the Latin morphological case system can now be construed as a reflex of the move away from dependent-marking. In part, and especially in the spoken varieties, the identification of argument functions has to varying degrees been taken over by the D-system (Vincent 1997c:164), where accusative, and especially dative, DPs are referenced by doubling clitic pronouns affixed to the verb (Lipski 1994:82–89; Gierling 1997; Motapanyane 2000:11–13; D'Introno 2001:100f.):

(40) a. *no* l'_i *havia*   *conegut*   [*a vostè*]$_i$ (Cat.)
         not   you=I-had   recognized   to you
         'I had not recognized you'

     b. [*copiilor*]$_i$ *nu* le_i *lipseşte*   *nimic* (Ro.)
         children.the.DAT not   them.DAT lacks   nothing
         'the children don't lack anything'

     c. *les*$_i$ *tengo*   *que*   *regalar*   [*a*   *los*   *niños*]   *la*
         them.DAT I-have   that   give.INF   to   the   children   the
         bicicleta nueva (Sp.)
         bike   new
         'I have to give the children a new bike'

     d. $c'_i a_j$ *dugnu*   [*'a   chiave*]$_i$ [*a   fratimma*]$_i$ (Cal.)
         him.DAT=it.F.ACC= I-give   the   key   to   brother=my
         'I'll give my brother the key'

Moreover, as we have seen (§3.3.1), in a number of Romance varieties, especially Gallo-Romance and Brazilian Portuguese (Thomas 1969:49; Campos and Rodrigues 1992:129; Azevedo 2005:226), the D position often emerges as the principal, and in many cases the sole, locus of grammatical information relating to its nominal dependent. For example, in (41a–e) the number and gender features of the NPs are exclusively spelt out in the accompanying D head:

(41) a. [$_{DP}$ **cette** / **ces** [$_{NP}$ *fenêtre/s* [fnɛtʁ]]] (Fr.)
　　　　　this.F / these　　　window/s.F

　　b. [$_{DP}$ **la** / **lɛ** [$_{NP}$ *søɾɛ*]] (Tor.)
　　　　　the.F.SG / F.PL　sister(s).F'

　　c. [$_{DP}$ **quella** / **quelle** [$_{NP}$ *lezione*]] (Tsc.)
　　　　　that.F / those.F　lesson(s).F

　　d. [$_{DP}$ **um** / **uma** [$_{NP}$ *estudante*]] (Pt.)
　　　　　a.M.SG / F.SG　student

　　e. [$_{DP}$ **as** [$_{NP}$ *primeira chuva*]] (BrPt.)
　　　　　the.F.PL　first.F.SG rain.F.SG

Turning now to the verbal I(nfl) head, this too emerges as a key marker of a number of head-dependent relations. For example, in Gallo- and Ræto-Romance varieties, as well as Tuscan, the object clitic referencing system observed above carries over to the subject function, where between the fifteenth and sixteenth centuries there emerges a series of subject clitics derived from weakened nominative subject pronouns (see Poletto 1995). These are affixed to the auxiliary or lexical verb under I, where they spell out (see 42a–b) and/or match (see 42c–d) the features of the subject in SpecIP:[60]

(42) a. [$_{IP}$ [$_{Spec}$ $\emptyset_i$] [$_{I'}$ **a_i** *vegne*]] (Gen.; a < ILLA 'she')
　　　　　　　　　　　　　F.SG comes
　　　'she comes'

　　b. [$_{IP}$ [$_{Spec}$ $\emptyset_i$] [$_{I'}$ **i_i** *dizen*]] (Bol.; i < ILLI 'they')
　　　　　　　　　　　　　3M.PL say.3PL
　　　'they say'

　　c. [$_{IP}$ [$_{Spec}$ *les enfants*]$_i$ [$_{I'}$ *ils$_i$* *veulent* [$_{VP}$ *tout bouffer*]]] (coll. Fr.)
　　　　　　　　　the children　3M.PL want　all　eat.INF
　　　'the children want to eat everything'

　　d. [$_{IP}$ [$_{Spec}$ *Cec*]$_i$ [$_{I'}$ **u_i** *travaja*]] (Pie.; u < ILLU 'he')
　　　　　　　　Ciccio　M.SG　works
　　　'Ciccio is working'

I(nfl) is also the head, at least historically, that encodes through the HABERE/ESSE auxiliary alternation a core distinction between the core participants of the sentence (Vincent 1982). More specifically, as we shall see in greater detail below (§6.2.1.1), historically in the compound perfective forms of the verb AGENT/EXPERIENCER subjects align with the auxiliary HABERE (e.g., It. *la regina **ha** ammazzato il re* 'the queen has killed the king'), whereas UNDERGOER subjects align with ESSE (e.g., *È morto il re* 'the king has (lit. is) died'). In a related development, a variant of I(nfl) dedicated to encoding and licensing the object features of the verb, generally referred to as light *v* in the generative literature, also spells out via participle agreement the same distinction between AGENT/EXPERIENCER participants (no/default agreement;[61] e.g., Occ. *elas auran perdut* 'they(F) will have lost.(M.SG)) and UNDERGOER participants (with agreement; e.g., Occ. *sun arribats* 'they(M) have (lit. are) arrived.M.PL'; see Loporcaro 1998a). Yet a further development is found in a number of varieties spoken in central-southern Italy, Piedmont (province of Alessandria) and northern Catalonia (Tuttle 1986b; Veny 1998:51; Ledgeway 2000:192–95, 204f.; Bentley and Eythórsson 2001), where the two perfective auxiliaries are now distributed according to grammatical person, with ESSE tending to occur in the first and second persons and HABERE in the third persons (e.g., EAbr. *so/ si scritto* lit. 'I.am/you.are written' vs. *a scritto* 'he.has/they.have written'; Cpc. *son vist* lit. 'I.am seen' vs. *ha(n) vist* 'he.has/they.have seen').[62] Synchronically, the I(nfl) head in these varieties can be said to license through auxiliary selection a system of person-marking (namely discourse participants vs. non-discourse participants).

Turning now to the C head, here too there is clear evidence for the rise of head-marking at the expense of dependent-marking. For example, in embedded contexts in southern Italian dialects and Romanian, the indicative/subjunctive distinction on the verb is only present in the third person (Salentino, Romanian) or has been entirely lost (remaining southern Italian dialects). However, the C head which selects the IP-VP dependent containing the verb now marks this same distinction through a complementizer alternation (see the discussion surrounding examples (37) above): Cal. *ca* or *chi* (IND) vs. *mi*, *mu* or *ma* (SBJV); Ro. *că* (IND) vs. *să* (SBJV); Sal. *ca* (IND) vs. *cu* (SBJV). By way of example, consider the following minimal pair in (43a–b) from the Calabrian dialect of Melicucco, where the declarative vs. jussive reading of the complement of *diri* 'to say' is marked by the differing lexicalization of the C head:

(43) a. *ti dicu*   **ca**   *staju*   *jendu*
         you=I.tell   that   I.am   going
         'I tell you that I'm leaving'
      b. *Ti rissi*   **'u**   *vai*   *rá*
         you=I.told   that   you.go   there
         'I told you that you should leave'

Finally, we may note that one of the consequences of either an extensive system of dependent- or head-marking is the emergence of a relatively free word order, albeit pragmatically constrained (Vincent 1997c:164f.). Indeed, we have already seen this to be the case in Latin, where rich case and agreement inflections on nominal dependents allows them, in principle, to occur in all possible positions within the clause. In a similar fashion, a rich system of head-marking in Romance should a priori lead us to expect a similar degree of freedom in word order. It is not, then, by chance that some linguists, notably Harris (1978; 1988:236), have argued that the rise in clitic-doubling structures in the less conservative spoken varieties allow the nominals they reference to occur in all possible positions (on a par with polysynthetic languages; Baker 1995). This is illustrated in the colloquial French examples (44a–f), where commas are purely conventional and the presence of the nominative (*je* 1SG), accusative (*le* 3M.SG) and dative (*lui* 3SG) clitics on the verbal head (*ai donné* 'I.have given') unambiguously identify all the verb's dependents (*moi* 'I', *le livre* 'the.M.SG book.M.SG', *à Pierre* 'to Pierre'). In view of evidence like this, Harris has even argued, though not without some controversy, that such freedom has led to VSO emerging as the unmarked order in colloquial French.

(44)   a. *je le lui ai donné* (V), *moi* (S), *le livre* (DO), *à Pierre* (IO)
       b. *je le lui ai donné, moi* (S), *à Pierre* (IO), *le livre* (DO)
       c. *je le lui ai donné* (V), *le livre* (DO), *moi* (S), *à Pierre* (IO)
       d. *je le lui ai donné* (V), *le livre* (DO), *à Pierre* (IO), *moi* (S)
       e. *je le lui ai donné* (V), *à Pierre* (IO), *moi* (S), *le livre* (DO)
       f. *je le lui ai donné* (V), *à Pierre* (IO), *le livre* (DO), *moi* (S)
          'I gave Pierre the book'

Other potential candidates for the reinforcement of the head-marking pattern in Romance, which limitations of space unfortunately do not allow us to explore further here, include the loss and replacement of ESSE with HABERE (or TENERE) in the possessive construction (in the former the possessor was marked by a dative dependent (e.g., PAUCA PECUNIA **UOBIS** ERAT 'you had little money'), whereas in the latter the pronominal possessor is primarily marked through the verb inflection of the copular head (e.g., It. *avev**ate** pochi soldi*, Pt. *vôces ten**ham** pouco dinheiro*)); the emergence of the Romance causative construction marked by the incorporation of the verbal head FACERE or LAXARE into the lexical infinitive (e.g., Fr. *l'eau bout* 'the water boils' vs. *je* [v ***fais bouillir***] *l'eau* 'I boil the water'; Kayne 1975; Zubizarreta 1985; Burzio 1986; Alsina 1992; 1996: ch. 6; Guasti 1993; 1996), replacing earlier dependent-marking constructions like EFFICERE + dependent UT clause (e.g., EFFICIO UT REMANEAT 'I make him stay'; Zamboni 2000:120f.); the marking of transitivity in the Romanian imperative through the inflectional alternation *-e/-i* (transitive/intransitive) on the verb head (e.g., *ard**e** toate documentele!* 'burn all the documents' vs. *arz**i**!*

'burn!'; see Motapanyane 2000:31; Pîrvulescu and Roberge 2000); and the replacement of semantically based case distinctions with the use of distinct prepositions (for example, in Latin the distinction between position (inessive, adessive) and motion (allative) in conjunction with the same preposition was often marked by the ablative/accusative alternation on the nominal dependent (e.g., IN UILLA (ABL)/UILLAM (ACC) 'in/into the country house', SUB MURIS (ABL)/MUROS (ACC) 'under/up to the walls'), whereas in Romance the same distinction is marked by the choice of prepositional head (e.g., Fr. *dans* le jardin 'in the garden' vs. *au/vers* le jardin 'to(wards) the garden')). Clearly, further research is necessary to determine the extent of this typological change in the transition from Latin to Romance, but the discussion above highlights some of the advantages that can be gained from adopting the head-/dependent-marking distinction in understanding a number of the fundamental changes in the morphosyntax of Latin and Romance.

5   Head parameter

It has long been noted that basic ordering of head and dependency in Latin and Romance are diametrically opposed (von Wartburg [1934] 1971:256; Harris 1978:16; Renzi 1985:131–37; Vincent 1988a:55f., 62f.; 1997c:166; Bauer 1995; Oniga 2004:52).[63] For instance, Ernout and Thomas (1953:162) highlight how in general the determiner tends to precede the determined in Latin, whereas 'Romance inclines more to put the modifier after the word modified' (Grandgent 1907:30) according to a typological distinction from which many other basic properties are said to follow (Schmidt 1926; Greenberg 1963; Lehmann 1974; Harris 1978:4–6; Bauer 1995:13). Thus, to take three simple examples (45a–c), we can see that, at least as a possibility (though for the various markedness patterns, see the discussion in §§3.1–2), Latin places the modifier before the nominal, verbal and clausal head, whereas in the corresponding Romance structures, here exemplified by Portuguese, the modifier typically follows its nominal, verbal and clausal head (heads appear in bold type in the following examples):

(45) a. MORTIS   **METUS**   / o   ***mêdo*** *da*   *morte*
          death.F.GEN fear.M.NOM / the.M.SG fear.M of.the.F.SG death.F
          'the fear of death'
      b. MORTEM   **TIMEO**   / ***temo***   *a*   *morte*
          death.F.ACC I.fear   / I.fear   the.F.SG   death.F
          'I fear death'

c. NE	MORIATUR	**TIMEO**	/ **temo**	*que*	*morra*
that.not	he.die.SBJV	I.fear	/ I.fear	that	he.die.SBJV

'I fear he may die'

As has already been noted above (§2), this simple observation regarding the basic ordering of head and modifier, which classifies Latin essentially as head-final and Romance as head-first, captures the essence and more of the traditional synthesis–analysis distinction. In particular, the head parameter is generally taken to characterize not only syntactic structure, but also morphological structure (von Wartburg [1934] 1971:256; Renzi 1985:132; Bauer 1995:4, 7, 24f.; Zamboni 2000:123f.; Oniga 1998; 2004: §3.3), witness Latin head-last compounds like UEXILLIFER 'flag-bearer', which contrast with Romance head-first compounds like It. *porta*bandiera (see Bauer, this volume, chapter 10: §2). In this way, we can bring under the same roof changes that took place in morphology and syntax, treating them as reflexes of the same overall development towards a consistent manifestation of the head parameter. Thus, in the transition from Latin to Romance, the principal change evident in morphosyntax was not the replacement of synthetic with analytic forms, but the reversal of the order of head and modifier, namely the substitution of *Postdeterminierung* by *Prädeterminierung* (Baldinger 1968:88). Consequently, in the same way that the complement comes to follow its verb (CICERES NON **HABENT** > Ext. *no* **tienin** *garbanzu* 'they don't have any chickpeas'), so the lexical element in an inflected nominal or verbal form comes to follow its preposition (e.g., ROMAM > Fr. *à Rome* 'to Rome') or auxiliary (e.g., CELEBRATUR > It. *viene* celebrato 'it is celebrated').

Although subsuming much of the synthesis–analysis distinction, the results of the head parameter do not appear to make any useful predictions about the rise of functional structure (see §3.3). At most, all that one can say is that head-last – or to borrow Bauer's (1995) terminology, left-branching – structures produce or align with autonomous morphologically complex words (e.g., LAUAUERAT 'wash.PLPF.3SG'), while head-first or right-branching structures yield syntactic phrases in which the grammatical categories of the construction as a whole are realized by a lexicalized functional head (e.g., Sp. [$_{IP}$ [$_{I'}$ **había** [$_{VP}$ *lavado*]]] 'he.had washed'). By this same line of reasoning, however, we will be forced to assume, given the nature of the head parameter, that the corresponding Latin construction contains the same functional head, albeit ordered head-finally (namely [$_{IP}$ [$_{I'}$ [$_{VP}$ LAU-]**AUERAT**]]), thereby losing our overall generalization, for which we saw that there was considerable empirical motivation (§3.3), that Latin, unlike Romance, lacked functional projections.

Interpreted in this manner as a syntactic constraint (see Bauer's (1995:35–39) definition of head, based in large part on X-bar theoretical assumptions), a priori the head parameter also proves incompatible with our previous conclusions in section 3 about the shift from a predominantly non-configurational syntax to a fully configurational syntax. If Latin syntactic structure is predominantly of an exocentric, 'flat' design in which all elements can, in principle, occur in all positions, then there is no way in which the strict generalizations of a head-final parameter setting, defined in both linear and hierarchical terms, can be formally stated. If, on the other hand, we interpret head and modifier in semantic terms – the head is the element which cannot be omitted (e.g., Cat. *taules (de fusta)* '(wooden) tables') and whose subcategorization frame determines which, if any, dependents may co-occur (e.g., Glc. *tódolos cidadáns teñen dereito ó traballo* 'all citizens have the right **to work**') – then the essence of the head parameter can still be retained:[64] the head-final directionality of the parameter setting for Latin represents a strong tendency, but not an inviolable principle, of the grammar given the freedom afforded by its non-configurational syntax. By contrast, the parameter assumes a much more rigid interpretation in Romance, where the design of a configurational syntax consistently aligns the 'semantic' head with a fixed 'syntactic' head-first position. This explains, among other things, why in Romance dependent genitives and relatives consistently follow nominals (see 46a–b), nominals follow adpositions (see 46c), objects and adverbs follow verbs (see 46d–e) and lexical verbs follows auxiliaries (see 46f):

(46) a. *sa*   **mákkina**   *ruja*   *de*   *Juanne* (Srd.)
        the   car   red   of   Juanne
        'Juanne's red car'

      b. **Guillermo** *quien*   *construyó*   *esta*   *casa* (Sp.)
        Guillermo who   built   this   house
        'Guillermo who built this house'

      c. **sui**   *mûrs* (Frl.)
        'on.the walls'

      d. **menèri** *las*   *vacas*   *a*   *l'abeurador* (Occ.)
        'I.led   the   cows   to   the.trough'

      e. u tʃøv   ˈtʃaŋ   tʃaˈniŋ (Cairo Montenotte, Pie.)
        it=rains   slow   slow.DIM
        'it is raining very lightly'

      f. **quere**   *chover* (Glc.)
        it.wants   rain.INF
        'it's about to rain'

In Latin, by contrast, the parameter is generally acknowledged to display a less than consistent setting (Grandgent 1907:31; Bauer 1995:4; Oniga 2004:52). As we have already observed above in section 3.1.1, the head-final setting is generally observed with demonstratives, quantifiers, intensifiers and pronominal genitives, which tend to precede nominals, as well as with auxiliaries and complements, which both precede their associated verb, not to mention noun and verb inflections, whereas the head-first setting already seems relatively well established with adnominal genitives and other adnominal complement types, possessives, relatives and verbal adjuncts. In other cases, such as the position of the adjective, for example, we saw that there is no consensus on an unmarked position, hence the impossibility of talking about a parameter setting in either direction. A similarly mixed situation is observable with Latin co-ordination structures, which can employ both an older head-last structure (e.g., SENATUS [[POPULUS]QUE] 'the senate and the people') and a more innovative head-first structure (e.g., SENATUS [ET [POPULUS]]).

In short, the overall conclusion to be drawn from the Latin evidence is that of a language drawn between two tendencies which contrast an archaic pattern of head-last/left-branching structures with an innovative pattern of head-first/right-branching structures. As Grandgent (1907:31) succinctly sums up the situation, 'Classic Latin may be said to represent an intermediate stage, while the revolution was in progress; there was a long struggle, and for centuries the ancient and the modern type were used side by side'. Indeed, on this point there is general consensus in the literature that Indo-European was predominantly head-last, whose grammatical structures in the transition to the daughter languages increasingly became head-first (Lehmann 1974; Bichakjian 1987:94; Bauer 1995:213f.; Oniga 2004:103). Adams (1976), however, convincingly argues that this change in directionality had already been largely completed as early as the Classical Latin period, but that its effects were in many cases masked by the deliberately archaizing patterns of the literary language.

To this it must be added that the relevant change in directionality of the parameter did not occur at the same time in all areas of the grammar, but, rather, displays a staggered development proceeding at different rates in different morphosyntactic domains. To begin with, it is widely acknowledged that head-first structures emerge much earlier in syntactic than in morphological structures (Oniga 2004:52, 103): in the area of derivational morphology, for example, Latin compounds, apart from a handful of rare and usually late exceptions (e.g., FULCIPEDIA 'harlot', UERSIPELLIS 'werewolf'), still strongly resist head-first formations, and the head-final patterns of Latin inflectional morphology are still relatively well preserved in Romance verbal and nominal formations (e.g., Srs. *ils fretgs* 'the.PL fruits', (literary) Pt. *chamara* (< CLAMAUERAT) 'he had called'). As for syntactic structures, the first signs of the head-first setting are to be observed in the nominal group, surfacing for the first time in the archaic Latin period (e.g., adjectives, adpositions, relatives), and only spreading to the verbal group at a later date, where a number of head-last constructions survive well into the Romance period (e.g., verb-final orders in French relatives until the seventeenth century) and, in some cases, even up until the present day (e.g., Sp. synthetic future *llorará* 'he will cry', though now rivalled by the right-branching GO-future *va a llorar* 'he's gonna cry') (Vincent 1988a:63; Bauer 1995:4, 11, 85, 89f., 168f.; Oniga 2004:94). Similarly, we have seen that there are generalized signs of head-first in conjunction with complementizers (§3.3.3.1) and adpositions (see note 56) since the earliest textual attestations (see §3.3.3.1).

There are, of course, a number of apparent exceptions to the generalization of the head-first parameter in Romance. For example, in section 3.1.2 it was noted that alongside the unmarked postnominal position of the Romance adjective, just about the only position available in some varieties such as Sardinian, a number of Romance varieties (with growing degrees of productivity the further one goes back in time; Huber 1933:148; Alisova 1967; Ledgeway 2007a:115–21; Vincent 2007a:61–64) also license prenominal adjectives under particular circumstances (e.g., Fr. *un ancien collègue* 'a former colleague'). Rather than constituting a genuine problem for the head parameter, it is, however, possible to maintain a head-first analysis even in these cases, if we assume that at an underlying level the adjective is always generated in postnominal position and that apparent prenominal adjectives constitute derived structures (see Vanelli 1980; Salvi 1985). Alternatively, others have maintained, both from a cross-linguistic perspective (Dryer 1988) as well as on the evidence of Romance-specific data (Berruto 1998; Pountain 1998b; Vincent 2007a:57f., n3), that there is no compelling correlation between the order of the adjective and other word patterns, in which case the Romance prenominal adjective would constitute a genuine exception to the parameter setting. Another potential counter-example to the head-first setting includes, according to Renzi (1985:135), Romance determiner + noun sequences (e.g., Vgl. *i* + *jáur* 'the hours'), in which he sees a continuation of the Latin head-last pattern (e.g., ILLE PUER 'that boy'). However, as noted above in section 3.3.1, with the rise of configurationality and functional structure, determiner + noun sequences should be considered DP structures (Longobardi 1994; Giusti 2002), in which the head of the construction is the determiner which selects for an NP complement (identical considerations carry over to the Romanian enclitic definite article, where its postnominal position is derived by N- or A-raising (see 19a–b)). On this view, Romance determiner + noun sequences represent canonical head-first structures. Indeed, whenever determiners such as demonstratives function as modifiers rather than heads in Romance, according to the archaic Latin pattern, a possibility preserved in Ibero- and Daco-Romance varieties (see 20a–d), they consistently follow their associated noun on a par with adjectives (e.g., Sp. *los ingleses **aquellos*** 'those English (people)').

More problematic for the head parameter, and indicative of a more general problem with the same, is the simple sentential negation of many Gallo-Romance varieties (Price 1962; 1986; Posner 1984; 1985a; 1985b; Schwegler 1990; Zanuttini 1991: ch. 3; Parry 1997:183–85) and northern Catalan (Veny 1998:51), where the negator does not precede its associated finite verb as in other Romance varieties (see 47a–b), but stands immediately after the finite verb (see 47c–f), the so-called Stage III in Jespersen's (1917) negation cycle:

(47) a. **no** *portarem* *armes* (Cat.)
          not   we.shall.carry   arms
          'we shall not bear arms'

      b. **nu** *gghioca* *cu* *ll'ate* (Nap.)
          not   he.plays with the.others
          'he does not play with the others'

      c. *elle* *fume* **pas** (coll. Fr.; cf. PASSUM 'step')
          she   smokes   not
          'she doesn't smoke'

      d. *mi* *capis* **miga** (Eml.; cf. MICAM 'crumb')
          I   understand   not
          'I don't understand'

      e. *esperèri* **pas** (Occ.)
          I-waited not
          'I didn't wait'

      f. *l'aiga* *és* **pas** *clara* (Ros.)
          the-water is   not   clear
          'the water is cloudy'

According to one view, canonical Romance negation structures like (47a–b) involve a head-first structure in which the negator constitutes the head that selects for a complement consisting of the verbal constituent (in generative terms, a NegP that selects for an IP complement). In this light, the structures in (47c–f) can be brought into line with those in

(47a–b), if we assume that they are derived from raising of the verb to a position higher than that of the negator (see Renzi 1985:136f.; Zanuttini 1991), as witnessed by the underlying position of the negator to the left of the verb in certain non-finite contexts (e.g., coll. Fr. *pour **pas** fumer* 'for not smoke.INF', Mil. *de **minga** credeg* 'of not believe.INF=it'). However, according to some analyses (see Rowlett 1998; Zanuttini 1991), postverbal negators like French *pas* represent, not the governing head of a NegP, but rather, its specifier position. If this is the case, then there is no obvious sense in which the negator can be formally considered the governing head of the construction. Moreover, this conclusion has a fundamental semantic, not to mention intuitive, appeal, in that negation is traditionally taken to be an operator that modifies the veracity of the verbal predicate (= the operand). Moreover, negators can be omitted without affecting the grammaticality of the remaining sentence, hence are improbable candidates for head status. We are thus forced to conclude, assuming the verb to be the head of the construction, that Romance negation is, somewhat unexpectedly, invariably head-final (namely Neg + **V**), but that the fixed linearization of head and modifier is often superficially disrupted in Gallo-Romance by the effects of verb raising in certain cases (namely **V** + Neg t_V).

Examples like this highlight the difficulties in providing a consistent definition of the term 'head' which, in some cases, is open to subjective interpretation or yields apparently counterintuitive results (La Fauci 1997:41–43). For example, in Bauer's (1995) analysis, the head of a comparative like DULCIOR 'sweet**er**' is taken to be the suffix -IOR on account of the parallel with other inflectional forms, where the lexical stem is the modifier and the inflection is the head consistently surfacing to the left in the corresponding Romance structure (e.g., PAULO > It. *a Paolo* 'to Paolo', CLAMAUI > **ho** *chiamato* 'I.have called'). However, in the case of the corresponding Romance comparative structure (e.g., It. **più** *dolce*), conventional X-bar structural representations of the phrase would represent the adverb *più* 'more' as the specifier of the AP headed by *dolce* 'sweet', hence not the head of the entire construction. In other cases, the parameter yields apparently conflicting results. For instance, whereas the emergence of Romance AUX + V sequences conforms to the expected head-first/right-branching pattern, the inflectional structure of the auxiliary itself displays a head-final/left-branching pattern (La Fauci 1997:42f.).

Similar problems for the head parameter result from a consideration of the development of word order. In sections 3.2.2 and 3.3.3.1 we identified in the passage from Classical Latin (S)OV to modern Romance (S)VO an intermediate stage of Top/FocV(X), namely a V2 syntax. Interpreting these developments in terms of the head parameter, at the very most one can only talk of a change from OV to VO at the start and end points, whereas the intermediate V2 stage proves more difficult to capture. Of course, one could, as we did above, argue that underlyingly the V2 stage is part of the new VO order, inasmuch as the sentential core presents a fixed SVO order. However, this VO characterization fails to reflect the fact that in root clauses the finite verb is invariably fronted to the left periphery, where it is frequently preceded, among other constituents, by a fronted complement yielding the older OV order. In short, what this intermediate V2 situation requires is a hybrid characterization of the head parameter, a setting, however, not envisaged by the theory.

6   Nominative/accusative vs. active/stative alignments

In this final section we shall discuss a number of core changes in the transition from Latin to Romance, many of which have already been discussed in detail above, in relation to an ongoing and as of yet unresolved conflict between two competing alignments in the marking of arguments (La Fauci 1988:48; Zamboni 1998:128). Although not necessarily providing direct support for our preceding formal approaches to the historical morphosyntax of Romance, much of what will be discussed below is entirely compatible with the conclusions of these approaches, especially those relating to the rise of configurationality and functional structure, whilst demonstrating how the core developments in the history of Romance morphosyntax can be integrated into a highly original and insightful theory of a centuries-old typological conflict between a nominative/accusative and an active/stative syntactic orientation (central to our discussion are the seminal works of La Fauci (1988; 1991; 1997; 1998) and Zamboni (1998; 2000)). In particular, it will be demonstrated that, despite both the start and the end points of our discussion, Classical Latin and modern Romance, displaying a predominantly nominative/accusative orientation in their morphosyntactic systems, this does not represent a case of uninterrupted continuity but, rather, masks an intermediate stage, only in part inferable from documented sources, of an active/stative orientation (Zamboni 1998:130).

Before we turn to look at the details of these developments, we must first establish some basic concepts and distinctions. Following a widely accepted typological distinction (Dixon 1994:6–8; see also Comrie 1989:110–16), we can distinguish three core sentential participants labelled A and O (see 48a), the subject and object, respectively, of a transitive construction, and S (see 48b–c), the subject of an intransitive construction (the following examples are from Spanish):

(48) a. **Guillermo** (A)   *perdió*   **la**   **llave** (O)
      'Guillermo   lost   the   key'
   b. **Guillermo** (S)   *perdió*
      'Guillermo   lost'
   c. *Se perdió* **la**   **llave** (S)
      self=lost   the   key
      'the key got lost'

In a number of cases, both Latin and Romance make a further distinction between two types of intransitive S(ubject), namely between: (i) an S with an agentive interpretation (see 48b) and hence, to all intents and purposes, identical to A(gent), bar the presence of an O(bject); and (ii) an S with an UNDERGOER interpretation (see 48c) and hence, to all intents and purposes, identical to O(bject), bar the presence of an A(gent). The former we may call S_A and the latter S_O.

To varying degrees, languages make available the means to encode these three core participants through nominal marking systems (case, adpositions), verb marking systems (agreement, auxiliaries and voice distinctions) and through sentential word order (La Fauci 1988:54). Together, these three mechanisms of argument marking variously place the three nuclear sentential participants into one of the following three typological organizations (La Fauci 1997:12):

(i)   A is formally distinguished from O and, in turn, shares the same formal marking as $S_{A/O}$;

(ii)   O is formally distinguished from A, and, in turn, shares the same formal marking as $S_{A/O}$;

(iii)   A is formally distinguished from O, but the formal marking of S is split between A (= S_A) and O (= S_O).

The arrangement described in (i) is traditionally termed a nominative/accusative alignment, while the arrangement described in (ii) yields an ergative/absolutive alignment. The third and final alignment represents a compromise between the two preceding alignments, in that S is formally aligned in part with A and in part with O, as illustrated in Table 8.5.

It is doubtful, however, that the full grammatical apparatus of any language can be consistently described in terms of just one of these three alignments (La Fauci 1988:31f.), although it is often possible to associate particular languages with one predominant orientation. For example, below

Table 8.5 *Typological alignments of A, S and O*

Nominative/Accusative	Active/Stative	Ergative/Absolutive
A	A	A
S	S_A	S
	S_O	
O	O	O

we shall see that Classical Latin combines a nominative/accusative orientation in the nominal system with a partially active/stative orientation in certain areas of the verb system (La Fauci 1997:17–19). In the later Latin period, and continuing into the early Romance period, this active/stative orientation expands further into the verb system, spreading even to the nominal system (and, in some cases, perhaps even to be considered an ergative/absolutive orientation), whereas at the level of the sentence there emerges a new nominative/accusative orientation in word order. However, in many cases and in some, especially southern Romance, varieties these new or expanded active/stative alignments were short-lived, coming to be replaced eventually by new nominative/accusative alignments.

Significantly, the complex vicissitudes in the morphosyntactic alignments of the late Latin and Romance nominal, verbal and sentential systems to be discussed below point to a new (though see Cremona 1970, and now also Green 2006) areal classification of Romània in terms of a northern–southern continuum (Zamboni 1998:128; 2000:86, 104f.), rather than the traditional western–eastern (von Wartburg 1950) or central–peripheral (Bartoli 1925; 1929; 1933) divisions based on predominantly phonological and lexical criteria, respectively. This northern–southern continuum contrasts a northern Romània, coinciding with the historical areas of *Gallia transalpina* (northern Gaul: *langue d'oïl*, southern Gaul: *langue d'oc*), *Gallia cisalpina* (northern Italian dialects) and *Raetia* (Raeto-Romance varieties) on the one hand, and a southern Romània made up of the (historical) areas of central-southern Italy (central-southern Italian dialects), Sardinia, Iberia (Galician, Portuguese, Spanish, Catalan), Istria/Illyria (Dalmatian) and Dacia (Romanian) on the other. Putting aside details for the moment, these northern/southern areas can be broadly, though not exhaustively, distinguished, respectively, in terms of the following structural oppositions: (i) prolonged retention/early loss of V2 syntax; (ii) marking of A/S (subject clitics, generalized preverbal position) vs. marking of O (prepositional accusative, object clitic doubling); (iii) prolonged retention/early loss of binary (or ternary) case system; (iv) HABERE/ESSE auxiliary alternation vs. generalized auxiliary (ether HABERE or ESSE depending on variety and/or syntactic context); (v) retention vs. loss of participial agreement; and (vi) loss vs. retention (and reinforcement) of preterite (Zamboni 2000:87).

6.1   Classical Latin

The nominal system of Classical Latin can unequivocally be described in terms of a nominative/accusative alignment (Zamboni 2000:103). By way of illustration, consider the three sentences in (49a–c):

49   a. **ROMANUS**   INIMICUM   NECAT
         Roman.NOM   enemy.ACC   kills
         'The Roman kills his enemy'
      b. **ROMANUS**   NAUIGAT
         Roman.NOM   sails
         'The Roman is sailing'
      c. **ROMANUS**   ABIT
         Roman.NOM   leaves
         'The Roman is leaving'

Whether the Latin grammatical subject corresponds to the A of a transitive predicate (see 49a), the S_A of an (intransitive) unergative predicate (see 49b) or the S_O of an (intransitive) unaccusative predicate (see 49c), it invariably surfaces in the nominative (indicated by the final inflection -s borne by the subject ROMANUS in the above examples). By contrast, the grammatical O(bject) of a transitive verb surfaces in the distinct accusative form (marked in (49a) above by final inflectional -M on INIMICUM). It follows, then, that the nominal system of Latin formally contrasts A and $S_{(A/O)}$ (marked nominative) with O (marked accusative) to yield a canonical nominative/accusative orientation which proves totally insensitive to the semantic characterization (AGENT vs. UNDERGOER) of the subject.

By contrast, the verb system of Classical Latin is less consistent in its morphosyntactic orientation. As the examples in (49a–c) have already clearly illustrated, in the active voice the verb system in the tenses of the IMPERFECTUM also operates according to a nominative/accusative alignment, in that the finite verb invariably agrees in person and number with the nominative subject (witness the final 3SG inflection -T in all three examples above), and not with the accusative object. However, Classical

Latin also boasts a middle voice (UOX MEDIA), which formally brings together intransitive UNDERGOER subjects variously drawn from the passive (see 50a) and deponent (see 50b) paradigms, which in the IMPERFECTUM align with verb-forms marked by the middle formant -R:

(50) a. INIMICUS   NECATUR
          enemy.NOM is-killed
          'The enemy is being killed'
      b. INIMICUS   MORITUR
          enemy.NOM dies
          'The enemy is dying'

As the active–passive alternation between (49a) and (50a) illustrates, the surface passive subject in the latter is underlyingly an O, hence its S_O status. Analogously, the overwhelming majority of deponents are unaccusative predicates, whose surface subject is analysed in many current formal frameworks as a derived subject moved from or related to the verb's complement position, hence its UNDERGOER interpretation and S_O status. In the tenses of the PERFECTUM, the middle is further marked with respect to the active: whereas the latter employs a synthetic verb construction (cf. the use of the perfective -UI- formative in 51a–b), the former makes recourse to a periphrastic conjugation consisting of auxiliary ESSE and participle, the latter agreeing in gender and number with nominative subject (see 52a–b):

(51) a. ROMANUS   INIMICUM   NECAUIT
          Roman.NOM enemy.ACC   killed
          'The Roman has killed his enemy'
      b. ROMANUS   NAUIGAUIT
          Roman.NOM   sailed
          'The Roman has been sailing'
(52) a. INIMICUS   NECATUS   EST
          enemy.M.NOM   killed.M.SG.NOM is
          'The enemy has been killed'
      b. INIMICUS   MORTUUS   EST
          enemy.M   died.M.SG.NOM   is
          'The enemy has died'

To conclude, the Classical Latin verb system combines a formal distinction between a nominative/accusative alignment in the tenses of the IMPERFECTUM of the active and middle voices, where in both cases the finite verb displays person and number agreement with its associated nominative subject (be it A, S_A or S_O), and an active/stative alignment in the tenses of the PERFECTUM (Zamboni 2000:103), where A and S_A are marked by a synthetic paradigm and S_O alone is marked by a periphrastic paradigm with number and gender features referenced in the agreement of the verbal participle (La Fauci 1997:20).

6.2 *Late Latin and conservative Romance: active/stative syntax*

In the passage from Classical Latin to Romance there is initially a notable decline in the nominative/accusative orientation of the nominal and verbal systems, paralleled by a corresponding expansion in the range of the active/stative alignment in the verbal and nominal domains. In the verb system, reflexes of an expanding active/stative alignment can be observed in the genesis of the perfective auxiliary construction and concomitant patterns of participle agreement, which, in turn, provide the necessary impetus for comparable realignments within the nominal system surfacing in the early Romance reduced case systems based on a binary opposition and, ultimately, in the gradual generalization of the accusative as the universal, unmarked, case-form. At the level of the sentence, too, the effects of an active/stative alignment are clearly observable in emergent word order patterns.

6.2.1 The verbal group

6.2.1.1 Perfective auxiliary constructions

Traditionally, the emergence of the HABERE + PP periphrasis is retraced to the grammaticalization of an original resultative aspectual periphrasis (Vincent 1982; Salvi 1982; 1987; Tuttle 1986b; Zamboni 2000:127f.):

(53) a. [VP [THEME [LOC IN   EA   PROUINCIA] PECUNIAS   MAGNAS
          in   that   province money.F.PL.ACC big.F.PL.ACC
[pp COLLOCATAS]] HABENT]
placed.F.PL.ACC they-have
'They have much money invested in that province'

b. [IP [VP [LOC IN EA PROUINCIA] [THEME PECUNIAS   MAGNAS]
         in that province   money.F.PL.ACC big.F.PL.ACC
COLLOCATAS]   HABENT]
placed.F.PL.ACC   they-have
'They have invested much money in that province'

The oft-cited Ciceronian sentence in (53a) is generally claimed to exemplify a resultative aspectual periphrasis (and not at this stage a temporal periphrasis), in that it foregrounds the present result of a backgrounded past action. Hence the meaning of (53a) is not that of a perfective past action 'they have invested much money in that province', but that of a present state or condition ensuing from a previous past action 'they have much money invested in that province'. Consequently, in (53a) HABENT '(they) have' is still a lexical predicate indicating possession which subcategorizes for a LOCATIVE subject (the possessor) encoded in the 3PL inflection -NT and a THEME direct object (the possessed), namely IN EA PROUINCIA PECUNIAS MAGNAS COLLOCATAS 'in that province much money invested'. Note, in particular, that the verbal participle COLLOCATAS 'placed, invested' simply functions as an adjectival modifier of the direct object MAGNAS PECUNIAS, hence its agreeing feminine plural form (in -AS) which, as part of its argument structure, subcategorizes for a LOCATIVE complement (namely IN EA PROUINCIA 'in that province') and an AGENT ('the investor'), whose identity is not made explicit in this structure, though possibly recoverable from the extra-linguistic context. Consequently, in (53a) the identity of the investor(s) can either coincide with the LOCATIVE subject of HABENT or is free to refer to another pragmatically salient, albeit implicit, individual or group of individuals. Given the nature of the resultative construction, it is thus only compatible with the participles of transitive predicates, hence the presence of an implied AGENT or, more rarely, EXPERIENCER (e.g., 'I have got something painted/written/prepared/thought out'), but is clearly not compatible with intransitive predicates (e.g., **'I have got cried/sung/gone/come').

Through time, however, resultative structures like (53a) became increasingly common and, given the frequent pragmatic inference that the LOCATIVE subject of HABERE and the implied AGENT or EXPERIENCER of the participle were one and the same – a pattern which apparently began with participles with EXPERIENCER subjects (cf. *I have got the lesson learnt, he had the plan thought out*, etc.), where it would have been impossible to interpret the implied EXPERIENCER and the LOCATIVE possessor of HABERE as disjoint in reference – this coreferential interpretation eventually became conventionalized. As a result of this conventionalization ('I have got much money invested in that province' ⇒ 'I have invested much money in that province'), the original resultative periphrasis in (53a) is transformed into a present perfective periphrasis with concomitant reanalysis of its structure (Harris and Campbell 1995:50f.), resulting in a modification in the underlying structure of the construction but with no overt surface manifestation (see 53b). In the new reanalysed structure in (53b), the identification of the implied AGENT (here the 'investor(s)') with the subject of HABENT entails that HABERE is no longer an independent lexical verb of possession, but now functions instead as an auxiliary referencing the person and number features of the participial subject and the tense and modal features of the entire construction. As such, auxiliary HABERE now simply inherits the argument structure, including the A/S_A subject, of its associated participle (see Harris and Campbell's (1995:193) *Heir-Apparent Principle*). Thus, COLLOCATAS no longer functions as an adjectival modifier of the nominal MAGNAS PECUNIAS, but now assumes fully-fledged verbal status as the head of the VP, selecting the latter nominal as its NP object. As a result of this categorial change from adjective to verb, agreement of the participle with its direct object is progressively weakened (cf. early examples like the sixth-century HAEC OMNIA PROBATUM HABEMUS 'we have tried.NEUT.SG all these things.NEUT.PL' (Oribas.); Väänänen 1982:255), since verbs in Romance canonically agree with subjects and not objects. Agreement disappears first in those contexts (e.g., with postverbal DPs) in which perceptual factors rendered its presence barely functionally relevant, but resists with greater resilience in those contexts (e.g., with preverbal DPs and (third person) clitics) in which its presence plays a significant functional role in sentence parsing (Smith 1993; 1995a; 1999b). Finally, as a genuine perfective construction no longer linked to the transitivity of lexical HABERE, the distribution of the periphrasis soon extends to include (intransitive) unergative participles (cf. seventh-century SICUT PARABOLATUM HABUISTIS 'Thus you had spoken' (*Form. Merkel.* 260,7)), ultimately emerging as a generalized perfective periphrasis for all predicates with A or S_A subjects irrespective of their transitivity. In Table 8.6, we sum up the principal changes involved in the reanalysis and grammaticalization of the temporal perfective periphrasis.

With the rise of the perfective HABERE periphrasis, there remained a residue of morphologically active intransitive verbs with UNDERGOER subjects, namely unaccusatives (e.g., IRE 'to go', UENIRE 'to come', (DE)SCENDERE 'to descend', SALIRE 'to leap', ENTRARE 'to enter', TORNARE 'to return', etc.) which proved semantically incompatible with the HABERE periphrasis on account of their subcategorization of a subject of the S_O, rather than the

Table 8.6 *Reanalysis and grammaticalization of* HABERE + *PP*

HABERE = lexical (+θ)	HABERE = auxiliary (−θ)
Resultative	Present perfective
2 subjects / biclausal	1 subject / monoclausal
Adjectival PP	Verbal PP
+ Participial Agr	± Participial Agr
Transitives	Transitives > Unergatives

A/S_A, type. This residue of unaccusatives is said to have been absorbed into the established ESSE perfective periphrasis for deponents and passives (e.g., *entratʊ sʊm), since they shared with the latter the property of subcategorizing for a subject of the S_O type. With the eventual loss of the middle morphology of the IMPERFECTUM, in some cases subsequently marked by the reflexive marker SE (e.g., MYRINA QUAE SEBASTOPOLIM SE UOCAT (= UOCATUR) 'Myrina which is called Sebastopol'; see Zamboni 2000:125f.), the original deponents (where they survive) and unaccusatives were no longer formally distinguished (e.g., MORI > *morire 'to die': ENTRARE 'to enter', MORITUR > *mɔrit 'he dies' : ENTRAT 'he enters'), and continued to converge with the passive in the perfective paradigms (e.g., *ɛst mɔrtʊ : *ɛst entratʊ : *ɛst kantatʊ).

The overall result, then, of these developments is a split in the perfective forms of the verb between a periphrasis with auxiliary HABERE for transitive/unergative predicates with A/S_A subjects on the one hand, and a periphrasis with auxiliary ESSE for unaccusative and passive predicates with S_O subjects on the other. In short, the verb system of late Latin and, in turn, (early) Romance develops an active/stative orientation (also often termed 'split intransitivity') in which intransitive S(ubjects) are formally distinguished according to their S_A–S_O characterization (La Fauci 1988:51f.).

While accepting the core developments of the HABERE/ESSE periphrasis outlined above, this analysis takes the genesis of the HABERE periphrasis as essentially unrelated to the already established ESSE periphrasis, situating its origins wholly in the fortuitous reanalysis of an erstwhile resultative periphrasis. An empirically and theoretically more satisfying alternative analysis is, however, to view the rise of the HABERE periphrasis as an integrated change in the verb system within a more general active/stative realignment already underway in Classical Latin (La Fauci 1988:46–50; 1997:26; 2006). Recall that above we observed in relation to (52a–b) that in the tenses of the PERFECTUM Classical Latin already displayed a specialized perfective auxiliary periphrasis (ESSE 'be' + PP) for a subset of intransitive predicates (passives and deponents), whose S(ubjects) at some underlying level of representation are also O(bjects), namely S_O. In the PERFECTUM, therefore, the Latin verb tends to contrast S_O (marked by a periphrastic formation: ESSE + PP) and A/S_A (marked by a synthetic formation: -UI-). The rise of HABERE + PP in the late Latin/early Romance period can then be seen as an analogical response to the ESSE + PP periphrastic conjugation, reinforcing through the auxiliary alternation of otherwise parallel structures the original active/middle distinction of Classical Latin to ultimately produce an active/stative alignment following the extension of ESSE to all constructions with S_O subjects (namely unaccusatives).

On this view, the emergence of HABERE to mark all A/S$_A$ subjects in the perfective paradigms does not involve the fortuitous grammaticalization of HABERE in an original resultative periphrasis, but simply represents the extension of an already existing active/middle distinction in the Latin possessive construction, a case of conservative innovation (Zamboni 2000:87). In this regard, La Fauci (1997:24) notes that Classical Latin had two possessive constructions, one involving ESSE (e.g., PECUNIA MIHI EST 'money.NOM me.DAT is') and the other HABERE (e.g., EGO PECUNIAM HABEO 'I.NOM money.ACC I.have'). Although ESSE is not usually labelled a possessive, a definition traditionally reserved for HABERE, the first example demonstrates that it can assume possessive function. This leads La Fauci to conclude that the possessive value of ESSE and HABERE, just like the perfective value they assume in the so-called auxiliary periphrasis, is a global property of the constructions in which they appear, and not an inherent property of the predicates themselves. Returning, then, to the two possessive constructions, that formed with ESSE should be considered a middle construction, in that the surface subject PECUNIA 'money' (the possessed) is semantically to be identified with the UNDERGOER role, hence a subject of the S$_O$ type, whereas the LOCATIVE argument (the possessor) surfaces as a dative. The HABERE possessive, by contrast, exemplifies an active construction in which the LOCATIVE and UNDERGOER arguments now surface, respectively, as the subject and object of a transitive construction (namely as A and O). It follows that the HABERE/ESSE alternation we find in the late Latin perfective construction is simply a direct extension of this original active/middle alignment of the possessive construction from nominal to verbal predicates.

Generalizing, we note that this original active/stative alignment of the two perfective auxiliaries proves most resilient in northern Romània (e.g., Fr. *tu **as** pleuré* 'you have cried' vs. *tu **étais** monté* 'you had (lit. 'were') gone up'; It. **ha** *dormito* 'he has slept' vs. *è venuto* 'he has (lit. 'is') come'; Pie. (Cairo Montenotte) *a i'**eu** drimì* 'I have slept' vs. *a **suma** partìi* 'we have (lit. 'are') left'; Occ. **ai** *vist* 'I have seen' vs. **soi** *vengut* 'I have (lit. 'am') come'). In the modern varieties of southern Romània, by contrast, there has been a tendency towards the gradual loss of the original active/stative alignment (see Loporcaro 2007b), with either the generalization of HABERE (e.g., Ast. **hubiéremos** *bebío/venío* 'we would have drunk/come'; Cat. *ja **havia** fumat/ arribat* 'I had already smoked/arrived'; Pt. **tinhas** *chorado / estado doente* 'you had cried/been ill'; Sic. **avianu** *manciatu/nisciutu* 'they had eaten/gone out'; Sp. **he** *comido/vuelto* 'I have eaten/returned'; Vgl. *i **ju** insegnut/venájt* 'they had taught/come') or the alternation of both auxiliaries according to: (i) grammatical person (First and second persons typically align with ESSE and third persons with HABERE (§4): Chieri (Pie.) *e' süma vistla* 'we have (lit. 'are') seen her' vs. *al a vistla* 'he has seen her'; Arielli (EAbr.) *so/si viste/ menute* lit. 'I am/you are seen/come' vs. *a viste/menute* lit. 'he/they has/have seen/come'); (ii) tense (e.g., Procida (Cmp.) *jo hó/fove parleto* lit. 'I have/ was spoken'; San Leucio del Sannio (Cmp.) *a/era venuto* lit. 'he has/was come'; see Ledgeway 2000:201–6); (iii) realis/irrealis modality (e.g., ONap. *ben che **avessero** puro foyuto per luongo spacio de via* / ***erano** fuyute a li templi* 'although they had (SUJBV) even run such a long way' / 'they had (lit. 'were.IND') run to the temples'; see Formentin 2001; Ledgeway 2003a); and (iv) finiteness (e.g., Ro. ***au** mâncat/plecat* 'they have eaten/left' vs. *a **fi** mâncat/plecat* 'to have (lit. 'be') eaten/left', *nu cred să **fi** mâncat/plecat* 'I don't believe that they have (lit. 'be.SBJV') eaten/left', *vor **fi** mâncat/plecat* 'they will have (lit. 'be') eaten/left', *ar **fi** mâncat/plecat* 'they would have (lit. 'be') eaten/left'; see Motapanyane 2000:16). Of course, there are some exceptions to these areal generalizations including, in northern Romània, the extension of HABERE to (most) unaccusative predicates in Jerriais, Acadian and Canadian French (e.g., Aca. *il **a** mny* 'he has come'; see Haden 1973:431; Canale *et al.* 1978; Sankoff and Thibault 1980; Jones 2001:109f.) and Venetian (e.g., *el **ga** invecià tanto* 'he has aged a lot'; see Marcato and Ursini 1998:251–54), and the retention of the active/stative HABERE/ESSE split in some parts of southern Romània, including Alguerès and Balearic Catalan varieties (e.g., Alg. ***he** caminat* 'I have walked' vs. *vengut **sés**?* 'have (lit. 'are') you come?'), Bal. (though not the Pitiuses) (e.g., *Què **has** trobat?* 'What have you found?' vs. ***som** tornada de Barcelona* 'I have (lit. 'am') returned from Barcelona'; Moll 1997:134; 2006:290; Veny 1998:68, 81), Sardinian (e.g., (Lula) ***at** faeddatu* 'he has spoken' vs. ***est** ghiratu* 'he has (lit. 'is') returned'), and some southern Italian dialects (e.g., Cos. ***amu** chiangiutu* 'we have cried' vs. ***simu** caduti* 'we have (lit. 'are') fallen'). Despite these variations in the distribution of the perfective auxiliaries, the original correlation between ESSE and S_O is still preserved in all modern varieties in the retention of ESSE as the passive auxiliary.[65]

6.2.1.2 Participle agreement

Together with the emergence of an active/stative split in the auxiliary alternation of the perfective paradigms, there emerges a parallel alignment in the novel system of participle agreement. In particular, in the ESSE periphrasis, the participle variously agrees in gender and number with the subject (see 54a), while in the HABERE periphrasis the participle agrees with the direct object (see 54b) but not with the subject (see 54c), as witnessed by the following examples from Majorcan:

(54) a. *ma   mareta   s'és   aufega**da***
     my   mother.DIM   self=is   suffocated.F.SG
     'my poor mother has suffocated'

  b. *Una   altra   cosa   m'ha   di**ta***   *aquella*
     an   other   thing.F   me=has   told.F.SG   that.one.F.SG
     'Another thing she told me'

  c. *vui   fer   lo   que   ha   fe**t***   *(**fe**ta***)   aquesta*
     I-want do.INF the   what   has   done.M.SG   done.F.SG this.one.F.SG
     'I want to do what she has done'

The agreement paradigm evidenced in (54a–c) is that of a classic active/
stative alignment, in which agreement marks all types of O (including those
which subsequently surface as S), but never A (including S_A).

Now, while there does seem to be a strong correlation with the
retention of the active/stative alignment in the auxiliary system and a
corresponding retention of the same alignment in participle agreement,
witness the evidence of Balearic Catalan (excluding the Pitiuses;
Villangómez i Llobet 1978:122), French, many Italo-Romance varieties (including Italian) and Occitan, there are some genuine counterexamples (Loporcaro 1998a:8–12; for standard Catalan, see §6.3).
Particularly revealing in this respect are many of the dialects of central
and southern Italy, where the original active/stative auxiliary alternation has been replaced by a nominative/accusative person-marking
system (ESSE: first and second vs. HABERE: third), but participle agreement still operates according to the original active/stative alignment.
For example, in the central Italian dialect of Cori spoken in Lazio,
whether HABERE (3PL) or ESSE (all other persons) is selected, the
participle only agrees with O (see 55a) and S_O (see 55b), but never
with A (see 55c) or S_A (see 55d):

55 a. *So   co**te***   *le*   *prunca*
      I.am   picked.F.PL   the.F.PL   plums.F
      'I've picked the plums'

   b. *issi   s'èo   vergognat**i***
      they.M   selves=have   shamed.M.PL
      'they've shamed themselves'

   c. *Maria   è   rut**to***   *jo*   *dindarolo*
      Maria   is   broken.M.SG   the.M.SG   piggy-bank.M
      'Maria's broken the piggy-bank'

   d. *issi   èo   magna**to***
      they.M   have   eaten.M.SG
      'they have eaten'

6.2.2 The nominal group

6.2.2.1 Extended and generalized accusatives

It has long been observed that,[66] apart from some very early examples, Latin texts from the southern provinces of the Empire (Italy, Iberian Peninsula, Africa and the Balkans) from the end of the second century AD, and with rapidly increasing frequency in subsequent centuries (Löfstedt 1933:329–34; Norberg 1944:21–32), frequently show an 'extended' use of the accusative in place of the nominative to mark the subject of finite clauses. This use of the 'extended' accusative (or 'restricted' nominative) does not involve, however, a random substitution of the nominative with the accusative, but rather is structurally determined (La Fauci 1988:54f.; Zamboni 1998:132; Cennamo 2001:4f., 10f.). In particular, it is found in unaccusative syntax, surfacing in middle constructions with deponents (see 56a), anticausatives (see 56b), passives (see 56c), impersonal passives (see 56d) and existentials (see 56e), as well as in active syntax in conjunction with unaccusatives denoting change of state and place (see 56f):

56 a. NASCITUR EI   GENUORUM **CONTRACTIONEM** AUT **CLAUDICATIONEM**
is.born   him.DAT knees.GEN contraction.F.ACC or limp.F.ACC
'his knees are developing a contraction or a limp' (*Chiron*)

b. **MULTOS**   **LANGUORES**   SANANTUR IN IPSIS LOCIS
many.M.PL.ACC weaknesses.M.PL.ACC are-healed in same places
'many weaknesses are healed in these places' (*Antonini Placentini Itinerarium*)

c. **IPSAS**   **PORTAS**   APERIUNTUR
sames.F.PL.ACC gates.F.PL.ACC are-opened
'the(se) gates are opened' (*Peregrinatio Aetheriae*)

d. ET SIC FIT **ORATIONEM** PRO OMNIBUS
and thus is-done prayer.F.SG.ACC for all.ABL.PL
'and thus the prayer is made for everyone' (*Peregrinatio Aetheriae*)

e. HABEBATDE CIUITATE FORSITAN **MILLE** QUINGENTOS PASSUS
had.3SG from city.F.ABL perhaps thousand five.hundred.M.PL.ACC steps.M.ACC
'it was perhaps 1500 paces from the city' (*Peregrinatio Aetheriae*)

f. **GRAUEM**   **HIEM**   FECIT
harsh.F.SG.ACC winter.F.ACC it.made
'It was a harsh winter' (Gregory of Tours)

This 'extended' use of the accusative, which increases greatly in frequency in later Latin texts, is to be construed as a gradual active/stative alignment of the nominal system (La Fauci 1988:54f.; Cennamo 2001:4, 7), parallel to that we have seen emerge in the compound perfective forms of the verb system. In the same way that the latter comes to formally distinguish A/S_A from S_O/O in auxiliary selection and participle agreement (namely HAB-ERE, −Agr vs. ESSE, +Agr), the nominal system too comes to mirror this distinction in the southern provinces with nominative reserved for A/S_A subjects and accusative for S_O subjects and O(bjects). Apart from some important exceptions to be discussed below (§6.2.2.2), by the time our written records begin, the Romance texts of this southern area no longer show such an intransitive split in the nominal system, inasmuch as accusative had generalized to all nominals, A, $S_{A/O}$ and O alike. Indeed, even in late Latin texts there is early evidence of this development (Cennamo 2001:8f.), with the extension in some cases of the accusative even to active, dynamic intransitive subjects (S_A) (e.g., **IPSOS LIOS** SEDEANT 'the(se) children were sitting' (*S. Vincente*)) and, more rarely, to transitive subjects (A) (e.g., IULIA CRESCENSA CUI **LIOS** ET NEPOTES OBITUM FECERUNT 'Iulia Crescensa to whom (her) sons.ACC and grandchildren.ACC death brought' (*ILCV* 3052 B)).

Moreover, this extension of the accusative is not limited to the verbal domain examined above, but also involves the nominal domain, where the nominative is increasingly replaced by the accusative in contexts such as lists, recipes, citation forms, appositions, exclamations and commands:[67]

(57) a. PUTEOLOS,   ANTIUM,   TEGEANUM,   POMPEIOS: HAE SUNT
       Pozzuoli. M.PL.ACC Antium.NEUT.Tegeanum.NEUT.Pompei.M.PL.ACC these are
       UERAE COLONIAE
       real   colonies
       'Pozzuoli, Anzio and Tegeanum are real colonies' (*Corpus Inscriptionum Latinarum* IV, 3525)

    b. ASPARAGOS,   PORROS,   TISANAM   UEL SUCUM
       asparagus.ACC leaks.ACC   pearl.barley(.drink).ACC   or   juice
       'asparagus, leaks, pearl-barley (drink) or juice' (Apicius)

    c. **AQUAM**   FORAS,   **UINUM**   INTRO
       water.ACC outside   wine.NEUT.   inside
       'water outside, wine inside' (Petr.)

    d. **POTIONEM**   AD   EOS,   QUI   SANGUINEM   MEIENT
       drink.ACC   to   those   who   blood   urinate
       'a drink for those who pass blood' (*Chiron* 822)

Significantly, it is generally claimed from a cross-linguistic perspective (Villar 1983:31; Zamboni 1998:131) that the case-form used in so-called a-syntactic functions such as those in (57a–d) above represents the unmarked case. In short, the late Latin evidence points to a gradual generalization of the accusative in verbal and nominal contexts as the unmarked case, a development already complete in the earliest texts of most of southern Romània, but not in those of northern Romània, where a residual nominative–accusative/oblique distinction continued until the fourteenth century (Gallo-Romance) or even the seventeenth/eighteenth century in the case of Ræto-Romance (namely Surselvan and Vallader).[68] Traditionally, the generalization of the accusative in Romance is simplistically claimed to be a consequence of the greater frequency of the accusative with respect to the nominative (Price 1971:96f.; Harris 1978:46; De Dardel and Wüest 1993:52). However, in a language assumed to operate on a nominative–accusative alignment, the near-exclusive survival of the accusative stands out as an unexpected development, since the accusative represents the marked case in such an alignment; as Penny (2002:119) succinctly puts it, 'the traditional argument, while morphologically adequate, is syntactically inadequate'. Rather, the extension and gradual generalization of the accusative in late Latin and Romance provides further proof for the loss of the original nominative/accusative orientation in the nominal system in favour of an active/stative or, better, ergative/absolutive orientation (recall the extension of the accusative to active, dynamic intransitive subjects), in which it is precisely the accusative (= absolutive/stative), and not the nominative (= ergative/active) which represents the unmarked case (La Fauci 1997:56–58; Zamboni 1998:131). Incidentally, this observation calls into question the traditional hypothesis that the loss of the case system was due (in large part) to phonetic erosion (Lakoff 1972:189; Vennemann 1975; Harris 1978:8; Bauer 1995:5). While perceptual saliency will undoubtedly have some impact on the survival of the case system, the evidence reviewed here suggests that the reduction and loss of the case system is fundamentally due to a typological realignment in the nominal system from an original nominative/accusative orientation towards an active/stative (or ergative/absolutive) orientation (La Fauci 1997:41; Zamboni 1998).

6.2.2.2 Early Romance binary case systems

Superficially, the Romance languages fall into two groups, those that from the earliest texts present a binary case distinction (Gallo-Romance, Ræto-Romance: nominative vs. accusative/oblique; Daco-Romance: nominative/accusative vs. dative/genitive) and those which have lost all case distinctions following the generalization of the accusative (southern Romance). De Dardel and Wüest (1993) interpret this distribution of case across Romance in terms of two areally and chronologically conditioned phases of simplification. Accordingly, in the first phase the case system of Latin would have been radically reduced to zero in all emergent Romance varieties on account of presumed creolization processes, in turn followed by a second phase of reconstruction which produced a ternary (nominative vs. accusative vs. oblique) case system. Consequently, the vast majority of southern Romance varieties with apparently no documentary evidence are assumed to be more archaic and belong to the first phase, whereas languages with (residual) case distinctions (Gallo-Romance, Ræto-Romance, Daco-Romance) belong to the second phase. The problems for this theory are numerous (for an overview, see Zamboni 1998:129f.); suffice it to note here two points. First, it is inconceivable that uneducated speakers would be able to reconstruct, even partially, the case system of a (literary) language which had long ceased to be spoken. Second, there is considerable residual evidence in southern varieties to suggest the existence of a binary (or ternary) case system here too.

Rather, all the available evidence from northern and southern Romània points to a binary case system,[69] whose original nominative–accusative orientation, as witnessed, for example, by early Gallo-Romance (see Salvi, this volume, chapter 7: §2, Smith, this volume, chapter 6: §2.2, and Sornicola, this volume, chapter 1: §3.1) where all subjects, be they A, S_A or S_O, are marked nominative in contrast to accusative-marked O(bjects), gradually develops into an active/stative orientation. Revealing in this respect is the observation that virtually all modern Romance residues of the nominative, including in southern Romance varieties where evidence has traditionally been deemed lacking, involve animate nouns:[70] AMITA > 'father's sister' > (O)Fr. (t)ante 'aunt' (cf. OFr. OBL antain); COMPANIO > Cat. company, It. compagno; *kompatre 'godfather' > OSp. cuémpadre; *dɛmʋ 'demon' > Pt. demo; DEUS 'God' > OCat./Pt. Deus, RæR. Dius, Sp. Dios; DOM(I)NUS 'master' > Cat. en 'the' (used before male proper names), Sp. don 'honorific title' (cf. ACC DOMINUM > dueño 'owner, landlord'); *drakʋs 'large serpent > dragon' (cf. DRACONEM) > Cat. drac, It. drago, Ro. drac 'devil'; FRATE(R) 'brother' (cf. ACC FRATREM) > It. frate 'monk', Ro. frate;[71] HOMO 'man' (cf. ACC HOMINEM) > Cat. hom 'one' (indefinite subject), It. uomo, Ro. om; HOSPES 'host, guest' (cf. ACC HOSPITEM) > Ro. oaspe 'guest' (alongside oaspete); JESUS > Fr./Pt. Jesus, Sp. Jésus; LATRO 'thief' (cf. ACC LATRONEM) > Cat. lladre, OGen. layro, It. ladro, ONap. latro; MAGISTE(R) 'master' (cf. ACC MAGISTRUM) > Nap. masto; MAIOR (cf. ACC MAIOREM) > Srd. mère 'boss'; MILES 'soldier' (cf. ACC MILITEM) > Ro. mire 'bridegroom'; MULIE(R) 'lady' > It. moglie 'wife' (cf. ACC MULIEREM > Cat. and Pt./Sp. mulher/mujer); NEMO 'nobody' + NOM -s > Log. nemos; NEPOS 'nephew' (cf. ACC NEPOTEM) >

SLig./Pie. *nevu,* OVnz. *nievo,* Rov. *nevo* (cf. PL *navaudi*); PATE(R) 'father' (cf. ACC PATREM) > Nap. *pate*; PAUO 'peacock' > Sp. *pavo* 'turkey' (cf. PAUONEM > Fr./It. *paon/pavone* 'peacock'); PRE(S)BYTE(R) 'priest' (cf. ACC PRESBYTEREM) > Cal. *prìevite,* OCat./OPt./OSp. *prestre,* Fr. *prêtre,* It. *prete,* Olmb. *prèvido,* Ro. *preot*; *[|]*pullitru 'colt' > Sp. *potro*; RES 'thing' (cf. ACC REM) > Srd. *arrèze* 'reptile, worm'; RE(X) 'king' (cf. ACC REGEM) > (O)Fr. *roi(s),* It. *re*; SARTO(R) 'tailor' (cf. SARTOREM) > Cat./Sp. *sastre,* It. *sarto*; SENIOR 'elder' > Cal. *segnu* 'master!' (VOC), Fr. *sire* 'sire', OOcc. *senher*; SERPE(NS) 'snake' (cf. ACC SERPENTEM) > Nap./OIt. *serpe*; SORO(R) 'sister' (cf. ACC SOROREM) > Fr. *soeur,* It. *suora* 'nun', Ro. *sorǎ,* Srd. *sòrre*; ? *tata* 'father' > Ro. *tatǎ* (cf. ORo. GEN–DAT *tătâni*).

Also to be included here are the agentive suffixes -ATO(R) (e.g., ADUOCA-TOR > OVto. *avogádro* 'lawyer', CURATOR > Cal./Sic./Tar. *curátulu* 'head shepherd', PASTOR > OBel. *pástro* 'pastor', *teksator 'weaver' > Trn. *tesádro,* TRADITOR > Fr. *traitre* 'traitor', PICTOR 'painter' > *peintre*), and -ONE + NOM -S (e.g., FILONES 'spinner' > Egd. *filunz,* Lmb. *filonz,* Egd. *tissunz* 'weaver', Mtv. *crivlonz* 'jigger'), *-a* (F)/-Ø (M) (with OBL -AN- (F)/-ON- (M); e.g., Lvl. *muta/mut* 'girl/boy' vs. *mutans/mutons* 'girls/boys'), many male first names in *-s* (e.g., Cat./Fr./Pt. and Sp. *Carles/Charles/Carlos,* Fr. *Jacques, Georges, Louis,* Fr./Pt./Sp. *Jésus/Jesus/Jesús,* (Pt./)Sp. *Marcos, Pablos, Pilatos*; cf. also Fr. *Eve, Berte* (OFr. ACC *Evain, Bertain*)) and in Italo-Romance in (-ES >) *-i* (e.g., Cal. *Biasi* 'Biagio' (< BIASES), It. *Gi(ov)anni* (< IOHANNES)). For a detailed discussion of the retention of the nominative in Italo-Romance masculine palatal plurals in *-ci/-gi* (e.g., It. *amici* 'friends', *greci* 'Greeks', *medici* 'doctors', *monaci* 'monks' *nemici* 'enemies', *porci* 'pigs'), see Maiden (2000a).

Within a typological perspective, the otherwise exceptional retention of a marked nominative in conjunction with animates clearly points to a pre-vious active/stative alignment in the late Latin/early Romance nominal system (Villar 1983:3–40; La Fauci 1991:149; 1997:56–58; Zamboni 1998:131), in which animate nouns, on account of their high dynamicity and definiteness, were typically encoded as A and S_A and consequently often fossilized in their nominative (= active) form in Romance, whereas inani-mates, on account of their low dynamicity and indefiniteness, were typically encoded as S_O and O and therefore usually fossilized in the accusative (= stative) form in Romance (Zamboni 2000:114). Exceptionally, in a small number of cases both the active and stative forms of the same animate noun have survived (Harris 1978:49), giving rise to lexically and/or syntac-tically differentiated doublets (see Smith, this volume, chapter 6), including COMPANIO/COMPANIONEM > *copain/compagnon* '(boy)friend/companion',

Frk. *wrakkjo/*wrakkjone 'vagabond' > Fr. *gars/garçon* 'lad/boy', HOMO/
HOMINEM > Cat. *hom/home*, Fr. *on/homme* 'one (indefinite NOM only)/
man', Fr. PASTOR/PASTOREM > Fr. *pâtre/pasteur* 'shepherd/pastor', SE(N)
IOR/SENIOREM > Fr. *sire/seigneur* 'sire/lord'.

6.2.3   The sentence: word order

Above (see §3.2.2) we have reviewed abundant evidence to demonstrate
that, following original Latin SOV and transient late Latin / early Romance
XV(X) orders, the Romance languages have broadly converged towards an
unmarked SVO word order. With the exception of some modern Gallo-
Romance varieties, typified by French (see §6.3), this SVO order masks in
most modern varieties an active/stative alignment, where S and O are to be
understood more broadly as A/S_A and O/S_O, respectively. This explains
why in the unmarked case (answering the question: *What happened?*)
transitive (see 58a) and unergative (see 58b) subjects occur preverbally,
whereas unaccusative subjects (see 58c) occur in a postverbal position
corresponding to that occupied by the complement in transitive constructions (following examples from Italian and Catalan):[72]

(58) a. *Il   treno bloccò la   stazione / Un desconegut portà la   bandera*
         the   train blocked the station / a   stranger   carried the flag
      b. *Il   treno fischiava   / Un desconegut passejava   en el pis*
         the   train was.whistling / a   stranger   was.walking in the flat
      c. *Arrivò   il   treno / Arribà   un desconegut*
         arrived   the train / arrived   a   stranger
         'the train/a stranger arrived'

Once again, evidence like this, with early attestations in late Latin
(Cennamo 2001:15f.), points to an active/stative orientation at the level
of the sentence to parallel at every level the identical orientations examined
above in the verbal domain (auxiliary selection, participle agreement) and
nominal domain (restricted nominative for A/S_A and extended accusative
for O_s).

6.2.4   Other patterns

Finally, we briefly review here how the active/stative alignment exemplified
above in relation to the nominal and verbal systems and the sentence finds
further support in a number of other phenomena which systematically
distinguish between A/S_A and O/S_O. Within the nominal system there is
some evidence to suggest that, in the relative pronoun systems of many early

Italo-Romance varieties, an original nominative/accusative distinction QUI vs. QUEM/QUOD > *qui/chi* vs. *que/che* was realigned according to an active/stative orientation (Formentin 1996; Parry 2007). In these varieties, headed subject relatives are typically marked by *qui* when the antecedent is high in the Animacy hierarchy (typically human and dynamic, cf. Genoese 59a), but marked by *que* when the antecedent is low in the Animacy hierarchy (typically non-human and stative; cf. Piedmontese 59b). However, even with human antecedents, the original accusative *que* form is encountered when the verb denotes a non-controlled event or state with a non-agentive subject. This situation typically obtains with unaccusatives (cf. Lombard 59c), but, under the appropriate circumstances, can also involve unergatives and transitives as in the Neapolitan and Piedmontese examples (59d–e), where the acts of urinating and carrying an unborn child, respectively, can readily be construed as involving a non-controlled event with a non-agentive subject.

(59) a. *a quela santa inperarixe* **chi** *de lo mundo è guiarixe* (*Anonimo genovese*)
to that holy empress who of the world is guide
'to that holy empress who leads the world'

b. *Aquesta città* **que** *avea num Iherico* (*Sermoni subalpini*)
this city which had name Jericho
'this city which was called Jericho'

c. *quilli* **ke** *sono andai* (*Purgatorio di S. Patrizio*)
those who are gone
'those who have gone'

d. *chillo* **che** *piscia raro* (*Bagni*)
that.one who pisses rarely
'he who urinates rarely'

e. *som quella* **che** *lo portay* (*Statuto della Compagnia di S. Giorgio*)
I.am that.one who him=I.carried
'I am the one who carried him (in my womb)'

In short, the *qui/que* alternation in the relative system of these early Italo-Romance varieties serves, not so much to mark a subject/object distinction, as is arguably the case in French, but rather to distinguish A/S$_A$ from O/S$_O$ (and even A from O/S according to an ergative/absolutive alignment).

Within the verb system, there are further reflexes of the active/stative alignment in, for example, the distribution of the absolute participle. In this construction, the accompanying DP must function as the direct object of a transitive participle (see 60a) or the subject of an unaccusative (see 60b), but not the subject of an unergative or (see 60c) or transitive (see 60d) participle, thereby aligning once again O with S$_O$ and A with S$_A$ (the following examples are from French):

(60) a. **La lettre**   *écrite,*   *Jean sabla*   *le*   *champagne*
the letter.F.SG written.F.SG Jean sanded the champagne
'Having written the letter, Jean opened the champagne'

b. **Les parents**   *partis,*   *Jean s'est*   *mis à organiser*   *la fête*
the parents.M left.M.PL Jean self=is put to organize.INF the party
'The parents having left, Jean began to organize the party'

c. ****Les amis**   *causé(s),*   *ils*   *se sont*   *embrassés*
the friends.M chatted.M(PL) they selves=are kissed
'The friends having chatted, they kissed'

d. ****Les amis**   *préparé(s)*   *le dîner, ils*   *se sont*   *misà manger*
the friends.M prepared.M(PL) the dinner they selves=are putto eat.INF
'The friends having prepared dinner, they began to eat'

An identical split in the verb system can be seen in the central Marchigiano dialect studied by Peverini (2008). In addition to the widely attested active/ stative alignment in the compound perfective paradigms, where HABERE aligns with A/S$_A$ and ESSE with S$_O$, simplex lexical verbs also display an identical alignment in the third person. Typically, in the third person lexical verbs do not mark a formal number distinction between the singular and the plural, where a form corresponding to the singular in most other Romance varieties marks both numbers (see 61a–b'). However, when the subject is left-dislocated, as is clearly shown when it precedes another topic or a focused phrase, full agreement in the 3PL becomes possible with unaccusatives (see 61c), but not with unergatives or transitives (see 61d):[73]

(61) a. *Marco*   **magna**   *siempre*   *i*   *biseje*
Marco eat.3SG always the peas
'Marco always eats peas'

a'. *Marco e*   *Checco*   **magna**   */ **magnano siempre i*   *biseje*
Marco and Checco eat.3SG / eat.3PL always the peas
'Marco and Checco always eat peas'

b. **Arvenia**   *Marco*
returned.3SG Marco
'Marco was coming back'

b'. **Arvenia**   */ **arveniano Marco e*   *Checco*
returned.3SG / returned.3PL Marco and Checco
'Marco and Checco were coming back'

c. *Marco e*   *Checco* DA LA SCOLA **arvenia**   */ arveniano*
Marco and Checco from the school returned.3SG / returned.3PL
'Marco and Checco were coming back from school'

d. *Marco e*   *Checco dae nonnesi*   **magna**   */ **magnano siempre (i biseje)*
Marco and Checco at grandparents=their eat.3SG / eat.3PL always the peas
'Marco and Checco, at their grandparents' house, always eat (peas)'

Finally, at the level of the sentence, the active/stative orientation surfaces in the distribution of INDE-cliticization (cf. Catalan examples in 62; Burzio 1986; Bentley 2006: ch. 6), bare plural NPs (cf. Sp. examples in 63; Zagona 2002:21f.) and the agreement of adjectives in adverbial function (cf. Cosentino examples in 64; Ledgeway 2000:273f.; 2003b:117–19; Maturi 2002:165). In all three cases, the licensing of the phenomenon in question is exclusively linked to the complement position, thus grouping together O and S_O and contrasting these with A and S_A. Consequently, only transitive objects (cf. (a) examples) and unaccusative subjects (cf. (b) examples), but not unergative/transitive subjects (cf. (c) examples), can be cliticized by INDE 'of it/them', surface as bare plural NPs, and license adverbial agreement:

(62) a. *He   vist   tres* [$_{NP}$ ***nois***] ⇒ ***N'he***   *vist   tres* [t_{en}]
          I.have seen three   boys of.them=I-have seen three
          'I've seen three boys' ⇒ 'I've seen three of them'

        b. *Han vingut   tres* [$_{NP}$ ***nois***] ⇒ ***N'han***   *vingut tres* [t_{en}]
          have   come   three   boys of.them=have come three
          'Three boys came' ⇒ 'Three of them came'

        c. *Tres* [$_{NP}$ ***nois***] *menjan (tomàquets)* ⇒ **Tres [t_{en}] ***en*** *menjan (tomàquets)*
          three   boys eat   (tomatoes)   three   of.them=eat (tomatoes)
          'Three boys are eating (tomatoes)' → 'Three of them are eating (tomatoes)'

(63) a. *Han   visto   **animales***
          they.have   seen   animals
          'They have seen animals'

        b. *Han   muerto   **animales***
          have   died   animals
          'Animals have died'

        c. *****Animales*** *han   comido (la hierba)*
          animals   have   eaten (the grass)
          'Animals have been eating (the grass)'

(64) a. *Ci avia   cunzatu **bbuoni**   i   capiddri*
          her.DAT=I.had prepared good.M.PL the.PL   hair.M.PL
          'I had styled her hair well'

        b. *Si eranu   priperati   **bbuoni***
          selves=they.were prepared.M.PL good.M.PL
          'They had prepared themselves well'

        c. ***Maria ha   studiatu **bbona**   (ssi fatti)*
          Maria   has   studied   good.F.SG (these facts)
          'Maria has been studying (these facts) well'

6.3   Innovative Romance: nominative/accusative syntax

In the preceding discussion we have seen how, in the transition from Latin to Romance, there arose a number of new active/stative orientations, replacing earlier nominative/accusative orientations. These, in turn, were countered in many cases by the emergence of new nominative/accusative alignments which, although clearly morphosyntactic innovations, recreate the conservative typological orientations of Latin, highlighting an ongoing, yet unresolved, conflict between opposing and incoherent argument-marking orientations (La Fauci 1988:59f.; Zamboni 1998:130). Although many of these new nominative/accusative orientations are often reported to affect predominantly southern Romània (Zamboni 2000:128), ostensibly on account of the subsequent changes in the systems of auxiliary selection and participle agreement, they are, as we shall see presently, just as prevalent in northern Romània.

Beginning with the verb system, the most notable development involves the loss of the split auxiliary system in favour of generalized HABERE (/TENERE) in Ibero-Romance and in numerous southern Italian varieties such as southern Calabrian, Neapolitan and Sicilian. Here, the perfective auxiliary therefore no longer encodes the A/S_A vs. S_O split of previous stages, but simply marks the agreement features of the nominative subject, be it A, S_A or S_O. In these same varieties, participle agreement too has generally seen a concomitant attrition (but see Loporcaro 1998a:8–12), such that in ModPortuguese, Spanish and Sicilian, for example, agreement has been lost in all cases except that of the passive participle (e.g., Sp. *la manzana la había comido/**-a* 'The apple.F.SG, I had eaten.M.SG/F.SG it', *Ana ha vuelto/**-a* 'Ana has returned.M.SG/F.SG', but *La carta fue escrita/**-o* 'The letter.F.SG was written.F.SG/M.SG'). The previous pattern which licensed stative-oriented agreement controlled by O and S_O, as still preserved to varying degrees in modern French, Italian and Occitan (see 54a–c), is thus lost. Significant in this respect is the situation found in the modern standard Catalan of Barcelona, where auxiliary ESSE has been lost from the active paradigms, as in Portuguese and Spanish, but participial agreement has been residually preserved in conjunction with (typically feminine) third person accusative clitics (Solà 1993:73–86; Smith 1995a; Moll 1997:135; Loporcaro 1998a:149–53):

(65) a. *L'Alícia   ja   ha   pujat(**a)*
        the=Alícia already   has   ascended.M.SG(F.SG)
        'Alícia has already gone up'

b. *Aquells   llibres   ja   els he   llegit(s)*
  those.M.PL books.M   already   them.M.PL=I-have read.M(PL)
  'Those books, I've already read them'

c. *Aquella   revista   ja   l'he   llegita*
  that.F.SG   magazine.F   already   it.F.SG=I-have read.F.SG
  'That magazine, I've already read it'

d. *Aquelles   revistes   ja   les he   **llegides***
  those.F   magazines.F   already   them.F.PL=I-have read.F.PL
  'Those magazines, I've already read them'

As La Fauci (1988:102f.) perceptively observes, what we have here is not a residue of the former active/stative alignment in the participle, but, rather, a new, albeit rather restricted, nominative/accusative alignment. In particular, the participle now simply marks certain types of O (see 65b–d), but never A or S (see 65a).

An even more radical and apparently unique development in participle agreement is highlighted by D'Alessandro and Roberts (2005; to appear) for the eastern Abruzzese dialect of Arielli. In this dialect, the auxiliary system in the present perfect operates on a classic person split (ESSE: first and second vs. HABERE: third) – also a nominative/accusative orientation replacing the earlier active/stative alignment – but the participle system displays neither an active/stative nor a nominative/accusative split. Rather, the active participle simply shows metaphonetic participial agreement with any plural DP, be it the subject (see 66a) or the object (see 66b):

(66) a. *seme   magnite   / **magna*te   *lu   biscotte*
  we.are   eaten.M.PL   / eaten.SG   the.M   biscuit.M
  'we have eaten the biscuit'

     b. *si   magnite   / **magna*te   *li   biscutte*
  you.are.SG   eaten.M.PL / eaten.SG   the.M.PL   biscuits.M
  'you have eaten the biscuits'

Moving now finally to the sentence, here too there are significant signs of new nominative/accusative alignments. In northern Romània, the active/stative-oriented word order discussed in relation to (58), which places A and S_A in preverbal position and O and S_O in postverbal position, has largely been replaced by a generalized SV(O) word order, in which all subjects, including those of the S_O type, now obligatorily occur in preverbal position (La Fauci 1988:57f.; 1997:29; Vincent 1988a:62), as illustrated in the French examples in (67a–b). This grammaticalization of the preverbal position as the dedicated 'subject' position, originally arising from the reanalysis of frequently fronted subjects within a V2 syntax (see §3.2.2), eventually leads to the reanalysis of preverbal subject pronouns as (obligatory) subject clitics (see §4) and the apparent reversal in the pro-drop parameter (see 67c).

(67) a. *la* *marine* *a* *coulé* *le* *navire*
   'the navy has sunk the ship'
  b. *le* *navire* *a* *coulé*
   'the ship has sunk'
  c. *il* /**Ø* *a* *coulé*
   'it   / Ø has sunk'

There thus arises in northern Romània an unresolved conflict in the markedness status of O(bjects). Postverbal O(bjects) can be considered marked in terms of a nominative/accusative word order typology which places O alone after the verb, but are to be considered unmarked in terms of the active/stative orientation of the perfective verb system, which formally identifies O with S_O in terms of auxiliary selection and participle agreement (La Fauci 1988:58). Consequently, the progressive restriction in the distribution of auxiliary ESSE and participle agreement, as witnessed in the recent history of French, can now be viewed as the gradual dominance of a nominative/accusative orientation over an earlier active/stative orientation.

In contrast to this northern Romance system of subject marking, varieties from southern Romània (including southern Occitan varieties) preserve the original active/stative word order, but tend to overlay this earlier alignment with an innovative (but typologically conservative) nominative/accusative alignment through a system of prepositional object marking (La Fauci 1997:55f.; Zamboni 1998:130; see also Sornicola, this volume, chapter 1: §3.3). In particular, highly particularized animate participants, which otherwise typically map onto the subject function (namely A and S_A), are differentially marked by a reflex of PER (Romanian; see 68a) or AD (elsewhere; see 68b–e) whenever they assume the O(bject) function. In short, southern Romance systematically contrasts O, whenever a potential candidate for subject status, with A and $S_{A/O}$ in accordance with a classic accusative/nominative orientation.

(68) a. *L-am* *văzut* **pe** **el** (Ro.)
   him=I.have seen on him
   'I have seen him'
  b. *Les* *monges* *no* *estimen* **a** **les** **nenes** (Cat.)
   the nuns not like to the girls
   'The nuns don't like the girls'

  c. *l'aimi*   ***a***   *mon*   *paire* (Pyrenean Occ.)
   him=I.love   to   my   father
   'I love my father'

  d. *Pedro*   *coroou*   *rainha*   ***à***   ***sua***   ***amante morta*** (Pt.)
   Pedro   crowned   queen   to.the   his   mistress   dead
   'Pedro crowned his dead mistress queen'

  e. *Chiamàu*   ***a***   ***Micheli*** (SCal.)
   he.called   to   Micheli
   'He called Micheli'

Together with the generalization of a single perfective auxiliary and the loss of participle agreement, the rise of the prepositional accusative in southern Romània therefore represents a consistent typological development towards an ever expanding nominative/accusative-oriented syntax at the expense of an ever dwindling active/stative syntax (La Fauci 1988:60–63).

9   PRAGMATIC AND DISCOURSE CHANGES

Maria M. Manoliu

1   Theoretical preliminaries

1.1   *Pragmatics*

Ever since Morris (1971) defined pragmatics as the study of the relationship between [the symbols of] language and its users, pragmatics has been seen as encompassing a number of informational levels considered incompatible with a description in terms of formal semantics. However, Morris's definition is too broad; in particular, it fails to offer any criteria for delimiting socio-linguistics as a separate discipline, despite the fact that the constraints imposed by social status and background constitute one type of relationship between speakers and their utterances. Another common definition, according to which pragmatics deals with 'language in context', is similarly too broad, since the definition of 'context' itself includes historical, social, individual and textual environments. I shall therefore adopt a narrower definition of prag-matics as 'the discipline dealing with linguistic choices constrained by speak-ers' attitudes towards the propositional content of utterances'. Consequently, in what follows, I shall examine the main types of change in some areas which are particularly relevant for encoding the speaker's point of view.[1]

1.2   *Discourse analysis*

I shall define discourse analysis as 'the study of constraints imposed by the organization of the discourse'. Word order and voice are the most general signals of discourse organization, since they mark the referents and/or events which correspond to the speakers' centre of attention (their cognitive viewpoint) and are consequently their preferred topics.[2] It should be noted that the relevant unit of analysis here is the *utterance* and not the *sentence*, which is the principal domain of syntax.

The existence of emphatic and/or focalized elements, which carry new information or the most important information in an utterance, can affect cross-sentential – and even sentential – structures in a variety of ways. Cross-utterance constraints have led to the incorporation of elements or features such as topic or cross-sentential anaphoric relations into the hierarchical structure of the sentence in a variety of generative models, with the aim of accounting for certain syntactic configurations; however, explaining the choices that speakers actually make amongst these configurations is the role of discourse analysis. I shall therefore deal here with the grammatical choices triggered by topic–comment information structure, namely:

(i)   word order (including the change from SOV to SVO);
(ii) Topic versus Comment;
(iii) voice: the development of a three-term paradigm.

I should emphasize at the outset that this chapter is somewhat programmatic in nature – it does no more than outline the direction research should take if significant progress is to be made in the diachronic characterization of pragmatic and discourse changes in Romance.

2 Pragmatic changes: deixis

Changes in demonstratives between Latin and Romance underline the important role of talk-interaction signals in accounting for grammaticalization.[3] I suggest that the evolution of these items is best viewed as a cyclical phenomenon, in which each demonstrative goes through several similar stages (although the final result may be different in each case). These stages may be briefly described as follows:

• The starting point is the use of the demonstrative as a conversation marker (focusing on the fact that the referent should already be in the addressee's activated knowledge, owing to its presence in either the context or the co-text). The demonstrative can function as an indexical or as an anaphor. It may introduce a definite description as an afterthought, in order to ensure that the referent can be identified (e.g., *Antiochus, Magnus ille, rex Asiae* 'Antiochus, the Great One, the king of Asia', Cic., *Deio.*, 36).

• It may then become a foregrounding marker before either a proper noun or a common noun followed by an appositional element (upgrading the discourse salience of the following description, regardless of whether or not this description is restrictive).[4]

- Finally, it loses its foregrounding value and comes to express only 'definiteness' (i.e., 'specificity and uniqueness, reference to an exhaustive set'). When it can no longer occur without a noun or an NP, it becomes a definite article: its head noun may have a specific or a generic referent.

As a result of these changes, another variant of the original demonstrative comes to be used with full demonstrative force, and may then undergo the same cycle of progressive weakening of its indexical value.

In order to explain why certain forms are more likely to survive than others, we must consider other factors:

(i)   In some areas, the parallelism between demonstratives and third person pronouns favours the development of a demonstrative pronoun from the distal deictic.[5]

(ii) The morphological split between adjectival and pronominal forms affects many types of pro-form, and not simply demonstratives.[6]

(iii) The loss of demonstrative forms functioning as topic-markers (such as the old French pronouns exhibiting an *i*-prefix – *icel* and *icest*) or as focalizers (e.g., Ro. *cesta* and *cela* + ADJ) may be related to the development of other means of marking similar functions.

2.1   *The opposition of 'distance'*

Latin demonstratives are usually classified according to their function, as follows:

(i)   purely endophoric (IS, which refers to either the previous or the following co-text);

(ii) deictics, which can be either exophors or endophors (HIC 'this, close to the speaker', ISTE 'this, close to the addressee', ILLE 'that');

(iii) intensive pronouns (IDEM 'same', IPSE 'self, same').

The most important changes in this system fall into the following categories:

- changes in the structure of the deictic paradigm, resulting in either a two- or a three-term system (in contemporary French, the system has arguably been reduced to a single term);
- the development of new pragmatic interpretations of demonstratives according to their position (pre- or postnominal);
- the development of a personal pronoun;

- the development of a definite article;
- a distributional and morphological split between demonstratives and intensive pronouns.

It should be stressed that, at this stage, there is insufficient discourse evidence to validate the hypothetical explanatory model which will be presented below. Such validation would require the analysis of larger corpora of texts, with particular reference to the differences between discourse types and between various registers (colloquial speech, dialogue, narrative, etc.), as well as the examination of more extensive co-texts (i.e., more than simply the analysis of NPs containing a demonstrative, a noun and its modifiers – which has been, and remains, the traditional approach). In spite of all this, we feel that the model, even at its current stage of development, offers real insights into the changes we shall discuss.[7]

2.1.1   Reference to the enunciation: exophora

(a)   *The first cycle.* What contexts might favour changes in deictic structure? It is highly likely that the opposition of distance was neutralized first of all in endophoric contexts, i.e., when the antecedent was a single noun and the difference between 'proximity' and 'remoteness' was redundant for purposes of identification. This hypothesis is supported by various so-called 'confusions' in a variety of late Latin texts. For example, in the Vulgate, HIC predominates as an exophor, referring to 'the one present in the context of uttering', whereas, in the case of reference to the text (endophor), there seems to be no sharp distinction between the uses of HIC, ISTE and ILLE (see Abel 1971; Bauer 2007). There are instances in which HIC is used as an anaphoric instead of IS; however, subsequently, HIC is no longer used as a pronoun but simply as an adverbial locative indicating proximity to the enunciation.[8] In referring to the enunciation, ISTE, the original second person demonstrative, took over the functions of HIC, which disappeared, probably as the result of several factors:[9] (i) *textual:* its endophoric focalizing (deictic) value was weakening, partly because it was used instead of IS, and partly because the double deictic construction HIC ... ILLE 'the latter ... the former' (when referring to two antecedents) came to be in free variation with HIC ... HIC and ILLE ... ILLE (Ernout and Thomas 1953/ 1993:188f.); (ii) *indexical:* as a consequence of (i), its value as a proximal exophor referring to the speaker was also weakened in conversational settings; both HIC and ISTE could refer to the enunciation, but ISTE seems to have been the extensive term, since it was also capable of referring to proximity to *both* interlocutors, and not only to the speaker (compare also the use of ISTIC 'there [near us]' *mortuos qui **istic** sepultus est, Corpus Inscriptionum Latinarum* (*CIL*), I², 1012 'the dead man who is buried here').[10]

IPSE, not being an indexical, could not have been confused with HIC, ISTE and ILLE in their exophoric function. Therefore, any confusion must have arisen with regard to its endophoric use. According to Ernout and Thomas (1953/1993:189), IPSE is, properly speaking, an intensifier, which involves the idea of a latent opposition. In familiar registers, IPSE could be used for ISTE (HIC) in an anaphoric function, with an adversative effect:

(1) ***Ipse** in colle medio triplicem aciem instruxit*
'**He [meanwhile]** organized the line of battle in three ranks in the middle' (Caes., *BG*, I, 24)

The basic difference between IPSE and ILLE can be described in pragmatic terms (Manoliu-Manea 1994:192–94). Consider the following example:

(2) *ualuae* [...]   *se*   *ipsae*   *aperuerunt*
doors   REFL   self   opened
'the doors opened by themselves'   (Cic., *Diu.*, I)

In (2) IPSAE (in addition to the simple reflexive accusative SE) has the function of an intensifier. According to what we assume to have been the prototypical cognitive model of the period in question, the event of a door opening by itself would be considered very unlikely. In pragmatic terms, *intensifiers* are markers confirming the truth-value of a statement which conflicts with the probability values assigned by the prototypical cognitive model characterizing a certain linguistic community. A prototypical cognitive model assigns probability values to events according to the results of the interaction between the community and its environment. Within this framework, certain events have a high probability and others have a lower probability. Intensifiers are then markers of the difference between the *factual world*, in which the actual event occurs, and the corresponding prototypical *cognitive model*, in which this type of event has a very low probability of happening (e.g., *I succeeded in solving this problem by myself, wow! can you believe it?!*).

An intensifier can be used even when a specific event is expected, in order to confirm the truth-value of a statement that an event does occur despite the low probability value assigned to it by the prototypical cognitive model in question. Compare, for example, the following sentences:

(3) a. *As everyone expected,* **the king** *attended the celebration.*
    b. *As everyone expected,* **the king himself** *attended the celebration.*

Sentence (3a) states: it is true that 'the king attended …'. Sentence (3b) conveys the implicature: 'it is not true that it was not the king who attended', in contrast to the predictions of the cognitive model of the community in question ('the fact that the king attends celebrations' is not a common event) – the celebration is a special one.[11]

When combined with other demonstrative pronouns (HIC IPSE, ISTE IPSE, ILLE IPSE), IPSE is synonymous with IDEM 'same'.[12] In late Latin, IPSE by itself could also carry the conversational implicature of IDEM, as shown by the following utterance:

(4) *non*   ***ipsa***   *parte*   *exire*   *habebamus*
     not   same   side   go:INF   had.to.we
     qua   *intraueramus*
     which:ABL   went.in.we.
     'we did not have to go out the same way we went in'   (*Aeth.,* 4. 5)

In late Latin, IPSE began to lose its pragmatic value (i.e., that of intensifier). This development had two consequences:

(i) In order to function as a reinforcing (intensive) pronoun, IPSE began to co-occur with other 'identity markers' such as -MET: e.g., EGOMET IPSE 'I myself' + 'self' or METIPSE 'self.self', sometimes in a 'superlative' form METIPSIMUM; compare the resulting forms in Romance languages: Fr. *même* 'self, same, even', Sp. *mismo*, Pt. *mesmo*, It. *medesimo* 'self, same'.

(ii) When its force of denying the addressee's expectation of non-identity weakened, its pragmatic function could be reinterpreted as a means of referring to the speakers (and not only to the addressee), as a mere indexical. IPSE then stands in opposition to ISTE, which is the marked term, since it comes to express the fact that the speaker is the *origo*. In spoken Latin, IPSE could replace other demonstratives indicating the addressee, such as ISTE or HIC, as shown by the corresponding Romance demonstratives: OSp. *eje*, Occ. *eis*, OPt. *eiso*, Sp. *ese*, Pt. *esse* 'this' (referring to the second person), ARo. *nîs*, *năs*, IRo. *ăns* 'this' (Puşcariu 1957: s.v. 870). In some areas, IPSE developed its anaphoric value even further and loosened its indexical value of referring to the speakers, which explains the fact that it became a personal pronoun (compare It. *essi* 'they'; ORo. *însu*, cf. also *dânsul*, a polite form of *el* 'he'), and then a focalizer pointing to a salient constituent in the co-text and even a definite article (compare Srd. *su* 'the').[13]

(b) *The second cycle.* If ISTE and ILLE had undergone a progressive loosening of their exophoric function, their indexical value could be reinforced, most commonly by one of the following means (which were probably already present in the language):

   (i) use of the interjection ECCE (or variants ECCUM/*ACCE/*ACCUM) 'here [it] is! behold!' as in ECCE + ISTE, which evolved into a proximal deictic (compare It. *questo*, OFr. *cest*, ORo. *cestŭ*) – vs. ECCE ILLE 'that', which became the exponent of distal deixis (compare OFr. *cel*, Fr. *celui*, It. *quello*, ORo. *celŭ* 'that');

   (ii) use of the adverbial deictics: HAC 'in this place, on this side, here, over here' and ILLAC 'on that side, there, over there': cf. Ro. *ăsta* (< ISTE + HAC) 'this one' and *ăla* (<*ille*+ ILLAC) 'that one' (cf. also the corresponding adverbial deictics in §2.4).

(c) *The third cycle.* In French, when *cest* was generalized as an adjectival deictic or determiner (e.g., *cet homme*), and *celui* as a pronominal demonstrative, the adverbs *ci* (< Lat. ECCE-HIC) and *là* (< ILLAC) served to express distance: *cet homme-ci* 'this man' / *cet homme–là* 'that man', *celui-ci* 'this one' / *celui-là* 'that one'. In old Romanian, *cestŭ* 'this' and *celŭ* 'that' also lost their indexical value and new variants developed by the addition of the adverbial deictics Lat. HAC or ILLAC (see above) – e.g., *cesta* 'this', *cela* 'that', which are very frequent in seventeenth- and eighteenth-century texts. At first, the adverbial deictic HAC could follow the pronominal proximal deictic in colloquial registers: e.g., ISTE HAC 'this one, here' (compare It. *questo qua*, Pt. *este aqui* 'this one, here'; 'this one'; and also Sp. *acá* 'here' and OFr. *ça* < Lat. ECCE-HAC 'here it is'; ARo. *aestu* (< ISTU)-*aoa* 'this one', where *aoa* is also an adverb 'here'). The distal adverb ILLAC 'through/in there' could follow the distal deictic: e.g., *ILLU-ILLAC (cf. It. *là*, Fr. *là*, ARo. *aṭelu* (< ECCE-ILLE)-*aclo* 'that [one]').

The co-ordinator AC 'and, and also' or the preposition AD 'to' (or possibly *ACCE or *ACCUM, variant forms of ECCE; see above) were also added to the deictics in some Romance varieties: preposed either to all or both deictics as in Romanian: *acest(a)* 'this', *acel(a)* 'that', Cat. *aquest, aqueix, aquel*, or only to the distal deictic: Sp. *aquel*, Pt. *aquele*.

(d) *The Romance demonstrative paradigm.* As a result of these morphological changes, two demonstrative paradigms emerged:

(i) *Two-term system*: [Reference to the speaker: proximal vs. distal]. The extended use of ISTE as the expression of 'proximity to the speakers' accounts for the reduced two-term system in French, in most varieties of Italian and in Romanian:[14]

(5) OFr. *cist* 'this' vs. *cil* 'that'; ModFr. *celui-ci* vs. *celui-là*
It. *questo* vs. *quello*.
ORo. *cest(a)* vs. *cel(a)*; ContRo. *acest(a)* vs. *acel(a)*.[15]

(ii) *Three-term system.* Spanish, Portuguese, Catalan and some Italian varieties (including Tuscan) recreated a three-term exophoric system:[16]

(6) [+reference to the speaker as the *origo*] [−reference to the speakers]

	[+1P]	[−1P]	
Sp.	este	ese	aquel
Pt.	êste	esse	aquele
Tsc.	questo	codesto[17]	quello
SIt.	chistu	chissu	chillu

Note that some neuter forms (Fr. *ceci, cela, ça*, It. *ciò*, Sp. *esto, eso, aquello*, Pt. *isto, isso, aquilo*) serve only as pronouns. They may refer to an abstract idea, to a whole event (an utterance or a set of utterances) or to an object whose name is not known.

2.1.2   Reference to the text: anaphora

As mentioned above, Lat. IS had an anaphoric function (see Ernout and Thomas 1953/1993:189):

(7) *Nam ego uos nouisse credo iam ut sit pater meus* [...] **Is** *amare occepit Alcumenam clam uirum,* [...] *Et grauidam fecit* **is eam** *compresu suo*
'But I think you know how my father is [...] He fell in love with Alcmena despite her husband, [...] And **he** made **her** pregnant thanks to his embraces'
(Pl., *Amph. Prologue*, 104–9)

As a mere indicator of coreference, IS encountered competition from other demonstratives and finally disappeared. In Romance, the markers of coreference have developed special forms, among them the third person pronouns and the definite article. But the referential identity of two nouns can also be expressed by the new demonstratives. The choice between personal pronouns and demonstratives has been attributed to differences in accessibility and foregrounding (see Corblin 1987; Ariel 1988; Tasmowski-De Ryck 1990). According to Gundel and Zacharski (1993:275), the choice of one item over the other can be predicted on the basis of a 'Givenness Hierarchy', namely:

> focus > activated > familiar > uniquely identifiable > referential > type identifiable.

The demonstrative introduces a break; it is a marker of a new vantage point in presenting the referent (for details, see Adam 1990:55f.; Kleiber 1992; Gundel and Fretheim 1996). According to Kleiber (1992), for example, if a speaker uses an indexical expression (that is, an expression that triggers a process of locating in space and/or time), it is either because he assumes that the addressee does not yet have the referent in mind (i.e., the referent is new) or because he intends to present the referent to the addressee in a new light (if the referent is already known).[18]

In pro-drop languages, the choice between zero-anaphors, personal pronouns and demonstratives can also be accounted for within a discourse framework. In pro-drop languages, the zero-anaphor is a marker of discourse continuity. It may operate across paragraph boundaries, either within the same narrative unit – specifically a foregrounded scene – even when other narrative units, belonging to the background, are inserted in between subunits of the foregrounded events. The condition is that the zero-anaphor and its coreferential NP must share the same semantic role. The coreferential personal pronoun is a marker of discourse discontinuity, originating in different kinds of shift (shifts in syntactic functions, in semantic roles, in character attributes, in expectations) or in the absence of the explicit corresponding NP in the preceding co-text (inferred coreferentiality; associative anaphor), etc. (Manoliu-Manea 1994:227–63). According to D'Introno's hypothesis (D'Introno 1989), 'in Spanish pronouns and anaphors in A-position (i.e., in subject position) are used, with few exceptions, when they are animate'.

Example (8) is a striking example of the use of a zero-anaphor in subject position which can be explained precisely by taking into account discourse organization, namely the camera-angle switch to the newly introduced topic, *la isla* 'the island':

(8)   *Los músicos pastores, invisibles u ocultos, calmaron levemente la angustia de la bella, le dieron fuerza para levantarse e iniciar su primer recorrido de la **isla**. [Ø] **Era** plana, un contorno de pocos kilómetros, la podría abarcar de una sola caminata.*

    'The shepherd musicians, invisible or hidden, tamed the nervousness of the beauty, gave her the strength to get up and begin her first tour of the island. [It] was level, a circuit of a few kilometres; she could do it in a single walk.'   (Manuel Puig, *Pubis angelical*, in Pellettieri, 1993:5–6)

When two NPs are referred to, the proximal deictic is used for retrieving the nearer NP (compare Eng. 'the latter') and the distal deictic for the one further away (compare Eng. 'the former'):

(9) Fr. *Marlborough et Eugène étaient presque comme deux frères; **celui-ci** avait plus d'audace, **celui-là** l'esprit plus froid et calculateur*

    'Marlborough and Eugene were almost like two brothers; the latter was more impetuous, the former more cold and calculating.'

    (Price 2008:166)

(10) It. *Insomma, sembra che il peccato sia regolato dalla stessa legge che regola la virtù; sia anche **quello**, non meno di **questa**, una forma di virtù*

    'So it seems that sin is regulated by the same law as virtue; that the former just as much as the latter is a kind of virtue.'

    (Maiden and Robustelli 2007:82)

(11) Sp. *Divididos estaban caballeros y escuderos, **éstos** contándose sus trabajos, y **aquéllos** sus amores.*

    'The knights and the esquires are divided, the latter counting their deeds, and the former their love affairs.'   (Cervantes, in Bello 1982:100)

(12) Pt. *Fala-se em acabar com as procissões, para dar lugar aos automóveis. Realmente, não há lugar para **estes** e **aquelas** na cidade atual*

    'There is talk of ending processions, to make room for cars. In fact, there is no room for either one of them [for neither the latter nor the former] in the present town.'

    (Carlos Drummond de Andrade, in Cunha 1981:237)

In both Spanish and Portuguese, demonstratives preserve their reference to the interlocutors even when used anaphorically (Bello 1982:99; Cunha 1981:236): Sp. *este*, Pt. *êste* are used when the speaker refers to what he or she has said; Sp. *ese*, Pt. *esse* refer to what the addressee has said; Sp. *aquel*,

Pt. *aquele* refer to something reactualized from memory. Some Spanish speakers find *aquel* more formal than *ese*.

(13) Sp. *No digo yo, Sancho, que sea forzoso a los caballeros andantes no comer en un mes [...] y **esto** se te hiciera cierto si hubieras leído tantas historias como yo.*
'It is not me who says, Sancho, that it is obligatory for knights errant not to eat for one month [...] and this would have become certain if you had read as many stories as I have.'
(Cervantes, in Bello 1982:99)

(14) Sp. *Me trae por estas partes el deseo de hacer en ellas una hazaña con que he de ganar perpetuo nombre; y será tal, que con ella he de echar el sello a todo **aquello** que puede hacer famoso un caballero.*
'I have been brought to these places by my desire to perform a great deed which will bring me an everlasting name; and it would be such [a great one], that with it I could achieve everything that could make a knight famous.'
(Cervantes, in Bello 1982:99)

In his question, Don Quixote's addressee uses *esa*:

(15) Sp. *¿ Y es de muy gran peligro **esa** hazaña?*
'And it is very dangerous, this deed?'
(Cervantes, in Bello 1982:99)

Compare also:

(16) Pt. *A boa vida é **esta**: O sossego normal deste meu quarto*
'A good life is this: The normal tranquility of my apartment'
(Mário Pederneiras, in Cunha 1981:236)

2.2 The distribution of demonstratives

In all the Romance languages, with the exception of Romanian, the adjectival demonstratives have traditionally been included in the paradigm of the predeterminers, because they occur in prenominal position. Romanian has both preposed and postposed demonstratives. Compare (17), from a seventeenth-century text:

(17) *Măria-sa vodă i-au tremis la noi să-ş aducă Saşa **acei** martori şi duhovnicul **acela***
'The King sent them to us for Saşa to bring his witnesses [lit. those witnesses] and his priest [lit. priest-the that]'
(*Document* 1646, in *Crest. Rom.*, 25)

Since this apparently idiosyncratic distribution has been the topic of many studies, it is worth briefly presenting some of the most recent hypotheses.[19] In most current histories of Romance in general, and Romanian in particular, the postposition of both the definite article and the demonstratives is accounted for in terms of the Balkan *Sprachbund*. But the 'Balkan hypothesis' is either unnecessary or incapable on its own of explaining the distribution of demonstratives in Romanian, for the following reasons:

(i) Postnominal demonstratives may in fact occur in other Romance languages: in Spanish, for instance, the demonstrative may occasionally follow the head noun when expressing contempt or disdain:

(18) Sp. *la muerta de hambre* **esa** ...
the dead of hunger this
'that despicable [girl]'

(Telenovela *Preciosa*, June 1999, Univisión, USA)

(ii) Prenominal demonstratives occur frequently in both old and Contemporary Romanian even when the noun is followed by an adjective (19):

(19) a. ORo. *această apă limpede*
this water limpid
'this limpid water'

(Coresi, *CÎ*, 5)

b. ContRo. *acest copil nevinovat*
this child innocent
'this innocent child'

On the other hand, the distribution of Romanian demonstratives can be explained without recourse to the 'Balkan hypothesis' if a variety of other factors are taken into consideration.

(a) *The discourse functions of demonstratives.* In the area where the different varieties of Romanian developed, both north and south of the Danube, during the early medieval period, socio-historical conditions favoured colloquial rather than written registers. Orality of this sort favours extensive use of discourse-coherence devices and markers of talk-interaction such as articles and demonstratives.[20] We assume that during the unattested period of Romanian, as in Latin, demonstratives followed by a definite description must have had the role of providing supplementary information, to ensure the correct identification of the referent.[21] On the basis of the attributive and appositive constructions found in old Romanian, the following reconstructions are possible: (i) DEM + N and (ii) N + DEM (see Densusianu 1961: II,112f.).

(20) DEM-GEN/DAT | N | Proper N
lui | *proroc* | *David*
the.GEN | prophet | David
'of the prophet David' (Coresi, *CÎ*, 54, in Densusianu 1961:II,112)

(21) N | DEM-GEN/DAT | ADJ
domnu – | *lŭ* | *romănescŭ*
king | the | Romanian
'the Romanian king' (*Cronograful Moxa*, in *Crest. Rom.* 17)

In seventeenth-century Romanian, the postnominal distal deictic -*lu(i)* is already specialized as both a definite article and a case marker. As a consequence of its cliticization and the weakening of its indexical value, other postnominal demonstratives (whether or not they are followed by a definite description) may be used to fulfil the same conversational function of providing supplementary information, introducing an afterthought. Compare ContRo.:

(22) *dă-mi* | *rochia* | *nouă,* | *aia* | *albastră!*
give-me | dress-the | new, | the one | blue!
'give me the new dress, the blue one!'

(b) *Typological factors and areal convergence.* Romanian generally conforms to the Romance pattern favouring preposed modifiers and markers; however, it is situated within an area characterized by a number of languages that favour postposition.[22] For this or other reasons, Romanian developed both prenominal and postnominal demonstratives, case markers and articles.

2.3 *Pragma-semantic exploitation of deictics*

2.3.1 Pejorative connotations

Fr. *ça* (a reduced form of the neuter distal pro-form *cela*) is often used in spoken registers for a variety of pragmatic reinterpretations. Generally speaking, *ça* (which does not agree in gender and number with its antecedent) introduces a certain affective/cognitive distance between the speaker and the referent in question, which can be exploited as an ironic connotation:[23]

(23) – *J'ai* | *entendu* | *la* | *musique* | *des* | *sphères.*
– I have | heard | the.FEM.SG | music | of.the | spheres
– *Et ça* | *fait* | *quel* | *bruit?*
– And it | makes | what | noise?
'– I heard the music of the spheres / – And it makes what noise?'
(Queneau, *Fleurs bleues*, 145)

It generally has a derogatory connotation after topics marked [+Person], since it carries the implication of 'non-person':

(24) *Vous connaissez ça l'«Argus de la Presse »?*
Non, dit le type.
Minable. Et ça veut discuter avec moi!
Do you know this.NEUT the.M 'Argus of the Press'?
No, says the:M chap.
Pitiful. And this.NEUT wants to have a talk with me! (Queneau, *Zazie*, 48)

It. *costui* may also have a pejorative connotation when used as an indexical in reference to a person:

(25) *Ma   chi   si   crede   de   essere   costui?*
But   who   REFL   think   of   be.INF   that?'
'But who does that [bloke] over there think he is?'

(Maiden and Robustelli 2007:87)

In Spanish, *ese* is the preferred demonstrative for introducing a pejorative connotation (see 18 above, repeated as 26):

(26) *la   muerta   de   hambre   esa*
the   dead   of   hunger   this
'that despicable [girl]'   (Telenovela *Preciosa*, June 1999, Univisión, USA)

2.3.2   Story-world and enunciation-world

In Romanian, the postposed demonstrative retains from its original deictic value the capacity of referring to the enunciation. This function predicts the fact that the postnominal demonstratives are used as exophors *par excellence* (see 27).

(27) – *Văz că tu ești voinică, fata mea, și bine ai făcut de ți-ai luat calul ăsta, căci fără dânsul te-ai fi întors și tu ca și surorile tale*
'– I see that you are courageous, dear girl, and you made the right decision when you took this horse [lit. **horse-the this**], because, without it, you would have gone back as your sisters did.'   (Ispirescu, *Op.*, 19)

When used as an endophor, the demonstrative overtly anchors the story-world in the speaker's hypothesis concerning the addressee's knowledge. In (28) *flăcăul acesta* 'this fellow' refers to the previously introduced referent and also establishes a relation between the story-world and the enunciation-world:

(28) *Bag de seamă   nu   era   așa de   căscăund* **flăcăul   acesta** [...]
     I realize   not   was   so   dumb   fellow-the *this* [...]
     'I realize that this fellow was not so dumb'.   (Ispirescu, *Op.*, 200)

Since they are neutral with regard to expressive function, the prenominal demonstratives are used primarily as anaphors. They carry the conventional implicature of 'separation between enunciation-world and story-world'. The distal prenominal endophor strongly activates the implicature of the difference between these two worlds, whereas the proximal endophor tends to blur it (see Manoliu-Manea 2001:197f.).

2.3.3   Foregrounding

In Italian, the demonstrative *codesto*, which formerly expressed proximity to the addressee, is reinterpreted as a focalizer with a phatic function (aimed at maintaining the connection with the addressee):

(29) *Mi stia a sentire un attimo, che le volevo proporre* **codesta** *idea che mi è venuta in mente l'altro giorno*
     'Just listen to me for a moment, because I wanted to show you this idea which I had the other day.'   (Maiden and Robustelli 2007:83)

2.4   Adverbial deictics

Adverbs that relate the action to the spatial/temporal circumstances of the utterance are organized along similar axes to the demonstratives, namely 'inclusion of the space of uttering' vs. 'non-inclusion of the space of uttering'. The point of reference (the *origo*) may be situated in the space of uttering or in the text. The Latin forms HIC 'here' and ILLAC 'there, over there' serve as the basis for many Romance formations, although the exact etymologies are often obscure. HIC could be preceded by the presentatives ECCE and its variant forms ECCUM, *ACCE and *ACCUM 'lo, behold', and also by the preposition AD 'to' and the co-ordinator AC 'and, also'; it could be followed by the reinforcing particle -CE. It is various combinations of these forms which underly, for instance, It. *qui, ci*, Fr. *ici*, Sp., Pt. *aquí, ahí*, Pt. *aqui, aí*, Ro. *ici, aici*. French *là* derives relatively uncontroversially from Latin ILLAC.

French represents the basic paradigm with three terms for spatial deixis:

'inclusion of the space of uttering' 'non-inclusion of the space of uttering'
ici 'here'   *là* 'there/here' –   *là-bas* 'over there'

Fr. *là* is the unmarked term as shown by (30) (see Kleiber 1992; Smith 1992, 1995b):

(30) a. *Viens ici!*
      'Come here!' (with insistence on the proximity to the speaker)
   b. *Assieds-toi là, près de moi!*
      'Sit here, close to me.'
   c. *Regarde là!*
      'Look there.'

In Spanish, Portuguese and Italian, each term has two forms:

(31) 'here'   'there'
   Sp. *aquí, acá*   *allí, allá*
   Pt. *aqui, cá*   *ali, lá*
   It. *qui, qua*   *lì, là*.

The difference between the series in *-a* and the series in *-i* corresponds to the opposition 'area' vs. 'point'.

Romanian encodes an opposition [±Movement], as follows: *încoace* and *încolo* are compatible only with verbs of movement, whereas *aici* 'here' and *acolo* 'there' represent the neuter term (see 32).

(32) a. *Vino încoace*
      'Come here (toward me)!' vs.
      stai aici!
      'stay here!', as well as
      vino aici!
      'come here!', but not
      *stai încoace! and
   b. *Du-te încolo!*
      'Go there (from here)!' vs.
      stai acolo!
      'stay there', as well as
      du-te acolo!
      'go there', but not
      *stai încolo!

Modern temporal deictics originate in a variety of Latin or old Romance forms:

(i) Lat. (HAC+) HORA 'hour' – Cat. *ara*, Sp. *ahora*, Pt. *agora* (compare also Cat. *aleshores*);
   Lat. AD ILLA(M) HORA(M) > Fr. *alors*
(ii) Lat. (AC/AD+) TUNC 'then'(+CE) > Ro. *atunci*
   Lat. (IN+) TUNC 'then' (+CE) > Sp. *entonces*

(iii) Lat. HOC DIE > HODIE 'today' > Sp. *hoy*, Pt. *hoje*
Lat. HAC DIE 'this day' > Cat. *avui*, Ro. *azi*;
Lat. [TEMPUS] DIURNUM 'day [time]' > Fr. *jour* 'day'
and *aujourd'hui* 'today'

(iv) Lat. (AC/AD+) MODO 'right away' > Ro. *amu*, SIt. *mo* 'now';
Lat. *ACCUM +MODO > Ro. *acum*

(v) Lat. (DE/AD+) MANE 'morning' > Fr. *demain*, Sp. *mañana*, Pt. *amanhã*,
It. *domani*, Ro. *mâine* 'tomorrow'

(vi) Lat. CRAS 'tomorrow' > Srd. *cras*, SIt. *crai* 'tomorrow'

(vii) Fr. *maintenant* (*main* + *tenant* lit. 'hand holding') 'now';
etc.

Deictics referring to time are organized in a similar manner according to the inclusion of the time of uttering, with the point of reference (*origo*) situated in the time of uttering or in the time created by the text:

	'inclusion of the time of uttering'		'non-inclusion of the time of uttering'	
	'now'	'today'	'yesterday'	'tomorrow'
Fr.	*maintenant*	*aujourd'hui*	*hier*	*demain*
Sp.	*ahora*	*hoy*	*ayer*	*mañana*
Pt.	*agora* (*ja*)	*hoje*	*ontem*	*amanhã*
It.	*adesso*	*oggi*	*ieri*	*domani*
Ro.	*acum*	*azi*	*ieri*	*mâine*

When referring to the time created by the text, the adverbial deictics may have different markers for the opposition of distance, since the point of reference is established within the text-world and has no relation to the time of uttering (writing or reading). The deictic axis EGO–HIC–NUNC ('I'–'here'–'there') becomes IBI–TUNC ('there'–'then'). Compare:

(33) a. Fr. *Le journaliste s'éloigna un peu, puis s'assit sur un banc et put les regarder à loisir Il s'aperçut **alors** qu'ils n'avaient sans doute pas plus de vingt ans.*
'The journalist moved a short distance away, [and] then he sat on a bench and could look at them. He **then** realized that, no doubt, they were no more than twenty years old.'
(Camus, *La Peste*, 123)

b. Sp. *Pedro nos dijo que aquél que estaba allí **entonces** era su amigo*

c. Ro. *Petru ne-a spus că omul care se afla **atunci** acolo era prietenul său*
'Peter told us that the one who was there **then** was his friend'

Special forms may exist for the expression of spatial relations of anteriority or posteriority when their point of reference is specified by the text, for instance:

(34) 'the day before'   'the following day'
    Fr. *la veille*   *le lendemain*
    It. *la vigilia*   *l'indomani*

2.5   From exophora to anaphora

The decay of the deictic value of the distal deictic ILLE 'that' gives rise to two developments, according to context: (i) when used as a pronoun, it becomes a third person personal pronoun; (ii) from its original adjectival use, it develops a specialized function as a definite article.

2.5.1   Personal pronouns

Latin had personal pronouns only for referring to the interlocutors: EGO 'I' for the speaker and TU 'you' for the addressee, with the corresponding plural forms NOS 'we' and UOS 'you'. For the third person, demonstratives were used. The Romance third person pronouns originate in either ILLE or IPSE. From its deictic textual use of referring to an antecedent in a more distant position (in opposition to HIC/ISTE), ILLE comes to refer to any previously mentioned NP and forms part of the paradigm of personal endophors, incapable of taking any determiner (adjectival or prepositional). As early as spoken Latin, IS as an anaphoric pronoun tended to be replaced by ILLE, or, less frequently, by IPSE:[24]

> (35) *Sed eccum Amphitruonem: aduenit* [...] | *Dein susum escendam in tectum,*
> *ut **illum** hinc prohibeam.*
> 'But look, Amphitryo is coming [...] | Then perched up on the roof, I
> shall keep **him** out of here.'   (Pl., *Amph.*, 3.2, 1008)

ILLE became the third person pronoun in most of the Romance languages, except Sardinian, Costa Brava and Balearic Catalan, and (historically) southern Italian dialects which adopted the forms originating in IPSE (Srd. *issu, issa, issos* and *issas*). In Italian, reflexes of ILLE and IPSE exist alongside one another, with a complex pattern of regional and stylistic variation. In Florentine, from the Renaissance period onwards, *esso* (< IPSUM) has tended to be used with reference to things and *egli* (<ILLE/*ILLI) as a subject pronoun with reference to males. But, unlike *esso*, the feminine singular and the plural forms (*essa, essi* and *esse*) may be used for both humans and non-humans (see Maiden and Robustelli 2007:82). In old Romanian, the form *însu* (< IPSU) also occurs instead of *el* (< ILLE) especially after prepositions. In some Romanian regional varieties (Muntenia), *dânsul* (< *de+îns+-l*) is considered more polite than *el*. [25]

2.5.2   Definite articles

In the majority of the Romance languages, the definite article derives from ILLE 'that'. In some varieties of the western Mediterranean, and in particular in Sardinian and Balearic Catalan, it was IPSE that developed into a definite article (Srd. *su, sa, sos, sas*, Bal. *es, sa, es, ses*), and occasional relics of similar forms are found in some varieties of Occitan (e.g., Gascon proper names such as *Sacase* = *la case* 'the house', *Sarrieu* = *la rieu* 'the river'). The development of a definite article in the Romance languages clearly involved a series of steps in which the deictic value of the original demonstrative weakened. It is very likely that, when accompanying NPs, as adjectival determiners, the demonstratives went through the following stages (see Renzi 1992b; Faingold 1996; Manoliu 2001):

(i)   The demonstrative is used to signal that the referent should be in the addressee's activated knowledge, because of its presence in either the context or the co-text.

(ii) It then becomes a foregrounding marker (upgrading the discourse salience of the following description, regardless of whether or not this is restrictive).

(iii) It ends by losing its foregrounding value and comes to express only 'definiteness'. [26]

There is ample evidence of the weakened deictic use of the adjectival demonstratives in late Latin texts. Relevant examples illustrating the stages of bleaching may be found in Faingold (1996). For example, ILLA in (36) and IPSA in (38) mark a prominent NP:

ILLE:

(36) ***Illa** autem **aqua**, quam persae auertarent*
      'The water which the Persians diverted.'   *(Aeth., 102, in Faingold, 1996:77)*

(37) *Iusso leonis inter his bisteis missa est vulpis* [...] ***Vulpis illa** forto ablato cor eius comedit*
      'At the lion's command the fox set upon these beasts [...] That/the fox, making off with what he had stolen, devoured its heart.'
      (Fredegar, sixth century, in Faingold 1996:77)

IPSE:

(38) *Quod cum dixisset, tenens minibus levatis* **epistolam ipsam apertam** *rex*
'And when the king had said this, holding up the open letter with uplifted
hands'
(*Aeth.*, 102 in Faingold, 1996:77)

In (39) ILLE introduces a definite description in order to trigger the correct
identification of the referent:

(39) *cito proferte mihi* **stolam illam primam** *et induite illum*
'Bring right away my ceremonial garment, that first [one], and put [it] on
him.'
(Luke 15, 22, in Mihăescu 1960: 163)

The development of a definite article implies more than a progressive loss of
the indexical function of a deictic and then of its capacity to foreground; it
also presupposes changes in its basic functions and syntactic status – in
short, it involves the creation of a new grammatical category. As Guillaume
(1975) points out, from a semantic point of view, articles have the capacity
of actualizing both the 'universal' and the 'integral' (the particular) according to the context (see also Pottier 1969:50). Compare the French utterances in (40) and (41):

(40) *L'enfant entra dans le jardin* (particular)
'The child entered the garden'

(41) *L'enfant est un symbole de la pureté* (universal)
'The child is a symbol of purity'

I turn now to the position of the definite article. In late Latin, demonstratives occur with almost the same frequency in either prenominal or postnominal positions. In all the Romance languages except Romanian, the
definite article patterns with predeterminers, and consequently it always
precedes the common noun.

(42) *Je cherche un/le livre, le vert.*
'I am looking for a/the book, the green [one].'

The position of the Romanian article has been the topic of extensive debate.
It is for this reason that I believe it is worth examining, if only briefly, the
factors that may have contributed to this deviation from the Romance type.
As I hope to have demonstrated elsewhere (Manoliu-Manea 1985), the
postposition of the definite article must have been related to the preservation of case markers in the first declension for the genitive/dative singular as
opposed to the nominative/accusative. Compare NOM/ACC *fată* 'girl' vs.
GEN/DAT *fete*. This unique phenomenon in the Romance domain may be

due to the fact that Romanian is situated in a wider European geographical area that preserved case inflection, regardless of language family (Romance, Slavic, Greek, Germanic and Finno-Ugric). The definite article also preserved the same case distinction as the noun and could be used as a new case marker, especially when nouns had no inflection at all. It was then attracted by the inherited case marker to the final position. In brief, the postposed variant was preferred in order to conform to the morphological pattern already in place (see Manoliu-Manea 1985): compare SG NOM/ACC *fata* 'the girl' vs. SG GEN/DAT *fetei*; PL NOM/ACC *fetele* vs. PL GEN/DAT/ VOC. *fetelor!* On the model of feminine nouns, the enclitic definite article spread to all types of noun: see, for example, the invariable noun *pui* 'chicken'. When the definite article is present, the noun displays the following case paradigm: SG NOM/ACC *puiul* 'the chicken', SG GEN/ DAT *puiului*; PL NOM/ACC *puii*, PL GEN/DAT/VOC *puilor*. Evidence in support of the case-marking hypothesis is provided by the following phenomenon present in sixteenth-century texts. Both variants of the definite article (that is *lui* < Lat.*ILLUI and *lu* < Lat. ILLO) can be found in either prenominal or postnominal position. Proper nouns prefer prenominal case markers. But masculine proper nouns ending in -*a* (like feminine nouns continuing the Latin first declension) may take an enclitic article as the genitive/dative marker, as in (43).

(43) **lu**   *Marco*   *și*   *Lucăei*
the:M.GEN   Mark   and   Luke.the: GEN
'to Mark and Luke'   (Coresi, *CÎ*, 2)

In contemporary oral registers, *lu(i)* is the preferred variant of the genitive–dative case marker before proper nouns and nouns denoting unique family members, regardless of their grammatical gender: e.g., *lu(i) Ion* 'of/to John', *lu tata* 'of/to my father', *lu(i) Carmen* 'of/to Carmen', *lu mama* 'of/to [my] mother' (see Graur 1968:302).[27]

The co-occurrence of definite articles with proper nouns is not limited to Romanian. It is also found in other Romance languages (see Ledgeway, this volume, chapter 8: §3.3.1.2), where it may be pragmatically marked, possibly providing support for the hypothesis that, at first, overdetermination was pragmatically exploited as a sign of intimacy and even empathy. For example, in Italian (in northern Italy and Tuscany, though generally only with feminine proper names) and in European Portuguese, it indicates a certain degree of familiarity (it has an affective connotation):

(44) It.   *è venuta la Maria*
'Maria came'

(45)   Pt.   *o Fernando sabe que a Maria não gosta dele.*
       'Ferdinando knows that Maria doesn't like him.'

It can be also found in spoken registers in Spanish (e.g., *el Luís*, *la María*), French (popular register: e.g., *le Louis*, *la Marie*), as well as in some varieties of Occitan (e.g., Languedoc *lo Joan*, *la Maria*) and in the Salentino dialects of south-east Italy (e.g., *'u Pascali*, *'a Rita*). In Catalan its use is regular and has no particular affective value (*l'Alfons*, *la Maria*); it is not generally found in Valencian.

2.5.3   Pronouns of politeness

Latin personal pronouns did not have special forms for expressing social relations between speakers. Expressions of politeness developed relatively late in the history of the Romance languages and display a variety of etymological patterns, which have in common that they can be seen as introducing a certain 'psychological distance' between the speaker and the addressee. In other words, the feature 'social distance between the speakers' originates in the reinterpretation of various features relating to distance within the domain of enunciation, such as: 'non-inclusion in the enunciation', i.e., third person, or 'inclusion of the speaker/addressee in a larger set', expressed either by the first person plural 'we' or the second person plural 'you-all' (less individuated). The sources of polite pronouns may thus be subclassified as follows:

(i)   The original Lat. plural form UOS 'you.PL' acquired a deferential singular value: Fr. *vous*, southern It. *voi*, Cat. *vós*. In Modern Portuguese, the second person plural pronoun, *vós*, has almost completely disappeared. It was replaced as the plural 'polite pronoun' by *vocês* (< *Vossas Mercês* 'Your Graces'; see below), which takes a third person plural verb. Later on *vocês* lost its social value of respect and so came to serve as the plural of *tu* 'you.SG'.

(ii) An original third person pronoun acquired the value of 'addressee': It. singular *Lei* (as opposed to neutral *tu* 'you') – plural *Loro* (the polite form – now conservative and very rare – of *voi* 'you.PL'). In spite of the fact that they refer to the addressee, the Italian polite pronouns take a third person verb:

(46) *Lei   canta   –   Loro   cantano*
     You   sing.3SG   You   sing.3PL
     'You sing'   'You (all) sing'

(iii) What were originally non-pronominal modes of address expressing respect have come to function as pronouns. Such forms combine a noun with the meaning of 'Grace' (Sp. *Merced*, Pt. *Mercê*) or 'Lordship' (Ro. *domnia*) with a possessive pronoun: e.g., Sp. *Usted* (< *Vuestra Merced*), Pt. *Você* (< *Vossa Mercê*) 'Your Grace' (compare also Cat. *vostè* Glc. *vostede*), Ro. *dumneata* (lit. 'lordship yours.2SG'), more polite *dumneavoastră* (lit. 'lordship yours.2PL') and *dumnealui* (< *domnia lui*) 'he [+Respect]' vs. *dumnealor* (< *domnia lor*) 'they [+respect]'.

(iv) The first person plural is used for the first person singular as the expression of either 'royalty' or 'modesty'. Kings or high-ranking officials may use 'we' instead of 'I' as a sign of the fact that they view themselves as representatives of their country/people. The authorial 'we' is used as a sign of 'modesty', diluting the reference to 'I'.

As a consequence of these developments, the Romance languages present two politeness paradigms. French, Spanish and standard Italian exhibit a two-term paradigm, and express only one degree of social distance:

(47) Fr. *tu* – *vous*
Sp. SG *tú* – *usted*; PL *vosotros* – *ustedes*
It. SG *tu* – *Lei*, PL *voi* – *Loro* (rare)

In contrast to French, in Spanish and Italian the verb takes the third person form. Compare:

(48) Fr. *Vous*   *êtes*   *très aimable*
'You   are.2PL   very kind.SG'

(49) It. *Quando*   *arriva Lei?*
When arrives.3SG   you
'When are you arriving?'

Sp. *Usted*   *se*   *engaña*
You.SG   REFL   mistakes.3SG
'You are mistaken.'

Pt. *Você*   *chegou*   *tarde.*
You   arrived.3SG   late
'You arrived late.'

Romanian, on the other hand, has a three-term paradigm, expressing two degrees of social distance:

second person: *tu – dumneata – dumneavoastră,*
and, in some Southern varieties,

third person: *el – dânsul – dumnealui.*

In Brazilian Portuguese (see Vásquez Cuesta and Mendes da Luz 1980:159–62; Cunha 1981:210–13) there is an opposition between a familiar form *você* (PL. *vocês*) and a non-pronominalized polite form, *o Senhor, a Senhora* 'the gentleman, the lady'. The forms *tu* and plural *vós* have largely gone out of use. In Peninsular Portuguese (Vásquez Cuesta and Mendes da Luz 1980:152–59), the situation is much more complicated, varying according to a number of sociolinguistic factors. Both *tu* and *você* occur as familiar forms, whilst there is also widespread use (in contexts where Spanish would use the familiar forms) of names or nouns indicating family relationships, with a third person verb: e.g., *O pái esta zangado?* 'Are you (i.e., father) annoyed?', or even of a third person verb without any specific mode of address: e.g., *Cale-se!* lit. 'let him/her be quiet!' The title of the person follows *o/a Senhor/a*: e.g., *O Senhor Arquitecto/Engenheiro/Capitão*; *Vossa Excelência* (lit. 'Your Excellency') is used when a person's title is unknown.

3   Discourse organization

Discourse structures have usually been described in terms of 'actualized known information' versus 'new, unknown information', as well as in terms of word order, such as 'left- versus right-dislocation' or 'emphatic versus normal linear order'. As Lambrecht (1994) points out, the 'information status' and the discourse-organizational distinction between topic and comment structures are separate levels. Roughly speaking, the ***topic*** represents the actualized information, the starting point of the discourse, what the discourse is about (see Donnellan 1966). ***Topicalization*** is to be taken as the overt marking of the discourse function 'topic'. It is true that most of the time topics correspond to known information, but this is not necessarily the case. For example, deictic markers may point to an actualized constituent *in præsentia* and not only to one that has been previously identified. The ***comment*** is the part of the utterance representing 'what is asserted about the topic'. ***Emphasis*** may be defined as an assertion of coreferentiality by which any other competitor for a given argument of the verb is excluded. In other words, emphasis is a form of denying an expectation of coreferentiality. ***Focus***, referring to the constituent bearing the highest discourse salience in the sentence/utterance, is not to be confused with the 'speaker's focus of attention', which naturally coincides with the 'element the speaker wants to talk about'.[28] We have to add the concept of ***rhematic sentence*** (sometimes called ***sentence-focus***), which is meant to cover situations in which an utterance does not make the distinction between topic and comment, but refers to a whole event presented as rhematic, usually as new information.

From a traditional perspective, such distinctions were considered to be 'stylistic phenomena', as represented by expressions such as Fr. *mise en relief*, 'expressivity', 'affectivity', 'the most important entity', etc. Theories of syntax have accounted for these phenomena in several ways: by a series of movement rules (right- or left-dislocations); by inserting symbols such as 'topic/theme' above or under categorial symbols such as NPs; by inserting a superordinate dummy verb such as 'it is about' in the initial structure; or by a redundancy rule (when the dislocated constituent is copied by a pronoun), etc. It is not our intention here to dwell on the syntactic models, but rather to present some of the more general changes in the linguistic means of signalling discourse organization.

3.1   Word order

Word order is an important means of encoding discourse organization: for example, fronting a constituent may mark it as a topic or serve as a focalization device. The literature dealing with word-order changes from Latin to French abounds in data described within both traditional and more recent frameworks.[29] Thanks to recent treatments of Latin word order and its evolution from PIE, we can reconstruct the broad outline of changes in configurationality from left-branching to right-branching (see Ledgeway, this volume, chapter 8: §5). In a nutshell, the branching model is based on a hypothesis concerning the linear position of the head (defined as the entity that assigns the function to the whole phrase) vis-à-vis its subordinate entities. Since the morphemes of case, number and gender carry the N function, they are classified as heads. As far as verbal constituents are concerned, grammatical morphemes such as tense, mood and voice (expressed either by bound morphemes or by auxiliaries) are also carriers of the V function and consequently are also classified as heads.

A caveat should be entered here: when reconstructing the evolution of word order, we must be aware of the fact that studies of Latin syntax are based on written texts, which cannot fully represent speakers' choices in conversational settings.

3.1.1   Latin

The hypothesis that left-branching was the unmarked structure of Latin is supported by the following phenomena:

(a)   Within the NP:
 (i)   The lexical entity precedes the grammatical morphemes (case, gender, number):

(50) a. *res publica*   *firma* **est**
   republic.NOM.SG strong is.IND.PRS.3SG
   'the republic is strong' (Sall., *Cat.*, in Marchello-Nizia, 1995:43)
  b. *de*   *libro*   *meo*
   from book.SG.ABL mine.SG.ABL
   'from my book' (Vulgate, *Exodus*, 32.33, 34)

 (ii)   The restrictive adjective precedes the noun, except when discourse factors such as topicalization or focalization entail its postposition. On the other hand, the preposed genitive was the marked variant mainly motivated by emphasis or the co-occurrence of a preposed adjective:

(51) *magni*   *ponderis* *saxa*
  heavy.GEN weight.GEN rocks.ACC
  'rocks of heavy weight' (Caes., *BG*, 2.29.3, in Bauer 1995:57)

(b)   Within the VP, the same distribution of heads and modifiers may be observed even in the earliest texts:
 (i)   *Morphologically:* The root precedes the grammatical entities: voice markers, mood, tense, person and number morphemes:

(52) *qui* *peccaverit …*
  who sin.ACT.IND.FUT.3SG
  'who will sin …' (Vulgate, *Exodus*, 32: 33)

 (ii)   *Syntactically:* In written texts, complements precede the verb; neutral Latin order is therefore typologically Verb final (SOV, SV, OV), and this order predominates in both main and subordinate clauses:

(53) *Tamen* *res publica firma* **est***: opulentia neglegentiam*
  tolerabat
  Nevertheless republic strong is: prosperity negligence
  tolerate.IND.IPF.3SG
  'Nevertheless the republic is strong: (its) prosperity could tolerate negligence.' (Sall., *Cat.*, in Marchello-Nizia, 1995:43)

(iii) The cases in which the verb may occur in other positions are governed by **discourse** or **pragmatic** factors:

(α) *Sentence-initial verb:* The verb may occur in initial position in a string of enumerations, when it is a marker of a deontic speech act (an imperative) or in rhematic sentences, such as (54).[30]

> (54) ***Accurrunt*** *serui … **uideo** alios festinare … nihil relinquo in aedibus …* 'Servants are running … I see others rushing … I leave nothing in the house …' (Ter. *HT*, in Marouzeau 1938:48)

(β) *Verb in medial position:* In view of the emergence of SVO as the neutral word order in the Romance languages, the most interesting phenomenon is the relatively rare occurrence of the verb in medial position (although see Ledgeway, this volume, chapter 8: §3.1.1). This pattern is considered to be an innovation in Latin; it seems to occur for the most part either when a highly discourse-salient preverbal item is present (see (54) above: ***nihil*** *relinquo in aedibus* '**nothing** I leave in the house') or, more commonly, in the presence of certain postverbal elements, such as multiple subjects, multiple direct and/or indirect objects, relative, infinitive or participial clauses, especially when these are adverbial expressions indicating goals or aims.

(55) *Scin tu[…] **ad te** attinere hanc omnem rem?*
Know.INT you[…] to you concern.INF this.ACC whole.ACC thing.ACC
'Don't you know […], it is you that this whole story/affair concerns?' (Ter., *Eun.*, 744, in Marouzeau 1938:52)

In later texts such as the *Aetheriae Peregrinatio* and the Vulgate, (S)VO order becomes more frequent and does not seem to be triggered by the same discourse conditions as in Classical Latin:

(56)
Cui	*respondit*	*Dominus:*	*qui*	***peccaverit***
mihi,	*delebo*	*eum*	*de*	*libro*
meo;	*tu autem*	*vade*	*et*	*dice*
populum	*istum*	*quo*	*locutus sum*	*tibi;*
angelus meus	***praecedet***	*te*		
Him.DAT	answered	God:	who will have sinned	
me.DAT	delete.FUT.1SG	him.ACC from	book.ABL	
mine.ABL;	you.NOM however	go and	tell	
people.ACC.SG	this.ACC.SG what	I told	you.DAT;	
angel mine	lead.FUT.3SG	you.ACC		

'to him God answered: who sinned against me, I shall delete him
from my books; you however go and tell to these people what I told
you; my angel leads you.'   (Vulgate, *Exodus*, 32: 33–34)

In short, in Latin, SOV (corresponding to the left-branching
organization of the utterance) constitutes the neutral order,
but the verb occurs in sentence-initial position when the entire
sentence or the verb itself bears the highest degree of discourse
salience. The verb occurs in medial position when a constituent other than the verb carries the highest degree of discourse
salience.

3.1.2   Early Romance

SVO order is increasingly present in early and medieval texts. Explanations
for the change from SOV to SVO have been sought mainly within the
following domains:

(i) *Language universals*. A move to SVO order corresponding to a shift
to right-branching structures is seen as a natural typological change
across a variety of language families (Bauer 1995). But it is difficult
to find a convincing explanation as to why this change should take
place to begin with.

(ii) *Morphological factors*.[31] Although quite widely accepted, the
hypothesis that the change in word order was a consequence of
the loss of morphological markers does not seem sufficient, for the
following reasons: (a) in some languages (such as old French, old
Occitan and Romanian) a two- or a three-case declension system
was preserved for centuries, even after the right-branching syntactic
pattern had become predominant; and (b) the Romance preference
for pre-position instead of postposition has often been seen as a
consequence of the change in word order.

(iii) *Information structure*. The change from SOV to SVO is often
thought to have been triggered by the conversational preference
for the syntax to conform to the informational structure, where the
known entity or the entity referring to the speaker's centre of
attention (theme or topic) precedes the unknown entity and/or
the rheme/comment (what the speaker says about the topic).[32] In
short, the order 'theme–transitional element', hence 'verb–rheme',
would be the preferred choice for spoken registers. Consequently,
since the subject mainly represented the theme (topic), it was

fronted, like any other topical entity. A transitive verb requires the presence of a completion (the affected or created object), so it occurs naturally in the transitional position. One cannot deny the importance of oral registers in the development of the Romance languages, but we need to find an explanation for the fact that earlier languages, such as the early IE languages, which had mainly spoken registers, appear to have had such a strong preference for V-final structures.

Although the change from SOV to SVO is already attested in Latin, medieval texts show some interesting intermediate stages (although in many cases stylistic choices and/or the model of the original language – Arabic, Hebrew, Slavic – may explain the different word order).

(a) *SVO*. The verb in medial position is well attested in all early Romance languages:

(57) Fr. *Li   quens   Rolant   se   jut desuz   un   pin*
   The count Roland REFL lay under a   pine tree
   'Count Roland lay down under a pine tree' (*Roland*, 2375)

(58) Sp. *El hermano del rey **desea** a su hermano la muerte.*
   'The king's brother desires his brother's death.'
         (Martínez de Toledo, *El corbacho*, 313, in Crabb 1969:43)

(59) Pt. *E este conde **ouue** muitas batalhas com os mouros e com os leoneses*
   'And this count had many battles with the Moors and with the people of León'
        (*Chron. Brev. E mem. Av.*, in Canaes and Pádua 1960:51)

(60) It. *Il re **vede** due case, una picola e una grande*
   'The king sees two houses, one small and one big'
        (M 135, 15, in Vanelli 1986:257)

(61) Ro. *Iară celŭ feciorŭ mai tânărŭ **văzù** ceriulŭ și Dumnezeu*
   'And the youngest son saw heaven [lit. the sky] and God'
        (Coresi, *Cî*, 24)

(b) *SOV. Verb in sentence-final position*:
  Verb-final order was more frequent in early Romance texts than it is nowadays.[33] It represented an archaic word order (see Salvi, this volume, chapter 7), but could also be triggered by the fronting of other constituents:

(62) OFr. *Dist   Oliver: 'Jo   ai   païens   veüz …'*
    Says: Olivier 'I   have   pagans   seen'
    'Olivier says "I have seen [the] pagans"' (*Roland*, 1048)

Another possibility is that this word order is due to the influence of other languages. In Romanian, for instance, it has been attributed to the influence of Serbian or Hungarian patterns. However, it is rather hard to believe that the high frequency of final verbs that characterizes, say, Coresi's sermons is merely an imitation of foreign syntax. It is very likely that the foreign pattern reinforced a pre-existing choice, as is often the case when syntactic patterns come into contact, especially since such inversions obey similar Romance rules: for example, when other focalized constituents (such as direct objects or prepositional phrases) precede the verb.

(63)   *cu   văşmântulŭ   dentâi,   celŭ   fără de păcate,*
     îmbrăcà-ne-va,   *şi   cu   făgăduirea   duhului   sfântŭ*
     dăruì-ne-va
     'with cloth-the   primordial, the-one   without of sins,
     put-on.he-us-will   and   with   promise-the spirit   holy
     give.he-us-will
     'he will put on us the primordial cloth, the one which is without sins, and he will give us the promise of the Holy Spirit'

(Coresi, CÎ, 33)

3.2   Topic versus Comment

3.2.1   Topicalized constituents

Marking the topic constitutes the most obvious reason for fronting an NP.

3.2.1.1   Early and medieval Romance

(a)   The topicalized object, usually preceded by a definite determiner (article, demonstrative, possessive pronoun) or an ordinal quantifier, is also fronted and then the subject follows the verb. The fronted object is not always copied as a pronoun:

- no pronominal copy:

(64) Fr.   **Grant duel**   *firent   et   li   povre   et   li*
       riche   por   le   roi   Artur.
       Great   mourning   made   both   the   poor   and   the
       rich   for   the   King   Arthur
       'Both poor and rich mourned King Arthur greatly.'

(La Mort le roi Artur, 136, in Marchello-Nizia 1995:89)

(65) Sp.   **todas   estas   cosas**   *otorga   el   Rey*
       all   these   things   grants   the   King
       'all these things the King grants'   (Crónicas, 30)

(66) Pt.   **Esta   espada**   *trouve   eu   aqui*
       This   sword   brought   I   here
       'This sword I brought here'

(Chron. Brev., in Canaes and Pádua, 1960:144)

(67) It. **Queste parole** l'insegnaro i   savi vecchi del   regno
These   words him taught the wise old   of.the kingdom
'These words, the wise old men of the kingdom taught him'

(N 76, in Vanelli 1986:259)

(68) Ro. **repedele**   îmblînzeaşte, iară **neputinciosul** mîngâie
untamed.the tames.he,   and weak-the   encourages-he
'he tames the untamed (people), and encourages the weak'

(*Texte*: 189)

- When left-dislocated, the NP is copied by a clitic pronoun.

(69) Fr. **Cette   bataille**   veirement **la**   ferum
This   battle   truly   it.F.SG   we shall make.
'This battle, truly we shall fight'

(*Roland*, 882, in Marchello-Nizia 1995:74, n81)

This construction is fairly frequent in Middle French:

(70) Fr. **Les seigneurs** je **les** vous nommerai
'The Lords, I shall name them to you'

(Froissart: 829. 1.3.7, in Marchello-Nizia 1995:105)

(71) It. e   tutti   coloro   de la terra   ch'   erano
colpevoli,   il   Grande Cane **li**   fece
uccidere,   e   a   tutti   gli   altri   perdonò
and   all those   of   the   land   who   were
guilty,   the   Great   Dog   them   made
kill.INF   and   to   all   the   rest   forgave
'and all those of the land who were guilty, the Great Dog had
[them] killed, and he forgave everyone else'

(M 130, in Vanelli 1986:262)

(72) Sp. E   **los   ángeles** del   inferno   crió**los**
Dios   de   fuego
And   the   angels   of.the   inferno   created.them
God   of   fire
'And the angels of Hell, the God of fire created them'

(Crabb 1969:111)

(73) Ro. şi au   tăiat   capetele   pârcălabilor   şi
muerile   lor   **le-**   au robit   [...] şi **cetatea**
o   au   arsu.
and have   cut.off heads   magistrates.GEN and
women.the their   them   have enslaved   [...] and castle-the
it.F   have   burnt-down
'and they cut off the heads of the chief magistrates and enslaved
their women [...] and burnt down the castle.'   (Ureche, *Let.*, 95)

(b)   The indirect object may also be fronted:

(74) It. **A voi** ree Marco e a tutta la vostra compagnia Tristano **vi** manda
salute e buono amore

'To you king Mark and to all your companions Tristan sends
[you] greetings and love'   (*Tristan* LXVI, in Vanelli 1986:263)

(75) Pt. **Deos** *e*   *homem* verdadeyro, *humilho-me* **a ty**
God   and   people   righteous,   humble-me   to   you
'My Lord and righteous people, I humble myself in front of
you'   (*Mort. De S. Jer.*, in Canaes and Pádua 1960:1139)

(c) The attribute may precede the noun if focalized:[34]

(76) Fr. *Mult* *orent* **grant** *joie* *li*   *cuens* *de* *Venise* *et*
li   *cuens* *Loeys* *de*   *Blois*
Much   had   great   joy   the   count   of   Venice   and
the   count   Louis   of   Blois
'The Count of Venice and the Count Louis de Blois had much
joy'   (Villehardouin, 288)

(77) Sp. **Nuevas** *cosas* *yo*   *fallo* *con* *las* *quales* *tu* *veras*
el   **grant** *poder* *del*   *rrey*
New   things I   find   with the which   you see.FUT
the   great power of.the king
'I find new things with [the help of] which you will see the
king's great power'   (Lopez de Ayala, *Rimado de Palacio*, 1–2)

(78) Pt. **Gran** *misericordia fez*   *o*   *Senhor* *Deos* *connoso*
Great mercy   makes the Lord   God with.us
'The Lord (God) bestows great mercy upon us'
(*Cron de D.J.I*, cap. CLI: 316, in Canaes and Pádua 1960:195)

(79) Ro. *la* *această* *luminată*   *carte*
to   this   enlightened book
'to this enlightened book'   (Coresi, *CÎ*, 5)

3.2.1.2 Modern Romance

In the modern Romance languages, topicalization mainly involves dislocation that leaves a pronominal trace.

(a) *Topicalized subject.* In modern Romance, even the subject may be
copied, when topicalized. Since the subject normally represents the
topic, copying by a personal pronoun has a conversational function, namely to serve as an overt signal of agreement with the
interlocutor's topic.

(80) Fr. *Ce*   *quartier*   *radieux,* **il** *a*   *bien*
jailli *de*   *vous*
This   neighbourhood dazzling, it   has   certainly
sprung from   you
'This dazzling neighbourhood, it has certainly sprung out of
you'   (Ionesco, *Tueur.* 88)

(81) It.   *I samoani,* **loro** *si coprono sempre le ginnocchia*
'The Samoans, they always cover their knees'
(Duranti and Ochs 1979:273)

(82) Sp.   *Aquélla, la del viejito,* **ésa** *sí que está aplastada*
'That one, the one of the old man, **this** one for sure is flattened'
(Contreras 1976:81)

(83) Ro.   *Aşijderea acest domnu* **el** *bea vin mai mult din oală roşie decât din pahar de cristal*
'Also this king, **he** used to drink from a red pot rather than from a crystal glass'
(Neculce, *Cronica*, 36)

(b)   *Topicalized direct or indirect object.* When a DO or IO is fronted in sentence-initial position as topicalized, then it is commonly copied as a pronoun, usually a clitic pronoun, whose purpose is to signal the syntactic function of the topicalized constituent, especially when the topic has no other syntactic marker (for example, a preposition such as Sp., Pt. *a*, Ro. *pe*).

(84) Fr. **Cette moto,**   *je*   **l'**   *ai*   *achetée hier.*
This motorbike,   I   **it.ACC**   have   bought yesterday
'This motorbike, I bought it yesterday.'

(85) It. **La pipa,**   **la**   *fumi?*
The pipe,   **it.F.SG.ACC**   smoke?
'The pipe, do you smoke it?'

(86) Ro. **Bicicleta**   **asta**   *mi-*   *a*   *cumpărat*   **-o** *bunicul.*
Bicycle.the   **this**   me.DAT   has bought   **it.F.SG.ACC** grandfather.the
'This bike, my grandfather bought it for me.'

(c)   *Topical objects and the part/whole relation.* The expression of the part/whole relation is also sensitive to the topic constituent. The noun of the possessor-topic is the subject, but the corresponding reflexive clitic is an indirect object, whilst the inalienable possession is expressed by a direct object:

(87) Fr.   *Pierre*   *se*   *lave*   *les*   *mains.*
Sp.   *Pedro*   *se*   *lava*   *las*   *manos.*
Peter   REFL.IO   wash   the   hands.DO
'Peter washes his hands.'

If the inalienable possession is the topic, then it becomes the subject and the possessor becomes the indirect object:

(88) Fr. *les   pieds   me   font   mal*
        the   feet   me.IO   make   hurt.DO
        'My feet ache'

In Romanian, with activity verbs, the topical Possessor/ Experiencer is expressed by a direct object, but the noun referring to the inalienable possession becomes a prepositional phrase:

(89) *mă-   spăl   pe   mâini*
        me.ACC   wash   on   hands
        'I wash my hands'

3.2.2   Rhematic postverbal subjects

Postverbal subjects may carry new information. Whether definite or indefinite, they remain within the lower verb phrase. According to some generative analyses, the order is not derived by moving the verb to the left of the subject (Alboiu 1999; Costa 2000:98).

(i) VOS is the only order possible when only the subject carries new information:[35]

(90) It. *La prossima settimana confluiranno a Roma **rappresentanti dei molti poli di crisi dell'industria italiana***
        'Next week representatives of the many poles of crisis in Italian industry will meet in Rome.'   (in Wandruska 1986:18)

(91) Pt. *Sabe   francês   **o Paulo**.*
        Knows   French   **the Paulo**
        'Paulo knows French.'

(92) Ro. *Maria nu   avea   rochiţe   de   vară,*
        *aşa că   i   a   cusut   una   **mama.***
        Maria not   had   dresses   of   summer,
        therefore   her.DAT   has   sewed   one   **mother**
        'Maria had no summer dresses, therefore her mother made one for her.'

Even in contemporary French, when expressed by a 'heavy' phrase (one which includes a relative clause, for example), the subject follows the verb in rhematic sentences:

(93) *Doivent mener la campagne **ceux qui** entendent incarner le mouvement socialiste, après mars 1993*
        'Those whose intention is to embody the socialist movement after March 1993 should lead the campaign'
            (Interview with François Hollande, *Le Nouvel Observateur*, 24–30 décembre 1992, in Marchello-Nizia 1995:37)

(ii) VSO order is felicitous (in Portuguese, Spanish and Romanian, but not in Italian or Catalan) when neither subject nor object is topical:[36]

(94) Pt. *Sabe*   *o Paulo*   *francês.*
Knows   the Paulo   French
'Paulo knows French.'

(iii) IOVS(IO). The choice between preverbal or postverbal positions is also determined by the semantics of the verb. For example, with a verb such as 'like' (Sp. *gusta*, It. *piace*, Ro. *place*) the dative clitic of the Experiencer precedes the verb and the subject follows.[37]

(95) Sp. *me*   *gusta*   **el vino**   **de Málaga**
me.DAT   pleases   **the wine**   **of Málaga**
'I like Málaga wine'

(96) It. *mi*   *piace*   **il Chianti**
me.DAT   pleases   **the Chianti**
'I like Chianti [wine]'

(97) Ro. *îmi*   *place*   **muzica**   **simfonică.**
me.DAT   pleases   **music.the**   **symphonic**
'I like symphonic music.'[38]

In Romanian, the possessor-topic (whether coreferential or not with the subject-initiator) takes the accusative case after certain categories of verbs expressing feelings:

(98) **mă**   *doare*   *capul*
me.ACC   aches   head.the
'I have a headache'

3.2.3   Rhematic sentences

The subject occurs after the verb and the verb occupies the initial sentence position in rhematic sentences both in medieval texts and in modern Romance.[39]

(a) Medieval texts:

(99) Fr. *Sunent*   *mil*   *grailles*   *por*   *ço*   *que*   *plus*
          bel   *seit*
Sound a   thousand bugles   for   that   that   more
beautiful   be.SUBJ
'A thousand bugles sound so that it may be more
beautiful'   (*Roland*, 1005) (rhematic sentence)

(100) Sp. *Erase*   *un*   *caçador …*
Was.REFL   a   hunter
'There was once a hunter …'
          (J. Ruiz de Hita, *Abutarda e Golondrina*, in *Crest.Rom.*, 1: 735)

(101) Pt. *Sabía porem isto o Meestre e os de seu Conselho*
Knew however this the Master and those of his Council
'However the Master and those of his Council knew this'

(*Cron. De D.J.*, in Canaes and Pádua 1960:104)

(102) Ro. *Deci   m-   au   prinsu   neşte   saşi*
So   me   have   captured   some   Saxons
'So a few [Transylvanian] Saxons captured me'

(*Scrisoare* 1660, in *Doc.*, 206)

(b)   Modern Romance:

(103) Sp. *¡Llegan   los   invitados!*
are.arriving   the   guests
'The guests are arriving!'

(104) Pt. *Vêm   os   hóspedes!*
are.coming   the   guests
'The guests are coming!'

(105) It. *Entravano   delle   donne.*
enter.IPFV   some   ladies
'Ladies were coming in.'

(106) Ro. *Vin   musafirii!*
are.arriving   guests.the.
'The guests are arriving!'

In French, the (obligatorily indefinite) rhematic subject in postverbal position must occur with a preverbal expletive in the canonical subject position controlling agreement on the verb:

(107) Fr.   a. plural postverbal subject
Il   *arrive*   **des   invités**
It.M.SG   arrives   INDF.ART   guests
'Guests are arriving'
Fr. b. feminine singular – postverbal subject
J'avais déjà   commencé à manger lorsqu'   **il**
est   entré   une bizarre   petite femme   qui
m 'a demandé si elle pouvait s'asseoir à ma table
I had   already   started   to eat   when   it.M.SG
is   entered.M.SG a   strange   little woman   who
me asked   if she could   sit   at my table
'I had already started to eat when a strange little woman came in
and asked me if she could sit at my table'   (Camus, *L'Étranger*, 36)

Berruto (1986:57) notes that in contemporary (standard) Italian the canonical preverbal subject position cannot be overtly filled since Italian does not have phonetically overt expletives.

According to several generative models, Romanian is a verb-initial language (see Dobrovie-Sorin 1994; Alboiu 1999; Cornilescu 2000). This hypothesis would predict that only subjects that represent salient discourse entities (topics, subtopics or focalized constituents) would move from their postverbal position to preverbal position. Rhematic utterances (where there is no contrast between topic and comment) would then have to be considered as the neutral discourse entities. This perspective would open up new avenues for explaining word-order changes in pro-drop Romance languages. It would also predict that, in such languages, subjects expressed by personal pronouns and demonstratives occur in preverbal position when representing discourse-salient entities and that the occurrence of a preverbal noun would occur at topic-switch or focalization (unifying the treatment of both subjects and objects). This hypothesis also offers a basis for explaining the difference between covert and overt topic-marking. The overt marking of topics (i.e., topicalization) is a specific conversational device aimed at signalling the acceptance of the interlocutor's topic.

3.2.4 Definite and indefinite NPs in the contemporary Romance languages

SVO order becomes the neutral, unmarked order, since the subject is usually associated with information which is known and topical. If the link between syntax, informational structure and discourse structure is broken, this can be marked linguistically in various ways.

Definite NPs are preferred candidates for topical subjects and for sentence-initial position. However, there are cases in which the preverbal subject is expressed by a definite NP that is not topical but announces the 'topic to be'. This is the case, for example, at the beginning of a story, when the author wants to attracts the reader's attention by presenting the character(s) as being already identified:

(108) Fr. ***Les cinq amis*** *achevaient de dîner, cinq hommes du monde mûrs,*
riches, trois mariés, deux restés garçons
'The five friends were just finishing their dinner, five mature men of the world, rich, three of them married, two of them still bachelors'
(Maupassant, *Les Tombales*, 107)

Even a personal pronoun can be used for narrative purposes at the beginning of a story (see Adam 1990:54f.):

(109) Fr. *L'écharde pointue du soleil transperça l'écale de la paupière [...]*
Elle *ouvrit les yeux sur la lumière du grand jour [...] Éblouie par*

> *tout cet éclat, elle ne sut plus pendant un moment où **elle** était.*
> *Tanya Marine Fernande, baptisée deux mois après la mort de son*
> *père des prénoms qu'il lui avait choisis avant de basculer dans*
> *l'invisible?*
> 'The sharp-pointed husk of the sun pierced the shell of her
> eyelid [...] She opened her eyes on broad daylight [...] Dazzled
> by all this light, she did not know for a moment where she was.
> T.M.F., christened two months after her father's death with the
> names that he had chosen for her before toppling into the
> invisible?' (Maryse Condé, *La Colonie du nouveau monde*, 9)

There are also subjects expressed by an indefinite NP or quantifier which occur in preverbal position. An interesting structural distinction between definite NPs and indefinite NPs in preverbal position is proposed by Costa (2000), who claims that, in pro-drop languages such as Portuguese, the definite subject must occur under the highest position within the sentential core (namely, SpecIP), whereas indefinite NPs, which are not topical, target a preverbal left-dislocated position within the left periphery, when they represent an identified referent. (110) and (111) will therefore have different structures.

(110) – *O Paulo sabe que línguas?* (one is talking about Paulo)
  '– Paulo knows which languages?'
  – *O Paulo sabe francês.*
  '– Paulo knows French.'

In (111) *um cão* belongs to the group of animals already visible in the surroundings (information activated by the context), but the information as a whole in B's utterance is rhematic (carries new information):

(111) A: *Estão imensos animais neste parque: cães, gatos, galinhas.*
  'There are lots of animals in this park: dogs, cats, chickens.'
  B: *Olha: **um cão** mordeu uma criança.*
  'Look! A dog bit a child.'

If the indefinite subject introduces new information, the SVO order is not felicitous:

(112) A: *O que é que mordeu o Paulo?*
  ' What bit Paulo?'
  B: ??*Uma cobra mordeu o Paulo.*
  'A snake bit Paulo.'
  rather B: *Uma cobra* (with gapping).
  'A snake'.

The highest position in the sentential core (SpecIP) is a position for subjects that carry known information but are not necessarily topical. However, the status of preverbal subjects is in fact more complicated, since definite NPs may be constituents of rhematic sentences and generic statements may contain topical indefinite NPs. It is for this reason that it seems more appropriate to represent the relations in question as tendencies rather than as obligatory combinations of features.

An indefinite NP which represents unknown information may nonetheless become the topic and occur in sentence-initial position when it carries the highest degree of communicative information:

(113) It. *Un giovanotto grasso, dagli occhi vivaci, si fermava sulla porta e li ascoltava*
'A fat youngster, with lively eyes, was standing at the door and was listening to them'   (Pavese, in Wandruska 1986:18)

4   Voice as a means of marking discourse organization

The Romance three-term category of voice constitutes another innovation in the area of topic-marking. Before outlining our discourse hypothesis, we shall briefly present the main descriptions of voice within cognitive and discourse frameworks.

4.1   *Theoretical preliminaries*

4.1.1   Psycho-mechanics

The first hypothesis concerning the role played by voice in the linguistic organization of information can be identified in the writings of Guillaume (see especially Guillaume 1971). In his opinion, voice encodes differences in discourse organization reflecting the movement of the speaker's thought from one participant to another participant in the event. The participants are characterized in terms of their 'degree of involvement' in the events, very much as in the Case Grammars developed in the 1960s. In Case Grammars and Generative Semantics (which introduced thematic roles in initial structures), participants are defined both by their role in the event and by their capacity for having an impact on syntactic constructions. The labels used are fairly transparent, indicating the function of the participant in the event: Agent, Experiencer, Cause, Instrument, Objective, Patient, Beneficiary, Locative, Goal, Space.

As Givón (1984:I,139–45) has pointed out, there is a relationship between these Cases/Roles and the degree of accessibility to topic position and, consequently, to the syntactic subject, which can be represented as a topic hierarchy. The topic hierarchy is a ranking of the various semantic Roles according to their probability of becoming the most continuous topic in discourse, and may be formulated as follows:

Agent > Dative > Patient > Locative > Instrument/Associate > Manner.

The Patient (also called the Undergoer) is the affected participant, 'being-in-a-state' or 'undergoing a change-in-state'. The Dative is an Experiencer (for example, the subject of verbs of knowledge or feeling) or a Beneficiary (when involved in receiving activities, etc.). In the Romance languages, the Agent corresponds most frequently to the subject (of an active construction), the Experiencer to the subject or to the indirect object (taking the dative case or a prepositional marker); the Patient is the prototypical role of the direct object in the accusative; and the Locative is chiefly found in prepositional constructions.

4.1.2   Cognitive Grammar

According to Langacker's Cognitive Grammar, the passive imposes a choice of the trajector that reverses the relation between the figure and the ground of the active construction (Langacker 1987:351f.). The figure is 'the structure perceived as "standing out" from the remainder, which is represented by the **ground**' (Langacker 1987:120). For example, the English past participle is defined by the following functions:

'(i)   it suspends the sequential scanning of the verb stem, converting it into a complex atemporal relation (hence the temporalizing *be* is required in a finite clause);
      and

(ii) it imposes a figure/ground alignment distinct from that of the stem, specifically with respect to the choice of trajector' (Langacker 1987:351).

In order to define the distinction between middle and reflexive constructions in Latin, Kemmer (1993:66) introduces two cognitive dimensions:

• the *relative distinguishability of participants in the event*, i.e., 'the degree to which a single physico-mental entity is conceptually distinguished into separate participants, whether body vs. mind, or Agent vs. unexpectedly contrasting Patient' and

- (ii) the *relative elaboration of events*, i.e., 'the degree to which the participants and component subevents in a particular verbal event are distinguished [...] The variation in elaboration of events reflects alternative conceptualizations by the speaker, who has the choice of either making reference to events as undifferentiated wholes, or making reference to their substructures or component parts' (Kemmer 1993:121).

The middle is characterized by *a low degree of elaboration of events, subsuming low participant and subevent distinguishability*.

4.1.3   Discourse organization

According to Touratier (1984:90), the category of voice is the effect of a structural organization of the sentence which corresponds to an orientation at the level of meaning. When defining the passive voice, for example, he stresses the fact that the reorganization of the sentence is triggered by the suppression of the first argument of the verb and the structural promotion of its second argument to subject function. This leads to a reorganization of the meaning, which now has a different orientation: although the semantic content is unchanged, it is now linked to the second argument and not the first, the suppression of which has ruled it out of consideration.

In his OT model of voice, Sells (2001) introduces topicality alongside the role of participants, agent and patient, in order to calculate the possibilities that voice can encode in any language. In fact, Sells speaks of a *scalar topicality*:

> **Scalar Topicality** is determined by the discourse measures of Referential Distance and Topic Persistence. **Referential Distance** is the measure of how far back in discourse the previous mention of a referent is, from a given point; the lower the measure of Referential Distance, the more topical the entity is. **Topic Persistence** measures how many times in succeeding discourse a referent is mentioned, from a given point; hence the higher the measure, the more frequent and topical the entity in question is.   (Sells 2001:360)

The possible combinations of these parameters may be summarized as follows (Sells 2001:363), where 'A' and 'P' represent 'high-prominence' Agents and Patients, respectively, and 'a' and 'p' represent 'low-prominence' Agents and Patients, whilst numerals represent 'weighting'.

Voice Type equivalent	*Expression*	*Linking*	*LRS*
Active	a1-p1	a_S1-p_O1	AP
Inverse–GR	a1-p1	a_O1-p_S1	
Antipassive	a1-p0	a_S1-$p_{OBL}0$	AP
Passive	a0-p1	$a_{OBL}0$-p_S1	aP
Super Active	a2-p1	a_S2-p_O1	
Super Inverse-GR	a1-p2	a_O1-p_S2	
Super Antipassive	a2-p0	a_S2-$p_{OBL}0$	
Super Passive	a0-p2	$a_{OBL}0$-p_S2	

This model, which takes into account only two roles, the A(gent) and the P(atient) (corresponding to the grammatical subject or to the oblique case), cannot account for languages in which there is a grammatical encoding of the difference between constructions with a subject referring to an Agent and those with a subject referring to an Experiencer. This is the case with Latin forms in -R (the so-called medio-passive) and the Romance reflexive, which can have an Experiencer as their subject, as distinct from active constructions (see (114) and (115)).

(114) Lat.   LAETOR (middle) 'I am happy', 'I rejoice', and

(115) Fr.   *je me réjouis*, Sp. *me alegro*, It. *mi rallegro*, Ro. *mă bucur* (reflexive)
'I rejoice/I am glad.'

Further evidence for the fact that Latin syntax was sensitive to the difference between Experiencer and Agent is to be found in constructions with the so-called 'impersonal verbs of feeling' such as: PUDET 'it shames', PIGET 'it irks', PAENITET 'it regrets', etc. These constructions have a dummy subject in the third person, the Experiencer is encoded in an accusative NP, and the noun referring to the cause takes the genitive case, as in (116):

(116) *me* [...]   *pigeat*   *stultitiae*   *meae*
me.ACC   irks.it.is.SUBJ   stupidity.GEN.SG   mine.GEN.SG
approx. 'I should be irked at my stupidity.'   (Cic., *Dom.*, 29)

In spoken and late Latin there is a preference for developing medio-passive forms (the so-called deponent forms) for verbs of feeling (*doleor, CIL*, 6. 23176 for *doleo* 'I suffer', GAUDEOR for GAUDEO 'I rejoice') and psychological verbs (DUBITOR beside DUBITO 'I doubt'), which also shows that the category 'Experiencer' was perceived as being different from the category 'Agent (active force)'. Romance syntax is still sensitive to the difference between Agent and Experiencer: see, for example, constructions in which the topical personal Experiencer is either in the dative or in the accusative and not in the subject case (nominative):

(117) dative:

> Sp. *me gusta*, It. *mi piace*, Ro. *îmi place* lit. 'to me pleases', i.e., 'I like ...';
> Sp. *me duele la cabeza* lit. 'to me hurts the head', i.e., 'my head hurts'
> Ro. *mi-e frig* lit. 'to me is cold', i.e., 'I am cold'

(118) accusative:

> Ro. *mă doare capul* lit. 'me.ACC hurts head', i.e., 'my head hurts'

4.1.4   Scenic strategies

Rather than adopting Kemmer's cognitive approach, we propose a discourse hypothesis, namely the *scenic strategy of highlighting*, because it can explain the use of the Latin forms in -R and the Romance reflexive constructions even when the referent of the subject does not fulfil two roles in the event (e.g., passive: Lat. AMOR 'I am loved' or impersonal DICITUR 'it is said'). Langacker's 'figure/ground alignment' is the basis for a staging strategy, which we propose to interpret metaphorically as 'highlighting'. Figuratively, it can be viewed as *directing light at the stage*. At this point it is necessary to specify that 'highlighting' and 'topicality', although coinciding most of the time, belong to different levels of information. As has already been mentioned, topic can be defined roughly as the 'entity speakers want to talk about'; the topic is usually identifiable across sentence boundaries (compare the notion of 'scalar topicality' in Sells (2001), discussed above). *Highlighting* does not preclude the repeated presence of a protagonist on the stage. See, for example, (119):

> (119) Fr.   *Raymond voulait fuir, mais, en même temps, se cacher, ne pas être vu.*
> 'Raymond wanted to flee, but at the same time, to hide, not to be seen.'
> (Mauriac, *Désert*, 44)

In (119) the topic is Raymond, as the subject of all the clauses. The first clause has an active construction and therefore highlights Raymond, the Experiencer, as the initial point of the trajectory; in the third clause the affected participant, Raymond, is highlighted, as the subject of a passive construction, but in the second clause the reflexive construction *se cacher* highlights the whole event of 'hiding', and not just Raymond.

4.2   *Latin voice*

4.2.1   The values of the forms in -R

Although there has been little discussion of the interpretation of the active voice, the Latin medio-passive has been subjected to a variety of interpretations, mostly conditioned by translations into a specific contemporary language. According to classic descriptions, the values of the medio-passive (the forms in -R) are characterized by a mosaic-like variety:

(a) impersonal (with either transitive or intransitive verbs):

(120) DICITUR lit. 'there is saying', 'it is said'; ITUR lit.' there is going', 'they go' (Ernout and Thomas, 1953:204f.);
dabitur tibi amphora
cf. Fr. *on te donnera une amphore*
'they will give you an amphora'[40]   (Pl., *Cas.*, 121)

(b) middle-reflexive (when the subject shares the roles of both Agent and Patient):

(121) *lauari, tergeri*
'to wash, to clean [oneself]' (intrinsic passive)   (Pl., *Poen.*, 219)

(c) middle/active (especially verbs of feeling) (the subject refers to an Experiencer, who is both the inner cause and the location of the feeling):

(122) LAETOR 'I rejoice', MIROR 'I am amazed [at], I am surprised, I admire', QUEROR 'I complain, I lament', compare also the semi-deponent GAUISUS SUM 'I rejoiced' and late Lat. *doleor* 'I suffer'
(*CIL*, 6. 23176; *CIL* 02, 03249)

(d) inchoative:

(i) change in position (the referent of the subject is the initiator of the movement and the entity that moves):

(123) FERRI 'to rush, to flee', MOUERI 'to move [oneself]', UEHI 'to transport [oneself]'

(ii) change in state (the referent of the subject is the initiator of the change and the object that changes):

(124) ALBISCOR 'I am becoming white', AEGROR 'I am falling sick'; IGNIS EXSTINGUITUR 'the fire goes out [by itself]'; compare also MORIOR 'I am becoming dead', i.e., 'I am dying, I die'[41]

(e) passive:

(125) AMOR 'I am loved'

(f) factitive-passive (the subject refers to the Patient acted upon and the one who lets it happen):

(126) *aduruntur* 'they let themselves be burnt'
(Cic., *Tusc.*, 5, 27, 77)
(cf. Fr. *ils se laissent brûler*)
(Touratier 1984:81)

(g) deponent:

(127) IMITOR 'I imitate'; SEQUOR 'I follow'

Owing to the preoccupations of current linguistic theory, more recent descriptions of the Latin medio-passive have been concerned only with their syntactic characteristics. Consequently, the medio-passive forms have been categorized as a means of *intransitivizing the verb*, in other words, of reducing the valency of the verb. But the syntactic hypothesis that the medio-passive forms were means of detransitivizing the verb cannot account for the behaviour of all forms in -R (see Touratier 1984). Several Latin verbs, including the deponents, were transitive. For example, DEXTERAS '[right] hands' is the object of COPULARI in (128) and *ferrum* 'the sword' is the direct object of *cingor* in (129):[42]

(128) COPULARI DEXTERAS
'to shake [the] right [hands]'

(129) *ferrum*   *cingitur*
      sword:ACC   girds.he/himself
      'He girds on his sword'   (Verg. *Aen.*, 7, 640)

Generative grammars have tended to provide a variety of initial structures for explaining the functions which have traditionally been assigned to the Latin forms in -R.[43] But it is hard to believe that a single morphological form could express so many values, some of which are contradictory. Rather, we should attempt to find some invariant that can account for all these uses. It is for this reason that I find cognitive and discourse approaches more convincing, because they offer a more unified description and have a better explanatory power both synchronically and diachronically. In what follows, I shall briefly present the most important results of these descriptions, which are more related to some of the views of classical grammarians (for further details, see Manoliu Manea 2000c).

4.2.2   Traditional grammars in support of a discourse hypothesis

4.2.2.1   Arguments against a passive interpretation

Even according to traditional grammarians, the impersonal interpretation (where the agent is not explicitly present) was more important than the passive value. For example, according to Meillet and Vendryes (1960:324), the impersonal meaning which merely indicates that the action is being accomplished or has been accomplished (depending on whether we are dealing with the infectum or the perfectum) is the predominant value of the Latin passive. According to Ernout and Thomas (1953[1]/93:206), the distinction between active constructions and the personal passive is secondary, since the passive does not necessarily imply that the subject is the Undergoer. They claim that in general only transitive verbs have a personal

passive, but take issue with the claim that the active and passive constructions (as represented by ME DILIGIT PATER '[my] father loves me' and A
PATRE DILIGOR 'I am loved by [my] father', respectively) are equivalent,
seeing any equivalence as imperfect and secondary. The personal passive
does not necessarily imply that the subject is the undergoer of the action; it
often retains an impersonal value, indicating a state or an action without
reference to any determinate subject, which also makes it an expression of
indefiniteness. They quote the following examples: Pl., *Cas.*, 121: ***dabitur
tibi amphora*** 'you will be given an amphora' (the identity of the giver is
irrelevant); Pl., *Mi.*, 674**:** *quod **sumitur*** 'what is being spent', contrasting
with 673: *sim quid **sumas*** with a second person indefinite subject. This
value may even appear in a first person context – see Ter., *Ad.*, 911: *iam
lepidus **uocor*** 'now I'm being called charming'. They further point out that
not all transitive verbs have a passive: thus FIO, corresponding to FACIO 'I
do', except for the gerund FACIENDUS and the past participle FACTUS; DISCO
'I am taught' corresponding to DOCEO 'I teach' (DOCEOR is postclassical);
INTEREO 'I die' pour INTERFICIO 'I kill'. Deponent verbs use periphrases to
form a 'passive': USUI ESSE 'to be useful, to be used', corresponding to UTI
'utiliser'; ADMIRATIONEM HABERE (MOUERE) 'to be admired', corresponding
to ADMIRARI 'to admire'.

A sentence such as:

(130) *cum   a   Cotta   resisteretur*
       as   by   Cotta   resist: medio-passive.past.3SG

(Caes., B.G., 5.30,1)

means something like: 'as there was resisting by Cotta' (in Meillet and
Vendryes's words, 'puisqu'il y avait de la résistance de la part de Cotta'),
rather than: 'as it was resisted by Cotta'. According to traditional grammars,
in Latin there was no real agentive complement; the forms in -R could be
determined by a 'dative of the author' or by a cause complement (see below,
§4.3.2). But, if the forms in -R cannot be considered as expressions of a true
passive, what functions did they fulfil?

4.2.2.2   Arguments for a middle interpretation

In our opinion, the forms in -R seem more closely related to the IE middle
voice than to the passive. Our hypothesis rests upon the following interpretations of the functions and values of the Latin forms in -R.

According to Ernout and Thomas (1953[1]/93:207f.), the characteristic function of the Latin passive construction was to stress (to give a
prominent position to) the verbal notion rather than the agent. They note

that the ablative preceded by A or AB is rare in old Latin, becoming frequent only in the late Republican period. This increase in frequency is accompanied by a semantic weakening of the preposition, so that the notion of 'origin' is now less prominent. Nonetheless, this construction is not always precisely equivalent to the corresponding active form with a nominative subject.[44] It often has the function of highlighting the verb rather than the Agent. They give the examples *sine controuersia ab dis solus diligere* 'you are without any doubt the only one who is cherished by the gods' (Ter., *Ph.*, 854) and *cursus incitato in summo colle ab hostibus conspiciebantur* 'after a rapid march, they were espied by the enemy at the top of the hill' (Caes., *BG*, 2, 26, 3), noting that the former stresses the idea of uniqueness and the latter that of a sudden event.

Guillaume (1971:II,189) offers an interesting comment on the 'impersonal meaning' of the middle. In the ancient languages, he claims, the middle, with its passive-like inflection, often involves a shift into impersonality, whereby the verb continues to have an active value, but with no underlying person. As a result, we can say that the middle voice in a sense turns the verb into its own subject. Thus, PUGNATUR comes to mean 'it is fought, fighting takes place'. For Flobert (1975:523), deponents mark the fact that the subject is profoundly implicated in and affected by the process; the active is more neutral and more commonplace, and there is less commitment on the part of the subject. When the forms in -R are used as passives, the agent is either missing or only present in a subsidiary role; he sees passive morphemes as completely altering the representation of the process.

It is also relevant to recall here the relation between the forms in -R and the so-called 'internal diathesis', defined as expressing the fact that the subject is 'affected' by the action. As Joffre (1995:236) puts it, the basic meaning of the forms in -R is internal diathesis (*la diathèse interne*): the two concepts (nominal and verbal) are superimposed on and implicated in one another ('les deux concepts (nominal et verbal) se superposent, ils sont impliqués l'un dans l'autre'). The two notions are closely linked; their reciprocal appropriateness is signalled ('les deux notions sont étroitement associées, leur adéquation réciproque est signalée'; Joffre 1995:195). In the case of impersonal constructions, the morpheme -TUR modifies the lexical content of the verb by adding a seme which emphasizes the existence of the process ('le morphème -**tur** modifie le contenu lexical du verbe en lui ajoutant un sème qui souligne l'existence du procès'; Joffre 1995:193). When analysing the deponents or the passive, she stresses (Joffre 1995:235) that the subject is always implicated in the process ('on note toujours une implication du sujet dans le procès').

As I have demonstrated elsewhere (Manoliu 2006), various interpretations of the Latin medio-passive support our *discourse hypothesis* that Latin diathesis (the semantic area expressed by morphologically or syntactically marked voice) was organized around *agency*, interpreted as the capacity to influence human life (which is not the same as the feature 'animate' referring to the property of 'living'). The active voice typically highlighted the participant that had the power of affecting human life in positive or negative ways as the initial point in the movement of thought when constructing the event linguistically, and this accorded with the most common perceptive strategy. The form in -R signalled the fact that the speaker did not want to highlight the initiator – because the speaker did not want to specify it; because it was not a Doer but an affected participant (Experiencer); or because it fulfilled two roles in the event. As such, the medio-passive could be used as a staging strategy for highlighting the whole event.

4.3   *The emergence of a three-term paradigm*

A change in orientation when constructing the event (or situation) mentally and linguistically cannot by itself account for the differences between the Latin category of voice and the Romance developments, in which a system of at least three voices (active, passive and reflexive) came into existence. The differences between the morphologically encoded voice of Latin and the corresponding Romance constructions must have been the result of the following phenomena:

(a)   *The loss of the inherent passive feature.* In our hypothesis, one has to consider *the changes that occurred in the encoding of various cognitive categories,* which are highly culture-dependent. Changes in cognitive categories have a significant impact on the process of reconfiguring the semantics of noun classes. In the case of the evolution of the category of voice, one has to consider the importance attached to an inherent semantic feature such as [±Capacity for being a Doer] in Latin,[45] and to [Person] rather than to [Agent] in Romance.[46] Once the feature [–Capacity for being a Doer] (i.e., an incapacity for doing things) was no longer considered as an inherent feature of nouns but as contextually assigned by the event, any noun could in principle refer to an active or to a passive participant, either living or not. It is the loss of this type of inherent feature in nouns that prompted the development of passive constructions as markers signalling that the result/the affected participant constitutes the centre of the speaker's attention (highlighting the affected participant).

(b) *Changes in the case system.* The vanishing case system could not offer any compensatory means for indicating which NP corresponded to the passive or to the active participant in a given event. Even in areas in which the subject ending -s was preserved, it tended to be generalized – even to the subject case of neuter nouns.[47]

(c) *Discourse factors.* The choice of a particular case (e.g., in Latin the nominative), agreement with the predicative verb in person and number, preference for sentence-initial position – all these syntactic markers of the nominal chosen as subject are surely connected with the fact that subjectivization was one of the means of overtly marking the topic. Note that the nominative was also the case used with topicalized NPs, as in (131):

(131) *tu,   si te   di   amant, agere   tuam   rem occasiost*
you.NOM if you.ACC gods love   do.IN   your   affair it.is.the.occasion
'as for you, if the Gods love you, it is the right occasion for you to do business'   (Pl., *Poen.*, 659)

4.3.1   Plain passives

Owing to the predominance of colloquial registers in late Latin and early Romance, marking the most salient discourse entity (the topic, the focalized entity, etc.) assumes even greater importance, and the syntactic subject tends to be even more closely linked to the topic of the discourse than to the Agent. Consequently, new linguistic means evolve for signalling which NP corresponds to the most dynamic participant and which to the least dynamic participant, especially when there is a change in the typical relation between topic, dynamicity and subject; for example, when the most dynamic participant is not the focus of the speaker's attention as the initial point in the movement of thought. Since the verb assigns various roles to its arguments, it is not surprising that the combination of topicality of an argument with a situationally assigned 'passive role' will affect the entire sentence structure, including the verbal markers: when topical, the noun referring to the 'inactive participant' becomes the subject and the verb develops a plain passive form (ESSE/STARE/UENIRE/IRE + passive participle).[48]

The key context favouring the development of a passive value from the impersonal construction can be described as follows:

(i) The NP referring to the less dynamic participant was a neuter noun and consequently had the same ending for direct object and for subject.

(ii) The neuter NP was topical and so occurred in sentence-initial position. For example, a resultative impersonal construction such as (132) is reinterpreted as a passive: 'the temple has been closed'.

> (132) *templum clausum est*
> 'the temple[, one] closed [it]' (it is therefore closed),
> rather, 'as for the temple, there was a closing [of it]'

Once (132) becomes a possible interpretation for resultative constructions, an agentive prepositional phrase of the type AB + NP can be added if the agent is focalized as in (133):

> (133) *templum clausum est ab uestalibus*
> 'the temple has been closed by the vestals'

4.3.2   Reflexive constructions

Several forms in -R and the reflexive constructions refer to a protagonist that has more than one Role (syntactically speaking, two NPs are coreferential): the pronominal construction **explicitly** expresses this coreference, whereas most of the forms in -R carry the **conventional implicature** of coreference (see (121) middle reflexive, (122) middle/active, (123), (124) inchoative, above).[49]

(a) *Latin reflexive versus middle.* In Classical Latin, the reflexive pronoun could be used with either active or medio-passive forms. When it co-occurred with active forms, the reflexive pronoun expressed the identity between the 'agent' (the most prominent participant, subsequently assimilated to the syntactic subject) and another participant. In Flobert's words (Flobert 1975:384), this is a reduplication of the subject, which is both acting and acted upon; the process reflects a deliberate and willed action of self on self; the reflexive is therefore dualist.[50]

> (134) SE   OCCIDERE
>   3.REFL   kill.INF
>   'to kill oneself'

The reflexive pronoun can also co-occur with verbs of change:

> (135) CONUERTIT   SE   IN   HIRUNDINEM
>   turned   himself   into   swallow
>   'He turned himself into a swallow'

With verbs of movement (such as SE MOUERE), the reflexive pronoun, according to Flobert (1975:387), stresses the fact that the subject has the initiative when it comes to the movement, whereas the intrinsic passive MOUERI merely indicates that the subject is implicated in a movement; the reflexive construction is therefore stronger and more expressive.[51]

(136) SE DUCERE

    lit. 'to lead oneself [away]', i.e., 'to leave'

(137) SE   MOUIT   EX   URBE

    3.REFL   moved   out-of   city

    'he left the city'

The reflexive pronoun could also co-occur with the forms in -R, even with deponent verbs. This means that the pronoun must have had (at least at the outset) a different function from that of the middle morphemes (Flobert 1975:386–98; Milner 1978). We have already noted Flobert's view (Flobert 1975), for example, that the reflexive pronoun has a certain stylistic function because it expresses a high degree of voluntarism – 'a deliberate and willed action of self on self'. But this description does not account for the cases where the subject refers to a thing, as in (138).[52]

(138) *ubi **se** uia findit in ambas*

    'where the road splits [itself] into two [parts]'   (Verg., *Aen.*, 6, 540)

As (139) and (140) below show, SE could also accompany a form in -R.

(139) *repens* [for *serpens*] *torquebatur **se***

    'the snake twisted (itself) around'   (*Vit Anton.*, 9) (middle)

(140) ***me** nunc commoror*

    'as for me, I now refrain [myself]'   (Pl., *Ps.*, 1131) (deponent)

In these cases, we suggest that the reflexive pronoun had a pragmatic value, similar to that of an intensifier expressing the denial of a highly probable non-identity by overtly expressing the fact that the referent of the subject had two roles at the same time. The reinforcing pronoun IPSE 'self' had a similar function when added to a reflexive construction with an active verb (see §2.1.1 above). Flobert (1975:387) further notes that this stylistic choice rapidly became commonplace, to the point at which it became necessary to reinforce the reflexive meaning ('le choix stylistique a vite entraîné la banalisation au point qu'il a fallu renforcer la réflexivité') by constructions such as SE IPSUM MOUERE. In other words, in colloquial and late Latin, SE started to lose its pragmatic function of intensifier, as did IPSE.

(b) *The Romance reflexive as a marker of event-highlighting.*[53] The forms in
-R carrying the conventional implicature of coreferentiality constituted the favourable contexts in which SE could replace the morphologically expressed Latin middle. From the contexts in which it
expressed the coreferentiality of the two Roles corresponding to the
syntactic subject, the Romance reflexive pronoun spread to cases in
which the subject did not refer to two Roles, namely impersonal and
passive constructions. Consequently, in the Romance languages the
reflexive pronoun is no longer just a signal of coreference, but has
acquired a new function, as a marker of an event-highlighted presentation (with or without coreferentiality) (see Manoliu-Manea
1988; 1994). This discourse hypothesis can account for various
syntactic and/or pragmatic characteristics of the reflexive passive:

(i) The reflexive construction can occur when any reference to
both the Doer and the Undergoer is eliminated; it is the
preferred construction for a sentence-focus type of utterance.

(141) Sp. *Aquí   se   come   bien; se   sale   hoy*
      Ro. *Aici   se   mănâncă   bine; se   pleacă azi*
          here   REFL   eats   well   REFL leaves today
          'Here one eats well'   'we are leaving today'

(ii) It has become the preferred means for expressing telic (and not
categorial) predicates. Even when functioning as a qualitative
reflexive (cf. Fr. *réfléchi facilitant*), it gives equal prominence to
both the subject and the verb, since the quality of the referent
favours the type of event.

(142) Fr. *Le   vin   rouge se   boit   chambré*
          the   wine   red   3.REFL   drinks   at.room.temperature
          'Red wine should be drunk at room temperature'

(143) Ro. *Portocalele   s-au   vândut   imediat.*
          Trebuie   să   comandăm   alt transport
          [*de portocale*]
          Oranges.the   3.REFL have sold   immediately.
          Needs   that   we.order   other transport
          [of oranges]
          'The oranges sold quickly. We need to order another
          consignment [of oranges]'

In (143), the first sentence highlights the whole process of 'something selling (better/fast)', since it refers to the cause for the
following conclusive sentence. But the topic encompassing both
sentences is 'the oranges'.

(iii) It is incompatible – even when it is interpreted as a passive reflexive – with an agentive phrase 'by + NP'. The agentive complement is limited to certain categories of verbs in old Portuguese, old Spanish, old Italian and Romanian, and has subsequently become largely unacceptable.

4.3.3   Supporting hypotheses for the pragmatic and discourse roles of Romance voice

Although the syntactic approach is a useful tool for disambiguation, especially in contrastive grammars and for purposes of translation, it has less explanatory power than the discourse hypothesis when it comes to accounting for the fact that the same construction can have so many functions.

After analysing the French passive, Gaatone (1998:213) concludes that it has five functions, as follows (note that his concept of 'orientation' is partly synonymous with the notion of 'highlighting' in our model):

(i)   avoidance (elimination) of the first argument;
(ii)   orientation towards the second argument;
(iii) focalization of the first argument;
(iv)   orientation towards the process;
(v)   cadence of the sentence.

The variety of interpretations of Spanish reflexives has been explored by Maldonado (1993) in interesting ways that support our hypothesis of an event-highlighted reflexive. He claims that, on the one hand, *se* may serve to focus on the characteristics of the process and background the participant who has the initiative; on the other hand, it favours the interpretation of the event as an unexpected happening. In short, according to Maldonado, the exact meaning that *se* brings to the construction depends greatly on the semantics of the verb involved. *Se* is a polysemic element, and not a meaningless detransitivizer as generative grammars claim. Let us examine Maldonado's explanations for the semantics of reflexive constructions:

(a)   *Focusing on the process and backgrounding the initiative source*: for example, constructions expressing a change in body posture (see 144) focus on the change of state that is undergone and not on the initiator or on the input. Maldonado calls this tendency 'terminal prominence'.

(144) Sp. María *se*   *arrodilló*
      Maria   REFL   knelt-down
      'Maria knelt down'

With intransitive verbs *se* also focuses on the change in state: Compare (145) and (146):

(145) *Cuando llegué   a   casa,   Juan ya   se   había   ido*
When   arrived.I at home Juan already REFL had   left
'When I arrived home, Juan had already left'

(146) *Juan   (*se)   va   al   cine   todos los   días*
Juan   (* REFL) goes at-the cinema all.PL the days
'Juan goes to the cinema every day' (habitual)

In (146), the speaker refers to the act of Juan going to the cinema every day as a whole, thus *irse* would be inappropriate. In (145), *irse* (*se había ido*) shows that the speaker is focusing on the moment of departure.

The impersonal passive focuses on the change of state, leaving the initiator in the background. The motivation for not referring to the Doer varies: this element may be conceptualized as a non-specified external entity or force either because the identity of the Doer is irrelevant (as in 147) or because the speaker wants to play down the responsibility of the Doer (as in 148).

(147) *se   habla   español*
REFL   speaks   Spanish
'we speak Spanish [Spanish is spoken]'

(148) *se   perdían   las   llaves*[54]
REFL   lost   the   keys
'the keys got lost'

(b)   In energetic–dynamic constructions, the relevant notion is that of 'unexpectedness'. The fact that these dynamic constructions downplay the role of the Initiator allows *se* to give the impression that events happen suddenly by overcoming or overriding some resisting force. Often the speaker's expectations refer to an abstract resisting force. Maldonado gives examples such as:

(149) *la   lluvia   (*se)   cae*
the   rain   (*3REFL) falls
'the rain is falling'

Since rain is expected to fall, *se* is unacceptable. But since human beings are expected to resist gravity and stay upright, the following situations require *se*:

(150) *Juan   se   (*Ø)   cayó al agua   con su mejor traje puesto*
John   REFL (*Ø)   fell   in the water   with his best suit on
'John fell in the water with his best suit on'

(151) *a pesar de que estos pantalones son prelavados,*   *se*   (*Ø)
encogieron.
despite that these trousers are pre-washed,   3REFL   (*Ø)
shrank
'despite the fact that these trousers are pre-washed, they shrank'.

(c) *Cognitive/Emotive Middle.* With verbs of cognition and emotion, *se* conveys the idea that the person experiences the mental or affective state in question. In such cases *se* also serves to deny an expectation, namely the fact that humans are seen as being in control of their mental activities. In order to depart from this expectation, one uses *se* to signal a lower degree of participation.[55]

(152) Agent —>   Experiencer   <— Patient
la olvidé—>   *me olvidé de ella*
'I forgot her'

me alegro de verte   <——— *me alegra verte*
'I am glad to see you'   'seeing you rejoices me'

(d) *Inherent* se. These verbs have only a reflexive form (no active counterpart): verbs which express a high degree of affective participation (compare Latin deponents, such as QUEROR 'I complain'). They differ from absolute verbs (such as *llorar, suspirar*) in that they involve more participation or control on the part of the participant.[56] Syntactic evidence for this distinction is that absolute verbs such as *llorar* do not easily combine with adverbs expressing the active participation of their subject referent.

In conclusion, Romance voice is no longer a morphologically marked category. An analytical passive, *result-highlighted* (marking the Undergoer as the initial point in the linguistic reconstruction of the event), developed in opposition to the active (*initiator/agent-highlighted*) and to the reflexive form, which is *event-highlighted*. Our discourse hypothesis assuming that voice is a means of a scenic strategy of highlighting has the advantage of accounting for the following phenomena in both Latin and Romance:

1. Synchronically, it provides a unified description of both the Latin forms in -R and the Romance reflexive constructions.

2. Diachronically, it provides an explanation for two important changes in the category of voice:

   (a) It accounts for the development of a plain passive, once the original inherent semantic feature [±Capacity for being a Doer] had become a contextually assigned feature.

   (b) It provides an explanation for the fact that the reflexive constructions could assume the functions of the forms in

-R. *Coreferentiality* of two Roles constituted a *conventional implicature* carried by several Latin medio-passive forms. This type of middle construction provided a favourable context in which the reflexive, *overtly* marking the coreferentiality of two Roles, could replace the morphological medio-passive in all its functions. In the Romance languages, the reflexive pronoun is not just a sign of coreference but has acquired a new function, as a marker of a linguistic construction which highlights the event (with or without coreferentiality: passives, impersonals).

Corpus

Aeth.: Siluiae uel potius Aetheriae Peregrinatio ad loca sancta, herausgegeben von W. Heraeus. Heidelberg, 2nd edn 1921.

Antonius of Piacenza: Antonius Placentinus *Itinerarium Antonini Placentini* in *Itinera hierosolymitana*. Recensuit et commentario critico instruxit Paulus Geyer, Pragae,-Vindobonae-Lipsiae, 1897 in C.S.E.L. 39, pp. 159–61.

Blatt, *Acta*: Blatt, Franz. *Die lateinischen Bearbeitungen der Acta Andreae et Matthiae apud anthropophagos. Mit sprachlichem Kommentar.* Giessen: Topelmann, 1930.

Caes., *BG*: *Caesars Bellum Gallicum*, ed. J. H. Schmalz. Leipzig & Berlin: B.G. Teubner, 1926.

Caes., *BG* 5: *Bellum Gallicum: liber quintus*, ed. Michel Rambaud. Paris: P.U.F., 1974.

Cic., *Cat.*: Cicero, Marcus Tullius. *In Catilinam* vols. 1–4, with English translation by C. MacDonald. Cambridge, MA: Harvard University Press, 1977.

Cic., *Deio.*: Cicero, *Pro Deiotaro*. In *M. Tullii Ciceronis Orationes Pro S. Roscio, Pro Lege Manilia, In Catilinam, Pro Archia Poeta, Pro Milone, Pro Marcello, Pro Ligario, Pro Deiotaro, Pro Murena*, ex codicibus regiis bavaricis atque parisinis nunc primum collatis, ceterisque recensuit et explicavit Ioannes Baptista Steinmetz, adiecta est varietas lectionis ernestianae. Maguntiaci [Mainz]: typis et sumptibus Floriani Kupferberg, 1832.

Cic., *Diu.*: *De diuinationem*, in Cicero, Marcus Tullius. *De natura deorum. De diuinationem. De legibus. Codex Heinsianus* (Leidensis 111) phototypice editus. Prefatus est Otto Plasberg, Luguduni Batavorum, A.W. Sijthoff's uitg.-mij., 1912.

Cic. *Dom.*: Cicero, *De domosua*. In Cicero, Marcus Tullius. *Speeches. English and Latin Selections. Pro Archia poeta; Post reditum in Senatu; Post reditum ad Ceuirites; De domo sua; De haruspicum responsis; Pro Plancio*; with an

English translation by H. N. Watts. Cambridge, MA: Harvard University Press/London: W. Heinemann, 1979.

Cic., *Fin.*: M. Tullii Ciceronis *De finibus bonorum & malorum* libri quinque. Ex recensione Joannis Davisii, … Cum ejusdem animadversionibus, et notis integris Petr. Victorii, P. Manucii, Joach. Camerarii, D. Lambini, ac Fulvii Ursini. Cantabrigiæ: typis academicis. Sumptibus Corn. & J. Crownfield, & J. & P. Knapton, 1741.

Cic., *Imp.*: Cicero, Marcus Tullius. *de Imperio Cn. Pompei*, in: *Orationes.* recognovit brevique adnotatione critica instruxit Albertus Curtis Clark, vol. 6, Oxonii: E. Typographeo Clarendoniano, 1905–18 (Scriptorum classicorum bibliotheca Oxoniensis). Reimp. 1957–60.

Cic., *Legibus*: Cicero, Marcus Tullius. *De republica, De legibus*, with an English translation by Clinton Walker Keyes. London: W. Heinemann, 1966 (1921[1]).

Cic., *Tusc.*: *Ciceronis Tusculanarum disputationum libri V.* Ex recensione Joannis Davisii, Cum ejusdem commentario Cantabrigiæ: typis academicis. Impensis Edm. Jeffery. Prostant venales Londini apud Jac. Knapton, 1708.

Cic., *Verr.*: Cicero. *The Verrine Orations*; L. H. G. Greenwood. Cambridge, MA: Harvard University Press, 1928–35 (Loeb Classical Library).

Fredegar: *Fredegarii et aliorum chronica.* Ed. Bruno Krusch. In *Scriptores rerum merouingicarum.* vol. 2. Hannouerae, 1888.

Plautus, *Macci Plauti Comoediae*, ed. W. M. Lindsay, Oxonii: E Typographe Clarendoniano, 1904–05.

Pl., *Amph.*: Plautus, *Amphitruo*, ed. David M Christenson. Cambridge and New York: Cambridge University Press, 2000.

Pl., *Cas.*: Plautus, *Casina*, ed. Ettore Paratore: Firenze, Sansoni [1959].

Pl., *Mi.*: Plautus, *Miles gloriosus*, ed. Mason Hammond. Cambridge MA: Harvard University Press, 1963.

Pl., *Mo.*: Plautus, *Mostellaria*, ed. Frank R Merrill: [London] Macmillan; [New York] St. Martin's Press [1972].

Pl., *Poen.*: Plautus, *Poenulus.* In [sic] *M. Acii. Plauti Comœdiae superstites xx accuratissime editæ*, Amstelodami: typis Ludovici Elzevirii, sumptibus Societatis, 1652.

Pl., *Ps.*: Plautus *Pseudolus*, ed. Malcolm M. Willcock. Bristol: Bristol Classical Press, 1987.

Plautus, *The Captives and Reinumus of Plautus*, ed. Edward Parmelee Morris. Boston & London: Ginn and Co., 1898.

Sall., *Cat.*: *Sallustius Crispus, De Catilinae Coniuratione*, ed. Joseph Hellegouarc'h. Paris: Presses Universitaires de France, 1972.

Seneca, *Controuersiae*: [*Controuersiae*] *Annaei Senecae tum rhetoris tum philosophi opera omnia*. Ab Andrea Schotto ad veterum exmplarium fidem castigata, Graecis etiam hiatibus expletis. Genevae: Sumptibus Samuelis Chouët, 1646.

Ter., *HT*: Terence *Heautontimoroumenos; Phormio*, ed. J. Marouzeau. Paris: Les Belles Lettres, 1947.

Ter., *Eun.*: Terence *Eunuchus*, ed. John Barsby. Cambridge and New York: Cambridge University Press, 1999.

Ter., *Ad.*: Terence *Adelphoe*, ed. Ronald H. Martin. Cambridge and New York: Cambridge University Press, 1976.

Ter., *Ph.*: *Phormio, a comedy by Terence*: manuscript reproduction, facing transcription; edited Latin texts, notes, vocabulary; ed. Elaine M. Coury. Chicago: Bolchazy-Carducci, 1982.

Ulpiani digesta: *Domitii Ulpiani e libro regularum singulari excerpta*: *eiusdem Ulpiani Institutionum fragmenta* recensuit Ioannes Vahlen. Bonnae: A. Marci, 1856.

Verg. *Aen.*: *P. Vergilius, Aeneis*; ed. M. J. Pattist. Amsterdam: Nederlandsche Keurboekerij, 1941.

Vit. Anton.: *Vitae Patrum*: *De vita et verbis seniorum libri X. Historiam eremiticam.* Antverpiae: ex officina Plantiniana, [1628] Editio secunda, variè aucta et illustrate.

Vulgate: *Nouum Testamentum Latinae*, Oxonii: Londini, 1911; see also *Novum Testamentum Latine: Novum Vulgatam Bibliorum Sacrorum.* Editionem secuti apparatibus titulisque additis, ediderunt Kurt Aland et Barbara Aland una cum Instituto studiorum textus Novi Testamenti Monasteriensi (Westphalia). Stuttgart: Deutsche Bibelgesellschaft, 1984.

Romance texts

Alexis: *La Vie de Saint Alexis*, Gaston Paris ed., Paris, 1933 (Classiques français du Moyen Age 4). Paris: Champion.

Arcipreste de Hita, *Libro de buen amor*. Edición y notas de Julio Cejador y Frauca. vol. 1–2, Madrid: Espasa-Calpe, 1954 (Clásicos Castellanos).

Camus, *La Peste*: Camus, Albert, *La Peste*. Paris: Gallimard (Livre de Poche), 1947.

Camus, *L'Étranger*: Camus, Albert, *L'Étranger*. Paris: Gallimard, 1942 [1968].

Creangă, *Op.*: Creangă, Ion. *Opere*, ediție îngrijită, prefață și glosar de Acad. Prof. G. Călinescu (Clasicii români). Bucharest: Editura de stat pentru literatură și artă, 1953.

Crest. Rom.: *Crestomație Romanică*, Iorgu Iordan (ed.), Mioara Avram, Nicolae Dănăilă, Florica Dimitrescu, Valeria Guțu-Romalo, Maria Iliescu, Liliana Macarie, Constant Maneca, Maria Manoliu, Alexandru Niculescu, Marius Sala, Florența Sădeanu, Sanda Stavrescu, Mirela Teodorescu, vol.I. Bucureștit: Editura Academiei, 1962.

Doc.: *Documente și însemnări românești din secolul al XVI-lea*. Text stabilit și indice de G. Chivu, M. Gerogescu, M. Ioniță, A. Mareș și A. Roman-Moraru. Intr. De A. Mareș. Bucharest: Editura Academiei, 1979.

Ionesco, *Tueur*: Ionesco, Eugène. *Tueur sans gages*, in *Théâtre*. Paris: Gallimard, 1961.

Ispirescu, *Op.*: Ispirescu, Petre. *Opere*. Ediție îngrijită, note și variante, glosar și bibliografie de Aristița Avramescu. Studiu introductiv de Corneliu Bărbulescu. București: Minerva, 1969.

Indovinello veronese: Monteverdi, A. Sull metro dell'indovinello veronese, in *Studi mediævali*, Nuova serie X, 1937, p. 39ff.

Lopez de Ayala, *Rimado de palacio*: López de Ayala. Pedro, *Libro de poemas o Rimado de palacio*; edición crítica, introducción y notas de Michel García. Madrid: Gredos, 1978.

Martínez de Toledo, *El corbacho*: Martínez de Toledo, Alfonso. *El corbacho*. Introd., notas y revisión del texto Consuelo Pastor Sanz. Madrid: Editorial Magisterio Español, 1971.

Maupassant, *Les Tombales*: Maupassant, Guy de. *Les Tombales,* in Maupassant, Guy de. *Boule de suif.* Texte établi avec introd., chronologie, bibliographie, appendice, et notes par M.-C. Bancquart. Paris: Garnier, 1971 [1986].

Mauriac, *Désert*: Mauriac, François, *Le Désert de l'amour*, 1925. Paris: Grasset (Livre de Poche): 44.

Neculce, *Cronica*: *Cronica lui Neculce*, copiată de Ioasaf Luca. Manuscrisul Mihail. Ediție îngrijită, studiu introductiv de Zamfira și Paul Mihail. Chișinău: Știința, 1993.

Neculce, *Op.*: Neculce, Ion. *Opere. Letopisețul Țării Moldovei și O samă de cuvinte*, ediție îngrijită și studiu introductiv, note și indici de Gabriel Strempel. București: Minerva, 1982.

Preda, *CMIP*: Preda, Marin. *Cel mai iubit dintre pământeni*. 3. 2nd edn Bucharest: Editura Cartea românească, 1984.

Queneau, *Fleurs bleues*: Queneau, Raymond. *Les Fleurs bleues*. Paris: Gallimard, 1965.

Queneau, *Zazie*: Queneau, Raymond. *Zazie dans le métro*. Paris: Gallimard, 1959.

Roland: *La Chanson de Roland*. Publiée d'après le manuscrit d'Oxford et traduite par Joseph Bédier. 36e éd. Paris: L'Édition d'art, H. Piazza,

1927; see also *La Chanson de Roland* commentée par Joseph Bédier. Paris: H. Piazza, 1968.

Texte: *Texte româneşti din secolul la XVI-lea*. 1. *Catehismul lui Coresi*, II *Pravila lui Coresi* III *Fragmentul Todorescu* IV *Glosele Bogdan* V *Prefeţe şi epiloguri*. Ediţii critice de Emanuel Buză, Gheorghe Chivu, Magdalena Georgescu, Ion Gheţie, Alexandra Roman-Moraru, Florentina Zgraon. Coordonator Ion Gheţie. Bucureşti: Editura Academiei, 1982.

Tristan: *Le Roman de Tristan* par Béroul et un anonyme, poème du XIIe siècle. Publié par Ernest Muret, Paris, 1903 (Société des anciens textes français).

Ureche, *Let*: Ureche, Grigore. *Letopiseţul Ţării Moldovei*. Texte stabilite, studiu introductiv, note şi glosar de Liviu Onu. Bucureşti : Editura Ştiin-ţifică, 1967.

Vian, *Bâtisseurs*: Vian, Boris. *Les Bâtisseurs d'empire ou Le Schmürz* : *Théâtre*: *Les Bâtisseurs d'empire*. Paris: J.-J. Pauvert [1965].

Villehardouin: *La Conquête de Constantinople par Geoffroi de Ville-Hardouin, avec la continuation de Henri de Valenciennes*. Texte original, accompagné d'une traduction par Natalis de Wailly. Paris, 1872 (Bibliothèque de l'École des Hautes Études).

IO   WORD FORMATION[1]

Brigitte L. M. Bauer

1   Derivation

1.1   Prefixation

Proto-Indo-European clearly had suffixes, but is sometimes assumed (e.g., Meillet 1964) to have lacked prefixes, an hypothesis that fits the relatively late process in Indo-European of univerbation, by which particles came to form a unit with a verb (e.g., Lat. OB UOS SACRO > UOS OBSECRO 'I beseech you'). Latin's few prefixes were predominantly prepositions in origin and often had aspectual value, cf. EDERE vs. COMEDERE 'eat (up)'. In vulgar and late Latin the increase in prefixed forms was often matched by loss of semantic nuances and replacement of the simplex forms by originally prefixed ones, such as Sp. *comer* 'eat' (see Väänänen 1966:106–8). The original prefixes are often unrecognizable, cf. *COM-INITIARE > Fr. *commencer*, It. *cominciare*, Sp. *comenzar*. Some underwent semantic shift: e.g., It. *rileggere* 'read again' vs. *riposare* 'rest'. Meyer-Lübke (1894) reports seventeen prepositions and three adverbs used as prefixes in Latin verbal derivation surviving in Romance; many of these also occur in nominal derivation. Verbal derivatives are most widespread, and the use of two opposing prefixes with an otherwise non-existent verbal base is common; Fr. *embarrasser* 'hinder', *débarrasser* 'clear', but no **barrasser*.[2]

Productive prefixes[3] tend to occur in learnèd formations. Originally prepositions (and adverbs) borrowed from Greek and Latin, they combine with nouns, adjectives and verbs, e.g., *auto-, hyper-, super-, extra-, anti-, inter-*. They primarily convey intensification, reversal, negation, iteration and – unlike suffixes – lack evaluative force. Prefixes may occasionally occur as independent elements, often with a specific meaning, e.g., Fr. *ex-député* 'former representative' and *mon ex* 'my ex-(husband)'. Overall Romance prefixes, which leave intact the morphosyntactic category of the base, are semantically and formally more independent than suffixes, tend to fuse less with the base and are more recognizable than suffixes.

1.2   Suffixation[4]

1.2.1   Latin/Romance suffixes

Some Latin and Romance derivational suffixes derive new categories from base words; others, such as diminutives and augmentatives, rather than affecting the category of the base, modify its meaning, indicating degree or quantity.

Verb derivation in Latin and Romance is less widespread and productive than nominal derivation. Primarily affected are nouns and adjectives, and – to a lesser degree – pronouns, numerals and adverbs. The overview of suffixes in verbal derivation presented by Meyer-Lübke (1894) shows an overwhelming predominance of Latin first conjugation suffixes and their Romance reflexes, which corresponds to the general productivity of the first conjugation in modern Romance (e.g., Fr. *solution* > 1CONJ *solutionner* competing with 3CONJ *résoudre* 'solve'). In Spanish, preference for 1CONJ *-ar* in modern verbal derivation leads to doublets, e.g., *promocionar* (< *promoción*) 'promote' vs. *promover*. Similarly *-ar* almost always occurs in borrowings (*fax* > Sp. *faxar*).

The number of verbal suffixes expressing diminutive value in Latin/ Romance is striking, and their survival in Romance may correspond to the importance of diminutives in the individual languages. Although denotative meanings predominate, verbal diminutives may be pejorative, e.g., spoken Fr. *criailler* 'grumble' (cf. *crier* 'shout'). Whereas many nominal diminutives eventually replaced the basic word, in verbal derivation original frequentatives did so, a process already underway in Latin, e.g., CANERE 'sing' vs. CANTARE 'sing (frequently)' > Sp./Pt. *cantar* 'sing'.

Suffixes used in nominal derivation in Romance convey a variety of semantic values including abstract notions, collectives, action, agent, instruments, state, location, and diminutive and augmentative force.

Whereas many suffixes disappeared in the shift from Latin to Romance because of formal identity with other suffixes, or phonological changes such as the phonological effects of loss of stress or loss of vowel length, several suffixes appear in (almost) all Romance languages, basically keeping their original meaning. The suffix *-bilis* typically combined with verb stems (or participles) to form adjectives expressing possibility or necessity (e.g., COMPREHENSIBILIS 'that can be understood'). It remains widespread in vulgar Latin and survives generally, except in Romanian. The semantic value remains but in Romance the suffix also combines with nouns, e.g., It. *favorevole* 'favourable' (cf. *favore*). There are varieties, such as French, where the originally learnèd *-able* (e.g., *mangeable* 'edible') is productive, rather than *-ible*, now primarily limited to learnèd (e.g., *transmissible*), or inherited, words (e.g., *lisible* 'readable'). Similarly, although the phonetically regular *-evole* (< -EBILEM) survived in Italian and came to be used with all conjugations, learnèd *-bile* is spreading today, e.g., *fattíbile*, replacing original *fattévole*, 'feasible'.[5]

The near-pan-Romance reflexes of -OSUS, forming adjectives from abstract nouns, expresses 'full of a given quality'. In late Latin it kept its value and combined with adjectives and verbs. It survives in inherited words (e.g., Pt. *formoso*, Ro. *frumos* < FORMOSUS 'beautiful') and in numerous new creations, with nouns (Sp. *oloroso* 'aromatic' < *olor* 'smell'), adjectives (It. *grandioso* < *grande* 'big') and verbs (It. *rincrescioso* 'regrettable' < *rincrescere* 'to cause regret').

The original meaning of other suffixes disappeared or became opaque, with corresponding loss of productivity. The semantic value of many diminutives in -ICULUS, for example, is no longer perceived, and the, now unrecognizable, suffix survives in inherited formations that have replaced the original word, e.g., *SOLICULUM 'sun-DIM' (from SOL) > Fr. *soleil* 'sun,' APICULAM 'bee-DIM' (from APIS) > Fr. *abeille* 'bee'. Similarly, AGNELLUS 'little lamb' (from AGNUS), survives with the meaning 'lamb', e.g., Fr. *agneau*, It. *agnello*, Ro. *miel*. Yet there are traces of original diminutive value: Sp. *candilejo* 'small lamp', *albarejo* 'whitish (of bread, wheat)'; Ro. *cântecel* 'song-DIM'; Pt. *rapazelho* (< *rapaz*) 'little boy'. Loss of the base may cause or reinforce opacity of the suffix: e.g., diminutive AUUNCULUS 'mother's brother' (> Ro. *unchiu*, Fr. *oncle* 'uncle') became opaque through loss of AUUS 'mother's father' and its counterpart PATRUUS 'father's brother'.

Opacity caused by loss of the original lexical element often occurs in derivatives in -IA. Whereas Latin had many nominal abstracts in -IA, Romance does not favour this derivation, and if formations survive, the original adjective does not. Vulgar and Christian Latin ANGUSTIA 'narrowness, straits, difficult circumstances' survives in some languages (e.g., Fr. *angoisse* 'anguish'), but the adjective ANGUSTUS 'narrow' does not (except Ro. *îngust*).

Whereas suffixes may survive in given geographical areas or linguistic registers, in some formations, the inherited and learnèd suffixes survive, often with specific sociolinguistic or pragmatic characteristics, as in Italian, where Latinizing *-izia*, e.g., (*giustizia* 'justice') coexists with inherited *-ezza* (*giustezza* 'justness, rightness') (cf. also Fr. *-ice* vs. *-esse* or Sp. *-icia* vs. *-ez*).

1.2.2 Morphological spread

The morphological scope of several suffixes expanded. Thus *-ata*, originally the ending of (feminine) perfective participles and limited to 1CONJ verbs, became very important in Romance, combining with nouns. It conveyed 'what is being affected, contained', and thence developed a meaning 'fully done', 'full of', e.g., It. *annata* (*anno* 'year'), 'what covers a time frame of one year', *boccata* (from *bocca* 'mouth') 'mouthful', Fr. *année* (from *an* 'year') 'full year'.

Romance languages may share developments and at the same time undergo language-specific changes. Diminutive -OTTUS, for example, originally combined with nouns, and in Italian and French combined with adjectives to convey attenuation (It. *vecchiotto* 'elderly', Fr. *vieillot* 'quaint') – with differences in productivity; moreover, it typically combines with names of animals in Italian (e.g., *aquilotto* 'eaglet') and of objects in French (*chariot* 'cart'). In Spanish it developed augmentative value, in addition to original diminutive force.

Other suffixes remained limited to a given semantic category of noun. Among -ITTUS, -OTTUS and -ATTUS, of unknown origin and widespread in vulgar Latin, -ATTUS is a secondary form that continued to be used for young animals, e.g., It. *lupatto*, OFr. *louvat* 'wolf cub', Sp. *mulato* 'young mule'.

Several suffixes were borrowed either in the Latin period (see André 1971) – mainly from Greek – or in the Romance period. Among Latin suffixes of Greek origin are, e.g., -ISTA and -IA (PHILOSOPHIA < φιλοσοφία). Transfer of the suffix is rooted in lexical borrowings. Borrowed words often adopted the Latin stress pattern, cf. ἱστορία, yielding HISTÓRIA 'history'. Subsequently 'a fashionable pronunciation -*ía*, doubtless favoured by Christian influence, penetrated popular speech (σοφία taken over as SOPHÍA "wisdom") and produced a new Latin ending -ÍA, which was used to form many new words' (Grandgent 1907:65).[6]

The vulgar and late Latin borrowing -*ista* was used in formation of agent nouns referring to the person able to perform the action (BAPTISTA 'baptizer' vs. BAPTIZATOR; André 1971:133). The activity involved tends to be intellectual or relates to a certain level of schooling. From the Renaissance, such formations increasingly indicate followers of philosophical schools, scientific approaches, etc.: It. *papista* 'papist', Fr. *calviniste*, Sp. *franquista* 'follower of Franco'; cf. Fr. *jardinier* vs. *jardiniste* 'gardener' vs. 'garden designer'.

In the Romance period, suffixes borrowed into individual languages mainly originated in other Romance languages or Germanic. Thus -*ard* is from Germanic, where it typically occurred in proper names, e.g., *Goedhard*, a bahuvrihi compound, comprising an adjective (*goed* 'good') and a noun (*hard* 'heart'), i.e., 'having a noble heart'. In the borrowing process *hard* was reinterpreted as a suffix. It is productive in French, and in Italian, and combined with adjectives typically indicates persons with a specific characteristic, e.g., Fr. *richard* 'very rich person'. Probably because of its inherent augmentative aspects, it developed a pejorative connotation and in that function is quite productive in modern French.

1.2.3 Semantic change

The majority of Romance suffixes undergo semantic shifts, usually closely related to the original meaning. An example of related diachronic and synchronic values is -TOR. The semantic link between its uses and meanings is the notion of activity expressed by the verbal base: the suffix originally conveys first the person who carries out the action (AMATOR 'lover' < AMARE), then the instrument with which it is performed (cf. It. *calcolatore* 'calculator', Sp. *calzador* 'shoehorn'). Subsequently in several languages it formed adjectives meaning 'capable of carrying out …' (e.g., Sp. *corredor* 'able to run' from *correr* 'run') or nouns referring to the space where the action is performed (OFr. *dormeour* 'bedroom' from *dormir* 'sleep', Sp. *obrador* 'workroom' from *obrar* 'work').

Diminutives typically develop endearment values, whereas augmentatives, and suffixes expressing similarity, tend to acquire pejorative force. Originally conveying similarity, -ACEUS developed augmentative and subsequently pejorative connotation, closely related to the notion of 'bigness', 'formlessness', 'sexlessness'. It is equally productive in Provençal and Catalan, but most productive in Spanish (-*azo*), primarily as augmentative. Similarly, the meaning of -ASTER shifted from 'resemblance' to pejorative (It./Pt. *medicastro* 'quack, sham doctor').

Combined with verbal and nominal stems, individualizing -O/-ONEM originally referred to the person who carries out an action with special predilection, or who has a striking characteristic, e.g., BIBONEM (from BIBERE) 'drunkard'. The semantics of 'well-developed characteristic' accounts for the shift to augmentative or intensifying value in vulgar Latin and Romance, where it is productive, e.g., It. *ragazzone* 'big boy', Sp. *casón* 'big house'. In its augmentative use, the suffix occurs in combinations with adjectives as well, e.g., It. *grandone* 'very big'. Yet the history of this suffix reflects a complex set of values because the original individualizing force developed further in different languages: most display a series of person indicators with individualizing value or agent reference (WRæR. *lavunts* 'washer', Fr. *bûcheron* 'woodcutter') and some include pejorative value (It. *buffone* 'buffoon'). Similarly, Sp. *-ón* conveys agent function, without pejorative value, but its Portuguese equivalent, *-ão*, often has pejorative value. The suffix occurs without pejorative value in formations indicating instruments or animals, which are often more recent, e.g., It. *stallone* 'stallion', Sp. *cabrón* 'goat' (although this word can often be used as a term of abuse), or Fr. *bouchon* 'cork' (from *boucher* 'to plug'). Despite differentiation of semantic values, the fundamental – and historical – meaning of the suffix in Romance, except French (see below), is 'enlargement': in this function the suffix is used unrestrictedly. This augmentative use accounts for additional shifts in meaning, such as pejoration: Pt. *beatão* 'great hypocrite' from *beato* 'blessed'.

Conversely, -INUS originally expressed manner, origin and resemblance, with the emerging connotation that something is similar 'but not quite', hence 'not as perfect' or 'smaller'. Thus, it eventually became a diminutive, cf. It. *ragazzino* 'little boy', Pt. *livro* 'book' > *livrinho* 'booklet,' Sp. *labrantín* 'small farmer'. Its diminutive use was reinforced by its attenuating meaning when combined with adjectives (e.g., Sp. *verdino* 'greenish', Pt. *branquinho* 'whitish') and occasional adverbs.

1.2.4 Diminutives and augmentatives

Derivational processes referred to above are productive in individual languages to varying degrees. The major suffixes, in use and diffusion, are diminutives: historically numerous, widespread and varied, they remain productive, often with specific semantic and pragmatic functions (see Hakamies 1951; Wagner 1952; Hasselrot 1957; 1972; Ettinger 1974; Dardano 1978; Dressler and Merlini Barbaresi 1994). Diminutives, whose use increased in vulgar and late Latin (see Grandgent 1907:18–22), are much more widespread than augmentatives and have wider functional range. In Italian in particular, the suffixes are numerous, convey a wide variety of values and uses (including several morphosyntactic categories), and may be concatenated, e.g., *casa* 'house' > *casetta* 'small house' > *casettina* 'house-DIM-DIM, still smaller house'. Moreover, diminutive suffixes often combine with other suffixes, cf. *-ina* vs. lengthened *-iccina*, *-sina*, or *-olina*, each with different degrees of frequency (see Rohlfs 1969:413f.). Finally, the importance of diminutives – and augmentatives – in Italian shows in that *-one*, *-accio* and *-ino* may occasionally be used as independent words under strong emphasis, e.g., *Questo è proprio ino* 'This is really tiny.'

Cross-linguistically, diminutives have been better analysed than other suffixes. There are three main approaches (Jurafsky 1996:538f.): the *abstractionist* attempts to define a single abstract meaning – 'like', 'resemblance' – that accounts for all semantic varieties.[7] In the *homonymic* approach, each meaning realizes an independent morpheme. This perspective avoids generalization and ignores underlying regularity, overlap, and even obvious evidence of semantic and pragmatic extensions attested diachronically and cross-linguistically. It assumes that there are no motivated relations – synchronic or diachronic – between the meanings of given identical morphemes. More recent analyses focus on the *polysemous* characteristics of diminutive suffixes to find a common denominator, a prototypical meaning which is its core value and from which other meanings are derived on the basis of metaphorical processes, inferential (contact-induced) reinterpretations or abstractive extensions (e.g., the radial hypothesis of Jurafsky 1996). These studies are inspired by advances in pragmatics. Works discussing the value of diminutives and/or augmentatives in relation to their context in Romance languages include Gooch (1967), Dressler and Merlini Barbaresi (1994), Lang (1990) and Hasselrot (1957; 1972).

Diminutives are a near-universal phenomenon (see Hasselrot 1972:283–321), and represent a complex semantic category often conveying contradictory functions or meanings (e.g., affection and contempt). Moreover, diminutive forms may develop a value in one language opposite to that developed in another: e.g., Mexican Spanish intensifying *ahorita* 'now-DIM, immediately' vs. Cuban and Dominican attenuating *ahorita* 'in a little while' (Jurafsky 1996:534). Similarly, augmentative -ONEM (see §1.2.3) developed diminutive value in French (e.g., *chaton* 'young cat') and subsequently became an endearment suffix in proper names, e.g., *Marion*.[8] Tuscan -*accio* can express endearment, while elsewhere -*accio*/-*azzo* are pejorative (e.g., in Tuscany Pope John Paul II was often referred to as *Wojtylaccio*). Moreover, geographical varieties of the same language may vary in the applicability of diminutives: in Latin American Spanish many more grammatical categories may be involved than in Peninsular Spanish (Stewart 1999:75).

Diminutives can convey meanings such as (1) small size, (2) imitation (e.g., DoSp. *boca* 'mouth', *boquete* 'mouth-DIM, hole'), (3) exactness, (4) approximation, (5) individuation, (6) intensification (MxSp. *ahorita* 'immediately') and (7) partitive (e.g., It. *cioccolato* 'chocolate', *cioccolatini* 'chocolates'). Intensifying diminutives typically combine with words meaning 'small', 'young', 'low', cf. Fr. *jeunet* 'very young', DoSp. *bajito* 'very low'. With other adjectives a more diminutive or attenuative value prevails, e.g., It. *azzurretto* 'a bit blue' (see, e.g., Jurafsky 1996).

Diminutives may also convey pragmatic force, such as affection, contempt and playfulness, and typically occur in child and pet language. In talk *with* children and pets (less so in talk *about* them) diminutives mark affection, sympathy and intimacy. Similarly, children tend to use relatively many diminutives, especially in combination with kinship terms and names for toys. In Spanish and Portuguese, the emotive value is stronger than elsewhere, according to Lang (1990). Moreover, diminutives may weaken the illocutionary force of utterances or translate metalinguistic comment (Jurafsky 1996:557; for pragmatic uses of diminutives, see Wierzbicka 1984).

This range of meanings recurs 'with astonishing regularity across languages' (Jurafsky 1996:535). In these semantic and pragmatic uses, the diminutive value 'smallness' may be absent. MxSp. *boquete* 'mouth-DIM, hole', for example, can be bigger than *boca* (Jurafsky 1996:538). Evidence for semantic and pragmatic extension of suffixes is obvious not only from cross-linguistic analysis, which shows a strong regularity in patterns, but also from diachronic analysis, which reveals cross-linguistic regularity in change as well. Moreover, recent interest in grammaticalization emphasizes the polysemy of diminutive suffixes as well as the notion of direction of change, the relative order of semantic and pragmatic value (what derives from what?), and direction in bleaching processes, 'more specific' > 'more abstract and vague'.

While diminutives are common in informal spoken languages, some linguists argue that they originate in child language or in semantics or pragmatics related to children (Jurafsky 1996:562), either because the suffix originally meant 'child' or 'son', or because the morpheme is pragmatically embedded in linguistic contexts related to children. From the notion 'child' other semantic and pragmatic meanings and functions developed, such as affection, hypocorism, contempt and smallness (Jurafsky 1996:566; for a hypocoristic origin of diminutive suffixes, see Petersen 1916; Hasselrot 1957).

Augmentative suffixes in Romance are rarer and show less dialectal variation. Moreover, they do not show the same variety in semantic and pragmatic functions as diminutives and, whatever their actual function, the notion 'big' is fundamental and may be related to their often pejorative value, conveying disgust or hatred, cf. It. *testone* 'head-AUG, blockhead', or the use of augmentative in words referring to politicians: e.g., *mascellone* 'jaw.AUG' referring to Mussolini (Dressler and Merlini Barbaresi 1994:434).

Not all augmentatives are pejorative: the suffix may intensify positive characteristics, even in humans, cf. It. *professorone* and *dottorone*, which convey 'increased professional value' (Dressler and Merlini Barbaresi 1994:444; also for limitations of its use; for pejorative lexicalized formations in -one, see Dressler and Merlini Barbaresi 1994:437). Moreover, whereas variation in diminutive suffixes affects pragmatics and deeper semantics, hence derived functions, variations in augmentative suffixes primarily affect the core value, enlargement. The augmentative may intensify different aspects of an object, e.g., in *librone* (< *libro*) 'book.AUG', width and length are intensified. In *volumone* 'volume.AUG', the suffix may reflect the number of pages. Italian *stanzone* (*stanza* 'room') refers to a room that is longer but not necessarily taller, whereas *stradone* refers to a very busy, noisy street, ignoring its dimensions (Dressler and Merlini Barbaresi 1994:436f.).[9] Similarly, in Sp. *españolón* (< *español*) 'typically Spanish', the ending indicates degree rather than shape. In contrast to diminutives, the original denotative value of augmentatives remains relevant in all uses, e.g., It. *figli-one* 'son.AUG, son who is grown up or big in size' vs. *figli-ol-ino*, which does not necessarily imply that the person referred to is small or young. Augmentatives are less frequent in child-related speech than diminutives. They are not normally used in reference to the child's body parts or belongings, and in speech directed at children (and pets) their use is mainly limited to emphasizing the contrast between the adult's and child's world (It. *lettone della mamma* 'mummy's big bed') and in ludic exaggeration, e.g., *il mio bimbo ha tanto sonnone* 'my baby is so sleepy'; semantic and pragmatic values of diminutives and augmentatives show that their use often depends on degree of intimacy (Dressler and Merlini Barbaresi 1994:445, 453).

Although suffixation is a common diminutivizing device, there are many more, among them periphrastic structures in which an adjective 'little' combines with a noun conveying semantic and pragmatic functions similar to those of diminutive suffixes. Thus Fr. *petit* has grammaticalized as a diminutive (Hasselrot 1972:87–90), replacing the suffix -et(te). Romance languages vary in the degree to which they prefer periphrastic structures over suffixes: in Italian and Spanish, diminutive suffixes are very productive. Jurafsky (1996:569) reports that in French, periphrastic diminutive structures with *petit(e)* are thirteen times more common than -et(te) and -ot(te), while in Spanish diminutive structures with *pequeño/a* are eight times less common than diminutive suffixes. Togeby (1958:198) points out that *petit(e)* + noun already existed in medieval French and stresses the prenominal position of *petit(e)* in these uses as opposed to NOUN–ADJ sequence in Italian and Spanish equivalent structures. Moreover, French *petit* not only conveys denotative quantification, but also – to a lesser extent – pejorative and endearment value: it occurs in first names, surnames, as lexicalized items with specific value (e.g., *petit-fils* 'grandson') and in euphemisms (*une petite minute* 'one little minute'). The ongoing regression of French derivational diminutives in denotational and connotational uses occurs in favour of analytic constructions where the serial element comes first. More recent (post 1960s) is use of *mini-* in diminutive function, originally calquing English, e.g., *minijupe* (< Eng. *miniskirt*), *minivacances* 'mini-holidays' (for comparison with *petit*, see Hasselrot 1972:93–106).

Whereas diminutive suffixes are preferred over periphrastic structures in Spanish and Italian, periphrasis may be preferred to express augmentative value, for example intense pain: *un forte dolore* is used rather than *dolorone* (Dressler and Merlini Barbaresi 1994:451). Conversely, in downplaying pain, a suffixal augmentative as well as diminutive suffix may be used.

2 Compounding

Compounds – ranging from nouns to conjunctions – involve inseparable fusion of (autonomous) lexical elements with a fixed order; they have independent meanings that may differ from the sum of the meanings of the elements. In Latin and Romance there are no nominalization or adjectivization suffixes, because compounding is done by juxtaposition. Among them compound nouns, adjectives and verbs represent an open class in modern Romance. Compounded prepositions are much less productive and have become formally and semantically opaque.

2.1 Latin compounds

Compared to other early Indo-European languages, Latin had few compounds, and these were rather archaic in nature (see Bader 1962; Klingebiel 1989:27–41). Moreover, many original compounds were opaque, cf. PRINCEPS 'leader' (< *PRIMO-CAPS), PAUPER 'poor' (< *PAU-PER-OS 'who produces little'; Ernout and Meillet 1959:535); others were seen as derived forms, e.g., BENIGNUS 'kind, friendly', OPIFEX 'maker, craftsman' (Väänänen 1966:105). They included nouns, adjectives, verbs, adverbs, prepositions, conjunctions, numerals and pronouns, especially in late Latin.

Latin compounds typically involved thematic stems rather than autonomous words, cf. AGRI-COLA (AGR-+-COL-) 'farmer' or MAGN-ANIMUS 'greathearted' vs. It. *apribottiglie* 'bottle-opener' or Fr. *aigredoux* 'bittersweet', which combine independent words (Darmesteter 1967; Meillet and Vendryes 1924:395). The occurrence in compounds of thematic stems rather than full words as in Romance has been related by some to the case system: with the loss of case the formal difference between a word in its free use and a word occurring in a compound disappeared. Yet this interpretation remains hypothetical as long as the exact nature of the verb in Romance compounds is not determined (see below).

If true compounds with nominal themes in apposition were rare in Latin, those that go back to grammatical phrases (NPs, VPs, APs, etc.) were widespread: syntactically related elements become fixed combinations with specific semantic value, e.g., MAGNOPERE (NP [ADJ+NOUN]) 'greatly', RESPUBLICA (NP [NOUN+ADJ]) 'republic', USUSFRUCTUS (NP [NOUN+NOUN]) 'usufruct', PRO CONSULE (PRO-CONSUL, PP [PREP +NOUN]) 'pro-consul', MALEDICERE (VP [ADV +VERB]) 'curse'. These compounds often survived in Romance as opaque simplexes (Meyer-Lübke 1894:588). Verb + complement compounds, widespread and very productive in Romance, were infrequent in Latin.

2.2   Chronology and types of compounds

An early type of compounding involves prepositions, which spread in vulgar and late Latin (Grandgent 1907:28f.). Their early origin accounts for their occurrence – as lexical relics – throughout Romance, e.g., DEINTRO 'inside' > It./Sp./Pt. *dentro*, Prv./Cat. *dintre*; INANTE 'before' > Ro. *înainte*, *AB-ANTE> It. *avanti*, Fr. *avant*. Later developments are more language-specific and generate prepositions from adverb + noun or adverb + participle combinations (e.g., It. *malgrado*, Fr. *malgré* (< fifteenth century *mal* + *gre*) and It. *nonostante*, Sp. *no obstante*, Fr. *nonobstant* 'despite'). Romance languages have also acquired prepositions including preposition + noun + preposition: Fr. *au sommet de* 'atop', It. *in mezzo a*, Sp. *en medio de* 'amidst'.

Compound adverbs represent a long-standing closed class, are fully lexicalized and relatively stable (Grandgent 1907:28). Conjunctions that are the result of compounding (It. *perché*, Sp. *porque* 'because') represent a very small but frequent group; like other conjunctions they do not go back to Latin and are generally not pan-Romance.

For other compounds the situation is less clear: several types are inherited from Latin and remain productive. Verb–noun nominal compounds, for example, were attested in Latin but became more frequent in Romance and underwent dramatic changes. Others were Romance creations. In the twentieth century, for example, a very common and productive nominal formation in Italian and elsewhere emerged, based on juxtaposition of nouns, e.g., It. *formato tessera* 'passport sized (photograph)' (see further Darmesteter 1967; Tekavčić 1972c:197–219; Dardano 1978:141–94).

This process also underlies serial composition of the type Fr. *classe pilote* 'pilot class', *industrie pilote* 'pilot industry', that shares a semantic feature conveyed by the common word. Found in all Romance languages, this formation is typically very productive, e.g., It. *viaggio-lampo, guerra-lampo, caffé-lampo*, expressing 'short, quick [lit. 'lightning'] journey/war/coffee', Sp. *buque escuela* 'training ship', *hotel escuela* 'hotel school', etc. A widespread variant includes an initial element 'woman' (It. *la donna* / Fr. *femme* / Ro. *doamnă*), followed by the name of a professional (e.g., Fr. *femme médecin*) to refer to women professionals. With the entry of women into the job market this formation has become increasingly important (see Maurice 2001:235f.; Beyrer *et al.* 1987). Italian has a second recent analytic device (*la donna* + name of professional coexists with *il* + name of professional + *donna*), but the derivational processes are still very strong and productive (Marcato and Thüne 2002). The productivity of this formation in Romance is shown in the creation and spread of the French analytic diminutive including the noun *bébé* (e.g., *bébé chien* 'very young dog') conveying young animals and – in advertising – small objects (see Hasselrot 1972:91f.).

Compounds attested in all Romance languages are adjectives based on combination of adjectives (ADJ–ADJ), and nouns formed by juxtaposition of a verb and a noun (VERB–NOUN), a noun and an adjective (NOUN–ADJ / ADJ–NOUN) and an adverb and an adjective (ADV–ADJ). These are widespread historically and cross-linguistically and represent a large open class. Compound nouns are most widespread, not only in number and productivity, but also in variety of formation.

The development of compounds not only involves the chronology of their emergence or spread, but changes in the underlying syntactic relation. Compounds including a verb and underlying subject, for example, became very rare, e.g., It. *tremacuore* (cf. *il cuore trema* 'the heart trembles') 'palpitations' (Giurescu 1975:142).

The most important innovation in Romance is the dramatic increase of adjectival and nominal compounds based on verb + complement noun. Attested in all Romance languages in all periods and representing an open class, they are the richest type. In early times they occur especially in placenames and proper names (see Lloyd 1968:20–30); today their number continues to increase, especially in the western languages in names of objects (It. *apribottiglie* 'bottle opener'). (For detailed analyses for modern languages, see Lloyd 1968:31–66; Klingebiel 1989:78–120; Dardano 1978:148f.) Moreover, there has been a change in the order of elements (see below) and the definite article came to be included in some compounds, especially in French, where use of articles is strongest; Fr. *pince-nez* vs. *trompe-l'œil*. Nominal formations including a noun and an adjective also became widespread.

Whereas Latin adjectival compounds favour numeral–noun combinations (e.g., BIPEDALIS 'two feet long'), Romance prefers compounds combining two adjectives (e.g., Sp. *agridulce* 'bittersweet', Fr. *sourd-muet* 'deaf-mute'): they occur in all languages at all periods. Moreover, they are often created in specific contexts and may spread or just be temporary creations, e.g., Sp. *relaciones colombo–venezolanas* 'Colombian–Venezuelan relations', Fr. *la guerre franco–allemande* 'the Franco–German war', Ro. (*teatru*) *german–maghiar* 'German-Hungarian (theatre)', Sp. *dominio político–miltar* 'politico–military domain' (see Giurescu 1975:85, 143–44). Compared with their nominal equivalents, adjectival VERB–NOUN compounds are relatively rare and limited to western Romance (e.g., Sp. *una fragata portamísiles* 'guided-missile frigate', Fr. *tape à l'œil* 'flashy').

Verb compounds have declined in frequency. NOUN–VERB verb compounds already existed in Latin and, with the exception of Romanian, are found in Romance as lexical fossils, e.g., Fr. *maintenir* 'maintain', It. *barcamenare* 'embark' (for their Indo-European background, see Klingebiel 1989:27–41). A similar word-order pattern appears in ADV–VERB compounds, predominantly including reflexes of MALE 'badly' or BENE 'well', e.g., It. *maledire* 'curse'. In this respect Italian and Spanish differ from French: they not only have more instances, but all of them have fully-fledged paradigms. (For verbal VERB–VERB compounds, see Marchello-Nizia 1979; Dardano 1978:146.)

Recently, many new compound verbs have been created, mainly with verb and noun in that order, e.g., Sp. *tener lugar*, Fr. *avoir lieu* 'take place', It. *far finta* 'pretend'. This group and compounds that are based on preposition + verb (e.g., Sp. *contradecir* 'contradict', Fr. *outrepasser* 'exceed'), which are inseparable combinations, represent open classes.

Even if specific types of compounds occur in several Romance languages, they may be excluded in others or their distribution may vary in the individual languages. Giurescu's overview (1975) of compounds in four languages (Spanish, Italian, French, Romanian) shows that Romanian is often the exception, generally by lacking a type of compound that other Romance language possess. Conversely, Italian tends to be the exception by having a type of compound not found elsewhere. Moreover, the special status of Romanian as the only Romance language retaining case is reflected in that it alone has nominal compounds of the type NOUN.ART.NOUN. GEN, such as *mătasea-broaştei* 'floating pond weed', lit. 'silk.DET frog.

DET.GEN' (Giurescu 1975:62f.). The other languages require a preposition (e.g., *de*) in these contexts with or without article, cf. Fr. *hôtesse de l'air* 'air hostess', It. *fior di latte* 'cream' [lit. 'flower of milk'], Sp. *lengua de gato* 'finger biscuit' [lit. 'cat's tongue'].

2.3   *Internal formal variation*

The spelling of compounds (one word, separate words, with or without hyphen) reflects particularities of the individual languages rather than the actual degree of composition. Although the orthographical history of the individual words reflects the successive stages (e.g., Fr. *gens d'armes* 'men of arms' > *gendarme*), the fact that a compound is not written as one word in a language does not necessarily imply that the word is less a compound than its one-word equivalent elsewhere, cf. Fr. *chef-d'œuvre*, It. *capolavoro* 'masterpiece'.

A crucial stage in the development of compounds arises when the individual meaning of the elements no longer prevails, e.g., *pomme* in Fr. *pomme de terre* 'potato' is no longer interpreted as 'apple'. Rather, the combination of words is a semantic unit in which the new unique meaning may not be the sum of the meanings of the elements. Application of grammatical rules – such as gender and number agreement – and stress patterns reflect the degree of compoundness as well.

In contrast to grammatical phrases, full compounds typically have primary and secondary stress: the compound Fr. *cordon-bleu* has primary stress on *bleu* and secondary stress on *cordon*, but in the NP *cordon bleu* both words have primary stress. Other phonological phenomena may reflect the autonomy of components, such as absence of word-internal voicing of intervocalic sibilants, across word boundaries within compounds in northern Italian: *camposanto* 'cemetery' [lit. 'holy field'] has no voiced sibilant, cf. [kamposanto] not **[kampozanto] (cf. *casa* [kaza] 'house').

Loss of the independence of the components may be reflected in number marking: originally affecting the individual elements, morphological marking *may* eventually affect the entire unit. Italian *pomodoro* 'tomato,' for example, originally had a plural *pomidoro*, reflecting its etymology 'fruit of gold', in line with regular plural formation of noun phrases. Similarly, apposition compounds of the type *capocuoco* 'head chef' form their plural according to the rules of nominal phrases and both elements have number marking, cf. *capicuochi*. Nominal compounds of the type NOUN–ADJ may also take plural markers on both elements, e.g., It. *cassaforte* 'strongbox' – *casseforti*, It. *mezzaluna* 'half moon' > *mezzelune*.

Similarly, Sp. *la casamata* 'casemate' – *las casasmatas*. Yet Spanish ADJ–NOUN compounds as a rule only have the plural marker on the final element, cf. *la altavoz* 'loudspeaker' – *las altavoces* (see Giurescu 1975:67). Similarly, Italian compounds have often been reanalysed as simplex words and their plural marking has become limited to the end of the unit as well, e.g., *pomodori, capocuochi, capolavori*, but *capigruppo* (from *capo di gruppo* 'head of group'). This change reflects the loss of the 'structural autonomy' of the component elements (Maiden 1995a:184), and the word becomes morphologically opaque. Similarly, in its 1990 report, the *Conseil supérieur de la langue française* recommended that several compounds be written as one word and that the plural marking follow the entire unit, cf. *arcboutant* 'flying buttress' and *arcboutants*, respectively (Grevisse 1993:811). Compounds that include two nouns and a preposition still respect the underlying syntactic relations, underlining the autonomy of the individual elements (e.g., Fr. *hôtesse de l'air*, PL *hôtesses de l'air*). Compounds including a verb and a noun are typically invariable in Romance, e.g., Fr. *un/des gratte-ciel*, It. *grattacielo* (SG/PL) 'skyscraper' [lit. 'scratch-sky']. Yet here too patterns are changing: in 1990 the *Conseil supérieur de la langue française* ruled that hyphenated compounds including a verb and a direct object take plural marking at the end of the unit if the entity is plural, but the hyphen has to be maintained, e.g., *des perce-neiges* 'snowdrops' [lit. 'pierce-snows'] (Grevisse 1993:811).

The grammatical category that prevails in Romance compounds is number, but the individual languages vary in its application. French applies number marking in ADJ–ADJ adjectives to both adjectives (e.g., *sourds-muets* 'deaf mute'), whereas in Italian number is only indicated at the end of the formation, e.g., *sordomuti*. French applies the gender marker to both components, thereby displaying their autonomy (*sourde-muette*); by contrast, the first element is invariable in Italian.[10]

2.4 Problems[11]

2.4.1 The grammatical nature of the verb

The verb in VERB–NOUN compounds has been interpreted as indicative (Tollemache 1945) and as imperative (Diez 1838; Darmesteter 1967:168–234; Meyer-Lübke 1894:581–83; for a critical overview, see Lloyd 1968:3–10; Klingebiel 1989:11–26). By contrast, Marouzeau (1955:93) argued that the verb does not represent a specific mood, but instead is unspecified in relation to mood, tense and person. The imperative interpretation is most widespread and although there seems to be formal support for it in Italian, Sardinian and Romanian (see also Maiden 2007b), evidence from French is inconclusive: compounds such as *un fait-tout* 'cooking-pot' (lit. 'makes-all') suggest an indicative.

2.4.2   Semantic and formal opacity

Not all compounds are equally transparent, and formal does not necessarily imply semantic transparency. Formal opacity is generally related to the age of the compound and often manifest in phonological and grammatical characteristics. Few native speakers will realize the compound origin of words such as It. *ot(t)arda* 'bustard' (< AUIS TARDA). Similarly most compound adverbs and prepositions are perceived as simplex. Compounds combining verb and noun or noun and adjective are relatively transparent because they reflect underlying grammatical relations. Conversely compounds resulting from apposition (e.g., It. *cavolfiore* 'cauliflower', lit. 'cabbage flower') are less transparent because the semantic relation between the components cannot be induced from the underlying grammatical relation. Formally transparent compounds may be semantically opaque: Fr. *cordon-bleu* does not mean 'blue cord', but 'excellent cook'. The meaning of many such compounds is opaque because it is based on metaphoric or metonymic relations, e.g., It. *grillo talpa* 'mole cricket' (so-called because this cricket lives underground), or *pescespada* 'swordfish' (so-called because part of its anatomy resembles a sword).

2.4.3   Relative order of elements: NOUN–VERB vs. VERB–NOUN and ADJ–NOUN vs. NOUN–ADJ

Word-order problems typically affect ADJ–NOUN / NOUN–ADJ and NOUN–VERB / VERB–NOUN compounds, cf. Fr. *rouge-gorge* 'redbreast' and *cordon-bleu* or It. *purosangue* 'thoroughbred' (lit. 'pure blood') and *gattamorta* 'person who conceals an aggressive or malevolent nature under a harmless exterior', lit. 'dead cat' (ADJ–NOUN vs. NOUN–ADJ) and Fr. *tout-puissant* 'almighty' and *allume-cigare* 'cigar lighter', or the Italian equivalents *onnipotente* vs. *accendisigari* (NOUN–VERB vs. VERB–NOUN). Compounds with the sequence NOUN–ADJ and VERB–NOUN, which predominate, reflect the common unmarked right-branching word order that developed in Romance (see Bauer 2001a). The change in word order is most systematic in compounds including a verb and object, with or without preposition, e.g., UINIFER 'wine-producing', AGRICOLA 'farmer', and in

Romance VERB–OBJ sequences (Fr. *tournedisque*, It. *giradischi*, Sp. *toca-discos*, Pt. *toca-discos* 'record player'). For VERB–OBJ sequences including pronominal elements or PPs, such as It. *mangia-tutto* 'person who will eat anything', Fr. *tape-à-l'œil* 'flashy', see Giurescu (1975:71); for OBJ–VERB compounds in Catalan, despite regular VERB–OBJ order, see Gràcia and Fullana (1999).

There is more variation in compounds containing noun and adjective, as there is more variation in Romance NPs comprising an adjective. Whereas NOUN–ADJ is frequent in abstract and concrete formations, ADJ–NOUN nominal compounds also occur in common registers, e.g., Ro. *primăvară* 'springtime' [lit. 'first summer (*vară*)'], It. *buongusto* 'good taste', etc. Adjectives used in these compounds tend to precede the noun in NPs as well (Bauer 2001a). The occurrence of ADJ–NOUN sequences may also be partly contact-induced, as witness northern French placenames, with strong Germanic substrate or adstrate influence: *Neufchâteau* lit. 'new castle' vs. southern *Châteauneuf*, etc. (see Rohlfs 1971b). For an overview of compounds including a participle with subject, a complement, or an adverb, see Giurescu (1975:74, 84, 87).

2.5 Names of days[12]

Names of days in Romance represent a complex type of compound: some are serial compounds with a recurrent component (e.g., It. *giovedì*, *venerdì* 'Thurs**day**, Fri**day**'), whereas others are opaque (e.g., Sp./Pt. *domingo* 'Sunday'). Cross-linguistic variation depends on the degree of Christian influence, possible ellipsis of the head noun, and the order of elements. The names of days in Romance combine Judeo-Christian and pagan traditions: they refer to the planets and came into use in Latin, with the exception of 'Saturday' and 'Sunday', which refer to the Jewish Sabbath and the Christian Lord's Day, respectively, cf. DIES DOMINICA or DIES DOMINICUS 'lord's day' > Sp./Pt. *domingo*, Cat. *diumenge*, Fr. *dimanche*, It. *domenica*, Ro. *duminică*.

The pagan forms disappeared in Portuguese, where an early Christian tradition prevailed, involving an ordinal number followed by a noun, *feria*, which originally referred to the days in the Holy Week, cf. SECUNDA (QUARTA, QUINTA) FERIA > Pt. *segunda (quarta, quinta) feira* 'Monday' ('Wednesday', 'Thursday'); see Baehr (1958:35–42); Tagliavini (1963:67–69, 78). Another exception is Sardinian 'Friday', *kenápura/cenábara* (< CENA PURA 'pure dinner'), which refers to Friday as a fasting day in the Church: see Rohlfs (1971b:191; also 1952a:43f.), for other variants, e.g., dialectal (Tuscany) *mezzèdima* 'Wednesday'.

There is cross-linguistic variation in the order of elements and presence or absence of reflexes of the word DIES 'day', cf. Sp. *jueves*, Ro. *joi* and It. *giovedì* 'Thursday'; Sp. *viernes*, Ro. *vineri* and It. *venerdì* 'Friday'. Since Italian dialects and early attestations favour formations without DIES (e.g., early Tuscan dialectal *vènere*), the *venerdì* formation in standard Italian may be a later creation, possibly under French influence (Rohlfs 1971b:189f.). Ellipsis also occurs in 'Saturday' and 'Sunday': Fr. *samedi* vs. It. *sabato* and Sp./Pt. *domingo* vs. Prv. *dimenche*, Cat. *diumenge* and Fr. *dimanche*.

Variation in order of elements is illustrated by the type DIES UENERIS (Cat. *divendres* and Prv. *divendre* 'Friday', and early Wln. and Pic. *deluns* 'Monday') vs. the type UENERIS DIES (Fr. *vendredi*), in French, WRaeto-Romance and Italian. In Latin, the sequence DIES + GEN prevailed: it is found throughout the Roman Empire, in all inscriptions, and for all day-names. Moreover, it parallels the tendency at that time to have the nominal genitive follow the noun in NPs (Bauer 1995:55–59). The type GEN + DIES is rare and exclusively literary. In OFrench (and early Spanish) the type *deluns* 'Monday' is attested, although the reverse order predominates (Rohlfs 1971b:190; Baehr 1958:48f.). This suggests that DIES + GEN was inherited and that its elliptic variant probably predominated in an area including Spain, Italy and Romania, but there is no independent evidence. It would follow that the GEN + DIES formation was correspondingly late and contact-induced, possibly calquing Germanic day-names.

3   Numerals

The Romance numeral system is largely inherited from Latin, but there are important innovations: (i) fundamental structural changes affecting the order of elements or the occurrence of 'and' vs. asyndetic forms; (ii) use of vigesimals; and (iii) occurrence of analytical forms of the type *unsprezece* 'one upon ten, eleven' in Romanian.

3.1   Latin[13]

Romance inherited via Latin the fully developed decimal numerals of Proto-Indo-European. Latin numerals below 'ten' are opaque: 'one', 'two' and 'three' distinguish case and (three) genders, e.g., NOM M/NEUT DUO, F DUAE. Despite being asyndetic, numerals above ten are rather transparent. The predominant underlying arithmetical processes are multiplication and addition; a few numerals are based on subtraction. The teens are *dvandva* compounds, based on addition, and the digit typically precedes the decad in an asyndetic structure, e.g., TREDECIM 'thirteen'. Yet throughout the teens 'the Latin compounds often occur as free forms' (Coleman 1992:397), often with the reverse order, e.g., QUINQUE DECEMQUE vs. DECEM ET QUINQUE 'fifteen'. The higher numbers are characterized by the same arithmetical operation and word order, but typically include an overt link, the conjunction ET, e.g., TRES ET TRIGINTA 'thirty-three'. The reverse order is also attested. The numbers 'eight' and 'nine' of each decad are exceptions: they are based on subtraction and have an explicit link, DE- 'from', reflecting regularities of subtraction numerals (Greenberg 1978:258f.): DUO DE UIGINTI 'eighteen', UNDEQUADRAGINTA 'thirty-nine'. Variants typically have the order decad–digit and are additional, e.g., DECEM ET OCTO 'eighteen'. Decads, hundreds and thousands are compounds based on multiplication without overt marking and the factor precedes the unit: e.g., UIGINTI 'twenty', QUINQUAGINTA 'fifty', CENTUM 'one hundred', DUCENTI 'two hundred', MILLE 'one thousand', QUATTUOR MILIA 'four thousand'.

3.2   Romance[14]

3.2.1   Inherited numerals

Most numerals are inherited. The majority of Romance languages have only one numeral, 'one', which distinguishes gender. The plural indefinite of UNUS survives in modern Occitan dialects (Prv. *ùni cisèu* 'a pair of scissors'), Ibero-Romance (Pt. *uns/umas*; Sp. *unos/unas*; Cat. *uns/unes*) and in OFrench, but here 'only with reference to objects considered in pairs or collectively' (Price 1992:448), e.g., *uns ganz* 'a pair of gloves'. 'Two' has gender inflection in Pt. (*dois/duas*), Cat. (*dos/dues*) and Ro. (*doi/două*) and in several early Romance languages: OOccitan, OSpanish, some dialects of OFrench, and OItalian. For (residues of) gender distinction for 'three' in Romanian, OFrench and Italian dialects, see Rohlfs (1969:310f.) and Price (1992:450f.).

The opacity of teens varies: non-transparent numerals often reflect underlying ordering 'digit–decad'. In several numerals the order is the reverse of that in Latin. In Italian and French the break is at 'sixteen' ('fifteen' in Spanish and Portuguese): with the exception of Surselvan (e.g., *scheniv* < DECEM NOUEM; Schmid 1964:228–33), numerals above sixteen are not opaque, and are characterized by the order decad + digit, as in Sp. *diez y siete*, Pt. *dezassete*, It. *diciassette*, Fr. *dix-sept* 'seventeen'.

The change in ordering patterns within numerals is related to the comprehensive shift from left- to right-branching in the development from Latin to Romance (see Bauer 1995). Languages favouring complement–head (or OBJ–VERB) sequences tend to include numerals with the sequence digit–decad; right-branching languages tend to prefer decad–digit ordering (Greenberg 1963): SEPTEMDECIM vs. Fr. *dix-sept*. When exactly the change in internal order occurred is unknown, but instances of decad–digit sequences are attested in Classical Lat. SEPTENDECIM and UNDEUIGINTI went out of use in vulgar and late Latin, where *dece et septe* occurs (Grandgent 1907:160). Moreover, although analytic forms in Romance vary in being asyndetic or non-asyndetic, all favour the order decad–digit, suggesting that they go back to innovative Latin structures of the type DECEM SEPTEM, with or without overt link.

The conjunctions *y* and *e(t)* go back to Lat. ET, whereas the conjunction *a* in It. *diciassette* 'seventeen' is from AC. Several languages that had a linking element in earlier stages in these numerals lost it (e.g., OFr. *dis e set* but ModFr. *dix-sept*) or they became synthetic (e.g., OPt. *dez e sete* > ModPt. *dezassete*). The variant DECEM ET NOUEM survived in OFr. (*dis e nuef*) until the sixteenth century, in OPt. (*dez e nove*) and ModSp. (*diez y nueve / diecinueve*).

The pattern characterized by addition, with the decad coming first, also spread to numerals that in Latin were based on subtraction: DUODEUIGINTI > Fr. *dix-huit*, Sp. *diez y ocho / dieciocho* 'eighteen'; UNDEUIGINTI > Fr. *dix-neuf*, It. *diciannove* 'nineteen'.

3.2.2   Non-inherited numerals

Vigesimals and Romanian teens were not inherited. Romanian differs from other Romance languages in (i) formation of teens and (ii) choice of decad suffixes. Romanian teens typically include an element referring to the decad, *zece* 'ten', and a preposition (*spre* < SUPER 'on'), an overall pattern probably borrowed from Slavic, e.g., *unsprezece* 'one upon ten, eleven'. The element *-zeci* (plural of *zece*) also occurs in Romanian decads, where other Romance languages use inherited *-anta/-ante/-enta* (e.g., QUADRAGÍNTA > **quadráinta > *quarranta >* Sp. *cuarenta*, Fr. *quarante*, It. *quaranta* vs. Ro. *douăzeci*, lit. 'two tens', *patruzeci*, lit. 'four tens').

The origin and motivation of vigesimals represent a traditional problem in Romance linguistics. Vigesimal numerals are attested in (early) French, in medieval and modern Occitan, in dialects of Savoy and in SItaly; there are reported instances in early twentieth-century Catalan (Alcover 1925–26), but not in later Catalan (Wheeler *et al.* 1999:150–59), and in Spanish and Portuguese. Among these languages, the formation has been most widespread in French. Contemporary standard French only has vigesimals for the numbers 'eighty' to 'ninety' (and semi-vigesimals for 'seventy' to 'seventy-nine'), but decimals were original in OFrench, and documents from the twelfth to the sixteenth centuries commonly include vigesimal numerals for 'sixty' to 'three hundred and eighty'. As in Italian dialects, they typically occur in informal registers and combine with nouns expressing objects that are frequently counted, such as agricultural products and years.[15]

Vigesimal numerals are cross-linguistically similar: they typically include a cardinal (two to twenty) which is the factor of multiplication with a unit 'twenty', generally rendered by a cardinal number (e.g., *quatre-vingt-dix* 'ninety'), but also by a noun representing the unit 'twenty' (e.g., SIt./Sic. *vintini* 'scores'). This segment is followed by a digit ('one' to 'nineteen') either in an asyndetic construction or with an element 'and'. Because of their absence in Latin, Romance vigesimals are generally ascribed to borrowing (for an historical explanation of French vigesimals, see Reichenkron 1958:171–73). Their spread in French has been ascribed to Gaulish substrate; since little is known about the Gaulish numerical system, this hypothesis is based primarily on data from modern Celtic, which does have vigesimals. Basque influence has also been invoked (e.g., Rohlfs 1971b:132; Araujo 1975), although Spanish has only isolated instances. Finally, vigesimals in the dialects of Sicily and in French have been ascribed to Viking settlements. While evidence does not seem to support these hypotheses (for an extensive discussion, see Reichenkron 1958; also Bauer 2004), comparative analysis of other Indo-European languages in that same area has revealed that these languages also developed vigesimal numerals in the Middle Ages, that they have their own characteristics (excluding direct borrowing) but similar (sociolinguistic) use. Their emergence has been related to the spread of monetary systems based on the notions 'twenty' and 'twelve', and other phenomena in European society (e.g., the development of markets at local, regional and national level) and arithmetical advantages (Bauer 2004).

4   **Adverbs in -*ment(e)***

The adverbial formation in -*ment(e)* seems a textbook example of grammaticalization, whereby a noun became a grammatical suffix. The formation can be traced back to Latin, but is not pan-Romance: with a few exceptions these adverbs are unattested in Romanian, for example, which continues to use neuter (now masculine) adjectives as adverbs.

Romance adverbial formations in -*ment*(*e*) conveying manner typically include a feminine form of the adjective in combination with a suffix -*ment*(*e*) which goes back to the Latin feminine noun MENS 'mind, way, fashion'. Suffixes with a unique adverbial function are rather unusual cross-linguistically (see Karlsson 1981:5–16) and the Romance formation contrasts with the variety of forms in Latin. Latin adverbial formation was similar to that in Indo-European: there was no unique form or suffix and the morphological processes lacked unity, system and coherence. Among them adverbial formations in -E and -ITER, derived from adjectives, were relatively consistent, but the variety of suffixes, degree of suffixation and their formal and semantic unpredictability (e.g., MULTUS > ADV MULTUM 'much, often' and ADV MULTO 'very') made Latin adverbial formations rather opaque (for an overview, see Hofmann *et al.* 1965; for etymology, Osthoff 1887).

4.1   *Formal variation*

Although adverb formation is widespread and strong in Romance territory, Romance languages and dialects present formal variation, as reflected in the presence or absence of -*r*-. Adverbs in -*mente* are found in almost all Romance languages, e.g., Fr. *longuement* 'long', Pt. *cruamente* 'cruelly', Sp. *distintamente* 'distinctly', It. *chiaramente* 'clearly', Cat. *bellament*, Occ. *bellamen* 'beautifully', Engadine *sulamaing* 'only', Ro. *finalmein*, Srd. *finalmenti(s)* 'finally'. For dialectal variation, e.g., in Italian, see Karlsson (1981:116–20). In several Romance varieties the suffix includes -*r*-: it may be traced to the adverbial suffix -*(i)ter* that spread in vulgar and late Latin and may have been added when the adjective–noun combinations did not yet have full adverbial value (as AEQUANIMITER 'calmly' < AEQUA 'even' + ANIMA 'mind' + ITER seems to suggest): OSp. *buena mientre* 'well', Ist. -*mentro* (with -*mento*), Frl. *stupidamentri* 'stupidly', Lad. *autramenter* 'otherwise', OVnz. *cotidianamentre* 'daily', Ro. *altminteri* 'otherwise' (*aimintre*) (Rohlfs 1969:245; Karlsson 1981). Replacement in Spanish of regular *mientre* by -*mente* can be traced to the thirteenth and fourteenth centuries, and is generally accounted for as contact-induced. The suffix -*ment* was possibly a borrowing from OProvençal, or OFrench, which at that time was a prestige language. For discussion of the origins of -*ment*, see Karlsson (1981:98–101); also Menéndez Pidal (1908:296); Meyer-Lübke (1894:638f., 643).

The Romance languages now write -*mente* formations as one word: several did so early (OFrench, OProvençal), others much later (for details, see Karlsson 1981:103, and 125 for stylistic and other motivation of two-word realizations). That the combination is looser in some languages than others is obvious from instances in several early and contemporary Romance languages where -*mente* may be dropped when occurring in a series of adverbs (e.g., Sp. *clara y sencillamente* 'clearly and simply'). There is a preference for dropping all but the last instance of -*mente* in the early varieties of Italian, Portuguese and French, and Raeto-Romance, and modern Portuguese and Spanish. In Italian they were always exceptional and died out in the fourteenth century, but were taken up again in the sixteenth and early seventeenth (Karlsson 1981:123). Instances where only the first -*mente* survives are found in sixteenth-century Spanish, in OCatalan, OProvençal and Aragonese from the thirteenth century (Karlsson 1981:107, 122–29; for contemporary dialectal variety, 1981:102f.).

4.2   *Problems*

The emergence of -*mente* presents a number of linguistic problems. Although -*mente* is a fully-fledged suffix, it combines with a feminine form of the adjective, thus strongly reflecting its nominal origin. Similarly, in Spanish, for example, formations that include adjectives with a stress pattern different from the norm have two separate tonic accents, one on the first syllable and a secondary accent on -*mente* (*fácil* – *fácilmente*) emphasizing the two-word origin of the formation. From a diachronic perspective, the emergence of these left-branching formations is at variance with the general tendency in late Latin and early Romance for left-branching to give way to analytic right-branching structures: -*mente* adverbs are left-branching synthetic formations that emerged when the left-branching morphological system of Latin was breaking down.

Moreover, adverbs in -*mente* are widespread but not pan-Romance, since they do not occur in Romanian, for example, which has few -*mente* adverbs, possible borrowings from Italian (*realmente* 'really', *literalmente* 'literally'). This distribution raises the problem of chronology: the absence of -*mente* adverbs in Romanian suggests that their emergence postdates the split-off of Dacia (AD 275), which is confirmed by our textual data (see below). Yet their emergence cannot be much later because it would then not have been the widespread phenomenon it has become. The picture is further complicated by the absence of indigenous -*mente* in Dalmatian and in modern southern Italian dialects. Some linguists argue that -*mente* adverbs in Dalmatian (e.g., *altramiante* 'otherwise', *fenalmiánt* 'finally') were probably borrowings (Bartoli 1906:418), whereas -*mente* formations in southern

Italy are sometimes asserted to be borrowed from Italian (see Rohlfs 1969:243–45): see, however, Ledgeway (2009) for evidence to the contrary for southern Italy. Finally, on the basis of vulgar and late Latin it is difficult to trace the emergence of the adverbs in -*mente* or even predict the choice of -*mente* in this context (as we see below).

4.3   Origin

The emergence of -*mente* is the result of a long process whereby the noun MENTE had come to be the only noun in ADJ–NOUN combinations conveying adverbial value. Whereas linguistic changes typically first occur in the spoken language, especially in popular registers, the earliest attestations of adverbial MENTE combinations occur in high registers of written Latin. Most instances before AD 200 occur in poetry (Karlsson 1981:45). Moreover, in poetry, adjective + MENTE combinations have lexical-adverbial value (vs. purely lexical value), suggesting that -*mente* adverbs originated in literature (Bauer 2001b).

The complexity of the grammaticalization process of -*mente* adverbs is not only related to the stability of the lexical value of MENTE and the absence of semantic bleaching, but to the variety of nouns in this context. MENTE was not the only noun in adjective–noun combinations. In fact, there was a great variety including abstract nouns (MODO 'way', PACTO 'agreement', GENERE 'kind', and so forth), in Classical, and vulgar and late, Latin. These nouns were frequent in these contexts and even occurred in fixed expressions (ALIQUO MODO 'in some way', NULLO MODO 'in no way') and compounds (e.g., OMNIMODO 'entirely', MULTIMODIS 'variously', MAGNOPERE 'greatly'); see McCartney (1920). We also find nouns referring to body parts (e.g., PEDE 'foot', ORE 'mouth'), concrete nouns conveying heart, mind, PECTORE 'breast', ANIMO 'spirit', CORDE 'heart', MENTE 'mind', and so forth: ARDENTI CORDE 'intensely'. ANIMO and ANIMIS were widespread, in analytic and compound expressions, e.g., STUDIOSO ANIMO 'impatiently', AEQUANIMITER 'calmly'. Recent analysis has shown that if ADJ + MENTE combinations are formally the forerunners of -*mente* adverbs, they are less frequent than combinations with, say, ANIMO and less often have lexical-adverbial, let alone adverbial, value. Nothing in the *Vulgate*, for example, leads one to expect that MENTE would be the Romance suffix. The restrictive use of MENTE – semantically and formally – may account for its survival (see further Bauer 2003).

Another important aspect of grammaticalized -*mente* is the order of elements. At all times and in all registers there is preference for ADJ-*mente* sequences, which increases with time. This left-branching preference is related to the type of adjective involved. Adjectives (predominantly descriptive) that combine with *-mente* typically occur in prenominal position in other contexts as well (see Bauer 1995:71–73; 2001b). Moreover, since left-branching morphological constructions tend to become synthetic, these combinations became synthetic even at a time when parts of the Latin inflectional system were being replaced by analytic right-branching constructions. A similar development – parallel in chronology and structure – occurs in future tenses, where infinitive–auxiliary combinations became synthetic. In both cases the head element occurred in second position.

5 Other word-formation processes

5.1 Conversion[16]

The most common type of conversion (change of grammatical category without formal changes to the base word) is nominalization, mainly involving adjectives and participles, e.g., It. *caldo* 'hot' > *il caldo* 'the heat', Sp. *habitar* 'dwell' > *habitante* 'inhabitant', Ro. *răed* 'bad' > *răul* 'the evil', *frumos* 'beautiful' > *frumosul* 'beauty'. Other lexical items may undergo nominal conversion: pronouns (Fr. *le moi*, Ro. *eul* 'the ego'), numerals (Ro. *un zece* 'a teen'), conjunctions (It. *il perché* 'the why, the reason'), infinitives (Fr. *le devoir* 'duty'). Nominalization of infinitives was productive in OFrench and ModFrench, but today involves lexicalized relics, e.g., *le dîner* 'dinner'.

Other processes include: nouns or phrases becoming adjectives (e.g., It. *rosa* 'rose' > *rosa* 'pink', Fr. *tête-de-nègre* 'dark brown'), phrases becoming conjunctions (e.g., Fr. *cependant* < *ce pendant* 'during this') or nouns becoming pronouns, which is obviously the result of grammaticalization, e.g., HOMO 'man' > Fr. *on* / medieval It. *uomo* 'one' (Rohlfs 1968:231f.).

Conversion of adjectives into adverbs is widespread in Romanian, which has very few *-mente* adverbs, but not elsewhere in Romance. Sixteenth-century French, for example, replaces *vitement* by deadjectival *vite* 'quickly' (Grevisse 1993:258), but the process has recently been quite productive in French and Spanish in commercials and the media, possibly in imitation of spoken argot, cf. Fr. *ne bronzez pas idiot* 'don't tan stupidly' (lit. NEG-'tan'-IMP.NEG 'idiot'-ADJ; Grevisse 1993:1360; for Spanish Stewart 1999:80).

In addition, conversion commonly arises from ellipsis of the head noun in an NP and subsequent nominalization of the adjective, e.g., Sp. *un coche deportivo* 'a sports car' > *deportivo*. The distinguishing semantic function of the adjective or genitive accounts for its selection as representing the entire NP, cf. ARBOR QUERCEA, ARBOR PALMAE > It. *quercia* 'oak', *palma* 'palm tree'. Similarly, *autonómico* in Sp. *la cadena de televisión de un gobierno general autonómico* 'TV channel of a general autonomous government' is semantically distinctive, hence its conversion into *autonómica* (Stewart 1999:79).

Whereas conversion is characterized by zero morphology, the resultant word undergoes the regular morphological and syntactic processes of the new category. Thus in nominalization, syntactic characteristics such as the presence of determiners and inflectional characteristics such as plural marking (Fr. VERB *rire* 'laugh' > NOUN *le rire* 'laughter' > *les rires*) reflect the change in category. The degree of lexicalization may appear in number marking, e.g., Fr. *des robes roses* 'pink dresses', in which *rose* is a full adjective, but *des chaussures marron* 'brown shoes'. Similarly, in Fr. *on a vendu trois Rembrandt* 'three Rembrandts have been sold', *Rembrandt* is a common noun, but the link with the proper name remains obvious and the noun has no plural marking. Yet not all grammatical categories may apply to the new formation: gender marking, for example, is very rare and if it occurs the meaning is specific, cf. Fr, *chaussures marron* 'brown shoes' vs. *une négresse marronne* 'a fugitive female slave' (Grevisse 1993:838).

5.2   Reduplication

The Romance languages may include reduplication as a lexical process by which the first syllable of a word is reduplicated, often with truncation of its final consonant, yielding C1V1(C2)C1V1C2, e.g., Fr. *pépère* 'grandfather' (< *père* 'father'), *joujou* 'toy' (< *jouet*). The process is widespread in (colloquial) French (for phonological details, see Morin 1972; Mayerthaler 1977:40–46), in communication with or by children (e.g., *dodo* 'sleep' < *dormir*), and in adult speech, conveying hypocoristic (*poupoule* 'pet' < *poule*), diminutive or attenuating value (*foufou/fofolle* 'foolish' < *fou* 'mad', *bébête* 'silly' < *bête* 'stupid'; see Morin (1972:104–47); Bollée (1978:323f.); Mayerthaler (1977:27–32)). Reduplication words may undergo further morphological processes, such as derivation, cf. *blabla* > *blablater* > *blablateur* 'blabber on'. French reduplication is a sort of prefixation process emphasizing the importance of CV syllabic structure frequent in the spoken registers (Frei 1971:96–105; Bollée 1978:321f.), and possibly the tendency to prefer right-branching structures.

Reduplication is less widespread in other Romance languages, which favour iteration. Iteration consists in repeating the entire word and may have intensifying, diminutive, endearment or repetitive value, e.g., It. *occhi neri neri* 'very black eyes', *parlava parlava* 'he talked continuously', Sp. *luego luego* 'immediately', Srd. *díe díe* 'all day' (Bourciez 1956:530f.; Wagner 1957; Rohlfs 1968:89–92; Bollée 1978). Iteration in Latin typically included adjectives and adverbs, cf. *liber, liber sum* (Hor.) 'I am very free', or late Latin *modo modo* 'right now' (Petr.). In these examples it has intensifying and 'superlative' value: *malus, malus* (= *pessimus* 'very bad') (Rönsch 1965 [1868]:280). Moreover, lexicalized examples of a repetition process are attested in Classical Latin in a few instances, with generalizing meaning, e.g., QUISQUIS 'whoever', UBIUBI 'wherever'.

Iteration is strongest in Italo-Romance and Sardinian, affecting nouns, verbs, adverbs and prepositional phrases. Greek influence may have been a consolidating factor in southern Italy, where the phenomenon is particularly widespread (see Rohlfs 1968:91f.). In NItalian dialects, iteration is integrated in derivational processes when the second element is reinforced by a suffix -*ent* (e.g., *novo novente* 'very new'); see Bourciez (1956:530); Rohlfs (1968:87); Bollée (1978:329). Iteration is frequent in Romanian and Portuguese, less so in Occitan. Some languages, e.g., Spanish, Portuguese and Occitan, may include *que*: ADJ *que* ADJ, often with concessive value (e.g., Occ. *paure que paure* 'poor as he may be ...'; Bollée 1978:332f.). Similarly, Italian includes structures of the type V *che* V especially with imperatives (*corri che tu corri* 'run as you may'). Adverbial iteration, found throughout Romance, also conveys confrontation (e.g., It. *a corpo a corpo* 'body to body', Fr. *face à face* 'face to face') and reciprocity, e.g., Fr. *être copain-copain* 'be friends' or *donnant-donnant* 'quid pro quo' (see Rohlfs 1968:88f.; Bollée 1978:334–36). Some of these formations are lexicalized, especially NOUN–NOUN combinations, which lexicalize in all languages (e.g., Pt. *luze-luze* 'firefly', *pisca-pisca* 'blinker'). French has relatively little iteration, but much lexicalized repetition with vowel variation ([i], [a], [u]), *clic-clac* 'click', *flic-flac* 'splash' (It. *ninnananna* 'lullaby') and consonant variation, e.g., *pêle-mêle* 'higgledy-piggledy', *tirelire* 'piggybank', respecting the cross-linguistic consonant hierarchy p < b < m < s < t < l < v < ... (Mayerthaler 1977:46–53).

Reduplication, often calquing African languages, is also found in Romance creoles conveying a variety of semantic, pragmatic and sociolinguistic functions (e.g., intensification, Hai. *rõ-rõ* 'very round'). It also conveys grammatical categories, such as plurality, Malayo-Pt. *gatu-gatu* 'cats' (Sylvain 1936:42; Holm 1988:88f.,147; 1989:291, 320; Green 1988b: 468f.).

5.3   *Truncation*

Although attested in the nineteenth century, truncation has spread in Romance since the early twentieth, originating in informal language. In truncation the last part of the base word is deleted and what remains is a segment of the original word, e.g., Sp. *bici* < *bicicleta* 'bicycle'. The process predominantly affects nouns and sometimes adjectives. It may entail abbreviation of 'learnèd' words that include Greek elements (*auto-, micro-, cinema-, taxi-*, etc.), Ro. *micro* < *microraion* 'small urban area' or *microradiologie* 'microradiology' (Beyrer *et al.* 1987:51). The base words are generally later creations, referring to recent inventions, and the truncated form, which tends to be bisyllabic and vowel-final, may have infiltrated the standard language. In Italian, the vowels are unstressed and uninflectable, e.g., *l'automobile – le automobili* vs. *l'auto – le auto*. In Spanish and French the new words do inflect for number, cf. Sp. *las fotos*, Fr. *les photos* vs. It. *le foto*. Alternatively, truncation typically occurs in colloquial, highly informal registers – especially of young people (e.g., teenage slang) – where the processes are less systematic: apocope predominates, but apheresis occurs too, e.g., Fr. *bac*(*calauréat*) 'exam', (*ca*)*piston* 'captain'. Although truncation is widespread in Romance, the concrete processes may vary locally. In Spanish, abbreviations may have three syllables and end in *-a* (e.g., *estupa* – *estupefacientes* 'narcotics', *forasta* < *forastero* 'foreigner' (Stewart 1999:81)). In French, words predominantly end in a consonant (Grevisse 1993:248f.). Between 1980 and 1995, there has been a tendency, however, to add a suffix *-os* to many truncated (and non-truncated) words – especially adjectives – often with intensifying value, e.g., *rapidos* 'quickly'. Spanish influence, related to a revival of Spanish interest in the 1980s, may be involved (Boyer 1997).

5.4   *Syllabic reversal*

A recent development is the spread of *verlan* in France, and its infiltration into the standard language. Verlan (< *l'envers* 'the reverse') is a sociolinguistic variety of modern French characterized by syllabic reversal. The exact forms depend on the number of syllables per word and their open or closed nature:

> CV > VC: *fou* 'crazy' > *ouf*
> C1V1C2V2 > C2V2C1V1: *pourri* 'rotten' > *ripou*
> C1VC2 > C1V1C2V2 > C2V2C1V1: *femme* [fam] > (**femmeu*
> [fam(ə)] by epenthesis) > (**meufeu*) > *meuf* (with truncation)

If the original word has three syllables, one ordering is selected for each word, with no apparent motivation, e.g., *ci-ga-rette* > *ga-ret-si*; *ta-bou-ret* >*re-bou-ta*; *vé-ri-té* > *té-vé-ri* (see Calvet 1993:42; Méla 1997:18–24). The base words are often argot (e.g., *pascal* '500 franc note' > *skalpa*). Although verlan typically affects the lexicon, short fixed expressions also appear, e.g., *comme ça* > *sakom*.

Primarily a spoken variety, verlan[17] is closely related to immigrant culture: it originated in its present form in parts of the Parisian *banlieue* inhabited by immigrants from the Maghreb. In the last ten years it has heavily infiltrated the language of younger French people; all classes use it to some degree, and isolated words are integrated in Standard French, e.g., the inclusion of several in the 2001 *Grand Robert* (*ouf, keum, ripou*). Although originally a secret language, it has become a means of group recognition and solidarity and a way of excluding outsiders. Since the original process – syllable reversal – is relatively simple, its products can be easily recognized and reproduced and the rules have consequently been made more complex through 'reverlanisation', involving ongoing reversing, e.g., *arabe* 'Arab' > (**beu-ara*) > (**beura*) > *beur* > (**beureu*) > *reubeu*. More complex is *Veul* which has phoneme reversal as well, e.g., *comme ça* > verlan *sakom* > Veul *asmok* or *asmeuk*; *choper* > verlan *pécho* > Veul *péoch* 'steal'; *rendez-vous* > verlan *dérenvou* >Veul *vourdé* (Calvet 1993).The numerous processes of reverlanisation show no regularity and the exact origin of many *Veul* words or the processes involved in their creation often remain obscure. In contrast, infixing *javanais* inserts infixes into the root (e.g., *poulet* 'chick' > *pavoulet*), while *Largonji* creates words by affixation and inversion (*poulet* > *louletpèm*, *le jargon* > *largonji*; Bullock (1996:180, 184).

Splitting words into syllables destroys morphological roots and stems and verlanisation therefore differs fundamentally from the word formation processes discussed hitherto, where the root or stem of the base word remained intact and elements were added. Because of verlanisation, stems become unrecognizable and paradigmatic words lose their morphological connection, cf. *videur* 'bouncer' > verlan *deurvi*, *tireur* 'shooter' > *reurti*.

Moreover, verlanisation affects major morphological processes, such as gender-, tense- or person-marking, overcoming the few remaining left-branching residues of French morphology. The basic form of the verb in verlan is the past participle and tense is conveyed by the auxiliary, cf. *sorti* 'gone out' > *je tisor* (present), *je vais tisor* (future) and *je suis tisor* (past); Méla (1997:28). Feminine gender is severely affected as well: there is no gender agreement between the noun and the adjective (*il/elle est ouf*) and only a few masculine–feminine nominal pairs survive as lexicalized items and not as the result of productive morphological processes (Méla 1997:28), e.g., *sezfrã – sefrã* (< *française – français*); *pinko – pɛko* (< *copine – copain* 'pal'). Feminine gender is expressed in determiners: *ma roem* 'my.-F mother'.

Other languages have their own *javanais*, e.g., Lunfardo – a variety of Argentine Spanish spoken in the under-privileged neighbourhoods of Buenos Aires. Originally closely related to immigrant Italian culture, it has spread to other parts of Argentina and abroad (Chamberlain 1981:425). Its main characteristics are lexical: vocabulary is based on borrowing (mainly from NItalian dialects), metaphorical usage and *vesre* (< *revés*) (reversal of syllables), e.g., *diome* < *medio* 'middle', *choma* (< *macho*), *estroma* (< *maestro*), etc. (Grayson 1964:66). Lunfardo was originally used cryptophasically, but other sociolinguistic motives have since become predominant. Other specialized lexicons, such as Gíria in Rio de Janeiro, which is closely related to Italian immigrant culture as well, may include morphological processes similar to those in verlan, but on a smaller scale (Chamberlain 1981:425), e.g., Gíria/Lunfardo *trompa* < Sp. *patrón*.

Syllable reversal and insertion in general are found in popular varieties of Romance languages used by youngsters, e.g., It. *capasa* for *casa* (Pelon 1997:118).

These word formation processes affect roots, stems and affixes and their status: suffixes no longer play a role in verlan morphology. In this respect, verlan and its equivalents are fundamentally different: derivational as well as inflectional processes in Indo-European languages, including Romance, have previously been based on the word stem or root. Further systematic research is needed, focusing on the processes involved in individual Romance varieties, their implications and motivation, and cross-linguistic differences and parallels. Since so many different languages seem to be involved (e.g., Italian and Maghreb influence), their existence cannot be uniquely contact-induced.

5.5   Acronyms

Whereas the processes discussed above are typical of spoken language or reflect subcultures, acronyms represent a word formation process closely related to literacy, in the standard language, and do not include dialectal or sociolectal varieties. The base words are combinations of nouns and adjectives (sometimes also prepositions) of which the initial letters or initial parts of syllables are combined into new formations, cf. It. *FIAT* (< *Fabbrica italiana automobili Torino*), *Polfer* < *Polizia ferroviaria* 'railway police', or Ro. *C.F.R.*

([tʃɛ fɛ rɛ])[18] < *Căile Ferate Române* 'Romanian Railways'. Their occurrence is motivated by shortness or euphemism, e.g., Fr. *I.V.G.* (< *interruption volontaire de grossesse* 'voluntary interruption of pregnancy'), a euphemism for abortion (Grevisse 1993:250). Acronyms are either pronounced as one word (e.g., Sp. *ovni* < *objeto volante no identificado* 'UFO' or *Otan* < *OTAN* < *O.T.A.N.* 'NATO'), or their component letters are pronounced separately, e.g., Fr. *H.L.M.* 'council flat' [aʃ ɛl ɛm] (< *habitation à loyer modéré*), Ro. *OZN* 'UFO' [o zɛ nɛ] (< *obiect zburător neidentificat*). Although acronyms are strongly influenced by English, Romance tends to adapt its own ordering patterns, hence *SIDA* < Eng. *AIDS*. The gender of acronyms corresponds to that of the head noun in the full form, e.g., Fr. *une H.L.M.*[19]

6   Conclusion

Whereas suffixal derivation used to be the predominant device in Latin, in modern Romance it is one process among others and has lost much of its vitality in favour of analytic devices and compounds.

Latin had numerous suffixes, a few of which survived as productive endings in Romance; others are easily recognizable but not productive; others are only etymological residues. Although surviving suffixes generally keep their main functions – creating new grammatical categories and expressing evaluative meanings – and as a group still convey the functions they had in Latin, there is also a strong shift towards connotative and pragmatic rather than denotative functions, e.g., in diminutives and augmentatives. Accordingly, there is a tendency – much stronger in French than Italian, Spanish or Portuguese – to express denotative values with right-branching analytic constructions.

Prefixation has grown in importance, and even more so compounding, which was not typically Latin but is now predominant in Romance. Strikingly, a similar development appears in the history of German (Pounder 2000). Both devices take over various functions of suffixes, e.g., increasing use of (serial) compounds in names of female professionals at the expense of feminine endings. Compounds that have become very productive are those that reflect a clear grammatical relation, VERB–NOUN nouns, nouns and adjectives based on apposition of nouns (NOUN–NOUN), adjectives (ADJ–ADJ) and compounds verbs, which in fact are analytic and include a verb followed by its direct object. Here again opacity is a matter of degree, closely linked to the underlying grammatical or semantic relation (e.g., metaphor or metonymy) and manifest in formal variation, such as number or gender agreement.

As a rule, the basic word order of Romance is reflected in the order of components in compounds, but also in a specific type of compound, numerals: in the inherited structures the digit–decad sequences have been replaced by the reverse, a shift well under way in late Latin and in accord with the word order change that affected Latin/Romance.

In contrast, Romance adverbs in -*mente* and names of days are exceptions to the general linguistic shift. In day-names the recurrent head is absent, or in second position, possibly due to language contact. Grammaticalization of -*mente* constructions is also exceptional by chronology, origin, lack of direct evidence, and structuring. Even if there is a structural explanation for the chronology of these synthetic forms, the persistence of this anachronism remains remarkable. Only recently have Romance languages increasingly used prepositional phrases in these contexts.

Whereas derivation and composition were productive in Latin, modern Romance displays processes (almost) unprecedented in Latin. Latin had a few instances of iteration, but little conversion or truncation, and apparently no syllabic reversal. Yet in a literate society with a well-developed administration, the Romans used many acronyms. Most of these processes emerged or spread dramatically in the twentieth century, predominantly in informal registers.

Romance word formation shows historical movement away from suffixal derivation and increasing use of compounds, analytic constructions and prefixes, or other devices. The diverse processes discussed above (except syllabic reversal) all respect the stem or root of the base word, and the new formation is eventually subject to regular grammatical operations of the language. Syllabic reversal however, does not. If syllabic reversal is not new – it is also a characteristic of *argot* – it is now much more widespread, if only because it is at the heart of verlan. These may be 'just word games' and the vocabulary – which tends to be ad hoc – may eventually disappear with the game. Yet this game affects the core of Romance morphology, which makes it exceptional.

Word formation has been an 'enfant pauvre' of comparative linguistics, and there are no comprehensive detailed comparative-historical analyses for Romance establishing chronological relationships between the productive processes, the role of analogy and the relationship between coexisting devices. The manuals tend to list, rather than analyse. Studies analysing aspects of word formation in a language or group of languages exist, but larger-scale diachronic analyses (e.g., Pounder 2000 for German) are needed.

II   LEXICAL STABILITY

Arnulf Stefenelli[†]

1   Introduction

At their core, the 'Romance languages' are the direct continuation of Latin or, to be more precise, they are those forms of speech that post-antique spoken Latin ('vulgar Latin') turned into in those areas of the former Roman Empire that had been Latinized permanently. Thus, the relationship between Latin and Romance is largely characterized by stability, in the lexicon as well. This means that there is direct ('lexically immediate') continuation of Latin vocabulary in all or some of the Romance languages.

This partial, but fundamental, lexical stability and agreement is so evident that even in the pre-scientific era, at the beginning of the fourteenth century, Dante in his *De Vulgari Eloquentia* (I, viii) was able to infer the common origin of the Romance languages he knew from the fact that they 'give the same names to many (almost all) things':

> Signum autem quod ab uno eodemque ydiomate istarum trium gentium progrediantur vulgaria, in promptu est, quia multa per eadem vocabula nominare videntur, ut 'Deum', 'celum', 'amorem', 'mare', 'terram', 'est', 'vivit', 'moritur', 'amat', alia fere omnia.
> 'But the sign that the popular languages of these three peoples originate in one and the same tongue is obvious: they seem to give the same names to many things, for example "God", "heaven", "love", "sea", "earth", "he is", "he lives", "he dies", "he loves", and to almost all other things.'

The content of Dante's examples embraces 'on the one hand the whole world and on the other the whole life of the individual in this world' (Gauger *et al.* 1981:8). From a modern, scientific and pan-Romance perspective, some of them exhibit unlimited lexical stability in the sense of a pan-Romance, semantically (largely) unchanged continuity. This is especially clear in the case of Latin CÆLUM 'heaven, sky', MARE 'sea' and MORI (vulgar Lat. *ˈmorere, *moˈrire) 'die':

Lat.	Ro.	It.	Srd.	RæR.	Fr.	Occ.	Cat.	Sp.	Pt.
CÆLUM	cer	cielo	kélu	tschêl	ciel	cel	cel	cielo	céu
MARE	mare	mare	máre	mar	mer	mar	mar	mar	mar
MORI	muri	morire	mòrrere	murir	mourir	morir	morir	morir	morrer

About the other examples, however, some reservations have to be made. With regard to the areal distribution over the Romance area, AMOR 'love' (noun) and AMARE 'love' (verb) are missing in Romanian, and UIUERE 'live' is lacking in modern SItalian (see Rohlfs 1971b:§130). Besides, the verbs continuing AMARE have only limited vitality, especially in Ibero-Romance (compared to QUÆRERE 'seek' > Sp., Pt. *querer*, which spreads as a replacement; see Rohlfs 1971b:109; Stefenelli 1992a:12). The equivalents of the infinitive ESSE (vulgar Lat. *ˈɛssere) 'be' have different sources: Ro. *fi* goes back to Lat. FIERI, and Sp. and Pt. *ser* presumably to a contamination with SEDERE 'sit'. From a semantic point of view, moreover, the Romanian continuation of TERRA 'land' (i.e., *țară*) has the meaning 'country, territory'. And finally, AMARE and AMICUS undergo a semantic extension because they also take on the functions of the non-surviving CLat. synonyms DILIGERE 'love (especially out of respect)' and FAMILIARIS 'intimate friend'. (By way of contrast, Ibero-Romance *ser* undergoes a semantic restriction because of *estar* < Lat. STARE 'stand', which takes over some of the functions of Lat. ESSE.)

This chapter aims at a refined, comprehensive overview of the extent and the kinds of lexical stability in the sense of the immediate continuation of Latin words in Romance on the one hand, and of the various factors that can govern the relationship between stability and change in the history of words on the other.

Immediate continuation means that the surviving forms are semantically stable and have merely undergone the regular sound changes. In contrast, various restrictions and specifications have to be made for some forms that do continue as such and are counted as 'stable' here. Apart from the 'semi-learnèd' forms discussed in section 3, they concern a few morphological normalizations that took place in vulgar Latin and numerous semantic changes.

Without exception, the highly irregular verbs of CLat., ESSE 'be', UELLE 'want', POSSE 'be able', are continued in their partially normalized forms *ˈɛssere, *voˈlere, *poˈtere; likewise, CLat. os, ossis 'bone' is normalized to its less ambiguous (see chapter 2: §1) variant OSSUM in all of the Romance domain (see *Thesaurus Linguae Latinae* 9,2, 1093):

vulgar Lat.	Ro.	It.	Srd.	RæR.	Fr.	Occ.	Cat.	Sp.	Pt.
*'ɛssere	(3SG *este*)	*essere*	*èssere*	*esser*	*être*	*èsser*	*ésser*	(*ser*)	(*ser*)
*vo'lere	*vrea*	*volere*	*bòliri*	*lair*	*vouloir*	*voler*	*voler*		
*po'tere	*putea*	*potere*	*pòtere*	*pudair*	*pouvoir*	*poder*	*poder*	*poder*	*poder*
*'ɔssu	*os*	*osso*	*óssu*	*öss*	*os*	*os*	*os*	*hueso*	*osso*

Semantic changes vis-à-vis the traditional and classical lexicon have already been mentioned in the example of AMARE, which shows the restriction or shift of synonyms. There are other types as well, namely survival confined to a partial meaning (e.g., FORTIS 'strong, brave' > only 'strong' in Romance), survival in the traditional and a new meaning (e.g., TEMPUS 'time' > poly-semous in Romance as 'time' + 'weather') and survival only in innovating meanings (e.g., CAUSA 'reason, matter, legal case' > 'thing' in Romance):

CLat.	Ro.	It.	Srd.	RæR.	Fr.	Occ.	Cat.	Sp.	Pt.
FORTIS	*foarte*[1]	*forte*	*fòrte*	*fort*	*fort*	*fort*	*fort*	*fuerte*	*forte*
TEMPUS	*timp*	*tempo*	*témpus*	*temp*	*temps*	*temps*	*temps*	*tiempo*	*tempo*
CAUSA		*cosa*	(*kása*)	*chosa*	*chose*	*causa*	*cosa*	*cosa*	*coisa*

The quantity of Latin words that are directly continued is discussed in section 2. There are fundamental differences in the proportions of the lexicon that are stable: distinctions can be drawn on the one hand between the Latin lexicon as a whole and the areas of it that are 'central' because of their high frequency of usage, and on the other hand – from a chronological and historical point of view – between what remains if only the more narrowly defined traditional lexicon of Classical Latin is considered, and what is left if the postclassical and vulgar Latin innovations are taken into account as well. Among other things, potential divergences in the degree of stability between the different classes of lexemes will have to be considered as well.

Concerning areal ('diatopic') distribution within Romance (at least in the early stages), the 'pan-Romance' lexemes, that is, those that survive in all languages (e.g., CÆLUM, MARE, MORI), are outnumbered by Latin words whose diachronic stability seems to be restricted to individual parts of the Romance domain, to judge from the transmitted texts. In this respect, our exposition differentiates between 'inter-Romance' continuation in the majority of the Romance languages (e.g., AMOR, AMARE) and 'regional Romance' continuation in the minority of them (e.g., SCIRE 'know' > only Ro. *şti*, Srd. *iskíre*; METUS 'fear' > only Sp. *miedo*, Pt. *medo*). Apart from survival in the early stages of the Romance tradition, which is of course important for judging the Latin–Romance continuity, the situation in the modern languages has to be looked at as well. In part, especially in Modern French, the number of inherited Latin words has been reduced severely.

Several factors, both extra-linguistic and intra-linguistic, can be adduced as preconditions and causes creating stability or lability among (traditional) Latin words in their development towards Romance.

These factors, which are discussed in section 4, can in individual cases often be effective at the same time. As a rule, they are not laws that determine the outcome of the developments, but merely tendencies that can explain them and probably had some influence on them.

From the beginning of Romance linguistics, the regionally divergent degree of continuation of the (traditional) Latin lexicon has been an important criterion for comparative characterization of the various Romance languages (for instance 'innovative' French vs. 'conservative' Ibero-Romance). This topic will be discussed in section 5 on the basis of a methodological critique. Finally, a special section (6) will be devoted to the relationship between the diatopic lexical separation of the Romance languages and the diasystemic complexity of the Latin lexicon, an issue which has mostly been neglected in older research.

The investigation of the history of Latin–Romance lexicon has long been a central area of historical Romance linguistics. Yet until very recently the main focus was the examination of individual words or designations, and here again more often than not the respective diachronic changes and thus divergences from traditional Latin. More general statements about the subject matter discussed here – stability and conformity – have remained rare and have hardly ever been more specific than Dante's intuitive observation cited above (*multa* 'many' or *alia fere omnia* 'and to almost all other things'). However, a justifiable position must take into account the aspects sketched out above and deal with the extent, kinds and conditioning factors of lexical Latin–Romance stability. It can only be reached on the basis of maximally systematic diachronic analyses of the (accessible) total lexicon and/or broad, representative areas thereof. With some necessary reservations, these requirements are met especially by the more recent studies by Moore (1989) and Stefenelli (1992a), on whose results the following exposition is based. Sala's 1988 book deals with the (synchronic) comparison between Latin and the modern Romance languages and is of only limited use when it comes to continuous diachronic developments (on this point, see also Koch 1997:5).

There are some basic restrictions and problems which mean that all the following figures have to be understood as approximate values. First, in individual cases it may be difficult to differentiate between continuous survival as inherited words and secondary, learnèd borrowings as 'Latinisms' (for example, in the relationship between Lat. CONTENTUS 'contented' or

PROMITTERE 'promise' and their Romance equivalents; see also section 3). Second, documentation of the early Romance lexicon is limited and varies from region to region with regard to age and previous lexicographical investigation. These and other reservations notwithstanding, it is the historical lexical comparison of Latin and Romance that also enables us to exploit unique possibilities. Through the selective criterion of survival versus non-survival we get substantiated, direct insights into the vitality of Latin words (in the spoken language) and into the degree of convergence between the lexicon of written and spoken Latin.

2 The quantitative extent of Latin–Romance lexical stability

2.1 The total lexicon

Even though the lexicon of the Romance languages is fundamentally Latin at its core, the total of Latin words taken over directly by the Romance languages turns out to be relatively small (Müller (1987:312) speaks of an 'extremely narrow inherited lexical basis'). In the lexeme corpus of the *Romanisches Etymologisches Wörterbuch* (*REW*) by W. Meyer-Lübke (1935), the number of Latin words continued directly amounts to barely 6000 (or about 7500 if unattested but reconstructed 'asterisked forms' are included). We should also consider the extensions that are necessary given the position of today's lexicographical research (e.g., following Wartburg's *Französisches Etymologisches Wörterbuch*; Moore 1989 does not include them). In this case, the figures can be increased to a good 7000 (9000). These slightly over 7000 attested words surviving directly in Romance could be compared to the exhaustive (but heterogeneous) total in the *Thesaurus Linguae Latinae* (1900–), which comprises about 50,000 lexemes. If we do this, we arrive at a Latin–Romance stability rate of at best 15 percent (see Stefenelli 1992a:22–32). However, we could also start from an inventory concentrating on the common traditional words of Latin (see §2.4), such as Cassell's *New Latin Dictionary* (Simpson (1964)) (14,848 lexemes), which was analysed by Moore (1989). This would mean that the figure rises to slightly more than 27 percent (4057 survivals versus 10,791 failures according to the *REW*; Moore 1989: 7).

2.2 The central lexicon

From the last figure above it emerges that there is an increase in the rate of stability if we look at the more common Latin lexemes. Again, this percentage rises very substantially if the direct continuation from Latin to Romance is examined especially with regard to the highly frequent words of the 'central lexicon' of (written) Latin.

To be sure, there is nothing that prevents several of the most frequent Latin words from being lost, to a great extent or even completely, as inherited lexemes in the development to Romance (see also Vincent 1988a:74). Examples include: ANIMUS 'soul, spirit, heart', BELLUM 'war', EQUUS 'horse', NATURA 'nature', SPES 'hope', URBS 'city', UIR 'man', UIS 'strength', FACILIS 'easy', PARUUS 'small', PULCHER 'beautiful', AGERE 'drive, act, do', DILIGERE 'love', EDERE 'eat', FERRE 'carry', FLERE 'weep', IUBERE 'order', LOQUI 'speak', PUTARE 'think, believe', RELINQUERE 'leave', UOCARE 'call', ETIAM 'also', NIHIL 'nothing', NUNC 'now', SAEPE 'often', UALDE 'very'.

Consequently, the Latin–Romance lexical stability cannot be extended to the intuitive 'almost all others' cited above, not even in the most narrowly defined core. Corresponding statements about the convergence between the central lexicon of spoken and written Latin, even in handbooks on Romance such as Tagliavini (1972:§47: 'undoubtedly the main nucleus of words must have been fundamentally common'), simply do not tally with the facts.

As a tendency, however, high frequency of usage seems to be a stabilizing factor (see §4) which increases the degree of convergence between the vocabulary of written and spoken Latin and furthers diachronic survival in Romance. The core lexicon, analysed systematically in Stefenelli (1992a) on the basis of the frequency dictionaries by Delatte *et al.* (1981) and Gardner (1971), comprises the thousand most frequent lexemes (nouns, adjectives and verbs) of traditional (written) Latin. If this is used as a basis, the percentage of direct continuation in Romance and consequently the (overall) rate of stability rises to roughly two thirds (67%; an analysis of the 1276 Latin words of the frequency list used by Moore (1989) yields a total of 769 survivals, i.e., around 60%). If only the five hundred or one hundred most frequent of these central lexemes are taken into account, the rate of stability increases to around 75% or 90%, respectively (see Stefenelli 1992a:36f.; 1996:370–72). Consequently, with the elements of the most common everyday vocabulary – as is shown by Stefenelli (1981:11) – even whole sentences can be formed whose words are in overwhelming agreement in the Latin and (most of) the Romance versions.

Apart from CÆLUM, MARE, MORI, which have already been given above, the following Latin words that survive in all of the Romance domain could be named as concrete examples of lexemes that are stable because they are frequentially 'central': ANNUS 'year', AQUA 'water', FILIUS 'son', MANUS 'hand', NOX 'night', UENTUS 'wind', BONUS 'good', BENE 'well', HERI 'yesterday', BIBERE 'drink', CREDERE 'believe', NASCI 'be born', RIDERE (vulgar Lat. 'ridere) 'laugh', UENIRE 'come', UIDERE 'see', IN 'in', AUT 'or':

Lat.	Ro.	It.	Srd.	RæR.	Fr.	Occ.	Cat.	Sp.	Pt.
ANNUS	*an*	*anno*	*ánnu*	*an*	*an*	*an*	*any*	*año*	*ano*
AQUA	*apă*	*acqua*	*ábba*	*aua*	*eau*	*aiga*	*aigua*	*agua*	*água*
FILIUS	*fiu*	*figlio*	*fídzu*	*figl*	*fils*	*filh*	*fill*	*hijo*	*filho*
MANUS	*mână*	*mano*	*mánu*	*ma(u)n*	*main*	*man*	*má*	*mano*	*mão*
NOX	*noapte*	*notte*	*nòtte*	*not*	*nuit*	*nuech*	*nit*	*noche*	*noite*
UENTUS	*vânt*	*vento*	*véntu*	*vent*	*vent*	*vent*	*vent*	*viento*	*vento*
BONUS	*bun*	*buono*	*bónu*	*bun*	*bon*	*bon*	*bo*	*bueno*	*bom*
BENE	*bine*	*bene*	*bene*	*bain*	*bien*	*be*	*be*	*bien*	*bem*
HERI	*ieri*	*ieri*	*eris*	*er*	*hier*	*er*	*hir*	*ayer*	*(heire)*
BIBERE	*bea*	*bere*	*bí(b)ere*	*baiver*	*boire*	*beure*	*beure*	*beber*	*beber*
CREDERE	*crede*	*credere*	*krèdere*	*crajer*	*croire*	*creire*	*creure*	*creer*	*crer*
NASCI	*naşte*	*nascere*	*náskere*	*nascher*	*naître*	*nàisser*	*néixer*	*nacer*	*nascer*
RIDERE	*râde*	*ridere*	*ridere*	*arir*	*rire*	*rire*	*riure*	*reir*	*rir*
UENIRE	*veni*	*venire*	*bènnere*	*gnir*	*venir*	*venir*	*venir*	*venir*	*vir*
UIDERE	*vedea*	*vedere*	*vídere*	*vere*	*voir*	*vèser*	*veure*	*ver*	*ver*
IN	*în*	*in*	*in*	*in*	*en*	*en*	*en*	*en*	*em*
AUT	*sau*[2]	*o*	*a*	*u*	*ou*	*o*	*o*	*o*	*ou*

2.3   The different word classes

The stability rates of the central vocabulary in Stefenelli (1992a) are valid in very much the same way for each of the word classes dealt with there, that is, for nouns, adjectives and verbs (with a slightly higher percentage for nouns with widespread continuation). By way of contrast, the rate of stability in the central area of the thousand most frequent lexemes turns out to be significantly lower for the adverbs (around 40%), but higher for the prepositions (around 78%).

Within the wider frame of the *New Latin Dictionary*, the total values differentiated according to word classes by Moore (1989:9f., 87) yield the highest rates of stability for the pronouns and prepositions, followed by the nouns (especially of the first, second and fifth declensions), verbs (especially of the first conjugation), conjunctions, adjectives and adverbs:

Word class	Total	Survivals (nominal values)	Survivals (percentage)
Nouns	5978	1967	33%
Verbs	4372	1197	27%
Adjectives	3723	753	20%
Adverbs	558	100	18%
Prepositions	24	16	67%
Conjunctions	32	7	22%
Pronouns	13	13	100%
Interjections	7	0	0%

Compared to the central area, adjectives are somewhat less stable here. The explanation must be that their frequency of usage is usually lower (see Moore 1989:12). The disappearance of traditional Latin adverbs, which is particularly thoroughgoing, is caused first and foremost by the morphological innovation in their formation in vulgar Latin and Romance (with -*mente*; see chapter 10). On the semantic side, Moore (1989:89) concludes: 'To sum up, adjectives and adverbs have a higher combined failure rate than other morphological categories, their semantic function tends towards vagueness and abstraction, and they lend themselves in literate societies to synonymic series considered unnecessary luxuries in primary oral societies.'

2.4   *The traditional, Classical vocabulary versus the postclassical, vulgar Latin innovations*

In section 2.1, a total of slightly more than 7000 Latin words was given as the approximate estimation of Romance words continued directly from Latin. This figure contains both traditional, Classical lexemes and postclassical, vulgar Latin innovations. According to Stefenelli (1992a:23), the traditional forms (i.e., those that are also Classical or attested since Classical times) prevail with a good 5000 units (around 4400 in the *REW*, cf. the above-mentioned, slightly lower figure of 4057 in Moore (1989)).

For part of the 'traditional' forms as well, diachronic lexical stability is restricted because of semantic changes in the vulgar Latin development leading on to Romance. In the course of an extensive reduction of synonyms (see among others Coseriu 1954:56–60; Elcock 1975:166; Stefenelli

1981:28–33; 1992a:119–24), many of the retained words undergo shifts in their semantic structures through the loss of traditional synonyms in vulgar Latin. Besides AMARE (> especially It., Srd. *amare*, Fr. *aimer*, Occ. *amar*), the following words have also been affected:

> FACERE 'make, do' (> Ro. *face*, It. *fare*, Srd. *fákere*, RæR. *far*, Fr. *faire*, Occ. *far*, *faire*, Cat. *fer*, Sp. *hacer*, Pt. *fazer*) through loss of AGERE
>
> PERDERE 'lose' (> Ro. *pierde*, It. *perdere*, Srd. *pèrdere*, RæR., Sp., Pt. *perder*, Fr., Occ., Cat. *perdre*) through loss of AMMITTERE
>
> MONSTRARE 'show' (> It. *mostrare*, Fr. *montrer*, Cat., Sp., Pt. *mostrar*) through loss of OSTENDERE
>
> OCCIDERE 'kill' (> Ro. *ucide*, It. *uccidere*, Srd. *okkídere*, OFr. *ocire*, Occ. *aucir*, OCat. *aucire*) through loss of INTERFICERE
>
> AMICUS 'friend' (> It. *amico*, Srd. *amíku*, RæR., Fr. *ami*, Occ., Cat. *amic*, Sp., Pt. *amigo*) through loss of FAMILIARIS
>
> HOMO 'man'[3] (> It. *uomo*, Srd. *ómine*, RæR. *om*, Fr. *homme*, Occ. *ome*, Cat. *home*, Sp. *hombre*, Pt. *homem*) through loss of UIR
>
> TRISTIS 'sad' (> Ro., RæR., Occ., Cat. *trist*, It., Fr., Sp., Pt. *triste*) through loss of MAESTUS.

Very many meaning shifts of vulgar Latin and proto-Romance come about because (often more expressive) variants with similar meanings prevail over the (usually colourless and neutral) terms of traditional Classical Latin. Compare:

> FABULARI 'chat, prattle' > 'speak' (> Sp. *hablar*, Pt. *falar*) for CLat. LOQUI
>
> PLORARE 'weep one's eyes out' > 'weep' (> Fr. *pleurer*, Occ., Cat. *plorar*, Sp. *llorar*, Pt. *chorar*) and PLANGERE 'mourn loudly' > 'weep' (> Ro. *plânge*, It. *piangere*, Srd. *prangere*) for CLat. FLERE
>
> PORTARE 'transport' > 'carry' (> Ro. *purta*, It. *portare*, RæR., Occ., Cat. *portar*, Fr. *porter*) for CLat. FERRE
>
> COMEDERE 'eat up' > 'eat' (> Sp., Pt. *comer*) and MANDUCARE 'munch' > 'eat' (> Ro. *mânca*, OIt. *manicare*, Srd. *mandigare*, RæR. *mangiar*, Fr. *manger*, Occ. *manjar*, Cat. *menjar*) for CLat. EDERE
>
> COMPARARE 'procure, acquire' > 'buy' (> Ro. *cumpăra*, It. *comprare*, Srd. *comporare*, RæR. *cumprar*, Occ., Cat., Sp., Pt. *comprar*) and ACCAPTARE (presumably ACCEPTARE + CAPTARE) > 'buy' (> especially Fr. *acheter*) for CLat. EMERE

AURICULA 'outer ear' > 'ear' (> Ro. *ureche*, It. *orecchia*, Srd. *orikra*, RæR. *uraglia*, Fr. *oreille*, Occ. *aurelha*, Cat. *orella*, Sp. *oreja*, Pt. *orelha*) for CLat. AURIS

CABALLUS 'hack' > 'horse' (> Ro. *cal*, It. *cavallo*, Srd. *kavaddu*, RæR. *chavagl*, Fr. *cheval*, Occ., Cat. *cavall*, Sp. *caballo*, Pt. *cavalo*) for CLat. EQUUS

CASA 'hut' > 'house' (> Ro. *casă*, It. *casa*, RæR. *chasa*, Occ., Cat., Sp., Pt. *casa*) for CLat. DOMUS (which survives only in Sardinian)

CIUITAS 'community of citizens' > 'city' (> It. *città*, Srd. *kitáde*, RæR. *cità*, Fr. *cité* (cf. *ville* < UILLA), Occ., Cat. *ciutat*, Sp. *ciudad*, Pt. *cidade*) for CLat. URBS

FORMOSUS 'well-formed' > 'beautiful' (> Ro. *frumos*, Sp. *hermoso*, Pt. *formoso*) and BELLUS 'pretty' > 'beautiful' (> It. *bello*, RæR. *bel*, Fr. *beau*, Occ. *bel*, Cat. *bell*) for CLat. PULCHER

GRANDIS 'huge' > 'great' (> It., Srd. *grande*, RæR., Fr., Occ. *grand*, Cat. *gran*, Sp., Pt. *grande*) for CLat. MAGNUS (survives only in Sardinian and OOccitan)

TOTUS 'the whole' > 'every' (> Ro. *tot*, It. *tutto*, Srd. *tottu*, RæR. *tuot*, Fr. *tout*, Cat. *tot*, Sp., Pt. *todo*) for CLat. OMNIS (survives only in Italian).

Meaning changes proper, which are more extensive, can partly be described as monosemizations when compared to the traditional and classical language, as in the type mentioned above, FORTIS 'brave', 'strong' > only 'strong'. Other examples are:

PARERE 'seem', 'obey' > only 'seem' (> Ro. *părea*, It. *parere*, Srd. *párrere*, RæR. *parair*, OFr. *paroir*, Occ., OCat. *pàrer*)

GRADUS 'step (pace)', 'step (of stair)' > only 'step (of stair)' (> It. *grado*, RæR. *gro*, OFr. *gré*, OOcc. *graza*, Cat. *grau*, Sp. *grado*, Pt. *grau*).

More frequently, however, polysemy arises, sometimes only temporarily, because new partial meanings are added – this is the type TEMPUS 'time' > 'time', 'weather'. Compare also:

ARDERE 'burn' (intransitive) > also transitively 'burn down' (> Ro. *arde*, It. *ardere*, Srd. *árdere*, RæR. *arder*, OFr. *ardoir*, *ardre*, Occ., OCat. *ardre*, Sp., Pt. *arder*)

DUBITARE 'doubt' > also 'fear' (> Fr. *douter*, Occ. *dobtar*, Cat. *dubtar*, Sp. *dudar*, Pt. *duvidar*)

MANERE 'stay' > also 'dwell, live' (> Ro. *mânea*, OIt. *manere*, OSrd. *manere*, RæR. *magnair*, OFr. *manoir*, OOcc., OSp. *maner*, OPt. *maer*)

SAPERE 'taste' > also (today sometimes exclusively) 'know' (> It. *sapere*, RæR. *savair*, Fr. *savoir*, Occ., Cat., Sp., Pt. *saber*)

TENERE 'hold' > also 'have' (> upper SIt. *tenere*, Srd. *tènnere*, Cat. *tenir*, Sp. *tener*, Pt. *ter*; see Rohlfs 1971b:§41)

RATIO 'calculation; understanding; rationale' > also 'reason, cause' and 'right' (> It. *ragione*, OSrd. *rathone*, RæR. *radschun*, Fr. *raison*, Occ. *rason*, Cat. *raó*, Sp. *razón*, Pt. *ração*)

MEDIUS 'middle' (adjective), MEDIUM 'middle' (noun) > also 'half' (adjective/noun) (> Ro. *miez*, It. *mezzo*, OSrd. *meiu*, RæR. *mez*, OFr. *mi*, Occ. *mieg*, Cat. *mig*, Sp. *medio*, Pt. *meio*).

Completely new, secondary meanings can also be found, of the type CAUSA 'reason, matter, legal case' > 'thing'. Other examples include:

MITTERE 'send' > 'set, lay, put (inside)' (> It. *mettere*, Srd. *míttere*, RæR. *metter*, Fr. *mettre*, Occ., OCat. *metre*, Sp., Pt. *meter*)

MINARI 'threaten' > 'lead' (> RæR. *manar*, Fr. *mener*, Occ., Cat. *menar*; see Koch 1997:150f., 204–6)

CAMPUS 'plain' > 'field' (> Ro. *câmp*, It. *campo*, Srd. *kámpu*, RæR., Fr. *champ*, Occ., Cat. *camp*, Sp., Pt. *campo*)

FOCUS 'fireplace' > 'fire' (> Ro. *foc*, It. *fuoco*, Srd. *fogu*, RæR. *fög*, Fr. *feu*, Occ., Cat. *foc*, Sp. *fuego*, Pt. *fogo*)

HOSTIS 'enemy' > 'army' (> Ro. *oaste*, OIt. *oste*, OFr., OOcc. *ost*, OCat. *host*, OSp. *hueste*, OPt. *hoste*).

However, among the one thousand most frequent central lexemes the quantity of the last category, i.e., forms of widespread continuation in only or almost only secondary meanings, remains relatively small, amounting to about 2.5%. On the other hand, the extent of all (more or less far-reaching) meaning changes reaches at least 15% (see Stefenelli 1992a:119–59, 160–78). For semantic changes and differentiations one should also compare the fundamental work by Koch (1997), containing detailed analyses especially of Latin LEUARE and its Romance continuations (Klein 1997:95–168), and of the verbs belonging to the semantic field 'physical activity exerted on objects' (Klein 1997:169–263).

Most of the morphological postclassical innovations (see Stefenelli 1992a:179–91), which often take the place of dwindling traditional forms, are affixal extensions. Compare:

AERAMEN (third century) as pan-Romance replacement of CLat. AES 'ore, copper': Ro. *aramă*, It. *rame*, Srd. *ramene*, RæR. *aram*, Fr. *airain*, Occ., OCat. *aram*, Sp. *alambre*, Pt. *arame*

APPERTINERE (sixth century), inter-Romance besides PERTINERE 'belong to': It. *appartenere*, Fr. *appartenir*, Occ. *apertener*

ABANTE (since the *Itala Bible*), inter-Romance beside ANTE 'before': ORo. *ainte*, It. *avanti*, RæR., Fr., Occ., Cat. *avant*.

Many new derivations that have been formed for reasons of morphological interconnection belong here as well. Cases in point are:

FORTIA 'strength' (third century), cf. FORTIS 'strong', as inter-Romance replacement of CLat. UIS 'strength' (perhaps via FORTIA FACTA): It., RæR., *forza*, Fr. *force*, Occ., Cat. *força*, Sp. *fuerza*, Pt. *força*

SEMINARE 'sow' (first century), cf. SEMEN 'seed', as pan-Romance replacement of CLat.

SERERE: Ro. *sem na*, It. *seminare*, Srd. *semenare*, RæR. *semnar*, Fr. *semer*, Occ. *semenar*, Sp. *sembrar*, Pt. *semear*

MENSURARE 'measure' (since the *Itala Bible*), cf. MENSURA 'measurement', as inter-Romance replacement of CLat. METIRI (> only Srd., Sp., Pt.): Ro. *măsura*, It. *misurare*, Srd. *mesurare*, RæR. *masürar*, Fr. *mesurer*, Occ., Cat. (Sp., Pt.) *mesurar*

PARABOLARE 'speak' (seventh century), cf. vulgar Lat. PARABOLA 'word', as central Romance replacement of CLat. LOQUI, or FABULARI (> Sp., Pt.): It. *parlare*, Fr. *parler*, Occ., Cat. *parlar*.

2.5   The areal distribution of surviving forms

The degrees of diachronic lexical stability given so far are reduced quite heavily if the areal distribution of surviving forms within the Romance-speaking world is taken into account as well. Only a minority of Latin words surviving as such exhibit regionally unrestricted stability in the sense of 'pan-Romance' distribution over all the Romance languages (at least in their early stages). According to the available documents, about three times as many are missing in individual or most languages and thus have to be classified as 'inter-Romance' or 'regional Romance' as regards their immediate continuation (see §5 below). If just the words found in all or most of the Romance languages are considered, the total number of lexemes continued directly from Latin decreases to the relatively low figure of about 2300 (c. 1750 traditional and slightly more than 500 postclassical words; see Stefenelli 1992a:24–31). Among the thousand most frequent Latin central lexemes the percentages of the three distributional types distinguished here are roughly (Stefenelli 1992a:35): 14% pan-Romance; 23% inter-Romance; 19% regional Romance.

Particularly frequent among the inter-Romance word types, as was pointed out above for AMOR and AMARE, are those which are absent solely from Romanian (in all, over 500 words see Gossen 1982; §5 below). If, therefore, this easternmost region were to be excluded, the share of 'pan-Romance' units of the basic lexicon would increase to over 20%.

2.6   The older forms of Romance versus the modern languages

The approximate figures given so far refer to Latin–Romance lexical stability in the sense of immediate continuation of inherited words in at least the older phases of documentation of the Romance languages. As some of these Latin words which at first are continued are lost in the subsequent internal lexical developments of the various Romance languages, the figures can sometimes be far lower if the measurements are based on the modern languages and consider continuous diachronic stability until the present. With regard to the thousand most frequent Latin central lexemes, for example, the rate of Latin–Romance stability drops from the approximately 67% mentioned above to around 50%, and the share of pan-Romance survivals is reduced from the roughly 14% above to merely about 8% today. The element of stability diminishes particularly strongly in the history of French. Here, more than a third of the traditional Latin lexemes continued at first in OFrench are lost completely during the development to Modern French (see Stefenelli 1981, especially 169–205; 1992a:97).

3   The 'semi-learnèd' forms

We call 'semi-learnèd' those Romance forms that have undergone only part of the expected sound changes, in other words, forms whose popular, native phonological developments have been impeded by the 'learnèd' influence of the Latin language of education and writing (see also Pountain, this volume, chapter 13: §3). Concrete examples are all or most of the Romance continuations of Latin EXEMPLUM 'example', PERICULUM 'danger' or LIBER 'book' (from which we would, for instance, expect *loivre instead of livre in French if the word had developed purely according to the sound laws):

Lat.	It.	Fr.	Occ.	Cat.	Sp.	Pt.
PERICULUM	pericolo	péril	perilh	perill	peligro	perigo
LIBER	libro	livre	libre	llibre	libro	libro

More often than not, the semi-learnèd forms have been treated as mere phonological aberrations or special cases by traditional researchers. But through their formal non-conformity they are in many cases important witnesses to the limited frequency with which these notions are expressed in the language of the people, or for the fact that the vitality of the words differed along socio-culturally definable lines. In the postclassical period, notions such as 'book' seem to have been expressed only sporadically in spontaneous Latin, especially among the lower classes. Consequently, their unstable designations were exposed to the formal influences of the traditional pronunciation of these words, which were actualized much more commonly in educated Latin. The forms could thus evade the sound changes in part. In other words, in such cases the differences in phonological 'stability' can reflect degrees of lexical stability that diverge socio-culturally and are, on the whole, only limited.

Regarding the socio-cultural diversity of the (vulgar) Latin on which the Romance languages are based, and the interferences between the different sociolectal varieties that can arise from time to time in this context, the development of Latin PENSARE is particularly illuminating. Following the general tendency that abstract, mental notions are given concrete, graphic designations (see Stefenelli 1992a:172–74), the verb, which had the concrete meaning 'weigh', also became used figuratively for the abstract concept 'think'. From a socio-cultural point of view, this new, postclassical usage seems to have primarily colloquial origins. As an interference 'from the bottom up' it is also taken over by educated circles and thus manages to replace the traditional, classical verb COGITARE everywhere (the latter survives almost only in secondary usages). Yet in its phonological development into Romance, vulgar Latin *pen'sare 'think' differs from 'weigh': it consistently exhibits a (semi-)learnèd character because it preserves the cluster /ns/ (It., Srd. *pensare*, RæR. *pensar*, Fr. *penser*, Occ., Cat., Sp., Pt. *pensar* 'think' vs. *pesare, peser, pesar*, etc. 'weigh'). This reflects the influence of the educated, socio-culturally elevated variant on the less current form, which was used relatively rarely in the colloquial language. Consequently, we are also dealing with an interference 'from the top down' (see Stefenelli 1995a:39f.).

4   Factors that can influence lexical stability

Accounting for the relationship between lexical stability and change in the development from Latin to Romance involves a multi-layered set of problems. The varying degrees of diachronic stability of Latin words seem to be governed by the interplay of several extra- and intra-linguistic factors. These different factors may function partly as general preconditions (for example, favouring stability), partly as actual causes. As a rule, however, they are not inevitable or predictable laws, but merely more or less marked tendencies that can give us likely (partial) explanations.

One extra-linguistic precondition for the lexical stability of a designation is, above all, the material stability of the extra-linguistic referent. Besides the obvious relationship between loss of the thing and loss of the word, it seems that certain changes in the history of the things, which do continue as such, can tend to lower the stability of the traditional words. Thus, it is plausible that the remarkably low stability of traditional Latin military terms is also caused by the material dissolution or change of the traditional Roman army and military systems. Among others, the following words are lost entirely, or to a large extent, as inherited lexemes: BELLUM 'war', MILES 'soldier', EXERCITUS 'army', AGMEN 'army on the march', CASTRA 'camp', PROELIUM 'battle', PUGNA 'fight' (noun), PUGNARE 'fight' (verb). On the other hand, the Latin–Romance lexical stability of IUDEX 'judge' (noun; > inter-Romance) and IUDICARE 'judge' (verb; continued throughout Romance) corresponds to the higher material stability of the legal system (see Stefenelli 1992a:41f.).

From the frequency-dependent divergences in the stability rate, which are discussed in sections 2.1 and 2.2, it becomes clear that high frequency of usage of a word or high frequency of actualization of the notion expressed by it is a factor that certainly furthers stability. However, for the development to Romance it is, of course, the frequency and vitality within the spontaneous discourse of (late) vulgar Latin that is decisive, and often it is the immediate continuation of lexemes into Romance that these can be deduced from. Yet this frequency sometimes stands in marked contrast to the word frequencies of Classical Latin (see also §2.4). Especially, many abstract nouns common in the classical written language are not continued as inherited words, for instance ELOQUENTIA 'eloquence', FELICITAS 'happiness', MEMORIA 'memory', SAPIENTIA 'wisdom', or also a general term such as NATURA 'nature'. The reason is that these abstract notions were not very popular in the spontaneous spoken language, that is, they were hardly ever actualized. (But many of these abstract nouns were later borrowed as learnèd 'Latinisms' by the newly developing Romance languages of writing and education.) The loss of several other Classical central lexemes has less obvious reasons, compare BELLUM 'war', or the verbs of motion ABIRE 'go away', PROFICISCI 'set off', PERGERE 'go on'. As a diachronically destabilizing factor we can assume that they were unnecessary and thus could be lost more or less without replacement to the extent that the terms in question seem to have been actualized relatively rarely in the spoken language – in stark contrast to the written language. In spoken discourse, a collective noun such as BELLUM was rare as compared to its concrete partial aspects ('combat', 'attack'). The same holds true for the specific verbs of motion mentioned above as opposed to the general verb for 'going', which is IRE or its successors, which are usually sufficient in oral communication (see Stefenelli 1992a:102–18; 1992b).

In those areas of the Roman Empire that were Latinized secondarily the vitality, and thus the diachronic stability, of some Latin words, especially for terms connected with 'the land', such as plants, can also be restricted by holding on to autochthonous, pre-Roman substrate terms. This happened, for example, with the names for the 'oak', where, besides Latin QUERCUS and ROBUR, five different words of pre-Roman languages are continued in individual parts of the Romània (see Rohlfs 1971b:§70). On the whole, however, an analysis such as that by Moore (1989) of twenty-two 'semantic categories' yields, as one might expect, that it is the materially very stable 'elementary' areas such as 'animals' or 'agriculture, vegetation' that have a particularly high rate of lexical stability. Moore (1989:107f.) writes:

> it is clear that the highest rates of lexical retention are in the areas of primal necessity, i.e., agriculture, animals, the natural world, family relationships, parts of the body, food and drink, clothing and the dwelling place.

To be sure, it is only natural that the stability of designation of the different terms should also vary according to the different degrees in which they are exposed to the forces of word change. In this respect, one possible influence is first and foremost the varying degrees of emotion that the various terms convey, and hence the different amounts of pressure that more expressive variants exert on their emotionally neutral counterparts. In this way, Rohlfs (1971b:158–61) explains, for instance, the contrast between (relative) stability of the words for 'great' (MAGNUS > regional Romance; GRANDIS > inter-Romance) or 'good' (BONUS > pan-Romance) and innovative multiplicity of designations among the more emotional antonyms 'little' and 'bad'. But the difference in closeness to an emotional mode of expression can, among other things, also explain the fact that Latin DICERE is retained almost throughout the Romance domain (except for Sardinian) as the designation of the emotionally quite neutral concept 'say', while LOQUI, being the (too) objective and neutral expression for the notion 'speak', which is a more emotional matter, is replaced especially by its more expressive synonym FABULARI 'chat, gossip' in vulgar Latin. An interpretation along the same lines might also seem to suggest itself for the vulgar Latin replacement of the traditional normal verbs EDERE 'eat' and FLERE 'cry' by (at first) more expressive variants (see §2.4) because these concepts are quite emotional. However, the comparable terms 'drink' (BIBERE > pan-Romance) and 'laugh' (RIDERE > pan-Romance) are stable, even though they can hardly be said to be less affective. Consequently, the factor 'emotion' should also be seen as a general precondition which in most cases becomes effective only in combination with other factors.

Other such stabilizing or destabilizing influences are especially the formal characteristics of Latin words. Further destabilizing factors involved in the above-mentioned decline of EDERE and FLERE seem to have been the formal handicaps of monosyllabic shortness of some forms and of irregularity, which do not exist, or do not do so to such an extent, in BIBERE and RIDERE. Shortness and irregularity in themselves are not cogent reasons for the loss or replacement of a form, especially if it is a frequent one. Still, their potentially destabilizing effect is particularly evident from two facts: in verbs like EDERE and FLERE it seems to be the monosyllabic forms in the paradigm that are being avoided and replaced first (see Stefenelli 1992a:73), and statistically, the rate of stability is considerably higher for the regular Latin verbs in -ARE than for the irregular forms (see Stefenelli 1992a:81; Moore 1989:10, 25). As other formal factors in the loss of individual forms we also ought to consider the potential disadvantage of homophony (see Stefenelli 1992a:67–72) and, in presumably many cases of replacement of a word, the lack of recognizable affinities to word families and thus of morphological motivation (see Stefenelli 1979). The replacement of the traditional verb SERERE 'sow' in vulgar Latin by the new derivation SEMI-NARE (cf. Lat. SEMEN 'seed') in all of the Romance domain, for example, can probably be explained by the interplay of the tendency towards motivation, the desire for non-homophonous clarity (cf. Lat. SERERE 'line up'), and the wish to achieve regular simplicity.

5   **The behaviour of the individual Romance linguistic areas or languages with regard to lexical stability**

In the majority of cases, as has already been explained in section 2.5, lexical stability in the sense of the immediate continuation of Latin words in Romance (at least in the early stages thereof) concerns only some partial areas of the Romance domain. In principle, almost all imaginable types of geolinguistic distribution are possible here, for example general ('inter-Romance') distribution except for Romanian (e.g., in the case of AMOR 'love'), Sardinian (e.g., DICERE 'say'), French (e.g., DARE 'give'), Spanish and Portuguese (e.g., UELLE 'want'):

Lat.	Ro.	It.	Srd.	RæR.	Fr.	Occ.	Cat.	Sp.	Pt.
AMOR		amore	amore	amur	amour	amor	amor	amor	amor
DICERE	zice	dire		dir	dire	dire	dir	decir	dizer
DARE	da	dare	dare	dar		dar	dar	dar	dar
UELLE	vrea	volere	bòliri	lair	vouloir	voler	voler		

Similarly, a word may survive as a popular form only in Romanian (e.g., FELIX 'happy' > *ferice*), Italian (OMNIS 'every' > *ogni*), Sardinian (FERRE 'carry' > *ferrere*), Raeto-Romance (DIU 'long' > Lad. *di*), French (MORES 'customs' > *mœurs*), Occitan (EUADERE 'escape' > *evasir*), Catalan (FRETUM 'straits' > *freu*), Spanish and Portuguese (METUS 'fear' > *miedo, medo*); see Stefenelli (1992a:92–97; 1996:381).

Some types of distribution, however, turn out to be comparatively frequent and can thus to a certain extent appear characteristic of the respective nature of the Latinity. First and foremost, the familiar gaps for Romanian belong here (see Gossen 1982). Examples besides AMOR, AMARE also include: AMICUS 'friend', COLOR 'colour', CONSILIUM 'advice', CORPUS 'body', MATER 'mother', CARUS 'beloved', DURUS 'hard', FALSUS 'false', MALUS 'bad', PAUPER 'poor', SOLUS 'alone', DEBERE 'must', FINIRE 'finish', LEGERE 'read'. The frequent occurrence of survivals exclusive or nearly exclusive to Sardinian is also relevant in this context (see Wagner 1951:84–88; Rohlfs 1971b:201). Besides FERRE compare also: DOMUS 'house' (> *domo*), IANUA 'door' (> *yánna*), ONUS 'burden' (> *ónus*), MAGNUS 'great' (> *mannu*), DECERE 'be appropriate' (> *dekere*), DISCERE 'learn' (> OSrd. *diskere*), INUENIRE 'find' (> *imbennere*), SCIRE 'know' (> *iskire*), UERBERARE 'beat' (> *verberare*), CRAS 'tomorrow' (> *kras*; see Rohlfs 1971b:§27; Elcock 1975:174, 178f.).

With regard to affinities over larger areas, we can, like Rohlfs (1971b:78–88), stress specific convergences of stability between Romanian and Ibero-Romance which, corresponding to Matteo Bartoli's 'areal norms', could be described as particularly conservative and 'archaic' Romance border areas (see also Stefenelli 1981:93–98; 1996:382f.). This can be seen, for example, in the continuation of: HUMERUS 'shoulder' > esp. Ro. *umăr*, Sp. *hombro*, Pt. *ombro*; MENSA 'table' > esp. Ro. *masă*, Srd., Sp., Pt. *mesa*; ANGUSTUS 'narrow' > esp. Ro. *îngust*, Sp., OPt. *angosto*; FERUERE 'boil' > esp. Ro. *fierbe*, Sp. *hervir*, Pt. *ferver*.

In several older works, the Spanish or Ibero-Romance Latinity, for instance, is described as particularly 'conservative', or the proto-French

Latinity of northern Gaul as particularly 'innovative' and distanced from Latin. Such characterizations are based on selected examples and are thus always over-schematic and problematic. The comparative characterization of languages can only reach adequate (and usually far more differentiated) results by observing certain methodological principles (see Stefenelli 1995b). Objective examination of a larger lexical corpus shows that in comparison with the traditional Latin lexicon, every area of the Romance domain generally exhibits both conservative or stable and innovative features which are, in each case, the results of diasystemically complex developmental processes (see §6). In this respect, the traditional features of Ibero-Romance, which do exist (for the divergences within Ibero-Romance, see Pötters 1970; for Catalan, see Koppelberg 1998), are counterbalanced by many specific, idiosyncratic developments and losses of stability in this linguistic area. Retention of the following words is characteristic of Ibero-Romance: AUIS 'bird' (> Srd., Sp., Pt. *ave*), METUS 'fear' (> Sp. *miedo*, Pt. *medo*), SENSUS 'sense, intelligence' (> Sp. *seso*, Pt. *siso*), FOEDUS 'ugly' (> Sp. *feo*, Pt. *feio*), METIRI 'measure' (> Srd. *medire*, Sp., Pt. *medir*), PARERE 'give birth' (> Sp., Pt. *parir*).

But there are also several specific semantic innovations and morphological extensions, such as: GERMANUS for FRATER 'brother' (> Sp. *hermano*, Pt. *irmão*; see Elcock 1975:177), PRIMUS for COSOBRINUS 'cousin' (> Sp., Pt. *primo*), QUAERERE for UELLE, AMARE 'want, love' (> Sp., Pt. *querer*), SPERARE for EXSPECTARE 'hope' (> Sp., Pt. *esperar*) or CAPITIA for CAPUT 'head' (> Sp. *cabeza*, Pt. *cabeça*), *kora'tjone for COR 'heart' (> Sp. *corazón*, Pt. *coração*), *ma'njana for MANE 'tomorrow' (Sp. *mañana*, Pt. *amanhã*). And the abovementioned conservative convergence between the Romanian and Ibero-Romance border areas does indeed find a counterpart in some conservative peculiarities of the 'central Romania', for example in the continuation of FLUMEN 'river' > (among others) It. *fiume*, OFr. *flun*.

If regional divergences in the degree of stability are not only to be judged by the idiosyncratic 'archaisms', but also by the total number of retained Latin lexemes, which is undoubtedly the more meaningful figure (provided there is comparable documentation), then taking into account the thousand most frequent central lexemes of (written) Latin, analysed systematically in Stefenelli (1992a:96f.), we get the following extensive rates of stability for the individual Romance languages, or at least their early stages (in order of increasing stability):

Ro.	Srd.	RæR.	Cat.	Pt.	Sp.	Fr.	Occ.	It.
273	346	376	405	420	428	454	486	527

These figures make the conservative and archaic character of Sardinian, usually emphasized in a special way, appear far less prominent (certainly also for reasons of documentation). It is the Italian and southern Gallic (Occitan) linguistic areas that turn out to be the lexically most 'stable' regions. However, we can also see that even the Latinity of proto-French, innovative though it is in many individual traits (see Stefenelli 1981:105–8), continues, on the whole, more traditional Latin words than the Ibero-Romance languages (see also Stefenelli 1981:110f.; on the lexical closeness to Latin of the oldest literary monument, the Eulalia Sequence, see Stefenelli 1981:124–27; 1998:62f.; on the inner-Gallo-Romance divergences, see Schmitt 1974; on Raeto-Romance, see Haiman and Benincà 1992:154–64).

Yet if the modern languages are compared, the rate of stability in French is diminished very clearly as a result of its comparatively strong internal changes (see §2.6). On the other hand, the salience of Italian as being the most conservative and lexically most 'stable' of the Romance languages is increased even further (see Stefenelli (1992c) on the resulting degrees of transferability of Latin vocabulary in learning the various Romance languages):

Ro.	Fr.	Srd.	RæR.	Sp.	Cat.	Occ.	Pt.	It.
230	288	301	315	341	345	366	368	412

6 The diasystemic complexity of Latin and the regional lexical separation of the Romance languages

The Latin language was a complex structure of varieties ('diasystem'). It also had lexical variation, especially in stylistic, socio-cultural, regional and diachronic respects. In a correspondingly complex process, the postclassical diachronic development to the Romance languages leads to far-reaching diasystemic shifts, for example concerning the relative strength of various competing synonyms. From this complex dynamic, the main preconditions arise both for the relationship between stability versus loss of the (traditional) Latin lexicon (see §2.4), and for the resulting divergences between the individual Romance languages separating in space.

Because of the specific conditions of oral communication (see §4), the lexemes of (written) Latin that are not continued have sometimes been lost more or less without substitutes, but in most cases they have been replaced by other, competing variants. These replacements are usually synonyms or near-synonyms within Latin that were preferred in the varieties of spontaneous speech (at first especially of the socio-culturally lower classes) because they had advantages with regard to their content or form (see §2.4).

In the diachronic development to Romance, this diasystemic interplay between different variants often results in regional divergences concerning the respective status of the competing lexemes. These divergences then end in the lexical separation and differentiation of the various areas of the Romània. In essence, two main types of regionally diverging behaviour, and thus of geographic Romance differentiation, can be distinguished here (note that the two types can be combined as well): first, the traditional Latin standard designation may be continued in part of the Romània, while being replaced in other regions (e.g., the word for 'know': CLat. SCIRE in Romanian and Sardinian versus the replacement from SAPERE elsewhere); and second, the Romance areas may each choose one of several competing replacements (which are at first common vulgar Latin), thus giving up the traditional term more or less completely (cf. the replacement of CLat. PULCHER 'beautiful' by FORMOSUS VS. BELLUS; of CLat. FLERE 'weep' by PLORARE VS. PLANGERE; or of EDERE 'eat' by COMEDERE VS. MANDUCARE).

However, it is essential to recognize that each of the regional varieties of Latin underlying the Romance languages (for example, 'proto-French' or 'proto-Spanish') at first also had complex diasystems; this has not been sufficiently taken into account in traditional research. Consequently, we must, for example, assume that in the proto-Romance history of the word 'eat' both of the replacements mentioned at first coexisted in all the regional diasystems (that is, COMEDERE could also be found in Gaul and MANDUCARE also in the Latinity of Spain). It is only in the period of change to Romance that this coexistence of synonyms led to mutually exclusive, geolinguistic oppositions. These oppositions had the different status of the forms in the diasystems as their starting point, and they depended on the regionally diverging interplay between the varieties (see Stefenelli 1992a:86–88; 1995a:37; 1996:369; 1998:61f.).[4]

12   LEXICAL CHANGE[1]

Steven N. Dworkin

Lexical change encompasses two distinct phenomena. The first involves changes in the semantic structure or meaning of the signifier, the area traditionally known as semantic change. Lexical change also includes the demise of lexical items with the passage of time, as well as the addition and incorporation of new vocabulary into the lexicon. Most neologisms result from inter-linguistic borrowing or from processes of internal derivational morphology. As borrowings and derivational processes are treated elsewhere in this work, I shall limit this presentation of lexical change in the Romance languages to issues in semantic change (at the level of the individual word) and lexical loss. However, the creation of new lexical items through processes of derivational morphology and through borrowings from other languages has implications for a description of the historical processes of semantic change (especially if viewed from an onomasiological perspective) as well as of lexical loss.

The analysis of semantic change differs from the study of change at other levels. Phonological and morphological change involve dealing at any given moment with a finite number of basic units (phonemes, inflectional and derivational morphemes). Phonological and morphological change essentially lead to the loss or addition of phonemes or morphemes. In contrast, semantic change deals with an infinite number of elements (words) and an infinite number of semantic features (meanings). The acquisition by a word of a new meaning often (perhaps usually) does not entail the (immediate) loss of its earlier meaning(s). Strictly speaking, words do not acquire new meanings; speakers simply end up using them in different ways. Nerlich and Clarke (1988) make a useful distinction between micro-dynamic/short-term semantic change, related to the actual speech event, and macro-dynamic/long-term semantic change with long-term consequences. It is this latter category which is studied in historical linguistics. Certainly the adage traditionally attributed to Jules Gilliéron, 'Each word has its own history', originally formulated as a reaction to the Neogrammarian concept of sound laws, seems applicable to traditional diachronic semantics at what Traugott and Dasher (2002:4) call the micro-level of the individual lexical item. In historical Romance linguistics, most relevant studies, until recently, have dealt with the specific details of the semantic evolution of individual words, lexical fields or concepts (*'Begriffsgeschichte'*), without systematically paying attention to broader theoretical issues concerning the causes and the nature of semantic change. The authors of the great Romance etymological dictionaries, Wilhelm Meyer-Lübke (*Romanisches Etymologisches Wörterbuch* 1935), Walther von Wartburg (*Französisches Etymologisches Wörterbuch* 1928–) and Juan Coromines (*Diccionario crítico etimológico de la lengua castellana* 1954–57, [with José Antonio Pascual] *Diccionario crítico etimológico castellano e hispánico* 1980–91) were all products of the period of Neogrammarian dominance. They placed greater emphasis on justifying the formal evolution of a word from its etymon than on its semantic history. The different stages in a word's semantic evolution may have been identified and illustrated in a typical dictionary entry, but rarely did the reader find description, much less analysis, of the relevant causes and mechanisms. At best, Romance etymological dictionaries have contributed raw data for the study of diachronic semantics. Even such a prolific scholar in the field of diachronic Romance lexicology as Yakov Malkiel, concerned as he was in his writings with issues of theory and methodology, chose not to treat questions concerning the nature of semantic change in the many etymological studies where he carefully traced the semantic history of the word(s) under study.

This chapter is not the appropriate place for a thorough and detailed critical review of research in the field of diachronic Romance lexical semantics (a task carried out in Baldinger 1991; Stefenelli 1996; Blank 2003). Until fairly recently, most work in historical Romance semantics tended to employ a philological/socio-historical approach based largely on the writings of Stephen Ullmann, especially as reflected in chapter 4, 'Historical Semantics,' of his influential book *The Principles of Semantics* (1957). In addition to changes brought about by external factors, Ullmann operated with several essentially binary taxonomies of processes of semantic change: generalization or broadening of meaning vs. specialization or narrowing of meaning; pejoration or development of a negative meaning vs. amelioration or development of a less negative meaning; change resulting from metaphor vs. change resulting from metonymy. Recently several specialists have called into question various facets of Ullmann's conclusions (Geeraerts 1997; Blank 1997 – prepared as a corrective to Ullmann, as well as Traugott and Dasher 2002). They observe that Ullmann's classifications of semantic change are in reality classifications of mechanisms and results or consequences, not of causes. Metaphor, metonymy, generalization, specialization, amelioration and pejoration indicate what happened in the semantics of a particular word, but do not explain the motivation for the change, a topic to which Blank returns later (Blank 1999:70; 2001:95–99). The same criticisms can be made with regard to diachronic structural semantics as outlined (with copious Latin and Romance exemplification) in Eugenio Coseriu's seminal paper 'Pour une sémantique diachronique structurale' (1964). This approach involved positing the loss or addition of semantic features to a given word's semantic structure and the possible consequences of such shifts on the semantic features of other members of the lexical field at issue. Diachronic structural semantics enjoyed a certain vogue in Spain, where Gregorio Salvador directed a number of doctoral dissertations which described and compared the lexical composition and structure of selected semantic fields (e.g., 'dimension', 'age', 'women', 'to speak', 'to seize') at given moments in the history of Spanish, including its Latin prelude (for bibliographic details, see Salvador 1988). Critiques of Coseriu's approach to diachronic semantics can be found in Blank (1996) and Lebsanft and Glessgen (2004).

Over the last two decades, fruitful new insights into the nature of semantic change have come from linguists operating within the related frameworks of prototype theory and cognitive semantics. Many areas of human activity and life are understood metaphorically, i.e., language and cognition very often operate metaphorically (Sweetser 1990:17). Recently, some specialists in historical linguistics (Sweetser, Traugott) have sought to identify overarching and predictable cross-linguistic (potentially universal) regularities in semantic change and have highlighted the extent to which meaning change, as well as meaning itself, is structured by cognition. Linguists have long known that very often the abstract senses of a word derive from earlier concrete meanings (rather than the other way round). Various workers have argued for the essential unidirectionality of many types of semantic change across languages. Recent work has shown that in certain semantic domains there is a 'deep cognitive predisposition' (Sweetser 1990:18) to turn to specific concrete domains to derive vocabulary for specific abstract domains. Metaphor seems to be one of the most important connections between such domains. By using the idea of systematic metaphorical structuring of one domain in terms of another, cognitive semantics purports to be able to throw light on the motivation for and processes of meaning change. Some linguists have spoken of the quest for 'cognitive principles that guide lexical change like an invisible hand' (Koch 1999:333), applying to semantic change the notion of the 'invisible hand' introduced into historical linguistics from the realm of economics by Rudi Keller. Kurt Baldinger (1989; 1993) has called into question the applicability of the notion of the 'invisible hand' to semantic change, and Koch prefers to speak of a weak version of the invisible hand hypothesis, with regard to semantic change (1999:331; 2005).

The role of metaphor and metonymy in semantic change has been recognized since the pioneering work of Michel Bréal and Arsène Darmesteter (the latter's 1886 treatise *La Vie des mots étudiée dans leurs significations* can be described as the first systematic study of Romance diachronic semantics). In traditional diachronic semantics, metaphor and metonymy were treated as rhetorical devices. According to cognitive semantics, metaphor is a major structuring force in semantic change, operating between domains. Although linguists have identified numerous cross-linguistic metaphorical and metonymic patterns observable in semantic change, one cannot predict whether a given word will actually undergo a specific semantic shift. The repertory of diachronic semantic processes exploited by speakers is limited and universal. To use an oft-cited example, in many languages the verb meaning 'seize, grasp' has metaphorically evolved the sense 'understand' (e.g., Lat. CAPERE 'grasp, seize' > It. *capire* 'understand'; It. *afferrare* 'grasp' > 'understand'; COMPRÆHENDERE 'take firmly, seize' > Fr. *comprendre*, Sp. *comprender* 'understand', Sp. *coger* 'grasp, seize (an idea)'; in contemporary colloquial Spanish *pillar* 'to seize, grasp' is undergoing the same evolution. However, it cannot be predicted with absolute certainty that all verbs meaning 'seize, grasp' will at some point in their history necessarily undergo this development. Such changes tend to be unidirectional: 'grasp, seize' > 'understand', but never 'understand' > 'grasp, seize'. In like fashion, other words for the notion 'to understand' originally denoted other types of physical action: e.g., Fr. *entendre*, Sp. *entender* < Lat. INTENDERE 'to stretch', as well as the metaphor underlying Eng. *to understand*, Ger. *verstehen*.

Geeraerts (1992), who operates within the framework of cognitive semantics with a prototype model of semantic structure, emphasizes the overlap between the historical–philological approach to historical lexical semantics (e.g., Ullmann) and cognitive semantics. He argues that 'prototypicality, as a principle organizing the semasiological structure of lexical items, plays an important functional role in the language and should therefore be properly incorporated into a functionally-oriented classification of lexical changes' (Geeraerts 1997:84). Unfortunately for us this author does not apply his principles of diachronic prototype semantics to the Romance languages. Koch (1995) seeks to show how prototype semantics can explain the workings of some processes of semantic change, especially the widening or narrowing of a word's semantic scope. His Romance examples include the acquisition by the descendants of Lat. PASSER 'sparrow' of the more general meanings '(small) bird' in Sp. *pájaro* and 'bird' in Ro. *pasăre*, as well as the evolution *ADRIPARE 'to reach the shore' > Fr. *arriver*, It. *arrivare* 'to arrive', and of the conflation of the meanings of Lat. HOMO 'human being' and VIR 'male human' in the semantic scope of the former in spoken Latin (Fr. *homme*, Sp. *hombre*, It. *uomo*, etc.). In these cases the sparrow represents the prototypical bird, travel by boat allegedly represented for some speakers of Latin the prototypical way of arriving at a destination, and the male is considered the prototypical human. Koch specifically states that the prototype model has its limitations as an explanatory tool and it cannot account for all instances of the widening or narrowing of a word's semantic range.

The application of the insights provided by cognitive semantics to Romance historical semantics is still very much in its infancy. In the first part of this chapter, devoted to issues of semantic change in the Romance languages, I shall examine some of the research into the motivations and mechanisms of semantic change carried out by Peter Koch and his student, the late Andreas Blank, as well as the findings of Santos Domínguez and Espinosa Elorza (1996), a work which seeks to apply to Spanish the insights on the role of conceptual metaphor in semantic change provided by Lakoff and Johnson in their seminal book *Metaphors We Live By* (1980).

Traditional historical Romance semantics has tended to stress the semasiological side of meaning change, i.e., how a given lexical item acquires a new meaning. In contrast, Koch advocates stressing the onomasiological side, i.e., how a given concept acquires new signifiers, or how speakers find a new expression for a given concept. Koch (2000) asks the following question: 'Y-a-t-il des universaux cognitifs suffisamment puissants pour guider, comme une "main invisible" les innovations de désignation des sujets parlants et par-là, même les changements de désignation?' ['Are there cognitive universals sufficiently powerful to guide, like an "invisible hand", speakers' innovations in designation and thereby even to guide changes in designation?']. Following Coseriu's dictum that speakers do not set out deliberately to change their language, Koch argues that they strive to designate concepts in an efficient and expressive way, and so initiate processes of onomasiological change to carry out these goals. The semasiological and onomasiological sides to meaning change are not mutually exclusive, as the need for finding expressive signifiers for existing concepts can lead to the introduction of a new sense in a word's semantic range. Koch wishes to stress the onomasiological level as the motivator for what seems to be on the surface semasiological change, i.e., a word's acquisition of a new meaning may reflect the result of onomasiological pressures. However, as he points out, change of meaning is not the only way speakers can bring about a change of designation. Creation of neologisms through word formation can also carry out this purpose (e.g., to use Koch's own examples, the coining through derivation in French of the noun *voleur* 'thief' from the verb *voler* 'to steal', as replacement for the inherited OFr. *lerre* 'thief' (< LATRO), or of OFr. *maschoire* to replace OFr. *maschiele* 'jaw', as can inter-language borrowing (including borrowings from written languages such as Classical Latin)). Within the Romance domain, can the analyst observe recurrent patterns of onomasiological change? If such patterns do exist, do they have their origins in spoken Latin, or do they arise independently in the daughter languages, in accord with cross-linguistic cognitive principles that guide or direct lexical change?

Koch and his colleagues at the University of Tübingen have been conducting diachronic semantic studies within the conceptual domain of the human body, its parts, functions and qualities. This domain is universal with regards to its extra-linguistic reality, and is central, given its crucial role as a locus and point of orientation for human cognition and the perception of spatial realities. It often becomes the basis for metaphorical evolutions. Semanticists have long recognized that the human body has been the central focal point for man's anthropocentric world view, and that cross-linguistically the relevant lexical items may show parallel and predictable semantic evolutions. Within the domain of Romance linguistics, Koch, Blank and their collaborators have begun with work on the body parts associated with the head. The semantic evolution of body-part terminology must be examined from two distinct perspectives: changes undergone by the (Latin) signifier in the transition to the Romance languages and further metaphoric and metonymic semantic developments undergone by the Romance terms at issue. It is well known that Fr. *tête*, It. *testa* reflect a metaphoric transfer that affected TESTA 'pot' in spoken Latin; cf. also Srd. *konka* < Lat. CONCHA 'shell'. Parallel metaphoric evolutions occur later in the history of the Romance languages: witness such Fr. slang terms for 'head' as *carafe, carafon, terrine*; also Sp. *casco* 'helmet', Argentine Sp. *mate*, Peruvian Sp. *tutuma* (of indigenous origin and meaning 'gourd'). These examples all show the evolution CONTAINER > HEAD. A different path is followed by the semantic development of *CAPITIA < CAPITIUM 'head covering, part of the tunic through which the head passes', ultimately the source of Sp. *cabeza*, Pt. *cabeça*. The terms for 'eye' and 'ear' in Romance show great semantic stability in the evolution from Latin to the various Romance languages. Whereas the word for 'nose' usually continues Lat. NASUS 'nose', Sp., Glc., Pt. *nariz* and Logudorese Srd. *nare* go back to NARICAE and NAS/NAREM 'nostrils'. In many Romance languages the terms for 'cheek', 'mouth', 'eyebrow', 'eyelash', 'jaw', 'chin' result from metonymic transfers due to physical contiguity; e.g., BUCCA 'puffed-out cheek' > Fr. *bouche*, Sp., Pt. *boca*, It. *bocca* 'mouth'; GULA 'throat' > Ro. *gură* 'mouth'; Fr. *cil* 'eyelash', Sp. *ceja* 'eyebrow' (cf. Fr. *sourcil* 'eyebrow') < CILIUM 'eyelid'; Sp., Pt., Cat., Occ. *barba* 'chin' that go back to Lat. BARBA 'beard'; whereas It. *mento*, Fr. *menton* (the latter historically an augmentative) continue Lat. MENTUM 'chin'. The distinct terms for 'cheek' in medieval Spanish all go back to terms which originally designated other parts of the face or head: OSp. *mexiella* < MAXILLA 'jawbone', OSp. *tienlla* < TEMPORA 'temples'; *cariello* originally meant 'jaw'. Indeed, the Romance languages all show a wide variety of semantic transfers and borrowings in the designations for 'cheek'; Lat. GENA survives only in some varieties of Romanian, Calabrian and Provençal (*REW*, 3727); Fr. *joue*, Occ. *gauta*, Cat. *galta*, Tsc. *gota* go back to a Celtic base, whereas It. *guancia* continues a Germanic base which meant 'curved surface'; Ro. *obraz* is of Slavic background (for details see Dworkin 1982:579–83; Krefeld 1999a:263; Wright 1994:74–94). As the eyes, nose, mouth, ears, and skull seem to be the most salient parts of the head, these terms often come to form the basis of metaphors; Fr. *nez d'un avion* 'nose of an airplane', *œil d'une aiguille* 'eye of a needle', Ro. *urechea acului* 'eye [lit. 'ear'] of the needle', Sp. *boca del metro* 'subway entrance [lit. 'mouth']'.

It would be worth examining closely the metaphorical evolution / semantic history of body parts that carry negative connotations or taboo associations. Such words seem to give rise to pejorative derivations or semantic extensions. A few examples: in addition to being used frequently in colloquial speech as an interjection, Sp. *coño* 'cunt' is the source of the noun *coñazo* 'stupid action or behaviour' and the verb *coñear*; likewise, in French *con* is used as a highly derogative slang term for a person, and is the base for the noun *connerie* 'idiocy, stupid behaviour'. Spanish *culo* 'arsehole' is the base for a number of negatively tinged expressions (e.g., *estar en el culo del mundo* 'to be in the middle of nowhere'). Expressions such as Sp. *tener cojones*, Fr. *avoir des couillons* 'to have balls, be bold', though perhaps coarse in tone, have positive connotations (at least from a male point of view); nouns such as *couillonade, couillonnerie* carry the same negative connotations as *connerie*. Compare also It. *cazzo* 'cock' > *cazzone* 'idiot', *cazzata* 'stupid action / thing said', *cazzeggiare* 'to bum around, waste time', *incazzare* 'to piss off', etc.

In like fashion, it would be worthwhile to study across the Romance languages (and other families) the semantic history of non-visible body parts, i.e., internal organs such as the liver, lungs, heart and brain. The names of internal organs seem less prone to (though not exempt from) further metaphoric or metonymic semantic evolution. In the Romance languages the name of the 'liver' (Fr. *foie*, Sp. *hígado*, It. *fegato*, Ro. *ficat*, etc.) goes back to FICATUM, a derivative of FICUS 'fig', a development which has its origin in the culinary practice of stuffing the duck's liver with figs. Lat. IECUR 'liver' seems to have fallen into disuse in spoken Latin (with the possible exception of OPt. and Judeo-Spanish *iguaria*). There seems to exist an association between the liver and the notion 'fear'; cf. Fr. *il a les foies* 'he is scared' (cf. Eng. 'lily-livered'). In the Romance languages, the designations for the heart (It. *cuore*, Fr. *cœur*, OSp. *cuer*, Sp. *corazón*, Pt. *coração*) go back to the family of Lat. COR, inherited from the Indo-European term; a notable exception is Ro. *inimă*, which illustrates a metonymic development of Lat. ANIMA 'soul'. According to Ernout and Meillet (1967, s.v. CEREBRUM), CEREBELLUM (whence Fr. *cerveau*, It. *cervello*) was used frequently as a culinary term, whereas CEREBRUM (Sp. *cerebro*) was not. To a large extent further semantic evolution of these terms reflects (culturally conditioned?) associations of behavioural attributes or emotions with the organ in question (see Matisoff (1978) for an enlightening discussion of the semantic evolution of internal body parts in Tibeto-Burman languages).

I wish to mention here briefly the project *Dictionnaire étymologique et cognitif des langues romanes*. It focuses on the terms in the Romance languages for the parts of the human body. Its primary goal is not to identify new etyma, but rather to discern and to describe the cognitive bases for the semantic evolutions undergone by the words in question (see Blank and Koch 1999:53–57; Blank *et al.* 2000; Gévaudan *et al.* 2003). Koch is also directing a parallel project in Tübingen ('Lexical Change – Polygenesis – Cognitive Constants: The Human Body') which is studying the genesis of the designation for the parts of the human body in a sample of fifty languages from different families (see Koch and Steinkrüger 2001).

Specialists in cognitively slanted diachronic semantics have not limited their purview to body-part terminology. Cross-linguistic studies have shown that temporal terms often derive from spatial/local terms (location > temporal). Koch (1997) sets out to investigate the origin of spatial/local terms to determine whether there might be any pattern in the evolution non-spatial, non-local > spatial/local. Koch investigates the metonymic mechanism by which non-spatial/non-local terms acquire spatial/local meanings. He provides, among others, the following Romance examples: OFr. *prison* 'captivity' > 'place of detention'; *pension* 'fact of being fed and housed' > 'place where one is fed and housed'; Fr. *séjour* 'staying' (from *séjourner* 'stay') > 'place where someone stays for a certain time'; Lat. *STANTIA 'staying, standing' (cf. Sp. *estancia*) > It. *stanza* 'room'; Fr. *stationnement* 'action of parking (a car)' > 'parking'; *garage* 'action of parking (a vehicle)' > 'building intended for parking (a vehicle)', Sp. *ayuntamiento*, It. *municipio* 'administration' > 'offices of that administration', Lat. CIVITAS 'citizenship', 'citizenry' > Fr. *cité*, Sp. *ciudad*, It. *città* 'town, city'; OFr. *burel* 'cloth of coarse wool' > 'counting table, work table, writing table' > 'workroom, office, bureau'. Koch goes on to affirm: 'Il n'y a qu'une conclusion possible : cette famille de métonymies doit être fondamentale du point de vue **cognitif**. Nous avons tendance à concevoir les LOCALITÉS dont nous parlons en termes de certaines contiguïtés **saillantes** qui les entourent dans un frame **prototypique**' (Koch 1997:113, original emphases) ['There is only one possible conclusion: this family of metonymies must be fundamental from a *cognitive* point of view. We tend to conceive of the LOCALITIES of which we speak in terms of certain *salient* contiguities which surround them in a *prototypical* frame']. Koch also provides examples of spatial/local terms which develop through semantic change non-spatial/ non-local meanings. For example, Fr. *cabinet* 'place of work, of study' > 'group of persons working around an eminent political figure'; Lat. FORUM 'public square, market' > OFr. *fuer* 'price', OPrv. *for* '(ecclesiastical) jurisdiction)', Sp. *fuero* 'municipal law code'; CLat. FOCUS 'hearth' > Fr. *feu*, Sp. *fuego*, It. *fuoco*, Ro. *foc* 'fire'; Fr. *bois* 'place covered by trees' > 'woody substance, wood', a development not undergone by Sp. *bosque*, It. *bosco*. The development of spatial/local terms seems to go in both directions.

In contrast, the metaphorical evolution spatial/local > temporal seems to be universally unidirectional. Andreas Blank (1997b) examines selected Romance examples of this cross-linguistic metaphor and notes that almost all Romance temporal adjectives historically go back to spatial terms. Blank claims that the metaphorical schema 'space > time' is an example of a narrow metaphoricity ('métaphoricité étroite'; Blank 1997b:26–27), i.e., that it represents 'une relation fondamentale de notre cognition, une liaison habituelle de deux champs conceptuels distincts, une similarité qui s'étend jusqu'au niveau des sèmes; voilà qui nous donne l'impression d'une similarité plus étroite que dans d'autres métaphores' (Blank 1997b:27) ['a fundamental relationship in our cognition, a habitual linking of two distinct conceptual fields, a similarity which extends all the way to the level of semes; this is why we get the impression of a closer similarity than in other metaphors'].

Patterns of semantic change that have their origin in human cognition can repeat themselves in language history. In the transition from Latin to the Romance languages, it can often be difficult (if not impossible) to determine whether the semantic make-up of a given Romance word reflects internal evolution or whether it reflects a semantic structure inherited from Latin. One example: Lat. LONGUS and BREUIS denoted both spatial and temporal length, whereas CURTUS, whose original meaning was 'shortened, truncated; castrated, circumcised', seems to refer only to the physical dimension. However, in many Romance languages the reflexes of these adjectives (Fr. *long*, OSp. *luengo*, Pt. *longo*, It. *lungo*; Fr. *court*, Sp. *corto*, Pt. *curto*, Fr. *bref*, It., Sp., Pt. *breve*) denote both space and time. It seems reasonable to claim that the descendants of LONGUS inherited both meanings from their Latin ancestor and that CURTUS had acquired the temporal meaning within the spoken Latin of the Roman Empire. Alternatively, one would have to posit that all the adjectives underwent the evolution 'spatial length' > 'temporal length' independently in each Romance language. In late medieval Spanish, *luengo* gave way to *largo* (originally 'wide, ample; generous'), which quickly came to be used to refer to temporal duration, a usage that it could not have inherited from Latin (see Dworkin 1997). The semantic evolution in question can be seen in the Latin and Romance histories of the families of the Latin prepositions ANTE 'before' and POST 'after'. I also wish to point out that in many languages (including the Romance languages) there occurs a similar unidirectional metaphorical evolution 'rapid, quick' (physical speed) > 'rapid, quick' (the passage of time); witness the development of OFr. *viste* (mod. *vite*), OSp. *aína*, and in late Medieval Romance of the Latinate reflexes of RAPIDUS (Dworkin 2002b).

Blank (1999; 2001:95–99) proposes a typology of the motivations (as opposed to mechanisms and consequences) for semantic innovation based on pragmatic and cognitive models. He proposes six main categories (of which some admit subdivisions). Their common denominator is the efficient enhancement of communicative effectiveness.

(1) New concept (need for a new name).
(2) The need to verbalize abstract, distant concepts which are difficult to seize intellectually; e.g., (metaphoric) verbalization of time,

understanding, sense perception, emotions. The verbalization of abstract concepts through metonymy occurs infrequently; Blank provides the example Lat. LUNA 'moon' > Ro. *lună* 'month'.

(3) Socio-cultural change, i.e., the need to express new social realities, which Blank exemplifies with the broadening of the semantic scope in Romance of Lat. AUUNCULUS 'maternal uncle' and AMITA 'paternal aunt' (cf. Fr. *oncle* 'uncle', *tante* 'aunt').

(4) Close conceptual or factual relation. According to the nature of the conceptual relation, three types of cognitive constellations favoring semantic change can be distinguished:

   (a) Frame relation, which occurs when there exists a strong relation between concepts in a frame so that speakers use one word for both. This is the source of many metonymies.

   (b) Prototypical change, by which a word comes to designate the prototype of the particular category, e.g., Lat. HOMO 'human being, person' > spoken Latin 'male human being' (cf. the meaning of its descendants in the Romance languages, 'man', except in Romanian, where the original meaning is well preserved).

   (c) Blurred concept, by which speakers transfer meanings from one word to another because they do not perceive the differences between them. Blank (1998) has studied in detail such transfers in the field of such small rodents as rats, mice and moles.

(5) Complexity and irregularity in the lexicon. Four different lexical constellations can be distinguished:

   (a) Lexical complexity.

   (b) 'Orphaned word'.

   (c) Lexical gap.

   (d) Untypical meaning / untypical argument structure, i.e., words whose meaning is somewhat untypical for the word class to which they belong.

(6) Emotionally marked concepts (e.g., eating and drinking, sex, death, fear, anger, beauty, hope, great quantity / intensity, the future, orientation in time, space, and discourse). Some of these domains are marked with taboo. Although what is taboo in a speech community is partially culture-specific, Blank suggests that it may be worth exploring the possibility that there is a supra-cultural, if not universal, core.

The book-length study by Santos Domínguez and Espinosa Elorza (1996) represents, to the best of my knowledge, the first monographic treatment from a cognitive perspective of semantic change based on an extensive body of data taken from a Romance language – Spanish (with emphasis on its medieval phase). The authors specifically seek to apply to Spanish the work on changes resulting from metaphor and metonymy carried out with regard to English by George Lakoff and Mark Johnson, both in their tone-setting collaborative *Metaphors We Live By* and in other separate books from their pens. The opening chapter discusses and exemplifies selected metaphorical patterns. The remaining six chapters examine and analyse the metaphorical and metonymical bases for patterns of semantic evolutions in Spanish under the following headings: 'Spatial orientation and movement'; 'From space to time and other extensions'; 'Causation'; 'From physical perception to intellectual perception'; 'Verbal communication'; 'Feelings and emotions'.

By way of exemplification, I shall briefly describe here their treatment of the concept 'the vertical dimension' (Santos Domínguez and Espinosa Elorza 1996:54–65). The section begins by summarizing how the vertical dimension can be used to designate such concepts as quantity, quality, intensity and evaluation. Medieval and modern Spanish examples (many of which have parallels in other Romance languages as well as in English) illustrate the vertical dimension as a cognitive point of reference underlying the conceptual metaphors 'More is Up / Less is Down', e.g., *el número de libros impresos subió en los últimos años* 'the number of printed books grew in the last years'; *mis ingresos se elevaron el año pasado*, 'my income climbed last year', *la actividad artística decayó* 'artistic activity declined'. They provide examples from medieval Spanish of association of quantity with the vertical dimension as seen in the uses of the adverbs *arriba, ayuso* 'upwards' and *abaxo* 'downwards' with the respective meanings 'more than, less than'. Descendants of the Latin locative preposition SUPER 'over, on, above' have acquired similar meanings from Latin through to late medieval / early modern Spanish: witness *sobrar* 'to be left over' < SUPERARE, OSp. *sobejo, sobejano*, 'excessive, too much', *sobre todo* 'above all', as well as the later borrowings *superlativo* and *superioridad*. Other relevant metaphors analysed by the authors include 'Important Social Status is Up / Less Important Social Status is Down'; 'To Praise is Up / to Insult is Down'; 'Virtue is Up / Vice is Down'. In general, positively valued concepts are 'Up' while negatively valued concepts are 'Down'. Among the examples provided, the reader finds *levantar el ánimo* 'raise [someone's] spirits', *colmo* 'height, upper limit, culmination' < CUMULUS vs. *deprimir* < DEPRIMERE 'to press down'; *humillar* 'humiliate' / *humilde* 'humble', based on HUMUS 'earth'; *abyecto* 'abject' < ABIECTUS < ABIICERE 'to throw down'. The section concludes with a description of the metaphoric evolutions of such verbs as OSp. *crescer* 'to grow upwards', *levantar* 'rise, raise', *erzer, alçar* (mod. *alzar*) 'raise', *(a)bajar* 'to lower, descend', *menguar* 'reduce in size, stature'. The authors also discuss various uses of the adjectives *alto* 'high' and *bajo* 'low', originally indicating vertical dimension. *Alto* can also be used to indicate physical depth (the extreme end of the negative scale) as in *alta mar* (cf. English 'the high seas'). There follows a discussion of the semantic evolution of the originally locative prepositions *sobre, so, bajo*. I also wish to draw attention here to Heinemann (2001), a study within the framework of diachronic cognitive semantics of the development of the Italian spatial prepositions originally indicating location along the vertical dimension (*sotto, sopra, su*), within a delimited space (*in, entro, dentro*), and distance/proximity with regard to a point (*da*).

From the perspective of cognitive semantics, a significant number of the semantic changes observable in the histories of the Romance languages in their evolution over time result from a quasi-universal set of possible processes and mechanisms governed by cognitively controlled principles. In such a case, one might argue that there exists no such thing as a specifically Romance historical semantics, with the possible exception of changes that reflect culturally governed conditions or culture-specific associations and taboos at the level of either spoken Latin or the individual Romance languages (e.g., the Romance designations for meals, the history of colour terms (Dworkin 2006), metaphors based on animal names). Nevertheless, cognitive semantics does not provide an algorithm by which the linguist can predict whether a given word will actually experience a specific semantic change. In this respect, it is still true that each word has its own history.

Not all Romanists who study the evolution of the lexicon have embraced the tenets and methods of diachronic cognitive semantics. There are still many students of diachronic lexicology who prefer to study in searching detail the formal and semantic history of individual lexical items as documented in the textual tradition of the various Romance languages. Some scholars of this ilk have criticized the practice of specialists in diachronic cognitive semantics who take their examples principally from standard manuals and reference works such as the various etymological dictionaries of the Romance languages or the pan-Romance *Romanisches Etymologisches Wörterbuch* without critically assessing their accuracy and validity, cf. Ernst (2004) and Pfister (2004), who question the value of diachronic cognitive semantics in the preparation of etymological dictionaries and lexical/philological studies of older texts. Their stance illustrates one of the problems

597

facing traditional historical Romance linguistics today, namely the tension between scholars who concentrate on individual details versus those who wish to stress more general issues pertaining to the nature of language change in its various manifestations (see the papers assembled in Dworkin 2003).

Cognitive semantics may have one important role to play in the resolution of etymological cruxes. Etymologists no longer engage in the sterile debate that raged at the beginning of the twentieth century as to whether phonological/formal or semantic criteria ought to carry greater weight in determining the validity of a proposed base. Diachronic cognitive semantics has stressed that many (abstract) concepts cross-linguistically may go back to the same or similar underlying conceptual bases. Such information garnered from accepted etymologies may help to cast some light on the semantic side of controversial etymologies (see Gsell 2004). Etymology seems not to be in vogue today, as many specialists seem to feel that, barring new data, currently unresolved etymologies will continue to remain so. Perhaps a cognitive cross-linguistic approach to long-standing etymological cruxes may help to revive this once venerable branch of Romance historical linguistics.

Obviously cognitive semantics is not the 'magic bullet' which will solve all questions on the evolution over time of word meanings. It may throw light on the processes of semantic innovation, but it does not explain how the innovation is accepted by and spreads through the speech community. To test the extent of its applicability, linguists will have to study other semantic areas beyond the fields studied so far in the Romance domain (body parts, verbs of intellectual perception, and adjectival/adverbial indicators of spatial and temporal extension). The analyst must seek to distinguish and strike a balance between the cognitive conditioning of a semantic change and the role of cultural factors, both of which may come into play, as I have attempted to demonstrate in a study on the semantic evolution of primary colour terms in Spanish and Romance (Dworkin 2006).

Lexical change includes several other phenomena. Throughout the course of a language's history, some words documented in earlier stages become obsolescent or disappear completely from the lexicon, while other lexical items enter, often at identifiable moments, usually as the result of processes of borrowing or internal creation. In what follows, I shall discuss some of the relevant issues raised by lexical loss, taking as a base my own work on that topic in late medieval and early modern Spanish.

I do not intend to offer here a thorough or critical survey of work done on lexical loss since the beginning of Romance linguistics as an organized scholarly discipline. As in the case of semantic change, there have been numerous articles and notes dealing with individual instances of lexical loss (especially with regard to French), but very few systematic studies of this phenomenon. Lexical loss can be viewed from two distinct chronological perspectives: the failure of lexical items documented in Latin to survive in all or some of the Romance languages, or the loss of a word documented within the recorded history of a particular variety of Romance. Much relevant data on the first category can be found in the writings of Arnulf Stefenelli (for an overview and relevant bibliography, see chapter 11 of this volume).

It is speakers who choose not to employ a lexical item any longer. Words by themselves do not become obsolete or die out. Linguists have long recognized the role of external and internal factors in these processes. The former include the loss of a given word's referent, taboo associations and rivalry from lexical items deemed more prestigious. Internal structural factors that have been identified are excessive phonetic erosion, (near-)homonymic clash, phonotactic awkwardness, excessive morphological complexity (especially with regard to verbs) and excessive polysemy (Dworkin 1989a). Lexical loss has been treated (implicitly at least) as a pathological phenomenon. All the potential causes listed above can be viewed as some sort of structural defect in the make-up of the affected lexical item. The presence of such structural conditions does not automatically doom a lexical item. The availability in the lexicon of possible substitutes can play a role in determining a word's fate. In most cases, several factors come together to eliminate a word from the lexicon; in other words, lexical loss is an excellent testing ground for demonstrating the validity of the concept of multiple causation in language change.

Several earlier papers of mine examine specific cases of lexical loss against the wider background of structural conditions of (late) Medieval Spanish. Building on an earlier paper (Dworkin 1978) which demonstrates the presence in the phonological system of Medieval Spanish of a constraint forbidding sequences of two back vowels or a central and a back vowel in hiatus, i.e., *áo, óa, óo, úo, úa*), Dworkin (1981) attempts to demonstrate how the presence of these phonotactically unacceptable sequences of vowels led to (or at least played a role in) the elimination from the medieval lexicon of OSp. *rúa* 'street', *lúa* (from earlier *luva*) 'glove', *loar* 'to praise', and of **llo-er, -ir*, the putative local descendant of CLAUDERE 'to close' (cf. OPt. *chouvir*, OGlc. *choer*, Cat. *claure*, and especially Santanderino *llosa* 'fenced enclosure' < CLAUSA, substantivized feminine past participle of CLAUDERE). The presence in the language of the time of handy substitutes, namely *calle*, *guante*, *alabar* (originally 'to boast') and *cerrar* rendered it unnecessary for speakers to attempt to salvage these lexical items through some form of therapeutic adjustment of their phonetic structures. Dworkin (1983;1992) attributes the loss of OSp. *toller* 'take away, remove', *decir* 'descend' and *trocir* 'go across' to the presence in their paradigms of highly unusual morphophonemic alternations viewed against the background of OSp. verbs in *-er* and *-ir*; once again, the availability of formally regular substitutes in the medieval language (*quitar, baxar, passar*, respectively) may have played a role in sealing the fate of the verbs in question. Dworkin (1986) explains the loss of OSp. *vellido* 'handsome, beautiful' as an example of the failure of a perceived derivative to conform to the canons of the language's derivational morphology. This adjective appears to have stood in isolation, as it could not be linked to any verb in *-ir* or *-(ec)er*. It seems reasonable to posit that speakers may have incorrectly associated this adjective with the noun *vello* 'body hair'. Yet the formation of a denominal adjective in *-ido* from *vello* would not have yielded an adjective denoting 'handsome, beautiful' (see Dworkin 1985). The anomalous status of *vellido* within the lexicon may have led to its demise.

Using as a test case the fate of many OSp. deadjectival abstracts coined by means of the suffixes *-dad, -dumbre, -eza* and *-ura*, and which failed to survive into the modern language, Dworkin (1989b) argues that it may be more insightful to study lexical loss across grammatical categories and/or semantic fields rather than on a word-by-word basis. This study concluded that the relative vitality of the given suffix and/or the perceived lack of semantic compatibility between the base and suffix can play a decisive role in the fate of the derivative. Dworkin (1995a) examines the history of several dozen primary adjectives documented in old Spanish which failed to survive beyond the late medieval / early modern period. He notes that more than half of the adjectives that fell into disuse carried a negative meaning. Indeed, do words (regardless of form class) that can be classed as semantically negative show a higher rate of loss? It is possible that languages have more words to carry negative messages than positive messages. On the basis of his study of the semantic field 'health' in early modern Spanish, Rasero Machón (1982) concluded that the number of terms denoting aspects of the negative concept 'ill' far outnumber those denoting the positive concept 'healthy'.

Except for the study of the impact of taboo associations on the history of a word (an issue which can be culture-specific), linguists have hardly examined the role of semantic factors in lexical loss. Dworkin (1997) attempts to demonstrate how the restructuring of the semantic field 'dimension' might have led to the elimination from the lexicon of the OSp.

adjective *luengo* 'long'. To judge by its vitality well into the second half of the fifteenth century, this adjective did not seem to be afflicted with any structural defect which might have motivated speakers to jettison it. Yet, within a short period of time *largo*, originally 'wide, ample; generous' replaced *luengo* in the meaning 'long'. The acquisition by *largo* of its new meaning may have begun with regard to temporal duration and is a logical outgrowth of its original sense. A growing preference on the part of speakers for *ancho* to signify 'wide' may have led to the further semantic evolution of *largo*, whose encroachment on the semantic space of *luengo* may have rendered the latter adjective superfluous. In the late fifteenth century, *largo* seemed to denote both 'wide' and 'long'. Speakers resolved this instance of what Ullmann called 'pathological polysemy' by completing the shift 'wide' > 'long' for *largo*. There is probably no way to determine why *luengo* failed to oust the usurper of its space.

The history of the vocabularies of French, Italian, Spanish and Portuguese is characterized by the influx of a large number of borrowings from written Latin in the late medieval and early modern periods. Not all these Latinisms were coined for the purpose of filling conceptual gaps in the lexicon of the Romance languages as the latter became more elaborated vehicles for the expression of scientific and abstract thought. Many Latinisms came to denote concepts for which linguistic expression already existed in the medieval stages of the languages at issue, and consequently ousted from the lexicon the earlier signifiers. It is worth investigating the extent to which the loss or obsolescence of a lexical item that enjoyed a high degree of vitality in the medieval language can be attributed to the entry and integration into the language of a semantically equivalent Latinism. With regard to Spanish, work along this line has been carried out by Eberenz (1998) and Dworkin (1998a; 2002a; 2002b). The former examined closely the introduction into fifteenth-century Spanish of the adjectives *fácil* 'easy' and *difícil* 'difficult' at the expense of the numerous terms employed in the medieval language to express these notions. The studies by Dworkin dealt with the adaptation of *débil* 'weak', *estéril* 'sterile', *leproso* 'leprous', *rápido* 'quick, swift', *último* 'last', *único* 'only' and *útil* 'useful' at the expense of the medieval designations for these states and conditions. In the case of *único* and *útil*, old Spanish did not have a specific signifier which clearly functioned with the appropriate meaning; rather, speakers had recourse to somewhat awkward periphrases. The predecessors of *estéril* and *leproso*, namely *mañero*, on the one hand, and *gafo*, *malato* and (rare) *mesiello*, on the other, may have been burdened (at least in part) by their negative semantic connotations. In the cases of the other adjectives listed above, the writers responsible for their introduction into literary and scientific discourse may have felt that the Latinisms offered greater semantic precision in comparison with the perceived imprecision, lack of clear boundaries, and polysemy displayed by the vernacular expressions. It is interesting to note that whereas Sp. *rápido*, rarely documented before 1600, ousted its principal rival, the OSp. adverb *aína*, Fr. *rapide/rapidement* did not displace *vite* (OFr. *viste*). A monographic investigation of the lexical changes brought about by the flood of Latinisms in early modern Romance as well as the processes of their integration into the lexicon, would be highly desirable.

From the time of Diez, homonymy has been recognized as an alleged cause of lexical loss. It was Gilliéron, with his classical (and controversial) study on the effects of the clash in Gascon between the local reflexes of GATTUS 'cat' and GALLUS 'cock' (both yielding *gat*), who stressed the role of homonymy in word loss. Steven (1983; a Cologne dissertation which, unfortunately, remains unpublished), re-examines the role of homonymy in lexical loss. The work offers a balanced and critical survey of the opinions of distinguished linguists (mainly Romanists) on the role and workings of homonymy. Steven raises the long-neglected question (with specific reference to old and modern French) of a language's tolerance of homonymy. She claims that some workers in French diachronic lexicology have often too hastily resorted to homonymy to account for the demise of some words for whose loss other explanations appear more feasible. As minimal conditions for the invocation of homonymy, the words in question must be of the same form class, display similar syntactic behaviour and belong to the same semantic field. In a string of two dozen lexical vignettes, Steven examines critically a series of word histories where homonymy has traditionally been accepted as a cause of lexical loss or change, often calling into question the analyses of her predecessors.

In a series of papers employing data culled from medieval Hispano-Romance, Dworkin seeks to add a new dimension to this question by studying the potential role of near-homonymy as a factor in lexical loss. Near-homonymy typically occurs when two items are differentiated by one (or at most two) sounds. Great caution must be exercised when seeking to attribute a case of lexical change to near-homonymy, since the lexicon of any language is full of words that differ from each other by only one or two phonemes. It is the distinctive role of the phoneme that serves to keep such items apart. My research has shown that near-homonymy may play a role in lexical change if the near-homonyms at issue belong to the same form class and to referentially opposite semantic fields, especially with regard to semantically positive and negative meanings. Dworkin (1990) attributes

the loss of OSp. *laido* 'ugly' (a Gallicism) to near-homonymy with semantically positive *ledo* 'joyful, happy' (an adjective which, in the long run, was
also to fall into disuse). Dworkin (1993b) seeks to demonstrate that near-
homonymy between verb stems may have played some role in the loss or
obsolescence of OSp. *trebejar* 'to dance, frolic, play', of OSp. *empeecer* 'to
harm, impede' and of OSp. *morar* 'to dwell' (alongside *trabajar* 'to suffer,
toil', *empeçar* 'to begin' and *morir* 'to die'). In like fashion, Dworkin (1993a)
examines near-homonymy with *acabar* 'to finish', *durar* 'to last' and *viejo*
'old' as possible factors in the loss of OSp. *acabdar* 'obtain, acquire', *aturar*
'to last, persevere' and *viedro* 'old'; see also Dworkin (1995b).

In addition to the study of individual old Spanish lexical items which fell
into disuse, Malkiel has approached the specific question of the loss of
adjectives from different angles, emphasizing in his analysis form rather
than meaning (for a critical overview, with relevant bibliography, see
Dworkin 1998b). As has long been known, the typical Spanish primary
adjective is characterized by the syllabic structure CVCV as a result of (i) the
survival of many Latin disyllabic primary adjectives and (ii) reduction
through syncope of proparoxytonic trisyllabic adjectives. Malkiel (1984)
suggests that old Spanish had a strong aversion to monosyllabic adjectives.
In many of the examples adduced, he stresses that monosyllabicity is just
one factor that may have a played a role in that item's demise. The case
histories presented are OSp. *rafez* 'vile, cheap, common' > *refez* (through
influence of the prefix *re-*) > *rehez* > **reez* > *rez*; apocopated OSp. *doç–duç*
'sweet' which were replaced by the Latinism *dulce*; the elimination of the
OSp. Gallicism *fol* and of *soez* when reduced to monosyllabic [swets]
(a process which may go hand in hand with that of the formally near-
identical and semantically similar *rez*); the alleged fossilization (though not
outright loss) in Spanish of *vil* and *ruin* 'vile, low'.

Linguists have long known that in many languages speakers have come to
link certain sound patterns (manifested through stress patterns, syllabic
configurations, and choice and distribution of vowels) with a given grammatical category or semantic field. Such iconic associations are at best
tendential or relative and in no way obligatory, much less universal within
the framework of the given language (see Jakobson and Waugh
1987:181–91). Within the Romance domain, it is Malkiel who over the
last two decades has studied (with the emphasis on Spanish) the workings of
this type of phonosymbolism; see the essays gathered together in Malkiel
(1990), especially the monograph-length 'Semantically-marked root morphemes in diachronic phonology' (Malkiel 1990:81–156). He has gone one
step further in suggesting the possibility of phonosymbolic causation in the

extinction of lexical items whose formal shape may fail to match a dominant pattern associated with the word's semantic field. He recognizes that such incompatibility between form and meaning does not automatically doom the word at issue; often the presence in the language of a handy substitute may be a decisive factor in sealing the fate of the relevant item.

In the broader context of the alleged phonosymbolic value in Spanish of the rising diphthongs, Malkiel has authored a series of papers dealing with the genesis and role of /jé/ and /wé/ (orthographically *ie, ue*) in Spanish. His hypotheses include a claim that speakers gradually came to associate the root diphthongs *ie, ue*, in primary adjectives with the notions 'vigor, energy, resistance, strength'. Such an adjective might acquire an historically unjustified diphthong, as in the case of *tieso* 'tense, taught' replacing *teso*, the regular reflex of Lat. TE(N)SUM. On the other hand, primary adjectives bearing such a diphthong but which did not express these semantic notions ran a greater risk of being discarded; e.g., *duendo* 'meek, tame', *luengo* 'long', *muelle* 'soft' (Malkiel 1980; 1982). At most we are dealing with a tendency. As Malkiel himself realizes, many adjectives of long standing in Spanish with central *ie, ue*, and semantic ranges far removed from 'vigor, energy, resistance' have survived; e.g., *bueno* 'good', *cierto* 'certain', *tierno* 'tender', *viejo* 'old'. Malkiel also claimed that disyllabic adjectives with tonic /e/ and /o/ in the long run tended to connote and be associated with the concepts 'inanity, sloth, weakness, idleness, apathy, passivity' (e.g., *chocho* 'doddering, senile', *flojo* 'weak, soft', *lelo* 'foolish, simple', *memo* 'simple, stupid', *ñoño* 'insipid; childish; outmoded', *soso* 'insipid, tasteless', *tonto* 'foolish, stupid', among others). Adjectives so structured that did not fit this semantic pattern might fall into disuse, as is illustrated, according to Malkiel (1981) by the demise of the Lusism *ledo* 'glad, happy, mirthful' (which itself had displaced native *liedo*; cf. Dworkin (1990) for an alternative explanation).

Lexical change is a large and complex field, involving as it does the open-ended vocabulary of a language. The study of such change in the Romance languages as a broad phenomenon is still in its infancy; most studies published to date have dealt with the details of individual word histories rather than the broad issues that define the nature of semantic change and lexical loss (and replacement). Lexical change has received little attention in recent introductions to historical linguistics and to processes of language change. This contribution has but scratched the surface, dealing as it does with only two specific phenomena that fall under the broad rubric of lexical change. The recent application to Romance data of the insights of cognitive semantics has sought to demonstrate that a series of quasi-universal principles may underlie what appears on the surface to be a large number of individual, unrelated changes. Traugott and Dasher (2002) have presented a model of what they label 'The Invited Interfacing Theory of Semantic Change'. Its main goal is 'to account for the conventionalizing of pragmatic meanings and their reanalysis as semantic meanings' (Traugott and Dasher 2002:35). To the best of my knowledge, Romance data have played no role in further work on this approach to semantic change. Recent work in such areas as lexical typology (see Gévaudan 2007 and Koptjevskaja-Tamm *et al.* 2007) and lexical motivation (Koch and Marzo 2007) bids fair to throw insights into the nature and processes of lexical semantic change in the Romance languages. Insufficient work has been done so far for linguists to determine whether cross-linguistic guiding principles may direct lexical loss. Are there some semantic categories or parts of speech that show a greater degree of lexical loss? Are words that carry a negative semantic load more prone to replacement? Has the role of homonymic clash in lexical loss been exaggerated? What is the role of the alleged quest by speakers to find more expressive designations for a given concept? Clearly much work remains to be done in many aspects of the study of lexical change in the Romance languages.

13 LATIN AND THE STRUCTURE OF WRITTEN ROMANCE

Christopher J. Pountain

1 Introduction: the written language in the history of Romance

The Romance languages are often seen as being a uniquely interesting language family because of our extensive knowledge of their parent, Latin, the wealth of medieval and modern texts which can serve as data in tracing their evolution (Malkiel 1974a) and the diversity revealed in the existence of a number of present-day standard Romance languages and the many local variants, some now defunct, recorded by dialect geographers from the early twentieth century onwards. Linguistic variation is evident in all these sources, yet their exploitation has largely been carried out within the context of techniques which were a legacy of comparative reconstruction, in which the history of discrete languages was envisaged as a successive series of 'states' (in the case of the Romance languages, from Latin to the present day). Such an approach is now increasingly acknowledged to depend on a naively monolithic view of language, and in Romance Linguistics it has had a number of undesirable consequences.

1.1 *Latin as a stage in the history of Romance*

In the first place, and most seriously for our present purposes, 'Latin', however this term is to be understood more precisely, has largely been equated with the first state of Romanist enquiry. Histories of the Romance languages are still entitled and construed as 'From Latin to modern Language X'. Etymologies of Latin-derived words are typically traced back from modern Romance to an attested Latin form, or, if that is not forthcoming, to a plausible reconstruction – the lack of correspondence amongst the Romance languages is largely what has given rise to a theory of Latin variety and necessitated the notion of 'vulgar Latin' as a hypothetical construct. Morphosyntactic histories are generally defined by gross contrasts between Classical Latin (i.e., the usage of Roman writers) and medieval and modern Romance, though here too there has been a growing realization that Romance constructions are often based on attested Latin variants. All this suggests that 'Latin' is a base which the Romance languages have now left far behind. However, I will argue that one of the most interesting features of the western European Romance-speaking areas is the ongoing maintenance and knowledge of, and esteem for, Latin, which continues thereby to exercise a powerful formative influence on the development of certain forms of Romance.

1.2   Ausbau *languages*

Second, the difference of status among the Romance languages has been insufficiently acknowledged. By this, I do not of course mean that any language is 'better' or 'worse' than another: the crucial factor here is standardization. Some Romance varieties became the basis of the national, or official, languages we know today: French, Spanish (Castilian), Portuguese, Galician, Catalan, Romansh, Italian and Romanian; and to this list could be added several others, such as Occitan, Asturian and Friulian, which have undergone a substantial process of standardization. Kloss (1967) makes a fundamental distinction between a standardized language, which has undergone reshaping and elaboration (an *Ausbau* language), and a language which is identified simply because it is recognizably different from other languages (an *Abstand* language). Romance linguistic atlases identified a potential plethora of Romance *Abstand* languages ('potential', because a weakness of Kloss's distinction is that it is not clear exactly how an *Abstand* language differs from a language variety: consideration of this problem, which probably has to do more with speaker attitudes than with objective linguistic data, is beyond the scope of this chapter). The data of the atlases has often been used alongside that derived from Romance standard languages, in many ways justifiably, since it facilitates reconstruction; but it is important to realize that the forces acting on an *Ausbau* language will be quite different in many respects from those acting on a language which does not have *Ausbau* status.

1.3   *Spoken and written language*

This leads on to my next two points. Twentieth-century linguistics was dominated by the axiom that spoken language is 'normal' and must constitute the primary object of linguistic investigation, while written records are secondary representations of language, artificial and often distorting (see, for example, Bloomfield 1935:21f.). For Romance linguists, the primacy of the spoken language was reinforced both by the realization that the basis of the early Romance vernaculars was 'vulgar', or spoken, Latin rather than the Classical, written language, and by the wealth of data collected in linguistic atlases and dialect studies from spoken Romance varieties which gave a fuller picture of Romance diversity than did the standardized languages (built into the methodology of dialect surveys was the aspiration that ideal informants were illiterate, thus preventing 'contamination' from other varieties, especially the Romance standard of the area). Initial focus on phonological and morphological phenomena also favoured concentration on the spoken language. Such attention to the spoken language, is, however, at odds with the other strand of investigation in Romance linguistics, the exploitation of the very rich (written) textual record of Latin and Romance; and it is both indicative and ironic that textual evidence, mediated by philological evaluation, has generally been regarded as emblematic of the spoken language rather than simply being recognized as a source of knowledge of the written language as such. A number of observations need to be made about this state of affairs. If Romance linguists lay claims to charting the history of *Ausbau* languages (which they do), then that history must include the written language, since one of the main reasons for developing an *Ausbau* language is to render a language appropriate for use in written documents. It is often implied that the *Ausbau* Romance languages are no more than privileged particular regional varieties of Romance (French corresponding to the vernacular of the Île-de-France, Castilian to that of Castile, Italian to Florentine Tuscan), but on closer inspection this is a naive view: not only is an *Ausbau* language subject to a more or less conscious process of corpus planning (see §1.4), but its users rapidly develop vocabulary and structures that are unlikely to have featured in a purely spoken register. Dante's notion of the *vulgare illustre*, a pan-Italian vernacular fit for literary purpose, but identifiable with no existing Italian vernacular, may be taken as an aspiration to the development of such a language (Mazzocco 1987:136). More than this, as I have pointed out in Pountain (2006a), an *Ausbau* language typically has a multiplicity of registers which develop as the language comes to be used for a large number of different purposes and in different text-types. (This is not to say that register variation as such is absent in an *Abstand* language, but simply that, because an *Abstand* language is used for fewer purposes, we would expect *prima facie* that the range of registers encountered would be more restricted.[1]) An *Ausbau* language routinely shows quite marked differences between its written and spoken varieties: this is clearly observable in the present day, and it may be supposed that things were no different in times which are not directly observable – see the uniformitarian principle, as articulated by, amongst others, Romaine (1982:123) ('there is no reason for claiming that language did not vary in the same patterned ways in the past as it has been observed to do today'). At the same time, the plain binary distinction between 'written' and 'spoken' language is oversimplistic. Written texts, especially literary texts, may hold more important evidence about spoken registers than is sometimes supposed (see Pountain 2006b): for example, the written language sometimes seeks to reproduce the spoken through the use of direct speech (even if conventionalized). Conversely, certain varieties of the spoken language, especially careful planned discourse, may in an *Ausbau* language be heavily dependent on the experience of written varieties. The inescapable conclusion is that the study of *Ausbau* languages cannot avoid concerning itself with a close study of such variation: that this is a feasible enterprise is demonstrated by Ayres-Bennett (2004).

1.4 The role of corpus planning

The establishment of an *Ausbau* language also brings into play a different kind of scenario concerning language change; to quote Kloss (1967:38): 'To a large and increasing extent language change is the result of innovational language planning. Innovational language planning … is a legitimate, permissible, and (in many cases) a necessary way of changing a language.' This is a head-on challenge to some of the established ways of looking at language change. Historical linguists applying the principles of structuralist analysis have generally concentrated much more on 'natural' or internal processes of change, and have been convinced that these are of primary, if not exclusive, interest: Martinet (1960:175), for example, claimed that only internal causation was of interest to the linguist ('seule la causalité interne intéresse le linguiste'). The pursuit of linguistic universals understandably reinforced this kind of view, since it is the identification of regular, structure-dependent changes which is most likely to illuminate our understanding of the psychological properties of human language: Lightfoot (1979) dismissed change due to chance cultural factors, foreign borrowing and stylistic and expressive force as being uninteresting and unpredictable. Accordingly, Romanists have not in general paid very much attention to the role of language planning (conscious or subconscious) in language change.

Yet the consequences of such puristic intervention can be very striking: to give just one example, although singular impersonal passive reflexive constructions with plural direct objects occur in the textual record of several Romance languages (e.g., Sp. *se vende coches* 'cars for sale', Pt. *vende-se estas casas* 'these houses are for sale', Tsc.-It. *si legge i libri* 'the books are read'), they are puristically castigated today, and only plural verbs are tolerated (Sp. *se venden coches*, Pt. *vendem-se estas casas*, It. *si leggono i libri*): see Pountain (2000:22). Highly formalized corpus planning is a relatively recent phenomenon associated with the formation of national language academies, the first of which was the Italian Accademia della Crusca in 1582. A degree of urgency to corpus planning in the present day has been given by the revival and consequent need for standardization of Romance varieties such as Catalan and Galician. But an awareness of planning has certainly been a feature of the Romance languages of western Europe since the early Renaissance; this is nowhere more apparent than in Italy, where Dante, Petrarch and Boccaccio set through their writings a literary standard which eventually provided a reference point for the establishment of a common language in Italy, which came to be cultivated in both writing and speech by speakers for whom the Tuscan on which it was based was a foreign language. In the sixteenth century, we find Italy at the forefront of prescriptivist discussion: Castiglione's influential *Il Cortegiano*, published in 1528, expounds the humanist preference for the avoidance of archaisms and the embracing of borrowings and linguistic innovation (Burckhardt 1990:242). More generally, in an *Ausbau* language, literary prose of several different periods may influence everyday usage (Blatt 1957:36). Not only does mass education create an awareness of such registers which generally informs speakers, but the culture of intertextuality, allusion and indirect citation positively encourages borrowing.

With the foregoing considerations in mind, we may now begin to examine the relationship between Latin and Romance.

2   Latin and Romance in written texts

In the evolution of the Romance *Ausbau* languages in western Europe, there is a close, even symbiotic, relationship between Latin and the vernacular. Nykrog (1957:92) envisages a sociolinguistic scenario consisting of: (a) the everyday Romance speech of the illiterate; (b) Romance speech of the cultivated, reminiscent of scholastic language; (c) conversational Latin, used among clerics with some degree of learning, but with some accommodation to Romance usage; and (d) the Latin of the sophisticated and well-educated.

2.1   *The coexistence of Latin and Romance*

According to such a view, there is therefore not a simple opposition between Romance inheritance and Latin borrowing. Throughout the Middle Ages, the emergent literary language based on the vernacular was generally seen as inferior to Latin, which continued to be cultivated for 'serious' purposes and was the historic language of the Roman Church, as well as being the language of the most accessible source of scripture in the form of the Vulgate Bible. Indeed, Latin was spoken, as well as written, amongst clerics and scholars: Montaigne (1533–92) was famously exposed only to Latin until the age of six (Picoche and Marchello-Nizia 1994:27). It also had the advantage of serving both as an élite lingua franca and as something of a cryptolect among the educated classes; since it was already an *Ausbau* language, it was also easier for those who knew it to achieve accurate intellectual expression in Latin than in the vernacular. It is worth pointing out that while today there is a long tradition, dating back to the humanists, of according substantial respect to authors of creative literature and of considering that the best authors use the 'best' language, this was not true of the Middle Ages, when diverting literature, being primarily introduced for the entertainment of the nobility, who did not form part of the literate scholarly class, was not considered a 'serious' purpose; this is why literary texts deliberately written in Romance rather than Latin exist from relatively early on in the Romance textual record. Indeed, the prime movers in the demand for various types of written Romance overall were the secular nobility. The modern respect accorded to creative literature, coupled with the easier availability of literary texts in critical editions (see Pountain 2001:4–5), has meant that chrestomathies of Romance texts have tended to concentrate on literary sources after the very earliest records, and we therefore have the (erroneous) impression of a sudden global substitution of Latin by Romance. But in areas of practical literacy (see Burke 1987), the movement towards the use of Romance was slower and proceeded at different rates and in different ways in the various Romance-speaking areas until the fifteenth–sixteenth centuries, at which point the humanist concern for the more accurate cultivation of classical Latin, coupled with a more scholarly interest in the vernacular as such, dealt a definitive blow to Latin. However, although Romance did steadily replace Latin in a number of text-types (legal, commercial, historical, didactic, moral, scientific), the models were generally Latin, and texts in the vernacular were for a long time drafted by people who were educated in Latin. Equally, even in creative literature, despite the apparent novelty of some literary creations, Latin models and inspiration were usually not far beneath the surface. Burckhardt

611

(1990:165) observed that 'Italian prose was written best of all by those to whom it cost an inward struggle not to write in Latin'.

2.1.1 France

The contest, as we may see it, between Latin and Romance in written text-types, followed a similar trajectory in the various Romance-speaking areas, though there are some differences in timing and circumstance. The very first Romance texts come from north of the Pyrenees, where there is early development of impressive verse literatures in *francien* (the Romance of the Île-de-France) and Occitan before the thirteenth century. There is evidence of Romance being represented in notarial documents in the Occitan area from the twelfth century (see §2.2.1.1), but this seems not to have been paralleled in the *francien* area until the thirteenth century (Ayres-Bennett 1996:88). In this century a number of Romance prose text-types also made their appearance: the recording of the Fourth Crusade in the chronicles of Robert de Clari and Geoffroi de Villehardouin, histories such as *Li Fait des Romains*, and the *Lancelot* prose romance. The rising prestige of *francien* is very evident from a number of well-known remarks by writers (see, for example, Rickard 1974:49–50); the growth in its use for purposes of practical literacy was concomitant with the territorial expansion of France, whose Capetian kings had made Paris their capital. A further measure of the importance of Romance is the appearance of translations into *francien*: the old French Bible dates from the first half of the thirteenth century and Jean de Meun's translation of Boethius's *Consolatio Philosophiae* from the end of the century (however, translation work in France would really burgeon in the fourteenth century; see §2.4). Despite this, it was some considerable time before French supplanted Latin in some spheres of activity, notably the law courts, schools and universities, and the Church (broadly in that order). The consistent use of French rather than Latin in legal proceedings was only established as late as the Ordonnance de Villers-Cotterêts of 1539, although the use of French had been growing steadily since the thirteenth century. The use of French in schools only began with the Protestants in the sixteenth century, and Jesuit schools continued to use Latin as the medium of instruction as late as the eighteenth century (Picoche and Marchello-Nizia 1994:27).

2.1.2 The Iberian Peninsula

In the Iberian Peninsula, legal documents from León and Castile predominantly written in the Romance way date from the twelfth century, but creative literature is later in making its appearance. Troubadour poets from Catalonia from the twelfth and thirteenth centuries seem to have been drawn into the Occitan sphere of influence and their works are not recorded in a distinctively Catalan mode of writing (Elcock 1975:451): this in itself is an interesting reflection of the fact that creative writing often takes place within rather artificial conventions and may be quite far removed from the regular speech of its authors. A similar literary convention is represented by the later Galician lyric (thirteenth–fourteenth centuries). The first piece of creative literature, the Castilian *Cantar de Mio Cid*, dates from the late twelfth–early thirteenth century, and the thirteenth century sees the beginning of the writing of prose text-types: the vernacular chronicles of the various northern states (the *Liber Regum* in Castile, the *Llibre dels feyts del Rey Jaume* from Catalonia, the *Corónicas navarras* and, moving into the fourteenth century, the Portuguese *Livro de Linhagens*), and didactic literature such as the Castilian *Los diez mandamentos*. The political climate of the Reconquest was not especially favourable to the use of Latin, since Latin was not widely known outside the Christian north and was in any case too closely associated with Christianity in what were in reality multicultural kingdoms. Furthermore, continuing close contact with Arab culture meant at first that Latin was not so obviously the language of greatest cultural prestige: Arab science was held in great esteem; much Greek and Roman learning had been transmitted in the Muslim world through the medium of Arabic, and Arabic itself had a venerable literary tradition. The significant Jewish community also provided contact with Hebrew (the Biblical references in *La Fazienda de Ultramar* (early thirteenth century), the first extensive prose work in Castilian, suggest translation direct from Hebrew rather than from the Vulgate; see Lapesa 1981:234); Jews also proved to be pivotal in the making of translations from Arabic, since, while familiar with Semitic languages, they were also Romance speakers. In twelfth-century Castile, Archbishop Raimundo of Toledo set up the working practice of having teams of translators, Jew and Christian cleric, making translations from Arabic into Latin via Castilian; such activity culminated in the concentration of a school of translators in Toledo under Alfonso X. Fernando III (reigned 1217–52) and Alfonso X (reigned 1252–84) effected a remarkable sponsorship of the Castilian vernacular. Fernando ordered the drawing up of legal codes (*fueros*) in Castilian for newly conquered territories; the Visigothic legal code, the *Forum Iudicum*, was also translated into Castilian as the *Fuero Juzgo*. Alfonso's great innovation was the decision to produce Castilian translations of Arabic scientific texts; he also commissioned (in common with many other monarchs) the drawing up of histories and chronicles in the vernacular, into which versions of parts of the Bible and the classics found their way. The overall consequence of this activity was the use of written Castilian in legal, historical and technical milieux to an extent that seems to have exceeded the use of Romance vernacular anywhere else in Europe at the time. The use of Castilian generalized among notaries in the first quarter of the thirteenth century (Lapesa 1981:187, 232); the Bible was translated into Castilian in c.1260. In parallel with Fernando III's initiation of the movement away from the use of Latin and towards Castilian was a similar phenomenon in Aragon-Catalonia, where Vic and Ripoll were important centres of translation; Jaume I (reigned 1213–76) commissioned the writing of chronicles in the vernacular, and Ramon Llull (c.1233–c.1315) produced a sizeable *œuvre* of poetry and philosophical, theological and scientific works in Catalan.

2.1.3   Italy

In Italy, Latin seems to have continued in use in law and administration for a little longer, though Tuscany led the move towards the vernacular as early as the fifteenth century, when there was a Florentine requirement that all documents relating to trade should be in the vernacular (Migliorini 1978:253). The scenario for the establishment of an *Ausbau* language in Italy is quite different from the situation in France and the Iberian Peninsula, where a state court language was the basis of vernacular usage both in creative literature and areas of practical literacy. Italy lacked such an association, and while the national literary standard was eventually set on the basis of Tuscan by the prestige of Dante, Boccaccio and Petrarch (see §2.3), other local Romance varieties were the alternative to Latin in everyday documents (Burke 1987:24), and indeed in creative literature. The Tuscan literary vernacular was just one of several competing literary vernacular traditions that had sprung up in different parts of medieval Italy (Migliorini and Griffith 1984: ch. 4). Although by the end of the fifteenth century a form of Tuscan dialect (notably Florentine) was beginning to emerge as a national literary language, numerous other regional literary traditions of the peninsula and islands continued to flourish. Latin continued to hold sway in the universities and in the Church, so that original technical and religious works in the vernacular were relatively few, though practical manuals of instruction, such as those designed for barbers, surgeons and apothecaries (Migliorini 1978:198,432), and devotional works such as hagiographies, were written in the vernacular. Galileo's (1564–1642) historic decision to write in Italian rather than Latin in the early seventeenth century is usually taken to be the first significant use of Italian in a scientific text, and is paralleled by a similar break with tradition on the part of Descartes (1595–1650) in the *Discours de la méthode* of 1637 (though Descartes's intended readership was women and 'gens du monde', i.e., the laity; see Picoche and Marchello-Nizia 1994:29). We should not underestimate the opposition to the vernacular and literacy in some areas of life. The Church was chronically nervous of the threat to orthodoxy posed by the laity having access to the Biblical text in the vernacular, and literacy was also seen as a threat to the security of state documents (Burke 1987:34).

Thus the relatively early appearance of texts written in Romance by no means implies the substitution of Latin as a written medium. The process of replacement of Latin by Romance was gradual and achieved in some text-types only as late as the seventeenth century. The continuing knowledge and use of Latin by the educated of western Europe – to a large extent, and especially in the Middle Ages, those who also wrote in Romance – cannot be too strongly emphasized.

2.2 Early written Romance

We turn now to look in greater detail at the relation between Latin and Romance in different text-types.

2.2.1 Romance used for material to be read aloud

2.2.1.1 Legal documents

The starting point for writing in Romance appears to be the medieval *prise de conscience* of the distinction between 'Latin' as a formal written medium, whose cultivation and correct usage was the preserve of an educated élite, and everyday spoken language. The Council of Tours (813), which provided that sermons should be preached in the vernacular for the purpose of conveying the meaning of the scriptures and the Church's teaching to all, is usually considered the defining landmark. Accordingly, the very earliest documents which are written in a distinctively Romance way appear to be motivated by the need to represent actual Romance speech. In all probability, this does not mean transcribing *post hoc* actual speech, but rather providing set formulae or an *aide-mémoire*. The real originality of the Strasbourg Oaths (sworn by Charles the Bald and Louis the German in 842), dating from just twenty-nine years after the Council of Tours and usually reckoned as the very first attempt at writing down Romance vernacular in a way which was distinctive from Latin, is the author's attempt at explicit representation of the vernacular in writing, though it is likely that there was already a tradition of making legal declarations orally in the vernacular on the basis of documents which preserved the traditional Latin way of writing (Wright 1982:124). (A similar motivation to that of the Oaths may be perceived in the *Placiti cassinesi* of 960–63, four of the earliest texts written in Romance from Italy, where such documents are relatively scarce. The Romance declarations in the *Placiti* may perhaps suggest the need for the formulaic text to be read out to the interested parties, who had to be clear what was being agreed on.) It is unnecessary to go into the fine detail of the many, and probably not mutually exclusive, hypotheses surrounding the Oaths.[2] Most important for our present purpose is the register to which they belong. The relation of the Oaths to Latin is patently a very close one. They are represented within a Latin narrative and must be based on antecedents in legal language (it may even be that the text of the oaths is actually a version of a Latin original which has not survived; see Ewert 1935). All commentators on the Oaths have pointed to what they call 'latinisms' in the *romana lingua* texts as if Latin and Romance can already be completely separated by virtue of this early attempt to represent the vernacular. Ayres-Bennett (1996:21) lists the words and phrases *Deus* 'God', *in damno sit* 'may be to the detriment' and *conservat* 'keeps' as latinisms and *in quant* 'in so far as' as a 'semi-latinism'; she also ascribes the use of S[ubject]–O[bject]–V[erb] word order in such sentences as *in quant Deus savir et podir me dunat* 'in so far as God grants me the knowledge and ability' to the influence of Latin (Ayres-Bennett 1996:30). But how can such 'influence of Latin' be construed? *Deus* may simply be an orthographical latinism: it is very variously represented later in old French, often with representation of a nominative inflection (*Diex*, *Dex*), and we have no comparable contemporaneous text to act as a control (the Eulalia Sequence contains only the oblique form *Deo* – as in the Oaths, where *pro Deo amur* 'for the love of God' corresponds to Latin PRO DEI AMORE). It is tempting, of course, to say that since this word belongs *par excellence* to the ecclesiastical register which would have been the source of many Latin borrowings into Romance, it must itself be a borrowing, or at least have some effect on the development of the Romance word (compare the debate on Castilian *Dios*, which appeals to the late preservation of a nominative/ vocative 'case'; see Corominas and Pascual 1980–91:II, 498–500); yet almost by the same token it is a word which must have been very frequent in popular speech, and it is odd to think that it would have been read in a non-vernacular way by Louis. *In damno sit*, coming right at the end of

Louis's oath, is more patent: it is not obviously the antecedent of a Romance phrase. But it may have been familiar within legal register as the opposite of *in lucro* 'to the advantage [of]', and as such readily understood (perhaps in the same way as *et cetera* is understood in modern English); in any case, *damno* was not very distant from its old French descendant *dam*. This is perhaps best interpreted, then, as a code-switch between Romance and Latin. *Conservat* is thought of as a latinism because the verb is not otherwise attested until the fourteenth century, when it has its modern meaning, while here it has the Classical Latin meaning of 'to observe, keep (a law)'. It is perhaps most appropriately construed as a 'technical' word belonging to legal register which has, perhaps fleetingly, been created for the vernacular. *In quant* appears to be a straight imitation of Latin IN QUANTUM, again taken from legal register; because of the apparent phonetic adaptation to Romance and the existence of *quant* in other functions in old French, we must see it more as a calque than as a code-switch, encouraged, we might suppose, by the complexity of the syntactic structure which, while familiar in legal register, might not have been so readily expressible in the vernacular (though having said that, we should note that *teudisca lingua* is able to express this notion without any resort to borrowing). The suggestion that verb-final word order is taken from Latin is motivated by the fact that in later old French this order is not usual, and that verb-final word order was used in deliberate imitation of Latin in the Renaissance; see section 4.2.4. However, in the particular context of this document, it may equally have been encouraged by a desire for parallelism with the *teudisca lingua* text (thus *savir et podir me dunat* parallels *so fram so mir Got geuuizci indi mahd furgibit*). In summary, it seems that these various 'latinisms' in fact represent slightly different phenomena and that it is not appropriate to make as clear-cut a distinction between 'Latin' and the vernacular as it has traditionally been thought. Despite this early attempt to write Romance in a different way from Latin, and the growing acceptance of the desirability of doing so, Latin and Romance were probably construable as different linguistic registers between which there was a clear historical relation. Educated speakers of Romance could code-switch between these registers and could very easily turn to Latin when they needed a word or phrase: an option which, it is apparent from the Oaths, was not available to speakers of *teudisca lingua*.

Lengthier legal documents permit more detailed insight into the relation between Latin and Romance. Brunel's (1926) collection of early legal documents in Provençal between 1034 and the end of the twelfth century apparently shows a transition from predominantly 'Latin' to almost exclusively 'Romance' draftings of what are quite plainly the same legal formulae.

Taking the texts of the earliest oaths (texts 2, 3, 4, 8, 18, 25), for instance, we can readily establish the following equivalences:

Latin	Romance	English
DE ISTA HORA IN ANTEA	*d'aquesta ora enant*	'from this hour onwards'
EGO *N*	*eu N*	'I *N*'
FILIUS *N*	*fil de N*	'son of *N*'
DE TUA PARTE	*de la tua part*	'on your part'
QUE IBI SUNT	*que i sun*	'which are there'
ANTEA ERUNT IBI FACTAS	*adenant faias i serant*	'before they will there be made'
NEC OMO NEC FEMINA	*ni om ne femena*	'neither man nor woman'
CUM MEO CONSILIO	*ab mun consel*	'on my advice'
ME SCIENTE	*meun escient*	'to my knowledge'

On closer inspection, however, we might be more suspicious about the apparent differences evidenced here. These phrases show word-for-word equivalences with what would appear to be different spellings of the 'same' word (HORA~*ora*, IN ANTEA~*enant*, EGO~*eu*, PARTE~*part*, IBI~*i*, SUNT~*sun*, FACTAS~*faias*, OMO~*om*, NEC~*ni*, FEMINA~*femena*, CONSILIO~*consel*, SCIENTE~*escient*). The Latin often seems to be coloured by Romance (the use of ISTA as a 'first person' demonstrative corresponding to its augmented derivative *aquesta*, and the preverbal use of IBI which parallels the Romance use of *i* and its congeners). Conversely, Romance is coloured by Latin: *meun escient* (cf. the survival of the phrase in ModFr. *à mon escient*, but with an added preposition) appears as an absolute phrase and is word-for-word parallel to the Latin ablative absolute construction MĒ SCĬENTĒ (see §4.2.3.1), even though the parts of speech are different (*meun* is in Romance a possessive adjective rather than a pronoun, and *escient* a noun instead of a participle). These correspondences would seem to support Wright's (1982) hypothesis that what we are seeing in such texts is not two different languages but rather two different ways of writing, the discrimination of which had originally been encouraged by the Carolingian reforms of Latin pronunciation, which insisted on the

Church's return to what was considered a more 'correct' way of reading Latin letter by letter, instead of in a way which reflected contemporary vernacular pronunciation. On the other hand, some Romance forms are substantially different from their Latin counterparts, which suggests that at the very least there is evidence of variation (e.g., ISTA~*aquesta*, ERUNT~*serant*) or a sense of two different languages. To understand the basis of choice it is again crucial to bear in mind the nature of this particular text-type. In legal documents of this time we can see a tension between, on the one hand, the need to represent formulae on which legal precedents were based and, on the other, the need for reading aloud which ensured that the parties to agreements were fully aware of what they were subscribing. The former must have favoured the retention of Latin writing as handed down by scribal tradition, while the latter required some kind of explicit representation of the vernacular. It is not surprising, then, that over the 150-year period represented by these Provençal texts we see a growing preference for overt representation of the vernacular as scribes gain in confidence and pick up the new tradition, whilst there is also a care to mirror Latin formulae as exactly as possible in vernacular writing. The ultimate product is a compromise which gradually evolves in the direction of the vernacular; this scenario, if correct, would account naturally for the impression of constant code-switching we get from these documents and for apparent Latin 'influence' on Romance, or rather, the conscious parallelism between Latin and Romance legal formulae which is specific to this particular text-type.

2.2.1.2 Religious texts

A second kind of early Romance text stems from the deliberate use of the vernacular for the benefit of the illiterate in a religious context. The early isolated example of the Jonah Fragment of the mid tenth century, from Saint-Amand near Valenciennes, a mixture of Romance and Latin notes on the Latin text of chapter 4 of the Book of Jonah, seems to provide evidence of preachers preparing to explain the Latin Biblical text to their congregations in the vernacular, as required by the Council of Tours. There are similar texts from the early documentation in Romance of other Romance-speaking areas (the Organyà Homilies from Catalonia of c.1200 and a twelfth-century compilation of sermons from Piedmont). While it is not clear whether the Romance part of such documents was intended to be read out verbatim, to have been a prompt to the preacher (Ayres-Bennett 1996:40) or simply to have been the preacher's informal drafting, some degree of correlation between the written text and the oral performance of the preacher seems obvious. The relation of the Romance text to Latin is again patent, since the Vulgate text goes hand in hand with the Romance commentary, and in the Jonah Fragment the writer seems to oscillate effortlessly between Latin and Romance. Unlike the language of legal documents, however, we may surmise that the register represented by these documents is deliberately more informal and accessible to the common people. Indeed, the Romance sections of these texts are strikingly lacking in 'latinisms', the preachers apparently quite deliberately concentrating on paraphrasing and explaining the original text rather than on translating it accurately word by word. In the Organyà Homilies especially we seem to hear an authentic authorial voice which catches the words and structures of everyday speech, deliberately avoiding complexity and unfamiliar vocabulary: note the inherited vocabulary and paratactic structure with frequent use of *e*.

> Mas ja veng una femna qi era en aqela terra, e avia un fila qi avia mal de demonis, e ela audí dir que Nostre Sèiner ere en aqela terra, e exí de sa tera e anà cercar lo Seinor per zo qe garís sa fila.   (Sampson 1980a:43)

> 'But there came a woman who was in that land, and had a daughter who was tormented by demons, and she heard tell that Our Lord was in that land, and left her land and went to seek out the Lord so that he would cure her daughter.'

2.3   *Artistic literature*

Romance literature in the sense of artistic composition may be said to begin with religious poetry, which was essentially a paraphrase of the Vulgate. The Eulalia Sequence, from St Amand like the Jonah Fragment, is dated to the late ninth century. The explicit use of such a vernacular sequence in the Mass (albeit as an 'add-on' rather than as an integral part of the liturgy) must have been revolutionary. The text itself derives its subject matter from a Latin model, Prudentius' hymn in honour of Eulalia; but there appears to be little straight imitation, the Latin poem being in any case much longer than the sequence. There are, however, some words written in the Latin way, which may again be variously construed as code-switches (the proper names *Eulalia* and *Christus*, *anima* 'soul', which rhymes with *Eulalia*, and *clementia* 'mercy') or Latinate spellings (possibly the preposition *post* 'after' for the vernacular *puis*). There is subsequently a steady stream of verse compositions on Biblical and hagiographical themes, beginning with the *Passion du Christ* and the *Vie de saint Léger* (Clermont, eleventh century), the *Boecis* fragment and the *Chanson de Sainte Foi* from the *langue d'oc* area (mid eleventh century). There are also religious verse plays: the *Sponsus* (Limoges, eleventh century), in which Latin and Romance alternate, the *Mystère d'Adam* (Anglo-Norman, mid twelfth century) and the *Auto de los Reyes Magos* (Toledo, late twelfth century), which are entirely in the vernacular. The motivation for such compositions is no doubt the desire to make the Christian message accessible to the uneducated, and once again they relate to oral (often sung) performance. Patent latinisms are not frequent in these texts overall; those that there are have been adjusted to Romance patterns, belong to expected semantic fields (religious, cultural, technical) and have probably been borrowed out of necessity to fill lexical gaps in Romance. A typical case is that of *escriptura* 'scripture' in the *Auto de los Reyes Magos*, identified as a latinism by Lapesa (1981:220), which, whilst reflecting in its spelling the Latin consonant group /pt/, which had been simplified in inherited words (cf. Lat. SEPTE(M) > Sp. *siete* 'seven'), also has a prothetic /e/ which suggests its adaptation to Romance phonological patterns (see §3.7.1). It clearly belongs to the ecclesiastical domain in its meaning of 'scripture, sacred writing', and it enables a more finely nuanced contrast of meaning with the formally related noun *escripto*, which is used in the sense of '(non-Biblical) writing'.

Secular literature, stimulated by secular patronage (see §2.1), is of later date. From the twelfth century we have the first examples of lyric love-poems in *langue d'oc*, a tradition continued in the thirteenth–fourteenth centuries in Gallego-Portuguese, and Marie de France's poetic work in *langue d'oïl*. The late twelfth century also saw the flowering of the Sicilian school of lyric poetry. In the *Chanson de Roland* (Norman, late eleventh century) and the *Cantar de Mio Cid* (Castile, late twelfth–early thirteenth century) we have examples of long epic poems commemorating historical events. Such text-types have often been considered linguistically to be pure Romance creations which owe nothing to the example of Latin. (Although some of the thematic material of the *Cantar de Mio Cid* is covered in the Latin chronicle *Historia Roderici* and the poetic fragment *Carmen Campidoctoris*, there is indeed no compelling evidence of any linguistic debt to these possible sources: the most that can be said is that the poet may sometimes echo Latin phraseology with which he was familiar; see Smith 1972:xlvi–xlvii.) But it was not long before creative literary texts based on readily identifiable Latin sources, and with imitation of Latin as part of the stylistic repertoire of their highly educated (and linguistically aware) authors, emerged. In the *Divina Commedia* (early fourteenth century), not only does Dante (1265–1321) generally use a number of Latin lexical borrowings and direct quotations from Latin, but the frequency of such borrowings has been shown to increase in direct proportion to the abstractness and seriousness of the subject matter (Migliorini 1978:192–93). The following stanzas from the *Paradiso* (Canto III, ll.73–81), in which Piccarda Donati explains why she and her companions are content with their situation, illustrate such a style. *Superno* 'exalted', *discordo* 'discord', *cernere* 'to separate', *natura* 'nature', *formale* 'formal' and *divino* 'divine' are borrowings from Latin; *necesse* and *esse* show direct quotation from, or code-switching with, Latin.

> Se disiassimo esser più superne,
> foran discordi li nostri disiri
> dal voler di colui che qui ne cerne;
>
> che vedrai non capere in questi giri,
> s'essere in carità è qui necesse,
> e se la sua natura ben rimiri.
>
> Anzi è formale ad esto beato esse
> tenersi dentro a la divina voglia,
> per ch'una fansi nostre voglie stesse...
>
> 'Should we desire a higher sphere than ours
> then our desires would be discordant with
> the will of Him who has assigned us here,
>
> but you'll see no such discord in these spheres;
> to live in love is here necessity
> if you think on love's nature carefully.
>
> The essence of this blessed life consists
> in keeping to the boundaries of God's will,
> through which our wills become one single will.'
>
> (translated by Allen Mandelbaum, 1980)

In the thirteenth-century Iberian Peninsula, the poets of the *mester de clerecía* composed works on the basis of Latin hagiographical narratives; despite Gonzalo de Berceo's (fl. first half of the thirteenth century) declared intention of writing in *roman paladino* in what amounted to a popularizing endeavour to make these stories accessible to the laity, he is nevertheless credited with having been a leading exploiter of Latin lexical borrowings (Lapesa 1981:227). It should be stressed that there remains much work to be done in this area in order to establish more accurately the debt of such authors to Latin and the true nature of their innovations, in particular the question of the extent to which Latin borrowings were the product of necessity in the labelling of concepts which were difficult or impossible to express in the existing vernacular, and how far they were manipulated for stylistic purposes (e.g., to indicate different registers, or to satisfy the demands of metre and rhyme); the difficult matter of assessing the possible impact of Latin on the syntax of these compositions also deserves closer study; see Vincent (2007b). It is probably not an exaggeration to say that the subsequent, and overall very substantial, debt of western Romance creative literature to Latin is simply a matter of degree, with some periods of very extensive and deliberate imitation of Latin. The fifteenth century in Castile, for example, represented a high point in such a fashion, with Latin serving not only as the source of lexical borrowings, but also as a model for syntax and style, as may be judged from the following extract from the *Siervo libre de amor* by Juan Rodríguez Padrón (first half of the fifteenth century):

> Por la semblante vía le mandó passar con otra breve de creençia, rogadora, en boz de aquel muy alto rey de Vngría, señor del Imperio, allende del triste caso, aver recomendadas la ynoçente ánima de Lyessa con la trabajada suya, en rremuneraçión de los grandes seruiçios que de[él] reçibiera, syendo ella la causa. En punto, affynada su voluntat postrimera, bolvió contra sy en derecho del coraçón la sotil y muy delgada espada, la punta que sallía de la otra parte del refriado cuerpo; e diziendo aquestas palabras en esquivo clamor: «¡Reçibe de oy más, Lyessa, el tu buen amigo Ardanlier a la desseada compañía!» E lançóse por la media espada, e dio con grand gemido el aquexado espíritu.
>
> (Edición de Antonio Prieto (Madrid, Castalia, 1980), p.95)

'In the same way he ordered him to go with another letter of credence which asked, in the name of the most high king of Hungary, lord of the Empire, in addition to this sad affair, that he should take into his charge Lyessa's innocent soul together with his own tortured one, as payment for the many services which he had received from him, the cause being herself. Immediately, his last wish having been made, he turned against himself on his heart the sharp and very slender sword, the point of which was protruding from the other side of her cold body; saying these words in a terrible cry: "Receive from this day forth, Lyessa, your good friend Ardanlier into your desired company!" And he threw himself on the half sword and gave up his grieving spirit with a mighty groan.'

There are many lexical borrowings from Latin (*imperio* 'empire', *ynoçente* 'innocent', *ánima* 'soul', *rremuneraçion* 'payment', *seruiçios* 'services', *causa* 'cause', *clamor* 'cry', *espíritu* 'spirit'), and two (*rremuneraçion* and *clamor*) are likely to have been innovations in this text. Especially striking are its syntactic features: the many instances of the preposing of 'qualificative' adjectives to the noun they modify (see §4.2.5); the high incidence of absolute constructions involving the gerund or the past participle (see §4.2.3.1), and the use of *rogadora* as a verbal element in the manner of a Latin gerundive governing the infinitival complement *aver recomendadas* (see §4.2.3).

2.4   Translations

There is a general opinion that Latin influence on Romance is greatest in translations (Pagliaro and Belardi 1963:148; Brunot 1905:295); from the fourteenth century onwards, the number of translations substantially increased. It would, however, be wrong to assume that such influence is brought about by slavish imitation of the original, or that all translators worked in the same way. As an illustration, below are two very short extracts from Jean de Meun's (c.1240–1305) version of Boethius's *Consolatio philosophiae* and Nicholas Oresme's (1320–82) translation of the Latin version of Aristotle's *Politics* (see also Schiaffini (1943:151–66) on the differing practice of Boccaccio):

De Meun (Dedeck-Héry, 1952: 175)	Boethius *Consolatio Philosophiae*, Prosa III, text taken from O'Donnell (1984:5)	English translation (W. V. Cooper, *Boethius: The Consolation of Philosophy*, London: Dent, 1902, p. 6)
Ainsi et non pas autrement les nubleces de tristece dissolues, je pris le ciel et reçui ma pensee a cognoistre la face de ma mirgece.	Haud aliter tristitiae nebulis dissolutis hausi caelum et ad cognoscendam medicantis faciem mentem recepi.	In such a manner were the clouds of grief scattered. Then I drew breath again and engaged my mind in taking knowledge of my physician's countenance.
Si que, puis que je oi mis mes yeulx en li et fiché mon regart, je regardé ma norrice es mesons de cui avoie esté conversanz de ma jeunesce, c'est a savoir Philosophie,	Itaque ubi in eam deduxi oculos intuitumque defixi, respicio nutricem meam, cuius ab adulescentia laribus obuersatus fueram, Philosophiam.	So when I turned my gaze towards her and fixed my eyes upon her, I recognised my nurse, Philosophy, in whose chambers I had spent my life from earliest manhood.

et dis: «O tu mestresse de toutez vertuz, descendue du souverain cardinal, pour quoy es tu venue en ces solitaires lieus de notre essil?	Et quid, inquam, tu in has exsilii nostri solitudines, o omnium magistra uirtutum, supero cardine delapsa uenisti?	And I asked her, 'Wherefore have you, mistress of all virtues, come down from heaven above to visit my lonely place of banishment?
Es tu donques pour ce venue que tu soies ainsi demenee coupable avec moi des faus blasmes?»	An ut tu quoque me cum rea falsis criminationibus agiteris?	Is it that you, as well as I, may be harried, the victim of false charges?'

De Meun generally remains very close to the Latin original, so that on the whole each Latin word has a single Romance equivalent (excluding verbal subjects and articles), even at the expense of what is likely to have been some unnaturalness: HAUSI CAELUM = *je pris le ciel* 'I took the sky', MENTEM RECEPI = *reçui ma pensee* 'I received my thought', SUPERO CARDINE = *du souverain cardinal* 'from heaven above' [lit. 'from the highest pivot']. Only occasionally is there expansion for the sake of explanation: SOLITUDINES 'solitudes' is rendered as *solitaires lieus* 'solitary places', and the identity between NUTRICEM 'nurse' and PHILOSOPHIAM 'Philosophy', which is apparent from the Latin accusative inflection, is made clear by the addition in French of *c'est a savoir* 'that is to say' [lit. 'know']. Latin syntax is not in general imitated in the French, apart from the absolute construction TRISTITIAE NEBULIS DISSOLUTIS = *les nubleces de tristece dissolues* 'the clouds of sadness [having been] dissipated', though De Meun is clearly challenged to find economical French equivalents in some cases: the relative CUIUS 'whose' is rendered as *de cui* 'of whom, of which' and the complex interrogative of the last sentence is completely reformulated.

Oresme (Menut 1970:51)	Latin Aristotle (Michaud-Quantin 1961:7)	English translation of original Greek by H. Rackham (Aristotle, *Politics*, London: Heinemann / Cambridge, Mass.: Harvard UP, 1932, p.15)
Nous dirons donques que possession est une partie de maison,	Quoniam igitur possessio pars domus est	Since therefore property is a part of a household

et art ou industrie de gouverner possessions est une partie de yconomie	et possessiva pars yconomie,	and the art of acquiring property a part of household management
pource que l'en ne peut vivre en maison sans les choses necessaires a vie humaine.	(sine enim necessariis impossibile e[s]t bene vivere et vivere),	(for without the necessaries even life, as well as the good life, is impossible),
Car en la maniere que en certains ars il convient avoir convenables instrumens se l'en doit parfaire son oeuvre,	quemadmodum autem determinatis artibus necessarium utique erit existere convenientia organa, si debeant perficere opus,	and since, just as for the definite arts it would be necessary for the proper tools to be forthcoming if their work is to be accomplished,
semblablement a celui qui est yconomique et gouverneur d'hostel ou de maison sunt necessaires certains instrumens.	sic et yconomico.	so also the manager of a household must have his tools…

Oresme then adds a gloss: 'Car aussi comme il convient au feivre marteau et au charpentier hache, semblabelment a celuy qui gouverne un hostel il luy convient possessions comme instrumens necessaires a son fait' ('For just as a smith requires a hammer and a carpenter an axe, so he who runs a household requires possessions as tools necessary for his job'). Oresme was quite clear that esoteric and original words had to be used in scientific prose (Pichoche and Marchello-Nizia 1994:343): *yconomie* is such a word, used for the first time in French in this text; *parfaire*, used earlier by Philippe de Thaon, is most likely a calque from Latin PERFĬCĔRE 'to complete'. He also takes great pains to make the somewhat terse original absolutely clear by lengthy paraphrase: POSSESSIVA is rendered as *art ou industrie de gouverner possessions*, and the final YCONOMICO, basically expanded to *celui qui est yconomique*, is set in the context of repeated material, not to mention the explanatory gloss. (For further comments on Oresme's work, see Chaurand 1977:40ff.) Borrowing from Latin (and Greek) was by far the easiest resource for a translator when a special term was needed to label a concept exactly, or to achieve semantic discrimination; this strategy was consistently encouraged even by Renaissance humanists like Du Bellay, Valdés and Castiglione.

The style of translations also seems to have served as an influential model for original prose: Rasmussen (1958:26) points to the use of pairs of near-synonyms in sixteenth-century French prose in imitation of the common translators' custom of giving more than one equivalent for Latin words.

2.5   'Technical' literature

In any specialized field there is a need to coin words to label concepts, and Latin (and Greek) have consistently supplied the Romance languages and other languages of Europe with technical words and the morphological constituents for original creations. The following is a technical description of saffron in present-day Spanish:

> Como ya se ha visto, esta planta tiene el aspecto general de una liliácea, pero produce un bulbo tuberoso y no escamoso o tunicado, del cual sale una larga espata que echa cierto número de hojas lineares y unas cuantas flores, cuyo perianto es de color violado pálido, con un tubo muy largo de seis divisiones derechas y casi iguales, los estambres tres, y el estilo terminado en tres estigmas cóncavos y en forma de cucurucho; el fruto es una cápsula trilocular.   (Source: www.madridejos.net/azafran2.htm)

> 'As has already been seen, this plant has the general appearance of a member of the Liliaceae family, but produces a bulb which is tuberous and not scaly or layered, from which emerges a long spathe which sends out a number of linear leaves and some flowers, whose perianth is pale violet in colour, with a very long tube with six straight and more or less equal divisions, three stamens, and the stylus ending in three concave stigmas in the form of a cone; the fruit is a trilocular capsule.'

Setting aside the Latin borrowings which are common to many registers of modern Spanish (e.g., *aspecto* 'appearance, aspect', *linear* 'linear', *cóncavo* 'concave', *cápsula* 'capsule'), it can be seen that there are other borrowings which are more specific to the field of botany: *liliácea*, referring to a family of plants as specifically identified and labelled in the Linnean classification; *bulbo*, the rounded part of a plant's stem, *tunicado* 'layered', *espata* 'spathe' (note also *perianto* 'perianth', from Greek). Some other words are familiar in other meanings but are here used more specifically: *estigma*, which although more general in its meaning of 'stigma', is here used in the precise botanical sense of part of a plant, as is *estilo* 'stylus', and the inherited *estambre* 'stamen'. *Trilocular* is a neologism formed from the prefix *tri-* 'three' and *locular* from the Latin adjective LŎCŬLARE(M), an adjective pertaining to LŎCU(M) 'place'.

3   Lexical borrowing

Lexical borrowings from Latin (and Greek) are usually termed 'learnèd', on the grounds that they are made by a learnèd, cultured, élite. There is the implicit suggestion in the use of this term that they are different from other kinds of borrowing; but that is not necessarily an appropriate view, since it is likely that borrowings from other languages, such as Italian, French and English, also entered the language in cultured registers in the first instance. There is also nothing particularly different about Latin as a source of borrowing, which, as we have seen, continued to be used fluently in certain sectors of Romance-speaking societies, and so was in many respects a living and dynamic language. Instead of making the traditional distinction between 'learnèd' and 'popular' words, therefore, I shall refer to 'borrowed' and 'inherited' words.

3.1   *Phonetic modification*

A relatively small number of Latin words are borrowed without formal modification into Romance, although their grammatical function is sometimes changed. The nouns Fr., Pt., It. *album*, Sp. *álbum*, Cat. *àlbum* 'album' derive from Lat. ALBU(M) 'white', which is originally an adjective and in normal usage is an ellipsis for ALBUM AMĪCŌRUM, denoting a white (plain) notebook used by travellers. Fr., Sp. *déficit*, Cat. *dèficit*, It. *deficit* 'deficit' is treated as a noun, though in origin it is the 3SG of Lat. DĒFĬCĬO 'I become weak, fail.' Some Latin phrases are also used, e.g., Fr., Sp., Pt., Cat., It. *statu quo* 'status quo', *sine qua non* 'sine qua non' (again treated as nouns).

It is more usual for Latin words to undergo some accommodation to the host language. Some examples of phonetic 'changes' undergone by Latin words (not usually described systematically in histories of the Romance languages since they are not relevant to inherited words) are:

- The reduction of geminate consonant groups in languages in which geminate consonants were simplified: Lat. COLLŎQUĬU(M) 'colloquium' > Fr. *colloque* (orthographic *ll* corresponds to a single /l/ phoneme), Sp. *coloquio*, Pt. *colóquio* (but Cat. *col·loqui*, It. *colloquio*).

- Reduction of the Lat. /ai/ (AE) diphthong: Lat. PAENĬTENTĬA 'regret' > Fr. *pénitence*, Sp. *penitencia*, Pt. *penitência*, Cat. *penitència*, It. *penitenza* 'penitence, penance'.

- Palatalization before a front vowel following historical developments in the host language: see the treatment of the Lat. /tia/ sequence of PAENĬTENTĬA above, which yields Fr. /s(ə)/, Sp. /θja/~/sja/ from medieval /tsja/, Pt. and Cat. /sjə/, It. /tsa/; Lat. GERMEN 'shoot, sprout, bud' > Fr. and Pt. *germe* /ʒ/, Cat. *germen* /ʒ/, It. *germe* /dʒ/ (Sp. *germen*, which displays /x/ from medieval /ʒ/, applies such a palatalization to Latin borrowings, though the development in inherited words is to /j/ or zero, cf. Lat. GĔLU(M) 'frost, cold' > Sp. *hielo* 'ice', Lat. GERMĀNU(M) '(blood)-brother' > Sp. *hermano* 'brother').

- Introduction of a prothetic /e/ in languages which prohibit an initial consonantal group beginning with 'impure' /s/: Lat. STRUCTŪRA 'structure' > Sp. and Cat. *estructura*, Pt. *estrutura*. The situation in French is more complex, since while 'impure' /s/ initially required a prothetic /e/, e.g., Lat. SPATHA > OFr. *espee*, learnèd borrowings first accommodated to this pattern, e.g., Lat. SPIRITU(M) > Fr. *esprit* (twelfth century) but later maintain the Latin cluster, e.g., Lat. STRUCTŪRA > Fr. *structure* (fourteenth century) (see also §3.4.3). This is in all probability connected with the tendency for implosive /s/ to fall in French, e.g., Lat. FESTA > Fr. *feste* > *fête*, eleventh–thirteenth century. Learnèd influence may even have inhibited this change, e.g., Fr. *espérer* retains its /s/ (Pope 1934:151f.). The Italian prothetic vowel variant (*scuola* but *in iscuola*) seems never to have formed a model for the adaptation of learnèd words.

- Movement of stress in French in words deriving from Latin proparoxytones: Lat. FĂCĬLE(M) 'easy' > Fr. *facile* (but Sp. and Pt. *fácil*, Cat. *fàcil*, It. *facile*).

Frequently occurring suffixes are treated consistently, in accordance with existing models. Infinitives lose their final /e/ in French, Spanish, Portuguese and Catalan; in French the /a/ of the -ARE infinitive and of the abstract nominal suffix -ĀTE(M) is changed to /e/, as occurred historically with inherited members of these classes: thus Lat. EXCĪTĀRE 'to excite' > Fr. *exciter* (Sp., Pt., Cat. *excitar*), Lat. AUCTŌRĬTĀTE(M) 'authority' > Fr. *autorité* (Sp. *autoridad*, Pt. *autoridade*, Cat. *autoritat*, It. *autorità*). The -TĬONE(M) suffix similarly is consistently adapted to -*ção* in Portuguese. We might also mention here a similar phenomenon in Romanian, where, on the analogy of inherited words such as *bunătate* from Lat. BŎNĬTĀTE(M) 'goodness', borrowings such as *autoritate* have been in a sense 'relatinized' by the use of the *-tate* suffix. On the other hand, not all changes known to have affected inherited words are mimicked in Latin borrowings – and this is of course an essential factor in recognizing borrowed words as such (see §3.4). Thus the initial Lat. /kl/ group, which is modified by palatalization in a large number of Romance varieties in inherited words (Lat. CLĀUE(M) 'key' > Sp. *llave* /ʎ/, Pt. *chave* /ʃ/, It. *chiave* /kj/), is preserved in borrowings (Lat. CLĀMŌRE(M) 'clamour' > Sp. and Pt. *clamor*, It. *clamore*).

It is an interesting and relatively unexplored question as to what motivates and constrains the adaptation of Latin borrowings into Romance. As we have seen, analogy with existing morphological forms must be a major factor. Accommodation to the phonological pattern of the host language is more difficult to judge. The palatalization of -TĬŌNE(M) to Fr. *-tion*, Sp. *-ción*, Cat. *-ciò*, It. *-zione*, while avoiding the atypical sequences Fr. /tjõ/, etc., is not analogical with the development of this suffix in inherited words, which is to Fr. /tsõ/ > /sõ/, Sp. /tson/ > /θon/ ~ /son/, Cat. /tso/ > /sə/, It. /dʒone/ (cf. Lat. RĂTĬŌNE(M) 'reckoning, calculation; reason' > Fr. *raison*, Sp. *razón*, It. *ragione*), and in fact creates a diphthongal result (/j/, etc.) which was previously not very frequent. The role of the continued oral use of Latin was also no doubt crucial, since borrowed words were introduced in the first instance by the Latin-speaking and writing élite. In the Iberian Peninsula, for example, such speakers may already have pronounced Lat. SPĂTĬUM 'space' as [espatsju(m)], thus giving the model for the use of the prothetic /e/ in Sp. *espacio*, rather as Eng. *stress* has been borrowed into Modern Spanish as *estrés*. Phonetic distance is probably another factor in the form of borrowings: while the difference between, say, geminate /ll/ and single /l/ is not significant in that these two items share a large number of features, and crucially that of laterality (see the results of Lat. COLLŎQUĬU(M) above), the systematic adaptation of Lat. /pl/ to Pt. /ʃ/ (e.g., Lat. PLĒNU(M) 'full' > Pt. *cheio*), even if the etymological identity had been recognized, was presumably too great a distance to bridge, and so borrowings such as Pt. *plenário* < Lat. PLĒNĂRĬU(M) 'plenary' preserve the /pl/ group.

3.2   Morphological modification

None of the Romance languages of western Europe retains all the distinctions of case and gender found in Latin. Latin borrowings generally derive, as do inherited words, from what we might call the minimum oblique form of nouns and adjectives, which is usually equatable with the accusative case (at least for the masculine and feminine genders) minus the final /m/: it is in that form that etyma are cited in this chapter, and the fact that this strategy is usually appropriate confirms the general rule. Thus, to take some examples of borrowings from third declension nouns and adjectives, in which the oblique forms are often formally significantly different from the nominative, we find:

Lat. nominative / 'minimum oblique'	Fr.	Sp.	Pt.	Cat.	It.
ĪMĀGO/ĪMĀGĬNE	*image* (F)	*imagen* (F)	*imagem* (F)	*imatge* (F)	*immagine* (F)
GĔNUS/GĔNĔRE	*genre* (M)	*género* (M)	*género* (M)	*gènere* (M)	*genere* (M)
PRAESENS/PRASENTE	*présent*	*presente*	*presente*	*present*	*presente*

Masculine and feminine genders are generally retained, though the force of analogy can sometimes run counter to this principle, as in the case of French abstract nouns ending in *-eur*, which, though deriving from Latin masculines in -OR, are treated as feminine, probably on the model of Fr. *chaleur, couleur*, etc.: thus Lat. PŬDŌRE(M) (M) 'shame' > Fr. *pudeur* (F) (but Sp., Pt., Cat. *pudor* and It. *pudore* are masculine; in Spanish, analogy seems to have operated the other way round, since very few nouns in *-or* are feminine: *calor* and *color*, which were usually treated as feminine in old Castilian, are masculine in the modern standard language).

The assignment of verbs to conjugation types is a good deal more random. -ĀRE verbs generally join the majority conjugation of Fr. *-er*, Sp., Pt., Cat. *-ar* and It. *-are* (e.g., Lat. CĔLĔBRĀRE 'to celebrate' > Fr. *célébrer*, Sp., Pt., Cat. *celebrar*, It. *celebrare*). With third conjugation verbs the results are variable: Lat. OPPRĬMĔRE 'to oppress' yields Fr. *opprimer*, Sp., Pt. Cat. *oprimir* (Spanish and Portuguese have no rhizotonic stems) and Italian *opprimere*. Again, analogy may play an important part: compounds of TĔNĒRE 'to hold' follow the fortunes of the simple verb: Lat. OBTĬNĒRE 'to obtain' > Fr. *obtenir*, Sp. *obtener*, Pt. *obter*, Cat. *obtenir*, It. *ottenere*; how-ever, compounds of MĬTTĔRE 'to send' are often converted to Sp. and Pt. *-mitir* (*emitir, transmitir, permitir*) – despite the development of MĬTTĔRE itself to the inherited form *meter* 'to put' – possibly owing the presence of a high vowel in the root (see Maiden, this volume, chapter 4). (Numbers of borrowings from Latin -ĒRE and -ĪRE verbs are too small to permit generalization.)

3.3   Semantic modification

Latin borrowings in general preserve a restricted set of their original Latin meanings, or even one very specific meaning. In this they contrast with inherited words, which often undergo substantial semantic change and can diversify their meanings considerably. Lat. CANDĬDU(M), for instance, has the following range of meanings: (a) 'shining white', the antonym of NĬGRU (M) 'black', applied to snow, flowers and clothes; (b) 'fair (in complexion)'; (c) 'fortunate'; (d) 'clear'; and (e) 'honest (in character)'. Only the last of these meanings is taken by the borrowings Fr. *candide*, Sp. *cándido*, Pt. *cândido*, Cat. *càndid* and It. *candido*. Of course, this has not meant that borrowed words do not subsequently change or extend their meaning as they diffuse into wider usage: Lat. OCCĀSĬŌNE(M) 'favourable moment, opportunity', borrowed as Fr. *occasion*, is used with the preposition *de* to denote such notions as 'second-hand' (*un livre d'occasion* 'a second-hand book') and 'casual' (*une amitié d'occasion* 'a casual friendship').

3.4   The identification of borrowings

Latin borrowings may be recognized by appeal to the phonetic and semantic properties discussed above (patterns of purely morphological adaptation are not significantly distinctive from those affecting inherited words). They typically constitute exceptions to sound change, are relatively restricted in meaning and close to at least one of their Latin meanings. Additionally, Latin borrowings can often be characterized according to semantic field, which is typically abstract or technical. Further confirmation of their status is provided by the occasional existence of an inherited doublet development. Chronological criteria may also be informative, since Latin borrowings often have a relatively late date of first attestation. However, we must be wary of this last apparently more objective diagnostic: the vocabulary of very early texts is not vast, and a date of first attestation in the thirteenth–fourteenth centuries may simply mean that the word is not recorded previously in written form. A typical example of a Latin borrowing is Lat. FRĪGĬDU(M) 'cold', which yields Fr. *frigide* (1706, see *TLF*, 8, 1260), Sp. (sixteenth century, see *CDE*) and Pt. *frígido* (sixteenth century, see Machado 1952–56:I, 1718), Cat. *frigid* (1911, see *GDLIC*, 804), It. *frigido* (fourteenth century, see Battisti and Alessio 1950–57:III, 1718). All these derivatives have been minimally adapted to the host language (in Catalan and French the final vowel is lost; in French the stress has typically been transferred to produce an oxytone). They all have the specialized meaning of 'frigid' (the English word is also a borrowing) meaning 'very cold' and can be applied figuratively to people to denote unfriendliness or lack of sexual appetite. They contrast with the inherited developments Fr. *froid*, Sp. *frío*, Pt. *frio*, Cat. *fred*, It. *freddo*, which have undergone the regular sound changes and have the broader generic meaning 'cold'.

3.4.1 'Semi-learnèd' words

A problem is posed, however, by words which meet these diagnostic criteria only partially. A well-known example (see, for example, Guiraud 1968:16; Lüdtke 1974:62) is the development of Lat. SAECŬLU(M) 'century', which develops to Fr. *siècle*, Sp. *siglo*, Cat. *segle* (Pt. *século* and It. *secolo* are more appropriately seen as straightforward borrowings). The regular developments which would be expected on the basis of comparable inherited words are: (a) the reduction of the proparoxytone (seen in French, Spanish and Catalan, but not in Portuguese and Italian); (b) the palatal development of the Latin /k(u)l/ group, which can be illustrated from Lat. ŏCŬLU(M) 'eye': Fr. /j/ (*œil*), Sp. /ʒ/ > /x/ (*ojo*), Pt. and Cat. /ʎ/ (*olho, ull*), It. /kj/ (*occhio*), seen nowhere; and (c) the diphthongization of Lat. /ai/ (which merged with /ɛ/) in an open syllable in French, Spanish and Italian (seen in French and in the common Castilian variant *sieglo*). Spanish and Catalan show voicing of /k/ by assimilation to the following /l/, which shows some adaptation to Romance sound patterns, and the form ultimately prevailing in Spanish has raising of the tonic vowel to /i/, which is also a process not normally encountered amongst the adaptive strategies of straight Latin borrowings. Such words have traditionally been classified as 'semi-learnèd', the hypothesis behind such a concept being that they were inherited words whose 'natural' phonetic development in Romance was impeded or skewed by a continuing use or awareness of Latin; SAECŬLU(M) is indeed a very plausible candidate for such a scenario, since it would have been very familiar from a religious context, not least the ending of the *Pater Noster*, IN SAECŬLA SAECŬLŌRUM 'for ever and ever'. However, such a view would imply that inherited derivations of SAECŬLU(M) were present in the spoken registers of Latin which formed the basis of Romance, and we cannot know for sure that this was so. An alternative scenario for French, Spanish and Catalan is therefore that in the developments of SAECŬLU(M) we are seeing evidence of early borrowing (possibly the result of code-switching between different social dialects or registers of Latin/Romance), with the diffusion of a word associated with a particular register to a wider usage in which spontaneous, and essentially unsystematic, sound changes could take place. Again, it is worth insisting on the close relationship between some registers of Latin and spoken Romance: Brunot (1905:293) went so far as to say that words like *angele* 'angel', *chrestien* 'Christian', *esperit* 'spirit' and *virgene* 'virgin' were not appropriately referred to as borrowings, since they could never have felt foreign to people who crossed themselves and recited the most common prayers ('[ils] n'ont jamais pu être étranges à des gens qui faisaient le signe de la croix, ou disaient les prières les plus communes'). Lüdtke (1974:274) envisages a diglossic situation within Latin in which 'spontaneous' and 'cultured' pronunciations coexisted, the cultured variants becoming the basis of 'semi-learnèd' words. Some confirmation of this kind of process is to be found in later borrowings from Latin, in whose variant developments evidence of such 'popular' evolution can be found. Lat. RESPECTU(M) 'respect', already attested as *respecto* in thirteenth-century Castilian, also has the variant form *respeto*, in which the complex consonantal group /kt/ has been simplified; another borrowed word producing variable results in Castilian was Lat. AFFECTĬŌNE (M) 'feeling, attitude, affection', which yields *afición* 'fondness, liking; hobby', in which the Latin /ktj/ group has been simplified to /ts/ > /θ/ ~ / s/ rather than adapted, as is more usual, to Sp. /kts/ > /kθ/ ~ /ks/ (cf. Lat. ACTĬŌNE(M) 'action' > Sp. *acción*), and *afección* or *aficción* (the latter has not survived into the modern language, though the former survives with the meaning of 'medical condition'. Such words as *respeto* and *afición* have sometimes been termed 'semi-popular'; see Pountain (2001:278). The existence of surviving triplet developments of some Latin words (e.g., Lat. LIMPĬDU(M) 'clear, transparent' > Sp. *lindo* 'pretty' (inherited) / *limpio* 'clean' / *límpido* 'limpid') also seems to support the notion of phases of borrowing in which one form (*limpio*) is borrowed at a time which predates the earliest texts and another (*límpido*) is borrowed much later. What we are envisaging here, then, is that some Latin borrowings either entered the Romance languages at a less élite level, or that, being of longer standing, they retained the vernacular pronunciation of the Latin; once we abandon the concept of a clear separation between Latin and Romance in the early Middle Ages and allow the possibility of social dialect borrowing within Latin/Romance, such phenomena can be readily accounted for.

3.4.2   Indirect Latin borrowings

Some Latin loanwords do not have their immediate origin in Latin but are borrowed from other languages, which in turn borrowed them from Latin first, e.g., the scientific use of Fr. *gravitation*, *attraction*, which are borrowed from English (Guiraud 1968:34f.). Such a route for Latin borrowings has been of considerable importance in shaping the modern Romanian vocabulary, which as a result of extensive borrowing from the general stock of Latinisms in western European languages, especially French and Italian, appears to share a large number of words borrowed from Latin with the other Romance languages even though they are of more recent introduction (Reinheimer Rîpeanu 2004: 2.2).

3.4.3 'Relatinization'

However, Latin influence on lexis is not restricted to straight borrowings. Gougenheim (1959) identifies a number of processes of what he calls 'relatinisation' in French, where Latin has a more indirect effect on vocabulary. Words may undergo remodelling to make them more similar to the Latin originals: the Lat. adjective STĂBĬLE(M) 'stable, firm' appears in early French texts in the form *estable*, but the 'relatinized' variant *stable* (see §3.1) eventually prevails (additional motivation for this choice may be homonymy at that time with the result of the Lat. noun STĂBŬLA(M) 'stable (for animals)', which further developed to *étable* 'byre, cowshed'), and Fr. *impétrer* 'to be granted (a legal right, etc.)', deriving from Lat. IMPĔTRĀRE, is eventually preferred over the earlier *empétrer*. The meaning of a Romance word may be extended or restricted in parallel with that of its Latin etymon: Fr. *loi*, originally restricted in meaning to 'law' in a religious sense, was extended to secular usage, mirroring the use of Lat. LĒGE(M) by thirteenth-century jurists. Fr. *raison*, which had the meanings 'speech' and 'account, calculation' in old French, lost these meanings and so was brought more firmly into line with the Classical Latin meaning of 'reason, motive' (see also Chaurand 1977:40) (but note the survival of the old French meaning in ModFr. *à raison de* 'at a rate of').

3.5 Downward migration

It is likely that Latin loanwords were in origin restricted to cultured written registers of the language, though this is not easy to demonstrate since we have little evidence of anything other than these registers prior to the sixteenth century, and only in the twentieth century do we have extensive access to the data of informal everyday speech. However, many of these loanwords are present today in the spoken language, which suggests that they have undergone downward migration. Migliorini's (1978:407) list of selected words borrowed into Italian in the fifteenth century contains a number which have since passed into everyday usage: *abolire* 'to abolish', *clinica* 'clinic', *comparabile* 'comparable', *continente* 'continent', *decoro* 'decorous', *dialetto* 'dialect', *eccentrico* 'eccentric', *entusiasmo* 'enthusiasm', *esagerare* 'to exaggerate', *obeso* 'obese', *plastico* 'plastic', *preferire* 'to prefer'. The same is true of borrowings into technical registers in the seventeenth century (Migliorini 1978:489): *elaborare* 'to elaborate, develop', *letale* 'lethal', *monotono* 'monotonous'. It is symptomatic of such a movement that even some Latin borrowings which were originally ridiculed as being excessive were eventually accepted into common usage: Gougenheim (1959:5) cites the example of Rabelais's Limousin scholar in chapter 6 of *Pantagruel* (1532), who uses such words as *crépuscule* 'twilight', *méritoire* 'deserving', *patriotique* 'patriotic' and *redondance* 'redundancy' (see Rickard 1968:88f., 276), which are now reasonably familiar in everyday spoken language. It is also notable how Latin borrowings were often preferred to inherited doublets: for example, Fr. *paradis* is eventually preferred to the inherited variants *pareïs, parvis* in the meaning of 'paradise' (Guiraud 1966:32; Picoche and Marchello-Nizia 1994:344).

3.6   Some statistics

Such anecdotal evidence can be reinforced by a consideration of the statistics obtained from modern corpora. De Mauro *et al.*'s (1993:437–540) frequency list of words for a corpus of spoken Italian displays the following 32 borrowings from Latin within the 400 commonest words in spoken Italian. (Those words marked with a dagger are Greek in origin, but were originally borrowed into Latin, which is their most likely immediate source.) Words are given in descending order of frequency, with their position in De Mauro *et al.*'s list indicated in brackets; items marked ¶ are described as semi-learnèd ('semidotte') by Battisti and Alessio (1950–57); first attestation is fourteenth century and earlier unless otherwise indicated:

> ¶*esempio* 'example' (115), *momento* 'moment' (119), *importante* 'important' (158), ¶*discorso* 'speech, discourse' (179), *eccetera* 'et cetera' (184), *ultimo* 'last' (198), *situazione* 'situation' (200), *questione* 'question' (246), *prossimo* 'next' (262), *politico* 'political' (280), *possibile* 'possible' (281), *continuare* 'to continue' (291), *probabilmente* 'probably' (305), *particolare* 'particular' (315), *titolo* 'title' (321), †*periodo* 'period' (323), *significare* 'to mean, signify' (330), *interessare* 'to interest' (341), *studio* 'study' (342), *possibilità* 'possibility' (347), *studiare* 'to study' (354), *linea* 'line' (356), *iniziativa* 'initiative' (362) (nineteenth century), *generale* 'general' (363), *difficile* 'difficult' (364), *considerare* 'to consider' (367),

attenzione 'attention' (371), *esistere* 'to exist' (373), *ordine* 'order' (375), *professore* 'teacher' (378) (eighteenth century), [†]*base* 'base' (388), *servizio* 'service' (396).

However, it is extremely difficult to obtain significant statistics concerning the entry of Latin loanwords into Romance. As an illustration of the problems, as well as some of the potential insights that statistical analysis may yield, I have analysed the vocabulary of the M section of Dauzat *et al.* (1971). This has the advantage of providing a significant but not overwhelming number of words (952 in all). Only headwords with an independent entry (i.e., excluding headwords which were cross-referenced to others) were considered, and morphological derivatives of headwords listed within an entry were excluded. Prefixes and 'grammatical' words such as personal pronouns were also excluded. The number of Latin borrowings exceeds the number of inherited words by a substantial margin. The figures obtained were as follows (based on Dauzat *et al.*'s own classification and dates of first attestation):

Total inherited words	141
Words which may be taken as part of 'common' Latin	72
Words deriving from diminutive 'common' Latin forms	5
Words from 'imperial' Latin	2
Words from 'popular' (i.e., non-literary) Latin	55
Words from 'low' (i.e., first–fifth-century) Latin	5
Words from Christian Latin	2

Total words borrowed from Latin (at all periods, and including a number of Greek borrowings which are described as entering French through Latin)		250	
Distribution by century of first attestation:		Register (as marked in the entry or as deduced from the nature of the source):	
10th	1	Religion	22
11th	4	Literary sources	22
12th	32	From translations	20

13th	28	Physical sciences or technology	19
14th	53	Medical and veterinary	19
15th	31	Historical	15
16th	48	Botanical	14
17th	15	Philosophical	10
18th	19	Zoological	6
19th	18	Legal	7
20th	1	Other	5
		Not classified	91

The predominance of borrowed over inherited words in the French vocabulary overall does not, however, correlate with their relative frequency of occurrence in the modern language. Examining our sample of French words against the frequency lists of the French Ministry of Education,[3] and of Picoche (1998), we find that in the former (based on the 1,500 most common words in written French), 49 of the inherited words and 14 of the borrowed words are listed, and in the latter (based on the 907 most frequently occurring words according to the data of the *Trésor de la langue française*), 31 of the inherited words and 10 of the borrowed words appear. Nonetheless, it is impressive that there are such a number of borrowed words in these lists: those occurring in both lists, in descending order of frequency, are: *monde* 'world', *moment* 'moment', *ministre* 'minister', *minute* 'minute', *médecin* 'doctor', *musique* 'music', *matière* 'matter' and *misère* 'wretchedness'.

Stefenelli (1992a) adopts the strategy of examining the fate of the thousand 'core words' (*Zentrallexeme*) of Latin. Of these thousand words, 419 are not inherited in the range of Romance languages he considers, and 106 of these are lost completely in that they supply neither borrowed nor inherited forms. A further 196 of the thousand appear in one or more Romance languages as clear borrowings (that is to say, excluding those Stefenelli identifies as 'occasional' or belonging to restricted registers: if these are included, this number rises substantially, to 415). Note that Latin words which are inherited may also be borrowed (see §3.4.1), e.g., CAUSA 'cause', which yields the inherited forms Fr. *chose*, Sp., Cat., It. *cosa*, Pt. *coisa* 'thing' but also the borrowed forms Fr. *cause*, Sp., Pt., Cat., It. *causa* 'cause';

or a Latin word may be inherited in some Romance varieties but be a borrowing in others, e.g., ălĭēnu(m) 'alien, foreign' which is inherited as Sp. *ajeno*, Pt. *alheio*, but borrowed as It. *alieno* (French has borrowed derivatives such as *aliéner* 'to alienate'): there are 101 such cases. It does not, of course, follow that a core word in Latin will also be a core word in Romance (see above), and the frequency of occurrence of the Romance words is not considered by Stefenelli. Nevertheless, it is interesting to see that the high proportion of Latin words which were not inherited (just over 40 percent) is almost exactly matched by the proportion which served in some way as borrowings (again it must be stressed that these two groups are not mutually exclusive). See also Stefenelli's contribution to this volume, chapter 11.

We should finally observe that the chronology of borrowings is not the same for all Romance languages (Nykrog 1957:113). (Blatt (1957:41) makes a similar point concerning syntax, observing that different constructions prevail in different areas.) Although French, Spanish and Italian coincide today in having borrowings from Lat. ACCĒDĕRE 'to approach', their date of first attestation and range of meaning varies. According to the *TLF* (I, 330), Fr. *accéder* is first attested in an astronomical treatise of 1270 as the present participle / adjective *accedenz* 'approaching', after which it does not surface again until the fifteenth century; only in the eighteenth century is it used in the meaning of 'to agree (to)', and is still restricted to 'technical' registers. This is also the date of the first attestation of Sp. *acceder* (Corominas, II, 12). In Italian, *accedere* is first used by Dante (late thirteenth–early fourteenth century, *LEI*, I, 249–51).

3.7 *The structural impact of lexical borrowing*

3.7.1 Phonological structure

As we have seen, the vast majority of Latin borrowings adapted to the sound patterns of their Romance hosts. Nevertheless, even though they did not cause innovation, they made a significant statistical impact. A clear example of this can be seen in the borrowings of Latin proparoxytones into the Ibero-Romance languages and Italo-Romance. Although there is a general tendency across Romance (and especially in western Romance) to syncopate the penultimate syllable of proparoxytones (e.g., Lat. MASCŬLU(M) 'male' > Fr. *mâle*, Pt. and Sp. *macho*, Cat. *mascle*, It. *maschio*), these languages, in contrast to French, appear to preserve enough proparoxytonically stressed words to keep the door open, so to speak, for the later Latin loans: the presence of the vowel /a/ in the penultimate syllabel seems particularly resistant to syncopation (Lat. SABBĂTU(M) 'Saturday' > Sp. and Pt. *sábado*,

Cat. *sàbat*, It. *sabbato*), and some verb-forms even seem to have acquired proparoxytonic stress (Lat. CANTABĀMUS 'we sang' > Sp. *cantábamos*, with change of stress position; Lat. CANTANT 'they sing' > It. *cantano*, with the addition of the vowel producing a proparoxytone). In the Iberian Peninsula, borrowings from Arabic such as *búnduqa* > Sp. *albóndiga* 'meatball' contribute to this stock; in Italy it may be that there was a 'restitution' of some proparoxytones (Maiden 1995a:45f.; following Tuttle 1974). The number of Latin proparoxytones in Spanish, Portuguese and Italian is very high (not only individual words such as Sp./It. *ánimo/animo* 'mind', *crédito/credito* 'credit', *décimo/decimo* 'tenth', *decrépito/decrepito* 'decrepit', *ética/etica* 'ethics', *mérito/merito* 'merit', but adjectives such as Sp./It. *práctico/pratico* 'practical', which form part of a significant class of words which are regularly related to nouns (*práctica/pratica* 'practice') and verbs (*practicar/praticare* 'to practise'), and many productive suffixes (*-ántico/-antico*, *-ánico/-anico*, *-éreo/-ereo*, etc.)). French, by contrast, consistently resists such stress patterns: cf. *crédit*, *décrépit*, *éthique*, *mérite*, *pratique*, *romantique*, *satanique*, *éthéré*, while Catalan, although often avoiding proparoxytones because of the loss of final vowels, maintains the position of the Latin stress: *crèdit*, *decrèpit(a)*, *ètic(a)*, *mèrit*, *pràctic(a)*, *romàntic(a)*, *satànic(a)*, *eteri (etèria)*. Latin loans have also changed the combinatorial possibilities of Romance phonemes. Spanish borrowings from Latin often contain complex consonantal clusters which are not found in inherited words (e.g., *práctica*, *admirar*); in Italian, by contrast, such groups have readily been assimilated as geminates (*prattica*, *ammirare*), which word-internally are totally alien to Spanish, despite the occasional maintenance of Latin geminate groups (e.g., Sp. *innato* 'innate', *obvio* 'obvious'). The complex consonantal groups and geminates present a problem for Spanish speakers as these words migrate into everyday usage, however, and strategies of weakening, syncopation or dissimilation are employed, with such pronunciations as ['pratika] ~ ['praθtika], [aθmi'ɾaɾ], [i'nato] and ['obβjo] being encountered (forms such as *inmenso*, *inmediato*, etc., have standardly undergone dissimilation).

3.7.2   Derivational morphology

Because Latin borrowings were assimilated relatively easily into Romance, they readily yielded derivatives: thus OFr. *figure*, which is attested as early as the tenth-century Eulalia Sequence, afforced by the later borrowings *figurer* (twelfth century), *figuratif* and *figuration* (thirteenth century), serves as the basis of *défigurer* as early as the twelfth century and the later forms *figurant* (fifteenth century), *figuriste* (seventeenth century), *figurisme* (eighteenth century) (cf. Brunot 1905:295). Perhaps the most far-reaching structural consequence of borrowing from Latin, however, is the exploitation of borrowed prefixes and suffixes and the consequent creation of an extensive derivational morphology. The suffix -ĀLE(M), for example, has been exceptionally productive in all the Romance languages; its borrowed status is most apparent in French (see Brunot 1906:239), where it can be distinguished from the popular development of -ĀLE(M) to -*el* (thus Lat. MORTĀLE(M)> Fr. *mortel*, but Sp., Pt., Cat. *mortal*, It. *mortale* 'mortal, fatal') – though -*el* is also productive today, and the two suffixes can be in meaningful contrast, as in *partial* 'partial = prejudiced' / *partiel* 'partial = not the whole' (see *TLF*, 12.1065). -ĀLE(M) was clearly also productive within Classical, late and medieval Latin, and a number of Romance words are borrowed from such essentially Latin creations, e.g., (Classical) COLLĒGIĀLE(M) > Fr. *collégial*, Sp., Pt. *colegial*, Cat. *col·legial*, It. *collegiale* 'collegial'; (late) MARGINĀLE(M) > Fr. *marginal*, Sp., Pt., Cat. *marginal*, It. *marginale* 'marginal'. But in Romance it goes much further, applied not only to borrowed Latin stems (e.g., Fr. *commercial*, Sp., Pt., Cat. *comercial*, It. *commerciale* 'commercial' on the basis of the various reflexes of COMMERCĬU(M)), but also to stems from other sources (e.g., Fr. *khalifal*, Sp., Pt., Cat. *califal* 'pertaining to a caliph'; Fr., Sp., Pt., Cat. *hexagonal*, It. *esagonale* 'hexagonal'). Some other common prefixal and suffixal elements widely shared among the Romance languages are: the negative DIS- > Fr., Sp., Pt., Cat., It. *dis-* (contrast the inherited Fr. *dés-*, Sp., Pt., Cat. *des-*); nominalizing -TĬŌNE(M) > Fr. -*tion*, Sp. -*ción*, Cat. -*ció*, It. -*zione* (contrast the inherited Fr. -*son*, Sp. -*zón*, Cat. -*ó*, It. -*zone*); -ĀRĬU(M) 'relating to' or 'receptacle for' > Fr. -*aire*, Sp. -*ario*, Pt. -*ário*, Cat. -*ari*, It. -*ario* (contrast the inherited Fr. -*ier*, Sp. -*ero*, Pt. -*eiro*, Cat. -*er*, It. -*aio*); the agentive -TOR > Fr. -*teur*, Sp., Pt., Cat. -*dor*, It. -*tore*; the adjectival -ŌSU(M) > Fr. -*eux*, Sp., Pt., It. -*oso*, Cat. -*ós*, and -ĪU(M) > Fr. -*if*, Sp., Pt. -*ivo*, Cat. -*iu*, It. -*ivo*. Compounding by juxtaposition of elements, following Latin models, is also more intensively exploited in Romance word formation: thus Latin formations like MĀTRĬCĪDA 'matricide', PARRĬCĪDA 'parricide, patricide', HŎMĬCĪDA 'homicide' form the basis for Fr. *régicide*, Sp., Cat., It. *regicida* 'regicide'; Fr. *suicide*, Sp., It. *suicida*, Cat. *suïcida* 'suicide'; Fr. *insecticide*, Sp., Cat. *insecticida*, It. *insetticida* 'insecticide' (see Guiraud 1968:42).

However, the introduction of Latin words also created a problem for morphological transparency. Often, Latin words drafted in to fill lexical gaps can be naturally related to inherited words in the Romance languages: an example of this is the borrowed form Sp. *novísimo* 'very new' (< Lat. NŎUISSĬMU(M); see §4.1.2). This form is regularly related to the adjective stem Sp. *nuevo* 'new', both semantically and formally; the vocalic alternation between Sp. /o/ and /ue/ corresponds to the diphthongization of Latin /ŏ/ in a stressed syllable, as in Sp. *morir* ~ *muere* 'to die ~ he/she dies', which is a very widespread feature in Spanish morphology. At the other extreme, there are groups of words which are plainly related semantically but cannot by any stretch of the imagination be part of the language's derivational morphology, e.g., Sp. *bélico*, It. *bellico* 'pertaining to war' as adjectives corresponding semantically to Sp. *guerra*, It. *guerra* 'war'; or Fr. *urbain*, Sp. *urbano*, It. *urbano* 'urban' corresponding semantically to Fr. *ville*, Sp. *ciudad*, It. *città* 'city, town'. In between, however, are words which are plainly related semantically, and also display some phonetic similarities; these relationships are synchronically semi-transparent, but become a good deal more transparent in the light of the history of the language. Thus Sp. *nocturno* 'nocturnal' is related semantically and phonetically to *noche* 'night', though the suffix *-urno* is not particularly productive and the /tʃ/ of the inherited Spanish word is distant from the /kt/ group of the Latin borrowing; however, we know from other Spanish–Latin correspondences that historically Lat. /kt/ and Sp. /tʃ/ are related: Lat. OCTŌ 'eight' > Sp. *ocho* (and the borrowed *octavo* 'eighth'), Lat. DICTU(M) 'said; saying (N)' > Sp. *dicho* (and the borrowed *dictar* 'to dictate'), etc. So while alternations of /tʃ/ ~ /kt/ are limited in Spanish, there are perhaps just enough to give speakers a consciousness of their relatedness: this at any rate was an assumption behind some of the early work in generative phonology, which drew on such examples.[4] Another interesting situation produced by Latin borrowing occurs when a borrowed morpheme is extremely productive as a bound form while the semantically corresponding inherited free morpheme is not productive at all. Devoto (1957:84f.) cites the example of the borrowed It. *puer-* 'boy, child', which is a constituent of such words as *puericultore* 'paediatric nurse', *puericultura* 'child welfare', *puerile* 'pertaining to children; childish', *puerilità* 'childishness', *puerizia* 'childhood', and refers to such morphemes as 'virtual elements' ('elementi virtuali').

3.7.3   Semantic discrimination

Of most interest to us in dealing with the literary language is the growth in the Romance vocabulary and the greater possibilities for semantic discrimination which this growth brings about.

This can be clearly demonstrated by a study of near-synonyms in any standard Romance language. For example, the synonyms of *répugnance* listed in Bailly (1947:507f.) are: *répulsion*, *dégoût*, *nausée*, *antipathie* and *aversion*. Of these, only *dégoût* is an inherited word. *Répugnance* and *aversion* are first attested in the thirteenth century, *répulsion* and *nausée* in the fifteenth century; *antipathie* is a sixteenth-century borrowing from Greek. What we now assume to be extremely common concepts are often first distinguished in this way. Fr. *famille*, Sp. *familia*, It. *famiglia* 'family' are borrowings from Lat. FĂMĬLĬA 'household establishment (including servants)'. The Romance word seems originally to distinguish the concept of 'people living under the same roof', as distinct from such notions as 'lineage, parentage', and only later takes on the meaning of blood relationship; it adds the abstract meaning of 'group'. Gougenheim (1959:6) suggests that its borrowing is due to cultural differences between Roman and medieval society. A great deal of work still needs to be done on the history of concepts and their expression to complement the vast etymological reference works at our disposal. In French especially, later borrowing has often been seen as a therapeutic for homonymic clash: thus Gougenheim (1959:15f.) suggests that Fr. *monde* replaces the expected *mont* (< Lat. MUNDU(M) 'world') to avoid identity with *mont* < Lat. MONTE(M) 'hill, mountain'.

Discrimination is especially striking in doublet developments of Latin words (see §3.4.1). Lat. SACRĀMENTU(M) in the Classical language has the meaning 'pledge, oath', and as such is inherited as Fr. *serment*; the borrowing Fr. *sacrement* 'sacrament' reflects the later Christian meaning of the word, which belongs to a more specialized field (for many other French examples, see Chaurand 1977:38ff.). Lexical gaps were sometimes morphological: Chaurand (1977:71) points out how the absence of of an adjective corresponding to the Germanic borrowing Fr. *renard* 'fox' may have led to the adoption of the Latin borrowing *vulpin* 'pertaining to the fox; fox-like'. Another motivation for lexical borrowing may have been economy: for example, the noun Fr. *quadrupede* (late fifteenth century), Sp. *cuadrúpedo* (seventeenth–eighteenth centuries), Cat. *quadrúpede* (seventeenth century), It. *quadrupede* 'quadruped' conveniently encapsulates the notion of 'having four legs', which could otherwise only be expressed periphrastically. Latin borrowings may also have been cultivated by those seeking an elevated style (Lüdtke 1974:280f.).

4 Syntactic borrowing

4.1 *Preliminary issues*

The identification of syntactic borrowing from Latin to Romance is altogether a more complex matter; I discuss a number of the relevant considerations in Pountain (1998a), which I will briefly recapitulate here.

4.1.1 Feasibility

There is much current controversy concerning syntactic borrowing: opinions range from an outright denial that it is possible, through the notion that syntactic borrowing is essentially a function of lexical borrowing, to the view that borrowing is possible at all levels. This variety of views is mirrored in the history of Romance linguistics: while Guiraud (1966:41) is able to assert that it would be hard to exaggerate the extent to which the syntax of literary French is essentially Latin ('on ne saurait trop dire … à quel point la syntaxe du français littéraire est essentiellement latine'), Devoto (1957) is much more circumspect.

4.1.2 Mechanism

Even if we admit syntactic borrowing proper as a possibility, its likely mechanisms do not make its study easy. It is unlikely, for instance, that syntactic borrowings completely supplant native constructions, or that they constitute major structural innovation. It is most likely that imitation of foreign models encourages a statistical increase in the use of host language structures, or that a host language structure is extended in some way. For this reason, those who wish to minimize the effects of Latin on written Romance can quite plausibly insist that such trends are purely internally motivated. All this means that we are not going to see the quantum changes in syntax that we see in vocabulary, and that it will be difficult, if not impossible, to give an exact date for a syntactic borrowing.

The issue of the extent to which syntactic borrowing is related to lexical borrowing should perhaps be explored a little. (For some relevant discussion, see Vincent 2007a.) Lexical borrowing is certainly closely linked to the success of what may be ultimately seen as morphological borrowings. The borrowing of a bound morpheme must depend on the accumulation of individual lexical borrowings which exhibit the feature, though there may come a point at which speakers, recognizing a regular relationship, begin to use the suffix independently, and it is at this point that we may speak of a morphological borrowing. Thus, in Italian and the Ibero-Romance languages (the latter probably at least in part as a result of Italian as well as Latin influence), where the Latin superlative -ISSĬMU(M) suffix has enjoyed favour to the point of becoming completely productive as an adjectival intensifier, we find such doublets as *malísimo* (an analogical formation from *malo* 'bad') and *pésimo*, borrowed from the suppletive Latin form PESSĬMU(M), which was the superlative of MǍLU(M) 'bad', both meaning 'very bad'. That the stage of independent use of a suffix borrowed in this way may not be reached is demonstrated by the borrowing of many Latin present participle forms in -NTE(M) (e.g., It. *esistente*, Sp. *existente* 'existing'). Since this suffix never achieved full productivity in Italian and Spanish, in this case, such words must continue to be considered purely lexical borrowings. Syntactic constructions which depend on 'grammatical words' (see §§4.2.1 and 4.2.2) may also involve an element of lexical calquing: thus the Romance formations Fr. *après que*, Sp. *después (de) que*, It. *dopo che* 'after' may be thought of as paralleling the defunct Lat. POSTQUAM (see §4.2.1) and Fr. *lequel*, Sp. *el cual*, It. *il quale* 'which' as paralleling the Latin inflected relative QUĪ (see §4.2.2).

4.1.3 Identification

For the identification of lexical borrowings, it was possible to draw up a diagnostic profile based on exceptionality to sound change, type of meaning, register and date of first attestation, and, despite the limitations of existing etymological dictionaries, we have these and other powerful reference tools at our disposal which make tracing such borrowings a relatively straightforward task. In syntax, however, there is no such clear distinction between the profile of an inherited feature and that of a borrowed feature; there are no dictionaries of syntactic features, and the tools needed to identify syntactic constructions automatically in texts (e.g., part-of-speech (POS) tagging) are only just being developed.

The most fruitful way forward for the identification of syntactic borrowings would appear to lie in a hypothesized association between particular text-types and syntactic features, it being expected that borrowed Latin syntax will be most prevalent in translations and documents that are most heavily dependent on Latin originals (so informal writing would be at the bottom of this scale and creative literature further down than, say, historical or legal texts: see Blatt 1957:38f.). We might also expect that text-types which are rich in lexical borrowings will also exhibit syntactic borrowings. Another strategy for the identification of syntactic borrowings lies in comparison of spoken and written language in the present day: since we would expect the incidence of borrowed constructions to be lower in the spoken language, such comparison may also provide indications as to which syntactic features of the written language are borrowed. (However, we must bear in mind that since in an *Ausbau* language community linguistic features can migrate downwards, it will not be the case that such comparison will successfully identify all borrowed constructions.)

4.2 Examples

Some of the syntactic features which have been attributed to Latin influence are discussed below. We can make no overall generalization about their motivation: while some appear to be favoured by a move towards greater accuracy and exactness of expression, others seem to represent no such gain, and if anything seem rather to be encouraged by economy. For one or two proposed borrowings there seems no motivation other than a gain in variety of expression or the élitist pursuit of an elevated style (see §3.7.3).

4.2.1 Subordinating constructions

An overall preference for subordinating syntax, as opposed to parataxis or conjunction (Blatt 1957:37, 55), is often cited as having developed in the written language under the influence of Latin. This claim is based on observable changes in the course of the textual record and on the fact that the Latin subordinating conjunctions show a high rate of loss in Romance. But enough of the latter survive to suggest that subordination was far from absent in the spoken language: the versatile subordinator Fr., Sp., Pt., Cat. *que*, It. *che* 'that' had multiple functions as a complementizer and general logical connective, functions which continue in the spoken language down to the present day, again showing the likely register-specific nature of Latin-inspired innovations. Conjunctions deriving from Lat. *sī* 'if' and QUANDŌ 'when' also survived, as did relative clauses (where again *que*, etc., sometimes distinguished from a personal-referring *qui*, etc., served as the relative pronouns). The changes instigated by Latin influence appear to have consisted, as in vocabulary, of finer functional discrimination carried out by essentially lexical means. A whole range of adverbial conjunctions consisting of adverbs, prepositions or participles, plus the ubiquitous *que*, etc., appeared, which made temporal distinctions in particular more nuanced (cf. Fr. *alors que, attendu que, afin que*, etc.).

Some more particular syntactic constructions have been attributed to Latin influence; since in most cases Romance cannot precisely imitate Latin elements, the parallelism lies in a general patterning. The temporal clause type known in Latin as *cum inversum*, which is unusual in that the subordinate clause introduced by the temporal connective marks a relation of posteriority to the main clause rather than of anteriority or simultaneity (see Pountain 1983:201), is paralleled in Romance by constructions such as the following, in which Lat. *cum*, in the absence of any etymological reflex in Romance, is substituted by *quand*, etc., and in French and Italian by *quel che*: *On servait le café, quand le temps se gâta* 'They were serving the coffee, when the weather worsened' (Blatt 1957:55); *Stavo per prendere il treno, quando mi accorsi che mi era stato rubato il portafoglio* 'I was about to get the train, when I realized that my wallet had been stolen' (Giusti 2001:722).

These constructions are reported as being rare before 1500 (Pagliaro and Belardi 1963:151; Blatt 1957:55) and today appear to be restricted to formal written register.[5] Accordingly, the case for regarding them as a borrowing seems strong. The motivation for such borrowing is likely to have been élitist imitation of Latin for its own sake rather than expressive need, since all *cum inversum* constructions can be alternatively expressed as 'normal' temporal sentences; the above sentences can be rendered as follows: *Le temps se gâta quand on servait le café* 'The weather worsened when they were serving the coffee'; *Mi accorsi che mi era stato rubato il portafoglio quando stavo per prendere il treno* 'I realized that my wallet had been stolen when I was about to get the train'.

4.2.2   Relatives

Fr. *lequel*, Sp. *el cual / el que*, Pt. *o qual* and Cat. *el qual* and It. *il quale* and *cui* came to be used as relative pronouns and adjectives before which prepositions could be placed, hence making the expression of case function more accurate. Lat. QUĀLE(M) 'which', on which Fr. *quel*, It. *quale*, etc., are based, was originally an interrogative or relative adjective, and its first use with the article in Romance seems to have been as an interrogative: Foulet (1968:183) notes that use of *li quels*, etc., as a relative is rare in old French. But the marking of these forms for gender had the advantage of making anaphoric reference less prone to ambiguity, and facilitated the extensive exploitation of relative constructions. Such examples of the use of *laquelle* in Froissart (Diller 1972) are:

Laquelle with subject function:

> *Et i tint son tinel et son estat, et la roine Phelippe sa fenme avoecques lui,*
> ***laquelle*** *estoit enchainte.*
> (p. 226)

'And he kept his soldiers and his retinue, and Queen Philippa his wife with him, **who** was pregnant.'

Laquelle with prepositional object function:

> *Ensi que li bourgois de Jugon avoit en convenant il fist, et desfrema la porte de*
> ***laquelle*** *il gardoit les clefs.*
> (p. 558)

'He did as the burgher of Jugon had agreed and opened the door of **which** he kept the keys.'

Laquelle used adjectivally with a noun which is a prepositional object:

> *Et fui en la compagnie dou roi, un quartier d'un an, et euch celle aventure que, ce que je fui en Escoce, il viseta tout son pais, par **laquelle** visitation je apris et comsiderai moult de la matere et ordenance des Escoçois, et sont de toute tele condition que chi desus vous est devisé.* (p. 128)[6]

> 'And I was in the King's company for a quarter of a year, and had the experience that, whilst I was in Scotland, he visited the whole of his country, through **which** visitation I learnt and pondered a great deal about what the Scots are made of and how they behave, and they are of just that condition that is described to you above.'

It cannot be claimed that these relatives are in themselves borrowings, but they seem to have been exploited in order to give written Romance something of the same accuracy in anaphoric reference as in Latin.

The adjectival use of relatives as in the third example of *laquelle* given above came to be particularly characteristic of formal written language, where it is sometimes referred to as the 'transition relative' (Brunot 1906:426; Blatt 1957:56). An early example is to be found in the *Glosas Emilianenses* (tenth century?), where the writer of the Romance gloss appears to be striving to make the reference absolutely clear:

> Latin: *abjubante* [sic] *domino nostro Jhesu Christo cui est honor et jmperium cum patre* ...

> Romance: *conoajutorio de nuestro dueno, dueno Christo, dueno Salbatore, **qual** dueno get ena honore, **equal** duenno tienet ela mandatjone cono Patre...*

> 'with the help of our Lord Jesus Christ, which Lord [= who] is in honour, and which Lord [= who] has power with the Father' (see Pountain 2001:23)

This function also continues in formal registers of the modern Romance languages: Battaglia and Pernicone (1965:269) comment that the following construction is specific to legal language and the language of notaries: 'linguaggio giuridico e notarile': *Tale è il principio che dobbiamo tener presente; **il quale** principio si fonda* ... 'Such is the principle which we must maintain sight of, which principle is based on ...'; and in formal Spanish and Portuguese *cuyo/cujo*, which in this usage has no genitive value, is used in this way:

> *Disponía de cincuenta destructores que el presidente Roosevelt le había vendido, con **cuyo** acto los Estados Unidos habían dejado prácticamente de ser neutrales* (J. M. Gironella, cited in De Bruyne 1995:200)

'He had at his disposal fifty destroyers which President Roosevelt had sold him, with **which** action the United States effectively stopped being neutral'

*A região vem passando por uma transformação urbanística com a desocupação dos galpões e antigas casas, em **cujos** locais há grandes possibilidades de surgirem emprendimentos*   (*Folha de S. Paulo*, cited in Neves 2000:369)

'The region is going through a transformation of the city fabric, with people moving out of warehouses and old houses, in **which** buildings there are great possibilities for businesses to spring up'

Again, the modern spoken language seems closer to the situation which predated such discrimination in the formal written language. Use of the 'exact' relatives is rare in everyday speech, and the marking of case function is often correspondingly vague: thus Pagliaro and Belardi (1963:151) call attention to the following differences between spoken and written French

Spoken	Written
C'est lui que je parle	*C'est lui dont je parle*
'It's he that I speak'	'It's he of whom I speak'
à l'endroit qu'il est	*à l'endroit où il est*
'at the place that he is'	'at the place where he is'

and Cinque (2001:512) characterizes as 'low, casual style' ('stile [...] basso, trascurato') the sentences: *I posti che sta bene sono ...* 'The places that it is good are ...'; *È il posto che siamo andati ieri* 'It's the place that we went yesterday'.

4.2.3   Verb-forms

Latin had a wealth of non-finite verb-forms (past, present and future participles, the gerund and the gerundive, present, perfect and future infinitives, both active and passive) expressing a wide range of functions which in modern Romance are generally covered either by full-clause constructions or by extensions in the use of the simple infinitive: thus, for example, Lat. AD URBEM CĂPĬENDAM, lit. 'to the city being taken', would be rendered in Romance by Fr. *pour prendre la ville*, Sp. *para tomar la ciudad*, It. *per prendere la città* 'in order to take the city'. However, where the corresponding verb-forms (the infinitive, gerund and past participle) have survived, some of these constructions appear to have been reutilized in Romance, and this apparent 'resurrection' in formal registers of Romance of non-finite verb-form constructions has often been perceived as a case of Latin syntactic influence. We must nonetheless exercise caution in establishing identities between Romance forms and their Latin models, since the case, tense and voice inflections of the Latin forms have been lost.

4.2.3.1 Absolute constructions

'Absolute' constructions with participles, characterized by the absence of a finite verb or any logical connective, were clearly marked in Latin by the ablative case, and although there is no such demarcatory device available in Romance, there is an obvious parallelism with Latin (see also §2.4). Some modern literary examples with past participles are:

> **Sa messe dite**, *il déjeunait d'un pain de seigle trempé dans le lait de ses vaches*
> '**His mass said**, he lunched on a rye loaf dunked in the milk from his cows'
>
> (Victor Hugo, Les Misérables, I, 5, consulted at www.livresse.com/
Livres-enligne/lesmiserables/010105.shtml)

> **Sabido esto**, *pocas hay que se puedan comparar con la policía.*
> '**That [being] known**, there are few that can be compared with the police.'
>
> (Mariano José de Larra, La Revista Española, 7 de febrero de 1835, consultado
at www.irox.de/larra/articulo/art_poli.html)

> **Ciò detto**, *scese con lei in cucina …*
> '**That said**, he went down to the kitchen with her'
>
> (Alessandro Manzoni, I Promessi Sposi, XV, consulted at www.crs4.it/
Letteratura/PromessiSposi/PromessiSposi.html)

A much-discussed question has been the extent to which such constructions are due to Latin influence; the various contributions to the debate once again illustrate the difficulties of assessing the reality of syntactic borrowing. It may be that they were already firmly associated with more formal registers in Latin: Adams (1977:60f.) notes that absolute constructions are already rare in the letters of Claudius Terentianus, yet they continue to be amply attested in the *Peregrinatio*, whose author appears to ape certain features of formal classical prose (Pagliaro and Belardi 1963:153). Brunot (1906:466) observes that the absolute construction with the past participle is not found in old French outside translations and other works in which there is overt Latin influence of other kinds, even though it became more widely accepted in Middle French. For Devoto (1957:83f.), they constitute the only clear example of Latin influence on Romance syntax. However, Nykrog (1957:99) rejects the idea of Latin influence in view of the fact that the 'popular' Romance adverbial formation in *-ment/-mente* derives from an absolute construction, e.g., LENTĀ MENTĒ 'with a slow mind' → 'in a slow way' → Fr. *lentement*, Sp., Pt., It. *lentamente*, Cat. *lentament* 'slowly'. Yet it would not have been impossible for such a turn of phrase modelled on a feature of formal register to have provided the model for an essentially idiomatic construction which diffused in speech and became productive.[7]

An associated construction which may also be modelled on Latin is the use of a participle after a preposition which marks more explicitly its adverbial function (cf. Lat., AB URBE CONDĬTĀ, lit. 'from the city having been founded', i.e., 'from the time at which the city was founded'). Temporal prepositions seem to be the most favoured, and indeed appear to antedate 'bare' absolute constructions used in a temporal sense; Nykrog (1957:96f.) observes that in old French such constructions as *puis le soleil couchant* 'after sunset', *ainz le soleil levé* 'before sunrise', *contre soleil levant* 'against, into the rising sun' are limited to the expression of times of day. Some examples from literary texts in modern French, Spanish and Italian are:

> *Chaque soir,* ***après le travail fini,*** *Jules et Jeanne s'empressaient de se rendre au rivage*
> 'Every evening, **after the work [was] finished**, Jules and Jeanne hurried to get to the shore'.
>
> (H. Beaugrand, Jeanne la Fileuse, VI, consulted at www.gutenberg.org/
files/14536/14536-h/14536-h.htm)

> *Por último,* ***después de terminado este minucioso reconocimiento del lugar en que se encontraba,*** *agazapóse en un ribazo junto a unos chopos de copas elevadas y oscuras …*
> 'Finally, **after the painstaking reconnaisance of the place where he found himself [was] finished**, he crouched down on a slope next to high dark poplar trees …'
>
> (Gustavo Adolfo Bécquer, La corza blanca (Leyendas), consulted at www.rae.es/)

> ***Dopo finito lo spettacolo e sfollata la gente che si accalcava d'intorno,*** *Golasecca sentì toccarsi in un braccio*
> '**After the show [was] finished and the people who were surging forward all around [had] dispersed**, Golasecco felt someone touch his arm'
>
> (Carlo Collodi, Storie allegre, 14, consulted at www.pelagus.org/it/libri/
STORIE_ALLEGRE,_di_Carlo_Collodi_10.html).[8]

4.2.3.2 'Accusative and infinitive'

I have discussed in some detail elsewhere (Pountain 1998a) the adoption in Castilian of the 'accusative and infinitive' with verbs of saying and thinking, which is broadly paralleled in other Romance languages (Brunot 1906:454–56). Again, strictly speaking, to talk of 'accusative' in the Romance languages is inappropriate; we mean that verbs of saying and thinking are followed by an infinitive and a noun, the noun being construed as the subject of the infinitive; the construction is thus the equivalent of a full-clause complement:

> Aristote dit *[appartenir]*$_{INFINITIVE}$ *aux beaux [le droit de commander]'*$_{ACCUSATIVE}$'
> (= Aristote dit que le droit de commander appartenait aux beaux)
> 'Aristotle says that the right to command belongs to the beautiful'
> (Montaigne, cit. Blatt 1957:52)

The fifteenth and sixteenth centuries appear to have been the heyday of the 'accusative and infinitive' construction in western Romance: for French see Haase (1969:215) and Blatt (1957:67). I have pointed out (Pountain 1998) that some practical advantage of economy attached to the 'accusative and infinitive', and it is significant in this regard that even in French, from which the construction has been largely eradicated under the force of the purist opposition which began with Vaugelas (see below 4.3), it survives in circumstances where otherwise there would only be a stylistically awkward double-clause alternative: thus *l'homme que je dis ressembler à un chat*, lit. 'the man whom I say to resemble a cat', would otherwise be rendered by a construction such as *l'homme que je dis qu'il ressemble à un chat*, lit. 'the man whom I say that he resembles a cat'. In very formal registers in Italian and Spanish such constructions are more readily available, the major restrictions being that the subject follows the infinitive and that the infinitive is an auxiliary or a stative verb (see, for Italian, Rizzi 1982: ch. III):

> *Affermava infatti **esser la famiglia** ... la maledizione dell uomo*
> 'He claimed indeed that **the family was** ... the curse of man'
> [lit. 'He claimed indeed **to be the family** ... the curse of man']
> (Morante, cited in Skytte and Salvi 2001:528)

> *Hubo, pues, una primitiva versión del antídoto en la que el autor de Orfeo afirmaba **haber empleado Garcilaso** «una sola vez el acusativo griego»*
> 'Then there was an original version of the antidote [=critical response] in which the author of Orpheus claimed that Garcilaso used "the Greek accusative only once"'
> [lit. '... in which the author of Orpheus claimed **to have used Garcilaso**...'] (Alonso, cited in Pountain 1998a:171)

In fifteenth-century Castilian, a 'nominative and infinitive' construction also enjoys some popularity:

> ***honestidad e continencia*** *non es dubda **ser** muy grandes e escogidas virtudes*
> 'There is no doubt that honesty and reserve are very great and select virtues'

[lit. '**honesty and reserve** there is no doubt **to be** very great and select virtues']

(Lapesa 1981:140)

It is not easy to judge how far this construction diffused. Some writers who are often thought of as reflecting 'popular' features of Romance, such as Santa Teresa (sixteenth century), use it, but they may have been consciously or unconsciously imitating high registers. Brunot (1906:455) observes similarly for French that it was used by writers who were not Latinists. As we have seen, different Romance languages seem subsequently to be tolerant of it to different degrees.

4.2.4 Word order

Modification of word order, or hyperbaton, is a Latinate feature (see Ledgeway, this volume, chapter 8: §§3.1, 3.2) that is very frequent in some Castilian authors. In the poetry of Góngora (1521–1627), for example, closely associated elements in noun phrases, such as nouns and adjectives, or nouns and dependent prepositional phrases, may be separated:

> *Tras la bermeja Aurora el Sol dorado*
> *por **las puertas** salía **del Oriente***
> (= salía por las puertas del Oriente)
> 'After the russet Dawn the golden Sun
> through **the gates** came out **of the East**'
> 'came out through the gates of the East'

(Luis de Góngora, Soneto 218, Obras completas (Madrid: Aguilar), p. 442)

This feature was imitated from high register Latin literature and seems not to have diffused even into formal Castilian prose. What literary prose does show, however, is a quite widespread tendency for main verbs to be placed at the end of the sentence, an order which was apparently not inherited in any Romance language, even in those (Castilian, Portuguese) which are said to have relatively 'free' word order, and must accordingly be thought of as an imitation of the default word order of a declarative Latin sentence, possibly even as a feature which stereotypically characterized Latin (see Salvi, this volume, chapter 7):

> *… à tous ceux qui **ces présentes lettres verront***
> '… to all those who **these present letters** will see'
> = '… to all those will see these present letters'

(Voiture, I, 337, cited in Haase 1969:434)

Haase observes that this construction (a relative clause with the relative pronoun as subject) is the most frequent type; placing the object between an auxiliary and dependent infinitive is also common, especially in Malherbe and La Fontaine's poetry. Schiaffini (1943:134) considered verb-final position to be a sure indicator ('spia acutissima') of latinizing prose; Wanner (1987:395) similarly regards verb-final position as 'a clear sign of Latin imitation'. It seems to have diffused enough to have become also one of a number of markers of formal or upper-class speech in sixteenth-century Spanish, although it has not survived in the present day: in the prose plays of Lope de Rueda, upper-class characters regularly place objects and prepositional phrases before the verb:

> *Cristina, hermana, ¿qué te paresce del olvido tan grande como Leonardo, mi querido hermano, ha tenido en escrebirme, que ya son passados buenos días que [letra d'él]*_{OBJECT} *no [he visto]*_{VERB}? (Lope de Rueda, *Eufemia*, c.1550)
> 'My dear Cristina, what do you think of my beloved brother Leonardo's great forgetfulness in writing to me, now that many days have passed since I have seen a letter from him?'

4.2.5   Adjective position

The influence of Latin can also be manifested less obviously. I have suggested (Pountain 1998b; see also Vincent 2007a) that an increase in the use of qualificative adjectives preposed to the noun from the fifteenth century onwards is likely to be due to Latin, where preposed position was the rule for qualificative adjectives (see also Haase 1969:441). Yet the situation is in fact more complex than the simple imitation of Latin: the increase is not simply in the use of preposed adjectives, but in the use of adjectives overall, due to the pursuit of varied lexis known to rhetoricians as *amplificatio verborum*, a stylistic feature of Latin prose which was approvingly encouraged in written registers in Romance (see also §5) and famously satirized in Cervantes's *Don Quijote*:

> *Apenas auia el **rubicundo** Apolo tendido por la faz de la **ancha y espaciosa** tierra las **doradas** hebras de sus **hermosos** cabellos, y apenas los **pequeños y pintados** paxarillos con sus **harpadas** lenguas auian saludado con **dulce y meliflua** armonia la venida de la **rosada** Aurora, que, dexando la **blanda** cama del **zeloso** marido, por las puertas y balcones del **manchego** orizonte a los mortales se mostraua, quando el **famoso** cauallero don Quixote de la Mancha, dexando las **ociosas** plumas, subio sobre su **famoso** cauallo Rozinante, y començo a caminar por el **antiguo y conocido** campo de Montiel.*
> (Miguel de Cervantes, *Don Quijote de la Mancha*, ed. Rodolfo Schevill and Adolfo Bonilla (Madrid: Gráficas Reunidas, 1928), p.58)

'Scarcely had fair-haired Apollo spread the golden strands of his lovely hair across the surface of the wide and spacious earth, and scarcely had the little painted birds with their tuneful tongues greeted with sweet and mellifluous harmony the arrival of the roseate Aurora, who, leaving her jealous huband's soft bed, was revealing herself to mortals through the doorways and balconies of the Manchegan horizon, than the famous knight Don Quixote of La Mancha, forsaking idle slumber, mounted his famous horse Rozinante, and began to ride through the ancient and celebrated plain of Montiel.'

This has had an interestingly far-reaching result, however, in that in the modern formal written *Ausbau* Romance languages (in the non-*Ausbau* Romance languages prenominal position is very restricted), a complex semantic contrast has arisen between preposed and postposed adjectives, preposed adjectives being broadly associated with 'expected' properties of nouns and incapable of receiving contrastive stress, while postposed adjectives express distinguishing characteristics and can be stressed. Battaglia and Pernicone (1965:191) contrast such pairs as

Egli è un am**i**co *caro* / Egli è un *caro* am**i**co
(Italics and bold original; bold type indicates stress)
Lit. 'He is a **friend dear** / He is a dear **friend**'

observing that when the adjective is placed after the noun, the qualifying sense is stronger, whereas when the order is the reverse the attribute loses some of its force ('nel costrutto con l'aggettivo posposto al nome, l'indicazione qualificativa risulta più vigorosa, mentre nella successione inversa l'attributo perde d'intensità e di valore'). Some common adjectives appear to have developed secondary meanings as a result of these possibilities (made all the more apparent by translation into a non-Romance language); the following French example could be paralleled in other *Ausbau* Romance languages:

un simple soldat 'an ordinary soldier'
un soldat simple 'a simple (not very intelligent) soldier'

4.2.6   Other

In the case of a number of other features that have sometimes been cited as examples of Latin borrowing or imitation, the case for Latin influence is far from proven, and further research is likely to be fruitful. For example, the relative infrequency of the *be*-passive (Fr. *être*, Sp., Pt. *ser*, Cat. *ésser*, It.

essere + past participle) in the modern spoken Romance languages and its restriction to certain written registers might suggest that Latin influence has a role to play in its use (in the modern period its use is often seen as a consequence of contact with English, but this is most likely to have affected journalistic register, and only in relatively recent times). Comparison with Romanian, where, in striking contrast, the reflexive extended to fulfil the passive role until the advent of the *be*-passive, which is probably modelled on French, suggests that some differential factor is at play in western Romance. This question needs to be stated in a more nuanced way, however. The Romance *be*-passive is not used in the full range of functions available to the Latin passive, which included use: (a) as a medio-passive (LAUATI SUNT IN FLUMEN 'they washed in the river'); (b) to express an indefinite subject for intransitive verbs (IN SILVAM VENITUR 'people come to the wood'); and (c) as a form available to deponent and semi-deponent verbs (PROFECTI SUMUS 'we set out'). Thus, the true point at issue is whether the *be*-passive in its dynamic function is a Latin borrowing. It is unlikely that the form itself is borrowed from Latin: the past participle was familiar from other constructions, such as the Romance perfect with descendants of Lat. HĂBĒRE, and in its adjectival function; there is also no reason to suppose that the stative passive function of the Latin perfective *be*-passive (PORTA CLAUSA EST 'the door is shut'), which is closely associated with the adjectival function of the past participle, fell into disuse.[9] If anything, then, it seems most likely that the example of Latin may have extended or reinforced an already existing construction; but more detailed investigation is needed.

4.3 The role of grammarians

As we have seen (§1.4), a crucial feature of *Ausbau* language communities is the activity of purist grammarians. Since grammars of the Romance vernaculars closely followed those of Latin, features of Latin have often been imposed on Romance.

We have already (§4.2.2) noted the greater precision achieved by the extension of the Romance system of relatives in partial imitation of Latin. The use of 'imprecise' relatives continues to be castigated today, even though they are a widespread feature of the spoken language: thus Butt and Benjamin (2000:502) correct the colloquial Sp. *el hotel que estuvimos el año pasado* to *el hotel en el que estuvimos el año pasado*. It is probably for this reason too that 'resumptive relatives' in relative clauses, though apparently universally attested in the spoken Romance languages, are castigated. Examples are:

French: *la gosse que je lui ai parlé chez toi hier*
  'the girl that I spoke to her at your place last night'
Spanish: *la muchacha que pensaba que Juan le regaló un libro*
  'the girl that I thought that Juan gave her a book'
Catalan: *l'home a qui creus que li han donat un llibre*
  'the man to whom I think that they gave him a book'
Italian: *questo incarico che non sapevo la novità che lo avrebbero affidato a te*
  'this task that I didn't know the newness that I would have entrusted it
  to you'   (Examples from Smits 1989:57)

It is again perhaps significant in this respect that in Romanian, which was so long immune from contact with Latin, such resumptive features are accepted as standard, e.g., *calul pe care l-am cumpărat* 'the horse which I have bought' (Posner 1996:169).

Nykrog (1957:106f.) points to the possibility of the distribution of the French past historic and imperfect tenses being 'corrected' so that they resembled usage in Latin. Although there appears to have been little change in the use of these tenses between Latin and modern French, Schaechtelin's (1911) work on their use in Villehardouin and Joinville showed that at this time the past historic had a much wider usage than either it had had in Latin or was subsequently to have in later French.

I traced in Pountain (1998c) the introduction of spurious rules for the use of the Spanish gerund. These amount to the stipulation that the subject of the gerund must be identical with that of the main verb unless the gerund is being used in an absolute construction or as the complement of a verb of perception. Despite the major syntactical differences between Latin and Romance in the use of the gerund, the purist insistence seems to be based on Latin, where the understood subject of a gerund was by default interpreted as being coreferential with that of the main verb, or as having an indefinite subject:

(Titus) equitandi peritissimus fuit
(Titus).NOM riding.GEN very-expert.NOM was
'Titus was very expert at riding'
(*Titus* is the subject of both *equitandi* and *fuit*)
            (Suet., *Tit.*, 3, cited in Gildersleeve and Lodge 1895:279)

Sapientia ars vivendi putanda est
knowledge.NOM art.NOM living.GEN thinking.NOM is
'Knowledge is to be considered the art of living'
(*vivendi* and *putanda* both have indefinite subjects)
            (C., *Fin.*, I. 13, 42, cited in Gildersleeve and Lodge 1895:279)

The purists did not include in this rule the absolute construction, where, as we have seen (§4.2.3.1), the expression of a non-coreferential subject was possible, in the general rule for the Castilian gerund, presumably because it was itself borrowed from Latin. Another exception to the purist rule, the construction with verbs of perception (e.g., *Vi a los niños cruzando la calle* 'I saw the children crossing the road'), was presumably already too firmly entrenched in Castilian to be reversed.

On the other hand, it should not be thought that prescriptive grammarians have uniformly favoured all things Latin. In periods of heavy imitation of Latin, such excesses have been the subject of criticism. Vaugelas attacked the 'accusative and infinitive' construction (Blatt 1957:67).

5   Stylistic latinisms

So far we have been discussing what we might call linguistic latinisms: essentially, lexical and syntactic borrowings from Latin. The written registers of Romance also display stylistic latinisms, which in creative literature are often difficult to distinguish from what we might see as the natural demands of literary expression. The use of a wide vocabulary is part and parcel of the pursuit of *variatio*, which excites a reader's interest and admiration; the addition of epithets to nouns and noun phrases is, as we have seen (§4.2.5), an instance of *amplificatio*. Planned discourse permits and exploits such devices as the preposing of adverbial clauses and the use of nested and parenthetical structures, such as relative clauses and adjectival phrases. Poetry makes extensive use of inversion and even hyperbaton, often to suit the demands of rhyme and metre. Creative writers also make extensive use of the rhetorical devices and figures of speech which were familiar from classical literature and amply described and exemplified by Latin grammarians. I have considered it beyond the scope of this article to explore these matters further, but the close relation between the 'linguistic' and 'stylistic' features of an *Ausbau* language deserves much fuller attention than linguists generally accord it. In Sørensen's (1957:138) words, à propos of the influence of Latin on English: 'What is style may become syntax.'

6   Conclusion

Overall, borrowing from Latin in the standardized Romance languages is substantial and worthy of much more rigorous and detailed analysis than it has hitherto received. While borrowing of vocabulary has long been recognized, there are still many important questions to be resolved regarding borrowings in syntax. However, Latin borrowing is extremely difficult to quantify. In tracing the impact of Latin through the textual record of Romance, future research should pay close attention to the discrimination of text-types and registers, and should investigate more extensively Latin models and originals and the knowledge and awareness of Latin that the authors of texts are likely to have possessed. The mechanisms of dialect borrowing and code-switching also need to be identified and examined more critically. More generally, the *Ausbau* status of the standardized Romance languages should be fully acknowledged, in particular with regard to the possibility of downward migration of originally élitist features. Above all, the assumption of a clear boundary between inherited ('popular') and borrowed ('learnèd') features should be challenged and reassessed against the background of what was in effect for many centuries a diglossic situation in the Romance speech communities of western Europe. Such recognition of the complexity and consequences of the influence of Latin on written (and indeed spoken) Romance will not make the work of Romance linguists any easier; but it will ensure that a more appropriate agenda for the study of the evolution of the Romance languages, based on linguistic variation, is set in place.

John Trumper

1   Romance terms for 'slang' and their history

1.1   *Gergon(s); jargon; gergo (gergone); jerga/jergón, jerigonza*

Cardona (1988:91) had hypothesized that OFr. *jargon* (vs. *jargonner* 'to chatter, to chirp'), Sp. *jerigonza*, etc., originated in a series of words that indicated the 'chirping' of small birds. However, the initial point in the chain is not OFr. *jargon*, as Wartburg [*FEW*] (1959–: IV, 59) would have it, but rather OPrv. *gergons*, which appears in the *Donatz Proensals* of the latter half of the twelfth century (cf. l.188 'gergons, gergons … vulgare trutanorum' ['jargon, jargon … beggars' talk']; l.2754 'gergons uulgare trutanorum' ['jargon [is] beggars' talk']). Marshall (1969:265, n) supposed that Spitzer's original etymology based on **gargonike < *garga* 'throat', accepted by Meyer-Lübke (*REW* 3685), was inappropriate, but since we now know that OPrv. *gergons* antedates the OFrench form and that Franco-provençal admits palatalization of velars before the low vowel /a/, there is no incongruency in postulating a development (*REW* 3685a) **garg- > *garga* 'throat', etc. > **gargonike* > OPrv., OFr. *gergons* (parallel to *REW* 7370 ROMĀNĬCE > OPrv./OFr. *romans/romanz*). Chronological priority must, then, be given to the OProvençal form, whence OFr. *gergon* (shortly after 1200) > ModFr. *jargon*, OSp. *girgonz* (> *gerigoniza*), Pt. *gerigonça*, etc. The more or less direct source of the OSpanish and Portuguese forms is obviously, however, OFr. *gergon/jargon*. Its first French appearance is dealt with in Godefroy (1885: IV, 636C), and, as Cardona stated, is occasionally (e.g., in *Marie de France*) associated with birdsong (cf. references to *jargon* in Godefroy 1885 and Tobler and Lommatzsch 1925). Otherwise it means: (1) 'thieves' slang', which takes us back to the beggars' slang of the *Donatz Proensals*; (2) 'a garbled, incomprehensible tongue' (the OFrench version of *Alexandre le Grand* D72: 198 'Un ris gitat de joie e dist une oreisun; Une charme en chaldeu, ne sai pas le jargun' ['He gave a joyful laugh and said a prayer, an incantation in Chaldaic, I know not in what slang']).

FEW (IV, 59) under the onomatopoeic base '*garg-* (Schallwort)' ['gargle; babble'] deals with the derivation of *jargon*, first treating *argotic* and dialect terms such as *gargue* 'mouth', *garga* 'throat' / *engargar* 'to choke', *garger* 'to shriek' as coming from this base, then OFr. *jargon* 'birds' chirping/warbling/twittering; noises proper to animals' (cf. reference to *Marie de France* above), and finally, with a lapse of almost 200 years (beginning of the fifteenth century), MidFr. *gergon* 'running rumours', *jargon* 'criminals' slang' (giving as starting point 1426, as in Schmitt 1990:288). As noted above, the source is the Lat. onomatopoeia *garga (*REW* 3685a) used for 'babbling, gargling, gurgling, making incomprehensible noises', with its derivatives in OProvençal and then OFrench. The Latin term is attested in early grammarians such as Varro (cf. GARGARISSĀRE in *De Lingua Latina* VI.10, 96, for which he gave a Greek origin, and GARGARIDIARE in Gramm. Fragments, Quæst. epist.: ac poemata gargaridians dices 'and you'll mumble reciting your verses'), later in Pliny (N. H. XXX. 11), Cornelius Fronto (Epist. IIII. 6) and then in medical works such as those of Pliny (N. H. XX, XXII, XXIII GARGARIZĀRI *passim*, the active form GARGARIZĀRE only once in N. H. XXIII. 80) and Celsus (*De Medicina* IV. 2. 8: gargarizare iis, quæ saliuam mouent 'to gargle things which provoke salivation'; in V.22.9 we have the plural noun GARGARIZATIONES 'gargling'). The derived verb GARGARIZĀRI/GARGARIZĀRE is rarely found in philosophical works. GARGULUS 'babbler; mumbler; incomprehensible' appears once in Boethius (*De Interpretatione Aristotelis*, the chapter De Signis: Uox enim quæ nihil designat, ut est gargulus … 'a voice saying nothing comprehensible, babbling on …'). Derivatives do not seem initially of frequent usage, though abound in later, more 'vulgarized', medical works. Its high frequency in works of a medical nature seems to be a direct consequence of pervasive Greek influence in this particular sphere of Roman life, strong enough, as well we know, to replace native Latin terms for body parts with Greek medical equivalents. The whole series probably goes back to the IE elementary theme *gar- 'call; shout'; 'throat' (Pokorny 1959: II, 352), with or without reduplication.

Corominas and Pascual (1991) deal with IbR. *jergón, jerigonza, jerigonce*, etc. under *Jerga* 2 (definition: 'special language difficult to understand, slang'). They first accept with reservations the explanation offered by Spitzer and Meyer-Lübke, only later to abandon it: 'Spitzer insinuates, with some reservation (MLN LXXI, 385), that to explain the -z- in

OCastilian one must imagine a Vulgar Latin or Early Romance *GARGO-NICE based on adverbs such as VASCONICE > *vascuence*, ROMANICE > *romance*. It is ingenious but too hypothetical. The fact that it does not exist in French, whence it is supposed to originate, forces one to abandon the idea.'[1] They seem convinced that Spanish (*girgonz, jerga*), Portuguese (*gerigonça*) and Italian (*gergo*) outcomes derive from the Provençal form: 'there is no doubt that this *girgonz*, like eighteenth-century *jerga*, derives from OPrv. *gergon'*. *The Donatz Proensals* and the *Libre de Vicis e Vertutz* of c. 1300 are quoted as relevant, while the Provençal form, according to these authors, must derive, because of its initial *ge-*, from an OFrench form. Thirteenth-century northern French forms such as *gargon, gargun, gargon-ner* still have the 'etymological' initial *ga-*, which French develops into *ge-, je-* (later *jer-* > *jar-* by regular process). As observed above (cf. Marshall 1969), the first *Donatz Proensals* manuscripts appear to antedate the 'French' documents, which would give priority to the Provençal form, while the phonological development assumes at least a Franco-provençal intermediary. The base is the onomatopoeia conveying the concept 'incomprehensible utterances'. Birdcalls, animal noises and trade slang would, then, all start from seemingly nonsensical noise-words.

1.2   Argot, argotique; argotico

The first appearance of *argot* is rather late, dating to the early seventeenth century and, in particular, the first 1628 edition of Chéreau's *Le jargon de l'argot réformé comme il est à present en usage parmy les bons pauvres*, where it appears to mean a beggars' association of sorts (cf. Rey 1995 [Le Robert] 'corporation de gueux' ['beggars' federation'] in the expression 'le royaume d'argot' ['beggars' kingdom'?]). Consequently, it would appear to be associated with a socially marked phenomenon. Possible etymologies are legion. Schmitt (1990:286) lists some twenty-three proposed etyma, some of which are out of the question formally and semantically, like those based on placenames (the first seven of his list), though this still leaves sixteen options open. Sainéan (1907) maintained *argot* < *argoter* 'to argue' < Lat. ERGO 'therefore'; Dauzat ([1917] 1976) took *argot* to be a derivative of OFr. *hargaut* < OPrv. *argaut, argelut* 'rags, tatters', though he later abandoned this in favour of a Spanish origin (< *arigote* 'despicable person'); Guiraud ([1953] 1973) proposed a deverbal derivation from MidFr. *hargoter*, a derivative of Lat. ARGŪTUS 'quick-witted', which seems phonologically wrong, given the Latin stressed vowel.[2] Yet others proposed *argot* < *ergot* = 'claw; talon', though the origin of this term is also obscure. Finally, Rey (1995: I, 108) hypothesized slang *gargote* 'throat' > **gargot* > *argot*, coming back to the same origin as *jargon*, *jerga*, *gergo* (< *garg-). Hence the remote origin of the word, which came to cover the lexicon of Parisian non-standard French, far beyond and above its original application, remains thus far an enigma.

Other terms used for 'slang' in the French situation include *jobelin*, a term associated in the 1500s with François Villon, Colin de Cayeux and other members of the criminal association called the *Coquillards*, a term which seems to be equivalent to *jargon* as the secret code of the *pègre* 'criminal class',[3] *baraguin* (1532), from Breton *bara gwenn* 'white-bread (eaters)' (rather than Schmitt's (1990:288) *bara [a] gwin* 'bread [and] wine'), and in the late sixteenth-century *blesquin*, possibly from the Nrm., Pic. *blesque* 'trader'. Later still, in Chéreau's *Jargon de l'argot reformé* (1628), we find with the same function the enigmatic *bigorne*. However, *argot* and *jargon* are never really ousted by any of these, which seem to have had an ephemeral existence.

2   The dating and functions of Romance slangs

The first appearance of Romance slangs *jargon* or *argot* is datable with the word itself to the 1150–1200 period (OProvençal) or, in the north of France, to around 1200–1250 (*Le Jeu de Saint Nicolas*). This dating confirms the general view of slang experts that the phenomenon is linked to economic crisis and collapse in the Middle Ages (roughly 1100–1300), with the emergence of a new class whose main occupations were metallurgy and the commerce of associated wares. This new class constituted a *continuum*, whose upper levels were composed of foundry owners, merchants, craftsmen connected with the working of precious metals – all these were to eventually become a new 'middle class', some proto-industrialists *ante litteram* – and, at its lowest levels, tinkers, wandering cheapjacks and other unstable elements, who were often a short remove from the criminal classes in the late Middle Ages. A new class structure of this type, extremely composite and socially ambiguous, implies various trade secrets to do with smelting, metallurgy and associated occupations. It also needed a system of elaborated signals to stress its new knowledge and unique situation. From these two preoccupations stem: (1) a cryptolalic function related to metal-naming and the possession of metallurgical knowledge; and (2) an identificatory function reflecting the need for mutual recognition of specific group members, a relatively stable function at lower levels, more transitory at the upper ones as more members become integrated into upper echelons of society. This 'fonction identémique' is stressed both in the French (Stein

1974:91f.) and Italian (Trumper 1996a:28f.) situations, and is later taken up in Valdman (2000:1189), who reiterates this fundamental aspect: 'All linguists who have dealt with slang have highlighted its mainly identificatory function.' One might add that 'technical necessity' (namely keeping trade secrets) is also bound up with this identificatory function. The group which possessed specific technical knowledge also needed a code for mutual identification between fellow technicians.

Valdman, like others, also emphasizes two other functions, first the purely cryptic or cryptolalic function, not necessarily bound to maintaining secrets about metal-working, and second a sort of children's code bound to a sense of playfulness, as well as secrecy. Probably too much stress has been placed on the cryptolalic function of slangs, both in the Romance situation and in others. In France, Sainéan (1912) wrote of *jargon* as an 'artificial creation' with a particular 'imaginary make-up'; Dauzat ([1917] 1976:9), although highlighting 'the cryptic function of these languages … [as] one of the means for collective group defence', denied that *jargons* were 'artificial, conventional languages' (Dauzat [1917] 1976:17). Guiraud ([1953] 1973:5) notes that 'up to Vidocq, all testimonies bear witness to jobelin's cryptic character', with ancient sources 'presenting *argot* as an artificial language whose words were consciously created for cryptic aims' (Guiraud [1953] 1973:26f.). Italian sources are just as insistent, witness Biondelli (1846:8f.) who talked of a 'conventional, secret code', a view subsequently echoed by Ascoli (1861) and Niceforo (1897). Rovinelli (1919:5) referred to it as an 'artificial speech, incomprehensible to the uninitiated' (cf. also Pellis 1929:546f.; 1930:8), whereas Giacomelli (1955:10) described it as *crittolalia* 'cryptic speaking' (see also Sabatini 1956:241, n3; Ferrero 1972; 1973; Marcato 1983:23). Marcato (1988:256f.), though recognizing 'that one characteristic of a slang is that of being a "group language", in the specific sense of an element of cohesion between members of a group first at the psychological then social and linguistic levels', quotes approvingly Pellis's (1929:546f.) definition of slang as any patois, language or dialect used with the intent of masking, and in the strict sense of the word for deliberate cryptic purposes such as a *furbesco* 'criminal slang'. This same insistence on the cryptic function, of which Pellis had written eighty years previously, is evidenced in Marcato (1994:760), who, although acknowledging Menarini's (1959:468) definition of *gergo* as an identifier (namely the code of a distinctive environment showing belonging to a category), concludes that 'the masking function, once overvalued by critics who now tend to ignore it, needs be considered one of the constituent elements of a slang'.

The sense in which the cryptic function forms part of the definition of a slang is undeniable in the historical metal and metallurgy lexicon in the period up until the First World War, with echoes as late as the 1960s and 1970s in Italy. The close association over the centuries between the lower echelons of trader society (tinkers and their ilk) and the lower grades of the criminal classes had led to a kind of osmosis between them, which has had linguistic consequences. Obviously, in the case of the criminal classes the *cryptolalia* function is paramount: secrecy is the motive for any code change; there are no identificatory or playful functions involved. To say that there is some sort of 'technical necessity' implicit in the use of a differing code, namely keeping trade and 'technical' secrets, involving, say, metallurgy, is pushing hypotheses rather far. The criminal classes in a country such as Italy, traditionally associated with closed criminal societies such as the *Mafia*, *'Ndrànghita* and *Camorra*, have inherited a brigand tradition of close contact with travelling tinkers and their like as contacts for the basics of their operations, but not for the 'serious stuff', and have, to some extent, taken over traditional 'slang', albeit with some modification. The *Mafia's baccàgghju*, intimately related to historical trade slangs, has slowly modified and become *mafiese*, though the Calabrian *'Ndrànghita's baccàgghju*-type still presents close affinities with erstwhile traders' slang. This does not seem to be the case in France, unless an in-depth analysis of Marseille-*Mafia* relations were to reveal otherwise.

In a spirit of playfulness which seems to characterize children in all societies across all periods, secrets between members of children's peer groups have always led to the development of back slangs. These usually involve mere phonological processes, but not the overdeveloped metonymic chains and overall lexical substitutions we find in historical trade or criminal slangs. As Baurens (2007:9) notes, such slangs involve 'a form of language characterized essentially by a specific lexicon which is renewed in accordance with differing tastes of different periods and the needs and the degree of specificity of the group involved'. The creation of ModFrench *verlan* is a case in point.[4] The basic case is *parler à l'envers* 'to talk backwards' [paʁle a lãˈvɛʁ] > *lepar verlan* [ləpaʁ vɛʁˈlã], whence the name *verlan* (see §3.1 for details, as well as Bauer, this volume, chapter 10: §5.4). There are complications, for instance: (1) functional grammatical words (such as prepositions) are eliminated, compromising grammatical functions; (2) syllabic restraints are involved, as well as the impossibility of specific consonant clusters (cf. Plénat's (1992) observation that verlan is not the product of a single mechanism); (3) complications are introduced by truncation and suffixation rules which may be modified and, in turn, modify. A case of simple truncation would, for example, be *chatte* 'cat' [ʃat] > [təʃa] (with schwa insertion to avoid unusual [tʃ]) > truncation [təʃ] *tech* or *tœuch*, creating cases of the stressed phoneme /ə/ with new distributional properties (and not just in the enclitic *-le*).

Suffixation creates new phonological problems, as in the case of butchers' slang, *louchébem*, studied in Plénat (1985) and Robert L'Argenton (1991). This involves substitution of the word-initial consonant with l- and suffixation of the substituted consonant in word-final position (e.g., *boucher* 'butcher' > *loucheb*), to which *-em* is finally suffixed producing *louchébem* [luʃebã]. The simplest form involves the transformaton of a structure C_1VC_2V initially into LVC_2VC_1, and successively into the structure LVC_2VC_1+-EM. Sometimes, though rarely, we do find simple kinds of metonymy (specific > generic) as in *clocher* 'limp' (> *clochard* 'tramp') > *clocher* 'to be defective, non-functional' (as in *ça cloche* 'it doesn't work') > *clochard* 'non-functional; useless' > by suffix changing *clodo* (same meaning) or by *verlanisation* ('back-slanging') *clochard* > *charclo* (same meaning). Such cases seem fairly rare in verlan-types. Over the last twenty-five years *verlan*, *tchatches* and *louchébem* have all been thoroughly investigated.

In the nineteenth to twentieth centuries, classical traditional *argot* seems to have permeated some literary genres, from Vidocq and Victor Hugo even up to Céline, and, in the last half of the twentieth century, Frédéric Dard (*San Antonio*), slowly dying out as an identificatory idiom. In this function, it has been slowly replaced by *verlan* and similar back slangs. The latter have changed function over the years from the typical secretive and playful code of the youth to become the *parler branché* (cf. *branché* 'trendy, cool, switched-on') or partial *argot* (Valdman 2000:1187), which Paul (1985) exaggeratedly terms a simil-Sabir, recognizing in its linguistic insecurity the social insecurity of the suburbs of Paris and the large cities. Baurens (2007) claims that this particular type of *parler branché* is no longer a back slang, but has now become a symbol of urban revolt, a new-wave, cool slang, even felt suitable for rap. The linguistic structure is that of a modified back slang, modified by some elements taken from traditional slang (though not many), while the sociolinguistic function would seem to be approaching that of the traditional *argot* or slang as an identificatory code, no longer of traders, metal-workers, tinkers, 'marginals' or even of the criminal classes, but a class-marker of those who do not know or ideologically refuse *le bon usage*.

2.1 Literary use

Apart from early beginnings, where the presence of tinkers' and tradesmen's jargon is occasionally documented, there is a later extension of a quasi-literary use of such slangs in order: (1) to convey an idea of a lower class or even criminal milieu; (2) to serve cryptolalic purposes to avoid being readily understood; (3) to add a literary 'tone' to the speech of intellectuals who certainly did not belong to such circles; and (4) to expose the so-called 'criminal mentality' in late nineteenth-century police and proto-psychological studies on the form of communication adopted by the 'criminal classes' (e.g., Vidocq and others in France; Lombroso, Niceforo in Italy). The rise to literary level in France is due more to the influence of nineteenth-century novelists such as Henri Sue or Victor Hugo, whereas in Italy the literary vogue was established much earlier in the late Renaissance (Magnani 1976:78f.). Schematically we can summarize such 'literary' or 'semi-literary' manifestations from about the middle of the fifteenth century by way of Table 14.1.

3 Linguistic structures and *déstructuration*

3.1 *Phonological and morphological processes*

In the previous section we briefly introduced the phonological mechanisms of a typical back slang, namely French *verlan*. The first phonological mechanism involved is syllabic inversion or metathesis of the type CV > VC for monosyllables (e.g., *fou* 'mad' > *ouf*) and $C_1V_1C_2V_2 > C_2V_2 C_1V_1$ for bisyllables (e.g., *bouffon* [bufõ] 'buffoon, clown' > *fonbou* [fõbu]), the commonest word types in ModFrench. Trisyllabic structures $C_1V_1C_2V_2C_3V_3$ have two possible solutions, either $C_3V_3 C_2V_2 C_1V_1$ or $C_2V_2C_3V_3 C_1V_1$, while four-syllable words present a single solution $C_1V_1C_2V_2C_3V_3C_4V_4 > C_4V_4C_3V_3C_2V_2C_1V_1$, exactly as in the first case. One must note, though, that the last two cases are much rarer than the first two, and that the most complex structure is limited in a similar way to the first two with a single obligatory solution. The apparent simplicity of a back slang like *verlan* is complicated, however, by at least four considerations: (1) the impossibility of concealing a vowel-initial word by backward masking makes suffixation practically obligatory, so *argot* [aʁgo] will have to become either *[laʁgoã]* or [laʁgomyʃ] *largomuche*; (2) trisyllabic structures may present two solutions, complicating the interpretation of such structures, though variation, even when it renders analysis more complex, is part and parcel of all language interplay; (3) aphaeresis and truncation, observed in all such types, complicate morphology and makes the relation between morphologically related types unrecognizable following extreme phonological *déstructuration* (e.g., *chatte* 'cat' [ʃat] > by 'verlanisation' [təʃa] > by truncation *tœuch* [təʃ] vis-à-vis *chat* 'tom-cat' [ʃa] > by 'verlanisation' [aʃ]);[5] (4) the phonological processes described above are

Table 14.1 *(Semi-)Literary manifestations of jargons/slangs*

DATING FRANCE	DATING ITALY
1453: François Villon's *Compagnon de la Coquille*, famous Dijon Trial. Poetry. *Argot* is termed 'jobelin'.	1460: *gergo* documented and used in correspondence between G. F. Soardi and F. Feliciano.
1510: In France the famous *Liber Vagatorum* appears.	1466: Luigi Pulci's famous letter to Lorenzo the Magnifico, where *gergo* masks unorthodox 'festicciole' and practices (Ageno 1962).
1547: Noël de Fail's *Propos rustiques* (ch. 8 has a part in *argot* dealing with the 'bon et sçavant gueux Tailleboudin'), published in Paris.	1471: The parts in *gergo* in L. Pulci's 'Morgante Maggiore' (Cantare XVIII. 122). About this time the anon. *Vocabolarietto furbesco* appears: slang is called 'lingua furbesca'.
1566: Henri Estienne's *Introduction au traité de la conformité des merveilles anciennes avec les modernes* published in Geneva.	1508: In Ariosto's *Cassaria* the pander and his 'servant' use *gergo* as a cover (Act I. Sc. 7; Act 3. Sc. 7).
1596: G. Jullieron's *La Vie Généreuse des Mercelots, Gueux et Boesmiens, contenant leur façon de vivre, subtilitez et jargon*, published in Lyon. Slang is termed 'blesquin'.	1514: The *Anonima Bulesca* is published. 1533: In Angelo Beolco's (Ruzante) play *La Piovana* some characters use *gergo* instead
1628: O. Chéreau's *Le Jargon de l'argot réformé comme il est à present en usage parmy les bons pauvres*, published in Paris. There are frequent successive editions until the last in 1850. Here 'argot' is originally that part of society which uses 'jargon'; it later becomes, metonymically, the 'code' used by that particular group.	of dialect (Act 3, Sc. 3). In the same year Aretino's *Ragionamenti* contains many slang elements. Around the middle of the century the *Barzelletta Stramboti Soneti de amore de diuersi auctori* appears in *gergo* (Cortelazzo 1976:225f.).
1725–26: Racot de Granval's *Le Vice puni du Cartouche* (Ambience is called 'argot', slang 'jargon').	1545–46: Antonio Brocardi's *Nuovo Modo de intendere la lingua zerga*. 1557: Parabosco's *Fantesca* and *Diporti* written in *gergo*.
1800: Leclair's testimony to the force and spread of *argot* as a code of the criminal classes at the trial of the 'Chauffeurs de Pieds d'Orgères'.	1598: Anon., *Il diletteuole Essamine de' Guidoni, Furfanti o Calchi, altramente detti Guitti nelle Carceri di Ponte Sisto di Roma*.
1836: The criminal Lacenaire's famous slang poems entitled *À la Pègre* (published posthumously).	1619: R. Frianoro's *Trattato de' Bianti* ('Il Vagabondo').
1837: Vidocq's slang dictionary entitled *Les Voleurs*.	1634: B. Bocchini's *Dialogo in furbesco* (slang still called 'lingua furbesca').

generally not applied to functional or grammatical words, which are either dropped or left in the linguistic chain in the position and with the function they assume in standard or non-standard French (e.g., *j'ai pas dit ça au boucher* [ʒɛ pa di sa o buʃe] 'I didn't say that to the butcher' in *verlan* becomes *èj ap id ass au chébou* [ɛʒ ap id as o ʃeˈbu]; *parler du boucher* [paʁle dy buˈʃe] 'to talk about the butcher' in *luchébem* becomes *larlépem du louchébem* [laʁlepã dy luʃeˈbã], where preposition + article *du* 'of-the' cannot undergo 'verlanisation' or back slang processes).[6]

The absolute insistence on such phonological processes as syllable inversion (the only exception being certain function words) seems but little used in traditional *argot* (although there are a few cases treated in all the classical works), while in Italian *gergo* the process proves marginal. In those southern slangs which have been investigated, only a few rare cases have been observed, including, for example, *puru > rùpu* 'also', *picca > ccàpi* 'a little', *quetu > tùque* 'tranquill, calm'. In fact such cases of inversion occur only in bisyllabic words,[7] although in southern dialects (unlike in French) three-, four-, five-, six- and seven-syllable words abound, and historical processes of aphaeresis and metathesis are far from uncommon (cf. Cal., Sic. examples such as CARBONE(M) > + -ARIUS > *cravunaru* or *carbunaru* 'hornet', MER-ULAM > *mìellura, mèllura* 'blackbird'), as is syllable inversion (e.g., as in ἐπίπλοον > *plippʊ[m]* > *chjippu* 'veil-membrane of a pig', MERGITE(M) > *germitʊ* > *j(i)ermitu* 'bale of hay', DIGITUM > *gid̪itʊ* > *jìditu* 'finger', AFFILARE > *alliffari* 'to smooth down'). That said, 'verlanisation' appears unimaginable in pentasyllabic words like Cal. *arrumazzatu* and Sic. *arru-mazzatu/arrimazzatu* 'having a cold' or the Calabrian hexasyllabic *appeda-mentari* 'to approach (of dogs); make a good marriage match' to produce such hypothetical forms as ****tuzzamarru*, ****tamendappari*, let alone in the structurally simpler trisyllabic Cal., Sic. *cìnnara* 'ash' (cf. ****rànnaci*). One might, however, expect slightly more 'verlanisation' in traditional slangs built on and around northern Italian dialects, yet even here one does not meet with a high degree of phonological inversion.

In traditional slangs there is no *déstructuration* at the phonological level, which seems, instead, to be typical of back slangs or *parlers branchés* 'partial slangs'. Nor do we find systematic phoneme substitutions, which might be different from the types found elsewhere in Romance or in interdialectal comparisons with dialects having higher social prestige. What we do find, however, are deforming morphological processes which confound the listener. Many years ago Dauzat ([1917] 1976:64–66) had already given a list of French slang deforming suffixes, including the denominal *-al, -ier, -erie, -elle, -et(te), -ot(te), -ost(e), -ust(e), -eux, -ol(e), -ou(e), -anche, -ache, -uche, -oche, -iche, -èche, -in (-igne)*; the deverbal nominal suffix in *-y* (e.g., *épier > épy*, 'spying, watching' > 'watch-post' > 'house'); the bare verb-root minus thematic vowel (e.g., *mouvoir > meuve/move* 'move' > 'earth', *béler > béle* 'bleat' > 'goat', some already present in French but only with the basic meaning, e.g., *branler* > *branle* 'shake; push; jog' > (naval) 'hammock' > (slang) 'chair'); deverbal adjectives in *-ant(e)* (e.g., *floquer* 'to rob' > *flocante(s)* 'playing cards'). In the south of Italy where historical trade slangs become the base for criminal slangs, it is possible to identify numerous deforming morphological processes, including the verbal suffixes *-ifici* (added to any Romance verbal root with intent to deform, e.g., *cuntu* > *cuntari* > *cuntìfici* > *fari cuntìfici* 'to count; assess; assay') and *-ella* (e.g., *stavella* 'to be', *cappella* 'to rob' (also *fari cappella*)), the nominal suffixes *-usa* (e.g., *jancu/-a* 'white' > *jancusa* 'milk; flour; snow' (and hence also 'dose of cocaine'), *carni* 'flesh' > *carnusu/-a* 'relative; godparent'), *-ignu*, *-aru* (e.g., *campana* 'bell' > *campanaru* 'lead' by metonymy), *-acchju*, *-ornia* (e.g., **pi-* 'drink' > *piòrnia* 'bar; wine-cellar'), *-èparu* (*cristianu* > *cristianèparu* 'person', *latinu* > *latinèparu* 'hocus-pocus; rubbish; nonsense'), *-anza* (e.g., *casa* 'house' > *casanza* 'police station; prison', *carni* 'flesh' > *carnanza* 'blood relation'), *-ante/-ente* (e.g., *carne* 'flesh' > *carnenti/carnanti* 'relative; parent'), the deadjectival suffixes (often with nominalized functions) in *-usu -a* (cf. *jancusa, carnusu* above), *-utu*, *-ante/-ente* (cf. *carnante* above), as well as cases like *-òpari* (added to numbers, e.g., *duòpari* 'two', *triòpari* 'three'), *-anu* or *-òdari* (added to pronouns, e.g., *mianu* 'I', *tuanu* 'you', *vostròdari/ 'ostròdari* 'you (pl. or respect)'), *-utru* (added to deictics, e.g., *chissutru, ssutru* 'this'), *-arma* (added to adverbs, e.g., dial. *'ntra* 'in(side)' > *'ntrarma, fora* 'out(side)' > *forarma*). In short, suffixes are legion, sometimes adding new meanings, sometimes merely deforming. All are traditional and can be traced back to the fifteenth–sixteenth century *jargon/argot* and *gergo/ furbesco*.

In the main, we may conclude that what is involved in possible deforming processes is derivational morphology, rather than inflectional morphology. We witness continuous changes due to prefixation (e.g., *mala-* in (*pezz'i*) *malacarni* 'informer', *caca-* (< dial. *cacari* 'to shit') in *cacafocu* 'firearm'), suffixation and sometimes drastic semantic changes effected by modification of the noun + adjective type (see discussion in §3.2). At the morphological level, three relevant points are to be observed. The first is that of Rom morphological intrusion in the verb system, where the base infinitive has a Rom ending *-ella* (< Rom *-el* 3SG of the present; cf. *stavella* above),[8] even though, contrary to popular belief, lexically Rom has but little influence on traditional slang. The second is the Albanian calque in the construction of negatives with *senza-* 'without' (cf. Alb. *pa-* 'without'), particularly common in eighteenth–twentieth-century traders' slang, prefixed to nouns and adjectives (e.g., southern tinkers' jargon *senzafilusi* 'bald' (< *filusi* 'hair' < *fili* 'threads; wires'), *senzandrappe* 'bare, naked' (< dial.

'*ndrappi* 'clothes'), *senzafinestri* 'blind' (< *finestra* 'window' > 'eye') on the model of Alb. *sy* 'eye' > *pasy* 'blind', *fatë* 'destiny; luck' > *pafatën* > *pafanë* 'luckless'). The third point involves verb conjugation, which displays three patterns: (1) the usual Romance formation through word-final inflections (e.g., *mi nn' [nd'] aùcciu, ti nn' [nd'] aùcci, si nn' [nd'] aùccia*, etc. 'I/you/(s)he go(es)'; *mi ndi aùcciài*, etc. 'I went'); (2) zero inflection whenever subject pronouns are used (e.g., **mianu** *aùccia,* **tuanu** *aùccia*, etc. 'I/you go'); (3) '*do-*support' through the use of *fari* 'to do' in conjunction with a deforming suffix like *-ifici* (e.g., *cuntari* 'to count; assess' > *cuntìfici* > *fari cuntìfici*: *fazzu cuntìfici, fai cuntìfici, fa [fàcia/faci] cuntìfici*, etc. 'I/you/(s)he count(s)').

The second case has strong implications for a conservative Romance language, which has long maintained a rich inflexional system for the verb: the system now loses personal inflections in the verb, keeping only tense markers, much along the lines of Mediterranean Sabir or lingua franca. In this case, the traditional slang undergoes a 'sabirizing' process, one might even say a sort of pidginization, with consequent total morphological simplification.[9] The third case is well known in the languages of the world (e.g., among others, Celtic and non-standard regional English), and its consequences are not as drastic for Romance as the second. It is also true that the third quite happily coexists with the other two strategies: the first only applies if the verb to be used is Italian or dialectal without metonymic shift; in other cases one of the other two strategies is used. Modern tendencies regarding this type of shift have not been analysed in depth.

3.2 Syntax

As far as syntax is concerned, Italian slangs apparently present no differences with respect to regional dialect varieties. For instance, in the case of unaccusative verbs the unmarked order is VS as in standard Italian (e.g., *è aùcciatu / aùcciàu l'avucatu* 'the lawyer has come / came', just like *è aùcciat(a) / aùcciàu (l)a jancusa* 'the cocaine's just come in'), whereas in transitive/unergative clauses the order is SV(O) (e.g., *nu turchjillu a (a)gghjagghjatu / agghagghjàu supr' i roti* 'a dog's just urinated on the wheels'). As far as one can see, traditional slang has maintained conservative southern Italian participle agreement patterns, such that past participles agree with objects, even when postverbal (e.g., *avivi allumati tutti ssutri fangusi novi c'aju aggallati/chi aggallài?* 'Had you seen.M.PL. all these new shoes.M.PL I bought?', *avivi allumata tutta ssutra jancusa c'amu sballata / chi sballammi?* 'Had you seen.F.SG all the cocaine.F.SG we've flogged?'). It is also interesting to note that recent bugging cases involving the *'Ndrànghita* have revealed that, when conversations are carried out in Italian mixed with *gergo*, typical central and southern Calabrian syntactic features such as the avoidance of the infinitive are systematically found.

Clearly, in-depth investigation of slang syntax is greatly needed, not only of traditional slangs, but also of back slangs like French *verlan*. For example, if in the latter case function markers are deleted from discourse, this implies that functions have to be re-established by other means, usually by syntactic positioning. When they are left in place without undergoing 'verlanisation', no problems arise and the syntactic strategies of so-called 'substandard' *français populaire* apply. Unfortunately, the whole question still awaits in-depth investigation.

3.3   Semantic processes and the slang lexicon

Originally, considerable emphasis was placed on the particular development of semantic 'deformation' and continuous metaphorization in historical slangs, the most important statements to this effect being in Guiraud ([1953] 1973:59) and Ferrero (1972; 1973:212). More recently this extreme position has been abandoned, initially in favour of the opposite hypothesis, namely that there is a passage of some 'characterizing' semantic feature rather than of any 'defining' one, the extension operating on the basis of mere superficial phonological or even phonetic similarity (cf. Ageno 1957:419, 421, 428; Stein 1974:283; Marcato 1983:133). Classical examples of similar semantic drift would include, for French *argot*, *fourbe* 'cunning' > *fourber* 'to steal' = *fourbir* 'to polish; clean', hence *polir* 'to polish' and *nettoyer* 'to clean' = 'to steal, to clean out'; and for Italian *gergo* or *furbesco*, *bianca* 'white' > property of paper > 'paper' = *fioccosa* 'snow' > 'paper' crossed with derivative *bianchina* 'snow; drug', hence *fioccosa* = 'snow' > 'paper; cocaine', now taking on *all* the connotations and secondary features of both *bianca* and *bianchina*.

Continuous metonymy rather than metaphor seems to snowball thanks to a phonological similarity trigger, yielding usual classical metonymy such as 'cause for effect', 'effect for cause', 'whole for the part', 'part for the whole' (synecdoche), or 'container' for 'contents', 'contents' for 'container', 'object made of X' > X, X > 'object made of X'. Classical Italian slang examples include *ruffo* 'fire'[10] > *arruffare* 'to set fire to something', whence *arruffente* 'hot peppers', *tufa* 'smoke' > effect for cause (a pistol when fired gives off smoke) > 'pistol', *lenza* 'water' > *lenzire* 'to water' > 'rain' (part for whole); 'tears (non-human > human)', with further extensions. However, Borello

(1976; 1978) and Trumper (1996a: ch. 5) show that the metonymic processes involved are more complex. Extensions involve a continuous passage between levels, namely both rising from the semantic 'genus' level to the intermediate and life-form levels, and being lowered, by modification (usually not morphological but by the mere addition of adjectival specifiers), to semantic specific and subspecific levels in Berlin's (1992) terminology. A case in point would be the extension of the Calabrian 'seed – pip – stone' partonymic lexicon to vegetable and fruit generics. One starts with *cocciu* 'pip; stone' (< Grk. diminutive κοκκίον with new Latin stress COCCIUM < COCCUM (*REW* 2009) κόκκον) which develops part of its connotation (pips and stones are usually 'roundish') and becomes the prototype of the 'round' characteristic, so that derived adjectives like *cocciuta* and *cocciusa* mean 'cherry' or other small round fruit. With modifiers we have *cocciuta janca* '(round) beans', *cocciuta niùra* 'olive', and thus begins a new series of extensions. Keeping to the masculine gender, we have a different extension, viz. *cocciutu* (1) 'rice' [generic] > (2) 'edible cereal' [intermediate] > (3) 'wheat' types (less inclusive intermediate, though not generic). What seems to be happening is that all the components and subcomponents of complex metonymical models are activated to allow 'characterizing' connotative features to become prototypical and to spread to other models, which incidentally possess these features at some component level. Slang processes thus merit more careful attention in new semantic models and are probably a good testing ground for post-Lakoff and post-Berlin semantic theorization.

There remains the important question of the role of borrowings in the life and development of trade slangs. From studies on slang corpora, it would appear that the three primary constituents are: (1) local and dialect items, with high metonymical extension potential, forming up to 45 percent of the total lexicon; (2) a 'common core' of Romance historical slangs, forming up to, say, 25 percent of all items; and (3) borrowings, which may constitute up to 30 percent of the whole, whether between different categories of slangs, different dialect slangs or across different Romance slangs, where probably French *argot* has dominated in more recent centuries. Amongst the external influences, Rom elements seem less prominent than might have been supposed, although a constant source of borrowing has been the cardinal numbers (e.g., *pancia*, *pancione* is consistently 'five', 'fifty' in Italy). However, the incidence of Rom seems greatest at the morphological level, including verb inflection (cf. discussion in §3.1) and word formation (e.g., the extended use of *sciórnïu* 'thing' in southern Italian slangs echoing the general spread of *səssò*, *sossòte* in the Rom spoken in Italy). The diffusion of

Albanian borrowings distinguishes Italian trade slangs from its French and Spanish counterparts, and occurs not just at the lexical level (e.g., *grèbin/cripine* 'salt' < Alb. *krypël kripë, jisima* 'ricotta cheese' < Alb. *gjizë*), but is also visible at the level of morphology (cf. discussion of negative prefix *senza-* in §3.1). The question of the relevance of historical Italo-Albanian has been debated in Trumper (1997). It even seems highly probable that Alb. *arbër* (originally 'Albanian', subsequently replaced by *shqiptar* in this sense in Albania), which is used as 'shepherd' in traditional Albanian trade and nomad jargon (cf. Haxhihasani 1964:110) and as 'man' in early eighteenth-century Italo-Albanian texts, is the starting point for traditional Italian names for such jargon, namely *arbaresca* (Sardinia), *arvâr* (Friuli), *ravaro* (Marche), *erbáru* (Calabria), literally 'man's language, human language'. Above and beyond this, it can reasonably be maintained, as did Pellis (1934:201), that the 'common core' evidenced between types of slang and jargon reflects manifest links between the different trade categories involved, as well as underlining what he terms the 'the common linguistic patrimony of our "minor criminals"', and this remains true for all the Romance cases discussed.

3.4 The 'hidden' lexicon as part of industrial history

Returning to the problem of slang as a 'secret language' from a socio-historical perspective, there is a sense in which the historical slang code is cryptolalic, its function being to hide knowledge. This is the case when one looks at the metal and metallurgy lexicon, as already briefly attempted in Trumper (1996a:32f.). The richness of this extremely sectorial lexicon, compared even with that of standard languages, stands out, leading one to speculate that this could well have constituted the pre-industrial seeds of an Italian industrial revolution which never took place. It is, however, true that their Lombard equivalents (in Como) represent what there is in Italy, from 1948 onwards, of an industrial economy. By way of illustration, consider the following central nucleus of metal items as specified in Calabrian traders' jargon or slang, around which other many elements are composed: *gritta* 'copper' (for a possible explanation, see Trumper and Straface 1998:244f.), > *bbruscijána 'e gritta* 'raw copper' (see Dauzat [1917] 1976:26) for the city of 'Bruges' as a famous production centre, possibly crossed with Cal. *vrusciáre/-i* 'to burn' (in the applied sense of 'smelting'), > *masséllu 'e gritta* 'treated copper ingot' (cf. Battisti and Alessio [DEI] 1950–57: III, 2384);[11] *mbrógliu* (1) 'copper roll', (2) 'standard metal roll ca. 1 kg. in weight'; *fuscáglia* 'copper pairings/dust (residual after working)';[12]

priciána 'metal strip (usually copper, though not always, used to mend pots and pans)'.

Other metals are: *culu níüru = trunánte níüru* 'iron'; *camággiu* 'zinc';[13] *campanáru* 'lead' (cf. *DEI* I. 705–6 *Campana*[1] 'bell' < Lat. CAMPANA UASA 'bronze vases made in Campania' > 'bronze bells', whence *campanaro* 'bell-tower', later 'bellringer', so the metonymy again is 'objects made of metal X' > 'metal X', though one would have expected 'bronze' rather than 'lead' as a possible metal meaning); *litáru = citáru* 'tin';[14] *mprácchja* (obviously from Cal. *mpracchjári = mpacchjári = mplacchjá* 'to stick; attach' (cf. Rohlfs 1977:429, 434); here the reference is 'metal that is stuck or welded on to pans', a property or characteristic that passes metonymically to the metal which possesses this property) = *scara-fílice* 'tin-roll'; *grisciólu = feriúlu* 'gold';[15] *grisciólu scáliu = grisciólu bbianchèparu* 'silver'. To these can be added *mortízzu* (*mu-*) any 'white' metal and *scòrza* 'mass' of any raw metal, both of rather obvious dialect origin. Some of the terms continue to remain historically obscure, as is the case with many slang items. On the whole, they give an idea of lexico–semantic development unrivalled by Italian, although we have only scratched the surface here (unfortunately informants used in the 1970s and early 1980s were already rather old and are no longer with us).

4   The functionality and history of slang

There is a decided difference between tinkers' and trade jargon and criminal slang, even though, down the centuries, they have known many points of contact. Pellis (1930) emphasizes that trade jargon is not the endpoint or end-product of a chain, but was, and is, an ever-open communicative system. The only points that could be labelled 'hidden knowledge' were constituted by the elements of its erstwhile trade secrets, while criminals' slang is an end in itself and constitutes a closed system, whose very existence depends on keeping secret its criminal manoeuvres. In this sense, historical jargon is an open system in close contact with all other trade slangs, as well as with a certain type of criminal slang, but also, in a historical sense, with decidedly open and ever-changing historical codes like Mediterranean Sabir and the well-known Romance types of lingua franca. Ferrero (1973) was also essentially in agreement with this kind of assessment, insisting that the various historical jargons were not characterized by an exasperated 'defor-mation' of the basic lexicon, nor even by exaggerated phonological 'defor-mation' like schoolboy slang or criminal secret codes. Criminals have further marked their condition of being 'different' and having 'secret elements' by even employing their own secret alphabets for writing on prison walls, a good example of which is discussed in Ferrero (1973) and given in full in Trumper (1996a:35).

Such codes as the ones we have discussed have been associated with criminal jargon since the nineteenth century for a very good reason, which involved the vaguely 'psychological' interests of both intellectuals and new police methodology towards the end of that century. As a result, we have not only the physiognomic (re)construction of criminals and their facial features on the part of Cesare Lombroso (1889), but also the compilation of criminal slang dictionaries (cf. Vidocq as an innovator) in an attempt to try to analyse the language of criminals. On this score, the private observations made to me by E. Ferrero on this positivist nineteenth-century trend or 'mania' prove instructive: 'the custom of editing pocket dictionaries ... occurs doubtlessly after Italian Unification, and is to be related more precisely with the flourishing of positivistic passions concerning "criminal man" following on from Lombroso's studies'. In Trumper (1996a:183–92) just such a small positivistically inclined pocket dictionary is discussed, in which a Calabrian parish priest confided to his diary the type of lexicon used by the last Calabrian *briganti* 'highway robbers' who came to him for confession in the period 1860–1880. In this case there is a meaningful overlap between criminal language and historical trade jargon.

4.1 *The future of Italian historical slang and criminal associations*

4.1.1 *Baccàgghju* and *mafiese*, camorra slang and writing

A random comparison of the letters A–C in Calvaruso's *'U baccàgghiu* with those in the main slang dictionary in Trumper (1996a) shows a fairly consistent number of ready equivalences such as Sic. *àcula 'i postu* 'custom's official' (because of the stylized eagle on the uniform) with Cal. *àgliulu/ àgghjula* 'money' (owing to the large identificatory predator on higher value nineteenth-century coins), Sic. *bianchettu, biancura* with Cal. *jancusa* 'cocaine', Sic. *bozza* 'prison warden' with Cal. *bbòzzu* 'ugly, deformed, hunchback', Sic. *caggiu* with Cal. *caggiúrru* 'farmworker; country bump-kin',[16] Sic. *cantanti* with Cal. *cantaturi* 'cockerel', Sic. *capatúfa* with Cal. *tufa* 'pistol', Sic. *carnenta* or *carnusu* with Cal. *carnenti/carnanti* 'parent; relative; godparent', Sic. *chiarenza* with Cal. *chiaru* 'wine', Sic. *chignu* with Cal. *chjignu* 'prick', as well as such shared items as Cal./Sic. slang *allippari* 'to fuck', *allumari* 'to see', *alluccari = alluscare* 'to look', *bbroccia* 'fork; horn', *cacafocu* 'firearm', *casanza* 'police station; prison', *cocciu, culleggiu* 'prison'. This continuous overlapping over long periods of time does not imply that tinkers, traders and similar people were criminals or that their trade *jargon* or *argot* had the same origins as the closed criminal code. Historical borrowing is almost always in the direction trade/tinkers' jargon > criminal code, and not the reverse. However, it is the case that the only groups which seem to regularly use at present what remains of this jargon are criminal groups and chiefly for cryptolalic purposes, the opposite of the historical origin of *argot* or *gergo*, whose main function seemed to have been identificatory.

In Italy, the situation is that of substitution as in France, but not as in the French case with a back slang that uses certain elements of traditional *argot*. In Italy the users change and most of the code remains, but with obvious changes due to criminal activity. The traditional forge-worker, foundry-man, smithy, trader or tinker no longer exists in the particular transformations that the Italian situation has undergone since the early 1950s. Individual cases still remained until the early 1980s, but employed their craft making traditional metal implements for the tourist trade. Most have gone into industry or other types of work, abandoning traditional crafts. However, the symbiosis between the lowest levels of such occupations (tinkers) and the criminal classes has produced its own fruits, the criminal classes taking over the traditional trade slang and developing it in a different manner.

The *Mafia* as a name identifying a criminal group seems to come into being in the mid eighteen hundreds, with Battaglia (2003: IX, 420) giving the Calabrian Arlia as the first writer to use the term before 1850. Its origins are thus fairly new: it may well be a phenomenon connected to local Sicilian rebellion against British control of the Mediterranean fruit, vegetable and wine markets as a consequence of the Treaty of Vienna (1815). Whatever its late origins, its regular use of *baccàgghju* (southern Italian *argot*) is attested by Calvaruso (1929), and the strong relationship between *baccàgghju* and traditional slang is well established. Similar conclusions might be reached about the beginnings of the *Camorra*, though slightly earlier, say 1780, from writers' comments on the use of the word (for which, see Battaglia 2003: II, 592). There is also a generalized southern negative use of *camurrìa* as (1) 'insistence; annoyance; boorishness', (2) 'gonorrhœa' (Sicilian variant also *camirrìa*; cf. Piccitto and Tropea 1977: I, 540), so the term and the phenomenon may well be earlier than 1780. The use on the part of Camorristi of modified traditional slang has so far not been subject to in-depth investigation, unlike the *Mafia*'s gradual transformation of *baccàgghju* into modern *mafiese* with, in a few cases, items finding their way into the writings of modern novelists like Camilleri, not to mention the *pizzini* ('short messages written by mafiosi') found in the bunkers of the *Mafia* bosses. On the other hand, the Camorristi seem to have been the first to invent a special alphabet for writing *gergo* (see Ferrero 1973; Trumper 1996a:35).

4.1.2   The *'Ndrànghita* and its *baccàgghju*

The *'Ndrànghita* is a different kettle of fish. Most commentators say the word first appears in newspaper reports from 1972, and in fact it does not appear in any classical Italian dictionary, though Martino (1988) rightly pointed out that fifteenth- and sixteenth-century Dutch and Italian cartographers used the expression *Andragathia Regio* to refer to Calabria and Lucania. Rejecting Mosino's (1972) and Falcone's (1983) attempts to etymologize, we might start from Martino's (1988) considerations. The basic term cannot be the noun *'ndrànghita* for the criminal association; rather this would seem to be a deverbal noun from the common Calabrian verb *'ndranghitijàri*, whose primary meaning is 'to behave courageously', its secondary one 'to be a member of the *'Ndrànghita*'.[17] If the origin is Greek, then it cannot be from Ἀνδράγαθος, which only exists as a personal name, though abstract nouns like ἀνδραγαθία 'courageous acts' = ἀνδρεία -αι have always existed in the history of Greek. From ἀνδραγαθία Middle Greek developed the denominal verb ἀνδραγαθίζω 'I behave courageously'. The latter would have as its direct outcome, with perfect morphological correspondence, the Calabrian verb *'ndranghatijàri,* or by reduction of unstressed vowels, *'ndranghitijàri,* the only unusual phonological development being the infixed or epenthetic nasal which, in the case of a southern Calabrian dialect source, would prevent deletion of /g/ in accordance with quite a regular process in such dialects. From the verb we would have by normal derivational processes the deverbal noun *'ndrànghita* and its derivatives *'ndranghitista* or *'ndranghitusu*. Although Rohlfs and others did not document a Calabrian Greek word ἀνδράγ[γ]αθη or similar, Crupi (1981), and later Violi (2001), recorded a local Bova district word ἀνδράγ[γ]ατη (F), transcribed *andràngati*, which Martino (1988) related to eastern Sicilian *dràngada* 'criminal association'. This criminal organization may well, then, exist from the period between Calabria's belonging to the Byzantine Empire and the coming of the Normans and the formation of the first Kingdom of the Two Sicilies, 1050–1100 being the relevant period. Their use of a particular *baccàgghju* which displays many elements of traders' and tinkers' *ammascanti* ('traders' jargon') is proof of considerable social movement effected by criminals and travelling traders and tinkers. This close relationship would explain the fairly substantial Greek element we find in the *gerghi* and their extension into other slangs outside the region. In the same way, intraregional contacts with arriving Albanian mercenaries in the fifteenth century, supported and integrated by the local nobility, would also explain the substantial Albanian element which seems to be present amongst all slang users in the south. On the other hand, Rom elements are at a minimum, amounting to less than ten lexical items and one verb morpheme. In the future, it may be possible to investigate traditional slang or *gergo* through *pizzini* ('short messages written by mafiosi'), writings on prison cell walls and the bugging of *'ndranghitisti,* but no longer by interviewing its original users.

4.2   The 'common core' of the slang lexicon

Is there a common 'core' to Romance historical slangs (*argot/jargon; gergo/ furbesco*), as many scholars claim? Comparing French *argot* in its many varieties and the manifold realizations of Italian *gergo*, one cannot but conclude with Sanga (1979; 1980) that there is a fairly large 'common core' to all such historical slangs, representing perhaps almost 25 percent of the lexicon of any one single slang (see also Trumper 1996a:55), although perhaps Spanish *germanía* has fewer 'common' elements than its French and Italian counterparts. In the case of southern and central Italian historical slangs, together with Sardinian manifestations (Isili), fairly detailed analysis shows similar lexical choices, probably in a non-random fashion, and in some cases spreading occurs from Calabria–Sicily to the centre of Italy and Sardinia (Trumper 1996a:48f., Table 1). Friulian and Lombard slangs also show a large number of common choices with southern varieties such as traditional Calabrian tinkers' slang (e.g., *berta* 'pocket', *biancosa* 'snow; cocaine', *calcosa/carcusa* 'shoe', as well as *fangosa/fangusa* 'shoe', *carnente* 'parent; relative', *chiaro* 'wine', *lustra* 'money', *lustro* 'day(light)', *lenza* 'water', *mùtria* 'face', *prosol-u* 'arse', *ruffo/-u* 'fire').[18] Spanish argot uses about a third of such cases. For example, it has *blanca, calcos, clara, proxeneta* with similar slang meanings, but not the other lexemes. By contrast, a large number of such elements form a 'common core' with their equivalents in historical French slangs (e.g., trade *argot*). Examples, which are far too numerous for us to provide an exhaustive list here, include Fr. *lumer* = It. *allumare, lumare* 'to look; see', Fr. *luer, reluquer* = It. *alluscare, alluccare* 'to look', Fr. *blanc* = It. *bianca, bianchina, bbiancusa, jancusa* 'snow; flour; drugs (cocaine)', OFr. *caym* (Villon) 'bricklayer' = It. *caino/-u* (and *gaino*) 'bricklayer', Fr. *cabeça* = It. *caversa* 'head' (of obvious Spanish origin), Fr. *chérance* = It. *chiaro* 'wine', OFr. *coys* = It. *cosco/-u* 'house', Fr. *frangin* = It. *frangino, frag[g]ello/-u* 'brother', Fr. *loffe* = It. *lòffio* 'ugly; nasty', Fr. *marque* = It. *marca* 'prostitute', Fr. *mourme* 'horse' = It. *marmotta, màrmoro/ màrmuru* 'donkey, ass; mule', Fr. *brune* = It. *bruna, mbruna* 'evening; night', Fr. *mon an, monnan* 'myself, I' = It. *monarca, monello, monel, miano/-u*, Fr. *mourmouse* = It. *morfosa, murfusa* 'sheep', Fr. *pier* 'drink', *piorne* 'bar; pub' = It. *piola, pioda, piòrnia*, Fr. *crie* = It. *crea, cria, criolfa, criorfa, triorfa* 'meat',[19] Fr. *tigner* = It. *tignare* 'to fuck', Fr. *troche* = It. *truscia* 'poverty' (> *trusciante* 'beggar; moneyless'), Fr. *boule* = It. *bolla, vulla* 'town; city; forge'.

Such close parallelism is not observed in the case of Spanish slang which, as already noted, uses about a third of the 'common-core' instances. For example, from the above it has only *blanca, cain* (semantically differenti-ated: *pasar las de cain* 'to suffer'), *cuesco* ('fart', not 'house', for which it has *cueva*, similar to SIt. *cubba*), *marmota* (= *chica, creada*, 'servant-girl')/ *marmolillo* (= 'stupid' < 'ass': asses are prototypically 'stupid') and *truja* (not 'poverty' but 'cigarette'), but certainly not the other cases.

4.3   *Modern slang trends: substitution and disappearance of argot*

Italian trends have already been discussed (cf. §4.1.2), showing that the main, perhaps only, development concerns the appropriation by the *Mafia, Camorra* and *'Ndrànghita* of mainstream historical slang elements, along-side its complete abandonment by erstwhile traditional users who have considerably changed their social roles in the course of the last century. Differently from the historical French situation and its developments, Italy has never developed any socially relevant slang which might compete, at the spoken level, with strong geographical dialect varieties. Such a slang, had it ever developed, would have formed part of the realm of diastratic variation. However, such variation in Italy is locally circumscribed and tightly bound to diatopic variation.

Obviously, the case of ModFrench *argot* is quite different from that of other Romance jargons and is now completely free of a dependent class or category conditioning, having first become the informal code of not just the Parisian lower classes, as in the past, but almost an '*identème*', to borrow Stein's terminology, of urban Paris itself at the end of the nineteenth and beginning of the twentieth centuries. However, the situation gradually changed in the second half of the twentieth century: *argot* lost ground as the code associated with the lower classes, or even a large proportion of urban populations, and was gradually replaced by back slangs like *verlan* as the language of urban revolt, the poor suburbs, rap and the new age. Diagrammatically this drift has been quite adequately captured in Schmitt (1990:295), which we simplify below in Scheme 1:

Scheme 1

	Argot	Regional French non-standard	Dialect	Standard
	↓	↓	↓	↓
Up to 1800s		Parisian non-standard (urban)	↓	↓
		↓		
1900s		↓	Ø	↓
2000	Ø	Verlan	Ø	

NOTES

INTRODUCTION

1 There are, of course, some very useful smaller-scale works, such as Hall (1974), Elcock (1960; 1975), Harris (1978), Harris and Vincent (1988); also of interest is Posner and Green (1980–93).

2 All cross-references have been introduced by the editors, and not the authors. Where the editors have added notes to individual chapters, these are indicated as such and followed by the initials MM, JCS or AL.

CHAPTER I: ROMANCE LINGUISTICS AND HISTORICAL LINGUISTICS: REFLECTIONS ON SYNCHRONY AND DIACHRONY

1 Thanks to Martin Maiden, Peter Matthews and David Trotter for reading and commenting on this chapter. Responsibility for any errors is wholly mine.

2 The term 'value' is obviously here used in the Saussurean sense.

3 'la méthode sterile et fictive de l'histoire des faits isolés'.

4 'car même dans un secteur envisagé synchroniquement existe la conscience du stade en voie de disparition, du stade présent et du stade en formation'.

5 Observations such as Herman (1978a; 1990: 358–61) should not be underestimated.

6 This is true of Meyer-Lübke's approach in the *Grundriss* (Gröber 1904–6) but, in the *Grammatik der Romanischen Sprachen*, he treats the development of form and function separately, revealing a sharp split between morphology and syntax/semantics, and between form and function in the linguistic sign.

7 See further Ascoli's (1876:416) critique of D'Ovidio, in which it is argued that the single outcome in the plural in, for example, Italian does not reflect survival of a particular case-form, but rather what is left after the operation of sound change and/or analogy.

8 CORPUS was a neuter noun. In neuters nominative and accusative forms were always identical.

9 See Dees (1980, maps 122–23, 150–54, 186, 206–8); Schøsler (1984:171–219); van Reenen and Schøsler (1988:508–12, 523–26).

10 See Stanovaïa (1993:179); but see Schøsler (1984:213f.).

11 Similar considerations have been advanced by Chambon (2003) for OPrv.

12 See Schøsler (1984:52); van Reenen and Schøsler (1988:513).

13 See Schuchardt (1874:163); Paris (1872:110); Meyer Lübke (1894, II:§21) and (1904–6:481).

14 See Meyer-Lübke (1904–6:481) and Paris (1872:110).

15 See Paris (1872:112); see also van Reenen and Schøsler (1988:507–21).

16 See Fichte (1879:76); Brekke (1884:23); also Paris (1872:112).

17 See Meyer-Lübke (1894, II:§22).

18 As Paris (1872:112f.) thought.

19 See Paris (1872:113f.) and Meyer-Lübke (1894:§22).

20 My calculations, based on Sas (1937).

21 See Schuchardt (1874:162); Meyer-Lübke (1894:§21; 1934, I:§244); Nyrop (1904–30, II:§249); Pope (1952:§§788, 790, 802, 803); Lausberg (1969, II:§620); Woledge *et al.* (1967–69:194f.); van Reenen and Schøsler (1988).

22 Brunot (1966–79, I: ch. 4); Lausberg (1969, II:§622).

23 See Meyer-Lübke (1894, II:§21); also Paris (1872:113); Pope (1952:§§788, 790); van Reenen and Schøsler (1988:512).

24 See van Reenen and Schøsler (1988:513).

25 See Paris (1872:113); Meyer-Lübke (1894:§21).

26 After observing that 'declension is certainly one of the ways forms are grouped in the feelings of speakers', he argues that 'It is the link between the postulated divisions which is missing', and wonders whether declensional paradigms have an 'existence' outside the constructions of the grammarian (Riedlinger, Quire IV [Komatsu and Wolf 1997:63]).

27 See also Coseriu (1973; 1981:94f.) and Herman (1987).

28 This is Herman's view, following Audollent (1904:304).

29 In the original Italian of this chapter, *carsismo*. This is a term for which there is no ready equivalent in English, but the notion it expresses is of such utility in historical linguistic discourse that it might well be worth adopting. The *Carso* is the 'Karst' area of modern Croatia, whose topography is characterized by 'areas of readily dissolved rock (usually limestone) and predominantly underground drainage and marked by numerous abrupt ridges, fissures, sink-holes and caverns' (*OED* 2, s.v. 'karst'). Just as rivers in karst terrain often sink underground only to reappear at the surface some distance away, so linguistic phenomena may seemingly vanish, only to come to the surface again at some later period (MM).

30 The concepts of 'law' and 'principle', although distinct, do overlap to some extent: see, for example, *OED* 1, 1545a and *OED* 2, 2356c.

31 See particularly Nerlich (1990).

32 See, e.g., the critique of Meillet (Coseriu 1973; 1981:81).

33 *Ibid.*, 107.

34 *Ibid.*, 98.

35 *Ibid.*, 79f.

36 *Ibid.*, 70f. and 79f. passim.

37 *Ibid.*, 105.

38 *Ibid.*, 110f.

39 The morphological explanation 'may explain the need to replace the synthetic future, but not its replacement with certain forms rather than others' (Coseriu 1973; 1981:113f.), while the other explanation 'reduces to mere affirmation of its original meaning'.

40 The term 'grammaticalization' is criticized in Coseriu (1973; 1981:124, n25).

41 Coseriu (1973; 1981:116).

42 *Ibid.*, 119.

43 *Ibid.*

44 *Ibid.*, 116.

45 Fleischman (1982:153f.) correlates the process of synthesis and agglutination in periphrastic constructions with the assumption of temporal value, and analyticity with the modal/aspectual character of the discourse.

CHAPTER 2: SYLLABLE, SEGMENT AND PROSODY

1 That the progressive subordination of VQ to stress was one of the causes of its eventual demise has been maintained by many scholars (e.g., Lüdtke 1956:127–31; Herman 1968:202; Porzio Gernia 1976–77:149f.; Castellani 1991:19).

2 Deletion of -D after a long, but not after a short, vowel provides a *terminus post quem* for the dating of *correptio iambica*. Deletion must have applied earlier, or it would have been bled by the shortening of the preceding vowel, resulting in **BĔNĬD, **MŎDŬD, instead of BĔNĔ, MŎDŎ, from reconstructed *dwĕnĕd, *mŏdōd (Kuryłowicz 1958:338f.; Allen 1973:181f.).

3 The change could easily be restated in nowadays more fashionable no-rule approaches, such as Optimality Theory formalism.

4 An alternative view maintains that *latinitas Balcanica*, remaining alive and well even after 271, could have served as a link for more recent innovations to reach the Daco-Romance area (thus Gsell 1996:568).

5 Claims to the contrary are deductively (and mostly implicitly) derived from 'higher' chronology of the demise of contrastive VQ (à la Pulgram 1975; cf. below): thus, for example, Alarcos Llorach (1951:13) assumes that Roman legionaries and colonists imported into Spain, from the outset (third century BC), a variety of Latin which had lost contrastive VQ.

6 More recently, Schürr's reductive interpretation has been followed by Crevatin (1992:30), Fanciullo (1992:178) and Mancini (1994:625; 2001).

7 For discussion of whether African Latin had a vowel system of Sardinian type, see Fanciullo (1992:178f.).

8 Mancini (2001:322) argues that Herman's deductions on the rise of OSL are inconclusive. He supports Pulgram's (1975) opinions (see below) on the early loss of VQ. However, by stating that he will not analyse the statistical implications of Herman's observations, nor the interesting comparisons between the testimony of the metrical epigraphs found in Africa and that of those found in Rome, he escapes the burden of proof incumbent on his refutation, and begs the fundamental question: if Herman's method is not sound, what else can explain the distributional contrasts between Africa and Rome in (10a–c)?

9 As Pulgram (1975:88) puts it, criticizing scholars who trust the grammarians, the latter are in his view but 'palpably incompetent plagiarist[s]'. Compare the more respectful judgement of the grammarians' testimony by Banniard (1992:34).

10 Some testimonies by Latin grammarians were interpreted as implying a 'melodic' (pitch) accent, and several scholars took these descriptions at face value (cf. Lepschy (1962) and Leumann (1977:248–54) for a discussion of different views). The prevailing interpretation, nowadays, seems to be that descriptions of this sort were simply lip service to the Greek model and that a pitch difference was never part of the genuine Latin system (cf. Allen 1973:151–69, and references quoted there), if perhaps superimposed on it by cultivated people, especially for literary performance. Latin stress is more faithfully described by later grammarians (around 400 BC) such as Servius or Pompeius. Pompeius also uses the Greek terminology, but with a clear shift in meaning, using *acutus* for 'stressed (vowel) in a closed syllable', *circumflexus* for 'stressed (vowel) in an open syllable' and *gravis* for 'unstressed'.

11 This variation, to be assumed not only for French, may have been affected by several external factors. Thus, if in Siena (AD 715) the form *madodinos* is documented, this does not exclude that MATUTINUM could have already given rise to Tuscan *mattino* 'morning' (parallel to Fr. *matin*, Cat. *matí*, etc.). As Gsell (1996:563) points out, this is just variation. And one can add that, in this specific case, the unsyncopated variant must have been a 'high' form, since here the word means 'matins', and it still survives today in the half-learnèd *mattutino*.

12 See Wagner (1941) and Camilli (1929).

13 The rest of southern Italy has reduced the system to a variable extent: some four-vowel systems (of the Tuscan kind, but with /u/ instead of /o/) occur in southern Salento and central-northern Calabria; Sicily, southern Calabria and northern Salento have a three-vowel system (/i a u/), while the central part of southern Italy merged all final vowels into /xə/ during the late Middle Ages.

14 Tuscan, furthermore, provides no evidence of metaphony, *pace* Schürr (1970).

15 Compare chapter 3, section 1.2.3 for further discussion.

16 On French final [ə] see §4.3. In Spanish, final *-u* marginally occurs in learnèd words like *espíritu* 'spirit', *tribu* 'tribe'. In Romanian, -o/-u were deleted (*orb* 'blind' < ORBUM, *ascult* 'I listen' < A(U)SCULTO) except when a preceding consonant cluster could not have been resyllabified as a coda: *aflu* 'I find' < *AFFLO 1SG. As for front vowels, while -E was preserved, -I was deleted, after causing palatalization and/or affrication of preceding consonants: e.g., *fraţi* 'brothers' [fratsʲ] vs. [ˈfratɛ] 'brother'.

17 According to Harris-Northall (1991), final vowel deletion was favoured by following vowels. Pensado Ruiz (2001) questions this interpretation.

18 This class was further fed by words in which a cluster in the last syllable had prevented final (non-low) vowel deletion: e.g., *veintre* 'win' < UINCERE, *diaule* 'devil' < DIABOLUM (St Eulalia), both with final [ə].

19 Data from Malagoli (1910–13b), Loporcaro *et al.* (2006) and Loporcaro (2005–6).

20 This also implies mutual intelligibility among Latin speakers from different areas of the former Roman Empire.

21 Straka (1953; 1956) assumes several rounds of syncope in different environments to have taken place between the third and the sixth centuries. If the criticism by Gsell (1996:560) and Morin (2003) is on right track, however, syncope might have been a variable process for a long time, and come to a conclusion at a point in time approaching final vowel deletion.

22 Herman (1996:373–35) points out that this reconstruction is incompatible with the view of Wright (1982), according to whom, prior to the Carolingian reform (in the last two decades of the eighth century), the only variety in spoken use was Romance, and medieval Latin was 'invented' by Alcuin and the intellectuals around Charlemagne through the introduction of systematic spelling pronunciations. To this construal, Herman (1996:374) objects that 'the gap in understanding emerged for linguistic reasons […], independently of the Carolingian reform and before it'.

23 These contrasts, actually, only occur under stress and are therefore described by some in terms of syllable cuts rather than vowel quantity (see Uguzzoni *et al.* 2003). However, I will use the traditional terminology in what follows. See Morin (2006) for the vowel quantity contrast in the history of French.

24 The newly created contrasts discussed in this section, just like the Latin one, are binary. One exception is reported for Burgundian French by Morin (1994:144), where several processes of vowel coalescence resulted in a three-way contrast.

25 In Milanese, final devoicing applies variably to the final obstruents in (23a) and (23c).

26 As shown in Loporcaro (2003b), the contrast eventually retreated even from oxytones in related varieties (eastern Lombard and some peripheral Friulian dialects).

27 In other words, reasons for the selection of one option or the other must be sought in the phonological system, not in phonetic (substantial) constraints. One factor might have been the existence of *raddoppiamento fonosintattico* (a proto-Romance phenomenon, see §5.1). Since geminates require shortness of the preceding stressed vowel, the vowel triggering *raddoppiamento* always surfaces as short. Consequently, it can be speculated that in the varieties of type (32), the prepausal allophone was generalized as underlying, whereas in those of type (31), the short allophone, conditioned by *raddoppiamento*, prevailed.

28 I adopt Roca's (1999) convention of inserting a stress mark 'immediately before the stressed vowel wherever stress is not signalled in orthography'.

29 Here only *L'evanto* and *'Agosta* stem from Latin. However, their outcomes in the respective dialects are fully regular: [le'vantu], ['au̯sta]. Their aberrant stress pattern arose in the process of Italianization.

30 Most dialects of central and northern Italy behave like standard Italian in not displacing stress under cliticization: e.g., Gen. ['metimegelu] 'put it onto it for me' (Toso 1997:29). Other strategies, however, like vowel deletion, occur to prevent violation of the 3SW or even the rise of proparoxytonic verb + clitic clusters (see (21b) above).

31 Phonologically non-integrated loans tend to be invariably stressed on the antepenult, even if the penult is heavy, e.g., *'internet, p'erformance, 'underground*. The same goes for Spanish, as shown by pronunciations like *W'ashington, M'anchester* (cf. Roca 1997:633).

32 Final stress is unpredictable, as shown by, e.g., *libertà* 'liberty' vs. *lib'erta* 'freedwoman', and so is antepenultimate stress, once the HPC is complied with: e.g., *f'atico* 'phatic', *fat'ico* 'toil.1SG', *faticò* 'toiled.3SG'.

33 These are learnèd words that did not undergo the proto-Romance stress shift discussed below.

34 Not all vowel insertion processes determine surface violations of the 3SW. Some are blocked where such a violation would be determined by their application, as is the case for the optional *i*-epithesis in Galician, described in Martínez Gil (1997b), that may apply in, e.g., *fuxir* [fu'ʃir]/[fu'ʃiri] 'to flee' but not in *Xúpiter*/**Xúpiter*[i].

35 In the spoken language, syncope can apply, resulting in e.g., *t'impurle* (Ulivi 1977:66).

36 Chitoran (2002:85) takes no stance on this, limiting herself to concluding that (some of) the preantepenultimate stressed words 'must be listed as exceptions'.

37 A comparable mobility of stress is found in the *-zeci* numerals, but in the symmetrical direction: here the basic form, occurring prepausally, carries stress on the penult (e.g., *douăz'eci* 'twenty'), but stress retraction occurs in compound numerals like *d'ouăzeci și trei* 'twenty-three', *ș'aptezeci de mii* 'seventy thousand' (Ulivi 1985:584).

38 The unease with antepenultimate stress is testified by stress shifts in several morphemes. In verbs like TREMULAT > *tremola* [tɾə'molə] 'tremble.3SG',

ROTULAT > rodola [ruˈðolə] 'roll.3SG', stress shift is analogical (Badia i Margarit 1984:170f.), whereas in other lexemes there may be contact influences (see Recasens 1996:353).

39 Here also, antepenultimate stress can occur, even in the D area, in verb plus clitic clusters: [ˈdunalus] 'give them' (Entraunes; Dalbera 1994:58). Dalbera also reports preantepenultimate stress in, for example, [ˈdunalume] 'give them to me' (Entraunes). On the other hand, several Occitan dialects display stress shift under cliticization (see Sauzet 1986:159) of the kind seen above in section 4.1. In Montepellierain, Bitterois, Aixois and Rouergat clitics always attract stress (*manja-lˈa* 'eat.SG-it.F' = *manjatz-lˈa* 'eat.PL-it.F'), whereas in Toulousain stress shift only applies when the verb-form involved is paroxytonic, not oxytonic: *manja-lˈa* 'eat.SG-it.F' vs. *manjˈatz-la* 'eat.PL-it.F'.

40 Martinet (1956:85) observes the strict compliance of the *patois* of Hauteville with a 2SW. On loss of proparoxytones in Occitan, see also Meyer (1920:iv), Quint (1998:8) and Wheeler (1988:251).

41 Recent generative phonology (or Optimality Theory) treatments of Romance stress diverge as to the details, but share the basic features focused on here discussing Serra (1997).

42 Descriptive generalizations (46a–e) apply, on the whole, for Spanish and Portuguese as well, except that pattern (46d) is quantitatively less prominent in modern Spanish and even more so in Portuguese, due to the more restricted application of apocope (cf. (18) above).

43 Analyses not recognizing this fact are compelled to 'adjust' the phonological representation to fit the allegedly phonological generalizations on stress: thus, for example, Iscrulescu (2006:134) assumes that Romanian consonant-final oxytonic nouns 'are underlyingly vowel-final': e.g., /împərat-u/ → [împəˈrat] 'emperor'.

44 The shift in syllabification described in §5.3 also affected word-internal heads.

45 Note that this can be extended to the strings where the preceding vowel was long. For UINDĒMIA, for instance, gemination in It. *vendemmia* as well as glide hardening in Fr. *vendange* suggest that a bad contact was repaired.

46 To the two main ones, a third type may be added, viz. the mora-counting one, as instantiated by Japanese.

47 This is not uncontroversial. Thus, Dufter (2004:152) denies that French is syllable-timed, although not on an experimental basis.

48 Matte's absolute chronology follows Richter's (1934) and Straka's (1953; 1956; 1959; 1964), on which see this volume, chapter 3, §1.2.1 (note 20). The idea that French was characterized at such an early date by such changes as diphthongization of Latin stressed Ĕ and Ŏ has since been revised (see, e.g., Morin 2003). So Matte's Gaulish substratum-based explanation for the prosodic changes at issue (1982:66), following Palermo's (1971) idea of a 'Gallo-Roman rhythm', does not seem consistent with the broader picture. See the following note.

49 In other words, while specific substrata might well have played a role (especially since prosody/rhythm is well known to belong to those aspects of phonetics–phonology most heavily affected by foreign accent), there seems to be an internal rationale for the shifts in prosodic/rhythmic organization which occurred in the change from Latin to Romance.

CHAPTER 3: PHONOLOGICAL PROCESSES

1 This paper is dedicated to Carmen Pensado Ruiz. I thank Martin Maiden for his help and patience. Thanks are also due to Marcello Barbato and Adam Ledgeway for their helpful comments on a previous draft. Unreferenced data stem from my own field notes.

2 The presentation of the Latin vowel system in (1) relies on some generally agreed assumptions, which is not to say that they are unanimously held. Thus, Pulgram (1975) maintained that spoken Latin had no distinctive VQ from the third century BC at least. In a different vein, Kaye (1989:151) claims that 'length distinctions can be removed from considerations of phonemic status and assigned to syllable structure, where they belong'. As to the loss of distinctive VQ in the daughter languages, several studies in generative phonology (from Saltarelli 1970a, 1970b to Burzio 1994) have postulated underlying (i.e., distinctive) vowel length for modern standard Italian.

3 See, for example, Servius *in Donat* (around AD 400, Keil IV 421, 16f.), who says that *e* and *o* sound different according as they are long or short, and that the lengthened *e* sounds similar to the sound of the letter *i*, while when it is short it is similar to the sound of what he calls a 'diphthong': 'ex (vocalibus) duae *e* et *o* aliter sonant productae, aliter correptae. nam *e* quando producitur, vicinum est ad sonum *i* litterae, ut *meta*; quando autem correptum, vicinum est ad sonum diphthongi, ut *equus*'. This and similar passages (by, for example, Sergius, cf. Keil IV 520) have been interpreted by, e.g., Fouché (1958:194), Wartburg (1950:82, n2), Spore (1972:270), Franceschi (1976:263n) and Mancini (1994b:617) as evidence for the phonetic realizations indicated in (1) (see note 20 for an alternative, but ill-founded, interpretation).

4 Lüdtke (1956:56), among others, recognized the relevance of the /ae̯/ > /ɛː/ change for the reshaping of the Latin vowel system, except that he overstated its consequences by making it responsible for the entire collapse of contrastive VQ. For the latter, however, an independent cause is available, viz. the rise of OSL (see chapter 2, §2).

5 Lejeune (1975:249f.) states that the loss of quantitative oppositions is in no sense a necessary consequence, at least in the short term, of the transformation of the system of vowel quality. The same can be assumed for Romance.

6 The change is due to the opacification of metaphony, a process which applies regularly to stressed mid vowels before high vowels in Logudorese (see §1.2) but was opacified in Campidanese through the raising of post-tonic /ɛ ɔ/, which spread from Cagliari towards the middle of the island from the eleventh century

(cf. Wagner 1941:36f.; Loporcaro 2005a:192f.). As a consequence, minimal pairs such as ['beːni] 'come.2SG.IMP'< UENI ≠ ['bɛːni] 'well' < BENE, ['olːu] 'oil' < OLEUM ≠ ['ɔlːu] 'want.1SG' < *UOLEO occur nowadays, which led scholars in the structuralist tradition (Virdis 1978:26; 1988:900; Piras 1994:208–17; Ferguson 1976:107) to assume phonologization of the /ɛ ≠ e/ and /ɔ ≠ o/ contrasts. Generative analyses, on the other hand, represent both Campidanese metaphony and unstressed vowel raising as synchronic processes, so that underlyingly the same five-vowel system is assumed as for Logudorese (see Bolognesi 1998:19–22).

7 The asymmetric vowel system of Sassarese (cf. Guarnerio 1892–93; Contini 1987:441) displays the following correspondences (Classical Latin vowel phonemes in the first row):

Sassarese vowel system

iː	i	eː	e	a(ː)	o	oː	u	uː
i	ɛ		e		a		ɔ	u

'fiːru	'pɛːra	'teːra	='feːri	ka'baɖːu	'noːβu	'soːri	'krɔdːzi	ka'dːʒudːu
'thread'	'pear'	'cloth'	'gall'	'horse'	'new.MSG'	'sun'	'cross'	'fallen.MSG'

As shown by Gartmann (1967), the rustic Sassarese dialect of Sorso, spoken on the border with Gallurese, provides evidence that, in Sassarese too, a Gallurese (i.e., Sardinian) system once occurred. In Sorso, the outcomes of Latin ĭ and ŭ split (in about equal proportions), with ['kiɖːu] < *ECCU+ ĬLLUM 'that.MSG', ['dʒuːβu] < IŬGUM 'pair of oxen' alongside ['frɛxːu] < FRĬSK(UM) 'cool.M', ['nɔdːzi] < NŬCEM 'walnut'. This is clear evidence for ongoing lexical diffusion of the substitution of [ɛ ɔ] for original [i u], finally resulting, in Sassari, in the asymmetrical pattern above.

8 See, however, Lüdtke (1956:88) for a different interpretation of these data, discussed in note 37. This evidence is counterbalanced by the existence of several other dialects of the area in which the metaphonic outcomes of ē ō and ĕ ŏ do merge: e.g., in Cersòsimo (province of Potenza) [a'tʃiə̯tə] < ACĒTUM 'vinegar' = ['piə̯tə] < PĔDĒS 'feet' and ['su̯ə̯rətʃə] < SŌRICĒM/-ES 'mouse/mice' = ['fuə̯kə] < FŎCUM 'fire' (Savoia 1997:371). Savoia concludes that this situation is primary and, hence, that the dialects of the Lausberg area did originally preserve a Sardinian vowel system.

9 Some doubts about ascribing a Sardinian vowel system to Africa have been expressed by, e.g., Fanciullo (1992:178–80) and Mancini (2001). Epigraphic evidence does not provide, for Africa, as strong support as for Sardinia, as epigraphic Latin offers here many examples of <i/e> <u/o> confusion (see Acquati 1971:159–65).

10 On the diphthongization of proto-Daco-Romance /ɛ/ and /ɔ/ (cf. below, section 1.2.3). As observed, for example, by Sánchez Miret (2001:377), some instances of ŭ > /o/ lowering do occur in Romanian (e.g., *scoate* < EXCŬTERE 'to

shake', *roşu* < RŬSSEUM 'red'), which shows that the claim (by, e.g., Straka 1959:180) that the change first arose after complete separation of Romanian from the rest of the Latin-speaking world is overstated.

11 Unlike Daco-Romance, in this area the outcomes of proto-Romance /ɛ/ merge with those of /e/.

12 Lüdtke (1956:175–85) pushed this line of argument to the extreme, claiming that even Portuguese, at the western periphery of the Romània, shows traces of the same successive layers in the development of stressed vowels, so that [ɛ ɔ] from ĕ ŏ in, e.g., *bod* [ɛ]*ga*, *f* [ɔ]*rma* evidence a 'Sardinian' stratum, whereas [u] from ŭ in, e.g., *jugo*, *sulco*, *cruz* are compatible with either a 'Sardinian' or a 'Romanian' layer, upon which the common Romance four-height vowel system was superimposed through lexical diffusion, as the product of later waves of colonization. There are alternative explanations for this evidence: for instance, the metaphonic alternation in the -*oso*/-*osa* suffix is explained by Lüdtke as a remnant of a Sardinian system but, as will be seen in section 1.2, it can also be attributed to analogy.

13 Although this fact has been emphasized by many scholars (e.g., Lüdtke 1956:293–95; Bonfante 1998:12), Bartoli himself observed that the evidence for [a] from checked ō is scanty. At any rate, a later stratum with 'common Romance' vowel system can be inferred for Dalmatian, as the Dalmatian loanwords into Slavic and Albanian (cf. Muljačić 2000:331–33) all show a common treatment of ō and ŭ (> /o/ > /u/) as opposed to ū (> /y/).

14 The same observation concerning the lack of merger of <o> vs. <u> in Pompeii is found in Bonfante (1983:417). On Herman's quantitative method, see chapter 2, section 2.

15 As for Dalmatia, Herman's results (1971:139–43) show that the <o/u> confusions, although not so frequent as <e/i> (as is the case in neighbouring Veneto), are not absent either (unlike in Dacia): this squares with the complex picture from the extinct Romance varieties of Dalmatia (see note 13).

16 In late Latin documents, the mergers <i/e> and <u/o> are attested up to the Iberian Peninsula; see Herman (1995:22).

17 There is evidence that the continental area(s) with Sicilian vowel system were broader in the Middle Ages and then shrank due to the prestige of Neapolitan, sharing the common Romance vowel system in (6).

18 A comparable inversion took place in the Galician dialect of Miranda do Douro (Lüdtke 1956:194) and, in southern Italy, in Bari and the surrounding area (cf. Loporcaro 1988:67–73). For this dialect area, however, since diphthongs from ĕ ŏ are subject to metaphonic conditioning (e.g., Altamurano [ˈlɪ°tːə] < LĔCTUM 'bed') and the inversion only affected non-metaphonic vowels (e.g., Altamurano [ˈlɛtːərə] < LĪTTERAM 'letter' vs. [ˈletːərə] < *LĔCT-ORA 'beds'), the assumption of a previous centralization (e.g., Lüdtke 1956:163) explains the lack of merger more plausibly.

19 Herman (1970:30) shows that two out of the three examples of alleged diphthongization from Latin inscriptions quoted in support of this chronology are indeed phantoms due to incorrect readings.

20 Richter (1934:138) and Wright (1982:59f.) capitalize on the expression *sonum diphthongi* in Servius' passage quoted in note 3 to argue that Latin short ĕ had dipthongized to [jɛ] by his time (around AD 400). This is a misinterpretation though, since *sonum diphthongi* here means, as recognized by the authors mentioned in note 3, the pronunciation [ɛ:] of the (long monophthongized) *graphical* diphthong <ae>.

21 Bourciez (1937:94) places French diphthongization 'around the sixth century', which seems more reasonable than the earlier chronologies just discussed.

22 See Castellani (1961:95) for the date of the two processes in Tuscany: late sixth / early seventh century for diphthongization, late seventh for AU > [ɔ]. Clearly, in Rovigotto diphthongization must have applied later, for it to be fed by AU-monophthongization.

23 The list of scholars maintaining that the metaphonic condition (12ii) underlies all Romance instances of ĕ ŏ-diphthongization includes, e.g., Lausberg (1976:207, 228, 230, for Tuscan and French) and Maiden (1995a:54f.).

24 Castellani's explanation can be refined in the light of what has been shown in chapter 2, section 3.5, so as to escape a possible objection (raised by M. Maiden, p.c., July 2008). According to this objection, if Castellani were right, Italian *bene, nove* should have a higher mid stressed vowel, as in unstressed position (e.g., [be'nis:imo] 'very well', [no'vanta] 'ninety'), which is not the case, as they sound ['bɛ:ne], ['nɔ:ve] instead. This objection can be rebutted through the following steps. Consider first that ĕ ŏ diphthongization can be conceived of as a further development of OSL (the position advocated for here). Consider secondly that, as argued in chapter 2, section 3.5, even in modern standard Italian OSL is not a strictly word-level process but is still sensitive to sentence phonetics. This provides evidence for reconstructing proto-Romance OSL as arising out of a natural process of prepausal lengthening. On this view, lack of diphthongization in standard Italian *bene, nove* can be explained because of their frequently occurring in non-prepausal position, as Castellani does, without this implying that those words had to be totally unstressed.

25 Throughout its history, Aretine was attained (with considerable delay) by innovations spreading from the north (e.g., degemination: cf. Castellani 1972:46) and from central-western Tuscany (e.g., deaffrication of /tʃ/ and /dʒ/: see Franceschi 1969:76). There is no evidence whatsoever of innovations having spread from Aretine west- and/or northwards.

26 For a rather different perspective on some of the facts discussed here, arguing that OAretine preserves a primitive stage at which metaphony itself was restricted to open syllables, and which historically underlies Florentine and other Tuscan varieties, as well as Gallo-Italian dialects, readers might also see Maiden (1987; 1988). (MM)

27 This distribution can already be observed in the earliest extant medieval documentation of Friulian: *pis* 'feet' < PĔDES, *dul* 'hurts' < DŎLET vs. *fiesto* 'feast' < FĔSTAM, *fuart* 'strong.SG' < FŎRTEM (see Formentin 2002:116).

28 Raeto-Romance behaves likewise, with metaphonic diphthongization irrespective of the syllabic context (see Lausberg 1976:226f.).

29 The latter, for instance, is only sporadically observed in the Gallo-Italian colonies of Sicily and Lucania (twelfth–thirteenth centuries).

30 OProvençal also shows instances of metaphonic diphthongs (before -ī): *ier* 'yesterday' < HERĪ, *vuelc* 'wanted.1SG' < UOLUĪ.

31 Surselvan has two distinct outcomes (examples for Tavetsch from Caduff 1952:33–37), with ['ie] before -ɪ- (['mieʦs] < MĔDIUM 'half.MSG') vs. ['e] before other palatal consonants (['lec] 'bed' < LECTUM, ['veʎ] 'old.MSG'), both distinct from the outcomes in closed syllable before non palatals, viz. ['iɐ] before-ŭ ([a'viɐrt] 'open.N') vs. ['ja] elsewhere ([a'vjartɐ] 'open.FSG').

32 This fact did not prevent generative phonologists from positing synchronic phonological rules here: Quicoli (1990:307–11) assumes different thematic vowels underlyingly in, e.g., /dorm+i+o/ vs. /mɔv+e+o/ to account for the different metaphonic alternations. Although this does not automatically prejudice the synchronic analysis, as for diachrony it has been shown (cf. Goldbach 2010) that the *durmo/dorme* 'sleep.1/3SG.PRS.IND', *fujo/foje* 'flee.1/3SG.PRS.IND' alternation occurs very rarely in medieval Galician-Portuguese. This kind of alternation was later extended to many more verbal lexemes in the process of normativization.

33 Similar sporadic cases of metaphonic raising before yod or -ī occur also in other Romance branches: cf. Spanish *cuña* 'cradle' < CUNEAM, *lluvia* 'rain' < PLUUIAM, *vendimia* 'grape harvest' < UINDEMIAM, or, in the preterite paradigm, *hize* 'do.1SG.PRET' < FĒCĪ (Menéndez Pidal 1953:64). Metaphony has also been posited in French to explain the raising of proto-Romance /e/ before -ī in a few morphologically defined contexts: preterite (*fis* < FĒCĪ), pronouns (*il* 'he' < ILLĪ).

34 Note that conservative varieties of Asturian-Leonese have *puirtu* 'port' < PORTUM, *fuibu* 'fire' < FOCUM, with metaphonic raising acting on the outcome of diphthongization (Zamora Vicente 1967:107), providing further evidence for the original distinctness of the two processes. Arias Cabal (1999) and Corbett (2000:124–26) argue that the contrast is one of number: Corbett distinguishes a 'second number system' in which singular and mass contrast with each other as well as with plural. Similarly, although without calling it number, several other scholars frame the contrast not in terms of gender but of other features such as mass/count (e.g., Hall 1968; Hualde 1992c; García Arias 2003:135) or continuous/discontinuous (Neira Martínez 1978). See also Fernández Ordóñez (2006–7) for a recent discussion of the Asturian facts, where it is shown, among other things, that they were not peculiar to Asturias but used to extend to a substantial part of the Iberian Peninsula.

35 Some cues that, even in Logudorese, metaphony is becoming opacified (although not yet morphologized) are discussed in Loporcaro (2003a). The fact remains that Logudorese metaphony differs from any other instances of the process across Romance in preserving a very high degree of transparency. In Campidanese, on the contrary, metaphony was fully opacified, as exemplified in note 6.

36 Those sceptical about the rise of metaphony as early as in Latin (e.g., Wartburg 1950:10) seem to be in the minority.

37 Among dubious arguments, one can list the entries from the *Appendix Probi* mentioned by Krefeld (1999b:95), who quotes *byzacenus non bizacinus, formonsus non formunsus, bipennis non bipinnis* and a couple of others as relevant examples since in none of those the raised vowel occurs before -*a*. However, most of the data can (or should) be interpreted otherwise: in *bipennis non bipinnis* what is at stake is the confusion between the lexical morphemes /penn-/ and /pinn-/ and the context is inappropriate, since the third declension ending of the derived noun has a short /i/ in the final syllable, which never induces metaphony in any Romance language. For *bizacinus*, too, there is a morphological explanation, standardly adopted in linguistic commentaries to the *Appendix* (see a recent overview in Quirk 2006:85), which regard this as an instance of suffix substitution. *Formunsus*, too, shows that Latin evidence does not quite square with the Romance metaphony facts. Lüdtke (1956:176) interpreted the etymologically unexpected metaphonic alternation in Portuguese *form*[o]*so* 'beautiful.MSG' vs. *form*[ɔ]*sa* 'beautiful.FSG' as a remnant of a 'Sardinian' system, which is at odds with *formunsus*, since Sardinian never displays metaphonic raising of ō. Lüdtke (1956:88) went as far as to claim that the application of metaphony must have preceded the loss of Latin contrastive vowel quantity, on evidence from southern Italian dialects from Lausberg's (1939) *Mittelzone* (e.g., Oriolo, *AIS* point 745). Here, as shown above in section 1.1 while discussing vowel systems of the Sardinian type (3), the non-metaphonic outcomes of Lat. ĕ and ē, ŏ and ō, respectively, merge, whereas under metaphony they are kept distinct. This need not imply, however, that metaphony antedated the loss of distinctive vowel quantity, if one assumes (like Fanciullo 1988:676f.) that those dialects went through a stage with a common Romance vowel system, in which proto-Romance /ɛ/ ≠ /e/, /ɔ/ ≠ /o/ had not merged yet.

38 'Metaphonic' is here in quotation marks, since, as made clear above, the analysis of those Romanian diphthongs as conditioned by the following vowel does not convince me.

39 Metaphonic diphthongization occurred in ORomanesco (cf. Merlo 1929b:47f.; Ernst 1970:31–53), before the dialect was Tuscanized during the fifteenth century.

40 See Vignuzzi and Avolio (1994:644f.) for the geographical details, although both authors adhere to (14bi) (Vignuzzi 2005:86; Avolio 1996:321). More

recently, Carosella (2005:73f.) reviews the geographical extension of the two kinds of metaphony: neither of those overviews mentions southern Salentino, which provides crucial data, as shown below.

41 That this was a synchronically active phonological rule throughout is shown by the fact that ['iə] diphthongs of different origin (e.g., in the suffix -iere, which owes its diphthong to Gallo-Romance influence all over Italy) were also affected: e.g., [ru var'viərə] 'the barber' / [ru var've:rə 'vuọnə] 'the good barber'.

42 For instance, the only point showing ['pjɛ:rə] 'feet' in AIS map 163 is S. Chirico Raparo (point 744), in Lucania. Everywhere else the diphthong, if retained, is ['pje:rə] (or, with stress retraction, ['piərə]).

43 A few dialects in the Tyrrhenian coastal area show diphthongization too, as seen in chapter 2. Some, like that of Pozzuoli (see Abete 2006:393), even in closed syllables.

44 Proparoxytones behave differently, as they tend not to host OSL (and, consequently, diphthongization or the other syllable-related colouring processes): e.g., Altamurano ['lɛmətə] 'path' < LĪMĬTE (Loporcaro 1988:33f.). In chapter 2, (28), proparoxytones were shown not to have undergone OSL in northern Italo-Romance: southern dialects also generally offer the same picture (see Carosella (2005:69–79) for a recent review of such facts in southern Italo-Romance, as well as Wartburg (1950) and Weinrich (1958) for an early account of the facts in a pan-Romance perspective).

45 This assumes, of course, the existence of such a process in varieties such as modern standard Italian, as discussed in chapter 2, section 1 (4)–(5). This has been denied recently, especially by research within phonetically grounded OT (cf. McCrary 2002; 2004; and Loporcaro 2007a, for a refutation).

46 In Emilian, A-fronting, like other processes affecting stressed vowels in open syllables, also occurs before r/l + C; see Loporcaro (1996:175f.).

47 Actually, ŏ > [ø] does obey a syllabic condition: e.g., French cœur 'heart' vs. corps 'body'. Also, in northern Italo-Romance, the change tends to apply in open, not in closed syllables. This can be explained under the view, defended among others by Rohlfs (1966:112–23, 139–50), that [ø] is the further evolution of a diphthong (which is indeed attested in OFr. cuer), since the open syllable conditioning of diphthongization has been shown (see §1.2.1) to be at work, among other factors, in northern Italo- and Gallo-Romance.

48 Had it been earlier, one would expect palatalization of velars (see §2.1) to apply before [y] < ū, which is, however, not the case in northern Gallo- and Italo-Romance (e.g., Fr. [ky], Mil. ['ky:] < CŪLUM 'arse'), as opposed to varieties in which arguably later palatalization processes took place, such as Acadian French ([tʃø] queue 'tail') or Dalmatian (['stʃor] < OBSCŪRUM 'dark'; cf. Migliorini 1929:287).

49 A wealth of information and insightful discussion concerning vowel nasalization in the Romance languages is found in Hajek (1997) and Sampson (1999).

50 That nasality may disappear without trace is demonstrated by diachronic evidence reviewed later: thus, (Latin) nasality cannot be excluded with certainty from Romance evidence. The opposite holds for length. Here, the hypothesis of contrastive lengthening of final -U(M) to -/u:/ due to weakening and loss of the final nasal, as proposed by Lüdtke (1965a), has been disproved by Campanile (1973).

51 There might be further constraints, a fairly widespread one in northern Italy being that the following consonant is voiceless.

52 Besides context, other (possible) hierarchies have been discussed. For the place of nasal consonants undergoing weakening and triggering nasalization, Tuttle (1991:77) assumes a scale [m] < [ɲ] < [n] < [ŋ] based on combined evidence from experimental phonetics and sound change, but this is not uncontroversial, as Sampson (1999:258) has a different scale. As for the influence of stress, there is agreement that nasalized vowels develop preferentially under stress rather than in unstressed position: for instance, in Campidanese some dialects have nasalization throughout (e.g., ['kãĩ] 'dog' and [kãĩˈɣeɖːu] 'little dog' in Villanova Truschedu), but others lack it before stress (e.g., ['tʃɛ̃ã] 'dinner' vs. [tʃɛˈnai] 'to have dinner' in Narbolia (see Contini (1987:457f.) for the Campidanese data and Hajek (1997:94–105) and Sampson (1999:251–53) for general discussion). The interaction of vowel quality with nasalization processes has also been extensively discussed, a point of general agreement being that nasalization affects low vowels preferentially (cf. Hajek 1997: ch. 5; Tuttle 1991:77). Tuttle also assumes that, *ceteris paribus*, back vowels are affected first ([a] > [o] > [e] > [u] > [i]), whereas Ruhlen (1973) assumes a hierarchy [a] > [e] > [o] > [i] > [u] (see Hajek (1997:116–36), who takes a stance against universalistic claims on the relevance of vowel height and frontness/backness for nasalization).

53 The palatal glide /j/ was the sole occupant of a fifth (palatal) place of articulation.

54 Retroflex consonants are reported as counterparts to Castilian [tʃ] (e.g., peṭŝu 'breast') in some Leonese varieties: see Zamora Vicente (1967:151, n70).

55 As for documentation, palatal consonants present special problems since Latin had no graphic device for them. This is an area in which huge variation in spelling is found, all along. Two basic solutions can be distinguished: etymological vs. phonetic spellings. Thus, in one of the earliest attestations of Romanesco (the eleventh-century San Clemente inscription; see Castellani 1976:118) *fili* 'sons' has to be read ['fiʎːi], although maintaining the Latin spelling *faute de mieux*. On the other hand, several phonetic spellings developed polygenetically, many of them involving <h>: cf., e.g., <lh> and <nh> for [ʎ] and [ɲ] in Occitan and Galician-Portuguese, <sh> for [ʃ] in Occitan, <th> for [tʃ] or [ʒ] and <hy> for [ʒ] in OSpanish (see Kramer 1995:587–88).

56 A passage by Consentius (Niedermann 1937:17.1–6), discussed in Adams (2007:203f.), seems to suggest that he regarded both spelling pronunciation and affrication as wrong, which leaves as the 'only possibility [...] that with yodisation of the second vowel such that the word were disyllabic (*etjam*)' (p. 204). In other words, this passage seems to be a witness for the starting point assumed on reconstructive grounds as well as on metric evidence for the i̯-induced changes in chapter 2, section 5.3.

57 The early date of yod-induced geminations may suggest a substratum influence from Oscan, possibly just as a concomitant factor as argued, e.g., by Castellani (1965:102f.).

58 Menéndez Pidal (1986[10]:235) adduces evidence from placenames (the overwhelmingly frequent spelling <ju> all over the Spanish territory, as opposed to <Ø/g/ch> before front vowels) in support of a differential treatment depending on the following vowel.

59 Even in the medieval documentation, the distribution of the outcomes does not seem to be amenable to any neat generalization. Dialectally, /j/ is the outcome of both -i̯- and -G$^{e/i}$- in Castilla La Vieja (Burgos area; see Menéndez Pidal 1986[10]:235) and the same was true of Mozarabic: *yana* < IANUAM 'door' = *yermanéllas* < GERMAN+ELLAS 'little sisters' (Corriente 1997:372); the irrelevance of the following vowel is confirmed here by occurrence of /j/ also before /u/, as witnessed by placenames like *Yuncos* (Toledo) and *Yunco* (Almería) (Zamora Vicente 1967:36f.). In the remaining Spanish dialects, palatal obstruents prevail.

60 A few still more conservative northern dialects preserve the previous stage [dʒ]: e.g., rural Ventimigliese and Monegascu (western Ligurian) (see Azaretti 1982:63f.; Toso 2000:233).

61 As expected, the same situation is observed in medieval texts, although those from the southern part of the island (OCampidanese) already show vacillation between <ge> and <je> < (-)G$^{e/i}$-. Modern Campidanese has merged the outcomes of (-)G$^{e/}$^{i}- and (-)i̯- into [dʒ] (Wagner 1941:83, 85, 88), whereas in most Logudorese dialects the distinction survives under a different form, since [j] changed to [(d)ʒ] (possibly with sentence-phonetic variation: [ˈunu ˈʒu]/[ˈtrɛr ˈdʒuɔzɔ] 'a yoke' / 'three yokes'), whereas [g] was replaced by [b]: [ˈbenːeru] 'son-in-law'.

62 Exceptions like *zace* < IACET and *zână* 'fairy' < DIANAM seem to continue that same variation, still mirrored in Italian doublets like *razzo* 'ray' *raggio* 'rocket', a vacillation whose origin is placed in the second century AD by Castellani (1980, I:113–18).

63 The same lack of affrication/palatalization is observed also for -CI̯-: Welsh. *Nadolig* 'Christmas' < NATALICIA, *benthyg* 'loan' < BENEFICIUM (Jackson 1953:402, n1).

64 The different chronology speaks against the substratum explanation (invoking ancient Umbrian influence for the Romance varieties of that area), at least in the form envisaged by Bonfante (1983:424), who adduces, on the one hand,

Umb. *taçez* (with <ç> possibly = [ʃ]), corresponding to Latin TACITUS, and on the other hand Umb. *façia* (= Latin FACIAT 'do.SBJV.3SG'). There would have been no reason for the substratum influence here to apply at different stages, much earlier for -CI̯- than for (-)c^{e/i}-.

65 Picard and Norman dialects were never affected by the change (cf. Gossen 1951:74f.): cf. [kary] 'plough' < CARRŪCAM, [kerke] 'load' < CARRĬCAM in the Picard variety of Saint-Pol, as opposed to standard Fr. *charrue, charge*.

66 In spite of this, Martinet (1952; 1955:257–96) assumed a (Celtic) substratum explanation for lenition (cf. also Tovar 1951; Ternes 1998:278). And indeed, there is compelling evidence, at least for the British Isles, that Celtic lenitions have been directly transferred into the local pronunciation of Latin (see Jackson (1953:70f.) and the more recent discussion by Harvey (1990)). In fact, compared with the scepticism nowadays prevailing about the Celtic substratum explanation for vowel changes such as ū > [y], A > [ɛ] (see §1.4), the substratic explanation of western Romance lenition still enjoys popularity (e.g., Di Giovine 2003:582). A Celtic substratum cannot be conceived of as a necessary condition for lenition, however, as shown by Sardinian, which also underwent lenition.

67 Straka (1964:237) and Zink (1999:154) propose a somewhat earlier date (seventh century), Bourciez (1956:§271) a later one (ninth century).

68 Geminate -LL- and -NN- (but not -MM-) escaped neutralization with their singleton counterparts not through lenition but through palatalization in most of Ibero-Romance (e.g., Cravens 2002:93–115): e.g., Sp. *año* 'year', *gallo* 'cock'. As for -RR- vs. -R-, it gave rise to a quality contrast (with different implementations) in many western Romance varieties: Sp. *pero* [ˈpero] 'but' vs. *perro* [ˈperːo] 'dog', Pt. *coro* [ˈkoɾu] 'coir' vs. *corro* [ˈkoʀu] 'run.1SG' (Mateus and d'Andrade 2000:21), Franco-Provençal (Hauteville) [baˈrõ] 'baron' vs. [baˈʀõ] 'window bar' (Martinet 1956:64).

69 On this feature of Belsetán, see also Cravens (1988).

70 Degemination even spread beyond the Apennines, into eastern Romance, reaching the area from northern Marche to northern Umbria and eastern Tuscany, e.g., in Ancona [kaˈpɛlo] 'hat', [ˈdɔna] 'woman' (Parrino 1967:20–25).

71 On the comparable situation of the other conservative areas on the Alps and the Apennines, see Loporcaro *et al.* (2005; 2006) and the previous literature cited there.

72 To be sure, graphical simplification of geminates is attested too, throughout the documented history of Latin: however, this is normally due to inaccurate rendering of the phonetics (cf. the examples from Pompeii discussed by Bonfante (1968:33) and Fanciullo (1997a:188)).

73 Politzer and Politzer (1953:13), from inspection of Langobardic documents, conclude that there is very scanty evidence at that time for lenition between the river Po and the Apennines: 'if there was indeed any line of dialectalization in the Eighth Century, it seems much more reasonable to suppose that it was the Po River, rather than the La Spezia-Rimini line'. See, however, Larson (2000: 160–1) for a critical reappraisal, casting doubt on the philological reliability of Politzer and Politzer's method.

CHAPTER 4: MORPHOLOGICAL PERSISTENCE

1 It is precisely the high degree of morphological complexity which is inherited from Latin that makes one dubious about any claims regarding early 'creolization' of Latin, such as has been suggested by De Dardel and Wüest (1993) to account for the apparent simplification involved in the disappearance of the case system (see also Ledgeway, this volume, chapter 8: §6.2.2.2). For appeals to formal simplification as one factor in the evolution of aspects of Romance inflectional morphology, see Elcock (1975:68f., 116); Väänänen (1963:§210–12); Herman (2000a:50, 57).

2 E.g., the passive endings of the present indicative of AMARE 'love': AMOR AMARIS AMATUR AMAMUR AMAMINI AMANTUR.

3 Romanian, the Romance variety where vestiges of an inflectional case system survive most robustly to this day, conserves one distinct case ending (apparently continuing the Latin first declension feminine genitive/dative ending), namely -e or -i, in the singular of feminine nouns and adjectives, and no distinct endings in masculines. The determiners have a common genitive/dative plural ending -or for both genders, derived from the masculine genitive plural -(ILL)ORUM, and corresponding singular forms in -ui and -ei from late Latin genitive/dative pronominal inflections M (ILL)UIUS/(ILL)UI and F (ILL)EIUS/(ILL)EI: e.g., *acestui băiat* 'of/to this boy', *acestei case* 'of/to this house', *acestor băieţi/case* 'of/to these boys/houses'.

4 Something of the kind is observable in the OTsc. 3PL.PRET *cantonno*, where plural -*no* is added to 3SG *cantò*. For interesting discussion of the -*no* morph in Italian, see Thornton (1999).

5 As often, the analysis of French is complicated by the deletion of original unstressed vowels such as -o, and later of [ə] (< -a).

6 First person singular in French is complicated by the generalization, in non-first conjugation present indicative, imperfect indicative and preterite, of -*s* (Pope 1934:§899–902; Price 1971:172–74).

7 Note that in the Spanish, Italian and Romanian examples cited, the continuant of the accusative form is clitic. French and Italian also have stressed continuants of the old accusative form (*moi* and *me,* respectively).

8 The Spanish singular possessives are stressed forms, with unstressed proclitic variants *mi* and *tu*. The French forms are clitic, with stressed counterparts (generally combined with the article to form possessive pronouns) *mien, tien, nôtre, vôtre.*

9 Classical Latin fourth declension neuters also had a distinctive dative singular inflection.

10 I indicate vowel length only where immediately relevant to the morphological argument.

11 In relatively recent times Romanian deleted word-final -u.

12 Those Romance varieties which conserved a 'nominative' form distinct from an 'oblique' form also inherited a distinctive trait of the third declension, the formal differentiation of the NOM.SG root from that of the rest of the paradigm. E.g., OFr. NOM.SG *lerre* < LATRO, OBL *larron* < LATRONEM; see also Price (1971:95).

13 See Savj-Lopez (1900:504–7), Rohlfs (1968:19), De Blasi (1986:382–84), Formentin (1998:298).

14 But fourth declension NURUS 'daughter-in-law' gave *noru* in ORo. (modern *noră*).

15 Of course, there are local details, such as attendant root-allomorphy, or the frequent loss of final -*e* in Portuguese and Spanish, which leads to -*es* being reanalysed as the plural inflection of words ending in consonants, but plural formation can generally be said to continue the Latin accusative masculine and feminine pattern.

16 E.g., D'Ovidio (1886:89f.), Hall (1962), Rohlfs (1966:178; 1968:25–27, 247f.), Densusianu (1938:166, 207), Puşcariu (1937), Rothe (1957:65, 66f., 68, 70f., 89), Rosetti (1986:131f., 142f.).

17 See chapter 1 for an account of the conceptual difficulties and dangers associated with this aspect of historical Romance morphology and syntax.

18 For a different view, arguing for phonetic derivation of -i from Latin -os, (via *-es), see Forner (2003).

19 In the case of *dio* – *dei* (note also F *dea* – *dee*), the plural, in a culture in which God is necessarily one, and male, is clearly semantically distinct from the *usual* meaning of the singular *dio*.

20 For a sophisticated and insightful new account of the theoretical status of the feminine plurals in -*a*, see Acquaviva (2008: esp. ch. 5). Acquaviva argues persuasively for the -*a* feminine plurals as lexical plurals, rather than inflectional plurals belonging to the same lexeme as the masculine singulars in -*o*. An important task facing Romance linguists in the light of Acquaviva's work will be to account for the historical emergence of such 'lexical plurals', and to establish the diachronic and synchronic status (lexical or inflectional?) of the more frequent -*a* and -*ora* forms in SItalian dialects and Romanian. See also Smith, this volume, chapter 6, for further considerations on the morphology and semantics of -*a* plurals.

21 See, however, Manoliu (2005) for the view that the Latin neuter expressed 'incapacity to act (in the sense of producing some effect on the world)': e.g., TEMPUS 'time', SAXUM 'stone'. The referents of inanimate nouns with masculine or feminine gender were typically capable of 'acting' in this sense (e.g., M. UENTUS 'wind', F. TERRA 'land, earth, soil').

22 The replacement of neuters by masculine forms (with distinctively masculine inflections) is already attested, sporadically, in Plautus (see Väänänen 1963:§214).

23 Cases where morphological form favours a change of gender, despite the sex of the referent, are rare in the extreme: Jensen (1976:76–84) describes OOccitan

nouns denoting males which acquired feminine gender because they ended in -a, e.g., *la vostra papa* 'your Pope'.

24 Masculine variants such as LACTEM (accusative) are also attested in early Latin.

25 But *mar* can also be feminine in certain expressions: e.g., *hacerse en la mar*, 'set sail'.

26 Feminine in parts of Andalusia.

27 See also Jensen (1976:84–89) for Occitan examples of fluctuating gender in such words.

28 The 'mass' subclass is often, and misleadingly, labelled 'neuter'.

29 Or even nouns: e.g., *lo mujer* 'femininity, being a woman'.

30 A richly documented survey of this phenomenon is Wilkinson (1985–91); also Santangelo (1981) for Italo-Romance.

31 There survives, however, some evidence of an earlier stage when agreeing determiners and adjectives also showed *-a* (e.g., ONap. *la bracia aperta* 'the open arms'). See further Russo (2002:130f.) for Neapolitan; also Loporcaro (1988) for the modern dialect of Altamura (Puglia). Ledgeway (2009) describes considerable vacillation in respect of such forms in ONeapolitan. For example, *la mura* shows signs of reanalysis as a feminine singular, but plural verb agreement.

32 In the northern Italian dialects of the Veneto, however, a different development occurs, such that some tree names remain feminine (but take the ending -a), while fruit names, continuing the old neuter singulars, are masculine (Marcato and Ursini 1998:58f.).

33 In French, fruit names are usually feminine but the corresponding tree names are derived by means of an affix from Lat. -ARIU(M), and are masculine (e.g., F. *pomme* 'apple', M. *pommier*). This may, in fact, be part of a wider phenomenon of systematic derivational gender-reversal associated with this suffix, and interestingly explored by Roché (2002). For example, Sp. F *ceniza* 'ash' vs. M *cenicero* 'ashtray'; M *cabello* 'hair' vs. F *cabellera* 'hairpiece'.

34 For the complexities of the situation in late Latin, where tree names could be either masculine or feminine and, when feminine, belong either to the second or the first conjugation, see Wilkinson (1988:47).

35 See further Kahane and Kahane (1948), Malkiel (1983b), Cano González (1981:98), Penny (1978:74), Fernández González (1981:97), Taboada (1979:99).

36 There are no grounds to say that any Romance language conserves from Latin a 'neuter gender'. While it is often claimed that Romanian in particular has a 'neuter', what Romanian really has is a class of nouns which have masculine endings (and show masculine agreement) in the singular but in the plural have the endings -e or -uri, and show morphologically feminine agreement. For a discussion, see Corbett (1991:150–53). It is worth mentioning that Romanian preserves Latin neuter morphosyntax in another respect. In Latin, plural adjectives agreeing with conjoined inanimate nouns of different genders

showed the neuter plural inflection: *Secundae res* (F.PL), *honores* (M.PL), *imperia* (NEUT.PL), *fortuita* (NEUT.PL.ADJ), *sunt* (Sall.) 'Good fortune, honours and power are a matter of luck'. In nearly all modern Romance languages, adjectives modifying conjoined nouns of different genders are masculine (e.g., It. *Il camion* (M.SG) *e la macchina* (F.SG) *sono rossi* (M.PL) 'The lorry and the car are red'), but Romanian has feminine plural agreement (reflecting the Latin neuter plural ending -A): *Uşa* (F.SG) *şi peretele* (M.SG) *sunt albe* (F.PL) 'The door and the wall are white'.

37 Remnants of such a system are also detectable in OFrench, with names of weights and measures preceded by a numeral – see Wilkinson (1986:163f.).

38 In parts of Sicily, northern Umbria and southern Corsica, the -a plurals have acquired the masculine gender of the singular; see Tuttle (1990).

39 A fact which tends to give rise to a 'gap' in the grammar. Italians usually experience difficulty in expressing 'one of the broken eggs': neither *uno* (M) *delle uova rotte* nor *una* (F) *delle uova rotte* seems acceptable.

40 In Istro-Romanian (Kovačec 1971:88), the -ure plural ending (= Ro. *-uri*) has been reanalysed as masculine, and has also been extended into animates as well as inanimates.

41 Although there are exceptions, e.g., *magnet – magneţi* 'magnet'.

42 There is a phonological constraint, in that words not stressed on the final syllable in the singular all take -e; but there are thousands of Romanian nouns with final syllable stress.

43 For a useful overview of Romance preterite morphology, see Mourin (1978).

44 As Ernout (1927:186) observes, conjugational distinctions are characteristic of imperfective verb-forms. In the perfective, distinctions between conjugations are much less clear.

45 Root-allomorphy in marking aspect is particularly frequent cross-linguistically, as a consequence of the high degree of 'relevance' of aspect to verb-meaning; see Bybee (1985:36, 63).

46 In the so-called 'sigmatic perfects' the [s] was originally a formative independent of the lexical root. But its idiosyncratic distribution in Latin means that it is properly viewed as a property of the root.

47 One result is 'retraction' of stress onto the thematic vowel – a feature which in Romance is extended even to first and second persons plural forms, e.g., DORMIUISSÉMUS > It. *dormíssimo*, Sp. *durmiésemos*. Vincent (1994) suggests an explanation in terms of Mester's (1994) notion of 'prosodic trapping', which asserts that trochees are bimoraic (while final syllables are extrametrical). In a form such as DORMIUISTI, UI is neither part of the stressed foot, nor is it extrametrical. It is a 'trapped' syllable and thereby liable to deletion.

48 But the functional distinction of aspect seems to have already been severely compromised in Latin; see Salvi, this volume, chapter 7.

49 Gamillscheg (1912:245f.) lists cases where the continuant of the pluperfect indicative allegedly had preterite value in early southern Italian dialects. None

of his examples seem to me to exclude a conditional (or past subjunctive) interpretation. The historical status of the use of conditional forms as preterites in some Campanian dialects (see Rohlfs 1968:329f.) is unclear.

50 I know just one case of Gallo-Romance extension of a present subjunctive root into the imperfect subjunctive which is unparalleled in the preterite. This occurs in *aller* 'go' in the Jersey French of St Ouën (Le Maistre 1966:xxx) – although this same verb also has an alternative, suppletive, root taken from the verb 'be', which *is* shared by preterite and imperfect subjunctive. It may be significant that this verb belongs to the first conjugation, unlike all other PYTA verbs. De Garis (1985:336, 341f.) records PRET *fis-* but IPF.SBJV *fa(i)ss-* in *faire* 'do', and PRET *bu-* 'drink' but IPF subjunctive *bév-* in Guernsey. Le Maistre's data from Jersey show certain verbs (e.g., *vivre* 'live') with apparently *optional* removal of the PYTA root in the imperfect subjunctive, but not with complete split between the two tense-forms, and this may in reality be the situation in Guernsey as well.

51 The distinctive vowel of *voil* actualy has a non-metaphonic origin; see Fouché (1967:276).

52 I am grateful to Paul O'Neill for alerting me to this problem.

53 See Egido Fernández (1996:411–41) for the situation in medieval Leonese, where the spread of the high vowels seems to have begun later than in Castilian (mid thirteenth century), and to have spread initially (as in OFrench) from the first person singular to other rhizotonic forms.

54 For Portuguese, see also Huber (1986:243, 246).

55 De Lima Coutinho (1958:330f.) reviews other interpretations.

56 Penny (2002:226) attributes *estude, andude* and even the occasional *tude* for *tuve* 'had', to the influence of *pude*. For *pude* < POTUI and *puse* < POSUI he postulates a double raising to /u/ by joint effect of the glide and final -i, but this seems a little speculative in the absence of more general evidence for such raising.

57 Rini (1999:51–68) believes he finds some propensity for the high vowel to occur particularly before yod, in OSpanish verbs where the diffusion of the high vowel was not yet complete. But the preference for [u] and [i] before yod seems to me to be tenuous and statistically marginal. Rini does not consider dissimilation as a motivation for forms such as *feziste* (see also Bustos Gisbert 1992:152, n89), and his analysis does not in fact compare like with like, since PYTA roots before [je] are always unstressed, while he computes stressed roots among the forms containing a high vowel and not followed by [je]. A comparison limited to unstressed PYTA roots becomes statistically problematic, because of the extremely low token frequency of the relevant forms (first person plural, second person plural and second person singular of the preterite). The only verb for which there is a fair number of such forms is *aver*, and while Rini's conclusions may be supported by comparing the unstressed roots of the preterite with the imperfect subjunctives, comparison with the future

subjunctive suggests that the incidence of [u] in unstressed preterites is ten times higher than that for the future subjunctive – although the relevant form, *oviere*, was perhaps already becoming a fossilized archaism; see Bustos Gisbert (1992:146). In any case, Rini himself prefers to analyse the phenomenon in terms of generalization of a metaphonic vowel originating in the first person singular preterite. The data surveyed by Rini already show 100% diffusion of [u] to the root-stressed forms of *poder* (*pude*, *pudo*), and over 80% in 3PL *pudieron*. *Pod-* predominates (over 75%) in the second person singular and is the only form found in first and second persons plural. The same general pattern is observable for *poner*, although the incidence of *pus-* in the second person singular is rather lower, and there is a small minority of *pus-* forms in first and second persons plural. The fact that [u] is best established in stressed syllables tends to belie any suggestion that the high vowel originated in unstressed syllables. Egido Fernández (1996:432, 441f.) is equally sceptical that closure of the vowel originated before [je], and favours an origin in the first person singular preterite; likewise Bustos Gisbert (1992:151f.).

58 Bustos Gisbert (1992:153) considers a similar line of argumentation, again overlooking the fact that in most of the paradigm the PYTA root is not associated with perfectivity. Lloyd also invokes the 'sound symbolism' of fourth conjugation verbs, typically characterized by high vowels and expressing actions, whence their introduction into the PYTA roots. But this seems to confuse aspect with Aktionsart. Compare also Montgomery (1976;1979) and Bustos Gisbert (1992:159f.).

59 For a critique of Montgomery's attempts (1976; 1979; 1985) to account for the high vowels in terms of 'sound symbolism', see Maiden (2001a).

60 De Poerck and Mourin (1961:225) report that sixteenth-century Engadine has six verbs with optional sigmatic perfect, while imperfect subjunctive never has the PYTA root. The relevant forms are root-stressed, and the distribution seems, therefore, to be the Italo-Romance one.

61 Penny reports that this pattern is 'rare' for this verb.

62 There is also a hybrid su'pjo, where for once stress and PYTA root do not coincide.

63 To ensure historical and comparative consistency in labelling conjugations, I use the labels first, second, third and fourth conjugations even for those varieties which now have fewer. Thus, despite loss of a distinctive third conjugation in Spanish, the original 'fourth' conjugation in *-ir* (e.g., *dormir*) will still be called 'fourth' (although grammars of Spanish traditionally classify this as the 'third').

64 It might be thought that this phonological neutralization between non-first conjugation verbs motivated other neutralizations which also affect non-first conjugation verbs only. That this is probably incorrect is shown by Sardinian, where the distinction between Latin short ĭ, and ĕ, is not phonologically neutralized, yet where non-first conjugation verbs nonetheless neutralize conjugational distinctions in the imperfect indicative (see Wagner 1939).

65 Ledgeway (2009) points out that there are southern Italian dialects in which the distinction between the non-first conjugations has become tenuous, and virtually limited to infinitives. The dialect of Cosenza (Calabria) comes very close to having only two, with virtually all non-first conjugation infinitives ending in unstressed -a (but there are a few infinitives in stressed -i, continuing the second conjugation, such as *avì* 'to have').

66 Third conjugation verbs were also characterized by a thematic vowel short ĭ, as opposed to long ē in the second. But, with the exception of Sardinian, the merger of these vowels has neutralized this distinction.

67 For strong criticism of the attempt by Davis and Napoli (1994) to explain these changes in terms of the phonological structure of the root, see Maiden (1995c) and Wright (1997).

68 Substitution of -IBA- for fourth conjugation -IEBA -is already attested in Latin (see Väänänen 1963:§244).

69 The Upper Engadine and Val Gardena varieties surveyed in Iliescu and Mourin (1991:212f.) stand out by neutralizing the distinction between the first three conjugations, but retaining a distinction between these and the fourth.

70 While this form survives in Balearic and Valencian varieties, the modern general variety of Catalan has *llevès,* neutralizing the distinction between non-first conjugations; see Wheeler *et al.* (1999:306).

71 Other non-first conjugation verbs have *-ût* (e.g., *connût, mourût*).

72 Except where the unaccusative past participle encodes number (and gender) agreement, and in varieties such as medieval Leonese, Galician, Portuguese, and ONeapolitan with inflected infinitives.

73 Romanian, unlike other Romance languages, conspicuously palatalizes *[k/g] from Latin [kw/gw] before a front vowel (see Ro. *ce* [tʃe] 'what', *sânge* ['sɨndʒe] 'blood', It. *che, sangue,* Sp. *quien, sangre* < QUEM, SANGUEN), and also applies palatalization before [e] or [i] derived from *-AS (Ro. *vaci* [vatʃ] 'cows', *largi* [lardʒ] 'wide', It. *vacche, larghe* < Lat. UACCAS, LARGAS). This extension of the process far beyond the phonological domain which it occupies elsewhere in Romance raises the suspicion that Romanian palatalization may have been a separate phenomenon, or at any rate continued to operate in Romanian long after its demise elsewhere. Interestingly, Romanian resists a later palatalization, that of [n] before [i], precisely in first conjugation verbs (see Graur 1968:34f.).

74 Bybee (2001:155f.) makes the same assumption, but seems unaware of my earlier work.

75 With the exception of the [ə] – [ɛ] alternation in verbs like *je l*[ɛ]*ve – nous l*[ə] *vons*; but see Grevisse (1964:610).

76 Exceptions are Megleno- and Istro-Romanian (Atanasov 2002:228; Kovačec 1971:130), where fourth conjugation verbs alone (plus the class of verbs in -*ui* in Istro-Romanian) are productive. The same was true historically of Daco-Romanian.

77 An exception is *oír* 'hear'. It is significant that this verb originally had [au̯] (<AUDIRE) in the root. The only other exceptions (see Togeby 1972:262f.) are a tiny handful of loanwords and Latinisms.

78 See chapter 5 for further discussion of the incidence of yod. Note that non-fourth conjugation verbs with root-final yod were generally transferred to the fourth (e.g., FERUEO FERUERE 'to boil' > *ˈfɛrvjo ferˈver > *hirvo hervir*).

79 For the possible reason for the outcome [i] rather than the diphthong, see Malkiel (1966).

CHAPTER 5: MORPHOPHONOLOGICAL INNOVATION

1 The term 'morphophonological' is a shorthand. The question whether there exists a separate domain of 'morpho(pho)nology' (see Dressler 1985; Maiden 1991a) is irrelevant to present concerns.

2 In neuters, the accusative shared the root-allomorph with the nominative.

3 For a critical review of the formal and functional problems associated with the continuation of Latin case-forms, see especially Sornicola in chapter 1 of this volume.

4 Exceptions were ESSE 'be', IRE 'go', UELLE 'want' and POSSE 'be able'. The highly erratic pattern of ESSE is described in Sihler (1995:548–54), and is well maintained in Romance. I shall not consider it here, nor will I deal with UELLE, which is continued in Romance by a single, originally undifferentiated root, *vol-. To IRE and POSSE, I return below.

5 It is sometimes suggested (e.g., Fanciullo 1998) that *fuggo*, etc. reflects early loss of yod: *ˈfugjo > * ˈfugo.

6 For discussion of the early history of these inflections (and especially of feminine plural -e, which probably derives from non-palatalizing *-as) and their morphological effects, see Maiden (1996a; 2000a).

7 Palatalization of [l] originally yielded [ʎ], which was subsequently deleted. Not all words show this alternation, however: *şacal – şacali* 'jackal', *şcoală – şcoli* 'school'.

8 See Loporcaro, this volume, chapter 3: section 1.1, for a more detailed account.

9 Final [s] is retained in this word when used pronominally, or stranded from its higher NP.

10 *Majeur* is of learnèd origin.

11 These are *abstract* labels invented by me to denote these morphomic entities, but they are (vaguely) suggested by the distribution of the alternation in the conventional layout of the paradigm. They have no phonological significance.

12 The modern language tends towards root uniformity throughout the relevant paradigms, but see Densusianu (1938:205–07, 211–13) and Rothe (1957:99, 109). The Romanian subjunctives have been replaced by the indicative, except in the third person (and throughout *fi* 'be').

13 That the same root alternant appears in the second person singular is due to a later change, in which most consonants were palatalized and/or affricated before [i].

14 The [z] found in first person plural and second person plural (and singular) is of different origin from that in first person singular and the subjunctive, reflecting later affrication of [d] before [i].

15 The absence of the root-final consonant reflects regular deletion of intervocalic [ɲ]. The second person singular reflects prior palatalization of [n] before [i], followed by deletion of the palatalized consonant.

16 For the status of the first and second persons plural roots in the subjunctive, see section 5.

17 This is recognized for Spanish by Bybee and Pardo (1981:958; also Bybee 1985:71–74), but nothing is explained by their arbitrary and diachronically unsupported assumption that a relatively 'autonomous' first person singular serves as a base from which the subjunctive is *derived*. They simply take for granted that the indicative must be a basis of derivation for the subjunctive. Appeals to the relative 'autonomy' of the first person singular and 'derivation' therefrom of the subjunctive root yield the observed distribution of allomorphy, but say nothing about *why* it subsists.

18 Note that the 'N-pattern' (discussed below) also appears here, as shown by the first and second persons plural.

19 Inspection of *AIS* maps 1694/5 shows clearly the correlation between the distribution of poss- and the L-pattern in northern Italy.

20 The [dʒ] alternants characterize second and third persons singular and first and second persons plural. There are other verbs in which *both* [g] and [dʒ] have been generalized (see Lombard 1955:1016–19).

21 Kovačec (1971:140, 152) and Pușcariu (1926:173f., 192) describe similar developments in Istro-Romanian.

22 I talk throughout this study as if the changes explored all involved modifications of the 'lexical root', which can be either paradigmatic, as with the introduction of root-final velars in Campanian 1SG ˈmɛkkə 3SG ˈmɛttə 'put' or Agnonese 1SG ˈʃeŋgə 3SG ˈʃeʎʎə 'choose', or syntagmatic, as with the augments (see §5.2). But is [g] a 'root-final' consonant, or has it been reanalysed as an empty affix appended to the root? In other words, in Spanish/Italian 1SG *salgo*, 3SG *sale*, do we have an alternation between lexical root-allomorphs [salg] and [sal], or a root [sal] + an affix [g]? The affixal (or 'interfixal') analysis is that preferred by Malkiel (1974b). It encounters obvious difficulties where the verb-form cannot be neatly broken into root + [g], although one might resort to special (but ad hoc) 'phonological' rules of the type ˈʃeʎʎ + g → ˈʃeŋgə, ˈmɛtt + g → ˈmɛkkə. In fact the whole question is of secondary importance, because what we have been describing are properties of paradigms, and more precisely of *arbitrary clusters of cells in inflectional paradigms*. True, to account for 'convergence' phenomena, some reference to the internal structure of the word-form seems inevitable, but this could be captured either in terms of a 'canonical shape' for the root, of the form 'root must end in a velar consonant in first person singular present indicative and present

subjunctive', or by saying that 'inflectional endings of first person singular present indicative and present subjunctive must be preceded by a velar'. It is not clear that there is any criterion for choosing, although the fact that the velar is often analyzable as replacing a root-final consonant must incline one to the former. Bybee (1985:128) takes the view that 'the velar consonants that appears in the 1SG Present Indicative and throughout the Present Subjunctive of some Spanish verbs […] is ambiguous in segmentation. It is in a sense part of the verb stem, restricted as it is to certain stems, but it is also part of the marker of certain inflectional categories. It would seem advantageous in such cases not to force a segmentation, but rather to use the notion of lexical connection developed in this model to associate the velar consonant to other instances of the velar in the same paradigm, as though it were part of the stem, and simultaneously to other instances of the velar in other paradigms, as though it were part of the inflectional affix.'

23 For meticulous surveys of the relevant phenomena, see Wilkinson (1978–83) and Malkiel (1974b).

24 There is considerable extension in Catalan of the alternation type PRS.IND 1SG *tinc* 'I hold' 2SG *tens*; SBJV *tingui* to other verbs in root-final nasals: e.g., *fonc fones*; *fongui* 'melt' (see Wilkinson 1982:118). The type *dic dius*; *digui*, also favours creation of *cloc, clous*; *clogui* 'close'. But such analogies are not so readily invoked for *puc pots* …; *pugui* 'be able'. For the type *visc vius* …; *visqui* 'live', under the influence of old first person singular and subjunctive forms of the veb 'be born' (*nasco*, etc.), see Malkiel (1974b:329, 331f., n50). Catalan (and Occitan) root-final velars (which also developed independently in the preterite) have been subject to wide-ranging generalization in the verb-paradigm outside the present tense. I have no space to explore these developments (see Wheeler 1993; Dalbera 1994:615–17), but they will provide fertile ground for further exploration.

25 There is a view (Wilkinson 1980:43; Elvira 1998:193) that *fago, fagas*, etc. was not remodelled on the *digo* type, but continues Latin *FACO, *FACAS, etc.

26 See Malkiel (1974b:326, n42, 328, n45).

27 In the modern language, root-invariance has re-established itself, carrying with it some originally alternating verbs: *vedo, vedi* …; *veda* …, etc.

28 See Capozzoli (1889); Freund (1933); Radtke (1997:87); Maiden (2001a). For an interestingly different view of how some southern Italian forms of this type emerged, see Tuttle (2001–2).

29 Subjunctive *mecca* occurs in ONeapolitan.

30 The novel allomorphy corresponding to the L/U-pattern rarely involves actual suppletion. However, Todoran (1960:43), states that in Vâlcele (near Turda, Romania) a ˈmere 'go' forms a suppletive paradigm with a sə ˈdutʃe also 'go', the latter appearing in the the 1SG.PRS.IND (məˈduk) and 3PL (sə ˈduku), and in the subjunctive (3PL sə ˈdukə), vs. 2SG merị, 3SG mere, etc. The example

comports a slight complication if we take Todoran at face value, for he states that the third person singular subjunctive is still ˈmargə, thereby violating an otherwise invariable syncretism between third person singular and third person plural subjunctive in Romanian.

31 Burzio (2004) also adopts a 'phonologizing' approach, appealing to the fact that the original triggering environment is still in many cases present on the surface in Italian. But his account fails to consider the full historical and comparative background. Beyond the observation that the U-pattern alternant often disappears before the first and second persons plural subjunctive endings -*iamo* and -*iate* (a change almost certainly attributable to the 'N-pattern', discussed below), he adduces no evidence that speakers actually make phonological generalizations about the conditioning of the alternants, beyond the theory-driven assertion that 'whatever identity relations have a statistical presence in the data, also have, ipso facto, a grammatical status, expressible as faithfulness constraints in the O[ptimality] T[heory] formalism'. While the OT model certainly provides the machinery for representing the alternations as a matter of 'syntagmatic' phonological conditioning whose exceptions could be simply a matter of constraint violation, what we lack is evidence that speakers actually make any such analysis; what we have instead is substantive evidence that they don't, as witness the massive incidence of counterexamples in the Italian phonological system in general, and the historical incidence within the verb of the velar alternants before inflectional front vowels, and the palatal alternants before non-front vowels. Worse, a gross anachronism is committed by Burzio in accounting for alternations such as *voglio* – *vuole* in terms of a phonological process triggered by /i/ allegedly following the root. There has been no such /i/ for centuries (save in the orthography!).

32 This label too is arbitrary (but inspired by a fancied resemblance of the pattern to the form of the letter 'N' in Morse code). It has no phonological significance.

33 Outside the present, rhizotonic stress was restricted to: (i) third and fourth conjugation futures (extinct in Romance); (ii) third (and some second and fourth) conjugation special 'perfective' roots; (iii) infinitives of third conjugation verbs (see chapter 6).

34 There are signs of something similar in Spanish (see Lathrop 1980:120f.), but the development is not systematic, and sometimes the reverse occurs (high mid vowels supplanting reflexes of low mid vowels).

35 In non-first conjugation verbs, the N-pattern intersects with the vocalic alternants characteristic of the L-pattern discussed above: so [e] and [o] appear in the first person singular and throughout the present subjunctive.

36 See Ledgeway (2009) for Neapolitan.

37 Alton and Vittur (1968:53); Mair (1973:109); Gartner (1883:138).

38 Alonso Garrote (1947:89); Chacón Berruga (1981:260).

39 See further Maiden (2004a). The augments are 'semantically empty' in the sense that they usually contribute nothing to the lexical or grammatical meaning of the verb: cross-dialectally (e.g., northern Romanian *lucră* 'he works' vs. southern *lucrează* 'he works') there is often vacillation between 'augmented' and 'non-augmented' forms.

40 Nineteenth-century Vegliote (Dalmatian) had this kind of augment only. It had become extremely widespread outside the first conjugation, and seems in fact to have replaced earlier -esk- (attested in Ragusan). See Bartoli (1906:390–92). See further Maiden (2004b).

41 A different type of creation of an N-pattern partly involving reflexes of this suffix in Spanish America is examined in Espinosa (1946:261–70).

42 Maurer (1951); Rohlfs (1968:242–4); Lausberg (1976:§921–23); Zamboni (1980/81; 1982/83); Iliescu (1990); Wolf (1998). Also Maiden (2004a).

43 For some examples of lexicalization of the two forms in Neapolitan, see Bichelli (1974:201–5). For a possible tendency to distribute the variants along morphosyntactic lines in ONeapolitan, see Barbato (2001:200).

44 In parts of southern Lazio and Calabria, the augment appears throughout the present, in indicative and subjunctive alike. Old Occitan as described by Anglade (1921:282) displayed the N-pattern, but with -isk- generalized through the present subjunctive (and into the gerund). The same pattern in the present tense allegedly occurs (Rohlfs 1968:243) in some Tuscan varieties. This may be a case of L/U-patterning, such that the non-palatalized alternant in -sk- characterizes the entire subjunctive and the first person singular (and third person plural) present indicative, in opposition to non-palatalized alternants elsewhere. The fact that in some southern Italian dialects the augment also appears in the infinitive appears due to frequent morphological identity between the infinitive and the third person singular present indicative (see Iannace 1983:69).

45 Lausberg (1976:§801); Rohlfs (1968:244f.); Väänänen (1963:§§95, 193); Tekavčić (1980:239f.); Zamboni (1980/81).

46 Rohlfs (1968:242); Bourciez (1956:78); Meyer-Lübke (1894:241); Tekavčić (1980:258); Lausberg (1976:§919); Iliescu (1990:161); Iliescu and Mourin (1991:455f.).

47 Zamboni simply takes it for granted that the N-pattern was the primitive early Romance pattern. Likewise Maurer (1951:144), Wolf (1998:443).

48 Claims that the N-pattern permits a neater delimitation of the boundary between roots and endings (e.g., Rudes 1980) are liable to similar objections.

49 Zamboni's suggestion (1980/81) that it may have retained a measure of 'ingressive' meaning in early Romance should not be ignored, although it is by no means true that all verbs with augments can be ascribed ingressive value. Zamboni (1982/83:128, n82) suggests the analogy of other 'N-pattern' verbs to account for the distribution of the augment. In that case, he has no need for the special explanation which he suggests (1982/83:106f.) for the absence of the phenomenon from the imperfect tense.

50 Vegliote also has the *vad- root, with N-pattern distribution (but a 2PL form vait is attested).

51 Bendel (1934:96); Ronjat (1930–41, III:296).

52 The fact that very high frequency verbs, such as 'go' or 'be' attract allomorphy is well known. There may even be advantages of 'economy' (see Werner 1989; Nübling 2001; Fertig 1998) in storing highly frequent verb-forms as phonologically distinct entities. But my concern here is not the *lexical distribution* of suppletion, but the distribution which suppletive forms assume within the paradigm.

53 I can find no evidence for the claim (*pace* Castellani 2000:5f., who recycles an earlier affirmation of Lüdtke's) that a 'Romance type' alternation between UAD- and I- already existed at the time of Vitruvius. Callebat *et al.* (1984) are able to find too few tokens of either verb for any safe conclusion to be drawn, and absolutely no sign of a 'Romance-type' distribution. For further discussion, and consideration of the hypothesis that an early tendency to replace monosyllabic forms of IRE with UADERE might have contributed in part to the N-pattern, see the discussion in Maiden (2005a).

54 For the Gallo-Romance future in *ir-*, see section 6.

55 Ive (1886:175); Bartoli (1906:203).

56 The first person singular, with the subjunctive, follows the L-pattern.

57 This development may have been facilitated by the fact that unstressed *tira- probably became *tra-, identical to the initial segments of *ˈtragere. See Decurtins (1958).

58 *AIS* 1691; Schmid (1949:118f.); Trumper (2001:540–42).

59 Leone (1980:31, n24) mentions another case, where the root krirr- 'believe', originating from phonetic and analogical developments affecting the infinitive, is generalized according to the N-pattern.

60 The conditional and future forms (and perhaps the infinitive) seem to contradict this, but the sample of tokens (just five) is too small to be significant.

61 Theories of suppletion generally attempt to ascribe the phenomenon to extra-morphological causation, but the cases examined here also seem refractory to the usual lines of explanation adduced to account for it (see Fertig 1998 for a survey), in terms of high token frequency, cognitive 'basicness' or communicative–functional 'economy'. The Romance examples discussed here show suppletion as an effect of competition between lexical synonyms or near-synonyms, resolved by the differential integration of the competing lexemes into a single paradigm.

62 Very often, stress and the N-pattern are so precisely coextensive that it can be very difficult to say which, if either, conditions the other. This is true, for example, of Anderson's deft illustration (2008) of the extensive N-pattern allomorphy found in the Savognin Surmiran variety of Romansh. Anderson analyses the facts as an example of morphological allomorphy conditioned by stress.

63 Conde Saiz (1978:177); Arnal Purroy (1998:355, 362); Alvar *et al.* (1995). See also Cano González (1981:156).

64 Alfonsi (1932:viif.); Santamarina (1974:72); Fernández Rei (1990b:85); Couceiro (1976:116); Cano González (1981:153f.).

65 There are similar examples involving the first conjugation augment in the subjunctive in Gallurese (a Sardinian variety influenced by Genoese; see Corda 1983:30).

66 Admittedly, verbs like *tenère* 'to hold' and some others listed do not have the diphthong in all N-pattern cells (*tengo tieni tiene teniamo tenete tengono*), but this reflects the rival influence of the U-pattern.

67 Compare also Ronjat's comments (1930–41, III:257f.) on the independence of vowel quality and stress in Limousin verbs.

68 To say that this alternation pattern was motivated by stress would require us to analyse *imos*, etc. as containing a zero-root + stressed inflectional ending (Ø+'imos). This analysis is counterintuitive: there is no other case of a zero-allomorph of a lexical root in Ibero-Romance. However, if we accept that *i* is a stressed root, it might then be claimed that the extension of the root *va-* in the first and second persons plural of this verb in modern Spanish supports the view that *va-* was analysed as a stressed alternant. The problem with this claim is that [i] remains in the second person plural imperative *id*, in the imperfect indicative *iba*, etc. And Portuguese has extended *va-* into the the first person plural present, but not the second person plural present.

69 The imperfect indicative of the verb 'to be' in many Italo-Romance varieties complicates the picture, in that it often has the stress pattern otherwise associated with the present, with associated root-allomorphy and even suppletion: It. *èro èri èra eravàmo eravàte èrano*, AIS Fara San Martino (Abruzzo) 'yerə 'yirə 'yerə sa'vamə sa'vat 'yerə. Since the verb 'be' is notoriously idiosyncratic in Romance, we might regard it as a special case. It seemingly contradicts the N-pattern in that imperfect forms are expected to share the roots of the first and second persons plural present. On the other hand, it does conform to the principle that first and second persons plural tend to be distinguished from other persons and numbers, and its exceptional resemblance to the present is manifested not only by its stress pattern, but by the desinences of the singular and third person plural forms, which are identical to those of a present tense first conjugation verb.

70 It may be significant that in Campidanese varieties of Sardinian one encounters occasional examples of the N-pattern in the verb 'go', with reflexes of UADERE and AMBULARE apparently 'blending' to yield band-: e.g., Villacidro (*AIS* 973) 'bandu 'bandas 'bandaða an'daus an'dais 'bandanta. Jones (1993:238) proposes that the b- forms incorporate the now extinct locative particle *bi*, but either way we have an N-pattern alternation. Now in Campidanese, the distinction between open and close mid vowels is not wholly predictable phonologically: raising of unstressed [e] and [o] to [i] and [u] has opacified the conditioning of

metaphonic alternation. As a result, alternation of vowel aperture between stressed and unstressed syllables is no longer fully predictable.

71 See also Loporcaro, this volume, chapter 3: § 3.

72 I am grateful to Louise Esher for recently drawing my attention to the fact that asymmetry between future and conditional in Occitan may in fact be much more widespread than I have indicated here.

73 Saying that N- and L/U-patterns, as well as the coherence, convergence and conflation phenomena that reveal them, are all a matter of signans–signatum relations in lexical signs does not undermine the claim that the patterns themselves are autonomously morphological. They are determined by aspects of paradigmatic structure peculiar to the paradigm.

74 For a formal account of the kind of 'top down' processes in the acquisition of morphological paradigms implicit here, see Pirrelli (2000).

CHAPTER 6: CHANGE AND CONTINUITY IN FORM– FUNCTION RELATIONSHIPS

1 My greatest debt is to Marion Glastonbury, who first drew my attention to the notion of skeuomorphy and encouraged me to investigate its applicability to language change. I am also grateful to J. N. Adams, Anders Ahlqvist, Sherry Ash, Richard Ashdowne, the late David Bain, Rachel Baker, Laurie Bauer, Paul Black, Kate Burridge, Michela Cennamo, the late Robert Coleman, Thomas D. Cravens, William Croft, Anna Morpurgo Davies, Ana Deumert, Mark Donohue, Wolfgang Ulrich Dressler, Martin Durrell, Louise Esher, K.-D. Fischer, Luciano Giannelli, Maria Teresa Greco, Camiel Hamans, Marc-Olivier Hinzelin, the late H. D. Jocelyn, Dieter Kastovsky, William Labov, Roger Lass, Adam Ledgeway, Jenny Lee, Michele Loporcaro, Martin Maiden, Sharon Millar, Sandra Paoli, Gillian Ramchand, Joel Rini, Suzanne Romaine, Gillian Sankoff, Masayoshi Shibatani, Rosanna Sornicola, Elizabeth Traugott, Alberto Varvaro, Theo Vennemann, Nigel Vincent, Max Wheeler, Werner Winter, Laura Wright and Roger Wright for discussing all or some of these issues with me. In pursuing biological analogies, I have benefited from the generous assistance of Richard Dawkins and David Raubenheimer, whilst David Cesarani has helped me refine my thoughts on some of the cultural parallels mentioned here. Errors and shortcomings are, of course, my own.

2 MIHI > MI, with loss of intervocalic [h], is an unproblematic development (Väänänen 1981:§§74, 101). The corresponding second-person singular dative, TI, cannot be derived by normal phonetic change from the Classical Latin dative TIBI, but was presumably created on the analogy of the first-person form (*ibid.*:§280). TIBI survives as *tibe* in some old Spanish texts, and as *teve* in some southern Italian dialects, and, in some of these varieties, gives rise to an analogical first-person form (old Spanish *mibe*; southern Italian *meve*) – see Menéndez Pidal (1956:§66) and Alvar and Pottier (1983:118f.) for Spanish,

and Rohlfs (1968:§442) for Italian (and compare the discussion of these and related forms by Sornicola, this volume, chapter 1: § 3.3). The existence of these various forms in no way affects the arguments put forward here. The discussion in this section might be extended to the third-person reflexive pronouns (undifferentiated for number), which parallel the first- and second-person singular forms morphologically. However, the semantic development of the third-person reflexive pronouns in Romance diverges significantly from that of the first- and second-person pronouns (for a discussion of the values of the atonic forms, see Lyons 1995; for the use of the French disjunctive form *soi*, see Grevisse and Goosse 2007:§664; for the vexed question of Italian *si*, see Brunet 1994). I therefore prefer to omit the third-person reflexives from consideration.

3 Languages can shift from one type to another. Medieval Occitan was a 'Type C' language; but in most varieties of modern Occitan, the dative derivative has disappeared and the original Latin accusative survives only as the conjunctive pronoun, whilst the Latin nominative, in addition to providing an emphatic subject pronoun, has now been drafted in as the disjunctive form – in terms of the accusative/dative opposition under discussion, Occitan has become a 'Type B1' language, although in some dialects we still find vestiges of 'Type C' free variation (Ronjat 1937:47–51). Some varieties of Spanish which were originally of Type D1 have extended the Latin nominative in a similar way to Occitan, and are now likewise of Type B1 (Penny 1991:120). The same development has affected the second-person singular pronoun of Catalan, but not the first-person forms (except in some Roussillonnais and Valencian dialects), so that Catalan, originally a 'Type D1' language, early on shifted to mixed type: D1 in the first-person and B1 in the second (Badia i Margarit 1951:§122). My main interest in this chapter is, of course, the evolution from Latin into Romance, not these subsequent shifts.

4 Compare Elcock (1975:91): 'this medieval allotment of function must have followed upon a long period of confusion in Vulgar Latin, since Spanish and Italian appeared with exactly opposite solutions'.

5 This note is omitted from the 1975 edition revised by John N. Green.

6 *Me* does not surface as the first element of all clitic clusters; thus, the rare combination of first- and second-person singular pronouns is always *mi ti*, never **me ti*. This points to a third hypothesis concerning the origin of conjunctive *me* in standard Italian. It seems to occur only in conjunction with pronouns which derive from a Latin form beginning with [ɪ] (subsequently [e]) – thus *me la* < ME ILLA(M), and *me ne* < ME INDE; just as *della* is arguably derived from DE ILLA(M) and *dello* from DE ILLU(M). In other words, rather than representing the simple juxtaposition of two Italian pronouns, the cluster itself may have evolved continuously from Latin; the final vowel of the first- (or second-)person pronoun may have been elided before the initial [ɪ] of the second element of the cluster, and this latter vowel may be the source of the [e]. If this is the origin of proclitic *me*, then the data from clitic clusters will be irrelevant to the claim that this form derives from Latin ME, but will not invalidate it.

7 Michela Cennamo (personal communication) has drawn my attention to three occurrences of INTER TIBI ET FISCO in the seventh-century texts published by Pirson (1913): page 1, line 16 (text 1); page 2, line 39 (text 4); and page 3, line 5 (text 5). In each instance, the expression appears to be formulaic. This is the only example I have come across of the use of the dative case of either the first- or second-person singular pronoun as the complement of a preposition in the Latin of any period. It may be the first attestation of the Romance refunctionalization discussed here.

8 Many other examples of skeuomorphy might be cited. Dresser (1996) notes that, in Britain, both umbrellas and the cords of roller-blinds may still bear small glandiform attachments, which are derived from acorns originally hung from these items in the belief that they would serve as lightning conductors (lightning was thought to strike oaks more frequently than other trees). Randy LaPolla (personal communication) describes an electric clock which has retained fixed plastic versions of the metal weights which drove its mechanical predecessors. It is often claimed that the rules of the road are determined by the dominance in the past of a form of locomotion which is no longer current. Countries which drive on the left allegedly do so because right-handed people mounted horses from the left-hand side (and mounted them from the side of the road rather than the centre), wore swords on the left and drew them with the right hand (and therefore needed to be on the left of potential assailants), or had to be in the centre of the road when controlling teams of horses driven from a wagon whilst sitting on the right-hand side of the seat in order to avoid injuring fellow-passengers with their whip. The origins of driving on the right are supposedly to be found in the need for a right-handed person leading a single animal or riding one horse in a team to control them from the left-hand side whilst occupying the centre of the road. (The topic is fraught with apocrypha and anecdote; but, for a scholarly survey, see Kincaid 1986.) This type of skeuomorphy may also become refunctionalized. At many road junctions controlled by traffic lights in the Australian city of Melbourne (where traffic keeps to the left), drivers turning right are required to do so from the left-hand lane. The modern effect of this manoeuvre is to allow free passage to the trams which run along tracks in the centre of the road; Ross Weber (personal communication) suggests to me that its original motivation was to accommodate the large turning circle of bullock carts. Likewise, the wine bottles traditionally used in Burgundy and Bordeaux are of different shapes (tapered in the case of Burgundy; 'shouldered' in the case of Bordeaux; for illustrations, see Beck 1973:38). Originally, then, the form of the bottle indicated the provenance of the wine, and, in the case of French wine, it still does. However, the bottle shape has come to be associated with the grapes typically used in the making of the wine (for instance, *pinot noir* and *chardonnay* for red and white Burgundy, respectively; *cabernet sauvignon*, *cabernet franc* and *merlot* for (red) Bordeaux), so that a given wine producer in, say, Australia, South Africa or California will generally use both types of bottle, selecting one or the other

simply on the basis of the grape variety. Robinson (1994:140) aptly summarizes this development as follows:

> [T]here are certain standard bottle shapes associated most commonly with certain regions or, increasingly, styles of wine associated with those regions. [...] Since the geographical provenance of most wines should be clear from the label, understanding bottle shapes is most useful for the clues they provide as to the intended style of the wines inside them.

Finally, some of the dietary (and other) precepts of Judaism, Islam and other religions have also been accounted for in essentially skeuomorphic terms, as originating in concerns of health and hygiene, but now having a purely symbolic value – that of defining membership of the religious group. However, this analysis is in many cases hotly disputed. For a summary, see Douglas (1966), who notes the belief of many nineteenth-century scholars that 'something of what we still do and believe is fossil; meaningless, petrified appendage to the daily business of living' (*ibid.*:13). Modern anthropology would, of course, reject the term 'meaningless'.

9 Except, as J. N. Adams and Sharon Millar point out to me, in studies of formal rhetoric.

10 In fact, Humphrey (1992:186) claims that, whilst biological skeuomorphs may persist as 'decoration', they may also survive as 'useless baggage' – the equivalent, presumably, of Lass's 'junk'. My own use of the term 'skeuomorphy' is restricted to instances in which the opposition does retain some content.

What might the linguistic equivalent of decoration be? There are morphological patterns which serve to define or identify without having any more obvious function. As Humphrey (1992:186) points out, copying an existing pattern, even after it may have ceased to be functional, is not only efficient and reassuring; it also sets a standard. Seen in this light, even the suppletion and irregularity which Lass (1990:82) describes as 'marginal garbage' may be skeuomorphic. Particularly relevant here is the suggestion by Maiden (1992:289f.) that '"irregularity", understood as a non-biunique relationship between meaning and form, is an autonomous abstract property of morphological paradigms which influences the implementation not only of phonetic changes, but also of purely morphological innovations'. Maiden (*ibid.*:308) argues for 'isolating allomorphy from exponence' in these cases, and gives examples from Romance verb conjugation to show that 'structurally redundant variation [...] may be "exapted" [...] and pressed into service as a means of highlighting abstract alternation patterns within paradigms' (*ibid.*:309f.). In like vein, Carstairs-McCarthy (1994:784) suggests that 'in their search for syntactic and morphological order, speakers will evidently pay attention even to form-'meaning' correlations of a purely intra-linguistic kind, with no obvious communicative benefits'. Considerations such as these have subsequently given rise to the concept of 'autonomous morphology' and the notion of the morphome (see, for instance, Aronoff 1994; Maiden 2000b; 2001a; 2004d; 2005b).

Another analogue of decoration might be when an opposition loses its semantic basis but acquires a stylistic or sociolinguistic value. I discuss some possible examples of this process in the section on defunctionalization (§5) below.

11 For possible mismatches between default status and unmarkedness, for example, see Marcus *et al.* (1995).

12 If we were able to analyse a corpus of spoken Latin (which for obvious reasons we cannot), we might even find that the vocative had pushed the dative into last position.

13 Relevant case forms occurring with the emphatic enclitic -MET, the interrogative enclitic -NE and the co-ordinating enclitic -QUE have all been counted towards the overall totals. However, the reduplicated forms MEME and TETE have not been taken into consideration, as it is not clear whether they actually constitute occurrences of ME and TE, or are separate lexical items. Neither have the comitatives MECUM and TECUM been included, since it is not certain that these forms were analysable at this stage of Latin (their evolution into Italian *meco*, *teco* (Rohlfs 1969:§443), Sardinian *mecus*, *tecus* (Jones 1993:199) and, albeit with an analogical change of vowel, Spanish *(con)migo*, *(con)tigo* (Penny 1991:120f.; Rini 1992:34–83), and Portuguese *(co)migo*, *(con)tigo* (Williams 1962:145f.), certainly implies that at some stage they became unanalysable), and the exact status of their pronominal element is therefore unclear. As all the forms mentioned are relatively infrequent, their inclusion or omission does not have a significant effect on the figures.

Delatte *et al.* (1981) do not distinguish between the different functions of a given form. It is therefore impossible to distinguish between the dative pronoun MI and the homographic masculine singular vocative case of the possessive MEUS. However, in view of the small figures involved and the comparative rarity of the vocative case (see above), all occurrences of MI have, for the sake of argument, been treated as dative pronouns.

14 We should, however, note that Romance conjunctive forms, even though cliticized to the verb, can be the complements of DPs (e.g., It. *Non gli sono più nemico* 'I'm not his enemy any more'; Ro. *Mi-am pierdut şosetele* 'I've lost my socks'), APs (e.g., It. *Mi sei molto caro* 'you are very dear to me'), PPs (e.g., It. *Mi viene incontro* 'he's coming towards me'; Fr. *Elle me court après* 'she's chasing after me'), and the subjects of small clauses (e.g., It. *Ti credevo malato* 'I thought you were ill'), as well as appearing in 'ethic dative' constructions (e.g., Glc. *Meu pai vaiche a peor, que a vellez no che ten cura* 'My father is getting worse, because there's no cure for old age', example from Álvarez *et al.* 1986:174f.; Fr. *Avez-vous vu comme je te vous lui ai craché à la figure* 'Did yer see how I went and spat in his face, then; did yer?', example from Grevisse 1993:§647e), in which they are arguably not complements at all (see Smith 2001b).

15 Although in some languages (e.g., Breton; see Stephens 2002:383–84) prepositions may take an object inflection.

16 Romanian has maintained a nominal case system up to the present day, but it does not reflect the nominative–accusative opposition; rather, there is a split between a form encoding both nominative and accusative and another which encodes the genitive and the dative. A vocative is also found, although this is at least partly the result of Slavonic influence, rather than a continuation of the Latin vocative. For a description of the Romanian case system, see Mallinson (1986:205–7, 223f.). For the view that a nominative–accusative distinction may have survived into pre-literary Italian, see Maiden (2000a). For a general discussion of the survival of case distinctions, see Hall (1980). It is occasionally claimed that the Romance oblique forms may, in some circumstances, be derived from the Latin ablative; but the Latin accusative is generally accepted as the etymon of the oblique case form; discussion can be found in Väänänen (1981:116f.).

17 These and other standard works on the language claim that Latin had six cases: nominative, vocative, accusative, genitive, dative, ablative, together with a rarely used locative. It is doubtful to what extent the vocative is a true case – see the arguments in Hjelmslev (1935:*passim*) and Blake (2001:8), who points out:

> Vocatives do not appear as dependents in constructions, but rather they stand outside constructions or are inserted parenthetically. They are unlike other cases in that they do not mark the relation of dependents to heads. For these reasons vocatives have not always been considered cases. In Ancient Greek and Latin the vocative's claim to being a case is structural. The vocative is a word-final suffix like the recognised case suffixes. However, modified forms of nouns used as forms of address also occur in languages that do not have case inflection. In Yapese (Austronesian), for instance, there is no morphological case marking on nouns, but personal names have special forms used for address. There is no reason to consider that these modifications of names constitute a vocative case.

18 'Si l'on met à part les plus anciens textes, ceux du IXe et du Xe siècle, comme *Sainte Eulalie* ou *Saint Léger*, les règles de la déclinaison n'apparaissent dans toute leur pureté que dans les grammaires modernes de l'ancien français.'

19 The conventional French terms for the nominative and oblique cases are '*cas sujet*' and '*cas régime*', respectively.

20 Note that, for reasons of space and clarity, the format adopted for the presentation of the data which follow represents a simplification, and should not be read as implying that the Latin nominative and accusative forms yield the Gallo-Romance items directly; there is, of course, an intervening stage in which

we find an opposition between a Gallo-Romance nominative form derived from the Latin nominative and a Gallo-Romance oblique form derived from the Latin accusative. Data cited from Occitan varieties are uniformly referred to as 'Occitan', regardless of the label used in the source of the data (which is often 'Provençal', *lato sensu*), with the exception of 'Gascon', which has the sanction of usage in reference to a distinct variety, and so has been retained as a separate term. However, the spelling of the Occitan examples is that given in the source from which they are taken; no attempt has been made to standardize or normalize orthography.

21 Although *chanteur* is commonly derived from CANTOREM, there exists the possibility that it may have originated later, as an agentive noun formed from the verb *chanter* 'sing'. If this were the case, then this example (but not, of course, the others) would be invalidated.

22 'la marque par excellence du sujet déterminé animé en position d'agent' (the context and Buridant's subsequent discussion make it clear that the subjects he is talking about have determined reference rather than necessarily being accompanied by a determiner).

23 Note that the original nominative provides the etymon for the proper name in all these cases, regardless of whether the proper name itself constitutes the original meaning of the item or is derived metonymically from an original common noun.

24 Here, and in the discussion which follows, it is important to recognize the distinction between grammatical functions, such as 'subject', and semantic or thematic roles, such as 'agent'. In claiming that the nominative is 'the more agentive case', I am not of course implying that all or even most nominatives encode agents. The nominative is the normal case of the subject, that which is predicated of the subject, and items in apposition to either. Subjects are often (but by no means always) agents; agents are characteristically (but not always) subjects – a point made succinctly by Pinkster (1990:16). However, given that agents are prototypically subjects and that the nominative is the prototypical case of the subject, whilst other cases encode agents rarely, if at all, then it is clear that the nominative is more agentive than any other case, in both Latin and Gallo-Romance. We may further note that there is evidence for a split in subject marking in late Latin, whereby agentive subjects continue to appear in the nominative, whilst non-agentive subjects tend to appear in the accusative (see Ledgeway, this volume, chapter 8: §6.2.2.1), a development which is not without relevance to the present discussion.

25 Other apparent examples of the lexicalization of the original opposition between nominative and accusative/oblique can be found, and not all of them are obvious examples of 'core-to-core' mapping. However, they tend to be problematic for other reasons too. Some cannot obviously (or at least uncontroversially) be traced back to a Latin distinction; and, in some cases, one member of the pair has undergone an irregular development – whether 'learnèd' or 'popular' – which the

other doublet has not, or may even be a loanword from another variety. In these circumstances we are probably not dealing with true refunctionalization. Examples are Fr. *sire* (< NOM SENIOR, with unexpected loss of medial /n/) vs. *seigneur* (< ACC SENIOREM), and Fr. *pâtre* (< NOM PASTOR) vs. *pasteur* (< ACC PASTOREM, with learnèd retention of /s/). For French, see Nyrop (1924:205–9); for Occitan, see Ronjat (1937:5–7, 373–77) and for Gascon, see Rohlfs (1977:175); and compare Mańczak (1969) and Spence (1971).

26 Further examples of the refunctionalization of what was originally a case distinction might be mentioned. Both Hall (1968) and Penny (1970) argue that the morphological distinction between count nouns and mass nouns found in some varieties of southern Italy and north-western Spain derives from an original opposition between, on the one hand, an accusative etymon and, on the other, an original dative or ablative serving as a partitive (for an alternative view, see Maiden, this volume, chapter 4: §3.2). Other examples are less systematic – compare Sp. *Marte* 'Mars' (< ACC MARTEM) vs. *martes* 'Tuesday' (< GEN MARTIS [DIES] '[day] of Mars') and possibly Fr. *chandelle* '(tallow) candle' (< ACC CANDELAM 'candle') vs. *Chandeleur* 'Candlemas' (< GEN *CANDELORUM [FESTA] lit. '[feast] of candles'), although here the name of the festival must be traced back to a masculine form of the genitive plural instead of the expected feminine.

27 UADERE is also the source of the 2SG IMP.

28 In Spanish, the reflex of the perfectum of Lat. ESSE(RE) 'be' also serves as the preterite, the past subjunctive, and (inasmuch as the form survives) the future subjunctive of the verb 'to go'. I shall not discuss this development here.

29 It may be for these reasons, amongst others, that, cross-linguistically, the first person is more likely to exhibit a distinct plural than other persons (see, for instance, Croft 1990:160f.). Many languages do not have morphological plural marking, and it is in any case perfectly plausible for the same form to refer to one or many addressees or to one or many non-discourse participants. However, the first-person plural does not normally refer to more than one speaker – in that sense, it is not a true plural, but rather has a distinct value (or values), and so requires a specific form (or specific forms).

30 The occurrence of second-person singular indicative forms may be overestimated, on account of the syncretism between the indicative and imperative in this person in the verbs selected. We should also note that, commonly in the singular and much more rarely in the plural, third-person forms may also be used to encode the 'formal' second person, and that this may lead to a slight inflation of the figures for this person. However, the figures are such that neither of these considerations is likely to have any impact on the rank order.

31 Compare, too, the frequency data for the indicative and subjunctive forms of second- and third-person plural in Italian contained in the tables above.

32 The functionalization of 'old' and 'new' plurals is not limited to Latin and Romance. A 'textbook' example (quite literally; see Hock and Joseph

1996:236) is the division of labour between earlier *brethren* and new *brothers* in modern English. The earlier form has become specialized in the sense of 'fellow-members of a church or guild', whilst the new, analogical, form serves as the unmarked plural, with the meaning of 'male siblings', as well as a variety of metaphorical values. Jespersen (1942:345) observes: 'Most 19th. c. grammarians would establish the distinction that *brothers* is used of blood-relations, *brethren* of spiritually connected people, but this distinction tends to be neglected, and *brothers* is often used in a figurative sense.' He quotes the arresting example from Byron: 'Call not thy brothers brethren.'

33 Note that these tables take late Lat. CORNUM, rather than CLat. CORNU, as the starting point.

34 In this connection, we may note the fact that collective plurals in one language frequently correspond to individuated singulars in another; compare Lat. plural CASTRA corresponding to Eng. singular *camp*, Fr. plural *élections législatives, transports en commun* corresponding to Eng. singular *general election, public transport*, etc.

35 'Du fait que *folia* comme sujet est souvent construit avec le verbe au singulier, il ne serait pas légitime d'inférer qu'il était déjà devenu un singulier féminin ; ce n'est encore qu'une espèce de σχῆμα κατα συνησιν, l'accord étant déterminé par le sens collectif «feuillage». Il s'agit donc d'un état transitoire.'

36 Possibly via a further stage similar to the situation observed in present-day Sardinian, where, for instance, *sa bira* can explicitly mean both 'the pear' and 'pears', in a collective sense; see Maiden, this volume, chapter 4: §3.2.

37 See, for example, *Harrap's Little French Dictionary* (Nicholson 2008), which glosses *cerveau* as 'organe, intelligence' ('organ, intelligence') and *cervelle* as 'substance, plat' ('substance, [culinary] dish').

38 Quinn (2004:903) observes: 'there is evidence indicating that information around the vertical axis is detected, identified, and remembered more efficiently, as well as perceived as more salient, than information around the horizontal axis […] The data on differences in the processing of vertical versus horizontal in adults are also consistent with the developmental literature on the emergence of orientation perception where children have been shown to distinguish upright (ie vertical) from non-upright (ie all other orientations) initially, and are only subsequently observed to parse the non-upright category into diagonal, upside-down, and horizontal […] Even young infants have demonstrated processing advantages for information presented about the vertical axis compared with information presented along the horizontal axis.'

39 Detailed discussion of this phenomenon lies outside the scope of this chapter. Following early work by Brown and Gilman (1960), the value of these forms has been dealt with by Bustin-Lekeu (1973), Claudel (2002), Gardner-Chloros (1991), Halmøy (2000), Hughson (2002), Maley (1974), Morford (1997), Peeters (2004) and Schoch (1978) for contemporary French, and by Foulet (1930:198–201), Hunt (2003), Nyrop (1925:§§192–203), Kennedy (1972) and Mason (1990) for earlier stages of the language.

40 I leave aside here the 'indefinite' use of *tu* and *vous*, discussed by, amongst others, Ashby (1992), Coveney (2003) and Williams and van Compernolle (2009).

41 The orthography <ai> in this and subsequent examples dates from the sixth edition of the *Dictionnaire de l'Académie française* (1835).

42 In a rather similar way, indeed, to Eng. *tell*, which formerly had the meanings 'narrate' and 'count' (see OED, s.v. *tell*), the latter retained in expressions such as *bank teller, all told* and *untold riches*.

43 If Pountain's analysis of how so-called 'semi-learnèd' words evolve (this volume, chapter 13: §3.4.1) is correct, then some of the examples of popular vs. semi-learnèd doublets discussed earlier in this section may also receive an explanation in these terms.

44 In essence, the situation described by Fishman (1967) as 'extended diglossia' (on the notion of 'diglossia', see Ferguson 1959; for a more recent discussion and further references, see Schiffman 1997).

45 By way of illustrative comparison, we may cite some examples from English. Myhill and Harris (1986:26) observe the decline of *-s* as a marker of the third-person singular present tense in African-American English Vernacular. As a result, the *-s*

> has no clear function; this creates the possibility of this morpheme being reinterpreted as having some other function. It is clear that for some speakers it has acquired a sociolinguistic function of marking speech as 'formal' (or in general more suitable for interaction with white people) so that in certain situations verbal /s/s are inserted regardless of the person of the subject.

Houston (1985) examines the pronunciation of final *-ing* in English, which may be realized with a velar nasal ([iŋ]) or with an alveolar nasal ([in]). She traces these two pronunciations back to the earlier nominal ending *-ing* and the earlier verbal ending *-ind* (*-ende, -and*), respectively, and finds some retention of the original categorial distinction in modern English, but also notes (Houston 1985:159) that the [in] pronunciation has a social value, being especially associated with working-class speech and with male speech. She concludes (Houston 1985:357f.):

> The expressive value which linguistic forms may acquire can be seen to influence their future place within the linguistic system. In this sense, processes of evaluation may not always be in accord with functional principles. The case of (ING) illustrates this divergence by showing on the one hand, that in some respects the phonological variation can be viewed as preserving a morphological contrast, but that such a functional contrast on the other hand, can be overridden by external social conditioning.

46 In practice, any opposition which can be defined in structural terms probably represents a refunctionalization, whilst purely stylistic oppositions represent defunctionalization.

47 Much the same type of development has taken place in other languages. For instance, English lost its distinctive second-person singular verb morphology (the inflectional ending *-st* or *-est*) with the disappearance from the standard language of the *thou* – *you* distinction by the eighteenth century (Denison 1998:134) and the southern third-person singular inflectional ending *-th* or *-eth* was supplanted by northern East Midlands *-s* during the sixteenth and seventeenth centuries (Lass 1999:162–65), but even now these endings are sometimes used, with no regard for their former function, to impart an archaic flavour to a text; compare, from recent newspaper articles: 'I sayeth, I sayeth, I sayeth: Ken Dodd tells Michael Billington why Shakespeare was a stand-up comic at heart' (Billington 2005) and 'And so it came to pass that my wife sayest: "This Telstra bill is an abomination ..."' (Glover 2004). As these examples show, the original southern English opposition *say* – *sayest* – *sayeth* in the singular is no longer an opposition between a first-person form, a second-person form and a third-person form, respectively, but between a non-third-person (singular) form and two cod archaisms which are used indiscriminately, with any person.

48 As Lass implies, this claim is principally associated with linguists who adopt a semiotic perspective. Amongst these is Henning Andersen, whose objections to the notion of linguistic 'junk' are summarized as follows by Nigel Vincent: 'The notion of linguistic junk is not coherent because languages are sign systems and no part of a sign system is without function, even if we as analysts have not worked out what the function in question is [...] Furthermore, since the scientific endeavor is never complete, one can never be sure that there is not a generalization still lurking out there waiting to be captured which will encompass just the piece of linguistic form that has heretofore been written off as junk' (Vincent 1995:435).

49 'Les innovations peuvent créer des homonymies, mais ne peuvent pas en détruire. Si deux mots ont été rendus identiques par un changement phonétique quelconque, ils ne peuvent plus jamais devenir différents par voie phonétique.'

CHAPTER 7: MORPHOSYNTACTIC PERSISTENCE

1 I thank the late József Herman, and Lorenzo Renzi, Ildikó Szijj and Laura Vanelli, whose comments on a first draft of this chapter helped considerably to improve it.

2 Unless otherwise indicated, sources of data are in part the result of personal research and in part taken from secondary sources. Particularly, for Latin: Ernout and Thomas (1953), Pinkster (1990), Bennett (1910–1914); old French: Foulet (1968), Moignet (1973), Jensen (1990), Buridant (2001); classical and modern French: Gamillscheg (1957), Grevisse (1980), Kelemen (1985); old Italian: Salvi and Renzi (2010), and *Enciclopedia Dantesca*; modern

Italian: Renzi *et al.* (2001); Italian dialects: Rohlfs (1968; 1969), Maiden and Parry (1997); old Spanish: Lapesa (1981); modern Spanish: Bosque and Demonte (1999); old Portuguese: Mattos e Silva (1989); classical and modern Portuguese: Dias (1918), Teyssier (1976), Perini (1995); Brazilian: Thomas (1969); Galician: Álvarez *et al.* (1986); old Romanian: Rosetti (1974), Niculescu and Dimitrescu (1970); modern Romanian: Lombard (1974), *Gramatica*; Sardinian: Jones (1993); Catalan: Fabra (1956), Badia i Margarit (1962); Occitan: Alibèrt (1976), Bec (1973); Raeto-Romance: Gartner (1910), Haiman and Benincà (1992), Spescha (1989).

For general reference see the relevant chapters in *LRL*, Meyer-Lübke (1899), Lausberg (1976), Harris and Vincent (1988); for the Latin – Romance transition: Herman (2000a), Väänänen (1974), Zamboni (2000).

3 For aspects of the gender and number system, see chapters 4 and 5.

4 Coromines (1997:310) cites a similar phenomenon in old Catalan.

5 The 2SG distinction between *che* (DAT) and *te* (ACC) found in much of Galician is an innovation (Ferreiro 1995:§155).

6 By 'Ladin' and 'Raeto-Romance' I mean, respectively, the varieties traditionally classified as central (or Dolomitic) Ladin/Raeto-Romance (German 'Ladinisch') and western Ladin/Raeto-Romance (German 'Bündnerromanisch').

7 Some varieties (spoken French, Romanian, NItalian dialects), by losing the old perfect form, lack this distinction.

8 The difference in (53e–e') is probably a matter of lexicalization.

9 Some Romance languages (Romanian, SItalian dialects in formerly Greek-speaking areas) are characterized by the recession of the infinitive and in these constructions generally use in most, if not all, verbs the subjunctive.

10 Use of the subjunctive in reported speech in Raeto-Romance is modelled on German (Grünert 2003).

CHAPTER 8: SYNTACTIC AND MORPHOSYNTACTIC
TYPOLOGY AND CHANGE

1 For exemplification from the different Romance varieties in their various diachronic, diatopic and diastratic manifestations, I have drawn on the following sources: Aragonese (Saralegui 1992), Asturian (Cano González 1992; Academia de la Llingua asturiana 1995), Catalan (Jordana 1933; Badia i Margarit 1951; 1962; 1991; 1995; Schlieben-Lange 1971; Yates 1975; Villangómez i Llobet 1978; Moll 1993; 1997; 2006; Sola 1993; 1994; Veny 1982; 1998; 2001; Blasco Ferrer 1984a; 1986; 1988; Wheeler 1988a; Wheeler *et al.* 1999; Hualde 1992a; Bernat i Baltrons 2007), Dalmatian and Istro-Romance dialects (Bartoli 1906; Doria 1989; Ursini 1989), Extremeño (García Santos 1992), French (von Wartburg [1934] 1971; Pope 1952; Désirat and Hordé 1967; Price 1971; Ewert 1978; Battye and Hintze 1992; Jones 1996;

Ayres-Bennett and Carruthers 2001; Fagyal *et al.* 2006; Rowlett 2007), Italian and the dialects of Italy (Rohlfs 1968–69; Tekavčić 1980; Durante 1981; Bruni 1984; Lepschy and Lepschy 1988; Graffi 1994; Marazzini 1994; Maiden 1995; 1998c; Maiden and Parry 1997; Ledgeway 2000; Maiden and Robustelli 2007), Leonese (Born 1992), Occitan dialects (Grandgent 1905; Ronjat 1930–41 (vol. III); Roncaglia 1965; Bec 1967; Lafont 1967; 1991; Schlieben-Lange 1971; Alibèrt 1976; Wheeler 1988b), Gallego-Portuguese (Huber 1933; Sten 1944; Thomas 1969; Mattoso Câmara 1972; Teyssier 1980; 1984; Nunes 1989; Costa 2000a; Azevedo 2005), Raeto-Romance varieties (Arquint 1964; Rohlfs 1975; Haiman 1988; Plangg 1989; Stimm and Linder 1989; Haiman and Benincà 1992), Romanian and dialects (Agard 1958; Guţia 1967; Rosetti 1968; Lombard 1974; Mallinson 1986; 1988; Dahmen 1989; Stati 1989; Manoliu Manea 1989; Dobrovie-Sorin 1994; Alboiu and Motapanyane 2000a; Motapanyane 2000), Sardinian dialects (Wagner 1951; Blasco Ferrer 1984b; 1986; 1988; 1994; Jones 1988; 1993; 1997), Spanish (García de Diego 1951; Menéndez Pidal 1966; Zamora Vicente 1967; Lapesa 1980; Lloyd 1987; Penny 2000; 2002; Alarcos Llorach 1994; Butt and Benjamin 1994; Lipski 1994; Stewart 1999; Pountain 2001; D'Introno 2001; Haulde, Olarrea and Escobar 2001; Zagona 2002). In what follows I do not consider creoles (for which, see Volume II).

2 For an historical overview of the use of the terms 'synthetic' and 'analytic', see Schwegler (1990: ch. 1).

3 The 'exceptional' accusative case of the infinitival subject is determined by the construction as a whole, as highlighted by the fact that CREDO canonically assigns dative to its complement (§3.3.3.1, and Pountain, this volume, chapter 13: §4.2.3.2).

4 The reversal in the head parameter is so pervasive that it equally surfaces in the area of derivational morphology (cf. Lat. SILUICOLA lit. forest.inhabitant ('forest dweller') vs. Cat. *guardabosc* lit. watch.forest ('forester'), although admittedly at a later date than in the areas of inflectional morphology and syntax (Oniga 2004:52f.)).

5 Harris (1978:16) too sees the emergence of a specified–specifier order as central to the developments in the syntax (e.g., SVO) and morphology (e.g., loss of inflection) of Romance. Yet, he does not try to subsume the shift from synthetic to analytic within this linear change but, rather, continues to treat it as an independent, albeit isolated, phenomenon, ultimately part of a general tendency towards more explicit structures (see also Bourciez 1956:23).

6 It is interesting to note that the Romance synthetic future and conditional paradigms which continue a reduced form of the present/imperfect (or, NCIt. preterite) of HABERE suffixed to the infinitive (e.g., PERDER(E)+*ˈajo/*aia > Occ. *perdrai/ perdriá* (+*ˈɛbwi > It. *perderei*; see Valesio 1968; Coleman 1971; Fleischman 1982; Pinkster 1987; Vincent 1987; Maiden 1996c; Nocentini 2001; La Fauci 2006) 'I will/would lose') must, given the postverbal position of the erstwhile auxiliary, represent an original early Latin, rather than Romance, innovation.

7 The future active, and especially passive, infinitive with auxiliaries ESSE and IRI (e.g., AUDITURUS ESSE 'to be about to hear' and AUDITUM IRI 'to be about to be heard') is most rare.

8 See Gildersleeve and Lodge ([1895] 1997:430, n1), Hale and Buck ([1903] 1994:§624), Fischer (1908), Marouzeau (1922:133), Muldowney (1937:73), Feix (1934:29f.), Ernout and Thomas (1953:162) and Bauer (1995:80, 166).

9 See Gildersleeve and Lodge ([1895] 1997:430), Hale and Buck ([1903] 1994:§624), Ernout and Thomas (1953:162), Vincent (1998:54) and Bauer (1995:64f., 79, 166).

10 See Kroll (1912), Kühner and Stegman (1912–14 II:611f.), Linde (1923), Perrochat (1926), Fankhänel (1938), Marouzeau (1938:47), Ernout and Thomas (1953:161), Adams (1976), Elerick (1989a), Pinkster (1990:168), Bauer (1995:90–92), Herman (2000a:86) and Oniga (2004:97). The clause-final position is also reported to be the unmarked position of the finite verb in Proto-Indo-European (Delbrück 1900:83; Leumann and Hofmann 1928:613; Watkins 1964:1039–41; Lehmann 1974:114; Konneker 1975:367; Adams 1976:92; Bauer 1995:88f.).

11 The exception here are subordinate clauses where the verb-final position proves most resilient, continuing even into early Romance (Foulet 1923:248, 268; Linde 1923; Bauer 1995:91, 108; Oniga 2004:99f.).

12 For the nominal group, see, among others, Gildersleeve and Lodge ([1895] 1997:431), Delbrück (1900:102), Rosenkranz (1933), Lehmann (1974:74), Konnecker (1975:370), Vincent (1988a:56) and Bauer (1995:51–53); and for the verbal group, Delbrück (1900:83), Leumann and Hofmann (1928:613), Watkins (1964:1039–41), Lehmann (1974:114), Konneker (1975:367), Adams (1976:92) and Bauer (1995:88f.).

13 Such discontinuous structures are traditionally termed *hyperbaton* in rhetoric (Hofmann and Szantyr 1965:11–19) and *scrambling* in the generative literature (Corver and van Riemsdijk 1994). See further Gildersleeve and Lodge ([1895] 1997:432f.), Hale and Buck ([1903] 1994:§624), Grandgent (1907:30), Ernout and Thomas (1953:162), Meillet (1977:156), Väänänen (1982:259), Pinkster (1990:184–86), Herman (2000a:82), Bolkestein (2001) and Oniga (2004:101f.).

14 See Gildersleeve and Lodge ([1895] 1997:432), Hale and Buck ([1903] 1994:§627), Marouzeau (1953:58–62,68), Vincent (1988a:54), Bauer (1995:131, 136) and Oniga (2004:102).

15 Even if such patterns represent a more archaic usage which was less and less typical of everyday speech in the classical and subsequent periods, this only pushes the apparent change in configurationality back to an even earlier stage, which still requires an explanation in the Latin to Romance transition.

16 Of course, it is possible to maintain a configurational representation, albeit at some quite considerable cost, if one assumes that the various surface orders of Latin are the result of a number of (costly and syntactically and semantically

unmotivated) scrambling operations which disrupt an underlying English-style configurational structure.

17 For the nominal group, see Väänänen (1982:260), Herman (2000a:81–84) and Bauer (1995:59–62), and for the verbal group, Linde (1923), Haida (1928), Leumann and Hofmann (1928), Adams (1976; 1977), Väänänen (1982:259f.), Vincent (1988a:62), Herman (2000a:86) and Bauer (1995:98–102).

18 Herman (1966), Pensado Ruiz (1986), Gerola (1949–50), Väänänen (1966:121), La Fauci (1988:54f.), Zamboni (1998:131f.), Bauer (1995:138), Cennamo (2001).

19 By way of illustration, one only has to compare the remarkable syntactic freedom of the Latin nominal and verbal groups observed in the permutations in (6a–d) and (7a–d) with the fixed order of the Romance NP and VP, as illustrated by the Italian strings in (ia–d; *un(o)* 'a', *scrittore/scrisse* 'writer/he wrote', *di* 'of', *gran(de)* 'great(/big)', *libro* 'book'):

(i) a. *Uno scrittore di un gran libro / Scrisse un gran libro*
     b. *Uno scrittore di un libro grande / Scrisse un libro grande*
     c. ***Di un gran libro uno scrittore / **Un gran libro scrisse*
     d. ***Grande uno scrittore di un libro / **Grande scrisse un libro*

Whereas the Latin strings in (6a–d) and (7a–d), pragmatic and stylistic effects aside, all mean the same thing, their exact Italian copies in (ia–d) do not. Assuming register and intonation to be neutral, excluding such marked processes as narrow focus and extraposition, the only strings which prove grammatical are (ia–b): (ic) is ruled out because the complement *(di) un gran libro* '(of) a great book' precedes rather than follows its head noun/verb *scrittore/ scrisse* 'writer/wrote', and (id) is excluded because the scope of the attributive adjective *grande* cannot be interpreted unless contiguous to its associated noun *libro*. Even in the case of the grammatical (ia–b), the prenominal and post-nominal orders of the adjective *gran(de)* give rise to a semantic distinction, namely the figurative *un gran libro* 'a great book' and the literal *un libro grande* 'a big book'.

20 As noted in §3.1.1, although some scholars do not recognize a semantic distinction between the pre- and postnominal positions in Latin (Gildersleeve and Lodge [1895] 1997:430; Hale and Buck ([1903] 1994:§624; Feix 1934:27; Coleman 1991a:326; Lehmann 1991:223; Oniga 2004:95; Herman 2000a:83), others already recognize a semantic distinction between the two positions largely similar to that found in modern Romance (Marouzeau 1922:15; 1953:1; Ernout and Thomas 1953:162; Väänänen 1982:260; Pinkster 1990:185; Bauer 1995:67–72; Devine and Stephens 2006:481f.; for an overview, see Vincent 2007:64f.). Whatever the correct interpretation, it is clear however that, contrary to modern Romance, the contrastive and non-contrastive interpretations are not exclusively associated with the post- and prenominal positions, a distinction which would only fully grammaticalize with the subsequent rise of full configurationality.

21 In a number of, especially non-standard, Romance varieties including Occitan (Wheeler 1988b:268), Sardinian (Jones 1988:335; 1993:42) and southern Italian dialects (Rohlfs 1969:330; Ledgeway 2007a), the prenominal adjectival position is extremely restricted and generally replaced by the postnominal position, which is neutral to the (non-/)contrastive distinction (e.g., Nap. *na (**piccerella) patana piccerella* 'a small potato', Srd. *una (**nova) mákkina nova* 'a new car'). In other cases the two positions appear to be lexicalized, as in Catalan where, unlike *mal* 'bad' which occurs in prenominal position, the synonymous *dolent* (cf. also Pt. *ruim* 'bad') always occurs in postnominal position even when interpreted non-restrictively (e.g., *una (mala) proposta (dolenta)* 'a (bad) suggestion').

22 See further Arnholdt (1916), Alisova (1967), Guția (1967:151–54), Reiner (1968), Lapesa (1975), Vincent (1986; 2007a:57–61), Stati (1989:123f.), Badia i Margarit (1995:433–36), Berruto (1998), Pountain (1998b), Scarano (1999; 2005), D'Introno (2001:418–21), Radatz (2001) and Ledgeway (2007a).

23 The same structural distinction also applies to adjectives like Cat. *xinès* 'Chinese' in the contrasting pair *l'invasió xinesa* 'the Chinese invasion' vs. *un cotxe xinès* 'a Chinese car'. In the former case, the adjective functions as a complement to the nominal head (hence a sister to N), whereas in the latter case it is an adjunct modifier (hence a sister to N').

24 We use here (O)bject as a shorthand notation to indicate all types of verbal complement, including direct, indirect and prepositional objects.

25 Hale and Buck ([1903] 1994:§627), Grandgent (1907:30), Ernout and Thomas (1953:162), Meillet (1977:156), Väänänen (1982:259), Pinskter (1990:164, 185f.).

26 For a discussion of parallel structures in the non-configurational central Australian language Warlpiri, in which the second-position AUX can follow both a complete NP or single constituent part of the NP, see Bresnan (2001:6) and Mereu (2004:120f.).

27 This empirical observation excludes a common view in the literature that the change in word order from SOV to SVO is a consequence of the weakening and eventual loss of case distinctions. For instance, Oniga (2004:96) hypothesizes that Classical Latin SOV can be derived from the necessity of raising the subject and object out of the VP to SpecAgrSP and SpecAgrOP, respectively, to check their strong Case features (directly reflected in their rich morphological case-forms). The rise and generalization of SVO in late Latin, by contrast, is related to a weakening and loss of case morphology, correlatively translated into a weak Case feature on AgrSP and AgrOP which can be checked covertly, allowing the subject and object to remain within the VP yielding the order SVO (see also Magni 2000).

28 See Price (1971:259f.), Skårup (1975), Vanelli *et al.* (1985), Vanelli (1986; 1998), Adams (1987), Dupuis (1989), Fontana (1993; 1997), Roberts (1993),

Benincà (1995; 2006), Lemieux and Dupuis (1995), Ribeiro (1995), Vance (1997), Lombardi and Middleton (2004), Salvi (2004) and Ledgeway (2007b; 2008). A clear exception to the general V2 nature of medieval Romance is OSardinian, which appears to be a VSO language (Lombardi 2007a).

29 However, some researchers have argued that preverbal (definite) lexical subjects in null subject languages, especially Ibero-Romance, are invariably left-dislocated (see, among others, Contreras 1991; Moro 1993; Alexiadou and Anagnostopoulou 1998; for an opposing view, see Cardinaletti 1997:§3; 2004:148f.).

30 See, among others, Pontes (1987), Benincà (1988:119), Doria (1989:527), Costa (2000b), Ayres-Bennett and Carruthers (2001: ch.9), Azevedo (2005:168f., 247f.). The principal exceptions here are Spanish and Romanian, where there is some controversy about the status of SVO as the unmarked order (Green 1976:26; Harris 1978:20; Stati 1989:122; Motapanyane 2000:24f.; Zagona 2002: ch.5) in view of the not uncommon occurrence of VSO. Particularly revealing in this respect is Vincent's (1998:62) observation that in modern Romance VSO, unlike VOS, proves extremely rare, inasmuch as it would involve interruption of the otherwise inseparable VP constituent. Therefore, when VSO obtains in Spanish and Romanian, it is generally argued to be a derived order involving raising of the verb out of the VP with subject *in situ* (Zagona 2002:214–16; Dobrovie-Sorin 1994; Motapanyane 1989).

31 The definite article in Asturian and some central and upper southern Italian dialects may also mark a non-count distinction (e.g., Ast./Srv. *lo* M non-count vs. *lu* M count; see Avolio 1996; Penny 2000:102f.), also marked on the accompanying noun/adjective in western Asturias (e.g., Srv. *lo pa* 'bread' vs. *lu pa* 'the loaf').

32 Recall that in many Romance varieties reflexes of IPSE came to mark addressee-related deixis (e.g., Sp./Pt. *ese/ësse*, SIt. dials ECCU+IPSU > *chisso* 'this/that (near you)'; see Ledgeway 2004b).

33 Parallels in the use of DOMINUS/DOMINA before first names are also found outside of Catalan, but do not have the status of articles, serving instead as honorifics variously used in conjunction with the aristocracy, clergy and notable dignitaries (e.g., SIt. dial. *Donn'Antonio* 'father Antonio (priest)', *(d)onna Marcella* '(Lady/Mistress) Marcella'; Sp. *Doña Sofía* 'Her Royal Highness Queen Sofía (wife of King Juan Carlos of Spain)', *Don Carlos* '(Lord) Carlos').

34 In Ibiza and Formentera the M.PL form is *es*, but *ets* in Majorca and Menorca (Villangómez i Llobet 1978:65).

35 See Badia i Margarit (1962 I:156; 1991:141f.; 1995:444–46), Villangómez i Llobet (1978:65–67), Wheeler (1988a:181), Moll (1993:40f., 69–71; 1997:182–84; 2006:182f.), Veny (1998:37f., 61–63), Wheeler *et al.* (1999:45f.), Bernat i Baltrons (2007:109f.). Historically, the IPSE-based forms were more prevalent (Aebischer (1948:189–93), including the

Catalonian mainland, as witnessed by their presence in numerous toponyms (e.g., *Sant Joan Despí* (< *d'es pí*), *Sant Just Desvern* (< *d'es vern*), *Sant Martí Sarroca* (< *sa roca*), *Sant Hilari Sacalm* (< *sa calm*), *Sant Martí Sesgueioles* (< *ses esglesioles*)). Exceptional are the Valencian dialects spoken around Tàrbena and the Vall de Gallinera, where, following a wave of Majorcan immigration in the seventeenth century, the *article salat* still remains robust (e.g., *as cavall* 'the horse', *s'home* 'the man'; Veny 1998:119). By contrast, the northern Majorcan coastal locality of Pollença stands out among the Balearic dialects in only employing forms derived from ILLE (namely *eu/eus cap/s* 'the head/s', *l'/us homo/s* 'the man/men', *la/les nina/-es* 'the girl/s', *amb los meus ulls* 'with my (own) eyes'; Moll 1993:40; 1997:184; Veny 1998:71).

36 As a general rule, the IPSE/ILLE articles can then be characterized in terms of the following featural specifications, respectively: [+definite, +particularized, ±given] vs. [+definite, – particularized, +given]. The distinction between the two articles is not, however, entirely robust as the following exceptions illustrate: *es sol* 'the sun', *sa lluna* 'the moon', *es Parlament* 'the (Balearic) Parliament'; cf. also Men. *en el camp* vs. Maj. *en es camp* 'in the country(side)'.

37 An apparent exception to this generalization is the behaviour of prepositional phrases, which in certain fossilized contexts and expressions take a syntactically indefinite NP complement, although assuming definite reference (e.g., Cat. *fora de casa* 'away from home'; Fr. *en Italie* 'in Italy', *par terre* 'on the floor'; It. *in montagna* 'in the mountains', *da capo* 'from the beginning'; Pt. *traduzir de português para italiano* 'to translate from (the) Portuguese into (the) Italian'; Sp. *en parlamento* 'in parliament', *a mediados de enero* 'in the middle of January'). Although this usage has a particularly non-productive feel to it in most Romance varieties, presumably reflecting the original tendency for the article to surface predominantly in subject NPs but not in object NPs or PPs (Vincent 1997c:162; Lyons 1999:335; Parry and Lombardi 2007:93), this archaic pattern appears to be well preserved in Romanian, where the general rule (except for *cu* 'with') is that unmodified definite NPs occur without the article when governed by a preposition (e.g., *după casă* 'behind the house', *sub pat* 'under the bed', but *după casa noastră* 'behind our house', *sub patul din dormitor* 'under the bed in the bedroom'). In all such cases, it seems plausible to assume that the prepositional head exceptionally selects for an NP, and not a DP, complement, despite the definite interpretation of the latter.

38 For reasons of space, in the following tree representations we omit all intermediate X′ categories, adopting a simple bare phrase structure representation (cf. Chomsky 1995).

39 Traditionally, the suffixal nature of the Romanian article is considered a consequence of Balkan areal influence, possibly reinforcing an original Latin order. However, as Martin Maiden (personal communication) points out, it is perfectly possible that this 'Balkan' feature starts with Romanian spreading subsequently, for example to Bulgarian and Macedonian.

40 The earlier adjectival paradigm of OFrench (e.g., *cist **meon** fradre Karle*, lit. 'this brother of mine Charles (or 'my brother Charles here present')' (*Strasbourg Oaths*)) has since been pressed into service as the pronominal paradigm in conjunction with the definite article (e.g., *le mien* 'mine').

41 See, among others, for the demonstrative article *cel*, Manoliu Manea (1989:105f.), Cornilescu (1992), Motapanyane (2000:3f.), and for the possessive article *al*, Dobrovie-Sorin (1987), Ştefănescu (1997), Motapanyane (2000:4–6), D'Hulst *et al.* (2000).

42 This explanation presumably carries over to superlatives, where the head of the superlative AP *mai* 'more' + ADJ equally blocks raising of the nominal head to the suffixal article under D (e.g., *cei mai buni copii* 'the best children').

43 This same analysis also accounts for the apparently optional use of the demonstrative article before postnominal adjectives (e.g., *studenţii (cei) inteligenţi* 'the intelligent students'), if we assume that, when present, the demonstrative article introduces a headless NP in apposition to the first DP (hence, the appositive reading 'the students, those (who are) intelligent').

44 In most Daco-Romanian dialects, however, the possessive article assumes the invariable form *a* (e.g., Mdv. [fiʃoru ista **a** ɲew] 'this boy of mine' (cf. *feciorul acesta **al** meu*)).

45 On the different extent of Romance verb movement, see Lois (1989), Pollock (1989), Belletti (1990:44f.), Kayne (1991), Cinque (1999:152), Cornilescu (2000:89–92), Motapanyane (2000:22–24), Zagona (2002:162–24, 168–70) and Ledgeway and Lombardi (2005:103–06).

46 See Marouzeau (1922), Panhuis (1982), Pinkster (1990:181f.), Ostafin (1986), Vincent (1998:418f.), Oniga (2004:97f.), Polo (2004) and Salvi (2004; this volume, chapter 7: §3.4.7).

47 According to Salvi (this volume, chapter 7: §3.4.7), fronting of both the verb and a focused element are in complementary distribution in Classical Latin, only co-occurring at a subsequent stage (his stage 1) in the transition to Romance when verb fronting becomes generalized.

48 Although the Latin clause provides for a fixed configurational CP structure with respective specifier and head positions, the non-configurationality of the other areas of the grammar is revealed by the observation (see Vincent 1998:420, 422) that SpecC can host indifferently both whole constituents (e.g., [$_{CP}$ [$_{Spec}$ ATER FAMILIAS] [$_{C'}$ UBI [$_{IP}$ AD UILLAM UENIT]]] 'When the father of the family arrived at the country house' (Cato)) and individual words (e.g., [$_{CP}$ [$_{Spec}$ PRATUM [$_{C'}$ SI [$_{IP}$ INRIGIUUM HABEBIS]]]] 'if you will have the meadowland irrigated').

49 See Ernout and Thomas (1953:§§304f.), Rohlfs (1969:189), Väänänen (1982:273), Bauer (1995:165), Herman (1989; 2000a:88f.) and Zamboni (2000:119f.).

50 See Benincà (1988; 1996; 2001; 2006), Campos and Zampini (1990), Dobrovie-Sorin (1994:93–111), Duarte (1996), Rizzi (1997; 2001), Alboiu

and Motapanyane (2000b:§4.2), Motapanyane (2000:20f., 26f.), Poletto (2000; 2001), Ledgeway (2004a; 2005; 2006; 2008; 2010; in press), Munaro (2002; 2003), Zagona (2002:208–29, ch. 6), Paoli (2003), Poletto and Zanuttini (2003), Benincà and Poletto (2004), Azevedo (2005:248f.) and Rowlett (2007: ch. 5).

51 The complex structure of the Focus field is further substantiated by Romanian which, exceptionally among the Romance languages, allows multiple *wh*-fronting in root interrogatives (e.g., **Cine ce** *spusese?*, lit. 'Who what had said?') on a par with the Slavonic languages (see Rudin 1988; Motapanyane 2000:29f.).

52 Unique within Romance is the situation encountered in Gascon, where the [+finite] feature of root clauses is exceptionally spelt out in the lexicalization of the lower complementizer position (Fin) with the complementizer *que* 'that' (Wheeler 1988b:272–74; Lafont 1991:16f.; Ravier 1991:90f.; Bec 1967:47f.), as illustrated in the following examples where *que* is preceded by a topicalized temporal adverbial (e.g., *auèi* **que** *hè calor* 'today (lit. 'that') it is warm') and a topicalized subject (e.g., *lo vesin* **qu'***ei vengut acqueste maitin* 'the neighour (lit. 'that') came this morning').

53 See for southern Italy Calabrese (1993), Lombardi (1997), Ledgeway (1998; 2004a; 2005; 2006), Roberts and Roussou (2003:88–97), Damonte (2005; in press) and Vecchio (2010), and for Romanian (Dobrovie-Sorin 1994:93–111), Alboiu and Motapanyane (2000b:§4.2) and Motapanyane (2000:32–35).

54 For an overview of the various positions, see Hale (1981; 1982; 1983), Jelinek (1984), Williamson (1984), Kiss (1987), Maracz and Muysken (1989), Speas (1990), Baker (1995), Bresnan (2001:5–15, 109–14) and Mereu (2004:119–79).

55 See Thomas (1969:98), Teyssier (1984:88), Raposo (1986), Schwenter and Silva (2002), Azevedo (2005:228f., 234–7) and Bachmann (2008).

56 Cuzzolin (1995), Vincent (1998:424, n11; 1999) and Oniga (2004:94) also note the precocious development of configurationality in the Latin preposi-tional group, where the order head + complement had become established since earliest times. Similarly, Bauer (1995:131f., 146f.), following Leumann and Hofmann (1928:495) and Marouzeau (1949:42; 1953:62, 67), stresses that prepositional disjunction and postposition of the adposition (so-called 'anastrophy') were extremely uncommon in Latin, occurring only in specific archaic styles and registers. As we saw to be the case for the precocious emergence of CP structure in §3.3.3.1, there are, however, residues of an earlier non-configurational arrangement of the prepositional group (Bauer 1995:137–39), especially those involving postposed CUM 'with' (e.g., MECUM/TECUM 'with me/you'), relative pronouns such as QUICUM, QUOCUM, QUACUM 'with who(m)', and QUO DE AGITUR 'the point in question' (Cic.).

57 In (39a–b) 'S' indicates 'flat' structure, standing for a non-projective exocentric 'sentence' or 'small clause', which lacks a categorial head dominating one or

more distinct categories 'C' that do not bear the typical branching relations of endocentricity (Bresnan 2001:110).

58 See, among others, Meyer-Lübke (1899:§50), Kalepky (1913), Reichenkron (1951), Meier (1948), Rohlfs (1969:§§632, 639; 1971a), Diaconesco (1970), Martin Zorraquino (1976), Villar (1983), Green (1988a:106), Nocentini (1985), Jones (1993:65–68; 1995), Zamboni (1992), Pensado Ruiz (1985; 1995), Trumper (1996b:354f.), Sornicola (1997; this volume, chapter 1: §3.3), Vincent (1997b:209), Torrego (1998; 1999), Ledgeway (2000:20f.) and Fiorentino (2003).

59 See Rohlfs (1968:§468), Jaeggli (1981), Suñer (1988), Demonte (1995), Schmitt (1998), Torrego (1998), Ledgeway (2000:37f.), Motapanyane (2000:11f.) and Zagona (2002:68f.).

60 See Kayne (1975), Renzi and Vanelli (1983), Vanelli *et al.* (1985), Vanelli (1987), Roberge (1990), Poletto (1993; 1995; 2000) and Cardinaletti (1997; 2004). For arguments that ModRomanian has developed a series of (doubling) postverbal subject clitics in the so-called double subject construction (e.g., *Ion vine el mai târziu,* lit. 'Ion comes=he more late'), see Cornilescu (2000).

61 In Aromanian (Kramer 1989:430) and Megleno-Romanian (Dahmen 1989:441) varieties, it is the feminine singular form of the participle that is the default form (e.g., *am mâncată* 'I have eaten.F.SG').

62 Auxiliary 'be' is also reported to occur with transitives, though in all six grammatical persons, in a number of Romanian dialects (e.g., MRo. *sam mănkát,* lit. 'I-am eaten.M.SG'), although the participle agreement here with the subject (e.g., *sam mănkátă,* lit. 'I-am eaten.F.SG') suggests that the participle be treated as a verbal adjective (Dahmen 1989:441; Avram and Hill 2007).

63 Head and dependent are also variously termed in the literature, albeit not with necessarily identical values, modified/modifier, qualified/qualifier, governing/governed, déterminé/déterminant (or déterminatif), operand/operator, specified/specifier (for an overview, see Bauer 1995:21f.).

64 It is less clear how these same informal semantic definitions of head can be carried over, if at all, to inflectional morphological structures.

65 The Apulian dialect of Altamura (Loporcaro 1988) is an apparent partial exception, in that the passive in this dialect can be constructed with both ESSE and HABERE.

66 See Löfstedt (1933:329–34), Norberg (1944:21–32), Gerola (1949–50), Bastardas Parera (1953:16–20), Herman (1966; 1987:102; 1995:72–75), Durante (1981:41), Pensado Ruiz (1986), Väänänen (1982:203f.), La Fauci (1988:54f.), Zamboni (1998:131f.), Cennamo (2001) and Rovai (2005).

67 Gerola (1949–50), Herman (1966), Väänänen (1982:203f.), Pensado Ruiz (1986), La Fauci (1997:34), Zamboni (1998:131f.).

68 In masculine adjectives in these Ræto-Romance varieties the original case distinction has been reinterpreted as a predicative (< nominative) vs. attributive

(< accusative/oblique) distinction (Haiman 1988:366f., 381–84; Haiman and Benincà 1992:141–52).

69 This binary case system (Gallo-/Ræto-Romance: nominative vs. accusative/ oblique; Daco-Romance: nominative/accusative vs. dative/genitive) is most likely derived from a preceding ternary nominative–accusative–oblique system (La Fauci 1997:37–53; Zamboni 1998:137–42; 2000:93, 110–15), evidence of which is still preserved in some pronominal systems (see Salvi, this volume, chapter 7: §2.2). In particular, this ternary system combined a subsystem of animate nouns operating on a nominative/accusative alignment incorporating a definite 'marked nominative' with three cases (nominative vs. accusative vs. oblique) and a sub-system of inanimate nouns operating on an active/stative alignment with two cases (nominative/accusative vs. oblique). It is this first subsystem, following the early neutralization of -u/-o and -i/-e producing the neutralization of accusative and oblique, which surfaces in Gallo- and Ræto-Romance varieties, whereas the second subsystem underlies the case system of ModDaco-Romance.

70 Cf. Rohlfs (1968:§344), Harris (1978:49), Tekavčić (1980:36f.), La Fauci (1988:55f.; 1991:149), Seidl (1995a), Formentin (1998:285f.) and Zamboni (1998:133–37, 139; 2000:95f., 108–12).

71 The nominative origin of forms derived from the lexemes FRAT-, MAT- and PAT- is not conclusive in all cases (Rohlfs 1968:6). Alongside a possible nominative etymological base (e.g., FRATE(R) > It. *frate* or FRAT(E)R > *fratre > Fr. *frère*), an accusative etymology is also possible, not to say preferable, in some cases (e.g., FRATRE(M) > OFr. *fradre* > Fr. *frère*).

72 For further detailed discussion, see Bentley (2006:§82). In literary/high regis-ters of ModFrench, a relic of this active/stative alignment is still observable in the postverbal position of indefinite S$_O$ subjects in construction with a pre-verbal 3M.SG expletive subject *il* (e.g., *il est arrivé **un prêtre*** 'there arrived a priest'), unavailable to indefinite transitive or unergative subjects (e.g., **il a chanté **un prêtre*** *(une chanson)*, lit. 'there has sung a priest (a song)').

73 For a further example of the active/stative alignment in late Latin pleonastic reflexives involving a SE/SIBI alternation, see Cennamo (1999).

CHAPTER 9: PRAGMATIC AND DISCOURSE CHANGES

1 For the evolution of other means of signalling the speaker's attitude (towards the propositional content of the utterances), see Salvi, this volume, chapter 7: §§2–3, and Ledgeway, this volume, chapter 8: §§3.3.2, 6.2.1.1.

2 Tenses are deictic means of organizing the discourse, since they present the speaker's view of the hierarchy of events, such as background vs. foreground, actualization of events, cinematographic effects, etc.

3 On changes in the demonstrative sysem, see especially Lyons (1999) and Vincent (1997c; 1998).

4 For the concept of *foregrounding* see Brown and Yule (1984). This is a process by which a particular referent is established in the foreground of consciousness while other discourse elements remain in the background.

5 This is the case with the French distal deictic, which became specialized as a pronoun *ce* (+*lui/elle*), whereas the proximity deictic functions only as a modifier (*cet* < ECCE-ISTE) (see Marchello-Nizia 1995). In Romanian, the short form *cel* (< ECCE+ILLE) 'that' remained as an article, introducing adjectives, whereas *cest* (< ECCE+ISTE) 'this' was marginalized and disappeared.

6 See, for example, the quantifiers: Fr. *quelque* but *quelqu'un, quelque chose*; *chaque* vs. *chacun*, etc.

7 For a recent presentation of the relations between anaphora, deixis and word order in Latin, see Spevak (2007).

8 Compare *Heraclius **ille** Syracusanus et hic Bidinus Epicrates* (Cic., Verr., 2.2.62.2). Epicrates has been discussed at length by Cicero in the preceding paragraphs (hence HIC), while Heraclius has been briefly mentioned on the preceding page (hence ILLE); see Bauer (2007). Reflexes of HIC are preserved in French deictic pronouns: *ce* (OFr. *ço*) and It. *ciò* (< Lat. ECCE HOC) and in certain adverbial deictics (e.g., HOC ANNO 'this year' > Sp. *hogaño* 'nowadays' (compare also OFr. *ouan*, OIt. *uguanno*, Cat. *enguany*); HAC HORA 'this hour' > Sp. *ahora*, Pt. *agora* 'now').

9 To the factors listed one might add the phonetic factor (extremely reduced phonetic form) in a period when the initial [h] was no longer pronounced and the final consonant was in a very weak position, especially when the following noun began with a consonant).

10 The new function of ISTE is recognizable in the Romanian short form of the proximity deictic *ăsta* 'this' as the opposite of the short distal deictic *ăla* (< Lat. ILLE). Although they were used first only as regional variants (Muntenia), Ro. *ăsta* 'this' and *ăla* 'that' are nowadays basic spoken standard variants (see §2.3.1 below).

11 According to Ekkehard König (personal communication), a sentence such as *As expected, the President himself attended the conference* conveys the meaning 'As expected, the President attended the conference (wow!) …'.

12 According to Ernout and Thomas (1953/93:191), in such contexts the meaning of IPSE was close to that of IDEM. For the functional difference between the two items, see Manoliu-Manea (1994:180–209).

13 IPSE used as an anaphoric adjective is attested in late Latin: *Sedens in eadem spelunca, quae in **ipsa** ecclesia est* (*Aeth.*, 123) 'He was sitting in the very cave which is in **the** church' (in Faingold 1996:78).

14 For recent presentations of French deixis, see Veland (1996) and Guillot (2006); for Romanian, see Hobjilă (2003).

15 Both Ro. *celŭ* and *cela* were then used mostly as foregrounding markers, enhancing the importance of the following definite description. Subsequently, *cel* became a clitic with a very restricted distribution (especially as a marker of the

relative superlative: *cel mai frumos copil* 'the prettiest child'), whereas *cela* remained only as a regional variant.

16 For more details on this three-term paradigm, see Lepschy and Lepschy (1988:120), Cifuentes (1989), Vanelli (1992), Gaudino-Fallegger (1992), Almeida (2000) and López Palma (2004).

17 *Codesto* is arguably not on the same footing as the other two members of the system; its status is discussed by Serianni (1989:276) and Ledgeway (2004b).

18 'Si un locuteur utilise une expression indexicale, c'est à dire une expression qui déclenche une procédure de repérage spatio-temporel, c'est qu'il juge que son interlocuteur n'a pas encore le référent à l'esprit (cas du référent nouveau) ou qu'il entend le lui faire découvrir sous un aspect nouveau (dans l'hypothèse où le référent est déjà connu).'

19 Recent studies of Romanian demonstratives have discussed several relevant phenomena belonging to various language levels, such as morphemic diversification according to position (Iordan *et al.* 1967:140f.), syntactic constraints (Giusti 1995), and pragmatic/discourse functions (Tasmowski-De Ryck 1990; Manoliu Manea 2000b; Iliescu 2007).

20 It may be worth recalling here that recent theoretical developments in the fields of discourse analysis and pragmatics have stressed the fact that demonstratives function as talk-interaction clues, which explains their overuse in conversation and the rapid weakening of their indexical value. In Romanian we find a greater variety of items originating in the Latin demonstratives than anywhere else in the Romance-speaking world (see Manoliu 2000b; 2001).

21 The construction was already used in Latin: *M. Drusus, ille clarissimus vir* (Cic., *Dom.*, 120.7); *Cato ille sapiens* (Cic., *Diu.*, 1.28.5). See also Renzi (1992b:173). Late Lat. *cito proferte mihi **stolam illam primam** e induite illum* (Luke 15, 22, in Mihăescu 1960:163) 'bring away my ceremonial garment, that first [one], and put [it] on him'. According to Löfstedt (1982:270–73), the use of a demonstrative with a proper noun was an emphatic device used to highlight an adjective conveying a judgement.

22 Greek, Slavonic, German, Finno-Ugric. See Malkiel (1985).

23 For various pragmatic functions of *ça* see also Corblin (1987), Klare (1987) and Manoliu-Manea (1990).

24 In many instances, especially when the subjects of co-ordinated sentences are coreferential, the zero-anaphor is the preferred choice. It would be interesting to examine in detail the constraints imposed on the choice of a zero-anaphor for subjects in classical as opposed to colloquial and late Latin, especially in Gaul, where the zero-anaphor is rare.

25 For their morphological evolution, see Salvi (this volume, chapter 7: §2).

26 As noted above, Löfstedt (1982:270–73) claims that the definite article has its origin in an emphatic device used to highlight an adjective that conveys a judgement. Drawing on hypotheses concerning the history of the article in

English, Faingold (1996) proposes the following stages for the development of a definite article in the Romance languages: NP in focus > prominent > accessible > identifiable.

27 This preference was interpreted as a way of encoding 'personal gender' (see Rosetti 1986:599).

28 For a detailed presentation of the concepts in question, see Lakoff (1971), Lambrecht (1994) and Manoliu-Manea (1994).

29 See, for example, Marouzeau (1938), Meillet and Vendryes (1960), Canaes and Pádua (1960), Marchello-Nizia (1995), Bauer (1995), Sornicola (2000) and Costa (2000).

30 For other cases in which the verb may be in initial position, see Marouzeau (1947) and Marchello-Nizia (1995).

31 See Marchello-Nizia (1995:67).

32 The two terms ***topic*** and ***theme*** are not in fact synonymous. The ***topic*** is a discourse concept, referring to 'the constituent the speaker wants to talk about', and can be repeated across utterance boundaries, whereas the ***theme*** is 'the sentence-constituent representing the topic'; see §3.2 below.

33 Compare verb-final position in Latin in Section 3.1.1, (53).

34 See Section 3.1.1 (51) above for the conditions governing the preposed noun modifier in Latin.

35 Compare Latin (54) in §3.1.1 above.

36 According to Kayne (1994) and Zubizarreta (1998), the postverbal subject occurring after the direct object is dislocated and clause external (see also Costa 2000:101).

37 Compare Lat.   PLACET   **HOC**   TIBI?
                  pleases   this   you.DAT
                  'Do you like this?'

38 Romanian also has the construction with the verb 'to be', which recalls the Latin dative construction. Compare Ro. *mi-e frig* 'I am cold', *mi-e foame* 'I am hungry' and Lat. MIHI EST PUDOR, CURA 'I am ashamed, worried' (see Manoliu-Manea 1985:101–4).

39 Compare Lat.   ME   PAENITET   DICTORUM
                  me.ACC   regret.3SG   words.GEN
                  'I regret my words' (Morwood 1999:107)

For a discourse explanation of the difference between the dative and accusative constructions of the possessor/eperiencer in Romanian, see Manoliu-Manea (1994:53–84).

40 See also Morwood (1999:106): CAPTIUIS PARCETUR, lit. 'there will be sparing of the prisoners', i.e., 'the prisoners will be spared'; Woodcock (2002:43): CURRITUR, lit. 'running is taking place', i.e., 'people are running', etc.

41 In the classical description, MORIOR was considered a deponent. However, in our opinion, it is clearly an inchoative.

42 See also other transitive medio-passive verbs: CONSPICOR 'I spot, I see [some-thing], I catch sight of '; AEMULOR 'I emulate [somebody], I rival'; AGGREDIOR 'I approach, I address, I attack'; SEQUOR 'I follow [somebody]', etc. A verb such as SUGGREDIOR changes its meaning according to its transitive or intransitive use, namely: when transitive, SUGGREDIOR means 'I board a ship, I tackle a question', compare Fr. *aborder* [*quelque chose*]; when intransitive, it means 'I get close to something'; compare Fr. *s'approcher* [*de quelque chose*].

43 For generative approaches, see, for instance, Vasiliu and Golopenția (1968), Vasiliu (1969), Saltarelli (1970b), Roldán (1971), Vincenz (1971), Ruwet (1972), Schroten (1972), Suñer (1974), Costa (1975), Cinque (1976), Luján (1976), Napoli (1976), Naro (1976), Zribi-Hertz (1978), Stéfanini (1982), Everaert (1986), Dobrovie-Sorin (1994) and Frajzyngier and Curl (2000).

44 See, for example, LEGIBUS   [A   BONIS   CIUIBUS]   PARETUR
                               law.DAT.PL   [by   good   citizens]   obey.Middle.PL,
    which is translated by Comrie (1977:53) as a true passive, 'The laws are obeyed [by good citizens]', although Lat. LEGIBUS is modified by a dative marker. Geniušienė (1987:232) discusses it under the heading 'Inventory of recessive diatheses for intransitive verbs'.

45 For the definition of the seme [Incapacity of doing], see Aristotle's *Metaphysics*, as discussed in Kirwan (1993) and Manoliu-Manea (2005). According to Aristotle (*Metaphysics,* Book Δ, chapter 12), objects are charac-terized by the features: δύναμις, δυνατόν – ἀδυναμία, ἀδύνατον (roughly 'capacity' – 'incapacity [for being active]'). 'We call a CAPACITY what originates a change or alteration either in another thing or *qua* other, as for instance housebuilding is a capacity which is not a constituent of the things being built, but doctoring, which is a capacity, might be a constituent of the thing being doctored, but not of it being doctored. […] INCAPACITY is lack of capacity, i.e. of the kind of origin described, either in general or by some-thing which characteristically possesses it or even at a time already characteristic of its possession. For people would not assert in the same way that a boy, a grown man, and a eunuch are incapable of begetting. Again, corresponding to each of the two capacities (for merely changing things, and for changing them satisfactorily) there is an opposite incapacity' (Kirwan 1993:46f.). It is to be noted at this point that the notion of CAPACITY is confined to a specific type of capacity, i.e., the capacity for doing something (change or alteration).

46 For the relation between topic and semes such as [+Person] and [+Dynamic] in Romance languages, see Manoliu-Manea (1987). For the hypothesis that the semantic feature [±Incapacity] was lost as an inherent feature in late Latin and Romance, see Manoliu (2007).

47 It is interesting to note that in old French texts, the nouns that best preserved their nominative forms were those carrying the feature [+Person] (see van Schøsler and Reenen 2020; Schøsler 1984). In western Romance, new forms without -s are reconstructed for neuter nouns that had an -s in Latin, probably

because *-s* became the plural marker *par excellence*: e.g., Sp. *cuerpo* 'body', *pecho* 'breast', but Lat. CORPUS, PECTUS. In the east (i.e., in Italian and Romanian), where not only the -M of the accusative singular is lost, as it is everywhere else, but the -s of the nominative singular also disappears (e.g., LUPUS 'wolf' > It. *lupo*, Rom. *lup(u)*), the distinction between nominative and accusative singular was lost in masculine nouns of the second declension. Consequently, the paradigm of masculine nouns fell into line with neuter nouns and feminine nouns (of the first declension), where this had happened earlier.

48 It is interesting to note Hewson's claim (Hewson 2007) that in Germanic the promotion of inanimates to the role of subject was a late development, which triggered the development of a passive voice.

49 For the concepts of 'conversational and conventional implicature', see Levinson (1983; 2000) and, more recently, the survey of various positions concerning Grice's 'Principle of Cooperation' in Jaszczolt (2002:207–23). ***Conventional implicatures*** are a type of non-truth-conditional inferences that are not derived from superordinate pragmatic principles like the maxims, but are simply attached by convention to particular lexical items or expressions. Their properties include the following: they are detachable; they depend on the particular lexical items used (in the present case: the reflexive clitics); they are not cancellable, because they do not rely on defeasible assumptions about the nature of the context; they are not calculated using pragmatic principles and contextually dependent knowledge, but are rather given by convention. Items carrying conventional implicatures do not seem to have radically different interpretations in different contexts.

50 See Flobert (1975: 387):

e.g., *mulier*   *quae*   ***se***   *suamque*   *aetatem*   *spernit* (Pl., *Mo.*, 250)
woman   who   REFL   her.and   age   hinders
'the woman who hinders herself and her age'

51 '[S]ouligne que l'initiative du mouvement appartient au sujet, tandis que le passif intrinsèque MOUERI "se mouvoir" marque seulement l'implication du sujet dans un mouvement. Le tour réfléchi est donc plus fort, plus expressif.'

52 Flobert (1975:389) notes that in Vergil one can find the beginning of a metaphorical use, the 'personification of inanimate subjects', a phenomenon that is frequently found in late Latin:

frangitur   *inque*   *sinus*   *scindit*   ***sese***   *unda* (Verg. *Aen.*, 1, 161)
breaks.MIDDLE   in-and   curves   divides   itself   wave
approx. 'the wave divides itself and breaks in curves'

53 Though Kemmer (1993:157) points to the fact that 'the reflexive marker was extended to express middle semantics on the strength of the semantic property shared by the reflexive and middle (Initiator and Endpoint are the same entity)', she does not make the distinction between the semantic interpretation (referential identity) and the pragmatic function (event-highlighting) of the middle. Consequently her hypothesis cannot account for the fact that the

reflexive pronoun also became the marker of impersonal and passive constructions.

54 Maldonado claims that this use of *se* has become quite productive in Hispanic countries. He mentions a comedian who included in his routine the words: 'It's *se*'s fault!' (precisely because he wanted to refer to the fact that one does not generally want to be held responsible for one's wrongdoings).

55 In such cases the label 'Agent' is inappropriate, since it is hard to imagine that such events involve voluntary actions. The idea of a more dynamic Experiencer therefore seems more appropriate.

56 They involve 'attitude': for example, *pavonearse* 'to strut' and *jactarse* 'to brag' differ from *caminar* 'to walk' and *hablar* 'to speak', in the sense that they define a way of walking or talking with a specific attitude.

CHAPTER 10: WORD FORMATION

1 I thank Martin Maiden for his very useful comments on an earlier version of this chapter.

2 For prefixes in Latin/Romance, see Meyer-Lübke (1894); Hofmann and Szantyr (1965:33, 304).

3 For prefixes in individual languages, see Rohlfs (1969:375–471); Dardano (1978:114–37, 165–69); Weidenbusch (1993:105–239).

4 The following (on which we have drawn extensively) present extensive overviews of suffixes in Romance or in individual languages: Meyer-Lübke (1894); Brunot (1922); Allen (1941); Menéndez Pidal (1958); Rohlfs (1969); Pattison (1975); for modern languages, Dardano (1978:21–107); Beyrer *et al.* (1987); Lang (1990); Grevisse (1993); Stewart (1999:68–78).

5 For details and semantic shift, see Kurschildgen (1983:16–73).

6 See further Meyer-Lübke (1894:452f.); Rohlfs (1969:397f.); Grandgent (1907:22f.).

7 E.g., Brugmann (1892:262).

8 For Provençal, see Meyer-Lübke (1894:499).

9 An interesting feature of It. *-one* is that when applied to objects it can only be used with reference to entities smaller than, or created by, human beings, e.g., *ditone* 'finger.AUG', *autostradone* 'motorway.AUG', but not **cielone* 'sky. AUG', or **spiaggione* 'beach.AUG' (see Maiden and Robustelli 2007:448).

10 See Maiden (1995a:185) for gender-related phenomena which reflect the autonomy of the elements in Italian.

11 For the origin of linking *-i-* in many compounds (e.g., It. *caprifoglio*, Fr. *chèvrefeuille* 'honeysuckle'), which is still a matter of discussion, see Meillet and Vendryes (1924:399); Giurescu (1975:83); Maiden (1995a:183f.); De Dardel and Zamboni (1999).

12 For further discussion, see especially Rohlfs (1952a; 1971b:95f., 189–91); Baehr (1958); Tagliavini (1963:74–114).

13 For (the etymology of) Indo-European and Latin numerals, see especially Brugmann (1890); Szemerényi (1960); Polomé (1968); Coleman (1992).

14 See especially Price (1992); Rohlfs (1952b).

15 See further Rösler (1910:198–201); Jaberg and Jud (1928–1940: maps 301–3); Rohlfs (1952b; 1969:314); Reichenkron (1958:167–71); Bauer (2004).

16 For conversion in individual languages, see Rohlfs (1968:80); Beyer *et al.* (1987:50, 56f.); Grevisse (1993:249); Stewart (1999:79f.).

17 Also discussed in chapter 14 of this volume (eds.).

18 Whence also the derived noun *ceferist* 'railway worker'.

19 This word has come widely to be used as a masculine as well, perhaps on the analogy of masculine nouns such as *appartement* 'flat, apartment'.

CHAPTER 11: LEXICAL STABILITY

1 This word means 'very' in Romanian, presumably via an earlier stage at which it meant 'strong(ly)' (cf. Fr. *fort* 'very'). (MM)

2 Professor Stefenelli's death deprived me of the opportunity to discuss this etymology with him. It has to be noted that other etymological authorities derive *sau* from Lat. SEU combined with AUT, or SEU alone, or SIUE. (MM)

3 The meaning in Latin was primarily 'person, human being', a sense which it preserves in Romanian. (MM)

4 This chapter was translated from the original German by Dr Wolfgarg De Melo.

CHAPTER 12: LEXICAL CHANGE

1 A revised and abbreviated Spanish version of the first part of this chapter has appeared as Dworkin (2006).

CHAPTER 13: LATIN AND THE STRUCTURE OF WRITTEN ROMANCE

1 The SAVI project (Vincent *et al.* 2002; 2003) has shown that *Abstand* languages can have long and rich written (including literary) traditions, and substantial register variation.

2 Cf. Woledge and Clive (1964:11), who argue that the text could be a scrupulously accurate historical account, an early example of political 'spin' or a sign of the growing prestige of the *lingua romana* and the *lingua teudisca*, and that these explanations are moreover not mutually exclusive, so that none of the three can be ruled out ('Scrupule d'un historien épris d'exactitude? Artifice d'un homme politique partisan des revendications de son cousin et seigneur? Ou bien reflet du prestige grandissant de la *lingua romana* et de la *lingua teudisca*? Ces explications ne s'excluent pas mutuellement et aucune des trois ne peut être rejetée').

3 Obtained from http://eduscol.education.fr/D0102/liste-mots-frequents.htm
4 Harris (1969:82) used 'alternations' such as *auricular~oreja* 'relating to the ear (ADJ)~ear (N)' to justify a rule whereby /au/ was the underlying form of /o/ 'under certain conditions', thus justifying the postulation of *ama+a+V** as the underlying form of the preterite *amó* 'he/she loved'.
5 In Pountain (1983:215) I recorded examples from Chrestien de Troyes and Dante, but this does not necessarily argue against a borrowed origin.
6 Data obtained from the *Base de français médiéval* (http://bfm.ens-lsh.fr/). The importance of text-type is very plainly shown by the distribution of *laquelle*, etc., in this database; it is most frequent in the chonicles and totally absent from poetry, grammar and hagiography:

(total words)	chronicle (423,326)	epic (25,283)	fabliau (24,636)	grammar (23,438)	hagiography (71,197)	legal (142,507)	lyric (9,372)	memoir (282,848)
liquels	80	0	0	0	0	0	0	0
lequel	114	0	0	0	0	23	0	216
laquelle	167	0	0	0	0	0	0	75
lesquels	39	0	0	0	0	0	0	0
lesquelles	39	0	0	0	0	0	0	17

7 Despite the availability of such an adverbial marking in Romance, there is a tendency in the spoken language to avoid such adverbial formations and to use adjectives or paraphrases to render the adverbial function.
8 See Mackenzie (2006:172–81) for an account and critique of the link often proposed between absolute constructions and unaccusative verbs.
9 The Ibero-Romance languages make to varying degrees a distinction between the stative passive and the dynamic passive by the use of different copular verbs (clearest in Spanish: *la puerta está cerrada* 'the door is shut (stative)' / *la puerta es cerrada* 'the door is (being) shut, is (regularly) shut (dynamic)'); but this is a relatively late development (Pountain 1985:350, 347 where the figures demonstrate the continuity of the dynamic ('action') passive in Castilian, at least in written texts).

CHAPTER 14: SLANG AND JARGONS

1 This and all following non-English quotes have been translated by the author.
2 *FEW* (I.138) treats OFr. *arguer*, OPrv. *arguar*, OSp. *argudar* as outcomes of late Lat. ARGŪTĀRE 'to confuse someone with chatter' (for usual (?) ARGŪTĀRI), which show regular outcomes of -ū- (cf. also Alb. *argëtoj*). As is well known, ARGŪTĀRI (< ARGŪTUS) is documented even in OLatin (see Ennius, *Tragedies* Fr. 312–13; Warmington 1988:332), but had to be explained in late commentaries, as in Nonius 245, 30 (Lindsay 1964: II, 369): Argutari dicitur loquacius proloqui. Ennius Phoenice: 'tum tu isti crede atque exerce linguam, ut

argutarier possis' 'ARGUTARI is said for prating. Ennius in the Phoenix (writes) "Then trust yourself to that fellow and give your tongue training so you'll be able to confuse with your chatter [= 'trick people']" .'

3 *Jargon* is used for the language of criminals in police reports of the first half of the fifteenth century. For example, a well-known report of 1426 states 'their way of speaking that they call "jargon", when they used to find some dupe or innocent they wanted to trick with a ruse or ruses and have his money'. *Jobelin* seems to be used as its equivalent, judging from the minutes of the famous Dijon Trial of 1455. No attempts to etymologize prove satisfactory.

4 First studied in the 1980s and 1990s in Walter (1984), Bachmann and Basier (1984), Paul (1985), Plénat (1985; 1992) and Duchêne (2002), and accompanied by a series of grammatical–phonological studies and dictionaries such as Andreini (1985), Merle (1986; 2006), Caradec (1988) and Goudailler (1998).

5 It would be possible to derive these outcomes from the following underlying structures [ʃat+Ø] (M) vs. [ʃatə] (F) by way of the two ordered rules (1) $C_x > Ø$ word-finally, (2) ə > Ø word-finally and where resulting consonant clusters are allowed. This allows us to relate the two forms morphologically and phonologically. Other solutions are, of course, possible. Clearly, [təʃ] and [aʃ] cannot be related in the same manner.

6 Although preposition + article is unaffected, it is striking that pronominal subject clitic *je* and perfective auxiliary *ai*, both standardly assumed to be function words, can undergo 'verlanisation'. The negative *pas*, though theoretically so considered, seems a distinct lexical element (cf. *le pas* 'the step, pace') rather than a function word from this perspective.

7 The only southern Italian exception of a three-syllable word so treated seems to be the designation of the police as *Viggiana*, an irregular 'verlanisation' of the name *Giovanna* (note the form *Viggiana*, rather than the expected **Viggianna*).

8 If one assumes *ker-* 'do; make' to derive from Hindi *kaṛṇa* (see Wolf 1960), then the singular persons of the present are *keraw, kerash, kerel*, where *-el* has been isolated as a base form along Romance lines, where, for example, *canta* 's/ he sings' might be considered the zero form of *cantare* 'to sing' and other personal and tense morphs being taken as suffixes to the stem. The suffix *-el* then becomes Romance *-ella*.

9 This represents an even more drastic reduction than ModFrench, where at least the plural forms *chantons* 'we sing', *chantez* 'you sing' are phonetically differentiated from the other persons.

10 Both for referential reasons ('fire' is in general 'red' to the sight) and for phonological similarity (a common frame [ru__o]), *ruffo* 'fire' becomes interchangeable with *russo* 'red', such that *russo* may assume the meaning 'fire' and take part in the extensions of *ruffo*. Consequently, on one hand, we have *russo > russetto* (1) 'blood', (2) 'tomato', (3) 'orange', (4) 'any red fruit' (becoming in

this last case not a lexical life-form nor a lexical generic, but, in Berlin's (1992) terminology, a lexical 'intermediate'), and, on the other, *russo > russetta* (1) 'cherry', (2) 'tomato sauce', where *russo* 'red' spreads to *russo* 'fire' and follows the *ruffo* model.

11 The first use of *massa* as 'ingot' is of considerable age. Rather than Vergil's use, one might pinpoint Pliny (NH 34.9), Ovid's *Fasti* (4.405), and Petronius' *Satyricon* (88); for 'molten metal', see also Juvenal (*Satura* 10.130). The basic sense 'ore' or 'crude metal' was also present, as highlighted in Forcellini's (1805 III: 386) definition. The most general extension 'ore' > 'metal' is implied in the Latin borrowing into Celtic, where it is the usual word for 'metal'. Lat. *massa* is also 'weight; ingot', though *massarius* as 'foundry foreman' (in Christian inscriptions) indicates use as both 'ingot' and 'raw metal'. The most generic meaning as 'metal' is, then, present in later Latin, starting, at least, with St Jerome.

12 Friulian trade slang (Tramonti) *biscàja* (Menegon 1950; Marcato 1983) and Sardinian trade slang (Isili) *biscàggia* seem to derive from this term, which was already documented for Calabrian trade slang by Vincenzo Padula in the middle of the nineteenth century. Its origin is the colour adjective for 'reddish', 'rust-colour' (see *REW* 3611: FŬSCUS > It. *fósco*, Cal. *fúscu* as a colour, in Calabrian used in bird names such as *capufúscu* 'redcap'). The presence of b- in other areas is probably due to northern Calabrian intervocalic voicing of short fricatives, such as f > v merging with b > v, with subsequent merger of /b/ and /f/ (for details, see Trumper and Chiodo 1999:207f.).

13 There is an obvious connection with Cal. *camaci* (Reggio Calabria) (1) 'rod', (2) 'pole', *camacina* (Catanzaro) 'shaft[s]', present also in Calabro-Greek dialects (for details, see Karanastasis 1988:48).

14 This looks suspiciously like a Calabrian outcome of Greek λιθάριον 'rock; large stone; mass', which is well represented in Calabro-Greek Byzantine and post-Byzantine texts. The slang item might represent, in its sense of 'mass' (< 'stone, rock'), the same kind of extension as Lat. MASSA > *massello, massella*, for which see slang *masséllu* 'copper ingot' above.

15 This is the usual dialect word for 'crucible' (cf. Cal. *grisciólu, grisciùolu*); the metonymic drift is 'crucible for melting metal X' > 'metal X', which was in origin the starting point ('gold'), with a 360 degree shift back to its origins (Grk. χρυσός).

16 Both are from Gypsy *gàgio/gagiò*, originally the Sindhi dialect term for 'cow-herder, cowboy', a fixed agricultural category vis-à-vis the nomadic Gypsy, viz. *Rom* 'man' or 'human' (< Hindi *Dom*).

17 In some parts of Calabria (south of Catanzaro), the verb *'ndranghitijari/-a* is often replaced by *baccagghjari/-a* with the same meaning ('to use the criminal code' > 'to behave like an 'ndranghitusu').

18 Wholesale listing would not be appropriate in the present case, but examples are truly legion.

19 Diffusion of an almost 'learnèd' Greek term χρέας. The problem of the spread of learnèd lexicon is also present in terms for 'bread' across all Romance slangs (< ἄρτος), e.g., *germancía*: *hartón*, *argot*: *arton*, *gergo*: *arto*, *arton[e]*. That similar terms might have spread from Calabrian Greek is a hypothesis suggested with some hesitation in Dauzat (1912:109), and with greater conviction in Schmitt (1990:286). The usual Bova word for 'bread' was σφωμί, στωμί; Apulo-Greek still has σφωμί, στωμί < ψωμίον 'piece; crumb', so ἄρτος was learnèd for Italo-Greeks as well, present in folk versions of the Lord's Prayer.

REFERENCES AND BIBLIOGRAPHICAL ABBREVIATIONS

Abel, Fritz 1971. *L'adjectif démonstratif dans la langue de la Bible latine*. Tübingen: Niemeyer.

Abete, Giovanni 2006. 'Sulla questione della sillaba superpesante: i dittonghi discendenti in sillaba chiusa nel dialetto di Pozzuoli', in Savy, R. and Crocco, C. (eds.), *Analisi prosodica. Teorie, modelli, sistemi di annotazione (Atti del 2° Convegno Nazionale AISV)*. Torriana: EDK Editore, pp. 379–98.

Academia de la llingua asturiana 1995. *La llingua asturiana*. Xixón: Academia de la llingua asturiana.

Acquati, Anna 1971. 'Il vocalismo latino-volgare nelle iscrizioni africane', *Annali della Facoltà di Lettere e Filosofia dell'Università degli studi di Milano* 24:155–84.

Acquaviva, Paolo 2002. 'Il plurale in *–a* come derivazione lessicale', *Lingue e linguaggio* 2:295–326.

    2005. 'The morphosemantics of transnumeral nouns', in Booij, Geert, Guevara, E., Ralli, A., Sgroi, S. and Scalise, S. (eds.), *Morphology and Linguistic Typology: On-line Proceedings of the Fourth Mediterranean Morphology Meeting*, pp. 251–65 (http://morbo.lingue.unibo.it/mmm/mmm-proc/MMM4/251–265-Acquaviva-MMM4.pdf).

    2008. *Lexical Plurals*. Oxford: Oxford University Press.

Adam, Jean-Michel 1990. *Éléments de linguistique textuelle. Théorie et pratique de l'analyse textuelle*. Liège: Mardaga.

Adams, James 1976. 'A typological approach to Latin word order', *IF* 81:70–99.

    1977. *The Vulgar Latin of the Letters of Claudius Terentianus*. Manchester: Manchester University Press.

    1991. 'Some neglected evidence for Latin *habeo* with infinitive: the order of the constituents', *TPS* 89:131–96.

    2003. *Bilingualism and the Latin Language*. Cambridge: Cambridge University Press.

    2007. *The Regional Diversification of Latin 200 BC–AD 600*. Cambridge: Cambridge University Press.

Adams, Marianne 1987. *Old French, Null Subjects, and Verb Second Phenomena*. UCLA: unpublished thesis.

Aebischer, Paul 1948. 'Contribution à la protohistoire des articles *ille* et *ipse* dans les langues romanes', *CN* 8:181–203.

Agard, Frederick 1958. *Structural Sketch of Romanian*. Baltimore: Linguistic Society of America.

Ageno, Franca 1957. 'Per una semantica del gergo', *SFI* 15:401–37.

    1962. 'La lettera in furbesco di Luigi Pulci', 'Tre studi quattrocenteschi', *SFI* 20:75–98.

    1964. *Il verbo nell'italiano antico. Ricerche di sintassi*. Milan-Naples: Ricciardi.

AGI = *Archivio glottologico italiano*.

Agostiniani, Luciano 1998. 'La defixio di Carmona (Siviglia) e lo sviluppo dei nessi consonantici con /j/', in Navarro Salazar, María Teresa (ed.), *Italica Matritensia. Atti del IV convegno SILFI*. Florence: Cesati, pp. 25–35.

AIS = Jaberg and Jud 1928–40.

Alameda, José Ramón and Cuetos, Fernando 1995. *Diccionario de frecuencias de las unidades lingüísticas del castellano*. Oviedo: Universidad de Oviedo.

Alarcos Llorach, Emilio 1951. 'Esbozo de una fonología diacrónica del español', in *Estudios dedicados a Ramón Menéndez Pidal*, II. Madrid: CSIC, pp. 9–39.

    1994. *Gramática de la lengua española*. Madrid: Espasa.

Alboiu, Gabriela 1999. '(De-)Focussing and object raising in Romanian', *Canadian Journal of Linguistics-Revue canadienne de linguistique* 44:1–22.

Alboiu, Gabriela and Motapanyane, Virginia (eds.) 2000a. *Comparative Studies in Romanian Syntax*. Amsterdam: Elsevier.

    2000b. 'The generative approach to Romanian grammar: An overview', in Alboiu and Motapanyane (eds.), pp. 1–48.

Alcover, Antoni 1925–26. 'Lo sistema de contar per vints a Catalunya', *Bolletí del Diccionari de la llengua catalana* 14:279–88.

Alcover, Antoni and Moll, Francesc 1929/30/32. 'La flexió verbal en el dialectes catalans', *Anuari de l'Oficina romànica de lingüística i literatura* 2:79–184; 3:73–168; 4:9–104; 5:9–72.

Alexiadou, Artemis and Anagnostopoulou, Elena 1998. 'Parametrizing AGR: word order, verb-movement and EPP checking', *NLLT* 16:491–539.

Alfonsi, Tommaso 1932. *Il dialetto còrso nella parlata balanina*. Livorno: Giusti.

Alibèrt, Loïs 1976. *Gramatica occitana*. Montpellier: Centre d'Estudis Occitans.

Alisova, Tatiana 1967. 'Studi di sintassi italiana. II. Le posizioni dell'aggettivo nel gruppo sintattico del sostantivo', *SFI* 25:250–313.

Allen, Joseph 1941. *Portuguese Word Formation with Suffixes*. Baltimore: Linguistic Society of America.

Allen, W. Sidney 1973. *Accent and Rhythm. Prosodic Features of Latin and Greek: a Study in Theory and Reconstruction*. Cambridge: Cambridge University Press.

Almeida, Maria Elisete 2000. *La deixis en portugais et en français*. Louvain: Peeters.

Alonso, Dámaso 1962. 'Metafonía, neutro de materia y colonización suditálica en la Península Hispánica', in *Enciclopedia lingüística hispánica, vol. I*. Madrid: CSIC, pp. 105–54.

Alonso Garrote, S. 1947. *El dialecto vulgar leonés hablado en Maragatería y tierra de Astorga*. Madrid: CSIC.

ALR = Puşcariu 1938.

Alsina, Alex 1992. 'On the argument structure of causatives', *LI* 23:517–55.
1996. *The Role of Argument Structure in Grammar*. Stanford: CSLI.

Alton, J. B. and Vittur, Franz 1968. *L ladin dla val Badia. Beitrag zu einer Grammatik des Dolomitenladinischen*. Bressanone: Weger.

Alvar, Manuel 1948. *El habla del Campo de Jaca*. Salamanca: CSIC.

Alvar, Manuel, Alvar, C. and Mayoral, J. A. 1995. *Atlas lingüístico y etnográfico de Cantabria*. Madrid: Arco Libros.

Alvar, Manuel and Pottier, Bernard 1983. *Morfología histórica del español*. Madrid: Gredos.

Álvarez, Rosário, Monteagudo, Henrique and Regueira, Xosé Luís 1986. *Gramática galega*. Vigo: Galaxia.

Álvarez Álvarez, M. 1990. *Estudio de la flexión verbal en la obra de Gonzalo de Berceo (siglo XIII)*. Logroño: Instituto de estudios riojanos.

Âmbar, Manuela 1988. *Para uma sintaxe da inversão sujeito verbo em português*. University of Lisbon: doctoral thesis.

Amsterdamski, Stefan 1981. 'Spiegazione', in Romano, Ruggiero (director), *Enciclopedia Einaudi 13*. Turin: Einaudi, pp. 358–95.

Anderson, Stephen 2008. 'Phonologically conditioned allomorphy in the morphology of Surmiran (Rumantsch)', *Word Structure* 1:109–34.

André, Jacques 1971. *Emprunts et suffixes nominaux en latin*. Geneva-Paris: Droz and Minard.

Andreini, Luc 1985. *Le Verlan. Petit dictionnaire illustré*. Paris: Veyrier.

Anglade, Joseph 1921. *Grammaire de l'ancien provençal ou ancienne langue d'oc. Phonétique et morphologie*. Paris: Klincksieck.

Araujo, Frank 1975. 'Counting sheep in Basque', *Anthropological Linguistics* 17:139–45.

Arias Cabal, Álvaro 1999. *El morfema de 'neutro de materia' en asturiano*. Santiago de Compostela: Universidad de Santiago de Compostela.

Ariel, M. 1988. 'Referring and accessibility', *JL* 24:65–87.

Aristotle 1993 (2nd edn). Aristotle's *Metaphysics. Books Γ, Δ, and E*. Translated with Notes by Christopher Kirwan. Oxford: Clarendon Press.

Arnal Purroy, M. 1998. *El habla de la Baja Ribagorzana occidental*. Zaragoza: CSIC.

Arnholdt, Karl 1916. *Die Stellung des attributiven Adjektivs im Italienischen und Spanischen*. Greifswald: Von Bruncken.

Aronoff, Mark 1994. *Morphology by Itself*. Cambridge, MA: MIT Press.

Arquint, Jachen 1964. *Vierv ladin*. Tusan: Lia rumantscha.

Ascoli, Graziadio Isaia 1861. 'Studj critici', *Studj orientali e linguistici* 3:379–420.
1864. 'Lingue e nazioni', *Politecnico* 21:77–102.
1873. 'Saggi ladini', *AGI* 1:1–556.

1876. 'Sull'origine dell'unica forma flessionale del nome italiano, studio di Francesco D'Ovidio', *AGI* 2:416–38.

1882. 'Lettere glottologiche: prima lettera', *Rivista di filologia e di istruzione classica* 10:1–71.

Ashby, William 1992. 'The variable use of *on* versus *tu/ vous* for indefinite reference in spoken French', *Journal of French Language Studies* 2:135–57.

Ashdowne, Richard and Smith, John Charles 2007. 'Some semantic and pragmatic aspects of case-loss in Old French', in Salmons, Joseph and Dubenion-Smith, Sharon (eds.), *Historical Linguistics 2005*. Amsterdam-Philadelphia: Benjamins, pp. 191–205.

Aski, Janice 1995. 'Verbal suppletion: an analysis of Italian, French, and Spanish "to go"', *Linguistics* 33:403–32.

Atanasov, Petar 2002. *Meglenoromâna astăzi*. Bucharest: Editura Academiei.

Audollent, Auguste 1904. *Defixionum Tabellae*. Frankfurt: Minerva.

Austin, Peter and Bresnan, Joan 1996. 'Non-configurationality in Australian aboriginal languages', *NLLT* 14:215–68.

Avolio, Francesco 1995. *Bommèsprə. Profilo linguistico dell'Italia centro-meridionale*. San Severo: Gerni.

1996. 'Il "neutro di materia" nei dialetti centro-meridionali: fonti, dati recenti, problemi aperti', *Contributi di filologia dell'Italia mediana* 10:291–337.

Avram, Laris and Hill, Virginia 2007. 'An irrealis *BE* auxiliary in Romanian', in Aranovich, Raúl (ed.), *Split Auxiliary Systems. A Cross-linguistic Perspective*. Amsterdam: Benjamins, pp. 47–64.

Ayres-Bennett, Wendy 1996. *A History of the French Language through Texts*. London: Routledge.

2004. *Sociolinguistic Variation in Seventeenth-Century France. Methodology and Case Studies*. Cambridge: Cambridge University Press.

Ayres-Bennett, Wendy and Carruthers, Janice 2001. *Problems and Perspectives. Studies in the Modern French Language*. London: Longman.

Azaretti, Emilio 1982. *L'evoluzione dei dialetti liguri esaminata attraverso la grammatica storica del ventimigliese*. Sanremo: Casablanca.

Azevedo, Milton 2005. *Portuguese. A Linguistic Introduction*. Cambridge: Cambridge University Press.

Bachmann, Christian and Basier, Luc 1984. 'Le verlan: argot d'école ou langues des keums?', *Mots* 8:169–87.

Bachmann, Iris 2008. 'Norm and variation in Brazilian TV: the case of hidden clitics'. Paper presented at *XXXVI Romance Linguistics Seminar*, Trinity Hall, Cambridge, January, 2008.

Bader, Françoise 1962. *La formation des composés nominaux du latin*. Paris: Les Belles Lettres.

Badia i Margarit, Antonio 1950. *El habla del Valle de Bielsa (Pirineo aragonés)*. Barcelona: Instituto de Estudios Pirenaicos.

1951. *Gramática histórica catalana*. Barcelona: Noguer.

1962. *Gramática catalana*. Madrid: Gredos.

1984 (2nd edn). *Gramàtica històrica catalana*. Valencia: Climent.

1991. 'Le catalan: evolución lingüística interna I. Grámatica', *LRL* (V, 2), pp. 127–52.

1995. *Gramàtica de la llengua catalana. Descriptiva, normativa, diatòpica, diastràtica*. Barcelona: Biblioteca universitària Edicions Proa.

Baehr, Rudolf 1958. 'Zu den romanischen Wochentagsnamen', in Lausberg, Heinrich and Weinrich, Harald (eds.), *Romanica. Festschrift für Gerhard Rohlfs*. Halle: Niemeyer, pp. 26–56.

Bailly, René 1947. *Dictionnaire des synonymes de la langue française*. Paris: Larousse.

Baist, Gustav 1888. 'Die spanische Sprache', in Gröber, G. (ed.), *Grundriss der romanischen Philologie*. Strasbourg: Trübner, pp. 698–714.

Baker, Mark 1995. *The Polysynthesis Parameter*. Oxford: Oxford University Press.

Baldi, Philip 1976. 'Remarks on the Latin *R*-form Verbs', *Zeitschfrit für vergleichende Sprachforschungen* 90:222–57.

Baldinger, Kurt 1968. 'Post- und Prädeterminierung im Französische', in Baldinger, Kurt (ed.), *Festschrift Walther von Wartburg zum 80. Geburtstag*. Tübingen: Niemeyer, pp. 87–106.

1989. 'Le problème du changement de sens: nouvelles perspectives', *Alfa* 2:3–25.

1991. 'Le changement de sens: problèmes anciens et perspectives nouvelles', *Bulletin de la Classe des lettres et des sciences morales et politiques, 6e série* 2:63–102.

1993. 'Ist die unsichtbare Hand wirklich unsichtbar? Kritische Betrachtungen zum Bedeutungswandel', in Schmidt-Radefeldt, Jürgen and Harder, Andreas (eds.), *Sprachwandel und Sprachgeschichte. Festschrift für Helmut Lüdtke zum 65. Geburtstag*. Tübingen: Narr, pp. 1–8.

Banniard, Michel 1992. *VIVA VOCE. Communication écrite et communication orale du IVe au IXe siècle en Occident latin*. Paris: Institut des Etudes Augustiniennes.

Barbato, Marcello (ed.) 2001. *Il libro VIII del Plinio napoletano di Giovanni Brancati*. Naples: Liguori.

2002. 'La formazione dello spazio linguistico campano', *Bollettino Linguistico Campano* 2:29–64.

2005–6. 'Un'ipotesi sul vocalismo corso', *ID* 66–67:7–27.

2008. 'Sistemi vocalici a contatto in area italo-romanza', in Heinemann, S. and Videsott, P. (eds.), *Sprachwandel und (Dis-)Kontinuität in der Romania*. Tübingen: Niemeyer, pp. 139–52.

2009. 'Metafonia napoletana e metafonia sabina', in De Angelis, A. (ed.), *I dialetti italiani meridionali tra arcaismo e interferenza*. Atti del Convegno internazionale di Dialettologia (Messina, 4–6 giugno 2008), Palermo: Centro di Studi filologici e linguistici siciliani, pp. 275–89.

Baroni, Marco and Vanelli, Laura 2000. 'The relationship between vowel length and consonantal voicing in Friulian', in Repetti (ed.), pp. 13–44.

Bartoli, Matteo 1906. *Das Dalmatische. Altromanische Sprachreste von Veglia bis Ragusa und ihre Stellung in der Apennino-Balkanischen Romania*, 2 vols. Vienna: Hölder.

1925. *Introduzione alla neolinguistica. Principi, scopi, metodi.* Geneva: Olschki.

1929 'La norma linguistica dell'area maggiore', *Rivista di filologia e d'istruzione classica* 57:333–45.

1933. 'Le norme neolinguistiche e la loro utilità per la storia dei linguaggi e dei costumi', *Atti della Società italiana per il progresso delle scienze* 21:157–67.

1943. *Lineamenti di linguistica spaziale.* Milan: Le Lingue Estere.

Bastardas Parera, Juan 1953. *Particularidades sintácticas del latín medieval.* Barcelona: Escuela de filología.

Battaglia, Salvatore (ed.) 2003. *Grande dizionario della lingua italiana.* Turin: UTET.

Battaglia, Salvatore and Pernicone, Vincenzo 1965. *La Grammatica Italiana.* Turin: Loescher.

Battistella, Edwin 1990. *Markedness. The Evaluative Superstructure of Language.* Albany: SUNY Press.

1996. *The Logic of Markedness.* New York-Oxford: Oxford University Press.

Battisti, Carlo 1926, 'Le premesse fonetiche e la cronologia dell'evoluzione di *á* in *é* nel ladino centrale', *ID* 2:50–84.

Battisti, Carlo and Alessio, Giovanni 1950–57. *Dizionario etimologico italiano*, 5 vols. Florence: Barbera.

Battye, Adrian and Hintze, Marie-Anne 1992. *The French Language Today.* London: Routledge.

Battye, Adrian and Roberts, Ian (eds.) 1995. *Clause Structure and Language Change.* Oxford: Oxford University Press.

Bauer, Brigitte 1995. *The Emergence and Development of SVO Patterning in Latin and French.* Oxford: Oxford University Press.

2001a. 'Variability in word order: adjectives and comparatives in Latin, Romance and Germanic', *Southwest Journal of Linguistics* 20:19–50.

2001b. 'Syntactic innovation in Latin poetry? The origins of the Romance adverbial formation in -*ment(e)*', in Orbán, A. and van der Poel, M. (eds.), *Ad Literas. Latin Studies in Honour of J. H. Brouwers.* Nijmegen: Nijmegen University Press, pp. 29–43.

2003. 'The adverbial formation in *mente* in Vulgar and Late Latin: a problem in grammaticalization', in Solin, H., Leiwo, M. and Halla-aho, H. (eds.), *Latin vulgaire – latin tardif VI.* Hildesheim: Olms, pp. 439–57.

2004. 'Vigesimal numerals in Romance: an Indo-European perspective', *General Linguistics* 41:21–46.

2007. 'The definite article in Indo-European: emergence of a new category?', in Stark, E., Leiss, E. and Abraham, W. (eds.), *Nominal Determination. Typology, Context Constraints, and Historical Emergence.* Amsterdam: Benjamins, pp. 103–39.

Baurens, Maryvonne 2007. *Du 'jargon' aux 'parlers des cités'.* Macerata: EUM.

Bazzanella, Carla 1991. 'Il passivo personale con e senza cancellazione d'agente: verso un approccio multidimensionale', in Giannelli, L., Maraschio, N.,

Poggi Salani, T. and Vedovelli, M. (eds.), *Tra Rinascimento e strutture attuali. Saggi di linguistica italiana.* Turin: Rosenberg & Sellier, pp. 371–85.

Bec, Pierre 1967. *La langue occitane.* Montpellier: PUF.

1973. *Manuel pratique d'occitan moderne.* Paris: Picard.

Beck, Doreen 1973. *The Book of Bottle Collecting.* London: Hamlyn.

Bédier, Joseph 1927. *La Chanson de Roland. Commentée par Joseph Bédier.* Paris: Piazza.

Belardi, Walter 1983. 'La formazione del plurale nominale in gardenese attraverso la documentazione scritta', *Ladinia* 7:129–91.

Belletti, Adriana 1990. *Generalized Verb Movement.* Turin: Rosenberg & Sellier.

Bello, Andrés 1982. *Gramática de la lengua castellana.* Madrid: EDAF Universitaria.

Bendel, Hugo 1934. *Beiträge zur Kenntnis der Mundart von Lescun (Basses Pyrénées).* Biberach: Biberacher Verlag.

Bender, Byron, Francescato, G. and Salzmann, Z. 1952. 'Friulian phonology', *Word* 8:216–23.

Benincà, Paola 1988. 'L'ordine degli elementi della frase: costruzioni con ordine marcato degli elementi', in Renzi, Lorenzo (ed.), *Grande grammatica italiana di consultazione I.* Bologna: il Mulino, pp. 129–94.

1994. *La variazione sintattica. Studi di dialettologia romanza.* Bologna: il Mulino.

1995. 'Complement clitics in medieval Romance: the Tobler-Mussafia law', in Battye and Roberts (eds.), pp. 325–44.

1996. 'La struttura della frase esclamativa alla luce del dialetto padovano', in Benincà, Cinque, De Mauro and Vincent (eds.), pp. 23–43.

2001. 'The position of topic and focus in the left periphery', in Cinque and Salvi (eds.), pp. 39–64.

2006. 'A detailed map of the left periphery of medieval Romance', in Zanuttini, R., Campos, H., Herberger, E. and Portner, P. (eds.), *Crosslinguistic Research in Syntax and Semantics. Negation, Tense, and Clausal Architecture.* Washington: Georgetown University Press, pp. 53–86.

Benincà, Paola, Cinque, G., De Mauro, T. and Vincent, N. (eds.) 1996. *Italiano e dialetto nel tempo. Saggi di grammatica per Giulio C. Lepschy.* Rome: Bulzoni.

Benincà, Paola, Mioni, Alberto and Vanelli, Laura (eds.) 1999. *Fonologia e morfologia dell'italiano e dei dialetti d'Italia, Atti del XXXI Congresso della Società di Linguistica Italiana.* Rome: Bulzoni.

Benincà, Paola and Munaro, Nicola (eds.) In press. *Mapping the Left Periphery.* Oxford: Oxford University Press.

Benincà, Paola and Poletto, Cecilia 2004. 'Topic, focus, and V2. Defining the CP sublayers', in Rizzi, Luigi (ed.), *The Structure of CP and IP. The Cartography of Syntactic Structures, vol. 2.* Oxford: Oxford University Press, pp. 52–75.

Benincà, Paola and Vanelli, Laura 1978. 'Il plurale friulano', *RLiR* 42:241–91.

Benjamin, Walter 1997. *Sul concetto di storia.* Turin: Einaudi.

Bennett, Charles 1910–14. *Syntax of Early Latin. I–II.* Boston: Allyn and Bacon. (Reprint: Hildesheim: Olms, 1982.)

Bentley, Delia 2006. *Split Intransitivity in Italian*. Berlin: Mouton de Gruyter.

2007. 'Relazioni grammaticali e ruoli pragmatici: siciliano e italiano a confronto', in Bentley and Ledgeway (eds.), pp. 48–62.

Bentley, Delia and Eyþórsson, Þórhallur 2001. 'Alternation according to person in Italo-Romance', in Brinton, Laurel (ed.), *Historical Linguistics 1999*. Amsterdam: Benjamins, pp. 63–74.

Bentley, Delia and Ledgeway, Adam (eds.) 2007. *Sui dialetti italoromanzi. Saggi in onore di Nigel B. Vincent, The Italianist* 27, Special supplement 1. Norfolk: Biddles.

Benveniste, Émile 1956. 'La nature des pronoms', in Halle, M., Lunt, H., McLean, H. and van Schooneveld, C. (eds.), *For Roman Jakobson. Essays on the Occasion of his Sixtieth Birthday*. The Hague: Mouton, pp. 34–37 (Reprinted in Émile Benveniste, 1966, pp. 251–57).

Berlin, Brent 1992. *Ethnobiological Classification*. Princeton: Princeton University Press.

Bernat i Baltrons, Francesc 2007. *Un estudi de dialectologia catalana al segle XIX. Les notes de Manuel Milà i Fontanals sobre el maonès*. Barcelona: Abadia de Montserrat.

Berruto, Gaetano 1986. 'Le dislocazioni a destra in italiano', in Stammerjohann (ed.), pp. 55–69.

1998. 'Sulla posizione prenominale dell'aggettivo in italiano', in Bernini, G., Cuzzolin, P. and Molinelli, P. (eds.), *Ars linguistica. Studi offerti a Paolo Ramat*. Rome: Bulzoni, pp. 95–105.

Bertinetto, Pier Marco 1977. 'Syllabic blood, ovvero l'italiano come lingua ad isocronismo sillabico', *Studi di Grammatica Italiana* 6:69–96.

1981. *Strutture prosodiche dell'Italiano*. Florence: Accademia della Crusca.

1999. 'La sillabazione dei nessi /sC/ in italiano: un'eccezione alla regola generale?', in Benincà *et al.* (eds.), pp. 71–96.

2001. 'Il verbo', in Renzi, Salvi and Cardinaletti (eds.), 13–163.

Bertinetto, Pier Marco and Bertini, Chiara 2008a. 'Modelización del ritmo y estructura silábica, con aplicación al italiano', in Sánchez Miret, F. (ed.), *Romanística sin complejos. Homenaje a Carmen Pensado*. Bern: Lang, pp. 259–87.

2008b. 'On modeling the rhythm of natural languages', *Proceedings of the 4th International Conference on Speech Prosody*, Campinas, Brazil, May 2008, pp. 427–30.

Bertinetto, Pier Marco and Loporcaro, Michele (eds.) 1988. *Certamen Phonologicum. Papers from the 1987 Cortona Phonology Meeting*. Turin: Rosenberg & Sellier.

Bertinetto, Pier Marco and Vékás, Domokos 1991. 'Controllo vs. compensazione: sui due tipi di isocronia', in Magno Caldognetto, E. and Benincà, P. (eds.), *L'interfaccia tra fonologia e fonetica*. Padua: Unipress, pp.155–62.

Bertocchi, Alessandra 1989. 'The role of antecedents of Latin anaphors', in Calboli, Gualtiero (ed.), *Subordination and other Topics in Latin*. Amsterdam: Benjamins, pp. 441–61.

Bertoni, Giulio 1909. 'Per la cronologia di "ä" da "á" nell'Emilia', *ZRPh* 33:581–85.

Beyrer, Arthur, Bochmann, K. and Bronsert, S. 1987. *Grammatik der rumänischen Sprache der Gegenwart*. Leipzig: VEB.

Bichakjian, Bernard 1982. 'La genèse de la subordination de l'indo-européen au français', in Ignatius, Quirinus, Mok, Maria, Spiele, Ina and Verhuyck, Paul (eds.), *Mélanges de linguistique. De littérature et de philologie médiévales*. Leiden: Brill, pp. 5–20.

1987. 'The evolution of word order: a paedomorphic explanation', in Giacalone Ramat, A., Carruba, O. and Bernini, G. (eds.), *Papers from the 7th International Conference on Historical Linguistics*. Amsterdam: Benjamins, pp. 87–107.

Bichelli, Pirro. 1974. *Grammatica del dialetto napoletano*. Bari: Pegaso.

Billington, Michael 2005. 'I sayeth, I sayeth, I sayeth: Ken Dodd tells Michael Billington why Shakespeare was a stand-up comic at heart'. *The Guardian* (London), Culture section, 15 September 2005, p. 22.

Biondelli, Bernardino 1846. *Studi sulle lingue furbesche*. Milan: Stabilmento di Civelli.

Birdsong, David and Montreuil, Jean-Pierre (eds.) 1988. *Advances in Romance Linguistics*. Dordrecht: Foris.

Bjerrome, Gunnar 1957. *Le patois de Bagnes (Valais)*. Stockholm: Almqvist och Wiksell.

Blake, Barry 2001. *Case*. Cambridge: Cambridge University Press.

Blank, Andreas 1996. 'Der Beitrag Eugenio Coserius zur historischen Semantik: "Für eine strukturelle diachrone Semantik" – 30 Jahre danach', in Weigand, Edda and Hundsnurscher, Franz (eds.), *Lexical Structures and Language Use. Proceedings of the International Conference on Lexicology and Lexical Semantics*, 2. Tübingen: Niemeyer, pp. 341–54.

1997a. *Prinzipien des lexikalischen Bedeutungswandels am Beispiel der romanischen Sprachen*. Tübingen: Niemeyer.

1997b. 'Les adjectifs temporels du type long/court dans les langues romanes: un cas de "métaphoricité étroite". L'organisation lexicale et cognitive des dimensions spatiale et temporelle', in Dupuy-Engelhardt, Hiltraud and Montibus, Marie-Jeanne, *Actes d'EUROSEM 1996*. Rheims: Presses Universitaires de Reims, pp. 15–37.

1998. 'Topo et al. Onomasiologie, Semasiologie und Kognition am Beispiel der bezeichnungen von Maus, Ratte und Maulwurf in der Italoromania', *ZRPh* 114:505–31.

1999. 'Why do new meanings occur? A cognitive typology of the motivation for semantic change', in Blank, Andreas and Koch, Peter (eds.), *Historical Semantics and Cognition*. Berlin-New York: Mouton de Gruyter, pp. 61–89.

2001. *Einführung in die lexikalische Semantik für Romanisten*. Tübingen: Niemeyer.

2003. 'Problemgeschichte der romanischen historischen Semantik', in Ernst *et al.* (eds.), pp. 318–29.

Blank, Andreas, and Koch, Peter 1999. 'Onomasiologie et étymologie cognitive: l'exemple de la TETE', in *Actas do 1.0 Encontro internacional de lingüística cognitiva*. Porto: Facultade de Letras do Porto, pp. 49–71.

Blank, Andreas and Koch, Peter (eds.) 2003. *Kognitive romanische Onomasiologie und Semasiologie*. Tübingen: Niemeyer.

Blank, Andreas, Koch, Peter and Gévaudan, Paul 2000. 'Onomasiologie, sémasiologie et l'étymologie des langues romanes: esquisse d'un projet', in Englebert, Annick, Piessard, Michel, Rosier, Lawrence and van Raemdonck, Dan (eds.), *Actes du XXIIe Congrès international de linguistique et philologie romanes. IV*. Tübingen: Niemeyer, pp. 103–14.

Blasco Ferrer, Eduardo 1984a. *Grammatica storica del catalano e dei suoi dialetti con speciale riguardo all'algherese*. Tübingen: Narr.

1984b. *Storia linguistica della Sardegna*. Tübingen: Niemeyer.

1986. *La lingua sarda contemporanea*. Cagliari: Edizioni della Torre.

1988. 'Sardisch: Interne Sprachgeschichte I. Grammatik', in *LRL* (IV), pp. 836–53.

1994. *Ello, ellus*. Nuoro: Poliedro.

Blatt, Franz 1957. 'Latin influence on European syntax', *TCLC* 11:33–69.

Bloomfield, Leonard 1935 [1933]. *Language*. London: Allen and Unwin.

Bolelli, Tristano 1940. 'Contributo allo studio dell'elemento celtico nella fonetica romanza', *Archivum romanicum* 24:188–205.

Bolkestein, Machtelt 2001. 'Random scrambling? Constraints on discontinuity in Latin noun phrases', in Moussy, Claude (ed.), *De lingua latina novae quaestiones. Actes du Xe colloque international de linguistique latine*. Louvain-Paris: Petters, pp. 245–58.

Bollée, Annegret 1978. 'Reduplikation und Iteration in den romanischen Sprachen', *Archiv für das Studium der neueren Sprachen und Literaturen* 215:318–36.

Bolognesi, Roberto 1998. *The Phonology of Campidanian Sardinian*. Dordrecht: HIL.

Bonfadini, Giovanni 1987. 'Il dialetto della Val Cavallina e zone adiacenti', in Sanga, G. (ed.), *Lingua e dialetti di Bergamo e delle valli*, 3 vols. Bergamo: Lubrina, pp. 317–95.

Bonfante, Giuliano 1968. 'Quando si è incominciato a parlare italiano? Criterii fonologici', in Baldinger, K. (ed.), *Festschrift Walther von Wartburg zum 80. Geburtstag, vol. I*. Tübingen: Niemeyer, pp. 21–46.

1983. 'La lingua latina parlata in età imperiale', in Haase, W. (ed.), *Aufstieg und Niedergang der römischen Welt. II. Principat. 29.1*. Berlin-New York: de Gruyter, pp. 413–52.

1998. *The Origin of the Romance Languages. Stages in the Development of Latin*. Heidelberg: Winter.

Bonnet, Max 1890. *Le Latin de Grégoire de Tours*. Paris: Hachette.

Borello, Enrico 1976. 'Meccanismi semantici del lessico gergale', *LN* 37:110–15.

Borello, Enrico 1978. 'Aspetti semantici del gergo', *Studi italiani di linguistica teorica e applicata* 7:383–407.

Borer, Hagit 1984. *Parametric Syntax. Case Studies in Semitic and Romance Languages*. Dordrecht: Foris.

Born, Joachim 1992. 'Leonesisch' in *LRL* (VI, 1), pp. 693–700.

Bortolini, Umberto, Tagliavini, C. and Zampolli, A. 1972. *Lessico di frequenza della lingua italiana contemporanea*. Milan: Garzanti.

Bosque, Ignacio and Demonte, Violeta (eds.) 1999. *Gramática descriptiva de la lengua española, I–III*. Madrid: Espasa.

Bossong, Georg 1991. 'Differential object marking in Romance and beyond', in Wanner and Kibbee (eds.), pp. 143–71.

Bourciez, Édouard 1937 (8th edn). *Précis de phonétique française*. Paris: Klincksieck.

   1956 (4th edn). *Eléments de linguistique romane*. Paris: Klincksieck.

   1967 (5th edn). *Eléments de linguistique romane*. Paris: Klincksieck.

Boyer, Henri 1997. 'Le statut de la suffixation en *-os*', *Langue française* 114:35–40.

Braudel, Fernand 1967–68. Introduction au *Traité de sociologie*. Paris: PUF.

   1969. 'Histoire et sociologie', in *Écrits sur l'histoire 1*. Paris: Flammarion, pp. 97–122.

Brekke, K. 1884. *Étude sur la flexion dans le voyage de S. Brandan*. Paris:Vieweg.

Brero, Camillo 1971. *Gramàtica piemontèisa*. Turin: Ij Brandé.

Bresnan, Joan 2001. *Lexical-Functional Syntax*. Oxford: Blackwell.

Brown, Gillian and Yule, George 1984. *Discourse Analysis*. Cambridge: Cambridge University Press.

Brown, R. and Gilman, A. 1960. 'The pronouns of power and solidarity', in Sebeok, Thomas (ed.), *Style in Language*. Cambridge, MA: MIT Press, pp. 253–76.

Brüch, Josef 1921. 'Zur Entwicklung der betonten Vokale im Volkslatein', *ZRPh* 41:574–82.

Brugmann, Karl 1890. 'Die Bildung der Zehner und der Hunderter in den indogermanischen Sprachen', *Morphologische Untersuchungen auf dem Gebiete der indogermanischen Sprachen* 5:1–61.

   1892. *Grundriß der vergleichenden Grammatik der indogermanishcen Sprachen* 2.2. Strasbourg: Trübner.

Brunel, Clovis 1926. *Les plus anciennes chartes en langue provençale. Recueil des pièces originales antérieures au XIIIe siècle, publiées, avec une étude morphologique*. Paris: Picard.

Brunet, Jacqueline 1994. *Grammaire critique de l'italien, vol. 12: Un si ou deux*. Saint-Denis: Presses universitaires de Vincennes.

Bruni, Francesco 1984. *L'italiano. Elementi di storia della lingua e della cultura*. Turin: UTET.

Brunot, Ferdinand 1905. *Histoire de la langue française des origines à 1900. Tome I: De l'époque latine à la Renaissance*. Paris: Colin.

   1906. *Histoire de la langue française des origines à 1900. Tome II: Le seizième siècle*. Paris: Colin.

1922. *Histoire de la langue française. 2.* Paris: Colin.

1966–79. *Histoire de la langue française des origines à nos jours.* Paris: Colin.

Buchholtz, H. 1889. 'Lockere und straffe italienische Perfektformen', *Archiv für das Studium neuren Sprachen* 82:133–66.

Bühler, Karl 1934. *Sprachtheorie. Die Darstellungsfunktion der Sprache.* Jena: Fischer.

Bullock, Barbara 1995a. 'Prosodic constraints and morphological alignment in French', *Lingua* 96:95–117.

1995b. 'The uneven trochee in French', *Rivista di linguistica* 7:273–92.

1996. 'Popular derivation and linguistic inquiry: les javanais', *The French Review* 70:180–91.

2001. 'Double prosody and stress shift in Proto-Romance', *Probus* 13:173–92.

Burckhardt, Jacob 1990 [1860]. *The Civilization of the Renaissance in Italy.* Translated by S. G. C. Middlemore; with a new Introduction by Peter Burke and Notes by Peter Murray. Harmondsworth: Penguin.

Burger, André 1928. 'Etudes de phonétique et de morphologie latines', *Recueil de travaux publiés par la Faculté des Lettres*, Université de Neuchâtel, 13.

Buridant, Claude 2001. *Grammaire nouvelle de l'ancien français.* Paris: SEDES.

Burke, Peter 1987. 'The uses of literacy in early modern Italy', in Burke, Peter and Porter, Roy (eds.), *The Social History of Language.* Cambridge: Cambridge University Press, pp. 21–42.

Burzio, Luigi 1986. *Italian Syntax.* Dordrecht: Reidel.

1994. *Principles of English Stress.* Cambridge: Cambridge University Press.

2004. 'Paradigmatic and syntagmatic relations in Italian verbal inflection', in Auger, J., Clancy Clements, J. and Vance, B. (eds.), *Contemporary Approaches to Romance Linguistics.* Amsterdam: Benjamins, pp. 17–44.

Bustin-Lekeu, Francine 1973. 'Tutoiement et vouvoiement chez les lycéens français', *The French Review* 46:773–82.

Bustos Gisbert, Eugenio 1992. 'La alternancia «OVE»/«PUDE» en castellano medieval y clásico', in Bartol Hernández, José Antonio, García Santos, Juan Felipe, De Santiago Guervós, Javier (eds.), *Estudios filológicos en homenaje a Eugenio de Bustos Tovar.* Salamanca: Universidad de Salamanca, I, pp. 137–65.

Butt, John and Benjamin, Carmen 1994 (2nd edn) / 2000 (3rd edn). *A New Reference Grammar of Modern Spanish.* London: Arnold.

Bybee, Joan 1985. *Morphology. The Relation between Form and Meaning.* Benjamins: Amsterdam.

2001. *Phonology and Language Use.* Cambridge: Cambridge University Press.

Bybee, Joan and Brewer, Mary 1980. 'Explanation in morphophonemics: changes in Provençal and Spanish preterite forms', *Lingua* 52:201–42.

Bybee, Joan and Pardo, E. 1981. 'On lexical and morphological conditioning of alternations: a nonce-probe experiment with Spanish verbs', *Linguistics* 19:937–68.

Byck, Jack and Graur, Alexander 1967. 'Influența pluralului asupra singularului substantivelor și adjectivelor în limba română', in Dimitrescu, F. (ed.) *Jack Byck, Studii și articole*. Bucharest: Editura științifică 1967, pp. 49–92.

Caduff, Léonard 1952. *Essai sur la phonétique du parler rhétoroman de la Vallée de Tavetsch (Canton des Grisons – Suisse)*. Bern: Francke.

Calabrese, Andrea 1993. 'The sentential complementation of Salentino: a study of a language without infinitival clauses', in Belletti, Adriana (ed.), *Syntactic Theory and the Dialects of Italy*. Turin: Rosenberg & Sellier, pp. 28–98.

Calboli, Gualtiero (ed.) 1989. *Subordination and Other Topics in Latin. Proceedings of the Third Colloquium on Latin Linguistics*, Bologna, April 1985. Amsterdam: Benjamins.

Callebat, Louis, Bouet, P., Fleury, P. and Zuinghedau, M. (eds.) 1984. *Vitruve. De Architectura. Concordance*. Hildesheim-Zurich-New York: Olms-Wedmann.

Calvaruso, Giuseppe 1929. *'U baccàgghiu*. Catania: Libreria Tirelli di F. Gautolini.

Calvet, Louis-Jean 1993. 'Le verlan en kit', *Le Français dans le monde* 256:42.

Cameron-Faulkner, Thea and Carstairs-McCarthy, Andrew 2000. 'Stem alternants as morphological signifiés: evidence from blur avoidance in Polish nouns', *NLLT* 18:813–35.

Camilli, Amerindo 1929. 'Il dialetto di Servigliano', *Archivum Romanicum* 13:220–71.
1946. 'Articoli, pronomi, preposizioni articolate', *LN* 6:89f.

Campanile, Enrico 1971. 'Due studi sul latino volgare', *ID* 34:1–64.
1973. 'Sulla quantità della vocale che precede *-m* in latino', *ID* 36:1–6.

Campos, Héctor and Zampini, Mary 1990. 'Focalization strategies in Spanish', *Probus* 2:47–64.

Campos, Odette and Rodrigues, Ângela 1992. 'Flexão nominal: indicação de pluralidade no sintagma nominal', in Ilari, Rodolfo (ed.), *Gramática do português falado, vol. 2: Níveis de análise lingüística*. Campinas: Editora da Unicamp, pp. 111–34.

Canaes, Maria de Piedade and de Pádua, Mariz 1960. *A ordem das palavras no português arcaico (frases de verbo transitivo)*. Coimbra: Faculdade de Letras da Universidade de Coimbra, Instituto de Estudos Românicos.

Canale, Michael, Mougeon, Raymond and Belanger, Monique 1978. 'Analogical levelling of the auxiliary *être* in French', in Suñer, Margarita (ed.), *Studies in Romance Linguistics*. Washington DC: Georgetown University Press, pp. 41–61.

Cano González, Ana María 1981. *El habla de Somiedo (Occidente de Asturias)*. Santiago de Compostela: Universidad de Santiago de Compostela.
1992. 'Asturiano. Evolución lingüística interna', *LRL* (VI, 1), pp. 652–80.

Capidan, Teofil 1925. *Meglenoromânii. I. Istoria și graiul lor*. Bucharest: Cultura națională.
1932. *Aromânii. Dialectul aromân. Studiu lingvistic*. Bucharest: Academia Română.

Capozzoli, Raffaele 1889. *Grammatica del dialetto napoletano*. Naples: Chiurazzi.

Caracausi, Girolamo 1986. *Lingue in contatto nell'estremo Mezzogiorno d'Italia. Influssi e conflitti fonetici*. Palermo: CSFLS.

Caradec, François 1988. *N'ayons pas peur des mots. Dictionnaire du français argotique et populaire*. Paris: Larousse.

Cardinaletti, Anna 1997. 'Subjects and clause structure', in Haegeman, Liliane (ed.), *The New Comparative Syntax*. London: Longman, pp. 33–63.

2004. 'Toward a cartography of subject positions', in Rizzi, Luigi (ed.), *The Structure of CP and IP. The Cartography of Syntactic Structures, vol. 2*. Oxford: Oxford University Press, pp. 115–65.

Cardona, Giorgio 1988. *I sei lati del mondo. Linguaggio ed esperienze*. Bari: La Terza.

Carosella, Maria 2005. *Sistemi vocalici tonici nell'area garganica settentrionale fra tensioni diatopiche e dinamiche variazionali*. Rome: Edizioni Nuova Cultura.

Carstairs-McCarthy, Andrew 1994. 'Inflection classes, gender, and the principle of contrast', *Language* 70:737–88.

Casella, Mario 1922. 'Studi sui dialetti della Valdarda. Fonologia del dialetto di Fiorenzuola'. *Studj romanzi* 17:5–71.

Castellani, Arrigo 1952. *Nuovi testi fiorentini del Dugento*. Florence: Sansoni.

1961. 'Sulla formazione del tipo fonetico italiano: fenomeni vocalici', *SLI* 2:24–45 [also in Castellani, 1980, I:73–95].

1962. 'Quelques remarques à propos de la diphtongaison toscane: réponse à M. Schürr', *ZRPh* 78:494–502 [also in Castellani, 1980, I:139–45].

1965. 'Sulla formazione del tipo fonetico italiano. Fenomeni consonantici. I. Raddoppiamento delle consonanti diverse da «r», «s» davanti a «i̯»', *SLI* 5:88–96 [also in Castellani, 1980, I:95–103].

1970a. 'Dittongamento senese e dittongamento aretino nei dialetti dell'Italia mediana (in epoca antica)', in *I dialetti dell'Italia mediana con particolare riguardo alla regione umbra. Atti del V Convegno di studi umbri, Gubbio, 28 maggio – 1 giugno 1967*. Gubbio: Centro di Studi Umbri presso la Casa di Sant'Ubaldo-Perugia. di Lettere e filosofia, 311–380 [also in Castellani, 1980, I:358–422].

1970b. 'Note sul dittongamento toscano', in *Mille I dibattiti del Circolo linguistico fiorentino*. Florence: Olschki, pp. 41–53 [also in Castellani, 1980, I:146–155].

1970c. 'Ancora sul dittongamento italiano e romanzo: seconda risposta a Friedrich Schürr', *CN* 30:117–130 [reprinted in Castellani, 1980, I:156–176].

1972. 'Frammenti d'un libro di conti castellano del Dugento', *Studi di filologia italiana* 30:5–58 [also in Castellani, 1980, II:455–513].

1976. *I più antichi testi italiani* (2nd edn). Bologna: Patron.

1980. *Saggi di linguistica e filologia italiana e romanza 1946–1976*. Rome: Salerno.

1985. *Capitoli d'un'introduzione alla grammatica storica italiana. II: L'elemento germanico. SLI* 11:1–26;151–81 [also in Castellani, 2000:29–94].

1991. *Sulla scomparsa dell'opposizione di quantità vocalica in latino volgare*, in Kremer, Dieter (ed.), *Actes du XVIIIe Congrès international de linguistique et philologie romanes, Université de Trèves (Trier) 1986, Tome III, Section V. Grammaire diachronique et histoire de la langue.* Tübingen: Niemeyer, pp. 10–21.

2000. *Grammatica storica della lingua italiana. I. Introduzione.* Bologna: il Mulino.

Catalán, Diego 1989. *El español. Orígenes de su diversidad.* Madrid: Paraninfo.

CDE = Mark Davies *Corpus del Español.* www.corpusdelespanol.org/.

Cennamo, Michela 1999. 'Late Latin pleonastic reflexives and the unaccusative hypothesis', *TPS* 97:103–50.

2001. 'L'*extended accusative* e le nozioni di voce e relazione grammaticale nel latino tardo e medievale', in Viparelli, Valeria (ed.), *Ricerche linguistiche tra antico e moderno.* Naples: Liguori, pp. 3–27.

Chacón Berruga, T. 1981. *El habla de la Rocha de la Mancha.* Albacete: Instituto de estudios albtecenses.

Chamberlain, Bobby 1981. 'Lexical similarities of lunfardo and gíria', *Hispania* 64:417–25.

Chambers, Jack and Trudgill, Peter 1998 (2nd edn). *Dialectology.* Cambridge: Cambridge University Press.

Chambon, Jean-Pierre 2003. 'La déclinaison en ancien occitan, ou: comment s'en débarrasser? Une réanalyse descriptive non orthodoxe de la flexion substantivale', *RLiR* 67:343–63.

Chaurand, Jacques 1977. *Introduction à l'histoire du vocabulaire français.* Paris: Bordas.

Chéreau, Olivier 1628. *Le Jargon de l'argot réformé comme il est à present en usage parmy les bons pauvres.* Paris: Veuve du Carroy.

Cherubini, Francesco 1839–43. *Vocabolario milanese-italiano.* Milan: Regia Stamperia.

Chitoran, Ioana 2002. *The Phonology of Romanian. A Constraint-Based Approach.* Berlin-New York: Mouton de Gruyter.

Chomsky, Noam 1986. *Barriers.* Cambridge, MA-London: MIT Press.

1995. 'Bare phrase structure', in Webelhuth, Gert (ed.), *Government and Binding Theory and the Minimalist Program.* Oxford: Blackwell, pp. 383–439.

Cifuentes, José Luis 1989. *Lengua y espacio. Introducción al problema de la deixis en español.* Alicante: Universidad de Alicante.

CIL = *Corpus Inscriptionum Latinarum*

Cinque, Guglielmo 1971. *La deissi nella lingua italiana.* Padua: Unipress.

1976. 'Appropriateness conditions for the use of passives and impersonals in Italian', *Italian Linguistics* 1:11–31.

1995. *Italian Syntax and Universal Grammar.* Cambridge: Cambridge University Press.

1999. *Adverbs and Functional Heads. A Cross-Linguistic Perspective*. Oxford: Oxford University Press.

2001. 'La frase relativa', in Renzi, Salvi and Cardinaletti (eds.), vol. I, pp. 457–517.

Cinque, Gugliemo and Kayne, Richard (eds.) 2005. *The Oxford Handbook of Comparative Syntax*. Oxford-New York: Oxford University Press.

Cinque, Guglielmo and Salvi, Giampaolo (eds.) 2001. *Current Studies in Italian Syntax. Essays Offered to Lorenzo Renzi*. Amsterdam: Elsevier.

Ciorănescu, Alexandru 2002. *Dicționarul etimologic al limbii române*. Bucharest: Editura Saeculum I. O.

Claudel, Chantal 2002. 'De l'utilisation du système d'adresse dans l'interview de presse écrite française'. Paper given at conference *Pronoms de 2e personne et formes d'adresse dans les langues d'Europe*, Institut Cervantes, Paris, March 2002. Downloadable from: http://cvc.cervantes.es/obref/coloquio_paris/ponencias/pdf/cvc_claudel.pdf

CN = *Cultura neolatina*

Coco, Francesco 1970. *Il dialetto di Bologna*. Bologna: Forni.

Coleman, Robert 1971. 'The origin and development of Latin *habeo* + infinitive', *Classical Quarterly* 21:215–32.

Coleman, Robert (ed.) 1991a. *New Studies in Latin Linguistics*. Amsterdam: Benjamins.

Coleman, Robert 1991b. 'Latin prepositional syntax in Indo-European perspective', in Coleman (ed.), pp. 323–38.

1992. 'Italic', in Gvozdanović, Jadranka (ed.), *Indo-European Numerals*. Berlin: Mouton de Gruyter, pp. 389–445.

Como, Paola 2002. 'Affinità grammaticale e variazione in alcune categorie lessicali del dialetto di Monte di Procida', *Bollettino linguistico campano* 1:169–96.

2007. *La variabilità del dialetto. Uno studio su Monte di Procida*. Naples: Liguori.

Comrie, Bernard 1977. 'In defense of spontaneous demotion: the impersonal passive', in Cole, P. and Saddock, J. M. (eds.), *Syntax and Semantics 8. Grammatical Relations*. New York: Academic Press, pp. 47–58.

1981. *Language Universals and Linguistic Typology. Syntax and Morphology*. Oxford: Blackwell.

1989 (2nd edn). *Language Universals and Linguistic Typology*. Oxford: Blackwell.

Conde Saiz, María Victoria 1978. *El habla de Sobrescobio*. Mieres del Camino: Instituto «Bernal de Quirós».

Contini, Gianfranco 1935. 'Per il trattamento delle vocali d'uscita in antico lombardo', *ID* 11:33–60.

Contini, Michel 1987. *Etude de géographie phonétique et de phonétique instrumentale du sarde*. Alessandria: Edizioni dell'Orso.

Contreras, Heles 1976. *A Theory of Word Order with Special Reference to Spanish*. Amsterdam-New York: North-Holland-Elsevier.

1991. 'On the position of subjects', in Rothstein, Susan (ed.), *Perspectives on Phrase Structure. Heads and Licensing.* San Diego: Academic Press, pp.63–79.

Corbett, Greville 1991. *Gender.* Cambridge: Cambridge University Press.

2000. *Number.* Cambridge: Cambridge University Press.

Corblin, Francesco 1987. 'CECI et CELA comme formes à contenu indistinct', *Langue française* 75:75–93.

Corda, F. 1983. *Saggio di grammatica gallurese.* Cagliari: Edizioni 3T.

Cornilescu, Alexandra 1992. 'Remarks on the determiner system of Romanian: the demonstratives *al* and *cel*', *Probus* 4:189–260.

2000. 'The double subject construction in Romanian', in Motapanyane (ed.), pp. 83–133.

Corominas, Juan 1954–57. *Diccionario crítico etimológico de la lengua castellana.* Madrid: Gredos.

Corominas, Juan and Pascual, José Antonio 1980–91. *Diccionario crítico etimológico castellano e hispánico.* Madrid: Gredos.

Coromines, Joan 1997. *Lleures i converses d'un filòleg.* Barcelona: Club.

Corpus Inscriptionum Latinarum, 17 vols. 1868–. Berlin: Wiedmann-De Gruyter.

Corriente, Federico 1997. *Poesía dialectal árabe y romance en Alandalús.* Madrid: Gredos.

Cortelazzo, Manlio 1976. *Avviamento critico allo studio della dialettologia Italiana, vol. 1: Problemi e metodi.* Pisa: Pacini.

Coseriu, Eugenio 1954. *El llamado 'latín vulgar' y las primeras diferenciaciones romances.* Montevideo: Universidad de la República.

1964. 'Pour une sémantique diachronique structurale', *Travaux de linguistique et de littérature* 2:139–86.

1968. 'Sincronía, diacronía y tipología'. *Actas del XI Congreso internacional de lingüística y filología románicas.* I. Madrid: CSIC, pp. 269–83.

1973. *Sincronía, diacronía e historia.* Madrid: Gredos.

1981. *Sincronia, diacronia e storia. Il problema del cambio linguistico.* Turin: Boringhieri.

1988. 'Linguistic change does not exist', in Albrecht, Jörn, Lüdtke, Jens and Thun, Harald (eds.), *Energeia und Ergon.* Sprachliche Variation – Sprachgeschichte – sprachliche Typologie: Studia in Honorem Eugenio Coseriu, pp. 147–57.

Costa, João 2000. 'Word order and discourse-configurationality in European Portuguese', in Costa, João (ed.), *Portuguese Syntax.* Oxford: Oxford University Press, pp. 94–115.

Costa, R. 1975. 'A functional solution for illogical reflexives in Italian', in Grossmand, R. E., San, J. and Vance, T. (eds.), *Papers from the Parasession on Functionalism.* Chicago: Chicago Linguistic Sociey, pp. 112–25.

Couceiro, José Luis 1976. *El habla de Feás.* Santiago de Compostela: Universidad de Santiago de Compostela.

Cours = Ferdinand de Saussure, *Cours de linguistique générale*, publié par Charles Bally et Alfred Sechehaye, avec la collaboration de Albert Riedlinger. Paris: Payot, 1916. Quotations from the English translation (1960) by Wade Baskin, *Course in General Linguistics*. London: Owen.

Coveney, Aidan 2003. 'Anything *you* can do *tu* can do better': *tu* and *vous* as substitutes for indefinite *on* in French', *Journal of Sociolinguistics* 7:164–91.

Crabb, Daniel 1969. *Comparative Study of Word Order in Old Spanish and Old French Prose Works*. New York: AMS Press.

Craddock, Jerry. 1983. 'Descending diphthongs and the regular preterite in Hispano-Romance', *Bulletin of Hispanic Studies* 60:1–14.

Cravens, Thomas 1988. 'Consonant Strength in the Romance Dialects of the Pyrenees', in Birdsong, D. and Montreuil, J.-P. (eds.), *Advances in Romance Linguistics*. Dordrecht: Foris, pp. 371–409.

1991. 'Phonology, phonetics and orthography in Late Latin and Romance: the evidence for early intervocalic sonorization', in Wright, R. (ed.), *Latin and the Romance Languages in the Early Middle Ages*. London-New York: Routledge, pp. 52–69.

2002. *Comparative Historical Dialectology. Italo-Romance Clues to Ibero-Romance Sound Change*. Amsterdam-Philadelphia: Benjamins.

Cremona, Joseph 1970. 'L'axe nord-sud de la Romania et la position du toscan', in Rosetti, Alexandru (ed.), *Actele celui de-al XII-lea Congres internaţional de lingvistică şi filologie romanică*. Bucharest: Editura Academiei, pp. 155–59.

Crevatin, Franco 1992. 'Intorno al vocalismo "protoromanzo"', in *Etymologie und Wortgeschichte des Italienischen. LEI. Genesi e dimensioni di un vocabolario etimologico*. Wiesbaden: Ludwig Reichert, pp. 26–31.

Croft, William 1990. *Typology and Universals*. Cambridge: Cambridge University Press.

Croft, William, Bat-Zeev Shyldkrot, Hava and Kemmer, Suzanne 1987. 'Diachronic semantic processes in the middle voice', in Giacalone Ramat, A., Carruba, O. and Bernini, G. (eds.), *Papers from the 7th International Conference on Historical Linguistics*. Amsterdam-Philadelphia: Benjamins, pp. 179–91.

Crupi, Giovanni 1981. *La glossa di Bova. Cento favole esopiche in greco calabro: schema grammaticale, lessico*. Roccella Ionica: Associazione Culturale Jonica.

Cruschina, Silvio 2006. 'Informational focus in Sicilian and the left periphery', in Frascarelli, Mara (ed.), *Phases of Interpretation*. Berlin: Mouton, pp. 363–85.

Cunha, Celso 1981 (9th edn). *Gramática do português contemporâneo. De acordo com a Nomenclatura gramatical brasileira*. Rio de Janeiro: Padrão.

Cuzzolin, Pierluigi 1994. *Sull'origine della costruzione* dicere quod. *Aspetti sintattici e semantici*. Florence: La Nuova Italia.

1995. 'A proposito di *sub vos placo* e della grammaticalizzazione delle adposizioni', *AGI* 80:122–43.

D'Alessandro, Roberta and Roberts, Ian 2005. 'Split ergativity in Abruzzese and the null-subject parameter'. Paper presented at *Going Romance 2005*, Utrecht, the Netherlands, 8–10 December 2005.

2008. 'Movement and agreement in Italian past participles and defective phases', *LI* 39:477–91.

(to appear). 'Past participle agreement in Abruzzese: split auxiliary selection and the null-subject parameter', *Natural Language and Linguistic Theory*.

D'Hulst, Yves, Coene, Martine and Tasmowski, Liliane 2000. 'Last resort strategies in DP: article reduplication in Romanian and French', in Motapanyane (ed.), pp. 135–75.

D'Imperio, Mariapaola 2000. 'Acoustic-perceptual correlates of sentence prominence in Italian', *Ohio State University Working Papers in Linguistics* 54:59–77.

D'Imperio, Mariapaola and Rosenthall, S. 1999. 'Phonetics and phonology of main stress in Italian', *Phonology* 16:29–64.

D'Introno, Francesco 1989. 'Empty and full pronouns in Spanish', *Hispanic Linguistics* 3:38–46.

2001. *Sintaxis generativa del español. evolución y análisis*. Madrid: Cátedra.

D'Ovidio, Francesco 1873. 'Sull'origine dell'unica forma flessionale del nome italiano', *Annali della reale Scuola Normale Superiore di Pisa. Filosofia e Filologia 1* 2:153–209.

1886. 'Ricerche sui pronomi personali e possessivi neolatini', *AGI* 9:25–101.

1905. 'Ricerche sui personali e possessivi neolatini', *AGI* 9:25–101.

Dahmen, Wolfgang 1989. 'Rumänisch: Arealinguistik III. Meglenorumänisch', *LRL* (III), pp. 436–47.

Dalbera, Jean-Philippe 1994. *Les parlers des Alpes-Maritimes: etude comparative, essai de reconstruction*. London: Association internationale d'études occitanes.

Dalbera, Jean-Philippe and Dalbera-Stefanaggi, Marie-José 1998. 'De la genèse des vocalismes corses', in Ruffino, G. (ed.), *Atti del XXI Congresso di Linguistica e Filologia Romanza, 1995, V. Dialettologia, geolinguistica, sociolinguistica*. Tübingen: Max Niemeyer, pp. 217–29 [also in Dalbera-Stefanaggi, 2001:149–62].

Dalbera-Stefanaggi, Marie-José 1990. 'L'évaluation de l'affinité en situation dialectale', *Travaux du Cercle Linguistique de Nice* 12:51–65 [also in Dalbera-Stefanaggi, 2001:139–48].

1991. *Unité et diversité des parlers corses. Le plan phonologique. Parenté génétique et affinité*. Alessandria: Edizioni dell'Orso.

1995a. 'La partition dialectale de la Corse: des données renouvelées', *Revue de linguistique romane* 59:141–58 [also in Dalbera-Stefanaggi, 2001:107–19].

1995b. 'Morsiglia et les parlers du Cap Corse: une strate dans l'espace insulaire?', *Travaux du Cercle Linguistique de Nice* 17:89–108 [also in Dalbera-Stefanaggi, 2001:121–38].

1995c. *Nouvel Atlas linguistique et ethnographique de la Corse*. Paris: CNRS.

2001. *Essais de linguistique corse*. Ajaccio: Editions Alain Piazzola.

Damonte, Federico 2005. 'La diffusione della particella "mi" in alcune varietà messinesi: problemi di metodo', in Marcato, Gianna (ed.), *Dialetti in città. Atti del convegno, Sappada/Plodn (Belluno)*. Padua: Unipress, pp. 237–42.

In press. '*Mood concord between CP and IP in Salentino and southern Calabrian subjunctive complements*', in Benincà and Munaro (eds.).

Daniliuc, Laura and Daniliuc, Radu 2000. *Descriptive Romanian Grammar*. Munich: Lincom Europa.

Dardano, Maurizio 1978. *La formazione delle parole nell'italiano di oggi*. Rome: Bulzoni.

Dardel, Robert de 1964. 'Considérations sur la déclinaison romane à trois cas', *Cahiers Ferdinand de Saussure* 21:7–23.

Dardel, Robert de and Wüest, Jacob 1993. 'Les systèmes casuels du protoroman. Les deux cycles de simplification', *VR* 52:25–65.

Dardel, Robert de and Zamboni, Alberto 1999. 'L'interfixe -i- dans les composés protoromans: une hypothèse de travail', *RLiR* 63:439–69.

Darmesteter, Arsène 1886. *La Vie des mots étudiée dans leurs significations*. Paris: Delgrave.

1967 [1875]. *Traité de la formation des mots composés dans la langue française comparée aux autres langues romanes et au latin*. Paris: Champion.

Dauzat, Albert 1900. *Morphologie du patois de Vinzelles*. Paris: Bouillon.

1912. *La Défense de la langue française. La Crise de la culture française. L'Argot. La Politesse du langage. La Langue internationale*. Paris: Colin.

[1917]1976. *Les argots de métiers Franco-Provençaux*. Paris: Slatkine.

Dauzat, Albert, Dubois, Jean and Mitterand, Henri 1971 (3rd edn). *Nouveau Dictionnaire Etymologique et Historique*. Paris: Larousse.

Davis, Stuart 1990. 'Italian onset structure and the distribution of *il* and *lo*', *Linguistics* 28:43–55.

Davis, Stuart and Napoli, Donna Jo 1994. *A Prosodic Template in Historical Change. The Passage of the Latin Second Conjugation into Romance*. Turin: Rosenberg & Sellier.

De Blasi, Nicola 1986. *Libro de la destructione de Troya. Volgarizzamento napoletano trecentesco da Guido delle Colonne*. Rome: Bonacci.

2006. *Profilo linguistico della Campania*. Bari: Laterza.

De Blasi, Nicola and Imperatore, Luigi 2002. *Il napoletano parlato e scritto. Con note di grammatica storica*. Nuova edizione. Naples: Libreria Dante e Descartes.

De Bruyne, Jacques 1995. *A Comprehensive Spanish Grammar*. Adapted and with Additional Material by Christopher J. Pountain. Oxford: Blackwell.

De Garis, Marie 1985. *Guernesiais. A Grammatical Survey*. Guernsey: La Société Guernesiaise.

De Gregorio, Iolanda 1939. 'Contributo alla conoscenza del dialetto di Bisceglie (Bari)', *ID* 15:31–52.

De Kok, Ans 1985. *La Place du pronom personnel régime conjoint en français. Une étude diachronique*. Amsterdam: Rodopi.

De Lima Coutinho, Ismael 1958. *Pontos de gramática histórica*. Rio de Janeiro: Académica.

De Mauro, Tullio, Mancini, Federico, Vedovelli, Federico and Voghera, Miriam 1993. *Lessico di frequenza dell'italiano parlato*. Milan: Etaslibri.

De Poerck, Guy and Mourin, Louis 1961. *Introduction à la morphologie comparée des langues romanes basée sur des traductions anciennes des actes des Apôtres ch. XX à XXIV. Tome I: Ancien portugais et ancien castillan*. Bruges: De Tempel.

Decurtins, Alexi. 1958. *Zur Morphologie der unregelmässigen Verben im Bündnerromanischen*. Bern: Francke.

Dedeck-Héry, V. L. 1952. 'Boethius' *De Consolatione* by Jean de Meun', *Medieval Studies* 14:165–275.

Dees, Anthonij 1980. *Atlas de formes linguistiques des textes littéraires de l'ancien français*. Tübingen: Niemeyer.

DEI = Battisti, Alessio and De Felice.

Delatte, Louis, Évrard, É., Govaerts, S. and Denooz, J. 1981. *Dictionnaire fréquentiel et index inverse de la langue latine*. Liège: L.A.S.L.A.

Delbrück, Berthold 1900. *Vergleichende Syntax der indogermanischen Sprachen. 3.* Strasbourg: Trübner.

Demonte, Violeta 1995. 'Dative alternation in Spanish', *Probus* 7:5–30.

Denison, David 1998. 'Syntax', in Romaine, S. (ed.), *The Cambridge History of the English Language, vol. IV: 1776–1997*. Cambridge: Cambridge University Press, pp. 92–329.

Densusianu, Ovid 1938. *Histoire de la langue roumaine. Tome II: Le seizième siècle*. Paris: Leroux.

   1961. *Istoria Limbii române. 1. Originile 2. Secolul al XVI-lea*. Bucharest: Editura Ştiinţifică.

Désirat, Claude and Hordé, Tristan 1967. *La Langue française au 20ème siècle*. Paris: Bordas.

Devine, A. M. and Stephens, Laurence 2006. *Latin Word Order. Structured meaning and information*. Oxford: Oxford University Press.

Devoto, Giacomo 1957. 'Le sopravvivenze linguistiche latine nel mondo moderno', *TCLC* 11:75–88.

Di Giovine, Paolo 2003. 'Sostrati, adstrati e superstrati e i loro effetti sulle lingue romanze: Italoromania e Alpi orientali', in Ernst *et al.*, pp. 578–93.

Diaconescu, Paula 1970. 'Acuzativul cu *pre* în textele traduse din secolul al XVI-lea', in Diaconescu, Paula (ed.), *Structură și evoluție în morfologia substantivului românesc*. Bucharest: Editura Academiei, pp. 259–63.

Dias, Augusto Epiphanio da Silva 1918. *Syntaxe histórica portuguesa*. Lisbon: Livraria Clássica.

Díaz González, O. 1979. *El habla de Candamo*. Oviedo: Universidad de Oviedo.

Diehl, Ernestus (ed.) 1925–31. *Inscriptiones Latinae Christianae Veteres*, 3 vols. Berlin: Weidmann.

Diez, Friedrich 1838. *Grammatik der romanischen Sprachen. 2.* Bonn: Weber.

Dijk, Teun Adrianus van 1977. *Text and Context. Explorations in the Semantics and Pragmatics of Discourse*. London-New York: Longman.

1979. 'Pragmatic connectives', *Journal of Pragmatics* 3:447–86.

Dixon, Robert 1980. *The Languages of Australia*. Cambridge: Cambridge University Press.

1994. *Ergativity*. Cambridge: Cambridge University Press.

Dobrovie-Sorin, Carmen 1987. *Syntaxe du roumain: chaînes thématiques*. Université de Paris 7: unpublished thesis.

1994. *The Syntax of Romanian*. Berlin: Mouton.

Donnellan, Keith 1966. 'Reference and definite description', *The Philosophical Review* 75:281–304.

Donohue, Mark and Smith, John Charles 1998. 'What's happened to us? Some developments in the Malay pronoun system', *Oceanic Linguistics* 37:65–84.

Doria, Mario 1989. 'Dalmatico: storia linguistica interna', *LRL* (III), pp. 522–30.

Douglas, Mary 1966. *Purity and Danger. An Analysis of Concepts of Pollution and Taboo*. London-Henley: Routledge and Kegan Paul.

Dresser, Norine 1996. 'An acorn for stormy weather', *Los Angeles Times*, 10 August, Metro, Part B, p. 7.

Dressler, Wolfgang 1980. 'A semiotic model of diachronic process phonology', in Lehmann, W. and Malkiel, Y. (eds.), *Perspectives on Historical Linguistics*. Amsterdam-Philadelphia: Benjamins, pp. 93–131.

1985. 'On the predictiveness of Natural Morphology', *JL* 21: 321–37.

1992. 'Confronti e contatti fonologici', in Mocciaro, A. and Soravia, G. (eds.), *L'Europa linguistica: contatti, contrasti, affinità di lingue. Atti del XXI congresso internazionale di studi della SLI, Catania, 1987*. Rome: Bulzoni, pp. 125–37.

1997. '"Scenario" as a concept for the functional explanation of language change', in Gvozdanović, Jadranka (ed.), *Language Change and Functional Explanations*. Berlin: Mouton de Gruyter, pp. 109–42.

Dressler, Wolfgang and Merlini Barbaresi, Lavinia 1994. *Morphopragmatics. Diminutives and Intensifiers in Italian, German and Other Languages*. Berlin-New York: Mouton de Guyter.

Dryer, Matthew 1988. 'Object-verb order and adjective-noun order: dispelling a myth', *Lingua* 74:185–217.

767

Duarte, Inês 1996. 'A topicalização em português europeu: uma análise comparativa', in Duarte, Inês and Leira, Isabel (eds.), *Actas do congresso internacional sobre o português, vol. 1*. Lisbon: Edições Colibri, pp. 327–60.

Duchêne, Nadia 2002. 'Langue, immigration, culture: paroles de la banlieue française', *Meta* 47:30–37.

Dufter, Andreas 2004. 'Ist das Französische eine silbenzählende Sprache?', in Meiselburg, T. and Selig, M. (eds.), *Nouveaux départs en phonologie. Les conceptions sub- et suprasegmentales*. Tübingen: Narr, pp. 139–59.

Duncan S. 1974. 'On the structure of Speaker-Auditor during speaker turns', *Language and Society* 3:161–80.

Duncan, S. and Fiske, D. 1977. *Face-to-Face Interaction*. Hillsdale, NJ: Erlbaum.

Dupuis, Fernande 1989. *L'expression du sujet dans les subordonnées en ancien français*. Université de Montréal: unpublished thesis.

Duraffour, Antonin 1932. 'Phénomènes généraux d'évolution phonétique dans les dialectes franco-provençaux étudiés d'après le parler de la commune de Vaux (Ain)', *RLiR* 8:1–280.

Durand, Jacques, Slater, Catherine and Wise, Hilary 1987. 'Observations on schwa in southern French', *Linguistics* 25:983–1004.

Durante, Marcello 1981. *Dal latino all'italiano moderno*. Bologna: Zanichelli.

Duranti, Alessandro and Ochs, Elinor 1979. 'La pipa la fumi? Uno studio sulla dislocazione a sinistra nelle conversazioni', *SGI* 8:269–301.

Dworkin, Steven 1978. 'Phonotactic awkwardness as an impediment to sound change', *Forum Linguisticum* 3: 47–56.

1981. 'Phonotactic constraints and lexical loss in old Spanish', *ZRPh* 97:86–92.

1982. 'From "temple" to "cheek": Old Spanish *tienlla* reconsidered (with sideglances at *carriello* and *sien*)', *RPh* 35:573–85.

1983. 'The fragmentation of the Latin verb tollere in Hispano- (including Luso-) Romance', *RPh* 37:166–74.

1985. *Etymology and Derivational Morphology. The Genesis of Old Spanish Denominal Adjectives in -ido*. Tübingen: Niemeyer.

1986. 'The etymology of hispanic vel(l)ido: a new approach to an old problem', *RPh* 40:328–37.

1989a. 'Factores lingüísticos operantes en la pérdida léxica', *Actes du XVIIIᵉ Congrès international de linguistique et de philologie romanes, vol. 4*. Tübingen: Niemeyer, pp. 379–84.

1989b. 'Studies in lexical loss: the fate of old Spanish postadjectival abstracts in -dad, -dumbre, -eza, and –ura', *Bulletin of Hispanic Studies* 66:335–42.

1990. 'The role of near-homonymy in lexical loss: the demise of OSp. laido "ugly, repugnant"', *La Corónica* 19:32–48.

1992. 'The demise of old Spanish *decir*: a case study in lexical loss', *RPh* 45:493–502.

1993a. 'La cuasi-homonimia y la pérdida léxica en el español antiguo', *Lexis* 17:57–74.

1993b. 'Near-homonymy, semantic overlap and lexical loss in medieval Spanish: three case studies', *Romanistisches Jahrbuch* 44:271–81.

1995a. 'The role of grammatical category and semantic features in lexical loss: old Spanish primary adjectives', in Hoinkes, Ulrich (ed.), *Panorama der lexikalischen Semantik. Thematische Festschrift aus Anlass des 60. Geburtstags von Horst Geckeler*. Tübingen: Narr, pp. 159–67.

1995b. 'Two studies in old Spanish homonymics', *Hispanic Review* 63:527–42.

1997. 'Semantic change and lexical loss: the case of OSp. *luengo* "long" ', *La Corónica* 26:53–65.

1998a. 'Lexical loss and neologisms in late medieval Spanish: two case studies', *Bulletin of Hispanic Studies* [Liverpool] 75:1–11.

1998b. 'Yakov Malkiel's contributions to the study of lexical loss: a critical overview', *Romanistik in Geschichte und Gegenwart* 5:3–19.

2002a. 'La introducción e incorporación de latinismos en el español medieval tardío: algunas cuestiones lingüísticas y metodológicas', in Saralegui, C. and Casado, M. (eds.), *Pulchre, Bene, Recte. Estudios en homenaje al Profesor Fernando González Ollé*. Pamplona: EUNSA, pp. 421–33.

2002b. 'Pérdida e integración léxicas: *aína* vs. *rápido* en el español premoderno', in Pöll, B. and Rainer, F. (eds.), *Vocabula et vocabularia. Etudes de lexicologie et de (méta-) lexicographie romanes en l'honneur du 60e anniversaire de Dieter Messner*. Frankfurt: Peter Lang, pp. 109–18.

(ed.) 2003. *Historical Romance Linguistics. The Death of a Discipline? La Corónica* 31:7–134.

2006. 'La naturaleza del cambio léxico', in Girón Alconchel, José Luis and de Bustos Tovar, José Jesús (eds.), *Actas del VI Congreso internacional de historia de la lengua española I*. Madrid: Arco Libros, pp. 67–84.

Eberenz, Rolf 1998. 'Dos campos semánticos del español preclásico: "fácil" y "difícil" ', in Andrés-Suárez, I. and López Molina, L. (eds.), *Estudios de lingüística y de filología españoles: Homenaje a Germán Colón*. Madrid: Gredos, pp. 167–83.

Egido Fernández, M. 1996. *El sistema verbal en el romance leonés*. León: Universidad de León.

Ekblom, R. 1908. *Etude sur l'extinction des verbes au prétérit en -si et en -ui en français*. Uppsala: Almqvist och Wiksell.

Elcock, William 1938. *De quelques affinités phonétiques entre l'aragonais et le béarnais*. Paris: Droz.

1960. *The Romance Languages*. London: Faber.

1975. *The Romance Languages*. Revised with a New Introduction by J. N. Green. London: Faber.

Elerick, Charles 1989a. 'Gapping, preemptive markedness, and word order in Latin', in Calboli, Gualtiero (ed.), *Subordination and Other Topics in Latin*. Amsterdam: Benjamins, pp. 559–71.

1989b. *Word order in Caesar. SOV/V-1*. University of Texas at el Paso: unpublished manuscript.

Elsner, Alfred von 1886. *Über Form und Verwendung des Personalpronomens im Altprovenzalischen*. Kiel: Fiencke.

Elvira, Javier 1994. '*Uno* en español antiguo', *Verba: Anuario galego de filoloxía* 21:167–82.

1998. *El cambio analógico*. Madrid: Gredos.

Elwert, W. Theodor 1943. *Die Mundart des Fassa-Tals*. Heidelberg: Winter.

Enciclopedia dantesca. 1970–8. Rome: Istituto della Enciclopedia italiana.

Ernout, Alfred 1927/1953 (3rd edn). *Morphologie historique du latin*. Paris: Klincksieck.

Ernout, Alfred and Meillet, Antoine 1959. *Dictionnaire étymologique de la langue latine*. Paris: Klincksieck.

1967 (4th edn). *Dictionnaire étymologique de la langue latine. Histoire des mots*. Paris: Klincksieck.

Ernout, Alfred and Thomas, François 1953/93. *Syntaxe latine*. Paris: Klincksieck.

Ernst, Gerhard 1970. *Die Toskanisierung des römischen Dialekts im 15. und 16. Jahrhundert*. Tübingen: Niemeyer.

2004. 'Lexikalische Analyse historischer Texte und semantische Theorie am Beispiel nonstandardsprachlicher französischer Texte des 17. und 18. Jahrhunderts', in Lebsanft and Gleßgen (eds.), pp. 153–61.

Ernst, Gerhard, Gleßgen, Martin-D., Schmitt, Christian and Schweickard, Wolfgang (eds.) 2003–9. *Romanische Sprachgeschichte. Ein internationales Handbuch zur Geschichte der romanischen Sprachen und ihrer Erforschung*, 3 vols. Berlin-New York: Mouton de Gruyter.

Eska, Joseph 2004. 'Continental Celtic', in Woodard, R. (ed.), *The Cambridge Encyclopedia of the World's Ancient Languages*. Cambridge: Cambridge University Press, pp. 857–80.

Espinosa, Aurelio 1946. *Estudios sobre el español de Nuevo Méjico II. Morfología. Notas de morfología dialectal*. Buenos Aires: Universidad de Buenos Aires.

Ettinger, Stefan 1974. *Form und Funktion in der Wortbildung. Die Diminutiv- und Augmentativmodifikation im Lateinischen, Deutschen und Romanischen. Ein kritscher Forschungsbericht 1900–1970*. Tübingen: Tübinger Beiträge zur Linguistik.

Everaert, Martin 1986. *The Syntax of Reflexivization*. Dordrecht: Foris.

Ewert, Alfred 1935. 'The Strasbourg Oaths', *TPS* 16–35.

1978. *The French Language*. London: Faber.

Fabra, Pompeu 1904. 'Les *e* toniques du catalan', *Revue Hispanique* 15:9–23.

1956. *Gramàtica catalana*. Barcelona: Teide.

Fagyal, Zsuzsanna, Kibbee, Douglas and Jenkins, Fred 2006. *French. A Linguistic Introduction*. Cambridge: Cambridge University Press.

Faingold, Eduardo D. 1996. 'Demonstrative pronouns and definite article in Latin and the Romance languages', *Papiere zur Linguistik* 54:67–82.

Falcone, Giuseppe 1983. 'Strutture organizzative, rituali e "baccagghju" della 'ndràngheta', in Di Bella, Saverio (ed.), *Mafia e Potere. Società civile, organizzazione mafiosa ed esercizio dei poteri nel Mezzogiorno contemporaneo.* Soveria Mannelli: Rubbettino, pp. 251–73.

Fanciullo, Franco 1984. 'Il siciliano e i dialetti meridionali', in Quattordio Moreschini, A. (ed.), *Tre millenni di storia linguistica della Sicilia. Atti del Convegno della SIG.* Pisa: Giardini, 139–59) [also in Fanciullo, 1996:11–29].

1988, 'Lucania', in *LRL* III, pp. 669–88.

1992. 'Un capitolo della Romania submersa: il latino africano', in Kremer, Dieter (ed.), *Actes du XVIIIe Congrès international de linguistique et philologie romanes*, I. *Romania submersa-Romania nova.* Tübingen: Niemeyer, pp. 162–87.

1994. 'Morfo-metafonia', in Cipriano, P., Di Giovine, P. and Mancini, M. (eds.), *Miscellanea di studi linguistici in onore di Walter Belardi.* Rome: Il Calamo, pp. 571–92.

1996. *Fra Oriente e Occidente. Per una storia linguistica dell'Italia meridionale.* Pisa: ETS.

1997a. 'Anticipazioni romanze nel latino pompeiano', *AGI* 82:186–98.

1997b. *Raddoppiamento sintattico e ricostruzione linguistica nel Sud italiano.* Pisa: ETS.

1998. 'Per una interpretazione dei verbi italiani a "inserto" velare', *AGI* 83:188–239.

Fankhänel, Herbert 1938. *Verb und Satz in der lateinschen Prosa bis Sallust.* Leipzig: Vogel.

Farkas, Donka 1982. *Intensionality and Romance Subjunctive Relatives.* Bloomington, IN: Indiana University Linguistics Club.

Farnetani, Edda and Kori, Shiro 1986. 'Effects of syllable and word structure on segmental durations in spoken Italian', *Speech Communication* 5:17–34.

Fava, Elisabetta and Magno Caldognetto, Emanuela 1976. 'Studio sperimentale delle caratteristiche elettroacustiche delle vocali toniche e atone in bisillabi italiani', in Simone, R., Vignuzzi, U. and Ruggiero, G. (eds.), *Studi di fonetica e fonologia.* Rome: Bulzoni, pp. 35–79.

Feix, Joseph 1934. *Wortstellung und Satzbau in Petrons Roman.* University of Breslau: unpublished thesis.

Felixberger, Joseph 2003. 'Sub-, Ad- und Superstrate und ihre Wirkung auf die romanischen Sprachen: Galloromania', in Ernst *et al.* (eds.), pp. 594–607.

Ferguson, Charles 1959. 'Diglossia', *Word* 15:325–40.

Ferguson, Thaddeus 1976. *A History of the Romance Vowel Systems through Paradigmatic Reconstruction.* The Hague: Mouton.

Fernández González, J. 1981. *El habla de Ancares (León).* Oviedo: Universidad de Oviedo.

Fernández Ordóñez, Inés 2006–7. 'Del Cantábrico a Toledo: el "neutro de materia" hispánico en un contexto románico y tipológico', *Revista de historia de la lengua española* 1:67–118; 2: 29–81.

Fernández Rei, Francisco (coord.) 1990. *Atlas lingüístico galego, vol. 1 Morfoloxía verbal*. La Coruña: Instituto da lingua galega.

Ferreiro, Manuel 1995. *Gramática histórica galega*. Santiago de Compostela: Laiovento.

Ferrero, Ernesto 1972. *I gerghi della malavita dal '500 a oggi*. Milan: Mondadori. 1973. 'I gerghi della malavita', in Beccaria, Gian Luigi (ed.), *I linguaggi settoriali in Italia*. Milan: Boringhieri, pp. 207–19.

Fertig, Daniel 1998. 'Suppletion, natural morphology and diagrammaticity', *Linguistics* 36:1065–91.

Festa, Giovan Battista 1916. 'Il dialetto di Matera', *ZRPh* 38:129–62.

FEW = Wartburg 1959

Fichte, Emil 1879. *Die Flexion im Cambridger Psalter – Grammatische Untersuchung*. Halle: Niemeyer.

Filimonova, Elena (ed.) 2005. *Clusivity: Typology and Case Studies of the Inclusive– Exclusive Distinction*. Amsterdam-Philadelphia: Benjamins.

Fillmore, Charles 1997. *Lectures on Deixis*. Stanford: CSLI.

Fiorentino, Giuliana 2003. 'Prepositional objects in Neapolitan', in Fiorentino, Giuliana (ed.), *Romance Objects. Transitivity in Romance Languages*. Berlin: Mouton, pp. 117–51.

Fischer, Anton 1908. *Die Stellung der Demonstrativpronomina bei lateinischen Prosaikern*. Tübingen: Heckenhauerschen Buchhandlung.

Fischer, Kerstin 2006. *Approaches to Discourse Particles*. Amsterdam-Boston-London: Elsevier.

Fishman, Joshua 1967. 'Bilingualism with and without diglossia; diglossia with and without bilingualism', *Journal of Social Issues* 23:29–38.

Fleischman, Suzanne 1982. *The Future in Thought and Language. Diachronic Evidence from Romance*. Cambridge: Cambridge University Press.

Flobert, David 1975. *Les verbes déponents latins des origines à Charlemagne*. Paris: Belles Lettres.

Flobert, Pierre 1987. 'La date de l'Appendix Probi', in *Filologia e forme letterarie. Studi offerti a F. Della Corte, IV*. Urbino: Università degli Studi, pp. 299–320.

Flutre, Louis-Ferdinand 1977. *Du Moyen picard au picard moderne*. Amiens: Musée de Picardie.

Fontana, Josep 1993. *Phrase Structure and the Syntax of Clitics in the History of Spanish*. University of Pennsylvania: doctoral dissertation. 1997. 'On the integration of second position phenomena', in (van) Kemenade and Vincent (eds.), pp. 207–49.

Formentin, Vittorio 1996. 'Flessione bicasuale del pronome relativo in antichi testi italiani centro-meridionali', *AGI* 81:133–76.

Formentin, Vittorio (ed.) 1998. *Loise De Rosa, Ricordi*. Rome: Salerno.

Formentin, Vittorio 2001. 'L'ausiliazione perfettiva in antico napoletano', *AGI* 86:79–117.

2002. 'L'area italiana medievale', in Boitani, P., Mancini, M. and Varvaro, A. (eds.), *Lo spazio letterario del Medioevo. 2. Il medioevo volgare, vol. II: La circolazione del testo*. Rome: Salerno, pp. 97–147.

Forner, Werner 1975. *Generative Phonologie des Dialekts von Genua*. Hamburg: Buske.

1988. *Ligurien, LRL* (IV) 453–69.

2003. 'Variationelle Evidenzen für eine monogenetische Theorie der romanischen Pluralmarkierung', *ZRPh* 121:197–245.

Fouché, Pierre 1929. 'Etudes de philologie hispanique. III. Le parfait en castillan', *Revue hispanique* 77:45–87.

1958. *Phonétique historique du français, vol. II, Les voyelles*. Paris: Klincksieck.

1967. *Le verbe français. Etude morphologique*. Paris: Klincksieck.

Foulet, Lucien 1923 (2nd edn)/1930(3rd edn)/1968 (3rd edn revised). *Petite syntaxe de l'ancien français*. Paris: Champion.

Frajzyngier, Zygmunt and Curl, Traci (eds.) 2000. *Reflexives: Forms and Functions*. Amsterdam–Philadelphia: Benjamins.

Francescato, Giuseppe 1966. *Dialettologia friulana*. Udine: Società Filologica Friulana.

Franceschi, Temistocle 1965. 'Postille alla Historische Grammatik der italienischen Sprache und ihrer Mundarten di G. Rohlfs', *AGI* 50:153–74.

1969. 'Il principio dell'esagerazione come criterio di ricerca linguistica', *AGI* 54:49–85.

1976. 'Sull'evoluzione del vocalismo dal latino repubblicano al neolatino', in *Scritti in onore di Giuliano Bonfante, vol. 1*. Brescia: Paideia, pp. 259–79.

Frâncu, Constantin 1980. 'Din istoria verbelor neregulate: perfectul simplu şi mai mult ca perfectul verbelor a da şi a sta', *Limba română* 29:307–18.

Frau, Giovanni 1984. *Friuli*. Pisa: Pacini.

Frei, Henri. 1971 [1929]. *La grammaire des fautes*. Geneva: Slatkine.

Freund, Ilse 1933. *Beiträge zur Mundart von Ischia*. Eberhart-Karls-Universität: dissertation.

Froissart, Jean 1972. *Chroniques. Début du premier livre. Édition du manuscrit de Rome Reg. lat. 869* (ed. George T. Diller). Geneva: Droz.

Gaatone, David 1998. *Le passif en français*. Paris-Brussels: Duculot.

Galves, Charlotte 1993. 'O enfraquecimento da concordância no português brasileiro', in Roberts, Ian and Kato, Mary (eds.), *Português brasileiro. Uma viagem diacrônica*. Campinas: Editora da Unicamp, pp. 387–408.

Gamillscheg, Ernst 1912. *Studien zur Vorgeschichte einer romanischen Tempuslehre*. Vienna: Sitzungsberichte der Akademie der Wissenschaften.

1957. *Historische französische Syntax*. Tübingen: Niemeyer.

Ganzoni, Gian Paul 1977. *Grammatica ladina. Grammatica sistematica dal rumantsch d'Engiadin' Ota per scolars e creschieus da lingua rumauntscha e tudas-cha*. Samedan: Lia Rumantscha.

García Arias, Xosé Lluis 2003. *Gramática histórica de la lengua asturiana*. Oviedo: Academia de la Llingua Asturiana.

García Bellido, Paloma 1997. 'Inherent and structural prominence in Spanish', in Martínez Gil and Morales-Front (eds.), pp. 469–513.

García de Diego, Vicente 1909. *Elementos de gramática histórica gallega (fonética – morfología)*. Burgos: Rodríguez.

1946. *Manual de dialectología española*. Madrid: Instituto de Cultura Hispánica.

1951. *Gramática histórica española*. Madrid: Gredos.

García Santos, Juan Felipe 1992. 'Extremeño'. *LRL* (VI, 1), pp. 701–708.

Garde, Paul 1961. 'Réflexions sur les différences phonétiques entre les langues slaves', *Word* 17:34–62.

Gardette, Pierre 1983. 'Le francoprovençal. Son histoire, ses origines', in *Etudes de géographie linguistique*. Strasbourg: Klincksieck, pp. 569–84.

Gardner, David 1971. *A Frequency Dictionary of Classical Latin Words*. Stanford University: dissertation.

Gardner, Rosalyn and Greene, Marion 1958. *A Brief Description of Middle French Syntax*. Chapel Hill: University of North Carolina Press.

Gardner-Chloros, Penelope 1991. 'Ni tu ni vous: principes et paradoxes dans l'emploi des pronoms d'allocution en français contemporain', *Journal of French Language Studies* 1:139–55.

Gartmann, Christian 1967. *Die Mundart von Sorso (Provinz Sassari, Sardinien)*. Zürich: Juris Verlag.

Gartner, Theodor 1883. *Raetoromanische Grammatik*. Heilbronn: Sammlung Romanischen Grammatiken.

1910. *Handbuch der rätoromanischen Sprache und Literatur*. Halle: Niemeyer.

Gaßner, Armin 1908. 'Die Sprache des Königs Denis von Portugal', *RF* 22:399–425.

Gaudenzi, Augusto 1889. *I suoni, le forme, le parole dell'odierno dialetto della città di Bologna*. Turin: Loescher.

Gaudino-Fallegger, Livia 1992. *I dimostrativi nell'italiano parlato*. Wilhelmsfeld: Egert.

Gauger, Hans-Martin, Oesterreicher, Wulf and Windisch, Rudolf 1981. *Einführung in die romanische Sprachwissenschaft*. Darmstadt: Wissenschaftliche Buchgesellschaft.

GDLlC = Diccionaris Enciclopèdia Catalana, 1998. *Gran Diccionari de la Llengua Catalana* Barcelona: Enciclopèdia Catalana (and at http://www.grec.net/home/cel/dicc.htm).

Geeraerts, Dirk 1992. 'Prototypicality effects in diachronic semantics: a roundup', in Kellermann, G. and Morrissey, M. D. (eds.), *Diachrony Within Synchrony. Language History and Cognition*. Frankfurt: Peter Lang, pp. 183–203.

1997. *Diachronic Prototype Semantics*. Oxford: Oxford University Press.

Geniušienė, Emma 1987. *The Typology of Reflexives*. Berlin-New York-Amsterdam: Mouton de Gruyter.

Gerola, Berengario 1949–50. 'Aspetti della sintassi del nominativo e dell'accustivo nel tardo latino', *Atti dell'Istituto Veneto di SS.LL.AA* 108:207–36.

Gess, Randall and Arteaga, Deborah 2006. *Historical Romance Lingusitics. Retrospective and Perspectives*. Amsterdam-Philadelphia: Benjamins.

Gévaudan, Paul 2007. *Typologie des lexikalischen Wandels. Bedeutungswandel, Wortbildung und Entlehnung am Beispiel der romanischen Sprachen*. Tübingen: Stauffenburg Verlag.

Gévaudan, Paul, Koch, Peter and Neu, Antonia 2003. 'Hundert Jahre nach Zauner: die romanische Namen der Körperteile im DECOLAR', *RF* 115:1–27.

Ghini, Mirco 2001. *Asymmetries in the Phonology of Miogliola*. Berlin-New York: Mouton de Gruyter.

Giacomelli, Roberto 1955. 'Il "ciàmbrico": gergo della meta', *Bollettino dell'Atlante linguistico italiano* 1:10–17.

Giammarco, Ernesto 1979. *Abruzzo*. Pisa: Pacini.

Gierling, Diana 1996. 'Further parallels between clitic doubling and scrambling', in Green, Anthony and Motapanyane, Virginia (eds.), *Proceedings of the 13th Eastern States Conference on Linguistics '96*. Ithaca, NY: Cornell University Press, pp. 113–23.

1997. 'Clitic doubling, specificity and focus in Romanian', in Black, James and Motapanyane, Virginia (eds.), *Clitics, Pronouns and Movement*. Amsterdam: Benjamins, pp. 63–85.

Gil, David 1987. 'Definiteness, noun phrase configurationality, and the count-mass distinction', in Reuland, Eric and ter Meulen, Alice (eds.), *The Representations of (In)definiteness*. Cambridge, MA: MIT Press, pp. 254–69.

Gildersleeve, Basil and Lodge, Gonzalez 1895. *Latin Grammar*. Basingstoke: Macmillan.

[1895] 1997. *Latin Grammar*, Bristol: Bristol Classical Press.

Gilliéron, Jules 1918. *Généalogie des mots qui désignent l'abeille d'après l'Atlas linguistique de la France*. Paris: Bibliothèque de l'Ecole des Hautes Études.

Giurescu, Anca 1975. *Les mots composés dans les langues romanes*. The Hague-Paris: Mouton.

Giusti, Giuliana 1993. 'Enclitic articles and double definiteness: a comparative analysis of nominal structure in Romance and Germanic', *The Linguistic Review* 11:231–55.

1995. 'Heads and modifiers among determiners: evidence from Rumanian', in Cinque, Guglielmo and Giusti, Giuliana (eds.), *Advances in Rumanian Linguistics*. Amsterdam-Philadelphia: Benjamins, pp. 103–25.

1997. 'The categorial status of determiners', in Haegeman, Liliane (ed.), *The New Comparative Syntax*. London: Longman, pp. 95–123.

2001. 'Le frasi temporali', in Renzi, Salvi and Cardinaletti, Anna (eds.), vol. II, pp. 720–38.

2002. 'The functional structure of noun phrases: a bare phrase structure approach', in Cinque, Guglielmo (ed.), *Functional Structure in DP and IP. The Cartography of Syntactic Structures, vol. 1*. Oxford: Oxford University Press, pp. 54–90.

Givón, Talmy 1984–90. *Syntax. A Functional Typologic Introduction, 1–2.* Amsterdam-Philadelphia: Benjamins.

Glover, Richard. 2004. 'And the 11th commandment was: shop around for the right price', *Sydney Morning Herald*, 1 May 2004.

Godefroy, Frédéric 1881–1902. *Dictionnaire de l'ancienne langue française et de tous ses dialectes du IXe au XVe siècle*, 10 vols. Paris:Vieweg.

Goldbach, Maria 2010 'Metaphony in Portuguese 3rd class -u(C)C-ir and -o(C)C-ir verbs – evidence from modern Galician and mediaeval Galician-Portuguese', in Goldbach, M., Hinzelin, M.-O., Maiden, M. and Smith, J.C. (eds.), *Morphological Autonomy: Perspectives from Romance Inflectional Morphology*, Oxford: Oxford University Press, 417–68.

Goldsmith, John 1995. *The Handbook of Phonological Theory.* Oxford: Blackwell.

Gooch, Anthony 1967. *Diminutive, Augmentative, and Pejorative Suffixes in Modern Spanish.* Oxford: Pergamon Press.

Gossen, Charles 1951. *Pétite grammaire de l'ancien picard.* Paris: Klincksieck.

1970. *Grammaire de l'ancien picard.* Paris: Klincksieck.

1982. 'Interromanisch außer Rumänisch', *VR* 41:13–45.

Goudailler, Jean-Pierre 1998. *Comment tu tchatches! Dictionnaire du français contemporain des cités.* Paris: Maisonneuve et Larose.

Gougenheim, Georges 1959. 'La relatinisation du vocabulaire français', *Annales de l'Université de Paris* 29:5–18.

Gould, Stephen Jay and Vrba, Elisabeth 1982. 'Exaptation – a missing term in the science of form', *Paleobiology* 8:4–15.

Grabe, Esther and Ee Ling Low 2002. 'Acoustic correlates of rhythm class', in Gussenhoven, C. and Warner, N. (eds.), *Papers in Laboratory Phonology 7.* Berlin: Mouton de Gruyter, pp. 515–46.

Gràcia, Lluïsa and Fullana, Olga 1999. 'On Catalan verbal compounds', *Probus* 11:239–61.

Graffi, Giorgio 1994. *Sintassi.* Bologna: il Mulino.

Gramatica limbii române. I–II 1966. Bucharest: Editura Academiei.

Grandgent, Charles 1905. *An Outline of the Phonology and Morphology of Old Provençal.* Boston: Heath.

1907. *An Introduction to Vulgar Latin.* Boston: Heath.

Grassi, Cesare 1966. *Problemi di sintassi latina.* Florence: la Nuova Italia.

Graur, Alexandru 1968. *Tendinţele actuale ale limbii române.* Bucharest: Editura Ştiinţifică.

Grayson, John 1964. 'Lunfardo, Argentina's unknown tongue', *Hispania* 47:66–68.

Green, John 1976. 'How free is word order in Spanish?', in Harris (ed.), pp. 7–32.

1982. 'The status of the Romance auxiliaries of voice', in Vincent and Harris (eds.), pp. 97–138.

1987. 'The evolution of Romance auxiliaries: criteria and chronology', in Harris and Ramat (eds.), pp. 255–67.

1988a. 'Spanish', in Harris and Vincent (eds.), pp. 79–130.

1988b. 'Romance Creoles', in Harris and Vincent (eds.), pp. 420–73.

2006. 'The north-south axis of Romance: contact reinforcing typology', in Lepschy and Tosi (eds.), pp. 73–86.

Greenberg, Joseph 1963. 'Some universals of grammar with particular reference to the order of meaningful elements', in *Universals of Languages*. Cambridge, MA: MIT Press, pp. 58–90.

1966. 'Language universals', in Sebeok, Thomas (ed.), *Current Trends in Linguistics, vol. III: Theoretical Foundations*. The Hague-Paris: Mouton, pp. 61–112.

1978. 'Numeral systems', in *Universals of Human Language*. Stanford, CA: Stanford University Press, pp. 250–95.

Grevisse, Maurice 1964. *Le bon usage*. Gembloux: Duculot.

1980. *Le bon usage*. Gembloux: Duculot.

1993. *Le bon usage. Grammaire française*. Refondue par André Goosse. Paris: Duculot.

Grevisse, Maurice and Goosse, André 2007. *Le Bon Usage. Grammaire française*. Bruxelles: De Boeck.

Grimaldi, Mirko 2003. *Nuove ricerche sul vocalismo tonico del Salento meridionale. Analisi acustica e trattamento fonologico dei dati*. Alessandria: Edizioni dell'Orso.

Griva, Guido 1980. *Grammatica della lingua piemontese*. Turin: Viglongo.

Gröber, Gustav 1904–6. *Grundriss der romanischen Philologie*. Strasbourg: Trübner.

Grosu, Alexander 1988. 'On the distribution of genitive phrases in Rumanian', *Linguistics* 26:931–49.

1994. *Three Studies in Locality and Case*. London: Routledge.

Grünert, Matthias 2003. *Modussyntax im Surselvischen. Ein Beitrag zur Erforschung der Morphosyntax des Verbs im Bündnerromanischen*. Tübingen: Francke.

Gsell, Otto 1996. 'Chronologie frühromanischer Sprachwandel', *LRL* (II, 1), pp. 557–84.

2004. 'Was haben historische Semantik und Etymologie voneinander zu erwarten?', in Lebsanft and Gleßgen (eds.) 2004a, pp. 119–27.

Gsell, Otto and Wandruszka, Ulrich 1986. *Der romanische Konjunktiv*. Tübingen: Niemeyer.

Guarnerio, Pier Enea 1892–3. 'I dialetti odierni di Sassari, della Gallura e della Corsica', *AGI* 13:125–40; 14:131–200, 385–422.

Guasti, Maria Teresa 1993. *Causative and Perception Verbs. A Comparative Approach*. Turin: Rosenberg & Sellier.

Guasti, Maria Teresa 1996. 'Semantic restriction in Romance causatives and the incoporation approach', *LI* 27:97–110.

Guillaume, Gustave 1971 [2005]. *Leçons de linguistique de Gustave Guillaume*, publiées par Roch Valin [1948–9]. *Psychosystématique du langage*.

Principes, méthodes et applications, 1, 2, 3. Québec-Paris: Presses de l'Université Laval.

1975. *Le problème de l'article et sa solution dans la langue française*. Paris: A.G. Nizet; Québec: Presses de l'Université Laval.

Guillot, C. 2006. 'Démonstratif et deixis discursive: analyse comparée d'un corpus écrit de français médieval et d'un corpus oral de français contemporain', *Langue française* 152:56–69.

Guiraud, Pierre 1965. *Le Français populaire*. Paris: PUF.

1966. *Le Moyen Français*. Paris: PUF.

1968. *Les Mots savants*. Paris: PUF.

[1953] 1973 (6th edn). *L'Argot*. Paris: PUF.

Gundel, Jeanette and Fretheim, Thorenstein (eds.) 1996. *Reference and Referent Accessibility*. Amsterdam-Philadelphia: Benjamins.

Gundel, Jeanette, Hedberg, Nancy and Zacharski, Ron 1993. 'Cognitive status and form of referring expressions', *Language* 69:274–307.

Guția, Ioan 1967. *Grammatica romena moderna*. Rome: Bulzoni.

Haase, Albert 1969 [1898]. *Syntaxe française du XVIIè siècle, traduite et remaniée par M. Obert*. Paris: Picard.

Haden, Ernest 1973. 'French dialect geography', in Sebeok, Thomas (ed.), *Current Trends in Linguistics, vol. 10*. The Hague: Mouton, pp. 422–44.

Haida, Roman 1928. *Die Wortstellung in der Peregrinatio ad Loca Sancta*. University of Breslau: unpublished thesis.

Haiman, John 1988. 'Rhaeto-Romance', in Harris and Vincent (eds.), pp. 351–90.

Haiman, John and Benincà, Paola 1992. *The Rhaeto-Romance Languages*. London-New York: Routledge.

Hajek, John 1997. *Universals of Sound Change in Nasalisation*. Oxford: Blackwell.

Hakamies, Reino 1951. *Etude sur l'origine et l'évolution du diminutif latin et sa survie dans les langues romanes*. Helsinki: Suomalaisen Tiedeakatemian Toimituksia – Annales Academiae Scientiarum Fennicae 71.

Hale, Ken 1981. *On the Position of Warlpiri in a Typology of the Base*. Bloomington, IN: Indiana University Lingusitics Club.

1982. 'Preliminary remarks on configurationality', *North Eastern Linguistic Society* 12:86–96.

1983. 'Warlpiri and the grammar of non-configurational languages', *NLLT* 1:5–47.

1994. 'Core structures and adjunctions in Warlpiri syntax', in Corver, Norbert and van Riemsdijk, Henk (eds.), *Studies on Scrambling. Movement and Non-movement Approaches to Free Word Order Phenomena*. Berlin-New York: Mouton de Gruyter, pp. 185–219.

Hale, William and Buck, Carl [1903] 1994. *A Latin Grammar*. Tuscaloosa, AL: University of Alabama Press.

Hall, Robert A. 1962 'Latin -s, -es, -as, -os in Italian', *RPh* 15:234–44.

1968. '"Neuters", mass-nouns, and the ablative in Romance', *Language* 44:480–86.

1974. *External History of the Romance Languages*. New York: Elsevier.

1980. 'The gradual decline of case in Romance substantives', in van Coetsem, Frans and Waugh, Linda (eds.), *Contributions to Historical Linguistics. Issues and Materials*. Leiden: Brill, pp. 261–69.

Halmøy, Odile 2000. 'Le vouvoiement en français: forme non marquée de la seconde personne du singulier', in Nystedt, Jane (ed.), *Actes du XIV Congrès des romanistes scandinaves, Stockholm, 10–15 août 1999*. Stockholm: Almqvist & Wiksel, pp. 556–65.

Hansen, Maj-Brit Mosegaard 1998. *The Function of Discourse Particles. A Study with Special Reference to Spoken Standard French*. Amsterdam-Philadelphia: Benjamins.

Hanssen, F. 1898. *Über die altspanischen Präterita vom Typus ove pude*. Valparaíso: Universo.

Harbert, Wayne 2007. *The Germanic Languages*. Cambridge: Cambridge University Press.

Harnisch, R. 1988. 'Natürliche Morphologie und morphologische Ökonomie: ein Vermittlungsversuch angesichts der Morphologien natürlicher Sprachen', *Zeitschrift für Phonetik, Sprachwissenschaft und Kommunikationsforschung* 41:426–37.

Harris, Alice and Campbell, Lyle 1995. *Historical Syntax in Cross-Linguistic Perspective*. Cambridge: Cambridge University Press.

Harris, James 1969. *Spanish Phonology*. Cambridge, MA: MIT Press.

Harris, Martin (ed.) 1976. *Romance Syntax. Synchronic and Diachronic Perspectives*. Salford: University of Salford.

Harris, Martin 1978. *The Evolution of French Syntax. A Comparative Approach*. London: Longman.

1988. 'French', in Harris and Vincent (eds.), pp. 209–45.

Harris, Martin and Ramat, Paolo (eds.) 1987. *The Historical Development of Auxiliaries*. Berlin: Mouton.

Harris, Martin and Vincent, Nigel (eds.) 1988. *The Romance Languages*. London: Croom Helm.

Harris, Roy 1966. 'Gallo-Romance third declension plurals', *Revue de linguistique romane* 30:57–70.

Harris-Northall, Ray 1991. 'Apocope in Alfonsine texts: a case study', in Harris-Northall, Ray and Cravens, Thomas (eds.), *Linguistic Studies in Medieval Spanish*. Madison, WI: The Hispanic Seminary of Medieval Studies, pp. 29–38.

Harvey, Anthony 1990. 'Retrieving the pronunciation of early insular Celtic scribes: towards a methodology', *Celtica* 21:178–90.

Haşdeu, B. P. 1983. *Cuvente den Bătrîni* I. Bucharest: Editura didactică şi pedagogică.

Haspelmath, Martin 2006. 'Against markedness (and what to replace it with)', *JL* 42:25–70.

Hasselrot, Bengt 1957. *Etudes sur la formation diminutive dans les languaes romanes.* Uppsala and Wiesbaden: Lundequist and Harrassowitz.

　　1972. *Etude sur la vitalité de la formation diminutive française au XXe siècle.* Uppsala: Almqvist och Wiksell.

Haudry, Jean 1973. 'Parataxe, hypotaxe et corrélation dans la phrase latine', *Bulletin de la Société de linguistique* 68:147–86.

Havet, Louis 1877. '*Colubra* en roman', *Romania* 6:433–36.

Haxhihasani, Qema 1964. 'Të folmet shoqnore', *Studime Filologjike* 1:99–125.

Heath, Jeffrey 1998. 'Hermit crabs: formal renewal of morphology by phonologically mediated affix substitution', *Language* 74:728–59.

Heine, Bernd 1993. *Auxiliaries.* Oxford: Oxford University Press.

Heinemann, Sabine 2001. *Bedeutungswandel bei italienischen Präpositionen. Eine kognitiv-semantische Untersuchung.* Tübingen: Gunter Narr.

Herman, József 1963. *La formation du système roman des conjonctions de subordination.* Berlin: Akademie-Verlag.

　　1966. 'Recherches sur l'évolution grammaticale du latin vulgaire: les emplois "fautifs" du nominatif', *Acta Classica Universitatis Scientiarum Debrecen* 2:109–12.

　　1968. 'Statistique et diachronie: essai sur l'évolution du vocalisme dans la latinité tardive', *Word* 24:242–51 [also in Herman (1990), pp. 196–203].

　　1970. 'Les particularités de l'évolution du latin provincial', in *Actele celui de-al XII-lea Congres internaţional de lingvistică şi filologie romanică.* Bucureşti: Editura Academiei, I, pp. 125–30 [also in Herman (1990), pp. 29–34].

　　1971. 'Essai sur la latinité du littoral adriatique à l'époque de l'Empire', in *Sprache und Geschichte. Festschrift Harri Maier,* Munich: Fink, pp. 199–226 [also in Herman (1990), pp. 121–46].

　　1978a. 'Language in time (on the theory of linguistic change)', *Acta Linguistica Academiae Scientiarum Hungaricae* 28:241–53.

　　1978b. 'Évolution *a* > *e* en latin tardif? Essai sur les liens entre la phonétique historique et la phonologie diachronique', *Acta Antiqua Academiae Scientiarum Hungariae* 26:37–48. [also in Herman (1990), pp. 204–16].

　　1982. 'Un vieux dossier réouvert: les transformations du système latin des quantités vocaliques', *BSL* 77:285–302 [also in Herman (1990), pp. 217–31].

　　1985a. 'La différenciation territoriale du latin et la formation des langues romanes' [also in Herman (1990), pp. 62–92].

　　1985b. 'La disparition de la déclinaison latine et l'évolution du syntagme nominal' [also in Herman (1990), pp. 326–37].

　　1985c. 'Témoignage des inscriptions latines et préhistoire des langues romanes: le cas de la Sardaigne', in *Mélanges Skok.* Zagreb: Jugoslavenska Akademija Znanosti i Umjetnosti, pp. 207–16 [also in Herman (1990), pp. 183–94]].

1987. 'La disparition de -*s* et la morphologie dialectale du latin parlé', in Herman, József (ed.), *Latin vulgaire – latin tardif. I.* Tübingen: Niemeyer, pp. 97–108.

1989. '*Accusativus cum infinitivo* et subordonné à *quod, quia* en latin tardif. – Nouvelles remarques sur un vieux problème', in Calboli (ed.), pp. 133–52 [also in Herman (2006), pp. 43–54].

1990. *Du latin aux langues romanes. Etudes de linguistique historique.* Tübingen: Niemeyer.

1991. 'On the grammatical subject in late Latin' [also in Herman (2006), pp. 55–64].

1995. 'Les ardoises wisigothiques et le problème de la différenciation territoriale du latin', in Callebat, Louis (ed.), *Latin vulgaire-latin tardif IV*. Hildesheim: Olms-Weidmann, pp. 63–76.

1996. 'The end of the history of Latin', *RPh* 49:364–82.

1998. 'La chronologie de la transition: un essai', in Herman, József and Mondin, Luca (eds.), *La transizione dal latino alle lingue romanze.* Tübingen: Niemeyer, pp. 5–25.

2000a. *Vulgar Latin.* Pennsylvania: The Pennsylvania State University Press.

2000b. 'Differenze territoriali nel latino parlato dell'Italia tardo-imperiale: un contributo preliminare', in Herman and Marinetti (eds.), pp. 123–35.

2006. *Du latin aux langues romanes II. Nouvelles études de linguistique historique.* Tübingen: Niemeyer.

Herman, József and Marinetti, Anna (eds.) 2000. *La preistoria dell'italiano. Atti della tavola rotonda di linguistica storica, Università Ca' Foscari di Venezia, 11–13 giugno 1998.* Tübingen: Niemeyer.

Hernández Campoy, Juan Manuel and Trudgill, Peter 2002. 'Functional compensation and southern peninsular Spanish /s/-loss', *Folia Linguistica Historica* 23:31–57.

Hewson, John 2007. 'Grammaticalization of the verbal diathesis of Germanic'. Paper presented at the *18th International Conference on Historical Linguistics*, Montréal, August, 2007.

Hilty, Gerold 1991. 'Problemas de metafonía en asturiano', *Lletres asturianes* 42:7–15.

2000. 'Das Zurückweichen des Rätoromanischen vom Bodensee bis Sargans (7.-14. Jahrhundert)', in *Actas dal Colloqui retoromanistic*. Chur: Societad Retorumantscha, pp. 29–42.

2001. 'I più antichi testi romanzi', in Boitani, Piero, Mancini, M. and Vàrvaro, A. (eds.), *Lo spazio letterario del Medioevo 2. Il Medioevo volgare.* Rome: Salerno, pp. 57–89.

Hirsch, L. 1886. 'Laut- und Formenlehre des Dialekts von Siena, VIII. Verb', *ZRPh* 10:411–46.

Hjelmslev, Louis 1935. *La Catégorie des cas: étude de grammaire générale. Première Partie.* (*Acta Jutlandica* 7,1.) Aarhus: Universitetsforlaget.

Hobjilă, Angelica 2003. *Microsistemul deicticelor în limba română vorbită neliterară actuală*. Iași: Demiurg.

Hock, Hans Henrich and Joseph, Brian 1996. *Language History, Language Change, and Language Relationship. An Introduction to Historical and Comparative Linguistics*. Berlin: de Gruyter.

Hoecke, Willy van 1996. 'The Latin dative', in Belle, William van and Langendonck, Willy van, *The Dative, vol. 1: Descriptive Studies*. Amsterdam-Philadelphia: Benjamins, pp. 119–51.

Hoenigswald, Henry 1949. 'A note on Latin prosody: initial *s* impure after short vowel', *Transactions of the American Philosophical Society* 80:270–80.

1960. 'On the history of the comparative method', *Anthropological Linguistics* 5:1–11.

Hofmann, Johannes and Szantyr, Anton 1965. *Lateinische Grammatik. II. Lateinische Syntax und Stilistik*. Munich: Beck.

Holm, John 1988. *Pidgins and Creoles. 1. Theory and Structure*. Cambridge: Cambridge University Press.

1989. *Pidgins and Creoles. 2. Reference Survey*. Cambridge: Cambridge University Press.

Holtus, Günter, Metzeltin, Michael and Schmitt, Christian (eds.) 1988. *Lexikon der romanistischen Linguistik. Band IV. Italienisch, Korsisch, Sardisch*. Tübingen: Niemeyer.

(eds.) 1989. *Lexikon der romanistischen Linguistik. Band III. Die einzelnen romanischen Sprachen und Sprachgebiete von der Renaissance bis zur Gegenwart. Rumänisch, Dalmatisch/Istroromanisch, Friaulisch, Ladinisch, Bündnerromanisch*. Tübingen: Niemeyer.

(eds.) 1990. *Lexikon der romanistischen Linguistik. Band V, 1. Französisch*. Tübingen: Niemeyer.

(eds.) 1991. *Lexikon der romanistischen Linguistik. Band V, 2. Okzitanisch, Katalanisch*. Tübingen: Niemeyer.

(eds.) 1992. *Lexikon der romanistischen Linguistik. Band VI, 1. Aragonesisch-Navarresisch, Spanisch, Asturianisch-Leonesisch*. Tübingen: Niemeyer.

(eds.) 1996. *Lexikon der romanistischen Linguistik. Band II, 1. Latein und Romanisch. Historisch-vergleichende Grammatik der romanischen Sprachen*. Tübingen: Niemeyer.

Hopper, Paul and Traugott, Elizabeth 1993. *Grammaticalization*. Cambridge: Cambridge University Press.

Houston, Ann Celeste 1985. *Continuity and Change in English Morphology: The Variable (ING)*. University of Pennsylvania: unpublished PhD dissertation.

Hualde, José Ignacio 1992a. *Catalan*. London: Routledge.

1992b. 'Compensatory lengthening in Friulian', *Probus* 2:31–46.

1992c. 'Metaphony and count/mass morphology in Asturian and Cantabrian dialects', in Laeufer, C. and Morgan, T. (eds.), *Theoretical Analyses in Romance Linguistics*. Amsterdam: Benjamins, pp. 99–114.

2001. *Introducción a la lingüística hispánica*. Cambridge: Cambridge University Press.

Huber, Joseph 1933. *Altportugiesisches Elementarbuch*. Heidelberg: Carl Winters Universitätsbuchhandlung.

1986. *Gramática do português antigo*. Coimbra: Fundação Gulbenkian.

Hughson, Jo-Ann 2002. 'Tu et vous: étude sociolinguistique dans la banlieue parisienne'. Paper given to conference on *Pronoms de 2e personne et formes d'adresse dans les langues d'Europe*, Institut Cervantes, Paris, March 2002. Downloadable from: http://cvc.cervantes.es/obref/coloquio_paris/ ponencias/pdf/cvc_hughson.pdf.

Humphrey, Nicholas 1992. *A History of the Mind*. London: Chatto and Windus.

Hunt, Tony 2003. 'The use of *tu/vous* in the Anglo-Norman *Seinte Resureccion*', in Taavitsainen, I. and Jucker, A. (eds.), *Diachronic Perspectives on Address Term Systems*. Amsterdam-Philadelphia: Benjamins, pp. 47–59.

Hurch, Bernhard and Rhodes, Richard A. (eds.) 1996. *Natural Phonology. The State of the Art*. Berlin-New York-Amsterdam: Mouton de Gruyter.

Iannace, Gaetano 1983. *Interferenza linguistica ai confini fra Stato e Regno. Il dialetto di San Leucio del Sannio*. Ravenna: Longo.

ID = *L'Italia dialettale*

IF = *Indogermanische Forschungen*

Ilari, Rodolfo 1999. 'Notas para uma semântica do passado composto em português', in Pál, Ferenc (ed.), *Actas do Congresso internacional organizado por motivo dos vinte anos do português no ensino superior*. Departamento de português da Universidade Eötvös Loránd de Budapeste, pp. 224–47.

ILCV = Diehl (1925–31)

Iliescu, Maria 1990. 'Les suffixes d'élargissement verbaux. (Etat de la question. Evolution sémantique de -esc- / -isc-.)', in Calboli, Gualtiero (ed.), *Latin vulgaire – latin tardif II*. Tübingen: Niemeyer, pp. 159–69.

2007. *Româna din perspectivă romanică. Le roumain dans la Romania. Rumanisch: die östlichste Sprache der Romania*. Bucharest: Editura Academiei Române.

2008. 'Das "possessive" Genitivattribut im Altfranzösischen und im Rumänischen', in Heinemann, Sabine and Videsott, Paul (eds.), *Sprachwandel und (Dis-)Kontinuität in der Romania*. Tübingen: Niemeyer, pp. 15–25.

Iliescu, Maria and Mourin, Louis. 1991. *Typologie de la morphologie verbale romane 1 Vue synchronique*. Innsbruck: Innsbrucker Beiträge zur Kulturwissenschaft.

Imbs, Paul (dir.) 1971. *Dictionnaire des fréquences. Vocabulaire littéraire des XIXe et XXe siècles*. Paris: CNRS-Klincksieck.

Iordan, Iorgu, Guțu-Romalo, Valeria and Niculescu, Alexandru 1967. *Structura morfologică a limbii române contemporane*. Bucharest: Editura Științifică.

Iscrulescu, Cristian 2006. 'The nominal stress system of Romanian (re)revisited', in Montreuil, J.-P. (ed.), *New Perspectives on Romance Linguistics, vol. II:*

Phonetics, Phonology and Dialectology. Amsterdam-Philadelphia: Benjamins, pp. 127–40.

Ivănescu, Gheorghe 1980. *Istoria limbii romîne*. Junimea: Iași.

Ive, Antonio 1886. 'L'antico dialetto di Veglia', *AGI* 9:114–87.

Jaberg, Karl and Jud, Jakob 1928–40. *Sprach- und Sachatlas Italiens und der Südschweiz*. Zofingen: Ringier.

Jackson, Kenneth H. 1953. *Language and History in Early Britain*. Edinburgh: Edinburgh University Press.

Jaeggli, Osvlado 1981. *Topics in Romance Syntax*. Dordrecht: Foris.

Jakobson, Roman, Fant, Gunnar and Halle, Morris 1952. *Preliminaries to Speech Analysis*. Cambridge, MA: MIT Press. (Reprinted 1972.)

Jakobson, Roman and Halle, Morris 1962. *Tenseness and Laxness* [appendix to the reprint of Jakobson *et al.*, (1952), pp. 57–61].

Jakobson, Roman and Waugh, Linda 1987. *The Sound Shape of Language*. Berlin-New York: Mouton de Gruyter.

Jaszczolt, Katarzyna 2002. *Semantics and Pragmatics. Meaning in Language and Discourse*. London: Pearson /Longman.

Jelinek, Eloise 1984. 'Empty categories, Case, and configurationality', *NLLT* 2:39–76.

Jenkins, Edgar 1932. *Index verborum Terentianus*. Chapel Hill: University of North Carolina Press.

Jennings, A. C. 1940. *A Linguistic Study of the Cartulario de San Vicente de Oviedo*. New York: Vanni.

Jensen, Frede 1976. *The Old Provençal Noun and Adjective Declension*. Odense: Universitetsforlag.

1990. *Old French and Comparative Gallo-Romance Syntax*. Tübingen: Niemeyer.

1994. *Syntaxe de l'ancien occitan*. Tübingen: Niemeyer. (Beihefte zur *Zeitschrift für romanische Philologie* 257).

Jespersen, Otto 1917. *Negation in English and Other Languages*. Copenhagen: A.F. Host.

1942. *A Modern English Grammar on Historical Principles, VI: Morphology*. London: Allen and Unwin / Copenhagen: Munksgaard.

JL = *Journal of Linguistics*

Joffre, Marie-Dominique 1995. *Le verbe latin. Voix et diathèse*. Louvain-Paris: Peeters.

Jones, Mari 2001. *Jersey Norman French. A Linguistic Study of an Obsolescent Dialect*. Oxford: Blackwell.

Jones, Michael 1988. 'Sardinian', in Harris and Vincent (eds.), pp. 314–50.

1993. *Sardinian Syntax*. London: Routledge.

1995. 'The prepositional accusative in Sardinian: its distribution and syntactic repercussions', in Smith, John Charles and Maiden, Martin (eds.), *Linguistic Theory and the Romance Languages*. Amsterdam: Benjamins, pp. 37–75.

1996. *Foundations of French Syntax*. Cambridge: Cambridge University Press.

1997. 'Sardinian', in Maiden and Parry (eds.), pp. 376–84.

Jordana, Cèsar August 1933. *El català i el castellà comparats*. Barcelona: Barcino.

Joseph, Brian 1998. 'Diachronic morphology', in Spencer, Andrew and Zwicky, Arnold (eds.), *The Handbook of Morphology*. Oxford: Blackwell, pp. 351–73.

Jud, Jakob. 1907. *Recherches sur la genèse et la diffusion des accusatifs en -ain et en -on*. Halle: Karras.

Juilland, Alphonse, Brodin, Dorothy and Davidovitch, Dorothy 1970. *Frequency Dictionary of French Words*. The Hague-Paris: Mouton.

Juilland, Alphonse and Chang-Rodriguez, E. 1964. *Frequency Dictionary of Spanish Words*. The Hague-Paris: Mouton.

Juilland, Alphonse and Traversa, Vicenzo 1973. *Frequency Dictionary of Italian Words*. The Hague-Paris: Mouton.

Jurafsky, Daniel 1996. 'Universal tendencies in the semantics of the diminutive', *Language* 72:533–78.

Kahane, Henry and Kahane, Renée 1948. 'The augmentative feminine in the Romance languages', *RPh* 2:135–75.

Kalepky, Theodor 1913. 'Präpositionale Passivobjekte im Spanischen, Portugiesischen und Rumänischen', *ZRPh* 37:358–64.

Karanastasis, Athanasios 1988. Ιστορικόν Λεξικόν των Ελληνικών Ιδιωμάτων της κατω Ιταλίας, 5 vols. Athens: Academy.

Karlsson, Keith 1981. *Syntax and Affixation. The Evolution of MENTE in Latin and Romance*. Tübingen: Niemeyer.

Kato, Mary Aizawa and Negrão, Esmeralda Vailati (eds.) 2000. *Brazilian Portuguese and the Null Subject Parameter*. Frankurt am Main-Madrid: Vervuert-Iberoamericana.

Kaye, Jonathan 1989. *Phonology. A Cognitive View*. Hillsdale-London: Lawrence Erlbaum Associates.

Kaye, Jonathan, Lowenstamm, Jean and Vergnaud, Jean-Roger 1990. 'Constituent structure and government in phonology', *Phonology* 7:193–231.

Kayne, Richard 1975. *French Syntax. The Transformational Cycle*. Cambridge, MA: MIT Press.

1976. 'French relative que', in Luján, Marta and Hensey, Fritz (eds.), *Current Studies in Romance Linguistics*. Washington: Georgetown University Press, pp. 255–99.

1991. 'Romance clitics, verb movement and PRO', *LI* 22:647–86.

1994. *The Antisymmetry of Syntax*. Cambridge, MA: MIT Press.

Keil = *Grammatici latini* ex recensione Henrici Keilii [reprinted Hildesheim: Olms, 1981]

Kelemen, J., Bárdosi, V., Kiss, S., Pataki, P. and Pálfy, M. 1985. *Grammaire du français contemporain*. Budapest: Tankönyvkiadó.

Keller, O. 1928. *La Flexion du verbe dans le patois genevois*. Geneva: Archivum Romanicum.

Kemenade, Ans (van) and Vincent, Nigel (eds.) 1997. *Parameters of Morphosyntactic Change*. Cambridge: Cambridge University Press.

Kemmer, Suzanne 1993. *The Middle Voice*. Amsterdam: Benjamins.

Kennedy, Elspeth 1972. 'The use of *tu* and *vous* in the first part of the Old French prose *Lancelot*', in Barnett, F., Crow, A., Robson, C. A., Rothwell, W. and Ullman, S. (eds.), *History and Structure of French. Essays in the Honour of Professor T. B. W. Reid*. Oxford: Blackwell, pp. 136–49.

Kincaid, Peter 1986. *The Rule of the Road. An International Guide to History and Practice*. New York: Greenwood Press.

Kiparsky Paul 1995. 'The phonological basis of sound change', in Goldsmith, J. (ed.), *The Handbook of Phonological Theory*. Oxford: Blackwell, pp. 640–70.

Kiss, Katalin 1987. *Configurationality in Hungarian*. Dordrecht: Reidel.

Kiss, Sándor 1972. *Les Transformations de la structure syllabique en latin tardif*. Debrecen: Studia Romanica Universitatis de Ludovico Kossuth nominatae.

1982. *Tendances évolutives de la syntaxe verbale en latin tardif*. Debrecen: Kossuth Lajos Tudományegyetem.

Klare, J. 1987. 'Zur sozialen und funktionalem Varianz von *ça* im modernen Französisch', in Neumand, W. and Techtmeier, B. (eds.), *Bedeutungen und Ideen in Sprachen und Texten*. Berlin: Akademie Verlag, pp. 344–52.

Kleiber, Georges 1992. 'Anaphore-deixis: deux approches concurrentes', in Morel and Danon-Boileau (eds.), pp. 613–23.

Klein Andreu, Flora 1991. 'Losing ground: a discourse-pragmatic solution to the history of *-ra* in Spanish', in Fleischman, S. and Waugh, L. (eds.), *Discourse Pragmatics and the Verb*. London: Routledge, pp. 164–78.

Klingebiel, Kathryn 1989. *Noun + Verb Compounding in Western Romance*. Berkeley: University of California Press.

Kloss, Heinz 1967. '"Abstand Languages" and "Ausbau Languages"', *Anthropological Linguistics* 9:29–41.

Koch, Peter 1995. 'Der Beitrag der Prototypentheorie zur historischen Semantik: Eine kritische Bestandsaufnahme', *Romanistisches Jahrbuch* 46:27–46.

1997. 'D'où viennent les substantifs spatio-locaux? L'organisation lexicale et cognitive des dimensions spatiale et temporelle', in Dupuy-Engelhardt, Hiltraud and Montibus, Marie-Jeanne (eds.), *Actes d'EUROSEM 1996*. Rheims: Presses Universitaires de Reims, pp. 107–22.

1999. 'Tree and fruit: a cognitive-onomasiological approach', *Studi italiani di linguistica teorica e applicata* 28:331–47.

2000. 'Pour une approche cognitive du changement sémantique lexical: aspect onomasiologique', in François, Jacques (ed.), *Théories contemporaines du changement sémantique* (=*Mémoires de la Société Linguistique de Paris*, N.S. 9), pp. 75–95.

2005. 'Ein Blick auf die unsichtbare Hand: Kognitive Universalien und historische romanische Lexikologie', in Stehl, Thomas (ed.), *Unsichtbare Hand und*

Sprecherwahl. Typologie und Prozesse des Sprachwandels in der Romania. Tübingen: Narr, pp. 245–75.

Koch, Peter and Marzo, Daniela. 2007. 'A two-dimensional approach to the study of motivation in lexical typology and its first application to French high-frequency vocabulary', *Studies in Language* 31:259–91.

Koch, Peter and Steinkrüger, Patrick 2001. 'Poligenesi lessicale e dati "empirici"', in Albano Leoni, Federico *et al.* (eds.), *Dati empirici e teorie linguistiche. Atti del XXXIII Congresso internazionale di studi della Società de linguistica italiana.* Rome: Bulzoni, pp. 527–43.

Komatsu, Eisuke and Harris, Roy (eds.) 1993. *Ferdinand de Saussure, Troisième Cours de linguistique générale 1910–1911, d'après les cahiers d'Emile Constantin.* Oxford-New York: Pergamon Press.

Komatsu, Eisuke and Wolf, George (eds.) 1996. *Ferdinand de Saussure, Premier Cours de linguistique générale 1907, d'après les cahiers d'Albert Riedlinger.* Oxford-New York: Pergamon Press.

  1997. *Ferdinand de Saussure, Deuxième Cours de linguistique générale 1908–1909, d'après les cahiers d'Albert Riedlinger et Charles Patois.* Oxford-New York: Pergamon Press.

Konneker, Beverly Hill 1975. 'Word order change in Italic', in Grossman, Robin, San, J. and Vance, T. (eds.), *Papers from the Eleventh Regional Meeting of the Chicago Linguistic Society.* Chicago: The Linguistic Society, pp. 366–70.

Koppelberg, Stephan 1998. *Untersuchungen zum lateinischen Erbwortschatz des Katalanischen. Aspekte der Klassifikierung und Differenzierung im Verhaltnis zu Gallo- und Hispano-Romania.* Münster: Nodus.

Koptjevskaja-Tamm, Maria, Vanhove, Martine and Koch, Peter 2007. 'Typological approaches to lexical semantics', *Linguistic Typology* 11:159–85.

Kovačec, August 1963. 'Notes de lexicologie istro-roumaine: sur la disparition des mots anciens et leur remplacement par des mots croates', *Studia Romanica et Anglica Zagabriensia* 15/16:3–39.

  1966. 'Quelques influences croates dans la morphosyntaxe istroroumaine', *Studia Romanica et Anglica Zagabriensia* 21/22:57–76.

  1968. 'Observations sur les influences croates dans la grammaire istroroumaine', *La Linguistique* 1:79–115.

  1971. *Descrierea istromânei actuale.* Bucharest: Editura Academiei.

Kramer, Johannes 1983. *Glossaria bilingua in papyris et membranis reperta.* Bonn: Habelt.

  1989. 'Areallinguistik II. Aromunisch', *LRL* (III), pp. 423–35.

  1995. 'Verschriftungsarten und -tendenzen in der Romania', *LRL* (II.ii), pp. 584–97.

Krefeld, Thomas 1999a. 'Cognitive ease and lexical borrowing: the recategorization of body parts in Romance', in Blank, Andreas and Koch, Peter (eds.), *Historical Semantics and Cognition.* Berlin-New York: Mouton de Gruyter, pp. 259–73.

1999b. *Wortgestalt und Vokalsystem in der Italoromania. Plädoyer für eine gestalt-phonologische Rekonstruktion des romanischen Vokalismus*. Kiel: Westensee Verlag.

Kroch, Anthony 1989. 'Reflexes of grammar in patterns of language changes', *Journal of Language and Variation and Change* 1:199–244.

Kroll, Wilhelm 1912. 'Der lateinische Relativsatz', *Glotta* 3:1–18.

Kuen, Heinrich 1923. 'Zur Chronologie des Uebergangs von *a > e* im Grödnischen', *ZRPh* 43:68–77.

Kühner, Raphael and Stegman, Carl 1912–14. *Ausführliche Grammatik der lateinischen Sprache*. Hannover: Hahnsche Buchhandlung.

Kurschildgen, Elke. 1983. *Untersuchungen zu Funktionsveränderungen bei Suffixen im Lateinischen und Romanischen*. Rheinische Beiträge zur lateinisch-romanischen Wortbildungslehre. Bonn: RHV.

Kuryłowicz, Jerzy 1958. *L'Accentuation des langues indo-européennes*. Wrocław-Kraków: Zakład Narodowy im. Ossolyńskich.

La Fauci, Nunzio 1988. *Oggetti e soggetti nella formazione della morfosintassi romanza*. Pisa: Giardini.

1991. 'La continuità nella diversità formale: aspetti di morfosintassi diacronica romanza', in Orioles, Vincenzo (ed.), *Innovazione e conservazione nelle lingue*. Pisa: Giardini, pp. 135–58.

1997. *Per una teoria grammaticale del mutamento morfosintattico. Dal latino verso il romanzo*. Pisa: ETS.

1998. 'Riflettendo sul mutamento morfosintattico: nel latino, verso il romanzo', in Ramat and Roma (eds.), pp. 519–45.

2006. 'Dinamiche sistematiche. Perifrasi perfettive e futuro sintetico: dal latino al romanzo', in Oniga, R. and Zennaro, L. (eds.), *Atti della Giornata di Linguistica Latina*. Venice: Libreria Editrice Cafoscarina, pp. 101–31.

Labov, William 1994. *Principles of Linguistic Change. Volume 1: Internal Factors*. Oxford: Blackwell.

Lacheret-Dujour, Anne and Beaugendre, Frédéric 1999. *La prosodie du français*. Paris: CNRS.

Lafont, Robert 1967. *La phrase occitane. Essai d'analyse systématique*. Montpellier: PUF.

1991. 'Okzitanisch: Interne Sprachgeschichte I. Grammatik-Histoire interne de la langue I. Grammaire', *LRL* (V, 2), pp.1–18.

Lahiri, Aditi, Riad, Tomas and Jacobs, Heike 1999. 'Diachronic prosody', in van der Hulst (ed.), pp. 335–422.

Lakoff, George 1971. 'On generative semantics', in Steinberg, D. D. and Jakobovits, L. A. (eds.), *Semantics. An Interdisciplinary Reader in Philosophy, Linguistics, and Psychology*. London-New York: Cambridge University Press, pp. 232–96.

Lakoff, George and Johnson, Mark 1980. *Metaphors We Live By*. Chicago: University of Chicago Press.

Lakoff, Robin 1968. *Abstract Syntax and Latin Complementation*. Cambridge, MA: MIT Press.

1972. 'Another look at drift', in Stockwell, Robert and Macauley, Ronald (eds.), *Linguistic Change and Generative Theory*. Bloomington, IN: Indiana University Press, pp. 172–98.

Lambrecht, Knud 1994. *Information Structure and Sentence Form*. Cambridge: Cambridge University Press.

Lambrior, A. 1878. 'L'*e* bref latin en roumain', *Romania* 7:85–93.

Lang, H. 1909. 'Zum Cancioneiro da ajuda', *ZRPh* 32:129–60; 290–311.

Lang, Mervyn 1990. *Spanish Word Formation*. London: Routledge.

Lang, R. Hamilton 1887. 'On archaic survivals in Cyprus', *Journal of the Anthropological Institute of Great Britain and Ireland* 16:186–88.

Langacker, Ronald 1977. 'Syntactic reanalysis', in Li, Charles (ed.), *Mechanisms of Syntactic Change*, Austin-London: University of Texas Press, pp. 57–139.

1987. *Foundations of Cognitive Grammar. 1. Theoretical Prerequisites*. Stanford, CA: Stanford University Press.

Lapesa, Rafael 1974. 'El sustantivo sin actualizador en español', in Cano, Rafael and Echenique, María Teresa (eds.), *Estudios de morfosintaxis histórica*. Madrid: Gredos, pp. 436–54.

1975. 'La colocación del calificativo atributivo en español', in *Homenaje a la memoria de Don Antonio Rodríguez-Moniño 1910–1970*. Madrid: Castalia, pp. 329–45.

1980 (8th edn)/1981 (9th edn). *Historia de la lengua española*. Madrid: Gredos.

Larson, Pär 2000. 'Tra linguistica e fonti diplomatiche: quello che le carte dicono e non dicono', in Hermand and Marinetti (eds.), pp. 151–66.

Lass, Roger 1984. *Phonology. An Introduction to Basic Concepts*. Cambridge: Cambridge University Press.

1990. 'How to do things with junk: exaptation in language evolution', *JL* 26:79–102.

1997. *Historical Linguistics and Language Change*. Cambridge: Cambridge University Press.

1999. 'Phonology and morphology', in Lass, R. (ed.), *The Cambridge History of the English Language vol. III: 1476–1776*. Cambridge: Cambridge University Press, pp. 56–186.

Lathrop, Thomas 1980. *The Evolution of Spanish. An Introductory Historical Grammar*. Newark: Cuesta.

Laurent, Richard 1999. *Past Participles from Latin to Romance*. Berkeley: University of California Press.

Lausberg, Heinrich 1939. *Die Mundarten Südlukaniens*. Halle (Saale): Niemeyer.

1947. 'Zum romanischen Vokalismus', *RF* 60:295–307.

1956–62. *Romanische Sprachwissenschaft* I: *Einleitung und Vokalismus*. II: *Konsonantismus*. III: *Formenlehre*. Berlin: de Gruyter.

1969. *Romanische Sprachwissenschaft*. Berlin: de Gruyter.

1971. *Linguistica romanza*. I. *Fonetica*. Milan: Feltrinelli.

1976 (2nd edn). *Linguistica romanza*. Milan: Feltrinelli.

Le Maistre, Frank. 1966. *Dictionnaire jersiais-français*. Jersey: Le Don Balleine.

Lebsanft, Franz and Gleßgen, Martin-Dietrich (eds.) 2004a. *Historische Semantik in den romanischen Sprachen*. Niemeyer: Tübingen.

2004b. 'Historische Semantik in den romanischen Sprachen: Kognition, Pragmatik, Geschichte', in Lebsanft and Gleßgen (eds.), pp. 1–28.

Ledgeway, Adam 1998. 'Variation in the Romance infinitive: the case of the southern Calabrian inflected infinitive', *TPS* 96:1–61.

2000. *A Comparative Syntax of the Dialects of Southern Italy. A Minimalist Approach*. Oxford: Blackwell.

2003a. 'L'estensione dell'ausiliare perfettivo *avere* nell'antico napoletano: Intransitività scissa condizionata da fattori modali', *AGI* 88:27–71.

2003b. 'Linguistic theory and the mysteries of Italian dialects', in Lepschy, Anna Laura and Tosi, Arturo (eds.), *Multilingualism in Italy. Past and Present*. Oxford: Legenda, pp. 108–40.

2004a. 'Il sistema completivo dei dialetti meridionali: la doppia serie di complementatori', *Rivista Italiana di Dialettologia* 27:89–147.

2004b. 'Lo sviluppo dei dimostrativi nei dialetti centromeridionali', *Lingua e stile* 39:65–112.

2005. 'Moving through the left periphery: the dual complementiser system in the dialects of southern Italy', *TPS* 103:336–96.

2006. 'The dual complementiser system in southern Italy: *Spirito greco, materia romanza?*', in Lepschy and Tosi (eds.), pp. 112–26.

2007a. 'La posizione dell'aggettivo nella storia del napoletano', in Bentley and Ledgeway, pp. 104–25.

2007b. 'Old Neapolitan word order: some initial observations', in Lepschy and Tosi, pp. 121–49.

2008. 'Satisfying V2: *Sì* clauses in old Neapolitan', *JL* 44:437–40.

2009. *Grammatica diacronica del napoletano*. Tübingen: Niemeyer.

2010. 'The clausal domain: CP structure and the left periphery', in D'Alessandro, Roberta, Ledgeway, Adam and Roberts, Ian (eds.), *Syntactic Variation. The Dialects of Italy*. Cambridge: Cambridge University Press, pp. 38–51.

in press. 'Subject licensing in CP: the Neapolitan double-subject construction', in Benincà, Paola and Munaro, Nicola (eds.), *Mapping the Left Periphery*. Oxford: Oxford University Press.

Lehiste, Ilse 1970. *Suprasegmentals*. Cambridge, MA: MIT Press.

Lehmann, Christian 1984. *Der Relativsatz*. Tübingen: Narr.

1991. 'The Latin nominal group in typological perspective', in Coleman (ed.), pp. 203–32.

Lehmann, Winfred 1968. 'Saussure's dichotomy between descriptive and historical linguistics', in Lehmann and Malkiel (eds.), pp. 5–20.

1971. 'On the rise of SOV patterns in New High German', in Schweistal, Klaus Günther (ed.), *Grammatik Kybernetik Kommunikation. Festschrift für Alfred Hoppe*. Sine Loco: Drümmler, pp. 19–24.

1972. 'Contemporary linguistics and Indo-European studies', *Publications of the Modern Language Association of America* 87:976–93.

1974. *Proto-Indo-European Syntax*. Austin: University of Texas Press.

1982. 'Introduction: diachronic linguistics', in Lehmann and Malkiel (eds.), pp. 1–16.

Lehmann, Winfred and Malkiel, Yakov (eds.) 1968. *Directions for Historical Linguistics*. Austin-London: University of Texas Press.

(eds.) 1982. *Perspectives on Historical Linguistics*. Amsterdam: Benjamins.

LEI = Pfister, Max 1979–. *Lessico Etimologico Italiano*. Wiesbaden: Reinhart.

Lejeune, Michel 1975. 'Réflexions sur la phonologie du vocalisme osque', *Bulletin dela Société de linguistique de Paris* 70:233–51.

Lemieux, Monique and Dupuis, Fernande 1995. 'The locus of verb movement in non-asymmetric verb-second languages: the case of Middle French', in Battye and Roberts (eds.), pp. 80–109.

Leone, Alfonso 1980. *La morfologia del verbo nelle parlate della Sicilia sud-orientale*. Palermo: Centro di Studi Filologici e Linguistici Siciliani.

Lepschy, Anna Laura and Lepschy, Giulio 1988. *The Italian Language Today*. London: Hutchinson.

Lepschy, Anna Laura and Tosi, Arturo (eds.) 2006. *Rethinking Languages in Contact. The Case of Italian*. Oxford: Legenda.

2007. *Histories and Dictionaries of the Languages of Italy*. Ravenna: Longo.

Lepschy, Giulio 1962. 'Il problema dell'accento latino: rassegna critica di studi sull'accento latino e sullo studio dell'accento', *Annali della SNS di Pisa, 2nd series*, 31:199–246.

Leumann, Manu 1977. *Lateinische Laut- und Formenlehre*. Munich: Beck.

Leumann, Manu and Hofmann, Johannes 1928. *Lateinische Grammatik*. Munich: Beck.

Levinson, Stephen 1983. *Pragmatics*. Cambridge: Cambridge University Press.

2000. *Presumptive Meanings. The Theory of Generalized Conversational Implicatures*. Cambridge, MA: MIT Press.

LI = *Linguistic Inquiry*

Lightfoot, David 1979. *Principles of Diachronic Syntax*. Cambridge: Cambridge University Press.

1999. *The Development of Language, Acquisition, Change and Evolution*. Oxford: Blackwell.

2003. 'Grammatical approaches to syntactic change', in Joseph, Brian and Janda, Richard (eds.), *The Handbook of Historical Linguistics*. Oxford: Blackwell, pp. 495–508.

Linde, P. 1923. 'Die Stellung des Verbs in der lateinischen Prosa', *Glotta* 12:153–78.

Linder, Karl Peter 1987. *Grammatische Untersuchungen zur Charakteristik des Rätoromanischen in Graubünden*. Tübingen: Narr.

Lindsay, Wallace 1894. *The Latin Language. An Historical Account of Latin Sounds, Stems, and Flexions*. Oxford: Clarendon.

Lindsay, Wallace (ed.) 1964. *Nonius Marcellus. De compendiosa doctrina*, 3 vols. Hildesheim: Olms.

Lipski, John 1994. *Latin American Spanish*. London: Longman.

Liver, Ricarda 1999. *Rätoromanisch*. Tübingen: Narr.

Lloyd, Paul 1968. *Verb-Complement Compounds in Spanish*. Tübingen: Niemeyer.

  1987. *From Latin to Spanish. Historical Phonology and Morphology of the Spanish Language*. Philadelphia: American Philosophical Society.

LN = *Lingua nostra*

Löfstedt, Bengt 1961. *Studien über die Sprache der Langobardischen Gesetze, Beiträge zur frühmittelalterlichen Latinität*. Stockholm: Almqvist och Wiksell.

Löfstedt, Einar 1911. *Philologischer Kommentar zur Peregrinatio Aetheriae. Untersuchungen zur Geschichte der lateinischen Sprache*. Uppsala: Almqvist och Wiksell.

  1933. *Syntactica*. Lund: C. W. K. Gleerup.

  1942. *Syntactica. Studien und Beiträge zur historischen Syntax des Lateins. Erster Teil: Über einige Grundfragen der lateinischen Nominalsyntax*. Lund: Gleerup.

Löfstedt, Leena 1982. 'À propos des articles et des articloïdes', in Rohrer, Christian (ed.) *Logos Semantikos. IV Gramática*. Berlin: de Gruyter, pp. 269–77.

Lois, Ximena 1989. *Aspects de la syntaxe de l'espagnol et théorie de la grammaire*. Université de Paris VIII: unpublished thesis.

Lombard, Alf 1955. *Le Verbe roumain*. Lund: Gleerup.

  1974. *La langue roumaine. Une présentation*. Paris: Klincksieck.

Lombardi, Alessandra 1997. *The Grammar of Complementation in the Dialects of Calabria*. University of Manchester: unpublished thesis.

  2007a. 'Posizione dei clitici e ordine dei costituenti nella lingua sarda medievale', in Bentley and Ledgeway (eds.), pp. 133–47.

  2007b. 'Definiteness and possessive constructions in medieval Italo-Romance', in Lepschy and Tosi (eds.), pp. 99–118.

Lombardi, Alessandra and Middleton, Roberta 2004. 'Alcune osservazioni sull'ordine delle parole negli antichi volgari italiani', in Dardano, Maurizio and Frenguelli, Gianluca (eds.), *SintAnt. La sintassi dell'italiano antico. Atti del Convegno internazionale di studi*. Rome: Aracne, pp. 553–82.

Lombroso, Cesare 1889. *L'uomo delinquente in rapporto all'Antropologia, alla Giurisprudenza ed alle Discipline carcerarie*. Turin: Bocca.

Longnon, Auguste (ed.) 1977. *François Villon. Œuvres* (quatrième édition revue par Lucien Foulet; nouveau tirage suivi de notes sur le texte par A. Lanly). Paris: Champion.

Longobardi, Giuseppe 1994. 'Reference and proper names: a theory of N-movement in syntax and Logical Form', *LI* 25:609–65.

2001. 'Formal syntax, diachronic minimalism and etymology: the history of French *chez*', *LI* 32:275–302.

López Palma, Helena 2004. *La deixis. Lecturas sobre los demonstrativos y los indiciales*. Lugo: Axac Editorial.

Loporcaro, Michele 1988. *Grammatica storica del dialetto di Altamura*. Pisa: Giardini.

1996. 'On the analysis of geminates in Standard Italian and Italian dialects', in Hurch and Rhodes (eds.), pp. 153–87.

1997. *L'origine del raddoppiamento fonosintattico. Saggio di fonologia diacronica romanza*. Basel-Tübingen: Francke.

1998a. *Sintassi comparata dell'accordo participiale romanzo*. Turin: Rosenberg & Sellier.

1998b. 'Syllable structure and sonority sequencing: evidence from Emilian', in Schwegler *et al.* (eds.), pp. 155–70.

1999. 'Il futuro CANTARE-HABEO nell'Italia meridionale', *AGI* 84:67–114.

2000. 'Stress stability under cliticization and the prosodic status of Romance clitics', in Repetti (ed.), pp. 137–68.

2001. 'Flessione a tre casi del pronome personale in un dialetto alle porte di Roma', in Zamboni, Alberto, Del Puente, Patrizia and Vigolo, Maria Teresa, (eds.), *La dialettologia oggi fra tradizione e nuove metodologie. Atti del Convegno Internazionale*, Pisa 10–12 Febbraio 2000. Pisa: ETS, pp. 457–76.

2003a. *Dialettologia, linguistica storica e riflessione grammaticale nella romanistica del Duemila. Con esempi dal sardo*, in Sánchez Miret (ed.), vol. I, pp. 83–111.

2003b. 'Rise and fall of contrastive vowel quantity in Northern Italo-Romance. Or: why comparison is better'. Paper given at the *International Congress of Historical Linguistics XVI*, Copenhagen, 10–16 August 2003.

2005a. 'Di una presunta reintroduzione preromanza di -US di accusativo plurale in Sardegna', *Studi e Saggi Linguistici* 40f:187–205.

2005b. 'La sillabazione di muta cum liquida dal latino al romanzo', in Kiss, S., Mondin, L. and Salvi, G. (eds.), *Etudes de linguistique offertes à József Herman à l'occasion de son 80ème anniversaire*. Tübingen: Niemeyer, pp. 419–30.

2005–6. 'I dialetti dell'Appennino tosco-emiliano e il destino delle atone finali nel(l'italo-)romanzo settentrionale', *ID* 66–67:69–122.

2007a. 'Facts, theory and dogmas in historical linguistics: vowel quantity from Latin to Romance', in Salmons, Joseph and Dubenion-Smith, Shannon (eds.), *Historical Linguistics 2005. Selected Papers from the 17th International Conference on Historical Linguistics*. Amsterdam-Philadelphia: Benjamins, pp. 311–36.

2007b. 'On triple auxiliation in Romance', *Linguistics* 45:173–222.

Loporcaro, Michele, Delucchi, Rachele, Nocchi, Nadia, Paciaroni, Tania and Schmid, Stephan 2006. 'La durata consonantica nel dialetto di Lizzano in Belvedere (Bologna)', in Savy, R. and Crocco, C. (eds.), *Analisi prosodica. Teorie, modelli e sistemi di annotazione, AISV 2005*. Torriana (RN): EDK, 98 [abstract], pp. 491–517 [cd-rom].

Loporcaro, Michele and Limacher-Riebold, Ute 2001. 'La sintassi nei lessici storici: sull'origine del costrutto *figlio a* nell'italo-romanzo', in Fábián, Zsuzsanna and Salvi, Giampaolo, *Semantica e lessicologia storiche. Atti del XXXII Congresso della Società di linguistica italiana*. Rome: Bulzoni, pp. 261–79.

Loporcaro, Michele, Nocchi, Nadia, Paciaroni, Tania and Schwarzenbach, Michael 2007. *Dittongazione e metafonia nel dialetto di Agnone (IS)*. Paper read at the *Fourth AISV Conference*, Cosenza, 3–5 December 2007.

Loporcaro, Michele, Paciaroni, Tania and Schmid, Stephan 2005. 'Consonanti geminate in un dialetto lombardo alpino', in Cosi, P. (ed.), *Misura dei parametri. Aspetti tecnologici ed implicazioni nei modelli linguistici, AISV 2004*, 1° Convegno Nazionale, Università di Padova. Brescia: EDK, 67 [abstract], pp. 579–618 [cd-rom].

Lowenstamm, Jean 1996. 'CV as the only syllable type', in Durand, Jacques and Laks, B. (eds.), *Current Trends in Phonology. Models and Methods*. Salford: University of Salford, 2, pp. 419–41.

LRL = Holtus, Metzeltin and Schmitt (eds.)

Lucci, Vincent 1972. *Phonologie de l'acadien (Parler de la région de Moncton, N. B., Canada)*. Montréal-Paris-Brussels: Didier.

Lüdi, Georges 1978. 'Die Alternanz zwischen Dativ und Akkusativ bei *prier, supplier, requérir* im 15. Und 16. Jahrhundert', *VR* 37:160–92.

1981. 'Sémantique, syntaxe et forme casuelle: remarques sur la construction *aider à qn.* en français romand', *VR* 40:85–97.

Lüdtke, Helmut 1956. *Die strukturelle Entwicklung des romanischen Vokalismus*. Bonn: Romanisches Seminar an der Universität.

1959. 'Zur bündnerromanischen Laut- und Formenlehre', *Romanistisches Jahrbuch* 10: 19–33.

1965a. 'Die lateinischen Endungen *-im, -um, -unt* und ihre romanischen Ergebnisse', in *Omagiu lui Alexandru Rosetti la 70 de ani*. Bucureşti: Editura Academiei, pp. 487–499.

1965b. 'Le vie di comunicazione dell'Impero romano e la formazione dei dialetti romanzi', in Straka (ed.), vol. III, pp. 1103–9.

1974 [1968]. *Historia del léxico románico*. Madrid: Gredos.

2005. *Der Ursprung der romanischen Sprachen. Eine Geschichte der sprachlichen Kommunikation*. Kiel: Westensee Verlag.

Luján, Martha 1976. 'The analysis of reflexive inchoatives', in Luján, M. and Hensy, Fr. (eds.), *Current Studies in Romance Linguistics*. Washington, DC: Georgetown University Press, pp. 377–87.

Lunn, Patricia and Cravens, Thomas 1991. 'A contextual reconsideration of the Spanish *-ra* indicative', in Fleischman, S. and Waugh, L. (eds.), *Discourse Pragmatics and the Verb*. London: Routledge, pp. 147–63.

Lupinu, Giovanni 2000. *Latino epigrafico della Sardegna. Aspetti fonetici*. Nuoro: Ilisso.

Lyons, Christopher 1986. 'On the origin of the Old French strong-weak possessive distinction', *TPS* 84: 1–41.

    1995. 'Voice, aspect, and arbitrary arguments', in Smith, John Charles and Maiden, Martin (eds.), *Linguistic Theory and the Romance Languages*. Amsterdam-Philadelphia: Benjamins, pp. 77–114.

    1999. *Definiteness*. Cambridge: Cambridge University Press.

Mac Cormac, Earl 1985. *A Cognitive Theory of Metaphor*. Cambridge, MA: MIT Press.

Machado, José Pedro 1952–56. *Dicionário etimológico da língua portuguesa com a mais antiga documentação escrita e conhecida de muitos dos vocábulos estudados*. Lisbon: Confluência.

Mackel, Emil 1896. 'Zur romanischen Vokaldehnung in betonter freien Silbe', *ZRPh* 20:514–19.

Mackenzie, Ian 2006. *Unaccusative Verbs in Romance Languages*. Basingstoke: Palgrave Macmillan.

Macrea, Dumitru 1965. 'La tradition de la langue roumaine littéraire et le phénomène phonétique de la palatalisation des labiales', in Straka (ed.), vol. III, pp. 1219–33.

Magnani, Franca 1976. 'Contributi gergali', *SGI* 5:177–94.

Magni, Elisabetta 2000. 'L'ordine delle parole nel latino pompeiano: sulle tracce di una deriva', *AGI* 85:3–37.

    2001. 'Paradigm organization and lexical connections in the organization of the Italian passato remoto', in Booij, G. and van Marle, J. (eds.), *Yearbook of Morphology 1999*, pp. 75–96.

Maiden, Martin 1987. 'New perspectives on the genesis of Italian Metaphony', *TPS* 85:38–73.

    1988. 'On the dynamics of low mid vowel diphthongization in Tuscan and Gallo-Italian', *Canadian Journal of Italian Studies* 11:1–37.

    1989. 'Sulla morfologizzazione della metafonesi nei dialetti italiani meridionali', *ZRPh* 105:178–92.

    1991a. *Interactive Morphonology. Metaphony in Italy*. London: Routledge.

    1991b. 'On the phonological vulnerability of complex paradigms: beyond analogy in Italo- and Ibero-Romance', *RPh* 54:284–305.

    1992. 'Irregularity as a determinant of morphological change', *JL* 28:285–312.

    1995a. *A Linguistic History of Italian*. London: Longman.

    1995b. 'A proposito dell'alternanza *esce, usciva*, in italiano', *LN* 56:37–41.

    1995c. [Review of Davis and Napoli 1994], *Forum Italicum* 29:391–93.

    1996a. 'On the Romance inflectional endings -i and -e', *RPh* 50:147–82.

    1996b. 'The Romance gerund and system-dependent naturalness in morphology', *TPS* 94:167–201.

    1996c. 'Ipotesi sulle origini del condizionale analitico come "futuro del passato" in italiano', in Benincà *et al.* (eds.), pp. 149–73.

1997. 'Inflectional morphology of the noun and adjective', in Maiden and Parry (eds.), pp. 68–74.

1998a. 'Towards an explanation of some morphological changes which "should never have happened"', in Schmid, M., Austin, J. and Stein, D. (eds.), *Historical Linguistics 1997*. Amsterdam: Benjamins, pp. 241–54.

1998b. 'Metafonesi, "parola", "morfema": alcune riflessioni metodologiche', *Italienische Studien* 19:44–63.

1998c. *Storia linguistica dell'italiano*. Bologna: il Mulino.

2000a. 'Il sistema desinenziale del sostantivo nell'italo-romanzo preletterario. Ricostruzione parziale a partire dai dialetti moderni (il significato storico di plurali del tipo amici)', in Herman and Marinetti (eds.), pp. 167–79.

2000b. 'Di un cambiamento intramorfologico: origini del tipo *dissi dicesti* ecc., nell'italoromanzo', *AGI* 85:137–71.

2001a. 'A strange affinity: perfecto y tiempos afines', *Bulletin of Hispanic Studies* 58:441–64.

2001b. 'Di nuovo sulle alternanze velari nel verbo italiano e spagnolo', *Cuadernos de filología italiana* 8:39–61.

2004a. 'Verb augments and meaninglessness in early Romance morphology', *SGI* 22:1–61.

2004b. 'Into the past: morphological change in the dying years of Dalmatian', *Diachronica* 21:85–111.

2004c. 'Perfect pedigree: the ancestry of the Aromanian conditional', in Ashdowne, Richard and Finbow, Thomas (eds.), *Oxford Working Papers in Linguistics, Philology and Phonetics* 9:83–98.

2004d. 'When lexemes become allomorphs: on the genesis of suppletion', *Folia Linguistica* 38:227–56.

2005a. 'La ridistribuzione paradigmatica degli «aumenti» verbali nelle lingue romanze', in Kiss, S., Mondin, L. and Salvi, G. (eds.), *Etudes de linguistique offertes à József Herman à l'occasion de son 80ème anniversaire*. Tübingen: Niemeyer, pp. 433–40.

2005b. 'Morphological autonomy and diachrony', *Yearbook of Morphology 2004*, pp. 137–75.

2006a. 'On Romanian imperatives', *Philologica Jassyensia* 2:47–59.

2006b. 'Endangerment as stimulus to innovation? Some observations on the Romance languages of the eastern Adriatic'. Unpublished paper given to the *Third Oxford-Kobe Linguistics Seminar: The Linguistics of Endangered Languages*, Kobe Institute, Kobe, April 2006.

2007a. 'La linguistica romanza alla ricerca dell'arbitrario', in Trotter, David (ed.), *Actes du XXIVe Congrès international de linguistique et de philologie romanes, III*. Tübingen: Niemeyer, pp. 505–18.

2007b. 'On the morphology of Italo-Romance imperatives', in Bentley, Delia and Ledgeway, Adam (eds.), *Sui dialetti italoromanzi. Saggi in onore di Nigel B. Vincent*. Norfolk: Biddles, pp. 148–64.

2009. 'Un capitolo di morfologia storica del romeno: preterito e tempi affini', *ZRPh* 125(2):273–309.

Maiden, Martin and Parry, Mair (eds.) 1997. *The Dialects of Italy*. London: Routledge.

Maiden, Martin and Robustelli, Cecilia 2007. *A Reference Grammar of Modern Italian*. London: Arnold.

Maingueneau, D. 1996. *Les termes clés de l'analyse du discours*. Paris: Seuil.

Mair, Walter 1973. *Ennebergische Morphologie. Analyse eines dolomitenladinischen Flexion-systems*. Innsbruck: Institut für romanische Philologie.

Malagoli, Giuseppe 1910–13a. 'Studi sui dialetti reggiani: fonologia del dialetto di Novellara', *AGI* 17:29–197.

1910–13b. 'L'articolo maschile singolare nel dialetto di Piandelagotti (Modena)', *AGI* 17:250–54.

1930. 'Fonologia del dialetto di Lizzano in Belvedere (Appennino bolognese)', *ID* 6:125–96.

Maldonado, Ricardo 1993. 'Dynamic construals in Spanish', *Studi italiani di linguistica teorica e applicata* 22:532–66.

Maley, Catherine 1974. *The Pronouns of Address in Modern Standard French*. Romance monographs no. 10. Mississippi: University of Mississippi.

Malkiel, Yakov 1960. 'Paradigmatic resistance to sound change: the Old Spanish preterite forms *vide*, *vido* against the background of the recession of primary -*d*-', *Language* 36: 281–346.

1968. 'The inflectional paradigm as an occasional determinant of sound change', in Lehmann and Malkiel (eds.), pp. 23–64.

1974a. 'Distinctive traits of Romance Linguistics', in Hymes, Dell (ed.), *Language in Culture and Society. A Reader in Linguistics and Anthropology*, New York: Harper and Row, pp. 671–88.

1974b. 'New problems in Romance interfixation (I) the velar insert in the present tense (with an excursus on -zer/-zir verbs)', *RPh* 27:304–55.

1980. 'The decline of Spanish *luengo* "long"; the disappearance of old Spanish *lueñ(e)* "far"', in d'Heur, Jean Marie and Cherubini, Nicoletta (eds.), *Etudes de philologie romane et d'histoire littéraire offertes à Jules Horrent*. Liège: [publisher unknown], pp. 267–73.

1981. 'The Old Spanish and Old Galician-Portuguese adjective *ledo*, archaic Spanish *liedo*', *La Corónica* 9:95–106.

1982. 'Morpho-semantic conditioning of Spanish diphthongization: the case of *teso* ~ *tieso*', *RPh* 36:154–84. (Reprinted in Malkiel, 1990: 199–229.)

1983a. 'Range of variation as a cue to dating', in *From Particular to General Linguistics*. Amsterdam-Philadelphia: Benjamins, pp. 87–125.

1983b. 'Gender, sex and size as reflected by the Romance languages', in *From Particular to General Linguistics*. Amsterdam-Philadelphia: Benjamins, pp. 155–75.

1984. 'La aversión al monosilabismo en los adjetivos del español antiguo y moderno', *Lingüística española actual* 6:5–27.

1985. 'Old and new problems in the Latinity of the Lower Danube', *Journal of the American-Romanian Academy of Arts and Sciences* 6/7:90–104.

1988. 'The Triple Janus Head of Romance Linguistics'. Lecture delivered in October 1988 in the Senate House of the University of Liverpool. Liverpool: Liverpool University Press [The Allison Peers Lectures Series].

1990. *Diachronic Problems in Phonosymbolism. Edita and Inedita, 1979–1988.* I. Amsterdam-Philadelphia: Benjamins.

Mallinson, Graham 1986. *Rumanian*. London: Croom Helm.

1988. 'Rumanian', in Harris and Vincent (eds.), pp. 391–419.

Mameli, Francesco 1998. *Il logudorese e il gallurese*. Villanova Monteleone: Soter.

Mancini, Marco 1994. 'Un passo del grammatico Pompeo e la dittongazione protoromanza', in Cipriano, P., Di Giovine, P. and Mancini, M. (eds.), *Miscellanea di studi linguistici in onore di Walter Belardi*. Rome: il Calamo, II, pp. 609–27.

2001. 'Agostino, i grammatici e il vocalismo del latino d'Africa', *Rivista di linguistica* 13:309–38.

Mańczak, Witold 1969. 'Survivance du nominatif singulier dans les langues romanes', *Revue romane* 4:51–60.

Manoliu-Manea, Maria 1985. 'Genetic type versus areal coherence: Rumanian case markers and the definite articles', in Deanović, M. *et al.* (eds.), *Zbornik u cast Petru Skoku o stotoj obljetnici rodenja (1881–1956) / Mélanges linguistiques dédiés à la mémoire de Petar Skok (1881–1956)*. Zagreb: Académie Yougoslave des Sciences et des Arts, pp. 301–308.

1987. 'The myth of the agent: roles and communicative dynamism in Romance', in Cazelles, B. and Girard, R. (eds.), *Alphonse Juilland. D'une passion l'autre.* Stanford, CA: Anma, pp. 261–75.

1988. 'Pragmatique et sémantique du passif: l'agent et le réfléchi roman', *Revue Romane* 23:198–210.

1989. 'Le roumain: morphosyntaxe', *LRL* (III), pp. 101–14.

1990. 'French neuter demonstratives: evidence for a pragma-semantic definition of pronouns', in Green, John and Ayres-Bennett, Wendy (eds.), *Variation and Change in French. Essays Presented to Rebecca Posner on the Occasion of her Sixtieth Birthday*. London-New York: Routledge, pp. 89–115.

1994. *Discourse and Pragmatic Constraints on Grammatical Choices. A Grammar of Surprises*. Amsterdam: Elsevier.

2000a. 'Interrogative utterances as non-questions: Romanian markers of talk-interaction', in *Romanistik in Geschichte und Gegenwart*. Trier-Hamburg: Helmut Buske Verlag, vol. 6, pp. 55–68.

2000b. 'Demonstratives, story-world, and talk-interaction', in Coene, M., Mulder, W., Dendale, P. and D'Hulst, Y. (eds.), *Traiani Augusti Vestigia*

Pressa Sequamur. Studia linguistica in Honorem Lilanae Tasmowski. Padua: Unipress, pp. 583–600.

2000c. 'Une hypothèse cognitive sur les formes latines en –R. A la recherche d'un invariant', in Schøsler, L. (ed.), *Le passif. Actes du colloque international*. University of Copenhagen: Museum Tusculanum Press, pp. 99–116.

2001. 'The conversational factor in language change. from prenominal to postnominal demonstratives', Brinton, Laurel (ed.), *Historical Linguistics 1999 Selected Papers from the 14th International Conference on Histoneri Linguistics, Vancouver, 9–13 August 1999*. Amsterdam-Philadelphia: Benjamins, pp. 187–205.

2005. 'The return of the goddess culture and gender in the history of Romance Languages', *Philologica Jassyensia* 1:69–85.

2006. 'Conventional implicature and grammatical change. from Latin middle to Romance reflexive', *Revue Roumaine de Linguistique* 51:245–66.

2007. 'The animacy fallacy: cognitive categories and noun classification'. Paper presented at the *18th International Conference on Historical Linguistics*, Montreal, 6–11 August 2007.

Maracz, Laszlo and Muysken, Pieter (eds.) 1989. *Configurationality. The Typology of Asymmetries*. Dordrecht: Foris.

Marazzini, Claudio 1994. *La lingua italiana. Profilo storico*. Bologna: il Mulino.

Marcato, Carla 1983. 'I gerghi veneti', in Cortelazzo, Manlio (ed.), *Guida ai dialetti veneti V*. Padua: CLEUP, pp. 123–52.

1988. 'Linguaggi gergali', *LRL* (IV), pp. 255–68.

1994. 'Il gergo', in Serianni, Luca and Trifone, Pietro (eds.), *Storia della lingua. II. Scritto e parlato*. Turin: Einaudi, pp. 757–91.

Marcato, Gianna and Thüne, Eva-Maria 2002. 'Gender and female visibility in Italian', in Hellinger, Marlis and Bußmann, Hadumod (eds.), *Gender Across Languages*, 2. Amsterdam-Philadelphia: Benjamins, pp. 187–217.

Marcato, Gianna and Ursini, Flavia 1998. *Dialetti veneti. Grammatica e storia*. Padua: Unipress.

March, H. Colley 1889. 'The meaning of ornament, or its archaeology and its psychology', *Transactions of the Lancashire and Cheshire Antiquarian Society* 7:160–92.

Marchello-Nizia, Christiane 1979. *Histoire de la langue française aux XIVe et XVe siècles*. Paris: Bordas.

1995. *L'évolution du français. Ordre des mots, démonstratifs, accent tonique*. Paris: Armand Colin.

1997. *La Langue française aux XIVe et XVe siècles*. Paris: Nathan.

Marcus, Gary, Brinkmann, Ursula, Clahsen, Harald, Wiese, Richard and Pinker, Steven 1995. 'German inflection: the exception that proves the rule', *Cognitive Psychology* 29: 189–256.

Marotta, Giovanna 1985. *Modelli e misure ritmiche. La durata vocalica in italiano*. Bologna: Zanichelli.

1993. 'Selezione dell'articolo e sillaba in italiano: un'interazione totale?', *SGI* 15:255–96.

1995. 'Proposte per l'interpretazione del cambiamento fonologico in area romanza nel segno della non linearità', in Ruffino (ed.), pp. 439–54.

Marouzeau, Jules 1922. *L'ordre des mots dans la phrase latine. I. Les groupes nominaux*. Paris: Champion.

1938. *L'ordre des mots dans la phrase latine. II. Le verbe*. Paris: Les Belles Lettres.

Marouzeau, Jules (ed.) 1947. *Térence. Heautontimoroumenos, Phormio*. Paris: Les Belles Lettres.

Marouzeau, Jules 1949. *L'ordre des mots dans la phrase latine. III. Les articulations de l'énoncé*. Paris: Les Belles Lettres.

1953. *L'ordre des mots en latin. Volume complémentaire*. Paris: Les Belles Lettres.

1955. *Notre langue*. Paris: Delagrave.

Marshall, John 1969. *The Donatz Proensals of Uc Faidit*. Oxford: Oxford University Press.

Martin, Jean-Baptiste 1990. 'Frankoprovenzalisch', *LRL* (V, 1):671–85.

Martín Zorraquino, María Antonia 1976. '*A* + objeto directo en el Cantar de Mio Cid', in Colòn, G. and Kopp, R. (eds.), *Mélanges offerts à C. Th. Gossen*. Bern–Liège: Francke, pp. 554–66.

Martinet, André 1952. 'Celtic lenitions and Western Romance consonants', *Language* 28:192–217.

1955. *Economie des changements phonétiques*. Berne: Francke.

1956. *La description phonologique avec application au parler franco-provençal d'Hauteville (Savoie)*. Geneva and Paris: Droz and Minard.

1960. *Eléments de linguistique générale*. Paris: Colin.

1969. 'Qu'est-ce que le "*e* muet"?', in *Le Français sans fard*. Paris: PUF, pp. 168–190.

1975. 'Remarques sur la phonologie des parlers francoprovençaux', in *Evolution des langues et reconstruction*. Paris: PUF, pp. 195–207.

Martínez, García Hortensia 1990. 'Del *pues* «temporal» al «causal» y «continuativo »', in Alvarez, A. (ed.), *Actas del Congreso de la Sociedad española de lingüística hispánica*. XX Aniversario, II, pp. 599–610.

Martínez Gil, Fernando 1997a. 'Obstruent vocalization in Chilean Spanish: a serial versus a constraint-based approach', *Probus* 9:167–202.

1997b. 'Word-final epenthesis in Galician', in Martínez-Gil and Morales-Front (eds.), pp. 269–340.

Martínez Gil, Fernando and Morales-Front, Alfonso (eds.) 1997. *Issues in the Phonology and Morphology of the Major Ibero-Romance Languages*. Washington, DC: Georgetown University Press.

Martino, Paolo. 1988. *Per la storia della 'Ndrànghita*. Dipartimento di studi glottoantropologici dell'Università di Roma La Sapienza (Roma).

Mason, Patricia 1990. 'The pronouns of address in Middle French', *Studia Neophilologica* 62:92–100.

Mateus, M. Helena and d'Andrade, Ernesto 2000. *The Phonology of Portuguese*. Oxford: Oxford University Press.

Matisoff, James 1978. *Variational Semantics in Tibeto-Burman*. Philadelphia: Institute for the Study of Human Issues.

Matte, Edouard Joseph 1982. *Histoire des modes phonétiques du français*. Geneva: Droz.

Matthews, Peter 1981. 'Present stem alternations in Italian', in Schlieben-Lange, Brigitte, Trabant, Jürgen, Weydt, Harald, Dietrich, Wolf, Geckeler, Horst and Rohrer, Christian (eds.), *Logos Semantikos: Studia Linguistica in Honorem Eugeniu Coseriu*. IV. Tübingen: Niemeyer, pp. 57–76.

  1982. 'Do languages obey general laws?' An inaugural lecture delivered before the University of Cambridge on 17 November 1981. Cambridge: Cambridge University Press.

  1991. *Morphology*. Cambridge: Cambridge University Press.

Mattos e Silva, Rosa Virgínia 1989. *Estruturas Trecentistas. Elementos para uma gramática do português arcaico*. Lisbon: IN-CM.

Mattoso Câmara, Joaquim 1972. *The Portuguese Language*. Chicago-London: University of Chicago Press.

Maturi, Pietro 2002. *Dialetti e substandardizzazione nel Sannio beneventano*. Frankfurt: Lang.

Maurer, T. 1951. 'The Romance conjugation in -esco, (-isco) -ire its origin in Vulgar Latin', *Language* 27:137–45.

Maurice, Florence 2001. 'Deconstructing gender – the case of Romanian', in Hellinger, Marlis and Bußmann, Hadumod (eds.), *Gender Across Languages*, 1. Amsterdan-Philadelphia: Benjamins, pp. 1229–52.

Mayerthaler, Eva 1996. 'Stress, syllables and segments: their interplay in an Italian dialect continuum', in Hurch and Rhodes (eds.), pp. 201–21.

Mayerthaler, Willi 1977. *Studien zur theoretischen und zur französischen Morphologie*. Tübingen: Niemeyer.

Mazzocco, Angelo 1987. 'Dante's notion of the *Vulgare Illustre*: a reappraisal', in Aarsleff, Hans, Kelly, Louis and Niederehe, Hans-Josef (eds.), *The History of Linguistics. Proceedings of the Third International Conference on the History of the Language Sciences*. Amsterdam-Philadelphia: Benjamins, pp.129–41.

McCartney, Eugene 1920. 'Forerunners of the romance adverbial suffix', *Classical Philology* 15:213–29.

McCrary, Kristie 2002. 'Syllable structure vs. segmental phonotactics: geminates and clusters in Italian revisited'. *Proceedings of the Texas Linguistics Society*. The University of Texas at Austin (http://uts.cc.utexas.edu/~tls/2002tls/TLS_2002_Proceedings.html).

  2004. 'Prosodic structure and segment duration in Italian revisited'. Paper presented at the *34th Linguistic Symposium on Romance Languages*, Salt Lake City, 12–14 March.

MedRom = Medioevo romanzo

Meier, Harri 1948. 'Sobre as origens do acusativo preposicional nas línguas românicas', in *Ensaios de filologia românica*. Lisbon: Edição da Revista de Portugal, pp. 115–64.

Meillet, Antoine 1921. *Linguistique historique et générale, Tome 1*. Paris: Champion.

1937. *Linguistique historique et générale, Tome 2*. Paris: Champion.

1964 [1937]. *Introduction à l'étude comparée des langues indo-européennes*. Alabama: University of Alabama Press.

1977. *Esquisse d'une histoire de la langue latine (avec une bibliographie mise à jour et complétée par J. Perrot)*. Paris: Klincksieck.

Meillet, Antoine and Vendryes, Joseph 1924. *Grammaire comparée des langues classiques*. Paris: Champion.

1960 (3rd edn). *Traité de grammaire comparée des langues classiques*. Paris: Champion.

Meiser, Gerhard 1998. *Historische Laut- und Formenlehre der lateinischen Sprache*. Darmstadt: Wissenschaftliche Buchgesellschaft.

Méla, Vivienne 1997. 'Verlan 2000', *Langue française* 114:16–34.

Melander, J. 1928. *Étude sur l'ancienne abréviation des pronoms personnels régimes dans les langues romanes*. Uppsala: Almqvist och Wiksell.

1929. 'L'origine de l'italien *me ne, me lo, te la*, etc.', *Studia Neophilologica* 2:169–203.

Ménard, Philippe 1994 (4th edn). *Syntaxe de l'ancien français*. Bordeaux: Bière.

Menarini, Alberto 1959. 'Il gergo della "piazza"', in Leydi, Roberto and Magnani, Franco (eds.), *La Piazza. Spettacoli popolari italiani*. Milan: Avanti, pp. 463–519.

Menegon, Pietro 1950. 'Gli stagnini di Tramonti e il loro gergo', *Ce fastu?* 26:63–72.

Menéndez Pidal, Ramón 1908. *Cantar de Mio Cid. Texto, gramática y vocabulario*. Madrid: Imprenta de Bailly-Baillière e Hijos.

1953 (9th edn)/1958 (10th edn)/1966 (12th edn)/1968 (13th edn). *Manual de gramática histórica española*. Madrid: Espasa Calpe.

1956 (4th edn)/1986 (10th edn). *Orígenes del Español. Estado lingüístico de la península ibérica hasta el siglo XI*. Madrid: Espasa Calpe.

Menut, Albert Douglas 1970. *Maistre Nicole Oresme. Le Livre de Politiques d'Aristote. Published from the Text of the Avranches Manuscript 223 with a Critical Introduction*. Philadelphia: The American Philosophical Society.

Mereu, Lunella 2004. *La sintassi delle lingue del mondo*. Rome-Bari: Laterza.

Merle, Pierre 1986. *Le Dictionnaire du français branché*. Paris: Seuil.

2006. *Argot, verlan et tchatches*. Toulouse: Milan.

Merlo, Clemente 1911–12. 'Note fonetiche sul parlare di Bitonto (Bari), parte Ia Vocalismo', *Atti R. Accad. delle Scienze di Torino* 47:907–32.

1926. 'Il vocalismo tonico del dialetto di Carbonara di Bari', *ID* 2:85–99.

1929a. 'Consonanti brevi e consonanti lunghe nel dialetto di Borgo S. Sepolcro', *ID* 5:66–80.

1929b. 'Vicende storiche della lingua di Roma. I. Dalle origini al sec. XV', *ID* 5:172–201.

1933. 'Il sostrato etnico e i dialetti italiani', *ID* 9:1–24.

Mester, Armin 1994. 'The quantitative trochee in Latin', *NLLT* 12:1–61.

Meyer, Paul 1920. *Remarques sur le patois de la vallée de l'Ubaye*, in Arnaud, F. and Morin, G. (eds.), *Le langage de la vallée de Barcelonette*. Paris: Champion, pp. i-xv.

Meyer-Lübke, Wilhelm 1890. *Grammatik der romanischen Sprachen. I. Lautlehre*. Leipzig: Reisland.

1894. *Grammatik der romanischen Sprachen. II. Formenlehre*. Leipzig: Reisland.

1899. *Grammatik der romanischen Sprachen. III. Syntax*. Leipzig: Reisland.

1901. *Einführung in das Studium der romanischen Sprachwissenschaft*. Heidelberg: Winter.

1902. *Grammatik der romanischen Sprachen. IV. Register*. Leipzig: Reisland.

1904–6. 'Die lateinische Sprache in den romanischen Ländern', in Gröber, G. (ed.), *Grundriss der romanischen Philologie*. Strasbourg: Trübner I, pp. 451–97.

1920 (3rd edn). *Einführung in das Studium der romanischen Sprachwissenschaft* Heidelberg: Winter.

1934 (5th edn). *Historische Grammatik der französischen Sprache. Erster Teil. Laut- und Flexionslehre*. Heidelberg: Winter.

1935. *Romanisches Etymologisches Wörterbuch*. Heidelberg: Winter.

1972. *Grammatica storica della lingua italiana e dei dialetti toscani*. Turin: Loescher.

1992 (6th edn). *Romanisches Etymologisches Wörterbuch*. Heidelberg: Winter.

Michaelis, Susanne 1998. 'Antikausativ als Brücke zum Passiv: *fieri*, *venire* und *se* im Vulgärlateinischen und Altitalienischen', in Dahmen, W., Holtus, G., Kramer, J., Metzeltin, M. and Shweickard, W. (eds.), *Neuer Beschreibungsmethoden der Syntax romanischer Sprachen*. Tübingen: Narr, pp. 69–98.

Michaud-Quantin, Petrus 1961. *Aristoteles Latinus XXIX I (Libri I-II, ii). Translatio prior imperfecta. Interprete Guillelmo de Moerbecka*. Bruges-Paris: Desclée de Brouwer.

Migliorini, Bruno 1929. 'L'intacco della velare nelle parlate romanze', *AGI* 22–23:271–301.

1978 [1960] (5th edn). *Storia della Lingua Italiana*. Florence: Sansoni.

Migliorini, Bruno and Griffith, T. Gwynfor 1984 [1960]. *The Italian Language*. Abridged, recast and revised by T. Gwynfor Griffith. London: Faber.

Mihǎescu, Haralambie 1960. *Limba latină în provinciile dunǎrene ale Imperiului Roman*. Bucharest: Editura Academiei.

Millardet, Georges 1933. 'Sur un ancien substrat commun à la Sicile, la Corse et la Sardaigne', *RLiR* 9:346–69.

Milner, Jean-Claude 1978. 'Le système du réfléchi latin', *Langages* 50:73–85.

Mistral, Frédéric 1932. *Lou Tresor dóu Felibrige, ou dictionnaire provençal-français embrassant les divers dialectes de la langue d'oc moderne, etc.* (édition du centenaire). Paris: Delagrave.

Möbitz, Otto 1924. 'Die Stellung des Verbums in den Schriften des Apuleius', *Glotta* 13:116–26.

Mocciaro, A. 1976. 'Le forme del passato remoto in siciliano', in *Problemi di morfosintassi dialettale. Atti del IX Convegno del Centro di studio per la dialettologia italiana.* Pisa: Pacini, pp.271–86.

Moignet, G. 1959. 'La forme en re(t) dans le système verbal du plus ancien français', *Revue des Langues Romanes* 73: 1–65.

    1965. *Le Pronom personnel français. Essai de psycho-systématique historique.* Paris: Klincksieck.

    1966. 'Sur le système de la flexion à deux cas de l'ancien français', in *Mélanges de linguistique et de philologie offerts à Mgr. Pierre Gardette à l'occasion de son soixantième anniversaire, le 13 juin 1966. Travaux de Linguistique et de Literature*, 4, 1. Strasbourg : Klincksieck, pp. 339–56.

    1973. *Grammaire de l'ancien français. Morphologie, syntaxe.* Paris: Klincksieck.

Molinu, Lucia and Roullet, S. 2001. 'Analisi strumentale e fonologica del vocalismo tonico di una varietà francoprovenzale valdostana', in Zamboni, A., Del Puente, P. and Vigolo, M. T. (eds.), *La dialettologia oggi fra tradizione e nuove metodologie, Atti del Convegno Internazionale.* Pisa: ETS, pp. 117–32.

Moll, Francesc de B. 1993. *El parlar de Mallorca.* Mallorca: Moll.

    1997. *Gramàtica catalana, referida especialment a les Illes Balears.* Mallorca: Moll.

    2006. *Gramàtica històrica catalana.* Valencia: Universitat de València.

Momigliano, Arnaldo 1974. 'Le regole del gioco nello studio della storia antica', *Annali della Scuola Normale Superiore di Pisa, serie III*, pp. 1183–92 [= 1987 *Storia e storiografia antica*. Bologna: il Mulino].

Monachesi, Paola 1995. *A Grammar of Italian Clitics.* Tilburg: ITK Dissertation Series.

Monaci, Ernesto 1955. *Crestomazia italiana dei primi secoli.* Rome-Naples-Città di Castello: Società Editrice Dante Alighieri.

Monteil, P. 1997. *Le parler de Saint-Augustin. Phonétique et phonologie; morphologie; syntaxe.* Limoges: PULIM.

Montgomery, Thomas 1976. 'Complementarity of stem-vowels in the Spanish second and third conjugations', *RPh* 29:281–96.

    1978. 'Iconicity and lexical retention in Spanish stative and dynamic verbs', *Language* 54:907–16.

    1979. 'Sound symbolism and aspect in the Spanish second conjugation', *Hispanic Review* 47:219–37.

    1985. 'Sources of vocalic correspondences of stems and endings in the Spanish verb', *Hispanic Linguistics* 2:99–114.

Montreuil, Jean-Pierre 1991. 'Length in Milanese', in Wanner and Kibbee (eds.), pp. 37–47.

1998. 'Vestigial trochees in Oïl dialects', in Schwegler *et al.* (eds.), pp. 183–95.

Moore, A. O. 1989. *Patterns of Lexical Loss from Latin to Romance*. Tulane University, Ann Arbor: dissertation.

Morais, Maria Aparecida 2003. 'EPP generalizado, sujeito nulo e línguas de configuração discursiva', *Letras de hoje* 38:71–98.

Morani, Moreno 2000. *Introduzione alla linguistica latina*. Munich: Lincom Europa.

Morel, Mary-Annick and Danon-Boileau, Laurent 1992. *La Deixis. Colloque en Sorbonne*. Paris: PUF.

Morford, Janet 1997. 'Social indexicality in French pronominal address', *Journal of Linguistic Anthropology* 7:3–37.

Morin, Yves-Charles 1972. 'The phonology of echo-words in French', *Language* 48:97–108.

1990. 'Parasitic formation in inflectional morphology', in Dressler, W., Luschützky, H., Pfeiffer, O. and Rennison, J. (eds.), *Contemporary Morphology*. Berlin-New York: Mouton de Gruyter, pp. 197–202.

1992. 'What are the historical sources of lengthening in Friulian?', *Probus* 4:155–82.

1994. 'Phonological interpretations of historical lengthening', in Dressler, W., Prinzhorn, M. and Rennison, J. (eds.), *Phonologica 1992. Proceedings of the 7th International Phonology Meeting*. Turin: Rosenberg & Sellier, pp. 135–55.

2003. 'Syncope, apocope, diphthongaison et palatalisation en gallo-roman: problèmes de chronologie relative', in Sánchez Miret, Fernando (ed.), *Actas del XXIII CILFR*, I, Tübingen: Niemeyer, pp. 113–69.

2006. 'On the phonetics of rhymes in Classical and Pre-classical French: a sociolinguistic perspective', in Gess and Arteaga (eds.), pp. 131–62.

Moro, Andres 1993. *I predicati nominali e la struttura della frase*. Padua: Unipress.

Morris, Charles 1971. *Writings on the General Theory of Signs*. The Hague: Mouton.

Morwood, James 1999. *A Latin Grammar*. Oxford: Oxford University Press.

Mosino, Franco 1972. ''Ndràngheta, la mafia calabrese', *LN* 33:87.

Motapanyane, Virginia 1989. 'La position du sujet dans une langue à l'ordre SVO/ VSO', *Rivista di grammatica generativa* 14:75–103.

1995. *Theoretical Implications of Complementation in Romanian*. Padua: Unipress.

Motapanyane, Virginia (ed.) 2000. *Comparative Studies in Romanian Syntax*. Amsterdam: Elsevier.

Mott, Brian. 1989. *El habla de Gistaín*. Huesca: Instituto de Estudios altoaragoneses.

Mourin, Louis 1978. 'La réélaboration structurelle des systèmes romans de conjugaison du parfait', *Studii și cercetări lingvistice* 29:19–43.

Muldowney, Mary 1937. *Word Order in the Works of St. Augustine*. The Catholic University of America, Washington, DC: unpublished thesis.

Muljačić, Žarko 1965. 'La posizione del dalmatico nella Romània', in Straka (ed.), III, pp. 1185–95.

2000. *Das Dalmatische. Studien zu einer untergegangenen Sprache*. Cologne-WeimarVienna: Böhlau.

Müller, Bodo 1987. 'Das Lateinische und das Latein der etymologischen Wörterbücher der romanischen Sprachen', in Dahmen, W., Holtus, G., Kramer, J. and Metzeltin, M. (eds.), *Latein und Romanisch. Romanistisches Kolloquium I*. Tübingen: Narr, pp. 311–22.

Muller, Henri and Taylor, Pauline 1932. *A Chrestomathy of Vulgar Latin*. Boston-New York: Heath.

Munaro, Nicola 1999. *Sintagmi interrogativi nei dialetti italiani settentrionali*. Padua: Unipress.

2002. 'Splitting up subject clitic-verb inversion', in Beyssade, C., Bok-Bennema, R., Drijkoningen, F. and Monachesi, P. (eds.), *Romance Languages and Linguistic Theory 2000*. Amsterdam: Benjamins, pp. 233–52.

2003. 'On some differences between exclamative and interrogative Wh-phrases in Bellunese: further evidence for a Split-CP hypothesis', in Tortora (ed.), pp. 137–51.

Munthe, Åke 1987. *Anotaciones sobre el habla popular de una zona del occidente de Asturias*. Oviedo: Biblioteca de filoloxía asturiana.

Murray, Robert and Vennemann, Theo 1983. 'Sound change and syllable structure in Germanic phonology', *Language* 59:518–28.

Mussafia, Adolfo 1868. 'Zur rumänischen Vokalisation', *Sitzungsberichte der Wiener Akademie der Wissenschaften. Philosophisch-historische Klasse* 58:125–54.

Myhill, John and Harris, Wendell A. 1986. 'The rise of the verbal -s inflection in BEV', in David Sankoff (ed.), *Diversity and Diachrony*. Amsterdam-Philadelphia: John Benjamins, pp. 25–31.

Nagore Lain, Francho 1986. *El aragonés de Panticosa. Gramática*. Huesca: Instituto de Estudios altoaragoneses.

NALC = Dalbera Stefanaggi, 1995c .

Nandriş, Octave 1963. *Phonétique historique du roumain*. Paris: Klincksieck.

Náñez Fernández, Emilio 1973. *El diminutivo. Historia y funciones en el español clásico y moderno*. Madrid: Gredos.

Napoli, Donna Jo 1976. *The Two si's of Italian. An Analysis of Reflexive Inchoatives, and Indefinite Subject Sentences in Modern Standard Italian*. Bloomington, IN: Indiana University Linguistics Club.

Naro, Anthony 1976. 'The genesis of reflexive impersonal in Portuguese', *Language* 52:779–810.

Navarro Tomás, Tomás 1967. *Manual de pronunciación española*. Madrid: CSIC.

Navone, G. 1922. 'Il dialetto di Paliano', *Studi romanzi* 17:73–126.

Neira Martínez, Jesús 1955. *El habla de Lena*. Oviedo: CSSIC.

1978. 'La oposición "contínuo"/"discontínuo" en las hablas asturianas', in *Estudios ofrecidos a Emilio Alarcos Llorach, III*. Oviedo: Universidad, pp. 255–79.

Nerlich, Brigitte 1990. *Change in Language. Whitney, Bréal and Wegener*. London-New York: Routledge.

Nerlich, Brigitte and Clarke, David 1988. 'A dynamic model of semantic change', *Journal of Literary Semantics* 17:73–90.

Nespor, Marina 1999. 'Stress domains', in van der Hulst (ed.), pp. 117–59.

Nespor, Marina and Vogel, Irene 1986. *Prosodic Phonology*. Dordrecht: Foris.

Neves, Maria Helena de Moura 2000. *Gramática de usos do português*. São Paulo: UNESP.

Niceforo, Alfredo 1897. *Il gergo dei normali, nei degenerati e nei criminali*. Turin: Bocca.

Nichols, Johanna 1986. 'Head-marking and dependent-marking grammar', *Language* 62:56–119.

Nicholson, Kate 2008. *Harrap's Little French Dictionary. English–French, français–anglais*. Edinburgh: Chambers Harrap.

Nicoli, Franco 1983. *Grammatica milanese*. Busto Arsizio: Bramante.

Niculescu, Alexandru and Dimitrescu, Florica 1970. *Testi romeni antichi (secoli XVI-XVIII)*. Padova: Antenore.

Niedermann, Max 1931 (2nd edn). *Historische Lautlehre des Lateinischen*. Heidelberg: Winter.

1937. *Consentii Ars de barbarismis et metaplasmis. Edition nouvelle suivie d'un fragment inédit de Victorius* De soloecismo et barbarismo. Neuchâtel: Secrétariat de l'Université.

1943–44. 'Les gloses médicales du Liber glosarum', *Emerita* 11:257–96; 12:29–83. (Reprinted in *Recueil Max Niedermann*. Neuchâtel: Secrétariat de l'Université, 1954, pp. 65–136.)

Niermeyer, Jan Frederik 1984. *Mediæ Latinitatis Lexicon Minus*. Leiden: Brill.

NLLT = Natural Language and Linguistic Theory

Nocentini, Alberto 1985. 'Sulla genesi dell'oggetto preposizionale nelle lingue romanze', in *Studi linguistici e filologici per Carlo Alberto Mastrelli*. Pisa: Pacini, pp. 299–311.

1990. 'L'uso dei dimostrativi nella *Peregrinatio Egeriae* e la genesi dell'articolo romanzo', in *Atti del convegno internazionale sulla Peregrinatio Egeriae*. Arezzo: Accademia Petrarca di Lettere e Arti e Scienze, pp. 137–58.

1992. 'Oggetto marcato vs oggetto non marcato: stato ed evoluzione di una categoria nell'area euro-asiatica', in *L'Europa linguistica. contatti, contrasti, affinità di lingue*, Atti del XXI Congresso della Società di linguistica italiana. Rome: Bulzoni, pp. 227–46.

2001. 'La genesi del futuro e del condizionale sintetico romanzo', *ZRPh* 117:367–401.

Norberg, Dag 1943. *Syntaktische Forschungen auf dem Gebiete des Spätlateins und des frühen Mittellateins.* Uppsala: Lundqvist; Leipzig: Harassowitz.

1944. *Beiträge zur spätlateinischen Syntax.* Uppsala: Almqvist och Wiksell.

Nordlinger, Rachel 1998. *Constructive Case. Evidence from Australian Languages.* Stanford, CA: Centre for the Study of Language and Information.

Nübling, Damaris 2001. 'The development of "junk": irregularization strategies of have and say in the Germanic languages', in Booij, G. and Van Marle, J. (eds.), *Yearbook of Morphology 1999*, pp. 53–74.

Nunes, José Joaquim 1975. *Compêndio de gramática histórica portuguesa. Fonética e morfologia.* Lisbon: Livraria Clássica Editora.

1989. *Compêndio de gramática histórica portuguesa.* Lisbon: Clássica.

Nykrog, Per 1957. 'L'influence latine savante sur la syntaxe du français', *TCLC* 5:89–114.

Nyrop, Kristoffer 1904–30. *Grammaire historique de la langue française.* Copenhagen–Kristiania: Gyldendalske Boghandel – Nordisk Forlag.

1914. *Grammaire historique de la langue française. Tome I.* Copenhagen: Gyldendal.

1924. *Grammaire historique de la langue française. Tome II.* Copenhagen: Gyldendal.

1925. *Grammaire historique de la langue française. Tome V.* Copenhagen: Gyldendal.

1960 (2nd edn). *Grammaire historique de la langue française. Tome II.* Copenhagen: Gyldendal.

O'Donnell, James 1984. *Boethius,* Consolatio Philosophiae, *with commentary by James J. O'Donnell.* Bryn Mawr: Bryn Mawr College (http://ccat.sas.upenn.edu/jod/boethius/jkok/list_t.htm).

OED = *The New Shorter Oxford English Dictionary.* Oxford: Clarendon Press, 1993.

OED 1989 = *The Oxford English Dictionary* (2nd edn). Prepared by J. A. Simpson and E. S. C. Weiner. Oxford: Clarendon Press.

Ojeda, Almerindo 1992. 'The mass-neuter in Hispano-Romance dialects', *Hispanic Linguistics* 5:245–77.

1995. 'The semantics of the Italian double plural', *Journal of Semantics* 12:213–37.

Oldfather, William Abbott, Carter, Howard Vernon and Perry, Ben Edwin 1934. *Index Apuleianus.* Middleton: American Philological Association.

Oniga, Renato 1998. *I composti nominali latini. Una morfologia generativa.* Bologna: Pàtron.

2004. *Il latino. Breve introduzione linguistica.* Milan: Franco Angeli.

Orr, John 1951. 'Le français aimer', in *Mélanges de linguistique et de littérature romanes offerts à Mario Roques par ses amis, ses collègues et ses anciens élèves de France et de l'étranger, vol. I.* Paris: Didier, pp. 217–27. (Reprinted in John

Orr, *Three Studies on Homonymics*. Edinburgh: Edinburgh University Press, 1962.)

1953. *Words and Sounds in English and French*. Oxford: Blackwell.

Osborne, Charles Roland 1974. *The Tiwi Language*. Canberra: Australian Institute of Aboriginal Studies.

Ostafin, David 1986. *Studies in Latin Word Order. A Transformational Approach*. University of Connecticut: unpublished thesis.

Osthoff, Herman 1887. 'Die lateinischen Adverbia auf –iter', *Archiv für lateinische Lexikographie und Grammatik* 4:455–66.

Otero Alvarez, Aníbal 1952. 'Irregularidades verbales del gallego', *Cuadernos de Estudios Gallegos* 7:399–405.

Pace, Anna 1993–94. *Ricerche di morfosintassi sui dialetti di Trebisacce e Castrovillari*. Università della Calabria: unpublished thesis.

Packer, David 1968. *A Concordance to Livy*, 4 vols. Cambridge, MA: Harvard University Press.

Pagliaro, Antonino and Belardi, Walter 1963. *Linee di storia linguistica dell'Europa*. Rome: Ateneo.

Palay, Simin 1961. *Dictionnaire du béarnais et du gascon modernes (Bassin aquitain), embrassant les dialectes du Béarn, de la Bigorre, des Landes et de la Gascogne maritime et garonnaise*. Paris: CNRS.

Palermo, Joe 1971.'Rythme occitan et rythme oxyton: clé de la scission gallo-romane', *RLR* 35:40–49.

Palmer, Leonard 1990 [1954]. *The Latin Language*. Bristol: Bristol Classical Press.

Panhuis, Dirk 1982. *The Communicative Perspective in the Sentence. A Study of Latin Word Order*. Amsterdam: Benjamins.

Paoli, Sandra 2003. *COMP and the Left-Periphery. Comparative Evidence from Romance*. University of Manchester: unpublished thesis.

Papa, Eugene 1986. *Two Studies on the History of Southern Italian Vocalism*. Indiana University: dissertation.

Papahagi, Tache 1974. *Dicționarul dialectului aromân*. Bucharest: Editura Academiei.

Paris, Gaston 1872. *La vie de saint Alexis. Poème du Xe siècle et renouvellement des XIIe, XIIIe et XIVe siècles*. Paris: Franck.

Parkinson, Stephen 1988. 'Portuguese', in Harris and Vincent (eds.), pp. 131–69.

Parlangeli, Oronzo 1952. 'Il dialetto di Loreto Aprutino', *Rendiconti dell'Istituto Lombardo* 85:113–76.

1953. 'Sui dialetti romanzi e romaici del Salento', *Memorie dell'Istituto lombardo di scienze e lettere. Cl. di Lettere, Sc. morali e storiche* 25–26 (Serie III):93-200.

1960. *Storia linguistica e storia politica nell'Italia meridionale*. Florence: Le Monnier.

Parrino, Flavio 1967. 'Per una carta dei dialetti delle Marche', *Bollettino della Carta dei Dialetti Italiani* 2:5–37.

Parry, Mair 1997. 'Negation', in Maiden and Parry (eds.), pp. 179–85.

2007. 'The interaction of semantics and syntax in the spread of relative *che* in the early vernaculars of Italy', in Bentley and Ledgeway (eds.), pp. 200–19.

Parry, Mair and Lombardi, Alessandra 2007. 'The interaction of semantics, pragmatics and syntax in the spread of the articles in the early vernaculars of Italy', in Lepschy and Tosi (eds.), pp. 77–97.

Pattison, David 1975. *Early Spanish Suffixes. A Functional Study of the Principal Nominal Suffixes of Spanish up to 1300*. Oxford: Blackwell.

Paul, Elisabeth 1985. *Études des régularités morpho-syntaxiques du verlan contemporain*. University of Paris 3: unpublished thesis.

Paulis, Giulio 1984. *Appendix to the Italian translation of Wagner (1941)*. Cagliari: Trois.

Peeters, Bert 2004. 'Tu ou vous?', *Zeitschrift für französische Sprache und Literatur* 114:1–17.

Pei, Mario 1932. *The Language of the Eighth-Century Texts in Northern France*. New York: Carranza.

Pellegrini, Astore 1880. *Il dialetto greco-calabro di Bova*. Turin: Loescher.

Pellegrini, Giovan Battista 1973. 'I cinque sistemi dell'italo-romanzo', *Revue roumaine de Linguistique* 18:105–29 [also in Pellegrini (1975), pp. 55–87].

1975. *Saggi di linguistica: storia, struttura e società*. Turin: Boringhieri.

Pellettieri, Jill 1993. 'Anaphora and choice in Spanish'. Paper presented at a workshop on Pragmatics, University of Calfornia, Davis.

Pellis, Ugo 1929. 'Il gergo dei seggiolai di Gosaldo', *AGI* 22–23:542–86.

1930. *Coi furbi*. Udine: D. Del Bianco.

1934. 'Il gergo d'Isili in Sardegna e quello di Tramonti del Friuli', *Ce fastu?* 10:201–203.

Pelon, Martine 1997. 'Le langage jeune en Italie', *Langue française* 114:114–22.

Penny, Ralph 1969. *El habla pasiega*. London: Thamesis.

1970. 'Mass nouns and metaphony in the dialects of North-Western Spain', *Archivum Linguisticum* 1:21–30.

1972. 'Verb-class as a determiner of stem-vowel in the historical morphology of Spanish verbs', *RLiR* 36:342–59.

1978. *Estudio estructural del habla de Tudanca*. Tübingen: Niemeyer.

1991. *A History of the Spanish Language*. Cambridge: Cambridge University Press.

2000. *Variation and Change in Spanish*. Cambridge: Cambridge University Press.

2002 (2nd edn). *A History of the Spanish Language*. Cambridge: Cambridge University Press.

Pensado Ruiz, Carmen, 1984. *Cronología relativa del castellano*. Salamanca: Universidad de Salamanca.

1985. 'La creación del objeto directo preposicional y la flexión de los pronombres personales en las lenguas románicas', *RRL* 30:123–58.

1986. 'Inversion de marcage et perte du système casuel en ancien français', *ZRPh* 102:271–96.

1988. 'How do unnatural syllabifications arise? The case of consonant + glide in Vulgar Latin', *Folia Linguistica Historica* 8:115–42.

1993. 'Consonantes geminadas en la evolución histórica del español', in Penny, Ralph (ed.), *Actas del I Congreso anglo-hispánico. Asociación de hispanistas de Gran Bretaña e Irlanda, vol. I Lingüística*. Madrid: Castalia, pp. 193–204.

Pensado Ruiz, Carmen (ed.) 1995. *El complemento directo preposicional*. Madrid: Visor Libros.

Pensado Ruiz, Carmen 1997. 'Spanish delalatalisation of /ɲ ʎ/ in rhymes', in Martínez Gil and Morales-Front (eds.), pp. 595–618.

2001. 'El valor de la toponimía en la reconstrucción de la fonética sintáctica', in Casanova, E. and Rosselló, V. M. (eds.), *Actas del Congrés Internacional de Toponimía e Onomastica, València 18–21 abril 2001*. Valencia: Denes.

Perini, Mário 1995. *Gramática descritiva do português*. São Paulo: Ática.

Perrochat, Paul 1926. 'Sur un principe d'ordre des mots: la place du verbe dans la subordonnée', *Revue des Études Latines* 4:50–60.

1932. *Recherches sur la valeur et l'emploi de l'infinitif subordonné en latin*. Paris: Les Belles Lettres.

Petersen, Walter 1916. 'Latin diminution of adjectives', *Classical Philology* 11:426–51.

Peverini, Claudia 2008. 'Subject-verb non-agreement in Marchigiano'. Paper presented at the *XXXVI Romance Linguistics Seminar*, Trinity Hall, Cambridge, 3–4 January 2008.

Pfister, Max 2004. 'Der "Kopf" im Italienischen und in den romanischen Sprachen', in Lebsanft and Gleßgen (eds.), pp. 141–51.

Pianese, Giovanna 2002. 'La variabile -LL- e le sue varianti in alcune aree dell'isola d'Ischia', *Bollettino linguistico campano* 1:237–60.

Piccitto Giorgio 1941. 'Fonetica del dialetto di Ragusa', *ID* 17:17–80.

Piccitto, Giorgio and Tropea, Giovanni 1977–. *Vocabolario Siciliano*, 4 vols. Catania-Palermo: Centro di studi filologici e linguistici siciliani.

Picoche, Jacqueline 1998. *Didactique du vocabulaire français*. Paris: Nathan.

Picoche, Jacqueline and Marchello-Nizia, Christiane 1994. *Histoire de la langue française*. Paris: Nathan.

Pike, Kenneth 1943. *The Intonation of American English*. Ann Arbor: University of Michigan Press.

Pinkster, Harm 1987. 'The strategy and chronology of the development of future and perfect tense auxiliares in Latin', in Harris and Ramat (eds.), pp. 193–223.

1990. *Latin Syntax and Semantics*. London: Routledge.

Piras, Marco 1994. *La varietà linguistica del Sulcis. Fonologia e morfologia*. Cagliari: Della Torre.

Pirrelli, Vito. 2000. *Paradigmi in morfologia Un approccio interdisciplinare alla flessione verbale dell'italiano*. Pisa-Rome: Istituti editoriali e poligrafici internazionali.

Pirson, Jules 1913. *Merowingische und Karolingische Formulare*. Heidelberg: Winters.

Pîrvulescu, Michaela and Roberge, Yves 2000. 'The syntax and morphology of Romanian imperatives', in Motapanyane, pp. 295–312.

Plangg, Guntram 1989. 'Ladinisch: Interne Sprachgeschichte I. Grammatik', *LRL* (III), pp. 646–67.

Plénat, Marc 1985. 'Morphologie du largonji des loucherbems', *Langages* 20:73–122.

1992. 'Note sur la morphologie du verlan: données et hypothèses', *Cahiers de Grammaire* 17:171–208.

Poghirc, Cicerone 1969. 'Pronumele personale şi reflexive', in Rosetti, Alexandru, Cazacu, Boris and Onu, Liviu (eds.), *Istoria limbii române, volumul II*, pp. 239–243. Bucharest: Editura Academiei Republicii Socialiste România.

Pokorny, Julius 1959. *Indogermanisches Etymologisches Wörterbuch*. Bern: Francke.

Poletto, Cecilia 1993. *La sintassi dei pronomi soggetto nei dialetti settentrionali*. Padua: Unipress.

1995. 'The diachronic development of subject clitics in northern eastern Italian dialects', in Battye and Roberts (eds.), pp. 295–324.

2000. *The Higher Functional Field*. Oxford: Oxford University Press.

2001. 'Complementizer deletion and verb movement in standard Italian', in Cinque and Salvi (eds.), pp. 265–86.

2005a. 'Sì and *e* as CP expletives in Old Italian', in Batllori, M., Hernanz, M.-L., Picallo, C. and Roca, F. (eds.), *Grammaticalization and Parametric Variation*. Oxford: Oxford University Press, pp. 206–35.

2005b. 'The left periphery of the low phase: OV orders in Old Italian'. Paper presented at the *XXI Incontro di Grammatica Generativa*, Rome.

in press. 'La struttura della frase', in Renzi, Lorenzo and Salvi, Giampaolo (eds.), *Grammatica dell'italiano antico*. Bologna: il Mulino.

Poletto, Cecilia and Zanuttini, Raffaella 2003. 'Making imperatives: evidence from central Rhaetoromance', in Tortora, Christina (ed.), *The Syntax of Italian Dialects*. Oxford: Oxford University Press, pp. 175–206.

Politzer, Frieda and Politzer, Robert 1953. *Romance Trends in 7th and 8th Century Latin Documents*. Chapel Hill: University of North Carolina Press.

Politzer, Robert 1951. 'On the chronology of the simplification of geminates in northern France', *Modern Language Notes* 56:527–31.

Pollock, Jean-Yves 1981. 'On case and impersonal constructions', in May, Robert and Koster, Jan (eds.), *Levels of Syntactic Representation*. Dordrecht: Foris, pp. 219–52.

1989. 'Verb movement, universal grammar, and the structure of IP', *LI* 20:365–424.

Polo, Chiara 2004. *Word Order in Latin, Italian and Slovene between Morphology and Syntax*. Padua: Unipress.

Polomé, Edgar. 1968. 'The Indo-European numeral for "five" and Hittite panku-"all"', in Heesterman, J., Schokker, G. and Subramoniam, V. (eds.), *Pratidanam. Indian, Iranian and Indo-European Studies Presented to Franciscus B. J. Kuiper on his Sixtieth Birthday*. The Hague–Paris: Mouton, pp. 98–101.

Pons, Teofilo and Genre, Arturo 1997. *Dizionario del dialetto occitano della val Germanasca*. Alessandria: Edizioni dell' Orso.

Pons Bordería, Salvador 1998. *Conexión y conectores. Estudio de su relación en el registro informal de la lengua*. Valencia: Universitat de València, Facultat de Filologia, Departamento de Filología Española.

Pop, Sever 1948. *Grammaire roumaine*. Bern: Francke.

Pope, Mildred 1934. *From Latin to Modern French with Especial Consideration of Anglo-Norman. Phonology and Morphology*. Manchester: Manchester University Press.

    1952. *From Latin to Old French, with Especial Consideration of Anglo-Norman*. Manchester: Manchester University Press.

Popper, Karl 1957. *The Poverty of Historicism*. London: Ark.

Porto Dapena, J. 1973. 'Alternancias vocálicas en los nombres y verbos gallego-portugueses: un intento de explicación diacrónica', *Thesaurus* 28:526–44.

Porzio-Gernia, Maria Luisa 1976. 'Tendenze strutturali della sillaba latina in età arcaica e classica', in Gendre, Renato (ed.), *Studi in onore di Giuliano Bonfante, II*. Brescia: Paideia, pp. 757–79.

    1976–77. 'Lo stato attuale degli studi di fonologia latina', *Incontri linguistici* 3:137–52.

Posner, Rebecca 1984. 'Double negatives, negative polarity, and negative incorporation in Romance: a historical and comparative view', *TPS* 82:1–26.

    1985a. 'Post-verbal negation in non-standard French: a historical and comparative view', *RPh* 39:170–97.

    1985b. 'L'histoire de la négation et la typologie romane', in *Linguistique comparée et typologie des langues romanes (Actes du XVIIème congrès international de linguistique et philologie romanes), vol. 2*. Aix-en-Provence: Université de Provence, pp. 265–71.

    1996. *The Romance Languages*. Cambridge: Cambridge University Press.

Posner, Rebecca and Green, John (eds.) 1980–93. *Trends in Romance Linguistics and Philology*, 5 vols. Berlin-New York: Mouton.

Pötters, Wilhelm 1970. *Unterschiede im Wortschatz der iberoromanischen Sprachen*. Köln: dissertation.

Pottier, Bernard 1961. 'Sobre el concepto de "verbo auxiliar"', *Nueva revista de filología hispánica* 15: 325–31.

    1969. *Grammaire espagnole*. Paris: PUF.

Pounder, Amanda 2000. *Processes and Paradigms in Word-Formation Morphology*. Berlin-New York: Mouton de Gruyter.

Pountain, Christopher 1982. '*ESSERE/STARE* as a Romance phenomenon', in Vincent and Harris (eds.), pp. 139–60.

    1983. *Structures and Transformations. The Romance Verb*. London: Croom Helm.

    1985. 'Copulas, verbs of possession and auxiliaries in Spanish: the evidence for structurally interdependent changes', *Bulletin of Hispanic Studies* 62:337–55.

    1998a. 'Learned syntax and the Romance languages: the "accusative and infinitive" construction with declarative verbs in Castilian', *TPS* 96:159–201.

    1998b. 'Nuevo enfoque de la posición del adjetivo atributivo', in Ruffino, Giovanni (ed.), *Atti del XXI Congresso internazionale di linguistica e filologia romanza II. Morfologia e sintassi delle lingue romanze*. Tübingen: Niemeyer, pp. 697–708.

    1998c. 'Gramática mítica del gerundio castellano', in Ward, Aengus (ed.), *Actas del XII Congreso de la Asociación Internacional de Hispanistas, Birmingham 1995. I. Medieval y Lingüística*. Birmingham: Birmingham University Press, pp. 284–92.

    2000. 'Pragmatic factors in the evolution of the Romance reflexive (with special reference to Spanish)', *Hispanic Research Journal* 1:5–25.

    2001. *A History of the Spanish Language through Texts*. London: Routledge.

    2006a. 'Syntactic borrowing as a function of register', in Lepschy, Anna Laura and Tosi, Arturo (eds.), *Rethinking Languages in Contact. The Case of Italian*. Oxford: Legenda, pp. 99–111.

    2006b. 'Towards a history of register in Spanish', *Spanish in Context* 3:5–24.

Pozas-Loyo, Julia 2008. 'On the evolution of *un* in Medieval and Classical Spanish'. Paper presented at the *XXXVI Romance Linguistics Seminar*, Trinity Hall, Cambridge, 3–4 January 2008.

Price, Glanville 1962. 'The negative particles *pas*, *mie*, and *point* in French', *Archivum Linguisticum* 14:14–34.

    1971. *The French Language. Present and Past*. London: Arnold.

    1986. 'Aspects de l'histoire de la négation en français', in *Morphsyntaxe des langues romanes (Actes du XXIIème congrès international de linguistique et philologie romanes), vol. 4*. Aix-en-Provence: Université de Provence, pp. 569–75.

    1992. 'Romance', in Gvozdanović, Jardanka (ed.), *Indo-European Numerals*. Berlin-New York: de Gruyter, pp. 447–97.

    2008 (6th edn). *A Comprehensive French Grammar*. Oxford: Blackwell.

Prieto, Pilar 1993. 'Historical vowel lengthening in Romance: the role of sonority and foot structure', in Mazzola, Michael (ed.), *Issues and Theory in Romance Linguistics*. Washington, DC: Georgetown University Press, pp. 87–107.

    2000. 'Vowel lengthening in Milanese', in Repetti (ed.), pp. 255–72.

814

Prosdocimi, Aldo 1986. 'Sull'accento latino e italico', in Etter, Annemarie (ed.), *o-o-pe-ro-si. Festschrift für Ernst Risch zum 75. Geburtstag*. Berlin-New York: de Gruyter.

Pulgram, Ernst 1975. *Latin-Romance Phonology Prosodics and Metrics*. Munich: Fink.

Pult, Gaspard 1897. *Le parler de Sent (Basse-Engadine)*. Lausanne: Payot.

Puşcariu, Sextil 1926. *Studii istroromâne*. Bucharest: Cultura naţională.

1937. *Etudes de linguistique roumaine*. Cluj-Bucharest: Imprimeria naţională.

1938. *Atlasul Lingvistic Romîn*, Partea I. Cluj: Muzeul Limbii Române.

1957. *Etymologisches Wörterbuch der rumänischen Sprache. Lateinisches Element mit Berücksichtigung aller romanischen Sprachen*. Heidelberg: Winter.

Quicoli, Antonio Carlos 1990. 'Harmony, lowering, and nasalization in Brazilian Portuguese', *Lingua* 80:295–331.

Quinn, Paul 2004. 'Visual perception of orientation is categorical near vertical and continuous near horizontal', *Perception* 33:897–906.

Quint, Nicolas 1998. *Le parler occitan alpin du Pays de Seyne, Alpes-de-Haute-Provence*. Paris: L'Harmattan.

Quirk, Ronald 2006. *The* Appendix Probi. *A Scholar's Guide to Text and Context*. Newark, NJ: Juan de la Cuesta.

Radatz, Hans-Ingo 2001. *Die Semantik der Adjektivstellung*. Tübingen: Niemeyer.

Radden, Günther and Panther, Klaus-Uwe 2004. 'Introduction: reflections on motivation', in Radden, Günther and Panther, Klaus-Uwe (eds.), *Studies in Linguistic Motivation*. Berlin: Mouton de Gruyter, pp. 1–46.

Radtke, Edgar 1997 (ed.). *I dialetti della Campania*. Rome: il Calamo.

Ramat, Anna Giacalone 1998. 'Testing the boundaries of grammaticalization', in Ramat, Anna Giacalone and Hopper, Paul (eds.), *The Limits of Grammaticalization*. Amsterdam–Philadelphia: Benjamins, pp. 227–70.

Ramat, Paolo 1980. 'Zur Typologie des pompejanischen Lateins', in Brettschneider, Günter and Lehmann, Christian (eds.), *Wege zur Universalienforschung*. Tübingen: Narr, pp. 187–91.

1987. 'Introductory paper', in Harris and Ramat (eds.), pp. 3–19.

Ramat, Paolo and Roma, Elisa (eds.) 1998. *Sintassi storica. Atti del XXX congresso internazionale della Società di linguistica italiana*. Rome: Bulzoni.

Ramsden, H. 1963. *Weak Pronoun Position in the Early Romance Languages*. Manchester: Manchester University Press.

Ramus, Franck 2002. 'Acoustic correlates of linguistic rhythm: perspectives', in Bel, B. and Marlien, I. (eds.), *Proceedings of the 1st International Conference on Speech Prosody*. Aix-en-Provence: Université de Provence, pp. 115–20.

Ramus, Franck, Nespor, Marina and Mehler, Jacques 1999. 'Correlates of linguistic rhythm in the speech signal', *Cognition* 73:265–92.

Raposo, Eduardo 1986. 'On the null object in European Portuguese', in Jaeggli, Osvaldo and Silva-Corvalán, Carmen (eds.), *Studies in Romance Linguistics*. Dordrecht: Foris, pp. 373–90.

Rasero Machón, José 1982. 'El campo semántico "salud" en el Siglo de Oro'. Universidad de Extremadura, Cáceres: thesis abstract.

Rasmussen, Jens 1958. *La prose narrative française du XVème Siècle*. Copenhagen: Munksgaard.

Ravier, Xavier 1991. 'L'occitan. Les aires linguistiques', in *LRL* (V, 2), pp. 80–105.

Real Academia Española 1989 (12th edn). *Esbozo de una nueva gramática de la lengua española*. Madrid: Espasa-Calpe.

Recasens, Daniel 1996 (2nd edn). *Fonètica descriptiva del català (Assaig de caracterització de la pronúncia del vocalisme i consonantisme del català al segle XX)*. Barcelona: Institut d'estudis catalans.

Reichenkron, Günter 1933. *Passivum, Medium und Reflexivum in den romanischen Sprachen*. Jena-Leipzig: Gronau.

　1951. 'Das präpositionale Akkusativobjekt im ältesten Spanisch', *Romanische Forschungen* 63:342–97.

　1958. 'Einige grundsätzliche Bemerkungen zum Vigesimalsystem', *Festgabe Ernst Gamillscheg zu seinem fünfundsechzigsten Geburtstag*. Tübingen: Niemeyer, pp. 164–85.

Reiner, Edwin 1968. *La place de l'adjectif épithète en français*. Vienna and Stuttgart: Wilhelm Braumüller.

Reinheimer Rîpeanu, Sanda 2004. *Les emprunts latins dans les langues romanes*. Bucharest: University of Bucharest (consulted at http://www.unibuc.ro/eBooks/filologie/Ripeanu/stanga.htm).

Remacle, Louis 1948. *Le problème de l'ancien wallon*. Liège: Faculté de Philosophie.

Remberger, Eva-Maria 2006. *Hilfsverben. Eine minimalistische Analyse am Beispiel des Italienischen und Sardischen*. Tübingen: Niemeyer.

Renier, Léon 1855–58. *Inscriptions romaines de l'Algérie*. Paris: Imprimerie Impériale.

Renzi, Lorenzo 1976. 'Grammatica e storia dell'articolo italiano', *SGI* 5:5–42.

　1984. 'La tipologia dell'ordine delle parole e le lingue romanze', *Linguistica* 24: 27–59.

　1985. *Nuova introduzione alla filologia romanza*. Bologna: il Mulino.

　1987. 'Essor, transformation et mort d'une loi: la loi de Wackernagel', in *Mélanges offerts à Maurice Molho, vol. III: Linguistique*. Paris: Editions hispaniques, Fontenay, pp. 291–302.

　1992a. 'I pronomi soggetto in due varietà substandard: fiorentino and français avancé', *ZRPh* 108:72–98.

　1992b. 'Le développement de l'article en roman', *RRL* 37:161–76.

　1993. 'Vestiges de la flexion casuelle dans les langues romanes', in Hilty, Gerold (ed.), *Actes du XXe Congrès International de Linguistique et Philologie Romanes* II. Tübingen: Francke, pp. 672–77.

　1994. *Nuova introduzione alla filologia romanza*. Bologna: il Mulino.

　1998. 'Pronomi e casi. La discendenza italiana del lat. *qui*', *SGI* 17:5–36.

2001. 'I dialetti italiani centro-meridionali tra le lingue romanze. Uno sguardo alla sintassi', *Lingua e stile* 36:81–96.

Renzi, Lorenzo and Salvi, Giampaolo (eds.) 1991. *Grande grammatica italiana di consultazione II. I sintagmi verbale, aggettivale, avverbiale. La subordinazione.* Bologna: il Mulino.

Renzi, Lorenzo, Salvi, Giampaolo and Cardinaletti, Anna 2001. *Grande Grammatica Italiana di Consultazione*, I–III. Bologna: il Mulino.

Renzi, Lorenzo and Vanelli, Laura 1983. 'I pronomi soggetto in alcune varietà romanze', in Benincà, P., Cortelazzo, M., Prosdocimi, A., Vanelli, L. and Zamboni, A. (eds.), *Studi in onore di Giovan Battista Pellegrini*. Pisa: Pacini, pp. 121–45.

Repetti, Lori 1992. 'Vowel length in northern Italian dialects', *Probus* 4:155–82.

Repetti, Lori (ed.) 2000. *Phonological Theory and the Dialects of Italy*. Amsterdam-Philadelphia: Benjamins.

REW = Meyer-Lübke (1935)

Rey, Alain (ed.) 1995. *Le Robert. Dictionnaire historique de la langue française*. Paris: Le Robert.

RF = Romanische Forschungen

Ribeiro, Ilza 1995. 'Evidence for a verb-second phase in old Portuguese', in Battye and Roberts (eds.), pp. 110–39.

Richter, Elise 1911. *Der innere Zusammenhang in der Entwicklung der romanischen Sprachen*. Halle (Saale): Niemeyer.

1934. *Beiträge zur Geschichte der Romanismen, I. Chronologische Phonetik des Französischen bis zum Ende des 8. Jahrhunderts*. Halle (Saale): Niemeyer.

Rickard, Peter 1968. *La langue française au seizième siècle. Etude suivie de textes.* Cambridge: Cambridge University Press.

1974. *A History of the French Language*. London: Hutchinson.

Riiho, Timo 1988. *La redundancia pronominal en el iberorromance medieval*. Tübingen: Niemeyer.

Rini, Joel 1991. 'Metathesis of yod and the palatalization of Latin medial /k'l/, /g'l/, /t'l/; /ks/, /ssj/, /sj/; /kt/, /ult/ in Hispano- and Luso-Romance', in Harris-Northall, Ray and Cravens, Thomas (eds.), *Linguistic Studies in Medieval Spanish*. Madison, WI: The Hispanic Seminary of Medieval Studies, pp. 109–33.

1992. *Motives for Linguistic Change in the Formation of the Spanish Object Pronouns*. Newark, NJ: Juan de la Cuesta.

1999. *Exploring the Role of Morphology in the Evolution of Spanish*. Amsterdam-Philadelphia: Benjamins.

Rix, Helmut 1966. 'Die lateinische Synkope als historisches und phonologisches Problem', *Kratylos* 11:156–65.

Rizzi, Luigi 1982. *Issues in Italian Syntax*. Dordrecht: Foris.

1986. 'Null objects in Italian and the theory of *pro*', *LI* 17:501–57.

1997. 'The fine structure of the left periphery', in Haegeman, Liliane (ed.), *Elements of Grammar*. Dordrecht: Kluwer, pp. 281–337.

2001. 'On the position "Int(errogative)" in the left periphery of the clause', in Cinque and Salvi (eds.), pp. 287–96.

RLiR = *Revue de Linguistique romane*

Roberge, Yves 1990. *The Syntactic Recoverability of Null Arguments*. Montreal-London: McGill-Queen's University Press.

Robert L'Argenton, Françoise 1991. 'Larlépem largomuche du louchébem: parler l'argot du boucher', *Langue Française* 90:113–25.

Roberts, Ian 1993. *Verbs and Diachronic Syntax. A Comparative History of English and French*. Dordrecht: Kluwer.

Roberts, Ian and Kato, Mary (eds.) 1993. *Português Brasileiro. Uma viagem diacrônica*. Campinas: Editora da Unicamp.

Roberts, Ian and Roussou, Anna 2003. *Syntactic Change. A Minimalist Approach to Grammaticalization*. Cambridge: Cambridge University Press.

Robinson, Jancis (ed.) 1994. *The Oxford Companion to Wine*. Oxford-New York: Oxford University Press.

Robinson, Lynda 1968. 'Etude du rythme syllabique en français canadien et en français standard', in Léon, Pierre (ed.), *Recherches sur la structure phonique du français canadien*. Montréal-Paris-Bruxelles: Didier, pp. 161–74.

Robson, C. A. 1954. [Review of Orr 1953.] *French Studies* 8:57–60.

Roca, Iggy 1986. 'Secondary stress and metrical rhythm', *Phonology Yearbook* 3:341–70.

1997. 'On the role of accent in stress systems: Spanish evidence', in Martínez Gil and Morales-Front (eds.), pp. 619–664.

1999. 'Stress in the Romance languages', in van der Hulst (ed.), pp. 659–811.

Roché, M 2002. 'Gender inversion in Romance derivatives with -arius', in Benjaballah, S., Dressler, W., Pfeiffer, O. and Voeikova, M. (eds.), *Morphology 2000*. Amsterdam: Benjamins, pp. 283–91.

Rodríguez Castellano, Lorenzo 1951. *La variedad dialectal del Alto Aller*. Oviedo: Instituto de estudios asturianos.

Rohlfs, Gerhard 1937. 'Mundarten und Griechentum des Cilento', *ZRPh* 57:421–61.

1938. 'Der Einfluß des Satzakzentes auf den Lautwandel', *Archiv für das Studium der neueren Sprachen* 174:54–56.

1952a. 'Les noms des jours de la semaine dans les langues romanes,' in Rohlfs, Gerhard (ed.), *An den Quellen der romanischen Sprachen*. Halle: Niemeyer, pp. 40–45.

1952b. 'Die Zählung nach Zwanzigern im Romanischen', in Rohlfs, Gerhard (ed.), *An den Quellen der romanischen Sprachen*. Halle: Niemeyer, pp. 238–44.

1966. *Grammatica storica della lingua italiana e dei suoi dialetti. Fonetica*. Turin: Einaudi.

1968. *Grammatica storica della lingua italiana e dei suoi dialetti. Morfologia.* Turin: Einaudi.

1969. *Grammatica storica della lingua italiana e dei suoi dialetti. Sintassi e formazione delle parole.* Turin: Einaudi.

1970. *Le gascon. Étude de philologie pyrénéenne.* Tübingen: Niemeyer.

1971a. 'Autour de l'accusatif prépositionnel dans les langues romanes', *RLiR* 35:312–33.

1971b. *Romanische Sprachgeographie. Geschichte und Grundlagen, Aspekte und Probleme mit dem Versuch eines Sprachatlas der romanischen Sprachen.* München: Beck.

1975. *Rätoromanisch.* Munich: Beck.

1977. *Nuovo dizionario dialettale della Calabria.* Ravenna: Longo.

Rokseth, Pierre 1921. 'La diphthongaison en catalan', *Romania* 47:532–46.

Roldán, Mercedes 1971. 'Spanish constructions with *-se*', *Language Sciences* 18:15–29.

Romaine, Suzanne 1982. *Socio-historical Linguistics. Its Status and Methodology.* Cambridge: Cambridge University Press.

Roncaglia, Aurelio 1965. *La lingua dei trovatori.* Rome: Edizioni dell'Ateneo.

Ronconi, Alessandro 1946. *Il verbo latino. Principi di sintassi storica.* Bologna: Zanichelli.

Ronjat, Jules 1930–41. *Grammaire istorique des parlers provençaux modernes*, 4 vols. Montpellier: Société des Langues Romanes.

Rönsch, Hermann 1965 [1868]. *Itala und Vulgata.* Munich: Hueber.

Rosenkranz, Bernhard 1933. 'Die Stellung des attributiven Genitivs im Italischen', *IF* 51:131–39.

Rosetti, Alexandru 1968. *Istoria limbii române de la origine pînă în secolul al XVII-lea.* Bucharest: Editura pentru literatură.

1974. *Istoria limbii române. I: De la origini pînă în secolul al XVII-lea.* Bucharest: Editura științifică și enciclopedică.

1986. *Istoria limbii române. De la origini pînă la începutul secolului al XVII-lea.* Bucharest: Editura științifică și academică.

Rösler, Margarete 1910. 'Das Vigesimalsystem im Romanischen', *Prinzipienfragen der romanischen Sprachwissenschaft.* Halle: Niemeyer, pp. 187–205.

Rossi, Maria Aparecida Garcia Lopes 1993. 'Estudo diacrônico sobre as interrogativas do português do Brasil', in Roberts, I. and Kato, M. A. (eds.), *Português brasileiro. Uma viagem diacrônica.* Campinas, SP: Editora da Unicamp, pp. 307–42.

Rossini, Giorgio 1975. *Capitoli di morfologia e sintasi del dialetto cremonese.* Florence: La Nuova Italia.

Rothe, Wolfgang 1957. *Einführung in die Laut- und Formenlehre des Rumänischen.* Halle: Niemeyer.

Rovai, Francesco 2005. 'L'estensione dell'accusativo in latino tardo e medievale', *AGI* 90:54–89.

Rovinelli, Attilio 1919. *Il gergo nella società, nella storia, nella letteratura con alcuni saggi di vocabolario di vari gerghi.* Milan: Sonzogno.

Rowlett, Paul 1998. *Sentential Negation in French.* Oxford: Oxford University Press.

2007. *The Syntax of French.* Cambridge: Cambridge University Press.

RPh = *Romance Philology*

RRL = *Revue roumaine de linguistique*

Rudes, Blair 1980. 'On the nature of verbal suppletion', *Linguistics* 18: 655–76.

Rudin, Catherine 1988. 'On multiple questions and multiple wh-fronting', *NLLT* 6:445–501.

Ruffino, Giovanni (ed.) 1995. *Atti del XXI Congresso Internazionale di Linguistica e Filologia Romanza,* Palermo, 18–24 settembre 1995, *vol. I: Grammatica storica delle lingue romanze.* Tübingen: Niemeyer.

Ruhlen, Merrit 1973. 'Nasal Vowels', *Working Papers on Language Universals* 12:1–36.

Russo, Michela 2002. 'La categoria neutrale nella diacronia del napoletano: implicazioni morfologiche, lessicali, semantiche', *VR* 61:117–49.

Ruwet, Nicholas 1972. 'Les constructions pronominales en français: restrictions de selections, transformations et règles de redondances', *Le Français moderne* 2:102–25.

Sabatini, Francesco 1956. 'La "lingua lombardesca" di Pescocostanzo (Abruzzo). contributo alla storia dei gerghi in Italia', *CN* 16:241–57.

1965. 'Sull'origine dei plurali italiani: il tipo in *–i*', *SLI* 5:5–39.

Safarewicz, J. 1974. *Linguistic Studies.* The Hague: Mouton.

Sainéan, Lazare 1907. *L'argot ancien (1455–1850).* Paris: Champion.

1912. *Les sources de l'argot ancien.* Paris: Champion.

Sala, Marius 1976. *Contributions à la phonétique historique du roumain.* Paris: Klincksieck.

Sala, Marius (ed.) 1988. *Vocabularul reprezentativ al limbilor romanice.* Bucharest: Editura științifică și enciclopedică.

Sala, Marius 2004. *Dal latino al romeno.* Alessandria: Edizioni dell'Orso.

Saltarelli, Mario 1970a. *A Phonology of Italian in a Generative Grammar.* The Hague: Mouton.

1970b. *La grammatica generativa trasformazionale. Con introduzione alla fonologia, sintassi e dialettologia italiana.* Florence: Sansoni.

Salvador, Gregorio 1988. 'Lexemática histórica', in Ariza, M., Salvador, A. and Viudas, A. (eds.), *Actas del I Congreso internacional de historia de la lengua española I.* Madrid: Arco Libros, pp. 635–46.

Salverda de Grave, J. J. 1920. 'Evolutions de certains groupes intervocaliques de consonnes en français', *Neophilologus* 5:1–11.

1930. 'Sur l'évolution des consonnes en italien', *Romania* 56:321–30.

Salvi, Giampaolo 1982. 'Sulla storia sintattica della costruzione romanza *habeo* + part. perf.', *Revue Romane* 17:118–33.

1985. 'L'infinito con l'articolo', in Franchi De Bellis, Annalisa and Savoia, Leonardo (eds.), *Sintassi e morfologia della lingua italiana d'uso*. Rome: Bulzoni, pp. 243–68.

1987. 'Restructuring in the evolution of Romance auxiliaries', in Harris and Ramat (eds.), pp. 225–36.

1990. 'La sopravvivenza della legge di Wackernagel nei dialetti occidentali della Penisola Iberica', *MedRom* 15:177–210.

1995. 'L'ordine delle parole nella frase subordinata in galego–portoghese antico', in Rákóczi, István (ed.), *Miscellanea Rosae. Tanulmányok Rózsa Zoltán 65. születésnapjára*. Budapest: Mundus, pp. 19–37.

1997. 'La posizione tipologica dell'italiano fra le lingue romanze', *Italienische Studien* 18:25–38.

2000. 'La formazione del sistema V2 delle lingue romanze antiche', *Lingua e Stile* 35:665–92.

2001a. 'La nascita dei clitici romanzi', *Romanische Forschungen* 113:285–319.

2001b. 'The two sentence structures of Early Romance', in Cinque, Gugliemo and Salvi, Giampaolo (eds.), *Current Studies in Italian Syntax*. Amsterdam: North-Holland, pp. 297–312.

2004. *La formazione della struttura di frase romanza. Ordine delle parole e clitici dal latino alle lingue romanze antiche*. Tübingen: Niemeyer.

2008. 'Imperfect systems and diachronic change', in Detges, Ulrich and Waltereit, Richard (eds.), *The Paradox of Grammatical Change. Perspectives from Romance*. Amsterdam: Benjamins, pp. 127–45.

Salvi, Giampaolo and Renzi, Lorenzo 2010. *Grammatica dell'italiano antico*. Bologna: Il Mulino.

Salvioni, Carlo 1884. *Fonetica del dialetto moderno della Città di Milano*. Turin: Loescher.

1886. 'Saggi intorno ai dialetti di alcune vallate all'estremità settentrionale del Lago Maggiore. I. Annotazioni fonetiche e morfologiche. Effetti dell'-*i* sulla tonica', *AGI* 9:188–260, 440 [also in Salvoni (2008), I, pp. 13–86].

1907. 'Lingua e dialetti della Svizzera italiana', *Rendiconti dell'Istituto Lombardo* 40 (s. II):719–36 [also in Salvoni (2008), I, pp. 151–68].

1919. 'Sul dialetto milanese arcaico', *Rendiconti dell'Istituto Lombardo* 52 (s. II):517–40 [also in Salvoni (2008), III, pp. 181–204].

1925. 'Etimologie valtellinesi', *ID* 1:213–28 [also in Salvoni (2008), IV, pp. 173–88].

2008, *Scritti linguistici*, Loporcaro, Michele, Pescia, Lorenza, Broggini, Romano and Vecchio, Paola (eds.), 5 vols. Locarno: Edizioni dello Stato del Cantone Ticino.

Sampson, Rodney 1980a. *Early Romance Texts*. Cambridge: Cambridge University Press.

1980b. 'On the history of final vowels from Latin to Old French', *ZRPh* 96:23–48.

1999. *Nasal Vowel Evolution in Romance*. Oxford: Oxford University Press.

Sánchez Miret, Fernando 1998. *La diptongación en las lenguas románicas*. Munich-Newcastle: LINCOM Europa.

2001. *Proyecto de gramática histórica y comparada de las lenguas romances*, 2 vols. Munich: LINCOM Europa.

(ed.) 2003. *Actas del XXIII Congreso internacional de lingüística y filología románica, vol. I*. Tübingen: Niemeyer.

2007. 'El papel de la fonética en la explicación de los cambios fonológicos dentro de *la gramática histórica de las lenguas románicas*', in Cunița, A., Lupu, Coman and Tasmowski, Liliane (eds.), *Studii de lingvistică și filologie romanică. Hommages offerts à Sandra Reinheimer Rîpeanu*. București: Editura Universității, pp. 484–93.

Sanga, Glauco 1979. 'I calderai di Castelponzone: da "diritti" a "proletari"', in Leydi, R. and Bertolotti, G. (eds.), *Cremona e il suo territorio, Mondo Popolare in Lombardia 7*. Milan: Silvana.

1980. 'Il gergo e il rapporto lingua-classe', in Albano Leoni, Federico (ed.), *I dialetti e le lingue delle minoranze di fronte all'italiano*. Rome: Bulzoni, pp. 99–116.

1984. 'La tensione nei dialetti lombardi', in Sanga, Glauco (ed.), *Dialettologia lombarda. Lingue e culture popolari*. Pavia: Aurora, pp. 45–67.

1988. 'La lunghezza vocalica nel milanese e la coscienza fonologica dei parlanti', *RPh* 41:290–97.

1997. 'Lombardy', in Maiden and Parry (eds.), pp. 253–59.

Sankoff, Gillian and Thibault, Pierrette 1980. 'The alternation between the auxiliaries *avoir* and *être* in Montréal French', in Sankoff, Ulrich (ed.), *The Social Life of Language*. Philadelphia: University of Pennsylvania, pp. 295–310.

Santamarina, Antonio 1974. *El verbo gallego*. Santiago: Verba Anejo 4.

Santangelo, Annamaria. 1981. 'I plurali italiani del tipo "le braccia"', *AGI* 66: 95–153.

Santos Domínguez, Luis Antonio and Espinosa Elorza, Rosa María 1996. *Manual de semántica histórica*. Madrid: Síntesis.

Sapir, Edward 1921. *Language*. New York: Harcourt Brace.

Saralegui, Carmen 1992. 'Aragonés-Navarro', *LRL* (VI, 1), pp. 37–54.

Sas, Louis 1937. *The Noun Declension System in Merovingian Latin*. Paris: André.

Sasse, Hans-Jürgen 1977. 'Gedanken über Worstellungsveränderung', *Papiere zur Linguistik* 9:82–142.

Saussure, Ferdinand de 1922. *Cours de linguistique générale, publié par Charles Bally et Albert Sechehaye*. Paris: Payot.

Sauzet, Patrick 1986. 'Les clitiques occitans: analyse métrique de leur variation dialectale', in *Actes du XVIIème CILPhR, vol. 4: Morphosyntaxe des langues romanes*. Marseille: Université de Provence – Jean Laffitte, pp. 153–80.

Savj-Lopez, P. 1900. 'Studi d'antico napoletano', *ZRPh* 24: 501–7.

Savoia, Leonardo 1980. 'Fonologia delle varietà apuane e garfagnine: consonantismo', *Studi urbinati di storia, filosofia e letteratura. Suppl. linguistico* 2:233–93.

1997. 'Il vocalismo a tre gradi dell'area calabro-lucana', in Catagnoti, A. (ed.), *Studi linguistici offerti a Gabriella Giacomelli dagli amici e dagli allievi*. Padua: Unipress, pp. 363–75.

Savoia, Leonardo and Maiden, Martin 1997. 'Metaphony', in Maiden and Parry (eds.), pp. 15–25.

Scarano, Antonietta 1999. *Gli aggettivi qualificativi in italiano. Uno studio su corpora di italiano scritto e parlato*. Department of Linguistics, University of Florence: unpublished thesis.

2005. 'Aggettivi qualificativi, italiano parlato e articolazione dell'informazione', in Burr, Elisabeth (ed.), *Tradizione e innovazione. Atti del VI convegno della Società di linguistica e filologia italiana*. Florence: Cesati, pp. 277–92.

Schädel, Bernhard 1903. *Die Mundart von Ormea*. Halle: Niemeyer.

Schaechtelin, Paul 1911. *Das passé défini und imparfait im altfranzösischen*. Halle: Niemeyer.

Schane, Sanford 1968. *French Phonology and Morphology*, Cambridge, MA: MIT Press.

Scheer, Tobias and Philippe Ségéral 2003. 'A look at the Gallo-Romance trouble with *muta cum liquida* through the positional prism'. Paper given at *Going Romance 2003*, Nijmegen, 20–22 November 2003.

Schiaffini, Alfredo 1943. *Tradizione e poesia nella prosa d'arte italiana dalla latinità medievale a G. Boccaccio*. Rome: Storia e Letteratura.

Schiffman, Harold 1997. 'Diglossia as a sociolinguistic situation', in Coulmas, Florian (ed.), *The Handbook of Sociolinguistics*. Oxford: Blackwell, pp. 205–16.

Schlegel, August Wilhelm von 1818. *Observations sur la langue et la littérature provençales*. Paris: Librairie grecque-latine-allemande.

Schlieben-Lange, Brigitte 1971. *Okzitanisch und Katalanisch*. Tübingen: Gunter Narr.

Schmid, E. 1964. 'Zur Entwicklungsgeschichte der romanischen Zahlwörtern', *VR* 23: 186–238.

Schmid, Heinrich 1949. *Zur Formenbildung von* dare *und* stare *im Romanischen*. Bern: Francke.

1951. 'Zur Geschichte der rätoromanischen Deklination', *VR* 12:21–81.

Schmid, Stephan 2004. 'Une approche phonétique de l'isochronie dans quelques dialectes italo-romans', in Meiselburg, T. and Selig, M. (eds.), *Nouveaux départs en phonologie. Les conceptions sub- et suprasegmentales*. Tübingen: Narr, pp. 109–24.

2007. 'Les occlusives palatales du vallader'. Paper presented at *XXV Congrès international de linguistique et de philologie romanes*, Innsbruck, Austria.

Schmidt, Johannes 1889. *Die Pluralbildung der indogermanischen Neutra*. Weimar: Böhlau.

Schmidt, Wilhelm 1926. *Die Sprachfamilien und Sprachenkreise der Erde*. Heidelberg: Winter.

Schmitt, Christian 1974. *Die Sprachlandschaften der Galloromania. Eine lexikalische Studie zum Problem der Entstehung und Charakterisierung.* Bern: Lang.

    1990. 'Französische: Sondersprachen-Jargons', *LRL* (V, 1):283–307.

Schmitt, Cristina 1998. 'Lack of iteration: accusative clitic doubling, participial absolutes and *have* + agreeing participles', *Probus* 10:243–300.

Schoch, Marianne 1978. 'Problème sociolinguistique des pronoms d'allocution: «tu» et «vous», enquête à Lausanne', *La Linguistique* 14:55–73.

Schøsler, Lene 1984. *La Déclinaison bicasuelle de l'ancien français.* Odense: Odense Universitetsforlag.

    2001a. 'The coding of the subject/object distinction from Latin to Modern French', in Faarlund, Jan Terje (ed.), *Grammatical Relations in Change.* Oslo-Amsterdam: Benjamins, pp. 273–302.

    2001b. 'From Latin to Modern French: actualization and markedness', in Andersen, Henning (ed.), *Actualization. Linguistic Change in Progress.* Amsterdam: Benjamins, pp. 169–85.

Schøsler, Lene and van Reenen, Pieter 2000. 'Declension in Old and Middle French: two opposing tendencies', in Smith, John Charles and Bentley, Delia (eds.), *Historical Linguistics 1995. Selected Papers from the 12th International Conference on Historical Linguistics*, Manchester, August 1995. Amsterdam-Philadelphia: John Benjamins, pp. 327–44.

Schroeder, Walter 1932. 'Die bedingte Diphthongierung betonter Vokale im südfranzösischen Alpengebiet', *Volkstum und Kultur der Romanen* 5:152–241.

Schroten, J. 1972. *Concerning the Deep Structures of Spanish Reflexive Sentences.* The Hague: Mouton.

Schuchardt, Hugo 1866–68. *Der Vokalismus des Vulgärlateins.* Leipzig: Teubner.

    1874. 'Zur romanischen Sprachwissenschaft: Lateinische und romanische deklination', *Zeitschrift für vergleichend Sprachforschung* 22:153–90.

Schürr, Friedrich 1919. *Romagnolische Dialektstudien, II. Lautlehre lebender Mundarten.* Vienna: Akademie der Wissenschaften.

    1936. 'Umlaut und Diphthongierung in der Romania', *RF* 50:275–316.

    1965. 'Grundsätzliches zu den Fragen der romanischen, insbesondere italienischen Diphthongierung', *Archiv für das Studium der neueren Sprachen* 201:321–39.

    1970. *La Diphthongaison romane.* Tübingen: Narr.

    1972. 'Epilogo alla discussione sulla dittongazione romanza', *RLiR* 36:311–21.

Schwegler, Armin 1990. *Analyticity and Syntheticity. A Diachronic Perspective with Special Reference to Romance Languages.* Berlin-New York: Mouton.

Schwegler, Armin, Tranel, Bernard and Uribe-Etxebarria, Myriam (eds.) 1998. *Romance Linguistics: Theoretical Perspectives. LSRL 27.* Amsterdam-Philadelphia: Benjamins.

Schwenter, Scott and Silva, Gláucia 2002. 'Overt vs null direct objects in spoken Brazilian Portuguese: a semantic-pragmatic account', *Hispania* 853:577–86.

Searle, John R. 1993 (2nd edn). 'Metaphor', in Ortony, Andrew (ed.), *Metaphor and Thought*. Cambridge: Cambridge University Press, pp. 83–111.

Seidl, Christian 1994. 'Gemeinsabellisch und Vulgärlateinisch: der Vokalismus', in Dunkel, G., Meyer, G., Scarlata, S. and Seidl, C. (eds.), *Früh-, Mittel-, Spätindogermanisch. Akten der IX. Fachtagung der Indogermanischen Gesellschaft*. Wiesbaden: Reichert, pp. 349–70.

1995a. 'Le système acasuel des protoromans ibériques et sarde: dogmes et faits', *Vox Romanica* 54:41–73.

1995b. 'Lingua latina in bocca italica? Uno sguardo critico dal punto di vista del sostrato', in Ruffino (ed.), pp. 371–83.

Selig, Maria 1992. *Die Entwicklung der Nominaldeterminanten im Spätlatein*. Tübingen: Niemeyer.

1998. 'Pseudoreflexivität im Altitalienischen: Voraussetzungen und Richtungen eines Grammatikalisierungsprozesses', in Geisler, Hans and Jacob, Daniel (eds.), *Diathese und Transitivität in den romanischen Sprachen*. Tübingen: Narr, pp. 21–42.

Sells, Peter 2001. 'Form and function in the typology of grammatical voice systems', in Legendre, Geraldine, Grimshaw, Jane and Vikner, Sten (eds.), *Optimality-Theoretic Syntax*. Cambridge, MA: MIT Press, pp. 355–91.

Serianni, Luca 1989. *Grammatica italiana. Italiano comune e lingua letteraria*. Turin: UTET.

1999. [Review of Maiden 1998c] *Studi linguistici italiani* 25:108–16.

Serra, Pep 1997. 'Prosodic structure and stress in Catalan', in Martínez Gil and Morales-Front (eds.), pp. 195–231.

SFI = *Studi di filologia italiana*

SGI = *Studi di grammatica italiana*

Șiadbei, I. 1930. 'Le sort du prétérit roumain', *Romania* 56:330–60.

Sihler, Andrew 1995. *A New Comparative Grammar of Greek and Latin*. Oxford–New York: Oxford University Press.

Silverstein, Michael 1976. 'Hierarchy of features and Ergativity', in Dixon, Robert (ed.), *Grammatical Categories in Australian Languages*. Canberra: Australian Institute of Aboriginal Studies, pp. 112–71.

Silvestri, Domenico 1977–79. *La teoria del sostrato. Metodi e miraggi*, 2 vols. Naples: Macchiaroli.

Simpson, D. (ed.) 1964. *Cassell's New Latin Dictionary Latin–English, English–Latin*. London: Cassell.

Skårup, Povl 1975. *Les premières zones de la proposition en ancien français*. Copenhagen: Akademisk Forlag.

1997. *Morphologie élémentaire de l'ancien occitan*. Copenhagen: Museum Tusculanum Forlag.

Skytte, Gunver and Salvi, Giampaolo 2001. 'Frasi subordinate all'infinito', in Renzi, Salvi and Cardinaletti, Anna (eds.), vol. II, pp. 483–569.

SLI = Studi linguistici italiani

Smith, Colin 1972. *Poema de Mio Cid.* Edited with Introduction and Notes by Colin, Smith. Oxford: Oxford University Press.

Smith, John Charles 1989. 'Actualization reanalyzed: evidence from the Romance compound past tenses', in Walsh, T. (ed.), *Synchronic and Diachronic Approaches to Linguistic Variation and Change.* Washington, DC: Georgetown University Press, pp. 310–25.

    1992. 'Traits, marques et sous-spécification: application à la deixis', in Morel, Mary-Annick and Danon-Boileau, Laurent (eds.), *La Deixis. Colloque en Sorbonne, 8–9 juin 1990.* Paris: Presses Universitaires de France, pp. 257–64.

    1993. 'La desaparición de la concordancia entre participio de pasado y objeto directo en castellano y catalán: aspectos geográficos e históricos', in Penny, Ralph (ed.), *Actas del primer congreso anglo-hispano I. Lingüística.* Madrid: Castalia, pp. 275–85.

    1995a. 'Perceptual factors and the disappearance of agreement between past participle and direct object in Romance', in Smith, J. C. and Maiden, M. (eds.), *Linguistic Theory and the Romance Languages.* Amsterdam: Benjamins, pp. 161–80.

    1995b. 'L'évolution sémantique et pragmatique des adverbes déictiques *ici, là* et *là-bas*', *Langue française* 107:43–57.

    1999a. 'The refunctionalization of a pronominal subsystem between Latin and Romance', in Folli, R. and Middleton, R. (eds.), *Oxford University Working Papers in Linguistics, Philology and Phonetics 4*, pp. 141–56.

    1999b. 'Markedness and morphosyntactic change revisited: the case of Romance past participle agreement', in Embleton, S., Joseph, J. and Niederehe, H.-J. (eds.), *The Emergence of the Modern Language Sciences. Studies on the Transition from Historical-Comparative to Structural Linguistics in Honour of E. F. K. Koerner. 2: Methodological Perspectives and Applications.* Amsterdam: Benjamins, pp. 203–15.

    2001a. 'Markedness, functionality, and perseveration in the actualization of a morphosyntactic change', in Andersen, Henning (ed.), *Actualization. Linguistic Change in Progress.* Amsterdam-Philadelphia: Benjamins, pp. 203–23.

    2001b. 'Illocutionary conversion, bystander deixis, and Romance "ethic" pro-nouns', *Working Papers in Functional Grammar 74.* Amsterdam: Vrije Universiteit Amsterdam.

    2005. 'Some refunctionalizations of the nominative-accusative opposition between Latin and Gallo-Romance', in Smelik, Bernadette, Hofman, Rijcklof, Hamans, Camiel and Cram, David (eds.), *A Companion in Linguistics. A Festschrift for Anders Ahlqvist on the Occasion of his Sixtieth Birthday.* Nijmegen: De Keltische Draak, pp. 269–85.

2006. 'How to do things without junk: the refunctionalization of a pronominal subsystem between Latin and Romance', in Montreuil, Jean-Pierre (ed.), *New Perspectives on Romance Linguistics, vol. II: Phonetics, Phonology and Dialectology*. Amsterdam-Philadelphia: Benjamins, pp. 183–205.

2008. 'The refunctionalisation of first-person plural inflection in Tiwi', in Bowern, Claire, Evans, Bethwyn and Miceli, Luisa (eds.), *Morphology and Language History. In Honour of Harold Koch*. Amsterdam-Philadelphia: Benjamins, pp. 341–48.

Smits, R. J. C. 1989. *Eurogrammar. The Relative and Cleft Constructions of the Germanic and Romance Languages*. Dordrecht: Foris.

Solà, Joan 1993. *Estudis de sintaxi catalana, 2*. Barcelona: Edicions 62.

1994. *Sintaxi normativa. Estat de la qüestió*. Barcelona: Empúries.

Sørensen, Knud 1957. 'Latin influence on English syntax', *TCLC* 11:131–55.

Sornicola, Rosanna 1995. 'Mutamenti di prospettiva culturale nelle lingue europee moderne: l'influenza del latino sulla sintassi', in Lönne, Karl-Egon (ed.), *Kulturwandel im Spiegel des Sprachwandels*. Tübingen-Basel: Francke, pp. 41–58.

1997. 'L'oggetto preposizionale in siciliano antico e in napoletano antico: considerazioni su un problema di tipologia diacronica', *Italienische Studien* 18:66–80.

2000. 'Stability, variation and change in word order: some evidence from the Romance Languages', in Sornicola, Rosanna, Poppe, Erich and Shisha-Halevy, Ariel (eds.), *Stability, Variation and Change of Word-Order Patterns Over Time*. Amsterdam-Philadelphia: Benjamins, pp. 101–18.

Spagnoletti, C. and Dominici, M. 1992. 'L'accent italien et la cliticisation de la terminaison verbale *–no*', *Revue Québecoise de Linguistique* 21:9–32.

Speas, Margaret 1990. *Phrase Structure in Natural Languages*. Dordrecht: Kluwer.

Spence, Nicol 1971. 'La survivance des formes du nominatif latin en français', *Revue romane* 6:74–84.

Spescha, Arnold 1989. *Grammatica sursilvana*. Chur: Casa editura per mieds d'instrucziun.

Spevak, Olga 2007. 'L'anaphore, la deixis et l'ordre des consituants en latin', *Latomus* 66:853–70. Bruxelles: Editions Latomus.

Spiess, Federico 1956. *Die Verwendung des Subjekt-Personalpronomens in den lombardischen Mundarten*. Bern: Francke.

Spitzer, Leo 1937. 'Du langage-écho en portugais', *Boletim de Filologia* 5:165–69.

Spore, Palle 1972. *La Diphtongaison romane*. Odense: Odense University Press.

Stammerjohann, Harro (ed.) 1986. *Tema-rema in italiano – Theme-Rheme in Italia-Thema-Rhema in Italienischen*. Tübingen: Narr.

Stampa, Gian Andrea 1934. *Der Dialekt des Bergell. I Teil. Phonetik*. Aarau: Sauerländer.

Stampe, David 1979. *A Dissertation on Natural Phonology*. Bloomington, IN: Indiana University Linguistics Club.

Stanovaïa, Lydia 1993. 'Sur la déclinaison bicasuelle en ancien français (point de vue scriptologique)', *Travaux de linguistique et de philologie* 23:163–82.

Stati, Sorin 1989. 'Le roumain: syntaxe', *LRL* (III), pp. 114–37.

Steadman, Philip 1979. *The Evolution of Designs. Biological Analogy in Architecture and the Applied Arts.* Cambridge: Cambridge University Press.

Steele, Susan, Akmajian, Adrian, Jelinek, Eloise, Kitagawa, Chisato, Oehrle, Richard and Wasow, Thomas 1981. *An Encyclopedia of AUX. A Study of Cross-Linguistic Equivalence.* Cambridge, MA: MIT Press.

Ştefănescu, Ioana 1997. *The Syntax of Agreement in Romanian.* City University of New York: thesis. Distributed as *MIT Occasional Papers in Linguistics no. 14.* Cambridge, MA: MIT Working Papers in Linguistics, MIT, Department of Linguistics.

Stéfanini, Jean 1982. 'Reflexive, impersonal, and passives in Italian and Florentine', in MaCaulay, M. and Gensler, O. (eds.), *Proceedings of the Eighth Annual Meeting of the Berkeley Linguistics Society.* Berkeley: University of California, pp. 97–107.

Stefenelli, Arnulf 1979. 'Remotivationstendenzen in der Geschichte des französischen Wortschatzes', in Ernst, Gerhard and Stefenelli, Arnulf (eds.), *Sprache und Mensch in der Romania. H. Kuen zum achtzigsten Geburtstag.* Wiesbaden: Steiner, pp. 179–92.

1981. *Geschichte des französischen Kernwortschatzes.* Berlin: Erich Schmidt.

1987. 'Die innerromanische Sonderstellung des Frühgalloromanischen hinsichtlich der Kasusflexion: ein Beitrag zur diachronischen Varietätenlinguistik', in Dahmen, W., Holtus, G., Kramer, J. and Metzeltin, M. (eds.), *Latein and Romanisch. Romanistisches Kolloquium I.* Tübingen: Narr, pp. 69–91.

1992a. *Das Schicksal des lateinischen Wortschatzes in den romanischen Sprachen.* Passau: Rothe.

1992b. 'Sprechsprachliche Universalien im protoromanischen Vulgärlatein (Lexikon und Semantik)', in Iliescu, M. and Marxgut, W. (eds.), *Latin vulgaire – latin tardif III.* Tübingen: Niemeyer, pp. 347–59.

1992c. 'Die Transferierbarkeit des lateinischen Wortschatzes beim Erwerb romanischer Sprachen', *Französisch Heute* 3:379–87.

1995a. 'Remarques sur la structure socioculturelle du latin protoroman', in Callebat, L. (ed.), *Latin vulgaire-latin tardif IV.* Hildesheim-Zurich-New York: Olms, pp. 35–45.

1995b. 'Methodologische Prinzipien der vergleichenden Sprachcharakterisierung', in Schmitt, C. and Schweickard, W. (eds.), *Die romanischen Sprachen im Vergleich. Der Sprachvergleich in der Romania. Anwendungsbereiche, Ziele, Methoden und Ergebnisse.* Bonn: Romanistischer Verlag, pp. 351–64.

1996. 'Gemeinromanische Tendenzen VIII: Lexikon und Semantik', in *LRL* (II, 1), pp. 368–86.

1998. 'La base lexicale des langues romanes', in Herman, J. (ed.), *La transizione dal latino alle lingue romanze. Atti della Tavola rotonda di linguistica storica. Università Ca'Foscari di Venezia.* Tübingen: Niemeyer, pp. 53–65.

Stein, A. 1974. *L'écologie de l'argot ancien.* Paris: Nizet.

Sten, Holger 1936. 'Zur portugiesischen Syntax', *Archiv für das Studium der neueren Sprachen* 170:229–34.

1944. *Les particularités de la langue portugaise.* Copenhagen: Cercle Linguistique.

1973. *L'emploi des temps en portugais moderne.* Copenhagen: Det Kongelige Danske Videnskabernes Selskab, Historisk-filosofiske Meddelelser 46.1.

Stephens, Janig 2002. 'Breton', in Ball, Martin (ed.), *The Celtic Languages.* London: Routledge, pp. 349–409.

Steriade, Donca 1984. 'Glides and vowels in Romanian', in Brugman, Claudia and Macaulay, Monica (eds.), *Proceedings of the Tenth Annual Meeting of the Berkeley Linguistics Society.* Berkeley: University of California, pp. 47–64.

1988. 'Gemination and the proto-Romance syllable shift', in Birdsong and Montreuil (eds.), pp. 371–409.

Steven, Eva-Marie 1983. *Worttod durch Homophonie im Französischen.* Inaugural-Dissertation zur Erlangung des Doktorgrades der philosophischen Fakultät der Universität Köln.

Stewart, Miranda 1999. *The Spanish Language Today.* London: Routledge.

Stimm, Helmut 1986. 'Die Markierung des direkten Objekts durch a im Unterengadinischen', in Holtus, G. and Ringger, K. (eds.), *Raetia antiqua et moderna, W. Th. Elwert zum 80. Geburtstag.* Tübingen: Niemeyer, pp. 407–48.

Stimm, Helmut and Linder, Karl Petere 1989. 'Bündnerromanisch. Interne Sprachgeschichte I. Grammatik', in *LRL* (III), pp. 764–85.

Straka, Georges 1953. 'Observations sur la chronologie et les dates de quelques modifications phonétiques en roman et en français prélittéraire', *Revue des Langues Romanes* 71:247–307.

1956. 'La dislocation linguistique de la Romania et la formation des langues romanes à la lumière de la chronologie relative des changements phonétiques', *RLiR* 20:213–94.

1959. 'Durée et timbre vocaliques: observations de phonétique générale appliquées à la phonétique historique des langues romanes', *Zeitschrift für Phonetik und allgemeine Sprachwissenschaft* 12:276–300 [also in Straka, 1979, pp. 167–91].

1964. 'L'évolution phonétique du latin au français sous l'effet de l'énergie, et de la faiblesse articulatoire', *Travaux de Linguistique et de littérature* 2:17–98 [also in Straka, 1979, pp. 213–94].

Straka, Georges (ed.) 1965. *Linguistique et philologie romane. Xe Congrès International de linguistique et philologie romanes,* 3 vols. Paris: Klincksieck.

Straka, Georges 1979. *Les sons et les mots. Choix d'études de phonétique et de linguistique.* Paris: Klincksieck.

Stricker, Hans 1981. *Die romanischen Orts- und Flurnamen von Grabs*. Chur: Greko.

Studer, Paul 1924. 'The Franco-Provençal dialects of Upper Valais (Switzerland) with texts', *Philologica* 2:1–43.

Stump, Gregory 2001. *Inflectional Morphology. A Theory of Paradigm Structure*. Cambridge: Cambridge University Press.

Stussi, Alfredo 1965. *Testi veneziani del Duecento e dei primi del Trecento*. Pisa: Nistri-Lischi.

Suñer, Margarita 1988. 'The role of agreement in clitic-doubled constructions', *NLLT* 6:391–434.

Suñer, Martha 1974. 'Where does impersonal *se* come from?', in Campbell, Joe, Goldin, Mark and Warg, Mary (eds.), *Linguistic Studies in Romance Languages*. Washington, DC: Georgetown University Press, pp. 146–57.

Sweetser, Eve 1990. *From Etymology to Pragmatics. Metaphorical and Cultural Aspects of Semantic Structure*. Cambridge: Cambridge University Press.

Sylvain, Suzanne 1936. *Le créole haïtien. Morphologie et syntaxe*. Port-au-Prince-Wetteren: Imprimerie de Meester.

Szemerényi, Oswald 1960. *Studies in the Indo-European System of Numerals*. Heidelberg: Winter.

Taboada, Manuel 1979. *El habla del Valle de Verín*. Santiago de Compostela: Verba Anejo 15.

Tagliavini, Carlo 1963. *Storia di parole pagane e cristiane attraverso i tempi*. Brescia: Morcelliana.

1972. *Le origini delle lingue neolatine: introduzione alla filologia romanza*. Bologna: Pàtron.

Tasmowski-De Ryck, Liliane 1990. 'Les démonstratifs français et roumain dans la phrase et dans le texte', in Cadiot, Pierre and Zribi-Hertz, A. (eds.), *Langages. Aux confins de la grammaire: l'anaphore*. Paris: Larousse, pp. 82–99.

TCLC = *Travaux du Cercle Linguistique de Copenhague* .

Tekavčić, Pavao 1972. *Grammatica storica dell'italiano. I. Fonematica. II. Morfonsintassi. III. Lessico*, 3 vols. Bologna: il Mulino.

1980. Grammatica storica della lingua italiana. *I. Fonematica. II. Morfosintassi*. Bologna: il Mulino.

Ternes, Elmar 1998. 'Keltisch und Romanisch / Le celtique et les langues romanes', *LRL* (VII), pp. 266–91.

Tessitore, Fulvio 1991. *Introduzione allo storicismo*. Bari: Laterza.

Teyssier, Paul 1980. *Histoire de la langue portugaise*. Paris: PUF.

1982. *História da língua portuguesa*. Lisbon: Sá da Costa.

1984. *Manuel de langue portugaise (Portugal-Brésil)*. Paris: Klincksieck.

Thèses: 1929. 'Thèses présentées au Ier Congrès des philologues slaves en octobre 1929 à Prague', *Travaux du Cercle linguistique de Prague* 1:5–29.

Thom, René 1975. *Stabilité structurelle et morphogénèse. Essai d'une théorie générale des modèles*. Reading, MA: W.A. Benjamin.

Thomas, Earl 1969. *The Syntax of Spoken Brazilian Portuguese*. Nashville: Vanderbilt University Press.

Thornton, Anna 1999. 'Diagrammaticità, uniformità di codifica e morfomicità nella flessione verbale italiana', in Benincà *et al.* (eds.), pp. 483–502.

Tiersma, Peter Meijes 1982. 'Local and general markedness', *Language* 58:832–49.

Timberlake, Alan 1977. 'Reanalysis and actualization in syntactic change', in Li, Charles (ed.), *Mechanisms of Syntactic Change*. Austin-London: University of Texas Press, pp. 141–77.

Timpanaro Sebastiano 1965. 'Muta cum liquida *in poesia latina e nel latino volgare*', in Paratore, Ettore (ed.), *Studi in onore di Alfredo Schiaffini*. Rome: Ateneo, pp. 1074–103.

TLF = Trésor de la langue française : dictionnaire de la langue du XIXe et du XXe siècle, 1789–1960, publié sous la direction de Paul Imbs 1971–94. Paris: CNRS.

Tobler, Adolf and Lommatzsch, Erhard 1925. *Altfranzösisches Wörterbuch*. Wiesbaden: Steiner.

Todoran, Romulus 1960. 'Graiul din Vîlcele (raionul Turda)', *Materiale şi cercetări dialectale* 1:29–126.

Togeby, Knud 1958. 'Les diminutifs dans les langues romanes du moyen âge', *Studia Neophilologica* 30:192–99.

    1966. 'Le sort du plus-que-parfait latin dans les langues romanes', *Cahiers Ferdinand de Saussure* 23:175–84.

    1972. 'L'apophonie des verbes espagnols et portugais en -ir', *RPh* 26:256–64.

    1980. 'Romance historical morphology', in Posner, R. and Green, J. (eds.), *Trends in Romance Linguistics and Philology I*. The Hague-Paris-New York: Mouton, pp. 105–55.

Tollemache, Federico 1945. *Le parole composte nella lingua italiana*. Rome: Rores.

Torrego, Esther 1998. *The Dependencies of Objects*. Cambridge, MA: MIT Press.

    1999. 'El complemento directo preposicional', in Bosque Muñoz, Ignacio and Demonte, Violeta (eds.), *Gramatica descriptiva de la lengua española*. Madrid: Espasa-Calpe, pp. 1779–807.

Tortora, Christina (ed.) 1998. *The Syntax of Italian Dialects*. Oxford: Oxford University Press.

Toscano, Reinat 1998. *Gramàtica niçarda*. Toulouse: Princi Néguer.

Toso, Fiorenzo 1997. *Grammatica genovese*. Genova: Le Mani.

    2000. 'Nota sul monegasco', *Plurilinguismo. Contatti di lingue e culture* 7:239–49 [also in Toso (2008) pp. 233–40]

    2008. *Linguistica di aree laterali ed estreme*. Recco–Genova: Le Mani.

Touratier, Christian 1984. 'Il y a un passif en latin; mais de quoi s'agit-il?', in Bresson, Daniel (ed.), *Le passif. Travaux 2*. Aix-en-Provence-Marseille: Laffite, pp. 75–92.

Tovar, Antonio 1951. 'La sonorisation et la chute des intervocaliques phénomène latin occidental', *Revue des études latines* 29:102–20.

TPS = Transactions of the Philological Society

Traugott, Elizabeth 2004. 'Exaptation and grammaticalization', in Akimoto, Minoji (ed.), *Linguistic Studies Based on Corpora*. Tokyo: Hituzi Syobo, pp. 133–56.

Traugott, Elizabeth and Dasher, Richard 2002. *Regularity in Semantic Change*. Cambridge: Cambridge University Press.

Trinchera, Francesco 1865. *Syllabus Græcarum Membranarum*. Naples: Cataneo.

Tropea, Giovanni 1988. *Lessico del dialetto di Pantelleria*. Palermo: CSFLS.

Trotter, David 2007. '"Tutes choses en sapience": la transmission du lexique biblique dans les Psautiers anglo-normands', in Bubenicek, V., Corbet, P. and Marchal, R. (eds.), *Gouvernement des hommes, gouvernement des âmes: mélanges Charles Brucker*. Nancy: Presses Universitaires, pp. 507–15.

Truman, James and Riddiford, Lynn 1999. 'The origins of insect metamorphosis', *Nature* 401:447–52.

Trumper, John 1996a. *Una lingua nascosta. Sulle orme degli ultimi quadarari calabresi*. Soveria Mannelli: Rubbettino.

  1996b. 'Riflessioni pragmo-sintattiche su alcuni gruppi meridionali: l'italiano "popolare"', in Benincà *et al.* (eds.), pp. 351–67.

  1997. 'Vindex verborum: aspetti importanti dell'elemento albanese nei gerghi italiani di mestiere', in Pellegrini, Giovan Battista (ed.), *Terza raccolta di saggi dialettologici in area italo-romanza*. Padua: CNR, pp. 109–24.

  2001. *Vocabolario calabro. Laboratorio del Dizionario etimologico calabrese. I. A-E*. Bari: Laterza.

Trumper, John and Chiodo, Giovanna 1999. 'La pertinenza degli eventi catastrofici naturali per la dialettologia e la linguistica romanza', *Rivista Italiana di Dialettologia* 23:9–38.

Trumper, John, Romito, Luciano and Maddalon, Marta 1991. 'Double consonants, isochrony and raddoppiamento fonosintattico: some reflections', in Bertinetto, P. M., Kenstowicz, M. and Loporcaro, M. (eds.), *Certamen phonologicum II Papers from the 1990 Cortona Phonology Meeting*. Turin: Rosenberg & Sellier, pp. 329–60.

Trumper, John and Straface, Ermanno 1998. 'Varia etymologica I', in Mioni, Alberto, Vigolo, Maria Teresa and Croatto, Enzo (eds.), *Dialetti, cultura e società*. Padua: CNR, pp. 225–54.

Tuaillon, Gaston 2006. 'Les neo-oxytons du francoprovençal', *Lingue e idiomi d'Italia* 1,2:7–35.

Tully, T., Cambiazo, V. and Kruse, L. 1994. 'Memory through metamorphosis in normal and mutant Drosophila', *Journal of Neuroscience* 14:68–74.

Tuttle, Edward 1974. '*Sedano, senero, prezzemolo* and the intertonic vowels in Tuscan', *RPh*. 27:451–65.

  1985. 'Morphologization as redundancy in central Italian dialects', *RPh* 39:35–43.

1986a. 'Alpine systems of Romance sibilants', in Holtus, G. and Ringger, K. (eds.), *Raetia antiqua et moderna. W. Elwert zum 80. Geburtstag*. Tübingen: Max Niemeyer, pp. 315–30.

1986b. 'The spread of ESSE as universal auxiliary in central Italo-Romance', *MedRom* 11:229–87.

1990. 'Parallelismi strutturali e poligenesi: l'estrapolazione di nuovi morfemi del plurale in alcuni dialetti italiani isolani e periferici', *Bollettino Centro di studi filologici e linguistici siciliani* 16:67–118.

1991. 'Nasalization in Northern Italy: syllabic constraints and strength scales as developmental parameters', *Rivista di linguistica* 3: 23–92.

1992. 'Comunità linguistiche chiuse o endocentriche e l'intensificazione delle nasali finali nel Norditalia', *RID* 16: 81–180.

2001–2. 'Ampliamenti velari nel verbo meridionale: le figure daco/staco "do/ sto", parco "parto", veco "vedo", kándeke "canto", jecco "getto"', *Bollettino linguistico campano* 1:41–88.

Uguzzoni, Arianna, Azzaro, Gabriele and Schmid, Stephan 2003. 'Short vs. long and/or abruptly cut vowels: new perspectives on a debated question', in Recasens, D. (ed.), *Proceedings of the XVth International Congress of the Phonetic Sciences, III*, pp. 2717–20.

Ulivi, Anca 1977. 'Quelques remarques sur la relation entre la syncope et l'accent dans les parlers dacoroumains', *RRL* 22:63–71.

1985. 'Quelques remarques sur l'accent secondaire dans les parlers dacoroumains', *RRL* 30:583–88.

Ullmann, Stephen 1957. *The Principles of Semantics*. Oxford: Blackwell.

Ursini, Flavia 1989. 'Istroromanzo: storia linguistica interna', *LRL* (III), pp. 537–48.

Väänänen, Veikko 1963/81 (3rd edn). *Introduction au latin vulgaire*. Paris: Klincksieck.

1966 (3rd edn). *Le latin vulgaire des inscriptions pompéiennes*. Berlin: Akademie-Verlag.

1967 (2nd edn). *Introduction au latin vulgaire*. Paris: Klincksieck.

1974/82. *Introduzione al latino volgare*. Bologna: Pàtron.

1987. *Le journal-épître d'Egérie. Etude linguistique*. Helsinki: Suomalainen Tiedeakatemia.

Vai, Massimo 1996. 'Per una storia della negazione in milanese in comparazione con altre varietà altoitaliane', *ACME. Annali della Facoltà di Lettere e Filosofia dell'Università degli Studi di Milano* 49: 57–98.

Valdman, Albert 2000. 'La Langue des faubourgs et des banlieues: de l'argot au français populaire', *The French Review* 73:1179–92.

Valesio, Paolo 1968. 'The Romance synthetic future pattern and its first attestations', *Lingua* 20:113–61.

1969. 'The synthetic future again: phonology and morphosyntax', *Lingua* 24:181–93.

van der Hulst, Harry (ed.) 1999. *Word Prosodic Systems in the Languages of Europe.* Berlin-New York: Mouton de Gruyter.

van Reenen, Pieter and Schøsler, Lene 1988. 'Formation and evolution of the feminine and masculine singular nouns in Old French *la maison(s)* and *li charbons*', in Fisiak, Jacek (ed.), *Historical Dialectology.* Berlin: Mouton de Gruyter, pp. 505–45.

1997. 'La declinaison en ancien et moyen français: deux tendances contraires', in *Le moyen français. Philologie et linguistique. Approches du texte et du discours.* Paris: Didier, pp. 595–612.

2000a. 'The pragmatic function of the Old French particles AINZ, AORES, DONC, LORS, OR, PUIS, and SI', in Herring, S., van Reenen, Pieter and Schøsler, L. (eds.), *Textual Parameters in Older Languages.* Amsterdam: Benjamins, pp. 59–105.

2000b. 'Declension in Old and Middle French: two opposing tendencies', in Smith, John Charles and Bentley, Delia (eds.), *Historical Linguistics 1995, vol. 1: General Issues and Non-Germanic Languages.* Amsterdam: Benjamins, pp. 327–44.

Vance, Barbara 1997. *Syntactic change in Medieval French. Verb-second and Null Subjects.* Dordrecht: Kluwer.

Vanelli, Laura 1979. 'L'allungamento delle vocali in friulano', *Ce fastu?* 55:66–76.

1980. 'A suppletive form of the Italian article and its phonosyntax', *Journal of Linguistic Research* 1:69–90.

1986. 'Strutture tematiche in Italiano antico', in Stammerjohann, Harro (ed.), *Tema-Rema in Italiano.* Tübingen: Narr, pp. 248–73.

1987. 'I pronomi soggetto nei dialetti italiani settentrionali dal Medio Evo a oggi', *MedRom* 12:173–211.

1992. *La deissi in italiano.* Padua: Unipress.

1993. 'Osservazioni sulla concordanza dei tempi in italiano', in Costelazzo, M. and Mergaldo, P. V. (eds), *Omaggio a Gianfranco Folena.* Padua: Programma, pp. 2345–73.

1998. 'Ordine delle parole e articolazione pragmatica nell'italiano antico: La "prominenza" pragmatica della prima posizione nella frase', in Renzi, Lorenzo (ed.), *Italant). Per una grammatica dell'italiano antico.* Padova: Università di Padova, Progetto Italant, pp. 73–89.

1999. 'Ordine delle parole e articolazione pragmatica nell'italiano antico: la "prominenza" pragmatica della prima posizione nella frase', *MedRom* 23:229–46.

Vanelli, Laura, Renzi, Lorenzo and Benincà, Paola 1985. 'Typologie des pronoms sujets dans les langues romanes', in *Actes du XVIIe congrès international de linguistique et philologie romanes, vol. 3: Linguistique descriptive, phonétique, morphologie et lexique.* Aix-en-Provence: Université de Provence, pp. 163–76.

Varvaro, Alberto 1968. *Storia, problemi e metodi della linguistica romanza.* Naples: Liguori.

1972–73. 'Storia della lingua: passato e presente di una categoria controversa', *RPh* 26:16–51; 509–31.

1984. 'Omogeneità del latino e frammentazione della Romània', in Vineis, E. (ed.), *Latino volgare, latino medioevale, lingue romanze. Atti del Convegno della Società italiana di glottologia*. Pisa: Giardini, pp. 11–22.

Vasiliu, Emanuel 1968. *Fonologia istorică a dialectelor dacoromâne*. Bucharest: Editura Academiei.

Vasiliu, Emanuel and Golopenţia, Sanda 1969. *Gramatica transformaţională a limbii române*. Bucharest: Editura Academiei.

Vasiliu, Laura 1969. 'Some grammatical and semantic remarks on the reflexive constructions', *RRL* 14:365–72.

Vasmer, Max 1971. Фасмер Макс. *Этимологический словарь русского языка (перевод с немецкого и дополнения О. Н. Трубачева). Том III*. Moscow: Progress. (Revised and expanded Russian version of *Russisches etymologisches Wörterbuch*. Heidelberg: Winter, 1955–58.)

Vásquez Cuesta, Pilar and Mendes Da Luz, Maria Albertina 1980. *Gramática da língua portuguesa*. Lisbon: Edições 70.

Vecchio, Paola 2010. 'The distribution of the complementizers /ka/ and /ku/ in the North Salentino dialect of Francavilla Fontana (Brindisi)', in D'Alessandro, R., Ledgeway, A. and Roberts, I. (eds.), *Syntactic Variation. The Dialects of Italy*. Cambridge: Cambridge University Press, pp. 312–22.

Veland, Reidar 1996. *Les marqueurs référentiels: celui-ci et celui-là: structure interne et déploiement dans le discours direct littéraire*. Geneva: Droz.

Vennemann, Theo 1974. 'Topics, subjects, and word order: from SXV to SVX via TVX', in Anderson, John and Jones, Charles (eds.), *Historical Linguistics*. Amsterdam: North Holland, pp. 339–76.

1975. 'An explanation of drift', in Li, Charles (ed.), *Word Order and Word Order Change*. Austin: University of Texas, pp. 269–305.

1988. *Preference Laws for Syllable Structure and the Explanation of Sound Change*. Berlin-New York-Amsterdam: Mouton de Gruyter.

Veny, Joan 1982. *Els parlars catalans (Síntesi de dialectologia)*. Mallorca: Moll.

1998. 'Katalanisch: Areallinguistik – Áreas lingüisticas', *LRL* (V, 1), pp. 243–61.

2001. *Llengua històrica i llengua estàndard*. Valencia: Universitat de València.

Videsott, Paul 2001. 'Vokallängen im Norditalienischen und im Dolomitenladinischen', in Wunderli, P., Werlen, I. and Grünert, M. (eds.), *Italica – Raetica – Gallica. Studia linguarum litterarum artiumque in honorem Ricarda Liver*. Tübingen-Basel: Francke, pp. 151–68.

Vidos, Benedek Elemér 1959. *Manuale di linguistica romanza*. Florence: Olschki.

Vignoli, Carlo 1925. *Il vernacolo di Veroli*. Rome: Società filologica romana.

Vignuzzi, Ugo 2005. 'La lingua e i dialetti', in *Lazio*. Milan: Touring Club Italiano, pp. 83–89.

Vignuzzi, Ugo and Avolio, Francesco 1994. *Per un profilo di storia linguistica «interna» dei dialetti del Mezzogiorno d'Italia*, in Galasso, G. and Romeo, R.

(eds.), *Storia del Mezzogiorno, vol. 9: Aspetti e problemi del Medioevo e dell'età moderna*. Rome: Editalia, pp. 631–99.

Vigolo, Maria Teresa 1992. *Ricerche lessicali sul dialetto dell'Alto Vicentino*. Tübingen: Niemeyer.

Villangómez i Llobet, Marià 1978. *Curs d'iniciació a la llengua. Normes gramaticals. Lectures eivissenques i formentereres*. Ibiza: Institut d'Estudis Eivissencs.

Villar, Francisco 1983. *Ergatividad, acusatividad y género en la familia lingüística indoeuropea*. Salamanca: Ediciones Universidad de Salamanca.

Vincent, Nigel n.d. *On Paradigmatic Stress*. University of Manchester, Department of Linguistics: manuscript.

1976. 'Perceptual factors and word order change in Romance', in Harris (ed.), pp. 54–68.

1982. 'The development of the auxiliaries *habere* and *esse* in Romance', in Vincent and Harris (eds.), pp. 71–96.

1986. 'La posizione dell'aggettivo in italiano', in Stammerjohann (ed.), pp. 181–95.

1987. 'The interaction of periphrasis and inflection: some Romance examples', in Harris and Ramat (eds.), pp. 237–56.

1988a. 'Latin', in Harris and Vincent (eds.), pp. 26–78.

1988b. 'Italian', in Harris and Vincent (eds.), pp. 229–313.

1992. 'Abduction and exaptation'. Paper delivered at the *Fifth Krems International Morphology Meeting*, Krems, Austria, 7–9 July 1992.

1993. 'Head- versus dependent-marking: the case of the clause', in Corbett, G., Fraser, N. and McGlashan, S. (eds.), *Heads in Grammatical Theory*. Cambridge: Cambridge University Press, pp. 140–63.

1994. *On the default case in Latin*. University of Manchester: manuscript.

1995. 'Exaptation and grammaticalization', in Andersen, Henning (ed.), *Historical Linguistics 1993*. Amsterdam-Philadelphia: Benjamins, pp. 433–45.

1997a. 'Synthetic and analytic structures', in Maiden and Parry (eds.), pp. 99–105.

1997b. 'Prepositions', in Maiden and Parry (eds.), pp. 208–13.

1997c. 'The emergence of the D-system in Romance', in Kemenade and Vincent (eds.), pp. 149–69.

1997d. 'Esiste un caso "default" in latino?' Unpublished paper delivered at *Giornata di studio sulla questione dei casi*, Università di Bergamo.

1998. 'Tra grammatica e grammaticalizzazione: articoli e clitici nelle lingue (italo)-romanze', in Ramat and Roma (eds.), pp. 411–40.

1999. 'The evolution of C-structure: prepositions and PPs from Indo-European to Romance', *Linguistics* 37:1111–53.

2000. 'Competition and correspondence in syntactic change: null arguments in Latin and Romance', in Pintzuk, S., Tsoulas, G. and Warner, A. (eds.), *Diachronic Syntax. Models and Mechanisms*. Oxford: Oxford University Press, pp. 25–50.

2007a. 'Learned vs popular syntax: adjective placement in early Italian vernac-ulars', in Lepschy and Tosi (eds.), pp. 55–75.

2007b. 'Tra latino e dialetto: riflessioni sulla sintassi di un testo padovano medievale', in Maschi, R., Penello, N. and Rizzolatti, P. (eds.), *Miscellanea di studi linguistici offerti a Laura Vanelli da amici e allievi padovani*. Udine: Forum, pp. 413–25.

Vincent, Nigel and Bentley, Delia 2001. 'On the demise of the Latin future periphrasis in -urus + esse', in Moussy, C. (ed.), *De lingua latina nouae quaestiones. Actes du Xe Colloque international de linguistique latine*. Louvain–Paris: Peeters, pp. 145–58.

Vincent, Nigel and Harris, Martin (eds.) 1982. *Studies in the Romance Verb*. London: Croom Helm.

Vincent, Nigel, Parry, M. and Hastings, R. (eds.) 2002. *Sintassi degli antichi volgari d'Italia. Saggi preliminari, vol. 1*. Universities of Manchester and Bristol.

2003. *Sintassi degli antichi volgari d'Italia: Saggi preliminari, vol. 2*. Universities of Manchester and Bristol.

Vincenz, Ileana. 1971. 'The reflexive voice in contemporary Romanian and the Romanian-English contrastive analysis', *RRL* 16:491–97.

Vineis, Edoardo 1984. 'Problemi di ricostruzione della fonologia del latino vol-gare', in Vineis, Edoardo (ed.), *Latino volgare, latino medioevale, lingue romanze. Atti del Convegno della Società italiana di glottologia*. Pisa: Giardini, pp. 45–62.

1993 (4th edn). 'Preliminari per una storia (ed una grammatica) del latino parlato', in Stolz, F., Debrunner, A. and Schmid, W. (eds.), *Storia della lingua latina*. Bologna: Pàtron, pp. xxxvii–lviii.

Violi, Filippo 2001. *Lessico grecanico-italiano, italiano-grecanico*. Bova: Apodiafazzi.

Viparelli, Valeria 1990. *Tra prosodia e metrica*. Naples: Loffredo.

Virdis, Maurizio 1978. *Fonetica storica del dialetto campidanese*. Cagliari: Della Torre.

1988. 'Sardo. Aree linguistiche', *LRL* (IV), pp. 897–913.

Vising, Johann 1882. *Étude sur le dialecte anglo-normand du XIIe siècle*. Uppsala: Edquist.

VR = Vox Romanica

Wagner, Max Leopold 1939. 'Flessionale nominale e verbale del sardo antico e moderno (II)', *ID* 15:207–47.

1941. *Historische Lautlehre des Sardischen* Halle (Saale): Niemeyer.

1951. *La lingua sarda. Storia, spirito e forma*. Bern: Francke.

1952. 'Das "Diminutiv" im Portugiesischen', *Orbis* 1:460–76.

1957. 'Die Iteration im Sardischen', in Reichenkron, Günter (ed.), *Syntactica und Stylistica. Festschrift für Ernst Gamillscheg*. Tübingen: Niemeyer, pp. 611–24.

1960–64. *Dizionario etimologico sardo*. Heidelberg: Winter.

Wahlgren, Ernst 1920. *Etude sur les actions analogiques réciproques du parfait et du participe passé dans les langues romanes.* Uppsala: Akademiska.

Walter, Henriette 1984. 'Verlan', in Olback, H., Soral, A. and Pasche, A. (eds.), *Les mouvements de mode expliqués aux enfants.* Paris: Laffont, pp. 397–406.

Wandruszka, Ulrich 1986. 'Tema e soggetto in italiano', in Stammerjohann (ed.), pp. 15–24.

Wanner, Dieter 1987. *The Development of Romance Clitic Pronouns. From Latin to Old Romance.* Berlin: Mouton de Gruyter.

1996. 'Second position clitics in medieval Romance', in Halpern, Aaron and Zwicky, Arnold (eds.), *Approaching Second. Second Position Clitics and Related Phenomena.* Stanford, CA: Center for the Study of Language and Information, pp. 537–78.

Wanner, Dieter and Kibbee, Douglas (eds.) 1991. *New Analyses in Romance Linguistics.* Amsterdam-Philadelphia: Benjamins.

Ward, Ralph 1951. 'Stops plus liquid and the position of the Latin accent', *Language* 27:477–84.

Warmington, Eric (ed.) 1988. *Remains of Old Latin 1. Ennius, Cæcilius.* Harvard: LOEB.

Wartburg, Walther von 1928–. *Französisches Etymologisches Wörterbuch.* Bonn: Klopp.

[1934] 1971. *Evolution et structure de la langue française.* Bern: Francke.

1950. *Die Ausgliederung der romanischen Sprachräume.* Bern: Francke.

1959–. *Französisches Etymologisches Wörterbuch.* Basel: Zbinden.

Watkins, Calvert 1964. 'Preliminaries to the reconstruction of Indo-European sentence structure', in Lunt, Horace (ed.), *Proceedings of the Ninth International Congress of Linguistics.* London: Mouton, pp. 1035–45.

Weidenbusch, Waltraud 1993. *Funktionen der Präfigierung. Präpositionale Elemente in der Wortbildung des Französischen.* Tübingen: Niemeyer.

Weil, Henri. [1844] 1978. *The Order of Words in the Ancient Languages Compared with that of the Modern Languages.* Amsterdam: Benjamins.

Weinrich, Harald 1958. *Phonologische Studien zur romanischen Sprachgeschichte.* Münster Westfalen: Aschendorff.

1960. 'Sonorisierung in der Kaiserzeit?', *ZRPh* 76:205–18.

Werner, O. 1989. 'Sprachökonomie und Natürlichkeit im Bereich der Morphologie', *Zeitschrift für Phonetik, Sprachwissenschaft und Kommunikationsforschung* 42:34–47.

Wheeler, Max 1988a. 'Catalan', in Harris and Vincent (eds.), pp. 170–208.

1988b. 'Occitan', in Harris and Vincent (eds.), pp. 246–78.

1993. 'Changing inflection: verbs in North West Catalan', in Mackenzie, D. and Michael, I. (eds.), *Hispanic Linguistic Studies in Honour of F. W. Hodcroft.* Langrannog: Dolphin, pp. 171–206.

Wheeler, Max, Yates, Alan and Dols, Nicolau 1999. *Catalan. A Comprehensive Grammar.* London: Routledge.

Widmer, Ambros 1959. *Das Personalpronomen im Bündnerromanischen in phonetischer und morphologischer Schau*. Bern: Francke.

Wierzbicka, Anna 1984. 'Diminutives and depreciatives: semantic representation for derivational categories', *Quaderni di semantica* 5:123–30.

Wilkinson, Hugh 1967. 'The Latinity of Ibero-Romance', *Ronshu* 8:1–34.
1969. 'The Vulgar Latin conjugation system', *Ronshu* 10:81–121.
1971. 'Vowel alternation in the Spanish -ir verbs', *Ronshu* 12:1–21.
1978/79/80/81/82/83. 'Palatal vs. velar in the stem of the Romance present', *Ronshu* 19:19–35; 20:19–35; 21:41–62; 22:67–85; 23:115–36; 24:177–99.
1985/86/87/88/89/90/91. 'The Latin neuter plurals in Romance (I–VII)', *Ronshu* 26:137–50; 27:157–71; 28:33–46; 29:47–61; 30:109–22; 31:113–27; 32:35–50.

Willems, Dominique 1985. 'La construction impersonnelle', in Melis, L., Tasmowski de Ryck, L., Verluyten, P. and Willems, D. (eds.), *Les constructions de la phrase française*. Ghent: Communication and Cognition, pp. 167–222.

Williams, Edwin Bucher 1962. *From Latin to Portuguese. Historical Phonology and Morphology of the Portuguese Language*. Philadelphia: University of Pennsylvania Press.

Williams, Lawrence and van Compernolle, Rémi 2009. '*On* versus *tu* and *vous*: pronouns with indefinite reference in synchronous electronic French discourse', *Language Sciences* 31:409–27.

Williamson, Janis 1984. *Studies in Lakhota Grammar*. University of California at San Diego: unpublished thesis.

Wilmet, Marc 1976. *Etudes de morpho-syntaxe verbale*. Paris: Klincksieck.

Winter, Werner 1971. 'Formal frequency and linguistic change: some preliminary comments', *Folia Linguistica* 5:55–61.

Woledge, Brian 1979. *La Syntaxe des substantifs chez Chrétien de Troyes*. Geneva: Droz.

Woledge, Brian, Beard, J. and Horton, C. H. M. 1967–69. 'La declinaison des substantifs dans la Chanson de Roland recherches mécanographiques', *Romania* 88:145–74; 90:174–201.

Woledge, Brian and Clive, H. 1964. *Répertoire des plus anciens textes en prose française depuis 842 jusqu'aux premières années du XIIIe Siècle*. Geneva: Droz.

Wolf, Heinz-Jürgen 1998. 'Du latin aux langues romanes: le sort de l'infixe inchoatif -sc- et la conjugaison des verbes en -scere', *Travaux de linguistique et de philologie* 36:441–54.

Wolf, Siegmund 1960. *Großes Wörterbuch der Zigeunersprache*. Mannheim: Bibliographisches Institut.

Woodcock, E. C. 2002 (1959[1]). *A New Latin Syntax*. Bristol Classical Press-Duckworth and Co., London.

Wright, Roger 1982. *Late Latin and Early Romance in Spain and Carolingian France*. Liverpool: Francis Cairns.

Wright, Roger (ed.) 1991. *Latin and the Romance Languages in the Early Middle Ages*. London-New York: Routledge.

Wright, Roger 1994. *Early Ibero-Romance. Twenty-one Studies on Language and Texts from the Iberian Peninsula between the Roman Empire and the Thirteenth Century*. Newark, NJ: Juan de la Cuesta.

1997. [Review of Davis and Napoli 1994], *Studies in Language* 21:169–74.

Wüest, Jakob 1979. *La dialectalisation de la Galloromania*. Berne: Francke.

Wunderli, Peter, Benthin, Karola and Karasch, Angela 1978. *Französische Intonationsforschung*. Tübingen: Narr.

Wurff, Wim (van der) 1993. 'Null objects and learnability: the case of Latin'. Paper presented at the *International Conference on Historical Linguistics 11*, UCLA.

Wurzel, Wolfgang 1987. 'System-dependent morphological naturalness in inflection', in Dressler, W., Mayerthaler, W., Panagl, O. and Wurzel, W. (eds.), *Leitmotifs in Natural Morphology*. Amsterdam: Benjamins, pp. 59–96.

Yates, Alan 1975. *Catalan*. Kent: Hodder and Stoughton.

Yngve, V. 1970. 'On getting a word in edgewise', in *Papers from the Sixth Regional Meeting. Chicago Linguistic Society*. Chicago: University of Chicago Press, pp. 567–78.

Zagona, Karen 2002. *The Syntax of Spanish*. Cambridge: Cambridge University Press.

Zamboni, Alberto 1974. *Veneto*. Pisa: Pacini.

1976, 'Alcune osservazioni sull'evoluzione delle geminate romanze', in Simone, R., Vignuzzi, U. and Ruggiero, G. (eds.), *Studi di fonetica e fonologia*. Rome: Bulzoni, pp. 325–36.

1980/1981. 'Un problema di morfologia romanza: l'ampliamento verbale in -idio, -idzo', *Quaderni patavini di linguistica* 2:171–88.

1982/1983. 'La morfologia verbale latina in -sc- e la sua evoluzione romanza: appunti per una nuova via esplicativa', *Quaderni patavini di linguistica* 3:87–138.

1983. 'Note aggiuntive alla questione dei verbi in -isco', *SGI* 12:231–37.

1992. 'Postille alla discussione sull'accusativo preposizionale', in Lorenzo, Ramón (ed.), *Actas do XIX Congreso internacional de lingüística e filoloxía románicas V: Gramática histórica e historia da lingua*. A Coruña: Fundación 'Pedro Barrié de la Maza, Conde de Fenosa', pp. 787–808.

1998. 'Dal latino tardo al romanzo arcaico: aspetti diacronico-tipologici della flessione nominale', in Ramat and Roma (eds.), pp. 127–46.

2000. *Alle origini dell'italiano. Dinamiche e tipologie della transizione dal latino*. Rome: Carocci.

Zamora Vicente, Alonso 1967. *Dialectología española*. Madrid: Gredos.

Zanuttini, Raffaella 1991. *Syntactic Properties of Sentential Negation. A Comparative Study of Romance Languages*. Oxford: Oxford University Press.

Zink, Gaston 1989. *Morphologie du français médiéval*. Paris: PUF.

1990. *Le Moyen Français: XIVe et XVe siècles*. Paris: PUF.

1996. *Phonétique historique du français*. Paris: PUF.

1997 (4th edn). *Morphologie du français médiéval*. Paris: PUF.

1999 (6th edn) *Phonétique historique du français*. Paris: PUF.

Zörner, Lotte 1998. *I dialetti canavesani di Cuorgné, Forno e dintorni. Descrizione fonologica, storico-fonetica e morfologica*. Cuorgné: CORSAC.

2008. *I dialetti occitani della Valle Po*. Turin: Valados usitanos.

Zribi-Hertz, Anne 1978. 'Economisons-nous: à propos d'une classe de formes réflexives métonymique en français', *Langue française* 39:104–22.

1984. 'Prépositions orphelines et pronoms nuls', *Recherches linguistiques* 12:46–91.

ZRPh = Zeitschrift für romanische Philologie

Zubizarreta, María-Luisa 1985. 'The relationship between morphophonology and morphosyntax: the case of Romance causatives', *LI* 16:247–89.

1998. *Prosody, Focus, and Word Order*. Cambridge, MA: MIT Press.

INDEX

842

Index

Index

Index

Index